Systems of Consanguinity and Affinity of the Human Family

Systems of Consanguinity and Affinity of the Human Family

LEWIS HENRY MORGAN

Introduction by Elisabeth Tooker

University of Nebraska Press
Lincoln and London

Introduction © 1997 by the University of Nebraska Press
Manufactured in the United States of America

☉ The paper in this book meets the minimum requirements of American National Standard
for Information Sciences—Permanence of Paper for Printed Library Materials,
 ANSI Z39.48-1984.

First Bison Books printing: 1997
Most recent printing indicated by the last digit below:
10   9   8   7   6   5   4   3   2   1

Library of Congress Cataloging-in-Publication Data
Morgan, Lewis Henry, 1818–1881.
Systems of consanguinity and affinity of the human family / Lewis H. Morgan; introduction
by Elisabeth Tooker.
p.   cm.
Originally published: Washington: Smithsonian Institution, 1870, in series: Smithsonian
contributions to knowledge; v. 218.
Includes bibliographical references (p.   ) and index.
ISBN 0-8032-8230-3 (pa: alk. paper)
1. Kinship.   2. Family.   I. Title.
GN487.M67   1997
306.83—dc21
96-53016   CIP

Reprinted from the original 1871 edition published by the Smithsonian Institution as volume
17 in its Contributions to Knowledge series.

CONTENTS.

PART I.

DESCRIPTIVE SYSTEM OF RELATIONSHIP.

ARYAN, SEMITIC, AND URALIAN FAMILIES.

PART II.

CLASSIFICATORY SYSTEM OF RELATIONSHIP.

GANOWÁNIAN FAMILY.

PART III.

CLASSIFICATORY SYSTEM OF RELATIONSHIP—Continued.

TURANIAN AND MALAYAN FAMILIES.

INTRODUCTION

ELISABETH TOOKER

Lewis H. Morgan's pioneering *Systems of Consanguinity and Affinity of the Human Family* is one of the most remarkable of all anthropological studies. Before Morgan, few observers had recorded the kinship terminologies of other peoples, except the words for husband, wife, father, mother, son, daughter, brother, and sister. *Systems* changed that. While doing field work among the Seneca Indians, Morgan learned that they had a system of kinship terminology quite different in plan from those of Western peoples. Believing that the kinship terminologies of other peoples might exhibit similar differences and that these might contribute to the understanding of history, Morgan undertook the extensive comparative study that resulted in the publication of *Systems*. Most anthropologists, however, did not accept all of Morgan's conclusions, and a number offered alternative explanations. The subject of "kinship" thus became one of the most central as well as most esoteric in anthropology.

Systems of Consanguinity and Affinity was published as volume 17 in the series *Smithsonian Contributions to Knowledge* early in 1871, just after John Lubbock's *The Origin of Civilisation* (1870) and just before Edward B. Tylor's *Primitive Culture* (1871). Morgan had submitted the manuscript to Joseph Henry, secretary of the Smithsonian Institution, six years before, in 1865, the year Lubbock's *Pre-historic Times*, Tylor's *Researches into the Early History of Mankind*, and John F. McLennan's *Primitive Marriage* all appeared. *Systems* was not published that same year in part because Henry, believing that it was rather too lengthy for the conclusions arrived at, suggested that Morgan condense it. After receiving the reviewers' and Henry's comments, Morgan did revise the manuscript, which Henry sent to a second set of reviewers, accepting it for publication in January 1868. It took three years to print and was the most expensive volume the Smithsonian had published up to that date.

Morgan had undertaken the study in the belief that a comparison of the kinship terminologies of the Old and New Worlds might provide evidence of the Asiatic origin of the American Indians. As the research progressed, it also became in Morgan's eyes—as he noted in the preface—a philological study, one, he suggested, that might contribute to recognition of relationships between two or more languages not previously known to be related. Morgan's suggestion that a comparative study of kinship terminologies could be of aid in ascertaining relationships between languages, however, was not accepted by linguists, and the idea that the Americas were peopled from across the Bering Straits came to be more generally accepted on other grounds.

I am indebted to Thomas R. Trautmann for many insights into Morgan's life and work and for his critical reading of an earlier draft of this introduction. I am also indebted to Karl Kabelac of the University of Rochester Library for much help in the course of my study of the Morgan papers there.

What did attract particular comment were two other aspects of the study that Morgan himself also regarded as major contributions: (1) what Morgan termed "a conjectural solution," a hypothesis regarding the evolutionary development of marriage and family forms and (2) the extensive data the volume contained. *Systems* is immensely long, containing as it does 600 pages, 200 of which are tables and 400 text. The tables contain information on 139 kinship terminologies, either data Morgan collected himself or data collected by others under his supervision by means of a schedule he had devised.

Morgan was not the first to notice that not all peoples had kinship terminologies organized on the plan familiar in European ones. Some data, albeit few and scattered, had already been published, and if more had not been, one reason may well have been that these data could be easily explained by reference to marriage, descent, and/or role—customs later invoked by those seeking a "better" solution to Morgan's conjectural one. The mass of data Morgan collected, then, was scarcely necessary to suggest that kinship terminology might have sociological significance. And, because it was not, some anthropologists came to regard *Systems* as the work of a pedant.

Morgan was not a pedant, as a careful reading of *Systems* reveals. *Systems* is not without its flaws, as might be expected of a pioneering work, and it requires rather more effort on the part of the reader than do most monographs. It seems unlikely, however, that the great riddle of kinship posed in *Systems* will be solved without close consideration of the data Morgan presented and his discussion of the significance of these data—a task that despite a century and a quarter of work has, I believe, only just begun.

The Research Program

Morgan was born on November 21, 1818, on a farm south of Aurora in central New York State. His family moved into Aurora when he was eight and he attended Cayuga Academy there. In 1838 he entered Union College. Graduating two years later, he returned to Aurora, read law, and was admitted to the bar. He also joined a secret society, composed largely of Cayuga Academy graduates, called the Gordian Knot. This fraternity was floundering and, in an effort to revive it, members decided to reorganize it as an "Indian society" and to change its name to the "Grand Order of the Iroquois," what they also termed the "New Confederacy of the Iroquois." Seeking to model its organization after that of the League of the Iroquois, they found little information on its structure in the literature and so turned to the Indians themselves. Although others of the order visited Iroquois on their reservations, it was Morgan who most avidly pursued field work, particularly among the Seneca living on the Tonawanda reservation. With the publication in 1851 of his *League of the Ho-dé-no-sau-nee, or Iroquois*, an ethnography that remains the best single description of these people, he abandoned ethnographic studies. Later that year, on August 13, 1851, he married his cousin, Mary Elizabeth Steele. For the next half-dozen years he devoted most of his time and energy to his family, his law practice in Rochester, New York, where he had moved in 1844, and his business ventures.

His interest in anthropology was revived at the 1856 meetings of the American Association for the Advancement of Science (AAAS) held that year in Albany,

New York, and the following year he gave a paper at the AAAS meetings in Montreal. Titled "Laws of Descent of the Iroquois" (1858), it proved to be a kind of research proposal for the work that was to engage him for the remainder of his life.

As he noted in this paper, he had found in the course of his research that the Iroquois laws of descent

> were unlike both the civil and canon law; but yet were original and well defined. The chief differences were two: first, descent among the Iroquois followed the female line, or passed through the mother, while in each of the former systems it follows the male, or passes through the father. In the second place, the collateral lines, with the Iroquois, were finally brought into or merged in the lineal; while in the other cases, every remove from the common ancestor separated the collateral lines from the lineal, until after a few generations actual relationship ceased among collaterals. (Morgan 1858: 133)

He also noted that the Iroquois were not alone in having matrilineal descent. A number of North American Indians were also reported to have matrilineal clans, as were some Micronesian peoples. Evidence of matrilineal descent was also to be found in the literature on the Aztec, the native tribes of Australia and South America, and in Herodotus's description of the Lydians of Asia Minor. This led Morgan to suggest that this code of descent might "be used as a test of the truthfulness of history" (that is, the accuracy of historical writings) and "as an instrument in the attempt to solve the great problem of the origin of our Indian races" (Morgan 1858: 139–40).

A business trip to Marquette, Michigan, in July 1858 offered Morgan an opportunity to collect more comparative data. Interviewing Mrs. William Cameron, an Ojibwa, and her husband, a Scotsman with one-quarter Ojibwa blood, he found that the Ojibwa had clans, albeit patrilineal ones, a fact he at first was reluctant to accept. More importantly, he collected kin terms sufficient to convince him that the Ojibwa and Iroquois systems of kinship terminology were essentially identical. On his return to Rochester, he developed a schedule and in November went to the Tonawanda Seneca reservation to obtain the terms called for on it. It proved to be a kind of pretest that led him to further expand his schedule. This Morgan had printed along with his "Laws of Descent" paper, copies of which he sent to missionaries, Indian agents, and others who might be able to provide information on both clans and kinship terminology.

In May and June of 1859, Morgan went on what proved to be the first of four trips west of the Mississippi to collect more data. Two months later, in August, he reported his findings in a paper titled "System of Consanguinity of the Red Race, in its Relations to Ethnology" at the Springfield meetings of the AAAS. Shortly after returning from these meetings, he received from Dr. Henry M. Scudder of the Arcot mission in southern India details of the Tamil system. Later that month he visited Scudder, then living in Milton, New York, obtaining information on the Telugu also. These data indicated that the Tamil and Telegu systems were similar to those of North American Indians, confirming Morgan's initial hypothesis and renewing his resolve to test it further.

Morgan rewrote his circular, including these new data, and in October had it printed along with a slightly revised schedule. In January 1860, Joseph Henry and Secretary of State Lewis Cass provided a cover letter. Several months later, Morgan's supply of circulars having been exhausted, the Smithsonian reprinted it. Later that year Morgan went on a second western field trip and the following year on his third. In 1862, while returning from his fourth such trip, he learned of the death of his two daughters. He gave up his law practice and began writing *Systems*, which he saw as a memorial to them and would have dedicated to them if Joseph Henry had not objected to having such in a scientific publication.

Writing Systems

Morgan had attempted to obtain, through both his own efforts and those of others under his direction, kinship terminologies from all parts of the world. His success was mixed. He obtained completed schedules from only Central America, South America and Africa. He did, however, have extensive data from North America, two-thirds of which he himself had collected; and somewhat less from Oceania and Asia. He also had a number of completed schedules for the peoples of Europe and the Near East.

These data confirmed to Morgan his initial hypothesis: that, although there was variation, there were only two fundamentally different systems of kinship terminology. As he wrote in *Systems*:

One of these is descriptive and the other classificatory. The first, . . . rejecting the classification of kindred, except so far as it is in accordance with the numerical system, describes collateral consanguinei, for the most part, by an augmentation or combination of the primary terms of relationship. These terms, which are those for husband and wife, father and mother, brother and sister, and son and daughter, to which must be added, in such languages as possess them, grandfather and grandmother, and grandson and granddaughter, are thus restricted to the primary sense in which they are here employed. All other terms are secondary. Each relationship is thus made independent and distinct from every other. But the second, . . . rejecting descriptive phrases in every instance, and reducing consanguinei to great classes by a series of apparently arbitrary generalizations, applies the same terms to all the members of the same class. It thus confounds relationships, which, under the descriptive system, are distinct, and enlarges the signification both of the primary and secondary terms beyond their seemingly appropriate sense. (Morgan 1871: 11–12)

Descriptive systems, Morgan concluded, were characteristic of the Aryan (Indo-European), Semitic, and Uralian (Ural-Altaic) language families. Classificatory systems were to be found among (1) Malayan (Malayo-Polynesian) speakers of the Pacific region, (2) Turanian speakers (in Morgan's classification, the Dravidian languages of southern India, the Gauran ones of northern India, Chinese, and Japanese; in current usage the term "Turanian" refers to Ural-Altaic languages), and (3) the Indians of North America, speakers of what Morgan termed languages of the Ganowánian family (a word and classification of Morgan's invention no longer used).

Because of this association Morgan applied the names of these language families to types of kinship terminology. Later anthropologists provided other names, and Morgan's terminology fell into disuse. His Ganowánian type of kinship terminology includes those now termed Iroquois, Crow, and Omaha. His Turanian type is now called Dravidian, and Malayan, Hawaiian.

The differences between the various types of classificatory systems, Morgan came to believe, could not be explained by clan organization. As Morgan (1871: 476) stated it in *Systems*: "when the tribal [clan] relationships [of the Seneca] are run parallel with those established by the system [of kinship terminology] . . . the former traverse the latter quite as frequently as they affirm the connection." Omitted from *Systems* is a sentence in the previous draft: "We cannot discover, therefore, that the tribal organization exercised any direct influence upon its formation." Also omitted is a sentence that follows the observation that among North American Indians the system of kinship terminology is fundamentally the same, irrespective of the existence or nonexistence of the clan organization or whether descent is in the male or in the female line: "It would seem to follow, therefore, that inasmuch as this system of relationship is a domestic institution independent in its objects and designs, it cannot be explained by other institutions which are equally independent in their objects and designs."

Marriage customs figured little in Morgan's early thinking about kinship terminology, perhaps because the Seneca were and are quite thoroughly monogamous and extend the incest taboo to all near relatives. The Seneca, then, had a marriage system like ours—albeit with also a rule of clan exogamy—but a kinship terminology organized on a quite different plan.

The differences between the descriptive and classificatory systems, Morgan suggested, might be the result of the growth of property: "Among nomadic stocks, especially, the respectability of the individual was measured, in no small degree, by the number of his Kinsman. The wider the circle of kindred the greater the assurance of safety, since they were the natural guardians of his rights and the avengers of his wrongs. Whether designedly or otherwise, the Turanian form of consanguinity organized the family upon the largest scale of numbers" (Morgan 1871: 14). With the growth of property, however, this changed: "It would be manifestly unjust to place . . . collateral sons upon an equality with my own son for the inheritance of my estate" (Morgan 1871: 14).

After Morgan submitted the manuscript of *Systems* in 1865, Joseph Henry sent it for review to two individuals, one of whom was the Reverend Joshua H. McIlvaine, then professor of belles-lettres at Princeton. McIlvaine, who had been pastor of the First Presbyterian Church in Rochester from 1848 to 1860, was a good friend of Morgan's and had often discussed Morgan's research with him. At least as early as 1864, McIlvaine had suggested to Morgan that the classificatory system might be explained as pointing back "to a state of promiscuous intercourse" (Trautmann 1987: 159), an idea Morgan rejected on the grounds that it could account for only the Malayan system, not the peculiarities of the Turanian and Ganowánian systems, the ways they differed from Malayan ones. McIlvaine next suggested polygyny and polyandry as explanations. These, too, Morgan rejected, as these practices could account for only some features of the system and, further, could not have been practiced by a majority in any society. Then, on reading the draft of *Systems* Henry had sent him, McIlvaine noticed that, in the notes he had sent Morgan on the Hawaiian system, Judge Lorrin Andrews of Honolulu had mentioned the former Hawaiian custom of *pinalua* (spelled *punalua* in *Ancient Society*): "that two or more brothers, with their wives, or two or more sisters with their husbands, were inclined to possess each other in common" (Morgan 1871: 453 n.26). On the basis of this and cross-cousin marriage, McIlvaine wrote out a long solution to the Turanian system. This Morgan revised, suggesting that *pinalua* could account for the Malayan system and cross-cousin marriage the difference between Turanian and Ganowánian systems, although he stated it in somewhat obscure language (Morgan 1871: 486). He added this "conjectural solution of the origin of the classificatory system of relationship" to the draft of *Systems*, and with the permission of Joseph Henry gave a lecture on it to the American Academy of Arts and Sciences on February 11, 1868, who published it in their *Proceedings* that year (Morgan 1868; see Trautmann 1987: 158–70 for a discussion of the influence of McIlvaine's ideas on the development of Morgan's conjectural solution).

Reception of Systems

Ever since its publication in 1871, *Systems* has been subjected to a series of critiques that often have misconstrued what Morgan wrote and to a series of new interpretations of Morgan's data purporting to be more adequate analyses than Morgan's own. The first of these to appear was one by Sir John Lubbock. Lubbock had received an advance copy of *Systems* and on February 14, 1871, at the first meeting of the Anthropological Institute of Great Britain and Ireland gave a paper on the subject. It was published as the first article in the first volume of the *Journal of the Anthropological Institute*. In this paper, titled "On the Development of Relationships" (1871), Lubbock used the data Morgan had presented to suggest that the development of kinship terminology had not involved a few, sudden, and radical changes as Morgan had implied, but a long series of small ones.

Although Lubbock included this interpretation in the third edition of *Origin of Civilisation* published in 1875, it little influenced the subsequent course of the study of kinship. More important was the work of John Ferguson McLennan, especially his *Primitive Marriage* (1970). In it, McLennan outlined his ideas regarding the growth of the idea of kinship—the earliest human groups, McLennan believed, having had no idea of it. *Systems* challenged these ideas, and McLennan chose to defend them as well as criticize Morgan's in an eighty-page chapter, "The Classificatory System of Relationships," in his *Studies in Ancient History* (1876).

In *Systems* Morgan had not addressed the question McLennan thought was the central one: How did the idea of kinship grow? This lack led McLennan to assert that Morgan had made "two radical mistakes." His first was that "he did not seek the origin of the system in the probable origin of the classification"; his second, that he "so lightly assumed the system to be a system of blood-ties"—an error, McLennan thought, from which Morgan "certainly would have been safe, had he not fallen into the first" (McLennan 1876: 360–61). The classificatory system could not be a system of blood ties, McLennan asserted, because the terms themselves do not refer to actual blood ties. "Mother," for example, does not mean "begetting mother," nor does "father" mean "begetting father." Further, McLennan adduced, all or almost all peoples having the classificatory system also have what is now termed a matrilineal descent system. A people, McLennan believed, cannot have two different "systems of blood relationship"—one given in the system of kinship terminology and the other in a system that traces descent through females only. The descent system of any society must be one or the other, not both, or at least only one can have any important practical consequences. The conclusion was obvious. In McLennan's now famous words, "The classificatory system is a system of mutual salutations merely" (McLennan 1876: 366).

Although, as McLennan saw it, Morgan's data did not support Morgan's conclusions, they did support his own as outlined in *Primitive Marriage*. Using Morgan's data on systems of kinship terminology, McLennan proceeded to reinterpret them as showing that the system of blood ties and the system of address grew up together.

If *Systems* had challenged McLennan's ideas, *Primitive Marriage* and McLennan's defense of it also challenged Morgan's. Morgan had received a copy of McLennan's *Studies in Ancient History* while *Ancient Society* was in press, and he took that occasion to append a thirteen-page "Note" on the controversy. In it, Morgan observed that McLennan denied that the kinship terminologies which the tables in *Systems* exhibit "are systems of consanguinity and affinity, thus going to the bottom of the subject" (Morgan 1877: 510). McLennan did so, Morgan suggested, because *Systems* refuted various of McLennan's major theories (Morgan 1877: 510). Not unexpectedly, Morgan also rejected McLennan's contention that he should have sought the origin of the system in the origin of the classification, maintaining that the system and the classification "mean the same thing, and cannot by any possibility be made to mean anything different. To seek the origin of one is to seek the origin of the other" (Morgan 1877: 520). It was a conclusion perhaps strengthened by the fact that Morgan had found no society that did not possess a true system of kinship terminology.

McLennan did not publish any reply to Morgan's rebuttal, perhaps because he was then in ill health (Peter Rivière in McLennan 1970: xiii). Morgan's own health also began to decline after publication of *Ancient Society*. Both men died in 1881, Morgan on December 17, six months after McLennan's death on June 16. Their dispute, however, did not end. It has echoed and reechoed in discussions of the nature of kinship terminology ever since.

The third of Morgan's British contemporaries, Edward B. Tylor, had shown relatively little interest in social organization until 1889 when he published a paper "On a Method of Investigating the Development of Institutions: Applied to Laws of Marriage and Descent." Among the topics he considered in it were "exogamy"—a term McLennan had coined—and Morgan's "classificatory system." These Tylor suggested were in fact two sides of one institution, the simplest form of exogamy being that between two classes or sections (moieties)—which, as Tylor also observed, was a conclusion reached by Lorimer Fison in *Kamilaroi and Kurnai* (Fison and Howitt 1880), a volume dedicated to Morgan and for which Morgan had written an introduction. Tylor found some confirmation of this idea in his statistical data, which showed an association between classificatory systems and exogamy and an even greater association between cross-cousin marriage and exogamy—leading Tylor to suggest that although McLennan and Morgan "believed themselves adversaries" they were, in fact, "all the while allies pushing forward the same doctrine from different sides" (Tylor 1889: 265). Others, however, took the position that both Morgan and McLennan were wrong, among them, C. Staniland Wake (1889), Carl Nicolai Starke (1889), and Edward Westermarck (1891).

About the same time, the discipline started to become professionalized. The first graduate students in anthropology in the United States entered in 1890: two at Harvard and one at Clark University. This generation of anthropologists had grown up in a social and intellectual climate quite different from that earlier in the century. To these Ph.D.s, formally trained in the discipline, the older anthropologists, all those who had founded the discipline and given it direction, were "amateurs." These younger anthropologists saw their task as putting anthropology on a "scientific" basis—as if those who had gone before them did not know what science is and how it is practiced.

Among those who early received a doctorate in anthropology was Alfred L. Kroeber. As is evident in his paper "Classificatory Systems of Relationship," published in 1909, Kroeber's interest in kinship was an interest in the principles underlying terminological systems. This concern led him to reject Morgan's distinction between descriptive and classificatory systems with the comment, "A moment's reflection is sufficient to show that every language groups together under single designations many distinct degrees and kinds of relationship" (Kroeber 1909: 77). To cite one of Kroeber's examples: "Our word brother includes both the older and the younger brother and the brother of a man and of a woman. It therefore embraces or classifies four relationships" (Kroeber 1909: 77). "Systems of terms of relationship," Kroeber thus asserted, "can be properly compared through an examination of the categories of relationship which they involve and of the degree to which they give expression to these categories." He listed eight such categories or principles, the first two of which were "the difference between persons of the same and of separate generations" and "the difference between lineal and collateral relationship" (Kroeber 1909: 78).

Further, Kroeber maintained, terms of relationship do not reflect sociology: "They are determined primarily by language and can be utilized for sociological inferences only with extreme caution" (1909:84). This position was directly opposite from that of W. H. R. Rivers, who, four years after Kroeber's paper appeared in the *Journal of the Royal Anthropological Institute*, gave a series of three lectures at the London School of Economics. These were published the following year under the title *Kinship and Social Organization*. The first sentence of the first lecture gives Rivers's position: "The aim of these lectures is to demonstrate the close connection which exists between methods of denoting relationship or kinship and forms of social organization, including those based on different varieties of the institution of marriage" (Rivers 1968: 39).

Rivers, an experimental psychologist, was twelve years older than Kroeber and had shown no interest in anthropology, let alone kinship studies, until he joined the Torres Straits expedition in 1899. He had been induced to go because of the opportunity to conduct psychological experiments on some non-Western peoples. The experiments he did led him to consider the possibility that the traits so tested might be inherited, and he and others on the expedition began collecting genealogies. Having collected these data, Rivers sought uses to which they might be put. They could, Rivers suggested, be a source of information on both vital statistics—data on average family size, sex and age ratio, female fertility, and the like—and social statistics—such matters as the frequency of exogamous and endogamous marriages, polygamy, the levirate, and sister exchange (Rivers 1900: 78–81). But of all the possibilities, Rivers came to believe, the most important was their use in the study of kinship terminology.

Ignoring the field methods advocated and used by Morgan (1871: 134–36), Rivers contended that the questions then raging in discussions of kinship terminology could only be resolved by a "scientific" method: his "genealogical method" (Rivers 1910). Morgan had collected data on kinship terminology by means of his lengthy schedule—a list of some two hundred kin types, obtaining from the individual he was interviewing the kin term for each kin type. Rivers's procedure was first to ask his informant for his pedigree and then to ask for the kin terms that he used for each of these relatives, optimally procuring three such separate genealogies (Rivers 1910: 3–4).

The data Rivers so collected was much less extensive than that Morgan had, and perhaps not unexpectedly Rivers suggested that Morgan's work might not have been so neglected or rejected by his contemporaries "if Morgan had been less industrious and had amassed a smaller collection of material which could have been embodied in more available form" and if he had been "content to demonstrate, as he might to some extent have done from his own material, the close connection between the terminology of the classificatory system of relationship and forms of social organization" (Rivers 1968: 41).

Just how the opposing positions of Rivers and Kroeber were to be reconciled was not clear to their contemporaries. Aspects of the question were treated in various books and articles, but no major statements appeared until mid-century, when virtually simultaneously three quite different solutions, each combining elements of Rivers's and Kroeber's contentions, were offered: one by George Peter Murdock, another by Claude Levi-Strauss, and a third most closely identified with the names of Ward H. Goodenough and Floyd G. Lounsbury.

Combining Rivers's idea that kinship terminology is "vigorously determined by social conditions" and Kroeber's idea that many factors determine kinship terminology, Murdock made an extended cross-cultural test of the relationship between various sets of kin terms and various social factors—among them, sororal and non-sororal polygyny, the levirate, the sororate, cross-cousin marriage, patrilineal and matrilineal descent groups, and neolocal, matrilocal, and patrilocal residence. He reported the results in his then widely acclaimed *Social Structure* (1949). They were perhaps the expectable ones. The tests showed positive correlations, many of them low or weak. Because they were statistically significant, however, they could be interpreted as vindicating both the idea that kinship terms are socially determined and the idea that "the causal factors actually operating in any particular situation are always multiple" (Murdock 1949: 126).

But the basic question remained. Were the correlations low or weak because "kinship terms mean different things," have a multiplicity of causes, or because "the hypothesis being tested is faulty" (David M. Schneider in Rivers 1968: 14)? It is, of course, in the nature of a statistical test only to confirm the probability of a relationship. It leaves the question of what caused what unanswered, and also the reasons for the exceptions. The resolution of these matters necessarily must be left to other kinds of analyses.

One such was offered by Lévi-Strauss in *Les Structures élémentaires de la parenté*, a volume dedicated to Morgan's memory and published the same year as Murdock's *Social Structure*, whose dedication also included mention of Morgan's name, among others. Enormously influential, a revised edition appeared in 1967, and an English translation of this edition in 1969 under the title *Elementary Structures of Kinship*. In it Lévi-Stauss combined a version of Kroeber's idea that kinship is to be studied as "logic" and "psychology" with Rivers's idea of it as social structure, concerned primarily with marriage and descent.

Like Rivers, Lévi-Strauss saw a relationship between kinship and marriage rules, but unlike Rivers did not seek to demonstrate that there is such a relationship. Rather, he was interested in the comparison of the structure of kinship systems. These structures, he suggested, may be divided into two major types: (1) elementary structures of kinship—"systems in which the nomenclature permits the immediate determination of the circle of kin and that of affines, that is, those systems which prescribe marriage with a certain type of relative, or, alternatively, those which, while defining all members of the society as relatives, divide them into two categories, viz., possible spouses and prohibited spouses" and (2) complex structures—"systems which limit themselves to defining the circle of relatives and leave the determination of the spouse to other mechanisms, economic or psychological" (Lévi-Strauss 1969: xxiii). As its title suggests, *Elementary Structures of Kinship* treats the former. Central in this discussion is Levi-Strauss's conclusion that "It is always a system of exchange that we find at the origin of rules of marriage" (Lévi-Strauss 1969: 478)—a conclusion that led him to a consideration of how the various forms of these systems of exchange between wife-givers and wife-takers work, or, more accurately, how the models of these systems work.

Not surprisingly, given its size, scope, and erudition, *Elementary Structures of Kinship* commanded much attention—an interest that waned following much discussion of Lévi-Strauss's analysis and presumptions on which it was based. Even Lévi-Strauss himself abandoned the project of writing a second volume, one on complex systems, when what he regarded as transitional cases, Crow and Omaha systems, proved intractable to his kind of analysis (Lévi-Strauss 1969: xxxv–xxxix).

Not long after Murdock and Lévi-Strauss offered their solutions to the impasse between Rivers and Kroeber, others came to advocate one or another form of semantic analysis, including those termed "componential analysis" and "formal analysis" (Goodenough 1951: 102–10, 1956; Lounsbury 1956, 1964a, 1964b). This and other methods of semantic analysis combined Kroeber's view that kinship terminology should be studied as logic and language with a more plausible version of Rivers's contention that natives cannot think abstractly: speakers of a language rely on rules of which they may not be consciously aware. It is, then, the business of the analyst to discover these rules that a speaker of a language must know in order to speak the language correctly, that is, to speak such that he is intelligible to other speakers of that language. In the case of kinship terminology in particular, semantic analysis seeks to learn what a speaker of the language has to know in order to correctly use each kin term.

In this type of analysis the task is to collect a list of all the kin terms used in a particular language and, for each kin term, all the kin types to which it refers. From inspection of these data, the "components" (what Kroeber termed "principles" or "categories") are ascertained and the definition of each kin term written as a combination ("paradigm") of the components ("factors," "dimensions," etc.) unique to that term.

Like those of earlier suggestions, the promise of this method faded when different analysts looking at essentially the same data came to different conclusions. As Goodenough (1965: 259) phrased it: "It is possible to devise at least several different models of the semantic structure of a terminological system, any one of which will predict adequately the permissible denotata of its terms." No particular agreement could be reached even in the case of our own terminology as the several analyses of it showed (Wallace and Atkins 1960; Romney and D'Andrade 1964; Goodenough 1965). The difficulty was the familiar one: differences over what data were to be chosen for analysis and differences as to what in these data were to be regarded as most significant.

Prospects

To date, then, it cannot be said that a truly satisfactory solution has been found to the great riddle of kinship Morgan posed a century and a quarter ago: Why should the various peoples of the world have the kinship terminologies that they do? Just what the answer ultimately will turn out to be cannot, of course, be predicted. More certain is that this riddle will continue to attract attention—for it involves a number of fundamental questions. These include not only those concerning that popular subject "marriage and the family" but also those respecting the wider human experience and its history. The study of "kinship" is thus also one that, perhaps more than any other, touches on matters of interest in the various subdisciplines: sociocultural, linguistic, and biological anthropology. Because it does, it gives concrete expression to that much discussed issue: the unity of the discipline of anthropology as a whole.

Bibliographic Note

The best general biography of Morgan is Carl Resek's *Lewis Henry Morgan: American Scholar* (1960). Bernhard J. Stern's earlier effort, *Lewis Henry Morgan: Social Evolutionist* (1931) is marred by factual error, although still useful for the quotes from the Morgan papers in the University of Rochester that it contains. Thomas R. Trautmann's *Lewis Henry Morgan and the Invention of Kinship* (1987) is an indispensable guide for understanding the course of Morgan's research that resulted in the publication of his *Systems of Consanguinity and Affinity*.

In "How Morgan Came to Write *Systems of Consanguinity and Affinity*" (1957), Leslie A. White publishes Morgan's journal entry of October 19, 1859, containing Morgan's reflections on his research to that date and general plans for future work. *Lewis Henry Morgan: The Indian Journals*, also edited by White (1959), publishes Morgan's journals of his four western field trips, somewhat edited.

References Cited

Fison, Lorimer, and A. W. Howitt
  1880   *Kamilaroi and Kurnai.* Melbourne: G. Robertson.
Goodenough, Ward H.
  1951   *Property, Kin and Community in Truk.* Yale University Publications in Anthropology 46.
  1956   Componential Analysis and the Study of Meaning. *Language* 32: 195–216.
  1965   Yankee Kinship Terminology: A Problem in Componential Analysis. *American Anthropologist* 67 (5, pt. 2): 259–87.
Kroeber, A. L.
  1909   Classificatory Systems of Relationship. *Journal of the Royal Anthropological Institute of Great Britain and Ireland* 39: 77–84.
Lévi-Strauss, Claude
  1949   *Les Structures élémentaires de la parenté.* Paris: Universitaires de France.
  1969   *Elementary Structures of Kinship.* Boston: Beacon Press.
Lounsbury, Floyd G.
  1956   A Semantic Analysis of Pawnee Kinship Usage. *Language* 32: 158–94.
  1964a A Formal Account of the Crow- and Omaha-type Kinship Terminologies. In *Explorations in Cultural Anthropology: Essays in Honor of George Peter Murdock,* edited by Ward H. Goodenough. New York: McGraw-Hill.
  1964b The Structural Analysis of Kinship Semantics. *Proceedings of the Ninth International Congress of Linguists,* edited by Horace G. Lunt, 1073–93.
Lubbock, John
  1865   *Pre-historic Times.* London and Edinburgh: Williams and Norgate.
  1870   *The Origin of Civilisation and the Primitive Condition of Man.* London: Longmans, Green. University of Chicago Press, Reprint, Chicago: 1978.
  1871   On the Development of Relationships. *Journal of the Anthropological Institute of Great Britain and Ireland* 1: 1–29.
  1875   *The Origin of Civilisation.* Third edition. London: Longmans, Green.
McLennan, John F.
  1970   *Primitive Marriage: An Inquiry into the Origin of the Form of Capture in Marriage Ceremonies.* Edinburgh: Adam and Charles Black. Reprint, Chicago: University of Chicago Press, 1970.
  1876   *Studies in Ancient History.* London: B. Quaritch.
Morgan, Lewis H.
  1851   *League of the Ho-dé-no-sau-nee, or Iroquois.* Rochester NY: Sage and Brother.
  1858   Laws of Descent of the Iroquois. *Proceedings of the American Association for the Advancement of Science* 11 (2): 132–48.
  1868   A Conjectural Solution of the Origin of the Classificatory System of Relationship. *Proceedings of the American Academy of Arts and Sciences* 7: 436–77.
  1871   *Systems of Consanguinity and Affinity of the Human Family.* Smithsonian Contributions to Knowledge 17.
  1877   *Ancient Society; or, Researches in the Lines of Human Progress from Savagery through Barbarism to Civilization.* New York: Henry Holt.
Murdock, George Peter
  1949   *Social Structure.* New York: Macmillan.
Resek, Carl
  1960   *Lewis Henry Morgan: American Scholar.* Chicago: University of Chicago Press.

Rivers, W. H. R.

1900 A Genealogical Method of Collecting Social and Vital Statistics. *Journal of the Anthropological Institute of Great Britain and Ireland* 30: 74–82.

1910 The Genealogical Method of Anthropological Inquiry. *The Sociological Review* 3: 1–12. (Reprinted in *Rivers* 1968: 97–109.)

1914 *Kinship and Social Organization*. London: Constable. Reprint, London: Althone Press, 1968.

Romney, A. Kimball, and Roy D'Andrade

1964 Cognitive Aspects of English Kin Terms. *American Anthropologist* 66 (3, pt. 2): 146–79.

Starke, Carl Nicolai

1889 *The Primitive Family in Its Origin and Development*. London: Kegan Paul, Trench. Reprint, Chicago: University of Chicago Press, 1976.

Stern, Bernhard J.

1931 *Lewis Henry Morgan: Social Evolutionist*. Chicago: University of Chicago Press.

Trautmann, Thomas R.

1987 *Lewis Henry Morgan and the Invention of Kinship*. Berkeley: University of California Press.

Tylor, Edward B.

1865 *Researches into the Early History of Mankind and the Development of Civilization*. London: J. Murray.

1871 *Primitive Culture*. 2 vols. London: J. Murray.

1889 On a Method of Investigating the Development of Institutions: Applied to Laws of Marriage and Descent. *Journal of the Anthropological Institute of Great Britain and Ireland* 18: 245–69.

Wake, C. Staniland

1889 *The Development of Marriage and Kinship*. London: George Redway. Reprint, Chicago: University of Chicago Press, 1967.

Wallace, Anthony F. C., and John Atkins

1960 The Meaning of Kinship Terms. *American Anthropologist* 62: 58–60.

Westermarck, Edward

1891 *The History of Human Marriage*. 2 vols. London and New York: Macmillan.

White, Leslie A.

1957 How Morgan Came to Write *Systems of Consanguinity and Affinity*. *Papers of the Michigan Academy of Science, Arts, and Letters* 42: 257–68.

1959 *Lewis Henry Morgan: The Indian Journals, 1859–62*. Ann Arbor: University of Michigan Press.

PREFACE.

PHILOLOGY has proved itself an admirable instrument for the classification of nations into families upon the basis of linguistic affinities. A comparison of the vocables and of the grammatical forms of certain languages has shown them to be dialects of a common speech; and these dialects, under a common name, have thus been restored to their original unity as a family of languages. In this manner, and by this instrumentality, the nations of the earth have been reduced, with more or less of certainty, to a small number of independent families.

Some of these families have been more definitely circumscribed than others. The Aryan and Semitic languages have been successfully traced to their limits, and the people by whom they are severally spoken are now recognized as families in the strict and proper sense of the term. Of those remaining, the Turanian is rather a great assemblage of nations, held together by slender affinities, than a family in the Aryan or Semitic sense. With respect to the Malayan it approaches nearer to the true standard, although its principal divisions are marked by considerable differences. The Chinese and its cognates, as monosyllabic tongues, are probably entitled upon linguistic grounds to the distinction of an independent family of languages. On the other hand, the dialects and stock languages of the American aborigines have not been explored, with sufficient thoroughness, to determine the question whether they were derived from a common speech. So far as the comparisons have been made they have been found to agree in general plan and in grammatical structure.

The remarkable results of comparative philology, and the efficiency of the method upon which as a science it proceeds, yield encouraging assurance that it will ultimately reduce all the nations of mankind to families as clearly circumscribed as the Aryan and Semitic. But it is probable that the number of these families, as finally ascertained, will considerably exceed the number now recognized. When this work of philology has been fully accomplished, the question will remain whether the connection of any two or more of these families can be determined from the materials of language. Such a result is not improbable, and yet, up to the present time, no analysis of language, however searching and profound, has been able to cross the barrier which separates the Aryan from the Semitic languages,—and these are the two most thoroughly explored,—and discover the processes by which, if originally derived from a common speech, they have become radically changed in their ultimate forms. It was with special reference to the bearing which the systems of consanguinity and affinity of the several families of mankind might have upon this vital question, that the research, the results of which are contained in this volume, was undertaken.

Kin terms

In the systems of relationship of the great families of mankind some of the oldest memorials of human thought and experience are deposited and preserved. They have been handed down as transmitted systems, through the channels of the blood, from the earliest ages of man's existence upon the earth; but revealing certain definite and progressive changes with the growth of man's experience in the ages of barbarism. To such conclusions the evidence, drawn from a comparison of the forms which now prevail in different families, appears to tend.

All the forms thus far discovered resolve themselves, in a comprehensive sense, into two, the *descriptive* and the *classificatory*, which are the reverse of each other in their fundamental conceptions. As systems of consanguinity each contains a plan, for the description and classification of kindred, the formation of which was an act of intelligence and knowledge. They ascend by the chain of derivation to a remote antiquity, from which, as defined and indurated forms, their propagation commenced. Whether as organic forms they are capable of crossing the line of demarcation which separates one family from another, and of yielding evidence of the ethnic connection of such families, will depend upon the stability of these forms, and their power of self-perpetuation in the streams of the blood through indefinite periods of time. For the purpose of determining, by ample tests, whether these systems possess such attributes, the investigation has been extended over a field sufficiently wide to embrace four-fifths and upwards, numerically, of the entire human family. The results are contained in the Tables.

evolutionism

A comparison of these systems, and a careful study of the slight but clearly marked changes through which they have passed, have led, most unexpectedly, to the recovery, conjecturally at least, of the great series or sequence of customs and institutions which mark the pathway of man's progress through the ages of barbarism; and by means of which he raised himself from a state of promiscuous intercourse to final civilization. The general reader may be startled by the principal inference drawn from the classificatory system of relationship, namely, that it originated in the intermarriage of brothers and sisters in a communal family, and that this was the normal state of marriage, as well as of the family, in the early part of the unmeasured ages of barbarism. But the evidence in support of this conclusion seems to be decisive. Although it is difficult to conceive of the ex-

barbarism had sibling incest

tremity of a barbarism, which such a custom presupposes, it is a reasonable presumption that progress through and out from it was by successive stages of advancement, and through great reformatory movements. Indeed, it seems probable that the progress of mankind was greater in degree, and in the extent of its range, in the ages of barbarism than it has been since in the ages of civilization; and that it was a harder, more doubtful, and more intense struggle to reach the threshold of the latter, than it has been since to reach its present status. Civilization must be regarded as the fruit, the final reward, of the vast and varied experience of mankind in the barbarous ages. The experiences of the two conditions are successive links of a common chain of which one cannot be interpreted without the other. This system of relationship, instead of revolting the mind, discloses with sensible clearness, " the hole of the pit whence [we have been] digged" by the good providence of God.

A large number of inferior nations are unrepresented in the Tables, and to that extent the exposition is incomplete. But it is believed that they are formed upon a scale sufficiently comprehensive for the determination of two principal questions: First, whether a system of relationship can be employed, independently, as a basis for the classification of nations into a family? and, secondly, whether the systems of two or more families, thus constituted, can deliver decisive testimony concerning the ethnic connection of such families when found in disconnected areas? Should their uses for these purposes be demonstrated in the affirmative, it will not be difficult to extend the investigation into the remaining nations.

In the progress of the inquiry it became necessary to detach from the Turanian family the Turk and Finn stocks, and to erect them into an independent family. It was found that they possessed a system of relationship fundamentally different from that which prevailed in the principal branches of the Southern division, which, in strictness, stood at the head of the family. The new family, which for the reasons stated I have ventured to make, I have named the *Uralian*. At the same time the Chinese have been returned to the Turanian family upon the basis of their possession, substantially, of the Turanian system of consanguinity. Still another innovation upon the received classification of the Asiatic nations was rendered necessary from the same consideration. That portion of the people of India who speak the Gaura language have been transferred from the Aryan to the Turanian family, where their system of consanguinity places them. Although ninety per centum of the vocables of the several dialects of this language are Sanskritic, against ten per centum of the aboriginal speech, yet the grammar as well as the system of relationship, follows the aboriginal form.[1] If grammatical structure is

---

[1] Caldwell's Dravidian Comp. Gram. Intro. p. 39.

the governing law in the classification of dialects and stock languages, and this is one of the accepted canons of philology,[1] then the "Dialects of India," as they are called in the Genealogical Table of the Aryan Family of Languages, do not, for this reason, properly belong in that connection, but in the Turanian. Their system of relationship, which has followed the preponderance of numbers or of the blood, is also Turanian in form, although greatly modified by Sanskritic influence. The Sanskritic people of India, notwithstanding their Aryan descent, and the probable purity of their blood to the present day, have been, in a linguistic sense, absorbed into an aboriginal stock. Having lost their native tongue, which became a dead language, they have been compelled to adopt the vernacular idioms of the barbarians whom they conquered, and to content themselves with furnishing, from the opulent Sanskrit, the body of the vocables, whilst the remainder and the grammar were derived from the aboriginal speech. If they are ever rescued from this classification it must be affected through reasons independent of their present language and system of consanguinity.

LEWIS H. MORGAN.

ROCHESTER, NEW YORK,
    January, 1866.

Acknowledgments.

For the materials, out of which the Tables were formed, I am indebted upon a scale which far outruns my ability to render a sufficient acknowledgment. The names attached to the list of schedules will afford some impression of the extent to which correspondents in foreign countries must have been taxed, as well as wearied, in studying through the intricate and elaborate forms they were severally solicited to investigate, and to develop in a systematic manner upon a schedule of printed questions. Without their co-operation, as well as gratuitous labor, it would have been impossible to present the Tables, except those relating to the American Indian nations. Each schedule should be received as the separate contribution of the person by whom it was made, and the credit of whatever information it contains is due to him. Without intending to discriminate, in the least, amongst the number of those named in the Tables, I desire to mention the fact that much the largest number of the foreign schedules were furnished by American missionaries. There is no class of men upon the earth, whether considered as scholars, as philanthropists, or as gentlemen, who have earned for themselves a more distinguished reputation. Their labors, their self-denial, and their endurance in the work to which

---

[1] Müller's Science of Language. Scribner's ed., p. 82.

they have devoted their time and their great abilities, are worthy of admiration. Their contributions to history, to ethnology, to philology, to geography, and to religious literature, form a lasting monument to their fame. The renown which encircles their names falls as a wreath of honor upon the name of their country.

I am also indebted to S. B. Treat, D. D., Secretary of the American Board of Commissioners for Foreign Missions; to Hon. Walter Lowrie, Secretary of the Board of Missions of the Presbyterian Church; to J. G. Warren, D. D., Secretary of the American Baptist Missionary Union; and to Rev. Philip Peltz, Secretary of the Board of Missions of the American Dutch Reformed Church, for their co-operation, and for the facilities which they afforded me during a protracted correspondence with the missionaries of their respective boards.

missionaries

In an especial manner I am indebted to the Smithsonian Institution for efficient co-operation in procuring materials for this work.

To the late Hon. Lewis Cass, Secretary of State of the United States, and to his immediate successor, Hon. William H. Seward, I am also under very great obligations for commending this investigation to the diplomatic and consular representatives of the United States in foreign countries; and for government facilities whilst conducting with them an equally extended correspondence.

U. S. Consulates p. 5

Among many others whom I ought to mention I must not omit the names of my friends J. H. McIlvaine, D. D., of the College of New Jersey, who has been familiar with the nature and objects of this research from its commencement, and from whom I have received many important suggestions; Chester Dewey, D. D., of the University of Rochester, now an octogenarian, but with undiminished relish for knowledge in all its forms, whose friendly advice it has been my frequent privilege to accept; and Samuel P. Ely, Esq., of Marquette, at whose hospitable home on Lake Superior the plan for the prosecution of this investigation was formed.

There is still another class of persons to whom my obligations are by no means the least, and they are the native American Indians of many different nations, both men and women, who from natural kindness of heart, and to gratify the wishes of a stranger, have given me their time and attention for hours, and even days together, in what to them must have been a tedious and unrelished labor. Without the information obtained from them it would have been entirely impossible to present the system of relationship of the Indian family.

Indians

PART I.

DESCRIPTIVE SYSTEM OF RELATIONSHIP.

ARYAN, SEMITIC, AND URALIAN FAMILIES.

WITH A TABLE.

CHAPTER I.

INTRODUCTION.

Causes which induced this Investigation—Peculiar System of Relationship among the Iroquois—Discovery of the same among the Ojibwas—Inferences from their Identity—Its prevalence throughout the Indian Family rendered probable—Plan adopted to determine the Question—Results Reached—Evidence of the existence of the same System in Asia obtained—Range of the Investigation Extended—Necessity for including, as far as possible, all the Families of Mankind—Method of Prosecuting the Inquiry—General Results—Materials Collected—Order of Arrangement—Tables of Consanguinity and Affinity—Systems of Relationship as a Basis of Classification—Their Use in Ethnological Investigations.

As far back as the year 1846, while collecting materials illustrative of the institutions of the Iroquois, I found among them, in daily use, a system of relationship for the designation and classification of kindred, both unique and extraordinary in its character, and wholly unlike any with which we are familiar. In the year 1851[1] I published a brief account of this singular system, which I then supposed to be of their own invention, and regarded as remarkable chiefly for its novelty. Afterwards, in 1857,[2] I had occasion to reëxamine the subject, when the idea of its possible prevalence among other Indian nations suggested itself, together with its uses, in that event, for ethnological purposes. In the following summer, while on the south shore of Lake Superior, I ascertained the system of the Ojibwa Indians; and, although prepared in some measure for the result, it was with some degree of surprise that I found among them the same elaborate and complicated system which then existed among the Iroquois. Every term of relationship was radically different from the corresponding term in the Iroquois; but the classification of kindred was the same. It was manifest that the two systems were identical in their fundamental characteristics. It seemed probable, also, that both were derived from a common source, since it was not supposable that two peoples, speaking dialects of stock-languages as widely separated as the Algonkin and Iroquois, could simultaneously have invented the same system, or derived it by borrowing one from the other.

From this fact of identity several inferences at once suggested themselves. As its prevalence among the Seneca-Iroquois rendered probable its like prevalence among other nations speaking dialects of the Iroquois stock-language, so its existence and use among the Ojibwas rendered equally probable its existence and use among the remaining nations speaking dialects of the Algonkin speech. If investigation should establish the affirmative of these propositions it would give to

---

[1] League of the Iroquois, p. 85.

[2] Proceedings of American Association for Advancement of Science for 1857, Part II., p. 132.

the system a wide distribution. In the second place, its prevalence among these nations would render probable its like prevalence among the residue of the American aborigines. If, then, it should be found to be universal among them, it would follow that the system was coeval, in point of time, with the commencement of their dispersion over the American continent; and also that, as a system transmitted with the blood, it might contain the necessary evidence to establish their unity of origin. And in the third place, if the Indian family came, in fact, from Asia, it would seem that they must have brought the system with them from that continent, and have left it behind them among the people from whom they separated; further than this, that its perpetuation upon this continent would render probable its like perpetuation upon the Asiatic, where it might still be found; and, finally, that it might possibly furnish some evidence upon the question of the Asiatic origin of the Indian family.

This series of presumptions and inferences was very naturally suggested by the discovery of the same system of consanguinity and affinity in nations speaking dialects of two stock-languages. It was not an extravagant series of speculations upon the given basis, as will be more fully understood when the Seneca and Ojibwa systems are examined and compared. On this simple and obvious line of thought I determined to follow up the subject until it was ascertained whether the system was universal among the American aborigines; and, should it become reasonably probable that such was the fact, then to pursue the inquiry upon the Eastern Continent, and among the islands of the Pacific.

The work was commenced by preparing a schedule of questions describing the persons in the lineal, and the principal persons embraced in the first five collateral lines, which, when answered, would give their relationship to *Ego*, and thus spread out in detail the system of consanguinity and affinity of any nation with fullness and particularity. This schedule, with an explanatory letter, was sent in the form of a printed circular to the several Indian missions in the United States, to the commanders of the several military posts in the Indian country, and to the government Indian agents. It was expected to procure the information by correspondence as the principal instrumentality. From the complicated nature of the subject the results, as might, perhaps, have been foreseen, were inconsiderable. This first disappointment was rather a fortunate occurrence than otherwise, since it forced me either to abandon the investigation, or to prosecute it, so far as the Indian nations were concerned, by personal inquiry. It resulted in the several annual explorations among the Indian nations, the fruits of which will be found in Tables II., which is attached to Part II. By this means all the nations, with but a few exceptions, between the Atlantic and the Rocky Mountains, and between the Arctic Sea and the Gulf of Mexico, were reached directly, and their systems of relationship procured. Some of the schedules, however, were obtained by correspondence, from other parties.

Having ascertained as early as the year 1859 that the system prevailed in the five principal Indian stock-languages east of the mountains, as well as in several of the dialects of each, its universal diffusion throughout the Indian family had become extremely probable. This brought me to the second stage of the investigation, namely, to find whether it prevailed in other parts of the world. To determine that question would require an extensive foreign correspondence, which a private individual could not hope to maintain successfully. To make the attempt effectual would require the intervention of the national government, or the co-operation of some literary or scientific institution. It is one of the happy features of American society that any citizen may ask the assistance of his government, or of any literary or scientific institution in the country, with entire freedom; and with the further consciousness that his wishes will be cheerfully acceded to if deserving of encouragement. This removed what might otherwise have been a serious obstacle. In this spirit I applied to Prof. Joseph Henry, Secretary of the Smithsonian Institution, for the use of the name of the latter in foreign countries in the conduct of the correspondence; and further desired him to procure a letter from the Secretary of State of the United States to our diplomatic and consular representatives abroad, commending the subject to their favorable attention. With both of these requests Prof. Henry complied in the most cordial manner. From January, 1860, until the close of the investigation, the larger part of the correspondence was conducted under the official name of the Institution, or under cover by the Secretary of State. By these means an unusual degree of attention was secured to the work in foreign countries, the credit of which is due to the influence of the Smithsonian Institution, and to the official circular of the late General Cass, then Secretary of State. In addition to these arrangements I had previously solicited and obtained the co-operation of the secretaries of the several American missionary boards, which enabled me to reach, under equally favorable conditions, a large number of American missionaries in Asia and Africa, and among the islands of the Pacific.

From the distinguished American missionary, Dr. Henry W. Scudder, of Arcot, India, who happened to be in this country in 1859, I had obtained some evidence of the existence of the American Indian system of relationship among the Tamilian people of South-India. This discovery opened still wider the range of the proposed investigation. It became necessary to find the limits within which the systems of the Aryan and Semitic families prevailed, in order to ascertain the line of demarcation between their forms and that of the eastern Asiatics. The circumscription of one was necessary to the circumscription of the other. In addition to this it seemed imperative to include the entire human family within the scope of the research, and to work out this comprehensive plan as fully as might be possible. The nearer this ultimate point was approximated the more instructive would be the final results. It was evident that the full significance of identity of systems in India and America would be lost unless the knowledge was made definite concerning the relations of the Indo-American system of relationship to those of the western nations of Europe and Asia, and also to those of the nations of Africa and Polynesia. This seeming necessity greatly increased the magnitude of the undertaking, and at the same time encumbered the subject with a mass of subordinate materials.

In the further prosecution of the enterprise the same schedule and circular were sent to the principal missions of the several American boards, with a request that the former might be filled out, according to its design, with the system of relationship of the people among whom they were respectively established; and that such explanations might be given as would be necessary to its interpretation. This class of men possess peculiar qualifications for linguistic and ethnological researches; and, more than this, they reside among the nations whose systems of consanguinity were relatively of the most importance for the purpose in hand. The tables will show how admirably they performed the task.

They were also sent to the diplomatic and consular representatives of the United States in foreign countries, through whom another, and much larger, portion of the human family was reached. By their instrumentality, chiefly, the system of the Aryan family was procured. A serious difficulty, however, was met in this direction, in a difference of language, which the official agents of the government were unable, in many cases, to surmount. In Europe and Asia the number of schedules obtained through them, in a completely executed form, was even larger than would reasonably have been expected; while in Africa, in South America, and in Mexico and Central America the failure was nearly complete.

To supply these deficiencies an attempt was made to reach the English missions in the Eastern Archipelago and in Polynesia; and also Spanish America through the Roman Catholic bishops and clergy of those countries; but the efforts proved unsuccessful.

The foregoing are the principal, but not the exclusive, sources from which the materials contained in the tables were derived.

A large number of schedules, when returned, were found to be imperfectly filled out. Misapprehension of the nature and object of the investigation was the principal cause. The most usual form of mistake was the translation of the questions into the native language, which simply reproduced the questions and left them unanswered. A person unacquainted with the details of his own system of relationship might be misled by the form of each question which describes a person, and not at once perceive that the true answer should give the relationship sustained by this person to *Ego*. As our own system is descriptive essentially, a correct answer to most of the questions would describe a person very much in the form of the question itself, if the system of the nation was descriptive. But, on the contrary, if it was classificatory, such answers would not only be incorrect in fact, but would fail to show the true system. The utmost care was taken to guard against this misapprehension, but, notwithstanding, the system of several important nations, thus imperfectly procured, was useless from the difficulty, not to say impossibility, of repeating the attempt in remote parts of the earth, where it required two years, and sometimes three, for a schedule to be received and returned. In some cases, where the correspondent was even as accessible as India, it required that length of time, and the exchange of several letters, to correct and perfect the details of a single schedule. Every system of relationship is intrinsically difficult until it has been carefully studied. The classificatory form is complicated in addition to being difficult, and totally unlike our own. It is easy, therefore, to perceive that when a person was requested to work out, in detail, the system of a foreign people he would find it necessary, in the first instance, to master his own, and after that to meet and overcome the difficulties of another, and, perhaps, radically different form. With these considerations in mind it is a much greater cause for surprise that so many schedules were completely executed than that a considerable number should have failed to be so.

The schedule is necessarily self-corrective as to a portion of the persons described, since the position of *Ego* and his or her correlative person is reversed in different questions. It was also made self-confirmatory in other ways, so that a careful examination would determine the question of its correctness or non-correctness in essential particulars. This was especially true with respect to the classificatory system. Notwithstanding all the efforts made to insure correctness, it is not supposable that the tables are free from errors; on the contrary, it is very probable that a critical examination will bring to light a large number. I believe, however, that they will be found to be substantially correct.

It was a matter of some difficulty to determine the proper order of arrangement of the materials thus brought together. The natural order of the subject has been followed as closely as possible. All the forms of consanguinity exhibited in the tables resolve themselves into two, the descriptive and the classificatory. Of these the former is the most simple in its structure, and for this reason should be first considered. It embraces the systems of the Aryan, Semitic, and Uralian families, which are identical in their radical characteristics. The classificatory system has one principal form, the Indo-American, and two subordinate forms, the Malayan and the Eskimo. Of these, the Malayan is the most simple, and probably underlying form, and, as such, would come first; after this in its natural order would be either the Turanian or the American Indian, at convenience, since each stands in the same relation to the Malayan; and after these the Eskimo, which stands disconnected from the systems of either of the families named. But it was found advisable to reverse this order, as to the classificatory form, on account of the preponderating amount of materials, and to consider, first, the American Indian, then the Turanian, and after all these the Malayan and Eskimo.

In Part I., after discussing the elements of a system of relationship considered in the abstract, the Roman form of consanguinity and affinity is taken up and explained with fulness and particularity, as typical of the system of the Aryan family. This is followed by a brief exposition of the forms which prevail in other branches of the family for the purpose of indicating the differences between them and the typical form; and also to ascertain the general characteristics of the system. The systems of the Semitic and Uralian families are then treated in the same manner, and compared with the Aryan form. By this means, also, the limits of the spread of the descriptive system of relationship are determined.

In Part II., after discussing certain preliminary facts, the Seneca-Iroquois form is first explained with minuteness of detail, as typical of the system of the American Indian family. After this the several forms in the remaining branches of this family are presented; confining the discussion, so far as could properly be done, to the points of difference between them and the typical system.

In Part III., the Tamilian form is first presented and explained as typical of the system of the Turanian family; after which the forms that prevail among the other Asiatic nations represented in the tables, are considered and compared with the typical form. These are necessarily presented with fulness of detail, particularly the Chinese, from the great amount of divergence from the typical form which they exhibit. After this the system of the Malayan family, of which the Hawaiian form is typical, is presented and explained in the same manner. The Eskimo system concludes the series.

Lastly, the general results of a comparison of these several forms, together with a conjectural solution of the origin of the classificatory system, furnish the subject of a concluding chapter.

The tables, however, are the main results of this investigation. In their importance and value they reach far beyond any present use of their contents which the writer may be able to indicate. If they can be perfected, and the systems of the unrepresented nations be supplied, their value would be greatly increased. The classification of nations is here founded upon a comparison of their several forms of consanguinity. With some exceptions, it harmonizes with that previously established upon the basis of linguistic affinities. One rests upon blood, the preponderance of which is represented by the system of relationship; the other is founded upon language, the affinities of which are represented by grammatical structure. One follows ideas indicated in a system of relationship and transmitted with the blood; the other follows ideas indicated in forms of speech and transmitted in the same manner. It may be a question which class of ideas has been perpetuated through the longest periods of time.

In Table I., which is appended to Part I., will be found the system of the Aryan, Semitic, and Uralian families; in Table II., which is likewise appended to Part II., that of the American Indian family; and in Table IV., which is appended to Part III., that of the Turanian and Malayan families. The plan adopted in framing these tables was to bring each specific relationship, among a certain number of affiliated nations, into the same column, so that their agreement or disagreement as to any particular relationship might be seen at a glance. This arrangement will facilitate the comparison. The names of the several nations, whose systems are brought together, will be found in a column on the left of the page; and the descriptions of the several persons, whose relationships to *Ego* are shown, are written in a consecutive series at the top of the several columns. In this series the lineal line is first given. This is followed by the first collateral line in its male and female branches; and this, in turn, by the second collateral line in its male and female branches on the father's side, and in its male and female branches on the mother's side; after which, but less fully extended, will be found the third, fourth, and fifth collateral lines. An inspection of the tables will make the method sufficiently obvious.

If these tables prove sufficient to demonstrate the utility of systems of relationship in the prosecution of ethnological investigations, one of the main objects of this work will be accomplished. The number of nations represented is too small to exhibit all the special capabilities of this instrumentality. The more thoroughly the system is explored in the different nations of the same family of speech, especially where the form is classificatory, the more ample and decisive the evidence will become which bears upon the question of their genetic connection. The threads of this connection between remotely affiliated nations are sometimes recovered in the most unexpected manner. These tables, therefore, as but the commencement of the work if this new instrument in ethnology invite the test of criticism. The remaining nations of the earth can be reached and their systems procured, should it seem to be desirable; and it may be found that this is the most simple as well as compendious method for the classification of nations upon the basis of affinity of blood.[1]

---

[1] In the appendix to this volume will be found a schedule of questions adapted to this work. Any person interested in the furtherance of this object, who will procure the system of any nation not represented in the tables, or correct or complete any deficient schedule therein, will render a special service to the author. The schedule may be sent to the Smithsonian Institution, at Washington; and when published full credit will be given to the person furnishing the same.

2   May, 1868.

CHAPTER II.

GENERAL OBSERVATIONS UPON SYSTEMS OF RELATIONSHIPS.

Marriage the basis of the Family Relationships—Systems of Consanguinity and Affinity—Each Person the Centre of a Group of Kindred—The System of Nature Numerical—Not necessarily adopted—Every System embodies Definite Ideas—It is a Domestic Institution—Two Radical Forms—The Descriptive, and the Classificatory—Aryan, Semitic, and Uralian Families have the former—Turanian, American Indian, and Malayan the latter—Divergence of Collateral Lines from Lineal, Characteristic of the First—Mergence of Collateral Lines in the Lineal, of the Second—Uses of these Systems depend upon the Permanence of their Radical Forms—Evidence of their Modification—Direction of the Change—Causes which tend to the Stability of their Radical Features.

IN considering the elements of a system of consanguinity the existence of marriage between single pairs must be assumed. Marriage forms the basis of relationships. In the progress of the inquiry it may become necessary to consider a system with this basis fluctuating, and, perhaps, altogether wanting. The alternative assumption of each may be essential to include all the elements of the subject in its practical relations. The natural and necessary connection of consanguinei with each other would be the same in both cases; but with this difference, that in the former the lines of descent from parent to child would be known, while in the latter they would, to a greater or less extent, be incapable of ascertainment. These considerations might affect the form of the system of consanguinity.

The family relationships are as ancient as the *family*. They exist in virtue of the law of derivation, which is expressed by the perpetuation of the species through the marriage relation. A system of consanguinity, which is founded upon a community of blood, is but the formal expression and recognition of these relationships. Around every person there is a circle or group of kindred of which such person is the centre, the *Ego*, from whom the degree of the relationship is reckoned, and to whom the relationship itself returns. Above him are his father and his mother and their ascendants, below him are his children and their descendants; while upon either side are his brothers and sisters and their descendants, and the brothers and sisters of his father and of his mother and their descendants, as well as a much greater number of collateral relatives descended from common ancestors still more remote. To him they are nearer in degree than other individuals of the nation at large. A formal arrangement of the more immediate blood kindred into lines of descent, with the adoption of some method to distinguish one relative from another, and to express the value of the relationship, would be one of the earliest acts of human intelligence.

Should the inquiry be made how far nature suggests a uniform method or plan for the discrimination of the several relationships, and for the arrangement of kindred into distinct lines of descent, the answer would be difficult, unless it was first assumed that marriage between single pairs had always existed, thus rendering definite the lines of parentage. With this point established, or assumed, a natural system, numerical in its character, will be found underlying any form which man may contrive; and which, resting upon an ordinance of nature, is both universal and unchangeable. All of the descendants of an original pair, through intermediate pairs, stand to each other in fixed degrees of proximity, the nearness or remoteness of which is a mere matter of computation. If we ascend from ancestor to ancestor in the lineal line, and again descend through the several collateral lines until the widening circle of kindred circumscribes millions of the living and the dead, all of these individuals, in virtue of their descent from common ancestors, are bound to the "*Ego*" by the chain of consanguinity.

The blood relationships, to which specific terms have been assigned, under the system of the Aryan family, are few in number. They are grandfather and grandmother, father and mother, brother and sister, son and daughter, grandson and granddaughter, uncle and aunt, nephew and niece, and cousin. Those more remote in degree are described either by an augmentation or by a combination of these terms. After these are the affineal or marriage relationships, which are husband and wife, father-in-law and mother-in-law, son-in-law and daughter-in-law, brother-in-law and sister-in-law, step-father and step-mother, step-son and step-daughter, and step-brother and step-sister; together with such of the husbands and wives of blood relatives as receive the corresponding designation by courtesy. These terms are barely sufficient to indicate specifically the nearest relationships, leaving much the largest number to be described by a combination of terms.

So familiar are these ancient household words, and the relationships which they indicate, that a classification of kindred by means of them, according to their degrees of nearness, would seem to be not only a simple undertaking, but, when completed, to contain nothing of interest beyond its adaptation to answer a necessary want. But, since these specific terms are entirely inadequate to designate a person's kindred, they contain in themselves only the minor part of the system. An arrangement into lines, with descriptive phrases to designate such relatives as fall without the specific terms, becomes necessary to its completion. In the mode of arrangement and of description diversities may exist. Every system of consanguinity must be able to ascend and descend in the lineal line through several degrees from any given person, and to specify the relationship of each to *Ego*; and also from the lineal, to enter the several collateral lines and follow and describe the collateral relatives through several generations. When spread out in detail and examined, every scheme of consanguinity and affinity will be found to rest upon definite ideas, and to be framed, so far as it contains any plan, with reference to particular ends. In fine, a system of relationship, originating in necessity, is a domestic institution, which serves to organize a family by the bond of consanguinity. As such it possesses a degree of vitality and a power of self-perpetuation commensurate with its nearness to the primary wants of man.

In a general sense, as has elsewhere been stated, there are but two radically distinct forms of consanguinity among the nations represented in the tables.   One of these is descriptive and the other classificatory. The first, which is that of the Aryan, Semitic, and Uralian families, rejecting the classification of kindred, except so far as it is in accordance with the numerical system, describes collateral consanguinei, for the most part, by an augmentation or combination of the primary terms of relationship.   These terms, which are those for husband and wife, father and mother, brother and sister, and son and daughter, to which must be added, in such languages as possess them, grandfather and grandmother, and grandson and granddaughter, are thus restricted to the primary sense in which they are here employed.   All other terms are secondary. Each relationship is thus made independent and distinct from every other.   But the second, which is that of the Turanian, American Indian, and Malayan families, rejecting descriptive phrases in every instance, and reducing consanguinei to great classes by a series of apparently arbitrary generalizations, applies the same terms to all the members of the same class.   It thus confounds relationships, which, under the descriptive system, are distinct, and enlarges the signification both of the primary and secondary terms beyond their seemingly appropriate sense.

Although a limited number of generalizations have been developed in the system of the first-named families, which are followed by the introduction of additional special terms to express in the concrete the relationships thus specialized, yet the system is properly characterized as descriptive, and was such originally.   It will be seen in the sequel that the partial classification of kindred which it now contains is in harmony with the principles of the descriptive form, and arises from it legitimately to the extent to which it is carried; and that it is founded upon conceptions entirely dissimilar from those which govern in the classificatory form. These generalizations, in some cases, are imperfect when logically considered; but they were designed to realize in the concrete the precise relationships which the descriptive phrases suggest by implication.   In the Erse, for example, there are no terms for uncle or aunt, nephew or niece, or cousin; but they were described as *father's brother*, *mother's brother*, *brother's son*, and so on.   These forms of the Celtic are, therefore, purely descriptive.   In most of the Aryan languages terms for these relationships exist.   My father's brothers and my mother's brothers, in English, are generalized into one class, and the term *uncle* is employed to express the relationship.   The relationships to *Ego* of the two classes of persons are equal in their degree of nearness, but not the same in kind; wherefore, the Roman method is preferable, which employed *patruus* to express the former, and *avunculus* to indicate the latter.   The phrase " father's brother" describes a person, but it likewise implies a bond of connection which *patruus* expresses in the concrete. In like manner, my father's brother's son, my father's sister's son, my mother's brother's son, and my mother's sister's son are placed upon an equality by a similar generalization, and the relationship is expressed by the term *cousin*.   They stand to me in the same degree of nearness, but they are related to me in four different ways.   The use of these terms, however, does not invade the principles of the descriptive system, but attempts to realize the implied relationships in a simpler manner.   On the other hand, in the system of the last-named families, while corresponding terms exist, their application to particular persons is founded upon very different generalizations, and they are used in an apparently arbitrary manner. In Seneca-Iroquois, for example, my father's brother is my father. Under the system he stands to me in that relationship and no other. I address him by the same term, *Hä-nih'*, which I apply to my own father. My mother's brother, on the contrary, is my uncle, *Hoc-no'-seh*, to whom, of the two, this relationship is restricted. Again, with myself a male, my brother's son is my son, *Ha-ah'-wuk*, the same as my own son; while my sister's son is my nephew, *Ha-yă'-wan-da*; but with myself a female, these relationships are reversed. My brother's son is then my nephew; while my sister's son is my son. Advancing to the second collateral line, my father's brother's son and my mother's sister's son are my brothers, and they severally stand to me in the same relationship as my own brother; but my father's sister's son and my mother's brother's son are my cousins. The same relationships are recognized under the two forms, but the generalizations upon which they rest are different.

In the system of relationship of the Aryan, Semitic, and Uralian families, the collateral lines are maintained distinct and perpetually divergent from the lineal, which results, theoretically as well as practically, in a dispersion of the blood. The value of the relationships of collateral consanguinei is depreciated and finally lost under the burdensomeness of the descriptive method. This divergence is one of the characteristics of the descriptive system. On the contrary, in that of the Turanian, American Indian, and Malayan families, the several collateral lines, near and remote, are finally brought into, and merged in the lineal line, thus theoretically, if not practically, preventing a dispersion of the blood. The relationships of collaterals by this means is both appreciated and preserved. This mergence is, in like manner, one of the characteristics of the classificatory system.

How these two forms of consanguinity, so diverse in their fundamental conceptions and so dissimilar in their structure, came into existence it may be wholly impossible to explain. The first question to be considered relates to the nature of these forms and their ethnic distribution, after the ascertainment of which their probable origin may be made a subject of investigation. While the existence of two radically distinct forms appears to separate the human family, so far as it is represented in the tables, into two great divisions, the Indo-European and the Indo-American, the same testimony seems to draw closer together the several families of which these divisions are composed, without forbidding the supposition that a common point of departure between the two may yet be discovered. If the evidence deposited in these systems of relationship tends, in reality, to consolidate the families named into two great divisions, it is a tendency in the direction of unity of origin of no inconsiderable importance.

After the several forms of consanguinity and affinity, which now prevail in the different families of mankind, have been presented and discussed, the important question will present itself, how far these forms become changed with the progressive changes of society. The uses of systems of relationship to establish the genetic connection of nations will depend, first, upon the structure of the system, and, secondly, upon the stability of its radical forms. In form and feature they must be found able, when once established, to perpetuate themselves through indefinite periods of time. The question of their use must turn upon that of the stability of their radical features. Development and modification, to a very considerable extent, are revealed in the tables in which the comparison of forms is made upon an extended scale; but it will be observed, on further examination, that these changes are further developments of the fundamental conceptions which lie, respectively, at the foundation of the two original systems.

There is one powerful motive which might, under certain circumstances, tends to the overthrow of the classificatory form and the substitution of the descriptive, but it would arise after the attainment of civilization. This is the inheritance of estates. It may be premised that the bond of kindred, among uncivilized nations, is a strong influence for the mutual protection of related persons. Among nomadic stocks, especially, the respectability of the individual was measured, in no small degree, by the number of his kinsmen. The wider the circle of kindred the greater the assurance of safety, since they were the natural guardians of his rights and the avengers of his wrongs. Whether designedly or otherwise, the Turanian form of consanguinity organized the family upon the largest scale of numbers. On the other hand, a gradual change from a nomadic to a civilized condition would prove the severest test to which a system of consanguinity could be subjected. The protection of the law, or of the State, would become substituted for that of kinsmen; but with more effective power the rights of property might influence the system of relationship. This last consideration, which would not arise until after a people had emerged from barbarism, would be adequate beyond any other known cause to effect a radical change in a pre-existing system, if this recognized relationships which would defeat natural justice in the inheritance of property. In Tamilian society, where my brother's son and my cousin's son are both my sons, a useful purpose may have been subserved by drawing closer, in this manner, the kindred bond; but in a civilized sense it would be manifestly unjust to place either of these collateral sons upon an equality with my own son for the inheritance of my estate. Hence the growth of property and the settlement of its distribution might be expected to lead to a more precise discrimination of the several degrees of consanguinity if they were confounded by the previous system.

Where the original system, anterior to civilization, was descriptive, the tendency to modification, under the influence of refinement, would be in the direction of a more rigorous separation of the several lines of descent, and of a more systematic description of the persons or relationships in each. It would not necessarily lead to the abandonment of old terms nor to the invention of new. This latter belongs, usually, to the formative period of a language. When that is passed, compound terms are resorted to if the descriptive phrases are felt to be inconvenient. Wherever these compounds are found it will be known at once that they are modern in the language. The old terms are not necessarily radical, but they have become so worn down by long-continued use as to render the identification of their component parts impossible. While the growth of nomenclatures of relationship tends to show the direction in which existing systems have been modified, it seems to be incapable of throwing any light upon the question whether a classificatory form ever becomes changed into a descriptive, or the reverse. It is more difficult, where the primitive system was classificatory, to ascertain the probable direction of the change. The uncivilized nations have remained substantially stationary in their condition through all the centuries of their existence, a circumstance eminently favorable to the permanency of their domestic institutions. It is not supposable, however, that they have resisted all modifications of their system of consanguinity. The opulence of the nomenclature of relationships, which is characteristic of the greater portion of the nations whose form is classificatory, may tend to show that, if it changed materially, it would be in the direction of a greater complexity of classification. It is extremely difficult to arrive at any general conclusions upon this question with reference to either form. But it may be affirmed that if an original system changes materially, after it has been adopted into use, it is certain to be done in harmony with the ideas and conceptions which it embodies, of which the changes will be further and logical developments.

It should not be inferred that forms of consanguinity and affinity are either adopted, modified, or laid aside at pleasure. The tables entirely dispel such a supposition. When a system has once come into practical use, with its nomenclature adopted, and its method of description or of classification settled, it would, from the nature of the case, be very slow to change. Each person, as has elsewhere been observed, is the centre around whom a group of consanguinei is arranged. It is my father, my mother, my brother, my son, my uncle, my cousin, with each and every human being; and, therefore, each one is compelled to understand, as well as to use, the prevailing system. It is an actual necessity to all alike, since each relationship is personal to *Ego*. A change of any of these relationships, or a subversion of any of the terms invented to express them, would be extremely difficult if not impossible; and it would be scarcely less difficult to enlarge or contract the established use of the terms themselves. The possibility of this permanence is increased by the circumstance that these systems exist by usage rather than legal enactment, and therefore the motive to change must be as universal as the usage. Their use and preservation are intrusted to every person who speaks the common language, and their channel of transmission is the blood. Hence it is that, in addition to the natural stability of domestic institutions, there are special reasons which contribute to their permanence, by means of which it is rendered not improbable that they might survive changes of social condition sufficiently radical to overthrow the primary ideas in which they originated.

These preliminary statements being made, it is now proposed to explain and compare the systems of relationship of the several nations and families represented in the tables. In doing this the order therein adopted will be followed. Invoking the patient attention of the reader, I will endeavor to perform this task with as much brevity and clearness as I may be able to command.

CHAPTER III.

SYSTEM OF RELATIONSHIP OF THE ARYAN FAMILY.

Roman System of Consanguinity and Affinity—Framed by the Civilians—Relationships of two kinds—By Consanguinity, or Blood—By Affinity, or Marriage—Lineal and Collateral Consanguinity—Diagram—Method of Description by Lines explained—Diagram of the Roman Civilians—Completeness and precision of the Roman System—Immense number of Consanguinei within the near Degrees—Computations—Rapid intermingling of the Blood of a People—Mode of Computing Degrees under the Civil Law—Under the Canon Law—Under the Common Law—Origin of the Variance—Marriage Relationships fully discriminated—English System barren of Terms—Opulence of the Roman Nomenclature of Relationships.

An understanding of the framework and principles of our own system of relationship is a necessary preparatory step to the consideration of those of other nations. It was originally strictly descriptive. After the settlement and civilization of the several branches of the Aryan family, there was engrafted upon it, among several of them, a method of description differing materially from the primitive form, but without invading its radical features, or so far overspreading them as to conceal the simple original. The new element, which came naturally from the system itself, was introduced by the Roman civilians to perfect the framework of a code of descents. Their improvements have been adopted into the system of the several branches of the family, to which the Roman influence extended. To obtain a knowledge historically of our present English form, we must resort to the Roman as it was perfected by the civilians, and left by them in its codified form. The additions were slight, but they changed materially the method of describing kindred. They consisted chiefly in the establishment of the relationships of uncle and aunt on the father's side, and on the mother's side, which were unknown in the primitive system, and in the adoption of a descriptive method based upon these terms, which, with proper augments, enabled them to systematize the relationships in the first five collateral lines. We are also indebted to the Latin speech for the modern portion of our nomenclature of relationships.

It is evident, however, that the elaborate and scientific arrangement of kindred into formally described lines of descent employed by the civilians, and which became the law of the State, was not adopted by the Roman people, except in its least complicated parts. There are reasons for believing that the ancient method, modified by the substitution of some of the new terms of relationship in the place of descriptive phrases, was retained for those nearest in degree, and that more distant relatives were described without any attempt to preserve the artificial distinctions among the several lines. This variance between the forms used by the people and by the State, whenever it occurs in this family of nations, is entirely immaterial, since the two do not conflict.

It should also be observed that it is impossible to recover the system of consanguinity and affinity of any people, in its details, from the lexicon, or even from the literature of their language, if it has ceased to be a living form. The Hebrew and Sanskrit are examples. If it had been reduced to a statute and thus had become a law of the State, it would be found in a codified form. In all other cases it can only be obtained, in its completeness, by a direct resort to the people.

In the Pandects[1] and in the Institutes[2] the system of relationship of the Roman civil law has been preserved with minuteness and precision, with full explanations of its provisions and method of arrangement. A careful examination of its details will furnish us the readiest knowledge of our own, as well as unfold the principles which must govern the formation of any strictly philosophical system.

Relationships are of two kinds: First, by consanguinity, or blood: second, by affinity, or marriage. Consanguinity, which is the relation of persons descended from the same ancestor, is also of two kinds, lineal and collateral. Lineal consanguinity is the connection which subsists among persons of whom one is descended from the other. Collateral consanguinity is the connection which exists among persons who are descended from a common ancestor, but not from each other. Marriage relationships exist by custom.

In every supposable plan of consanguinity, where marriage between single pairs exists, there must be a lineal and several collateral lines. Each person, also, in constructing his own table becomes the central point, or *Ego*, from whom outward is reckoned the degree of relationship of each kinsman, and to whom the relationship returns. His position is necessarily in the lineal line. In a chart of relationships this line is vertical. Upon it may be inscribed, above and below any given person, his several ancestors and descendants in a direct series from father to son, and these persons together will constitute his right lineal male line, which is also called the trunk, or common stock of descent. Out of this trunk line emerge the several collateral lines, male and female, which are numbered outwardly. It will be sufficient for a perfect knowledge of the system to limit the explanation to the main lineal line, and to a single male and female branch of each of the collateral lines, including those on the father's side and on the mother's side, and proceeding in each from the parent to one only of his or her children, although it will include but a small portion of the kindred of *Ego* either in the ascending or descending series. An attempt to follow all the divisions and branches of the several collateral lines, which increase in number in the ascending series in a geometrical ratio, would embarrass the reader without rendering the system itself more intelligible. The first collateral line, male, consists of my brother and his descendants, and the first, female, of my sister and her descendants. The second collateral line, male, on the father's side, consists of my father's brother and his descendants, and the second, female, of my father's sister and her descendants; the second collateral

---

[1] Pand., Lib. XXXVIII. tit. x. "De gradibus et adfinibus et nominibus eorum."

[2] Inst. Just., Lib. III. tit. vi. "De gradibus cognationum."

3   May, 1868.

line, male, on the mother's side, is composed of my mother's brother and his descendants, and the second, female, of my mother's sister and her descendants. The third collateral line, male, on the father's side, consists of my grandfather's brother and his descendants, and third, female, of my grandfather's sister and her descendants; on the mother's side, the same line, male, is composed of my grandmother's brother and his descendants, and the same, female, of my grandmother's sister and her descendants.   It will be noticed, in the last case, that we have turned out of the lineal line on the father's side into that on the mother's side.   The fourth collateral line, male, on the father's side, consists of my great-grandfather's brother and his descendants; and the fourth, female, of my great-grandfather's sister and her descendants; the same line, male, on the mother's side, is composed of my great-grandmother's brother and his descendants; and the same, female, of my great-grandmother's sister and her descendants.   In like manner, the fifth collateral line, male, on the father's side, consists of my great-great-grandfather's brother and his descendants; and the fifth, female, of my great-great-grandfather's sister and her descendants; the same line, male, on the mother's side is composed of my great-great-grandmother's brother and his descendants; and the same, female, of my great-great-grandmother's sister and her descendants.   These five lines embrace the great body of our kindred who are within the range of practical or even necessary recognition.

Where there are several brothers and sisters of each ancestor, they constitute so many branches of each line respectively.   If I have several brothers and sisters, they and their descendants constitute as many lines, each independent of the other, as I have brothers and sisters; but all together they form my first collateral line in two branches, a male and a female.   In like manner the several brothers and sisters of my father and of my mother, with their respective descendants, make up as many lines, each independent of the other, as there are brothers and sisters; but all unite in forming my second collateral line in two divisions, that on the father's side and that on the mother's side, and in four principal branches, two male and two female.   If the third collateral line were run out fully in the ascending series, it would give four general divisions of ancestors and eight principal branches; and the number of each would increase in the same ratio in each successive collateral line.   With such a maze of branches, lines, and divisions, embracing such a multitude of consanguinei, it will be seen at once that a method of arrangement and description which should maintain each distinct, and render the whole intelligible, would be no ordinary achievement.   This work was perfectly accomplished by the Roman civilians, and in a manner so entirely simple as to elicit admiration.   It will be seen, however, in the sequel, that the development of the nomenclature to the requisite extent must have been so extremely difficult that it would probably never have occurred except under the stimulus of an urgent necessity.   The absence, from the primitive system, of the relationships of uncle and aunt, in the concrete form, was the first want to be supplied to render the new method attainable.   Nor was this alone sufficient; it was also necessary to discriminate those on the father's side from those on the mother's side, and to elaborate independent terms for each, an achievement made in a limited number only of the languages of mankind. These indispensable terms finally appeared in *patruus* and *amita* for uncle and aunt on the father's side, and in *avunculus* and *matertera* for uncle and aunt on the mother's side, which, with suitable augments, enabled the civilians to indicate specifically the first person in the second, third, fourth, and fifth collateral lines on the father's side and on the mother's side. After these were secured, the improved Roman method of describing collateral consanguinei became possible, as well as established. The development of these relationships, in the concrete, was the principal, as well as the greatest advance in the system of relationship, made by any of the members of the Aryan family.

All languages are able to describe kindred by a combination of the primary terms; and this method is still used, to the exclusion of the secondary terms, when it becomes necessary to be specific, unless the Roman method is employed. In the description we commence at *Ego*, and ascend first to the common ancestor, and then down the collateral line to the person whose relationship is sought, as in the English; or, reversing the initial point, commence with the latter, and ascend to the common ancestor, and then descend to the former as in the Erse. To describe a *cousin*, in the male branch of the second collateral line, we use in English the phrase *father's brother's son;* or, in Erse, *son of the brother of my father;* for a *second cousin*, in the same branch of the third collateral line, we say, in English, *father's father's brother's son's son;* in Erse, *son of the son of the brother of the father of my father.* Where the relationship of grandfather is discriminated by a specific or a compound term, we may say *grandfather's brother's grandson;* but as this would fail to show whether the person was on the father's side or on the mother's side, a further explanation must be added. The inconvenience of this method, which was the primitive form of the Aryan family, is sufficiently obvious. It was partially overcome, in process of time, by the generalization of the relationships of uncle and aunt, nephew and niece, and cousin, and the invention of special terms for their expression in the concrete. A little reflection upon the awkwardness and cumbersomeness of a purely descriptive system of relationship will illustrate the necessity, first, for common terms for the nearest collateral degrees, and, secondly, of a scientific method for the description of consanguinei. It will also enable us to appreciate the serious difficulties overcome, as well as the great advance made, by the Romans in the formal system which they established, or, rather, engrafted upon the original form.

If, then, we construct a diagram of the right lineal line, male, and the first five collateral lines, male and female, on the father's side, and limit each collateral line at its commencement to a single brother and sister of *Ego*, and to a single brother and sister of each of the lineal ancestors of *Ego*, and these several lines are projected from parent to child, the collateral lines will be parallel with each other and divergent from the lineal in the actual manner of the outflow of the generations. The diagram (Plate I.) will afford a more distinct impression of the relation of the lineal and several collateral lines to each other, and of the nomenclature of the Roman system, than could be given by a description. It exhibits the lines named, arranged with reference to a central person, or *Ego*, and indicates the relationship to him of each of the persons in these several lines. The great superiority of its nomenclature over those of the remaining Aryan nations will be recognized at once, as well as the thoroughly scientific method of description by which it is distinguished above all other systems which have ever been framed.

From *Ego* to *tritavus*, in the lineal line, are six generations of ascendants, and from the same to *trinepos* are the same number of descendants, in the description of which but four radical terms are used. If it were desirable to ascend above the sixth ancestor, *tritavus* would become a new starting-point of description; thus, *tritavi pater*, the father of *tritavus*, and so upward to *tritavi tritavus*, who is the twelfth ancestor of *Ego* in the lineal right line, male. In our rude nomenclature the phrase *grandfather's grandfather* must be repeated six times to express the same relationship, or rather to describe the same person. In like manner *trinepotis trinepos* carries us to the twelfth descendant of *Ego* in the right lineal line, male. He is the great-grandson of the great-grandson of *trinepos*, the great-grandson of the great-grandson of *Ego*.

The first collateral line, male, which commences with brother, *frater*, is composed of him and his lineal descendants, proceeding in the right line from father to son; thus, *fratris filius*, literally son of brother, *fratris nepos*, grandson of brother, and on to *fratris trinepos*, the great-grandson of the great-grandson of the brother of *Ego*. If it were necessary to extend the description to the twelfth generation, *fratris trinepos* would become a second starting-point, from which we should have *fratris trinepotis trinepos*, the great-grandson of the great-grandson of *fratris trinepos*, the great-grandson of the great-grandson of the brother of *Ego*. By this simple method *frater* is made the root of descent in this line, and every person within it is referred to him by the force of this term in the description; and we know at once that each person described belongs to the first collateral line, male. It is, therefore, in itself complete as well as specific. In like manner, and with like results, the first collateral line female commences with sister, *soror*, giving for the series *sororis filia*, sister's daughter; *sororis neptis*, sister's granddaughter; and on to *sororis trineptis*, her sixth, and to *sororis trineptis trineptis*, her twelfth descendant. While these two branches of the first collateral line originate, in strictness, in the father, *pater*, who is the common bond of connection between them, yet by making the brother and sister the root of descent of their respective branches in the description, not only this line, but, also, its two branches, are maintained distinct; and the relationship of each person to *Ego* is specialized by force of the description. This is one of the chief excellencies of the system as a purely scientific method of distinguishing and describing kindred.

The second collateral line, male, on the father's side, commences with father's brother, *patruus*, and is composed of him and his descendants, limited in the diagram to the right line. Each person, by the terms used to describe him, is referred with entire precision to his proper position in the line, and his relationship is indicated; thus, *patrui filius*, son of paternal uncle, *patrui nepos*, grandson of paternal uncle, and on to *patrui trinepos*, the sixth descendant of *patruus*. If it became necessary to extend this line to the twelfth generation we should have, after passing through the intermediate degrees, *patrui trinepotis trinepos*, the great-grandson of the great-grandson of *patrui trinepos*, the great-grandson of the great-grandson of *patruus*. It will be observed that the term for cousin is rejected in the diagram, as it is, also, in the formal method of the Pandects. He is described as *patrui filius*, but he was also called a brother patruel, *frater patruelis*, and among the people at large by the common term for cousin, *consobrinus*. The second collateral line, female, on the father's side commences with father's sister, *amita*, paternal aunt; and her descendants are described according to the same general plan; thus, *amitæ filia*, paternal aunt's daughter, *amitæ neptis*, paternal aunt's granddaughter, and so on to *amitæ trineptis*, and to *amitæ trineptis trineptis*. In this branch of the line the term for cousin, *amitinus, amitina*, is also set aside for the formal phrase *amitæ filia*, although the former indicates specifically, by its etymology, this particular one of the four cousins.[1] Among the people the term *consobrinus, consobrina* was applied to this cousin, as it was indiscriminately to each of the four.[2]

In accordance with the same general plan the third collateral line, male, on the father's side commences with grandfather's brother, who is styled *patruus magnus*, or great-uncle. At this point in the nomenclature special terms fail and compounds are resorted to, although the relationship itself is in the concrete, the same as grandfather. It is evident that this relationship was not discriminated until a comparatively modern period. No existing language, so far as this inquiry has been extended, possesses an original or radical term for great-uncle, although without the Roman method the third collateral line cannot be described except by the Celtic. In the Turanian, Malayan, and American Indian forms, where the classification of consanguinei is altogether different, he is a grandfather. If he were called simply *grandfather's brother*, the phrase would describe a person, leaving the relationship as a matter of implication; but if great-uncle, it expresses a relationship in the concrete, and becomes equivalent to a specific term. The specialization of this relationship was clearly the work of the civilians to perfect a general plan of consanguinity. With the first person in this branch of the line thus made definite as a great-uncle, all of his descendants are referred to him, in their description, as the root of descent; and the line, the side, whether male or female, and the degree of the relationship of each person, are at once severally and jointly expressed. This line may be extended, in like manner, to the twelfth descendant, which would give for the series *patrui magni filius*, son of the paternal great-uncle; *patrui magni nepos*, grandson of paternal great-uncle; and thus on to *patrui magni trinepotis trinepos*, the great-grandson of the great-grandson of *putrui magni trinepos*, the great-grandson of the great-grandson of paternal great-uncle. The third collateral line, female, on the same side commences with grandfather's sister, who is styled *amita magna*, or great-aunt; and her descendants are described in like manner, and with the same effect.

---

[1] Amitæ tuæ filii consobrinum te appellant, tu illos amitinos. Inst. Just., Lib. III. tit. vi. § ii.

[2] Item fratres patrueles, sorores patrueles, id est qui quæ-ve ex duobus fratribus progenerantur; item consobrini consobrinæ, id est qui quæ-ve ex duobus sororibus nascuntur (quasi consorini); item amitini amitinæ, id est qui quæ-ve ex fratre et sorore propagantur; sed ferè vulgus istos omnes communi appellatione consobrinos vocat. Pand., Lib. XXXVIII. tit. x.

The fourth and fifth collateral lines, male, on the father's side, commence, respectively, with great-grandfather's brother, who is styled *patruus major*, greater paternal uncle, and with great-great-grandfather's brother, who is called *patruus maximus*, greatest paternal uncle.   In extending the series we have in the fourth line, *patrui majoris filius*, *patrui majoris nepos*, and on to *patrui majoris trinepos ;* and in the fifth, *patrui maximi filius*, *patrui maximi nepos*, and thus onward to *patrui maximi trinepos.*   On the same side the corresponding female collateral lines commence, respectively, with *amita major*, greater paternal aunt, and *amita maxima*, greatest paternal aunt; and the description of persons in each follows in the same order.

Both the diagram and the description of consanguinei have thus far been limited to the lineal line male, and to the several collateral lines on the father's side. Another diagram with an entire change of terms, except in the first collateral line, is required to exhibit the right lineal line, female, and the four collateral lines, male and female, beyond the first.   The necessity for independent terms for uncle and aunt on the mother's side to complete the Roman method is now apparent, the relatives on the mother's side being equally numerous, and entirely distinct. These terms were found in *avunculus*, maternal uncle, and *matertera*, maternal aunt.   The first collateral line, as before stated, remains the same, as it commences with brother and sister.   In the second collateral line, male, on the mother's side we have for the series *avunculus*, *avunculi filius*, *avunculi nepos*, and on to *avunculi trinepotis trinepos*, if it were desirable to extend the description to the twelfth descendant of the maternal uncle.   In the female branch of the same line we have for the series *matertera*, *materteræ filia*, *materteræ neptis*, and on to *materteræ trineptis*.   In the third collateral line, male, same side, we have for the series *avunculus magnus*, *avunculi magni filius*, *avunculi magni nepos*, and on as before ; and the female branch of the same line, commencing with *matertera magna*, maternal great-aunt, is extended in the same manner.   The fourth and fifth collateral lines, male, on the same side commence, respectively, with *avunculus major*, and *avunculus maximus ;* and the corresponding female branches with *matertera major*, and *matertera maxima*, and their descendants, respectively, are described in the same manner.

Since the first five collateral lines embraced as wide a circle of kindred as it was necessary to include for the practical purposes of a code of descents, the ordinary diagram used by the Roman civilians did not extend beyond this number.   In the form of description adopted by Coke and the early English lawyers, and which was sanctioned by the same use of the terms in the Pandects, we find *propatruus magnus* instead of *patruus major*, and *abpatruus magnus* instead of *patruus maximus*. By adopting this mode of augmentation, which is also applied to *avus* in the lineal line, we have for the commencement of the sixth and seventh collateral lines, male, on the father's side, *atpatruus magnus* and *tripatruus magnus*, with corresponding changes of gender for the female branches.   This would exhaust the power of the nomenclature of the Roman system.   For collateral lines beyond the seventh it was necessary to resort again to the descriptive form which followed the chain of consanguinity from degree to degree.

The diagram (Plate I.) is not in the form of that used by the civilians. It is framed in accordance with the form adopted by Blackstone[1] for the purpose of showing the several persons in the lineal and collateral lines, who stand at equal distances in degree from their respective common ancestors, in the same horizontal plane. Since the movement downward is with equal step in each of the lines, the common law method has an advantage over that of the civil law in illustrating to the eye the relative position of consanguinei. In the Institutes of Justinian[2] the original diagram of the civilians is given and verified in the text (Plate II.). It arranges the several collateral lines at right angles with the lineal, which makes them transverse instead of collateral, and, at the same time, furnishes the reasons why they are described both in the Pandects and in the Institutes, as the transverse rather than the collateral lines.[3] In this diagram three lines meet in each ancestor, one of which is lineal, and the other two, consisting of a male and female branch, are transverse. With a slight examination it becomes perfectly intelligible. In some respects it is the most simple form in which the system can be represented. But since it does not show the relative position of consanguinei in the lineal and collateral lines with reference to their distance with *Ego* from the common ancestor, the first form appears to be preferable. This diagram is a venerable relic of the all-embracing Roman jurisprudence. It is interesting, even impressive, to us, as the chart with which that greatly distinguished class of men, the Roman jurists, "illustrated to the eye," as well as explained to the understanding, the beautiful and perfect system of consanguinity we have been considering.

It is obvious, as before remarked, that these diagrams include but a small portion of the immediate consanguinei of each individual, as the right line only is given proceeding from the parent to one only of his or her children, while there might be several brothers and sisters of *Ego*, and of each of his several ancestors, each of whom would send off as many additional lines as he or she left children, each leaving descendants. This might be true also of every person in each of the collateral lines. Beside this, the number of common ancestors increases at each degree, ascending, in geometrical progression, which multiplies indefinitely the number of ascending lines. It would be entirely impossible to construct a diagram of the lineal and first and second collateral lines alone, which would show all the possible consanguinei of *Ego* within six degrees of nearness. These considerations will serve to illustrate the complexity of the problem which the civilians solved by furnishing a logical and comprehensive system of relationship. It is the singular merit of the Roman form that, without being obscure or complicated, it contains all the elements of arrangement and description which are necessary to resolve any given case, and all that is material to a right understanding of descents.

---

[1] Blackstone's Commentaries; Tables of Consanguinity, II. 254. Watkins adopts the same method; Laws of Descent, Table of Con., p. 123. And Domat also substantially; Civil Law, Strahan's Trans. Table on Con. II. 210.

[2] Lib. III. tit. vii.

[3] The usual phrase is "Ex transverso sive à latere."

If we should follow the chain of relationship beyond the diagrams, and compute the number of the kindred of *Ego*, it would produce remarkable results. In strictness two lines commence at *Ego*, one ascending to his father and one to his mother; from these last the number is increased to four, one of which ascends to the father and one to the mother of his father, another to the father and another to the mother of his mother; and again from these four common ancestors the lines are increased to eight; and so upwards in geometrical progression. As a matter of computation it will be seen that at the fifth degree each person has thirty-two ancestors, at the tenth a thousand and twenty-four, and at the twentieth upwards of a million.[1] Carried to the thirty-first degree, or generation, it would give to each person a greater number of ancestors than the entire population of the earth. Such a marvellous result, although correct as a matter of computation, is prevented by the intermarriage of these common ancestors, by which a multitude of them are reduced to one. In the collateral lines the relatives are quadrupled at each generation. "If we only suppose each couple of our ancestors to have left, one with another, two children, and each of those on an average to have left two more (and without such a supposition the human species must be daily diminishing), we shall find that all of us have now subsisting near two hundred and seventy millions of kindred at the fifteenth degree, at the same distance from the several common ancestors as ourselves are; besides those that are one or two descents nearer to or farther from the common stock, who may amount to as many more."[2] But, as in the former case, the intermarriage of these collateral relatives would consolidate many thousands of these relationships into one, while others would, from the same cause, be related to *Ego* in many thousand different ways. The rapidity with which the blood of a people is interfused, or, in other words, tends to intermingle throughout the entire mass of the population, with the progress of the generations,

---

[1] In Black. Com. II. 204, note, is the following :—

Lineal Degrees.	Number of Ancestors.	Lineal Degrees.	Number of Ancestors.	Lineal Degrees.	Number of Ancestors.
1	2	8	256	15	32768
2	4	9	515	16	65536
3	8	10	1024	17	131072
4	16	11	2048	18	262144
5	32	12	4096	19	524288
6	64	13	8192	20	1048576
7	128	14	16384		

[2] Black. Com. II. 207, note, *vide* as follows:—

Collateral Degrees.	Number of Kindred.	Collateral Degrees.	Number of Kindred.	Collateral Degrees.	Number of Kindred.
1	1	8	16384	15	268435456
2	4	9	65536	16	1073741824
3	16	10	262146	17	4294967296
4	64	11	1048576	18	17179869184
5	256	12	4194304	19	68719476736
6	1026	13	16777216	20	274877906944
7	4096	14	67108864		

is forcibly illustrated by these computations.[1] It is both a singular and an extraordinary fact, that the blood and physical organization of so many millions of ancestors should be represented in the person of every human being. The specific identity of the individual of the present with the ancestor of the past generation illustrates the marvellous nature of a structural organization, which is capable of transmission through so many ancestors, and of reproduction as a perfect whole in one individual after the lapse of indefinite periods of time.

In the mode of computing the degrees of consanguinity the Aryan nations differ among themselves. It is apparent that the relationships which collaterals sustain to each other are in virtue of their descent from common ancestors. It is also obvious that each step in ascending from ancestor to ancestor in the lineal line, and in descending from parent to child, in either of the collateral lines, is a degree. Hence in tracing the connection between *Ego* and any given person in a collateral line, we must first ascend from *Ego* to the common ancestor, and then descend to the person whose relationship is sought, counting each intervening person as one degree, or unit of separation; and the aggregate of these units will express, numerically, the nearness, and, upon this basis, the actual value of the relationship. The difference made was upon the starting-point, whether it should commence with *Ego*, or with the common ancestor. The Roman civilians reckoned from the former; thus, if the degree of the relationship of the first cousin were sought, it would be estimated as follows: From *Ego* to father, *pater*, is one; from father to grandfather, *avus*, who is the common ancestor, is two; from grandfather down to paternal uncle, *patruus*, is three; and from paternal uncle to cousin, *patrui filius*, is four; therefore he stands to *Ego* in the fourth degree of consanguinity. Under this method the first person is excluded and the last is included. This was also the manner of computing degrees among the Hebrews.[2] But the canon law, and after it the common law, adopted the other method. It commenced with the common ancestor, and counted the degrees in the same manner, down to the person most remote from the latter, whether *Ego* or the person whose relationship was to be determined; thus, a first cousin stands in the second degree, since both the cousin and *Ego* are removed two degrees from the common ancestor; the son of this cousin is in the third degree, as he is three degrees from the common ancestor, which

---

[1] These figures bear directly upon one of the great problems in ethnology; namely, the multiplicity of the typical faces and forms of mankind. If a fragment of a people became insulated, as the Erse in Ireland, or repelled immigration to their territories by peculiar manners and customs, as the Hebrews, it matters not whether the original elements of population were simple or mixed, if the blood was left free to intermingle, the physical peculiarities of the people would rapidly assimilate, so that in a few centuries there would be developed a national face and form, which would be common, distinctly marked, and typical. The only conditions necessary to produce this result, in any number of cases, are an absolute respite from foreign admixture, with freedom of intermarriage among all classes. Under these conditions, which have been occasionally attained, typical faces and forms, such as the Hebrew, the Irish, and the German, could be multiplied indefinitely; and the differences among them might become very great, in the course of time, through congenital peculiarities, modes of subsistence, and climatic influences; not to say, processes of degradation of one branch or family, and of elevation in another.

[2] Selden's Uxor Hebraica, I. c. 4.

4   May, 1868.

corresponds with the fifth of the civil law. These two methods will be more fully understood by consulting the diagram, Plate I., on which the degrees are numbered according to the civil law, and the diagram of English descents, Chapter IV. Plate III., on which they are given according to the common law. Our English ancestors, at an early day, adopted the canon law mode of computation, in which they clearly made a mistake, if the matter were of any particular consequence. It is sufficiently obvious that the civil law method of computation is the only one which is consistent and logical.

Relationship, or cognation, was further distinguished by the civilians into three kinds, superior, inferior, and transverse; of which the first relates to ascendants, the second to descendants, and the third to collaterals. It results, also, from the civil law method of estimating degrees, that several persons in the lineal and collateral lines stand in the same degree of nearness to *Ego*, which rendered necessary some qualification of the relative value of the numerical degrees. The consanguinei of *Ego* were classified into six grades, according to their degree of nearness, all those who were in the same degree being classified in the same grade, whether ascendants, descendants, or collaterals; but they were distinguished from each other by these three qualifications.[1]

---

[1] DE GRADIBUS COGNATIONUM.—Hoc loco necessarium est exponere, quemadmodum gradus cognationis numerentur. Quare inprimis admonendi sumus, cognationem aliam supra numerari, aliam infra, aliam ex transverso, quæ etiam à latere dicitur. Superior cognatio est parentum: inferior liberorum: ex transverso fratrum sororumve, et eorum, qui quæve ex his generantur; et convenientèr patrui, amitæ, avunculi, materteræ. Et superior quidem et inferior cognatio à primo gradu incipit; et ea, quæ ex transverso numeratur, à secundo.

§ I. Primo gradu est supra pater, mater: infra filius, filia. Secundo gradu supra avus, avia: infra nepos, neptis: ex transverso frater, soror. Tertio gradu supra proavus, proavia: infra pronepos, proneptis: ex transverso fratris sororisque filius, filia: et convenientèr patruus, amita, avunculus, matertera. Patruus est patris frater, qui Græcis Πατραδελφος appellatur. Avunculus est frater matris, qui Græce Μητραδελφος dicitur; et uterque promiscuè Θειος appellatur. Amita est patris soror, quæ Græce Πατραδελφη appellatur: matertera vero matris soror, quæ Græce Μητραδελφη dicitur: et utraque promiscuè Θεια appellatur.

§ II. Quarto gradu supra abavus, abavia: infra abnepos, abneptis: ex transverso fratris sororisque nepos neptisve: et convenientèr patruus magnus, amita magna, id est, avi frater et soror: item avunculus magnus et matertera magna, id est, aviæ frater et soror: consobrinus, consobrina, id est, qui quæve ex sororibus aut fratribus procreantur. Sed quidam rectè consobrinos eos propriè dici putant, qui ex duabus sororibus progenerantur, quasi consororinos: eos verò, qui ex duobus fratribus progenerantur, propriè fratres patrueles vocari: si autem ex duobus fratribus filiæ nascuntur, sorores patrueles appellari. At eos, qui ex fratre et sorore progenerantur, amitinos propriè dici putant. Amitæ tuæ filii consobrinum te appellant, tu illos amitinos.

§ III. Quinto gradu supra atavus, atavia: infra atnepos, atneptis: ex transverso fratris sororisque pronepos, proneptis: et convenientèr propatruus, pròamita, id est, proavi frater et soror: et proavunculus et promatertera, id est, proaviæ frater et soror: item fratris patruelis, vel sororis patruelis, consobrini et consobrinæ, amitini et amitinæ filius, filia: proprior sobrino, proprior sobrina; hi sunt patrui magni, amitæ magnæ, avunculi magni, materteræ magnæ filius, filia.

§ IV. Sexto gradu supra tritavus, tritavia: infra trinepos trineptis: ex transverso fratris sororisque abnepos abneptis: et convenientèr abpatruus abamita, id est, abavi frater et soror: abavunculus, abmatertera, id est, abaviæ frater et soror: item propatrui, proamitæ, proavunculi, promaterteræ filius, filia: item proprius sobrino sobrinave filius, filia: item consobrini consobrinæ nepos, neptis: item sobrini, sobrinæ; id est, qui quæve ex fratribus vel sororibus patruelibus, vel consobrinis, vel amitinis progenerantur.—*Institutes of Justinian*, Lib. III. tit. vi.

It will not be necessary to pursue further the minute details of the Roman system of consanguinity. The principal and most important of its features have been presented, and in a manner sufficiently special to have rendered it perfectly intelligible. For simplicity of method, felicity of description, distinctness of arrangement into lines, truthfulness to nature, and beauty of nomenclature, it is incomparable. It stands pre-eminently at the head of all the systems of relationship ever perfected by man, and furnishes one of the many illustrations that whatever the Roman mind had occasion to touch, it placed once for all upon a solid foundation.

From its internal structure it is evident that this system, in its finished form, was the work of the civilians. We have reasons, also, for believing that it was not used by the people except within narrow limits. Its rigorous precision and formality, not to say complication of arrangement, tends to this conclusion; and the existence and use of common terms for near kindred, after its establishment, is still more decisive. It is not even probable that the common people employed either of the four special terms for uncle and aunt, or that either term for uncle or for aunt was used promiscuously. The disappearance of all of these terms from the modern Italian language, and the reappearance in it of the Greek common term for uncle and aunt, θειος, θεια, in the Italian *Zio, Zia*, renders it conjecturable at least, that the Greek term, in a Latinized form, was used among the ancient Romans; or, it may have been, that they retained the original descriptive phrases. *Consobrinus*, we know, was in use among the people as a common term for cousin,[1] and *nepos* for a nephew[2] as well as a grandson. In addition to the special terms heretofore named were *sobrinus, sobrina*,[3] a contraction of *consobrinus* for cousin, which were sometimes applied to a cousin's children; and *proprior sobrinus, sobrina*, to indicate a great uncle's son and daughter. If the people used the common terms, while the civilians and scholars resorted to the formal legal method, it would not create two systems, since one form is not inconsistent with the other, and the latter was developed from the former. From the foregoing considerations it may be inferred that the Roman form was not perfected merely to describe the several degrees of consanguinity, but for the more important object of making definite the channel, as well as the order of succession to estates. With the need of a code of descents, to regulate the transmission of property by inheritance, would arise the further necessity of specializing, with entire precision, the several lines, and the several degrees of each. A descriptive method, based upon particular generalizations, became indispensable to avoid the more difficult, if not impossible, alternative of inventing a multitude of correlative terms to express the recognized relationships. After the kindred of *ego* had been arranged in their appropriate positions, by the method adopted by the civilians, a foundation was laid for a code of descents for the transmission of property by inheritance.

It remains to notice briefly the affineal relationships. The Latin nomenclature

---

[1] Pandects, Lib. XXXVIII. tit. x.   [2] Eutropius, Lib. VII. cap. i.

[3] Nam mihi sobrina Ampsigura tua mater fuit, pater tuus, is erat frater patruelis meus. Plautus. Com. Pœnulus, Act V. Scene II. 109.

of the marriage relationships, unlike our own, which is both rude and barren, was copious and expressive.   For the principal affinities special terms were invented, after this language became distinct, and it contributed materially to the perfection of the system.   It contains even more radical terms for the marriage relationships than for that of blood.   Our English system betrays its poverty by the use of such unseemly phrases as father-in-law, son-in-law, brother-in-law, step-father, and step-son, to express some twenty very common and very near relationships, nearly all of which are provided with special terms in the Latin nomenclature.   On the other hand, the latter fails to extend to the wives of uncles and nephews, and to the husbands of aunts and nieces the corresponding designations, which the principal European nations have done.   The absence of terms for these relatives is the only blemish upon the Latin system.   The wife of the paternal uncle, for example, was described as *patrui uxor*, and the husband of the paternal aunt as *amitœ vir*.   A reason against the use of the principal terms existed in their fixed signification, which would render their use in the English manner a misnomer.

In the Latin nomenclature, as given in the table, there are thirteen radical terms for blood kindred and fourteen for marriage relatives.   These, by augmentation to express the different grades of what is radically the same relationship, and by inflection for gender, yield twenty-five additional terms, making together fifty-two special terms for the recognized relationships.   In this respect it is the most opulent of all the nomenclatures of relationship of the Aryan nations, except the Grecian.

CHAPTER IV.

SYSTEM OF RELATIONSHIP OF THE ARYAN FAMILY—Continued.

Forms of Consanguinity of the remaining Aryan Nations—Reasons for their ascertainment—Original System determined by a comparison of their Radical Characteristics—I. Hellenic Nations : Ancient Greek—System less accessible than the Roman—Descriptive in Form—Modern Greek—System founded upon the Roman—II. Romaic Nations—Italian System—Illustrations of its Method—French—Illustrations of same—Spanish and Portuguese, not exceptional—III. Teutonic nations—English System—Illustrations of its Method—Prussian and Swiss—Illustrations of their Forms—Holland Dutch—Method Imprecise—Belgian—The same—Westphalian—Illustrations of its Form—Danish and Norwegian—Free from Roman Influence—Illustrations of its Form—Swedish— Agrees with the Danish—Icelandic—Its form purely Descriptive—Illustrations—IV. Sanskrit—Illustrations of its Method—V. Sclavonic Nations—Polish System—Peculiar Method of designating Kindred—Presence of a Non-Aryan Element—Illustrations of its Form—Bohemian—Bulgarian—Illustrations of its Method—Russian—Illustrations of its Method—Special Features in 'the Slavonic System—Their Ethnological Uses—Lithuanian—Presumptively Original Slavonic Form—Schedule Imperfect—VI. Celtic Nations—Erse System—Purely Descriptive—Typical Form of Aryan Family—Illustrations of its Method—Gaelic and Manx—The same—Welsh—Its Nomenclature developed beyond Erse and Gaelic— VII. Persian Nation—System Descriptive—Illustrations of its Method—VIII. Armenian Nation—System Descriptive—Identical with the Erse in its minute Details—Illustrations of its Method—Results of Comparison of Forms—Original System of the Aryan Family Descriptive—Limited amount of Classification of Kindred not Inconsistent with this Conclusion—Secondary Terms represent the amount of Modification—System Affirmative in its Character—A Domestic Institution—Stability of its Radical Forms.

THE several forms of consanguinity which prevail among the remaining Aryan nations will be presented and compared with the Roman, and also with each other, for the purpose of ascertaining whether they are identical. After this the common system, thus made definite, can be compared with those of other families of mankind. It will be sufficient for the realization of these objects to exhibit, with the utmost brevity, the characteristic features of the system of each nation, and to indicate the points of difference between them and the Roman. This method will supersede the necessity, except in a few cases, of entering upon details.

I. Hellenic nations. 1. Ancient Greek. 2. Modern Greek.

1. *Ancient Greek.*—The same facilities for ascertaining the classical Greek method of arranging and designating kindred do not exist, which were found in the Institutes and Pandects, for the Roman. An approximate knowledge of the Grecian form can be drawn from the nomenclature, and from the current use of its terms in the literature of the language. For the most part these terms are compounds, and still indicate, etymologically, particular persons, as well as express particular relationships. They were evidently developed subsequently to the separation of the Hellenic nations from their congeners, since they are not found in the cognate languages. The multiplication of these terms also tends to show that che Greeks of the classical period had no formal scientific method of designating consanguinei like the Roman, but attempted, as a substitute, the discrimination

of the nearest relationships by special terms. This, carried far enough, would realize the Roman plan, but it would render the nomenclature cumbersome.

Several of the Greek terms are inserted in the table as conjectural; but a sufficient number are certain to show that consanguinei were arranged, by virtue of them, in accordance with the natural order of descents; and that the collateral lines were maintained distinct and divergent from the lineal line. This is a material characteristic.

The method for indicating the relationships in the first collateral line was irregular. *Kasis*, the ancient term for brother, gave place to *adelphos*; in like manner *anepsios*, which was originally the term for nephew, and probably like *nepos* signified a grandson as well, was superseded by *adelphidoûs*. This gave for the series *adelphos*, brother, *adelphidoûs*, nephew, and *anepsiadoûs*, nephew's son. After the substitution of *adelphidoûs* for *anepsios* the latter was restricted to cousin.

Whether consanguinei in the second collateral line were described by the Roman or the Celtic method, or were designated by special terms, does not clearly appear. The form in the table must, therefore, be taken as in a great measure conjectural. The tendency to specialize the principal relationships is shown by the opulence of the nomenclature; thus, for paternal uncle there are *patrōs*, *patradelphos*, and *patrokasignētos*; and for maternal uncle *mētrōs*, *mētradelphos*, and *mētrokasignētos*; and also common terms, *theios theia* and *nannos nannē*, for uncle and aunt, which were used promiscuously. *Patrokasignētos* and *nannos* appear to have fallen out of use after the time of Thucydides, but *theios* and *theia* remained in constant use among the people, and probably to the exclusion of the other more recent terms. This fact is noticed in the Institutes of Justinian as follows: "Patruus est patris frater, qui Græcis Πατραδελφος appellatur. Avunculus est frater matris, qui Græce Μητραδελφος dicitur; et uterquæ promiscuè Θειος appellatur. Amita est patris soror, quæ Græce Πατραδελφη appellatur. Matertera vero matris soror, quæ Græce Μητραδελφη dicitur; et uterquæ promiscuè Θεια appellatur."[1] It is worthy of mention that all of these terms have disappeared from the modern Greek language,[2] except *theios theia*, which reappear, as has elsewhere been stated, in the Italian *Tio Tia*, and in the Spanish *Tis Tia*, uncle and aunt. There was but a single term for cousin, which shows that the four classes of persons, who stand in this relationship, were generalized into one. The same amount of classification here indicated is found in the system of several of the branches of the Aryan family. It is evident that the special terms were used as far as they were applicable, and that the remaining kindred were described by a combination of the primary terms.

It is not necessary to trace further the details of the Grecian system, since it is not exceptional to the plan of consanguinity of the Aryan family. The great expansion of the nomenclature in the classical period, to avoid the inconvenience of

---

[1] Lib. III. tit. vi. § 1.

[2] Glossary of Later and Byzantine Greek, by E. A. Sophocles. Memoirs of the American Academy of Arts and Sciences. New series, vol. vii.

descriptive phrases, tends to the inference that the original system was purely descriptive.

There are twenty-two specific terms in this language given in the table for blood kindred, and nineteen for marriage relatives. These, by augmentation to express degrees of the same relationship, and by inflection for gender, yield forty-four additional, making together eighty-three special terms for the recognized relationships.

2. *Modern Greek.*—The schedule in the table was taken from the glossary, before cited, of Prof. Sophocles.[1] It was compiled by him according to the Roman method. In the later period of the Empire the two systems, in their legal form, doubtless became identical. It does not, therefore, require special notice. One of its interesting features is the contraction of the nomenclature which it exhibits in the direction of original terms.

II. Romaic Nations. 1. Italian. 2. French. 3. Spanish. 4. Portuguese.

1. *Italian.*—The Italian system is not fully extended in the table. It presents the popular rather than the legal form, the latter of which was doubtless based upon the Roman. The collateral lines are maintained distinct from each other and divergent from the lineal line, with the exception of the first collateral, in which respect the Italian form agrees with the Holland Dutch, Belgian, Anglo-Saxon, and early English. The nephew and grandson are designated by the same term, *nipote;* in other words, my nephew and grandson stand to me in the same relationship. This classification merges the first collateral line in the lineal, and in so far agrees with the Turanian form.

The readiest manner of showing the characteristic features of the system of the Aryan nations will be to give illustrations of the method of designating kindred in one of the branches of each of the first three collateral lines. This will make it apparent, first, that the connection of consanguinei is traced through common ancestors; secondly, that the collateral lines are maintained distinct from each other, and divergent from the lineal line, with some exceptions; thirdly, how far the system is descriptive, and how far the descriptive form has been modified by the introduction of special terms; and, lastly, whether the systems of these nations are radically the same. The illustrations will be from the first collateral line, male branch, and the male branch of the second and third collateral lines on the father's side. For a more particular knowledge of the details of the system of each nation reference is made to the table.

In the Italian the first collateral line gives the following series, *brother, nephew,* and *great-nephew,* and thus downward with a series of nephews. This is a deviation from the Roman form. The second collateral runs *uncle, cousin,* and *cousin's son,* which is also a deviation from the Roman.

2. *French.*—The French method is also unlike the Roman. My brother's descendants are designated as a series of nephews, one beyond the other, *e. g., neveu, petit-neveu,* and *arrière-petit-neveu.* The second collateral line likewise employed a different method, *e. g., oncle, cousin, cousin-sous-germain.* In the first

---

[1] Article Βαθμε Ουγγεναις.

the uncle is made the root of this branch of the line, and afterward the cousin is made the second starting-point. As *uncle* and *cousin* are common terms, explanatory words are required to show whether they belonged to the father's or to the mother's side. The following is the series in the third collateral: *Grand-oncle, fils du grand-oncle,* and *petit-fils du grand-oncle.* In the fourth and fifth collateral lines the descriptive method was necessarily adopted.

Among the Aryan nations the French alone, with the exception of the ancient Sanskrit speaking people of India, possess original terms for elder and younger brother, and for elder and younger sister. It is a noticeable feature for the reason that in the Turanian, Malayan, and American Indian families the fraternal and sororal relationships are universally conceived in the twofold form of elder and younger.

3. *Spanish.* 4. *Portuguese.*—There is nothing in the systems of these nations which is exceptional to the general plan of consanguinity of the Aryan family, or that requires special notice.

III. Teutonic Nations. 1. English. 2. Prussian, and German-Swiss. 3. Holland-Dutch. 4. Belgian. 5. Westphalian. 6. Danish and Norwegian. 7. Swedish. 8. Icelandic.

These nations possess the same system of relationship. Presumptively they commenced with the same primitive form, wherefore a comparison of their several forms, as they now exist independently of each other, should show, first, what is still common among them all, and consequently radical; secondly, that which has been developed independently in each; thirdly, the portion that has been borrowed from the Roman; and, lastly, the true character of the original system.

1. *English.*—The English legal method of indicating relationships is founded upon the Roman. It has followed the latter very closely, borrowing a portion of its nomenclature, and also its method. In the Diagram Plate III. this form is shown in detail, but limited to the relatives on the father's side. A similar diagram, with slight changes, would show the same lines on the mother's side.

In daily life, however, this formal plan is not resorted to for the near relationships. The common terms are employed in all cases as far as they are applicable; while for such kindred as are not thus embraced, descriptive phrases are used. The first collateral line gives for the series *brother, nephew, great-nephew,* and *great-great-nephew;* the second, *uncle, cousin, cousin's son,* and *cousin's grandson;* the third collateral, *great-uncle, great-uncle's son, second cousin,* and *second cousin's son.* These illustrations reveal a tendency to avoid the full descriptive phrases. If, however, the terms *uncle, aunt,* and *cousin,* which are borrowed, through Norman sources, from the Latin speech, were struck out of the nomenclature, *nephew* alone of the secondary terms would remain; and their loss would render compulsory the original descriptive form by a combination of the primary terms. Of discarded Anglo-Saxon terms one, at least, *eam*[1], uncle, was in general use before

---

[1] The word *nephew,* as used by our early English ancestors, must have had two correlatives, *uncle* and *grandfather,* or the difference in these relationships, as in the case of *nephew* and *grandson,* was not discriminated. In King Alfred's Orosius *eam* is used as frequently for *grandfather* as for *uncle. Vide* Bohn's Ed., pp. 297, 284, 497.

the Norman period. Whether *federa*, paternal uncle, and *fathe*, aunt, were in common use among the Saxons, or were developed by scholars with the first attempts at Saxon composition, is not so clear.

It is evident from the present structure and past history of the English system, that its original form was purely descriptive; thus, an uncle was described as *fathers's brother*, or *mother's brother*; a cousin as a *father's brother's son* or a *mother's brother's son*, as the case might be, these relationships in the concrete being then unknown.

In the English language there are but eleven radical terms for blood relatives, of which three are borrowed; and but two in practical use for marriage relatives.

2. *Prussian, and German-Swiss.*—The German-Swiss form, as given in the table, presents the legal system of the people speaking the German language. It is founded upon the Roman form of which it is nearly a literal copy, and, therefore, it does not require a special explanation.[1]

On the other hand, the Prussian exhibits more nearly the common method of the German people for designating their kindred. There are original German terms for uncle and aunt, grandson and granddaughter, and male and female cousin,

---

[1] After receiving the carefully prepared German-Swiss Schedule given in the table, which was filled out by Mr. C. Hunziker, attorney-at-law of Berne, Switzerland, I addressed to this gentleman some questions in reference thereto through the Hon. Theodore S. Fay, U. S. Minister Resident in Switzerland, and received from him through the same channel the following answers. The translation was by Samuel J. Huber, Esq., Attaché of the Legation.

Translation of the Report of Mr. Hunziker by Sam. J. Huber.

Question 1. Is the wife of a nephew now called a niece (*Nichte*), in common speech; and, in like manner, is the husband of a niece called a nephew (*Neffe*)?

Answer. No.

Question 2. Are the foreign terms *Onkel* and *Tante* also applied by a portion of the people both to the paternal and maternal uncles and aunts as well as *Oheim* and *Muhme*?

Answer. Yes. The terms are identical, only the denominations *Onkel* and *Tante* are of more recent [French] origin, while the terms *Oheim* (abbreviated *Ohm.*) and *Muhme* are German. So, in French, *Onkel* is called *oncle*, in old French *uncle*, derived from the Latin *avunculus*. *Tante* is the French word for *Muhme*; old French *ante* from the Latin *amita*. Before the aforesaid terms *Onkel* and *Tante* were adopted a portion of the people, for *Oheim* and *Muhme*, used the term *Vetter* and *Base*. This is still the case, even at present, with many, particularly country people, who not unfrequently apply the term *Vetter* and *Base* to all collateral relatives.

Question 3. Are my father's sister's son, my mother's brother's son, and my mother's sister's son described by the term *cousin* (*Vetter*), the same as marked on the schedule for my father's brother's son? And, in like manner, is each of the four female cousins called *Base*?

Answer. Yes. The terms *Vetter* and *Base* are often used in common life not in a strict sense (*in einem uneigentlichen Sinne*), and, indeed, their application has nothing actually fixed; the rule, however, may be fixed that no nearer relative but the descendants of brothers and sisters to each other (*Geschwisterkinder*) are called *Vettern* and *Basen* (cousins), and that, therefore, these terms embrace the first and second cousins, and, perhaps, even more remote collateral relations.

Question 4. Was the term *Muhme*, in ancient times, used to describe a niece and a cousin as well as an aunt, or either of them?

Answer. No. The term *Muhme* never described anything but an aunt.

Question 5. Did the term *Neffe* originally signify a grandson as well as a nephew?

Answer. No. Even our most ancient legal sources contain but the term *Enkel* for *Grosssohn*

which appear to have been developed, with the exception of the first, after the separation of this dialect from the common Teutonic stem. These terms greatly improve the nomenclature and consequently the method of the system.

(grandson), and in no instance that of *Neffe*. Even this last mentioned term was but recently adopted in legislative documents, having been in former times circumscribed by the term *Bruder's* or *Schwesterkind*.

Question 6. Desired: a list of obsolete terms of relationship, and the persons they were employed to describe.

6. Report on the obsolete terms of relationship.

After the defeat of the Romans in the fifth century ancient Helvetia formed a part of the great Germanic nation, and later a part of the Germanic empire. Though the Helvetian territory, and particularly the towns, were governed by their own national legislation, it is not to be mistaken that, besides the domestic legal sources, the laws of the Germanic family (the so-called *Leges Barbarorum*, of which, particularly, the *Lex Allemannorum* and the *Lex Burgundionum*, and, later, the *Sachsen-* and *Schwaben-Spiegel*) enjoyed a high authority, and that the domestic law has been amended and completed from that source. If we, therefore, now give a brief statement of the views of the ancient Germans with regard to relationship and their terms, it is thereby to be understood that throughout ancient Helvetia the same views had been adopted.

1. The term *parentela*, in ancient legal documents, is used to describe the family as a separate fellowship (*geschlossene Rechtsgenossenschaft*) as well as a number (*Mehrheit*) of relatives united under the same pair of parents as their next common stock (*Stamm*). The following expressions are remarkable :—

2. *Lippschaft, Magschaft* (kin), means, in its larger sense, the kindred in general; in its proper sense the law distinguishes between *Busen* (bosom), comprehending only the descendants of a deceased, and the *Magschaft* (kin proper), comprehending only the remote relatives. (According to the "*Sachsenspiegel*") the kin begins at the cousinship.

3. *Schwermagen, Speermagen, Germagen* (male issue), are called the male persons united by but male generation (*Zeugung*). In its real sense it means the blood-cousins upon whom rests the propagation of the family name and of the house-coat. Opposite to them are the—

4. *Spillmagen, Spindelmagen, Kunkelmagen* (female issue), that is, all the rest of kindred whose consanguinity, either in the ascending or in the descending line, is founded upon the birth from a woman, or who, although relatives by but male generation, for their female issue are not born for the sword and lance, but only for the spindle. (*Spillmagen* is also called *Niftel*)

5. To count the degrees of consanguinity two different ways have been used—the one representing them by a tree with branches, the other by the form of a human body. The following representation is from the "Sachsenspiegel:" Husband and wife, united in marriage, belong to the head; the children, born as full brothers and sisters from one man and one wife, to the neck. Children of full brothers and sisters occupy that place where the shoulders and arms join. These form the first kindred of consanguinity, viz., the children of brother and sister. The others occupy the elbow, the third the hand, &c. For the seventh degree there is an additional nail, and no member and the kin, which ends here, is then called *Nagelmagen*.

6. *Schooss* are often called the ascendants.

7. *Lidmagen* is often used for consanguineous with

8. *Vatermagen*. This term is more comprehensive than that of *Schwertmagen*, for it embraces all the relatives from the father's issue and descent, and it also includes all the women issuing from the fathers immediately, for instance, the sister and the aunt from the father's grandfather; and further, in the descending line, also the degrees of consanguinity arising from women, because, in the ascending line, fathers are at the head of *parentelas*. In certain cases this term can even comprehend all consanguineous with the father.

9. *Muttermagen* are called the relatives from *the* mother's side, or, according to circumstances, from *a* mother's side.

In the first collateral line, male, the series is as follows: *Brother, nephew, great-nephew*, and *great-great-nephew*; or a series of nephews, one beyond the other, which is analogous to the common English and French usage. The second collateral runs as follows: *Uncle, cousin, cousin's son*, and *cousin's grandson*. Cousin is thus made a second starting point, and his descendants are referred to him as the root, instead of the uncle. In the third, and more remote collateral lines, the Roman form is followed. The German is a very perfect system, but its excellence is due to its fidelity to its Roman model.

3. *Holland Dutch.* — As presented in the table the manner of designating kindred is rather the common form of the people than the statutory method. It will be perceived, by consulting the table, that the system is defective in arrangement, and imprecise in the discrimination of relationships. The absence of Roman influence, which has been so apparent in the previous cases, is quite observable. The terms *neef* and *nicht* are applied indiscriminately to a nephew and niece, to a grandson and granddaughter, and to each of the four classes of cousins.[1] These

---

[1] The term *nepos*, and its cognates, in the dialects of the Aryan language has a singular history, which if fully elaborated would be found instructive. Some of the facts are patent. This term exists in nearly all the dialects of the language, from which it is inferable that it was indigenous in the primitive speech. The terms for grandfather and uncle are different in the several stock-languages, from which it is also inferable that the terms for these relationships, where found, were developed subsequently to the separation of these nations from each other, or from the parent stem. Consequently *nepos*, and its cognates, must have existed as a term of relationship without a correlative. While the relationships of grandfather and grandson, and of uncle and nephew, were in process of being separated from each other, and turned into proper correlation, the use of *nepos* must have fluctuated. Among the Romans, as late as the fourth century, it was applied to a nephew as well as a grandson, although both *avus* and *avunculus* had come into use. Eutropius in speaking of Octavianus calls him the nephew of Cæsar, "*Cæsaris nepos*" (Lib. VII. c. i.). Suetonius speaks of him as *sororis nepos* (Cæsar, c. lxxxiii.), and afterwards (Octavianus, c. vii.), describes Cæsar as his greater uncle, *major avunculus*, in which he contradicts himself. When *nepos* was finally restricted to grandson, and thus became the strict correlative of *avus*, the Latin language was without a term for nephew, whence the descriptive phrase *fratris vel sororis filius*. In English *nephew* was applied to grandson as well as nephew as late as 1611, the period of King James' translation of the Bible. Niece is so used by Shakspeare in his will, in which he describes his granddaughter, Susannah Hall, as "my niece." But in English, and likewise in French and German, *nephew, neveu*, and *neffe* were finally restricted to the sons of the brothers and sisters of *Ego*, and thus became respectively the correlative of uncle. This, in turn, left these dialects without any term for grandson, which deficiency was supplied by a descriptive phrase, except the German, which in *enkel* found an indigenous term. In Greek, however, *anepsios* appears to have been applied to a nephew, a grandson, and a cousin, and finally became restricted to the last. *Neef* in Holland Dutch still expresses these three relationships indiscriminately. In Belgian and Platt Dutch *nichte* is applied to a female cousin as well as niece. These uses of the term tend to show that its pristine use was sufficiently general to include grandson, nephew, and cousin, but without giving any reason to suppose that it was ever as general as the words *relative* or *kinsman*. The difference in the relationships of these persons to *Ego* was undoubtedly understood, and each made specific by description. A term of relationship once invented and adopted into use becomes the repository of an idea; and that idea never changes. Its meaning, as indicated by its use, may become enlarged or restricted among cognate nations after their separation from each other, or in the same nation in the course of ages; but the subversion of its meaning or use is next to impossible. A term invented to express a particular relationship cannot be made to express two as distinct and dissimilar as those for grandson and nephew; and, therefore, its exclusive

several relationships were made definite, when necessary, by a description of the persons.

In the first collateral line, male, the following is the series : *Brother, nephew,* and *nephew,* which is the popular form ; and *brother, brother's son,* and *brother's grand-child,* which is the formal method.   The second collateral runs as follows : *Uncle, nephew,* and *nephew ;* or formally *uncle, uncle's son,* and *uncle's grand-child.* The novel feature here revealed of holding grandson, nephew, and cousin in the same identical relationship still records the first act in the progress of the Aryan system from a purely descriptive form.

4. *Belgian.*—The Belgian system of consanguinity is closely allied to the preceding.   It has the same defects and nearly the same peculiarities. *Nĕvĕ* and *nichte* are applied to the children of the brothers and sisters of *Ego ;* but not to his grand-children.   *Nichte* is also applied to a female cousin ; and it is probable that *nĕvĕ* was used to designate a male cousin prior to the adoption of *kozyn* into the Belgian dialect.   Where terms are found in a dialect cognate with our own, which are employed in a manner not sanctioned by our usage, it does not follow that it is either a vague or improper use of the term ; but it shows, on the contrary, that the several relationships to which a particular term is applied are not discriminated from each other ; and they are regarded as one and the same relationship.   In the primitive system of the Aryan family the relationship of cousin was unknown.

5. *Westphalian or Platt Dutch.*—The schedule in the table presents the common form of the people.   In the absence of special terms for nephew and niece the first collateral line is described, *e. g.,* *brother, brother's son,* and *brother's grand-child.* The second collateral gives the following series : *Uncle, cousin, cousin's son,* and *cousin's grand-child.*   *Nichte* still remains in the Westphalian dialect ; but it is restricted to female cousin.   In the third collateral the series is still more irregular from the absence of a term for great-uncle, *e. g., father's uncle, father's cousin,* and *father's cousin's son.*   This is simply a modification of the old descriptive method by the use of secondary terms.

6. *Danish and Norwegian.*—The system of these nations is entirely free from Roman influence, from which we have been gradually receding, and is, therefore, presumptively nearer the primitive form of the Aryan family.   The presence of German influence, however, is seen in the use of the term *fatter,* cousin, which introduces into the system the only feature that distinguishes it from the Celtic.

With the exception of the term last named there are no terms of relationship in this dialect but the primary.   For uncle and aunt on the father's side it has *far-broder* and *faster ;* and on the mother's side *morbroder* and *moster,* which it will be noticed are contractions of the terms father, mother, brother, and sister, and, therefore, describe each person specifically.   In the cities the borrowed terms *onkel* and *tante* are employed to a great extent, as they are in all German cities ; but the

application to one would render it inapplicable to the other.   It follows that *nepos* did not originally signify either a nephew, grandson, or cousin, but that it was used promiscuously to designate a class of persons next without the primary relationships.

rural populations in Denmark, Norway, and Germany as well, still adhere to the native term.

The first collateral line male gives the series, *brother, brother's son,* and *brother's grand-child ;* the second, *father's brother, cousin,* and *cousin's grand-child ;* and the third, *far-father's brother, father's cousin, father's cousin's son,* and *father's cousin's grand-child.* These illustrations reveal the character of the system.

7. *Swedish.*—The Swedish form agrees so closely with the Danish and Norwegian that it does not require a separate notice.

8. *Icelandic.*—The insulation of the Icelandic Teutons would tend to preserve their form of consanguinity free from foreign influence. It has original terms for grandfather and grandmother in *afi* and *amma*, and a term *nefi* for nephew, which is given in the Mithridates, but does not appear in the Table. It has terms, also, for first and second cousin, which are used concurrently with the descriptive phrases. In form and method, however, it approaches nearer to a purely descriptive system than any yet presented.

In the first collateral line, male, the series is as follows: *Brother, son of brother, son of son of brother,* and *son of son of son of brother.* It agrees with the Celtic in commencing the description at the opposite extreme from *Ego*, which, although it may be an idiomatic peculiarity, is yet significant, and will reappear in the Armenian and also in the Arabic. For the second collateral we have *father's brother, son of father's brother, son of son of father's brother,* and *son of son of son of father's brother.* The same form, which is seen to be purely descriptive, runs through the several lines. It follows strictly the natural streams of descent, and makes each relationship specific. This realizes what we understand by a descriptive system. It is evidently nearer the primitive form of the Aryan family than that of any other nation of the Teutonic branch. The advances made by some of the nations, which it is the object of this comparison to trace, are seen to be explainable. They have not proceeded far enough to obscure the original form with which they severally commenced.[1]

---

[1] Nomenclatures of relationship develop from the centre outward, or from the near to the more remote degrees. The primary terms would be first invented since we cannot conceive of any people living without them; but when the nomenclature had been carried to this point it might remain stationary for an indefinite period of time. The Celtic never passed beyond this stage. By means of these terms consanguinei, near and remote, can be described, which answered the main end of a nomenclature. Further progress, or the development of secondary terms, would result from a desire to avoid descriptive phrases. The first of these reached would, probably, be *nepos*, as elsewhere stated, and made to include several classes of persons. Next to this would, probably, be terms for grandfather and grandmother. In the Romaic, Hellenic, and Slavonic stock languages there are terms for these relationships, which, it is somewhat remarkable, are distinct and independent of each other. In the other dialects they are wanting. It would seem to follow that no terms for these relationships existed in the primitive speech, and that the persons were described as "father's father," and so on.

Next in order, apparently, stand the relationships of uncle and aunt. These do not appear to have been discriminated, in the concrete, in the primitive speech. A common term for paternal uncle is found in the Sanskrit *patroya*, Greek *patrōs*, and Latin *patruus ;* but this term seems to be

IV. Sanskrit.   Very naturally the Sanskrit would be regarded as one of the most important systems of consanguinity in the Aryan connection, from the weight of its authority in determining what the original form of the family may have been.   It is to be regretted that the system, as given in the Table, is so incomplete, although it is shown as fully as competent scholars were able to reproduce it from the remains of the language.   Where the special terms are numerous, and their etymologies apparent, as in the Greek, it facilitates the attempt; but where the language is barren of radical terms, and the compounds are limited in number, as in the Sanskrit, a failure to recover an ancient, after it has ceased to be a living system, is not surprising.

There is, however, another view of the case which is not without significance. The absence of radical terms for collateral relatives, and the presence of a limited number of compound terms which are descriptive of particular persons, tend to show that kindred were described, among them, by a combination of the primary terms; and that the system, therefore, was originally descriptive.

The following diagram exhibits a fragment of the original method of arranging and designating kindred:—

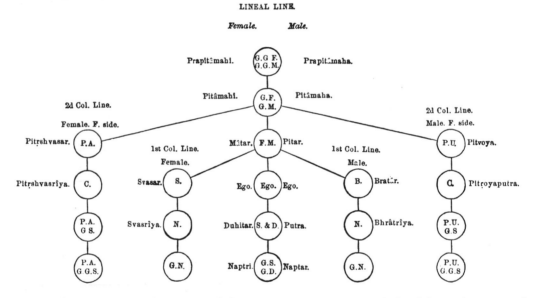

It will be observed that most of these terms are compounded of the primary, and describe persons.   They also indicate the line and branch, and whether on the

---

made from the term for *father*, by the addition of a termination, and might have come into use independently, after the separation of these dialects from each other, as *fædera*, paternal uncle, from *fæder*, father, in Anglo-Saxon.   The same remarks apply to *mátula*, *mētrōs*, and *matertera*, for maternal aunt.   There are also common terms for uncle and aunt in the Greek *theios theia*, German *Oheim* and *Muhme*, English *uncle* and *aunt*, derived the last two from *avunculus* and *amita*.   In Slavonic we have *stryc* and *ujec* for paternal and maternal uncle, and *tetka*, common for aunt.   From the fact that the same terms do not run through the several dialects of the Aryan language, the inference is a strong one that these relationships, in the concrete, were not discriminated in the primitive language.

Uncle is a contraction of *avunculus*, the literal signification of which is a "little grandfather."

father's side or on the mother's side. *Naptar* and *naptri* are restricted to grandson and grand-daughter, although, without much doubt, they were originally applied to a nephew and niece as well. From the diagram it is a proper inference that the remaining persons in the several lines are described in a similar manner. The Sanskrit system appears to agree with the general form prevalent in the Aryan family. In its development it took the same direction before noticed in the Grecian, and, to a great extent, in the other dialects of the Aryan language, but without changing essentially its original form.[1]

This term, together with that of aunt from *amita*, has been adopted with dialectical changes into several of the branches of the Aryan family, and promises ultimately to displace indigenous terms developed since the separation of its branches from each other.

In the order of time a term for cousin would be the last invented, on the supposition of a growth of the nomenclature outward from *Ego*. It is the most remote collateral relationship discriminated in any language or dialect represented in the tables, unless the Slavonic is regarded as an exception. A special term for this relationship must be founded upon a generalization of four different classes of persons into one class; and, therefore, it is more difficult than either of those previously named. This term cousin, which seems to be from the Latin *consobrinus*, was in strictness limited to the children of sisters; but it became a common term, and from this source it has been propagated into several branches of the Aryan family. With these facts before the mind it becomes more and more apparent that the original system of the family as to its present form was purely descriptive.

[1] Note on Sanskrit Schedule by Fitz Edward Hall, D. C. L. :—

1. The prescribed scheme of vowel-sounds being very inadequate for the Sanskrit, I have adhered to that more usually followed by Orientalists. According thereto, á is like a in "father;" a, like a in "America;" e, like our alphabetic a; i, like i in "pin;" í, like i in "machine;" o, like o in "no;" u, like u in "bull;" ú, like oo in "fool;" ai and au, as in the Italian. A peculiar vowel is represented by ri, which is sounded somewhat like the ri in "rivalry." Sh, s', and s, indicate three different sibilants.

2. In consequence of prefixing *mama*, "my," to each word, I have had to give it a case. I have selected the nominative. The crude form, that found in the dictionaries, of the words for "father," "mother," "son," "brother," &c., are *pitri*, *mátri*, *bhrátri*, *putra*, &c.

3. It requires great credulity to believe that the Hindus know much of the origin of Sanskrit words. Generally, they can only refer words to verbal themes, which are, of course, the invention of the grammarians. *Putra*, "son," for instance, is fancifully derived from *pu*, one of the "hells," and the etymon "tra," "to draw out;" quasi, "an extractor from hell." *Duhitri*, "daughter," is thought, with more of reason, to mean "the milker." See Prof. Max Müller on Comparative Mythology, in the Oxford Essays. *Pautra*, "grandson," is from *putra*, "son." To *pautra*, the preposition *pra*, "before," is prefixed in *prapautra*, "great-grandson." "Elder brother" and "younger brother," *agraja* and *anuja*, mean, when analyzed, "foreborn" and "after-born." In *pitámaha* and *mátámaha*, "paternal grandfather" and "maternal grandfather," and so of the feminines, *maha* and *mahi* are inseparable affixes. The *vriddha*, in the word for "great-great-grandfather," imports "old." *Pati*, "husband," "lord," we have in the post-Homeric δεσπότης, the first syllable of which is the same as the Sanskrit *drsá*, "country." The feminine of *pati*, *patui*, occurs in the Homeric and later δέσποινα. *Dhava*, "husband," is seen in the Latin *vidua*, in Sanskrit, *vidhavá*, "without husband." Hence appears the absurdity of the masculine *viduus*, and so of our "widower." *Vimátri*, "step-mother," means "a different mother;" for *vi* has numerous senses in Sanskrit. *Dattaka*, "adopted son," = "given." In *vimátreya*, "half-brother," we see *vi* and *mátri*, "mother."

4. Degrees of relationship representable only by compounds of other degrees have been omitted. And here I should mention that *pitrivya*, "father's brother," is the only word for "paternal uncle" in Sanskrit. It contains *pitri*, "father," and an ending. Compare *bhrátrivya* and *bhágineya*. *Mátula* is connected, not very obviously, with *mátri*.

V. Slavonic Nations.   1. Polish.   2. Slovakian or Bohemian.   3. Bulgarian.
4. Russian.   5. Lithuanian.

Among the nations of Slavonic lineage the method of designating kindred is, in
some respects, original and distinctive.   There appears to be a foreign element in
their system of consanguinity which finds no counterpart in those of the remaining
Aryan nations.   The same ideas, both of classification and of description, run
through all the forms heretofore presented in a manner so obvious as to leave no
doubt that they sprang from a common original.   But a new element is found in
the Slavonic which is unexplainable by the hypothesis that it has departed, like the
Roman, from an original form in all respects common.   The schedules in the Table
are neither sufficiently numerous nor perfect to illustrate the system fully in its stages
of growth; but enough may be gathered from a comparison of them to encourage
belief that a full knowledge of the system, in its several forms, would tend to
explain the order of the separation of the Slavonic nations from each other, as well
as their relative position in the Aryan family.   It would also demonstrate a non-
Aryan source of a portion of the Slavonic blood.

1. *Polish.*—The Polish system has an opulent and expressive nomenclature,
inferior only to the Roman; and in the fulness of its development it stands at the
head of the several Slavonic forms.

There are two terms for nephew applied to a brother's son, *bratanec* and *synowiec*,
with their feminine forms for niece; also a separate term *siostrzenca* for nephew
applied to a sister's son, with its feminine for niece.   The opulence of the nomenclature is still further shown by the presence of special terms, evolved from the
foregoing, for the husbands and wives of these nieces and nephews: namely,
bratancowa and *siostrzencowa*, for the two former; and *synowice* and *siostrzenin*, for
the two latter.   In the first collateral line, male, we have for the series: *brother,
nephew, son of nephew,* and *grand-son of nephew.*   In so far there is nothing
peculiar in the Polish system.

There are separate terms for uncle on the father's and on the mother's side, and
a common term for aunt.   The members of the second collateral line are thus
indicated: *stryj*, paternal uncle, *stryjecznybrat*, " brother through paternal uncle;"
and *stryjecznywnuk*, " grandson through paternal uncle."   That is to say: my
father's brother's son is not my cousin, for there is no term in the Slavonic

---

5. All Sanskrit dictionaries hitherto published, whether Indian or European, are very defective;
and the Pundits of the present day are, ordinarily, most indifferent scholars.   For some of the words
I have given, I am indebted to neither of these sources.   My own reading has furnished them to me;
and I dare say I might, at a future time, fill up a number of the many blanks which the paper still
exhibits.   Among words indicative of kin which I have met with in Hindu law-books, but which
you do not require, are *atyáryas'was'ura*, " paternal great-grandfather of a woman's husband;"
atyáryavriddhaprapitámaha, " paternal great-grandfather's paternal great-grandfather;" &c. &c.

6. The remarriage of widows not having been current in old times in India, a number of words
expressive of relationship that might be counted on, do not exist in the Sanskrit.

7. Should any further information be required in connection with the accompanying table, I would
refer you to Prof. W. D. Whitney, of Yale College.   Mr. Whitney's knowledge of the Sanskrit
is acknowledged, by the best of living Sanskrits, to entitle him to rank fully on a level with themselves.

stock-language for this relationship: but he is my *brother* through this uncle—my brother in a particular way. The son of this collateral brother is my nephew, and the son of the latter is my *grandson* in the same peculiar sense, since these terms express the relationship which comes back to *Ego*. But for the qualification here placed upon the terms for brother, nephew, and grandson, the mode of classification would be identical with one of the Asiatic forms hereafter to be presented. How the Polish made such a wide departure from the primitive descriptive method is a suggestive question.

The following diagram will make more familiar the lineal and first three collateral lines on the father's side:—

LINEAL LINE.

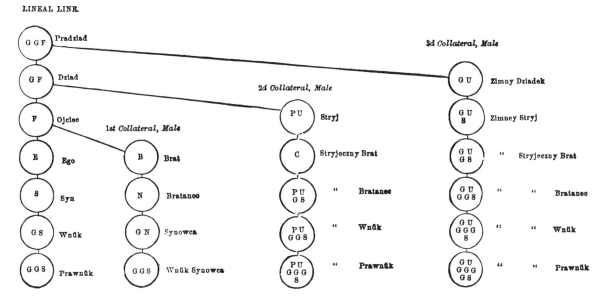

Having no term for great uncle, my grandfather's brother is my grandfather; but to distinguish him from the real ancestor, and to express, at the same time, the difference in the relationship, the word, *zimny* = cold, is prefixed, which qualification is continued to each of his descendants. This gives for the series, in the third collateral, as shown in the diagram, *cold grandfather, cold paternal uncle, brother through cold paternal uncle, nephew through cold paternal uncle,* and *grandson through cold paternal uncle*. For a further knowledge of this interesting system reference is made to the Table.

2. *Slovakian* or *Bohemian*.—The Bohemian schedule seems to have been imperfectly filled in consequence of following a variant translation of the questions from English into German, by means of which the learned Professor it would seem was misled in all the branches of the second collateral line. In this line the most remarkable features of the Slovakian system appear. It exhibits the nomenclature, and some portion of each line in agreement with the Polish or Russian, and it is given entire in the Table as furnished, as it is at least possible that it may be correct. Since the Bohemians and Poles are of the western Slavonic branch, and the Bulgarians and Russians of the eastern, the forms of consanguinity that now prevail in these

6   December, 1868.

nations would probably exhibit all the diversities in the system of the Slavonic nations. For this reason the incompleteness referred to, and which is true, to nearly the same extent, of the Bulgarian, is the more to be regretted. The Bohemian form, as it appears in the Table, is nevertheless worthy of a careful examination.

3. *Bulgarian.*—Two schedules of the Bulgarian are given in the Table. It agrees with the Polish in a part of the first and second collateral lines. When both forms are fully investigated, they will doubtless be found in full agreement. The series of the first collateral line, male, is as follows: *Brother, nephew, little grandson,* and *little great-grandson.* In the second collateral is found the same extraordinary series before given in the Polish; namely, *chicha,* "paternal uncle;" *otchicha brat,* "brother through paternal uncle;" *otchicha bratanetz,* "nephew through paternal uncle;" and *otchicha vnook,* "grandson through paternal uncle." this remarkable classification of kindred, and which is the same in the other branches of these lines, is peculiar to the Slavonic nations within the limits of the Aryan family.[1] In the remaining branches of this line the persons, as shown in the Table, are described, which was not to have been expected. It probably indicates that both forms are used.[2]

4. *Russian.*—In some respects the Russian differs from the Polish and Bohemian. The following diagram exhibits these differences, as well as all that is peculiar in the Russian method :—

LINEAL LINE.

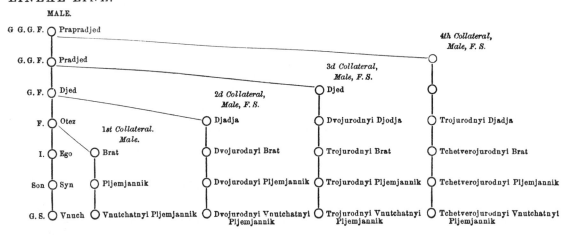

---

[1] The fulness of the Bulgarian nomenclature is further shown by the possession of terms not called out by the questions in the Table: as *bratetz,* "husband's younger brother;" *malina* and *sestritza,* "husband's younger sister;" *nahranenitz,* "adopted son;" nahraneitza, "adopted daughter;" streekovi, "the children of brothers.

[2] Mr. Morse, in his letter to the author, remarks: "The only things peculiar which I have noticed are the three following: First, *otchicha brat,* brother from paternal uncle, for father's brother's son, or cousin ; but in eastern Bulgaria uncle's son is used; second, *vnook* is used both for one's grandson, and for a brother's and sister's grandson; third, *deda* is both grandfather and great-uncle. This is the reciprocal of the preceding. If I call my brother's grandson my grandson, it is proper that he should call me grandfather." Elsewhere he states that *vnook* was used in the twofold sense of grandson and nephew, and that the distinction, in the last use, was sometimes made by prefixing *mal* = little.

The first collateral line, male, gives the following series: *Brother, nephew,* and *nephew-grandson.* The second: *Paternal uncle, double-birth brother, double-birth nephew,* and *double-birth nephew-grandson.* The same peculiarity runs through the other branches of this line, and also through the several branches of the third and more remote collateral lines. Thus, in the third we have for the series, *grandfather, double-birth uncle, triple-birth brother, triple-birth nephew,* and *triple-birth nephew-grandson.* A reference to the Table will show that the same form of designation runs through the entire system. It will be observed that in the Russian, as in the Polish, the terms for brother and sister are applied to first, second, third and fourth cousins, male and female: thus the double-birth brother is in the second collateral line, the triple in the third, and the quadruple in the fourth. The son of each of these collateral brothers is a nephew of *Ego*, and the son of each of these nephews is his nephew-grandson of a certain birth. This realizes, in part, the classification of consanguinei which is found in the Hindi and Bengali, and in other forms in the several dialects of the Gaura language. It appears to be its object to bring collateral kindred within the near degrees of relationship, instead of describing them as persons; leaving the relationship to be implied from the force of the description. The same idea repeats itself in calling a grandfather's brother a grandfather, which he is not, instead of great-uncle, or describing him as grandfather's brother.

Special features, such as these, incorporated in a system of relationship, are of great value for ethnological purposes. Where not essentially foreign to the system they may be explained as deviations from uniformity which sprang up fortuitously in a particular branch of a great family of nations, after which they were transmitted with the blood to the subdivisions of such branch; or, if fundamentally different from the original system of the family, they may have resulted from a combination of two radically distinct forms, and, therefore, indicate a mixture of the blood of two peoples belonging to different families. These special features of a system, when as marked as in the Polish and the Russian, have a history capable of interpretation which reaches far back into the past. They are worthy of investigation for the possible information they may yield upon the question of the blood affinities of nations which concur in their possession, however widely separated they may be from each other. If the divergent element is unexplainable as a development from the materials of the common system of the family, its foreign origin, through mixture of blood, will become a strong presumption. The peculiar features of the Sclavonic system cannot be explained as arising by natural growth out of a form originally descriptive. There is a distinct element of classification of kindred applied to collaterals which does not seem to spring by logical development from the ideas that underlie the common system of the Aryan family. It falls far below the comprehensive method of classification which distinguishes the Turanian system; but it finds its counterpart to some extent, as before stated, in the Hindi and Bengali forms, which have been placed in the Turanian connection.

5. *Lithuanian.*—The Lithuanian system of relationship is not fully extended in the Table. So much of it only is given as could be drawn from the lexicon or vocabulary of the dialect. It is therefore limited to the special terms. The

method of designating collateral kindred, which is the most important part of the system, is wanting. It is for this reason of but little value for comparison. Since both the Lithuanian and Lettish dialects are still spoken, the system of relationship of each of these nations is still a living form. The absence of the Lithuanian, therefore, is the more to be regretted, since it might have shown the original Slavonic form, and thus tended to explain its peculiar features.

VI. Celtic Nations. 1. Erse. 2. Gaelic. 3. Manx. 4. Welsh.

1. *Erse.*—The forms in the Gaelic and Manx are in so near agreement with the Erse that they will be considered together; but the illustrations will be taken from the latter.

The Celtic system, as it appears in the forms of these three nations, is purely descriptive. It is more strictly the typical form of the Aryan family than the Roman, and on some accounts should have been first presented. But as the Roman was based upon the same original, and embodies all the developments from it subsequently made, it furnished a better starting-point for the exposition of the descriptive system. Whilst the Turanian and American Indian systems employ special terms for every recognized relationship, and are therefore non-descriptive, the Celtic, possessing no special terms except the primary, is descriptive, pure and simple; and thus holds the opposite extreme. The difference, as will appear in the sequel, is fundamental. There is every probability that the Erse and Gaelic forms have remained as they now are from a very early period.

Where relatives by blood and marriage are described, without exception, by a combination of the primary terms, it might be supposed to indicate the absence of any positive system of relationship; but this would be an erroneous inference. Such a form is essentially affirmative. To describe kindred in this manner we must ascend step by step, by the chain of consanguinity, from *Ego* to the common ancestor, and then descend in the same definite manner in each collateral line to the particular person whose relationship is sought; or, we must reverse the process, and ascend from this person to the common ancestor, and then down to *Ego*. By this means the natural outflow of the generations is recognized, the several collateral lines are preserved distinct from each other and divergent from the lineal, and absolute precision in the description of kindred is reached. So far it contains a positive element. In the second place, to resist for ages the invention or adoption of special terms for the near collateral relationships which are so constantly needed in domestic life, evinces a decisive, not to say pertinacious, preference for the descriptive method. Although this form suggests from within itself a certain number of generalizations of kindred into classes, with the use of special terms for these relationships in the concrete, yet a system must be developed up to and beyond the Roman standard form to render the use of these common terms definitely expressive; or, in other words, to secure the precision of the purely descriptive method. As a domestic institution the system necessarily possesses the elements of permanence; and its modifications are the slow products of time and growth. Beside the adoption of the Roman as our legal form, the only changes in the English system within the last five centuries, so far as the writer is aware, is the restriction of the terms *nephew* and *niece* to the children of the brother and sister of *Ego*, and the substitution of *grandson* and *granddaughter* in their places in the lineal line. It is not probable that it will be changed as much as this within the same period of time in the future.

The following diagram exhibits the Erse form:—

LINEAL LINE.

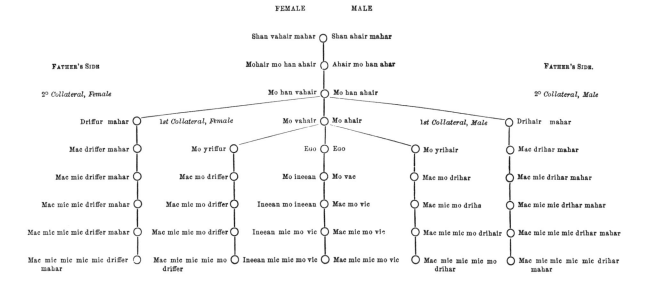

For consanguinei and marriage relatives the Erse and Gaelic have but eight, and these the primary terms.[1] By means of these terms, which exhaust the nomenclature, all of their kindred, near and remote, are described. The diagram represents the lineal line, male and female, and the first and second collateral lines, male and female. Each relationship is made personal to Ego by the use of the pronoun *my* in the description of each person.

In the first collateral the series is as follows: *Brother, son of my brother* and *son of son of my brother;* the second collateral, *brother of my father, son of brother of my father,* and *son of son of brother of my father.* In the third collateral the description is modified by the use of *shan ahair*, "old father," in the place of "father of father," which gives for the series, *brother of my old father, son of brother of my old father* and *son of son of brother of my old father*, and so downward as far as the line is followed. The description, as in the Icelandic, commences at the opposite extreme from *Ego.* In the Table, the Erse, Gaelic and Manx forms will be found fully extended.

4. *Welsh.*—It is probable that the Welsh form of describing kindred was originally the same as the present Erse; but it is now distinguished from it by the

---

[1] The term *uncle* has been naturalized in the Erse dialect in *ūncail*, pronounced *Oonchail*.

possession of several special terms for collateral relations, which were evidently indigenous in the Welsh dialect. The use of these terms, as a part of the nomenclature, modified the method of describing kindred in the same manner as it did in other Aryan dialects. They were evolved by generalizing certain persons into classes, and were used as common terms to express the corresponding relationships.

In the first collateral line, male, the series is as follows : *brother, nephew,* and *grandson of brother ;* in the second, *uncle, male cousin, son of male cousin,* and *grandson of male cousin.* The cousin, as in other forms, is made a second starting-point. Which uncle, or which cousin is intended, does not appear; and the defect in the statement could only be corrected by resorting to the Erse method, or general words explaining the line and branch to which each person belonged. The prevalence of a concurrent as well as anterior descriptive method, is plainly inferrible.[1]

VII. Persian. The modern Persian dialect of the Aryan language has a remarkable history : not so much from the changes through which it has passed, as from its having been a literary language from the earliest period, nearly, of authentic history. After passing through several forms of speech, the Zend, the Pahlevi, and the Parsee, each of which is permanent in written records, it still remains a lineal descendant of the Zend, as well as a closely allied dialect of the Sanskrit.

---

[1] In the " Ancient Laws and Institutes of Wales," there is a curious diagram illustrative of the Welsh system of consanguinity, of which the following is a copy. (*Vide* British Records, Commission Series, Ancient Laws and Institutes of Wales, book xi, ch. iv, p. 605.)

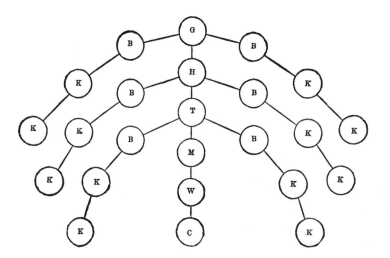

If *Ego* is placed between the father and son the lineal and first collateral lines would become intelligible, and would be in the same form as the Holland Dutch; but the remainder would be unintelligible. The same result follows each change of *Ego* upon the lineal line. But it shows that the arrangement of the lines was correctly apprehended.—G. = *Gorhendad* = great-grandfather ; H. = *Hendad* = grandfather ; T. = *Tad* = father ; M. = *Mab* = son ; W. = *Wyr* = grandson ; B. = *Brawt* = brother ; K. probably represents either *Nai*, nephew, or *Nghfnder* (pronounced hevender), cousin, under a different orthography. C. probably *Goroyr* = great-grandson.

It is the only Aryan dialect which can point to more than one antecedent form in which it was established by a literature, and from which it successively broke away. It still retains its grammatical structure as an Aryan dialect, whilst it has drawn its vocables so largely from Semitic and other sources as to seriously alter its family complexion.

For many reasons the Persian system of relationship was very desirable for comparison with those of the remaining branches of the family. It is given with tolerable fulness in the table. Its nomenclature has been augmented by the adoption of several terms from the Arabic, which in turn have introduced a change in the mode of designating kindred; but it is still evident, notwithstanding the foreign element, that its original form was descriptive. The following diagram exhibits the material parts of the system.

LINEAL LINE.

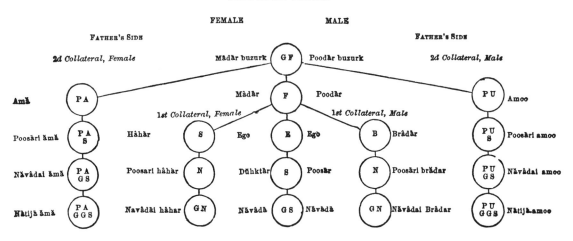

There is no term in the Persian for grandfather; he is described as an " elder father." The term *nätijä*, great-grandchild, was either borrowed from the Nestorian, or the latter obtained it from the former. In the Persian terms for paternal uncle and aunt *ămoo, ămă,* are recognized the Arabic *'amm, 'ammet,* for the same relationships; and in *hăloo, hălä,* maternal uncle and aunt, the Arabic *'Khăl, 'Khălet,* also for the same. From the presence of these foreign terms in the Persian it is inferrible that these relationships were not discriminated either in the Zend, Pahlevi or Parsee, nor in the Persian until after they were borrowed. These several persons, therefore, must have been described by the Celtic method.

In the first collateral line, male, the series is as follows: *brother, son of brother* and *grandchild of brother;* and in the second: *paternal uncle, son of paternal uncle, grandchild of paternal uncle,* and *great-grandchild of paternal uncle.* The other branches follow in a similar form.[1]

---

[1] The pronoun *my* is a suffix in the Persian, as it is in the Finn and also in the Arabic.

Father.	Mother.	Son.	Daughter.	Paternal Uncle.
My Poodărăm,	Mădărăm,	Poosăăm,	Dŭhktărăm,	Amooyăm.
Our Poodărimă,	Mădărima,	Poosăima,	Dŭhktărima,	Amooyămă.
His Poodărioo,	Mădărioo,	Poosăioo,	Dŭhktăroo,	Amooyăoo.

VIII. Armenian. The great antiquity of the Armenians as a people, and their intimate connection, at different periods, with members of the three great families of mankind, which have held dominion in Asia Minor, invests their system of consanguinity with some degree of interest. It is a simple and yet complete system. In its radical features, and in its minute details, it is substantially identical with the Erse and Gaelic forms. One more term is found in its nomenclature than the Erse contains, namely, *tor*, grandson; but this was probably borrowed either from the Osmanli-Turkish, or the Nestorian, in both of which it is found. The Armenian system is purely descriptive, the description of kindred being effected by a combination of the primary terms.

In the first collateral line, male, the following is the series: *brother*, *son of my brother*, and *son of son of my brother;* in the second collateral: *brother of my father*, *son of brother of my father*, and *son of son of brother of my father;* and in the third collateral: *brother of my old-father*, *son of brother of my old-father;* and *son of son of brother of my old-father*. These illustrations are sufficient to exhibit the character of the system, and also to show its identity of form with the Erse and Gaelic. There is also a seeming identity of some of the terms in their nomenclatures of relationship. With the Armenian the series of Aryan nations represented in the Table is closed.

Very little reference has been made to the marriage relationships as they exist in the several nations of this family. They are not material in the descriptive system, except for comparison of the terms as vocables. They will be found in the Table to which the reader is referred for further information.

From this brief review of the more prominent features of the system of relationship of the Aryan nations it has been rendered apparent that the original form of each nation, with the possible exception of the Slavonic nations, was purely descriptive. It is also evident that it is a natural system, following the streams of the blood, and maintaining the several collateral lines distinct from each other, and divergent from the lineal line. In several of the subdivisions of this great family it is still exclusively descriptive as in the Armenian, the Erse, and the Icelandic, while in others, as the Roman, the German, and the English, it is a mixture of the descriptive, with a limited amount of classification of kindred by means of common terms. These terms embrace but a fraction of our kindred. Their use, in describing more distant relations, in combination with the primary terms is but a further expansion of the original system. The origin of these secondary terms, which represent the extent of the modification made, must be found in the constantly recurring desire to avoid the inconvenience of descriptive phrases. Such modifications as have been made are neither inconsistent with the inference that the original form of each nation was descriptive, nor such a departure from it as to render it other than a descriptive system at the present time. This general conclusion, I think, must be considered established.

It may be farther remarked that certain persons who stand in the same degree of nearness to *Ego* were classed together, and a common term invented to express the relationship; but some of these terms, as *oheim* and *uncle*, *vedder* and *cousin*, are radically distinct, and are yet applied to the same persons. At the same time descriptive phrases are used concurrently to designate each respectively. It might be a reasonable supposition that an elaborate nomenclature of relationships was developed in the formative period of the primitive speech of the family, yielding synonyms more or less in number; and that some of these terms had fallen out of certain dialects of the language after their separation, and had been retained by others. But the constancy of the primary terms in all these dialects, and the ascertained subsequent development of several of the secondary, such as *uncle* and *cousin*, forbid this supposition. There is nothing in the original nomenclature, or in its subsequent growth, which seems to favor an assumption that the present has advanced or receded from a primitive form that was radically different. On the contrary, the evidence from the Sanskrit and Scandinavian, and conclusively from the Celtic and Armenian, tends to show that the system of the Aryan family, immediately before its subdivision commenced, was purely descriptive, whatever it might have been at an anterior epoch. The changes that have occurred are explainable by the changes of condition through which the branches of this family have passed. And when the amazing extent of these changes is considered it is chiefly remarkable that the primitive system of consanguinity should still so clearly manifest itself.

If each distinct idea or conception embodied in the common system of relationship of the Aryan family were detached by analysis from its connections, and placed as a separate proposition, the number would not be large; and yet when associated together they are sufficient to create a system, and to organize a family upon the bond of kindred. A system thus formed became, when adopted into practical use, a domestic institution, which, after its establishment, would be upheld and sustained by the ever-continuing necessities that brought it into being. Its mode of transmission, like that of language, was through the channels of the blood. It becomes, then, a question of the highest moment whether its radical forms are stable; and whether they are capable of self-perpetuation through indefinite periods of time. The solution of these problems will decide the further, and still more important question, whether or not these systems, through the identity of their radical features, can deliver any testimony concerning the genetic connection of the great families of mankind, as well as of the nations of which these families are severally composed. Without entering upon the discussion of these topics, which is reserved until the facts with reference to the systems of other families have been presented, it may be observed that the perpetuation of the descriptive system through so many independent channels, and through the number of centuries these nations have been separated from each other, was neither an accidental nor a fortuitous occurrence. There are sufficient reasons why the Erse, the Icelandic, and the Armenian forms are still identical down to their minute details; why the system of the remaining nations of this family has departed so slightly from the original common form; and why it has moved independently, in each dialect and stock-language, in the same definite direction.

The systems of the Semitic and Uralian families remain to be noticed, which, as they are also descriptive, properly precede the classificatory.

7   January, 1869.

CHAPTER V.

SYSTEM OF RELATIONSHIP OF THE SEMITIC FAMILY.

Arabic System—Illustrations of its method—Nearly identical with the Celtic—Druse and Maronite—Agrees with the Arabic—Hebrew System—Restoration of its Details difficult—Illustrations of its Method—Agrees with the Arabic—Neo-Syriac or Nestorian—Illustrations of its Method—Agrees with the Arabic—System presumptively follows the Language—Comparison of Aryan and Semitic Systems—Identical in their Radical Characteristics—Originally Descriptive in Form—Probable Inferences from this Identity.

THE Semitic language, in its three principal branches, is represented in the Table, with the system of consanguinity and affinity peculiar to each. First, the Arabic, by the Arabic and Druse and Maronite; second, the Hebraic, by the Hebrew; and third, the Aramaic, by the Neo-Syriac or Nestorian. Since the Arabic and Nestorian are spoken languages, and their systems of relationship are in daily use, and as the Hebrew exhibits the Jewish form as it prevailed when this language ceased to be spoken, the schedules in the Table present, without doubt, the ancient plan of consanguinity of that remarkable family which has exercised such a decisive influence upon the destiny of mankind. Although the influence of the Semitic family has been declining for centuries, before the overmastering strength of the Aryan civilization, the family itself will ever occupy a conspicuous position in human history. These schedules are the more interesting because they reveal, with so much of certainty, not only the present but also the ancient system which prevailed in the Semitic kingdoms of Babylon, Nineveh and Jerusalem, and in the Commonwealth of Carthage. They are likewise important for comparison for the purpose of ascertaining the nature and ethnic boundaries of the descriptive form of consanguinity, and its relations to the forms in other families of mankind.

The two distinguishing characteristics of the system of the Aryan family are present in the Semitic. In the first place, it is substantially descriptive in form, with the same tendency to a limited number of generalizations to relieve the burdensomeness of this method; and in the second, it maintains the several collateral lines distinct from each other and divergent from the lineal line. In other words, it follows the streams of the blood, as they must necessarily flow where marriage exists between single pairs.

Whilst the Semitic system separates the family by a distinct and well defined line from the Asiatic nations beyond the Indus, it places it side by side with the Aryan and Uralian. So far as the descriptive system of relationship can deliver any testimony through identity of radical forms, which is worthy of acceptance, it tends to show, that while there is no traceable affinity from this source between the Semitic and Turanian families, there is a positive convergence of the Aryan, Semitic and Uralian families to a common point of unity, the evidence of which is still preserved (if it can be said to amount to evidence) in their several modes of indicating the domestic relationships.

I. Arabic Branch. 1. Arabic. 2. Druse and Maronite.

1. *Arabic Nation.*—There are original terms in this language for grandfather and grandmother, which is the more singular as there are none in Hebrew. Ascendants above these degrees are described by a combination of these terms with those for father and mother, in which respect the Arabic is variant from the Aryan form. While we would say grandfather's father or great-grandfather, an Arab would say, father of grandfather. It is a slight difference, and yet it reveals a usage with respect to the manner of expressing this relationship. There are no terms in Arabic for grandson or granddaughter, nephew or niece, or cousin. These persons are described by the Celtic method.

The following is the series in the first collateral line, male: *brother, son of my brother, son of son of my brother,* and *son of son of son of my brother.* It is in literal agreement with the Roman and Erse.

It is a noticeable feature of the Arabic system that it has separate terms in *'amm 'ammet* for paternal uncle and aunt, and in *'khâl 'khâlet* for maternal uncle and aunt. By means of these terms the manner of describing the four branches of the second collateral line was carried up fully to the Roman standard in convenience and precision, and became identical with it in form. It also tends to show that the development of a system originally descriptive has a predetermined logical direction. With the exception of the discrimination of the relationships named, and the changes thereby introduced in the method of indicating consanguinei, the Arabic form is identical with the Erse.

In the second collateral line, male branch, the series gives *paternal uncle, son of paternal uncle,* and *son of son of paternal uncle.* The third, which is variant from the Roman, is as follows: *paternal uncle of father, son of paternal uncle of father,* and *son of son of paternal uncle of father.* This line is described as a series of relatives of the father of *Ego.* In like manner the fourth collateral line is described as a series of relatives of the grandfather of *Ego,* e. g., *paternal uncle of grandfather, son of paternal uncle of grandfather,* and so downward as far as the line was traceable. For a further knowledge of the details of the Arabic system reference is made to the Table.

No attempt is made in this system to classify kindred by the generalization of those who stand in the same degree of nearness to *Ego* into one class, with the use of a special term to express the relationship. On the contrary, the four special terms for collateral kindred, above named, are each applied to a single class of persons who are brothers and sisters to each other, which is the lowest form of generalization in any system of consanguinity. It is the same as the generalization of the relationship of *brother* or *son,* each of which terms is applied to several persons who stand in an identical relationship. Nephew, in our sense, on the contrary, involves the generalization of two classes of persons into one class, and cousin that of four into one. Neither does the Arabic employ the Sanskritic or Grecian method of compounding terms by contraction to express specific relationship; but it adheres closely to a purely descriptive method by the use of the primary terms. The Erse and Gaelic are nearer to the Arabic in their minute forms than they are to any form of any Aryan nation, except the Armenian and the Scandinavian.

It is quite probable that the words for uncle and aunt are of comparatively modern use in Arabic as terms of relationship, as they have other meanings, which for a period of time may have been exclusive. In answer to an inquiry upon this point the distinguished American missionary Dr. C. V. A. Van Dyck, of Beirut, Syria, writes: " The Arabic words for uncle and aunt, *'amm 'ammet, 'khâl 'khâlet,* are derived from pure Arabic roots, but are not necessarily of very ancient use in the above meanings, as they have several other meanings. Their use in describing degrees of relationship may be somewhat later than the early history of the language, yet they are found as far back as we have any remains of the language. If the Himyaritic were sufficiently restored to be of use, it might throw some light upon what you remark concerning the Erse and Gaelic."

The presence of two of these terms in the Hebrew, and of the four in the Nestorian, gives to them necessarily a very great antiquity as terms of relationship; but it may be possible to reach beyond the period of their first introduction.

The marriage relationships are quite fully discriminated, and reveal some peculiarities. For an inspection of them reference is again made to the Table.

2. *Druse and Maronite.*—This form is so nearly identical with the last that it does not require a separate notice. The fact of its identity, both in form and terms, is important, however, since it furnishes a criterion for determining the stability of the system during the period these nations have been politically distinct.

II. Hebraic Branch. Hebrew Nation. The same difficulty that prevented the restoration of the Sanskrit system of relationship in its full original form exists also with reference to the Hebrew. It ceased to be a living form when the language ceased to be spoken, and from the remains of the language it can only be restored conjecturally beyond the nearest degrees.

In the lineal line all persons above father and below son must have been described by a combination of the primary terms. This is inferable also from the general tenor of the Scripture genealogies. There are special terms for descendants of the third and fourth generation which were applied to each specifically.

The series in the first collateral line, male, as given in the Table, is limited to two persons, namely, *brother* and *son of brother*. It is to be inferred that the remaining descendants were described as *son of son of brother*, and so downward as far as the relationship was to be traced.

In this language the term for paternal uncle is *dōdhī*, the literal signification of which is " beloved." Is it to be inferred that this relationship was not discriminated until after the Hebrew became a distinct dialect, or that it superseded the original of the Arabic *'amm?* The first two members of this branch of the line only are given in the table, namely, *paternal uncle* and *son of paternal uncle*. Without doubt the remaining persons were described as in the Arabic. The analogy of the system suggests this inference. In *ªkhi* and *ªkhoth*, maternal uncle and aunt, we find words from the same root as *khâl* and *khâlet* for the same relationships. The description of persons in these branches is the same as in the last case, namely, *maternal uncle* and *son of maternal uncle; maternal aunt* and *son of maternal aunt.* This fragment is all that remains of the Hebrew system as it is shown in the table. The nature, and to some extent the form, of the system may be gathered from the Scripture genealogies, in which it is found to be descriptive.

So far as the characteristic features of the Hebrew form of consanguinity are given in the Table, they are seen to be identical with the Arabic substantially. This fact becomes important when it is remembered that the Hebrew system is shown as it existed when the language ceased to be spoken, which event is generally placed at the period of the Babylonian captivity 720 B. C. At the commencement of the Christian era the Aramaic dialect of the Semitic language had become substituted for the Hebrew among the Jews. The slight differences between the Arabic of to-day and the Hebrew form of twenty centuries and upwards ago, is a fact of some significance in its bearing upon the question of the stability of the radical features of descriptive systems of relationship.

There are several points concerning the use of terms of consanguinity in the New Testament Scriptures, as well as in the Old, which it would be instructive to investigate. This is particularly the case with reference to the term for *brother*, which appears to have been applied to a *cousin* as well, and which use finds its parallel in the Turanian form. But with the radical features of the Hebrew system before us, these uses of the term must either find their explanation in some particular custom; or point to a different and still more primitive form.

III. Aramaic Branch. Neo-Syriac, or Nestorian.

The Syriac and Chaldee are the two principal dialects of the Aramaic branch of the Semitic language. Of these, the Nestorian is the modern form of the Syriac, and stands to it in the same relation Italian does to Latin. It is a lineal descendant of the ancient language of Babylon and Nineveh. We are indebted to the American missionaries for rendering the dialect accessible.

The Nestorian nomenclature of relationships has been developed slightly beyond the Arabic and the Hebrew. It has original terms for grandfather and grandmother, by means of which, and in combination with the terms for father and mother, ascendants are described in the same manner as in the Arabic; also, original terms for grandson and granddaughter, and for the next degree beyond, by means of which descendants are distinguished from each other. This is the extent of the difference, but it introduces a slight variation in the method of describing kindred.

The first collateral line, male, gives the following series: *Brother, son of brother, grandson of brother,* and *great grandson of brother.* The form is the same as in the Arabic, but with the substitution of the new terms. In the second collateral we have *paternal uncle, son of paternal uncle,* and *grandson of paternal uncle;* and in the third, *brother of grandfather, son of brother of grandfather,* and *grandson of brother of grandfather.* The remaining branches of these lines are described, with corresponding changes, in the same manner.

In the Nestorian there are no terms for nephew or niece or cousin, consequently *ámŭwee* and *umte, Khâlŭwee* and *Kâhleh,* uncle and aunt, and which are from the same root as the corresponding Arabic words, were without any correlatives except in the form of descriptive phrases. Notwithstanding the slight deviations between the Nestorian and the Arabic forms, after an independent and separate existence of many centuries, they are still identical in their radical characteristics.

Terms for the marriage relationships are less numerous in the Semitic than in the Aryan language. From their limited number and the manner of their use they are of but little importance as a part of the general system of relationship, except for comparison as vocables. In the systems of the Turanian and American Indian families they enter more essentially into their framework, and are of much greater significance from the manner of their use.

The system of relationship of the Semitic family has a much wider range than is indicated in the Table. It will doubtless be found wherever the blood and language of this family have spread. Among the Abyssinians, who speak a Semitic dialect, it probably prevails; and most likely among the people who speak the Berber dialects of North Africa, which are said to be Semitic. Traces of it exist in the system of the Zulus or Kafirs of South Africa, which, Malayan in form, has adopted Semitic words into its nomenclature. The Himyaritic dialect, if investigated with reference to this question, would probably disclose some portion of the primitive form.

A comparison of the systems of relationship of the Semitic and Aryan families suggests a number of interesting questions. It must have become sufficiently obvious that in their radical characteristics they are identical. Any remaining doubt upon that point is removed by the near approach of the Arabic and Nestorian to the Erse and Icelandic. It is rendered manifest by the comparison that the system of the two families was originally purely descriptive, the description being effected by the primary terms; and that the further development of each respectively, by the same generalizations, limited to the same relationships, was, in each case, the work of civilians and scholars to provide for a new want incident to changes of condition. The rise of these modifications can be definitely traced. Whether the system in its present form is of natural origin, and the two families came by it through the necessary constitution of things; or whether it started at some epoch in a common family and was transmitted to such families as now possess it by the streams of the blood, are the alternative questions. Their solution involves two principal considerations: first, how far the descriptive system is affirmative, and as such is a product of human intelligence; and secondly, how far its radical forms are stable and self-perpetuating. It is not my purpose to do more than make a general reference to the elements of those propositions which will require a full discussion in another connection.

The descriptive system is simple rather than complex, and has a natural basis in the nature of descents, where marriage subsists between single pairs. For these reasons it might have been framed independently by different families, starting with an antecedent system either differing or agreeing; and its perpetuation in such a case might be in virtue of its foundation upon the nature of descents. And yet these conclusions are not free from doubt. With the fact established that the plan of consanguinity of the two families is identical in whatever is radical, and with the further fact extremely probable that it had become established in each at a time long anterior to their civilization, the final inference is encouraged that it prevailed in the two original nations from which these families were respectively derived. Standing alone, without any contrasting form, the descriptive system of the two families would scarcely attract attention. But it so happens that in other portions of the human family a system of relationship now exists radically different in its structure and elaborate and complicated in its forms, which is spread out over large areas of human speech, and which has perpetuated itself through equal periods of time as well as changes of condition. The conditions of society, then, may have some influence in determining the system of relationship. In other words, the descriptive form is not inevitable; neither is it fortuitous. Some form of consanguinity was an indispensable necessity of each family. Its formation involved an arrangement of kindred into lines of descent, with the adoption of a method for distinguishing one kinsman from another. Whatever plan was finally adopted would acquire the stability of a domestic institution as soon as it came in general use and had proved its sufficiency. A little reflection will discover the extreme difficulty of innovating upon a system once established. Founded upon common consent, it could only be changed by the influence of motives as universal as the usage. The choice of a descriptive method for the purpose of specializing each relationship, by the Semitic family, and the adoption of the classificatory by the Turanian, for the purpose of arranging consanguinei into groups, and placing the members of each group in the same relationship to *Ego*, were severally acts of intelligence and knowledge. A system of relationship is to a certain extent necessarily affirmative. Those parts which embody definite ideas and show man's work are capable of yielding affirmative testimony concerning the ethnic connection of nations among whom these ideas have been perpetuated. The descriptive system is simple in its elements, and embraces but a few fundamental conceptions. It is therefore incapable of affording such a body of evidence upon these questions as the classificatory: but it does not follow that it is entirely without significance. It is something that the Aryan and Semitic families have a system which can be definitely traced to the same original form, and to a period of time when each family, in all probability, existed in a single nation. It is something more that this system has positive elements as a product of human intelligence; and that it has perpetuated itself through so many centuries of time, in so many independent channels, and under such eventful changes of condition. To these may be added the further fact that the several systems of the Aryan nations, taken in connection with the terms of relationship as vocables, demonstrate the unity of origin of these nations, and their descent from the same stem of the human family. In like manner, the systems of the several Semitic nations, considered in connection with the terms as vocables, demonstrate the unity of origin of the latter nations, and perform this work in the most simple and direct way. Upon the present showing it will not be claimed, against the testimony of the vocables, and in the face of the radical differences in the grammatical structure of the Aryan and Semitic languages, that it affords any positive evidence of the unity of origin of the two families.[1] It will be sufficient to say that the descriptive system separates these families and the Uralian from all the other families of mankind by a clearly defined line; and that it seems to point to a nearer connection among them than either has with any other family of man.

---

[1] "It is impossible to mistake a Semitic language, and what is more important, it is impossible to imagine an Aryan language derived from a Semitic, or a Semitic from an Aryan language. The grammatical framework is totally distinct in these two families of speech. This does not preclude, however, the possibility that both are divergent streams of the same source; and the comparisons that have been instituted between the Semitic roots, reduced to their simplest form, and the roots of the Aryan languages, have made it more than probable that the material elements with which both started, were originally the same."—*Müller's Science of Language*, Lec. viii. p. 282.

CHAPTER VI.

SYSTEM OF RELATIONSHIP OF THE URALIAN FAMILY.

Reasons for Detaching Ugrian and Turk Nations from the Turanian Connection—Their System of Relationship Descriptive — Uralian proposed as a Name for the New Family — I. Ugrian Nations — Their Subdivisions — System of the Finns—Illustrations of its Method—Marriage Relationships—Limited Amount of Classification —System of the Esthonians—Purely Descriptive—System of the Magyars—Illustrations of its Method— Peculiar Features—Chiefly Descriptive—II. Turk Nations—Closely Allied to the Ugrian—Their Subdivisions —Area of Uralian Family—Osmanli-Turks—An Extreme Representative of the Turkic Class of Nations— Relative Positions of the Aryan, Semitic, and Uralian Families—Osmanli-Turkish System of Relationship— Illustrations of its Form — Kuzulbashi—A Turkic People—System of Relationship — Illustrations of its Form—Descriptive in Character—Identity of System in the Branches of this Family—Its Agreement with that of the Aryan and Semitic Families—Objects gained by Comparisons—Ascertainment of the Nature and Principles of the Descriptive System—Ethnic Boundaries of its Distribution—Concurrence of these Families in its Possession—Subordinate in Importance to the Classificatory—Exposition of the Classificatory System the Main Object of this Work.

IT is proposed to detach from the assemblage of nations, distinguished as the Turanian family, the Ugrian and Turk branches, and to erect them into an independent family under the name of the Uralian. All of the Asiatic dialects which fell without the Aryan and Semitic connections, have been gathered into the Turanian family of languages, with the exception of the Chinese and its cognates. This classification, however, philologists have regarded as provisional. These dialects are not parts of a family speech in the same sense as are the Aryan and Semitic dialects.[1] The latter respectively agree with each other in their minute as well as general grammatical forms, and this, in turn, is corroborated by the identity of a large number of vocables in the several branches of each. On the other hand, in the Turanian dialects, in addition to morphological similarities, which are inconclusive, there is a partial identity of grammatical forms, and also of vocables which serve to connect particular groups, but fail to unite the several groups as a whole. In other words, the Turanian family of languages, as now constituted, cannot hold together if subjected to the same tests upon which the Aryan and Semitic were established; or upon which a new dialect would now be admitted into either.

The introduction of this new family does not contravene any established philological conclusion. In the formation of a family of languages the method of the philologists was rigidly scientific. Such dialects as were derived from the same immediate source, the evidence of which was preserved in the vocables, were first brought together in a stock-language, such as the Slavonic. A further comparison

---

[1] Science of Language, p. 289.

of these stock languages with each other was then made, to find how far the root forms of their vocables were identical; and also to discover another class of affinities which the grammatical structure of these stock languages might reveal. It was early ascertained that grammatical structure was the ultimate criterion by which the admission of a doubtful language must be determined, since the number of constant vocables became smaller in the extreme branches of a family ethnically connected, and the subtile process of naturalization might explain their presence in each without being indigenous in either. In this manner a true family of languages was bound together by common grammatical forms, and by the more simple and conclusive bond of common vocables. The Turanian dialects, so called, have been much less investigated, and are less thoroughly known than the Aryan or Semitic, in consequence of their great numbers, their inaccessible position, and the vast extent of the areas over which they are spread. It is not claimed that the same coincidences in grammatical forms, or identity of vocables exist in the several branches of the Turanian speech. A limited number of common words and of common roots, running, not through all the branches of the Turanian speech, but here and there through certain portions, furnished some evidence of original unity, but not enough, standing alone, to sustain the classification. These dialects also agree with each other with respect to their articulation. They are agglutinated in their structure, and this common feature has entered, to some extent, into the basis upon which they have been organized into a family of languages. If, however, agglutination is a stage of growth or development through which all languages must pass after emerging from the monosyllabic and before reaching the inflectional, which is the received opinion, it does not furnish any basis for the organization of these dialects into a family of speech. Beside this, the use of this common feature of agglutination, as a ground of classification, forces the Chinese and its cognate dialects into a position of isolation, and interposes a barrier between them and the proper Turanian dialects where none such may exist. For these reasons the reduction of this great body of languages, under a Northern and Southern division, into one common family, the Turanian, could not be other than a provisional arrangement. The science of language is impeded rather than advanced by raising to the rank of a family of languages such an incongruous assemblage of dialects as are now included in the Turanian. The Aryan and Semitic standard is much to be preferred.

Upon the basis of the systems of consanguinity and affinity of the Asiatic nations, they divide themselves into at least two distinct families, each of which, it seems probable, will ultimately become as clearly distinguished from the other as the Aryan now is from the Semitic. A comparison of the systems of a limited number of these nations has led to singular and rather unexpected results. The system of the Turanian family proper, which will be presented in a subsequent part of this work, separates it from the Aryan and Semitic by a line of demarcation perfectly distinct and traceable. Such a result furnishes no occasion of surprise. On the other hand, it excludes from the Turanian connection, by a line not less distinct and unmistakable, the Ugrian and Turk stocks, which are the principal members of the Northern division of the family, as now constituted. In other words, the Ugrian and Turk nations detach themselves, through their system of relationship, from the Turanian family, and stand independent. Such a result was not to have been expected. Their system of consanguinity is not classificatory, but descriptive. If any inference can be drawn from the joint possession of such a system it would be that these nations are nearer akin to the Aryan and Semitic nations than they are to the Turanian; and that the blood of the Finn, the Magyar, and the Turk, if traced back to its sources, will be found to revert to the common stream from which issued the Semitic and Aryan currents before it can approach the still older Turanian channel.

The Ugrian and Turk nations represented in the Table are few in number. A much larger number is fairly necessary to substantiate the claims of these nations to the rank of a family; but nevertheless, the indications revealed in their system of relationship are unmistakable. It will be quite satisfactory to leave the final recognition of the Uralian family dependent upon the concurrence of the unrepresented nations in the possession of the same system of consanguinity. For the present it will suffice to present the system as it now exists in some of the branches of the proposed family as a justification of their removal from the Turanian connection.

The term Uralian, which is suggested for this family, has some advantages of a positive character. Ugrian and Turkic have definite significations in ethnology; and Mongolian, which was formerly applied to both, as well as to other and more Eastern nations, includes stocks not represented in the Table, whose system of relationship when procured may be variant. Uralian has been used in various connections, but without becoming limited to any exclusive use. The Ural chain of mountains traverses the areas of the Ugrian and Turk nations, and with it they have been territorially associated from time immemorial. Uralian, therefore, as an unappropriated term, is not only free from objection, but there are general reasons commending it to acceptance.

I. Ugrian Nations. 1. Finn. 2. Esthonian. 3. Magyar.

Under the general name of Ugrians are now included the Laps, Samoyeds, Yeniscians, and Yukahiri; the several subdivisions of the Permians, and of the Finns of the Baltic and the Volga; and the Voguls, Ostiaks, and Magyars.[1] They hold the chief part of the polar area both of Europe and Asia, and spreading southward through several parallels of latitude, they are confronted on the south by the Slavonic and Turk nations. The Ugrians are believed to be older occupants of Northeastern Europe than the Slavonians,[2] and stand to this area in the same relation that the Celts do to Western Europe. The southern portion of their area lies between that of the Turk stock on the east, and the Slavonic on the west, by both of whom it has been encroached upon and reduced from century to century. It seems probable that they have been forced northward to the Arctic region from a much lower primitive area; and that they have become a polar people from necessity rather than choice. They are still a numerous, and, in many respects, an

---

[1] For the systematic classification of these nations, see Latham's Descriptive Ethnology, I, 461.
[2] Latham's Native Races of the Russian Empire, p. 5.

interesting race of men. Their capabilities for future improvement may be inferred from the progress made by the Magyars and Finns. The system of relationship of the Ugrian nations, so far as it is given in the Table, is limited to that form of it which now prevails among the Finns of Finland, the Esthonians, and the Magyars. Of these, the first two belong to the same and the third to a different subdivision of the Ugrian stock. Presumptively, the system of the remaining nations is the same in fundamental characteristics; but a knowledge of their forms is necessary to the determination of that fact.

1. *Finns.*—Two schedules were received, fully and minutely filled out with the system of consanguinity and affinity of the Finns. One of them was prepared by Mr. G. Selin, a student in the University of Helsingfors, at the request of the late President Retzius; and the other by Dr. Urjo Koskinen, one of the Faculty of the University of Jacobstad, both of them Finns. The differences between the two schedules were so slight, although made without any knowledge of each other's work, that they are given in the Table as one under their joint names. A special notation was furnished with each schedule, but the pronunciation of the words is indicated by the common characters.[1]

As it is important to know the precise character of the Finn system, it will be presented with more fulness than in previous cases.

There are no terms in this language for ancestors above father and mother, except *eukko*, grandmother; or for descendants below son and daughter. They are described, with the exception named, by an augmentation or reduplication of the primary terms. Among the Turanian nations the relationship of brother and sister is conceived in the twofold form of elder and younger, as is shown by the possession of separate terms for these relationships, and the absence, usually, of terms for brother and sister in the abstract. The Finns, in this respect, follow the usage of the Aryan and Semitic families.

In the first collateral line male, the series is as follows: *Brother, son of brother, son of son of brother,* and *son of son of son of brother.* There is a term for nephew, *nepää,* but none for niece; while the female branch of this line necessarily employs the descriptive method, the male has the same, and also a second form, as follows: *Brother, nephew, son of nephew,* and *son of son of nephew.*

There are separate terms for paternal and maternal uncles, a common term for aunt, and two terms for cousin, which give to the Finn nomenclature quite a full development, and to its form a sensible approach to the Roman.

---

[1] Mr. Selin, in his letter, remarks: " The information relating to the ancient condition of the Finnish nation is scarce and defective, which is not surprising, the nation having been for seven centuries subjected to foreign influence and subdued, before they had brought forth a history of their own, or reached any high degree of culture. The ancient national songs, proverbs, and fables, which have been gathered of late, with great zeal and application, are almost the only source from which we derive any knowledge of the life, customs, and institutions of our ancestors. Among these monuments of times gone by, the celebrated cycle of songs called "Kalevala" stands foremost. Concerning most of the circumstances of which you desire to be informed, all positive knowledge is wanting. . . . . No division into tribes has as yet been traced among the Finns. We call ourselves Susmalaisct."

The second collateral line male on the father's side runs as follows: *Paternal uncle, son of paternal uncle,* and *son of son of paternal uncle.* Another, and perhaps more common form, is the following: *Paternal uncle, cousin, son of cousin,* and *son of son of cousin.* The other branches of this line show the same forms with corresponding changes of terms.

Assuming that the Finn system was originally purely descriptive, it will be seen that it has developed in the precise direction of the Roman form and of the forms among some other Aryan nations. In this respect the comparison is instructive, as it tends to show: first, that however simple the ideas may be which express the connection of consanguinei, they serve to organize a family upon the bond itself, and thus assume the form of a domestic institution; secondly, that it is extremely difficult to change essentially an established system, whether descriptive or classificatory; thirdly, that the inconvenience of the descriptive form tends to suggest the use of the common terms found in the Finn, and English as well, which arise out of the system by logical development; and lastly, that the direction this development would take was predetermined by the logical trend of the ideas embodied in the system. The phrase " father's brother" describes a person, but it also implies, as elsewhere remarked, a bond of connection between that person and myself, which is real and tangible. When the idea suggested by the phrase found a new birth in *patruus* or *seta*, these terms superseded the former, and became the living embodiment of the idea itself. It was not so much an overthrow of the descriptive method as the realization of the conception it suggested in an improved as well as concrete form. Centuries of time may have elapsed before this much of advance was made. Having thus gained the relationship of paternal uncle, the Finns could say, *setani poĭkä,* " son of my paternal uncle," instead of " son of my father's brother," which is slightly more convenient. The same remarks apply to the relationships of nephew and cousin.

The third collateral line gives the following series: *Paternal uncle of my father, son of paternal uncle of my father,* and *son of son of the same;* or, in another form, *brother of my great father, cousin of my father,* and *son of cousin of my father.* The relatives of *Ego* in the remaining branches of this line are designated in a similar manner.

The marriage relationships are quite fully discriminated. There are special terms for husband and wife, father-in-law, and mother-in-law, son-in-law and daughter-in-law; and also three different terms for the several brothers-in-law, and two for the several sisters-in-law. Its nomenclature, therefore, is nearly equal to the Roman. Fulness in the discrimination of the marriage relationships is also a characteristic of the Turanian system.

There are but five generalizations in the system of relationship of the Finns. First, the several brothers of a father are generalized into a class, and the term *setä,* parental uncle, is used to express the relationship; secondly, the several brothers of the mother of *Ego* are generalized into another class, and a different term, *eno,* maternal uncle, is employed to distinguish it from the former; thirdly, the several sisters of his father and mother are generalized into a class, and a common term, *täte,* aunt, is used to indicate the relationship; fourthly, the sons of the brothers and sisters of *Ego* are brought into a common class, and the term *nepää*, nephew, indicates the relationship; and lastly, the children of these several uncles and aunts are generalized into one class, and the common term *serkku*, and another, *orpänä*, cousin, were used to express this relationship. Such an amount of classification, and following so closely in the direction of the Roman, suggests a presumption of influence from that source. But it is difficult to see how it can be sustained. At the same time there is a striking similarity, not to say affinity, between several of the Finnish terms of consanguinity, and the corresponding terms in the Aryan dialects: for example, *sīsär*, sister; *tytär*, daughter; *poīkä*, son; *nepää*, nephew; *täte*, aunt; *setä*, parental uncle; and *eno*, paternal aunt. The terms for collateral consanguinei may have been borrowed from Aryan sources, which is not improbable, but this could not be affirmed of *sisar*, *tytar*, and *poīkä*. What the explanation of these affinities may be, I am unable to state. As the Turanian system has not yet been presented, it cannot be contrasted with that here shown. It may be premised, however, that the Finn system does not contain a single characteristic of the Turanian, the two former being the reverse of each other in every respect, as will appear in the sequel.

From what has been seen of the gradual development of special terms in the Aryan languages, and of the modification, by means of them, of the descriptive form; and from what now appears on the face of the Finnish system, it is a reasonable, if not a necessary inference, that the latter was also originally descriptive, and that the special terms for collateral consanguinei were of comparatively modern introduction. This view will be materially strengthened by the present condition of the Esthonian form.

2. *Esthonians.*—The system of relationship of the Esthonians was furnished by Charles A. Leas, Esq., United States Consul at Revel, Russia. It is the more valuable and interesting from the fact that this people are rude and uncultivated, and still possess their native language, usages, and customs, although surrounded by Slavonic and German populations.[1] It is, therefore, presumptively nearer to the

---

[1] From the instructive letter of Mr. Leas, which accompanied the schedule, the following extracts are taken. "The Esthonians who inhabit this province, and who for the past seven hundred years have constituted its peasantry, were found a comparatively wild and uncultivated people by the German Knights, when they invaded and took possession of the country, A.D. 1219. This people were at that time divided into a number of tribes, each being governed by a chief. At that period they had, to some extent, abandoned their nomadic life, and a portion of them had commenced the cultivation of the land, by making farms; but they have preserved no traditions, nor have they the slightest conception as to their origin, or from whence they came. And although they have lived among a highly intelligent and cultivated people (the Germans) for the past six hundred years, they have persistently and obstinately refused to adopt or learn their language, habits, customs, or dress; but to this day have preserved with tenacity the language, habits, customs, and even dress of their fathers, living in the same condition substantially in which they were found in 1219. No traditions are known or related among them which throw any light upon their origin or ancient history; nor have the Germans preserved any knowledge of their civil organization or mode of government, beyond the simple fact that they were divided into tribes, and that these tribes were governed by chiefs. From 1219 to about fifty years ago, this people were held as slaves by the German nobility; and they now constitute the peasantry of that province. Until lately they had no written language; and

primitive form of consanguinity of this branch of the Uralian family than that of the Finns. The two peoples speak closely allied dialects of the same stock language.

Mr. Leas remarks upon the system as follows: "The system of relationship now in use among the Esthonians is nearly the same as our own, the terms being few, and extending only to the nearest kindred. You will notice from the annexed schedule that the native Esthonian has no condensed form of expression, as with us, for the principal relationships. For example, instead of calling his father's brother his *uncle*, he says, 'my father's brother;' and instead of calling his father's or his mother's sister his *aunt*, he says, 'my father's sister,' or 'my mother's sister;' and instead of condensing the phrase, 'mother's sister's husband' into *uncle*, he says, 'my mother's sister's husband.' In like manner, instead of calling his son's wife his daughter-in-law, he would say, *minu poeg naine*, that is, 'my son's wife;' and so on with the other relationships."

He thus gives, in a few words, the substance and the characteristics of the Esthonian system. Having no terms in their language for uncle or aunt, nephew or niece, or cousin, and no classification of kindred of any kind, they describe them by a combination of the primary terms. It is, therefore, the Erse and Gaelic method, pure and simple, and the only instance in which it has been found without the circle of the Aryan family. The terms of relationship are, for the most part, the same, under dialectical changes, as the Finnish; from which the inference arises that the system, with the terms, came down to each from the same original source. Since the Esthonian form is the simpler of the two, it seems to be a

---

even now are extremely ignorant and uneducated, abounding in superstitions, and bitterly opposed to all modern improvements. That the line of succession in their original chiefs was from the father to his eldest son (and not elective), seems probable from the fact that to this day all the property of the father descends to the eldest son, the other children inherited nothing; and this rule prevails outside of the Russian law. The people are 'hewers of wood and drawers of water,' having no part whatever either in making laws, or in the administration of the general or provincial government. The old German nobility make and execute all the laws of the province, under the Emperor, who permits them to do so; nor are the peasantry possessed of any wealth worth mentioning. The land of the province is owned by the German nobles, who have divided it into estates of immense dimensions, called Knights' Estates, some of which are twenty and thirty miles square; and none, I believe has less than eight or ten miles square. These estates can neither be reduced below what is called a Knight's estate, which is some three or four thousand acres; nor can any man purchase an estate in the province except he be an Esthonian nobleman. The most distinguished Russian, of whatever rank, could not purchase an Esthonian estate, unless the Esthonian nobility first admitted him as a member of their body; and as the Esthonians proper are peasants, and none of them noblemen, so none possess estates. They rent the land and cultivate it, and in payment give either work or money. Each estate has one, two, or three thousand acres of land immediately around the residence of the nobleman, which he cultivates himself through the labor of the peasants, the balance being parcelled out in peasant farms of one or two hundred acres. The peasant farmers, if they pay in work, which is generally the case, send their sons, wives, and daughters to work for the nobleman, who, in this manner, without personal labor, secures the ample cultivation of that part of the estate which remains for his own use, as first stated. The peasants live in small wood houses without chimneys, which are filled with smoke the entire winter, and live on black bread, milk, and salt. They have stoically resisted all the kind efforts of the nobility to give them chimneys to their houses, declaring, as they do, that it is a destructive innovation, only tending to destroy their lives."

further necessary inference that it still exhibits the system of the original stock from which both were derived; thus tending to confirm, by an independent argument, a conclusion previously formed, that the system of the Finns was originally purely descriptive. The two forms are identical in their radical conceptions, the difference consisting in the limited amount of classification of kindred which is found in the latter. In like manner, the absence from the Esthonian dialect of several of the terms of relationship now existing in the Finnish, tends to show that the latter have been developed in the Finnish, or introduced from external sources, with the modifications of form thereby produced, since the separation of these nations from each other, or from the parent stem. The same system of consanguinity being thus found in two parallel streams of descent, carries back its existence, as a distinct system, to the time when the Finns and Esthonians, or their common ancestors, were one people. It can therefore claim an antiquity in the Uralian family of many centuries.

It will not be necessary to take up the Esthonian system in detail after this general explanation of its character. For a further knowledge of its form reference is made to the Table. Although not fully extended, the remainder, from what is given, can be readily inferred.

3. *Magyars.*—The ethnic connection of the Magyars with the Ugrian nations is well established. Since their irruption into Hungary they have been surrounded by Slavonic populations, of whose progress they have, to some extent, partaken; but their system of consanguinity appears to have remained uninfluenced from this source. The schedule in the Table, by some misconception, was filled out as far only as special terms are used, leaving all the remaining questions unanswered. Of this omission the following explanation was given in a note. "The degrees of relationship left unfilled, or marked with [a wave line] have no popular nouns [terms] in the Hungarian or Magyar language, and are circumscribed [described] as in English." It would have been more satisfactory to have had the full details of the system, since the method of description is material; but yet it will be sufficient for general purposes to know that it is descriptive in all cases where special terms are not used.

Grandfather is expressed by prefixing *oreg*, old, to the term for father, and great-grandfather by prefixing *ded*, the signification of which is not given. A grandson is described as "son of my son."

The relationships of brother and sister are concieved in the twofold form of elder and younger, and not in the abstract. It is one of the remarkable features of the Magyar system, and one which may be expected to reappear in the forms of other nations belonging to this branch of the family. The four terms are radically distinct from each other, and as follows: *batyam*, "my elder brother;" *ocsem*, "my younger brother;" *nenem*, "my elder sister;" and *hugom*, "my younger sister." This is the first, and the only Turanian characteristic in the Magyar system.

I call my brother's son, *kis ocsem*, kis = little, literally, "my little younger brother;" and my brother's daughter, *kis hugom*, "my little younger sister." My brother's grandson and great-grandson are described, but the form of description is not given.

In the second collateral line the same peculiarity reappears. I call my father's brother, *nagy batyam*, nagy = grand, literally, "my grand elder brother," and my father's sister, *nagy nenem*, "my grand elder sister." My mother's brother and sister are designated by the same phrases; and therefore, which branch was intended must be indicated, when necessary, by additional words. In what way the children and descendants of these several uncles and aunts are described, does not appear.

No explanation is given in the schedule of the manner of indicating the series of relatives in the third, and more remote collateral lines, except that they are described.

The novel method found in the Magyar system for expressing the relationships of uncle and nephew, aunt and niece, has not before appeared, and does not appear again in the system of any nation represented in the Tables. The nearest approach to it occurs in the system of the Minnitaree and Upsaroka Indian nations of the Upper Missouri, among whom uncle and nephew stand in the relation of elder and younger brother. This form, however, is exceptional, and confined to these cases in the Indian family. Such deviations as these from the common form are important, since they are apt to reappear in other branches of the same stock, and thus become threads of evidence upon the question of their ethnic connection, and also with reference to the order of their separation from each other, or from the parent stem. When such a method of indicating particular relationships comes into permanent use to the displacement of a previous method, the offshoots of the particular nation in which it originated, are certain to take it with them, and to perpetuate it as an integral part of their system of consanguinity. A feature of the same kind has been noticed in the Slavonic, and still others will appear in the systems of other families. The most unexpected suggestions of genetic connection present themselves through such deviations from uniformity, when it reappears in the systems of other nations.

In Magyar, the marriage relationships are not fully discriminated by special terms. There are terms for husband and wife, father-in-law and mother-in-law, son-in-law and daughter-in-law, and one term for sister-in-law. All others are described.

Notwithstanding the absence of full details of the Magyar system of relationship, enough appears to show that it is not classificatory in the Turanian sense, but chiefly descriptive. The generalizations which it contains are: first, that of brothers and sisters into elder and younger; secondly, that of the brothers of the father and of the mother into one class, as grand elder brothers; thirdly, that of the sisters of the father and of the mother into one class, as grand elder sisters; and fourthly, that of the children of the brothers and sisters of *Ego* into two classes, as his little younger brothers and little younger sisters. The last three, while they exhibit a novel method of description, failed to develop in the concrete form the relationships of uncle and aunt, or nephew and niece. It gives to the system a certain amount of classification; but it is in accordance with the principles of the descriptive form.

9   February, 1869.

II. Turk Nations.   1. Osmanli-Turks.   2. Kuzabbashi.

The Turk stock is allied to the Ugrian.[1] It is one of the most important in Asia, both with respect to its past history and its future prospects. More highly endowed, and more energetic in impulse than other Asiatic nomades, their migratory movements, and military and civil achievements have been more conspicuous than those of other nomadic nations. The principal subdivisions of the Turk stock are the Kirgiz, the Bashkers, and the Nogays, on the north and west; the Yakuts, or Sokhalars, detached geographically and established on the Lena within the Arctic circle; the Osmanli-Turks on the west; and the inhabitants of Bokhara, Chinese Tartary, and Turkistan on the east and south.[2] The differences among the several dialects of these nations are said to be less than among the Ugrian.

It is thus seen that the Uralian family, in its several branches, occupies an immense, a compact, and a continuous area, extending from the Arctic Sea to the Mediterranean and Caspian, and from China and Mongolia to the territories of the Aryan family.[3] This fact is equally true of all the great linguistic families of mankind. Reasons for this are found in the causes which control the migrations of nations,

---

[1] "Those writers, in short, who adopt the nomenclature of Blumenbach, place the Ugrians and Turks in the same class, that class being the Mongol. So that, in the eyes of the anatomist, the Turks and the Ugrians belong to the same great division of mankind."—*Latham's Native Races of the Russian Empire*, p. 30.

[2] "It suggests the idea of the enormous area appropriated to the Turkish stock. It is perhaps the largest in the world, measured by the mere extent of surface; not, however, largest in respect to the number of inhabitants it contains. In respect to its physical conditions, its range of difference is large. The bulk of its surface is a plateau—the elevated table-land of Central Asia—so that, though lying within the same parallels as a great part of the same area, its climates are more extreme. But then its outlying portions are the very shores of the icy sea; whilst there are other Turks as far south as Egypt."—*Native Races of Russian Empire*, p. 29.

[3] Lamartine describes the prairie or table-lands of Asia between the Caspian Sea and the frontiers of China, the home country of the pastoral tribes of the Turks, as follows. "This basin, which extends, uncultivated, from the frontiers of China to Thibet, and from the extremity of Thibet to the Caspian Sea, produces, since the known origin of the world, but men and flocks. It is the largest pasture-field that the globe has spread beneath the foot of the human race, to multiply the milk which quenches man's thirst, the ox that feeds him, the horse that carries him, the camel that follows him, bearing his family and his tent, the sheep that clothes him with its fleece. Not a tree is to be seen there to cast its shade upon the earth, or supply a covert for fierce or noxious animals. Grass is the sole vegetable. Nourished by a soil without stones, and of great depth, like the slimy and saline bottom of some ocean, emptied by a cataclysm; watered by the oozings of the Alps of Thibet, the loftiest summits of Asia; preserved during the long winters by a carpet of snow, propitious to vegetation; warmed in spring by a sun without a cloud; sustained by a cool temperature that never mounts to the height of parching, grass finds there, as it were, its natural climate. It supplies there all other plants, all other fruits, all other crops. It attracted thither the ruminant animals—the ruminant animals attracted man. They feed, they fatten, they give their milk, they grow their hair, their fur, or their wool for their masters. After death they bequeath their skin for his domestic uses. Man, in such countries, needs no cultivation to give him food and drink, nor fixed dwellings, nor fields inclosed and divided for appropriation. The immeasurable spaces over which he is obliged to follow the peregrinations of his moving property, leads him in its train. He takes with him but his tent, which is carried from steppe to steppe, according as the grass is browsed upon a certain zone around him; or he harnesses his ox on to his leather-covered wagon, the movable mansion of his family."—*History of Turkey*, I, 181 (Book II, S. xix.) Appleton's edition, 1855.

of which the principal are physical; but among the moral are those relating to the sympathy and mutual protection which flow from community of blood.

1. *Osmanli-Turks.*—In many respects the Osmanli-Turks are an extreme representative of the Turkic class of nations. Their language, originally scant in vocables, has drawn largely, as is well known, from Persian, Arabic, and other incongruous sources, but without yielding its primitive grammatical forms. Their blood, also, has become intermixed, in the course of centuries, with that of the Semitic and Aryan families, without disturbing, however, the influence of the preponderating Turk element, or infusing, to any perceptible extent, Aryan or Semitic ideas. As a people they are still under the guidance of the same impulses and conceptions which existed in their brains when they left the table-lands of Asia to enter upon their eventful migration for the possession of one of the ancient seats of Aryan civilization. Their civil and domestic institutions, which are still oriental, have proved incapable of developing a State of the Aryan type, because the elements of such a political organism did not exist in the conceptions of the Turk mind. It is impossible to develop from the primary ideas deposited in the intellectual and moral life of a people, and transmitted with the blood, a series of institutions which do not spring logically from them. There is a fixed relation between rudimentary institutions and the State which rises out of them by the growth of centuries. These institutions are developments from pre-existing ideas, conceptions, and aspirations, and not new creations of human intelligence. Man is firmly held under their control, and within the limits of expansion of which they are susceptible. It is by the free admixture of diverse stocks, or, better still, of independent families of mankind, that the breadth of base of these primary ideas and conceptions is widened, and the capacity for civilization increased to the sum of the original endowments and experiences of both. Where the intermixture of blood is greatly unequal, the modifications of institutions are relatively less than the quantum of alien blood acquired; since, in no case, will the preponderating stock adopt any conceptions that do not assimilate and become homogeneous with the prevailing ideas. Hence, the most favorable conditions for a new creation, so to express it, of mental and moral endowments is the consolidation of two diverse and linguistically distinct peoples into one, on terms of equality, that they may become fused in an elementary union.

The Aryan family unquestionably stands at the head of the several families of mankind. Next to the Aryan stands the Semitic, and next to the latter the Uralian; and they are graduated at about equal distances from each other. Each has its points of distinguishing excellence; but taken in their totalities, the Aryan family has the greatest breadth and range of intellectual and moral powers, and has made the deepest impression upon human affairs. By what combination of stocks this immense mental superiority was gained we are entirely ignorant. The same may be said of the Semitic as compared with the Uralian, and of the Uralian, though in a less degree, as compared with the Turanian.

In the light of these suggestions the failure of the Osmanli-Turks to reach or even to adopt the Aryan civilization is not remarkable. Six hundred years of experience, of civilizing intercourse with Aryan nations, and of localized government have failed to raise them to the necessary standard of intelligence. Instead of working their way up to civilization by the slow process of internal growth, as each of the Aryan nations has done independently of each other, they attempted to seize it ready-formed at the point of the scimitar. .It cannot be won in this manner; neither can it be acquired by formal attempts to practise its arts and usages. It has an older and deeper foundation in the mental constitution of the people. These suggestions have a direct bearing upon systems of relationship, which are under the same law as to their development, and share the same elements of permanence which inhere in domestic institutions.

The Osmanli-Turkish system, having borrowed a portion of the Arabic nomenclature, is not the best type of the system of this branch of the family. That of the Kirgiz or Bashkirs would have been much better had it been procured. It is inferior to the Kuzulbashi which follows.

There are terms in this language for grandfather and grandmother, and a term in common gender for grandchild. Ascendants and descendants beyond these are described by a combination of terms.

I call my brother's son and daughter *yĕyĕnim*, which is a term in common gender for nephew and niece. The children of the latter are described.

The term for paternal uncle, *ämmĭm* or *ämŭjäm*, and paternal aunt, *häläm*, appear to be from the Arabic. It has terms also for maternal uncle, *däyĕm*, and for paternal aunt, *diäzäm*. These terms determine the form for the designation of kindred in the second collateral line, at least in part. The series, in the male branch used for illustration, is as follows: *paternal uncle, son of paternal uncle, and son of son of paternal uncle*. Of the next degree below this, Dr. Pratt remarks in a note that " the same form of description, if any, is employed." This is a novel feature in the system, since it appears that all the descendants of an uncle, near and remote, are designated as uncle's sons and uncle's daughters, and all the descendants of an aunt as an aunt's sons and daughters.

Of the third collateral line Dr. Pratt remarks, " that no account is made of these degrees," which is repeated as to each of its branches. This is a significant statement, as it shows that they are not classified, and thus brought within the near degrees of relationship, as in the Turanian system; but are left without the system, and to the descriptive method for their designation.

It would seem from the present features of the Osmanli-Turkish system, barren as it is in its details, that it must have been originally purely descriptive. The changes that have occurred are limited to the same generalizations which have been found in those of the Aryan and Semitic families. On the other hand, the Turanian form does not admit of the description of a solitary kinsman, however remote in degree he may stand from *Ego*. Each and all, so far as the connection can be traced, are brought into one of the recognized relationships for the indication of which a special term exists. It will be found in the sequel that the Osmanli-Turkish form separates itself, by a clearly-defined line, from the Turanian in its fundamental characteristics. The degree of importance which rightfully attaches to this radical difference will be hereafter considered.

2. *Kuzulbashi.*—Our knowledge of this people, and of their proper linguistic position, is not altogether definite, if they are identical with the Tajicks referred

to by Dr. Prichard, who speaks of them as "genuine Persians."[1] Max Müller sets them down as a Turkish nation. The latter remarks: "The northern part of Persia, west of the Caspian Sea, Armenia, the south of Georgia, Sherwan and Dagestan, harbor a Turkic population known by the general name of *Kisel-bash* (Red Caps). They are nomadic robbers, and their arrival in these countries dates from the eleventh and twelfth centuries."[2]

The late Rev. George W. Dunmore, formerly a missionary of the American Board at Diarbekir, in Turkey, speaks of them in his letter which accompanied the schedule, as Kuzulbashi-Koords. He remarks, "Not being myself familiar with the language of the Kuzulbashi, I am indebted [for the filling out of the schedule] chiefly to an educated native, whose vernacular may be said to be that of the Kuzulbashi-Koords, among whom he spent his early days. * * * None of the missionaries, however, know the language of the Kuzulbashi, and all intercourse with them is through converted Armenians familiar with their language, or by means of the Turkish, which many of them know."[3]

There are special terms in this language for grandfather and grandmother, and for grandchild.

In the first collateral line male, the series is as follows: *brother, son of my brother, grandchild of my brother, and son of grandchild of my brother.* There is a special term for nephew, which is applied by a man to the children of his sister, and restricted to that relationship.

The Arabic terms for uncle and aunt reappear in the Kuzulbashi language in *aph, ammeh,* for those on the father's side, and in *kálleh,* a term in common gender, for those on the mother's. From the presence of these terms it is inferable that the relationships named were not discriminated among this people until a comparatively recent period. The series in the branch of the second collateral line, usually cited, is the following: *paternal uncle, son of paternal uncle, grandchild of paternal uncle, and son of grandchild of paternal uncle.*

In the third collateral line the form is similar, namely: *brother of grandfather, son of brother of grandfather, and grandson of brother of grandfather.* The persons in the fourth collateral line, in the several branches, are similarly described.

From these illustrations it is evident that the system of relationship of the Kuzulbashi is descriptive. With the exception of the terms borrowed from Arabic sources, and the term for nephew, applied to a sister's son, it is purely descriptive. The method of description is such, both in this and in the Osmanli-Turkish, as to imply the existence of an earlier form substantially identical with the Celtic.

---

[1] "The modern Tajicks, or genuine Persians, called by the Turks Kuzulbashes, are well known as a remarkably handsome people, with regular features, long oval faces, black, long, and well-marked eyebrows, and large black eyes."—*Prichard's Nat. Hist. of Man,* 173, c. f. *Latham's Descrip. Eth.* II, 191.

[2] Science of Language, Lec. VIII. p. 302.

[3] I cannot forbear to mention the manner in which this estimable missionary laid down his life. At the date of his letter (July, 1860) he was at Constantinople, but he returned to his native country the following year, and in April, 1862, enlisted as a chaplain in the Union army. In August of that year he fell mortally wounded at Helena, Arkansas, in an engagement in which he participated, and while defending the place against an assault of the rebel forces. Thus perished, in the prime of life, a brave, patriotic, and Christian citizen, in the service of his country.

The Kuzulbashi closes the series of nations comprised in the Uralian family, whose system of consanguinity is given in the Table. A comparison of their several forms shows them to agree in their fundamental characteristics. Upon the basis of this agreement, but more particularly upon the ground of total variance between the system of the Turanian family proper and that of the Ugrian and Turk nations, the Uralian family has been constituted. Although the number of nations, whose system has been procured, is small in comparison with the number unrepresented, and for this reason may seem inadequate to establish properly the foundations of a new family, it will be found, in the sequel, that they are entitled to an independent position.

The system of consanguinity and affinity of the Aryan and Semitic families, and of the Uralian, so far as it is given in the Table, is one and the same in general plan and in fundamental conceptions. In each family, the system, as it now prevails, is in accordance with the nature of descents where marriage subsists between single pairs, and the family in its proper sense exists. It recognizes the distinction between the several lines, and the perpetual divergence of those which are collateral from that which is lineal, together with the bond of connection through ascertainable common ancestors. Advancing a step beyond this, such generalizations of kindred into classes as it contains, limit the members of each class to such persons as stand in the same degree of nearness to *Ego*. These generalizations are suggested, with more or less distinctness, by the principles of the system with which they are in harmony, and out of which they rise by natural development. In so far as nature may be said to teach this form of consanguinity, the nations comprised in each of these great families have read her lessons alike. It is not, however, a necessary inference that the descriptive system springs up spontaneously, and consequently that all nations must inevitably gravitate toward this form; since it is known that much the largest portion of the human family, numerically, have a system radically different, the forms of which have stood permanently for ages upon ages. It is far easier to conceive of the formation of the descriptive than of the classificatory system; but when once formed and adopted into use, each is found to possess, to an extraordinary degree, the power of self-perpetuation.

In the foregoing exposition of the descriptive system of relationship, the utmost brevity, consistent with an intelligible presentation of the subject, has been sought. At best it is but a superficial discussion of the materials contained in the Table. It was necessary to show: first, the nature and principles of the system; secondly, the ethnic boundaries of its distribution; and thirdly, the concurrence of these three great families in its possession. To these propositions the discussion has been chiefly confined. The bearing which the joint possession of the descriptive system by these families may have upon the question of their ethnic connection, and which is believed to be deserving of consideration, is entirely subordinate to another, and that the main object of this work, to which attention will now be directed. It is to present the classificatory system of relationship of the American Indian and Turanian families, to show their identity, and to indicate some of the conclusions which result therefrom. Having ascertained the nature and limits of the descriptive system, it will be much easier to understand the classificatory, although it rests upon conceptions altogether different.

APPENDIX TO PART I.

TABLE OF CONSANGUINITY AND AFFINITY OF THE SEMITIC ARYAN AND URALIAN FAMILIES.

APPENDIX TO PART I.

GENEALOGICAL TABLE OF THE SEMITIC, ARYAN, AND URALIAN NATIONS, WHOSE SYSTEM OF CONSANGUINITY AND AFFINITY IS CONTAINED IN THE TABLE HERETO ANNEXED.

Families.	Classes.	Branches.	Peoples.
SEMITIC	ARABIC	SOUTHERN	1. Arabic,
			2. Druse and Maronite.
	HEBRAIC	MIDDLE	3. Hebrew.
	ARAMAIC	NORTHERN	4. Neo-Syriac, or Nestorian.
ARYAN			5. Armenian.
	CELTIC	GAELIC	6. Erse, or Irish,
			7. Gaelic, or Highland Scotch,
			8. Manx.
		CYMRIC	9. Welsh.
	IRANIC		10. Persian.
	INDIC		11. Sanskrit.
	TEUTONIC	SCANDINAVIAN	12. Danish and Norwegian,
			13. Icelandic.
			14. Swedish.
		LOW GERMAN	15. Anglo-Saxon,
			16. English,
			17. Holland Dutch,
			18. Belgian.
			19. Westphalian, or Platt Dutch.
		HIGH GERMAN	20. German (Prussian),
			21. German (Swiss).
	ROMAIC	ITALIC	22. French,
			23. Spanish,
			24. Portuguese,
			25. Italian.
			26. Latin.
	HELLENIC	ANCIENT	27. Ancient Greek.
		MODERN	28. Modern Greek.
	SLAVONIC	LETTIC	29. Lithuanian.
			30. Polish,
			31. Slovakian, or Bohemian,
			32. Bulgarian,
			33. Bulgarian,
			34. Russian.
URALIAN	TURKIC		35. Osmanli-Turk,
			36. Kuzulbashi.
	UGRIC		37. Magyar.
		FINNIC	38. Esthonian,
			39. Finn.

LIST OF SCHEDULES IN TABLE I.

Nations.	Names of Persons by whom, and places where Schedules were filled.
1. ARABIC. . .	Rev. C. V. A. Van Dyck, D. D., Missionary of the American Board of Commissioners for Foreign Missions, Beirut, Syria, May, 1860.
2. DRUSE and MARONITE	Hon. J. Augustus Johnson, U. S. Consul at Beirut, Syria, May, 1860.
3. HEBREW . .	Prof. W. Henry Green, D. D., Theological Seminary, Princeton, New Jersey, June, 1861.
4. NEO-SYRIAC or NESTORIAN	Austin K. Wright, M. D., Missionary of the American Board above named, Ooromiah, Persia, July, 1860.
5. ARMENIAN .	Lewis H. Morgan, with the aid of John D. Artin and James Thomason, native Armenians, residents of Rochester, N. Y., 1859.
6. ERSE . . .	Prof. D. Foley, D. D., Trinity College, Dublin, Ireland, March, 1860. Procured through Hon. Samuel Talbot, U. S. Consul at Dublin.
7. GÆLIC.	Rev. Duncan McNab, Glasgow, Scotland, April, 1860, through Hon. George Vail, U. S. Consul, Glasgow.
8. MANX . . .	John Moore, Esq., Rochester, N. Y., December, 1864.
9. WELSH . . .	Evan T. Jones, Esq., Palmyra, Portage Co., Ohio, August, 1861.
10. PERSIAN . .	Rev. G. W. Coan, D. D., Missionary of the American Board, Ooromiah, Persia, April, 1863.
11. SANSKRIT . .	1. Prof. W. D. Whitney, Yale College, New Haven, March, 1860. 2. Fitz Edward Hall, D. C. L., Saugor, North India, August, 1861.
12. DANISH and NORWEGIAN	Hon. W. De Rasloff, Chargé d'Affairs of Denmark in the United States. At New York, April, 1861.
13. ICELANDIC . .	Prof. Sigwrdsson, Copenhagen, Denmark, May, 1862, through Prof. C. C. Raffn, Secretary of the Royal Society of Northern Antiquarians, Copenhagen.
14. SWEDISH . .	Edward Count Piper, Minister Resident of Sweden in the United States, Washington, February, 1864.
15. ANGLO-SAXON	Compiled from Bosworth's Anglo-Saxon Dictionary, from Orosius and other sources.
16. ENGLISH . .	Lewis H. Morgan, Rochester, N. Y.
17. HOLLAND DUTCH	Gerard Arink, M. D., Rochester, N. Y., January, 1861.
18. BELGIAN . .	Rev. P. J. De Smet, S. J. St. Louis, Missouri, June, 1862.
19. WESTPHALIAN or PLATT DUTCH	Lewis H. Morgan, with the aid of M. Wischemier, Rochester, N. Y., April, 1862.
20. GERMAN (PRUSSIAN)	Joseph Felix, Esq., Rochester, N. Y., May, 1860.
21. GERMAN (SWISS)	C. Hunziker, Attorney at Law, Berne, Switzerland. Prepared at the request of the Hon. Theodore S. Fay, U. S. Minister Resident at Berne, March, 1860.
22. FRENCH . .	Lewis H. Morgan, Rochester, N. Y.
23. SPANISH . .	The Counsellor Señhor Miguel Maria Lisboa, Minister Plenipotentiary of Brazil in the United States. Washington, December, 1862.
24. PORTUGUESE .	The Counsellor Señhor M. M. Lisboa, above named. December, 1862.
25. ITALIAN . .	Lewis H. Morgan, Rochester, N. Y.
26. LATIN . . .	" " " "
27. CLASSICAL GREEK	" " " "
28. MODERN GREEK	Glossary of Later and Byzantine Greek, by Prof. E. A. Sophocles. Memoirs Am. Acad. N. S., vol. vii. Article Βαθμε Συγγενείας.

LIST OF SCHEDULES IN TABLE I.—*Continued.*

Nations.	Names of Persons by whom, and places where Schedules were filled.
29. LITHUANIAN .	Prof. Francis Bopp, Berlin, Prussia, April, 1860. Procured through Hon. Joseph A. Wright, U. S. Minister Resident in Prussia.
30. POLISH . . .	Augustus Plinta, Esq , Civil Engineer, Albany, N. Y., January, 1861.
31. SLOVAKIAN or BOHEMIAN	Prof. Kanya, Pesth, Hungary, February, 1861. Procured through Hon. J. Glancy Jones, U. S. Minister Plenipotentiary in Austria. Vienna.
32. BULGARIAN .	Rev. Elias Riggs, D. D., Missionary of the American Board at Constantinople, Turkish Empire, February, 1862.
33. BULGARIAN .	Rev. Charles F. Morse, Missionary of same Board, Sophia, Turkey, January, 1863.
34. RUSSIAN . .	By a Russian gentleman.
35. OSMANLI-TURK	Rev. Andrew T. Pratt, Missionary of the American Board, Aleppo, Syria, August, 1860.
36. KUZULBASHI .	Rev. George W. Dunmore, Missionary of the same Board, at Kharpoot, Turkish Empire. July, 1860.
37. MAGYAR . .	Prof. Paul Hunfalvy, Member of the Hungarian Academy, Pesth, Hungary, January, 1861. Procured through Hon. J. Glancy Jones, U. S. Minister Plenipotentiary in Austria.
38. ESTHONIAN .	Hon. Charles A. Leas, U. S. Consul Revel, Russia, February, 1861.
39. FINN . . .	1. G. Selin, Student of the Physico-Mathematical Faculty in the University of Helsingfors, Russia, April, 1860. Prepared at the request of President A. Retzius, President of the Academy of Sciences, Stockholm, Sweden. 2. Urjo Koskinen, Prof. in the University of Jacobstad, Finland, September, 1860. Procured through Hon. B. F. Angel, U. S. Minister Resident in Sweden.

TABLE I.—Systems of Consanguinity and Affinity.

Families.	Classes.	Branches.			Dialects.	Author of Schedule.	Pronoun My.
SEMITIC	ARABIC	Southern	{	1	Arabic	C. V. A. Van Dyck, D.D. .	Suffix i.
				2	Druse and Maronite . . .	Hon. J. A. Johnson . . .	" i.
	HEBRAIC	Middle . . .		3	Hebrew	Prof. W. Henry Green . .	" i.
	ARAMAIC	Northern . .		4	Neo-Syriac or Nestorian . .	Austin H. Wright, M.D. . .	" e.
	——	——		5	Armenian	John De Artin (Native Arm.)	Im.
ARYAN			{	6	Erse or Irish	D. Foley, D.D.	Mo.
	CELTIC	Gadhelic . .	{	7	Gaelic or Highland Scottish,	Rev. Duncan McNab . . .	Mo.
				8	Manx	John Moore	My.
		Cymric . .		9	Welsh	Evan T. Jones, Esq. . . .	Fy.
	IRANIC	——		10	Persian	Rev. George W. Coan, D.D.	Suffix ăm.
	INDIC	——		11	Sanskrit	{ Prof. W. D. Whitney } 2 S. { Fitz Ed. Hall, D.C.L. }	Mama.
		Scandinavian {		12	Danish and Norwegian . .	Hon. W. Raasloff	Post { minn { mas. { min { fem.
				13	Icelandic	Prof. I. Sigwrdson . . .	" { mim { mas. { min { fem.
				14	Swedish	Edward Count Piper . . .	Min.
				15	Anglo-Saxon	Lewis H. Morgan	
	TEUTONIC			16	English	" " "	My.
		Low German .		17	Holland Dutch	Gerard Arink, M.D. . . .	{ My { mas. { Myne { fem.
				18	Belgian	Father P. J. De Smet, S. J.	{ Myn { mas. { Myuen { fem.
				19	Platt-Deutsh	Lewis H. Morgan	{ Me { mas. { Mene { fem.
		High German	{	20	German	Joseph Felix, Esq.	{ Mein { mas. { Meine { fem.
				21	German-Swiss	Herr C. Hunziker	{ Mein { mas. { Meine { fem.
		Modern . . {		22	French	Lewis H. Morgan	{ Mon { mas. { Ma { fem.
				23	Spanish	Senhor Miguel Maria Lisboa	Mi
	ROMAIC			24	Portuguese	" " " "	{ Min { mas. { Mia { fem.
				25	Italian	Prof. Paul Marzolo . . .	{ Mio { mas. { Mia { fem.
				26	Latin	Lewis H. Morgan	{ Meus { mas. { Mea { fem.
	HELLENIC	Ancient . .		27	Classical Greek	" " "	{ Emos { mas. { Emē { fem.
		Modern . .		28	Modern Greek	Glossary of Prof. Sophocles .	
		Lettic . . .		29	Lithuanian	Prof. F. Bopp	
			{	30	Polish	Augusta Plinta, Esq. . . .	{ Moj { mas. { Moja { fem.
	SLAVONIC	——	{	31	Slovakian or Bohemian . .	Prof. Kanya	{ Moj { mas. { Moja { fem.
				32	Bulgarian	Elias Riggs, D.D.	Post mi.
				33	Bulgarian	Rev. Charles F. Morse . .	" mi.
				34	Russian	By a Russian	{ Moi { mas. { Maja { fem.
URALIAN	TURKIC	——	{	35	Osmanli-Turk	Rev. Andrew T. Pratt . .	Suffix m.
			{	36	Kuzulbashe	Rev. George W. Dunmore .	Post mun.
		——		37	Magyar	Prof. Paul Hunfalvy . . .	Suffix m.
	UGRIC	Finnic . . . {		38	Esthonian	Hon. Chas. A. Leas . . .	Minn.
				39	Finn	{ Dr. Urjo Koskinen } 2 Sch. { Mr. G. Selin }	Suffix ni.

NOTATION IN TABLE I.

VOWEL SOUNDS.

a as a in ale. o as o in tone.

ä " " " father. ŏ " " " got.

ă " " " at. u " u " unit.

e " e " mete. ŭ " oo " food.

ĕ " " " met. { ē and ō in Greek

i " i " ice. { are long e and o.

ĭ " " " it.

The literary languages represented in the Table, with two or three exceptions, have their own diacritical marks.

TABLE I.—Systems of Consanguinity and Affinity of the Semitic, Aryan, and Uralian Families.

	1. Great-grandfather's great-grandfather.	Translation.	2. Great-grandfather's grandfather.	Translation.
1	Jidd jidd jiddi......................	Grandfather of g. f. of g. f. my.	Jidd jidd ăbi......................	Grandfather of g. f. of father my.
2	Jădd jădd jăddi	" " " "	Jadd jadd ăbi	" " "
3				
4	Săwŭnă d'sawŭă d'săwŭnee	" " " "	Săwŭnă d'săwŭnă d'babee	" " "
5				
6				
7				
8				
9				
10				
11				
12	Tip tip tip olde fader.................	Great gd. father's gt. gd. father.	Tip tip oldefader....................	Great grandfather's grandfather.
13				
14	Farfars farfars farfar..................	Grandfather's grandfather's grandfather.	Farfars farfars far...................	Grandfather's grandfather's father.
15	Eald eald eald eald eald faeder ...	Gt. gd. father's gt. gd. father.	Eald eald eald faeder	Gt. grandfather's grandfather
16	Gt. grandfather's gt. grandfather..	" " " "	Great grandfather's grandfather	" " "
17	Over over over oud groot vader....	" " " "	Over over oud groot vader........	" " "
18	Groot groot groot groot groot vader	" " " "	Groot groot groot groot vader....	" " "
19	Antke vader's antke vader	" " " "	Antke vader's bess vader.........	" " "
20	Urururur grossvater..................	Gt. gt. gt. gt. grandfather.	Ururur grossvater..................	Great gt. gt. grandfather.
21	Urururururgrossvater	" " "	Urururgrossvater	" " "
22	L'aïeul de l'aïeul de mon aïeul....	The grandfather of the gd. f. of my g. f.	Le père de l'aïeul de mon aïeul.	The father of the g. f. of my g. f.
23				
24				
25				
26	Tritavus......................	Great grandfather's great grandfather.	Atavus......................	Great grandfather's grandfather.
27	Tripappos	" " " "	Dispappos	" " "
28	Trispappos	" " " "	Dispappos...................	" " "
29				
30	Moj prapraprapra dziadek..........	My great gt. gt. gt. grandfather.	Moj praprapra dziadek	My great gt. gt. grandfather.
31				
32				
33				
34	Moi praprapraradjed	My great gt. gt. gt. grandfather.	Moi praprapradjed.................	My great gt. gt. grandfather.
35				
36	Bävkäleh bävkäleh bävkäleh mun	Grandfather of g. f. of g. f. my.	Bävkäleh bävkäleh baveh mun.	Grandfather of g. f. of father my.
37				
38				
39				

	3. Great grandfather's father.	Translation.	4. Great grandfather's mother.	Translation.
1	Jidd jiddi....................	Grandfather of grandfather my.	Sitt sitti......................	Grandmother of grandmother my.
2	Jăd jăddi......................	" " " "	Sitt sitti......................	" " " "
3				
4	Săwŭnă d'săwŭnee	Grandfather of grandfather my.	Năna d'nănee......................	Grandmother of grandmother my.
5	Metzhorus metzhoră hiră............	" " " "	Metzmorus metzmoră miră.......	" " " "
6	Shan ahair mahar....................	The old father of my father.	Shan vahair mahar...............	The old mother of my father.
7	Mo shin sin seanair..................	My great grandfather's father.	Mo shin sin sear mhathair	My great grandfather's mother.
8				
9	Fy ngororhendad	" " " "	Fy Ngororhenfam...................	" " " "
10				
11	Vriddhaprapitámahah[1]	My great great grandfather.	Vriddhaprapitámahí.....	My gt. gt. grandfather's mother
12	Tip oldefader.......................	Great great grandfather.	Tip oldemoder......................	Great grandfather's mother.
13	Langalangafi minn....................	" " " my.	Langalangamma min...............	" " " my.
14	Farfars farfar.......................	Grandfather's grandfather.	Farfars mormor.....................	Grandfather's grandmother.
15	Eald eald eald faeder	Great grandfather's father.	Eald eald eald modor............	Great grandfather's mother.
16	Great-grandfather's father	" " "	Great grandfather's mother......	" " "
17	Over oud groot vader...............	" " "	Over oud groot moeder...........	" " "
18	Groot groot groot vader.............	" " "	Groot groot groot moeder	" " "
19	Antke vaders vader..................	" " "	Antke vader's mohder	" " "
20	Ururgrossvater	Great great grandfather.	Ururgrossmutter	Great great grandmother.
21	Ururgrossvater	" " "	Ururgrossmutter	" " "
22	Mon trisaïeul.......................	My great great grandfather.	Ma trisaïeule......................	My great great grandmother.
23	Tatarabuelo..........................	" " " "	Tatarabuela	" " " "
24	Tataravô.............................	Great great grandfather.	Tataravó	Great grandfather's mother.
25				
26	Abavus	Great great grandfather.	Abavia.............................	Great great grandmother.
27	Epipappos	" " "	Epitēthē	" " "
28	Apopappos	" " "	Apommē...........................	" " "
29				
30	Moj prapra dziadek..................	My great great grandfather.	Moja praprabka...................	My great great grandmother.
31	Mŭj prapraded.......................	" " " "	Ma praprababa	" " " "
32	Prepredyed...........................	" " " "	Preprebaba mi......................	Great great grandmother my.
33	Preprededa...........................	" " " "	Preprebaba mi......................	" " " "
34	Moi prapradjed.......................	" " " "	Moja praprabka....................	" " " " "
35				
36	Bävkäleh Bävkäleh mun............	Grandfather of grandfather my.	Däpeereh däpeereh mun..........	Grandmother of grandmother my.
37				
38				
39				

[1] The Sanskrit terms are in the nominative case.   "Mama," my is omitted.

TABLE I.—*Continued.*

	5. Great grandfather.	Translation.	6. Great grandmother.	Translation.
1	Jidd ăbi	Grandfather of father my.	Sitt ăbi	Grandmother of father my.
2	Jad ăbĭ	" " " "	Sitt ăbĭ	" " " "
3				" " " "
4	Säwŭnä d' bäbä	" " " "	Yimmä d' säwunee	" " " "
5	Metzhorus hirä	" " " "	Metzmorus mirä	" " " "
6	Ahair mo han ahar	Father of my old father.	Mahair-mo han vahair	My old father's mother.
7	Mo shin sin sean athar	My ancestral old father.	Mo shin sin sean mhathar	My ancestral old mother.
8	My shen shanar	My old ancestor.	Moir moir my moir	Mother of mother of my mother.
9	Fy ngorhendad	My great grandfather.	Fy ngorhenfam	My great grandmother.
10				
11	Prapitámahah	" " "	Prapitámahí	" " "
12	Oldefader	Great grandfather.	Oldemoder	Great grandmother.
13	Langafi minn	Great grandfather my.	Langamma minn. b Edda min	Great grandmother my.
14	Farfars far	" " "	Mornors mor	" " "
15	Eald eald faeder	Great grandfather.	Eald eald modor	Great grandmother.
16	Great grandfather	" "	Great grandmother	" "
17	Over groot vader	" "	Over groot moeder	" "
18	Groot groot vader	" "	Groot groot moeder	" "
19	Antke vader	" "	Antke mohder	" "
20	Urgrossvater	" "	Urgrossmutter	" "
21	Grossgrossvater	" "	Grossgrossmutter	" "
22	Mon bisaïeul	My great grandfather.	Ma bisaïeule	My great grandmother.
23	Bisabuelu	" " "	Bisabuela	" " "
24	Bisavô	Great grandfather.	Bisavó	Great grandmother.
25	Bisavo	" "	Bisava	" "
26	Proavus	" "	Proavia	" "
27	Propappos	" "	Protéthé	" "
28	Propappos	" "	Promammé	" "
29				
30	Moj pradziad	My great grandfather.	Moja prababka	My great grandmother.
31	Muj praded	" " "	Ma prababa	" " "
32	Predyed mi	Great grandfather my.	Prebaba mi	Great grandmother my.
33	Prededa mi	" " "	Prebaba mi	" " "
34	Moi pradjed	My great grandfather.	Moja prababka	My great grandmother.
35	Dĕdĕmin bäbäzŭ	My grandfather's father.	Dĕdĕmin änäsŭ	My grandmother's mother.
36	Baveh bävkäleh mun	Grandfather of father my.	Deeyä däpeereh mun	Grandmother of father my.
37	Ded atyam	" " " "	Ded anyam	Grandfather's mother my.
38	Minu esä esä esä	My father's father's father.	Minu emä emä emä	My mother's mother's mother.
39				

	7. Grandfather.	Translation.	8. Grandmother.	Translation.
1	Jiddi	Grandfather my.	Sitti	Grandmother my.
2	Jăddi	" "	Sitti. b Jŭdătti	" "
3				
4	Säwŭnee	" "	Nänee	" "
5	Mitz hire	" "	Metz mire	" "
6	Mo han ahair. b Mohair ereeno	My old father.	Mo han vahair	My old mother.
7	Mo shean Athar	" "	Mo shean mhathair	" " "
8	Ayr my ayr. b Jezig moir	Father of my father.	Moir my moir. b Woavey	Mother of my mother.
9	Fy hendad	My grandfather.	Fy henfam	My grandmother.
10	Poodar buzurk	Father elder.	Mädär buzurk	Mother elder.
11	Pitámahah	Grandfather.	Pitámahi	Grandmother.
12	Bedstefader	"	Bedstemoder	"
13	Afi minn	" my	Amma min	Grandmother my.
14	Farfader. b Farfar	"	Mormor	Grandmother.
15	Eald faeder	"	Eald modor	"
16	Grandfather	"	Grandmother	"
17	Groot vader	"	Groot moeder	"
18	Groot vader	"	Groot moeder	"
19	Bess vader	"	Bess mohder	"
20	Grossvater	"	Grossmutter	"
21	Grossvater	"	Grossmutter	"
22	Mon aïeul. b Grandpère	My grandfather.	Mon aïeule. b Ma grand'mère	My grandmother.
23	Abuelo	" "	Abuela	" "
24	Avô	Grandfather.	Avó	Grandmother.
25	Avo	"	Ava	"
26	Avus	"	Avia	"
27	Pappos	"	Téthé	"
28	Pappos	"	Mammé	"
29	Mano sĕnutĭs	"	Măno sĕnutĕ	"
30	Moj dziad. b Dziadek dziadunio	My grandfather.	Moja babka. b Babunia	My grandmother.
31	Mŭj ded	" "	Ma baba	" "
32	Dyed mi	Grandfather my.	Baba mi	Grandmother my.
33	Deda mi	" "	Baba mi	" "
34	Moi djed	My grandfather.	Moja babka	My grandmother.
35	Dĕdĕ-m	Grandfather my.	Nĕnĕ-m	Grandmother my.
36	Bävkäleh mun		Däpeereh mun	
37	Oreg atyam	Old father my.	Oreg anyam	Old mother my.
38	Minu esä esä	My father's father.	Minu emä emä	My mother's mother.
39	Tso ĭsănĭ. b Tsanĭ isä	Father of fath. my. b Father my great.	Tsăn aĭtĭ. b Eukko	Great mother my.

TABLE I.—*Continued.*

	9. Father.	Translation.	10. Mother.	Translation.
1	Abi	Father my.	Ummi	Mother my.
2	Abī	" "	Ummi	" "
3	Abhī	" "	Immī	" "
4	Bäbee	" "	Yimmee	" "
5	Hire	" "	Mire	" "
6	Mo ahair	My father.	Mo vahair	My mother.
7	M'athaīr	" "	Mo mhathair	" "
8	My ayr	" "	My moir. ᵇ Voir	" "
9	Fy nhad. ᵇ Tad	" "	Fy marn	" "
10	Poodär	Father.	Mådär	Mother.
11	Pitá. ᵇ Janitar	"	Matá. ᵇ Janitri	"
12	Fader	"	Moder	
13	Fathir minn	Father my.	Mothir min	Mother my.
14	Fader	Father.	Moder	Mother.
15	Faeder	"	Modor	"
16	Father	"	Mother	"
17	Vader	"	Moeder	"
18	Vader myn	Father my.	Moeder myne	Mother my.
19	Vader	Father.	Mohder	Mother.
20	Vater	"	Mutter	"
21	Vater	"	Mutter	"
22	Mon père	My father.	Ma mere	My mother.
23	Padre	" "	Madre	Mother.
24	Páe	Father.	Mõe	"
25	Padre	"	Madre	"
26	Pater	"	Mater	"
27	Pater	"	Mater	"
28	Pater	"	Mammē	"
29	Măno tërräs	My father.	Măno mŏmá	My mother.
30	Moj ojciec. ᵇ Rodziciet	" "	Moja matka. ᵇ Rodzicietka	"
31	Mūj otec	" "	Ma matka	" "
32	Otets. ᵇ Bashtami	Father my.	Maika mi	Mother my.
33	Bashta mi	" "	Maika mi	" "
34	Moi otez	My father.	Maja matj	My mother.
35	Bäbä-m	Father my.	Anä-m	Mother my.
36	Bäveh mun	" "	Deeyä mun	" "
37	Atya-m		Anyá-m	" "
38	Minu esä	My father.	Minu emä	My mother.
39	Tsänī	Father my.	Aītīnī. ᵇ Emoni	Mother my.

	11. Sòn.	Translation.	12. Daughter.	Translation.
1	Ibni	Son my.	Ibneti. ᵇ Binti	Daughter my.
2	Ibni	" "	Binti	" "
3	B'nī	" "	Bittī	" "
4	Brŭnee	" "	Brätee	" "
5	Vorete	" "	Tooster	" "
6	Mo văc	My son.	Mo ineean	My daughter.
7	Mo mhăc	" "	Mo neeghean	" "
8	My mac	" "	My inneen	" "
9	Fy mab	" "	Fy merch	" "
10	Poosär	Son.	Dŭkhtär	Daughter.
11	Putráh. ᵇ Sănuh. ᶜ Sutah	"	Putrá. ᵇ Suta. ᶜ Duhiti	"
12	Sön	"	Datter	"
13	Sönr minn	Son my.	Dottir min	Daughter my.
14	Son	Son.	Dotter	Daughter.
15	Sunu	"	Dohtor	"
16	Son	"	Daughter	"
17	Zoon	"	Dochter	"
18	Zoon	"	Dochter	"
19	Soohn	"	Dochter	"
20	Sohn	"	Tochter	"
21	Sohn	"	Tochter	"
22	Mon fils	My son	Ma fille	My daughter.
23	Hijo	Son.	Hija	" "
24	Filho	"	Filha	Daughter.
25	Figlio	"	Figlia	"
26	Filius	"	Filia	"
27	Huios	"	Thugatēr	"
28	Huios	"	Thugatēr	"
29	Măno sŭnŭs	My son.	Măno duktē	My daughter.
30	Moj syn	" "	Moja corka	" "
31	Mūj syn	" "	Ma dura	" "
32	Sin mi	Son my.	Dshteria mi	Daughter my.
33	Sin mi	" "	Dushtera mi	" "
34	Moi sin. ᵇ Syn	My son.	Moja dotch	My daughter.
35	Oghl-ŭm	Son my.	Kûs-ûm	Daughter, my girl.
36	Läveh mun	" "	Keezä mun	" "
37	Fia-m	" "	Leanyo-m	" "
38	Minu Poeg	My son.	Minue tutär	My daughter.
39	Poïkanī	Boy my.	Tyttäreni	Daughter my.

TABLE I.—*Continued.*

	13. Grandson (common term).	Translation.	14. Grandson (descriptive phrase).	Translation.
1	Ibn ibni...............	Son of son my.	Ibn ibneti...............	Son of daughter my.
2	Ibn ibni. ᵇ Hafidi........	" " "	Ibn binti	" " " "
3	Bĕn b'nĭ................	" " "	Bĕn bĭttĭ	" " " "
4	Närrigee...............	Grandson my	Närrigee...............	Grandson my.
5	Tor...................	Grandson.	Toostris voretin	My daughter's son.
6	Mäc mo vic...........	Son of my son.	Mac mo ineean........	Son of my daughter.
7	M'ogha...............	My grandchild.	M'ogha...............	Grandchild.
8	Mac my vac	Son of my son.	Mac my inneen.......	Son of my daughter.
9	Fy wyr...............	My grandson.	Fy wyr...............	My grandson.
10	Năvădä...............	Grandchild.	Năvădä...............	Grandchild.
11	Naptá...............	Grandson.	Pautráh. ᵇ Dauhitrah	Son's son. ᵇ Daughter's son.
12	Barnebarn.............	"	Sönne son. ᵇ Dattersön	" " " "
13	Sonar sonr minn.......	Son's son my.	Dottur sonr. ᵇ Sonar sonr min	Daughter's son and son's son my.
14	Souson................	" "	sonson. ᵇ Dottterson	Son's son, daughter's son.
15	Nefa. ᵇ Genefa.......	Grandson.	Nefa	Grandson.
16	Grandson.............	"	Son's son. ᵇ Daughter's son....	"
17	Klein zoon. ᵇ Neef........	Grandson. ᵇ Nephew.	Zoon's zoon. ᵇ Dochter's zoon .	Son's son. ᵇ Daughter's son.
18	Groot zoou............	"	Zoon's zoon. ᵇ Dochter's zoon .	Son's son. ᵇ Daughter's son.
19	Kinds kind...........	Grandchild.	Kinds kind	Grandchild.
20	Enkel	Grandson.	Sohn's sohn. ᵇ Tochter sohn...	Son's son. ᵇ Daughter's son.
21	Enkel	"	Sohn's sohn. ᵇ Tochter sohn...	" " " "
22	Mon petit-fils.........	My grandson.	Mon petit-fils.........	My grandson.
23	Nieto	Grandson.	Nieto	" "
24	Neto	"	Neto	Grandson.
25	Nipote...............	Grandchild.	Nipote...............	Grandchild.
26	Nepos	Grandson.	Nepos	Grandson.
27	Eggonos...............	"	Huiōnos. ᵇ Thugatridous.......	Son's son. ᵇ Daughter's son.
28	Eggonos...............	"	Eggonos	Grandson.
29	Sūnaus sūnūs............	Son of my son.	Dukter's sūnūs.........	Daughter's son.
30	Moj wnŭk............	My grandson.	Moj wnŭk............	My grandson.
31	Mŭj wnŭk............	" "	Mŭj wnŭk............	" "
32	Vnuk mi...............	Grandson my.	Vnuk mi	Grandson my.
33	Vnook mi.............	" "	Vnook mi.............	" "
34	Moi vnŭk.............	My grandson.	Moi vnŭk.............	My grandson.
35	Torŭn-ŭm.............	Grandchild my.		
36	Törneh mun............	"	Törneh mun............	Grandchild my.
37	Fiam fija...............	Son of my son.	Lanyon fija............	Son of my daughter.
38	Minu poeg poeg.........	My son's son.	Minu tutar poeg.........	My daughter's son.
39	Poĭkani poĭkä. ᵇ Tyttäreuĭ poĭkä	Son's son. ᵇ Daughter's son.	Minu tutar poeg.........	My daughter's son.

	15. Granddaughter (common term).	Translation.	16. Granddaughter (Descriptive phrase).	Translation.
1	Ibnet ibni...............	Daughter of son my.	Ibnet binti...............	Daughter of daughter my.
2	Bint ibni	" " "	Bint binti...............	" " " "
3	Bath b'nĭ...............	" " "	Bath bĭttĭ	" " " "
4	Närrigtee	My granddaughter.	Närrigtee...............	My granddaughter.
5	Voretees tooster........	Son's daughter.	Toostris toostra........	Daughter of my daughter.
6	Ineean mo vic........	Daughter of my son.	Ineean mo ineean	" " " "
7	M'ogha...............	My grandchild.	M'ogha...............	My grandchild.
8	Inneen my vac	Daughter of my son.	Ineen my ineen	Daughter of daughter.
9	Fy wyres.............	My granddaughter.	Fy wyres...............	My granddaughter.
10	Năvădä...............	Grandchild.	Năvădä...............	Grandchild.
11	Naptrí...............	Granddaughter.	Pautri. ᵇ Dauhitrí...............	Son's daughter. ᵇ Daught.'s daugh.
12	Barnebarn.............	Grandchild.	Sönnedatter. ᵇ Datterdatter ...	" " " "
13	Sonar dottir minn.......	Son's daughter my.	Dottur Dottir min......	Daughter's daughter my.
14	Dotter dotter	Daughter's daughter.	Son's dotter . ᵇ Dotter dotter...	Son's daughter, daughter's daugh.
15	Nefane...............	Granddaughter.	Nefane	Granddaughter.
16	Granddaughter........	"	Son's daught. ᵇ Daught. daught.	"
17	Klein dochter. ᵇ Nicht........	Little daughter. ᵇ Niece.	Zoon's dochter. ᵇ Dochter's doch.	Son's daughter. ᵇ Daught.'s daugh.
18	Groote dochter........	Granddaughter.	Zoon's dochter. ᵇ Dochter's doch.	" " " "
19	Kinds kind...........	Grandchild.	Kinds kind	Grandchild.
20	Enkelinn	Granddaughter.	Sohn's tochter. ᵇ Tochter kind	Son's daughter. ᵇ Daughter's child.
21	Enkelin...............	"	Sohn's tochter. ᵇ Tochter kind	" " " "
22	Ma petite-fille.........	My granddaughter.	Ma petite-fille.........	My granddaughter.
23	Nieta...............	" "	Nieta...............	" "
24	Neta	Granddaughter.	Neta	Granddaughter.
25	Nipote	Grandchild.	Nipote...............	Grandchild.
26	Neptis...............	Granddaughter.	Neptis...............	Granddaughter.
27	Eggonē...............	"	Huionē. ᵇ Thugatride............	Son's daughter. ᵇ Daught.'s daugh.
28	Eggonē...............	"	Eggonē...............	Granddaughter.
29	Sūnaus dukter........	Son's daughter.	Dūkters dūkter........	Daughter's daughter.
30	Moja wnŭczkä........	My granddaughter.	Moj wnŭczka........	My granddaughter.
31	Ma wnŭcka...........	" "	Ma wnŭcka...........	" "
32	Vnuka mi...............	Granddaughter my.	Vnuka mi...............	Granddaughter my.
33	Vnooká mi.............	" "	Vnooka mi.............	" "
34	Moja vnutchka........	My granddaughter.	Maja vnutchka........	My granddaughter.
35	Torŭn-ŭun.............	Grandchild my.		
36	Törnee mun............	"	Törnee mun............	Grandchild my.
37	Fiam lanya...........	Daughter of my son.	Leanyon lanya	Daughter of my daughter.
38	Minu tutär tutär.......	My daughter's daughter.	Minu poeg tutär........	My son's daughter.
39	Poĭkanĭ tytär. ᵇ Tyttäreuĭ tytär..	Son's daughter. ᵇ Daughter's daughter.		

TABLE I.—*Continued.*

	17. Great-grandson.	Translation.	18. Great-granddaughter.	Translation.
1	Ibn ibn ibni	Son of son of son my.	Bint bint binti	Daught. of daught. of daught. my.
2	Ibn ibn ibni	" " " "	Bint bint binti	" " " "
3	Shĭllĕshīm	Descendants of the third generation.	Shĭllĕshīm	Descendants of third generation.
4	Natejee	Great grandson my.	Natigta	Great granddaughter my.
5	Voretees voretein voretin	Son's son's son.	Toostris toostriu toostra	Daughter's daughter's daughter.
6	Măc mic mo vic	The son of the son of my son.	Ineean mic mo vic	The daughter of the son of my son.
7	M'iär ogha	My great grandchild.	M'Eear ogha	My great grandchild.
8	Mac vac my vac	Son of son of my son.	Inneen inneen my inneen	Daught. of daught. of my daught.
9	Fy orwyr	My great grandson.	Fy orwyres	My great granddaughter.
10	Nätijä	Great grandchild.	Nätijä	Great grandchild.
11	Pratnaptár. ᵇ Prapautrah	Great grandson.	Pratinaptri. ᵇ Prapautri	Great granddaughter.
12	Barnebarn's barn	Great grandchild.	Barnebarn's barn	" grandchild.
13	Sonar sonar sonr minn	Son's son's son my.	Dottur dottur dottir min	Daughter's daughter daughter my.
14	Son's son's son	" " "	Dotter dotter dotter	" " " "
15				
16	Great grandson	Great grandson.	Great granddaughter	Great granddaughter.
17	Achter klein zoon. ᵇ Neef	After little son. ᵇ Nephew.	Aihter klein dochter. ᵇ Nicht.	After little daughter. Niece.
18	Groot groot zoon	Great grandson.	Groote groote dochter	Great granddaughter.
19	Kinds kinds kind	" grandchild.	Kinds kind kind	Child's child's child.
20	Urenkel	" grandson.	Urenkelinn	Great granddaughter.
21	Grossenkel	" "	Grossenkelinn	" " "
22	Mon arrière petit fils	My great grandson.	Mon arrière petit fille	My great granddaughter.
23	Bisnieto	Great grandson.	Bisnieta	" " "
24	Bisneto	" " "	Bisneta	Great granddaughter.
25	Secundo Nipote	" grandchild.	Secunda nipote	" grandchild.
26	Pronepos	" grandson.	Proneptis	" granddaughter.
27	Triteggonos. ᵇ Apeggonos	" "	Triteggonē	" " "
28	Proeggonos	" "	Proeggonē	" " "
29				
30	Moj prawnŭk	My great grandson.	Moja Prawnŭczka	My great granddaughter.
31	Mŭj Prawnŭk	" " "	Ma prawnucka	" " "
32	Prevnuk mi	Great grandson my.	Prevnuka mi	Great granddaughter my.
33	Prevnook mi	" " "	Prevnooka mi	" " "
34	Moi pravnuk	My " "	Moja pravnutchka	My " "
35	Torŭnŭmŭn	Grandchild of my child.	Torŭnŭmŭn	Grandchild of my child.
36	Läveh törneh mun	Son of grandchild my.	Keezäh törneh mun	Daughter of grandchild my.
37				
38	Minu poeg poeg poeg	My son's son's son.	Minu tutär tutär tutär	My daughter's daughter's daughter.
39	Poïkanï poïan poïka. ᵇ Tyttäreni tyttären poïka	My son's son's son. Daughter's daughter's son.	Poïkanï poïan tytär. ᵇ Tyttäreni tyttäreu tytär	The son's daughter of my son. The daughter's daught. of my daught.

	19. Great-grandson's son.	Translation.	20. Great-grandson's daughter.	Translation.
1	Ibn ibn ibn ibni	Son of son of son of son my.	Bint bint bint binti	Daughter. of dt. of dt. of dt. my.
2	Ibn ibn ibn ibni	" " " "	Bint bint bint binti	" " " "
3	Rĭbbĕïm	Descendants of the fourth generation.	Rĭbbĕïm	Descendants of fourth generation.
4	Närriga d'narrigee	Grandson of grandson my.	Närrigta d'narrigtee	Grand daught. of g daught. my.
5	Voretees voretein voretein voretin	Son's son's son's son.	Toostris toostriu toostrin toostra	Daught.'s daught.'s daught.'s dt.
6	Măc mic mic mo vic	The son of the son of the son of my son.	Ineean mic mic mo vic	The dt. of son of son of my son.
7	M'iar iar ogha	My great great grand child.	M'iar iar ogha	My great great grandchild.
8	Mac vac vac my vac	Son of son of son of my son.	Inneen inneen inneen ny inneen.	Dt. of dt. of dt. of my daught.
9	Fy ororwyr	My great great grandson.	Fy ororwyres	My great great granddaughter.
10	Näbirä	Great great grandchild.	Näbirä	Great great grandchild.
11	Parapratinapta	Great great grandson.	Parapratinaptri	Great great granddaughter.
12	Barnebarns barnebarn	Grand child's grand child.	Barnebarns barnebarn	Grandchild's grandchild.
13	Sonar sonar sonar sonr minn	Son's son's son's son my.	Dottur dottur dottur dottir min.	Daught.'s dt. dt. dt. my.
14	Son's son's son's son	" " " " "	Dotters dotters dotter dotter	" " " " "
15				
16	Great grandson's son	Great grandson's son.	Gt. grandson's daught. [ᵇ Neef.	Great grandson's daughter.
17	Achter klein zoon's zoon. ᵇ Neef.	After little son's son. ᵇ Nephew.	Achter klein zoon's klein docht.	After little son's little dt. ᵇ Nephew.
18	Groot groot groot zoon	Great great grandson.	Groote groote groote dochter	Great great granddaughter.
19	Kinds kinds kinds kind	Child's child's child's child.	Kinds kinds kinds kind	Child's child's child's child.
20	Urgrossenkel	Great great grandson.	Urgrossenkelinn	Great great granddaughter.
21	Urgrossenkel	" " "	Urgrossenkelin	" " "
22				
23	Tercer nieto	Third grandson.	Tercera nieta	Third granddaughter.
24	Tataraneto	Great great grandson.	Tataraneta	Great great granddaughter.
25	Terzo nipote	" " grandchild.	Terza nipote	" " grandchild.
26	Abnepos	" " grandson.	Abneptis	" " granddaughter.
27	Tetartos apogonos	" " "	Tetarte eggonē	" " "
28	Apeggonos	" " "	Appeggonē	" " "
29				
30	Moj praprawnŭk	My great great grandson.	Moja praprawnŭczka	My great great granddaughter.
31	Mŭj praprawnŭk	" " " "	Ma praprawnŭcka	" " " "
32	Preprevnuk mi	Great great grandson my.	Preprevnuka mi	Great great granddaughter my.
33	Preprevnook mi	" " " "	Preprevnooka mi	" " "
34	Moi prapravnuk	My great great grandson my.	Moja prapravnutchka	My " "
35	Torŭnŭmŭn torŭnŭ	Grandchild of my grandchild.	Torŭnŭmŭn torŭnŭ	Grandchild of my grandchild.
36	Törneh törneh mun	Grandchild of grandchild my.	Törneh törneh mun	Grandchild of grandchild my.
37				
38				[of my son.
39	Poïkanï poïan poïan poïka	The grandson of my grandson.	Poïkanï poïan poïan tytär	The daughter of the son of the son

TABLE I.—*Continued.*

	21. Great-grandson's grandson.	Translation.	22. Great-grandson's granddaughter.	Translation.
1	Ibn ibn ibn ibn ibni	Son of son of son of son of son my.	Bint bint bint bint binti	D. of d. of d. of d. of daughter my.
2	Ibn ibn ibn ibn ibni	" " " " " "	Bint bint bint bint binti	" " " " " " "
3				
4	Nateja d'näwigee	Great grandson of grandson my.	Näwigtä d'nawigtee	Gt. gd. daughter of grandson my.
5	Voretees voretein vn. vn. voretin.	Son's son's son's son's son.	Toostris toostrin t. t. toostra	Daughter's d. d. d.
6	Mic mic mic mic mo vic	The son's son of the son's son of my son.	Ineean mic mic mic mo vic	The d. of the son's s. of my son's s.
7	M'iar iar iar iar ogha	My great grandchild's grandchild.	M'iar iar iar ogha	My great grandchild's grandchild.
8	Mac vac vac vac my vac	Son of son of son of son of my son.	Inneen in. in. in. my inneen	
9	Fy orororwyr	My great grandson's grandson.	Fy orororwyres	My gt. grandson's granddaughter.
10	Näbirä	Great great great grandchild.	Näbirä	Great great great grandchild.
11				
12	Barnebarns barnebarns barn	Great grandson's grandchild.	Barnebarns barnebarn barn	Great grandson's grandchild.
13	Sonar sonar sonar sonar sonr minn.	Son's son's son's son's son my.	Dottur d. d. d. dottir min	Daughter's d. d. d. d. my.
14	Sons son sons son son	" " " " "	Dotters dotters dotter dotter	" " " "
15				
16	Great grandson's grandson	Great grandson's grandson.	Gt. grandson's g. d. [b Nicht.	Gt. grandson's granddaughter.
17	Achter klein zoons k. z. b Neef	After little son's little son. b Nephew.	Achter klein zoons kn. dochter.	After little son's little d. b Niece.
18	Groot groot groot groot zoon	Great great great grandson.	Groote g. g. g. dochter	Great great great granddaughter.
19	Kinds kinds kinder	" " " grandchild.	Kinds kinds kinder	" " " grandchild.
20	Ururgrossenkel	" " " grandson.	Ururgrossenkelinn	" " " granddaughter.
21	Ururgrossenkel	" " "	Ururgrossenkelin	" " " "
22				
23	Cuarto nieto	Fourth grandson.	Cuarta nieta	Fourth granddaughter.
24	Cuarto neto	" "	Cuarta neta	" "
25	Quarto nipote	" "	Quarta nipote	" "
26	Atnepos	Great grandson's grandson.	Atneptis	Great grandson's granddaughter.
27	Pemptos apogonos?	" " "	Pempte eggoné?	" " "
28	Diseggonos	" " "	Diseggoné	" " "
29				
30	Moj prapraprawnük	My great great great grandson.	Moja prapraprawnŭczka	My gt. gt. gt. granddaughter.
31	Müj prapraprawnük	" " " " "	Ma prapraprawnücka	" " " "
32	Prepreprevnuk mi	Great great great grandson my.	Prepreprevnuka mi	Gt. gt. gt. granddaughter my.
33				
34				
35				
36	Läveh törneh törneh mun	Son of grandchild of grandchild my.	Keeza törneh törneh mun	Daughter of g. child of g. child my.
37				
38				
39				

	23. Great grandson's great grandson.	Translation.	24. Great grandson's g't granddaughter.	Translation.
1	Ibn ibn ibn ibn ibn ibni	Son of son of s. of s. of s. of s. my.	Bint bint bint bint bint binti	D. of d. of d. of d. of d. of d. my.
2	Ibn ibn ibn ibn ibn ibni	" " " " " " "	Bint bint bint bint bint binti	" " " " " " "
3				
4	Nateja d' natejee	Great grandson of great grandson my.	Natejta d' natejee	Great granddaughter of g. grandson.
5	Voretees voretein v. v. v. voretin.	Son's son's son's son's son's son.	Toostris toostrin t. t. t. toostra	Daughter d. d. d. d. daughter.
6	Mäc mic mic mic mo vic	The son's son of s. of s. of my s.	Ineean mic mic mic mo vic	The d. of son's s. of s. s. of my s.
7	M'iar iar iar iar ogha	My great grandchild's great grandchild.	M'iar iar iar iar ogha	My gt. grandchild's gt. grandchild.
8	Mac vac vac vac vac my vac	" " " " "	Inneen in. in. in. in. my in	" " " "
9	Fy ororororwyr	My great grandson's great grandson.	Fy orororwyres	My gt. grandson's gt. granddaugh.
10				
11				[barn.
12	Barnebarns barnebarns barnebarn	Great grandchild's great grandchild.	Barnebarns barnebarns barne-	Gt. grandchild's gt. grandchild.
13	Sonar sonar sonar s. s. sonr minn.	Son's son's son's son's son's son my.	Dottur d. d. d. d. dottir min	Daughter's d. d. d. d. daughter my.
14	Sonson sonson sonson	" " " " " "	Dotter' dotter's dotter's dotter [dotter dotter.	" " " "
15				
16	Great grandson's great grandson	Great grandson's great grandson.	G't granddau's g't granddaught.	Gt. grandson's gt. granddaughter.
17	Achter klein zoons a. k. z. b Neef	" " " grandson's neph.	A. k. zoons a. k. dochter. b Nicht	" " niece.
18	Groot groot groot groot groot zoon	Great great great grandson.	Groote g. g. g. groote dochter	Gt. gt. gt. gt. granddaughter.
19	Kinds kinds kinds kinder	" " " grandchild.	Kinks kinds kinds kinder	" " " grandchild.
20	Urururenkel	Great great great grandson.	Urururenkelinn	" " " granddaughter.
21	Grossenkels grossenkel	Great grandson's great grandson.	Grossenkelins grossenkelin	Gt. granddaughter's gt. gd. daugh.
22				
23	Cuinto Nieto	Fifth grandson.	Cuinta nieta	Fifth granddaughter.
24	Cuinto Neto	" "	Cuinta neta	" "
25	Quinto Nipote	" "	Quinta Nipote	" "
26	Trinepos	Great grandson's great grandson.	Trineptis	Gt. grandson's gt. granddaughter.
27	Hektos Apogonos	" " " "	Hehté eggoné	" " " "
28	Triseggonos	" " " "	Triseggoné	" " "
29				
30	Moj praprapraprawnük	My great great great great grandson.	Moja praprapraprawnŭczka	My gt. gt. gt. gt. granddaughter.
31	Müj praprapraprawnük	" " " " " "	Ma praprapraprawnüka	" " " "
32	Prepreprevnuk mi	Great great great great grandson my.	Prepreprevnuka ni	Gt. gt. gt. gt. granddaughter my.
33				
34				
35				
36	Törneh törneh törneh mun	Grandchild of grandchild of g. c. my.	Törneh törneh törneh mun	Grandchild of g. c. of g. c. my.
37				
38				
39				

TABLE I.—*Continued.*

	25. Elder brother.	Translation.	26. Younger brother.	Translation.
1	Akhi akbia minni......................	Brother my older than me.	Akhi asghar minni......................	Brother my younger than me.
2	Akhi il ăkbar........................	Brother my the greatest.	Akhi il asghär........................	Brother my the smallest.
3	Akhī hăggădhŏl mĭmmĕnnĭ........	Brother my great from me.	Akhī hăkkaton mĭmmĕnnĭ........	Brother my small from me.
4	Akhonee gora........................	Brother my the greater.	Akhŏnee sŭra........................	Brother my the younger.
5	Yakepire	My brother.	Yakepire	My brother.
6	Mo yrihair-as-shŭne	My brother the eldest.	Mo-yrihair-as-oggĭ........	My brother the younger.
7	Mo bhrathair as sinne..............	" " "	Mo bhrathair asoige..............	" " "
8	My braar shinnay....................	" " "	My braar saah....................	" " "
9	Fy mrawd henaf......................	" " "	Fy mrawd jeangaf......................	" " "
10	Brädär bûzûrk	Brother elder.		
11	Agrajar........................	Elder brother.	Amujar........................	Younger brother.
12	Oldre broder........................	" "	Yngre broder........................	" "
13	Eldri brodir........................	" "	Yngri brodir........................	" "
14	Aldre broder........................	" "	Yngre broder........................	" "
15				
16	Elder brother........................	" "	Younger brother........................	" "
17	Audste broeder........................	" "	Jongste broeder........................	" "
18	Vredsten broeder........................	" "	Jonger broeder........................	" "
19	Oelste brohr........................	" "	Jŭngster brohr........................	" "
20	Aelterer bruder	" "	Jŭngerer bruder........................	" "
21	Aelterer bruder........................	" "	Jŭngerer bruder........................	" "
22	Mon aîné	My elder brother.	Mon cadet. ᵇ Pûné........	My younger brother.
23				
24				
25	Fratello maggiore........................	Brother the elder.	Fratello minore	Brother the younger.
26	Frater major	Elder brother.	Frater minor........................	Younger brother.
27			Adelphidion	A little brother.
28				
29				
30	Moj starszy brat........................	My elder brother.	Moj mtodszy brat	My younger brother.
31	Mŭj sarsi bratr........................	" " "	Mŭj mladsi bratr........................	" " "
32	Brat........................	Brother.	Brat........................	Brother.
33	Baye. ᵇ Nane........	Elder brother.	Byname	Younger brother.
34	Moi starshi brat........................	My elder brother.	Moi mladshi brat	My younger brother.
35	Kärndäsh ūm	Brother my. ᵇ Womb companion.	Kärndäsh-ūm	Brother my. ᵇ Womb companion.
36	Brä mun e mĕzun	Brother my the elder.	Brä mun e pŭchook........................	Brother my the younger.
37	Batyam........................	Elder brother my.	Oosem........................	Younger brother my.
38	Mĭnu vänem vend	My old brother.	Minu nohrem vend........................	My young brother.
39	Vän hempĭ veljenĭ........................	Elder brother my.	Nuorempĭ veljenĭ........................	Rounger brother my.

	27. Elder sister.	Translation.	28. Younger sister.	Translation.
1	Akhti akbia minni........................	Sister my older than me.	Akhti asghar minni........................	Sister my younger than me.
2	Akhti il kubrä........................	Sister my the greatest.	Akhti il sughrä	Sister my the smallest.
3	ᵃ Khōthī hagg'dhōlā mĭmmĕnnĭ ...	Sister my great from me.	ᵃ Khŏthī hăkkitănnā mĭmmĕnnĭ ..	Sister my small from me.
4	Khätee görta	Sister my the greater.	Khätee Sŭrta........................	Sister my the small.
5	Kooere	My sister.	Kooere	My sister.
6	Mo yriffŭr as shŭne	My sister the eldest.	Mo yriffŭr as oggĭ........................	My sister the younger.
7	Mo phiŭthar as sinne..............	" " "	Mo phiŭsthar as ŏige..............	" " " "
8	My shuyr shinnay....................	" " " "	Ma shuyr saah........................	" " " "
9	Fy chwaer henaf......................	My sister the elder.	Fy chwaer ieangaf......................	" " " "
10	Hähär bûzûrk	Sister elder.		
11	Agrajri.	Elder sister.	Amujri........................	Younger sister.
12	Oldre söster........................	" "	Yngre Söster	" "
13	Eldri systir........................	" "	Yngri systir........................	" "
14	Aldre syster........................	" "	Yngre syster........................	" "
15				
16	Elder sister........................	" "	Younger sister........................	" "
17	Audste zuster........................	" "	Jongste zuster........................	" "
18	Vredste sister........................	" "	Jonger Sister	" "
19	Oelste sister........................	" "	Jŭngste sister........................	" "
20	Aeltere schwester...	" "	Jŭngere schwester........................	" "
21	Aeltere schwester........................	" "	Jŭngere schwester........................	" "
22	Mon aînée........................	My elder sister.	Ma cadette. ᵇ Puînée	My younger sister.
23				
24				
25	Sorella maggoire........................	Sister the elder.	Sorella minore........................	Sister the younger.
26	Soror Major........................	Elder sister.	Soror minor........................	Younger sister.
27				
28				
29				
30	Moja starsza siostra........................	My elder sister.	Moja Mtodsza siostra................	My younger sister.
31	Ma starsa sestra........................	" " "	Ma mladsa sestra........................	" " "
32	Sestra........................	Sister.	Sestra........................	Sister.
33	Kaka........................	Elder sister.	Byname........................	Younger sister.
34	Maja starshaja sestra........................	My elder sister.	Maja mladshaja sestra........................	My younger sister.
35	Kus kärndäsh-ūm	Sister my. ᵇ Girl womb companion.	Kus kärndäsh-ūm	Sister my. ᵇ Girl womb companion.
36	Khōoshkeh mun eh mĕzun..........	Sister my the elder.	Khŏoshkeh mun eh pŭchook.......	Sister my the younger.
37	Nenem........................	Elder sister my.	Hugom........................	Younger sister my.
38	Minu vanem odde........................	My elder sister.	Minu nohsem odde....................	My young sister.
39	Vanhempĭ sisärenĭ	Elder sister my.	Nuorempĭ veljenĭ........................	Younger sister my.

TABLE I.—*Continued.*

	29. Brothers.	Translation.	30. Sisters.	Translation.
1	Ahwati	Brothers my.	Ahwâti	Sisters my.
2	Akwati	" "	Akhăwăti	" "
3	Akhai	" "	Akhyŏthai	" "
4	Akhonwätee	" "	Khawatee	" "
5	Yakepire narse	" "	Kooere-räris	" "
6	Mo yriharacha	My brothers.	Mo yriffĕracha	My sisters.
7	Mo bhräthrean	" "	Mo phethrichean	" "
8	My braaraghyn	" "	My shuyraghyn	" "
9	Fy mrodyr.	" "	Fy chwaeriorydd	" "
10	Brâdârâni	Brothers.	Hâhârâni	Sisters.
11	Bhrätarah	"	Swasärah. ᵇ Bhaginyah	"
12	Broders	"	Sösters	"
13	Broetr minir	Brothers my.	Systur minar	Sisters my.
14	Bröder	Brothers.	systrar	Sisters.
15	Brodors	"	Swusters	"
16	Brothers	"	Sisters	"
17	Broeders	"	Zusters	"
18	Broeders	"	Sisters	"
19	Brohrs	"	Sisters	"
20	Brüder	"	Schwestern	"
21	Brüder	"	Schwestern	"
22	Mes frères	My brothers.	Mes sœurs	My sisters.
23	Hermanos	Brothers.	Hermanas	Sisters.
24	Irmanõs	My brothers.	Irmans	My sisters.
25	Fratelli	Brothers.	Sorelle	Sisters.
26	Fratres	"	Sorores	"
27	Adelphoi	"	Adelphai	"
28	Adelphoi	"	Adelphai	"
29	Măno brŏlei	My brothers.	Măno sessers	My sisters.
30	Moj bracia	" "	Moje siostry	" "
31	Moji bratri	" "	Moje sestry	" "
32	Bratia mi	Brothers my.	Sestri mi	Sisters my.
33	Bratie mi	" "	Sestri mi	" "
34	Moi bratja. ᵇ Bratia	My brothers.	Moi sestri	My sisters.
35	Kärndäshlär ūm	Brothers my.	Kus kärndäshlär ūm	sisters my.
36	Brŏugeh mun		Kooshkä mun	
37	Atyam fijai. ᵇ Testvreim	Sons of my father.	Atyam lanyai. ᵇ Testverein	Daughters of my father sisters.
38	Minu vennäd	My brothers.	Minu odded	My sisters.
39	Weljenĭ	Brothers my.	Sisareni	Sisters my.

	31. Brother. (Male speaking.)	Translation.	32. Brother's son. (Male speaking.)	Translation.
1	Akhi	Brother my.	Ibn äkhi	Son of brother my.
2	Akhi	" "	Ibn äkhi	" " " "
3	Akhĭ	" "	Bĕn akhĭ	" " " "
4	Akhŏnee	" "	Brūna d'äkhŏnee	" " " "
5	Yäkepire	" "	Yakeporus voretin	Brother's son my.
6	Mo yrihair	My brother.	Măc mo drihär	Son of my brother.
7	Mo bhräthäir	" "	Mac hhräthäir	" " " "
8	My braar	" "	Mac my braar	" " " "
9	Fy mrawd	" "	Fy Naï	My nephew.
10	Brâdär	Brother.	Poosäri brâdär	Son of brother.
11	Bratar. ᵇ Sodare	"	Bhrátrivyah. ᵇ Bhrâtroya	Brother's son.
12	Broder	"	Brodersön	" "
13	Brodir minn	Brother my.	Brodursonr minn	Brother's son my.
14	Broder	Brother.	Brorson	Brother's son.
15	Brodor. ᵇ Brothor	"	Nefa	Nephew.
16	Brother	"	Nephew	Nephew
17	Broeder	"	Neef	Nephew or grandson.
18	Broeder	"	Nĕvĕ	Nephew.
19	Brohr	"	Brohrs soohn	Brother's son.
20	Bruder	"	Neffe	Nephew.
21	Bruder	"	Neffe	"
22	Mon frère	My brother.	Mon neveu	"
23	Hermano	Brother.	Sobrino	My nephew.
24	Irmano	"	Sobrinho	Nephew.
25	Fratello	"	Nipote	Nephew. ᵇ Grandchild.
26	Frater	"	Fratris filius..........[phopais	Son of a brother.
27	Adelphos. ᵇ Kasignētos. Kasis?	"	Adelphidous. ᵇ Kasignētos 'adel-	Nephew.
28	Adelphos	"	Adelphidous. ᵇ Anepsios	"
29	Brolis	"	Brŏtuszĭs	Brother's son.
30	Moj brat	My brother.	Moj bratanek. ᵇ Synowiec	My nephew.
31	Mŭj bratr	" "	Mŭj bratranec	" "
32	Brat mi	Brother my.	Bratanets mi	Nephew my.
33	Brat mi	" "	Bratanetz. ᵇ Bratovchad	Nephew.
34	Moi brat	My brother.	Moi pljemiannik	My nephew.
35			Yĕyĕn ĭm	Nephew my.
36	Brä mun	Brother my.	Läveh brä mun	Son of brother my.
37	Batyam. ᵇ Ocsem	Brother elder. ᵇ Younger.	Kis ocsem	Little younger brother my.
38	Minu vennä	My brother.	Minu vennä poeg	My brother's son.
39	Veljeni	Brother my.	Veljen poikä. ᵇ Nepaa	Brother's son. ᵇ Nephew.

TABLE I.—*Continued.*

	33. Brother's son's wife. (Male speaking.)	Translation.	34. Brother's daughter. (Male speaking.)	Translation.
1	Amrât ibn äkhi	Wife of son of brother my.	Bint äkhi	Daughter of brother my.
2	Zanjat ibn äkhi	" " " "	Bint äkhi	" " " "
3	Eshĕth bĕn äkhî	" " " "	Bâth äkhî	" " " "
4	Calta d'Akhŏnee	Daughter-in-law of my brother.	Bräta d'äkhŏnee	" " " "
5	Yäkeporus voretien gena	Brother's son's wife my.	Yäkeporus toostra	Brother's daughter.
6	Ban-mic mo drihâr	Wife of the son of my brother.	Ineean mo drihâr	Daughter of my brother.
7	Bean mic bhrăthăir	" " " " "	Neegheau bhrăthăir	" " " "
8	Ben mac my braar	" " " " "	Inneen my braar	" " " "
9	Fy nith .	My niece.	Fy nith	My niece.
10	Zăni poosäri brădär	Wife of son of brother.	Dûkhtäri brâdär	Daughter of brother.
11			Bhratrivyá	Brother's daughter.
12	Broderson's hustrue	Brother's son's wife.	Broderdatter	"
13	Kona brodursnor minn	Wife of brother's son my.	Brodur dottir minn	Brother's daughter my.
14	Brorsons hustru	Brother's son's wife.	Brorsdotter	Brother's daughter.
15			Nefane	Niece.
16	Niece	Niece.	Niece .	Niece. ᵇ Brother's daughter.
17	Nicht	"	Nicht	Niece's granddaughter.
18	Nichtĕ	"	Nichte	Niece.
19	Brohrs soohns frau	Brother's son's wife.	Brohr's dochter	Brother's daughter.
20	Nichte	Niece.	Nichte	Niece.
21	Gattin des neffen	Wife of nephew.	Nichte	"
22	Ma nièce	My niece.	Ma nièce	My niece.
23	Sobrina politica	Niece (by courtesy).	Sobrina	Niece.
24	Sobrinha por affinidade	Niece by affinity.	Sobrinha	"
25	Aquistella nipote	Acquired niece.	Nipote	Niece. ᵇ Grandchild.
26	Fratris filii uxor	Wife of the son of a brother.	Fratris filia	Daughter of a brother.
27	Adelphidou gunē	Wife of nephew.	Adelphidē. ᵇ Kasignĕtē	Niece.
28			Adelphidē. ᵇ Anepsia	"
29				
30	Moja bratankowa	My niece-in-law.	Moja synowica	My niece.
31	Ma bratrancowa	" " " "	Ma sestrena	" "
32			Bratanetsa mi	Niece my.
33			Bratanitza. ᵇ Bratoochoctka	Niece.
34	Shena moego pljemiannitza	My called niece.	Moja pljemiannitza	My niece.
35	Yĕyĕnum karŭsŭ	Nephew's my wife.	Yĕyĕn im	Niece my.
36	Bookeh brä mun	Daughter-in-law of brother my.	Keesä brä mun	Daughter of brother my.
37			Kis hugom	Little younger sister my.
38	Minu venna poeg naine	My brother's son's wife.	Minu vennä tutär	My brother's daughter.
39	Nepaan vaimo	Nephew's wife.	Veljen tytär .	Brother's daughter.

	35. Brother's daughter's husband. (Male speaking.)	Translation.	36. Brother's grandson. (Male speaking.)	Translation.
1	Zôj bint äkhi	Husband of daughter of brother my.	Ibn ibn äkhi	Son of son of brother my.
2	Zauj bint äkhi	" " " " " "	Ibn ibn äkhi	" " " "
3	Ish bath äkhî	" " " " " "		
4	Gora d'bräta d'Akhŏnee	Son-in-law of brother my.	Näwiga d'äkhŏnee	Grandson of brother my.
5	Yäkeporus toostrin arega	Brother's daughter's husband.	Yäkeporus voretein voretin	Brother's son's son.
6	Far ineeni mo drihâr	Husband of daughter of my brother.	Mac mic mo drihâr	Son's son of my brother.
7	Fear pŏsda nghen brathair	Brother's daughter's husband.	Ogha brăthar	Brother's grandchild.
8	Sheshey inneen my braar	Husband of daughter of my brother.	Mac vac my braar	Son of son of my brother.
9	Fy nai	My nephew.	Wyr fy mrawd	Grandson of my brother.
10	Shŏhäri dûkhtäri brâdär	Husband of daughter of brother.	Năvădär brädär	Grandchild of brother.
11			Bhrătrnaptar	Brother's grandson.
12	Broder datter's husbond.	Brother's daughter's husband.	Broders barnebarn	Brother's grandchild.
13	Madr brodur dottur minn	Husband of brother's daughter my.	Sonar sonr brodur minn	Son's son of brother my.
14	Brorsdotters man	Brother's daughter's husband.	Brorsons son	Brother's son's son.
15				
16	Nephew .	Nephew.	Great nephew	Great nephew. Brother's grandson.
17	Neef	"	Broeders klein zoon. ᵇ Neef	Brother's grandson, nephew.
18	Nĕvĕ .	"	Groot Nĕvĕ	Great nephew.
19	Brohrs dochters man	Brother's daughter's husband.	Brohrs kinds kind	Brother's child's child.
20	Neffe	Nephew.	Gross neffe	Great nephew.
21	Gatte der nichte	Husband of niece.	Bruders enkel	Brother's grandson.
22	Mon neveu	My nephew.	Mon petit-neveu	My little nephew.
23	Sobrino politico	Nephew by courtesy.	Sobrino	My grandson.
24	Sobrinho por affinidade	Nephew by affinity.	Sobrinho neto	Nephew's grandson.
25	Aquistata nipote	Acquired nephew.	Pronipote	Great nephew. Great grandson.
26	Fratris filiae vir	Husband of a daughter of a brother.	Fratris nepos	Grandson of a brother.
27	Adelphidēs anēr	Husband of a niece.	Adelphou eggonos. ᵇ Anepsiadous?	" " "
28			Adelphou eggonos	" " "
29				
30	Moj synowice	My nephew-in-law.	Moj synowca	My nephew's son.
31	Mŭj sestrin	" " "		
32				
33			Mal vnook mi	Little grandson my.
34	Shena moega pljemiannik	My called nephew.	Moi vnutchatnyi pljemiannik	My nephew's grandson.
35	Yĕyĕnum kojäsŭ	Niece's my husband.	Kärndäshmŭn torŭ .	Brother's my grandchild.
36	Zävä brä mun	Son-in-law of brother my.	Tŏneh brä mun	Grandchild of brother my.
37				
38	Minu vennä tutär mees	My brother's daughter's husband.	Minu vennä poeg poeg	My brother's son's son.
39	Veljen tyttären mies	Brother's daughter's husband.	Nepaan poika	Nephew's my son.

TABLE I.—*Continued.*

	37. Brother's granddaughter. (Male speaking.)	Translation.	38. Brother's great grandson. (Male speaking.)	Translation.
1	Bint ibn äkhi	Daughter of son of brother my.	Ibn ibn ibn äkhi	Son of son of son of brother my.
2	Bint ibn äkhi	" " " "	Ibn ibn ibn äkhi	" " " " " "
3				
4	Näwigata d'äkhönee	Granddaughter of brother my.	Nateja d'äkhönee	Great grandchild of brother my.
5	Yäkeporus toostrin toostra	Brother's daughter's daughter.	Yäkeporus voretein v. voretin	Brother's son's son's son.
6	Ineean mic mo drihăr	Daughter of son of my brother.	Mac mic mic mo drihăr	Son of the son of the son of my b'ther.
7	Egha brăthar	Brother's granddaughter.	Iar iar ogha brathar	Brother's great grandchild.
8	Inneen inneen my braar	Daughter of daughter of my brother.	Mac mac mac my braar	Son of son of son of my brother.
9	Wyres fy mrawd	Granddaughter of my brother.	Orwyr fy mrawd	Great grandson of my brother.
10	Năvâdâr brådär	Grandchild of brother.	Nätijăr brådär	Great grandchild of brother.
11	Bhrâtrnaptri	Brother's granddaughter.		
12	Broders barnebarn	Brother's grandchild.	Broders barnebarns barn	Brother's great grandchild.
13	Dottur dottir brodur minn	Daughter's daughter of brother my.	Sonar sonar sonr brodur minn	Son's son's son of brother my.
14	Brorsdotter dotter	Brother's daughter's daughter.	Brosons sonson	Brother's son's son's son.
15				
16	Great niece.	Great niece, brother's granddaughter.	Great great nephew	Brother's great grandson.
17	Broeder's klein dochter. b Nicht.	Brother's granddaughter, niece.	Broeders achter klein zoon. b Neef	Brother's great grandson. b Nephew.
18	Groote nichte.	Great niece.	Groot groot nečě	Great great nephew.
19	Brohrs kinds kind	Brother's child's child.	Brohrs kinds kinds kind	Brother's child's child's child.
20	Tochter meiner nichte	Daughter of my niece.	Urgross neffe	Great great nephew.
21	Bruders enkelin	Brother's granddaughter.	Bruders grossenkel	Brother's great grandson.
22	Ma petite-nièce	My little niece.	Mon arrière-petit-neveu	My great little nephew.
23	Sobrina	My granddaughter.	Sobrino	My grandson.
24	Sobrinho neta	Nephew's granddaughter.		
25	Pronipote	Great niece. Great granddaughter.	Pronipote	Great nephew.
26	Fratris neptis	Granddaughter of a brother.	Fratris pronepos	Great grandson of a brother.
27	Adelphou Huiŏnē. b Anepsiadēs?	" " "	Adelphou apogonos tritos	" " " "
28	Adelphou eggonē	" " "	Adelphou proeggonos	" " " "
29				
30	Moja corka synowca	My nephew's daughter.	Moj wnŭk synowca	My nephew's grandson.
31				
32				
33	Mal vnooka mi	Little granddaughter my.	Mal prevnook mi	Little great grandson my.
34	Moja vnutchatnaja pljemiannitza	My niece granddaughter.	Moi pravnutchatnyi pljemannik	My nephew great grandson.
35	Kärndäshmŭn torŭ	Brother's my grandchild.	Kärndäshmŭn torŭnŭm torŭnŭ	Brother's my great grandchild.
36	Törneh brä mun	Grandchild of brother my.	Lăveh törneh brä mun	Son of grandchild of brother my.
37				
38	Minu vennä poeg tutär	My brother's son's daughter.	Minu vennä poeg poeg poeg	My brother's son's son's son.
39	Nepaan tytär	Nephew's my daughter.	Nepaan poiăn poïka	Nephew's my grandson.

	39. Brother's great granddaughter. (Male speaking.)	Translation.	40. Sister. (Male speaking.)	Translation.
1	Bint bint bint äkhi	Daughter of d. of d. of brother my.	Akhti	Sister my.
2	Bint bint bint äkhi	" " " " "	Ikhti	" "
3			a Khŏthī	" "
4	Natijta d'äkhönee	Great granddaughter of brother my.	Khätee	" "
5	Yäkeporus toostrin t. toostra	Brother's daught. daught. daught.	Kovere	My sister.
6	Ineean mic mic mo drihăr	Daughter of son of son of my brother.	Mo yriffür	" "
7	Iar Iar ogha brăthăr	Brother's great grandchild.	Mo phiuthar	" "
8	Ineen mac mac my braar	Daughter of son of son of my brother.	My shuyr	" "
9	Orwyres fy mrawd	Great granddaughter of my brother.	Fy chwaer	" "
10	Nätijäi brådär	Great grandchild of brother.	Hâhâr	Sister.
11			Svasar. b Jami. c Bhaginî	"
12	Broders barnebarns barn	Brother's great grandchild.	Söster	"
13	Dottur dottur dottir brodir minn	Daughter's d. d. of brother my.	Systur minn	Sister my
14	Brorsons sons dotter	Brother's son's son's daughter.	Syster	Sister.
15				
16	Great great niece	Brother's great granddaughter.	Sister	"
17	Broeders achter klein doch. b Nicht	Brother's gt. granddaught. b Niece.	Zuster	"
18	Groote groote nichte	Great great niece.	Sister	"
19	Brohrs kinds kinds kind	Brother's child's child's child.	Sister	"
20	Urgross nichte	Great great niece.	Schwester	"
21	Bruders grossenkelin	Brother's great granddaughter.	Schwester	"
22	Mon arrière-petite fille	My great little niece.	Ma sœur	My sister.
23	Sobrina	My granddaughter.	Hermana	Sister.
24			Irman	"
25	Pronipote	Great niece.	Sorella	"
26	Fratris proneptis	Great granddaughter of a brother.	Soror	"
27	Adelphou apogonē tritē	" " " "	Adelphē. b Kasignētē. c Kasē?..	"
28	Adelphou preggonē	" " " "	Adelphē	"
29			Sěsŭ	"
30	Moja wnuczka synowca	My nephew's granddaughter.	Moja Siostra	My sister.
31			Mŭj Sestra	" "
32			Sestra mi	Sister my.
33	Mal prevnooka mi [nitza	Little great granddaughter my.	Sestra my	" "
34	Moja pravnutchatnaja pljemian-	My niece great granddaughter.	Moja sestra	My sister.
35	Kärndäshmŭn torŭnŭm torŭnŭ	Brother's my great grandchild.		
36	Keezä törneh brä mun	Daughter of g. d. of brother my.	Khoôshkeh mun	Sister my.
37			Nenem. b Hugom	Sister elder. b Younger.
38	Minu vennä poeg poeg tutär	My brother's son's son's daughter.	Minu odde	My sister.
39	Nepaan poïän tytär	Nephew's my son's daughter.	Sisareni	Sister my.

TABLE I.—*Continued.*

	41. Sister's son. (Male speaking.)	Translation.	42. Sister's son's wife. (Male speaking.)	Translation.
1	Ibn äkhti	Son of sister my	Amrât ibn äkhti	Wife of son of sister my.
2	Ibn ïkhti	" " "	Zaujat ibn ikhti	" " " " "
3	Běn. ᵃ Khŏthī	" " "	Esheth běn. ᵃ Kŏthī	" " " " "
4	Brūnă d'khätee. ᵇ Khwärză	Son of sister my. ᵇ Nephew.	Calta d'khätee	Daughter-in-law of my sister.
5	Crochus voretin	Son of sister my.	Crochus voretin gena	Wife of son of sister my.
6	Mac mo driffer	Son of my sister.	Ban mic mo driffer	Wife of son of my sister.
7	Mac pethair	" " "	Bean mic pethar	" " " " "
8	Mac my shuyr	" " "	Ben mac my shuyr	" " " " "
9	Fy nai	My nephew.	Fy nith	My niece.
10	Poosäri hâhär	Son of sister.	Zăni poosäri hâhär	Wife of son of sister.
11	Svasrîya	Sister's son.	Söstersöns hustrue	Sister's son's wife.
12	Söstersön	" "		
13	Systur sonr minn	Sister's son my.	Kona systur sonar minn	Wife of sister's son my.
14	Systersou	Sister's son.	Systersons hustru	Sister's son's wife.
15	Nefa. ᵇ Swester sunu	Nephew. ᵇ Sister's son.		
16	Nephew	" " "	Niece	Niece.
17	Neef	Nephew. ᵇ Grandson.	Nicht	"
18	Něvě	Nephew.	Nichte	"
19	Sisters soohn	Sister's son.	Sister's soohns frau	Sister's son's wife.
20	Neffe	Nephew.	Nichte	Niece.
21	Neffe	"	Gattin des neffen	Wife of nephew.
22	Mon neveu	My nephew.	Ma nièce	My niece.
23	Sobrino	Nephew.	Sobrina politica	My niece (by courtesy).
24	Sobrinho	"	Sobrinha por affinidad	Niece by affinity.
25	Nipote	Nephew. ᵇ Grandchild.	Aquistella nipote	Acquired niece.
26	Sororis filius ....[epsios ?]	Son of a sister.	Sororis filii uxor	Wife of a son of a sister.
27	Adelphidous. ᵇ Kasignētos. ᶜ An-	Nephew.	Adelphidou gunē	" " " "
28	Adelphidous. ᵇ Anepsios	"		
29				
30	Moj siostrzeniec	My nephew.	Moja siostrzencowa	My niece-in-law.
31	Mŭj sestrinec	" "	Ma sestrincowa	" "
32	Sestrinets mi	Nephew my.		
33	Sestrenik mi	" "		
34	Moi pljemiannik	My nephew.	Shoena moego pljeminnitza	Wife of my nephew.
35	Yěyěn-mi	nephew my.	Yěyěnum kärüsü	Nephew's my wife.
36	Khooärzeh mun		Zhuneh khooärzeh mun	Daughter-in-law, nephew my.
37	Kis öcsem	Little younger brother.		
38	Minu odde poeg	My sister's son.	Minn odde poeg naine	My sister's son husband.
39	Sĭsären poïkä. ᵇ Nepaa	Sister's my son, nephew.	Nepaan vaino	Nephew's my wife.

	43. Sister's daughter. (Male speaking.)	Translation.	44. Sister's daughter's husband. (Male speaking.)	Translation.
1	Bint äkhti	Daughter of sister my.	Zôj bint äkhti	Husband of daughter of sister my.
2	Bint ikhti	" " "	Zauj bint ikhti	" " " " "
3	Băth. ᵃ Khŏthī	" " "	Ish băth. ᵃ Khŏthī	" " " " "
4	Brätä d'khätee. ᵇ Khwärzätä	Daughter of sister my. ᵇ Niece.	Khutnä d'khätee	Son-in-law of sister my.
5	Crochus toostra	Sister's daughter.	Crochus toostrin arego	Sister's daughter's husband.
6	Ineean mo driffer	Daughter of my sister.	Far ineenĭ mo driffer	Husband of the daught. of my sister.
7	Neeghean pethar	" " "	Fear pòsda neeghin pethar	Husband of daughter of my sister.
8	Inneen my shuyr	" " "	Sheshey ineen my shuyr	" " " " "
9	Fy nith	My niece.	Fy nai	My nephew.
10	Dûkhtäri hâhär	Daughter of sister.	Shŏhäri dûkhtäri hâhär	Husband of daughter of sister.
11	Svasriyâ	Sister's daughter.		
12	Sösterdatter	" "	Sösterdatter husbond	Sister's daughter's husband.
13	Systur dottir minn	Sister's daughter my.	Madr systur dottur minn	Husband of sister's daughter my.
14	Syster dotter	Sister's daughter.	Systerdotters man	Sister's daughter's husband.
15	Nefane	Niece, sister's daughter.	Nephew	Nephew.
16	Niece	Niece, sister's daughter.	Neef	"
17	Nicht	Niece. ᵇ Granddaughter.	Něvě	
18	Nichte	Niece.	Sisters dochter man	Sister's daughter's husband.
19	Sister's dochter	Sister's daughter.	Neffe	Nephew.
20	Nichte	Niece.	Gatte der nichte	Husband of niece.
21	Nichte	"	Mon neveu	My nephew.
22	Ma nièce	My niece.	Sobrino politico	My nephew (by courtesy).
23	Sobrina	" "	Sobrinho por affinidade	Nephew by affinity.
24	Sobrinha	Niece.	Aquistata nipote	Acquired nephew.
25	Nipote	Niece or grandchild.	Sororis filiae vir	Husband of a daughter of a sister.
26	Sororis filia	Daughter of a sister.	Adelphidēs anēr	Husband of a niece.
27	Adelphidē. ᵇ Kasignētē. ᶜ Anepsiē	Niece.		
28	Adelphidē. ᵇ Anepsia	"		
29				
30	Moja siostrzenica	My niece.	Moj siostrzenin	My nephew-in-law.
31	Ma sestrenice	" "	Mŭj sestrennin	" " "
32	Sestrinitsa mi	Niece my.		
33	Sestrenitza mi	" "		
34	Moja pljemiannitza	My niece.	Mush moego pljemiannik	Husband of my niece.
35	Yěyěn-mi	Niece my.	Yěyěnŭm kojäsü	Niece's my husband.
36	Khooärzeh mun	" "	Měreh khooärzeh mun	Husband of niece my.
37	Kis hugom	Little younger sister my.		
38	Minu odde tutär	My sister's daughter.	Minu odde tutar mees	My sister's daughter's husband.
39	Sĭsaren tytär	Sister's my daughter.	Sĭsaren tyttären miès	Sister's my daughter's husband.

TABLE I.—*Continued.*

	45. Sister's grandson. (Male speaking.)	Translation.	46. Sister's great grandson. (Male speaking.)	Translation.
1	Ibn ibn äkhti	Son of son of sister my.	Ibn ibn ibn äkhti	Son of son of son of sister my.
2	Ibn ibn ikhti	" " " "	Ibn ibn ibn ikhti	" " " " " "
3				
4	Näwiga d' khätee	Grandson of sister my.	Natija d'khätee	Great grandson of sister my.
5	Crochus voretein voretin	Sister's son's son.	Crochus voretein v. voretin	Son of son of son of sister my.
6	Mac mic mo driffer	Son of the son of my sister	Mac mic mic mo driffer	Son of the son of the son of a sister.
7	Ogha pethar	Grandson of my sister.	Iar ogha pethar	Great grandson of my sister.
8	Mac mac my shuyr	Son of son of my sister.	Mac mac mac my shuyr	Son of son of son of my sister.
9	Wyr fy chwaer	Grandson of my sister.	Orwyr fy chwaer	Great grandson of my sister.
10	Nåvåadäi hâhär	Grandchild of sister.	Nätijär hâhäi	Great grandchild of sister.
11	Svasrnaptar	Sister's grandson.		
12	Sösters barnebarn	Sister's grandchild.	Sösters barnebarns barn	Sister's great grandchild.
13	Sonar sonr systur minn	Son's son of sister my.	Sonar sonar sonr systur minn	Son's son's son of sister my.
14	Systersons son	Sister's son's son.	Syster's son's sonson	Sister's son's son's son.
15				
16	Great nephew	Grand nephew. Sister's grandson.	Great grand nephew	G't grandneph. Sister's g't g'dson.
17	Zusters klein zoon. b Neef	Sister's grandson. b Nephew.	Zuster's achter klein zoon. b Neef	Sister's great grandson. b Nephew.
18	Groot nēvĕ	Great nephew.	Groot groot nēvĕ	Great great nephew.
19	Sisters kinds kind	Sister's child's child.	Sister's kinds kinds kind	Sister's child's child's child.
20	Gross neffe. b Schwester enkel	Great nephew. b Sister's grandson.	Urgross neffe	Great great nephew.
21	Schwester enkel	Sister's grandson.	Schwester grossenkel	Sister's great grandson.
22	Mon petit-neveu	My little nephew.	Mon arrière-petit neveu	My great little nephew.
23				
24	Sobrinho neto	Nephew's grandson.		
25	Pronipote	Great nephew.	Pronipote	Great nephew.
26	Sororis nepos [dous	Grandson of a sister.	Sororis pronepos	Great grandson of a sister.
27	Adelphēs. b Eggonos. c Anepsia-	" " "	Adelphēs tritos apogonos	" " " "
28	Adelphēs eggonos	" " "	Adelphēs proeggonēs	" " " "
29				
30	Moj syn siostrzenca	My nephew-son.	Moj wnuk siostrzenca	My nephew-grandson.
31				
32				
33	Mal vnook mi	Little grandson my.	Mal prevnook mi	Little great grandson my.
34	Moi vnutchatnyi pljemiannik	My nephew grandson.	Moi prevnutchatnyi pljemiannik	My nephew-great grandson.
35	Kŭs kärndüshmŭn torŭ	Sister's my grandchild.	Kŭs kärndäshmŭn torŭ	Sister's my grandchild.
36	Läveh khooärzeh mun	Son of nephew my.	Läveh khooärzeh mun	Son of nephew my.
37				
38	Minu odde poeg poeg	My sister's son's son.	Minu odde poeg poeg poeg	My sister's son's son's son.
39	Sïsaren poïan poïka	Sister's my son's son.	Sïsaren poïan poïan poïkä	Sister's my son's son's son.

	47. Sister's great granddaughter. (Male speaking.)	Translation.	48. Brother. (Female speaking.)	Translation.
1	Bint bint bint akhti	D. of d. of d. of sister my.	Akhi	Brother my.
2	Bint bint bint akhti	" " " " "	Akhi	" "
3				
4	Natijta d'khätee	Great granddaughter of sister my.	Akhōnee	" "
5	Crochus toostrin t. toostra	Dau. of dau. of dau. of sister my.	Yäkepire	" "
6	Ineean mic mic mo driffer	Dau. of the son of the son of my sist.	Mo yrihair	My brother.
7	Iar ogha pethar	Great grandchild of my sister.	Mo bhrăthair	" "
8	Inneean mac mac my shuyr	Daughter of son of son of my sister.	My braar	" "
9	Orwyres fy chwaer	Great granddaughter of my sister.	Fy mrawd	" "
10	Nätijäi hâhär	Great grandchild of sister.	Brådär	Brother.
11			Bràtar. b Sodare	"
12	Sösters barnebarns barn	Sister's great grandchild.	Broder	"
13	Dottur dottur dottir systur minn	Daughter's d. d. of sister my.	Brodir min	Brother my.
14	Systerdotters dotter dotter	Sister's daughter's daught. daught.	Broder	Brother.
15				
16	Great grandniece [Nicht	Gt. grandniece, sister's gt. granddau.	Brother	"
17	Zuster's achter klein dochter. b	Sister's great granddaughter. Niece.	Broeder	"
18	Groote groote nichte	Great great niece	Broeder	"
19	Sister's kinds kinds kind	Sister's child's child's child. b Neph.	Brohr	"
20	Urgross nichte	Great great niece.	Bruder	"
21	Schwester grossenkelin	Sister's great granddaughter.	Bruder	"
22	Mon arrière-petite-fille	My great little daughter.	Mon frère	My brother.
23			Hermano	Brother.
24			Irmano	My brother.
25	Pronipote	Great niece.	Fratello	"
26	Sororis pronepti s	Great granddaughter of a sister.	Frater	Brother.
27	Adelphēs tritō eggonē	" " " "	Adelphos. b Kasignētos. c Kasis?	"
28	Adelphēs proeggonē	" " " "	Adelphos	"
29			Brōlis	"
30	Moja wnuczka siostrzenca	My nephew-granddaughter.	Moj brat	My brother.
31			Mŭj bratr	" "
32			Brat mi	Brother my.
33	Mal prevnooka mi [nitza	Little great granddaughter my.	Brat mi	" "
34	Moja prevnutchatnaja p'jemian-	My niece great granddaughter.	Moi brat	My brother.
35	Kŭs kärndäshmŭn torŭ	Sister's my great grandchild.	Kärndäsh-um	Brother my.
36	Törneh khooärzeh mun	Grandchild of nephew my.	Brä mun	Brother my.
37			Batyam. b Ocsem	Brother elder. b Younger.
38	Minu odde poeg poeg tutar	My sister's son's son's daughter.	Minu vennä	My brother.
39	Sïsaren poïan poïan tytär	Sister's my son's son's daughter.	Veljeni	Brother my.

TABLE I.—*Continued.*

	49. Brother's son. (Female speaking.)	Translation.	50. Brother's son's wife. (Female speaking.)	Translation.
1	Ibn ăkhti	Son of brother my.	Amrât ibn ăkhi	Wife of son of brother my.
2	Ibn ăkhi	" " "	Zaujat ibn ăkhi	" " " " "
3	Bĕn akhī	" " "	Eshĕth bĕn akhī	" " " " "
4	Brŭnă d'ăkhŏnee	" " "	Caltă d'ăkhŏnee	" " " " "
5	Yăkeporus voretin	Brother's son.	Yăkeporus voretin gena	Brother's son's wife.
6	Mac mo drihar	Son of my brother.	Ban mic mo drihar	Wife of son of my brother.
7	Mac mo brăthar	" " "	Bean mac mo brăthar	" " " " "
8	Mac my braar	" " "	Ben my braar	" " " " "
9	Fy nai	My nephew.	Fy nith	My niece.
10	Poosări brâdăr	Son of brother.	Zăni poosări brâdăr	Wife of son of brother.
11	Bhrâtrîya. b Bhrâtroya	Brother's son.		
12	Brodersön	" "	Brodersöns hustrue	Brother's son's wife.
13	Brodursour min	Brother's son my.	Kona brodursonar min	Wife of brother's son my.
14	Brorson	Brother's son.	Brorsons hustru	Brother's son's wife.
15	Nefa	Nephew.	Niece	Niece.
16	Nephew	Nephew. Brother's son.	Niece	"
17	Neef	Nephew and grandson.	Nicht	"
18	Nĕvĕ	Nephew.	Nichte	"
19	Brohrs Soohn	Brother's son.	Brohrs soohns frau	Brother's son's wife.
20	Neffe	Nephew.	Nichte	Niece.
21	Neffe	"	Frau des neffen	Wife of nephew.
22	Mon neveu	My nephew.	Ma nièce	My niece.
23	Sobrino	Nephew.	Sobrina politica	My niece (by courtesy).
24	Sobrinho	My nephew.	Sobrinha por affinidade	Niece (by affinity).
25	Nipote	Nephew. b Grandchild.	Aquistella nipote	Acquired niece.
26	Fratris filius	Son of a brother.	Fratris filii uxor	Wife of a son of a brother.
27	Adelphidous. b Kasignētēs	Nephew.	Adelphidou Gunē	Wife of nephew.
28	Adelphidous. b Anepsios			
29	Brŏtŭszis	Brother's son.		
30	Moj siostrzeniec	My nephew.	Moja bratankowa	My niece-in-law.
31	Mŭj sestrenec	" "	Ma Sestrencowa	" "
32	Bratanets mi	Nephew my.		
33	Bratanetz. b Bratovchad	Nephew.		
34	Moj pljemiannik	My nephew.	Shena moego pljemiannitza	Wife of my nephew.
35	Yĕyĕn im	Nephew my.	Yĕyenŭma kărŭsŭ	Nephew, my wife.
36	Lăveh brä mun	Son of brother my.	Bookeh brä mun	Daughter-in-law of brother my.
37	Kis öcsem	Little younger brother my.		
38	Minu vennä poeg	My brother's son.	Minu vennä poeg naine	My brother's son's wife.
39	Veljen poĭkä. b Nepaa	Brother's son. b Nephew.	Nepaan vaimo	Nephew's my wife.

	51. Brother's daughter. (Female speaking.)	Translation.	52. Brother's daughter's husband. (Female speaking.)	Translation.
1	Bint ăkhi	Daughter of brother my.	Zôj bint ăkhi	Husband of daughter of brother my.
2	Bint ăkhi	" " " "	Zauj bint ăkhi	" " " " " "
3	Băth akhī	" " " "	Ish băth akhī	Husband of sister of brother my.
4	Brătä d'ăkhŏnee	" " " "	Gora d'brätee d'ăkhŏnee	Son-in-law of my brother.
5	Yăheporus toostra	Brother's daughter.	Yăkeporus toostra arega	Brother's daughter's husband.
6	Ineean mo drihar	Daughter of my brother.	Far ineeni mo drihar	Husband of daughter of my brother.
7	Neeghan mo brăthar	" " "	Cleeamhuin mo brăthar	Son-in-law of my brother.
8	Inneen my braar	" " "	Sheshey ineen my braar	Husband of daughter of my brother.
9	Fy nith	My niece.	Fy nai	My nephew.
10	Dûkhtări brâdăr	Daughter of brother.	Shôhări dûkhtări brâdăr	Husband of daughter of brother.
11	Bhrâtrûyă	Brother's daughter.		
12	Broderdatter	" "	Broderdatters husbond	Brother's daughter's husband.
13	Brodur dottir min	Brother's daughter my.	Madr brodur dottur min	Husband of brother's daughter my.
14	Brorsdotter	Brother's daughter.	Brorsdottors man	Brother's daughter's husband.
15	Nefane	Niece.	Nephew	Nephew.
16	Niece	Niece. Brother's daughter.	Neef	"
17	Nicht	Niece. b Granddaughter.	Nĕvĕ	"
18	Nichte	Niece.		
19	Brohrs dochter	Brother's daughter.	Brohrs dochters man	Brother's daughter's husband.
20	Nichte	Niece.	Neffe	Nephew.
21	Nichte	"	Gatte der nichte	Husband of niece.
22	Ma nièce	My niece.	Mon neveu	My nephew.
23	Sobrina	Niece.	Sobrino politico	My nephew (by courtesy).
24	Sobrinha	My niece.	Sobrinho por affinidade	Nephew by affinity.
25	Nipote	Niece. b Grandchild.	Aquistata nipote	Acquired nephew.
26	Fratris filia	Daughter of a brother.	Fratris filiæ vir	Husband of a daughter of a brother.
27	Adelphidēs. b Kasignētē	Niece.	Adelphidēs anēr	Husband of a niece.
28	Adelphidē. b Anepsia	"		
29				
30	Moja siostrzenica	My niece.	Moj synowiec	My nephew-in-law.
31	Ma sestrina	"	Mŭj Sestrin	" "
32	Bratanitsa mi	Niece my.		
33	Bratanitza. b Bratovchactka	Niece.		
34	Moja pljemiannitza	My niece.	Mush moego pljemiannik	Husband of my niece.
35	Yĕyĕn-im	Niece my.	Yĕyĕnŭm kojäsŭ	Niece's my husband.
36	Keezä brä mun	Daughter of brother my.	Zävä brä mun	Son-in-law of brother my.
37	Kis hugom	Little younger sister my.		
38	Minu vennä tutar	My brother's daughter.	Minu vennä tutar mees	My brother's daughter's husband.
39	Veljen tytär	Brother's my daughter.	Veljen tyttären mies	Brother's my daughter's husband.

TABLE I.—*Continued.*

	53. Brother's grandson. (Female speaking.)	Translation.	54. Brother's granddaughter. (Female speaking.)	Translation.
1	Ibn ibn ākhi	Son of son of brother my,	Bint ibn ākhi	Daughter of son of brother my.
2	Ibn ibn ākhi	" " " "	Bint ibn ākhi	" " " " "
3				
4	Näwiga d'äkhŏnee	Grandson of brother my.	Näwigta d'äkhŏnee	Granddaughter of brother my.
5	Yäkeporus voretein voretin	Brother's son's son.	Yäkeporus toostrin toostra	Brother's daughter's daughter.
6	Mac mic mo drihar	Son of son of my brother.	Ineean mic mo drihar	Daughter of son of my brother.
7	Ogha mo bräthar	Grandchild of my brother.	Ogha mo bräthar	Grandchild of my brother.
8	Mac mac my braar	Son of son of my brother.	Inneean mac braar	Daughter of son of my brother.
9	Wyr fy mrawd	Grandson of my brother.	Wyres fy mrawd	Granddaughter of my brother.
10	Nävâdäi brâdär	Grandchild of brother.	Nävâdäi brâdär	Grandchild of brother.
11	Bhrâtrnaptar	Brother's grandson.	Bhrâtrnaptri	Brother's granddaughter.
12	Broders barnebarn	Brother's grandchild.	Broders barnebarn	Brother's grandchild.
13	Sonar sonr brodur min	Son's son of brother my.	Dottur dottir brodur min	Daughter's daughter of brother my.
14	Brorsons son	Brother's son's son.	Brorsdotters dotter	Brother's daughter's daughter.
15				
16	Great nephew. Cousin-nephew	Great nephew. Brother's grandson.	Great niece. b Cousin-niece	Grandniece. Brother's granddaught.
17	Broeders klein zoon. b Neef	Brother's grandson. b Nephew.	Broders klein dochter. b Nicht	Brother's granddaughter. Niece.
18	Groot nĕvĕ	Great nephew.	Groote nichte	Great niece.
19	Brohrs kinds kind	Brother's child's child.	Brohrs kinds kind	Brother's child's child.
20	Gross neffe. b Bruders enkel	Great nephew. b Brother's grandson.	Bruders enkelinn	Brother's granddaughter.
21	Bruders enkel	Brother's grandson.	Bruders enkelin	" " "
22	Mon petit-neveu	My Little nephew.	Ma petite-fille	My little niece.
23				
24	Sobrinho neto	Nephew-grandson.	Sobrinha por affinidade	Niece by affinity.
25	Pronipote	Great nephew.	Pronipote	Great niece.
26	Fratris nepos	Grandson of a brother.	Fratris neptis	Granddaughter of a brother.
27	Adelphou eggonos. b Anepsiadous?	" " "	Adelphou huionē. b Anepsiades ?	" " "
28	Adelphou eggonos	" " "	Adelphou eggonē	" " "
29				
30	Moj syn synowca	My nephew's son.	Moja corka synowca	My nephew's daughter.
31				
32				
33	Mal vnook mi	Little grandson my.	Mal vnooka mi	Little granddaughter my.
34	Moi vnutchatnyi pljemiannik	My nephew-grandson.	Meja vnutchatnaja pljemiannitza	My niece granddaughter.
35	Kärndäshmün torü	Brother's my grandchild.	Kärndäshmün torü	Brother's my grandchild.
36	Törneh brä mun	Grandchild of brother my.	Törneh brä mun	Grandchild of brother my.
37				
38	Minu vennä tutar poeg	My brother's daughter's son.	Minu vennä tutar tutar	My brother's daughter's daughter.
39	Nepaan poïka	Nephew's my son.	Nepaan tytär	Nephew's my daughter.

	55. Brother's great grandson. (Female speaking.)	Translation.	56. Brother's great granddaughter. (Female speaking.)	Translation.
1	Ibn ibn ibn ākhi	Son of son of son of brother my.	Bint bint bint ākhi	Daughter of d. of d. of brother my.
2	Ibn ibn ibn ākhi	" " " " " "	Bint bint bint ākhi	" " " " " "
3				
4	Natija d'äkhŏnee	Great grandson of brother my.	Natijta d'äkhŏnee	Great granddaughter of brother my.
5	Yäkeporus voretein v. voretin	Brother's son's son's son.	Yäkeporus toostrin t. toostra	Brother's daughter's daught. daught.
6	Mac mic mic mo drihar	Son of son of son of my brother.	Ineean mic mic mo drihar	Daughter of son of son of my brother.
7	Iar ogha mo bräthar	Grandchild of my brother.	Iar ogha mo bräthar	Great grandchild of my brother.
8	Mac mac mac my braar	Son of son of son of my brother.	Inneen mac mac my braar	Daughter of son of son of my brother.
9	Orwyr fy mrawd	Great grandson of my brother.	Orwyres fy mrawd	Great granddaughter of my brother.
10	Nätijääi brâdär	Great grandchild of brother.	Nätijäi brâdär	Great grandchild of brother.
11				
12	Broders barnebarns barn	Brother's great grandchild.	Broders barnebarns barn	Brother's great grandchild.
13	Sonar sonar sonr brodur min	Son's son's son of brother my.	Dottur dottur dottir bro tur min	Daughter's d. d. of brother my.
14	Brorsons sonson	Brother's son's son's son.	Brorsdotters dotter dotter	Brother's daughter's daught. daught.
15				
16	Great great nephew	G't g't nephew, bro. g't grandson.	Great great niece............[Nicht	G't g't niece, brother's g. g. daughter.
17	Broeders achter klein zoon. Neef.	Brother's g't grandson. b Nephew.	Broeders achter klein dochter. b	Brother's g't granddaughter. b Niece.
18	Groot groot nĕvĕ	Great great nephew.	Groote groote nichte	Great great niece.
19	Brohrs kinds kinds kind	Brother's child's child's child.	Brohrs kinds kinds kind	Brother's child's child's child.
20	Urgross neffe	Great great nephew.	Bruders urenkelinn	Brother's great granddaughter.
21	Bruders grossenkel	Brother's great grandson.	Bruders grossenkelin	" " "
22	Mon arrière-petit-ueveu	My great little nephew.	Mon arrière-petite-niece	My great little niece.
23				
24				
25	Pronipote	Great nephew.	Pronipote	Great niece.
26	Fratris pronepos	Great grandson of a brother.	Fratris proneptis	Great granddaughter of a brother.
27	Adelphou apogonos tritos	" " " "	Adelphou eggonē tritē	" " " "
28	Adelphou proeggonos	" " " "	Adelphou proeggonē	" " " "
29				
30	Moj wnuk synowca	My nephew-grandson.	Moja wnuczka synowca	My nephew-granddaughter.
31				
32				
33	Mal prevnook	Little great grandson.	Mae prevnooka mi...........[nitza	Little great granddaughter.
34	Moi pravnutchnayi pljemiannik	My nephew-great grandson.	Moja pravnutchatnaja pljemian-	My niece great granddaughter.
35	Kärndäshmün torünüm torüñ	Brother's my great grandchild.	Kärndäshmün torünüm torünü	Brother's my great grandchild.
36	Läveh törneh brä mun	Son of grandchild of brother my.	Keezä törneh brä mun	Daughter of grandchild brother my.
37				
38	Minu vennä poeg poeg poeg	My brother's son's son's son.	Minu vennä poeg poeg tutar	My brother's son's son's daughter.
39	Nepaan poïan poïka	Nephew's my son's son.	Nepaan poïan tytär	Nephew's my son's daughter.

TABLE I.—*Continued.*

	57. Sister. (Female speaking.)	Translation.	58. Sister's son. (Female speaking.)	Translation.
1	Akhti	Sister my.	Ibn äkhti	Son of sister my.
2	Ikhti	" "	Ibn ikhti	" " "
3	ª khŏthĭ	" "	Bĕn. ª Khŏthĭ	" " "
4	Khätee	" "	Brŭnä d'khatee	" " "
5	Kooere	" "	Crochus voretin	Sister's soñ.
6	Mo yriffŭr	My sister.	Mac mo driffer	Son of my sister.
7	Mo phiŭthăr	" "	Măc peathar	" " "
8	My Shuyr	" "	Mac my shuyr	" " "
9	Fy chwaer	" "	Fy nai	My nephew.
10	Håhär	Sister.	Poosäri håhär	Son of sister.
11	Svasar. ᵇ Iămi. ᶜ Bhagini	"	Svasrîya	Sister's son.
12	Söster	"	Sösterson	" "
13	Systur min	Sister my.	Systursonr min	Sister's son my.
14	Syster	Sister.	Systerson	Sister's son.
15	Swuster. ᵇ Theoster	"	Nefa	Nephew.
16	Sister	"	Nephew	Nephew, sister's son.
17	Zuster	"	Neef	Nephew. ᵇ Grandson.
18	Sister	"	Nĕvŏ	Nephew.
19	Sister	"	Sisters soohn	Sister's son.
20	Schwester	"	Neffe	Nephew.
21	Schwester	"	Neffe	"
22	Ma sœur	My sister.	Mon neveu	My nephew.
23	Hermana	Sister.	Sobrino	" "
24	Irman	My sister.	Sobrinho	Nephew.
25	Sorella	Sister.	Nipote	Nephew. ᵇ Grandchild.
26	Soror	"	Sororis filius .... [epsios?	Son of a sister.
27	Adelphē. ᵇ Kasignētē. ᶜ Kasē? ...	"	Adelphidous. ᵇ Kasignatos. ᶜ An-	" " "
28	Adelphē	"	Adelphidous. ᵇ Anepsios	" " "
29	Măno sŭsē	My sister.		
30	Moj siostra	" "	Moja siostrzenice	My nephew.
31	Mŭj sestra	" "	Mŭj sestrenec	" "
32	Sestra mi	Sister my.	Sestrinets mi	Nephew my.
33	Sestra mi	" "	Sestrenik mi	" "
34	Moja sestra	My sister.	Moj pljemiannik	My nephew.
35			Yĕyĕn-im	Nephew my.
36	Khoôshkeh mun	Sister my.	Liveh khoôshkeh mun	Son of brother my.
37	Nenem. ª Hugom	Sister elder. ᵇ Younger.	Kis ŏcsem	Little younger sister my.
38	Minu odde	My sister.	Minu odde poeg	My sister's son.
39	Sisareni	Sister my.	Sîsaren poïka. Nepaa	Sister's my son. ᵇ Nephew.

	59. Sister's son's wife. (Female speaking.)	Translation.	60. Sister's daughter. (Female speaking.)	Translation.
1	Amrât ibn äkhti	Wife of son of sister my.	Bint äkhti	Daughter of sister my.
2	Zaujat ibn ikhti	" " " " "	Bint ikhti	" " " "
3	Eshĕth bĕn ª Khŏthĭ	" " " " "	Băth ª Khŏthĭ	" " " "
4	Caltă d'Khätee	Daughter-in-law.	Brătä d'Khätee	" " " "
5	Crochus voretin gena	Daughter-in-law of my sister.	Crochus toostra	Sister's daughter.
6	Ban mac mo driffer	Wife of son of my sis er.	Ineean mo driffer	Daughter of my sister.
7	Bean mic pethar	" " " " "	Nighean mo phiŭthăr	" " " "
8	Bĕn mac my shuyr	" " " " "	Inneen my shuyr	" " "
9	Fy nith	My niece.	Fy nith	My niece.
10	Zăni poosäri håhär	Wife of son of sister.	Dŭkhtäri håhär	Daughter of sister.
11			Svasrîyă	Sister's daughter.
12	Söstersöns hustrue	Sister's son's wife.	Sösterdatter	" "
13	Kona systur sonar min	Wife of sister's son my.	Systur dottir min	Sister's daughter my.
14	Systersons hustru	Sister's son's wife.	Systerdotter	Sister's daughter.
15			Nefane	Niece.
16	Niece	Niece.	Niece	Niece. Sister's daughter.
17	Nicht	"	Nicht	Niece. ᵇ Granddaughter.
18	Nichte	"	Nichte	Niece.
19	Sisters soohns frau	Sister's son's wife.	Sisters dochter	Sister's daughter.
20	Nichte	Niece by marriage.	Nichte	Niece.
21	Gattin des neffen	Wife of nephew.	Nichte	"
22	Ma nièce	My niece.	Ma nièce	My niece.
23	Sobrina politica	My niece (by courtesy).	Sobrina	Niece.
24	Sobrinha por affinidade	Niece by affinity.	Sobrinha	My niece.
25	Aquistella nipote	Acquired nephew.	Nipote	Niece. ᵇ Grandchild.
26	Sororis filii uxor	Wife of a son of a sister.	Sororis filia	Daughter of a sister.
27	Adelphidou gunē	Wife of a nephew.	Adelphidē. ᵇ Kasignētē. ᶜ Anepsia?	Niece.
28			Adelphidē. ᵇ Anepsia	"
29				
30	Moja siostrzencowa	My niece-in-law.	Moja siostrzenica	My niece.
31	Ma sestrencowa	" " "	Ma sestrina	" "
32			Sestrinitsa mi	Niece my.
33			Sestrinitsa mi	" "
34	Shena moego pljemiannitza	Wife of my nephew.	Moja pljemiannitza	My niece.
35	Yĕyĕnum kărŭ-ŭ	Nephew's my wife.	Yĕyĕn-im	Niece my.
36	Zhŭneh khoôshkeh mun	Daughter-in-law of sister my.	Keezä khoôshkeh mun	Daughter of sister my.
37			Kis hugom	Little younger sister my.
38	Minu odde poeg naine	My sister's son wife.	Minu odde tutär	My sister's daughter.
39	Nepaan vaimo	Nephew's my wife.	Sîsaren tytär	Sister's my daughter.

TABLE I.—*Continued.*

	61. Sister's daughter's husband. (Female speaking.)	Translation.	62. Sister's grandson. (Female speaking.)	Translation.
1	Zôj bint ăkhti..........................	Husband of daughter of sister my.	Ibn ibn ăkhti	Son of son of sister my.
2	Zauj bint ikhti........................	" " " " " "	Ibn ibn ikhti	" " " " "
3	Ish băth ʰ Khôthĭ................			
4	Khutna d'Khätee......................	Son-in-law of my sister.	Năwigă d'khätee......................	Grandson of sister my.
5	Crochus toostrin arega...............	Sister's daughter's husband.	Crochus voretein voretin............	Sister's son's son.
6	Far ineeni mo driffer................	Husband's daughter of my sister.	Mac ineeni mo driffer.............	Sister's daughter of my sister.
7	Cleeamhiun mo phiuthar............	" " " "	Egha mo phiuthar...................	Grandchild of my sister.
8	Sheshey inneen my shuyr..........	" " " "	Mac mac my shuyr..................	Son of son of my sister.
9	Fy nai.................................	My nephew.	Wyr fy chwaer.....................	Grandson of my sister.
10	Shôbări dûkhtäri hâhär............	Husband of daughter of-sister.	Năvădăi hâhär......................	Grandchild of a sister.
11			Svasrnaptar........................	Sister's grandson.
12	Sösterdatter husbond................	Sister's daughter's husband.	Sösters barnebarn..................	Sister's grandchild.
13	Madr systur dottur min............	Husband of sister's daughter my.	Sonar sönr systur min..............	Son's son of sister my.
14	Systerdotters man	Sister's daughter's husband.	Systersons son.....................	Sister's son's son.
15				
16	Nephew	Nephew.	Great nephew. Cousin-nephew...	Great nephew. Sister-grandson.
17	Neef	"	Zusters klein zoon. ᵇ Neef.......	Sister's grandson. ᵇ Nephew.
18	Nĕvĕ	"	Groot nĕvĕ..........................	Great nephew.
19	Sisters dochters man	Sister's daughter's husband.	Sisters kinds kind.................	Sister's child's child.
20	Neffe................................	Nephew.	Gross neffe. ᵇ Schwester enkel...	Great nephew. ᵇ Sister's grandson.
21	Gatte der nichte....................	Husband of niece.	Schwester enkel....................	Sister's grandson.
22	Mon neveu..........................	My nephew.	Mon petit-neveu...................	My little nephew.
23	Sobrino politico.....................	My nephew (by courtesy).	Sobrino............................	My nephew.
24	Sobrinho por affinidade.............	Nephew by affinity.	Sobrinho neto......................	Nephew's grandson.
25	Aquistata nipote....................	Acquired nephew.	Pronipote..........................	Great nephew.
26	Sororis filiæ vir....................	Husband of a daughter of a sister.	Sororis nepos......................	Grandson of a sister.
27	Adelphidĕs aner....................	Husband of a niece.	Adelphĕs eggonos. ᵇ Anepsiades ?	" " "
28			Adelphĕs eggonos..................	" " "
29				
30	Moj siostrzenin.....................	My nephew-in-law.	Moj syn siostrzenca...............	My nephew's son.
31	Mŭj sestrin........................	" " "		
32				
33			Mal vnook mi......................	Little grandson my.
34	Mush moego pljemiannik..........	Husband of my niece.	Moi vnutchatnyi pljemiannik......	My nephew's grandson.
35	Yĕyĕn-um kojasŭ...................	Niece's my husband.	Kuz kärndäshmŭn torŭ............	Sister's my grandchild.
36	Mĕreh keezä khoôshkeh mun......	Husband of daughter of sister my.	Tôrneh khoôshkeh mun............	Grandchild of sister my.
37				
38	Minu odde tutar mees...............	My sister's daughter's husband.	Minu odde poeg poeg..............	My sister's son's son.
39	Sisären văvy	Sister's my son-in-law.	Sïsaren poĭan poĭka	Sister's my son's son.

	63. Sister's granddaughter. (Female speaking.)	Translation.	64. Sister's great grandson. (Female speaking.)	Translation.
1	Bint ibn ăkhti........................	Daughter of son of sister my.	Ibn Ibn ibn ăkhti	Son of son of son of sister my.
2	Bint ibn ikhti.......................	" " " "	Ibn ibn ibn ikhti.	" " " " "
3				
4	Năwigtă d'khätee...................	Granddaughter of sister my.	Nătija d'khätee.....................	Great grandson of sister my.
5	Crochus toostrin toostra............	Sister's daughter's daughter.	Crochus voretein v. voretin.......	Sister's son's son's son.
6	Ineean mic mo driffer...............	Daughter's son of my sister.	Mac mic mic mo driffer............	Son's son's son of my sister.
7	Ogha mo phiuthar..................	" " " "	Iar ogha mo phiuthar..............	Great grandchild of my sister.
8	Inneen mac my shuyr	" " " "	Mac mac mac my shuyr............	Son of son of son of my sister.
9	Wyres fy chwaer....................	Granddaughter of my sister.	Orwyr fy chwaer...................	Great grandson of my sister.
10	Năvădăi hâhär.....................	Grandchild of sister.	Nătijäi hâhär.......................	Great grandchild of sister.
11	Svasrnaptrĭ	Sister's granddaughter.		
12	Sösters barnebarn	Sister's grandchild.	Sösters barnebarns barn...........	Sister's great grandchild.
13	Dottur dottir systur min...........	Daughter's daughter of sister my.	Sonar sonar son systur min.......	Son's son of sister my.
14	Systersons dotter...................	Sister's son's daughter.	Systersons sonson.................	Sister's son's son's son.
15				
16	Great niece. Cousin-niece....	Great niece. Sister's granddaughter.	Great grand nephew...............	G't grandnephew. Sister's g. g. son.
17	Zusters klein dochter. ᵇ Nicht...	Sister's granddaughter. ᵇ Niece.	Zusters achter klein zoon. ᵇ Neef	Sister's great grandson. ᵇ Nephew.
18	Groote nichte......................	Great niece.	Groot groot nĕvĕ...................	Great great nephew.
19	Sisters kinds kind..................	Sister's child's child.	Sisters kinds kinds kind...........	Sister's child's child's child.
20	Schwester enkelinn.................	Sister's granddaughter.	Urgross neffe......................	Great great nephew.
21	Schwester enkelin..................	" "	Schwester grossenkel..............	Sister's great grandson.
22	Ma petite-nièce....................	My little niece.	Mon arrière-petit-neveu...........	My great little nephew.
23	Sobrina.............................	My niece.		
24	Sobrinha neta......................	Niece's granddaughter.		
25	Pronipote..........................	Great niece.	Pronipote..........................	Great nephew.
26	Sororis neptis......................	Granddaughter of a sister.	Sororis pronepos..................	Great grandson of a sister.
27	Adelphĕs eggonĕ. ᶜ Anepsiade ?...	" " "	Adelphĕs tritos apogonos..........	" " " "
28	Adelphĕs eggonĕ..................	" " "	Adelphĕs proeggonos..............	" " " "
29				
30	Moja corka siostrzenca..............	My nephew's daughter.	Moj wnuk siostrezenca............	My nephew-grandson.
31				
32				
33	Mal vnooka mi......................	Little granddaughter my.	Mal prevnook mi...................	Little great grandson my.
34	Moja vnutchatnaja pljemiannitza..	My niece's granddaughter.	Moi pravnutchatnyi pljemiannik..	My nephew's great grandson.
35	Kuz kärndäshmŭn torŭ............	Sister's my grandchild.	Kärndäshm ŭn torŭnŭm torŭnŭ..	Sister's my great grandchild.
36	Tôrnch khoôshkeh mun	Grandchild of sister my.	Läveh tôrneh khoôshkeh mun.....	Son of grandchild of sister my.
37				
38	Minu odde poeg tutär...............	My sister's son's daughter.	Minu odde poeg poeg poeg	My sister's son's son's son.
39	Sïsaren poĭan tytär.................	Sister's my son's daughter.	Sïsaren poĭan poĭan poĭkä.........	Sister's my son's son's son.

TABLE I.—*Continued.*

	65. Sister's Great granddaughter. (Female speaking.)	Translation.	66. Father's brother.	Translation.
1	Bint bint bint ăkhti...................	Daughter of d. of d. of sister my.	Ammi.....................................	Paternal uncle my.
2	Bint bint bint ikhti..................	" " " " "	Ammi.....................................	" " "
3			Dŏdhī.....................................	" " "
4	Natigta d'khătee......................	Great granddaughter of sister my.	Amŭwee..................................	" " "
5	Crochus toostrin t. toostra..........	Sister's daughter's d. daughter.	Horus yăkepira.......................	Father's brother.
6	Ineean mic mic mo driffer...........	Daughter's s. son my sister.	Drihar m'ahar........................	Brother of my father.
7	Iar ogha mo phiuthar................	Great grandchild of my sister.	Brăthăir m'ăthair...................	" " "
8	Inneen mac mac my shuyr.........	Daughter of son of son of my sister.	Braar my ayr..........................	" " "
9	Orwyres fy chwaer....................	Great granddaughter of my sister.	Fy ewyrth (pr. aworth)............	My uncle.
10	Nătijăi hăhăr.........................	Great grandchild of sister.	Amoo....................................	Paternal uncle.
11			Pitroya. b Pitrbhrătar............	" "
12	Sösters barnebarns barn.............	Sister's great grandchild.	Farbroder...............................	
13	Dottur dottur dottir systur min...	Daughter's d. d. of sister my.	Fodur brodir minn...................	Father's brother my.
14	Systerdotters dotter dotter.........	Sister's daughter's daught. daught.	Farbroder. b Farbror.............	Father's brother.
15				
16	Great grandniece..............[b Nicht	G't g'ndniece. Sister's g. g. daught.	Paternal uncle.......................	Uncle (father's side.)
17	Zusters achter klein dochter	Sister's g't granddaughter. b Niece.	Oom	"
18	Groote groote nichte...................	Great great niece.	Oom	"
19	Sisters kinds kinds kind	Sister's child's child's child.	Ohm. b Onkel.......................	"
20	Schwester urenkelinn...............	Sister's great granddaughter.	Oheim. b Onkel....................	"
21	Schwester grossenkelin..............	" " "	Oheim. b Onkel....................	"
22	Mon arrière-petite-nièce.............	My great little niece.	Mon oncle..............................	My uncle.
23			Tio.......................................	Uncle.
24			Tio carnal..............................	Blood uncle.
25	Pronipote...............................	Great niece.	Tio.......................................	Uncle.
26	Sororis proneptis......................	Great granddaughter of a sister.	Patruus.................................	Paternal uncle.
27	Adelphēs tritē eggonos...............	" " " "	Patrōs. b Patradelphos. c Theios	Uncle.
28	Adelphēs proggonē....................	" " " "	Theios.[d nannos? e Patrokasignatos	Uncle.
29			Măno dŏdē..............................	My father's brother.
30	Moja wnuczka siostrzenca.........	My nephew-granddaughter.	Moj stryj	My paternal uncle.
31			Mŭj stryc.............................	" " "
32			Chicha. b Strika mi..............	Paternal uncle my.
33	Mal prevnooka mi........... [nitza	Little great granddaughter my.	Chicha. b Streeka.................	" " "
34	Moja pravnutchatnaja plemian-	My niece, great granddaughter.	Moi djadja..............................	My uncle.
35	Kărndăshmŭn torŭnŭm torŭnŭ....	Sister's my great grandchild.	Ammī-m. b Amŭjă-m	Uncle·my (paternal).
36	Keeză tŏrneh khoôshkeh mun......	Daughter of grandchild of sister my.	Apeh mun..............................	Paternal uncle my.
37			Nagy batyam..........................	Grand elder brother.
38	Minu odde poeg poeg tutăr.........	My sister's son's son's daughter.	Minu esä vend........................	My father's brother.
39	Sïsaren poïan poïan tytăr...........	Sister's my son's son's daughter.	Setănï...................................	Uncle my.

	67. Father's brother's wife.	Translation.	68. Father's brother's son.	Translation.
1	Amrăt ammi..........................	Wife of paternal uncle my.	Ibn ammi...............................	Son of paternal uncle my.
2	Zoujat ammi..........................	" " " " "	Ibn ammi...............................	" " " " "
3	Dŏdhăthī..............................	Aunt my.	Bĕn dŏdhī.............................	Son of uncle my.
4	Băkhtă d'ămŭmee....................	Wife of paternal uncle my.	Brŭnă d'ămŭwee.....................	Son of paternal uncle my.
5	Horus yăkepora gena................	Father's brother's wife.	Horus yăkepora voretin	Father's brother's son.
6	Ban drihăr mahar....................	Wife of the brother of my father.	Mac drihar mahar....................	Son of brother of my father.
7	Bean brăthar m'ăthair	" " " " "	Măo brăthar m'ăthair...............	" " " " "
8	Ben braar my ayr	" " " " "	Măc brear my ayr....................	" " " " "
9	Fy mòdrib.............................	My aunt.	Fy nghefnder (pr. hevender).......	My cousin.
10	Zări amoo..............................	Wife of paternal uncle.	Poosari amoo..........................	Son of paternal uncle.
11			Pitroyaputra..........................	Paternal uncle's son.
12	Farbroders hustrue...................	Uncle's wife (father's side).	Fatters södskendebarn..............	Cousin.
13	Kona fodur brodur min..............	Wife of father's brother my.	Brodur sonr fodur min..............	Brother's son of father my.
14	Farbroders hustru....................	Father's brother's wife.	Farbrors son. b Sysling..........	Father's brother's son. b Cousin.
15			(Swor ?)...............................	Cousin germain.
16	Aunt....................................	Aunt.	Cousin. Uncle's son.................	First cousin. Uncle's son.
17	Ooms vrouw. b Moej...............	Uncle's wife. b Aunt.	Ooms zoon. b Neef.................	Uncle's son. b Nephew.
18	Moej	Aunt.	Kozyn. b Ooms zoon..............	Cousin. b Uncle's son.
19	Möhn. b Tante.....................	"	Vedder.................................	Cousin.
20	Muhme. b Tante...................	"	Vetter. b Geschwister kind	Cousin. b Relative's child.
21	Oheims frau...........................	Uncle's wife.	Oheims sohn. b Vetter...........	Uncle's son. b Cousin.
22	Ma tante...............................	My aunt.	Mon cousin-germain.................	My cousin germain.
23	Tia politica	My aunt by courtesy.	Primo hermano.......................	My cousin-brother.
24	Tia por affinidade....................	Aunt by affinity.	Primo irmão	Cousin-brother.
25	Tia.......................................	Aunt.	Cugino.................................	Cousin.
26	Patrui uxor............................	Wife of paternal uncle.	Patrui filius. b Frater patruelis.	Son of pat. uncle. b Bro. patruel.
27	Patrōs gunē. b Thiou gunē.......	" " " "	Anepsios. b Kasis?................	Cousin.
28			Prōtos exadelphos....................	"
29	Măno dedēnē	My father's brother's wife.		
30	Moja stryjenka.......................	My aunt.	Moj stryjeczny brat..................	My brother through paternal uncle.
31	Ma stryna.............................	" "		
32	Strinka mi.............................	Aunt my.	Bratooche mi	Uncle's son my. [b Uncle's son.
33	Streena. b China	Aunt.	Otchicha brat. b Chicher sin.....	Brother through paternal uncle.
34	Moja tjotka............................	My aunt.	Moi dvoiurodnyi brat................	My double birth brother.
35		Uncle's wife.	Amŭjämun oghlŭ.....................	Son of uncle my.
36	Amje mun..............................	Wife of paternal uncle my.	Lăveh ăpeh mun......................	Son of paternal uncle my.
37	Nagy angyom	Grand sister-in-law.		
38	Minu esä vennä naine	My father's brother's wife.	Minu esä vennä poeg................	My father's brother's son.
39	Setănï vaïmŏ...........................	Wife of my uncle.	Serkkunï. Orpanani.................	Cousin my.

TABLE I.—*Continued.*

	69. Father's brother's son's wife.	Translation.	70. Father's brother's daughter.	Translation.
1	Amrât ibn ammi......	Wife of son of paternal uncle my.	Bint ammi......	Daughter of paternal uncle my.
2	Zaujat ibn ămmi	" " " " " "	Bint ammi......	" " " "
3			Băth dödhĭ......	Daughter of uncle my.
4	Calta d'âmŭwee......	Daughter-in-law of patern. uncle my.	Brätä d'âmŭwee......	Daughter of paternal uncle my.
5	Horus yäkeporee voretin gena.....	Father's brother's son's wife.	Horus yäkepora tooster......	Father's brother's daughter.
6	Ban mic drihar mahar......	Wife of the son of my father's bro.	Ineean drihar mahar	Daughter of my father's brother.
7	Bean mâo brăthar m'athair......	Wife of the son of the bro. of my fa.	Nighean brăthar m'athair......	Daughter of the brother of my father.
8	Ben mac braar my ayr......	" " " " " "	Inneen braar my ayr......	" " " " " "
9	Fy cyfnither (pr. kefnether)......	My cousin.	Fy cyfnither......	My cousin.
10	Zăni poosäri ămoo......	Wife of son of paternal uncle.	Dŭkhtäri ammoo......	Daughter of paternal uncle.
11			Pitroyaputri......	Paternal uncle's daughter.
12	Fatters hustrue......	Cousin's wife.	Farbrodersdatter. ᵇ Södskendebarn	Cousin.
13	Sonar kona fodur brodur mins.....	Son's wife of father's brother my.	Dottir fodurbrodur mins......	Daughter of father's brother's my.
14	Farbrors sonhustru......	Father's brother's son's wife.	Farbrors dotter. ᵇ Syssling......	Father's brother's daught. Cousin.
15				
16	Cousin	Cousin.	Cousin. Paternal uncle's daught.	First cousin.
17	Ooms zoons vrouw......	Uncle's son's wife.	Ooms dochter. ᵇ Nicht......	Uncle's daughter. ᵇ Niece.
18	Nichte	Cousin.	Nichte. ᵇ Ooms dochter......	Niece. ᵇ Uncle's daughter.
19	Nichte	"	Nichte	Cousin.
20	Base	"	Base. ᵇ Gerschwisterkind......	"
21	Oheims sohnsfrau......	Uncle's son's wife.	Oheims tochter. ᵇ Base......	Uncle's daughter. ᵇ Cousin.
22	Ma cousîne......	My cousin.	Ma cousine germaine......	My cousin germain.
23	Prima politica......	My cousin (by courtesy).	Prima hermana......	My cousin sister.
24	Prima por affinidade......	Cousin by affinity.	Prima	Cousin.
25	Aquistella cugina......	Acquired cousin.	Cugina	"
26	Patrui filii uxor......	Wife of son of paternal uncle.	Patruĭ filia. ᵇ Soror patruelis......	Daught. of pat. uncle. ᵇ Sist. pat.
27	Anepsiou gunê......	Wife of cousin.	Anepsia. ᵇ Kasë?......	Cousin.
28			Prötë exadelphë......	"
29				
30	Moja stryjeczna bratowa......	My sister-in-law through p. uncle.	Moja stryjeczna siostra......	My sister through paternal uncle.
31			Bratovchetka mi......	Uncle's daughter my.
32			[tera	[daughter.
33			Otchicha sestra. ᵇ Chichev dush-	Sister through pat. uncle. ᵇ Uncle's
34	Shena moego dvoinrodnaja brata..	Wife of my double birth. brother.	Maja dvoiurodnaja sestra......	My double birth sister.
35	Amŭjämun oghlŭnŭm kărŭsă......	Wife of the son of my uncle.	Amŭjämŭn küsü......	Daughter of uncle my.
36	Thŭmeh läveh äpeh mŭn......	Daughter-in-law son of pater. uncle.	Keesä äpeh mun......	Daughter of paternal uncle my.
37				
38	Minu esä venna poeg naine......	My father's brother's son's wife.	Minu esä vennä tutär......	My father's brother's daughter.
39	Serkkunĭ vaimo......	Wife of my cousin.	Serkkunĭ orpanani......	Cousin my.

	71. Father's brother's daughter's husband.	Translation.	72. Father's brother's grandson.	Translation.
1	Zöj bint ammi......	Husband of daught. of pat. uncle my.	Ibn ibn ammi......	Son of son of paternal uncle my.
2	Zauj bint ămmi......	" " " " "	Ibn ibn ămmi......	" " " " " "
3				
4	Khutnă d'âmŭwee......	Son-in-law of paternal uncle my.	Näwiga d'âmŭwee......	Grandson of paternal uncle my.
5	Horus yäkepora toostrin arega	Father's brother's daught. husband.	Horus yäkepora voretein voretin...	Father's brother's son's son.
6	Far ineeni drihar mahar......	Husb. of daught. of bro. of my husb.	Mac mic drihar mahar......	Son of the s. of the broth. of my fath.
7	Cleeamhuin brăthar m'athair......	" " " " "	Egha brăthar m'athair......	Grandchild of brother of my father.
8	Sheshey inneen braar my ayr......	" " " " "	Mac mac braar my ayr......	Son of son of brother of my father.
9	Fy nghefnder	My cousin.	Mab fy nghefnder......	Son of my cousin.
10	Shōbäri dŭkhtäri ämoo......	Husb. of daught. of paternal uncle.	Năvädäi ämoo......	Grandchild of paternal uncle.
11				
12	Farbrodersdatters mand......	Uncle's daughter's husband.	Farbroders barnebarn......	Uncle's grandchild.
13	Dottur madr fodurbrodur mins....	Daughter's husb. of fath. bro. my.	Sonar sonr fodurbrodur mins......	Son's son of father's brother my.
14	Farbrors dotters man......	Father's brother's daughter's husb.	Farbrors sonson......	Father's brother's son's son.
15				
16	Cousin	Cousin.	Paternal uncle's grandson	Uncle's grandson (father's side).
17	Ooms dochter man......	Uncle's daughter's husband.	Ooms klein zoon. ᵇ Neef......	Uncle's granson. ᵇ Nephew.
18	Kozyn	Cousin.	Ooms groot zoon. ᵇ Kozyn......	Uncle's grandson. ᵇ Cousin.
19	Vedder	Cousin.	Vedders soohn	Cousin's son.
20	Vetter......	"	Vetters sohn......	" " "
21	Oheims tochter mann	Uncle's daughter's husband.	Oheims enkel......	Uncle's grandson.
22	Mon cousin......	My cousin.	Mon cousin sous-germain......	My cousin's son.
23	Primo politico......	My cousin by courtesy.	Sobrino......	My nephew.
24	Primo por affinidade	Cousin by affinity.	Primo distante......	Distant cousin.
25	Aquistata cugino......	Acquired cousin.	Secondo cugino?......	Second cousin.
26	Patrui filiæ vir......	Husband of son of paternal uncle.	Patrui nepos......	Grandson of paternal uncle.
27	Anepsias aner......	Husband of cousin.	Anepsiades?......	Cousin's son.
28			Theiou eggonos......	Uncle's grandson.
29				
30	Moj stryjeczny szwagier......	My broth.-in-law through pat. uncle.	Moj stryjeczny bratanek......	My nephew through paternal uncle.
31				
32				
33			Otchicha bratanetz......	From paternal uncle nephew.
34	Mush moego dvoiurod naja sestra..	My double-birth sister's husband.	Moi dvoiurodbyi plemiannik......	My double birth nephew.
35	Amŭjämun küsŭnŭmk ojäsu......	Uncle's my daughter's husband.	Amŭjämŭn oghlŭ......	Son of uncle my.
36	Keezä äpeh mun......	Son-in-law of paternal uncle my.	Törneh äpeh mun......	Grandchild of paternal uncle my.
37				
38	Minu esä vennä tutär mees......	My father's brother's daught. husb.	Minu esä vennä poeg......	My father's brother's son's son.
39	Serkkunĭ mies	Cousin's my husband.	Sŏrkkunĭ poĭka......	Son of my cousin.

	TABLE I.—*Continued.*			

	73. Father's brother's granddaughter.	Translation.	74. Father's brother's great grandson.	Translation.
1	Bint ibu ammi..............	Daughter of son of pat. uncle my.	Ibn ibn ibn ammi	Son of son of son of pat. uncle my.
2	Bint ibn ammi..............	" " " " " " "	Ibn ibn ibn ămmi	" " " " " " " " "
3				
4	Näwigta d'ămŭwee..............	Granddaughter of pat. uncle my.	Natija d'ămŭwee..............	Great grandson of pat. uncle my.
5	Horus yăkepora toostrin toostra...	Father's brother's dau. dau.	Horus yăkeporee voretein v.voretin	Father's brother's son's son's son.
6	Ineean mio drihar mahar..........	D. of the son of the bro. of my dau.	Mac mic mio drihar mahar	Son of son of son of bro. of my fa.
7	Egha brăthar m'ăthar	Grandchild of brother of my father.	Iar ogha brăthar m'ăthair...........	Great grandchild of bro. of my fa.
8	Iunneen mac braar my ayr...........	Daughter of son of bro. of my father.	Mac mac mac braar my ayr........	Son of son of son of bro. of my fa.
9	Merch fy nghefnder.............	Daughter of my cousin.	Wyr fy ngnefnder	Grandson of my cousin.
10	Nävâdäi ămoo..........................	Grandchild of paternal uncle.	Nätijäi ămoo	Grandchild of paternal uncle.
11				
12	Farbroders barnebarn.................	Uncle's grandchild.	Farbroders barnebarns barn........	Uncle's great grandchild.
13	Sonar dottir fodurbrodur mins.....	Son's daughter of father's bro. my.	Sonar sonar sonr fodurbrodur mins	Son's son's son of father's bro. my.
14	Farbrors dotter dotter................	Father's brother's daughter's daught.	Farbrors sonsons son..................	Father's brother's son.
15				
16	Paternal uncle's granddaughter...	Uncle's grandda . ('ather's side).	Paternal uncle's great grandson...	U. great grandson (father's side).
17	Ooms klein dochter. ᵇ Nicht......	Uncle's granddaught r. ᵇ Niece.	Ooms achter klein zoon. ᵇ Neef...	Uncle's great grandson. ᵇ Nephew.
18	Ooms groote dochter. ᵇ Nichte....	" " "	Kyzyn. ᵇ Oomes groot groot zoon	Cousin. ᵇ Uncle's great grandson.
19	Vedders dochter.......................	Cousin's daughter.	Vedders kinds kind..................	Cousin's child's child.
20	Vetters tochter	" "	Vetters enkel.........................	Cousin's grandson.
21	Oheims enkelin......................	Uncle's granddaughter.	Oheims grossenkel...................	Uncle's great grandson.
22	Ma cousine sous-germaine...........	My cousin's daughter.	Petit-fils de mon cousin.............	Grandson of my cousin.
23	Sobrina...............................	My niece.	Sobrino................................	My nephew.
24	Prima distante	Distant cousin.	Primo distante........................	Distant cousin.
25	Seconda cugina ?......................	Second cousin.	Terzo cugino ?........................	Third cousin.
26	Patrui neptis.......................	Granddaughter of paternal uncle.	Patrui pronepos......................	Great grandson of paternal uncle.
27	Anepsiadē ?...........................	Cousin's daughter.	Anepsiou eggonos ?....................	Cousin's grandson.
28	Thiou eggone........................	Uncle's granddaughter.	Thiou proeggonos.....................	Uncle's great grandson
29				
30	Moja stryjeczna siostrzenca.........	My niece through paternal uncle.	Moj stryjeczny wnuk...............	My grandson through paternal uncle.
31				
32				
33	Otchicha bratanitza...............	From paternal uncle niece.	Otchicha vnook ....[annik	From paternal uncle grandson.
34	Moja dvoiurodnaja plemiannitza..	My double birth niece.	Moi dvoiurodnyi vnutcha plemi-	
35	Amŭjamŭn kŭsŭ.......................	Daughter of uncle my.		
36	Tŏrneh äpeh mun...,.................	Grandchild of paternal uncle my.	Läveh tŏrneh äpeh mun.............	Son of grandchild of pat. uncle my.
37				
38	Minu esä vennä poeg tutăr.........	My father's brother's son's daughter.	Minu esä venna poeg poeg poeg...	My father's brother's son's son's son.
39	Serkkunĭ tytăr......................	Cousin's my daughter.	Serkkunĭ poïan poika...............	Cousin's my son's son.

	75. Father's brother's great-granddaughter.	Translation.	76. Father's sister.	Translation.
1	Bint bint bint ammi..................	D. of d. of d. of paternal uncle my.	Ammeti...............................	Paternal aunt my.
2	Bint bint bint ămmi..................	" " " " " " " "	Ammăti...............................	" " "
3			Dŏdhăthĭ. ᵇ Akhoth ăbhĭ..........	Aunt my. ᵇ Sister of father my.
4	Natijta d'ămŭwee....................	G't granddaught. of pat. uncle my.	Umtee................................	Paternal aunt my.
5	Horus yăkepora t. t. toostra.......	Father's brother's d. d. daughter.	Horus koverä.........................	Father's sister.
6	Ineean mic mio drihar mahar......	D. of the son of son of bro. of my fa.	Driffur mahar........................	Sister of my father.
7	Iar ogha brăthar m'ăthair...........	Great grandchild of bro. " " "	Phiuthar m'ăthair....................	" " " "
8	Inneen mac mac braar my ayra...	" " " " " "	Shuyr my ayr.........................	" " " "
9	Wyres fy nghefnder..................	Granddaughter of my cousin.	Fy modryb	My aunt.
10	Nätijäi ămoo.........................	Great grandchild of paternal uncle.	Aмă	Paternal aunt.
11			Pitrshvasar...........................	Father's sister.
12	Farbroders barnebarns barn.[mins	Uncle's great grandchild.	Faster.................................	Aunt (father's side).
13	Dottur dottur dottir fodurbroder	Daughter's d. d. of f. b. my.	Fodursyster min.....................	Father's sister my.
14	Farbrors dotters dotter dotter......	Father's brother's daughter's dau.	Faster.................................	Father's sister. Aunt.
15			Fathe.................................	Aunt.
16	P. uncle's gt. granddaughter.......	Uncle's gt. granddau. (fa.'s side).	Paternal aunt........................	Aunt (father's side).
17	Oom achter klein docht. ᵇ Nicht	Uncle's great granddaught. ᵇ Niece.	Moeje. ᵇ Tante	"
18	Nichte. ᵇ Ooms groote g. dochter	Cousin. ᵇ Uncle's great granddau.	Moej	"
19	Vedders kinds kind..................	Cousin's child's child.	Mŏhn. ᵇ Tante	"
20	Vetters enkelin......................	Cousin's granddaughter.	Muhme. ᵇ Tante.....................	"
21	Oheims grossenkelin.................	Uncle's great granddaughter.	Muhme. ᵇ Tante.....................	"
22	Petite-fille de ma cousine...........	Granddaughter of my cousin.	Ma tante..............................	My aunt.
23	Sobrina..............................	My niece.	Tia	Aunt. ᵇ Blood aunt.
24	Prima distante.......................	Distant cousin.	Tia. ᵇ Tia carnal....................	My aunt.
25	Terza cugina ?.......................	Third cousin.	Tia	
26	Patrui proneptis.....................	Great granddaughter of pat. uncle.	Amita.................................	Paternal aunt.
27	Anepsiou eggone ?....................	Cousin's granddaughter.	Patradelphē. ᵇ Theia. ᶜ Nannō ?	Paternal aunt. Aunt.
28	Theiou proeggonē....................	Uncle's great granddaughter.	Theia.................................	Aunt.
29			Mīno tētä............................	My father's sister.
30	Moja stryjeczna wnuczka............	My granddaughter through p. u.	Moja ciotka..........................	My aunt.
31			Ma tetka..............................	" "
32			Lyelya mi.............................	Paternal aunt my
33	Otchicha vnooka.....................	From paternal uncle granddaughter.	Lelya mi..............................	" " "
34	Moja dvoiurodnaja vnutchatnaja		Moja tjotka..........................	My aunt.
35	[plemiannitza		Hälä-m	Aunt my (paternal).
36	Keezä tŏrneh äpeh mun	Dau. of grandchild of pat. u. my.	Ammeh mun..........................	Paternal aunt my.
37			Nagy nenem..........................	Grand elder sister my.
38	Min esä venna poeg poeg tutăr....	My father's brother's son's son's dau.	Minu esä odde........................	My father's sister.
39	Serkkunĭ poïan tytăr.................	Daughter of the son of my cousin.	Tatīnĭ	Aunt my.

TABLE I.—*Continued.*

	77. Father's sister's husband.	Translation.	78. Father's sister's son.	Translation.
1	Arât ammeti	Husband of paternal aunt my.	Ibn ammeti	Son of paternal aunt my.
2	Zauj ămmăti	" " " " "	Ibn ammati	" " " "
3			Běn dōdhăthĭ	Son of aunt my.
4	Gorä d'umtee		Brŭnă d'umtee	Son of paternal aunt my.
5	Horus crocha arega	Father's sister's husband.	Horus crocha voretin	Father's sister's son.
6	Făr driffur mahar	Husband of sister of my father.	Mac driffer mahar	Son of sister of my father.
7	Fear phiuthar m'athair	" " " " "	Măc phiuthar m'athair	" " " "
8	Sheshey shuyr my ayr	" " " " "	Mac shuyr my ayr	" " " "
9	Fy ewyrth	My uncle.	Fy nghefnder	My cousin.
10	Shōhări amă	Husband of paternal aunt.	Poosări amă	Son of paternal aunt.
11			Pitrshvasrīya	Father's sister's son.
12	Faster's husbond	Father's sister's husband.	Fatter. b Södskendebarn	Cousin.
13	Madr fodursystur mins	Husband of father's sister my.	Systur sonr fodur mins	Sister's son of father my.
14	Fasters man	Father's sister's husband.	Faster's son. b Syskonbarn	Father's sister's son. Cousin.
15			(Swor ?)	Cousin germain.
16	Uncle	Uncle.	Cousin. b Paternal aunt's son.	First cousin.
17	Moejes man. b Oom	Aunt's husband. Uncle.	Moejes zoon. b Neef	Aunt's son. b Nephew.
18	Oom	Uncle.	Kozyn. b Moejes zoon	Cousin. b Aunt's son.
19	Ohm. b Onkel	"	Vedder	Cousin.
20	Oheim. b Onkel	Uncle.	Vetter. b Geschwisterkind	"
21	Gatte meiner muhme	Husband of my aunt.	Muhme sohn. b Vetter	Aunt's son. b Cousin.
22	Mon oncle	My uncle.	Mon cousin	My cousin.
23	Tio politico	My uncle (by courtesv).	Primo hermano	My cousin's brother.
24	Tio. b Tio por affinidade	Uncle. b Uncle by affinity.	Primo irmao	Cousin's brother.
25	Aquistata tio	Acquired uncle.	Cugino	Cousin.
26	Amitae vir	Husband of paternal aunt.	Amitae filius. b Amitinus	Son of paternal aunt. b Cousin.
27	Patradelphē anēr	" " " "	Anepsios. b Kasis ?	Cousin.
28			Prŏtēs exadelphos	"
29	Măno tēterŭs	My father's sister's husband.		
30	Moj stryj	My uncle.	Moj cioteczny brat	My brother through paternal aunt.
31	Mŭj stryc	" "		
32	Lyelin mi	Uncle my.	Bratovche mi	Aunt's son my.
33	Lelin mi	" "	Lelin sin mi	Paternal aunt's son my.
34	Moi djadja	My uncle.	Moi dvoiurodnyi brat	My double birth brother.
35	Ҡ nĭshtĕ-m	Brother-in-law my.	Hălăm oghlŭ	Son of paternal aunt.
36	Mĕreh ămmeh mun	Husband of paternal uncle my.	Lăveh ămmeh mun	Son of paternal aunt my.
37				
38	Minu esä odde mees	My father's sister's husband.	Minu esä odde poeg	My father's sister's son.
39	Tatīnĭ mies	Aunt's my husband.	Serkkunĭ. b Orpanani	Cousin my.

	79. Father's sister's son's wife.	Translation.	80. Father's sister's daughter.	Translation.
1	Amrât ibn ammeti	Wife of son of paternal uncle my.	Bint ammeti	Daughter of paternal aunt my.
2	Zaujat ibn ămmăti	" " " " "	Bint ammati	" " " "
3			Bath dōdhăthĭ	Daughter of aunt my.
4	Keltă d'umtee	Daughter-in-law of paternal aunt my.	Brätă d'umtee	Daughter of paternal aunt my.
5	Horus crocha voretin gena	Wife of son of sister of my father.	Horus crocha toostra	Father's sister daughter.
6	Ban mic driffur mahar	Wife of son of sister of my father.	Ineean mo driffer mahar	Father's sister of my father.
7	Bean măc phiuthar m'athair	" " " " " "	Nighean phiuthar m'athair	" " " "
8	Ben mac shuyr my ayr	" " " "	Inneen shuyr my ayr	" " " "
9	Fy nghefnither	My cousin.	Fy nghefnither	My cousin.
10	Zăni poosări ămă	Wife of son of paternal aunt.	Dŭkhtări ămă	Daughter of paternal aunt.
11			Pitrshvasrīyâ	Father's sister's daughter.
12	Södskendebarns hustrue	Cousin's wife.	Södskendebarn	Cousin.
13	Kona systur sonar fodur mins	Wife of sister's son of father my.	Systur dottir fodur mins	Sister's daughter of father my.
14	Fasters sonhustru	Father's sister's son's wife.	Fasters dotter. b Syskonbarn	Father's sister's daughter. b Cousin.
15				
16	Cousin	Cousin.	Cousin. b Paternal aunt's daught.	First cousin.
17	Moejes zoons vrouw	Aunt's son's wife.	Moejes dochter. b Nicht	Aunt's daughter. b Niece.
18	Nichte	Niece.	Nihhte. b Moejes dochter	Niece. b Aunt's daughter.
19	Nichte	Cousin.	Nichte	Cousin.
20	Base	"	Base. b Mühmehen	Cousin (father's-side).
21	Muhme sohnsfrau	Aunt's son's wife.	Muhme tochter. b Base	Aunt's daughter. g Cousin.
22	Ma cousine	My cousin.	Ma cousine	My cousin.
23	Prima politica	My cousin by courtesy.	Prima hermana	My cousin-sister.
24	Prima por affinidade	Cousin by affinity.	Prima	Cousin.
25	Aquistella cugina	Acquired cousin.	Cugina	
26	Amitae filii uxor	Wife of son of paternal aunt.	Amitae filia. b Amitina	Daughter of paternal aunt. b Cousin.
27	Anepsiou gunē	Wife of cousin.	Anepsia. b Kase ?	Cousin.
28			Prŏtē exadelphē	"
29				
30	Moja cioteczna bratowa	My sister-in-law through pat. aunt.	Moja cioteczna siostra	My sister-in-law through pat. aunt.
31				
32			Bratovchetka mi	Aunt's daughter my.
33			Lelina dushtera	Paternal aunt's daughter.
34	Shena moega dvoiurodnaja brata	Wife of my double birth brother.	Moja dvoiurodnaja sestra	My double birth sister.
35	Hălăm oglŭuŭm karŭsŭ	Wife of son of aunt my.	Halăm kŭsŭ	Daughter of paternal aunt my.
36	Bookeh ămmeh mun	Daughter-in-law of pat. aunt my.	Keeza ămmeh mun	" " " " "
37				
38	Minu esä odde poeg naine	My father's sister's son's wife.	Minu esä odde tutär	My father's sister's daughter.
39	Serkkunĭ vaimo	Cousin's my wife.	Serkkunĭ. b Orpadani	Cousin my.

TABLE I.—*Continued.*

	81. Father's sister's daughter's husband.	Translation.	82. Father's sister's grandson.	Translation.
1	Zôj bint ammeti......................	Husband of daught. of pat. aunt my.	Ibn ibn ammeti	Son of son of paternal aunt my.
2	Zauj bint ămmăti......................	" " " " " "	Ibn ibn ămmăti	" " " " " "
3				
4	Khutnă d'umtee......................	Son-in-law of paternal aunt my.	Năwigee d'umtee......................	Grandson of paternal aunt my.
5	Horus crocha toostra arega	Father's sister's daughter's husband.	Horus crocha voretein voretin......	Father's sister's son's son.
6	Far ineeni mo driffer mahar.......	Husband of d. of sister of my father.	Mac mic driffer mahar..............	Son of son of brother of my father.
7	Cleeamhiun phiuthar m'ăthair....	" " " " "	Egha phiuthar m'ăthair..............	" " " " " "
8	Sheshey inneen shuyr my ayr......	" " " " "	Mac mac shuyr my ayr..............	" " " " " "
9	Fy Nghefnder......................	My cousin.	Mab fy nghefnder	Son of my cousin.
10	Shōhäri dûkhtäri ămă..............	Husband of daughter of pat. aunt.	Năvâdăi ămă......................	Grandchild of paternal aunt.
11				
12	Södskendebarns husbond............	Cousin's husband.	Fasters barnebarn......................	Aunt's grandchild.
13	Madr systurdottur fodur mins......	Husb. of sister's daught. of fath. my.	Sonar sonr fodursystur minnar....	Son's son of father's sister my.
14	Fasters dotters man..................	Father's sister's daughter's husband.	Fasters sonson......................	Father's sister's son's son.
15				
16	Cousin	Cousin.	Paternal aunt's grandson............	Aunt's grandson (father's side).
17	Moejes dochters man..................	Aunt's daughter's husband.	Moejes klein zoon. ᵇ Neef.........	Aunt's grandson. ᵇ Nephew.
18	Kozyn......................	Cousin.	Kozyn. ᵇ Moejes groot zoon	Cousin. ᵇ Aunt's grandson.
19	Vedder......................	"	Vedders Soohn. ᵇ Nichtes Soohn..	Cousin's son. ᵇ Cousin's son (f.)
20	Vetter......................	Cousin.	Vetters Sohn.	Cousin's son.
21	Muhme tochtermann..................	Aunt's daughter's husband.	Muhme enkel......................	Aunt's grandson.
22	Mon cousin......................	My cousin.	Mon cousin sous-germain............	My cousin's son.
23	Primo politico......................	My cousin by courtesy.	Sobrino	My nephew.
24	Primo por affinidade..................	Cousin by affinity.	Primo distante......................	Distant cousin.
25	Aquistata cugino......................	Acquired cousin.	Secondo cugino......................	Second cousin.
26	Amitae filiae vir......................	Husband of daught. of pat. aunt.	Amitae nepos......................	Grandson of paternal aunt.
27	Anepsias anĕr......................	Husband of cousin.	Anepsiadēs	Cousin's son.
28			Theias eggonos......................	Aunt's grandson.
29				
30	Moj cioteczny szwagier..............	My brother-in-law through p. aunt.	Moj cioteczny bratanek..............	My nephew through paternal aunt.
31				
32				
33			Lelina vnook......................	Paternal aunt's grandson.
34	Mush moego dvoiurodnaja sestra..	Husband of my double birth sister.	Moi dvoiurodnyi plemiannik.......	My double birth nephew.
35	Häläm kŭsŭnŭm kojäsŭ	Aunt's my daughter's husband.	Häläm oghlŭ	Son of paternal aunt my.
36	Zävä ämmeh mun	Son-in-law of paternal aunt my.	Törneh ämmeh mun..............	Grandchild of paternal aunt my.
37				
38	Minu esä odde tutär mees............	My father's sister's daughter's husb.	Minu esä odde poeg poeg...........	My father's sister's son's son.
39	SerkkunI mies......................	Cousin's my husband.	SerkkunI poïka	Cousin's my son.

	83. Father's sister's granddaughter.	Translation.	84. Father's sister's great grandson.	Translation.
1	Bint ibn ammeti......................	Daught. of son of paternal aunt my.	Ibn ibn ibn ammeti......................	Son of son of son of pat. aunt my.
2	Bint ibn ămmăti......................	" " " " "	Ibn ibn ibn ămmăti......................	" " " " " "
3				
4	Năwigtee d'umtee......................	Granddaughter of paternal aunt my.	Natija d'umtee......................	Great grandson of paternal aunt my.
5	Horus crocha voretin toostra.......	Father's sister's son's daughter.	Horus crocha voretein v. voretin..	Father's sister's son's son's son.
6	Ineean mic driffer mahar............	Daughter of son of sister my father.	Mac mic mic driffer mahar..........	Son's son's son's sister of my father.
7	Ogha phiuthar m'ăthair............	Grandchild of sister of my fa.	Iar ogha phiuthar m'ăthair........	Great grandchild sister of my father.
8	Inneen mac shuyr my ayr............	daughter of son of sister of my father.	Mac mac mac shuyr my ayr.......	Daught. of son of son of son of my fa.
9	Merch fy nghefnither..............	Daughter of my cousin.	Mab wyr fy nghefnder..............	Grandson of my cousin.
10	Năvâdăi ămă......................	Grandchild of paternal aunt.	Nătijai ămă......................	Great grandchild of paternal aunt.
11				
12	Fasters barnebarn......................	Father's sister's grandchild.	Fasters barnebarns barn.......[nar	Father's sister's great grandchild.
13	Dottur dottir fodursyster minnar..	Daughter's daught. of fa. sister my.	Sonar sonar sonr fodursystur min-	Son's son's son of father's sister my.
14	Fasters dotter dotter..................	Father's sister's daughter's daught.	Fasters sonson son..................	Father's sister's son's son's son.
15				
16	Paternal aunt's granddaughter....	Aunt's granddaughter (father's side).	Paternal aunt's great grandson....	Aunt's great grandson (fath. side).
17	Moejes klein dochter. ᵇ Nicht....	Aunt's granddaughter. ᵇ Niece.	Moejes achter klein zoon. ᵇ Neef	Aunt's great grandson. ᵇ Nephew.
18	Nichte. ᵇ Moejes groote dochter..	Niece. ᵇ Aunt's granddaughter.	Kozyn. ᵇ Moejes groot groot zoon	Cousin. ᵇ Aunt's great grandson.
19	Vedders dochter. ᵇ Nichter doch.	Cousin's daughter.	Vedders kinds kind..................	Cousin's child's child.
20	Vetters tochter......................	"	Vetters enkel......................	Cousin's grandson.
21	Muhme enkelin......................	Aunt's granddaughter.	Muhme grossenkel......................	Aunt's great grandson.
22	Ma cousine sous-germaine............	My cousin's daughter.	Petit-fils de mon cousin	Grandson of my cousin.
23	Sobrina......................	My niece.	Sobríno......................	My nephew.
24	Primă distante......................	Distant cousin.	Primo distante......................	Distant cousin.
25	Seconda cugina......................	Second cousin.	Teszo cugino......................	Third cousin.
26	Amitae neptis......................	Granddaughter of paternal aunt.	Amitae pronepos......................	Great grandson of paternal uncle.
27	Anepsiadē......................	Cousin's daughter.	Anepsiou eggonos ?......................	Cousin's grandson.
28	Theias eggonē......................	Aunt's granddaughter.	Theias proeggonos......................	Aunt's great grandson.
29				
30	Moja cioteczna synowíec..............	My niece through paternal aunt.	Moj cioteczny wnuk	My grandson through paternal aunt.
31				
32				
33	Lelína vnooka......................	Paternal aunt's granddaughter.	Lelin prevnook.............[miannik	Paternal uncle's great grandson.
34	Moja dvoiurodnaja plemiannitza...	My double birth niece.	Moi dvoiurodnyi vnutchatnyi ple-	
35	Häläm kŭsŭ......................	Daughter of paternal aunt my.		
36	Törneh ämmeh mun..................	Grandchild of paternal aunt my.	Läveh törneh ämmeh mun	Son of grandchild of pat. aunt my.
37				
38	Minu esä odde poeg tutär............	My father's sister's son's daughter.	Minu esä odde poeg poeg poeg.....	My father's sister's son's son's son.
39	SerkkunI tytär......................	Cousin's my daughter.	SerkkunI poïan poïka..............	Cousin's my son's son.

TABLE I.—*Continued.*

	85. Father's sister's great grandson's daughter.	Translation.	86. Mother's brother.	Translation.
1	Bint bint bint ammeti.............	Daught. of d. of d. of paternal aunt.	Khâli....................	Maternal uncle my.
2	Bint bint bint ămmâti.............	" " " " "	Khâli....................	" " "
3			ᵃ Khĭ immĭ..............	" " "
4	Natijta d'umtee	Great granddaught. of pat. aunt my.	Khâlŭme	" " "
5	Horus crocha t. t. toostra............	Father's sister's daughter's dau. dau.	Morus yäkepira	Mother's brother.
6	Ineean mic mic driffer mahar......	Son of son of son of sister of my fa.	Drihar mo vahar	Brother of my mother.
7	Iar ogha phiuthar m'ăthair......	Gt. grandchild of sister of my father.	Brăthair mo m'hăthair.........	" " "
8	Inneen mac mac mac shuyr my ayr	Daught. of son of s. of sister of my fa.	Braar my moir..........	" " "
9	Wyres fy nghefnither..............	Granddaughter of my cousin.	Fy ewyrth................	My uncle.
10	Nătijäi ămă......................	Great grandchild of paternal aunt.	Hâloo...................	Maternal uncle.
11			Mâtula. ᵇ Matrbhrâtar......	" "
12	Fasters barnebarns barn............	Father's sister's great grandchild.	Morbroder................	Uncle (mother's side).
13	Dottur d. dottir fodursystur minnar	Daughter's d. of fath. sister my.	Modurbrodir minn..........	Mother's brother my.
14	Fasters dotters dotters dotter.	Father's sister's dau. dau. dau.	Morbroder. ᵇ Morbror.......	" " "
15			Eam....................	Uncle.
16	Paternal aunt's gt. granddaughter	Aunt's gt. granddaught. (fath. side).	Maternal uncle.........	Uncle (mother's side.)
17	Moejes achter klein doch. ᵇ Nicht	Aunt's gt. granddaught. ᵇ Niece.	Oom	Uncle.
18	Nichte. ᵇ Moejes groote g. docht.	Cousin. ᵇ Aunt's gt. granddaught.	Oom	"
19	Vedders kinds kind	Cousin's child's child.	Ohm. ᵇ Onkel........	"
20	Vetters enkelinn...............	Cousin's granddaughter.	Oheim. ᵇ Onkel. ᶜ Ohm	"
21	Muhme grossenkelin............	Aunt's great granddaughter.	Oheim. ᵇ Onkel.......	My uncle.
22	Petite-fille de mon cousin............	Granddaughter of my cousin.	Mon oncle.............	My uncle maternal.
23	Sobrina............................	My niece.	Tio materno	Uncle. ᵇ Blood uncle.
24	Prima distante....................	Distant cousin.	Tio. ᵇ Tio carnal.........	Uncle.
25	Terza cugina	Third cousin.	Tio	Maternal uncle. ᵇ Uncle.
26	Amitae proneptis.................	Gt. granddaughter of paternal aunt.	Avunuclus...............	Maternal uncle.
27	Anepsiou eggonĕ?.................	Cousin's granddaughter.	Mĕtrōs. ᵇ Metradelphos. ᶜ Thios.	Uncle.
28	Theias proggonĕ.................	Aunt's great granddaughter.	Theios..[ᵈ Patrokosignetos nannos?]	My mother's brother.
29			Măno awynăs	My uncle.
30	Moja cioteczna wnuczka............	My granddaughter through pat. aunt.	Moj wuj	" "
31			Mŭj ujec..............	Uncle my.
32			Vuyka mi..............	" "
33	Lelina prevnooka..................	Paternal aunt's great granddaughter.	Ooika mi..............	My uncle.
34	Moja dvoiurodnaja vnutchatnaja [plemiannitza	My double birth grandchild niece.	Moi djadja..............	Maternal uncle my.
35			Dăyi-m...............	" " "
36	Keeză törneh ămmeh mun..........	Dau. of grandchild of pat. aunt my.	Khăleh mun...........	Grand elder brother my.
37			Nagy batyam	My mother's brother.
38	Minu esă odde poeg poeg tutăr......	My father's sister's son's son's dau.	Minu emă vennă..........	Maternal uncle my.
39	Serkkunĭ tyttăren tytăr	Cousin's my daughter's daughter.	Enönĭ	

	87. Mother's brother's wife.	Translation.	88. Mother's brother's son.	Translation.
1	Amrăt khâli.............,.....	Wife of maternal uncle my.	Ibn khâli..............	Son of maternal uncle my.
2	Zaujat khâli...................	" " " " "	Ibn khăli..............	" " " " "
3	Eshĕth ᵃ khĭ fummĭ...........	Wife of brother of mother my.		
4	Bakhtă d'khâlŭmee	Wife of maternal uncle my.	Brŭnă d'khâlŭmee.........	Son of maternal uncle my.
5	Morus yäkepora gena...........	Mother's brother's wife.	Morus yäkepora voretin......	Mother's brother's son.
6	Ban drihar mo vahar............	Wife of brother of my mother.	Mac drihar mo vahar...............	Son of brother of my mother.
7	Bean b'răthăr mo m'hăthar	" " " " " "	Măo brăthair mo m'hăthair........	" " " " " "
8	Ben braar my moir.............	" " " " " "	Mac braar my moir.........	" " " " " "
9	Fy modryb	My aunt.	Fy nghefnder	My cousin.
10	Zăni hăloo	Wife of maternal uncle.	Poosări hăloo............	Son of maternal uncle.
11			Mătulaputra.............	Maternal uncle's son.
12	Morbroders hustrue.................	Uncle's wife.	Fatter. ᵇ Södskendebarn..........	Cousin.
13	Kona modurbrodur mins............	Wife of mother's brother my.	Sonr modurbrodur mins.........	Son of mother's brother my.
14	Morbrors hustru...................	Mother's brother's wife.	Morbrors son. ᵇ Syskonbarn......	Mother's brother's son. ᵇ Cousin.
15				
16	Aunt...........................	Aunt.	Cousin. ᵇ Maternal uncle's son..	First cousin.
17	Ooms vrouw. ᵇ Tante...........	Uncle's wife. ᵇ Aunt.	Ooms zoon. ᵇ Neef............	Uncle's son. ᵇ Nephew.
18	Moej	Aunt.	Kozyn. ᵇ Ooms zoon..............	Cousin. ᵇ Uncle's son.
19	Möhn. ᵇ Tante	"	Vedder...............	Cousin.
20	Muhme. ᵇ Tante.............	"	Vetter. ᵇ Geschwisterkind........	"
21	Meins oheims gattin	My uncle's wife.	Oheims sohn. ᵇ Vetter............	Uncle's son. ᵇ Cousin.
22	Ma tante......................	My aunt.	Mon cousin............	My cousin.
23	Tia politica....................	My aunt by courtesy.	Primo hermano..........	Cousin-brother.
24	Tia. ᵇ Tia por affinidade............	Aunt. ᵇ Aunt by affinity.	Primo irmão.............	" "
25	Aquistella tia...................	Acquired aunt.	Cugino................	Cousin.
26	Avunculi uxor..................	Wife of maternal uncle.	Avunculi filius. ᵇ Consobrinus..	Son of maternal uncle. ᵇ Cousin.
27	Mĕtradelphou gunĕ...............	" " "	Anepsios. ᵇ Kasis ?..........	Cousin.
28			Prōtos exadelphos...............	"
29	Măno awynĕnĕ...............	My mother's brother's wife.		
30	Moja wujenka.................	My aunt.	Moj wujeczny brat...........	My brother through maternal uncle.
31	Ma tetka......................	" "		
32	Vuyna mi....................	Aunt my.	Bratovche mim...........	Uncle's son my.
33	Ooina mi	" "		
34	Moja tjotka...................	My aunt.	Moi dvoiurodnyi brat..............	My double birth brother.
35		My uncle's wife.	Dăyim oghlŭ	Son of maternal uncle my.
36	Khăl zhŭneh mun	Wife of maternal uncle my.	Lăveh khăleh...........	" " " " "
37				
38			Mimu emă vennă poeg.............	My mother's brother's son.
39	Enönĭ răimŏ.................	Wife of maternal uncle my.	Serkunĭ. ᵇ Orpanani...........	Cousin my.

TABLE I.—Continued.

	89. Mother's brother's son's wife.	Translation.	90. Mother's brother's daughter.	Translation.
1	Amrât ibn khâli	Wife of son of maternal uncle my.	Bint khâli	Daughter of maternal uncle my.
2	Zaujat ibn khäli	" " " " " " "	Bint khäli	" " " " "
3				
4	Caltä d'khâlŭwee	Daughter-in-law of maternal uncle.	Brätä d'khâlŭwee	" " " " " "
5	Morus yäkepora voretin gena	Mother's brother's son's wife.	Morus yäkepora toostra	Mother's brother's daughter.
6	Ban mic drihar mo vahar	Wife of son of bro. of my mother.	Ineean drihar mo vahar	Daughter of brother of my mother.
7	Bean mic brăthar mo m'hăthair...	" " " " " " "	Nighean brăthair mo m'brathair...	" " " " "
8	Ben mac braar my moir	" " " " " " "	Inneen braar my moir	" " " " "
9	Fy Nghefnither	My cousin.	Fy Nghefnither	My cousin.
10	Zăni poosäri hâloo	Wife of son of maternal uncle.	Dûkhtäri hâloo	Daughter of maternal uncle.
11			Mătulaputrî	Maternal uncle's daughter.
12	Fatter's hustrue	Cousin's wife.	Södskendebarn	Cousin.
13	Sonar kona modurburodur mins...	Son's wife of mother's brother my.	Dottir modurbrodur mins	Daughter of mother's brother my.
14	Morbrors sons hustru	Mother's brother's son's wife.	Morbrors dotter. ᵇ Syskonban....	Mother's brother's daughter. Cous.
15				
16	Cousin	Cousin.	Cousin. ᵇ Mat. uncle's daughter.	First cousin.
17	Ooms zoons vrouw	Uncle's son's wife.	Ooms dochter. ᵇ Nicht	Uncle's daughter. ᵇ Niece.
18	Nichte	Niece by marriage.	Nichte. ᵇ Ooms dochter	Niece. ᵇ Uncle's daughter.
19	Nichte	Cousin.	Nichte	Cousin.
20	Base	"	Base. ᵇ Mühmchen	"
21	Oheims schwiegertochter	Uncle's daughter-in-law.	Oheims tochter. ᵇ Base	Uncle's daughter. ᵇ Cousin.
22	Ma cousine	My cousin.	Ma cousine	My cousin.
23	Prima politica	My cousin by courtesy.	Prima hermana	Cousin-sister.
24	Prima por affinidade	Cousin by affinity.	Prima	Cousin.
25	Aquistella cugina	Acquired cousin.	Cugina	"
26	Avunculi filii uxor	Wife of son of maternal uncle.	Avunculi filia. ᵇ Consobrina	Daughter of mat. uncle. ᵇ Cousin.
27	Anepsiou gune	Wife of cousin.	Anepsia. ᵇ Kasē?	Cousin.
28			Prōtē exadelphē	"
29				
30	Moja wujeczna bratowa	My sister-in-law through mat. unc.	Moja wujeczna siostra	My sister through maternal uncle.
31				
32			Bratoochetka mi	Uncle's daughter my.
33				
34	Shena moega dvoiurodnaja brata..	Wife of my double birth brother.	Moja dvoiurodnaja sestra	My double birth sister.
35	Däyine oghlŭnŭm kărŭsŭ	Wife of son of uncle my.	Däyine kŭsŭ	Daughter of maternal uncle my.
36	Bookeh khäleh	Daughter-in-law of mat. unc. my.	Keezä khäleh mun	" " " " "
37				
38				
39	Serkkunĭ vaĭmŏ	Wife cousin's my.	Sarkunĭ. ᵇ Orpanani	Cousin my.

	91. Mother's brother's daughter's husband.	Translation.	92. Mother's brother's grandson.	Translation.
1	Zôj bint khâli	Husband of daught. of m. uncle my.	Ibn ibn khâli	Son of son of maternal uncle my.
2	Zauj bint khäli	" " " " " "	Ibn ibn khäli	" " " " " "
3				
4	Khutnä d'khâlŭwee	Son-in-law of maternal uncle my.	Näwiga d'khâlŭwee	Grandson of maternal uncle my.
5	Morus yäkepora toostra arega	Mother's brother's daught. husband.	Morus yäkepora toostra voretin...	Mother's brother's son's son.
6	Fär ineeni drihar mo vahar	Husband of dau. of bro. of my husb.	Mac mio drihar mo vahar	Son of son of brother of my mother.
7	Cleeamhuin brăthair mo m'hăthar	" " " " "	Ogha brăthair mo m'hăthair	Grandchild of brother of my mother.
8	Sheshey inneen braar my moir....	" " " " "	Mac mac braar my moir	Son of son of brother of my mother.
9	Fy Nghefnder	My cousin.	Mab fy nghefnder	Son of my cousin.
10	Shöhäri dûkhtäri hâloo	Husband of daught. of mat. uncle.	Năvâdäi hâloo	Grandchild of maternal uncle.
11				
12	Södskendebarns husbond	Cousin's husband.	Morbroders barnebarn	Uncle's grandson (mother's side).
13	Madr brodurdottur modur mins...	Husband of brother's d. of m. my.	Sonar sonr modurbrodur mins	Son's son of mother's brother my.
14	Morbrors dotters man	Mother's brother's daughter's husb.	Morbrors sonson	Mother's brother's son's son.
15				
16	Cousin	Cousin.	Maternal uncle's grandson	Uncle's grandson (mother's side).
17	Ooms dochters man	Uncle's daughter's husband.	Ooms klein zoon. ᵇ Neef	Uncle's grandson. ᵇ Nephew.
18	Kozyn	Cousin.	Kozyn. ᵇ Ooms groot zoon	Cousin. ᵇ Uncle's grandson.
19	Vedder	"	Vedders soohn. ᵇ Nichtes soohn.	Cousin's son.
20	Vetter	"	Vetters sohn	" "
21	Oheims schwiegersohn	Uncle's son-in-law.	Oheims enkel	Uncle's grandson.
22	Mon cousin	My cousin.	Men cousin sous-germain	My cousin's son.
23	Primo politico	My cousin by courtesy.	Sobrino	My nephew.
24	Primo por affinidade	Cousin by affinity.	Primo distante	Distant cousin.
25	Aquistata cugino	Acquired cousin.	Secondo cugino	Second cousin.
26	Avunculi filiae vir	Husband of dau. of maternal uncle.	Avunculi nepos	Grandson of maternal uncle.
27	Anepsias anēr	Husband of cousin.	Anepsiadēs	Cousin's son.
28			Theiou eggonos	Uncle's grandson.
29				
30	Moj wujeczny szwagier	My brother-in-law through m. uncle.	Moj wujeczny bratanek	My nephew through mat. uncle.
31				
32				
33				
34	Mush moego dvoiurodnaja sestra..	Husband of my double birth sister.	Moi dvoiurodnyi plemiannik	My double birth nephew.
35	Dayim kŭsŭnŭm kojäsu	Husband of daughter of uncle my.	Däyim oghlŭ	Son of maternal uncle my.
36	Zävä khäleh mun	Son-in-law of maternal uncle my.	Törneh khäleh mun	Grandchild of maternal uncle my.
37				
38			Minu emä vennä poeg poeg	My mother's brother's son's son.
39	Serkunĭ mies	Cousin's my husband.	Serkkunĭ poĭkä	Cousin's my son.

TABLE I.—*Continued.*

	93. Mother's brother's granddaughter.	Translation.	94. Mother's brother's great grandson.	Translation.
1	Bint ibn khâli	Daughter of son of mat. uncle my.	Ibn ibn ibn khâli	Son of son of son of mat. uncle my.
2	Bint ibn khäli	" " " "	Ibn ibn ibn khäli	" " " " " "
3				
4	Näwigta d'khälûwee	Granddaught. of maternal uncle my.	Natija d'khälûwee	Gt. grandson of maternal uncle my.
5	Morus yäkepora toostrin toostra	Mother's brother's daught. daught.	Morus yäkepora voretein v. voretin	Mother's brother's son's son's son.
6	Ineean mic drihar mo vahar	Daught. of son of bro. of my mother.	Mac mic mic drihar mo vahar	Son of son of s. of bro. of my mother.
7	Ogha bräthar mo m'hathair	Grandchild of brother of my mother.	Iar ogha bräthar mo m'hathair	Gt. grandchild of bro. of my mother.
8	Inneen mac braar my moir	Daughter of son of my mother.	Mac mac mac braar my moir	Son of son of s. of bro. of my mother.
9	Merch fy nghefnither	Daughter of my cousin.	Wyr fy nghefnder	Grandson of my cousin.
10	Nävädäi hâloo	Granddaughter of maternal uncle.	Nätijäi hâloo	Gt. grandchild of maternal uncle.
11				
12	Morbroders barnebarn	Uncle's grandchild.	Morbroders barnebarns barn	Uncle's great grandchild.
13	Dottur dottir modurbrodur mins	Daughter's d. of mother's bro. my.	Sonar sonar sonr modurbrodur mins	Son's son of mother's bro. my.
14	Morbrors dotter dotter	Mother's brother's daught. daught.	Morbrors sonsons son	Mother's brother's son's son's son.
15				
16	Maternal uncle's granddaughter	Uncle's granddaughter (m. s.)	Maternal uncle's great grandson	Uncle's gt. grandson (mother's side)
17	Ooms klein dochter. b Nicht	Uncle's granddaughter. b Niece.	Ooms achter klein zoon. b Neef	Uncle's gt. grandson b Nephew.
18	Nichte. b Ooms groote dochter	Niece. b Uncle's granddaughter.	Kozyn. b Ooms groot groot zoon	Cousin. b Uncle's great grandson.
19	Vedders dochter. b Nichtes doch.	Cousin's daughter.	Vedders kinds kind	Cousin's child's child.
20	Vetters tochter	" "	Vetters enkel	Cousin's grandson.
21	Oheims enkelin	Uncle's granddaughter.	Oheims grossenkel	Uncle's great grandson.
22	Ma cousin sous-germaine	My cousin's daughter.	Le petit-fils de mon cousin	The grandson of my cousin.
23	Sobrina	My niece.	Sobrino	My nephew.
24	Prima distante	Distant cousin.	Primo distante	Distant cousin.
25	Seconda cugina	Second cousin.	Terzo cugino	Third cousin.
26	Avunculi neptis	Granddaughter of maternal uncle.	Avunculi pronepos	Gt grandson of maternal uncle.
27	Anepsiadē	Cousin's daughter.	Anepsiou eggonos ?	Cousin's grandson.
28	Theiou eggonē	Uncle's granddaughter.	Theiou proeggonos	Uncle's great grandson.
29				
30	Moja wujeczna synowica	My niece through maternal uncle.	Moj wujeczny wnuk	My grandson through mat. uncle.
31				
32				
33				
34	Moja dvoiurodnaja plemiannitza	My double birth niece.	Moi dvoiurodnyi vnutchatnyi ple-[miannik.	My double birth grandson nephew.
35	Däyine kûsû	Daughter of maternal uncle my.		
36	Törneh khäleh mun	Grandchild of maternal uncle my.	Läveh törneh khäleh mun	Son of grandchild of mat. uncle my.
37				
38				
39	Serkkunï tytär	Cousin's my daughter.	Serkkunï poïan poïkä	Cousin's my son's son.

	95. Mother's brother's great granddaughter.	Translation.	96. Mother's sister.	Translation.
1	Bint bint bint khâli	Daught. d. of d. of mat. uncle my.	Khâleti	Maternal aunt my.
2	Bint bint bint khäli	" " " " " "	Khäläti	" " "
3			a Khoth immï	" " "
4	Natijta d'khälûwee	Gt. granddaugnt. of mat. uncle my.	Khultee	" " "
5	Morus y. toostrin t. tooster	Mother's brother's dau. dau. dau.	Morus kovera	Mother's sister.
6	Ineean mic mic drihar mo vahar	Dau. of son of s. of bro. of my moth.	Driffür mö vahar	Sister of my mother.
7	Iar ogha bräthar mo m'hathair	Great grandchild of my mother.	Phiuthar mo m'hathair	" " "
8	Inneen mac mac braar my moir	Daught. of son of son of my mother.	Shuyr my ayr	" " "
9	Wyres fy nghefnither	Granddaughter of my cousin.	Fy modryb	My aunt.
10	Nätijäi hâloo	Great grandchild of mat. uncle.	Hälä	Maternal aunt.
11			Mätershvasar	Mother's sister.
12	Morbroders barnebarns barn	Uncle's great grandchild.	Moster	" "
13	Dottur d. dottir modurbrodur mins	Daughter's d. d. of m. brother my.	Modursystir min	Mother's sister my.
14	Morbrors dotters dotter dotter	Mother's brother's dau. dau. dau.	Moster	Mother's sister.
15			Moddrie. b Modrie	Maternal aunt.
16	Maternal uncle's gt. granddaught.	Uncle's great granddaughter (m. s.).	Maternal aunt	Aunt (mother's side).
17	Ooms achter klein dochter. b Nicht	Uncle's gt. granddaughter. b Niece.	Moeje. b Tante	Aunt.
18	Nichte. b Ooms groote g. dochter	Niece. b Uncle's gt. granddaughter.	Moej	"
19	Vedders kinds kind	Cousin's child's child.	Möhn. b Tante	"
20	Vetters enkelinn	Cousin's granddaughter.	Muhme. b Tante	"
21	Oheims grossenkelin	Uncle's great granddaughter.	Muhme. b Tante	"
22	La petite-fille de mon cousin	The granddaughter of my cousin.	Ma tante	My aunt.
23	Sobrina	My niece.	Tia materna	My aunt maternal.
24	Prima distante	Distant cousin.	Tia. b Tia carnal	Aunt. b Blood aunt
25	Terza cugina	Third cousin.	Tia	Aunt.
26	Avunculi proneptis	Great granddaughter of mat. uncle.	Matertera	Maternal aunt.
27	Anepsiou eggonē	Cousin's granddaughter.	Mētrapdelphē. b Theia	" "
28	Theiou proeggonē	Uncle's great granddaughter.	Theia	Aunt.
29			Mäno tētä	My mother's sister.
30	Moja wujeczna wnuczka	My granddaughter through m. uncle.	Moja ciotka	My aunt.
31			Ma tetka	" "
32			Tetka mi	Aunt my.
33			Tetka mi	" "
34	Moja dvoiurodnaja vnutchatnaja [plemiannitza.		Moja tjotka	My aunt.
35			Diäzä-m	Maternal aunt my.
36	Keezä törneh khäleh mun	Dau. of grandchild of m. uncle my.	Khäleh mun	" " "
37			Nagy nenem	Grand elder brother my.
38			Minu ennä odde	My mother's sister.
39	Serkkunï tyttären tytär	Cousin's my daughter's daughter.	Tati	Aunt.

TABLE I.—*Continued.*

	97. Mother's sister's husband.	Translation.	98. Mother's sister's son.	Translation.
1	Zôj khâleti..................................	Husband of maternal aunt my.	Ibn Khâleti....................	Son of maternal aunt my.
2	Zauj khälăti..............................	" " " " "	Ibn Khälăti....................	" " " "
3	Ish ᵃ khoth ïmmï........................	" " " " "		
4	Gorä d'khultee...........................	" " " " "	Brünä d'khultee.............	" " " "
5	Morus crochus arega..................	Mother's sister's husband.	Morus crocha voretin...............	Mother's sister's son.
6	Fär driffür mo vahar...................	Husband of sister of my mother.	Mac driffur mo vahar...............	Son of sister of my mother.
7	Fear phiuthar mo m'hathair.......	" " " " "	Măc phiuthar mo m'hathair........	" " " " "
8	Sheshey shuyr my moir	" " " " "	Mac shuyr my moir........	" " " "
9	Fy ewyrth................................	My uncle.	Fy Nghefnder.....................	My cousin.
10	Shŏhäri hâla.............................	Husband of maternal aunt.	Poosäri hâla....................	Son of maternal aunt.
11			Mătershvasrïya.................	Mother's sister's son.
12	Mosters husbond......................	Mother's sister's husband.	Fatter. ᵇ Sŏdskendebarn..........	Cousin.
13	Madr modursytur minnar............	Husband of mother's sister my.	Systur sonr modur minnar....	Sister's son of mother my.
14	Mosters man............................	Mother's sister's husband.	Mosters son. ᵇ Syskonbarn........	Mother's sister's son. ᵇ Cousin.
15			(Swor?) Modrigan sunu........	(Cousin?) Maternal aunt's son.
16	Uncle......................................	Uncle.	Cousin. Maternal aunt's son......	First cousin.
17	Moejes man. ᵇ Oom.................	Aunt's husband. ᵇ Uncle.	Moejes zoon. ᵇ Neef...............	Aunt's son. ᵇ Nephew.
18	Oom	Uncle.	Kozyn. ᵇ Moejes zoon............	Cousin. ᵇ Aunt's son.
19	Ohm. ᵇ Onkel..........................	"	Vedder..........................	Cousin.
20	Oheim. ᵇ Onkel. ᶜ Ohm	"	Vetter. ᵇ Geschwisterkind........	"
21	Meiner muhme gatte..................	My aunt's husband.	Muhme sohn. ᵇ Vetter...........	Aunt's son. ᵇ Cousin.
22	Mon oncle................................	My uncle.	Mon cousin......................	My cousin.
23	Tio politico	My uncle by courtesy.	Primo hermano..................	My cousin-brother.
24	Tio. ᵇ Tio por affinidade...........	Uncle. ᵇ Uncle by affinity.	Primo irmão.....................	Cousin-brother.
25	Aquistata tio............................	Acquired uncle.	Cugino...........................	Cousin.
26	Materteræ vir...........................	Husband of maternal aunt.	Materteræ filius. ᵇ Consobrinus..	Son of maternal aunt. ᵇ Cousin.
27	Mĕtradelphē anēr	" " " "	Anepsios. ᵇ Kasis?...............	Cousin.
28			Protōs exadelphos.................	"
29				
30	Moj wuj..................................	My uncle.	Moj cioteczny brat.................	My brother through maternal aunt.
31	Mŭj ujec.................................	" "		
32	Tetin mi..................................	Uncle my.	Bratovche mi.....................	Aunt's son my.
33	Tetin mi..................................	" "	Tetun sin. ᵇ Sestrenche............	Maternal aunt's son. ᵇ Cousin.
34	Moi djadja	My uncle.	Moi dvoiurodnyi brat...........	My double birth brother.
35	Enishtĕ-m................................	Brother-in-law my.	Diäzämeoghlŭ.....................	Son of maternal aunt my.
36	Mĕreh khäleh mun....................	Husband of maternal uncle my.	Läveh khäleh mun.................	" " " "
37				
38				
39	Tatïuï mies.............................	Husband of my aunt.	Minu emä odde poeg.................	My mother's sister's son.
			Serkkunï. ᵇ Orpanani...............	Cousin my.

	99. Mother's sister's son's wife.	Translation.	100. Mother's sister's daughter.	Translation.
1	Amrât ibn khâleti	Wife of son of maternal aunt my.	Bint khâleti....................	Daughter of maternal aunt my.
2	Zaujat ibn khälăti....................	" " " " " "	Bint khülăti....................	" " " " "
3				
4	Caltä d'khultee........................	Daughter-in-law of mater. aunt my.	Brätä d'khultee	" " " " " "
5	Morus crocha voretein gena........	Mother's sister's son's wife.	Morus crocha toostra..................	Mother's sister's daughter.
6	Ban mic driffer mo vahar........	Wife of son of sister of my mother.	Ineean driffer mo vahar..........	Daughter of sister of my mother.
7	Bean mic phiuthar mo m'hathair..	" " " " " "	Nighean phiuthar mo m'hathair...	" " " " "
8	Ben mac shuyr my moir............	" " " " "	Inneen shuyr my moir..............	" " " " "
9	Fy nghefnither........................	My cousin.	Fy nghefnither....................	My cousin.
10	Zăni poosäri hälä	Wife of son of maternal aunt.	Dŭkhtäri hâlä....................	Daughter of maternal aunt.
11			Mätrshvasrïyâ....................	Mother's sister daughter.
12	Fatters hustrue.......................	Cousin's wife.	Sŏdskendebarn....................	Cousin (mother's side).
13	Sonar kona modursystur minnar..	Son's wife of mother's sister my.	Systurdottir modur minnar........	Sister's daughter of mother my.
14	Mosters sons hustru................	Mother's sister's son's wife.	Mosters dotter. ᵇ Syskonbarn.....	Mother's sister's daughter. ᵇ Cousin.
15				
16	Cousin	Cousin.	Cousin. Maternal aunt's daught.	First cousin.
17	Mojes zoons vrouw...................	Aunt's son's wife.	Moejes dochter. ᵇ Nicht............	Aunt's daughter. ᵇ Niece.
18	Nichte..................................	Niece.	Nichte. ᵇ Moejes dochter	Niece. ᵇ Aunt's daughter.
19	Nichte..................................	Cousin.	Nichte............................	Cousin.
20	Base....................................	"	Base. ᵇ Mühmchen. ᶜ Bäschen..	"
21	Muhme schwiegertochter............	Aunt's daughter-in-law.	Muhme tochter. ᵇ Base............	Aunt's daughter. ᵇ Cousin.
22	Ma cousine............................	My cousin.	Ma cousine.......................	My cousin.
23	Prima politica.........................	My cousin by courtesy.	Prima hermana....................	Cousin-sister.
24	Prima por affinidade.................	Cousin by affinity.	Prima............................	Cousin.
25	Aquistella cugina.....................	Acquired cousin.	Cugina	"
26	Materteræ filii uxor..................	Wife of son of maternal aunt.	Materteræ filia. ᵇ Consobrina.....	Daughter of mat. aunt. ᵇ Cousin.
27	Anepsiou gunē........................	Wife of cousin.	Anepsiä. ᵇ Kasē?....................	Cousin.
28			Prōtē exadelphē...................	"
29				
30	Moja cioteczna bratowa.............	My sister-in-law through mat. aunt.	Moja cioteczna siostra.............	My sister through maternal aunt.
31				
32			Bratovchetka mi..................	Aunt's daughter my.
33			Tetuna dushtera..................	Maternal aunt's daughter.
34	Shena moego dvoiurodnaja brata..	Wife of my double birth brother.	Moja dviourodnaja sestra...........	My double birth sister.
35	Diäzäm oghlünün kärüsü..........	Wife of son of maternal aunt.	Diäzäm küzü....................	Daughter of paternal aunt my.
36	Bookeh khäleh mun.................	Daughter-in-law of maternal aunt.	Keesä khäleh mun.................	" " " " "
37				
38				
39	Serkkunï vaimo........................	Wife of my cousin.	Minu emä odde tütär...............	My mother's sister's daughter.
			Serkkunï. ᵇ Orpanani............	Cousin my.

TABLE I.—*Continued.*

	101. Mother's sister's daughter's husband.	Translation.	102. Mother's sister's grandson.	Translation.
1	Zōj bint khâleti	Husband of daught. of mat. aunt my.	Ibn ibn khâleti	Son of son of maternal aunt my.
2	Zauj bint khälăti	" " " " " "	Ibn ibn khälăti	" " " " " "
3				
4	Khutnä d'khultee	Son-in-law of maternal aunt my.	Näwiga d'khultee	Grandson of maternal aunt my.
5	Morus crocha toostrin arega	Mother's sister's daughter's husband.	Morus crocha voretein voretin	Mother's sister's son's son.
6	Für ineenī driffer mo vahar	Husb. of daught. of sist. of my moth.	Mac mic driffer mo vahar	Son of son of sister of my mother.
7	Cleeamhiun phiuthar mo m'hathair	" " " " "	Ogha phiuthar mo m'hathair	Grandchild of sister of my mother.
8	Sheshey inneen shuyr my moir	" " " " "	Mac mac shuyr my moir	Son of son of sister of my mother.
9	Fy nghefnder	My cousin.	Mab fy nghefnder	Son of my cousin.
10	Shōhäri dûkhtäri hälä	Husband of daughter of mat. aunt.	Năvâdäi hälä	Grandchild of maternal aunt.
11				
12	Södskendebarns husbond	Cousin's husband.	Mosters barnebarn	Mother's sister's grandchild.
13	Madr systurdottur modur minnar	Husb. of sister's daught. of mo. my.	Sonar sonr modursystur minnar	Son's son of mother's sister my.
14	Mosters dotters man	Mother's sister's daughter's husband.	Mosters sonson	Mother's sister's son's son.
15				
16	Cousin	Cousin.	Maternal aunt's grandson	Aunt's grandson (mother's side).
17	Moejes dochters man	Aunt's daughter's husband.	Moejes klein zoon. ᵇ Neef	Aunt's grandson. ᵇ Nephew.
18	Kozyn	Cousin.	Kozyn. ᵇ Moejes groot zoon	Cousin. ᵇ Aunt's grandson.
19	Vedder	"	Vedders soohn. ᵇ Nichtes soohn	Cousin's son.
20	Vetter	"	Vetters sohn	" " "
21	Muhme schwiegersohn	Aunt's son-in-law.	Muhme enkel	Aunt's grandson.
22	Mon cousin	My cousin.	Mon cousin sous-germain	My cousin's son.
23	Primo politico	My cousin by courtesy.	Sobrino	My nephew.
24	Primo por affinidade	Cousin by affinity.	Primo distante	Distant cousin.
25	Aquistata cugino	Acquired cousin.	Secondo cugino	Second cousin.
26	Materteræ filiae vir	Husband of daught. of mat. aunt.	Materteræ nepos	Grandson of maternal aunt.
27	Anepsiou anēr	Husband of cousin.	Anepsiades	Cousin's son.
28			Theias eggonos	Aunt's grandson.
29				
30	Moj cioteczny szwagier	My broth.-in-law through mat. aunt.	Moj cioteczny bratanek	**My nephew through maternal aunt.**
31				
32				
33			Tetum vnook	Maternal aunt's grandson.
34	Mush moego dvoiurodnaja sestra	Husband of my double birth sister.	Moi dvoiurodnyi plemiannik	**My double birth nephew.**
35	Diazam kûzûnûm kojäsu	Aunt's my daughter's husband.	Diäzäm oghlû	Son of maternal aunt my.
36	Zäväh khäleh mun	Son-in-law of maternal aunt my.	Törneh khäleh mun	Grandchild of maternal aunt my.
37				
38			Minu emä odde poeg poeg	**My mother's sister's son's son.**
39	Serkkunï mies	Cousin's my husband.	Serkkunï poïka	Cousin's my son.

	103. Mother's sister's granddaughter.	Translation.	104. Mother's sister's great grandson.	Translation.
1	Bint ibn khâleti	Daughter of son of mat. aunt my.	Ibn ibn ibn khâleti	Son of son of son of mat. aunt my.
2	Bint ibn khälăti	" " " " "	Ibn ibn ibn khälăti	" " " " " "
3				
4	Näwigta d'khultee	Granddaughter of maternal aunt my.	Natija d'khultee	Great grandson of mat. aunt my.
5	Morus crocha toostrin toostra	Mother's sister's daughter's daught.	Morus crocha voretein v. voretin	Mother's sister's son's son's son.
6	Ineean mic driffer mo vahar	Daught. of sist. of sist. of my moth.	Mac mic mic driffer mo vahar	Son of son of s. of sist. of my moth.
7	Ogha phiuthar mo m'hathair	Grandchild of sister of my mother.	Iar ogha phiuthar mo m'hathair	Gt. grandchild of sist. of my mother.
8	Inneen mac shuyr my moir	Daught. of son of sist. of my mother.	Mac mac mac shuyr my moir	Son of son of s. of sist. of my mother.
9	Mereh fy nghefnither	Daughter of my cousin.	Wyr fy nghefnder	Grandson of my cousin.
10	Năvâdäi hälä	Daughter of maternal aunt.	Nätijäi hâlä	Great grandchild of maternal aunt.
11				
12	Mosters barnebarn	Mother's sister's grandchild.	Mosters barnebarns barn [nar.	Mother's sister's great grandchild.
13	Dottur dottir modursystur minnar	Daughter's d. of maternal sister my.	Sonar sonar sonr modursytur min-	Son's son's son of mater. sister my.
14	Mosters dotters dotter	Mother's sister's daughter's daught.	Mosters sonsons son	Mother's sister's son's son's son.
15				
16	Maternal aunt's granddaughter	Aunt's granddaughter (moth. side).	Maternal aunt's great grandson	Aunt's gt. grandson (mother's side).
17	Moejes klein dochter. ᵇ Nicht	Aunt's granddaughter. ᵇ Niece.	Moejes achter klein zoon. ᵇ Neef	Aunt's great grandson. ᵇ Nephew.
18	Nichte. ᵇ Moejes groote dochter	Niece. ᵇ Aunt's granddaughter.	Kozyn. ᵇ Moejes groot groot zoon	Cousin. ᵇ Aunt's great grandson.
19	Vedders dochter. ᵇ Nichte docht.	Cousin's daughter.	Vedders kinds kind	Cousin's child's child.
20	Vetters tochter	" "	Vetters enkel	Cousin's grandson.
21	Muhme enkelin	Aunt's granddaughter.	Muhme grossenkel	Aunt's great grandson.
22	Ma cousine sous-germaine	My cousin's daughter.	Le petit-fils de mon cousin	The grandson of my cousin.
23	Sobrina	My niece.	Sobrino	My nephew.
24	Prima distante	Distant cousin.	Primo distante	Distant cousin.
25	Seconda cugina	Second cousin.	Terzo cugino	Third cousin.
26	Materteræ neptis	Granddaughter of maternal aunt.	Materteræ pronepos	Great grandson of maternal aunt.
27	Anepsiadē	Cousin's daughter.	Anepsiou eggonos ?	Cousin's grandson.
28	Theias eggonē	Aunt's granddaughter.	Theias proggonos	Aunt's great grandson.
29				
30	Moja cioteczna siostrzenica	My niece through maternal aunt.	Moj cioteczny wnuk	**My grandson through maternal aunt.**
31				
32				
33	Tetuna vnooka	Maternal aunt's granddaughter.	Tetun prevnook	Maternal aunt's great grandson.
34	Moja dvoiurodnaja plemiannitza	My double birth niece.	Moi dvoiurodnyi vnutchatnyi ple- [miannik	My double birth grandson-nephew.
35	Diäzäm kûsû	Granddaughter of maternal aunt my.		
36	Törneh khäleh mun	Grandchild of maternal aunt my.	Läveh törneh khäleh mun	Son of grandchild of mat. aunt my.
37				
38				
39	Serkkunï tytär	Cousin's my daughter.	Serkkunï poïan poïkä	Son's son of my cousin.

TABLE I.—*Continued.*

	105. Mother's sister's great granddaughter.	Translation.	106. Father's father's brother.	Translation.
1	Bint bint bint khâleti...............	Daught. of d. of d. of mat. aunt my.	Amm ăbi...............................	Paternal uncle of father my.
2	Bint bint bint khălăti...............	" " " " " "	Akhu jăddi............................	" " " "
3				
4	Natijta d'khultee......................	Gt. granddaughter of mat. aunt my.	Akhŏnä d'säwŭnee....................	Brother of grandfather my.
5	Morus crocha toostrin t. toostra....	Mother's sister's dau. dau. dau.	Metz horus yäkepira...............	Grandfather's brother.
6	Ineean mic mic driffer mo vahar...	Daught. of s. of s. of sist. of my mo.	Drihär mo han ahar..................	Brother of my grandfather.
7	Iar ogha phiuthar mo m'hathair...	Gt. grandchild of sist. of my mother.	Brathair mo sheanair.................	" " " "
8	Inneen mac mac shuyr my moir...	Dau. of son of son of bro. of my mo.	Braar ayr my ayr....................	" " " "
9	Wyres fy nghefnither................	Granddaughter of my cousin.	Brawd fy hendad	" " " "
10	Nätijäi hâlä.........................	Gt. grandchild of maternal aunt.		
11				
12	Mosters barnebarns barn..[minnar	Aunt's great grandchild.	Farfaders broder......................	Grandfather's brother.
13	Dottur dottur dottir modursystur	Daughter's d. d. of mat. sister my.	Afa brodir minn.......................	Grandfather's brother my.
14	Mosters dotters dotter dotter........	Mother's sister's dau. dau. dau.	Farfars bror..........................	Grandfather's brother.
15				
16	Maternal aunt's gt. granddaught.	Aunt's gt. granddaughter (m. s.)	Paternal great uncle.................	Great uncle (father's side).
17	Moejes achter klein doch. ᵇ Nicht	Aunt's gt. granddaughter. ᵇ Niece.	Oud oom..............................	Great uncle.
18	Nichte. ᵇ Moejes groote g. docht.	Niece. Aunt's gt. granddaughter.	Groot oom............................	Great uncle.
19	Vedders kinds kind...................	Cousin's child's child.	Bess vaders brohr. ᵇ Vaders öhm	Grandfather's bro. ᵇ Father's uncle.
20	Vetters enkelinn......................	Cousin's granddaughter.	Gross oheim...........................	Great uncle.
21	Muhme grossenkelin................	Aunt's great granddaughter.	Gross oheim. ᵇ Gross onkel.......	" "
22	La petite-fille de ma cousine........	The granddaughter of my cousin.	Mon grand-oncle......................	My great uncle.
23	Sobrina	My niece.	Tio abuelo...........................	My uncle-grandfather.
24	Prima distante.......................	Distant cousin.	Tio avô..............................	Uncle-grandfather.
25	Terza cugina.........................	Third cousin.	Provo................................	Great uncle.
26	Materteræ proneptis	Gt. granddaughter of maternal aunt.	Patruus magnus......................	Great paternal uncle.
27	Anepsiou eggone ?	Cousin's granddaughter.		
28	Theias proeggonē	Aunt's gt. granddaughter.	Megas theios	Great uncle.
29				
30	Moja cioteczna wnuczka............	My granddaught. through mat. aunt.	Moj Zimny dziadek	My cold grandfather.
31			Mŭj prestryc.........................	My great uncle.
32				
33	Tetuna prevnooka.....................	Maternal aunt's great granddaughter.	Deda mi..............................	Grandfather my.
34	Moja dvoiurodnaja vnutchatnaja		Môi djed.............................	My grandfather.
35	[plemiannitza.		Dědemĭn kärndäshu	Grandfather's my brother.
36	Keezä törneh khäleh mun...........	Dau. of grandchild of mat. aunt my.	Brä bävkäleh mun....................	Brother of grandfather my.
37				
38				
39	Serkkunĭ poïan tytär.................	Daughter of the son of my cousin...	Tso setanĭ............................	Great uncle my.

	107. Father's father's brother's son.	Translation.	108. Father's father's brother's daughter.	Translation.
1	Ibn ammi ăbi	Son of paternal uncle of father my.	Bint ammi ăbi.........................	Daught. of pat. uncle of father my.
2	Ibn akhi jăddi...........................	Son of brother of grandfather my.	Bint akhi jăddi.......................	Daught. of bro. of grandfather my.
3				
4	Brŭnä d'äkhŏnä d'säwŭnee..........	Son of the brother of grandfather my.	Brätä d'äkhŏna d'säwŭnee..........	Daught. of the bro. of grandfath. my.
5	Metz horus yäkepora voretin.......	Grandfather's brother's son.	Metz horus yäkepora toostra.......	Grandfather's brother's daughter.
6	Mac drihär mo han ahar..............	Son of brother of my old father.	Ineean drihar mo han ahar.........	Daught. of brother of my grandfath.
7	Măc brăthar mo sheanair.............	" " " "	Nighean brăthar mo sheanair.......	" " " " "
8				
9				
10				
11				
12	Faders fatter..........................	Father's cousin.	Faders södskendebarn................	Father's cousin.
13	Brodur sonr afa mins.................	Brother's son of grandfather my.	Brodur dottir afa mins..............	Brother's daught. of grandfath. my.
14	Farfars brorson........................	Father's father's brother's son.	Farfar brosdotter......................	Father's father's brother's daughter.
15				
16	Paternal great uncle's son.	Great uncle's son (father's side).	Paternal gt. uncle's daughter......	Great uncle's daught. (father's side).
17	Oud ooms zoon.......................	" " " "	Oud ooms dochter	" " " "
18	Groot ooms zoon......................	Great uncle's son.	Groot ooms dochter..................	Great uncle's daughter.
19	Vaders vedder.........................	Father's cousin.	Vaders nichte........................	Father's cousin.
20	Gross oheims sohn....................	Great uncle's son.	Gross oheims tochter................	Great uncle's daughter.
21	Gross oheims sohn....................	" " "	Gross oheims tochter................	" " "
22	Le fils de mon grand-oncle.........	The son of my great uncle.	La fille de mon grand-oncle........	The daughter of my great uncle.
23				
24				
25				
26	Patrui magni filius....................	Son of great paternal uncle.	Patrui magni filia....................	Daughter of great paternal uncle.
27				
28	Megalou theiou pais..................	Son of great uncle.	Megalou theiou pais..................	Daughter of great uncle.
29				
30	Moj zimny stryj.......................	My cold uncle.	Moja zimna ciotka...................	My cold aunt.
31				
32				
33				
34	Moi dvoiurodnyi djadja..............	My double birth uncle.	Moja dvoiurodnaja tjotka...........	My double birth aunt.
35				
36	Läveh brä bävkäleh mun.............	Son of the brother of grandfather my.	Keezä brä bävkäleh mun............	Daught. of the bro. of my grandfath.
37				
38				
39	Tsănĭ serkku...........................	Father's my cousin.	Tsănĭ my serkku......................	Father's my cousin.

14   November, 1869.

TABLE I.—*Continued.*

	109. Father's father's brother's grandson.	Translation.	110. Father's father's brother's grand-daughter.	Translation.
1	Ibn ibn ammi ăbi......................	Son of son of pat. uncle of father my.	Bint ibn ammi ăbi...................	Dau. of son of p. uncle of father my.
2	Ibn ibn akhi jăddi...................	Son of son of bro. of grandfather my.	Bint ibn akhi jăddi...................	Dau. of son of bro. of gd. father my.
3				
4	Näwiga d'äkhönä d'säwŭnee..[tin	Grandson of the bro. of gd.father my.	Näwigtä d äkhönä d'säwŭnee..[tra	Gd. dau. of the bro. of gd. father my.
5	Metz horus yäkepora voretein vore-	Grandfather's brother's son's son.	Metz horus yäkepora toostrin toos-	Grandfather's brother's dau. dau.
6	Mac mic drihar mohan ahar........	Son of s. of s. of bro. of my gd.father.	Ineean mic drihar mo han ahar...	Dau. of son of bro. of my old father.
7	Ogha brŏthar mo sheanair..........	Grandchild of s. of bro. of my gd.fath.	Ogha brăthar mo sheanair..........	Grandchild of bro. of my gd. father.
8				
9				
10				
11				
12	Faders fatters sön.....................	Father's cousin's son.	Faders fatters datter.................	Father's cousin's daughter.
13	Sonar sonr brodur afa mins.........	Son's son of bro. of grandfather my.	Dottur dottir brodur afa mins......	Daughter's dau. of bro. of gd.fath. my.
14	Farfars brorsons son.................	Father's father's brother's son's son.	Farfars brorsons dotter..............	Father's father's bro. son's daughter.
15	[uncle's grandson		[uncle's granddaughter.	
16	Second cousin. ᵇ Paternal great	Second cousin.	Second cousin. ᵇ Paternal great	Second cousin.
17	Oud ooms klein zoon. ᵇ Neef.	Great uncle's grandson. ᵇ Nephew.	Oud ooms klein dochter. ᵇ Nicht	Gt. uncle's granddaughter. ᵇ Niece.
18	Kozyn. ᵇ Groot ooms groot zoon..	Cousin. ᵇ Gt. uncle's grandson.	Nichte. ᵇ Groot ooms groote doch.	Niece. ᵇ Gt. uncle's granddaughter.
19	Vadders vedders soohn..............	Father's cousin's son.	Vadders vedders dochter............	Father's cousin's daughter.
20	Gross oheims enkel..................	Great uncle's grandson.	Gross oheims enkelinn..............	Great uncle's granddaughter.
21	Gross oheims enkel..................	" " "	Gross oheims enkelin...............	" " "
22	Le petit-fils de mon grand-oncle...	The grandson of my great uncle.	La petite-fille de mon grand-oncle	The granddaughter of my gt. uncle.
23	Primo segundo......................	Second cousin.	Prima segunda	Second cousin.
24	Primo segundo......................	" "	Prima segunda	" "
25	Secondo cugino....................	" "	Seconda cugina	" "
26	Patrui magni nepos..................	Grandson of great paternal uncle.	Patrui magni neptis	Granddaughter of gt. paternal uncle.
27				
28	Deuteros exadelphos.................	Second cousin.	Deutera exadelphē....................	Second cousin.
29				
30	Moj zimny stryjeczny brat.........	My brother through cold uncle.	Moja zimna stryjeczna siostra......	My sister through cold uncle.
31				
32				
33				
34	Moi trojurodnyi brat..................	My treble birth brother.	Moja trojurodnaja sestra.............	My treble birth sister.
35				
36	Törneh brä bävkäleh mun..........	Grandchild of the bro. of gd. fath. my.	Törneh brä bävkäleh mun..........	Grandchild of the bro. of gd.fath. my.
37				
38				
39	Tsănĭ serkkuni poĭkä................	Son of cousin of father my.	Tsănĭ serkkuni tytăr..................	Daughter of cousin of father my.

	111. Father's father's brother's great grandson.	Translation.	112. Father's father's brother's great granddaughter.	Translation.
1	Ibn ibn ibn ammi ăbi................	Son of son of son of p. u. of fath. my.	Bint bint bint ammi ăbi.............	Dau. of d. of d. of p. u. of fath. my.
2	Ibn ibn ibn akhi jăddi...............	Son of s. of s. of bro. of gd. fath. my.	Bint bint bint akhi jăddi...........	Dau. of d. of d. of bro. of gd. fath. my.
3				[grandfather my.
4	Natijä d'äkhönä d'säwŭnee........	Gt. gd. son of the bro. of gd. fath. my.	Natijä d'äkhönä d'säwŭnee	Gt. granddaughter of the brother of
5	Metz horus y. voretein v. voretin	Gd. father's brother's son's son's son.	Metz horus y. toostrin t. toostra ...	Grandfather's bro. dau. dau. dau.
6	Mac mic mic drihar mo han ahar	Son of s. of s. of bro. of my gd. fath.	Ineean mic mic drihar mo han ahar	Dau. of s. of s. of bro. of my gd. fath.
7	Iar ogha brathar mo shenair.........	Gt. grandchild of bro. of my gd. fath.	Iar ogha brathar mo sheanair......	Great grandchild of brother of my
8				[grandfather.
9				
10				
11				
12	Faders fatters barnebarn..............	Father's cousin's grandchild.	Faders fatters barnebarn............	Father's cousin's grandchild.
13	Sonar sonar sonr brodur afa mins	Son's son's son of bro. of gd. fath. my.	Dottur d. dottir brodur afa mins..	Daughter's d. d. of bro. of gd. f. my.
14	Farfars brorsons sonson..............	Father's father's bro. son's son's son.	Farfars brorson dotter dotter.......	Father's father's bro. son's dau. dau.
15				
16	Paternal gt. uncle's gt. grandson	Gt. uncle's gt. grandson (fath. side).	Pat. gt. uncle's gt. granddaughter	Gt. uncle's gt. granddaughter (f. s.).
17	Oud ooms achter klein zoon. ᵇ Neef.	Gt. uncle's gt. grandson. ᵇ Nephew.	Oud ooms achter k. doch. ' Nicht	Gt. uncle's gt. granddaught.. ᵇ Niece.
18	Kozyn. ᵇ Groot ooms gt. gt. zoon	Cousin. ᵇ Gt. uncle's gt. grandson.	Nichte. ᵇ Gt. ooms gte. gte. doch.	Niece. ᵇ Gt. uncle's gt. granddau.
19	Vaders vedders kinds kind.	Father's cousin's child's child.	Vaders nichtes kinds kind.	Father's cousin's child's child.
20	Gross oheims urenkel	Great uncle's great grandson.	Gross oheims urenkelinn............	Great uncle's great granddaughter.
21	Gross oheims grossenkel	" " " "	Gross oheims grossenkelin..........	" " " "
22	L'arrière petit-fils de mon grand-	The great grandson of my gt. uncle.	L'arrière-petite-fille de mon grand-	The gt. granddaught. of my gt. uncle.
23	[oncle		[oncle	
24				
25				
26	Patrui magni pronepos...............	Gt. grandson of gt. paternal uncle.	Petrui magni proneptis...............	Gt. granddau. of gt. paternal uncle.
27				
28	Megalou theiou proeggonos.........	Great grandson of great uncle.	Megalou theiou proeggonē..........	Gt. granddaughter of great uncle.
29				
30	Moj zimny stryjeczny bratanec....	My nephew through cold uncle.	Moja zimna stryjeczna siostrzenica	My niece through cold uncle.
31				
32				
33				
34	Moi trojurodnyi plemiannik........	My treble birth nephew.	Moja trojurodnaja plemiannitza...	My treble birth niece.
35				
36	Läveh törneh btä bävkäleh mun...	Son of the grandchild of the brother	Keezä törneh brä bävkäleh mun...	Daughter of grandchild of the bro-
37		[of grandfather my.		ther of grandfather my.
38				
39	Tsănĭ serkkun poĭan poĭkä	Father's my cousin's son's son.	Tsănĭ serkkun poĭan tytăr..........	Father's my cousin's son's daughter.

TABLE I.—*Continued.*

	113. Father's father's sister.	Translation.	114. Father's father's sister's son.	Translation.
1	Ammet ăbi...............	Paternal aunt of father my.	Ibn ammet ăbi..................	Son of paternal aunt of father my.
2	Ikht jăddi...............	Sister of grandfather my.	Ibn ikhti jăddi..............	Son of sister of grandfather my.
3				
4	Khätä d'säwŭnee................	" " " "	Brünä d'khätä d'säwŭnee..........	" " " " "
5	Metz horus kooera.............	Grandfather's sister.	Metz horus crocha voretin..........	Grandfather's sister's son.
6	Driffŭr mo han ahar.........	Sister of my grandfather.	Mac driffer mo han ahar............	Son of sister of my grandfather.
7	Phiuthar mo han sheanair.........	Sister of my ancestral old father.	Mac phiuthar mo shean ăthar......	" " " "
8	Shuyr ayr my ayr.	Sister of the father of my father.		
9				
10				
11				
12	Farfaders söster................	Grandfather's sister.	Faders fatter................	Father's cousin.
13	Afa systur min..............	Grandfather's sister my.	Systur sonr afa mins................	Sister's son of grandfather my.
14	Farfars syster...............	Father's father's sister.	Farfars systerson................	Father's father's sister's son.
15				
16	Paternal great aunt............	Great aunt (father's side).	Paternal great aunt's son...........	Great aunt's son (father's side).
17	Oud moeje..............	" " " "	Oud moejes zoon..................	" " " " "
18	Groot moej..............	Great aunt.	Groote moejes zoon..............	Great aunt's son.
19	Bess vaders sister. b Vaders möhn	Grandfather's sister. b Father's aunt.	Vaders vedder.........	Father's cousin.
20	Gross muhme. b Grosstante.......	Great aunt (father's side).	Gross mume sohn..................	Great aunt's son.
21	Gross muhme. b Grosstante.......	" " " "	Gross mume sohn.................	" " "
22	Ma grand 'tante...............	My great aunt.	Le fils de ma grand' tante..........	The son of my great aunt.
23	Tia abuelo.............	My grandfather-aunt.		
24	Tia avô.............	Grandfather-aunt.		
25	Tia provo.............	" "		
26	Amita magna	Paternal great aunt.	Amitæ magnæ filius...............	Son of paternal great aunt.
27				
28	Megalē theia...............	Great aunt.	Megalēs theias pais....................	Son of great aunt.
29				
30	Moja zimna babka..............	My cold grandmother.	Moj zimny stryj?	My cold paternal uncle.
31	Ma prestyna................	My great aunt.		
32				
33	Baba mi................	Grandmother my.		
34	Moja babka................	My great aunt.	Moi dvojurodnyi djadja............	My double birth uncle.
35	Dědĕmĭn kuzkärndäshu............	Grandfather's sister my.		
36	Khooshkeh bävkäleh	Sister of grandfather my.	Läveh khooshkeh bävkäleh mun	Son of the sister of grandfather my.
37				
38				
39	Tso tătĭnĭ...............	Great aunt my.	Tso tătĭnĭ poïkä	Great aunt's my son.

	115. Father's father's sister's daughter.	Translation.	116. Father's father's sister's grandson.	Translation.
1	Bint ammet ăbi................	Daughter of pat. aunt of father my.	Ibn ibn ammet abi................	Son of son of pat. aunt of father my.
2	Bint ikhti jăddi................	Daughter of sister of grandfather my.	Ibn ibn ikhti jăddi................	Son of son of sister of grandfath. my.
3				[my.
4	Brätä d'khätä d'säwŭnee...........	" " " " "	Näwigä d'khätä d'säwŭnee	Grandson of the sister of grandfather
5	Metz horus crocha toostra..........	Grandfather's sister's daughter.	Mets horus crocha voretein voretin	Grandfather's sister's son's son.
6	Ineean driffer mo han ahar.........	Daughter of sister of my grandfather.	Mac mic driffer mo han ahar.......	Son of son of sister of my grandfath.
7	Nighin phiuthar mo shean ăthar..	" " " "	Ogha phiuthar mo sheen athar....	Grandchild of sister of my grandfath.
8				
9				
10			Cyfferder. (Pro. Keverdther)......	Second cousin.
11				
12	Faders södskendebarn...............	Father's cousin.	Faders fatters sön......................	Father's cousin's son.
13	Systur dottir afa mins...............	Sister's daughter of grandfather my.	Sonar sonr systur afa mins.........	Son's son of sister of grandfather my.
14	Farfars systers dotter...............	Father's father's sister's daughter.	Farfars systers sonson...............	Father's father's sister's son's son.
15			[aunt's grandson	
16	Paternal great aunt's daughter....	Great aunt's daughter (father's side).	Second cousin. b Paternal great	Second cousin.
17	Oud moejes dochter..................	" " " " "	Oud moejes klein zoon. b Neef....	Great aunt's grandson. b Nephew.
18	Groote moejes dochter...............	" " " " "	Kozyn. b Groote moejes groot zoon	Cousin. b Great aunt's grandson.
19	Vaders nichte..........	Father's cousin (father's side).	Vaders Vedder soohn.................	Father's cousin's son.
20	Gross muhme tochter...............	Great aunt's daughter.	Gross muhme enkel..................	Great aunt's grandson.
21	Gross muhme tochter...............	" " "	Gross muhme enkel..................	" " "
22	La fille de ma grand' tante.........	The daughter of my great aunt.	Le petit-fils de ma grand' tante....	The grandson of my great aunt.
23			Primo segundo........................	Second cousin.
24			Primo segundo........................	" "
25			Secondo cugino.......................	" "
26	Amitæ magnæ filia..................	Daughter of paternal great aunt.	Amitæ magnæ nepos................	Grandson of paternal great aunt.
27				
28	Megalēs theias pais..................	Daughter of great aunt.	Deuteros exadelphos................	Second cousin.
29				
30	Moja zimna ciotka?..................	My cold aunt.	Moj zimny cioteczny brat............	My brother through cold aunt.
31				
32				
33				
34	Moja dvojurodnaja tjotka............	My double birth aunt.	Moi trojurodnyi brat................	My treble birth brother.
35				
36	Keezä kooshkeh bävkäleh mun....	Daughter of the sister of grandfather	Törneh kooshkeh bävkäleh mun...	Grandchild of the sister of grand-
37		[my.		[father my.
38				
39	Tso tătĭnĭ tytär......................	Daughter of great aunt my.	Tsănĭ serkkun poïkä..................	Son of cousin of father my.

TABLE I.—*Continued.*

	117. Father's father's sister's grand-daughter.	Translation.	118. Father's father's sister's great grand-son.	Translation.
1	Bint bint ammet ăbi	Dau. of d. of pat. aunt of father my.	Ibn ibn ibn ammet abi	S. of s. of s. of pat. aunt of fath. my.
2	Bint bint ikhti jăddi	Dau. of d. of sister of gd. father my.	Ibn ibn ibn ikhti jăddi	S. of s. of s. of sister of gd. fath. my.
3				
4	Năwigtä d'khätä d'säwŭnee'	Ga. dau. of the sister of gd. fath. my.	Natijä d'khätä d'säwŭnee......[tin	Gt. gd. son of the sister of g. f. my.
5	Metz horus crocha toostra	Grandfather's sister's dau. daut.	Metz horus crocha voretein v. vore-	Grandfather's sister's son's son's son.
6	Ineean mic driffer mo han ahar...	Daut. of sister of sister of my gd. fa.	Mac mic mic driffer mo han ahar	S. of s. of s. of sister of my gd. fath.
7	Ogha phiuthar mo shean ăthar....	Grandchild of sister of my gd. father.	Iar ogha phiuthar mo shean ăthar	Gt. grandchild of sister of my gd. f.
8				
9	Cyfferders	Second cousin.		
10				
11				
12	Faders fatters datter	Father's cousin's daughter.	Faders fatters barnebarn	Father's cousin's grandchild.
13	Dottur dottir systur afa mins	Daughter's d. of sister of gd. fath. my.	Sonar sonar sour systur afa mins	Son's son of son of sister of gd. f. my.
14	Farfars systers dotter dotter	Father's father's sister's dau. dau.	Farfars systers sonsons son	Father's father's sisters's son's son's
15	[granddaughter			[son.
16	Second cousin.　ᵇ Pater. gt. aunt's	Second cousin.	Paternal gt. aunt's gt. grandson...	Gt. aunt's gt. grandson (fath. side).
17	Oud moejes klein dochter.　ᵇ Nicht	Gt. aunt's granddaughter.　ᵇ Niece.	Oud moejes achter k. zoon.　ᵇ Neef	Gt. aunt's gt. grandson.　ᵇ Nephew.
18	Nichte.　ᵇ Gte. moejes gte. docht.	Niece.　ᵇ Gt. aunt's granddaughter.	Kozyn.　ᵇ Groote moejes gt. gt. zoon	Cousin.　ᵇ Gt. aunt's gt. gt. gd. son.
19	Vaders nichtes dochter	Father's cousin's daughter.	Vaders vedders kinds kind	Father's cousin's child's child.
20	Gross muhme enkelinn	Great aunt's granddaughter.	Gross muhme urenkel	Great aunt's great grandson.
21	Gross muhme enkelin	"　　"　　"	Gross muhme grossenkel	"　　"　　"　　"
22	La petite-fille de ma grand' tante	The granddaughter of my great aunt.	L'arrière-petit-fils de ma grand'	The gt. grandson of my great aunt.
23	Prima segunda	Second cousin.	[tante	
24	Prima segunda	"　　"		
25	Seconda cugina	"　　"		
26	Amitæ magnæ neptis	Granddaughter of pat. great aunt.	Amitæ magnæ pronepos	Gt. grandson of paternal great aunt.
27				
28	Deutera exadelphē	Second cousin.	Megalou theia proeggonos	Great grandson of great aunt.
29				
30	Moja zimna cioteczna siostra	My sister through cold aunt.	Moj zimny ciotneczny siostrzeniec	My nephew through cold aunt.
31				
32				
33				
34	Moja trojurodnaja sestra	My treble birth sister.	Moi trojurodnyi plemiennik	My treble birth nephew.
35				
36	Törneh khooshkeh bävkäleh mun	Grandchild of the sister of gd. fa. my.	Lǎveh törneh khooshkeh bavka-	Son of grandchild of the sister of
37			[leh mun	[grandfather my.
38				
39	Tsănĭ serkkun tytăr	Father's my cousin's daughter.	Tsănĭ serkkun tyttären poĭkă	Father's my cousin's daughter's son.

	119. Father's father's sister's great grand-daughter.	Translation.	120. Mother's mother's brother.	Translation.
1	Bint bint bint ammi ăbi	D. of d. of d. of pat. aunt of fath. my.	Khâl ŭmmi	Uncle of mother my.
2	Bint bint bint ikhti jăddi	D. of d. of d. of sist. of gd. father my.	Akhu sitti	Brother of grandmother my.
3				
4	Natijtä d'khätä d'säwŭnee....[tra	Gt. granddaught. of sister of g. f. my.	Akhŏnä d'nänee	"　　"　　"　　"
5	Metz horus crocha toostrin t. toos-	Grandfather's sister's dau. dau. dau.	Metz morus yäkepira	Grandmother's brother.
6	Ineean mic mic driffer mohan ahar	Dau. of s. of s. of sister of my gd. f.	Drihar mo han vahar	Brother of my grandmother.
7	Iar ogha phiuthar mo shean ăthar	Gt. grandchild of sister of my gd. f.	Brăthair mo shean m'hathar	"　　"　　"
8			Braar moir my moir	"　　"　　"
9			Brawd fy henfan	"　　"　　"
10				
11				
12	Faders fatters barnebarn	Father's cousin's grandchild.	Mormoders broder	Grandmother's brother.
13	Dottur d. dottir systur afa mins...	Daughter's d. d. of sister of gd. f. my.	Ommubrodir min	Grandmother's brother my.
14	Farfars systers sonsons dotter	Father's father's sister's son's son's	Mormors bror	Mother's mother's brother.
15		daughter.		
16	Pat. gt. aunt's gt. granddaughter	Gt. aunt's gt. granddaughter (f. s.)	Maternal great uncle	Great uncle (mother's side).
17	Oud moejes acht. k. doch.　ᵇ Nicht	Gt. aunt's gt. granddaught.　ᵇ Niece.	Oud oom	"　　"　　"　　"
18	Nichte.　ᵇ Gte. moejes gte. gte. doch.	Niece.　ᵇ Gt. aunt's gt. granddaught.	Groot oom	Great uncle.
19	Faders nichtes kinds kind	Father's cousin's child's child.	Bess mohders brohr.　ᵇ Moders öhm	Grandmother's bro.　ᵇ Mother's uncle.
20	Gross muhme urenkelinn	Great aunt's gt. granddaughter.	Gross oheim	Great uncle (mother's side).
21	Gross muhme grossenkelin	"　　"　　"　　"	Gross oheim.　ᵇ Grossonkel	"　　"　　"　　"
22	L'arrière-petite fille de ma grand'	The gt. granddaught. of my gt. aunt.	Mon grand oncle	My great uncle.
23	[tante		Tio abuela	My grandmother-uncle.
24			Tio avó	Grandmother-uncle.
25			Tio ava	"　　"
26	Amitæ magnæ proneptis	Gt. gd. daughter of pat. great aunt.	Arunculus magnus	Maternal great uncle.
27				
28	Megalou theias proeggonē	Gt. granddaughter of great aunt.	Megas theios	Great uncle.
29				
30	Moja zimna cioteczna siostrzenica	My niece through cold aunt	Moj zimny dziadek	My cold grandfather.
31			Mŭj predujec	My great uncle.
32				
33			Deda mi	Grandfather my.
34	Moja trojurodnaja plemiannitza...	My treble birth niece.	Moi djed	My great uncle.
35			Nĕnĕnim	Grandmother's my brother.
36	Keezä törneh kooshkeh bävkäleh	Dau. of d. d. of sister of gd. f. my.	Brä däpeereh mun	Brother of grandmother my.
37	[mun			
38				
39	Tsănĭ serkkun tyttären tytär	Father's my cousin's daught. daught.	Tso ĕnonĭ	Great uncle's my.

TABLE I.—*Continued.*

	121. Mother's mother's brother's son.	Translation.	122. Mother's mother's brother's daughter.	Translation.
1	Ibn khâl ŭmmi.........................	Son of maternal uncle of mother my.	Bint khâl ŭmmi.........................	Daught. of mat. uncle of mother my.
2	Ibn ăkhi sitti	Son of brother of grandmother my.	Bint ăkhi sitti...........................	Daught. of bro. of grandmother my.
3				
4	Brŭnä d'äkhŏnä d'nänee.............	" " " " "	Brätä d'äkhŏnä d'nänee.............	" " " " "
5	Metz morus yäkepora voretin.......	Grandmother's brother's son.	Metz morus yäkepora toostra.......	Grandmother's brother's daughter.
6	Mac drihar mo han vahar...........	Son of brother of my grandmother.	Ineean drihar mo han vahar.......	Daught. of brother of my gd. mother.
7	Măc brăthar mo shean m'hather...	Son of brother of my mother.	Nighin brathar mo shean mhathar	" " " "
8				
9				
10				
11				
12	Moders fatter...........................	Mother's cousin.	Moders södskendebarn	Mother's cousin.
13	Brodur sonr ommu minna...........	Brother's son of grandmother.	Brodur dottir ommu minna.........	Brother's daughter of gd. mother my.
14	Mormors brorson......................	Mother's mother's brother's son.	Mormors brorsdotter..................	Mother's mother's brother's daught.
15				
16	Maternal great uncle's son..........	Great uncle's son (mother's side).	Maternal great uncle's daughter...	Gt. uncle's daughter (mother's side).
17	Oud ooms zoon.........................	" " " " "	Oud ooms dochter......................	" " " " "
18	Groot ooms zoon.......................	" " " " "	Groot ooms dochter....................	" " " " "
19	Mohders vedder........................	Mother's cousin (mother's side).	Mohders nichte.........................	Mother's cousin (mother's side).
20	Gross oheims sohn.....................	Great uncle's son.	Gross oheims tochter..................	Great uncle's daughter.
21	Gross oheims sohn.....................	" " "	Gross oheims tochter..................	" " "
22	Le fils de mon grand oncle..........	The son of my great uncle.	La fille de mon grand oncle.........	The daughter of my great uncle.
23				
24				
25				
26	Avunculi magni filius	Son of maternal great uncle.	Avunculi magni filia...................	Daughter of maternal great uncle.
27				
28	Megalou theiou pais...................	Son of great uncle.	Megalou theiou pais...................	Daughter of great uncle.
29				
30	Moj zimny wuj	My cold maternal uncle.	Moja zimna ciotka.....................	My cold aunt.
31				
32				
33				
34	Moi dvojurodnyi djadja..............	My double birth uncle.	Moja dvojurodnaja tjotka............	My double birth aunt.
35				
36	Läveh brä däpereh mun.............	Son of brother of grandmother my.	Keezä brä däpeereh mun.............	Daught. of brother of gd. mother my.
37				
38				
39	Tso ĕnonĭ poĭkä.........................	Great uncle's my son.	Tso ĕnonĭ tytär.........................	Great uncle's my daughter.

	123. Mother's mother's brother's grandson.	Translation.	124. Mother's mother's brother's grand-daughter.	Translation.
1	Ibn ibn khâl ŭmmi....................	S. of s. of mat. uncle of mother my.	Bint ibn khâl ŭmmi..................	Dau. of s. of mat. uncle of moth. my.
2	Ibn ibn ăkhi sitti.....................	S. of s. of brother of grandmother my.	Bint ibn ăkhi sitti....................	Dau. of s. of bro. of gd. mother my.
3				
4	Näwigä d'äkhŏnä d'nänee...[retin	Gd. son of the bro. of gd. mother my.	Näwigtä d'äkhŏna d'nänee.....[tra	Gd. dau. of the bro. of gd. mo. my.
5	Metz morus yäkepora voretein vo-	Grandmother's brother's son's son.	Metz morus yäkepora toostrin toos-	Gd. mother's brother's dau. dau.
6	Mac mic drihar mo han vahar......	Son of son of bro. of my gd. mother.	Ineean mic drihar mo han vahar..	Dau. of son of bro. of my gd. mother.
7	Ogha brăthar mo shean m'hathar	Grandchild of bro. of my gd. mother.	Ogha brăthar mo shean mhathar..	Gd. child of bro. of my grandmother.
8				
9	Cyfferder................................	Second cousin.	Cyfferders..............................	Second cousin.
10				
11				
12	Moders fatters sön....................	Mother's cousin's son.	Moders fatters datter.................	Mother's cousin's daughter.
13	Sonar sonr ommubrodur mins......	Son's son of gd. mother's bro. my.	Dottur dottir ommubrodur mins...	Daughter's d. of g. m. brother my.
14	Mormors brorsons son................	Mother's mother's brother's son's s.	Mormors brorsons dotter.............	Mother's mother's bro. son's dau.
15				
16	Second cousin. ᵇ M. g. u. g. son...	Second cousin.	Second cousin. ᵇ M. g. u. gd. dau.	Mat. gt. uncle's gd. daughter (m. s.)
17	Oud ooms klein zoon. ᵇ Neef......	Great uncle's grandson. ᵇ Nephew.	Oud ooms klein dochter. ᵇ Nicht	Gt. uncle's granddaughter. ᵇ Niece.
18	Kozyn. ᵇ Groot ooms groot zoon..	Cousin. ᵇ Great uncle's grandson.	Nichte. ᵇ Gt. ooms groote dochter	Niece. ᵇ Great uncle's gd. daughter.
19	Mohders vedders soohn...............	Mother's cousin's son.	Mohders nichte dochter..............	Mother's cousin's daughter.
20	Gross oheims enkel	Great uncle's grandson.	Gross oheims enkelin	Great uncle's granddaughter.
21	Gross oheims enkel	" " "	Gross oheims enkelin	" " "
22	Le petit-fils de mon grand oncle...	The grandson of my great uncle.	La petite-fille de mon grand oncle	The gd. daughter of my gt. uncle.
23	Primo segundo.........................	Second cousin.	Prima segunda	Second cousin.
24	Primo segundo.........................	" "	Prima segunda	" "
25	Secondo cugino........................	" "	Seconda cugina........................	" "
26	Avunculi magni nepos................	Grandson of maternal great uncle.	Avunculi magni neptis...............	Gd. daughter of mat. great uncle.
27				
28	Deuteros exadelphos..................	Second cousin.	Deutera exadelphē.....................	Second cousin.
29				
30	Moj zimny wujeczny brat............	My brother through cold mat. uncle.	Moja zimna wujeczna siostra.......	My sister through cold mat. uncle.
31				
32				
33				
34	Moi trojurodnyi brat..................	My treble birth brother.	Moja trojurodnaja sestra.............	My treble birth sister.
35				
36	Törneh brä däpeereh mun...........	Grandchild of the brother of grand-	Törneh brä däpeereh mun...........	Grandchild of the brother of grand-
37		[mother my.		[mother my.
38				
39	Aïtĭnĭ serkkun poĭkä..................	Mother's my cousin's son.	Aïtĭnĭ serkkun tytär..................	Mother's my cousin's daughter.

TABLE I.—*Continued.*

	125. Mother's mother's brother's great grandson.	Translation.	126. Mother's mother's brother's great granddaughter.	Translation.
1	Ibn ibn ibn khâl ŭmmi..............	S. of s. of s. of mat. uncle of mo. my.	Bint bint bint khâl ŭmmi..........	D. of d. of d. of mat. uncle of mo. my.
2	Ibn ibn ibn ăkhi sitti................	S. of s. of s. of bro. of gd. mo. my.	Bint bint bint akhi sitti.............	D. of d. of d. of bro. of gd. mo. my.
3				
4	Natijä d'äkhŏnä d'nänee...........	Gt. grandson of the bro. of g. m. my.	Natijtä d'äkhŏnä d'nänee..........	Gt. gd. d. of the bro. of gd. mo. my.
5	Metz morus yäkepora v. v. v.......	Grandmother's brother's son's s. s.	Metz morus yäkepora t. t. toostra	Gd. mother's brother's dau. dau. dau.
6	Mac mic mic drihar mo han vahar	S. of s. of s. of bro. of my gd. mo.	Ineean mic m. drihar mo han vahar	D. of s. of s. of bro. of my gd. mo.
7	Iar ogha brăthar mo shean m'hat- [har	Gt. gd. child of bro. of my gd. mo.	Iar ogha brăthar mo shean m'hat- [har	Great grandchild of brother of my [grandmother.
8				
9				
10				
11				
12	Moders fatters barnebarn............	Mother's cousin's grandchild.	Moders fatters barnebarn............	Mother's cousin's grandchild.
13	Sonar sonar sonr ommubrodur mins	Son's son's son of g. m. brother my.	Dottur d. dottir ommubrodur mins	Daughter's d. d. of g. m. bro. my.
14	Mormors brorson sonson............	Mother's mother's brother's son's [son's son.	Mormors brorsons dotter dotter....	Mother's mother's brother's son's [daughter's daughter.
15				
16	Maternal gt. uncle's gt. grandson	Gt. uncle's gt. grandson (m. s.).	Mat. gd. uncle's gt. gd. daughter	Pat. uncle's gt. granddaught. (m. s.)
17	Oud ooms achter k. zoon. ᵇ Neef	Gt. uncle's gt. grandson. ᵇ Nephew.	Oud ooms achter k. doch. ᵇ Nicht	Pat. uncle's gt. granddau. ᵇ Niece.
18	Kozyn. ᵇ Gt. ooms gt. groot zoon	Cousin. ᵇ Gt. uncle's gt. grandson.	Nichte. ᵇ Gt. ooms gte. gte. doch.	Niece. ᵇ Gt. uncle's gt. gd. dau.
19	Mohders vedders kinds kind.......	Mother's cousin's child's child.	Mohders nichtes kinds kind.........	Mother's cousin's child's child.
20	Gross oheims urenkel................	Great uncle's great grandson.	Gross oheims urenkelinn...........	Great uncle's great granddaughter.
21	Gross oheims grossenkel.............	" " " "	Gross oheims grossenkelin...........	" " " "
22	L'arrière petit-fils de mon gr. oncle	The gt. grandson of my great uncle.	L'arrière petite fille de mon grand [oncle	The great granddaughter of my great [uncle.
23				
24				
25				
26	Avunculi magni pronepos...........	Gt. grandson of mat. great uncle	Avunculi magni proneptis..........	Great granddaughter of mat. great [uncle.
27				
28	Megalou theiou proeggonos.........	Great grandson of great uncle.	Megalou theiou proeggonē..........	Great granddaughter of great uncle.
29				
30	Moj zimny wujeczny bratanec......	My nephew through cold mat. uncle.	Moja zimna wujeczna siostrzenica	My niece through cold mat. uncle.
31				
32				
33				
34	Moj trojurodnyi p'emiannik........	My treble birth nephew.	Moja trojurodnaja plemiannitza ...	My treble birth niece.
35				
36	Läveh tŏrneh brä däpeereh mun...	Son of grandchild of the brother of [grandmother my.	Keezä tŏrneh brä däpeereh mun...	Daughter of grandchild of brother of [grandmother my.
37				
38				
39	Aïtīnī serkkun poïan poikä.........	Mother's my cousin's son's son.	Aïtīnī serkkun poïan tytăr.........	Mother's my cousin's son's daughter.

	127. Mother's mother's sister.	Translation.	128. Mother's mother's sister's son.	Translation.
1	Khâlet ŭmmi...............	Maternal aunt of mother my.	Ibn khâlet ŭmmi.......................	Son of maternal aunt of mother my.
2	Ikht sitti	Sister of grandmother my.	Ibn ikhti sitti........................	Son of sister of grandmother my.
3				
4	Khätä d'nänee......................	" " "	Brünä d'khätä d'nänee..............	" " " " "
5	Metz morus kooera...................	Grandmother's sister.	Metz morus crocha voretin........	Grandmother's sister's son.
6	Driffür mo han vahar..............	Sister of my grandmother.	Mac driffür mo han vahar...........	Son of sister of my grandmother.
7	Phiuthar mo shean m'hathar......	" " "	Măc phiuthar mo shean m'hathar	" " " "
8	Shuyr moir my moir................	" " "		
9	Chwaer fy henfam	" " "		
10				
11				
12	Mor moders söster....................	Grandmother's sister.	Moders fatter	Mother's cousin.
13	Ommusystir min	Grandmother's sister my.	Systur sonr ommu minnar.........	Sister's son of grandmother my.
14	Mormors syster.....................	Mother's mother's sister.	Mormors systerson...................	Mother's mother's sister's son.
15				
16	Maternal great aunt.................	Great aunt (mother's side.)	Maternal great aunt's son..........	Great aunt's son (mother's side).
17	Oud moeje........................	" " " "	Oud moejes zoon...................	" " " " "
18	Groote moej.................[möhn	" " " "	Groote moejes zoon.................	" " " " "
19	Bess mohders sister. ᵇ Mohders	Gd. mother's sister. ᵇ Mother's aunt.	Mohders vedder.....................	Mother's cousin (mother's side).
20	Gross muhme. ᵇ Grosstante	Great aunt (mother's side).	Gross muhme sohn...................	Great aunt's son (mother's side).
21	Gross muhme. ᵇ Grosstante	" " "	Gross muhme sohn..................	" " " "
22	Ma grand' tante......................	My great aunt.	Le fils de ma grand' tante.........	The son of my great aunt.
23	Tia abuela............................	Grandmother-aunt.		
24	Tia avá............................	" "		
25	Tia ava............................	" "		
26	Matertera magna	Maternal great aunt.	Materteræ magnæ filius.............	Son of maternal great aunt.
27				
28	Megalē theia......................	Great aunt.	Megalēs theias pais	Son of great aunt.
29				
30	Moj zimna babka....................	My cold grandmother.	Moj zimny wuj ?.....................	My cold maternal uncle................
31	Ma stara tetka.......................	My great aunt.		
32				
33	Baba m............................	Grandmother my.		
34	Moja babka........................	My great aunt.	Moi dvojurodnyi djadja..............	My double birth uncle.
35	Nĕnĕnim kuzkärndäshu...........	Grandfather's my sister.	Läveh khoôshkeh däpeereh mun	Son of sister of grandmother my.
36	Khoôshkeh däpeereh mun..........	Sister of grandmother my.		
37				
38				
39	Tso tätīnī.......................	Great mother my.	Tso tätīnī poïka.......................	Great mother's my son.

Table I.—Continued.

#	129. Mother's mother's sister's daughter.	Translation.	130. Mother's mother's sister's grandson.	Translation.
1	Bint khâlet ŭmmi......	Dau. of mat. aunt of mother my.	Ibn Ibn khâlet ummi......	S. of son of mat. aunt of mother my.
2	Bint ikhti sitti......	Dau. of sister of grandmother my.	Ibn ibn ikhti sitti......	S. of s. of sister of grandmother my.
3				
4	Brätä d'khätä d'nänee......	" " " " "	Näwigä d'khätä d'nänee......	Gd. son of the sister of gd. mother my.
5	Metz morus crocha toostra......	Grandmother's sister's daughter.	Metz morus crocha voretein voretin	Grandmother's sister's son's son.
6	Ineean driffer mo han vahar......	Daught. of sister of my grandmother.	Mac mic driffür mo han vahar......	S. of s. of sister of my grandmother.
7	Nighin phiuthar mo shean m'hat- [har	" " " "	Ogha phiuthar mo shean m'hathar	Gd. child of sister of my gd. mother.
8				
9			Cyfferder......	Second cousin.
10				
11				
12	Moders södskendebarn......	Mother's cousin's daughter.	Moders fatters sön......	Mother's cousin's son.
13	Systur dottir ommu minnar......	Sister's daughter of grandmother my.	Sonar sonr ommu systur minnar..	Son's son of g. m. sister my.
14	Mormors systurdotter......	Mother's mother's sister's daughter.	Mormors systers sonson...... [aunt's grandson	Mother's mother's sister's son's son.
15				
16	Maternal great aunt's daughter...	Gt. aunt's daught. (mother's side).	Second cousin. ᵇ Maternal great	Great aunt's grandson (moth. side).
17	Oud moejes dochter......	" " " " "	Oud moejes klein zoon. ᵇ Neef.	Great aunt's grandson. ᵇ Nephew.
18	Groote moejes dochter......	Great aunt's daughter.	Kozyn. ᵇ Groote moejes groot zoon	Cousin. ᵇ Great aunt's grandson.
19	Mohders nichte......	Mother's cousin.	Mohders vedders soohn......	Mother's cousin's son.
20	Gross muhme tochter......	Great aunt's daughter.	Gross muhme enkel......	Great aunt's grandson.
21	Gross muhme tochter......	" " "	Gross muhme enkel......	" " "
22	La fille de ma grand' tante......	The daughter of my great aunt.	Le petit fils de ma grand' tante...	The grandson of my great aunt.
23			Primo segundo......	Second cousin.
24			Primo segundo......	" "
25			Secondo cugino......	" "
26	Matertæ magnæ filia......	Daughter of maternal great aunt.	Matertæ magnæ nepos......	Grandson of maternal great aunt.
27				
28	Megalēs theias pais......	Daughter of great aunt.	Deuteros exadelphos......	Second cousin.
29				
30	Moja zimna ciotka ?......	My cold aunt.	Moj zimny cioteczny brat......	My brother through cold aunt.
31				
32				
33				
34	Moja dvjurodnaja tjotka......	My double birth aunt.	Moi trojurodnyi brat......	My treble birth brother.
35				
36	Keezä khôshkeh däpeereh mun...	Daughter of sister of gd. mother my.	Törneh khooshkeh däpeereh mun	Grandchild of the sister of g. m. my.
37				
38				
39	Tso tätïnï tytär......	Great mother's my daughter.	Aïtïnï serkkun poïkä......	Mother's my cousin's son.

#	131. Mother's mother's sister's grand-daughter.	Translation.	132. Mother's mother's sister's great grandson.	Translation.
1	Bint ibn khâlet ŭmmi......	D. of s. of mat. aunt of mother my.	Ibn ibn ibn khâlet ŭmmi......	S. of s. of s. of mat. aunt of mo. my.
2	Bint ibn ikhti sitti......	D. of s. of sister of grandmother my.	Ibn ibn ibn ikhti sitti......	S. of s. of s. of sister of gd. mo. my.
3				
4	Näwigtä d'khätä d'nänee......	Gd. d. of the sister of gd. mother my.	Nätijä d'khätä d'nänee......	Gt. gd. son of the sister of g. m. my.
5	Metz morus crocha toostrin toostra	Gd. mother's sister's dau. dau.	Metz morus crocha v. voretin......	Gd. mother's sister's son's son's son.
6	Ineean mic driffer mo han vahar..	D· of s. of sister of my grandmother.	Mac mic mic driffer mo han vahar	S. of s. of s. of sister of my gd. mo.
7	Ogha phiuthar mo shean m'hathar	Gd. child of sister of my gd. mother.·	Iar ogha phiuthar mo m'hathar...	Gt. gd. child of sister of my gd. mo.
8				
9	Cyfferders......	Second cousin.		
10				
11				
12	Moders fatters datter......	Mother's cousin's daughter.	Moders södskendebarns barnebarn	Mother's cousin's grandchild.
13	Dottur dottir ommusystur minnar	Daughter's dau. of g. m. sister's my.	Sonar s. sonr ommusystur minnar	Son's son's son of g. m. sister my.
14	Mormors systers dotter dotter......	Mother's mother's sister's daughter's [daughter	Mormors systers sonsons son...... [son	Mother's mother's sister's son's son's [son.
15				
16	Second cousin. ᵇ Maternal great	Gt. aunt's gd. daughter (moth. side).	Maternal great aunt's great grand-	Gt. aunt's gt. grandson (moth. side).
17	Oud moejes klein dochter. ᵇ Nicht	" " " " " "	Oud moejes acht. kl. zoon. ᵇ Neef	Gt. aunt's gt. grandson. ᵇ Nephew.
18	Nichte. ᵇ Gte. moejes gte. dochter	Niece. ᵇ Gt. aunt's granddaughter.	Kozyn. ᵇ Gte. moejes gt. zoon	Cousin. ᵇ Gt. aunt's gt. grandson.
19	Mohders nichtes dochter......	Mother's cousin's daughter.	Mohders vedders kinds kind......	Mother's cousin's child's child.
20	Gross muhme enkelinn......	Great aunt's granddaughter.	Gross muhme urenkel......	Great aunt's great grandson.
21	Gross muhme enkelin......	" " "	Gross muhme grossenkel......	" " " "
22	La petite fille de ma grand' tante	The granddaughter of my gt. aunt.	L' arrière-petit-fils de ma grand' [tante	The great grandson of my great aun..
23	Prima segunda......	Second cousin.		
24	Prima segunda......	" "		
25	Seconda cugina......	" "		
26	Matertæ magnæ neptis......	The gd. daughter of mat. gt. aunt.	Matertæ magnæ pronepos......	Great grandson of mat. great aunt.
27				
28	Deutera exadelphē......	Second cousin.	Megatēs theias proeggonos......	Great grandson of great aunt.
29				
30	Moja zimna cioteczna siostra......	My sister through cold aunt.	Moj zimny cioteczny siostrzeniec	My nephew through cold aunt.
31				
32				
33				
34	Moja trojurodnaja sestra......	My treble birth sister.	Moi trojurodnyi plemiannitz......	My treble birth nephew.
35				
36	Törneh koôshkeh däpeereh mun...	Gd. child of the sister of gd. mo. my.	Läveh törneh koôshkeh däpeereh [mun	Son of grandchild of sister of grand- [mother my.
37				
38				
39	Aïtïnï serkkun tytär......	Mother's my cousin's daughter.	Aïtïnï serkkun poïan poïkä......	Mother's my cousin's son's son.

TABLE I.—*Continued.*

	133. Mother's mother's sister's great granddaughter.	Translation.	134. Father's father's father's brother.	Translation.
1	Bint bint bint khâlet ŭmmi........	D. of d. of d. of mat. aunt of mo. my.	Amm jiddi	Paternal uncle of grandfather my.
2	Bint bint bint ikhti sitti............	D. of ... of d. of sister of gd. mo. my.	Akha jadd ăbi.................	Brother of grandfather of father my.
3				
4	Nätijtä d'khätä d'nänee ....[tra	Gt. gd. d. of the sister of g. m. my.	Akhŏnă d'bäbä d'säwŭnee.........	" " " "
5	Metz morus crocha toostrin t. toos-	Gd. mother's sister's dau. dau. dau.	Metz horus horă yăkepira..........	Great grandfather's brother.
6	Ineean mic m. driffer mo han vahar	D. of s. of s. of sister of my gd. mo.	Dribăr ahar mo han ahar............	Brother of father of my grandfather.
7	Iar ogha phiuthar mo shean m'hat-	Gt. gd. child of sister of my gd. mo.	Brăthair mo shin sean air............	Brother of my ancestral grandfather.
8	[har		Braar shen shanner................	" " " "
9			Brawd fy ngorhendad	Brother of my great grandfather.
10				
11				
12	Moders södskendebarns barnebarn	Mother's cousin's grandchild.	Oldefaders broder................	Great grandfather's brother.
13	Dottur d. dottir ommusyst. minnar	Daughter's d. d. of g. m. sister my.	Langafi brodir minn	Great grandfather's brother my.
14	Mormors systers dotters dotter	Mother's mother's sister's daughter's	Farfars farbror.....................	Father's father's father's brother.
15	[dotter	[daughter's daughter.		
16	Mat. gt. aunt's gt. granddaughter	Gt. aunt's gt. gd. daughter (m. s.).	Paternal great great uncle.........	Great great uncle (father's side).
17	Oud moejes acht. kl. doch. ᵇ Nicht	Gt. aunt's gt. gd. daughter. ᵇ Niece.	Over oud oom......................	" " " " "
18	Nichte. ᵇ Gte. moejes gte. gte. doch.	Niece. ᵇ Gt. aunt's gt. gd. daughter.	Groot groot oom...................	Great great uncle.
19	Mohders nichtes kinds kind........	Mother's cousin's child's child.	Antke vaders brohr................	Great grandfather's brother.
20	Gross muhme urenkelinn..........	Great aunt's great granddaughter.	Urgross oheim....................	Great great uncle.
21	Gross muhme grossenkelin.........	" " " "	Urgross oheim. ᵇ Urgross onkel..	" " " "
22	L'arrière-petite-fille de ma grand'	The great granddaughter of my great	Le frère de mon bisaïeul.............	The brother of my great grandfather.
23	[tante	[aunt.	Tio bisabuelo	Uncle-great grandfather.
24			Tio bisavó	" " "
25			Tio bisavo......................	" " "
26	Materteræ magnæ proneptis.........	Great granddaughter of mater. great	Patruus major....................	Paternal great great uncle.
27		[aunt.		
28	Megalēs theias proeggonē...........	Great granddaughter of great aunt.	Meizōn theios....................	Great great uncle.
29				
30	Moja zimna cioteczna siostrzenica	My niece through cold aunt.	Moj zimny pradziad..................	My cold great grandfather.
31			Mŭj pra stryc.......................	My great great uncle.
32				
33			Prededa mi......................	Great grandfather my.
34	Moja trojurodnaja plemiannitza...	My treble birth niece.	Moi pradjed......................	My great great uncle.
35			Dĕdĕmïn bäbäsŭnnum karndashu..	Grandfather's my father's brother.
36	Keezä törneh kooshkeh däpeereh	Daughter of grandchild of the sister	Brä băveh băvkaleh mun............	Brother of father of grandfather my.
37	[mun	[of grandmother my.		
38				
39	Aïtïnï serkkun tyttären tytär......	Mother's my cousin's dau. dau.	Tso tsănï setă.........................	Grandfather's my uncle.

	135. Father's father's father's brother's son.	Translation.	136. Father's father's father's brother's grandson.	Translation.
1	Ibn amm jiddi..................	Son of pat. uncle of gd. father my.	Ibn ibn amm jiddi....................	Son of s. of pat. uncle of g. fa. my.
2	Ibn akhi jădd ăbi.....................	Son of bro. gd. father of father my.	Ibn ibn ibn akhi jădd ăbi	Son of s. of bro. of g. fa. of fa. my.
3				
4				[tin
5	Metz horus hora yăkepora voretin	Great grandfather's brother's son.	Metz horus hora yăkepora v. vore-	Gt. gd. father's brother's son's son.
6	Mac drihar ahar mo han ahar......	Son of bro. of father of my gd. father.	Mac mic drihar ahar mo han ahar-	Son of son of bro. of fa. of my g. fa.
7	Măc brăthar mo shin sean air......	" " " " " "	Ogha brăthar mo shin sean air....	Gd. child of bro. of my ancestral g. f.
8				
9				
10				
11				
12	Oldefaders broders sön..............	Great grandfather's brother's son.	Oldefaders broders barnebarn......	Gt. gd. father's brother's gd. child.
13	Brodur sonr langafa minn..........	Brother's son of gt. grandfather my.	Sonar sonr brodur langafa minn...	Son's son of bro. of gt. g. father my.
14	Farfars farbrors son	Father's father's father's brother's	Farfars farbrors sonson.............	Father's father's father's brother's
15		[son.		[son's son.
16	Paternal great great uncle's son..	Great great uncle's son (fath. side).	Paternal gt. gt. uncle's grandson	Gt. gt. uncle's grandson (fa. side).
17	Over oud ooms zoon..................	" " " " " "	Over oud ooms klein zaon. ᵇ Neef	Gt. gt. uncle's grandson. ᵇ Nephew.
18	Groot groot ooms zoon................	Great great uncle's son.	Groot groot ooms groot zoon.......	Great great uncle's grandson.
19	Antke vaders brohrs soohn........	Great grandfather's brother's son.	Antke vaders brohrs kinds kind...	Gt. gd. father's brother's child's child.
20	Urgross oheims sohn..................	Great great uncle's son.	Urgross oheims enkel................	Great great uncle's grandson.
21	Urgross oheims soon................	" " " "	Urgross oheims enkel............ ...	" " " "
22				
23				
24				
25				
26	Patrui majoris filius	Son of paternal great great uncle.	Patrui majoris nepos..................	Grandson of paternal gt. gt. uncle.
27				
28	Meizonos theiou pais...................	Son of great great uncle.	Meizonos theiou eggonos	Grandson of great great uncle.
29				
30				
31				
32				
33				
34			Moi trojurodnyi djadja ?............	My treble birth uncle.
35				
36	Läveh brä băveh băvkäleh mun...	Son of brother of father of grand-	Törneh brä băveh băvkäleh mun	Grandchild of the brother of father of
37		[father my.		[grandfather my.
38				
39	Tso tsănï setan poïkä.................	Great father's my uncle's son.	Tso tsănï setan poïan poïkä.........	Great father's my uncle's son's son.

TABLE I.—*Continued.*

	137. Father's father's father's brother's great grandson.	Translation.	138. Father's father's father's sister.	Translation.
1	Ibn ibn ibn amm jiddi...............	Son of s. of s. of p. uncle of g. f. my.	Ammet jiddi........................	Paternal aunt of grandfather my.
2	Ibn ibn ibn akhi jădd ăbi	Son of s. of s. of bro. of g. f. of f. my.	Ikht jădd ăbi........................	Sister of grandfather of father my.
3				
4				
5	Metz horus hora yäkepora v. v. v.	Gt. gd. father's bro. son's son's son.	Metz horus hora kooera.............	Great grandfather's sister.
6	Mac m. m. drihar ahar mo han ahar	Son of s. of s. of bro. of f. of my g. f.	Driffür ahar mo han ahar...........	Sister of father of my grandfather.
7	Iar ogha brăthar mo shin sean air	Gt gd. son of bro. of fa. of ancestral [grandfather.	Phiuthar mo shin sean air.........	Sister of fa. of my ancestral gd. fa.
8			Shuyr shen shaner.................	" " " " " " " " "
9			Chwaer fy ngorhendad..............	Sister of my great grandfather.
10				
11				
12	Oldefaders broders barnebarns barn	Gt. gd. father's brother's gd. child.	Oldefaders söster......................	Great grandfather's sister.
13	Sonar s. sonr brodur langafa minn	Son's son's son of bro. of gt. g. f. my.	Langafa syster min...................	Great grandfather's sister my.
14	Farfars farbrors sonsons son.......	Father's father's father's brother's [son's son's son.	Farfars faster......................	Father's father's father's sister.
15				
16	Third cousin. ᵇ Pat. gt. gt. uncle's	Gt. gt. uncle's gt. gd. son (fa. side).	Paternal great great aunt............	Great great aunt (father's side).
17	Over oud ooms ach. kl. zoon. ᵇ Neef	Gt. gt. uncle's gt. gd. s. ᵇ Neph. (f.s.)	Over oud moeje	" " " " "
18	Kozyn groot gt. ooms groot gt. zoon	Cousin. ᵇ Gt. gt. uncle's gt. gd. son.	Groote groote moeje...................	Great great aunt.
19	Antke vaders brohrs kinds k. k.	Gt. gd. father's brother's gt. gd. child.	Antke vaders sister..................	Great grandfather's sister.
20	Urgross oheims urenkel............	Great great uncle's great grandson.	Urgross muhme. ᵇ Urgrosstante	Great great aunt.
21	Urgross oheims grossenkel.........	" " " " "	Urgross muhme. ᵇ Urgrosstante	" " "
22				
23	Primo terceiro........................	Third cousin.	Tia bisabuelo	Aunt-great grandfather.
24	Primo terceiro........................	" "	Tiă bisavô............................	" "
25	Terzo cugino............................	" "	Tia bisavo............................	" " "
26	Patrui majoris pronepos..............	Great gd. son of pat. gt. gt. uncle.	Amita major............................	Paternal great great aunt.
27				
28	Tritos exadelphos	Third cousin.	Meizōn theia........................	Great great aunt.
29				
30			Moja zimna prababka..................	My cold great grandmother.
31			Ma prastryna	My great great aunt.
32				
33			Prebaba mi............................	Great grandmother my.
34	Moi tchetverojurodnyi brat.........	My quadruple birth brother.	Moja prababka.................[dashu	My great great aunt.
35			Dĕdĕmin bäbäsumun kuzkarn-	Grandfather's my father's sister.
36	Läveh törneh brä bävkäleh mun...	Son of grandchild of brother of [father of grandfather my.	Khoôshkeh bäveh bävkaleh mun	Son of father of grandfather my.
37				
38				
39	Tso tsănĭ setan poiăn poiăn poĭkä	Gt. fa's. my uncle's son's son's son.	Tso tsănĭ tati...............	Grandfather's my aunt.

	139. Father's father's father's sister's son.	Translation.	140. Father's father's father's sister's grandson.	Translation.
1	Ibn ammet jiddi........................	Son of pat. aunt of grandfather my.	Ibn ibn ammet jiddi.................	Son of son of pat. aunt of gd. fa. my.
2	Ibn ikht jădd ăbi......................	Son of sister of gd. father of fa. my.	Ibn ibn ikht jădd ăbi...............	Son of son of sister of grandfather [of father my.
3				
4				
5	Metz horus hora crocha voretin....	Great grandfather's sister's son.	Metz horus hora crocha v. voretin	Great grandfather's sister's son's son.
6	Mac driffür ahar mo han ahar......	Sister of sister of fa. of my gd. fa.	Mac mic driffer ahar mo han ahar	S. of s. of s. of fa. of my gd. father.
7	Măc phiuthar mo shin sean air....	Sister of sister of my ancestral gd. [father.	Ogha phiuthar mo shean sean air	Grandson of sister of my ancestral [grandfather.
8				
9				
10				
11				
12	Oldefaders sösters son..............	Great grandfather's sister's son.	Oldefaders sösters barnebarn.......	Gt. gd. father's sister's grandchild.
13	Systar sonr längafa mins............	Sister's son of great gd. father my.	Sonar sonr systur langafa mins....	Son's son of sister of gt. gd. fa. my.
14	Farfars fasters son..................	Father's father's father's sister's son.	Farfars fasters sonson..............	Father's father's father's sister's [son's son.
15				
16	Paternal great great aunt's son...	Great great aunt's son (fa's side).	Paternal gt. gt. aunt's grandson...	Great great aunt's grandson (f. s).
17	Over oud moejes zoon...............	" " " " " "	Over oud moejes klein zoon........	" " " " "
18	Groote groote moejes zoon..........	Great great aunt's son.	Groote groote moejes groot zoon...	Great great aunt's grandson.
19	Antke vaders sisters soohn........	Great grandfather's sister's son.	Antke vaders sisters kinds kind...	Gt. gd. father's sister's grandchild.
20	Urgross muhme sohn...............	Great great aunt's son.	Urgross muhme enkel...............	Great great aunt's grandson.
21	Urgross muhme sohn...............	" " " "	Urgross muhme enkel...............	" " " "
22				
23				
24				
25				
26	Amitæ majoris filius..................	Son of paternal great great aunt.	Amitæ majoris nepos.................	Grandson of pat. great great aunt.
27				
28	Meizonos theias pais.................	Son of great great aunt.	Meizonos theias eggonos............	Grandson of great great aunt.
29				
30				
31				
32				
33				
34				
35				
36	Laveh khoôshkeh bäveh bävkäleh [mun	Son of sister of father of gd. fa. my.	Törneh khoôshkeh bäveh bävkä[leh mun	Grandchild of sister of father of [grandfather my.
37				
38				
39	Tso tsănĭ serkku......................	Grandfather's my cousin.	Tso tsănĭ serkkun poĭkä.............	Grandfather's my cousin's son.

TABLE I.—*Continued.*

	141. Father's father's father's sister's great grandson.	Translation.	142. Mother's mother's mother's brother.	Translation.
1	Ibn ibn ibn ammet jiddi...........	S. of s. of s. of p. a. of gd. fa. my.	Khâl sitti......................	Maternal uncle of grandmother my.
2	Ibn ibn ibn ikht jădd ăbi..........	S. of s. of s. of sist. of gd. fa. of f. my.	Akha sitt ŭmmi.....................	Brother of gd. mother of mother my.
3				
4				
5	Metz horus hora crocha v. v. voretin	G. g. father's sister's son's son's son.	Metz morus mŏră yăkepira.........	Great grandmother's brother.
6	Mac mic m. driffer ahar mo han ahar	S. of s. of s. of fa. of my gd. fa.	Drihar mahar mo han v. ahar......	Brother of mother of my gd. mother.
7	Iar ogha phiuthar mo shin sean air	Great grandson of sister of my an- [cestral grandfather.	Brăthair mo shin sean m'hathar...	" " " " " "
8			Braar moir moir my moir............	" " " " " "
9			Brawd fy ngorhenfam...............	Brother of my great grandmother.
10				
11				
12	Oldefaders sösters barnebarns barn	Gt. gd. fa.'s sister's great grandchild.	Oldemoders broder....................	Great grandmother's brother.
13	Sonar s.sonr systur langafa mins..	Son's s. s. of sister of gt. gd. fa. my.	Langommu brodir mınn............	Great grandmother's brother my.
14	Farfars fasters sonson son...........	Father's father's father's sister's [son's son's son.	Mormors morbror....................	Mother's mother's mother's brother.
15	[aunt's great grandson.			
16	Third cousin. ᵇ Paternal great gt.	Gt. gt. aunt's gt. grandson (f. s.).	Maternal great great uncle..........	Great great uncle (mother's side).
17	Over oud moejes ach. k. z'n. ᵇ Neef	Gt. gt. aunt's gt. gd. son. ᵇ Nephew.	Over oud oom......................	" " " " "
18	Kozyn. ᵇ Gte.gte. moejes gt.gt. z'n	Cousin. ᵇ Gt. gt. aunt's gt. gd. son.	Groot groot oom......................	Great great uncle.
19	Antke vaders sisters kinds k. kind	Gt. gd. father's sister's gt. gd. child.	Antke mohders brohr..............	Great grandmother's brother.
20	Urgross muhme urenkel.............	Great great aunt's great grandson.	Urgross oheim......................	Great great uncle.
21	Urgross muhme grossenkel.........	" " " " "	Urgross oheim. ᵇ Urgross onkel..	" " "
22				
23	Primo terceiro..........................	Third cousin.	Tio bisabuela......................	Uncle-great grandmother.
24	Primo terceiro..........................	" "	Tio bisava.......................	Uncle-great grandmother.
25	Terzo cugino...........................	" "	Tio bisavá........................	" " "
26	Amitæ majoris pronepos.............	Gt. grandson of pat. gt. gt. aunt.	Avunculus major....................	Maternal great great uncle.
27				
28	Tritos exadelphos.....................	Third cousin.	Meizōn theios.......................	Great great uncle.
29				
30			Moj pradziad ?.....................	My cold great grandfather.
31			Mŭj babinec.....................	My great great uncle (mother's side).
32				
33				
34	Moi tchetverojurodnyi brat.........	My quadruple birth brother.	Prededa mi.......................	Great grandfather my.
35			Moi pradjed.....................	My great great uncle.
36	Lăveh törneh khoŏshkeh băveh	Son of grandchild of sister of father	Dĕdĕmin băbăsunum karndashu..	My grandmother's mother's brother.
37	[bävkăleh mun	[of grandfather my.	Brä deeyä dăpeereh mun...........	Brother of mother of gd. mother my.
38				
39	Tso tsănĭ serkkun poiăn poïkă....	Grandfather's my cousin's son's son.	Tso tsănĭ enŏ.....................	Grandfather's my uncle.

	143. Mother's mother's mother's brother's son.	Translation.	144. Mother's mother's mother's brother's grandson.	Translation.
1	Ibn khâl sitti.....................	Son of mat. uncle of grandmother my.	Ibn ibn khâl sitti.....................	Son of s. of mat. uncle of g. m. my.
2	Ibn akhi sitt ŭmmi....................	Son of bro. of gd. mo. of mother my.	Ibn ibn akhi sitt ŭmmi..............	Son of s. of brot. of g. m. of m. my.
3				
4				
5	Metz morus mŏră yakepora voretin	Gt. grandmother's brother's son.	Metz morus mŏră yăkepora v. v.	Gt. gd. mother's brother's son's son.
6	Mac drihar mahar mo han vahar..	Son of bro. of mother of my g. m.	Mac m. drihar mahar mo han vahar	Son of son of bro. of m. of my g. m.
7	Măc brăthar mo shin sean m'hathar	" " " " "	Ogha brathar mo shin sean m'hat- [har	Grandchild of bro. of m. of my g. m.
8				
9				
10				
11				
12	Oldemoders broders sön............	Gt. grandmother's brother's son.	Oldemoders broders barnebarn.....	Gt. gd. mother's brother's gd. child.
13	Brodur sonr langommu mins.......	Brother's son of gt. grandmother my.	Sonar sonr brodur langommu minn	Son's son of bro. of g. g. mother my.
14	Mormors morbrors son	Mother's mother's mother's brother's [son.	Mormors morbrors sonson............	Mother's mother's mother's brother's [son's son.
15				
16	Maternal great great uncle's son..	Gt. gt. uncle's son (mother's side).	Maternal great great uncle's grand-	Great great uncle's grandson (m. s.).
17	Over oud ooms zoon	" " " " " "	Over oud ooms klein zoon..........	" " " " " "
18	Groot groot ooms zoon...............	" " " " " "	Groot groot ooms groot zoon........	" " " " "
19	Antke mohders brohrs soohn.......	Great grandmother's brother's son.	Antke mohders brohrs kinds kind	Gt. gd. mother's brother's gd. child.
20	Urgross oheims sohn..................	Great great uncle's son.	Urgross oheims enkel................	Great great uncle's grandson.
21	Urgross oheims sohn	" " " "	Urgross oheims enkel................	" " " "
22				
23				
24				
25				
26	Avunculi majoris filius...............	Son of maternal great great uncle.	Avunculi majoris nepos...............	Grandson of maternal gt. gt. uncle.
27				
28	Meizonos theiou pais...................	Son of great great uncle.	Meizonos theiou eggonos............	Grandson of great great uncle.
29				
30				
31				
32				
33				
34				
35				
36	Lăveh brä deeyä dăpeereh mun...	Son of brother of mother of grand- [mother my.	Törneh brä deeyä dăpeereh mun..	Grandchild of brother of mother of [grandmother my.
37				
38				
39	Tso aïtĭnĭ serkku......................	Grandmother's my cousin.	Tso aïtĭnĭ serkkun poïkă...........	Grandmother's my cousin's son.

TABLE I.—*Continued.*

	145. Mother's mother's mother's brother's great grandson.	Translation.	146. Mother's mother's mother's sister.	Translation.
1	Ibn ibn ibn khâl sitti...............	Son of s. of s. of mat. u. f. g. m. my.	Khâlet sitti.............................	Maternal aunt of grandmother my.
2	Ibn ibn ibn akhi sitt ümmi.........	S. of s. of s. of bro. of g. m. of m. my.	Ikht sitt ümmi........................	Sister of grandmother of mother my.
3				
4				
5	Metz morus morä yäkepora v. v. v.	Gt. gd. mother's brother's son's s. s.	Metz morus morä kooera...........	Great grandmother's sister.
6	Mac m. m. drihar mahar mo h'n v'r	Son of s. of s. of bro. of m. of my g. m.	Driffür mahar mo han vahar.......	Sister of mother of my grandmother.
7	Iar ogha brathar mo shin sean	Gt. gd. child of bro. of m. of my g. m.	Phiuthar mo shin sean m'hathar	" " " "
8	[m'hathar		Shuyr moir moir my moir...........	" " " "
9			Chwaer fy ngorhenfam..............	Sister of my great grandmother.
10				
11	[barn	[grandchild.		
12	Oldemoders broders barnebarns	Great grandmother's brother's great	Oldemoders söster	Great grandmother's sister.
13	Sonar s. sonr brodur langommu m.	Son's s. s. of bro. of gt. gd. mo. my.	Langommu syster min..............	Great grandmother's sister my.
14	Mormors morbrors sonsons son.....	Mother's mother's mother's brother's	Mormors moster......................	Mother's mother's mother's sister.
15		[son's son's son.		
16	Third cousin................... [b Neef	Gt. gt. uncle's gt. grandson (m. s.).	Maternal great great aunt...........	Great great aunt (mother's side).
17	Over oud ooms achter klein zonn.	Gt. gt. uncle's gt. grandson. b Neph.	Over oud moeje	" " " " "
18	Kozyn. b Gt. gt. ooms gt. gt. zoon	Cousin. b Gt. gt. uncle's gt. gd. son.	Groote groote moej...................	Great great aunt.
19	Antke mohders brohrs kinds k. k.	Gt. gd. mother's bro. gt. gd. child.	Antke mohders sister...............	Great grandmother's sister.
20	Urgross oheims urenkel	Great great uncle's great grandson.	Urgross muhme. b Urgrosstante..	Great great aunt.
21	Urgross oheims grossenkel..........	" " " " "	Urgross muhme. b Urgrosstante..	" " "
22				
23	Primo terceiro...........................	Third cousin.	Tia bisabuela.............................	Aunt-great grandmother.
24	Primo terceiro...........................	" "	Tia bisava..............................	" "
25	Terzo cugino		Tia bisava..............................	" "
26	Avunculi majoris pronepos..........	Great grandson of maternal great	Matertera major......................	Maternal great great aunt.
27		[great uncle.		
28	Tritos exadelphos......................	Third cousin.	Meizön theia..........................	Great great aunt.
29				
30			Moja prababka ?......................	My cold great grandmother.
31			Ma babinka............................	My great great aunt.
32				
33			Prebaba mi..............................	Great grandmother my.
34	Moi tchetverojurodnyi brat..........	My quadruple birth brother.	Moja prababka...................[shu	My great great aunt.
35			Dĕdĕmin bäbäsunnum kuzkarnda-	My grandmother's mother's sister.
36	Läveh törneh brä deeyä däpeereh	Son of gd. child of brother of mother	Khöoshkeh deeyä däpeereh mun..	Sister of mother of grandmother my.
37	[mun	[of grandmother my.		
38				
39	Tso aïtïnï serkkun poiän poïkä....	Grandmother's my cousin's son's son.	Tso aïtïnï tätï...........................	Grandmother's my aunt.

	147. Mother's mother's mother's sister's son.	Translation.	148. Mother's mother's mother's sister's grandson.	Translation.
1	Ibn khâlet sitti..........................	Son of mat. aunt of grandmother my.	Ibn ibn khâlet sitti....................	Son of s. of mat. aunt of g. m. my.
2	Ibn ikht sitt ümmi......................	Son of sister of gd. mother of m. my.	Ibn ibn ikht sitt ümmi..............	Son of s. of sister of g. m. of m. my.
3				
4			[tin	
5	Metz morus morä crocha voretin...	Gt. grandmother's sister's son.	Metz morus morä c. voretein vore-	Gt. grandmother's sister's son's son.
6	Mac driffer mahar mo han vahar..	Son of sister of m. of my gd. mother.	Mac m. driffer mahar mo h'n vah'r	Son of s. of sister of m. of my g. m.
7	Mäc phiuthar mo shin sean m'hat-	" " " " "	Ogha phiuthar mo shin sean m'hat-	Gd. child of sister of m. of my g. m.
8	[har		[har	
9				
10				
11				[child.
12	Oldemoders sösters son...............	Great grandmother's sister's son.	Oldemoders sösters barnebarn......	Great grandmother's sister's
13	Systur sonar edda minn.............	Sister's son of great grandmother my.	Sonar sonr systur edda minn	Son's son of sister of g. g. m. my.
14	Mormors mosters son.................	Mother's mother's mother's sister's	Mormors mosters sonson.............	Mother's mother's mother's sister's
15		[son.		[son's son.
16	Maternal great great aunt's son....	Great gt. aunt's son (mother's side).	Maternal great great aunt's grand-	Gt. gt. aunt's gd. son (mother's side).
17	Over oud moejes zoon................	" " " " " "	Over oud ooms klein zoon...........	" " " " " "
18	Groote groote moejes zoon..........	Great great aunt's son.	Groote groote moejes groot zoon...	Great great aunt's grandson.
19	Antke mohders sisters sooln.......	Great grandmother's sister's son.	Antke mohders sisters kinds kind	Gt. gd. mother's sister's grandchild.
20	Urgross muhme sohn.................	Great great aunt's son.	Urgross muhme enkel..............	Great great aunt's grandson.
21	Urgross muhme sohn................	" " " "	Urgross muhme enkel..............	" " " "
22				
23				
24				
25				
26	Matertěræ majoris filius	Son of maternal great great aunt.	Matertěræ majoris nepos............	Grandson of mat. great great aunt.
27				
28	Meizonos theias pais...................	Son of great great aunt.	Meizonos theias eggonos............	Grandson of great great aunt.
29				
30				
31				
32				
33				
34				
35				
36	Läveh khoâshkeh deeyä däpeereh	Son of sister of mother of gd. mother	Törneh khooshkeh deeyä däpeereh	Grandchild of sister of mother of
37	[mun	[my.	[mun	[grandmother my.
38				
39	Aïdïnï aïtï serkku.....................	My grandmother's cousin.	Aïdïni aïtï serkkun poïkä...........	Grandmother's my cousin's son.

TABLE I.—*Continued.*

	149. Mother's mother's mother's sister's great grandson.	Translation.	150. Father's father's father's father's brother.	Translation.
1	Ibn ibn ibn khâlet sitti.............	Son of s. of s. of mat. a. of g. m. my.	Amm jidd ăbi......................	Pat. uncle of the gd. fath. of fath. my.
2	Ibn ibn ibn ikht sitt ümmi.........	Son of s. of s. of sister of g. m. of m.	Akha jădd jăddi......................	Brother of grandfather of gd. father
3		[my.		[my.
4	[voretin			
5	Metz morus morā crocha v. v.	G. g. mother's sister's son's son's son.	Metz horus metz horā yăkepira...	Grandfather's grandfather's brother.
6	Mac m. m. driff. m'h'r mo h'n v'h'r	S. of s. of s. of sister of m. of my g. m.	Dribăr mo han ahar mo han ahar	Brother of gd. fath. of my gd. fath.
7	Iar ogha phiuthar mo shin sean	Gt. gd. child of sist. of m. of my g. m.	Brathar mo shin sin sean air.......	" " " " " "
8	[m'hathar		Braar ayr my shen shanner........	" " " " " "
9				
10				
11	[barn.			
12	Oldemoders sösters barnebarns	Gt. gd. mother's sister's gt. g. child.	Tip oldefaders broder...............	Great grandfather's father's brother.
13	Sonar sonar sonr systur edda mins	Son's s. son of sister of g. g. m. my.	Langa langafi brodir minn..........	Gt. grandfather's gd. fa. brother my.
14	Mormors mosters sonsons son......	Mother's mother's mother's sister's	Farfars farfars bror...............	Father's father's father's father's
15		[son's son's son.		[brother.
16	Third cousin...................[b Neef	Gt. gt. aunt's gt. grandson (m. s.).	Paternal great great great uncle...	Great gt. gt. uncle (father's side.)
17	Over oud ooms achter klein zoon.	Gt. gt. aunt's gt. gd. son. b Nephew.	Over over oud oom...............	" " " " " "
18	Kozyn. b Gte. gte. moejes gt. zoon	Cousin. b Gt. gt. aunt's gt. gd. son.	Groot groot groot oom...............	Great great great uncle.
19	Antke mohders sisters kinds k. k.	Gt. gd. mother's sister's gt. gd. child.	Antke vaders vaders brohr.........	Great grandfather's father's brother.
20	Urgross muhme urenkel.............	Great great aunt's great grandson.	Ururgross oheim...............	Great great great uncle.
21	Urgross muhme grossenkel.........	" " " " "	Ururgross oheim......................	" " " " "
22				
23	Primo terceiro..........................	Third cousin.		
24	Primo terceiro..........................	" "		
25	Terzo cugino............................	" "		
26	Materteræ majoris pronepos.........	Great grandson of mat. great great	Patruus maximus......................	Paternal great great great uncle.
27		[aunt.		
28	Tritos exadelphos......................	Third cousin.	Megistos theios........................	Great great great uncle.
29				
30				
31				
32				
33				
34	Moi tchteverojurodnyi brat.........	My quadruple birth brother.		
35				
36	Törneh koóshkeh deeyä däpeereh	Grandchild of sister of mother of	Brä bävkäleh bävkäleh mun.......	Brother of grandfather of grandfather
37	[mun	[grandmother my.		[my.
38				
39	Aïdïn aïtï serkkun poïăn poïkä....	Grandmother's my cousin's son's son.		

	151. Father's father's father's father's brother's son.	Translation.	152. Father's father's father's father's brother's grandson.	Translation.
1	Ibn amm jidd ăbi......................	Son of pat. unc. of g. f. of fath. my.	Ibn ibn amm jidd ăbi..............	Son of s. of pat. unc. of g. f. of f. my.
2	Ibn akhi jadd jăddi..................	Son of brother of grandfather of gd.	Ibn ibn akhi jădd jăddi............	Son of s. of bro. of g. f. of g. f. my.
3		[father my.		
4	[voretin			
5	Metz horus metz hora yakepora	Grandfather's grandfather's bro. son.	Metz h. metz h. y. voretein voretin	Gd. father's gd. father's bro. son's s.
6	Mac drih. mo h'n ah'r mo h'n ah'r	Son of bro. of gd. fath. of my gd. fa.	Mac mic drih. mo han ahar m. h. a.	Son of s. of bro. of gd. fa. of my g. f.
7	Măc brathar mo shin sin sean air	" " " " " "	Ogha brăthar mo shin sin sean air	Gd. child. of bro. of gd. fa. of my g. f.
8				
9				
10				
11				
12	Tip oldefadders broders sön.........	Gt. gd. father's father's brother's son.	Tip oldefaders broders barnebarn	Gt. gd. father's fath. bro. gd. child.
13	Brodur sonr langa langafi minns...	Brother's son of gd. fa. gd. fa. my.	Sonar sonr brod. langa langafi mins	Son's son of bro. of gd. fa. gd. fa. my.
14	Farfar farfars brorson...............	Father's father's father's father's	Farfars farfars brorsons son.........	Father's father's father's father's
15		[brother's son.		[brother's son's son.
16	Paternal great gt. gt. uncle's son	Gt. gt. gt. uncle's son (father's side)	Paternal great great great uncle's	Gt. gt. gt. uncle's grandson (f. s.)
17	Over over oud ooms zoon............	" " " " " "	Over over oud ooms klein zoon....	" " " " " "
18	Groot groot groot ooms zoon........	Great great great uncle's son.	Groot groot groot ooms groot zoon	Great great great uncle's grandson.
19	Antke vaders vaders brohrs sohn	Gt. gd. father's father's bro. son.	Antke vaders v. brohrs kinds kind	Gt. gd. father's fath. bro. gd. child.
20	Ururgross oheims sohn...............	Great great great uncle's son.	Ururgross oheims enkel...............	Great great great uncle's grandson.
21	Ururgross oheims sohn...............	" " " " "	Ururgross oheims enkel............	" " " " "
22				
23				
24				
25				
26	Patrui maximi filius..................	Son of pater. great great great uncle.	Patrui maximi nepos..................	Grandson of pat. gt. gt. gt. uncle.
27				
28	Megistou theiou pais..................	Son of great great great uncle.	Megistou theiou eggonos.............	Grandson of great great great uncle.
29				
30				
31				
32				
33				
34				
35				
36				
37				
38				
39				

TABLE I.—*Continued.*

	153. Father's father's father's father's brother's great grandson.	Translation.	154. Father's father's father's father's sister.	Translation.
1	Ibn ibn ibn amm jidd ăbi..........	Son of s. of s. of p. u. of g. f. of f. my.	Ammet jidd ăbi........................	Pat. aunt of gd. father of father my.
2	Ibn ibn ibn akhi jădd jăddi.......	Son of s. of s. of brother of gd. father	Ikht jădd jăddi........................	Sister of gd. father of gd. father my.
3		[of grandfather my.		
4				
5	[mo han ahar	[of my grandfather.	Metz horus metz horus kooerä.....	Grandfather's grandfather's sister.
6	Mac mic mic drihar mo han ahar	Son of s. of s. of brother of gd. father	Diffür mo han ahar mo han ahar..	Sister of gd. father of my gd. father.
7	Iar ogha brathar mo shin sin sean	Gt. gd. child of brother of gd. father	Phiuthar mo shin sin sean air.....	" " " " "
8	[air	[of my grandfather.	Shuyr moir my shen shauner......	" " " " "
9				
10				
11	[barn	[grandchild.		
12	Tip oldefaders broders barnebarns	Gt. gd. father's father's brother's gt.	Tip oldefaders söster..................	Gt. grandfather's father's sister.
13	Sonar s. s. bro. langa langafi mins	Son's s. s. of bro. of g. f. g. f. my.	Langa langafa systur min..........	Gd. father's grandfather's sister my.
14	Farfars farfars brorsons sonson....	Father's father's father's father's	Farfars farfars systur.................	Father's father's father's father's
15	[great grandson	[brother's son's son's son.		[sister.
16	Paternal great great great uncle's	Gt. gt. gt. uncle's gt. gd. son (f. s.).	Paternal great great great aunt....	Great great great aunt (father's side).
17	Over o. oud ooms acht. klein zoon	" " " " " "	Over over oud moeje..................	" " " " "
18	Kozyn. ᵇGt. gt.gt ooms gt.gt. zoon	Cousin. ᵇ Gt. gt. gt. uncle's gt. gd. s.	Groote groote groote moeje.........	Great great great aunt.
19	Antke vaders v. brohrs. kinds k. k.	Gt. gd. fath. fath. bro. gt. gd. child.	Antke vaders vaders sister........	Gt. grandfather's father's sister.
20	Ururgross oheims urenkel...........	Great gt. gt. uncle's gt. grandson.	Ururgross muhme..................	Great great great aunt.
21	Ururgross oheims urenkel...........	" " " " "	Ururgross muhme..................	" " " " "
22				
23				
24				
25				
26	Patrui maximi pronepos.............	Great grandson of pater. great great	Amita maxima........................	Paternal great great great aunt.
27		[great uncle.		
28	Mogistou theiou proggonos..........	Great grandson of great great great	Megiotē theia	Great great great aunt.
29		[uncle.		
30				
31				
32				
33				
34				
35				
36			Koôshkeh bävkäleh bävkäleh mun	Sister of gd. father of gd. father my.
37				
38				
39				

	155. Father's father's father's father's sister's son.	Translation.	156. Father's father's father's father's sister's grandson.	Translation.
1	Ibn ammet jidd ăbi....................	Son of pat. aunt of gd. fa. of fa. my.	Ibn ibn ammet jidd ăbi..............	Son of s. of pat. aunt of g. f. of f. my.
2	Ibn ikht jădd jăddi....................	Son of sister of gd. fa. of gd. fa. my.	Ibn ibn ikht jădd jăddi.............	Son of s. of sister of g. f. of g. f. my.
3				
4				[tin
5	Metz horus metz h. crocha voretin	Gd. father's gd. father's sister's son.	Metz horus metz h. crocha v. vore-	Gd. father's gd. father's sister's son.
6	Mac driffür mo han ahar m. h. a.	Son of sister of gd. fa. of my gd. fa.	Mac mic driffür mo han ahar m.h.a.	Son of s. of sister of g. f. of my g. f.
7	Măc phiuthar mo shin sin sean air	Son of sister of my old father of old	Ogha phiuthar mo shin sin sean	Gd. child of sister of my old father's
8		[father.	[air	[old father.
9				
10				
11				
12	Tip oldefaders sösters sön...........	Gt. gd. father's father's sister's son.	Tip oldefaders sösters barnebarn...	Gt. gd. father's fath. sist. gd. child.
13	Systur sonr langa langafi mins.....	Sister's son of gd. fath. gd. fath. my.	Sonar sonr syst. langa langafi min	Son's son of sister of g. f. g. f. my.
14	Farfars farfars syster son............	Father's father's father's father's	Farfars farfars systersons son......	Father's father's father's father's
15		[sister's son.		[sister's son's son.
16	Paternal gt. gt. gt. aunt's son......	Gt. gt. gt. aunt's son (father's side).	Pat. gt. gt. gt. aunt's grandson....	Great great gt. gt. aunt's gd. son (f. s.).
17	Over over oud moejes zoon..........	" " " " " "	Over over oud moejes klein zoon..	" " " " " "
18	Groote groote groote moejes zoon	" " " " " "	Groote groote gte. moejes gt. zoon	" " " " " "
19	Antke vaders vaders sisters soohn	Gt. gd. father's father's sister's son.	Antke vaders vaders sisters k. k.	Gt. gd. father's fath. sist. gd. child.
20	Ururgross muhme sohn..............	Great great great aunt's son.	Ururgross muhme enkel.............	Great great great aunt's grandson.
21	Ururgross muhme sohn.............	" " " " "	Ururgross muhme enkel.............	" " " " "
22				
23				
24				
25				
26	Amitæ maximæ filius.................	Son of pat. great great great aunt.	Amitæ maximæ nepos	Grandson of pat. gt. gt. gt. aunt.
27				
28	Megiotes theias pias	Son of great great great aunt.	Megiotēs theias eggonos..............	Grandson of great great great aunt.
29				
30				
31				
32				
33				
34				
35				
36				
37				
38				
39				

TABLE I.—*Continued.*

	157. Father's father's father's father's sister's great grandson.	Translation.	158. Mother's mother's mother's mother's brother.	Translation.
1	Ibn ibn ibn ammet jidd ăbi........	S. of s. of s. of p. a. of g. f. of f. my.	Khâl sitt ŭmmi.....................	Mat. uncle of gd. mo. of mother my.
2	Ibn ibn ibn ikht jădd jăddi........	S. of s. of s. of sist. of g. f. of g. f. my.	Akha sitt sitti.....................	Brother of gd. mo. of gd. mother my.
3				
4		[son.		
5	M. h. m. h. c. voretein v. voretin	Gd. father's gd. fa. sister's son's son's	Metz morus metz morus yäkepira	Gd. mother's gd. mother's brother.
6	Mac m. m. driff. mo han ahar m.h.a.	S. of s. of s. of sist. of g. f. of my g. f.	Drihăr mo han vahair m. h. v.....	Brother of gd. mother of my gd. mo.
7	Iar ogha phiuthar mo shin sin sean	Great grandchild of sister of my old	Brăthar mo shin sin sean m'hat-	Brother of my old mother's old mo.
8	[air	[father's old father.	[hair	[hair
9				
10				
11	[barn	[great grandchild.		
12	Tip oldefaders sösters barnebarns	Great grandfather's father's sister's	Tip oldefaders broder.................	Gt. grandmother's môther's brother.
13	Sonar s. s. syst. langa langafi mins	Son's son's s. of sist. of g. f. f. my.	Langa langommu brodir minn......	Gd. mother's gd. mother's bro. my.
14	Farfars farfars systersons son......	Father's father's father's father's sis-	Mormors mormors bror............	Mother's mother's mother's mother's
15	[great grandson	[ter's son's son.		[brother.
16	Paternal great great great aunt's	Gt. gt. gt. aunt's gt. gd. son (f. s.).	Maternal great great great uncle..	Great gt. gt. uncle (mother's side).
17	Over o. oud moejes acht. kl. zoon	" " " " " " "	Over over oud oom................	" " " " " "
18	Kozyn. ᵇ Gte. gte. gte. moejes g.g.z.	Cousin. ᵇ Gt. gt. gt. aunt's gt. gd. s.	Groot groot groot oom...............	" " " " " "
19	Antke vaders v. sisters kinds k. k.	Gt. gd. fa. fa. sister's gt. gd. child.	Antke mohders mohders brohr....	Great gd. mother's mother's brother.
20	Ururgross muhme urenkel..........	Gt. gt. gt. aunt's great grandson.	Ururgross oheim..................	Great great great uncle.
21	Ururgross muhme grossenkel......	" " " " " "	Ururgross oheim.....................	" " " " "
22				
23				
24				
25				
26	Amitæ maximæ pronepos...........	Great grandson of paternal great gt.	Avunculus maximus................	Maternal great great great uncle.
27		[great aunt.		
28	Megiotēs theias proeggonos........	Great grandson of great great great	Megistos theios.....................	Great great great uncle.
29		[aunt.		
30				
31				
32				
33				
34				
35				
36			Brä däpeereh däpeereh mun.......	Brother of grandmother of gd.mother
37				[my
38				
39				

	159. Mother's mother's mother's mother's brother's son.	Translation.	160. Mother's mother's mother's mother's brother's grandson.	Translation.
1	Ibn khâl sitt ŭmmi.....................	Son of mat. unc. of g. m. of mo. my.	Ibn ibn khâl ŭmmi	Son of s. of m. u. of g. m. of m. my.
2	Ibn akhi sitt sitti.....................	Son of brother of g. m. of g. m. my.	Ibn ibn akhi sitt sitti	Son of s. of bro. of g. m. of g. m. my.
3				
4				[son's son.
5	M. m. m. m. yäkepora voretin......	Gd. mother's gd. mother's bro. son.	M. m. m. m. y. voretein voretin	Gd. mother's gd. mother's brother's
6	Mac drihăr mo han vahair m. h. v.	Son of bro. of gd. mo. of my gd. mo.	Mac mic drihar mo h. v. mo h. v.	Son of s. of bro. of g. m. of my g. m.
7	Măc brăthar mo shin sin sean m'	Son of brother of my old mother's	Ogha brathar mo shin sin sean	Grandchild of brother of my old mo-
8	[hathar	[old mother.	[m'hathar	[ther's old mother.
9				
10				
11				[grandchild.
12	Tip oldemoders broders sön.........	Gt. gd. mother's mother's bro. son.	Tip oldemoders broders barnebarn	Great gd. mother's mother's brother's
13	Brodur sonr langa langommu mins	Brother's son of gd. mo. gd. mo. my.	Sonar s. bro. langa langommu mins	Son's son of bro. of g. m. g. m. my.
14	Mormors mormors brorson.........	Mother's mother's mother's mother's	Mormors mormors brorsons son....	Mother's mother's mother's mother's
15		[brother's son.	[grandson	[brother's son's son.
16	Mat. great gt. gt. uncle's son......	Great great great uncle's son (m. s.).	Maternal great great great uncle's	Gt. gt. gt. uncle's grandson (m. s.).
17	Over over oud ooms zoon............	" " " " " "	Over over oud ooms klein zoon...	" " " " " "
18	Groot groot groot ooms zoon........	" " " " " "	Groot groot groot ooms groot zoon	" " " " " "
19	Antke mohders moh. brohrs soohn.	Gt. gd. mother's mother's bro. son.	Antke mohders m. bro kinds k.	Gt. gd. mo. mother's bro. gd. child.
20	Ururgross oheims sohn...............	Great great great uncle's son.	Ururgross oheims enkel	Great great great uncle's grandson.
21	Ururgross oheims sohn............	" " " " " "	Ururgross oheims enkel.............	" " " " " "
22				
23				
24				
25				
26	Avunculi maximi filius..............	Son of maternal great great great	Avunculi maximi nepos.............	Gd. son of maternal great great great
27		[uncle.		[uncle.
28	Megistou theiou pais..................	Son of great great great uncle.	Megistou theiou eggonos............	Grandson of great great great uncle.
29				
30				
31				
32				
33				
34				
35				
36				
37				
38				
39				

TABLE I.—*Continued.*

	161. Mother's mother's mother's mother's brother's great grandson.	Translation.	162. Mother's mother's mother's mother's sister.	Translation.
1	Ibn ibn ibn khâl sitt ŭmmi........	S. of s. of s. of m. u. of g. m. of m. my.	Khâlet sitt ŭmmi......................	Mat. aunt of gd. moth. of moth. my.
2	Ibn ibn ibn akhi sitt sitti...........	S. of s. of s. of bro. of g. m. of g. m. my.	Ikht sitt sitti..................	Sister of gd. moth. of gd. moth. my.
3				
4		[son's son's son.		
5	Metz m. metz m. y. v. v. voretin	Gd. mother's gd. mother's brother's	Metz morus metz morä kooerä.....	Grandmother's grandmother's sister.
6	Mac m. m. drihar m. h. v. m. h. v.	S. of s. of s. of bro. of g. m. of my g.m.	Driffür mo han vahair mo han v'r	Sister of gd. moth. of my gd. moth.
7	Iar ogha brathar mo shin sin sean	Gt. gd. child of brother of my old	Phiuthar mo shin sin sean m'hat-	Sister of my old mother's old mother.
8	[m'hathar	[mother's old mother.	[har	
9				
10				
11	[barns barn	[great grandchild.		
12	Tip oldemoders broders barne-	Gt. gd. mother's brother's	Tip oldemoders söster.................	Great grandmother's mother's sister.
13	Sonar s. s. bro. langa l'mmu mins	Son's s. s. of bro. of g. m. g. m. my.	Langa langommu systirr min......	Gd. mother's gd. mother's sister my.
14	Mormors mormors brorson sonson	Mother's mother's mother's mother's	Mormors mormors syster	Mother's mother's mother's mother's
15		[great grandson		[sister.
16	Maternal great great great uncle's	Gt. gt. gt. uncle's gt. gd. son (m. s.).	Maternal great great great aunt...	Great great gt. aunt (mother's side).
17	Over o. oud ooms achter klein zoon	" " " " " " "	Over over oud moeje.................	" " " " " "
18	Kozyn. b Gt. gt. ooms gt. gt. zoon	Cousin. b Gt. gt. uncle's gt. gd. s.	Groote groote groote moeje.........	" " " " " "
19	Antke mohders ·m. brohrs k. k. k.	Gt. gd. mo. mo. bro. gt. gd. child.	Antke mohders mohders sister....	Great grandmother's mother's sister.
20	Ururgross oheims urenkel...........	Great gt. gt. uncle's gt. grandson.	Ururgross muhme...................	Great great great aunt.
21	Ururgross oheims grossenkel.......	" " " " " "	Ururgross muhme..................	" " " "
22				
23				
24				
25				
26	Avunculi maximi pronepos.........	Great grandson of mater. great great	Matertera maxima....................	Maternal great great great aunt.
27		[great uncle.		
28	Megiston theiou proggonos..........	Great grandson of great great	Megistē theia....................	Great great great aunt.
29		[uncle.		
30				
31				
32				
33				
34				
35				
36				
37			Khoôshkeh däpeereh däpeereh mun	Sister of grandmother of grandmother
38				[my.
39				

	163. Mother's mother's mother's mother's sister's son.	Translation.	164. Mother's mother's mother's mother's sister's grandson.	Translation.
1	Ibn khâlet sitt ŭmmi..................	Son of mat. aunt of g. m. of mo. my.	Ibn ibn khâlet sitt ŭmmi...........	S. of s. of mat. u. of g. m. of m. my.
2	Ibn ikht sitt sitti......................	Son of sister of g. m. of g. m. my.	Ibn ibn ikht sitt sitti................	S. of s. of sister of g. m. of g. m. my.
3				
4				
5	Metz m. metz m. crocha voretin...	Gd. mother's gd. mother's sist. son.	M. m. m. m. c. voretein voretin...	Gd. mo. gd. mo. sister's son's son.
6	Mac driffür mo han vahair m. h. v.	Son of sister of gd. mo. of my gd. mo.	Mac mic driffer m. h. v. m. h. v.	S. of s. of sister of g. mo. of my g. m.
7	Mãc phiuthar mo shin sin sean	Son of sister of my old mother's old	Ogha phiuthar mo shin sin sean	Gd. child of sister of my old mother's
8	[m'hathar	[mother.	[m'hathar	[old mother.
9				
10				
11				[grandchild.
12	Tip oldemoders sösters sön.........	Gt. gd. mother's mother's sist. son.	Tip oldemoders sösters barnebarn	Gt. grandmother's mother's sister's
13	Systur sonr langa langommu mins	Sister's son of gd. mo. gd. mo. my.	Sonar s. syst. langa l'ommu mins	Son's son of sister of g. m. g. m. my.
14	Mormors mormors systerson........	Mother's mother's mother's mother's	Mormors mormors systers sonson..	Mother's mother's mother's mother's
15		[sister's son.		[sister's son's son.
16	Maternal gt. gt. gt. aunt's son.....	Gt. gt. gt. aunt's son (mother's side).	Mat. gt. gt. gt. aunt's grandson...	Gt. gt. gt. aunt's grandson (m. s.)
17	Over over oud mojes zoon...........	" " " " " " "	Over over oud moejes klein zoon..	" " " " " "
18	Groote groote groote moejes zoon..	" " " " " "	Groote groote gte. moejes klein zoon	" " " " " "
19	Antke mohders mohders sist. soohn	Gt. gd. mother's mother's sist. son.	Antke mohders m. sisters kinds k.	Gt. gd. mother's sister's grandchild.
20	Ururgross muhme sohn..............	Great great great aunt's son.	Ururgross muhme enkel............	Great great great aunt's grandson.
21	Ururgross muhme sohn.............	" " " " "	Ururgross muhme enkel............	" " " " "
22				
23				
24				
25				
26	Materteræ maximæ filius	Son of mat. great great great aunt	Materteræ maximæ nepos............	Grandson of matern. gt. gt. gt. aunt.
27				
28	Megistēs theias pais...................	Son of great great great aunt.	Megistēs theias eggonos.............	Grandson of great great great aunt.
29				
30				
31				
32				
33				
34				
35				
36				
37				
38				
39				

Table I.—*Continued.*

	165. Mother's mother's mother's mother's sister's great grandson.	Translation.	166. Husband.	Translation.
1	Ibn ibn ibn khâlet sitt ŭmmi........	S. of s. of s. of m. a. of g. m. of m. my.	Zôji	Husband my.
2	Iqn ibn ibn ikht sitt sitti............	S. of s. of s. of sist. of g. m. of g. m. my.	Zauji	" "
3			Ishī	Husband my (lit. man my).
4	[tin		Goree	Husband my.
5	Metz m. metz m. crocha v. v. vore-	Gd. mo. gd. mo. sist. son's son's son.	Aregă................	" "
6	Mac mic m. driffer m. h. v. m. h. v.	S. of s. of s. of sis. of g. m. of my g. m.	Mo arh. b Mar	My husband.
7	Iar ogha phiuthar mo shin sin sean	Great grandchild of sister of my old	M'fhear pósda................	" "
8	[m'hathar	[mother's old mother.	My sheshey................	" "
9			Fy gwr (pr. goor)................	" "
10			Shōhăr................	Husband.
11	[barn	[great grandchild.	Pati. b Bhartar. c Dhavar........	"
12	Tip oldemoders sösters barnebarns	Great grandmother's mother's sister's	Husbond. b Mand. c Gemal......	
13	Sonar s. s. syst. langa l'ommu mins	Son's s. s. of sist. of g. m. g. m. my.	Madr (bondi) min................	Husband my.
14	Mormors mormors systersons son-	Mother's mother's mother's mother's	Man................	Man.
15	[son	[sister's son's son's son.	Huv. b Wir. c Bonda............	Husband.
16	Mat. gt. gt. gt. aunt's grandson...	Gt. gt. gt. aunt's gt. gd. son (m. s.).	Husband. Consort.	"
17	Over o. oud moejes acht. kl. zoon	" " " " " " "	Man. b Gade. c Gemaal............	"
18	Kozyn. b Ge. ge. ge. moejes g. g. z.	Cousin. b Gt. gt. gt. aunt's gd. s.	Man................	"
19	Antke mohders m. sisters k. k. k.	Gt. gd. mother's sister's gt. gd. child.	Man................	"
20	Ururgross muhme urenkel..........	Great gt. gt. aunt's great grandson.	Mann. b Gatte. c Gemahl........	"
21	Ururgross muhme grossenkel......	" " " " " "	Gatte................	"
22			Mon mari. b Monépoux............	My husband.
23			Marido................	" "
24			Marido................	Husband.
25			Marito................	
26	Materteræ maximæ pronepos.......	Great grandson of maternal great	Vir. b Maritus................	"
27		[great great aunt	Anēr................	"
28	Megistēs theias proeggonos.........	Great grandson of great great	Rum................	"
29		[aunt.	Măno pats................	My husband.
30			Moj maz. b Matzonek............	" "
31			Mŭj manzel................	" "
32			Mŭzh mi................	Husband my.
33			Muzh mi................	" "
34			Moi mush................	My husband.
35			Kojä-m................	Husband my. b Old man.
36			Mĕreh mun................	Husband my.
37			Ferjem. b Uram................	Lord my.
38			Mees................	Husband.
39			Mĭehenĭ................	Man my. b Consort.

	167. Husband's father.	Translation.	168. Husband's mother.	Translation.
1	Ammi................	Uncle my.	Amrât ammi................	Wife of uncle my.
2	Ammi. b Hami................	" "	Hamati................	Mother-in-law my.
3	Khāmī................	Father-in-law my.	Kh' mōthī................	" " " "
4	Khumyänee................	" " " "	Khmätee................	" " " "
5	Geshire................	Half father.	Ges sure................	Half mother.
6	Ahair mo chēlī................	My other's father.	Mahair mo chēlī................	My other's mother.
7	M'athar ceille................	" " "	Mo mhathair cheille................	" " "
8	Ayr sy laigh................	" " "	Moir si laigh................	" " "
9	Tad fy ngwr................	Father of my husband.	Mam fy ngwr................	Mother of my husband.
10				
11	Çvaçura. b Pûjya................	Father-in-law.	Gurupaturī................	Mother-in-law.
12	Svigerfader................	" " "	Svigermoder................	" " "
13	Tengdafadir min................	Father-in-law my.	Tengdamodir min................	Mother-in-law my.
14	Svärfar................	Father-in-law.	Svärmor................	Mother-in-law.
15	Sweor. b Stheor................	" " "	Sweger................	" " "
16	Father-in-law................	" " "	Mother-in-law................	" " "
17	Behuwd vader................	" " "	Behuwd moeder................	" " "
18	Schoon vader................	" " "	Schoone moeder................	" " "
19	Vader................	Father.	Mohder................	Mother.
20	Schwiegervater. b Schwäher......	Father-in law.	Schwiegermutter................	Mother-in-law.
21	Schwiegervater................		Schwiegermutter................	
22	Mon beau-père................	My father-in-law.	Ma belle-mère................	My mother-in-law.
23	Suegro................	Father-in-law.	Suegra................	Mother-in-law.
24	Sōgro................	" " "	Sogra................	" " "
25	Suecero................	" " "	Suocera................	" " "
26	Socer................	" " "	Socrus................	" " "
27	Pentheras. b Hekuros............	" " "	Penthera. b Hekura................	" " "
28				
29	Măno szēszuras................	My husband's father.	Măno anytă................	My husband's mother.
30	Moj swicker................	My father-in-law.	Moja swickra................	My mother-in-law.
31	Mŭj swoker................	" " " "	Ma swokra................	" " " "
32	Svekr mi................	Father-in-law my.	Svekŭrva mi................	Mother-in-law my.
33	Svekur mi................	" " " "	Svekurva mi................	" " " "
34	Moi sveker................	My father-in-law.	Moja svekror................	My mother-in-law.
35	Kayni băbăm................	" " " "	Kayni änäm................	" " " "
36	Băveh mĕreh mun................	Father of husband my.	Kheshäreh mun................	Mother-in-law my.
37	Ipam................		Napam................	
38				
39	Appīnĭ................	Father-in-law my.	Anopīnĭ................	Mother-in-law my.

TABLE I.—*Continued.*

	169. Husband's grandfather.	Translation.	170. Husband's grandmother.	Translation.
1	Jidd zôji.............................	Grandfather of husband my.	Sitt zôji.............................	Grandmother of husband my.
2	Jadd zauji........................	" " " "	Sitt zauji.............................	" " " "
3				
4	Säwŭnä d'goree......................	" " " "	Säwŭnta d'goree....................	" " " "
5	Geshirze metz hirä..................	Father of my half father.	Gessrochchus metz mirä..........	" " " "
6	Mo han ahair mo chĕlĭ..............	Father of my husband.	Mo han mahair mo chĕlĭ............	Grandmother of my husband.
7				
8				
9	Hendad fy ngwr......................	Grandfather of my wife.	Henfam fy ngwr......................	" " "
10				
11				
12	Svigerfaders fader..................	Father-in-law's father.	Svigerfaders moder..................	Father-in-law's mother.
13	Afi manns min.......................	Grandfather of man my.	Amma manns minnar................	Grandmother of man my.
14	Mans farfar.........................	Husband's grandfather	Mans mormor........................	Husband's grandmother.
15				
16	Father-in-law's father..............	Father-in-law's father.	Mother of mother-in-law..........	Mother of mother-in-law.
17	Behuwd groot vader.................	Husband's grandfather.	Behuwd groot moeder...............	Husband's grandmother.
18				
19	Mans bess vader....................	" "	Mans bess mohder...................	" "
20	Meines mannes grossvater..........	My husband's grandfather.	Meines mannes grossmutter.......	My husband's grandmother.
21	Meines mannes grossvater..........	" " "	Meines mannes grossmutter.......	" " "
22	L'aïeul de mon mari................	The grandfather of my husband.	L'aïeule de mon mari..............	The grandmother of my husband.
23				
24				
25	Ante suocero.......................	Great father-in-law.	Ante suocera........................	Great mother-in-law.
26	Socer magnus......................	" " . " "	Socrus magna.......................	" " " "
27	Propentheros.......................	Father of father-in-law.	Propenthera........................	Mother of father-in-law.
28				
29				
30	Moj dziadek........................	My grandfather.	Moja babka..........................	My grandmother.
31	Mŭj ded............................	" "	Ma baba............................	" "
32				
33	Deda mi............................	Grandfather my.	Babă mi............................	Grandmother my.
34				
35	Kayni dĕdĕm.......................	My grandfather-in-law.	Kayni nĕnĕm.......................	My grandmother-in-law.
36	Bävkäleh mĕreh mun...............	Grandfather of husband my.	Däpereh mĕreh mun................	Grandmother of husband my.
37				
38				
39	Tso appĭnĭ..........................	Great father-in-law my.	Tso anoppĭnĭ........................	Great mother-in-law my.

	171. Wife.	Translation.	172. Wife's father.	Translation.
1	Amrâti..............................	Woman my.	Ammi..............................	Uncle my.
2	Zaujati.............................	Wife my.	Ammi..............................	" "
3	Ishtĭ...............................	Wife my (lit. woman my).	Khôth' mĭ..........................	Giver in marriage my (masculine).
4	Bäkhtee............................	Wife my.	Khumyanee........................	Wife's father my.
5	Gena...............................	" "	Ahnare.............................	Father-in-law my.
6	Mo van.............................	My woman.	Ahair mo chĕlĭ.....................	My other's father.
7	Mo bhean...........................	" "	M'athair ceille.....................	" " "
8	My ben.............................	" "	Ayr si laigh........................	" " "
9	Fy ngwraig.........................	My wife.	Tad fy ngwraig.....................	My father-in-law.
10	Zän.................................	Wife.		
11	Patuî. b Bhâṛyâ. c Jûyâ...........	"	Çvaçura............................	Father-in law.
12	Hustrue. b Viv. c Kone............	"	Svigerfader........................	" " "
13	Kona (husfrayja) min...............	Wife my.	Tengdafadir min....................	Father-in-law my.
14	Hustru.............................	Wife.	Svärfar.............................	Father-in-law.
15	Wif.................................	"	Sweor. b Stheor....................	" " "
16	Wife. Spouse......................	"	Father-in-law......................	" " "
17	Vrouw. b Gemalin..................	"	Behuwd vader......................	" " "
18	Vrouw..............................	"	Schoon vader.......................	" " "
19	Frau................................	"	Frauen vader.......................	Wife's father.
20	Weib. b Frau. c Gattin. d Gemah-	"	Schwiegervater.....................	Father-in-law.
21	Gattin......................[lin	"	Schwiegervater.....................	" " "
22	Mon épouse. b ma femme.	My wife. b My woman.	Mon beau-père.	My father-in-law.
23	Epose. b Mujir. c Consorte.......	Spouse. b Wife. c Consort.	Suegro.............................	Father-in-law.
24	Espôsa. b Mulher..................	Wife.	Sôgro.............................	" " "
25	Moglie. b Consorti................	Wife. b Consort.	Suocero............................	" " "
26	Uxor. b Marita....................	Wife.	Socer..............................	" " "
27	Gunĕ...............................	"	Pentheros. b Kĕdestĕs.............	" " "
28				
29	Mäno mötĕ..........................	My wife.	Mäno öszwĭs........................	My wife's father.
30	Moja zona. b Matzonka.............	" "	Moj tesc...........................	My father-in-law.
31	Ma manzelka.......................	" "	Mŭj tehan..........................	" " " "
32	Zhena mi...........................	Wife my.	Test mi............................	Father-in-law my.
33	Zhena mi...........................	" "	Tust mi............................	" " " "
34	Moja shena.........................	My wife.	Moi tjest..........................	My father-in-law.
35	Käru-m.............................	Wife my. b Woman.	Kayin bäbäm........................	" " " "
36	Zhunäy mun........................	Wife my.	Khesäreh mun......................	Father-in-law my.
37	Felesege-m.........................	Half my.	Ipam...............................	
38	Naine..............................	Wife.		
39	Waïmonĭ............................	Woman my. b Consort..	Appĭnĭ.............................	Father-in-law my.

TABLE I.—*Continued.*

	173. Wife's mother.	Translation.	174. Wife's grandfather.	Translation.
1	Amrât ammi	Wife of uncle my.	Jidd amrâti	Grandfather of wife my.
2	Imraât ämmi	" " " "	Jadd zauji	" " " "
3	Khôth ª 'ăntĭ	Giver in marriage my (fem.).		
4	Khmätee	Wife's mother my.	Säwŭnä d' bakhtee	" " " "
5	Ahnarochus mirä	Mother of wife my.		
6	Mahair mo chēli	My other's mother.	Mo han ahair mo chēli	Grandfather of my wife.
7	Mo mhathair cheille	" " "		
8	Moir si laigh	" " "		
9	Marn fy ngwraig	My mother-in-law.	Hendad fy ngwraig	" " " "
10				
11	Çvaçura	Mother-in-law.	Kones bedstefader	Wife's grandfather.
12	Svigermoder	" " "	Afi gonu minnar	Grandfather of wife my.
13	Tengdamoder min	Mother-in-law my.	Hustrus farfar	Wife's grandfather.
14	Syärmor	Mother-in-law.		
15	Sweger	" " "		
16	Mother-in-law	" " "	Wife's grandfather.	" "
17	Behuwd moeder	" " "	Behuwd groot vader	" "
18	Schoon moeder	" " "		
19	Frauen mohder	Wife's mother.	Frauen bess vader	" "
20	Schwiegermutter	Mother-in-law.	Der grossvater meiner frau	The grandfather of my wife.
21	Schwiegermutter	" " "	Der grossvater meiner frau	" " " " "
22	Ma belle-mère	My mother-in-law.	L'aïeul de ma femme	" " " " "
23	Suegra	Mother-in-law.		
24	Sogra	" " "		
25	Suocera	" " "	Ante suocero	Great father-in-law.
26	Socrus	" " "	Socer magnus	" " " "
27	Penthera	" " "	Propenthiros	Wife's grandfather.
28				
29	Măno ŏszwē	My wife's mother.		
30	Moj tesciowa	My mother-in-law.	Moj dziadek	My grandfather.
31	Ma tchyne	" " " "	Muj ded	" "
32	Tushta mi	Mother-in-law my.		
33	Tushta mi	" " " "	Deda mi	Grandfather my.
34	Moja tjestcha	My mother-in-law.		
35	Kayni änäm	" " " "	Kayni dĕdĕm	My grandfather-in-law.
36	Deyä zhunäy mun	Mother of wife my.	Bävkäleh mĕreh mun	Grandfather of wife my.
37	Napam			
38				
39	Anoppĭnĭ	Mother-in-law my.	Tso appĭnĭ	Great father-in-law my.

	175. Wife's grandmother.	Translation.	176. Step-father.	Translation.
1	Sitt amrâti	Grandmother of wife my	Ammi	Uncle my.
2	Sitt zaujati	" " "	Ammi	" "
3			Ish ĭmmĭ	Husband of mother my.
4	Säwŭntä d' bakhtee	" " "	Bäbeĕ ŭgä	Father my (step).
5			Horthire	My step-father.
6	Mo han mahair mo chĕlï	My other's old mother.	Mo las ahair	" " "
7			M'oide	" " "
8			Lhias yezg	" " "
9	Henfam fy ngwraig	Grandmother of my wife.	Fy llus tad	" " "
10				
11				
12	Kones bedstemoder	Wife's grandmother.	Stedfader	Step-father.
13	Amma gonu minnar	Grandmother of wife mine.	Styupfadir min	Step-father mine.
14	Hustrus mormor	Wife's grandmother.	Styffar	Step-father.
15			Steop faeder	" "
16	Wife's grandmother	" "	Step father	" "
17	Behuwd moeder	" "	Stief vader	" "
18			Step vader	" "
19	Frauen bess mohder	" "	Stief vader	" "
20	Die grossmutter meiner frau	The grandmother of my wife.	Stiefvater	" "
21	Die grossmutter meiner frau	" " " " "	Stiefvater	" "
22	L'aïeule de ma femme	" " " " "	Mon beau-père	My step-father.
23			Padrastro	Step-father.
24			Padrastro	" "
25	Ante luocera	Great mother-in-law.	Patrigna	" "
26	Socrus magna	" " " "	Vitricus	" "
27	Propenthira	Wife's grandmother.	Patruios. ᵇ Mĕtruios	" "
28				
29			Măno pătēwis	My step-father.
30	Moja babka	My grandmother.	Moj ojczym	" " "
31	Ma baba	" "	Muj otcim	" " "
32				
33	Baba mi	Grandmother my.	Otchoov mi	Step-father my.
34			Moi otchim	My step-father.
35	Kayni mĕnĕm	My grandmother-in-law.	Bäbälukum	My fatherhood.
36	Däpeereh zhumay	Grandmother of wife my.	Zur bäveh	My step-father.
37			Mostoha atyam	
38				
39	Tsă anoppĭnĭ	Great mother-in-law my.	Tsă puolenĭ	My father half.

TABLE I.—*Continued.*

	177. Step-mother.	Translation.	178. Step-son.	Translation.
1	Khâleti...............................	Aunt my.	Karŭti...............................	Step-son my.
2	Khălăti...............................	" "	Kăbibi...............................	Son of wife my.
3	Eshĕth ăbhĭ............................	Wife of father my.	Ben ĭshĭ ᵒʳ ben ĭshtĭ.................	Son of husband or wife my.
4	Ymmee ŭgă............................	Mother my (step)	Brŭnee ŭga............................	Son my (step).
5	Hortmire...............................	My step-mother.	Horte voretin.......................	My step-son.
6	Mo las vahair.......................	" " "	Mo las vac...........................	" " "
7				
8				
9	Fy llus fam............................	" " "	Fy llus fab............................	" " "
10				
11	Vimátá...............................	Step-mother.	Bhartr suta.........................	Husband's son.
12	Stedmoder............................	" "	Stedsön...............................	Step-son.
13	Styupmodir min....................	Step-mother mine.	Styupsonr minn....................	Step-son mine.
14	Styfmor...............................	Step-mother.	Styfson...............................	Step-son.
15	Steop modor.........................	" "	Steop sunu.........................	" "
16	Step mother.........................	" "	Step son.............................	" "
17	Stief moeder.........................	" "	Stief zoon...........................	" "
18	Step moeder.........................	" "	Step zoon...........................	" "
19	Stief mohder........................	" "	Stief soohn.........................	" "
20	Stiefmutter...........................	" "	Stief sohn...........................	" "
21	Stiefmutter...........................	" "	Stief sohn...........................	" "
22	Ma belle-mère.......................	My step-mother.	Mon beau-fils.......................	My step-son.
23	Madrastra............................	Step-mother.	Hijastro...............................	Step-son.
24	Madrastra............................	" "	Enteado...............................	" "
25	Matrigna..............................	" "	Figleastro............................	" "
26	Noverca...............................	" "	Privignus............................	" "
27	Matruia...............................	" "	Progenos............................	" "
28				
29	Măno mŏczekă.......................	My step-mother.	Măno-pŏsŭnis.......................	My step-son.
30	Moja macocha.......................	" " "	Moj pasierb.........................	" " "
31	Ma macocha.........................	" " "	Mŭj pastorek.......................	" " "
32	Mashteha mi.........................	Step-mother my.	Dovedenik mi.......................	Step-son my.
33	Mashteha mi.........................	" " "	Paistrook mi.........................	" " "
34	Maja matchikha....................	My step-mother.	Moi pasinok........................	My step-son.
35	Anălŭkum............................	My motherhood.	Oghŭlŭkŭn. ᵇ Eoyĕ oghŭl.........	My sonhood. ᵇ Not own son.
36	Dămĕereh mun.......................	Step-mother my.	Lăveh muneh khŏrt.................	My step-son.
37	Mostoha anyam.....................		Mostoha fiam.......................	
38				
39	Aïtĭ puolenĭ...........................	My mother half.	Poïkă puolenĭ.......................	Son half my.

	179. Step-daughter.	Translation.	180. Step-brother.	Translation.
1	Karŭteti...............................	Step-daughter my.	Akhi...................................	Brother my.
2	Kabibati..............................	Daughter of wife my.	Akhi...................................	" "
3	Băth ĭshĭ ᵒʳ băth ĭshtĭ...............	Daughter of husband or wife my.	Bĕn ăbhĭ ᵒʳ ben ĭmmĭ...............	Son of father or mother my.
4	Brătee ŭgă............................	Daughter my (step).	Brŭnă d'yemmee ŭgă.................	Son of mother my (step).
5	Horte tooster........................	My step-daughter.	Horte yăkepire.......................	My step-brother.
6	Mo las ineean.......................	" " "	Mo las drihair.......................	" " "
7			Mo leth brathair....................	" " "
8				
9	Fy llus ferch.........................	" " "	Fy llus frawd........................	" " "
10				
11	Bhartr sută...........................	Husband's daughter.	Vâimâtra.............................	Step-brother.
12	Steddatter............................	Step-daughter.	Stedbroder...........................	Step-brother.
13	Styupdottir min.....................	Step-daughter my.	Styupbrodir minn..................	Step-brother mine.
14	Styfdotter............................	Step-daughter.	Styfbror..............................	Step-brother.
15	Steop dohter.........................	" "	Steop brodor.........................	" "
16	Step daughter.......................	" "	Step brother.........................	" "
17	Stief dochter.........................	" "	Stief broeder........................	" "
18	Step dochter.........................	" "	Step broeder.........................	" "
19	Stief dochter.........................	" "	Stief brohr..........................	" "
20	Stieftochter...........................	" "	Stiefbruder...........................	" "
21	Stieftochter...........................	" "	Stiefbruder...........................	" "
22	Ma belle-fille........................	My step-daughter.	Mon beau-frere......................	My step-brother.
23	Hijastra...............................	Step-daughter.	Medio-hermano.....................	My step-brother or half brother.
24	Enteada...............................	" "	Meio irmão..........................	Step-brother.
25	Figleastra............................	" "	Fratellastro..........................	" "
26	Privigna..............................	" "	Frater.................................	" "
27	Progenĕ...............................	" "		
28				
29	Măno pŏdukră.......................	My step-daughter.	Măno pŭsbrolis......................	My half brother.
30	Majo pasierbica.....................	" " "		
31	Ma pastorkynĕ......................	" " "	Mŭj newlastny bratr................	" " "
32	Dovedenitsa mi......................	Step-daughter my.	Zavaruik mi.........................	Step-brother my.
33	Paisterka mi.........................	" " "		
34	Maja padtcheritza..................	My step-daughter.	Kărndăshlukun.....................	My brotherhood.
35	Kŭzlukum. ᵇ Eoyĕ kŭzŭm.........	My daughterhood. ᵇ Not own dau.	Bră muneh khŏrt....................	My step-brother.
36	Keeză muneh khŏrt.................	My step-daughter.	Atyam fija...........................	Son of father my.
37	Mostoha leanyom...................			
38				
39	Tytăr puolenĭ........................	Daughter half my.	Veli puolenĭ..........................	Brother half my.

TABLE I.—*Continued.*

	181. Step-sister.	Translation.	182. Son-in-law.	Translation.
1	Akhti.	Sister my.	Khatan. b Saha	Son-in-law. b Bridegroom.
2	Ikhti.	" "	Suhri	" " "
3	Băth ăbhĭ or băth ĭmmĭ	Daughter of father or mother my.	Kh'thănĭ	" " "
4	Brätä d'yemmee-ugä	Daughter of mother my (step).	Khutnă	" " "
5	Horte kooeris	My step-sister.	Pessar	Son-in-law my.
6	Mo las driffür	" " "	Mo chliavain	My son-in-law.
7	Mo leth phiuthar	" " "	Mo chliamhiun	" " "
8			Mac sy laigh	" " "
9	Fy llus ferch	" " "	Mabnnghy fraith	" " "
10				
11	Vâimatrî	Step-sister.	Iâmatâr	Son-in-law.
12	Stedsöster	" "	Svigersön	" "
13	Styupsystir min	Step-sister my.	Tengdasonr minn	Son-in-law my.
14	Styfsyster	Step-sister.	Mag	Son-in-law.
15	Steop swuster	" "	Athum	" "
16	Step-sister	" "	Son-in-law	" "
17	Stief zuster	" "	Schoon zoon	" "
18	Step-sister	" "	Schoon zoon	" "
19	Stief sister	" "	Dochters man	Daughter's husband.
20	Stiefschwester	" "	Schwiegersohn. b Tochtermann	Son-in-law. b Daughter's husband.
21	Stiefschwester	" "	Schwiegersohn. b Tochtermann	" " " "
22	Ma belle-sœur	My step-sister.	Mon gendre. b Beau-fils	My son-in-law.
23	Medio hermana	My step-sister or half-sister.	Yerno	Son-in-law.
24	Meia irman	Step-sister.	Genro	" "
25	Sorellastra	" "	Genero	" "
26	Soror	" "	Gener	" "
27			Gambros	" "
28				
29	Măno pŭssesŭ (ŭnno)	My half-sister.	Zentas	" "
30			Moj ziec	My son-in-law.
31	Ma newlastna sestra	" " "	Mŭj zet	Son-in-law.
32			Zet mi	Son-in-law my.
33	Zavarnitza mi	Step-sister my.	Zet me	" " "
34			Moi Ziatj	My son-in-law.
35	Eoyĕ kuzkärndäshum	My not own sister.	Ginvĕyeïn	" " "
36	Khooshkee muneh khôrt	My step-sister.	Lävăreh mun	Son-in-law my.
37	Testverein		Vejem. b Vom	" " "
38				
39	Sĭsar puolenĭ	Sister half my.	Wăvynĭ	" " "

	183. Daughter-in-law.	Translation.	184. Brother-in-law (husband's brother).	Translation.
1	Kinnet	Daughter-in-law.	Ibn ămmi	Son of uncle my.
2	Kinnati	" "	Silfi	Husband's brother my.
3	Kăllăthĭ	Daughter-in-law. b Bride.	Y'bhămĭ	Brother-in-law my.
4	Keltä	" " "	Idmee	Husband's brother my.
5			Dakris	Brother-in-law.
6	Ban mo vic	My son's woman.	Drihair mo chĕli	My other's brother.
7			Mo bhrathair ceille	" " "
8	Inneen sy laigh	My daughter-in-law.	Sheshey my braar	Husband of my brother.
9	Merch ynnghy fraith	" " "	Brawd ynnghy fraith	My brother-in-law.
10	Aroos	Daughter-in-law.		
11	Snuska	" "	Devă. b Devarah	Brother-in-law.
12	Svigerdatter	" "	Svoger. b Kones söster	" "
13	Tengdadottir min	Daughter-in-law mine.	Tengdabrodir. b Magr minn	Brother-in-law mine.
14	Sonhustru	Daughter-in-law.	Svager	Brother-in-law.
15	Snor. b Snoru	" "	Sacor	" "
16	Daughter-in-law	" "	Brother-in-law	" "
17	Schoon dochter	" "	Zwager	" "
18	Schoon dochter	" "	Schoon broeder	" "
19	Soohns frau	Son's daughter.	Swoger	" "
20	Schwiegertochter. b Schnur	Daughter-in-law.	Schwager	" "
21	Schwiegertochter		Schwager	" "
22	Ma bru	My daughter-in-law.	Mon beau-frère	My brother-in-law.
23	Nuera	Daughter-in-law.	Cuñado	Brother-in-law.
24	Nora	" "	Cunhado	" "
25	Figliastra	" "	Cognato	" "
26	Nurus	" "	Levir	" "
27	Nuos	" "	Daër	" "
28				
29			Dĕwĕris	Husband's brother.
30	Mojă ziec	My daughter-in-law.	Moj szwagier	My brother-in-law.
31	Ma nevesta	" " "	Mŭj swat (swăgor)	" "
32	Snuha mi	Daughter-in-law my.	Dever mi	Brother-in-law my.
33	Snuha mi	" " "	Dever mi	" "
34	Moja snokha. b Nevestka	My daughter-in-law.	Moi dever	My brother-in-law.
35	Gĕlĭnim	" " "	Käyinim	" " "
36	Bookeh mun	Daughter-in-law my.	Vustăoorä	Husband's brother my.
37	Menyem	" " "		
38				
39	Mĭnĭănĭ	" " "	Kytynĭ	" " "

TABLE I.—*Continued.*

	185. Brother-in-law (sister's husband).	Translation.	186. Brother-in-law (wife's brother).	Translation.
1	Zôj äkhti	Husband of sister my.	Ibn ammi	Son of uncle my.
2	Suhrí	" " "	Ibn ämmi	" " "
3				
4	Khutnee	" " "	Akhŏnä d'bakhtee	Brother of wife my.
5			Anareh yaks	Brother-in-law.
6	Fär mo yriffür	My sister's man.	Drihair mo chĕli	My other's brother.
7	Fear mo phiuthar cheille	" " "	Mo bhrathair ceille	
8	Sheshey my shuyr	Husband of my sister.	Braar my ben	Brother of my wife.
9	Brawd ynnghy fraith	My brother-in-law.	Brawd ynnghy fraith	My brother-in-law.
10				
11	Avutta. [b] Svasrpati	Brother-in-law.	Syâlah. [b] Syálakah	Brother-in-law.
12	Svoger. Sösters mand	Brother-in-law (sister's man).	Svoger. [b] Kones broder	" "
13	Tengdabrodïr. [b] Magr min	Brother-in-law mine.	Tengdabrodir. [b] Magr min	Brother-in-law mine.
14	Svager	Brother-in-law.	Svager	Brother-in-law.
15	Athum	" "	Sacor	" "
16	Brother-in-law	" "	Brother-in-law	" "
17	Zwager	" "	Zwager	" "
18	Reihtswaer	" "	Reihtswaer	" "
19	Swoger	" "	Swoger	" "
20	Schwager	" "	Schwager	" "
21	Schwager	" "	Schwager	" "
22	Mon beau-frère	My brother-in-law.	Mon beau-frère	My brother-in-law.
23	Hermano politico	Brother by courtesy.	Cuñado	Brother-in-law.
24	Cunhado	Brother-in-law.	Cunhado	" "
25	Cognati	" "		
26	Maritus sororis	" "		
27	Kēdestēs	" "	Uxoris frater	" "
28			Kēdestēs	" "
29			Laigonăs	Wife's brother.
30	Moj szwagier	My brother-in-law.	Moj Szwagier	My brother-in-law.
31	Mŭj swat	" " "	Mŭj swat	" " "
32	Zet mi	Brother-in-law my.	Shura mi	Brother-in-law my.
33	Zet mi	" " "	Shura mi	" " "
34	Moi dever	My brother-in-law.	Moi svojak. [b] Shurin	My brother-in-law.
35	Enïshtïm	" " "	Käyïnïm	" " "
36	Lävä mun	Brother-in-law my.	Läveh kheeoreh mun	Son.
37				
38				
39	Lankonï	Sister's husband my.	Năălănï	Wife's brother my.

	187. Brother-in-law (wife's sister's husband).	Translation.	188. Sister-in-law (wife's sister).	Translation.
1	Zôj bint ammi	Daughter of uncle my.	Bint ammi	Daughter of uncle my.
2	Andili	Sister's husband of wife my.	Bint ämmi	" " " "
3				
4	Yăeesee	Husband of my wife's sister.	Baräkhmätee	Sister of my wife.
5			Gunauchris kooera	Sister of my wife.
6	Fär driffür mo chĕlï	My other's sister's man.	Driffür mo chĕli	My other's sister.
7	Brathair ceille mo mhua	" " " "	Mo phiuthar cheille	" " "
8			Shuyr my ben	Sister of my wife.
9			Chwaer ynnghy fraith	My sister-in-law.
10				
11				
12			Syâlika	Sister-in-law.
13	Systur madr konu minnar	Sister's husband of wife mine.	Svigerinde. [b] Kones söster	" "
14	Svägerskars man	Sister's husband of wife.	Maggona. [b] Tengdasystur min	Sister-in-law my.
15			Svägerska	Sister-in-law.
16			Sister-in-law	" "
17			Zwagerin	" "
18			Schoon sister	" "
19			Swigerin	" "
20	Meiner frau schwestec man	Wife's sister's husband.	Schwägerin	" "
21	Der mann meiner schwägerin	The husband of my sister-in-law.	Schwägerin	" "
22			Ma belle-sœur	My sister-in-law.
23	Concuñado	Wife's sister's husband.	Cuñada	Sister-in-law.
24	Concunhado	" " "	Cunhada	" "
25				
26				
27	Aelivi	Husbands of two sisters.	Uxoris soror	" "
28			Kēdestria	" "
29			Swainē	Wife's sister.
30			Moja szwagrowa	My sister-in-law.
31			Ma swatine	" " "
32	Badjanak (Turkish)	Brother-in-law my.		
33	Bajenak (Turkish)	Brother-in-law.	Balduza	Sister-in-law (Turkish).
34			Maja Svojatchina	My sister-in-law.
35	Bäjänäk um	My brother-in-law.	Bälduzum	" " "
36	Bäjänäkheh mun	Husband of my wife's sister.	Bältoozeh	Sister-in-law my.
37			Angyom	" " "
38				
39	Lankonï	Wife's sister's husband my.	Natonï	

TABLE I.—*Continued.*

	189. Sister-in-law (husband's sister).	Translation.	190. Sister-in-law (brother's wife).	Translation.
1	Bint ammi....	Daughter of uncle my.	Amrât äkhi....	Wife of brother my.
2	Hami....	" " "	Silfati....	" " " "
3			Y'chïmtï....	Sister-in-law my.
4	Khätä d'goree....	Sister of husband my.	Khätee....	Sister my.
5	Dälles....	Sister-in-law my.	Havse....	Sister-in-law.
6	Driffür mo chĕlï....	My other's sister.	Ban mo yrihär....	My brother's woman.
7	Mo phiuthar cheille....		Bean mo bhrathair....	Wife of my brother.
8	Shuyr my sheshey....	Sister of my husband.	Ben my braar....	" " " "
9	Chwaer ynnghy fraith....	My sister-in-law.	Chwaer ynnghy fraith....	My sister-in-law.
10				
11	Nânanda....	Sister-in-law.	Prajâvatî....	Brother's wife.
12	Svigerinde. b Mands söster....	Sister-in-law. (b Man's sister.)	Svigerinde. b Broders kone....	Sister-in-law. b Brother's wife.
13	Maggona. b Systur Manns mins..	Sister-in-law mine.	Maggona. b Brŏdur kóna mins...	Sister-in-law mine.
14	Svägerska....	Sister-in-law.	Svägerska....	Sister-in-law.
15				
16	Sister-in-law....	" "	Sister-in-law....	" "
17	Zwagerin....	" "	Zwagerin....	" "
18	Schoon sïster....	" "	Schoon sister....	" "
19	Swigerin....	" "	Swigerin....	" "
20	Schwägerin....	" "	Schwägerin....	" "
21	Schwägerin....	" "	Schwägerin....	" "
22	Ma belle-sœur....	My sister-in-law.	Ma belle-sœur....	My sister-in-law.
23	Cuñada politica....	My sister-in-law by courtesy.	Cuñada....	Sister-in-law.
24	Cunhada....	Sister-in-law.	Cunhada....	" "
25				
26	Glos....	" "	Fratria....	" "
27	Galōs....	" "		
28				
29	Mösză....	Husband's sister.	Moja bratowa....	My sister-in-law.
30	Moja zolovka....	My sister-in-law.	Ma swatine....	" " "
31	Ma swatine. b Swagrina....	" " "	Snuha mi....	Sister-in-law my.
32	Zolovka. b Sestritza....	Sister-in-law my.	Snuha mi....	" " "
33	Zulva*....	Sister-in-law.		
34	Moja zolovka....	My sister-in-law.	Moja nevestka....	My sister-in-law.
35	Georum um....	" " "	Kärndäshmun kärusu....	My brother's wife.
36	Gorŭmeh mun....	Sister-in-law my.	Zhŭneh brä mun....	Wife of brother my.
37	Augyom....	" " "		
38				
39	Natonï....	Husband's sister my.	Veljenï vaimo....	Brother's my wife.

	191. Sister-in-law (husband's brother's wife).	Translation.	192. Two father's-in-law to each other.	Translation.
1	Amrât ibn ammi....	Wife of son of uncle my.	Ammi ibni....	Uncle of son my.
2	Silfati....	" " " " "	Nasibi....	Marriage relations.
3	Y'chïmtï....	Sister-in-law my.		
4	Idemtee....	Wife of my husband's brother.		
5	Nare ess....	Sister-in-law.		
6	Ban drihär mo chĕlï....	My other's brother's woman.	Cleavnas....	Marriage relations.
7				
8				
9				
10				
11	Yátä....	Sister-in-law.		
12				
13	Kona brodur manns mins....	Wife of brother of man my.	Magar....	(If not of same family.)
14	Svägerska....	Wife of brother.		
15				
16				
17				
18				
19				
20	Meines schwagers frau....	My brother-in-law's wife.		Not related.
21	Die frau meines schwagers....	The wife of my brother-in-law.	Die väterder ehegatten....	The fathers of the married pair.
22				
23	Concuñada....	Husband's brother's wife.		
24	Concunhada....	" " "		
25				
26	Jamitrices....	" " "		
27	Einateres....	Wives of brothers.	Suggenis....	Marriage relations.
28				
29				
30				
31				
32	Eturva mi....	Sister-in-law my.	Svat....	
33	Iturva....	Sister-in-law.	Svat....	Father-in-law.
34				
35	Eltï-m....	My sister-in-law.		
36	Idemta....	Sister-in-law.	Khunämeh....	
37				
38				
39	Kalynï....	Brother's wife my.		

TABLE I.—Continued.

	193. Two mothers-in-law to each other.	Translation.	194. Widow.	Translation.
1	Amrât ibn ammi...............	Wife of uncle of son my.	Armelet...............	Widow.
2	Nasibati...............	Marriage relations.	Armalat...............	"
3			Almānā...............	"
4			Armilta...............	"
5			Oorpavawy...............	"
6	Cleavnas...............	Marriage relations.	Bointriuch...............	"
7			Bantrach...............	"
8			Ben freoghe...............	"
9			Gwaraig weddw...............	Widow (wedder—single).
10			Zăni br wah...............	"
11			Vidhava...............	"
12			Enke...............	"
13	Magkonur...............	(If not of same family.)	Ekkya...............	"
14			Enka...............	"
15			Laf...............	"
16			Widow...............	"
17			Weduwe...............	"
18			Weduwe...............	"
19			Widdefrau...............	"
20		Not related.	Wittfrau. b Wittwe...............	"
21	Die mütterder ehegatten............	The mothers of the married pair.	Wittwe...............	"
22			Une veuve...............	A widow.
23			Vidua...............	Widow.
24			Viuva...............	"
25			Vedova...............	"
26			Vidua...............	"
27			Chēra...............	"
28				
29			Năszlē...............	"
30			Wdowa...............	"
31			Wdowa...............	"
32	Svaha...............		Vdovitsa...............	"
33	Svaha...............	Mother-in-law.	Vdovitza...............	"
34			Vedova...............	"
35			Dŭl kăru...............	"
36	Khunämeh...............		Zhunĕbee...............	"
37			Ozvegy assiony...............	"
38				
39			Leski'...............	"

	195. Widower.	Translation.	196. Twins.	Translation.
1	Armel...............	Widower.	Tôme...............	Twins.
2	Armal...............	"	Taum...............	"
3	Almān...............	"	T'ōmīm...............	"
4	Armeela...............	"	Zogee...............	Pairs.
5	Oorpavawy...............	"	Yergorcyarg...............	Twins.
6	Bointriuch...............	"	Beirth. b Deesh...............	A pair.
7	Bantrack fher...............	"	Leth oan...............	Twins.
8	Sheshey freoghe...............	"	Daa lhiannoo...............	"
9	Gwydmon...............	"	Efilliaid...............	"
10				
11			Yamalau...............	"
12	Enkemand...............	"	Tvillinger...............	"
13	Ekkill...............	"	Tviburar...............	"
14	Enkling...............	"	Tvillengar...............	"
15	Widower...............	"	Twins...............	"
16				
17	Weduwnaar...............	"	Tweelinger...............	"
18	Weduwer...............	"	Zwelling...............	"
19	Widdeman...............	"	Twiskes...............	"
20	Wittmaun. b Wittwer...............	"	Zwillinge...............	"
21	Wittwer...............	"	Zwillinge...............	"
22	Un veuf...............	A widower.	Jumeaux. b Jumelles...............	"
23	Viduo...............	Widower.	Gemelli. b Mellizi...............	"
24	Viuvo...............	"	Gemeos...............	"
25	Vedovo...............	"	Gemelli...............	"
26	Viduus...............	"	Gemini...............	"
27	Chēros...............	"	Didumoi...............	"
28				
29	Năszlys...............	"	Dwyni...............	"
30	Wdowiec...............	"	Btiznieta. b Btizniaki...............	"
31	Wdowec...............	"	Blizenei...............	"
32	Vdovets...............	"	Blezhwatsi...............	"
33	Vdovitz...............	"	Blinatzi...............	"
34	Vdovetz...............	"	Dvoini...............	"
35	Dŭl...............	"	Ekiz...............	"
36	Zhunĕbee...............	"		
37	Ozvegy ember...............	"	Iker...............	"
38				
39	Leski...............	"	Kaksoset...............	"

PART II.

CLASSIFICATORY SYSTEM OF RELATIONSHIP.

———

GÁNOWÁNIAN FAMILY.

WITH A TABLE.

CHAPTER I.

SYSTEM OF RELATIONSHIP OF THE GANOWANIAN FAMILY.

GENERAL OBSERVATIONS, TOGETHER WITH AN ANALYSIS OF THE SYSTEM.

Evidence of the Unity of Origin of the Indian Family—Name proposed for this Family—Their System elaborate and complicated—Opulence of Nomenclatures—Usages tending to its Maintenance—American Indians, when related, salute by Kin—Never address each other by Personal Name—Manner of Procuring their System of Relationship—White Interpreters—Indians speaking English—Their Progress in this respect—Many Languages now accessible—Others which are not—The Table—Dialectical Variation—Less than has been supposed—Advantages of a Uniform Notation—Of Using same Pronominal Forms—Etymologies of Terms lost—Identity of the System throughout the Family—Deviations from Uniformity—Their Uses—The Tribal Organization—Prohibition of Intermarriage in the Tribe—Descent in the Female Line—Exceptions—Two Great Divisions of the Family—Roving Indians—Village Indians—Intermediate Nations—Three Stages of Political Organization—The Tribe, the Nation, and the Confederacy of Nations—Founded upon Consanguinity, Dialect, and Stock Language—Numbers of the American Aborigines overestimated—Analysis of their System of Relationship.

THE recognized families of mankind have received distinctive names, which are not only useful and convenient in description, but serve to register the progress of ethnology as well. Up to the present time the linguistic evidence of the unity of origin of the American aborigines has not been considered sufficiently complete to raise them to the rank of a family, although the evidence from physical characteristics, and from institutions, manners, and customs, tends strongly in the direction of unity of origin. Altogether these currents of testimony lead so uniformly to this conclusion that American ethnologists have very generally adopted the opinion of their genetic connection as the descendants of a common parent nation. In the ensuing chapters additional and independent evidence, drawn from their system of relationship, will be produced, establishing, as we believe, their unity of origin, and, consequently, their claim to the rank of a family of nations. The name proposed for this family is the Ganowánian; to consist of the Indian nations represented in the table, and of such other nations as are hereafter found to possess the same system of relationship. This term is a compound from *Gä'-no,* an arrow, and *Wä-ä'-no,* a bow, taken from the Seneca dialect of the Iroquois language, which gives for its etymological signification the family of " the Bow and Arrow."[1] It follows the analogy of "Aryan," from *arya,* which, according to Müller, signifies " one who ploughs or tills," and of " Turanian," from *tura,* which, according to the same learned author, " implies the swiftness of the horseman." Should the family thus christened become ultimately merged in the Turanian or Indo-American,

---

[1] Gä-no-wä'-ni-an : ä, as a in father ; ă, as a in at; a, as a in ale.

which is not improbable, the term would still remain as an appropriate designation for the American division.

There are several features in the elaborate system of relationship about to be presented that will arrest attention, and, perhaps, prompt inquiries, some of which it may be advisable to anticipate.

It may be premised, first, that every relationship which is discriminated by the Aryan family, as well as a large number unnoticed, is recognized by the Ganowanian; secondly, that the nomenclatures of relationship in the dialects of the latter family are more opulent than those of any other, not excepting the Turanian; and thirdly, that their system is so diversified with specializations and so complicated in its classifications as to require careful study to understand its structure and principles. Upon the strength of these statements it may be asked how rude and uncultivated Indians have been able to maintain such a system of relationship as that unfolded in the table? and, lastly, how it was possible to prosecute, through so many unwritten dialects, the minute inquiries necessary to its full development, and to verify the results? The answers to these questions have such a direct bearing upon the truthfulness of the table, upon which the final results of this research must depend, as to overcome, in a great measure, the repugnance of the author to refer to his personal labors in tracing out this extraordinary system of relationship amongst the American Indian nations; and he trusts that the necessity which impels him to such a reference will be received as a sufficient apology.

A single usage disposes of the first of the proposed questions. The American Indians always speak to each other, when related, by the term of relationship, and never by the personal name of the individual addressed. In familiar intercourse, and in formal salutation, they invariably address each other by the exact relationship of consanguinity or affinity in which they stand related. I have put the question direct to native Indians of more than fifty different nations, in most cases at their villages or encampments, and the affirmance of this usage has been the same in every instance. Over and over again it has been confirmed by personal observation. When it is considered that the number of those who are bound together by the recognized family ties is several times greater than amongst ourselves, where remote collateral relatives are practically disowned, the necessity for each person to understand the system through all its extent to enable him to address his kinsman by the conventional term of relationship becomes at once apparent. It is not only the custom to salute by kin, but an omission to recognize in this manner a relative, would, amongst most of these nations, be a discourtesy amounting to an affront. In Indian society the mode of address, when speaking to a relative, is the possessive form of the term of relationship; e. g., *my father, my elder brother, my grandson, my nephew, my niece, my uncle, my son-in-law, my brother-in-law*, and so on throughout the recognized relationships. If the parties are not related, then *my friend*. The effect of this custom in imparting as well as preserving a knowledge of the system through all of its ramifications is sufficiently obvious. There is another custom which renders this one a practical necessity. From some cause, of which it is not necessary here to seek an explanation, an American Indian is reluctant to mention his own personal name. It would be a violation of good manners for an Indian to speak to another Indian by his name. If I ask one to tell me his name he will probably comply with my request after a moment's hesitation, because, as an American, the question is not singular from me; but, even then, if he has a companion with him, the latter will at once relieve him from embarrassment by answering in his place.[1] In repeated instances I have verified this peculiarity in widely separated localities. This reserve in the use of personal names has tended to prevent the relaxation of the usage of addressing by kin, whilst, at the same time, it has contributed powerfully to the knowledge and maintenance of the system. It may also be stated, as a summary of the causes which have contributed to its perpetuation, that it is taught to each in childhood, and practised by all through life. Amongst the numerous and widely scattered nations represented in the table the system of consanguinity and affinity therein unfolded is, at this moment, in constant practical daily use.

To the second question the answer is equally plain. Thirty years ago it would have been impossible to work out this system of relationship, in its details, in any considerable number of the languages named, from the want of a medium of communication. There are nations still on the Pacific side of the continent whose languages are not sufficiently opened to render them accessible, except for the most common purposes. The same difficulty, also, exists with respect to some of the nations of New Mexico, Arizona, Nevada, and of the Upper Missouri. The trapper and the trader who spend their lives in the mountains, or at the posts of the Fur Companies, usually acquire so much only of each language as is necessary to their vocation, although there are instances among this class of men where particular languages have been fully acquired after a residence of twenty or thirty years in the Indian country; as in the case of Robert Meldrum, of the Crow language, of Alexander Culbertson, of the Blackfoot, and of James Kipp, of the Mandan. Even the Missionaries do not acquire the complete range of an Indian language until after a residence of fifteen or twenty years among the people expended in its constant study and use. The difficulty of filling up one of the schedules was by no means inconsiderable when perfectly competent white interpreters were employed. The schedule used contains two hundred and thirty-four distinct questions, all of which were necessary to develop the system without passing beyond the third collateral line except to elicit the indicative relationships. To follow it through without confusion of mind is next to impossible, except by persons accustomed to investigation. With a white interpreter the first obstacle was the want of a systematic knowledge of our own method of arranging and describing kindred. He had, perhaps, never had occasion to give the subject a

---

[1] Indian names are single, and in almost all cases significant. When a nation is subdivided into tribes, the names are tribal property, and are kept distinct. Thus, the Wolf Tribe of the Senecas have a class of names which have been handed down from generation to generation, and are so well known that among the Iroquois the tribe of the person can generally be determined from his or her name. As their names are single, the connection of brothers and sisters could not be inferred from them, nor that of father and son. Many of the nations have a distinct set of names for childhood, another for maturity, and still another for old age, which are successively changed.

moment's reflection; and when he was taken through the second or more remote collateral line, with a description of each person by the chain of consanguinity, he was first bewildered and then confounded in the labyrinth of relationships. It was necessary, in most cases, to explain to him the method of our own system; after which the lineal and first collateral line, male and female, and the marriage relationship in this line, were easily and correctly obtained from the native through him; and also the first relationships in the second collateral line in its several branches. But, on passing beyond these, another embarrassment was encountered in the great and radical differences between the Indian system and our own, which soon involved the interpreter in new difficulties more perplexing than the first. Suffice it to state that it required patient and often repeated attempts to prosecute the questions successfully to the end of the schedule; and when the work was finally completed it was impossible not to be suspicious of errors. The schedule, however, is so framed as, from its very fulness, to be, in many respects, self-corrective. It was also certain to develop the indicative relationships of the system however defective it might prove to be in some of its details. The hindrances here referred to were restricted to cases where white interpreters were necessarily used.

Another and the chief answer to the supposed question is found in the progress made, within the last thirty years, in the acquisition of our language by a number of natives in the greater part of the Indian nations represented in the table. The need of our language as a means of commercial and political intercourse has been seriously felt by them; and, within the period named, it has produced great changes amongst them in this respect. At the present time among the emigrant Indian nations in Kansas, in the Indian territory occupied by the Cherokees, Creeks, and Choctaws, in the territories of Nebraska and Dakota, and also among the nations still resident in the older States, as the Iroquois in New York, the Ojibwas on Lake Superior, and the Dakotas in Minnesota, there are many Indians, particularly half-bloods, who speak our language fluently. Some of them are educated men. The Indian has proved his linguistic capacities by the facility and correctness with which he has learned to speak the English tongue. It is, also, not at all uncommon to find an Indian versed in several aboriginal languages. To this class of men I am chiefly indebted for a knowledge of their system of relationship, and for that intelligent assistance which enabled me to trace out its minute details. Knowing their own method of classification perfectly, and much better than we do our own, they can, as a general rule, follow the branches of the several collateral lines with readiness and precision. It will be seen, therefore, that with a native sufficiently versed in English to understand the simple form used in the schedule to describe each person, it was only necessary to describe correctly the person whose relationship was sought to ascertain the relationship itself. In this way the chain of consanguinity was followed step by step through the several branches of each collateral line until the latter were merged in the lineal. With a knowledge, on my own part, of the radical features of the Indian system, and of the formulas of our own, there was no confusion of ideas between my interlocutor and myself since we were able to understand each other fully. If, at times, he lost the connection in following the thread of consanguinity, we commenced again; recording the several degrees, as we advanced, by counting the fingers on each hand, or resorting to some other device to preserve the continuity of the line we were following. If his knowledge of English was limited, which was frequently the case, it was always manifest whether or not he understood the question, in a particular instance, by his answer. It will thus be seen that to obtain their system of relationship it was far preferable to consult a native Indian, who spoke English even imperfectly, rather than a white interpreter well versed in the Indian language. Every question on the schedule was made personal to obtain the precise term of relationship used by *Ego*, when addressing the person described. Aside from the reason that this is the true method of ascertaining the exact relationship, the Indian sometimes uses, when speaking *of* a relative, a different term from the one used when speaking *to* him; and if he employs the same term in both cases the pronominal form is usually different. The following are illustrations of the form of the question: " What do I call my father's brother when I speak to him." If the question is asked a Seneca Indian he will answer "*Hä'-nih*," my father. " What do I call my father's brother's son if he is older than myself?" He will answer " *Hä'-je*," my elder brother. " What do I call my father's brother's son's son?" He will answer " *Ha-ah'-wük*," my son. " What should I call the same person were I a woman?" He will reply " *Ha-so'-neh*," my nephew. After going through all of the questions on the schedule in this manner, with a native speaking English, settling the orthography, pronunciation, and accent of each term by means of frequent repetitions, and after testing the work where it appeared to be necessary, I was just as certain of the correctness of the results as I could have been if a proficient in this particular Indian language. The same mode of procedure was adopted, whether a native speaking English or a white interpreter speaking Indian was employed. Such schedules as were obtained through the former agency were always the most satisfactory, and procured with the least labor.

It is a singular fact, but one which I have frequently verified, that those Americans who are most thoroughly versed in Indian languages, from a long residence in the Indian country, are unacquainted with their system of relationship except its general features. It does not appear to have attracted their attention sufficiently to have led to an investigation of its details even as a matter of curiosity. Not one of the number have I ever found who, from his own knowledge, was able to fill out even a small part of the schedule. Even the missionaries, who are scholars as well as proficients in the native languages, were unfamiliar with its details, as they had no occasion to give the matter a special examination. The Rev. Cyrus Byington, who had spent upwards of forty years of missionary life among the Choctas, wrote to me that " it required the united strength of the mission" to fill out correctly the Chocta schedule in the table; but the difficulty was not so much in the system of consanguinity, although it contained some extraordinary features, as in following the several lines and holding each person distinctly before the mind as formally described in the schedule. The same is also true of the returned missionaries from Asia, Africa, and the islands of the Pacific, as to the system of relationship which prevailed among the people with whom they had severally resided for years.   The attention of many of them had been arrested by peculiarities in the classification of kindred, but the subject, from its very nature, was without the range of their investigations.   But with native assistance this class of men possess peculiar qualifications for reaching the details of the system.   The most perfectly executed schedules in the tables were furnished by the American Home and Foreign Missionaries.   On the other hand, the rudest Indian is familiar with the system of his own nation, having used it constantly throughout its entire range from early childhood.   He will follow you through the several branches of each line with but little embarrassment if you can manage to engage him in the work.   It requires experience, as well as a knowledge of the Indian character, to hold a native to a protracted labor of such a tedious character, and to overcome his aversion to continuous mental exertion.   He is, also, suspicious of literary investigations unless he understands the motive which prompts them; and sensitive to ridicule, when their peculiar usages are sought, from his knowledge of their great unlikeness to our own.   After answering a few questions he may abruptly turn away and refuse to be interrogated further unless his interest is awakened by a sufficient inducement.   It was not always possible to complete a schedule without consulting the matrons of the tribe.   They are skilled in relationships beyond the males, and can resolve, with facility, questions of remote consanguinity, if the person is described with sufficient accuracy to show who is intended.   A sketch of the incidents connected with the procurement of such of the schedules as were worked out by the writer in the Indian country would furnish a number of singular illustrations of Indian character.

Another fact will become apparent upon a close examination of the table, namely, the near approach of the terms of relationship to each other in the several dialects of the same stock-language; or, in other words, the small amount of dialectical change these words have undergone, as compared with other words in the published vocabularies of the same dialects.   This was a matter of no slight surprise to the author.   It may be accounted for in part by the constant use of these terms in every family, and among the members of different families which would tend to preserve uniformity of pronunciation; but the chief reason is that these dialects, in reality, are much nearer to each other than is shown by the ordinary vocabularies. The greater portion of the schedules in Table II attached to Part II were filled out by the writer, using the same notation, and after hearing the words, or terms of relationship, many times repeated by native speakers.   This, of itself, would tend to keep the amount of dialectical variation within its actual limits.   On the contrary, the published vocabularies were made by different persons, using notations not uniform, and in many cases none at all, which, of itself, would tend to exaggerate the amount of change.   The words in the table are also given with the pronoun *my* in combination with the root, which in Indian languages is a matter of much importance where the words are to be used for philological purposes.   The pronoun *my* or *mine*, if not in every case inseparable, enters so constantly into combination with terms of a personal kind, and with names for objects which are personal, that a very marked change is produced in the word itself when the pronominal form is changed.   The following may be taken as illustrations:—

	Kenistenaux or Cree.	Cherokee.	Seneca–Iroquois.
My father.	Noh·-täh-we′.	A-do′-dä.	Hä′-nih.
Thy "	Koh·-tä-we′.	Tṣa-do′-dä.	Yä′-nih.
His "	Oh·-tä-we′.	Oo-do′-dä.	Ho′-nih.
Our "	Kooh·-tä-we′.	E-ge-do′-dä.	Sa-dwä′nih.
Your "	Koh·-tä-we-woo′.	E.-tṣe-do-dä.	Sez-wä′-nih.
Their "	Ooh·-tä-we-woo-wä′	Oo-ne-do′-dä.	Hä-go′-nih.
My mother.	N'-gä′-we.	A′-tṣe.	Noh-yeh′.
Thy "	Ke-gä′-we.	Is-huh′-tṣe.	Gä-no′-eh.
His "	Oh·-gä′-we-ä.	Oo′tṣe.	Hoo-no′-eh.
Our "	Ke-gä-we-nan′.	E-ge′tṣe.	A-te′no-eh.
Your "	Ke-gä-we-woo′.	E-tṣe′-tṣe.	A-che′-no-eh.
Their "	Oh·-gä′-we-woo-a′.	Oo-ne′-tṣe.	Ho-un-de-no′-eh.

These pronominal inflections are carried much further in the Ganowanian languages than philologists have generally supposed, although this characteristic has been fully recognized.[1] From the fact that the terms of relationship almost universally involve the pronoun it became important—to secure the advantages which would result from a comparison of these terms as well as for ascertaining the direct relationship to *Ego* of his blood kindred—that all the answers to the questions in the table should be in the same pronominal form. These questions, therefore, are to be understood as made in the direct form. " What do I call the person (described in the question) when I speak to him by the relationship which he sustains to me?" and the term given in the table is to be understood as responsive to the question in this form; *e. g.*, " my father," " my son," " my nephew." It would be impossible for an American Indian, in most of the nations, to use one of these terms in the abstract.[2] There are some exceptions.

---

[1] There are specializations in the dual and plural numbers which, so far as the writer is aware, have never been presented by Indian grammarians. My attention was first called to these additional inflections by the Rev. Evan Jones, who for upwards of forty years has been a missionary among the Cherokees, and who during this period has fully mastered the structure and principles of this language. The pronoun *myself* in the Cherokee is perfect and independent; the pronoun *my*, as also in Iroquois, is capable of a separate inflection; and all the terms of relationship pass through the same form. The following illustrations are from the Cherokee :—

Person.		Myself.		My or mine.		My elder sister.
Singular.	1.	A-gwä′-suh,	Myself.	A-gwä-tṣa′-le,	Mine.	Uṇ′-ge-do.
	2.	Tṣä′-suh,	Thyself.	Tṣa-tṣa′-le,	Thine.	Tsuh′-doh.
	3.	Oo-wä′-suh,	Himself.	Oo-tṣa′-le,	His.	Oo-doh′.
Dual.	1 & 2.	Ge′-nä-suh,	Ourselves, thou and I.	Gin-e-tṣa′-le,	Ours, thine and mine.	Gin-e-doh′.
	1 & 3.	O-ge-nä′-suh,	Ourselves, he and I.	O-gin′-ä-tṣa-le,	His and mine.	O-gin′-e-doh.
	2.	Sdä′-suh,	Yourselves, you two.	Stä-tṣa′-le,	Yours, you two.	Stä-doh′.
Plural.	1 & 2.	E-gä′-suh,	Ourselves, three or more of you and me.	E-gä-tṣa′-le,	Ours, yours and mine.	E-ge-doh′.
	1 & 3.	O-gä′-suh,	Ourselves, three or more of them and me.	O-gä-tṣa′-le,	Ours, thine and mine.	O-ge-doh′.
	2.	E-tṣa′-suh,	Yourselves, three or more.	E-gä-tṣa -le,	Yours, three or more.	E-tṣe-doh′.
	3.	O-nä′-suh,	Themselves.	Oo-tṣa′-le,	Theirs.	Oo-ne-doh′.

[2] Many of the words used in the formal vocabularies of the philologists are inferior for comparison, particularly such as are generic, as *tree, fish, deer;* such as relate to objects which are personal, as

It was found impossible to recover the etymological signification of the terms of relationship. This signification has long since disappeared beyond retrieval. In a few instances the terms are still significant; but we know at once, from that fact, that these terms are of modern introduction. The preservation of the meanings of this class of words in languages which have been simply oral from time immemorial would have been more remarkable than the loss, since presumptively the larger portion of these terms must have originated in the primitive speech.

A comparison, in detail, of the forms of consanguinity which prevail in the nations represented in the table (Table II, Part II) will disclose a number of deviations from uniformity. These deviations, since they do not invade the radical features of the system, are invested with special importance. They are insufficient to lessen the number of fundamental characteristics which should be common in order to demonstrate, by internal evidence, the common origin of the system. In general plan, minute details, and apparent design it is one and the same throughout, with the exception of the Eskimo, which detaches itself from the Ganowánian connection. It will be seen and recognized that it is far more difficult to maintain unchanged a complicated and elaborate system of relationship than one which is free from complexity; although it may be found to be as difficult for one as the other to depart essentially from its radical form. Absolute uniformity in such a system of relationship as the one about to be considered is a naked impossibility. Where we know that the period of separation of the several branches of the family from each other must be measured by centuries, not to say by decades of centuries of time, it would be to exclude at once development and modification, both of which, within narrow limits, are inseparable from all systems of relationship. When this comparison has been made, the inconsiderable amount of deviation and the constancy of the indicative features of the system will occasion the greater surprise. These diversities were, for a time, a source of much perplexity; but as the range of investigation widened their limits began to be circumscribed. They appeared to have taken their rise far back in the past, and to have perpetuated themselves in the several subdivisions of that branch of the family in which they originated It was perceived at once that they might envelop a record still decipherable of the immediate genetic connection of those nations, however widely separated geographically, in whose domestic relationship these diversities were common. If they could deliver any testimony upon such questions, they were worthy of careful investigation. These deviations thus become attractive

---

head, mouth, nose, or which are subject to personal ownership, as *hat, pipe, tomahawk*, and so on. In most of our Indian languages there are names for the different species of trees, and of animals, but no generic name for tree, or fish, or deer. The pronoun also is usually,found incorporated with the names of the different organs of the body, and with the names of objects which are personal. If, for example, I ask an Indian, "What do you call this?" touching the hat of a person standing near me, he will reply, "His hat;" if I point to mine, "Your hat," and if to his own, he will say, "My hat." This element of change tends to impair the usefulness of these words for comparison. Such terms as are founded upon generalizations, as *spring, summer, morning, evening*, are of but little value. Many of the words commonly used, however, are free from objection, such as *fire, water, rain, hail, hot, cold, pigeon, crow, elk*; the names of the *colors*, the *numerals*, and other words of that character.

rather than repellent as blemishes upon the system. They also furnish some independent testimony concerning the migrations of the Ganowanian family.

A brief explanation of the tribal organization as it now prevails amongst the American aborigines is necessary to a right understanding of the terms *tribe* and *nation*, as used in American Ethnology. This organization has some connection with the origin of some portion of the classificatory system of relationship. It is generally found that all the people speaking the same *dialect* are under one independent political government. For this reason they are called a *nation*, although numbering but a few hundred, and at most but a few thousand persons. Dialect and nation, therefore, are coextensive, as employed in Indian ethnography. Such is usually the case with respect to civilized nations where language becomes the basis of the distinction. The use of the term *nation* instead of *tribe*, to distinguish such small communities was rendered the more necessary, because the greater proportion of these so called Indian nations were each subdivided into a number of tribes, which were such in the strict generic sense of the term. The Seneca-Iroquois, for example, are subdivided into eight tribes, the Wolf, Bear, Beaver, Turtle, Deer, Snipe, Heron, and Hawk. Each tribe is a great family of consanguinei, the tribal name preserving and proclaiming the fact that they are the lineal descendants of the same person. It embraces, however, but a moiety of such person's descendants. The separation of a portion, and their transference to other tribes, were effected by the prohibition of intermarriage between individuals of the same tribe, and by limiting tribal descent to the female line. None of the members of the Wolf or other tribes were allowed to intermarry in their own tribe. A woman of the Wolf tribe might marry a man of any other tribe than her own, but the children of the marriage were of her tribe. If she married a Cayuga or even an Alien, her children would be Senecas of the Wolf tribe, since the mother confers both her nationality and her tribal name upon her children. In like manner her daughters must marry out of the tribe, but the children would nevertheless belong to the Wolf tribe. On the other hand, her sons must also marry women of other tribes, and their children, belonging to the tribes of their respective mothers, are lost to the Wolf connection. The eight tribes are, in this manner, intermingled throughout the nation, two tribes being necessarily represented in the heads of every family.

A tribe may be defined as a group of consanguinei, with descent limited either to the male or to the female line. Where descent is limited to the *male line*, the tribe would consist of a supposed male ancestor and his children, together with the descendants of his sons in the male line forever. It would include this ancestor and his children, the children of his sons, and all the children of his lineal male descendants, whilst the children of the daughters of this ancestor, and all the children of his female descendants would be transferred to the tribes of their respective fathers. Where descent is limited to the *female line*, the tribe would consist of a supposed female ancestor and her children, together with the descendants of her daughters in the female line forever. It would include the children of this ancestor, the children of her daughters, and all the children of her lineal female descendants, whilst the children of the sons of this ancestor, and all the children of her male descendants would be transferred to the tribes of their respective mothers. Modifications of this form of the tribe may have existed, but this is the substance of the institution.

Each tribe thus becomes territorially coextensive with the nation, since they were not separated into independent communities.[1] For the reason, therefore, that there are several tribes of the Senecas, they cannot be called collectively the Seneca tribe; but inasmuch as they all speak the same dialect and are under one political organization, there is a manifest propriety in calling them the Seneca nation. Among the nations whose institutions were the most developed, the office of sachem or chief was hereditary in the female line. Each tribe had the right to furnish its own civil ruler, and consequently the office could never pass out of the tribe. One singular result of this institution relating to the descent of official dignities was the perpetual disinheritance of the sons of sachems. As father and son were necessarily of different tribes, the son could not succeed to his father's office. It passed to the sachem's brother, who was of the same tribe, or to one of the sons of one of his sisters, who was also of the same tribe, the choice between them being determined by election. This was the rule among the Iroquois, among a portion of the Algonkin nations, and also among the Aztecs. In a number of Indian nations descent is now limited to the male line, with the same prohibition of intermarriage in the tribe, and the son succeeds to the father's office. There are reasons for believing that this is an innovation upon the ancient custom, and that descent in the female line was once universal in the Ganowánian family.

The aboriginal inhabitants of North America, when discovered, were divided into two great classes, or were found in two dissimilar conditions; each of which represented a distinct mode of life. The first and lowest condition was that of the *Roving Indians*, who lived chiefly upon fish, and also upon game. They were entirely ignorant of agriculture. Each nation inhabited a particular area which they defended as their home country; but roamed through it without being stationary in any locality. They spent a part of the year at their fishing encampments, and the remainder in the mountains, or in the forest districts most favorable for game. Of this class the Athapascans, west of Hudson's Bay, the nations of the valley of the Columbia, the Blackfeet, Shoshonees, Crees, Assiniboines, and Dakotas, and the Great Lake and Missouri nations are examples. The second and highest condition was that of the Village Indians, who were stationary in villages, and depended exclusively upon agriculture for subsistence. They lived in com-

---

[1] Among the nations, besides the Iroquois, who are subdivided into tribes, are the Wyandotes, Winnebagoes, Otoes, Kaws, Osages, Iowas, Omahas, Punkas, Cherokees, Creeks, Choctas, Chickasas, Ojibwas, Otawas, Potawattamies, Sauks and Foxes, Menominies, Miamas, Shawnees, Delawares, Mohegans, Munsees, Shoshonees, Comanches, the Village Indians of New Mexico, the Aztecs, and some other ancient Mexican nations. Some of the Algonkin and Dakotan nations have lost the tribal organization, which presumptively they once possessed, as the Crees and the Dakotas proper. It is not found among the Athapascas, nor amongst the nations in the valley of the Columbia, although it is said to prevail amongst the nations of the northwest coast. In addition to the Iroquois tribes above mentioned, the following may be named: Crane, Duck, Loon, Turkey, Musk-rat, Sable, Pike, Sturgeon, Carp, Buffalo, Elk, Reindeer, Eagle, Hare, Rabbit, and Snake.

munal houses constructed of adobe brick, or of rubble-stone and mud mortar, or of stone and mortar, and several stories high. This class had made considerable progress in civilization, but without laying aside their primitive domestic institutions. The Village Indians of New Mexico, of Mexico, and Yucatan are examples of this class. Between these two great divisions of the American aborigines there was a third or intermediate class, which exhibited all the gradations of condition between them, apparently forming the connecting links uniting them in one great family. The gradations were so uniform as to be substantially imperceptible, unless the extremes were contrasted. These intermediate nations were the partially Roving and partially Village Indians, who united agricultural subsistence with that upon fish and game, and resided for the greater part of the year in villages. Of this class the Iroquois, the Hurons, the Powhattan Indians of Virginia, the Creek, Choctas, Natches, Sauks and Foxes, Mandans, and Minnetaries, are examples. The two classes of nations, with those intermediate in condition, represent all the phases of Indian society, and possess homogeneous institutions, but under different degrees of development.

In their civil organizations there are, and have been, but three stages of progressive development, which are represented by the *tribe*, the *nation*, and the *confederacy* of nations. The unit of organization, or the first stage, was the tribe, all the members of which, as consanguinei, were held together by blood affinities. The second stage was the nation, which consisted of several tribes intermingled by marriage, and all speaking the same dialect. They were held together by the affinities of an identical speech. To them, as a nation, appertained the exclusive possession of an independent dialect, of a common government, and of territorial possessions. The greater proportion of the Ganowanian family never advanced beyond the national condition. The last, and the ultimate stage of organization was the confederacy of nations. It was usually, if not invariably, composed of nations speaking dialects of the same stock-language. The Iroquois, Otawa, Powhattan, and Creek Confederacies, the Dakota League of the Seven Council Fires, the Aztec Confederacy between the Aztecs, Tezcucans, and Tlacopans, and the Tlascalan Confederacy are familiar examples. It thus appears, that whilst we have for our own political series, the *town*, the *county*, the *state*, and the *United States*, which are founded upon territory, each in turn resting upon an increasing territorial area circumscribed by metes and bounds, the American aborigines have for theirs, the *tribe*, the *nation*, and the *confederacy* of nations, which are founded respectively upon *consanguinity*, *dialect*, and *stock-language*. The idea of a state, or of an empire in the proper sense of these terms, founded upon territory, and not upon persons, with laws in the place of usages, with municipal government in the place of the unregulated will of chiefs, and with a central executive government in the place of a central oligarchy of chiefs, can scarcely be said to have existed amongst any portion of our aboriginal inhabitants. Their institutions had not developed to this stage, and never could have reached it until a knowledge of property and its uses had been formed in their minds. It is to property considered in the concrete that modern civilization must ascribe its origin.

With respect to their numbers, there are no reasons for believing that they were ever very numerous, even in the most favored localities. Although spread over immense areas and in the occupation of many fruitful regions, still, without field agriculture, or flocks and herds, it was impossible that they should develop a large, much more a dense population. They possessed neither flocks nor herds, and their agriculture never rose above garden-bed culture, performed with no better implements than those of wood and bone. In the valley of Mexico, where there are reasons for supposing that irrigation upon a large scale was practised, production was greater than in other areas. But notwithstanding the exception to some extent of this region, the current statements with reference to the numbers of the American aborigines are unsupported by trustworthy evidence. The history of the human family does not afford an instance of a large population without ample pastoral subsistence or field agriculture. It may also be safely affirmed that the real distance in social condition between the Aztecs, as one of the highest representatives of the Village Indians, and the Iroquois, as one of the highest representatives of the Northern Indians, was not as great as has been generally supposed, although the former had reached a state considerably more advanced. If the civil and domestic institutions, arts, inventions, usages, and customs of the Northern Indians are compared with those of the Southern Village Indians, so far as the latter are reliably ascertained, whatever differences exist will be found to consist in the degree of development of the same homogeneous conceptions of a common mind, and not of ideas springing from a different source. With the common origin of the Village and Northern Indians established, there is no further problem of much difficulty in American Ethnology.

It now remains to present an analysis of the Indian system of relationship; and after that to take up in detail the system of the several nations represented in the Table; and to trace its radical characteristics as well as the extent of its distribution. It will be found that a common system prevails amongst all the nations named therein, with the exception of the Eskimo.

The system of relationship considered in Part I was characterized as descriptive because, in its original form, the collateral and a portion of the lineal consanguinei of every person were described by a combination of the primary terms. For example, the phrase "father's brother" was used to designate an uncle on the father's side; "brother's son" for a nephew, and "father's brother's son" for one of the four male cousins. The discrimination of these relationships, in the concrete, was an aftergrowth in point of time, and exceptional in the system. After it was effected and special terms had been introduced to express those relationships, in some of the branches of the great families named, they were sufficient for the designation of but a small portion of the blood kindred of each individual. At least four-fifths within the limits of the first five collateral lines, and within six degrees from the common ancestor, could only be indicated by means of descriptive phrases. At the present time, therefore, it is a descriptive system. It has also been called a natural system, because it is founded upon a correct appreciation of the distinction between the lineal and several collateral lines, and of the perpetual divergence of the latter from the former. Each relationship is thus specialized and separated from every other in such a manner as to decrease its nearness. and diminish its value according to the degree of the distance of each person from the central *Ego*. By this formal recognition of the divergence of the streams of the blood and the connection of consanguinei through common ancestors, the numerical system suggested by the nature of descents was affirmed. It also assumed the existence of marriage between single pairs.

In contradistinction from *descriptive* the term *classificatory* will be employed to characterize the system of consanguinity and affinity of the Ganowanian, Turanian, and Malayan families, which is founded upon conceptions fundamentally different. Among the latter families consanguinei are never described by a combination of the primary terms; but on the contrary they are arranged into great classes or categories upon principles of discrimination peculiar to these families. All the individuals of the same class are admitted into one and the same relationship, and the same special term is applied indiscriminately to each and all of them. For example, my father's brother's son is my *brother* under the system about to be considered; and I apply to him the same term which I use to designate an own brother: the son of this collateral brother and the son of my own brother are both my *sons*. And I apply to them the same term I would use to designate my own son. In other words, the person first named is admitted into the same relationship as my own brothers, and these last named as my own sons. The principle of classification is carried to every person in the several collateral lines, near and remote, in such a manner as to include them all in the several great classes. Although apparently arbitrary and artificial, the results produced by the classification are coherent and systematic. In determining the class to which each person belongs, the degrees, numerically, from *Ego* to the common ancestor, and from the latter to each kinsman, are strictly regarded. This knowledge of the lines of parentage is necessary to determine the classification. As now used and interpreted, with marriage between single pairs actually existing, it is an arbitrary and artificial system, because it is contrary to the nature of descents, confounding relationships which are distinct, separating those which are similar, and diverting the streams of the blood from the collateral channels into the lineal. Consequently, it is the reverse of the descriptive system. It is wholly impossible to explain its origin on the assumption of the existence of the family founded upon marriage between single pairs; but it may be explained with some degree of probability on the assumption of the antecedent existence of a series of customs and institutions, one reformatory of the other, commencing with promiscuous intercourse and ending with the establishment of the family, as now constituted, resting upon marriage between single pairs.

From the complicated structure of the system it is extremely difficult to separate, by analysis, its constituent parts and present them in such a manner as to render them familiar and intelligible without close application. There are, however, several fundamental conceptions embodied in the system, a knowledge of which will contribute to its simplification. The most of them are in the nature of indicative characteristics of the system, and may be stated as follows: First, all of the descendants of an original pair are not only, theoretically, consanguinei, but all of them fall within the recognized relationships. Secondly, relations by blood or marriage are never described by a combination of the primary terms, but a single special term is applied to each of them. Persons who stand to *Ego* in unequal degrees, and who are related to him in different ways, are thus placed upon the same level in the rank of their relationship. It makes no difference that it is a false use of terms, for example, to call my father's brother *my father*, when he is not my father in our sense of progenitor, since it is the Indian method of classification, and with that alone we are now concerned. Thirdly, the several collateral lines in every case are ultimately merged in the lineal line, by means of which the posterity of my collateral consanguinei become my posterity. Fourthly, the relationship of cousin is the most remote collateral degree which is recognized: consequently, none of the descendants of an original pair can fall without this collateral relationship. The number of recognized consanguinei is exceedingly multiplied by the operative force of the last two provisions. Fifthly, the children of brothers are brothers and sisters to each other; the children of sisters are brothers and sisters to each other; but the children of a brother and sister stand to each other in a different and more remote relationship. Sixthly, the relationship of uncle is restricted to the mother's brothers, and to the brothers of such other persons as stand to *Ego* in the relation of a mother. Seventhly, the relationship of aunt is restricted to the sister of a father, and to the sisters of such other persons as stand to *Ego* in the relation of a father. Eighthly, the relationships of nephew and niece are restricted, where *Ego* is a male, to the children of his sisters, and to the children of such collateral persons as stand to him in the relation of a sister. But when *Ego* is a female they are restricted to the children of her brother, and to the children of such other persons as stand to her in the relation of a brother. Ninthly, the correlative relationships are strictly applied; the person whom I call grandson calls me grandfather; the one I call nephew calls me uncle; the one I call father-in-law calls me son-in-law; and so on through every recognized relationship. To each of the foregoing propositions there are some exceptions, but they are few in number. Lastly, whilst this system of relationship recognizes and upholds the bond of consanguinity to an unprecedented extent, it contradicts, and attempts apparently to thwart, the natural outflow of the streams of the blood. At the same time the principles upon which it rests are enforced with rigorous precision.

An analysis of this system of relationship will develop its fundamental conceptions in the form of independent propositions, by means of which a comparison can be made between the several forms as they now exist in the branches of the family. This comparison will determine whether or not the system is one and the same throughout the family. At the same time the features in which there is a deviation from uniformity will be separated from those which are constant. It will then be seen whether these deviations invade any characteristics of the system which must be regarded as fundamental, or simply represent an amount of contraction and expansion which must be considered inseparable from its complicated structure. It is, therefore, important that this analysis should be rigorous and exact; and that the points of disagreement should be not less definitely traced. Among the more important questions involved in the final comparison to be made are the two following: first, whether or not the forms which prevail in the several branches of the Ganowánian family are identical in whatever is ultimate or radical; and secondly, if identical throughout all these nations, whether or not it was transmitted to each with the blood, involving, consequently, the genealogical connection of the nations themselves.

The following propositions develop all of the material characteristics of the system of relationship of the nations represented in the Table. They are severally true of each and every form in each and every nation, with the exceptions stated.

I. Consanguinei are not described by a combination of primary terms, but are classified into categories under some one of the recognized relationships, each of which is expressed by a particular term.

II. The several collateral lines, in their several branches, are ultimately merged in the lineal line.

III. In familiar intercourse and in formal salutation, consanguinei, near and remote, address each other by the term of relationship.

IV. From *Ego* a male to the children of his brother a male, and from *Ego* a female to the children of her sister a female, the relationship of these children to *Ego* approaches in the degree of its nearness; but from *Ego* a male, to the children of a female, and from *Ego* a female to the children of a male, it recedes. There are some exceptions to these rules.

V. Ascending one degree above *Ego* in the lineal line, and crossing over to the first members of the four branches of the second collateral line, it follows again that from male line to male line, and from female to female, the relationship to *Ego* approaches in the degree of its nearness, while from male line to female line, and from female to male, it recedes, and that irrespective of the sex of *Ego*. To these rules there are a few exceptions. The father's sister, in some cases, is a mother instead of an aunt, and the mother's brother, in two instances, is an elder brother instead of an uncle.

VI. There are original terms for grandfather and grandmother, father and mother, son and daughter, and grandson and granddaughter in all of the languages represented in the Table without an exception. In a few instances some of these terms are in common gender. These, with those of brother and sister, are called the primary relationships.

VII. All of my ancestors above grandfather and grandmother, are my grandfathers and grandmothers, without further distinction, except that in some of the nations they are discriminated as second, third, and more remote grandfathers and grandmothers. In common usage, however, the former are the recognized relationships. The Pawnee form is an exception.

VIII. All the brothers and sisters of my grandfather and of my grandmother, and all the brothers and sisters of my several ancestors above the latter, are, without distinction, my grandfathers and grandmothers, with the occasional modifications stated in the seventh proposition.

IX. All my descendants below grandson and granddaughter, are, without distinction, my grandsons and granddaughters, with the occasional modifications named in the seventh proposition. The Pawnee form is also an exception.

X. There is one term for elder brother and another for younger brother, one term for elder sister and another for younger sister; and no term for brother or

19   December, 1869.

sister in the abstract, except in the plural number. These terms are not applied to the oldest and youngest specifically, but to each and all who are older than the brother or sister speaking. In several languages there is a double set of terms, one of which is used by males, and the other by females. In some cases the term for elder and younger sister is common. There are also a few instances in which additional terms for brother and sister in the abstract are found.

XI. All the children of my several own brothers, and of my several collateral brothers, myself a male, are my sons and daughters, and all the children of the latter are my grandsons and granddaughters. There are exceptions to the first branch of this proposition. In a few nations they are step-sons and step-daughters.

XII. All the children of my several own sisters, and of my several collateral sisters, myself a male, are my nephews and nieces, and all the children of the latter are my grandsons and granddaughters. The exceptions are few in number.

XIII. All the children of my several own brothers, and of my several collateral brothers, myself a female, are my nephews and nieces. There are many exceptions. The children of these nephews and nieces are my grandsons and granddaughters.

XIV. All the children of my several own sisters, and of my several collateral sisters, myself a female, are my sons and daughters. The exceptions are few, and chiefly confined to those cases where the relationship is that of step-son and step-daughter. The children of these sons and daughters are my grandsons and grand-daughters.

XV. All the brothers of my own father, and all the brothers of such other persons as stand to me in the relation of a father, are my fathers; and all the sisters of my own mother, and of such other persons as stand to me in the relation of a mother, are severally my mothers, the same as by own mother. In several nations they are step-fathers and step-mothers; in some others they are little fathers and little mothers.

XVI. All the brothers of my own mother, and all the brothers of such other persons as stand to me in the relation of a mother, are severally my uncles; and all the sisters of my own father, and all the sisters of such other persons as stand to me in the relation of a father, are severally my aunts. In a few nations the relationship of aunt is not recognized, in which cases my father's sisters are my mothers. In two nations that of uncle is unknown, in which cases my mother's brothers are my elder brothers.

XVII. All the children of several brothers are brothers and sisters to each other; and they use, in each case, the respective terms for elder and younger brother, and for elder and younger sister, which they do in the case of own brothers and sisters. Exceptions exist in the limited number of nations in which step-father and step-son are used. Among them the relationship is that of step-brother and step-sister.

XVIII. All the sons of the sons of several brothers are brothers to each other, elder or younger; all the sons of the latter are brothers again, and the same relationship of males in the male line continues downward indefinitely, so long as each of these persons stands at the same degree of remove from the original brother. But when one is further advanced, by a single degree, than the other, the rule which turns the collateral line into the lineal at once applies: thus, the son of either of these my collateral, elder/or younger, brothers, myself being a male, be-comes my son, and the son of the latter is my grandson.

XIX. All the children of several sisters are brothers and sisters to each other; and the terms of relationship are applied as in the last case. The exceptions also are the same.

XX. All the daughters of the daughters of several sisters are sisters to each other, elder or younger, and the daughters of the latter are sisters again; and the relationship of females in the female line continues to be that of sisters, elder or younger, at equal removes, downward indefinitely, with the same result as in the former case, where one is further removed than the other from the original sisters.

XXI. All the children of several brothers on the one hand, and of the several sisters of these brothers on the other, are cousins to each other among some of the nations. Among other nations the males of the former class are uncles to the males and females of the latter class; and the males and females of the latter are nephews and nieces to those of the former; whilst to still others the females of the former class are mothers to the males and females of the latter class, and the males and females of the latter are sons and daughters to the females of the former. To illustrate: my father's sister's son and daughter, *Ego* a male, are my nephew and niece, each of them calling me (their mother's brother's son) uncle; but with *Ego* a female, the same persons are my son and daughter, each of them calling me mother. Among other nations these relationships are still different, and they can be easier expressed by an illustration than by a rule; namely, my father's sister's son, *Ego* a male, is my father, and he calls me his son; my father's sister's daughter is my aunt, and she calls me her nephew; but with *Ego* a female, my father's sister's son is my father, and calls me his daughter; whilst my father's sister's daughter is my grandmother, and calls me her granddaughter. Among still other nations the children of brothers on the one hand, and of sisters on the other, are brothers and sisters to each other. Upon this relationship occurs the most important, as well as the principal, deviation from uniformity.

XXII. All the children of several cousins are cousins again; the children of the latter are also cousins; and this relationship continues downward indefinitely. Where the relationship of the children of a brother and sister is that of uncle and nephew, the son of this uncle is an uncle again; and this relationship continues downwards in the male line indefinitely. Where, in the same case, it is that of son and father, the son and grandson of this father are each my father, and this relationship continues downward in the male line indefinitely. In all other cases the collateral line is brought into the lineal.

XXIII. As a general result the descendants of brothers and sisters, or of an original pair, can never pass, in theory, beyond the degrees of cousin and grand-child, these being the most remote collateral and descendant relationships; nor in the ascending series beyond the degree of grandfather. Hence the bond of con-sanguinity which can never, in fact, be broken by lapse of time or distance in degree, is not permitted, by the fundamental provisions of the Ganowanian system, to be broken in principle.

XXIV. All the wives of my several nephews and collateral sons are my daughters-in-law; and all the husbands of my several nieces and collateral daughters are my sons-in-law; and I apply to them the same terms respectively which I use to designate the husbands and wives of my own sons and daughters. There are some exceptions to this proposition.

XXV. All the wives of my several collateral brothers and of my several male cousins are my sisters-in-law; and all the husbands of my several collateral sisters and of my several female cousins are my brothers-in-law, without regard to the degree of nearness. There are some exceptions.

XXVI. In all of the preceding relationships the correlative terms are strictly applied; thus, the one I call my son calls me father; the one I call grandson calls me grandfather: the one I call nephew calls me uncle; the one I call brother-in-law calls me the same; the one I call father-in-law calls me son-in-law; and so on throughout the entire series, whether of affinity or of consanguinity.

When the foregoing propositions have been verified by passing through one of the schedules in the Table, the system itself will become perfectly familiar, and any deviations from the standard form in other schedules will at once be recognized wherever they occur. A number of discrepancies will also be discovered, falling below the character of permanent deviations; but they relate to subordinate details, and do not disturb the general plan of consanguinity. Some of them may represent a misapprehension of the question to be answered; others an ignorance of the true relationship, and still others a discrepancy in some part of the form of the particular nation. In the details of a system so complicated and elaborate, drawn out from uncultivated languages, and with a nomenclature so opulent, a large amount of variation would not only be unavoidable, but an exemption from it would excite surprise. A sufficient number of features, which may be called indicative of the typical form, are so constant as to leave no doubt of the identity of the system as it now prevails in the several branches of the family, with the exception of the Eskimo. The fundamental conceptions upon which the system rests are simple and clearly defined, and work out their results with logical accuracy.

The deviations from uniformity may be recapitulated as follows:—

I. Relationship of Uncle and Aunt. In the Crow and Minnitaree, and in one or more of the Athapascan nations, these relationships are wanting. These nations form an exception, in this respect, to the entire Ganowánian family. In a number of other nations the relationship of aunt is unknown, and that of mother usually takes its place.

II. Relationships of Nephew and Niece. In four or five dialects terms for nephew and niece are wanting. These relationships limited, with *Ego* a male, to the children of his sister, and with *Ego* a female, usually to the children of her brother, is one of the most striking of the indicative features of the system. But a failure of five out of seventy-five Indian nations upon these relationships is not sufficient to require an explanation, even if it could be made.

III. Double Set of Terms. The use of one set of terms by the males, and another set by the females in some nations for certain relationships; also the use of step-father, step-brother, and step-son, among other nations in the place of the full terms; and finally the use, in still other nations, of little father and little mother for the brother of a father and the sister of a mother, must be regarded in the light of modifications of the primitive form by particular usage rather than as deviations from uniformity.

IV. Relationships of the Children of a Brother and Sister. It is evident that the relationship of a cousin was unknown in the original system, and that it was an aftergrowth, or further development, designed to remove a blemish. The four different forms in which the relationships of the children of a brother and sister appear, render it difficult to determine which was the primitive form, only that *cousin* was not. The principles of the system required that they should stand in a more remote relationship than that of brother and sister; and thus we are led to the inference that it was either that of uncle and nephew, or that of son and father.

V. Marriage Relationships. There are a number of diversities in these relationships, but a sufficient number are constant to establish the unity of the system from this source of evidence alone.

VI. Mergence of Collateral Lines. In a few of the nations some branches of the collateral lines are more abruptly merged in the lineal than the common form allows; but of this peculiarity no explanation can be given.

We are now the better prepared to take up the system of relationship of the Ganowánian family in its several branches; and by an examination of its structure and details, to verify the preceding propositions, and also to trace this form of the classificatory system to its limits. In no other manner can its remarkable character, as a domestic institution, be understood or appreciated, or its value estimated for ethnological purposes.

CHAPTER II.

SYSTEM OF RELATIONSHIP OF THE GANOWANIAN FAMILY—Continued.

Position of the Iroquois—Area of their Occupation—Their Home Country—Epoch of the Establishment of the League—Hodenosaunee, their Proper Name—Other Nations of the same Lineage—the Hurons or Wyandotes—Neutral Nation—Eries—Susquehannocks—Nottoways—I. Iroquois—Their System of Relationship—Seneca Form adopted as typical; also as typical of the System of the Ganowánian Family—Lineal Line—First Collateral Line—Diagrams—Second Collateral Line—Diagrams—Indicative Relationships—Marriage Relationships—Third and Fourth Collateral Lines—Diagrams—Methods of Verifying same.—Other Marriage Relationships—Necessary Knowledge of Numerical Degrees—Consanguinei not allowed to Intermarry—Systems of Remaining Iroquois Nations—Identical with the Seneca—One Deviation from Uniformity—II. Hurons, or Wyandotes—Their System identical with the Seneca—Common Origin of the System—Coeval with their Existence as one People.

Dakotan Nations.

I. Hodenosaunian Nations.   1. Iroquois.   2. Hurons.

Among the Indian nations found in possession of the North American continent, north of New Mexico, the Iroquois deservedly hold the highest rank.   In energy and intelligence, and the degree of development of their civil institutions they are far in advance of the Northern Indian nations.   At the period of their discovery (1609), or within fifty years of that event, they reached their culminating point. It found them in acknowledged supremacy from the Hudson on the east, to the Wabash on the west, and from the St. Lawrence, and lakes Ontario and Erie on the north, to the Tennessee and the Upper Potomac on the south.   After the overthrow of the Hurons and Neutral Nation in the peninsula between lakes Huron, Erie, and Ontario, their dominion was extended northward to the Otawa[1] River and Lake Nipessing.   Within the boundaries named there were areas of several thousand square miles which were unbroken solitudes, except as they were occasionally traversed by war parties, or visited for hunting and fishing.   Other portions of the same area were occupied by Indian nations recognizing their supremacy.   The present State of New York was the home country of the Iroquois, first to the Genesee, and afterwards to Lake Erie.   Their presence, as an intrusive population, so near the centre of the Algonkin area, sufficiently attests their superiority over the Algonkin nations.   It also serves to explain the otherwise eccentric spread of the latter along the Atlantic coast to the southern limits of North Carolina, implying that the Iroquois area was originally Algonkin.   The Iroquois were, as there are reasons for believing, an early offshoot, and one of the advanced bands of the

---

[1] Pronounced O-tä'-wa

great Dakota stock, who first made their way eastward to the valley of the St. Lawrence, near Montreal, where they were once established, and afterwards into the lake region of Central New York, where they were found at the epoch of their discovery.

The prominent position of the Iroquois among the Northern nations was acquired subsequently to the establishment of the league under which they were consolidated into one political family. That tendency to disintegration, from the secession of successive bands which has ever been the chief element of weakness in Indian society, was counteracted by the federative principle, retaining, as it did, the natural increase of their population to the largely increased development of their intelligence, and to the great augmentation of their military strength. Such a league was rendered possible by a limited agricultural cultivation through which their means of subsistence had become permanently enlarged. Their superiority over their cotemporaries in the art of government is demonstrated by the structure and principles of the league itself, which for originality and simplicity of plan, for efficiency in organizing the power of the people, and for adaptation to military enterprises is worthy of commendation.[1] Since the commencement of European intercourse they have passed through a novel and severe experience, in the progress of which they have produced a greater number of distinguished men than any other Northern nation.

As near as can now be ascertained the league had been established about one hundred and fifty years, when Champlain, in 1609, first encountered the Mohawks within their own territories on the west shore of Lake George. This would place the epoch of its formation about A. D. 1459, or one hundred and thirty-four years subsequent to the foundation of the pueblo of Mexico, according to the current representations.[2] At the time the Iroquois nations confederated they were independent bands, speaking dialects of the same stock-language, but each having its own distinct previous history; with the exception of the Oneidas, who separated themselves from the Mohawks after their settlement in New York, and the Cayugas who, in like manner, separated themselves from the Onondagas. According to their traditions, which are confirmed to some extent by other evidence, they had resided in this area for a long period of time before the league was formed, and had at times made war upon each other. The Tuscaroras, who were of kindred descent, were admitted into the Confederacy about the year 1715, upon their expulsion from North Carolina.

There were but five other nations of the same immediate lineage of whom we have any knowledge. First among these, in numbers and importance, were the Hurons, the ancestors of the present Wyandotes, who occupied the shores of the Georgian Bay and ranged southward toward Lake Erie. Their principal villages were along the Georgian Bay and around Lake Simcoe. Although divided

---

[1] In another work, "The League of the Iroquois," I have presented and discussed the structure and principles of their civil and domestic institutions.

[2] "The foundation of Mexico happened in the year 2 Calli, corresponding with the year 1325 of the vulgar era."—*Clavigero's Hist. of Mexico*, I, 162. (*Cullen's Trans*. 1817.)

into several bands they spoke a common dialect. With these near kinsmen the
Iroquois waged a savage and unrelenting warfare, continued with slight intermis-
sions from the commencement of European intercourse down to 1650, when they
captured and destroyed their principal villages, and forced the remnant into exile.
A portion of them afterwards established themselves near Quebec, where their
descendants still remain. But much the largest portion, after several changes,
settled near the Sandusky, in Ohio, where they were known under their Iroquois
name of Wyandotes;[1] and from thence were finally removed, about thirty years
ago, to Kansas, where their descendants now reside.[2]

Next in importance was the Neutral Nation, who were established upon both
banks of the Niagara River, and spread from thence westward along the north shore
of Lake Erie. They were called by the Iroquois the Wild-cat nation (*Je-go'-sä-sa*),
which is the same name applied by Charleroix to the Eries.[3] It seems probable
that the two were bands of the same nation, not as yet entirely distinct, although
known to the Iroquois under different names, the latter being called *Ga-kwä-ga-o-no*.
The Eries, here treated as a third nation, were seated upon the southeast shore of
Lake Erie, and ranged eastward towards the Genesee. Both the Eries and the
Neutral Nation spoke dialects so near the Seneca that the three could understand
each other's speech. With the acknowledged political astuteness of the Iroquois
it seems remarkable that these nations, together with the Hurons, were not incorporated together in a common confederacy, which would have saved as well as
greatly augmented their strength. They were fully sensible of its importance; and
we have the testimony of the Senecas that the Iroquois offered both to the Eries
and to the Neutrals the alternative of admission into the League or of extermination before the final conflict. After the overthrow of the Hurons they turned next
upon the Neutrals and immediately afterwards upon the Eries, both of whom were
defeated and expelled between 1650 and 1655. A portion of the Eries, after their
defeat, voluntarily surrendered to the Senecas, and were incorporated with them.

On the south were the Susquehannocks, who occupied the lower part of the
Susquehanna River, in Southern Pennsylvania and Northern Maryland. The Iroquois were as relentless and uncompromising towards the Susquehannocks, as they
had been towards their other kinsmen. In 1673, a delegation of Iroquois chiefs
met Count Frontenac, Governor of Canada, near Kingston, and amongst other things
asked him " to assist them against the Andastiguez (Andastes or Susquehannocks),

---

[1] *Wane-dote'* in Seneca-Iroquois.

[2] Since the completion of this work, Francis Parkman, Esq., has given to the public "The Jesuits
in North America," which contains the most complete account of the Hurons ever published. It is a
work of rare excellence, founded upon accurate and comprehensive researches, and written in the most
attractive style. Whilst the ferocious characteristics of the Iroquois, as displayed in many a scene
of carnage, are delineated with graphic power, and are not exaggerated, there is another side of the
picture which should not be overlooked. The Iroquois displayed many virtues in their relations
with each other, both in the family and in political society, which tend to relieve the otherwise harsh
judgment upon their national character and name. Mr. Parkman derives the Wyandotes chiefly
from the Tionnontates, the southernmost band of the Hurons. (*Jesuits in North America*, Intro. xliii.

[3] Hist. of New France, II, 162.

the sole enemies remaining on their hands."[1] About the year 1676, the Susque-hannocks made their submission to the Senecas.[2]

Last were the Nottoways of Virginia, an inconsiderable band, who, with several Algonkin nations, occupied a part of the area between the Potomac and Roanoke Rivers. They are mentioned in treaties between the Colonial Governors of Virginia and the Iroquois as late as 1721.[3] The foregoing are the only branches of the Iroquois stock of which any knowledge has been preserved. The last three named are now extinct, or rather have been dispersed and incorporated with other nations. Above Montreal on the St. Lawrence, there is a small band called the "Two Mountain Iroquois," who were colonists chiefly from the Mohawks and Oneidas.

In addition to what has been stated of the probable immediate blood connection of the Eries and Neutral nation with each other and with the Senecas, there is some evidence that the Hurons and Senecas were subdivisions of one original nation. It is contained in their systems of relationship, both of which agree with each other in the only particular in which the Seneca form differs from that of the other Iroquois nations, except the Tuscarora; and, therefore, tends to show that the Seneca and Hurons were one nation after the Mohawks and Onondagas had become distinct from the Senecas. If this be so, the original Iroquois stock before their occupation of New York, and whilst they resided north of the St. Lawrence and the Lakes, consisted of but four subdivisions, the Hurons or Senecas, the Tuscaroras, the Onondagas, and the Mohawks; or, in short, Senecas and Mohawks.

At the formation of the league the Iroquois called themselves *Ho-dé-no-sau-nee*, " The People of the Long House," which term, notwithstanding its inconvenient length, will furnish a proper name for this branch of the Ganowánian family.[4] They symbolized their political structure by the figure of a " Long House," and were always partial to this name, which was, in fact, their only designation for themselves as one people.[5] They were Village Indians to a very considerable extent, although not exclusively such. In this respect they were in advance of most of the northern Indian nations. In the drama of colonization the influence of this Indian confederacy was conspicuously felt, and cast upon the side of the English colonists. It is made clear by the retrospect that France must ascribe, in no small degree, to the Iroquois, the overthrow of her great plans of empire in North America.

---

[1] Journal of Frontenac's Voyage to Lake Ontario, Col. His., N. Y., ix, 110.

[2] Ib., ix. 227, Note 2. [3] Ib , v. 673.

[4] The primitive bark house of the Iroquois was usually from forty to sixty feet in length, by about fifteen to eighteen in width, comparted at equal distances, but with a common hall through the centre; and with a door at each end of the hall, which were the only entrances. There were from six to ten fire pits in each house, located in the centre of the hall, and so as to give a fire to each compartment. There were two families to each fire, one upon each side of the hall. A house with ten fires would thus accommodate twenty families. In ancient times these houses were clustered together and surrounded with a stockade. The size of the village was estimated by the number of houses, (eighty to one hundred and fifty forming the largest of their villages); and also by the number of fires. The idea revealed in this communal house of the Iroquois runs through all the architecture of the Indian family.

[5] League of the Iroquois, p. 51.

20   December, 1869.

The Iroquois language, which is the proper representative of their intellectual life, compares favorably with that of any other in the circle of the family, with respect to the fulness of its vocables, and to the regularity of its grammatical forms. In the table will be found favorable specimens of its vocables, of its inflections for gender, and of the flexibility of its pronouns.

I. Iroquois. 1. Mohawks. 2. Oneidas. 3. Onondagas. 4. Cayugas. 5. Senecas. 6. Tuscaroras. 7. Two Mountain Iroquois.

From the prominent position of the Iroquois in the Ganowánian family their system of consanguinity and affinity possesses a proportionate value. It is so fully developed in all of its parts that it may be taken as typical of the system of this family. The nomenclature of relationships is opulent, the classification of kindred systematic, and the plan itself, although complicated, and apparently arbitrary and artificial, is yet simple, and in logical accordance with the principles of discrimination upon which it is founded. As the standard form, it is advisable to examine it minutely. When traced out step by step, through its entire range, a perfect knowledge of the system will be obtained, as well as of the fundamental conceptions upon which it rests, which will render an examination of the remaining forms comparatively easy.

For convenience of reference a table of the Seneca-Iroquois and the Yankton-Dakota forms is appended to this chapter. It contains the lineal and first, second, third, and fourth collateral lines, in their several branches, in which are given the terms of relationship applied to the several persons described in the questions, with a translation of each term into equivalent English. This method of arrangement for presenting the system of a single nation is preferable to the one necessarily used in the comparative Table, since it is brought out in a continuous form and separate and apart from other forms. With the aid of this special table, and of the diagrams which follow, all the facilities are afforded that can be necessary for the illustration and explanation of the system. As the Seneca system is developed as to one of the indicative relationships, beyond that of the remaining Iroquois nations, with the exception of the Tuscarora, theirs will be adopted as the standard form of the Iroquois. The terms of relationship used in the illustrations, as well as in the diagrams, are also in the Seneca dialect.[1]

There are terms for grandfather and grandmother, *Hoc'-sote* and *Oc'-sote*; for father and mother, *Hä'-nih* and *No-yeh'*; for son and daughter *Ha-ah'-wuk* and *Ka-ah'-wuk*; and for grandson and daughter *Ha-yä'da* and *Ka-yä'-da*[1]; and no terms for ancestors or descendants beyond those named. All above, without distinction, are grandfathers or grandmothers; and all below are grandsons or granddaughters. When it is necessary to be more specific the person is described.

The relationships of brother and sister are conceived in the twofold form of elder and younger, for each of which there are special terms, namely: *Hä'-je*, my elder brother; *Ah'-je*, my elder sister; *Ha'-gä* my younger brother; *Ka'-gä*, my younger sister. These terms are applied, respectively, to each and all of the brothers and sisters who are older or younger than the person who speaks. There

---

[1] For notation see Fly Leaf to table appended to part II.

is no term either for brother or sister in the abstract; but there is a compound term in the plural number, and in common gender, *Da-yä'-gwä-dan'-no-dä* for brothers and sisters in general.

In the diagrams (Plates IV and V) the lineal and first collateral line, male and female, are represented; in the first with *Ego* a male, and, in the second, with *Ego* a female. The relationships of the same persons in certain clearly defined cases, are entirely different to *Ego* a female, from what they are to *Ego* a male. It is, therefore, imperative that the sex of *Ego* be noted in every case. To exhibit fully these discriminations double diagrams are used, and in the table double questions, the necessity for which will be seen by comparing the diagrams, and also by comparing the questions and answers in the table. In these diagrams the connecting lines follow the chain of descent from parent to child, and the figures which stand in the same horizontal or transverse line show, that the several persons represented are equally removed in degree from the common ancestor. The relationship expressed in each figure is that which the person sustains to *Ego* and no other. A single person is represented by each figure, with the exception of the lowest, upon which the several branches of the collateral line converge. This figure represents as many persons, all of whom are the grandsons and granddaughters of *Ego*, as there are lines terminating in it. In reading the diagrams we ascend by the chain of consanguinity from *Ego* first to the common ancestor, and then down to the person whose relationship is sought; thus, my father's son who is my brother, elder or younger, is upon the right of *Ego*; and my father's daughter, who is my sister, elder or younger, is upon the left of *Ego*; the three, as they are equally removed in degree, being on the same horizontal line. Again the son and daughter of this brother and of this sister, are placed one degree lower down in the diagram, and in the same horizontal line with my own son, since they are equally removed from my father who is their common grandfather. And lastly, if a son and daughter are allowed to each of the persons last named, as well as to my own son, it would require ten figures below these to represent them separately in their proper positions; but inasmuch as they are all alike the grandsons and granddaughters of *Ego*, they are represented by a single figure, as above explained; and for the further object of illustrating the mergence of both branches of the first collateral line in the lineal line, which results from the classification of persons.

With these explanations made, it is now proposed to take up the several collateral lines in detail, and to trace them throughout, in their several branches, until they are finally brought into the lineal line.

In the first collateral line male with myself a male (Plate IV), I call my brother's son and daughter my son and daughter, *Ha-ah'-wuk* and *Ka-ah'-wuk*; and each of them calls me father, *Hä'-nih*. This is the first indicative feature of the system. It places my brother's children in the same category with my own children. Each of their sons and daughters I call severally my grandson and granddaughter, *Ha-yä'-da* and *Ka-yä'-da*, and they call me grandfather, *Hoc-sote*. The relationships here given are those actually recognized and applied, and none other are known.

Certain relationships are here called indicative. They are those which are determinative of the character of the system; and which, when ascertained, usually control those that follow   They are the decisive characteristics which, when they agree in the systems of different nations, embrace so much that is material and fundamental, both in the Turanian and Ganowánian forms, as to render the remaining details subordinate.

In the female branch of this line, myself still a male, I call my sister's son and daughter my nephew and niece, *Ha-yă'-wan-da* and *Ka-yă'-wan-da;* each of them calling me uncle, *Hoc-no'-seh*. This is a second indicative feature. It restricts the relationships of nephew and niece to the children of a man's sisters, to the exclusion of the children of his brothers. The son and daughter of this nephew and of this niece are my grandson and granddaughter as before; each of them addressing me by the correlative term. It will be noticed that, in the male branch, on crossing from *Ego* a male to his brother a male, the relationships of the children of the latter approach in the degree of their nearness to *Ego*, while, in the female branch, on crossing from *Ego* a male to his sister a female, the relationships of her children to *Ego* recede in the degree of their nearness, as compared with the former case.

In the same line, male branch, *Ego* being supposed a female (Plate V), I call my brother's son and daughter my nephew and niece, *Ha-soh'-neh* and *Ka-soh'-neh;* each of them calling me aunt, *Ah-ga'-huc*. It will be observed that the terms for nephew and niece which are used by females are different from those used by males. The son and daughter of this nephew and niece are my grandson and granddaughter, *Ha-yä'-da* and *Ka-yä'-da*, and each of them calls me grandmother, *Oc'-sote*.

Supposing myself still a female, I call my sister's son and daughter my son and daughter, *Ha-ah'-wuk*, and *Ka-ah'-wuk;* each of them calling me mother, *No-yeh'*. Having crossed in the male branch from *Ego* a female to her brother a male, the relationships of the children of the latter to *Ego* recede; whilst, in the female branch, having crossed from *Ego* a female to her sister a female the relationships of the children of the latter approach in the degree of their nearness to *Ego*, also as before. The children of this son and daughter are my grandchildren; each of them addressing me by the correlative term.

Irrespective of the sex of *Ego*, the wife of each of these collateral sons, and of each of these nephews is my daughter-in-law, *Ka'-sä;* and the husband of each of these collateral daughters, and of each of these nieces is my son-in-law, *Oc-na'-hose;* and I stand to each of them in the correlative relationship. This disposes of the first collateral line, including the relationships both of consanguinity and affinity.

Diagram, Plate VI, represents the lineal and second collateral line, male and female, on the father's side, with *Ego* a male; and Diagram, Plate VII, represents the same lines and branches on the mother's side, with *Ego* also a male. It would require two other diagrams of the same kind to represent the relationships of the same persons to *Ego* a female; but these will be sufficient for the purposes of illustration. They are constructed on the same principles as those previously explained.

In the male branch of this line, on the father's side, Plate VI, with myself a male, my father's brother I call my father *Hä'-nih;* and he calls me his son. Here we find a third indicative feature of the system. All of several brothers are placed in the relation of a father to the children of each other. My father's brother's son is my elder or younger brother; if older than myself I call him my elder brother, *Hä'-je*, and he calls me his younger brother, *Ha'-gă* ; if younger, these terms are reversed. My father's brother's daughter is my elder or younger sister ; if older than myself, I call her my elder sister, *Ah'-je*, and she calls me her younger brother, *Ha'-gă* ; but if younger I call her my younger sister, *Ka'-gă*, and she calls me her elder brother. This constitutes a fourth indicative feature. It creates the relationships of brother and sister amongst the children of several brothers. To distinguish these from own brothers and sisters they will hereafter be called *collateral* brothers and sisters. The son and daughter of this collateral brother are my son and daughter, and I apply to them the same terms, *Ha-ah'-wuk* and *Ka-ah'-wuk*, I would to my own children. In turn they call me father. The children of the latter are my grandchildren, each of them addressing me by the correlative term. On the other hand, the son and daughter of this collateral sister are my nephew and niece, *Ha-yă'-wan-da* and *Ka-yă'-wan-da*, and call me uncle ; their children are my grandchildren, each of them calling me grandfather. With myself a female, the preceding relationships are the same until the children of these collateral brothers and sisters are reached, when they are reversed. The son and daughter of this brother are my nephew and niece, *Ha-soh'-neh* and *Ka-soh'-neh*, each of them calling me aunt ; and their children are my grandchildren, each of them calling me grandmother ; whilst the son and daughter of this sister are my son and daughter, each of them calling me mother, and their children are my grandchildren each of them addressing me by the correlative term. It thus appears that the principle of classification in the first collateral line is carried into the second ; and it shows that my father's brother's sons and daughters are admitted to all intents and purposes into the same relationships as my own brothers and sisters, the same being equally true of the children and descendants of each.

In the female branch of this line, with myself a male, my father's sister is my aunt, *Ah-ga'-huc*, and she calls me her nephew. This is a fifth indicative feature of the system. The relationship of aunt is restricted to the sisters of my father, and, as will hereafter be seen, to the sisters of such other persons as stand to me in the relation of a father, to the exclusion of the sisters of my mother. My father's sister's son and daughter are each my cousin, *Ah-găre'-seh*, each of them calling me cousin ; the son and daughter of my male cousin are my son and daughter, each of them calling me father, and their children are my grandchildren, each of them calling me grandfather : but the children of my female cousins are my nephews and nieces, each of them calling me uncle ; and their children are my grandchildren, each of them applying to me the proper correlative. With myself a female, the relationships of the children of my male and female cousins are reversed, whilst all the others in this branch of the line are the same. The relationship of cousin does not form an indicative feature of the system, although its existence is remarkable. It would seem to be intended as a part of this plan of consanguinity that the children of a brother and sister should stand to each other in a more remote relationship than the children of brothers, on one hand, and the children of their sisters on the other, but without prescribing the relationship itself. As there are ruder forms, in many of the nations, than that of cousin and cousin, it is to be inferred that the latter relationship did not exist in the primitive system, but was developed subsequently by the more advanced nations to remove an irregularity which amounted to a blemish. It was, however, pre-determined by the elements of the system that, if ever invented, it would be restricted to the children of a brother and sister. The admission of the children of my cousins into the same relationships as the children of my own brothers and sisters seems to be entirely arbitrary, and yet it is not a departure from the general principles of the system.

On the mother's side, in the same line, I being a male (Plate VII), my mother's brother is my uncle, *Hoc-no'-seh*, and calls me his nephew. Herein is found a sixth indicative feature. The relationship of uncle is restricted to the brothers of my mother, to the exclusion of those of my father. It is also applied to the brothers of such other persons, and no other. as stand to me in the relation of a mother. My mother's brother's son and daughter are my cousins, *Ah-găre'-seh*, and call me the same; the son and daughter of my male cousin are my son and daughter, each of them calling me father, and their children are my grandchildren. On the other hand, the son and daughter of my female cousin are my nephew and niece, each of them calling me uncle; and their children are my grandchildren, each of them addressing me by the correlative term. Supposing myself a female, the relationships of the children of these cousins are reversed as in the previous cases, whilst, in other respects, there is no change.

The relationship of uncle in Indian society is, in several particulars, more important than any other from the authority with which he is invested over his nephews and nieces. He is, practically, rather more the head of his sister's family than his sister's husband. It may be illustrated in several ways from present usages. Amongst the Choctas, for example, if a boy is to be placed at school his uncle, instead of his father, takes him to the mission and makes the arrangement. An uncle, among the Winnebagoes, may require services of a nephew, or administer correction, which his own father would neither ask nor attempt. In like manner with the Iowas and Otoes, an uncle may appropriate to his own use his nephew's horse or his gun, or other personal property, without being questioned, which his own father would have no recognized right to do. But over his nieces this same authority is more significant, from his participation in their marriage contracts, which, in many Indian nations, are founded upon a consideration in the nature of presents. Not to enlarge upon this topic, the facts seem to reveal an idea familiar as well on the Asiatic as the American Continent, and nearly as ancient as human society, namely, the establishment of a brother in authority over his sister's children.[1] It finds its roots in the tribal organization, and that form of it which limits descent to the female line, under which the children of a man's sister are of the same tribe with himself.

In the fourth and last branch of this line, myself a male, my mother's sister I call my mother, *No-yeh'*, and she calls me her son. This constitutes a seventh indicative feature of the system. All of several sisters are placed in the relation of a mother to the children of each other. My mother's sister's son and daughter

---

[1] Amongst the Zulus or Kafirs of South Africa an uncle occupies a similar position of authority.

are respectively my elder or younger brother, or elder or younger sister as they are older or younger than myself: and we apply to each other the same terms we would use to designate own brothers and sisters. This is an eighth indicative feature. It establishes the relationships of brother and sister amongst the children of sisters. The son and daughter of this collateral brother are my son and daughter, *Ha-ah'-wuk* and *Ka-ah'-wuk*, each of them calling me father; and their children are my grandchildren, each of them calling me grandfather. On the other hand, the children of this collateral sister are my nephews and nieces, *Ha-yă'-wan-da* and *Ka-yă'-wan-da*, each of them calling me uncle; and their children are my grandchildren, each of them applying to me the proper correlative. With myself a female, the relationships of the children of this collateral brother and sister are reversed, the others remaining the same.

It will be observed that the female branch of this line, on the mother's side through which we have just passed, is an exact counterpart of the male branch on the father's side, the only difference being in the first relationship in each, one commencing with a father to *Ego*, and the other with a mother. The same is also true of the two remaining branches of this line, as to each other, and with the same single difference, one of them commencing with an uncle and the other with an aunt.

To exhibit the relationships of the same persons on the last two diagrams to *Ego* a female, it would only be necessary to substitute nephew and niece in the place of son and daughter, wherever they occur, and son and daughter in the place of nephew and niece. All other relationships would remain as they now are. These diagrams are easily read by observing the figures upon the right and left of the father of *Ego*. The first, for example, in Plate VI, represents my father's father's son, who is my father's brother, and therefore my father; and the second my father's father's daughter, who is my father's sister, and therefore my aunt. The other figures, except those in the lineal line, represent their descendants, proceeding from parent to child.

If we ascend one degree above *Ego* in the lineal line, and then cross over in turn to the first figure on the right and on the left in the same horizontal line in each diagram, the rules stated as to the first collateral line will also be found to hold true in the second. From my father to my father's brother, or from male line to male line, and from my mother to my mother's sister, or from female line to female line, the relationships of their children, as well as their own relationships, approach in their comparative nearness to *Ego* ; but from my father to my father's sister, or from male line to female line, and from my mother to my mother's brother, or from female to male, the relationships of the children of this uncle and aunt, as well as their own, recede in the degree of their nearness to *Ego*. The object of this minute analysis of the system is to show that it is founded upon clearly established principles of classification which are carried out harmoniously to their logical results. It is the constantly operative force of these ideas which gives to the system its vitality.

We have also seen that the first collateral line in its two branches, and the second in its four branches, are finally brought into and merged in the lineal line;

and the same will hereafter be found to be the case with each of the remaining collateral lines as far as the fact of consanguinity can be traced. This constitutes a ninth indicative feature of the system. It prevents consanguinei, near and remote, from falling without the relationship of grandfather in the ascending series, that of grandson in the descending, and that of nephew and cousin in the greatest divergence of the collateral lines from the lineal line.

Each of the wives of these several collateral brothers, and of these several male cousins, is my sister-in-law, *Ah-ge⌒ah'-ne-ah*, each of them calling me brother-in-law, *Ha-yă'-o*. In like manner, each of the husbands of these several collateral sisters, and of these several female cousins, is my brother-in-law, *Ah-ge-ah'-ne⌒o*, each of them calling me brother-in-law, *Ha-yă'-o*, if I am a male, and *Ka-yă'-o*, if a female. There are several different relationships which are classified together in our system under the descriptive phrases brother-in-law and sister-in-law, which are discriminated from each other in the Indian system, and distinguished by independent terms.

The foregoing explanations dispose of the second collateral line in its four branches, whether *Ego* be considered male or female, together with the marriage relationships. It provides a place and a term for each and every person connected with either of these branches, and holds them all within the degree of cousin and grandchild. Not one is allowed to pass beyond the recognition of this all-embracing system of relationship.

Among ourselves our nearest kindred, as well as the greater portion of those whose connection is recognized under our system, are found in the lineal and first and second collateral lines. After they are properly classified the system would answer the ordinary requirements of domestic life. Those beyond, as remote collaterals, might have been placed under general terms outside of the near degrees; but the theory of the Indian system is averse to the rejection of collaterals however remote, and insists upon the unqualified recognition of the bond of consanguinity. Kindred are bound together in the family relationships in virtue of their descent from common ancestors; so that the differences in the degrees of nearness, which are accidental, are subordinated to the blood-connection, which is indissoluble. Wherever, then, the chain of consanguinity can be traced, and the connection of persons ascertained, the system at once includes them in its comprehensive grasp. Such at least is the system as it now appears considered in the light of existing institutions. There may have been a state of society, as will be seen in the sequel, when the relationships we have been considering were true to the nature of descents as they actually existed when the system, in its present form, came into use. These results, as they now exist, were apparently effected by adopting the principle of classification established in the first and second collateral lines and extending it to the third, fourth, and even others more remote, theoretically, without limit. This established another principle equally fundamental in the system, which is the following: The children of own brothers, as has been shown, are brothers and sisters to each other, elder or younger, and so are the children of own sisters. In like manner the children of these collateral brothers are also brothers and sisters to each other, and so are the children of these collateral sisters. Advancing downwards another degree the children of such persons as were thus made brothers, are in like manner, brothers and sisters to each other, and the same is true of such of them as were thus made sisters. This relationship of brother and sister amongst the male descendants of brothers, and the female descendants of sisters, continues downward theoretically *ad infinitum* at the same degree of remove from the common ancestor. But with respect to the children of a brother and sister the relationship is more remote and not uniform. Amongst the Senecas, whose system is now under consideration, they are cousins to each other; the children of these cousins are cousins again; the children of the latter are cousins also; and this relationship continues downward theoretically *ad infinitum*. And, lastly, whenever the relationship of brother and brother, or of sister and sister at any one of these degrees is found, it determines at once the relationships of the descendants of each one of them to the other; thus, the son of either one of these, my collateral brothers, is my son if I am a male, and my nephew if I am a female; and the son of either one of these my collateral sisters is my nephew if I am a male, and my son if I am a female; and the children of these sons and nephews are my grandchildren. These several relationships do not exist simply in theory, but they are practical, and universally recognized amongst the Iroquois.

Diagram, Plate VIII, represents the lineal, and the second, third, and fourth collateral lines, male and female, on the father's side; and Diagram, Plate IX, represents the lineal and same collateral lines on the mother's side, with *Ego* in both cases a male. Each line in these diagrams proceeds from the parent to one only of his or her children, for greater simplicity, as well as from actual necessity in its construction. The first collateral line is omitted, and the second, which is presented in full in Plates VI and VII, is retained for comparison with the third and fourth. It requires no further explanation, except such as it may receive incidentally.

In the third collateral line male on the father's side, with myself a male (Plate VIII) my father's father's brother is my grandfather, *Hoc'-sote*, and calls me his grandson. This is a tenth indicative feature of the system, and the last of those which are treated as such. It places the several brothers of my grandfather in the relation of grandfathers, and thus prevents collateral ascendants from falling out of this relationship. In other words, the principle by which the collateral lines are merged in the lineal works upwards as well as downwards. The son of this collateral grandfather is my father *Hä'-nih*, and calls me his son. At first sight this relationship seems to be entirely arbitrary, but in reality it is a necessary consequence of those previously established. This will be made clear by reversing the question, and inquiring whether I am his son. This has already been shown in the male branch of the second collateral line, where my father's brother's son's son is found to be my son. The son of this collateral father is my brother, elder or younger. Our grandfathers are own brothers, and our fathers are collateral brothers, either of which determines our relationship to be that of brothers. Again the son of this collateral brother is my son, and calls me father, and the son of the latter is my grandson, and calls me grandfather.

My father's father's sister is my grandmother, *Oc'-sote*, her daughter is my aunt,

21   January, 1870.

Ah-ga-'huc, her daughter is my cousin, *Ah-găre'-seh*, her daughter is my niece, *Ka-yă'-wan-da*, and the daughter of the latter is my granddaughter, *Ka-yä'-da*, each of them addressing me by the proper correlative.

On the mother's side (Plate IX) my mother's mother's brother is my grandfather, *Hoc'-sote*, his son is my uncle, *Hoc-no'-seh*, his son is my cousin, *Ah-găre'-seh*, his son is my son, *Ha-ah'-wuk*, and the son of the latter is my grandson, *Ha-yä'-da*, each of them addressing me by the proper correlative.

My mother's mother's sister is my grandmother, *Oc'-sote*, her daughter is my mother, *No-yeh'*, her daughter is my sister, elder or younger, *Ah'-je* or *Ka'-gă*, the daughter of this sister is my niece, *Ka-yă'-wan-da*, and her daughter is my granddaughter, *Ka-yä'-da*, each of them addressing me by the proper correlative.

In the fourth collateral line male on the father's side, my father's father's father's brother is my grandfather, *Hoc'-sote*, his son is my grandfather also, his son is my father, his son is my brother, elder or younger; his son is my son, and the son of the latter is my grandson; each of them, as before, applying to me the proper correlative. With the exception of one additional ancestor, the three remaining branches of this line agree with the corresponding branches of the third collateral line, as will be seen by a reference to the diagram.

There are two methods of verifying every relationship upon these diagrams. The first is by commencing in each with the highest transverse line of figures, in one of which there are three children of a common father, and in the other three children of a common mother, who are, respectively, own brothers and sisters to each other. In Plate VIII, two of them are males and one a female; and in Plate IX two of them are females and one a male. Thus in the former there are two own brothers, with their descendants, one constituting the lineal, and the other the fourth collateral line, male of *Ego*; and in the other there are two own sisters, with their descendants, one constituting the lineal, and the other the fourth collateral line, female; those in the same horizontal line of figures being at equal removes from the common ancestor. There are, also, in both diagrams, a brother and sister and their descendants in corresponding positions. All of the elements are, therefore, contained in these diagrams for testing their own correctness, and also for resolving any question of consanguinity. In doing either it is only necessary to apply the rules before given, namely: that the children of brothers are themselves brothers and sisters to each other, that the children of sisters are also brothers and sisters to each other; and that the children of cousins are themselves cousins to each other; and, finally, that the same relationships continue downwards, as before explained, amongst their respective descendants, at equal removes, indefinitely. To illustrate from Plate VIII *Hoc'-sote* and *Hoc'-sote* are own brothers; the three *Hoc-so'-do* below them are brothers to each other as the children of brothers; the four fathers of *Ego* below them are also brothers to each other by the same rule, and three of them are also fathers to *Ego* because they are brothers of his own father. The four below the last are brothers, in like manner because they are the children of brothers. Having now reached the transverse line of figures to which *Ego* belongs, and ascertained that they are all brothers to each other, this, of itself, determines the relationships of the ascendants and descendants of each of these collateral brothers to *Ego* himself. The sons and grandsons of my collateral brothers are my sons and grandsons; the father of each of these brothers is my father because he is the brother of my own father; and so is the grandfather of each my grandfather, because he is the brother of my own grandfather. If *Oc'-sote* and *Oc'-sote* in Plate IX are taken, and the diagram is gone through with, the same results will be obtained; and so, also, if *Oc'-sote* and *Hoc'-sote* in the diagram, or *Hoc'-sote* and *Oc'-sote* in the other, are taken, the several relationships as given will be fully verified.

The other method is by shifting the position of *Ego* to that of each person on the diagram in turn, and then ascertaining the correlative relationship. It can be illustrated most conveniently by examples. In Plate VIII there are three figures to the right of my own father, each marked *Hä'-nih*. If it is desired to prove that the person represented by the middle of these figures is my father, under the system, we may reverse the question and ascertain whether I am the son of this person. In so doing the position of *Ego* and this *Hä'-nih* are exchanged, and the description of intermediate persons is reversed, whence the figure formerly occupied by *Ego* is found to represent " my father's brother's son's son," who, as before shown, is my son, I am therefore, the son of this *Hä'-nih*. Again, in Plate IX, if the middle figure marked *Hoc-no'-seh* to the right of *No'-yeh* be taken, and the description of intermediate persons be reversed, it will make the person represented by the figure formerly occupied by *Ego* " my father's sister's daughter's son," who is my nephew. He is the son of my female cousin, myself a male. Thus it is seen that *Ego* and *Hoc-no'-seh* are nephew and uncle. In this manner the correlative relationship will be found to be the true one in every case.

For each collateral line beyond the fourth as far as relationships can be traced the classification is the same. Wheresoever the chain of consanguinity can be followed, the principles of the system are rigorously applied; but the first four collateral lines, which include third cousins under the Aryan system, is as far as they have occasion to apply it in ordinary intercourse. It has before been stated, and the statement is here repeated, that the system of consanguinity and affinity just described is not only theoretically the system of the Ganowánian family, but the form as detailed is, at the present moment, in constant daily use amongst the Seneca Indians of New York, and has been in use by them from time immemorial. It is thoroughly understood by the rudest amongst them, and can be fully explained by the more intelligent of their number. They still address each other, when related by the term of relationship, and never by the personal name. To be ignorant of the relationship which another person sustains to the speaker, and to show it by an omission of the proper address is a discourtesy, and is regarded as such. In this usage is found a sufficient explanation of the manner in which a knowledge of the system is imparted as well as preserved from generation to generation.

It follows, from the nature of the system, that a knowledge of the degrees of consanguinity, numerically, is essential to the proper classification of kindred. Consanguinity in its most complicated ramifications is much better understood by these Indians than by ourselves. Our collateral kindred, except within the nearest degrees, are practically disowned. The more creditable Indian practice of recognizing their relatives, near and remote, and of addressing by kin, tends to preserve the integrity of the blood connection.

The marriage relationships, other than those named, are fully discriminated. There are two terms for father-in-law, *Hä-ga'-sä*, for the husband's father, and *Oc-na'-hose*, for the wife's father. This last term is also used to designate a son-in-law, and is therefore a reciprocal term. There are also terms for stepfather and stepmother, *Hoc-no'-ese* and *Oc-no'-ese*, which are also applied, respectively, to the husband of my father's sister, and to the wife of my mother's brother: and for stepson and stepdaughter, *Ha'-no* and *Ka'-no*. In a number of nations two fathers-in-law are related to each other, and so are two mothers-in-law, and there are terms to express the relationships. The opulence of the nomenclature, although rendered necessary by the elaborate discriminations of the system, is nevertheless remarkable.

None of the persons indicated in the diagrams, or in the Table, as consanguinei, however remote, can intermarry. Relatives by marriage, after the decease of their respective husbands or wives, are under no restriction. Against the intermarriage of consanguinei the regulations are very stringent amongst the greater part of the American Indian nations.

We have now passed step by step through the lineal, and the first, second, third, and fourth collateral lines in their several branches, with *Ego* a male, and also a female, and have exhibited every feature of the system with great minuteness of detail. The analysis of the system presented in the previous chapter has been confirmed in every particular. If the reader has been sufficiently patient to follow the chain of consanguinity, and to observe the operation of the principle which determines each relationship, the contents of this extraordinary system will have been fully mastered. It will be comparatively easy, hereafter, to follow and identify its characteristic features in the forms prevailing in other branches of the family; and also to detect, on bare inspection, the slightest deviations which they make from the typical or standard form.

It remains to notice the plan of consanguinity amongst the other Iroquois nations. With the exception of one indicative feature, and of a few inconsiderable and subordinate particulars, they all agree with each other in their domestic relationships. It will not, therefore, be necessary to take them up in detail. A reference to the Table (Table II) will show that the terms of relationship, with unimportant exceptions, are the same original words, under dialectical changes, in the six dialects. The presence in each of all of its indicative characteristics save one, and their minute agreement in subordinate details, establish the identity of the system, as well as its derivation by each nation from a common original source.

The discrepancy to which reference has been made consists in the absence, among the Cayugas, Onondagas, Oneidas, and Mohawks, of the relationship of *aunt*, and in supplying its place with that of *mother*, wherever the former occurs in the Seneca form. As a consequence, the relationships of nephew and niece are unknown to the females, and are supplied by those of son and daughter. This deviation from uniformity upon an indicative relationship is difficult of explanation. It is, also, not a little singular that after four hundred years of intimate political intercourse, and constant intermarriage, this diversity has been maintained to the present time.[1] On the other hand, the relationship of aunt, applied and restricted to the father's sister, is found in the system of the Tuscaroras and Wyandotes. In the former it is *Ahk-kaw'-rac*, in the latter *Ah-rä'-hoc*, which are evidently the Seneca *Ah-ga'-huc* dialectically changed. This fact suggests the question, before stated, whether the Wyandotes, Tuscaroras, and Senecas, are not more immediately connected, genetically, than the Senecas and other Iroquois nations. The Tuscarora and Wyandote dialects are much further removed from the Seneca than the latter is from those of the remaining nations: but it is possible that this may be explained by the long separation of the former from the Iroquois, which would tend to increase the variation, whilst the constant association of the Senecas with their confederates would tend to retard their dialectical separation. It is one thing to borrow a term of relationship and substitute it in the place of a domestic term of equivalent import, but quite a different undertaking to change an established relationship and invent a new term for its designation. The first might occur and not be extraordinary, but the latter would be much less likely to happen. Among the traditions of the Senecas there is one to the effect that they had a distinct and independent history anterior to the epoch of their confederation with the other Iroquois nations. This feature in their system of relationship, and which is shared by the Tuscaroras and Wyandotes, and not by their immediate associates, tends to confirm the tradition, as well as to suggest the inference that the Senecas, Tuscaroras, and Wyandotes, were of immediate common origin. It has been referred to, not so much for its intrinsic importance as for the illustration which it furnishes of the uses of systems of consanguinity and affinity for minute ethnological investigations through periods of time far beyond the range of historical records

7. Two Mountain Iroquois.

The location and antecedents of this fragment of the Iroquois stock were referred to in the early part of this chapter. Their system agrees substantially with that of the Oneidas and Mohawks; and is chiefly interesting as an illustration of the ability of the system to perpetuate itself in disconnected branches of the same stock.[2]

---

[1] Descent amongst the Iroquois is in the female line both as to tribe and as to nationality. The children are of the tribe of the mother. If a Cayuga marries a Delaware woman, for example, his children are Delawares and aliens, unless formally naturalized with the forms of adoption: but if a Delaware marries a Cayuga woman, her children are Cayugas, and of her tribe of the Cayugas. It is the same if she marries a Seneca. In all cases the woman confers her tribe and nationality upon her children. She will also adhere to the Cayuga system of relationship on the point under consideration. For seventy years the Cayugas, still living in Western New York, have resided with the Senecas, and constantly intermarried with them; but they still retain their dialect, tribes, nationality, and relationships. In 1858 I asked a Cayuga woman on one of the Seneca reservations in what relationship her father's sister stood to her. She replied, " My mother." I expressed a doubt of her correctness, but she adhered to her answer. She gave me the Seneca name for aunt in the Cayuga dialect, but denied the relationship. I afterwards found the same deviation from the Seneca form amongst the Onondagas, Oneidas, and Mohawks.

[2] There are Mohawks, Onondagas, Oneidas, and Cayugas now residing upon the Thames River in Canada West. Besides these, there are Oneidas and Onondagas near Green Bay in Wisconsin, and also Senecas in Kansas. The Iroquois in New York now number about 4000.

II. Hurons.   1. Wyandotes.

A brief notice of the Hurons and of their descendants, the Wyandotes, has already been given.   They were called *Wane'-dote* by the Iroquois, which name they afterwards adopted for themselves.[1]   The Wyandotes affirm that the Dakotas are descended from them, which must be understood simply as an assertion of their genetic connection.   They call the Dakotas *Tŭn-da'-no*.   This was the name, still preserved in Wyandote tradition, of the chief under whom the Dakotas separated themselves from the Wyandotes.   It signifies " Big Stomach."   The Dakotas themselves, it is said, still recognize the relationship, and style the Wyandotes Brothers.

Their system of relationship will be found in the Table.   It has all of the indicative features of the common system, and agrees with the Seneca so completely that its presentation in detail would be, for the most part, a literal repetition of the description just given.   The terms of relationship, in nearly every instance, are from the same roots as the Seneca; and although the dialectical variation, in some cases, is quite marked, their identity is at once recognized.   This, however, is of less importance than the coincidence of the radical features of their respective systems.   A comparison of the two forms shows that the system in all its precision and complexity, with the same original terms of relationship, now prevails in both nations; and that it has descended to each, with the streams of the blood, from the same common source.   For two hundred and fifty years, within the historical period, these nations have been separate and hostile, and were for an unknown period anterior to their discovery, and yet the system has been preserved by each, through the intervening periods, without sensible change.   The fact itself is some evidence of the stability and persistency of its radical forms.   Its existence in the Hodenosaunian branch of the Ganowánian family carries it back to the time when these several nations were a single people.

The most remarkable fact with reference to this system of relationship yet remains to be mentioned, namely, that indicative feature for indicative feature, and relationship for relationship, almost without an exception, it is identical with the system now prevailing amongst the Tamil, Telugu, and Canarese peoples of South India, as will hereafter be fully shown.   The discrepancies between them are actually less, aside from the vocables, than between the Seneca and the Cayuga.

The comparative table of the Seneca-Iroquois and Yankton-Dacota systems of relationship, referred to at page 154, is appended to this chapter.

---

[1] It signifies " calf of the leg," and refers to their manner of stringing strips of dried buffalo meat.

TABLE EXHIBITING THE SYSTEM OF CONSANGUINITY AND AFFINITY OF THE SENECA-IROQUOIS, AND OF THE YANKTON-DAKOTAS.

Description of persons.	Relationships in Seneca.	Translation.	Relationships in Yankton.	Translation.
LINEAL LINE.				
1. My great grandfather's father.................	Hoc'-sote..................	My grandfather.	Toon-kä'-she-nä.	My grandfather.
2. " great grandfather's mother...............	Oc'-sote..................	" grandmother.	O-che'...................	" grandmother.
3. " great grandfather.........................	Hoc'-sote..................	" grandfather.	Toon-kä'-she-nä............	" grandfather.
4. " great grandmother.......................	Oc'-sote..................	" grandmother.	O-che'...................	" grandmother.
5. " grandfather.............................	Hoc'-sote..................	" grandfather.	Toon-kä'-she-nä............	" grandfather.
6. " grandmother............................	Oc'-sote..................	" grandmother.	O-che'...................	" grandmother.
7. " father...................................	Hä'-nih..................	" father.	Ah-ta'....................	" father.
8. " mother..................................	No-yeh'..................	" mother.	E'-nah....................	" mother.
9. " son.....................................	Ha-ah'-wuk..............	" son.	Me-chink'-she.............	" son.
10. " daughter...............................	Ka-ah'-wuk..............	" daughter.	Me-chounk'-she............	" daughter.
11. " grandson...............................	Ha-yä'-da...............	" grandson.	Me-tä'-ko-zhä.............	" grandchild.
12. " granddaughter..........................	Ka-yä'-da...............	" granddaughter.	Me-tä'-ko-zhä.............	" "
13. " great grandson.........................	Ha-yä'-da...............	" grandson.	Me-tä'-ko-zhä.............	" "
14. " great granddaughter....................	Ka-yä'-da...............	" granddaughter.	Me-tä'-ko-zhä.............	" "
15. " great grandson's son....................	Ha-yä'-da...............	" grandson.	Me-tä'-ko-zhä.............	" "
16. " great grandson's daughter..............	Ka-yä'-da...............	" granddaughter.	Me-tä'-ko-zhä.............	" "
17. " elder brother (*male speaking*)	Hä'-je..................	" elder brother.	Che-a'...................	" elder brother.
18. " elder brother (*female speaking*)..........	Hä'-je..................	" " "	Chim'-a-do..............	" " "
19. " elder sister (*male speaking*)	Ah'-je..................	" younger sister.	Ton-ka'.................	" elder sister.
20. " elder sister (*female speaking*)...........	Ah'-je..................	" " "	Chu-ih'.................	" " "
21. " younger brother (*male speaking*)	Ha'-gä..................	" "	Me-soh'-kä..............	" younger brother.
22. " younger brother (*female speaking*)......	Ha'-gä..................	" " "	Me-soh'-kä..............	" " "
23. " younger sister (*male speaking*)	Ka'-gä..................	" younger sister.	Me-tänk'-she............	" younger sister.
24. " younger sister (*female speaking*)........	Ka'-gä..................	" " "	Me-tun'-kä..............	" " "
25. " brothers (*male speaking*)	Da-yä'-gwä-dan'-no-dä	" brothers.	Me-hun'kä-wan-zhe........	" brothers.
26. " brothers (*female speaking*)	Da-yä'-gwä-dan'-no-dä	" "		" sisters.
27. " sisters (*male speaking*)	Da-yä'-gwä-dan'-no-dä	" "		" "
28. " sisters (*female speaking*)...............	Da-yä'-gwä-dan'-no-dä	" "	Me-tä-we-noh'-tin..........	" "
First Collateral Line.				
29. " brother's son (*male speaking*)......	Ha-ah'-wuk..............	" son.	Me-chink'-she.............	" son.
30. " brother's son's wife " "	Ka'-sä.................	" daughter-in-law.	Me-tä'-koash..............	" daughter-in-law.
31. " brother's daughter " "	Ka-ah'-wuk.............	" daughter.	Me-chounk'-she............	" daughter.
32. " brother's dau. husb. " "	Oc-na'-hose............	" son-in-law.	Me-tä'-koash..............	" son-in-law.
33. " brother's grandson " "	Ha-yä'-da..............	" grandson.	Me-tä'-ko-zha.............	" grandchild.
34. " brother's gd.daughter " "	Ka-yä'-da..............	" granddaughter.	Me-tä'-ko-zha.............	" "
35. " brother's gt. gd. son " "	Ha-yä'-da..............	" grandson.	Me-tä'-ko-zha.............	" "
36. " brother's gt. gd. dau. " "	Ka-yä'-da..............	" granddaughter.	Me-ta'-ko-zha.............	" "
37. " sister's son " "	Ha-yä'-wan-da.........	" nephew.	Me-to⌢us'-ka.............	" nephew.
38. " sister's son's wife " "	Ka'-sä.................	" daughter-in-law.	Me-tä'-koash..............	" daughter-in-law.
39. " sister's daughter " "	Ka-yä'-wan-da.........	" niece.	Me-to⌢us'-zä.............	" niece.
40. " sister's daught. husb. " "	Oc-na'-hose............	" son-in-law.	Me-tä'-koash..............	" son-in-law.
41. " sister's grandson " "	Ha-yä'-da..............	" grandson.	Me-tä'-ko-zä..............	" grandchild.
42. " sister's granddaught. " "	Ka-yä'-da..............	" granddaughter.	Me-tä'-ko-zä..............	" "
43. " sister's gt. grandson " "	Ha-yä'-da..............	" grandson.	Me-tä'-ko-zä..............	" "
44. " sister's gt. gd. daught. " "	Ka-yä'-da..............	" granddaughter.	Me-tä'-ko-zä..............	" "
45. " brother's son (*female speaking*)......	Ha-soh'-neh...........	" nephew.	Me-to⌢us'-kä.............	" nephew.
46. " brother's son's wife " "	Ka'-sä.................	" daughter-in-law.	Me-tä'-koash..............	" daughter-in-law.
47. " brother's daughter " "	Ka-so'-neh.............	" niece.	Me-to⌢us'-zä.............	" niece.
48. " brother's dau. husb. " "	Oc-na'-hose............	" son-in-law.	Me-tä-koash...............	" son-in-law.
49. " brother's grandson " "	Ha-yä'-da..............	" grandson.	Me-tä-ko-zhä.............	" grandchild.
50. " brother's gd.daughter " "	Ka-yä'-da..............	" granddaughter.	Me-tä-ko-zhä.............	" "
51. " brother's gt. grandson " "	Ha-yä'-da..............	" grandson.	Me-tä-ko-zhä.............	" "
52. " brother's gt. gd. dau. " "	Ka-yä'-da..............	" granddaughter.	Me-tä'-ko-zhä.............	" "
53. " sister's son " "	Ha-ah'-wuk.............	" son.	Me-chink'-she-...........	" son.
54. " sister's son's wife " "	Ka'-sä.................	" daughter-in-law.	Me-tä'-koash..............	" daughter-in-law.
55. " sister's daughter " "	Ka-ah'-wuk.............	" daughter.	Me-chounk'-she...........	" daughter.
56. " sister's daught. husb. " "	Oc-na-hose.............	" son-in-law.	Me-tä'-koash..............	" son-in-law.
57. " sister's grandson " "	Ha-yä'-da..............	" grandson.	Me-tä'-ko-zhä.............	" grandchild.
58. " sister's granddaughter " "	Ka-yä'-da..............	" granddaughter	Me-tä'-ko-zhä.............	" "
59. " sister's gt. grandson " "	Ha-yä'-da..............	" grandson.	Me-tä'-ko-zhä.............	" "
60. " sister's gt. gd.daught. " "	Ka-yä'-da..............	" granddaughter.	Me-tä'-ko-zhä.............	" "
Second Collateral Line.				
61. " father's brother.....................	Hä'-nih.................	" father.	Ah-ta'...................	" father.
62. " father's brother's wife..............	Oc-no'-ese	" step-mother.	E'-nah	" mother.
63. " father's bro. son (*older than myself*)	Hä'-je..................	" elder brother.	Che-a'..................	" elder brother.
64. " father's bro. son (*younger* " ")....	Ha'-gä.................	" younger brother.	Me-soh'-kä..............	" younger brother.
65. " father's brother's son's wife (*m. s.*)	Ah-ge-ah'-ne-ah	" sister-in-law.	Hä'-ka.................	" sister-in-law.
66. " father's brother's son's wife (*f. s.*)	Ah-ge⌢ah'-ne⌢o.......	" " "	E-shä'-pä..............	" " "
67. " father's bro. dau. (*older than myself*)	Ah'-je.................	" elder sister.	Ton-ka'................	" elder sister.
68. " father's bro. dau. (*younger* " ")	Ka'-gä.................	" younger sister.	Me-tänk'-she............	" younger sister.
69. " father's bro. daught. husb. (*m. s.*)	Ah-ge⌢ah-ne⌢o	" brother-in-law.	Tä-huh'................	" brother-in-law.
70. " father's bro. daught. husb. (*f. s.*)	Ha-yä'-o	" " "	She-cha'...............	" " "
71. " father's brother's son's son (*m. s.*)	Ha-ah'-wuk	" son.	Me-chink'-she...........	" son.
72. " father's brother's son's son (*f. s.*)	Ha-soh'-neh............	" nephew.	Me-to⌢us'-kä...........	" nephew.
73. " father's brother's son's dau. (*m. s.*)	Ka-ah'-wuk............	" daughter.	Me-chounk-she..........	" daughter.
74. " father's brother's son's dau. (*f. s.*)	Ka-soh'-neh............	" niece.	Me-to⌢us'-zä...........	" niece.
75. " father's broth. daught. son (*m. s.*)	Ha-yä'-wan-da.........	" nephew.	Me-to⌢us'-zä...........	" nephew.
76. " father's broth. daught. son (*f. s.*)	Ha-ah'-wuk............	" son.	Me-chink'-she..........	" son.
77. " father's broth. daught. dau. (*m. s.*)	Ka-yä'-wan-da..........	" niece.	Me-to⌢us'-zä...........	" niece.
78. " father's broth. daught. dau. (*f. s.*)	Ka-ah'-wuk	" daughter.	Me-chounk'-she..........	" daughter.

TABLE EXHIBITING THE SYSTEM OF CONSANGUINITY AND AFFINITY OF THE SENECA-IROQUOIS AND YANKTON-DAKOTAS—*Continued.*

	Description of persons.	Relationships in Seneca.	Translation.	Relationships in Yankton.	Translation.
79.	My father's brother's great grandson...........	Ha-yä'-da.................	My grandson.	Me-tä'-ko-zhä	My grandchild.
80.	" father's brother's great gd.daughter.........	Ka-yä'-da.................	" granddaughter.	Me-tä'-ko-zhä.............	" "
81.	" father's sister.....................................	Ah-ga'-huc..............	" aunt.	Toh'-we...................	" aunt.
82.	" father's sister's husband......................	Hoc-no'-ese..............	" step-father.	Dake'-she.................	" uncle.
83.	" father's sister's son (*m. speaking*)......	Ah-gäre'-seh.............	" cousin.	Tä'-she	" male cousin.
84.	" father's sister's son (*fem. speaking*)........	Ah-gäre'-seh.............	" "	She-chä'-she.............	" " "
85.	" father's sister's son's wife (*male speaking*)	Ah-ge-ah'-ne-ah	" sister-in-law.	Hä-kä'....................	" sister-in-law.
86.	" " " " " (*fem. speaking*)	Ah-ge͡-ah'-ne͡-o...........	" " "	E-shä'-pä.................	" " "
87.	" father's sister's daughter (*male speaking*)	Ah-gäre'-seh.............	" cousin.	Hä-kä'-she...............	" female cousin.
88.	" " " " (*fem. speaking*)	Ah-gäre'-seh.............	" "	E-cha'-pä-she.............	" " "
89.	" father's sister's dau. husb. (*male speaking*)	Ah-ge͡-ah'-ne͡-o.........	" brother-in-law.	Tä-hä'....................	" brother-in-law.
90.	" " " " " (*fem. speaking*)	Ha-yä'-o.................	" " "	She-cha'..................	" " "
91.	" father's sister's son's son (*male speaking*)	Ha-ah'-wuk..............	" son.	Me-chink'-she............	" son.
92.	" " " " " (*fem. speaking*)	Ha-soh'-neh	" nephew.	Me-to͡us'-kä	" nephew.
93.	" father's sister's son's dau. (*male speaking*)	Ka-ah'-wuk..............	" daughter.	Me-chunk'-she	" daughter.
94.	" " " " " (*fem. speaking*)	Ka-soh'-neh	" niece.	Me-to͡us'-zä	" niece.
95.	" father's sister's daughter's son (*m. s.*)	Ha-yä'-wan-da	" nephew.	Me-to͡us'-kä.............	" nephew.
96.	" " " " " " (*f. s.*)	Ha-ah'-wuk..............	" son.	Me-chink'-she............	" son.
97.	" father's sister's daughter's daught. (*m. s.*)	Ka-yä'-wan-da	" niece.	Me-to͡us'-zä	" niece.
98.	" " " " " " (*f. s.*)	Ka-ah'-wuk..............	" daughter.	Me-chounk'-she...........	" daughter.
99.	" father's sister's great grandson.............	Ha-yä'-da.................	" grandson.	Me-tä'-ko-zhä........	" grandchild.
100.	" father's sister's great granddaughter.......	Ka-yä'-da.................	" granddaughter.	Me-tä'-ko-zhä.............	" "
101.	" mother's brother................................	Hoc-no'-seh..............	" uncle.	Dake'-she.................	" uncle.
102.	" mother's brother's wife........................	Ah-gä'-ni-ah..............	" aunt-in-law.	Toh'-we...................	" aunt.
103.	" mother's brother's son (*male speaking*)	Ah-gäre'-seh.............	" cousin.	Tä'-she	" male cousin.
104.	" " " " (*female speaking*)	Ah-gäre'-seh.............	" "	She-cha'-she.............	" " "
105.	" mother's brother's son's wife (*m. s.*)	Ah-ge-ah'-ne-ah	" sister-in-law.	Hä-kä'....................	" sister-in-law.
106.	" " " " " (*f. s.*)	Ah-ge͡-ah'-ne͡-o	" " "	E-shä'-pä.................	" " "
107.	" mother's brother's daughter (*m. s.*)	Ah-gäre'-seh.............	" cousin.	Hä-kä'-she...............	" female cousin.
108.	" " " " (*f. s.*)	Ah-gäre'-seh	" "	E-cha'-pä-she.............	" " "
109.	" mother's brother's daughter's husb. (*m. s.*)	Ah-ge͡-ah'-ne͡-o..........	" brother-in-law.	Tä-huh'...................	" brother-in-law.
110.	" " " " " (*f. s.*)	Ha-yä'-o.................	" " "	She-cha'..................	" " "
111.	" mother's brother's son's son (*m. s.*)	Ha-ah'-wuk..............	" son.	Me-chink'-she............	" son.
112.	" " " " " (*f. s.*)	Ha-soh'-neh..............	" nephew.	Me-to͡us'-kä..............	" nephew.
113.	" mother's brother's son's daughter (*m. s.*)	Ka-ah'-wuk..............	" daughter.	Me-chounk'-she...........	" daughter.
114.	" " " " " (*f. s.*)	Ka-soh'-neh	" niece.	Me-to͡us'-zä	" niece.
115.	" mother's brother's daughter's son (*m. s.*)	Ha-yä'-wan-da	" nephew.	Me-to͡us'-kä.............	" nephew.
116.	" " " " " (*f. s*)	Ha-ah'-wuk..............	" son.	Me-chink'-she............	" son.
117.	" mother's brother's daught. daught. (*m. s.*)	Ka-yä'-wan-da	" niece.	Me-to͡us'-zä	" niece.
118.	" " " " " (*f. s.*)	Ka-ah'-wuk..............	" daughter.	Me-chounk'-she...........	" daughter.
119.	" mother's brother's great grandson..........	Ha-yä'-da.................	" grandson.	Me-tä'-ko-zhä.............	" grandchild.
120.	" mother's brother's great granddaughter...	Ka-yä'-da.................	" granddaughter.	Me-tä'-ko-zhä.............	" "
121.	" mother's sister..................................	No-yeh'...................	" mother.	E'-nah....................	" mother.
122.	" mother's sister's husband......................	Hoc-no'-ese..............	" step-father.	Ah-ta'....................	" father.
123.	" mother's sister's son (*older than myself*)	Hä'-je....................	" elder brother.	Che-a'....................	" elder brother.
124.	" " " " (*younger than myself*)	Ha'-gä...................	" younger brother.	Me-soh'-kä...............	" younger brother.
125.	" mother's sister's son's wife (*m. s.*)	Ah-ge-ah'-ne-ah	" sister-in-law.	Hä-kä'...................	" sister-in-law.
126.	" " " " " (*f. s.*)	Ah-ge͡-ah'-ne͡-o	" " "	E-shä'-pä.................	" " "
127.	" mother's sister's dau. (*older than myself*)	Ah'-je....................	" elder sister.	Ton'-ka...................	" elder sister.
128.	" " " " (*younger than myself*)	Ka'-gä...................	" younger sister.	Me-tänk-she...............	" younger sister.
129.	" mother's sister's daughter's husb. (*m. s.*)	Ah-ge͡-ah'-ne͡-o..........	" brother-in-law.	Tä-hä'....................	" brother-in-law.
130.	" " " " " (*f. s.*)	Ha-yä'-o.................	" " "	She'-cha..................	" " "
131.	" mother's sister's son's son (*m. s.*)	Ha-ah'-wuk..............	" son.	Me-chink'-she............	" son.
132.	" " " " " (*f. s.*)	Ha-soh'-neh..............	" nephew.	Me-to͡us'-kä..............	" nephew.
133.	" mother's sister's son's daughter. (*m. s.*)	Ka-ah'-wuk..............	" daughter.	Me-chounk'-she...........	" daughter.
134.	" " " " " (*f. s.*)	Ka-soh'-neh..............	" niece.	Me-to͡us'-zä..............	" niece.
135.	" mother's sister's daughter's son (*m. s.*)	Ha-yä'-wan-da	" nephew.	Me-to͡us'-kä.............	" nephew.
136.	" " " " " (*f. s.*)	Ha-ah'-wuk	" son.	Me-chink'-she............	" son.
137.	" mother's sister's daught. daught. (*m. s.*)	Ka-yä'-wan-da	" niece.	Me-to͡us'-zä..............	" niece.
138.	" " " " " (*f. s.*)	Ka-ah'-wuk..............	" daughter.	Me-chounk-she............	" daughter.
139.	" mother's sister's great grandson	Ha-yä'-da.................	" grandson.	Me-tä'-ko-zhä.............	" grandchild.
140.	" mother's sister's great granddaughter......	Ka-yä'-da	" granddaughter.	Me-tä'-ko-zhä.............	" "
	Third Collateral Line.				
141.	" father's father's brother.....................	Hoc'-sote.................	" grandfather.	Toon-kä'-she-nä	" grandfather.
142.	" father's father's brother's son...............	Hä'-nih..................	" father.	Ah-ta'....................	" father.
143.	" father's fa. bro. son's s. (*older than myself*)	Hä'-je...................	" elder brother.	Che-a'....................	" elder brother.
144.	" " " " " (*younger than myself*)	Ha'-gä...................	" younger brother.	Me-soh'-kä	" younger brother.
145.	" father's fath. bro. son's son's son (*m. s.*)	Ha-ah'-wuk..............	" son.	Me-chink'-she............	" son.
146.	" " " " " " (*m. s.*)	Ha-soh'-neh..............	" nephew.	Me-to͡us'-kä	" nephew.
147.	" father's fath. bro. son's son's dau. (*m. s.*)	Ka-ah'-wuk..............	" daughter.	Me-chounk'-she...........	" daughter.
148.	" " " " " " (*f. s.*)	Ka-soh'-neh..............	" niece	Me-to͡us'-zä..............	" niece.
149.	" father's father's brother's gt. gt. grandson	Ha-yä'-da.................	" grandson.	Me-tä'-ko-zhä.............	" grandchild.
150.	" father's father's brother's gt. gt. gd. dau.	Ka-yä'-da	" granddaughter.	Me-tä'-ko-zhä.............	" "
151.	" father's father's sister.......................	Oc'-sote..................	" grandmother.	O-che'....................	" grandmother.
152.	" father's father's sister's daughter............	Ah-ga'-huc..............	" aunt.	Toh'-we	" aunt.
153.	" father's father's sister's dau. dau. (*m. s.*)	Ah-gäre'-seh	" cousin.	Hä-kä'-she	" female cousin.
154.	" " " " " " (*f. s.*)	Ah-gäre'-seh	" "	E-cha'-pä-she.............	" " "
155.	" father's father's sist. dau. dau. son (*m. s.*)	Ha-yä'-wan-da	" nephew.	Me-to͡us'-kä..............	" nephew.
156.	" " " " " " " (*f. s.*)	Ha-ah'-wuk.............	" son.	Me-chink'-she	" son.
157.	" father's father's sist. dau. dau. dau. (*m. s.*)	Ka-yä'-wan-da	" niece.	Me-to͡us'-zä..............	" niece.
158.	" " " " " " (*f. s.*)	Ka-ah'-wuk..............	" daughter.	Me-chounk'-she...........	" daughter.
159.	" father's father's sister's great grandson....	Ha-yä'-da.................	" grandson.	Me-tä'-ko-zhä.............	" grandchild.
160.	" father's father's sister's gt. granddaughter	Ka-yä'-da.................	" granddaughter.	Me-tä'-ko-zhä.............	" "

TABLE EXHIBITING THE SYSTEM OF CONSANGUINITY AND AFFINITY OF THE SENECA-IROQUOIS AND YANKTON-DAKOTAS—*Continued.*

	Description of persons.	Relationships in Seneca.	Translation.	Relationships in Yankton.	Translation.
161.	My mother's mother's brother	Hoc'-sote	My grandfather.	Toon-kä'-she-nä	My grandfather.
162.	" mother's mother's brother's son	Hoc-no'-seh	" uncle.	Dake'-she	" uncle.
163.	" mother's mother's bro. son's son *(m. s.)*	Ah-gare'-seh	" cousin.	Tä'-she	" male cousin.
164.	" " " " " " *(f. s.)*	Ah-gare'-seh	" "	She-chä'-she	" "
165.	" mother's mother's bro. son's s. s. *(m. s.)*	Ha-ah'-wuk	" son.	Me-chink'-she	" son.
166.	" " " " " " *(f. s.)*	Ha-soh'-neh	" nephew.	Me-to͡us'-kä	" nephew.
167.	" mother's moth. bro. son's s. dau. *(m. s.)*	Ka-ah'-wuk	" daughter	Me-chounk'-she	" daughter.
168.	" " " " " " " *(f. s.)*	Ka-soh'-neh	" niece.	Me-to͡us'-zä	" niece.
169.	" mother's mother's brother's gt. grandson	Ha-yä'-da	" grandson.	Me-tä'-ko-zhä	" grandchild.
170.	" mother's mother's bro. gt. granddaughter	Ka-yä'-da	" granddaughter.	Me-tä'-ko-zhä	" "
171.	" mother's mother's sister	Oc'-sote	" grandmother.	O-che'	" grandmother.
172.	" mother's mother's sister's daughter	No'-yeh	" mother.	E"-nah	" mother.
173.	" mother's mo. sis. dau. d. *(older than myself)*	Ah'-je	" elder sister.	Chim'-a-do	" elder sister.
174.	" " " " " *(younger than myself)*	Ka'-gä	" younger sister.	Me-soh'-kä	" younger sister.
175.	" mother's moth. sist. dau. son's son *(m. s.)*	Ha-yä'-wan-da	" nephew.	Me-to͡us'-kä	" nephew.
176.	" " " " " " " *(f. s.)*	Ha-ah'-wuk	" son.	Me-chink'-she	" son.
177.	" mother's mother's sist. dau. dau. *(m. s.)*	Ka-yä'-wan-da	" niece.	Me-to͡us'-zä	" niece.
178.	" " " " " " *(f. s.)*	Ka-ah'-wuk	" daughter.	Me-chounk'-she	" daughter.
179.	" mother's mother's sister's great grandson	Ha-yä'-da	" grandson.	Me-tä'-ko-zhä	" grandchild.
180.	" mother's mother's sister's gt. gd. daught.	Ka-yä'-da	" granddaughter.	Me-tä'-ko-zhä	" "
	Fourth Collateral Line.				
181.	" father's father's father's brother	Hoc'-sote	" grandfather.	Toon-kä'-she-nä	" grandfather.
182.	" father's father's father's brother's son	Hoc'-sote	" "	Toon-kä'-she-nä	" "
183.	" father's father's father's broth. son's son	Hä'-nih	" father.	Ah'-ta	" father.
184.	" father's fa. fa. br. s. s. *(older than myself)*	Hä'-je	" elder brother.	Che'-a	" elder brother.
185.	" father's fa. fa. broth. son's s. s. *(m. s.)*	Ha-ah'-wuk	" son.	Me-chink'-she	" son.
186.	" father's fa. fa. brother's son's son's s. s. s.	Ha-yä'-da	" grandson.	Me-tä'-ko-zhä	" grandchild.
187.	" father's father's father's sister	Oc'-sote	" grandmother.	O-che'	" grandmother.
188.	" father's father's father's sister's daughter	Oc'-sote	" "	O-che'	" "
189.	" father's father's father's sister's dau. dau.	Ah-ga'-huc	" Aunt.	Toh'-we	" aunt.
190.	" father's father's fath. sist. dau. dau. dau.	Ah-gäre'-seh	" Cousin.	Hä-kä'-she	" female cousin.
191.	" father's fa. fa. sist. dau. d. d. *(m. s.)*	Ka-ah'-wuk	" daughter.	Me-chounk'-she	" daughter.
192.	" father's fa. fa. sist. dau. d. d. d. "	Ka-yä'-da	" granddaughter.	Me-tä'-ko-zhä	" grandchild.
193.	" mother's mother's mother's brother	Hoc'-sote	" grandfather.	Toon-kä'-she-nä	" grandfather.
194.	" mother's mother's mother's brother's son	Hoc'-sote	" "	Toon-kä'-she-nä	" "
195.	" mother's mother's mother's bro. son's son	Hoc-no'-seh	" uncle.	Dake'-she	" uncle.
196.	" mother's mo. mo. bro. son's son's s. *(m. s.)*	Ah-gäre'-seh	" cousin.	Tä'-she	" male cousin.
197.	" mother's mo. mo. bro. son's s. s. s. "	Ha-ah'-wuk	" son.	Me-chink'-she	" son.
198.	" mother's mo. mo. bro. son's son's s. s.	Ha-yä'-da	" grandson.	Me-tä'-ko-zhä	" grandchild.
199.	" mother's mother's mother's sister	Oc'-sote	" grandmother.	O-che'	" grandmother.
200.	" mother's mother's mother's sister's dau.	Oc'-sote	" "	O-che'	" "
201.	" mother's mother's mo. sister's dau. dau.	No-yeh'	" mother.	E'-nah	" mother.
202.	" mother's mother's sister's dau. dau. dau.	Ah'-je	" elder sister.	Ton-ka'	" elder sister.
203.	" mo. m. m. sis. d. d. d. d. *(older than myself)*	Ka-ah'-wuk	" daughter.	Me-chounk'-she	" daughter.
204.	" mo. mo. mo. sis. dau. dau. dau. dau.	Ka-yä'-da	" granddaughter.	Me-tä'-ko-zhä	" grandchild.
	Marriage Relatives.				
205.	" husband	Da-yake'-ne	" husb. (two joined).	Ma-e-gin'-nä	" husband.
206.	" wife	Da-yake'-ne	" wife (two joined).	Me-tä'-we-che	" wife.
207.	" husband's father	Hä-ga'-sä	" father-in-law.	To-kä'-she	" father-in-law.
208.	" husband's mother	On-ya'-sä	" mother-in-law.	O-che'-she	" mother-in-law.
209.	" husband's grandfather	Hä-ya'-sä	" father-in-law.	Toon-kä'-she-nä	" grandfather.
210.	" husband's grandmother	On-ya'-sä	" mother-in-law.	O-che'	" grandmother.
211.	" wife's father	Oc-na'-hose	" father-in-law.	To-kä'-she	" father-in-law.
212.	" wife's mother	Oc-na'-hose	" mother-in-law.	O-che'-she	" mother-in-law.
213.	" wife's grandfather	Hoc'-sote	" grandfather.	Toon-kä'-she-nä	" grandfather.
214.	" wife's grandmother	Oc'-sote	" grandmother.	O-che'	" grandmother.
215.	" son-in-law	Oc-na'-hose	" son-in-law.	Me-tä'-koash	" son-in-law.
216.	" daughter-in-law	Ka'-sä	" daughter-in-law.	Me-tä'-koash	" daughter-in-law.
217.	" step-father	Hoc-no'-ese	" step-father.	Ah-ta'	" father.
218.	" step-mother	Oc-no'-ese	" step-mother.	E'-nah	" mother.
219.	" step-son	Ha'-no	" step-son.	Me-chink'-she	" son.
220.	" step-daughter	Ka'-no	" step-daughter.	Me-chounk'-she	" daughter.
221.	" step-brother	Hä'-je(o) ha'-gä(y)	" elder or y'nger bro.	Che-a'(o)me-soh'-kä(y)	" Elder or y'nger bro.
222.	" step-sister	Ah'-je(o) ka'-gä(y)	" elder or y'nger sist.	Ton-kä'(o)me-tänk'-she	" " "
223.	" brother-in-law *(husband's brother)*	Ha-yä'-o	" brother-in-law.	She-cha' [(y)	" brother-in-law.
224.	" " " " *(sister's husband (m. s.)*	Ah-ge͡ah'-ne͡o	" " "	Tä-huh'	" " "
225.	" " " " *(f. s.)*	Ha-yä'-o	" " "	She-cha'	" " "
226.	" " " " *(wife's brother)*	Ah-ge͡ah'-ne͡o	" " "	Tä-hä'	" " "
227.	" " " " *(wife's sister's husband)*	....	Not related.	Che-a'(o)me-soh'-kä(y)	" Elder or y'nger bro.
228.	" " " " *(husband's sister's husband)*		" "	Che-a(o) me-soh-kä (y)	" " "
229.	" sister-in-law *(wife's sister)*	Ka-yä'-o	My sister-in-law	Hä-kä'	" sister-in-law.
230.	" " " " *(brother's wife (m. s.)*	Ah-ge-ah'-ne-ah	" " "		
231.	" " " " *(f. s.)*	Ah-ge͡ah'-ne͡o	" " "	E-shä'-pä	" " "
232.	" " " " *(husband's sister)*	Ah-ge͡ah'-ne͡o	" " "	E-shä'-pä	" " "
233.	" " " " *(wife's brother's wife)*	....	Not related.	Hä-kä'	" " "
234.	" " " " *(husband's brother's wife)*			E-shä'-pä	" " "
235.	Widow	Go-no-kwä'-yes-hä-ah..	Widow.	We-tä'-she-na	Widow.
236.	Widower	Ho-no-kwä'-yes-hä-ah..	Widower.	Ta-zhe'nä-ho	Widower.
237.	Twins	Tä-geek'-hä	Twins..	Chek'-pä	Twins.
238.	Two fathers-in-law to each other	....	....	O-mä'-he-to	
239.	Two mothers-in-law to each other	....	....	O-mä'-he-to	

22   January, 1870.

CHAPTER III.

SYSTEM OF RELATIONSHIP OF THE GANOWÁNIAN FAMILY—CONTINUED.

II. Dakotan Nations.—1. Dakota Nations Proper—Their Area and Dialects—Their Transfer to the Plains—Federative Principle among them—System of Relationship of the Yanktons taken as the Standard—Indicative Relationships—System identical with the Seneca—Increasing Evidence of the Self-perpetuation of the System—2. Missouri Nations—Their Area and Dialects—System of the Kaws adopted as the Standard—Indicative Relationships—Principal Deviation from Uniformity—It occurs invariably on the Relationships between the Children of a Brother and Sister—System identical with the Yankton—3. Winnebagoes—Their Original Area—Nearest Affiliation of this Dialect with those of the Missouri Nations—Their System identical with the Yankton—4. Mandans—Agricultural and Village Indians—Indicative Relationships—System identical with the Yankton—5. Minnitarees and Upsarokas or Crows—Separation of the Crows from the Minnitarees—Their Migration northward to the Siskatchewun—Their Dialect—Observations upon the Divergence of Dialects—Minnitaree System—Indicative Relationships—Identical with the Yankton—Principal Deviation from Uniformity. III. Gulf Nations Proper—Their Area and Dialects—System of the Choctas adopted as Standard—Indicative Relationships—System identical with the Yankton—Principal Deviation from Uniformity—It agrees with the Minnitaree—Minnitarees a connecting link between Gulf and Missouri Nations—2. Cherokees—Their Language and Area—System of Relationship identical with the Chocta—Observations upon the Dakotan Dialects. IV. Prairie Nations—Their Area and Dialects—1. Pawnees—Republican Pawnee System taken as Standard—Its indicative Relationships—Identical with the Yankton—Principal Deviation from Uniformity—It agrees with the Chocta—2. Arickarees—Their Area and Dialect—Their System agrees with the Pawnee—Reasons for attaching Gulf and Prairie Nations to the Dakotan Stem—Results of Comparison of Systems—One System in Fundamental Characteristics found among all these Nations—Their Unity of Origin—System of Relationship as a Basis for the construction of a Family of Nations.

1. Dakota Nations Proper.   2. Missouri Nations.   3. Winnebagoes.   4. Mandans.   5. Minnitarees and Upsarokas or Crows.

The two leading subdivisions of the Ganowánian family north of New Mexico are the Dakotan and the Algonkin. They have held this position from the earliest period to which our knowledge extends. It is probable that all of the nations south of the Siskatchewun River and Hudson's Bay, and east of the Missouri and Mississippi Rivers will ultimately be resolved by linguistic affiliations, into these two great divisions. A large number of nations west of the Missouri also belong to the Dakotan Stem. The two groups of languages occupied about equal areas, and are respectively broken up into about the same number of dialects. Among the dialects of the former language, which is the oldest of the two in the area if the Gulf nations belong to this branch, the amount of deviation is much the greatest, the vocables of many of them having changed beyond the reach of identification, although they still wear a family resemblance. It is also extremely probable, not to say certain, that the two original languages from which these dialects respectively have emanated had become distinct and entirely changed in their vocables, on the Pacific side of the Continent, before the two streams of migration commenced to the eastward, the Dakotan to the valley of the Mississippi by some southern route, and the Algonkin to the chain of Lakes, and the valley of the St. Lawrence by some northern route. The classification of nations adopted in the Table is founded chiefly upon their system of relationship, which contains some evidence bearing upon their inter-relations that will appear as we proceed.

A *stock language*, as the term is here used, includes such dialects as have a sufficient number of vocables for common objects susceptible of identification to establish their immediate derivation from each other, or from a common parent language. *Branch*, when applied to a group of nations, is coextensive with stock language as applied to a group of dialects. The term *stem*, or *stem-people*, is used in a more comprehensive sense. It includes several branches or groups of nations, whose systems of relationship possess features showing affinity of blood. It also includes several stock languages, the vocables of which have a family resemblance, although changed beyond immediate identification.

I. Dakota Nations Proper. 1. Isaunties. 2. Yanktons. 3. Yanktonais. 4. Sissetons. 5. Ogalallas. 6. Brulés. 7. Unkpappas. 8. Blackfoot Dakotas. (9. Ohenonpas. 10. Minnikanyes. 11. Sansarcs. 12. Itazipcoes, these are not represented in the Table.) 13. Asiniboines.

At the period of European discovery, the Dakotas proper were found established upon the head waters of the Mississippi in the present state of Minnesota. Their home country extended from the head of Lake Superior to the Missouri River, the greater part of which, along the margins of the rivers, streams and lakes, was in their continuous occupation. When first known to the colonists, through the early explorers, they were subdivided into a number of independent bands, living more or less in tent villages,[1] and were supposed to be more numerous than any other northern Indians who spoke mutually intelligible dialects. The first accounts were favorable concerning their intelligence, their hospitality, and their manliness.

The Dakota language has assumed two, if not three, distinctly marked dialectical forms, but the variance is not sufficient to interrupt free communication. These dialects may be distinguished as the Isauntie, the Teeton, and the Yankton. Between the first two the amount of variation is considerable; but the third, the Yankton, is in the process of formation out of the first.[2] As two forms of the same speech, they may be called the Isauntie, or the Mississippi, and the Teeton or Missouri Dakota. For philological purposes they are extremely interesting, since the variance is still in the incipient stages of its development.

---

[1] Carver's Travels, p. 51 (Philadelphia edition 1796), shows that this was the case in 1766.

[2] "The chief peculiarity of the Ihanktonwan [Yankton] as compared with that of the Dakotas of Minnesota [Isaunties] is the almost universal substitution of *k* for *h*. The Titonwan [Teeton] exhibits more striking differences. In it *g* hard is used for *h* of the Isanties and *k* of the Ihanktonwans, and rejecting *d* altogether, they used *l* in its stead. * * * Thus, to illustrate the foregoing. * * * '*Hda*,' *to go home* of the Isantes, is '*kda*' of the Ihantonwans dialect, and '*gla*' in the Titonwan. Many words, too, are entirely different, as for example, '*isan*', a knife; the Titonwans say '*milla*', and the Ihanktonwans *minna*." Smithsonian Con. IV. Gram. and Dic. of Dakota Language, Intro. XVII. This last difference may probably be explained by the absence of a term for knife in the primitive language.

Since the period of their discovery, when the Dakotas occupied a territory of small dimensions, a great change has taken place in their condition, ascribable, in part, to the retro-migration westward of the Indian nations; but chiefly to the possession of the horse, which has proved by far the most important material gift of Americans to the American aborigines. After they had learned to rear and tend this valuable domestic animal, in which they have been eminently successful, they gradually spread over the vast prairies of the interior of the continent, which never before had been capable of human occupation, until at the present time their range extends over the immense area from the western head branches of the Mississippi to the foot of the Rocky Mountain chain. The change thus wrought in their condition has been chiefly for the worse, although it seems probable that they are now more numerous than at any former period. They have ceased altogether to live in villages, in which the first germs of social progress originate, and have betaken themselves to camps on the plains, where they now lead a life of unrelieved hardship, and of incessant conflict with adjacent nations, although acknowledged masters within their own area. They have now become nomades in the full sense of the term, depending for subsistence upon the buffaloes, whose migrations they follow. When first known to us they were not agriculturalists in the slightest particular, but depended exclusively upon fish, wild rice, and game. The innumerable lakes in central and northern Minnesota were well stocked with fish, and the mixture of forest, lake, and prairie, which make this one of the most strikingly beautiful regions within the limits of the United States, also rendered it an excellent game country. The exchange was greatly to their disadvantage. Their transfer to the plains, where the greater part of them now dwell, was much more from necessity than choice. The steady and irresistible flow of the white population westward necessarily forced the Dakotas in this direction, so that their retrogression was but the realization of their portion of the common destiny of all the nations east of the Mississippi.

The Dakotas have long enjoyed the advantages imparted by a consciousness of strength from superior numbers.[1] They have had the sagacity and wisdom to maintain a species of alliance among the several subdivisions into which they had fallen by the inevitable law of Indian Society, although each band was practically an independent nation. Friendly relations have subsisted among them from time immemorial with the single exception of the Asiniboines, who became detached shortly before the year 1600, as near as can be ascertained, and incurred, in consequence, the hostility of their congeners. The important uses of the federal principle to arrest the constant tendency to denationalization was understood by the Dakotas, although it never ripened into a permanent and effective organization. Their name *Lä-ko'-tä* in the dialects of the western nations, and *Dä-ne-ko'-tä* in that of the eastern, signifies *leagued* or *allied*, and they also called themselves, by a figure of speech, "*The Seven Council Fires*," from the seven principal bands which formed

---

[1] They are estimated at the present time, to number about twenty-three thousand.

the compact.[1] We have no knowledge of any important acts of legislation for the general welfare, by this Dakotan Confederacy, but there can be no doubt that even a nominal league would tend to promote and preserve harmony among them, as well as to increase their influence among Indian nations. Every trace of the federative principle in the Ganowánian family possesses some degree of importance, as it reveals in each case the development of the first germ of progress from the monotonous level of the roving bands.

Intellectually the Dakotas compare favorably with the most advanced of their contemporaries. Intractable and independent in their dispositions they have, for the most part held themselves aloof from government influence; but generous and just to each other, they have maintained among Indian nations a favorable reputation for energy, hardihood, and courage.[2] Their chiefs in council are bold, graceful, and fluent speakers. In this respect they compare favorably with the Iroquois, who have reached some distinction in eloquence. At different times I have heard the chiefs and orators of many Indian nations speak in council, but none of them impressed me more strongly than the Dakota chiefs. Clearness of thought and energy of will characterized their speech, and a free untameable spirit their demeanor.

It is impossible to save the Dakotas, or any Indian nation, in the strictly aboriginal condition. They must either become agricultural or pastoral, or disappear from the continent. With this great change even it is a formidable struggle for existence. The Dakotas have seized the principal part, or rather the northern half of the interior prairie area, no considerable portion of which, it seems probable, can ever be occupied by our people. It is throughout poorly watered, and substantially destitute of forest. On the Upper Missouri for two thousand miles, and until you reach the foot slopes of the mountains, the timber is confined to the bottom lands of the river, and is very scanty even there. It is the same with all of its tributaries. A civilized and agricultural population can never inhabit any portion of this inland region, except a narrow margin upon the rivers. On the plains, the Dakotas, if they maintain peaceful relations, will interfere with no interests of the American people. When the Buffalo ceases from diminished numbers to afford them subsistence, which will be the case at no distant day, they will be compelled to rear domestic cattle to supply their place. In this there is every reason to suppose they may be entirely successful, from their experience in raising horses, from their knowledge of the buffalo ranges, and from their familiarity with the life of the camp. Should

---

[1] These were, 1. The Mediwanktons; 2. Walipekutes; 3. Wabipetons; 4. Sissetons; 5. Yanktons; 6. Yanktonais; 7. Teetons. The first three are collectively the Isaunties of the Table; and the Teetons are now subdivided into, 1. Ogalallas; 2. Brulés; 3. Uncpappas; 4. Blackfoot Dakotas; 5. Ohenonpas; 6. Itazipcoes; 7. Minekanyes, and 8. Sansarcs.

[2] In the year 1862, at Fort Pierre in Nebraska Territory, at a council held by the United States Indian agent with the chiefs of several bands of the Dakotas, I witnessed the refusal of a chief of one of them to receive any annuity whatever from the government; and he alleged as a reason that the acceptance of the goods, which were in a pile before him as he spoke, would compromise the independence of his people.

they make the experiment and succeed in becoming a pastoral people, they will reach a higher degree of prosperity and numbers in the future than they have known in the past. In the course of events their removal to the plains may prove the means of their preservation, and secure to them a more hopeful future than awaits any other branch of the family.

Of the thirteen distinct and independent Dakota bands or nations named, eleven are represented in the Table (Table II, Part II). Their system of consanguinity and affinity is one and the same among them all, in every feature which is material, and in nearly every minute particular.

This would be expected from the near approach of their dialects to a common speech; but it is also important as a fact, since it tends to illustrate the living power of the system, and its ability to perpetuate itself among geographically separated nations. One form will be sufficient to present, and that of the Yanktons will be selected as the standard system of these nations.

It will not be necessary to take up the Yankton system of relationship as we did the Seneca and present the several lines in detail, since it is material only to know wherein it agrees with the Seneca, and wherein it differs. This may be shown by pointing out the differences in the Yankton, leaving it to be inferred that in other respects it agrees with the Seneca; or it may be shown by stating the *indicative relationships*, which not only reveal the fundamental characteristics of the system, but which also control the several relationships that follow. There are upwards of seventy different forms given in the Table in as many dialects of the Ganowánian language; and that which is true with respect to the Yankton is also equally true with reference to the others. Whilst it is important to know the actual present condition of the system among all of these nations to appreciate its nature and principles as a domestic institution, its power of self-perpetuation, and its bearing upon the question of the unity of origin of these nations, it would be too great a tax upon the reader to go through the minute details of each. The Table contains the full particulars. To this he is referred for a more minute knowledge of the system of each nation. Some plan, however, must be adopted for presenting so much of the system of each nation, or of groups of closely affiliated nations, as will exhibit its material characteristics. A statement of the general results of a comparison would be less satisfactory than a comparison of the material characteristics themselves; because the latter will reveal the positive elements of the system. In most cases the result desired can be secured by stating the indicative relationships, from which its agreement or disagreement with the Seneca will be at once perceived. These relationships disclose the radical features of the system. When they are found to agree with the Seneca the identity of the two becomes established. In other cases, where the differences are greater, it will be preferable to state the differences; and in still others it may be necessary to give details. The utmost brevity will be sought, under either form of explanation, in the survey about to be made of the system of relationship of the remaining nations of the Ganowánian family.

There are separate terms in the Yankton for grandfather and grandmother, *Toon-kä'-she-nä* and *O'-che*; for father and mother, *Ah-ta'* and *E'-nah*; for son and daughter, *Me-chink'-she* and *Me-chounk'-she*; and a term in common gender for grandchild, *Me-tä'-ko-zhä*. All above the former are grandfathers and grand-mothers, and all below the latter are grandchildren.

The fraternal and sororal relationships are in the twofold form of elder and younger, for which there is a double set of terms, one of which is used by the males and the other by the females; for brother and sister in the abstract there is no term in the dialect, except in the plural number. There are two terms for cousin (male and female), used by the males, and two for the same used by the females.

The following are the indicative relationships in the Yankton-Dakota system:—

First Indicative Feature. My brother's son and daughter, with *Ego* a male, are my son and daughter, *Me-chink'-she* and *Me-chounk' she*; with *Ego* a female they are my nephew and niece.

Second. My sister's son and daughter, *Ego* being a male, are my nephew and niece, *Me-to-us'-kä* and *Me-to-us'-ză*; with *Ego* a female they are my son and daughter.

Third. My father's brother is my father, *Ah-ta'*.

Fourth. My father's brother's son is my elder or younger brother *Che'-a* or *Me-soh'-kä*, as he is older or younger than myself; and his daughter is my elder or younger sister, *Ton-kä'* or *Me-tank'-she*.

Fifth. My father's sister is my aunt, *Toh'-we*.

Sixth. My mother's brother is my uncle, *Dake'-she*.

Seventh. My mother's sister is my mother, *E'-nah*.

Eighth. My mother's sister's son is my elder or younger brother, and her daughter is my elder or younger sister.

Ninth. My grandfather's brother is my grandfather, *Toon-kä'-zhe-nä*.

Tenth. The grandchildren of my brothers and sisters, and the grandchildren of my collateral brothers and sisters, and of my cousins are my grandchildren without distinction. This merges the several collateral lines in the lineal line.

In these the indicative relationships, the Yankton and Seneca are identical. It may be stated in addition that the children of my uncle and aunt are my cousins; that the children of my collateral brothers, and of my male cousins, *Ego* being a male, are my sons and daughters, and that the children of my collateral sisters, and of my female cousins, are my nephews and nieces; with *Ego* a female, these relationships are reversed. A comparison of the two forms, as they are found at the end of Chapter II, will show that they are in minute agreement throughout, the marriage relationships included.

It has before been stated that the system of relationship of the remaining Dakota nations is the same in all material respects as the Yankton. A reference to the Table will show how entirely they agree, not only in general characteristics, but also in minute details. It will also be noticed that the terms of relationship are the same words, in nearly every instance, under dialectical changes. This shows that the terms have come down to each nation as a part of the common language; and that the system, also, was derived by each from the common source of the language. The system is thus made coeval with the period when these nations spoke a single dialect, and were one people.

The Asiniboines, as has been elsewhere remarked, had become detached from the Dakotas when first known to Europeans. Their range was from near the northwest shore of Lake Superior, along the Rainy Lake, and Lake of the Woods towards Lake Winnipeg. They formed an alliance with the Crees for mutual defence against the Dakotas, which has been maintained with more or less constancy to the present time. They are now west of the Red River of the North, and north of the Missouri, their range including a portion of the Hudson's Bay Territory. In their system of relationship they agree so closely with the Yankton that whatever is said of one is equally applicable to the other. A greater difference in dialect is found between the Asiniboine and Yankton than is found among the remaining Dakota dialects as to each other, which is explained by the isolation of the former from the Dakota speech for two hundred and fifty years and upwards. But the amount of dialectical variation in the terms of relationship is still inconsiderable.

It thus appears that every indicative feature of the Seneca system is not only present in that of the Dakota nations; but that they are coincident throughout. The diagrams used to illustrate the Seneca-Iroquois form will answer for either of the Dakota nations as well. Every relationship I believe, without exception, would be the same in the six diagrams. This identity of systems is certainly an extraordinary fact when its elaborate and complicated structure is considered. The significance of this identity is much increased by the further fact that it has remained to the present time, after a separation of the Iroquois from the Dakota nations, or from some common parent nation, for a period of time which must be measured by the centuries required to change the vocables of their respective stock languages beyond recognition. The maintenance of a system which creates such diversities in the domestic relationships, and which is founded upon such peculiar discriminations, is the highest evidence of its enduring nature as a system. Ideas never change. The language in which they are clothed is mutable, and may become wholly transformed; but the conceptions which it embodies, and the ideas which it holds in its grasp, are alone exempt from mutability. When these ideas or conceptions are associated together in such fixed relations as to create a system of consanguinity, resting upon unchangeable necessities, the latter is perpetuated by their vital force, or the system, in virtue of its organic structure, holds these ideas in a living form. We shall be led step by step to the final inference that this system of relationship originated in the primitive ages of mankind, and that it has been propagated like language with the streams of the blood.

II. Missouri Nations. 1. Punkas. 2. Omahas. 3. Iowas. 4. Otoes. (5. Missouris, not in the Table.) 6. Kaws. 7. Osages. (8. Quappas, not in the Table.[1])

This name is proposed for the above group of nations whose dialects are closely allied with each other, and all of which were derived from the same immediate source as the dialects of the Dakota language proper. These nations, when first

---

[1] The orthography of some of these names is not in accordance with the common pronunciation in the Indian country. To conform with it they should be written: Punkaws, Omahaws, and Quappaws. Otoe is not the original name of this nation. Their own name, which has a vulgar signification, was changed to Otoe at the suggestion of the traders.

known to Europeans occupied the banks of the Missouri River from the mouth of the Punka on the north, to the junction of the Missouri and Mississippi, and thence down the latter river to the mouth of the Arkansas on the south. In their dialects they arrange themselves into three classes, as follows: 1. Punka and Omaha; 2. Iowa, Otoe, and Missouri; and 3. Kaw, Osage, and Quappa. The system of relationship of all these nations is given in the Table, with the exception of the Quappa, which is believed to be identical with the Osage. The remains of the Missouri nation are now intermingled with the Otoes, and the system of the latter nation represents both. These nations were originally three, as their dialects still demonstrate, and were afterwards increased to eight by subdivision. It is not now ascertainable whether the three were one when they separated from the parent stem, or broke off at three different times. The fact that the eight dialects are now nearer to each other than either is to the Dakota proper, favors the former supposition. It is at least clear that they broke off in one body, or quite near the same epoch in separate bodies. The Dakota dialects including the Asiniboine, are very much nearer to each other than the dialects of the Missouri nations are among themselves, as will be seen by consulting the Table. It would seem, therefore, that unless we assume the existence of some intermediate nation from which both were derived, and which has since disappeared, the greater relative age must be assigned to the Missouri Nations. There is, however, a serious philological difficulty encountered in deriving the Dakotas from the Missouri Nations, or the reverse. It must be considered, as a part of the problem, that the latter nations were scattered along the banks of the Missouri, and below on the Mississippi, for more than a thousand miles, which would tend to increase the amount of dialectical variation; whilst the former occupied a compact area upon the head waters of the Mississippi, and from thence across a narrow belt of country to the Missouri, which would tend in the first instance to prevent the formation of dialects and afterwards to repress the amount of dialectical variation.[1] On comparing their respective systems of relationship it will be found that the Missouri form deviates in one important particular, from that of the Dakota nations, in which respect it is the rudest, and therefore the oldest. But this fact does not yield any evidence with respect to relative age, since the supposition intervenes that the Dakota form

---

[1] A comparison of the Punka and Yankton vocables reveals a large amount of variation, although the identity of many of the words is obvious on mere inspection. These dialects were geographically contiguous. The Punka is one of the rudest dialects of the Dakotan stock language. It would scarcely be supposed from the vocables that a Punka and Yankton native could understand each other, and yet the contrary is the fact. While on the Punka reservation in Nebraska in 1862, I obtained the Punka system of relationship from a native, with the assistance of a Yankton half blood glrl, who spoke English and Yankton fluently, but could not speak the Punka. Neither could the Punka Indian speak the Yankton. With some difficulty they were able to understand each other while using their respective dialects. They were undoubtedly able to detect and follow common root forms, however much disguised. The actual amount of dialectical change is, in reality, much less than the vocabularies seem to show.

23 February, 1870.

was originally the same; and that it has been advanced, by development, from this lower to a higher stage.

The system of consanguinity and affinity of the Missouri Nations is one and the same among them all. They also agree with each other in those particulars in which they diverge from the Dakota form. It will be sufficient to present the system of one of these nations, and that of the Kaws will be taken as the standard.

It will be understood hereafter unless the contrary is stated, that each nation has special terms for the relationships of grandfather and grandmother, father and mother, brother and sister, son and daughter, and grandson and granddaughter; and that the fraternal and sororal relationships are in the twofold form of elder and younger.

First Indicative Feature. My brother's son and daughter, *Ego* a male, are my son and daughter. With *Ego* a female, they are my nephew and niece.

Second. My sister's son and daughter, *Ego* a male, are my nephew and niece. With *Ego* a female, they are my son and daughter.

Third. My father's brother is my father.

Fourth. My father's brother's son and daughter are my brother and sister, elder or younger.

Fifth. My father's sister is my aunt.

Sixth. My mother's brother is my uncle.

Seventh. My mother's sister is my mother.

Eighth. My mother's sister's son and daughter are my brother and sister elder or younger.

Ninth. My grandfather's brother is my grandfather.

Tenth. The grandchildren of my brothers and sisters, and the grandchildren of my collateral brothers and sisters, are my grandchildren. This merges the several collateral lines in the lineal line.[1]

The other relationships follow as in the Seneca and Yankton, until we come to that which subsists between the children of a brother and sister, where the principal deviation from uniformity in the system of the Ganowánian family occurs, as has elsewhere been stated. It is very necessary to understand the several forms of this divergence, since the knowledge will tend to explain some part of the internal history of the system. It also has a direct bearing upon the question of the stability of its radical characteristics. Among the Iroquois and Dakota nations as has been seen, the children of a brother and sister are cousins to each other; but among the Missouri nations they are uncle and nephew to each other if males,

---

[1] In the Omaha dialect there are two terms for son and two for daughter, one of which is used by the males, and the other by the females. It is probable that there are two sets of terms in the other Missouri dialects, although I did not discover them. *She-me-she-ga* in Kaw signifies *my girl*. It is formed differently from the corresponding term in the other Missouri dialects, *e. g.*, Kaw, *Be-she'-gä*, my son; *She-me'-she-gä*, my daughter; Osage, *We-she'-kä*, my son; *We-shon'-kä*, my daughter, which is analogous to the Yankton; *Me-chink'-she*, *Me-choonk'-she*, and the Winnebago, *E-neke'*, *E-nook'*. Where a term originally in common gender takes on a masculine and feminine form, the latter retains the original form.

and mother and daughter if females. When run out in detail the relationships are as follows:—

My father's sister is my aunt, *Be-jé'-me ;* her son and daughter are my nephew and niece, *Be-chose'-kă* and *Be-che'-zho*, each of them calling me uncle; and their children are each my grandchild, *Be-chose'-pä*, each of them calling me grandfather, *Be-che'-go*. With *Ego* a female, my father's sister's son and daughter are my son and daughter, *Be-she'-gä* and *She-me'-she-gä*, each of them calling me mother; and their children are my grandchildren, each of them calling me grandmother.

My mother's brother is my uncle, *Be-ja'-ga*, and calls me nephew; his son is my uncle again, and calls me nephew; and his descendants in the male line are severally my uncles, theoretically, in an infinite series.[1] My mother's brother's daughter is my mother *E'-naw*, and calls me her son; the son and daughter of this mother are my brother and sister, elder or younger according to our relative ages, and they address me by the correlative terms. The son and daughter of this collateral brother are my son and daughter; of this collateral sister my nephew and niece; and the children of each are my grandchildren. With *Ego* a female these relationships are the same, except that those who are sons and daughters are changed to nephews and nieces, and those who are the latter are changed to the former.

A mother's brother and his lineal male descendants are thus placed in a superior relationship over her children with the authority the avunculine relationship implies in Indian society. In its practical application the infant becomes the uncle of the centenarian.

The terms of relationship in the eight dialects of the Missouri nations are, for the most part, the same words under dialectical changes; and, inasmuch as the system of the several nations is identical, it follows that both the terms and the system were derived by each nation from the common source of the language. The system can also claim an antiquity coeval with the period when these nations were a single people. It has also been made evident that the system of the Missouri, the Dakota, and the Iroquois nations is identical.

With respect to the relationship of cousin, it will become more and more apparent, as the investigation progresses, that it was unknown in the primitive system of the Ganowánian family. It seems to have been developed at a later day, by the more advanced nations, to remove a blemish in the system and to improve its symmetry. All the nations which have advanced to a knowledge of this relationship have restricted it in every instance, to the children of a brother and sister; thus showing, as we have previously seen in the system of the Aryan family, that if it

---

[1] Of the actual existence and daily recognition of these relationships, as stated, novel as they are, there is no doubt whatever. I first discovered this deviation from the typical form while working out the system of the Kaws in Kansas in 1859. The Kaw chief from whom I obtained it, through a perfectly competent interpreter, insisted upon the verity of these relationships against all doubts and questionings; and when the work was done I found it proved itself through the correlative relationships. Afterwards in 1860, while at the Iowa reservation in Nebraska, I had an opportunity to test it fully, both in Iowa and Otoe, through White Cloud a native Iowa well versed in English. While discussing these relationships he pointed out a boy near us, and remarked that he was his uncle, and the son of his mother's brother who was also his uncle.

was developed at all, the direction of the advance was predetermined by the elements of the system. In other words, it is under the absolute control, like other domestic institutions, of the primary ideas upon which it is founded. Whilst it cannot be changed by the arbitrary introduction of new elements from without, it may be advanced by development from within, in which case it must move in logical accordance with the principles of the system. What the original form, as to these relationships, may have been, it is extremely difficult to determine. There are four different methods of disposing of them found among the Ganowánian nations; by the first the children of a brother and sister are cousin and cousin; by the second uncle and nephew when males, and mother and daughter when females; by the third, son and father when males, and granddaughter and grandmother when females; and of the fourth, brother and sister. The first appears to be an advance, and the last a lapse, from the primitive system. At present the choice lies between the second and third. It is also an interesting fact that the first, second, and fourth forms are found among the Algonkin nations. These deviations from uniformity have an important bearing upon the question of the order of the separation from each other of nations speaking independent stock languages.

3. Winnebagoes. When discovered this nation was established at the head of Green Bay, and around Winnebago Lake, in the present state of Wisconsin, surrounded by Algonkin populations. They are the Puants of the early French explorers. In 1840 they were removed by the national government to a tract of land assigned to them in Iowa, and in 1846 they were again removed to their present reservation on Long Prairie River in the State of Minnesota. The first census, taken in 1842, showed their numbers to be something over two thousand.

It has long been known that the Winnebago dialect belonged to the Dakotan speech; but the variation was so marked as to leave it in a state of isolation. When compared with the dialects of the Missouri nations it will be seen that it affiliates with them more closely than with the Dakota proper. Their ethnic position is near the latter nations. They call themselves *Ho-chun-'gä-rä*, the signification of which is lost.

The Winnebago system of relationship follows that of the Kaws so closely that it will be unnecessary to present it specially. It has all of the indicative features of the common system, and agrees with the Kaw in the greater part of its subordinate details. It is noticeable, also, that it agrees with that of the Missouri nations in placing the children of a brother and sister in the relationships of uncle and nephew and mother and daughter; thus tending to show that the Winnebagoes became detached from the parent stem while that form prevailed. It is also inferrible from their dialect that they are one of the oldest branches of the Dakotan stem.[1]

---

[1] Independently of the relationships given in the Table, and of the names borne by individuals, there is a series of terms applied to the first five sons in the order of their birth, and another to the first five daughters. These special designations are used by the Dakota nations, and doubtless by still other nations; but they appear to be names expressive of the order of birth, as first and second

4. Mandans. The Mandans have been brought into more prominent and favorable notice than any other Indian nation of the interior. The accounts of Lewis and Clark, who spent the winter of 1804–1805 at their principal village; of Catlin, who resided for several months in the year 1832, in the same village; and of Prince Maximilian, who visited the place in 1833, have furnished a larger amount of information concerning this nation than has been given of any other upon the Missouri River. When first discovered they were agricultural, and Village Indians. Their advanced condition in resources and intelligence is to be ascribed to their stationary life, and to their agricultural habits. The change from a roving life in the tent to permanency in large communities, and from fish and game to bread in connection with animal food produces a marked improvement in the social condition of any Indian nation. It also affords a better opportunity to witness their domestic life, from which, as a stand point, they should be judged. This has rarely been the combination of circumstances under which our knowledge of the American Indians has been acquired. The highly favorable representations of Lewis and Clark, Catlin, and Maximilian are due, in some measure, to their unusual opportunities for observation.

It is questionable whether the Mandans originated the partial civilization of which they were found possessed. There are strong reasons for believing that they obtained both their knowledge of agriculture and of house building from the Minnitarees, a people who migrated to the Upper Missouri after the Mandans had become established in the same region, and of whom the early accounts are not less favorable than of the Mandans themselves. Both of these nations constructed a house of a peculiar mode, usually called the "Dirt Lodge," although this designation fails to express the advance which it represents in the architecture of the Ganowánian family. It was a house on the communal principle, thoroughly constructed with a timber frame, commodious in size, and extremely neat and comfortable.[1] It is a question of some interest from what source this house, and agriculture, found their way to the Upper Missouri.

---

born, and so on, rather than terms of relationship. In Winnebagoe and Isauntie Dakota they are as follows :—

	Winnebagoe.	Isauntie Dakota.		Winnebagoe.	Isauntie Dakota.
First son,	Koo-no'-kä.	Chä-was'-kä.	First daughter,	E-noo'-kä.	We-no'kä.
Second "	Ha-na'-kä.	Ha-paŋ'-nä.	Second "	Wa-huŋ'-kä.	Hä'-paŋ.
Third "	Hä-kä'-kä.	Ha-pe'-na.	Third "	Ah-kse-ä'-kä.	Hä'-pes-teŋ-nä.
Fourth "	Nä-kh·e'-kä.	Chä-nä'-taŋ.	Fourth "	E-nŭk-ha'kä.	Wan'-ska.
Fifth "	Nä-kh·ä-kh·o'-no-kä.	Hä-kä'.	Fifth "	Ah-kse-gä-ho'-no-kä.	We-hä'-ka.

[1] In 1862 I visited the ruins of the Mandan village above referred to. It was abandoned by them in 1838, after the visitation of the pestilence which nearly depopulated the village. The Arickarees soon after occupied it, and held possession until the spring of 1862, when the inroads of the Dakotas forced them to abandon it in turn. It contained the remains of about forty houses, most of them polygonal in form, and about forty feet in diameter. The village was situated upon a bluff about fifty feet high at a bend in the Missouri River, which afforded a site of much natural beauty. Some miles above, on the opposite or east side of the river, we found the present Mandan and Minnitaree village, which they occupy together. The situation is upon a similar bluff at a bend, and the houses are constructed upon the same model. Both the old and the new village were stockaded. The Mandans, who now number but two hundred and fifty souls, were estimated by Lewis and Clarke

The dialects of the Dakota and Missouri nations, and of the Winnebagoes and Mandans, all belong to the same stock language. A sufficient number of vocables are common to render this certain upon bare inspection. At the same time the Minnitaree and Crow dialects contain a large number of words for common objects which are found in the dialects of the former nations. The connection of the latter nations with the Mandans, which is known to have been intimate for more than two hundred years, might explain the presence of some of these words in the Minnitaree and Crow dialects, particularly the words for the numerals; but the number of vocables for common objects renders it extremely probable, not to say certain, that all of these dialects belong to the same stock language. The subjoined comparative vocabulary, taken in connection with the terms of relationship in the Table, shows the degree of the correspondence in a list of forty ordinary words.[1] It also discloses a sensible family resemblance between these dialects and those of the Gulf nations, with the exception of the Cherokee.

(1804–1805) at three hundred and fifty fighting men, which would give a total of about eighteen hundred (Travels, London edition, 1814, p. 96), and by Catlin in 1832 at two thousand. (North American Indians, I, 287.) In their personal appearance they are still among the best specimens of the American Indian.

COMPARATIVE VOCABULARY.

		Mandan. (Morgan.)	Kaw. (Morgan.)	Otoe. (Morgan.)	Isauntie-Dakota. (Riggs, Lex.)	Winnebagoes. (Gallatin's vocabulary.)
1	Father,	Tä-tay′	E-dä′-je	Hin′-ka	At-tay′	E-in-cha′
2	Mother,	Nä-a′	E′-naw	He′-nah	E-nah′	E-oo-ne′
3	Head,	Pän	Be-a′-hä-be	Nä′-to	Pä	Nä-sah-ha
4	Hair,	Pä-he′	Pä-hu′-ya	Nä′-too	Hiŋ	
5	Eye,	In-stä′	Eshe-tä′	Ish′-tä	Is-tä	Ish-chah-suh-hä
6	Nose,	Pä′-ho	Pä′-shee-sha	Pä	Po′-ga	Pä-hä
7	Ear,	Nä-go′-he	Ha′-yu-ja	Nä′-twä	No′-ga	Nä-chä-wä-hä
8	Mouth,	E′-ha	E′-hä	E′-hä	We-chä′-e	Ee-hä
9	Arm,	Ah′-le	Ah-le′-tä	Ah-krä′-cha	We′-pa	
10	Foot,	Shee	See	The	Si-hä′	See-hä
11	Heart,	Not′-kä	No′-ja	Nä′-che	Chaŋ-te	
12	Tobacco,	Mä-nä′-she	Nä′-ne	Dä-ri′-ye	Chaŋ-di′	[hä (sun)
13	Sun,	Me′-nä-ke	Me′-yo-bä	Pee	An-pa-tŭ-we	Hau·nip (day), wee-
14	Moon,	Me′-nä-ke	Me′-yo-bä	Pee′-tä	Haŋ-ya′-tŭ-we	Hä-nip (night), wee
15	Star,	Hä-kä′-ka	Me-kä′-ga	Pe-kä-kä	Wi-chaŋ′-h·pe·	Kohsh-keh [hä(sun)
16	Day,	Häm′-pa	Hä′-ome-pä	Ah′-wa	Aŋ-pä′-tŭ	Haum-pee-hä
17	Night,	Ese-tŭ-sha	Hä-nope′-pä-sa	Ah′-ha	Haŋ-ye′-tŭ	
18	Fire,	Wä′-lä-la		Pai′-ye	Pe′-tä	Ped-ghä
19	Water,	Mä-ne′	Ne	Knu	Me-ne′	Ni-hä
20	Ice,	Ho′-lee	No′-hä	No′-ka	Cha′-gä	
21	Snow,	Mä′-h·a	Bä	Pow	Wa	Wä-hä
22	Black,	Pse	Sa′-bä	Skä	Sä′-pä	Seb-hä
23	White,	Shote′-ho	Skä	Tha′-wa	Skä	Skä
24	Red,	Sa-zhe	Shu′-ja	Soo′-che	Shä	Shoosh
25	Yellow,	See′-ro	Se′-hä	Che	Ze	
26	Blue,	Toh′-ho	To′-ho	To-ho′-ja	To	
27	Green,	Toh·	Mä-he′-a-go	To	To	
28	Moccasin,	Hom′-pa		Ah′-kooch	Haŋ′-pä	
29	Beaver,	Wä′-lä-pe		Pä-kuh′-thä	Cha′-pä	Nä-a-pä
30	Buffalo,	Bä-ro′-kä	Chä-do′-ga	Chä	Zä-taŋ′-kä	
31	Pigeon,		Eu-ete′-ta	Lute′-ja	Wä-ki′-ya-daŋ	
32	Arrow,	Mä′-he	Mä	Mä	Wäŋ-heŋk′-pe	
33	One,	Mä′-han-nä	Me-ikh′-je	E′-yunk	Wäŋ-the	Jun-ki-hä
34	Two,	Nope	No′-bä	No′-wä	Noŋ′pä	Nom-pi-wi
35	Three,	Nä′-min-ne	Ya′-bar-le	Tä′-nye	Yäm′-ne	Tä-ni-wi
36	Four,	Tope	To′-bä	To′-weh	To′-pä	Tsho-pi-wi
37	Five,	Ke′-ho	Sä′-tun	Thä′-tä	Zap′-täŋ	Sä-tshä
38	Six,	Kee′-nä	Shak′-pe	Shä′-gwa	Shak′-pe	Ah-ke-we
39	Seven,	Koo′-pä	Pa′-yo-bä	Shä′-ma	Shä′-ko-wiŋ	Shä-ko
40	Eight,	Ta-to-ke	Pa′-yü-ba-da	Grä-rä′-pen-ne	Shä-do′-gaŋ	A-oo-ougk

When the Minnitarees reached the Upper Missouri they found the Mandans, as the traditions of the latter affirm, in the possession of the country; and they were allowed to take up their residence apart, but near them, on the river as a friendly people. Although the Mandan tradition asserts that the Minnitarees "came out of the water to the east," it seems highly probable that they were originally from the region of the Gulf of Mexico, and that they are one of the connecting links between the Choctas and Creeks, and the Dakota nations. There is some evidence in their respective systems of relationship tending to the same conclusion. On the other hand, the Mandans were not intrusive, but established on the north of their nearest congeners, the Dakota and Missouri nations. They had been forced in later years by the hostility of the Dakotas further up the river, as the remains of their old villages, still to be seen, as well as their own accounts attest. The Mandans now call themselves *Me-too'-ta-häk*, "South Villages," which implies their displacement from a more southern location. They could have learned neither agriculture nor house building from the Dakotas, as the latter knew nothing of cultivation, or of house architecture; nor yet of the

COMPARATIVE VOCABULARY.

		Minnitaree. (Morgan.)	Crow. (Morgan.)	Chocta. (Byington.)	Creek. (Casey.)	Cherokee. (Morgan.)	Wyandote. (Morgan.)
1	Father,	Tä-ta'	Ah·-ha'	A'-kĭ	Chuhl'-ke	A-do'-dä	Hi-ese'-tä
2	Mother,	Ih'-kä	E'-kee-ä	Ush'-kĭ	Chutch-ke'	A-tse'	Nä-uh'
3	Head,	Ahk-too'	Ah-shu'-ä	Nĭsh-ko-bo	Ik-ah	Tse-sko'-le	Sku-tä
4	Hair,	Ah-rä'	E-she'-ä	Pä-shi	E-kä'-is-see	Ge-t'lä	A-ru'-shä
5	Eye,	Ish-tä'	Is-tä'	Ash-kin	Tothl'-wä	Tse-gä-to'-lih	Yone'-geh
6	Nose,	Ah-pä'	Bä-de-ä	I-bi-shak-ni	U-po'	Go-yä-so'-lih	Ah-ho'-tä
7	Ear,	Ah-päsh'	Ah'-pa	Hak-so-bish	Hats-ko'	Tse-lä'-ne	A-ska'-rent
8	Mouth,	Ee	E'-ah	I'-tih	Chok-wä'	Tse-di-lih	A-ska'-rent
9	Arm,	Ar-rä'	Ah'-ra	Shak'-ba	Sak'-pä	Tse-no-ga'-nee	A-zhä-shä
10	Foot,	E-che'	Ih'-cha	I-yi	E'-le	Dä'-tse-nä-sä-dä'-ih	A-she'-tä
11	Heart,	Nä-tä'	Nä-sä	Chuh'-kush	Fay'-kee	Ah-ge-no-wih	Tone-ta'-shrä
12	Tobacco,	Oh-pe	O'-pa	Hak-chu'-ma	Hee'-che	Tso'-lä	
13	Sun,	Mä-pa'-we-re	Ah'-h·kä-zha	Hŭ'-shi	Has'-see	Nän' doh'. Sä-no'-yih-a-heh	Yän-de'-shä
14	Moon,	Mä-ko'-we-re	Min-ne-tä'-cha	Hush-ni'-nak-a-ya	Has'-see	Wä-sun-ta-yeh yän-de'-shä	Wä-sun-ta-yeh yän-de'-shä
15	Star,	O-kä'	E-ka'	Fi-chik	Ko-tso-tsum-pi	Noh'·-kwe'-se	
16	Day,	Mä'-pih	Mä'-pa	Ni'-tak	Nit-tä'	E'-gä	Met-ta'-yeh
17	Night,	Ch·k'-che	O'-che-a	Ni-nak	Nith-le'	Sä-no-yeh	Wä-sun-ta'-[yeh
18	Fire,	Be-dä'	Be-dä'	Lu'-ak	Tate'-kä	Ah-des'-luh	Sä-nuse'-te
19	Water,	Min-ne'	Me-na'	O'-ka	Ne'-wä	Um'-mä	Oan-un-de'-
20	Ice,	Bä-ro'-h·e	Boo-roo'-h·a	Ok'-ti	He'-to-tee	O-nase'-tä-lä	De-ne-tä' [sha
21	Snow,	Mä'-pe	Be'-pa	Ok-tu'-sha	He-to-te-thlok-	Goo-te'-ah	De-ne-tä' [sha
22	Black,	She-pish'-shä	Che-pä'-sha	Lu'-sa	Lus-tee [lai-ye	Gä-h'nä'-yä-hi	Te-hese'-tä-ya
23	White,	Ah-tä'-ke	Che'-ä-kä-te	Toh·'-bi	Hat-kee	Oo-na'-gä	De-ne⁻yit'
24	Red,	Ish'-she	Hish'-shä	Hom'-ma	Isä-tse	Ge-gä-ga'-ih	Me-tä'-ya
25	Yellow,	She-re	She-re-kä'-ta	Lak-na	Lä-me	Dä-lo'-nih	Kan-ya'-tä-ya
26	Blue,	Toh·-he	Shu'-ä-kä-ta	Ok-cha-ma'-li	Ok-ko-lä-tee	Sä-ko'-ne-ga	Roan-ya
27	Green,	Ka-to'-gh·e-ka	Me-nis'-ta	Ok-cha'-ko	Pä-he-lä-nee	E-dsa'-ih	Ze-in-gwä'-ra
28	Moccasin,	Mä-tä-pä'	Hoom-pa'	Shu'-lush	Ist'-clee-'pi-kä		Ah-rä'-shu
29	Beaver,	We-rä'-pä	Be-rup'-pa	Kin'-ta	Its-has'-wä	Do'-yä	Tsu-ti'-e
30	Buffalo,	Ke'-rup-pe	Che'-rup-pa	Yä'-nŭsh	Yä-no-sä	Yaṇ'tsa	
31	Pigeon,	[-shä	Main-pä'-tse-sä	Pŭ-chi	Pa-chy [voc.]	Ah-dsä'-te	
32	Arrow,	Bed-ä-roo'-che	Ah-no'-ä-ta	Os-ke-no-ke	Khl-li(Gallatin	Gan'-na	Oon-dä'
33	One,	Ne-wat'-zä	Ah-mut'-tuk	A-chŭ'-fa	Hom-ma-ye	Sa-gws'	Scot
34	Two,	Doo'-putz	No'-puk	Tuk'-lo	Hok-k'o	Tä-lih'	Ten'-de
35	Three,	Nä'-wetz	Nä'-ma	Tu-chi'-na	Tot-cheh	Tso'-ih	Shaik
36	Four,	To'-putz	Sho'-puk	Ush-ta	Os-teh	Nuk'-ee	Daak
37	Five,	Kä-hotz'	Chuh-hook'	Ta-hla-pi	Chahg-kie	His-ke	Wish
38	Six,	Ah-kä'-wutz	Ah-kä'-muk	Ha-na-li	Eb-bah	Soo-dä'-le	Wä-zuh'
39	Seven,	Shä'-po-utz	Sä'-poo-uk	Un-tuk-lo	Koo-lo-ba	Guh'l-guo-ge	Ze-tä'-re
40	Eight,	Nä'-pä-pitz	No-pä'-pa	Un-tu-chi-na	Chin-na-bä	Tso-na'-lä	Ah-ter'-re

Missouri nations, for neither of these were agricultural, except the Quappas, at the mouth of the Arkansas, more than fifteen hundred miles below them; and possibly the Osages, who were south of the mouth of the Missouri. At a later period the Omahas and Iowas occasionally constructed houses upon the Mandan and Minnitaree model;[1] but they were never Village Indians in any proper sense. Finally, we must either suppose that the Minnitarees carried both agriculture and the art of constructing a timber framed house to the Upper Missouri, and taught them to the Mandans, or that the latter formerly resided as far south as the Arkansas. The former is the most probable.

The Mandan language is not accessible except for the most ordinary purposes. When I visited the Mandan village there was but one person there who spoke both Mandan and English. This was a half-blood Mandan, Joseph Kipp, a son of the well-known interpreter James Kipp, to whom Catlin was indebted for his means of communication with this people. I had no difficulty in procuring a vocabulary; but found it impossible to obtain their system of relationship complete. The Mandans have very generally learned the Minnitaree language, as they now live together, and the traders and trappers have done the same; but neither the one nor the other has learned the Mandan. For reasons beyond my control I was unable to reach the Mandan through the Minnitaree. Enough, however, of their system of relationship was obtained to establish the identity of its radical characteristics with those of the common system.

First Indicative Feature. My brother's son and daughter, *Ego* a male, are my son and daughter. With *Ego* a female, they are the same. This last is a deviation from the usual form. It shows that females have no aunt, the father's sister being a mother. In this respect it agrees with the Cayuga and Mohawk, and also with the Chocta and Creek.

Second. My sister's son and daughter, *Ego* a male, are my nephew and niece. Mr. Kipp was unable to recall the terms for these relationships, although assured of their existence in the language, which was also confirmed by the presence of the correlative *uncle*. With *Ego* a female, they are my son and daughter.

Third. My father's brother is my father.

Fourth. My father's brother's son and daughter are my brother and sister, elder or younger. There is a double set of terms for these relationships, and probably some inaccuracy in their use as given in the Table, since they make elder and younger sister the same.

Fifth. My father's sister is my aunt, *Ego* being a male; but my mother, *Ego* being a female.

Sixth. My mother's brother is my uncle.

Seventh. My mother's sister is my mother.

Eighth. My mother's sister's son and daughter are my brother and sister, elder or younger.

Ninth. My grandfather's brother is my grandfather.

---

[1] This fact was communicated to the author by Rev. S. M. Irwin, who for the last thirty years has been a missionary among the Omahas and Iowas in Nebraska.

Tenth. The grandchildren of my brothers and sisters, and the grandchildren of my collateral brothers and sisters, are my grandchildren.

The relationship which subsisted between the children of a brother and sister I was unable to ascertain. There can be no doubt whatever of the identity of the Mandan form with those previously presented, although its details are incomplete.

5. Minnitarees, and Upsarokas or Crows. These nations are immediate subdivisions of the same people. When they first appeared on the Upper Missouri they were, according to the Mandan tradition, agricultural and Village Indians. They were found by Lewis and Clarke living in Villages on Knife River, near their present town. These explorers furnish the following account of the original separation from each other. " The Mandans say that this people came out of the water to the east, and settled near them in their former establishments in nine villages; that they were very numerous, and fixed themselves in one village on the south side of the Missouri. A quarrel about a buffalo divided the nation, of which two bands went into the plains, and were known by the name of Crow and Paunch Indians, and the rest removed to their present establishment."[1] On the contrary, the Minnitarees now claim to be autochthones, a very common conceit among Indian nations, although the name by which they still distinguish themselves as a nation, *E-năt'-zä*, signifying "people who came from afar," expressly contradicts the assertion. This claim, however, may be received as some evidence of a long continued occupation of this particular area. Indian nations usually retain a tradition of their last principal migration, and when that has faded from remembrance the autochthonic claim is often advanced. If we adopt the Mandan tradition, as to the first appearance of the Minnitarees upon the Upper Missouri, they have remained during the intervening period Village Indians, and residents upon, and near this river; but the Crows changed their mode of life from the village to the camp, and from an agricultural basis of subsistence, to the products of the chase. They advanced northward by routes now unknown, until a part of them reached the south branch of the Siskatchewun River, more than fifteen hundred miles north of the present Minnitaree area. Their range was between the Siskatchewun and the Missouri. One of the tribes of the Crows resided along the Bear's Paw Mountain, in what is now the Blackfoot Country, near the base of the Rocky Mountain chain. The name *Ship-tet'-zä*, which this tribe still bears, signifying " Bear's Paw Mountain,"[2] commemorates the fact. The Crows have a distinct and well-preserved tradition, which was communicated to the author by Robert Meldrum (the highest authority in the language and domestic history of this nation), that while they resided around this mountain, the Shoshonee or Snake Indians were in possession of the present Crow Country upon the Yellowstone River; and the Comanches, now of Western Texas, then occupied the present Shoshonee area west of the Moun-

---

[1] Lewis and Clarke's Travels, &c., p. 96.

[2] This beautiful mountain range rises out of the plains about fifty miles east of the Falls of the Missouri, and stretches from near the Missouri to Milk River. Its highest peaks are about twenty-five hundred feet high. Although quite near the foot of the Rocky Mountains, it is entirely detached, and forms a conspicuous and striking object in the landscape of the prairie.

24   February, 1870.

tains, upon the south branch of the Columbia River.   If we may adopt this tradition, the truth of which is not improbable, it suggests the probability that the separation of the Crows from the Minnitarees antedates the conquest of Mexico. In the course of events the Crows have again become territorial neighbors to their former brethren.

The dialects of the two nations are not yet sufficiently changed to prevent them from conversing with each other, although it is attended with considerable difficulty.   The amount of change is about the same, or perhaps greater, than the divergence of the Wyandote from the Iroquois after a separation, in the latter case of at least four centuries.   If these dates could be authenticated absolutely, they would afford some criterion, now greatly desired, for determining the degree of rapidity or slowness with which the dialects of unwritten languages depart from each other.[1]

---

[1] At different times and places I have endeavored to obtain facts bearing upon this question, where the means of observation of particular persons, in the Indian Country, had been favorable. The results of the investigation have not furnished a basis upon which any general rule may be grounded, but they may serve in some measure to illustrate the subject.   The testimony of Robert Meldrum, above mentioned, is to the point concerning the Crow language.   In the year 1827, he became identified with this nation by adoption and marriage, and in 1830 he was raised to the rank of a chief.   Although one of the traders of the American Fur Company, he joined the Crows in their military adventures, shared their hardships, and became in every respect one of their number. During the entire period from 1827 to 1862, when I met him at the mouth of the Yellowstone, he had resided in the Crow Country, but without losing his connection with the Company, first as a trader, and afterwards as one of the factors in charge of different posts.   He had mastered the language in its entire range, thought in it, held his knowledge in it, performed his mental labor in it, and, as he affirmed, could speak the language better than his native tongue.   His observations were as follows : that the Crow and Minnitaree had not widened much in the last thirty-five years ; that many of the words of the Minnitaree dialect he did not understand ; but of most of them he could catch the meaning ; that the first noticeable change was in the loss of a syllable, and sometimes of half of a word ; that the principal element of change was the addition of new words with the progress of their knowledge or wants ; that this had been particularly the case since their intercourse with the whites commenced ; that the old words stood well, but the new ones made for the occasion fluctuated, and might or might not become permanently adopted ; that he had himself added quite a number to the Crow language (*Ah-hä'-sha* below is a specimen), that the new words were developed from radicals in the language, and were usually significant, while the etymological signification of the bulk of the old words was lost, *e. g.*

Corn,	Hó-hă-she, meaning lost,		Coffee,	Min-ne-she-pit'-ta, Black water.
Bean,	Ah-mä'-sa,	" "	Sugar,	Bat-see-koo'-a, Sweet.
Squash,	Ho'-ko-ma	" "	Tea,	Mä-nä'-pa, Leaves of bushes.
Tobacco,	O'-pa	" "	Watch,	Ah-hä'-sha, Follows the sun.

That the new words were not limited to new objects brought to their attention by American intercourse, but followed the extension of their own knowledge and wants ; that the gutturals when mastered so far from being objectionable were a source of pleasure in the use of the speech ; and finally that the Crow was a noble language.   He further observed that the Minnitarees could adopt and speak the Crow dialect with much more facility than the Crows could the former ; that when he wished to converse with a Minnitaree he induced the latter to talk poor Crow, rather than attempt himself to speak poor Minnitaree ; and finally that the amount of dialectical variation was such that

It seems probable that five centuries would be insufficient to render dialects of the same language incapable of being understood colloquially by the two peoples; and that twice or thrice that length of time would not destroy all trace of identity in the vocables for common objects. This is as much, perhaps, as can be safely suggested. There is one important fact, with reference to the American Indian languages, which should not be overlooked, tending to show that change would be more rapid, comparatively, among them, than in other verbal languages. In no part of the earth, not excepting the islands of the Pacific, are dialects and even stock languages intrusted for their preservation to such a small number of people. The Mandan, for example, which for colloquial purposes is an independent speech, is now in the exclusive keeping of two hundred and fifty persons; and so the Munsee, which is one of the oldest forms of the Algonkin, is in the custody of about two hundred persons. The Iroquois, which is a stock language, and now spoken in seven dialects, including the Wyandote, is dependent for its preservation, as a whole, upon less than eight thousand people, and they in widely separated localities. In like manner, the Pawnee, another stock language, spoken in four dialects, including the Arickaree and excluding the Hueco, and its immediate cognates, is in the keeping of about five thousand persons. If we take particular dialects, the number of people, by whom they are severally spoken, will be found to range from two hundred persons, which is the minimum, to one thousand which is about the average, and on to twenty-five thousand, which is the maximum number now speaking any one so called stock language within the limits of the United States. This is the number of the Cherokees, whose language, it is somewhat remarkable, is contained in but two dialects, the standard and the mountain Cherokees, or the modern and the ancient. When the people who speak a certain dialect advance in prosperity and multiply in numbers, the increased intellectual power invariably expends a portion of its strength upon the language; in the increase of the number of its vocables, in the advancement of its grammatical forms to a higher stage of development, and in imparting nerve and tone to the plastic and growing speech. On the other hand, when the same people meet with reverses, and decline in numbers and prosperity, their dialect necessarily impoverishes in its vocables, and recedes in its strength, although it does not follow that its grammatical forms must wither. At best these dialects are in a constant flux and oscillation.

There is another consideration which connects itself with the question of the stability of the American Indian dialects, namely; to what extent are words propagated by adoption from one language into another? It is impossible, with our present knowledge, to answer this question; but it is not improbable that this and other equally important problems will ultimately be solved. These languages are becoming more open, and are growing more accessible each and every year. There

---

he found it difficult to understand the Minnitaree. His impression was that the change had been of slow and gradual growth.

It is not a little singular that the Mandans should learn the Minnitaree; and the Minnitarees the Crow with comparative ease; while the reverse is attended with difficulty. Can those who speak the mother tongue learn a derived dialect with more ease than those who speak the latter can learn the former, or the reverse?

are now persons, especially missionaries, who understand particular languages in all their range, methods, and structure, and who are competent to present their minute mechanism. The difficulty with most grammars of Indian languages, besides their brevity, arises from a method too exclusively analytical, whereas a synthetical method, if more cumbersome, would be more efficient. We learn analytically, but teach synthetically. A grammar, therefore, should put together, as well as resolve a language, and be so complete in both of its processes that the philologist might learn, if need be, to speak the language from the grammar and vocabulary. Some modification of the Ollendorff method would be a sensible improvement upon the usual form of presenting an Indian language. A knowledge more special than has yet been reached is needed to detect a foreign element in an aboriginal language. It is a reasonable supposition that contiguous nations, and especially such as intermarry and maintain friendly intercourse, are constantly contributing of their vocables to each other's dialects. The identity of a limited number of vocables for common objects tends to show a near connection of the Minnitarees and Upsarokas or Crows with the Missouri and Dakota nations; whilst there are special features in their systems of consanguinity which reveal a more remote, but not less certain connection with the Gulf Nations.

Their systems of relationship are in agreement with each other in their radical characteristics. They possess one feature which is anomalous, and another which deviates from every form yet presented, but which finds its counterpart in the system of the Gulf nations, and that of the Pawnee or Prairie nations as well. The Minnitaree will be adopted for presentation.

First Indicative Feature. My brother's son and daughter, *Ego* a male, are my son and daughter. With *Ego* a female, they are my grandchildren. These last relationships are a deviation from the common form.

Second (wanting). My sister's son and daughter, *Ego* a male, are my younger brother and younger sister, *Mat-so'-gä* and *Mă-tä-ka'-shä*. This remarkable deviation from uniformity is restricted to these two nations, among whom the relationships of uncle and aunt, and nephew and niece, are unknown, their places being supplied by elder and younger brother, and by elder and younger sister.

Third. My father's brother is my father.

Fourth. My father's brother's son and daughter are my brother and sister elder or younger. There is a double set of terms for these relationships, one of which is used by the males, and the other by the females, with the exception of the terms for younger brother and sister, which are common.[1] In this respect the Minnitaree and Upsaroka agree with the Dakota, Missouri, and Gulf nations.

Fifth (wanting). My father's sister, among the Minnitarees is my grandmother, *Kä-rŭ'-hä*, and among the Crows my mother, *Ik'-hä*.

Sixth (wanting). My mother's brother is my elder brother, and calls me his

---

[1] My elder brother, male speaking, *Me-ä-kä'*.　　Female speaking, *Mä-tä-roo'*.
　" younger "　　"　　"　　*Mat-so'-gä*.　　"　　"　　*Mat-so'-gä*.
　" elder sister,　"　　"　　*Mat-tä-we'-ă*.　　"　　"　　*Mä-roo'*.
　" younger sister, "　　"　　*Mä-tä-kä'-shä*.　　"　　"　　*Mä-tä-kä'-shä*.

younger brother. This is the anomalous relationship in which the system of these nations differs from that of all the remaining nations of the Ganowánian family.[1]

Seventh. My mother's sister is my mother.

Eighth. My mother's sister's son and daughter are my brother and sister, elder or younger.

Ninth. My grandfather's brother is my grandfather.

Tenth. The grandchildren of my brothers and sisters, and of my collateral brothers and sisters, are, without distinction, my grandchildren.

A third form of the relationship which subsists between the children of a brother and sister is found among the Minnitarees and Crows. Among the Iroquois and Dakotas, they are cousins, among the Missouri nations they are uncle and nephew if males, and mother and daughter if females, as has been shown: but in the system now under consideration they are son and father if males, and daughter and mother if females. This form will reappear in the system of the Gulf and Prairie nations. When more particularly indicated they are as follows: my father's sister's son is my father, *Tä-ta'*, and calls me his son; my father's sister's daughter is my mother, *Ih'-kä*, and calls me her son; and reversed, my mother's brother's son and daughter are my son and daughter; each of them calling me father.

There is a term in Minnitaree for aunt, *Mä-sa'-we*, applied by a male to his father's sister; but it is without a correlative, and of uncertain use.

A sufficient number of the radical features of the common system are found in the Minnitaree and Crow forms to establish beyond a doubt their original identity, and that it was derived by them from the common source of the system.

III. *Gulf Nations.*

I. Gulf Nations Proper. 1. Choctás. 2. Chickasás. 3. Creeks. (4. Seminoles, not in the Table.) II. Cherokees. 1. Cherokees. 2. Mountain Cherokees.

There were five principal nations east of the Mississippi, occupying the area between the Gulf of Mexico and the Tennessee River, together with some parts to the north and east of it, which collectively are here called the Gulf branch of the Ganowánian family. They were the Choctas and Chickasas, who were immediate subdivisions of the same people; the Creeks; the Seminoles, who were derived from the Creeks; and the Cherokees. The latter nation in strictness constitutes an independent branch of the Dakotan stem upon the basis of language; but their system of relationship justifies this connection. The dialects of the first two are closely allied. The Creeks consist of five confederated nations, each having an independent dialect, namely: the *Mŭs-co'-kees* or Creeks proper, the *Hit'-che-tees*, the *Yoo'-chees*, the *Ah-lä-bä'-mäs*, and the *Nat'-ches*. Between the *Mŭs-co'-kee* and Seminole dialects the affinity is close; but between the former and the Chocta the dialectical variation is very great. Out of six hundred words in these dialects,

---

[1] There is a trace of this same form among the Blackfeet, but it is not the usual relationship.

compared by Mr. Gallatin, there were but ninety-three having some affinity.[1]   All of the Creek dialects, however, should be compared with each other, and with the Chocta and Chickasa, to determine their mutual ethnic relations.   As to the Cherokees, they were the mountaineers of this area, and presumptively the most ancient in the possession of the country.   Like the Iroquois, they appear to have been an advance band of the Dakotan stock.   Their range included the highland districts between South Carolina and the Mississippi.   Up to the present time the vocables of their language have not been identified with those of any existing Indian speech.   It still holds the rank of a stock language, spoken in two partially defined dialects, the standard and the mountain Cherokee.

In addition to these nations, the Catawbas inhabited the Gulf region, and also the Natchez Indians.   Remains of the former nation are still found in South Carolina, and of the latter in the *Nat-ches* of the Creek confederation.   Between the old Natchez and the Catawba dialects there are some affinities; but how far the present Natchez affiliates with the old or with any of the remaining Creek dialects the writer is unable to state.   When perfect vocabularies are obtained and compared, it seems probable that all the original dialects of the Gulf region will be resolved, at most, into two stock languages, the Creek and the Cherokee.

These nations have been so well known historically from the earliest period of European intercourse, that it is unnecessary to refer to their general history.   Since their removal to the Indian Territory, west of Arkansas, they have organized elective civil governments, and have made considerable progress in agriculture and civilization.   They now number collectively seventy-three thousand five hundred.[2]

In the Table will be found the system of relationship of the Choctas, Chickasas, Muscokee-Creeks, and Cherokees, which together exhibit with fulness and particularity the plan of consanguinity and affinity of the Gulf nations.   The several forms which prevail among these nations possess the radical forms of the common system, and also agree with each other in those respects in which they differ from those before considered.   Such discrepancies as exist are confined to subordinate details.   It will be sufficient to present one form, and the Chocta will be taken as the standard.   There are two schedules of the Chocta in the Table, one of which was furnished by the Rev. Jonathan Edwards and Rev. Dr. Cyrus Byington, and the other by the Rev. Charles C. Copeland.   These veteran missionaries, who have resided with this people, both in their old and new homes, from thirty to forty years, were abundantly qualified to investigate and explain this complicated system to its utmost limits.   It was also a fortunate circumstance that this, one of the most difficult forms of the system, fell into their hands for its elucidation, since the existence as well as verification of its peculiar features was of some importance.

First Indicative Feature.   My brother's son and daughter, *Ego* a male, are my son and daughter.   With *Ego* a female, they are my grandson and granddaughter. This last is a derivation from the typical form, but it agrees with the Minnitaree.

---

[1] Trans. Am. Eth. Soc., II, Intro. cxi.

[2] Cherokees, 26,000; Creeks, 25,000; Seminoles, 1500· Choctas, 16,000; Chickasas, 5000. (Schoolcraft's Hist. Cond. and Pur. Indian Tribes, I, 523.)

Second. My sister's son and daughter, *Ego* a male, are my nephew and niece. With *Ego* a female, they are my son and daughter.

Third. My father's brother is my father.

Fourth. My father's brother's son and daughter are my brother and sister, elder or younger.

Fifth. My father's sister is my aunt, with *Ego* a male; but my grandmother with *Ego* a female. In other words, the female has neither aunt or nephew or niece. This is also a derivation from the typical form, but it agrees with the Minnitaree.

Sixth. My mother's brother is my uncle.

Seventh. My mother's sister is my mother.

Eighth. My mother's sister's son and daughter are my brother and sister, elder or younger. Among all the Gulf nations there are separate terms, in common gender, for brother and sister in the abstract, which are applied by males to their collateral brothers, and by females to their collateral sisters; but the former use the full terms for their collateral sisters, and the latter the same for their collateral brothers. The first-named terms, however, are used concurrently with these for brother and sister, elder and younger.

Ninth. My grandfather's brother is my grandfather.

Tenth. The grandchildren of my brothers and sisters, and of my collateral brothers and sisters, are, severally, my grandchildren.

We come next to the relationship which subsists between the children of a brother and sister. My father's sister's son is my father, *Ah'-kĭ*, whether *Ego* be a male or a female; his son is my father again; the son of the latter is also my father; and this relationship, theoretically, continues downward in the male line indefinitely. The analogue of this is found in the infinite series of uncles among the Missouri nations, applied to the lineal male descendants of my mother's brother. My father's sister's daughter, *Ego* a male, is my aunt, *Ah-huc'-ne*, and calls me *her son*; the son and daughter of this aunt are my brother and sister, elder or younger; the son and daughter of this collateral brother are my son and daughter, while the son and daughter of this collateral sister are my nephew and niece; and the children of each and all of them are my grandchildren. With *Ego* a female, my father's sister's daughter is my grandmother, *Up-puk'-nĭ;* her son and daughter are my brother and sister, elder and younger; the children of this collateral brother are my grandchildren, of this collateral sister are my sons and daughters; and their children are my grandchildren. Notwithstanding the complexity of the classification in this branch of the second collateral line, the method is both simple and coherent.

On the reverse side, my mother's brother's son and daughter are my son and daughter, whether *Ego* be a male or a female; and their children are my grandchildren. In Creek and Cherokee my mother's brother's daughter, *Ego* being a female, is my granddaughter. It is probably the same in Chocta, although not so given in the Table.

The third and fourth collateral lines, male and female, on the father's and on the mother's side, are counterparts of the second, branch for branch, with the exception of additional ancestors.

There are some discrepancies in the forms of the four Gulf nations, which it is unnecessary to trace. In a system so elaborate and complicated, absolute agreement in minute details would not be expected. Whatever is fundamental in the common system is found in the most unmistakable manner in the Chocta form. Its identity with the Seneca or typical system is undoubted ; and we are again led to the same inference found in the previous cases, that it was derived by these nations, with the blood, from the same common original source.

II. Cherokee. The Cherokee system of relationship, in its two forms, agrees so fully with that last presented, that it is unnecessary to consider it separately. There are some general observations, however, upon this and other Indian languages, and upon the bearing of the deviations from uniformity in their systems of relationship upon the question of their near or remote ethnic affiliations, which may be made in this connection. In grammatical structure all of the Ganowánian, languages are believed to agree. But our knowledge concerning them is neither sufficiently extensive nor minute to raise these languages to the rank of a family of languages in the sense of the Aryan and Semitic upon the basis of ascertained linguistic affinities. Very few of the whole number comparatively have been studied. No common standards of evidence upon which particular dialects shall be admitted into the family, or rejected from the connection, have been adopted. They have been reduced with tolerable accuracy to a number of stock languages upon the basis of identity of vocables ; but the basis and principles upon which these stock languages shall be united into a family of languages remain to be determined. These dialects and languages have passed through a remarkable experience from the vast dimensions of the areas over which they have spread. By that inexorable law which adjusts numbers to subsistence in given areas, the Ganowánian family has been perpetually disintegrated, through all of its branches, at every stage of increase of numbers above this ratio. In the progress of ages they have been scattered, in feeble bands, over two entire continents, to the repression and waste of their intellectual powers, and to the sacrifice of all the advantages that flow from civil and social organization in combination with numbers. Every subdivision, when it became permanent, resulted in the formation of a new dialect, which was intrusted to the keeping of a small number of people. Although nations speaking dialects of the same stock language have in general maintained a continuity of territorial possession, it was impossible to prevent subdivision, displacement, and overthrow in the course of ages ; so that the end of each thousand years would probably find no stock language in the same geographical location. As a result of these subdivisions and its train of influences, these languages have been in a perpetual flux. The advance and decline of nations, the development and impoverishment of particular dialects, the propagation of words from one dialect into another by intermarriage, and by the absorption into one nation of the broken fragments of another, have contributed, with other causes not named, to the diversities which now exist. Their system of relationship, however, has survived the mutations of language, and still delivers a clear and decisive testimony concerning the blood affinity of all these nations. It is not at all improbable that it will be found a more efficient as well as compendious instrument, for demonstrating their original unity, than the grammatical structure of their dialects could that be comprehensively ascertained. If identity of system proves unity of origin, all of the Indian nations thus far named are of one blood. In addition to this general conclusion some evidence may be gained through the deviations from uniformity which it contains concerning the order of separation of these stock languages from each other or from the parent stem.

It has been seen from the comparative vocabulary, *supra*, that the Crow and Minnitaree dialects contain a number of words for common objects which are also found in the Mandan, the Dakota, and the Missouri dialects. A comparison of two hundred words, in unpublished vocabularies of the author, shows about twenty per centum which are common between the Minnitaree and Crow, and one or more of the remaining dialects. In the terms of relationship, which are words of a higher class, the percentage is less. This agreement, however, is perhaps sufficient to justify the classification of all these dialects in the same stock language. On the other hand, there are striking peculiarities in the system of relationship of the first two nations which are not found in that of the remaining nations, but which reappear in the system of the Gulf and Prairie nations. It is found in the relationship between the children of a brother and sister, which, as a variable, is not a radical portion of the system. Where nations of immediate blood affinity, as the Dakota and Missouri nations, are found to differ among themselves upon these relationships, it would be certain that one or the other had modified their system in this respect; and if one, then both may have done the same. It becomes necessary, then, to compare these forms and ascertain which is the highest and most perfect; and when that fact is determined, the inference arises that the rudest and least perfect is the oldest form. Among the Dakota they are cousin and cousin, among the Winnebagoes and Missouri nations they are uncle and nephew if males, and mother and daughter, if females. There can be no doubt that the former is the most perfect form, and that of the two the latter as the rudest is nearest to the primitive. The inference, therefore, is unavoidable, that the Dakota nations modified their system in this respect. If we now compare the oldest of the two forms with that which now prevails among the Minnitarees, Crows, Creeks, Choctas, Chickasas and Cherokees, and also with that of the Prairie nations, not yet presented, it will be seen that the form of the latter is ruder still, and presumptively older than either. They are son and father if males, and granddaughter and grandmother if females. If this conclusion is well taken, it will follow that it was the original form, as to those relationships which prevailed in the parent nation from which these several stocks or branches were mediately or immediately derived, and that all of them, except the Mandan, the Winnebago, the Dakota and the Missouri nations have retained it until the present time. And finally that the excepted nations modified it from the first or original to the second form, after which it was raised to the third and most perfect by the Dakota and Hodenosaunian nations alone, in this stem of the Ganowánian family. A critical examination of all the forms of the system of relationship will show that its development is under the control of principles within itself; and that the direction of the change when attempted, was predetermined by the elements of the system. We are yet to meet the second and third forms, as to these relationships, in the system of the Algonkin nations. It likewise follows, as a further inference that the Minnitaree, Crow, Mandan, Winnebagoe and Missouri nations may have been derived mediately or immediately from a single nation; that the Gulf and Prairie nations may each have been derived from a single nation; and that the three original nations may have sprung from a common stem-people still further back. In this manner the evidence from special features contained in the system is reconciled with the evidence from identity of vocables in the dialects first-named; leaving it probable that the Minnitarees and Crows form the nearest connecting link between the nations of the Gulf, and those upon the Missouri.

In this connection, attention may be directed to the dialects thus far named, taken collectively, as they appear in the Table. The people are classified together as belonging to the Dakotan stem. There is such a thing in the Ganowánian dialects as contrast and similarity in vocables; as excessive deviation and family resemblance; and as ancient and modern separation of stock languages. It can be detected and traced long after the vocables themselves have lost their identity. From first to last, among the great branches thus far considered, the terms of relationship have a family cast; a tendency, so to express it, to reveal their identity, although deeply concealed; a certain similarity of aspect which arrests attention while it baffles the scrutiny thereby invited. On the other hand, the same terms in the Algonkin dialects, when compared, are in sharp contrast. They wear an unfamiliar appearance, expressive of long-continued separation. The change has become so excessive as to repel the supposition of their identity within a comparatively modern period, or that they could have been spoken in the same household for many ages. The following terms will illustrate the similarity to which reference has been made:—

	Seneca.	Wyandote.	Yankton.	Mandan.
Uncle,	Hoc-no'-seh	Hä-wä-te-no'-rä	Dake'-she	Tä-wä'-rä-to-ra
Aunt,	Ah-ga'-huc	Ah-rä'-hoc	Toh'-we	
Cousin,	Ah-găre'-seh	Jä-rä'-seh	Hä-kä'-she	
Nephew,	Ha-yä'-wan-da	Ha-shone'-drä-ka	Me-to͡us'-kä	
Father,	Hä'-nih	Hi-ese'-tä	Ah-ta'	Tä-tay'
Mother,	No-yeh'	Ah'-nä'-ah·	E'-nah	E-oo-ne'
Son,	Ha-ah'-wuk	A-ne'-ah	Me-chink'-she	Me-ne'-ka
Daughter,	Ka-ah'-wuk	E-ne'-ah	Me-chounk'-she	Me-no' hä-ka
Grandmother,	Oc'-sote	Ah·-shu-tä'	O-che	Nah·'-ke-a.

	Kaw.	Otoe.	Chocta.	Cherokee.
Uncle,	Be-ja'-ga	Hin-chä'-kä	Um-ush'ĭ	E-dŭ'-tsĭ
Aunt,	Be-je'-me	E-tŭ'-me	A-huc'-ne	E-hlau'-gĭ
Cousin,				
Nephew,	Be-chose'-kä	Hin-tose'-ke	Sŭb-ai'-yih	Un-ge-wĭ-naɳ
Father,	E-dä'-je	Hiɳ'-kä	A'-kĭ	E-dau'-dä
Mother,	E'-naw	He'-nah	Ush'-kĭ	E-tsĭ'
Son,	Be-she'-gä	He-ne'-cha	Suh'-sŭh	A-gwae-tsĭ'
Daughter,	She-me'-she-ga	He-yuɳ-ga	Suh-sŭh'-take	A-gwae-tsĭ'
Grandmother,	E-ko'	Hiɳ-kŭ'-ne	Up-puk'-nĭ	E-nĭ-sĭ'

These terms represent four stock languages. To say there is a striking similarity among them is hardly sufficient. There is more or less of affinity among them all, which might be raised, by the recovery of a few intermediate links, to demonstrated identity. In a few instances the identity seems to be apparent; *e.g.*, the terms for cousin in Seneca and Yankton; the terms for uncle in Seneca, Yankton, Chocta, and Cherokee; the term for aunt in Seneca, Chocta, and Cherokee; and the term for mother in Wyandote, Yankton, Mandan, and Kaw. From the present relation of these dialects to each other, and more especially from the particular points of agreement in their several systems of relationship, there appears to be sufficient reason for classifying them together as branches of a common stem. This, for sufficient reasons, has been called the Dakotan.

IV. Prairie Nations. 1. Pawnees. 2. Arickarees. (3. Witchitas. 4. Kichais. 5. Huecos. Not in the Table.)

Our limited knowledge of this branch of the Ganowánian family is explained by their residence in the interior of the continent. The Pawnees and Arickarees are the only nations belonging to this branch which have ever reached a locality as far east as the Missouri River, and they were never known to reside upon its east side. Having obtained and domesticated the horse at an early day, they have been prairie Indians from the earliest period to which our knowledge of their existence extends. The range of the Pawnees was upon and between the upper waters of the Kansas and Platte Rivers, in Kansas and Nebraska; whilst the Arickarees, who are a subdivision of the Pawnees, moved northward and established themselves upon the Missouri, next south of the Mandans, where they became, to some extent, agricultural and Village Indians. Their congeners, the Witchitas, Kichais, and Huecos or Waccoes, held as their home country the region upon the Canadian River, and between it and the Red River of Louisiana. Gregg was one of the first to point out the connection of the last three nations named with the Pawnees.[1] They have sometimes been called the Pawnee-Picts, from their habit of "profuse tattooing."[2] The late Prof. William W. Turner established the identity of their dialects with the Pawnee by the selection of vocables in the note.[3] I have taken

---

[1] Commerce of the Prairie, II, 251, note.   [2] Ib., II, 305.
[3] Explorations for a Railroad Route, &c. to the Pacific, III, 68. Rep. on Indian Tribes.

	Grand Pawnee. Morgan.	Arickaree. Prince Maximilian.	Kichai. Lieut. Whipple.	Witchita. Capt. Marcy.	Hueco. Lieut. Whipple.
Woman,	Chä′-pä	Sa-pa′	Che-quoike	Kah-haak	Cah-he-ic
Mother,	A-te′-rä	Schách-ti	Cha′-che	Nut-ti-co-hay′-he	Ats′-iä
Ear,	Ut-kä-hä′-ro	At-ka′-ahn	A′-tik-a-ro-so		Ortz
Nose,	Chose	Sin-iht	Chus-ka-rai-o	Duts-tis′-toc	Tisk
Mouth,	Ah′-kow	Ha-káu	Hok-in-nik	Haw′-coo	Ah′-cok
Tongue,	Hät	Háh-tu	Hah′-toh	Huts-ke	Hotz
Hand,	Eck′-so	E′-schu	Ich-shen-e	Sim-he′-ho	Isk′-te
Foot,	Os′-sŭ		Us-in-ic	Dats′-oske	Os
Sun,	Sak-o′-rŭ	Scha-kùhn		Kee′-shaw	Sah′-ki
Water,	Kates′-so	Stoh-cho	Ki′-o-koh	Keet-che	Kits′-ah
Dog,	Ah-sä′-ke	Chah-tsch		Kéetch′-ah	Kit-si′-el
Black,	Kä′-tit	Te-ca-téh		Co′-rash	A-ha′-cod-e
One,	Os′-ko	Ach-ku	A-rish-co	Cha′-osth	Che-os
Two,	Pit′-ko	Pitt-cho	Cho′-sho	Witch	Witz
Three,	Tä′-weet	Táh-wit	Tah′-with-co	Taw-way	Tow

the liberty to substitute the Pawnee words from an unpublished vocabulary of my own in the place of Dr. Say's used by him.

I. Pawnees. 1. Grand Pawnees. 2. Republican Pawnee. 3. Loup Pawnee. 4. Tappas Pawnee.

The Pawnees are now divided into four bands, named as above, each of them having a dialect distinctly marked, but the four being mutually intelligible. The first call themselves *Chä'-ne*; the second call themselves *Kit'-kä*; the third, *Skee'-de*, signifying wolf; and the fourth, *Pe-tä-hä'-ne-rat*. Whatever may have been their former condition, the Pawnees are now among the most demoralized of our Indian nations. Within the past fifty years they have diminished in numbers from causes entirely independent of American intercourse.[1] They have no friends among the Indians of the plains. If a Pawnee and a Dakota, or a Pawnee and any other Indian, of whatever nationality, meet upon the buffalo ranges, it is a deadly conflict from the instant, without preliminaries and without quarter. In fighting qualities they are not inferior to the best of their enemies, but the warfare is unequal, and they are yielding before its influence. Indian nations speaking dialects of the same stock language, though not perfectly intelligible to each other, are much better able to keep the peace than those who speak dialects of different stock languages, and who are thus unable to communicate with each other except through interpreters, or by the language of signs which prevails throughout the interior of the continent. The greatest blessing that could now be bestowed upon the Indian family would be a common language. Difference of speech has undoubtedly been the most fruitful cause of their perpetual warfare with each other.

The system of relationship of the Grand and Republican Pawnees and of the Arickarees will be found in the Table. It prevails, without doubt, in the remaining nations comprising this branch of the family. That of the Republican Pawnee will be taken as the standard form. There is a peculiar series in the lineal line which has not yet been found in any other nation, and which appears to be limited to these nations. It is also repeated in the collateral lines. From its singularity, it deserves a special notice.

My great-great-grandfather.	Ah-te'-is.	My father.
" great-grandfather.	Te-wä-chir'-iks.	" uncle.
" grandfather.	Ah-te'-put.	" grandfather.
" father.	Ah-te'-is.	" father.
Myself.	Läte.	I.
My son.	Pe'-row.	My child.
" grandson.	Lak-te'-gish.	" grandson.
" great-grandson.	Te-wat.	" nephew.
" great-great-grandson.	Pe'-row.	" child.

It will be observed that the principle of correlative relationship is strictly pursued; *e. g.*, the one I call son, calls me father; the one I call nephew, calls me uncle; and the second one I call son, calls me father. This series must be explained as a refinement upon the common form, designed to discriminate the several ances-

---

[1] They now number less than 4000 souls.

tors above grandfather and the several descendants below grandson from each other. It is repeated both in the lineal and collateral lines as far as you choose to follow the chain of consanguinity.

Another peculiarity of the Pawnee consists in the absence of separate terms for elder and younger brother, and for elder and younger sister. There are terms for brother and sister in the abstract which are used by the males, and another set used by the females; besides which there is a series of terms, as in the Dakota and Winnebagoe, for each of several sons, and for each of several daughters, according to the order of their birth. The plural number is wanting, not only as to the terms of relationship, but it is also said to be entirely wanting in the language itself.[1] It is formed by adding the number, or the word for *all*.

First Indicative Feature. My brother's son and daughter, *Ego* a male, are my son and daughter. With *Ego* a female, they are the same.

Second. My sister's son and daughter, *Ego* a male, are my nephew and niece. With *Ego* a female, they are my son and daughter.

Third. My father's brother is my father.

Fourth. My father's brother's son and daughter are my brother and sister, *E-dah'-deh* and *E-tä'-heh*. With *Ego* a female they are the same, but different terms are used, *E-rats'-teh* and *E-dä'-deh*.

Fifth (wanting). My father's sister is my mother.

Sixth. My mother's brother is my uncle.

Seventh. My mother's sister is my mother.

Eighth. My mother's sister's son and daughter are my brother and sister.

Ninth. My grandfather's brother is my grandfather.

Tenth. The several collateral lines follow the series established in the lineal line; *e. g.*, the son and daughter of my collateral brother, *Ego* a male, are my son and daughter; of my collateral sister, are my nephew and niece; and the children of each are my grandchildren. The children of the latter—that is, of my grandchildren—are my nephews and nieces; their children are, again, my sons and daughters; and the children of the latter are my grandchildren.

With respect to the relationships between the children of a brother and sister, they are as follows: My father's sister's son and daughter, *Ego* a male, are my father and mother; the son and daughter of this father are my brother and sister; and the series below is the same as in the case of the descendants of my other collateral brothers. The son and daughter of this mother are my father and mother again, and their respective descendants continue to be fathers and mothers in an infinite series. This is variant from the Chocta form in some particulars. With *Ego* a female these relationships are the same.

---

[1] This fact was communicated to me by Rev. Samuel Allis, who for twenty-five years was a missionary of the American Board among the Pawnees. The pronouns *my* or *mine, they,* and *his* are separate, *e. g.* :—

My head,	Pak'-so ko'-tä-te.	My face,	Skä'-o ko'-tä-te.
Thy "	Pak'-so ko'-tä-se.	Thy "	Skä'-o ko'-tä-se.
His "	Pak'-so ko'-tä.	His "	Skä'-o ko'-tä.

On the reverse side, my mother's brother's son and daughter, *Ego* male or female, are my son and daughter; and their children are my grandchildren.

The third and more remote collateral lines are the same as the second in the classification of persons, but with additional ancestors.

Upon the basis of the presence in the Pawnee of nine out of ten of the indicative characteristics of the typical system, there can be no doubt of its identity with it, and that it was transmitted to them with the blood from the common original source.

2. Arickaree. When Lewis and Clarke ascended the Missouri River in 1804—1805, they found the Arickarees living in villages below the mouth of the Cannon Ball River, and consequently below the Mandans. Their lodges were constructed upon the Minnitaree model, and they were then, as now, agricultural and Village Indians. " They cultivate," say these explorers, " maize or Indian-corn, beans, pumpkins, watermelons, squashes, and a species of tobacco peculiar to themselves."[1] From the Mandans and Minnitarees they undoubtedly learned the arts of cultivation and of housebuilding. The Pawnees, with whom they immediately affiliate, were neither Village nor agricultural Indians until after they became established upon a reservation under government protection, which was quite recently effected. Mr. Gallatin observes that " it is said of the Pawnees that they raised no more maize than was necessary to whiten their broth,"[2] and he might have added a doubt whether even this was of their own producing. The Arickarees were never numerous. Their present village is on the west side of the Missouri, a short distance above that of the Minnitarees. At the time they made their last change of residence, in 1862, the latter nation urged them to settle with them in their village, as the Mandans had done, for mutual protection against the Dakotas, their common enemies; but they declined to live upon the east side of the river, alleging as a reason that their ancestors had always refused to establish themselves upon that side, and that they were fearful of evil consequences if they crossed their traditionary eastern boundary.

The Arickaree schedule in the Table is incomplete. This language is not accessible, except with extreme difficulty. A few of the traders have partially acquired the language, but not sufficiently for the prosecution of minute inquiries. When at the Arickaree village, I found but one man, Pierre Garrow, a half-blood, who spoke both that language and English. He was sufficiently qualified, but averse to giving information. Through the friendly offices of Mr. Andrew Dawson, chief factor of the American Fur Company, who was there at the time, the little that was obtained was secured. Incomplete as the schedule is, it is quite sufficient to establish the identity of the Arickaree and Pawnee forms, as will be seen by consulting the Table.

Notwithstanding the great divergence of the dialects of the Prairie nations from the others in the Table, these nations have been placed, provisionally, in the Dakotan connection. The agreement of their system of relationship with that of the Gulf nations, and of the Minnitarees and Crows, in those respects in which it is

---

[1] Travels, p 78.   [2] Trans. Am. Eth. Soc., Intro. xlviii.

variant from that of the remaining nations, furnishes sufficient grounds to justify the classification. These dialects, however, stand upon the outer edge of the Dakotan speech, without any connection in their vocables, and depending for this connection linguistically upon the grammatical structure of the language. The Pawnee and its cognate dialects still hold the position of an independent stock language.

The marriage relationships have been passed over. They will be found in the Table fully extended, and to be in general agreement with the Seneca marriage relationships. They are sufficient in themselves to demonstrate the unity of the system; but this conclusion is believed to be sufficiently substantiated without the additional strength which their concurrence affords. The people of all of these nations address each other, when related, by the term of relationship.

We have now considered the system of relationship of thirty-five Indian nations, contained, with more or less completeness of detail, in the Table. These carry with them, by necessary implication, the system of a number of other immediately affiliated nations, named herein in their proper connections. They represent five stock languages, namely: the Hodenosaunian, the Dakota, the Creek, the Cherokee, and the Pawnee. The nations named also include all the principal branches of the Ganowánian family east of the Rocky Mountain chain, which were found south of the Siskatchewun and Hudson's Bay, and north of the Gulf of Mexico and the Rio Grande, with the exception of the Algonkin, the Shoshonee, and a few inconsiderable nations whose linguistic affiliations are not well established. The constancy and uniformity with which the fundamental characteristics of the system have maintained themselves appear to furnish abundant evidence of the unity of origin of these nations, and to afford a sufficient basis for their classification together as a family of nations. The testimony from identity of systems in these several stocks, when judged by any proper standard, must be held to be conclusive upon this question. It is of some importance to have reached the assurance that upon this system of relationship we may commence the construction of an Indian family, and that it contains within itself all the elements necessary to determine the question whether any other nation is entitled to admission into the family.

The Algonkin and Athapasco-Apache branches, together with the nations upon the Pacific slopes, will next claim our attention.

CHAPTER IV.

SYSTEM OF RELATIONSHIP OF THE GANOWANIAN FAMILY.—Continued.

Algonkin Nations.

Area occupied by the Algonkin Nations—Nearness of their Dialects—Classification of these Nations into Groups—
I. Gichigamian Nations—Their Area and Dialects—1. Ojibwas—Their System of Consanguinity—Indicative
Relationships—Identical with the Seneca and Yankton—2. Otawas—3. Potawattamies—Their System agrees
with the Ojibwa—4. Crees—Their Dialects—Their System—Indicative Relationships—Agree with the Ojibwa.
II. Mississippi Nations—Their Area and Dialects—1. Miamis—2. Illinois (Weaws, Piankeshaws, Kaskaskias, and
Peorias)—Miami System taken as the Standard Form of these Nations—Indicative Relationships—Deviation
from Uniformity—Identical with Ojibwa in Radical Characteristics—3. Sawks and Foxes—Their Area and Dia-
lect—Agricultural Habits—4. Kikapoos—Their Area and Dialect—5. Menominees—Their Area and Dialect—The
System of these Nations agrees with the Miami—6. Shiyans—Their former Area and Dialect—Their System of
Consanguinity—Indicative Relationships—Agree with the Miami—7. Shawnees—Original Area—Migrations—
Improved State of Dialect—Indicative Relationships—Agree with the Miami. III. Atlantic Nations—Their Area
and Dialects—1. Delawares—One of the Oldest of Algonkin Nations—Their System of Consanguinity—Indicative
Relationships—Deviation from Uniformity—Their System in Radical Agreement with the Ojibwa—2. Munsees—
Indicative Relationships—Agree with the Delaware—3. Mohegans—Indicative Relationships—4. Etchemins—
Indicative Relationships—5. Micmacs—Indicative Relationships—System of these Nations in Radical Agreement
with the Delaware and Ojibwa. IV. Rocky Mountain Nations—1. Blackfeet—Their Area and Dialect—Piegau
System—Indicative Relationships—Agree with the Ojibwa—2. Ahahnelins—Former Area, and Dialect—Indicative Relationships—Agree with the Blackfoot—Concluding Observations—Unity of the System of Relationship
of the Algonkin Nations—Systems of the Algonkin and Dakotan Nations Identical.

THE limits of the Algonkin speech have been definitely ascertained.   Its numerous dialects are nearer to each other than those of any other Indian stock language
of equal spread.   This stem of the Ganowánian family contains but a single stock
language, which will be seen, as well as the nearness of its dialects, by consulting
the Table (Table II).   To such an extent is this nearness still preserved, that it
suggests the probability that the Algonkins are comparatively modern upon the
eastern side of the continent.   The area occupied by these nations was immense
in its territorial extent.   At the period of European discovery they were found
thinly scattered along the Atlantic seaboard from Labrador to the southern limits
of North Carolina; and as the interior was subsequently explored, they were found
continuously along the St. Lawrence, north of the chain of lakes, along the Red
River of the North, and the Siskatchewun,[1] quite to the foot of the Rocky Mountain
chain.   All of Canada was Algonkin, except a narrow fringe upon the north, held
by the Eskimo; and the peninsula between Lakes Huron, Erie, and Ontario, occupied by the Hurons and Neutral Nation.   The southern portion of the Hudson's

---

[1] The orthography of the word is taken from the original name in the Cree language, *Kis-sis
katch'-e-wun,* "Swift Water."

Bay Territory, south of the Siskatchewun and Nelson's River, was the same. New England, New Jersey, Delaware, Maryland, and the eastern parts of Pennsylvania, Virginia, and North Carolina, formed a part of the area of occupancy of this branch of the Ganowánian family. Along the Mississippi, from Lake Pepin to the mouth of the Ohio, and eastward to Indiana, including a part of the latter State, Illinois, Michigan, and the greater part of Wisconsin, the same people were distributed; while one nation, the Shawnees, occupied south of the Ohio, in the western part of the present State of Kentucky. Their eccentric spread southward along the Atlantic coast was forced by the development of the Iroquois nations within the central part of their area; and their spread down the Mississippi was, in like manner, probably due to the pressure of the Dakota nations upon the western boundaries of their area. The Algonkins were essentially a northern people, the main thread of their occupancy being the chain of lakes and the St. Lawrence.

In its development, the Algonkin ranks as the equal of the Dakotan languages. The more advanced dialects of the former are less vigorous and rugged in their pronunciation and accentuation than the equally improved dialects of the latter, and consequently are smoother and softer, as may be seen, to some extent, by a comparison of their respective vocables in the Tables. In the Shawnee, the Cree, and the Ojibwa are found the highest specimens of the Algonkin speech.

There is one peculiarity of Indian languages deserving of attention. It is found in the individualization of each syllable. In each word every syllable is pronounced with a distinctness so marked as to tend to its isolation. Instead of an easy transition of sound from one syllable into the next, the change is so abrupt as to result in hiatus rather than coalescence. The general effect is heightened by the vehemence of the accent, which is another characteristic of the most of the Ganowánian languages. This may be illustrated by the word *Gä-sko'-sä-go*, which is the name for Rochester in the Seneca-Iroquois. It would be difficult to form and put together four syllables which would maintain to a greater extent the individuality of each in their pronunciation. Between the penult and antepenult the transition is the easiest; but the effect is arrested by the intervention of the accent. These two features are strongly impressed upon the principal dialects east of the Rocky Mountain chain. If the Ganowánian languages were characterized as syllabical rather than agglutinated, the term would be more accurate.[1]

---

[1] The present classification of the languages of mankind into monosyllabical, agglutinated, and inflectional does not seem to be well founded. The principal objection lies to the last term as distinctive of the Aryan and Semitic languages. Inflection is a not less striking characteristic of the Ganowánian languages than agglutination. Conjugation, which is the all-controlling principle of these languages, together with agglutination, are continually submerging the word; whilst in the Aryan and Semitic languages the word is more definite and concrete. There is a decisive tendency in the inflectional languages, so called, to lessen inflection, and, so to speak, to solidify its words. This is shown by the development of the present Aryan languages into their modern forms. They are languages of complete and perfect words, as distinguished from the monosyllabical and polysyllabical, which are yet, in some sense, in the syllable stage. The three forms appear to give—1. The language of single syllables; 2. The language of many syllables; and 3. The language of words.

I. Gichigamian, or Great Lake Nations. II. Mississippi Nations. III. Atlantic Nations. IV. Rocky Mountain Nations.

The Algonkin nations fall naturally into the foregoing groups. As an inter-classification it is sustained by dialectical affinities, and by special features in their respective systems of relationship. Under the operation of the same inexorable law that produced the repeated subdivision of the Dakotan stem, and scattered its parts over wide areas, they have been broken up into a large number of politically distinct nations. Relying chiefly upon fish and game for subsistence, when an excess of population appeared within a particular area, the surplus were forced to spread abroad in search of a new seat, where, in due time, they established an independent nationality. Their form of government, which was incapable of following the people by expansion from a fixed centre, was perfect in every band; whence every band was a nation in embryo. The subdividings and the migrations of the Ganowánian nations were pre-eminently under the control of physical causes, the unbroken supremacy of which continued from the commencement of their career upon the North American continent down to the period of European colonization. It is still possible to retrace to a very considerable extent, the lines of the outflow of these nations from each other; and the direction of the spread of the several stocks from a common initial point. Were it not for the breaking up and absorption of nations that would have constituted the intermediate links, the precise relations of these stocks and stems of peoples to each other, as members of a common family, might not be beyond hope of recovery. At least the family may be resolved into great branches represented by stock languages, and the branches into groups represented by closely affiliated dialects. More than this is material only to establish the unity of these stock languages. Upon this last question their system of relationship offers an independent testimony which seems to be sufficient for its determination in the affirmative.

I. Gichigamian,[1] or Great Lake Nations.

1. Ojibwas. 2. Otawas. 3. Potawattamies. 4. Crees.

When the Jesuit missionaries first reached Lake Superior (1641) they found the principal establishment of the Ojibwas at St. Mary's Falls or rapids, at the outlet of this lake, and spread for some distance above upon both its northern and southern shores. At the same time the Otawas[2] inhabited the Manitoulin Islands scattered along the north side of the Georgian Bay, of Lake Huron, and the islands in the straits of Mackinaw; while a portion of them were then spreading southward over lower Michigan. Their previous home country was upon the Otawa River of Canada, and between it and Lake Superior, north of the Huron area; but they had been forced to leave this region by the irruptions of the Iroquois, who had extended their forays to the Otawa River, and thence to the shores of Lake Superior. With respect to the Potawattamies[3] their precise location is not

---

[1] Gï-chi-gä-me, "the Great Lake," from the Ojibwa, Gï'-chi, or Gï-tchï, great, and gä'-me, lake. They applied this name to each of the great lakes; Ma-she-gä'-me to all large lakes; and Sa-gä-e'-gäs to the small lakes.

[2] Pronounced O-tä'-wä.

[3] Pronounced Po-tă-wät'-tă-me.

as well ascertained. They were frontagers of the Dakotas, and occupied some part of Northern Wisconsin, ranging eastward towards Lake Michigan, and the occupancy of the Ojibwas on Lake Superior. Between these nations, whose dialects closely affiliate, there was a political alliance, which existed to as late a period as 1767, when they were called by Sir William Johnson "the Otawa Confederacy." In the Otawa dialect, this league was styled *Na-swä'-bă-ne-zid'*, signifying "Three Council Fires in One." Among confederated Indian nations there is usually an order of precedence in council established which indicates their relative rank, and not unfrequently the parent nation. In the Otawa confederacy the Ojibwas were styled the "Elder Brother," the Otawas, "Next Oldest Brother," and the Potawattamies, "Younger Brother."[1] These nations were probably subdivisions of one original nation; and the immediate progenitors of four other nations, called collectively, at one time, the Illinois, namely, the Kaskaskias, Peorias, Weas, and Piankeshaws, who occupied the quadrangle between the Mississippi, the Ohio, and the foot of Lake Michigan.

On the earliest map of Lake Superior in the relations of the Jesuits (1641–1667) the Kenistenaux or Crees are placed northwest of this lake, between it and Lake Winnipeg. They were afterwards found to spread eastward as far as the regions north of Montreal; and to hold the area between Lake Superior and Hudson's Bay, and thence westward to the Red River of the North and the Siskatchewan. They were evidently drawing westward at the epoch of the discovery, the causes of which may be traced to the rapid growth of the power and influence of the Iroquois. It is also probable that a portion of the New England Algonkins retired in this direction.

The four nations named are designated the Gichigamian or Great Lake Nations. Collectively they form one of the most conspicuous groups of this branch of the Ganowánian family; and from the earliest period, to which their traditions extend, they have been identified with these lakes. It is also extremely probable, from the great fisheries they afford, that these lakes have been the nursery of this stem of the family, and the secondary initial point of migration to the valley of the Saint Lawrence, and thence to the Atlantic seaboard; and also to the valleys of the Mississippi and the Ohio. They seem to stand intermediate between the eastern, the southern, and the western Algonkins.

The system of consanguinity and affinity of the four groups of nations will be considered in the order in which they are arranged.

1. Ojibwas. Under the more familiar name of Chippewas, this nation has become so well known, historically, that a reference to their civil affairs will be unnecessary. Small bands of this people still inhabit the south shore of Lake Superior, at the Sault St. Mary, and around Marquette and L'Anse Bays; but the great body of them now occupy the country around Leach and Red Lakes, in Western Minnesota. They number about ten thousand. Their system of relationship agrees intimately

---

[1] A similar order of precedure in council existed among the Iroquois; the Mohawks, Onandagas, and Senecas were collectively styled "Fathers," and the Cayugas, Oneidas, and Tuscaroras "Sons," and the nations were named in this relative order.—*Cf. League of the Iroquois*, pp. 96 and 118.

with that of the Otawas, Potawattamies, and Crees.   It also contains certain special features in which these nations agree with each other, but differ from the other Algonkin nations.   The Ojibwa system will be adopted as the standard.   Four complete schedules of this form are given in the Table—first, to show the slight amount of dialectical variation which has arisen in the Ojibwa, notwithstanding the geographical separation of their numerous bands; and secondly, the permanence of the special features of the system.   No other form has been more thoroughly explored, and it appears to exhaust all the capabilities for specialization which the fundamental conceptions of the system render possible.

There are original terms for grandfather and grandmother, *Ne-ma-sho-mis'* and *No'-ko-mis'*; for father and mother, *Nōss* and *Nin-gah'*; for son and daughter, *Nin-gwis'* and *Nin-dä'-niss*; and a term in common gender for grandchild, *No-she-shă'*. All ancestors above the first are grandfathers and grandmothers, and all descendants below the last are grandchildren.

The relationships of brother and sister are held in the twofold form of elder and younger, and there are separate terms for each; *Nĭ-sä-yă'*, elder brother, and *Ne-mis-să'*, younger brother; but the term for younger brother and younger sister, *Ne-she'-mă*, is in common gender, and applied to both.

It will be understood that what is stated in each of the last two paragraphs is also true with respect to every other Algonkin nation, unless the contrary is mentioned.

First Indicative Feature.   My brother's son and daughter, *Ego* a male, are my step-son, *N'-do'-zhim*, and my step-daughter, *N'-do'-zhe-mĭ-kwame*.   With *Ego* a female, they are my nephew and niece, *Ne-nin'-gwi-nis'* and *Ne-she-mis'*.

Second.   My sister's son and daughter, *Ego* a male, are my nephew and niece, *Ne-nin'-gwi-nis'* and *Ne-she-mis'*.   With *Ego* a female, they are my step-son and step-daughter.

Third.   My father's brother is my step-father, *Ne-mish'-sho-mă*.

Fourth.   My father's brother's son and daughter, *Ego* a male, are my step-brother, *Ne-kä'-na*, and my step-sister, *Nin-dä-wa'-ma*.   With *Ego* a female, they are my brother, elder or younger, and my sister, elder or younger.

Fifth.   My father's sister is my aunt, *Ne-see-gŭs'*.

Sixth.   My mother's brother is my uncle, *Ne-zhish-shă'*.

Seventh.   My mother's sister is my step-mother, *Ne-no-shă*.[1]

Eighth.   My mother's sister's son and daughter, *Ego* a male, are my step-brother and step-sister; but the latter, if younger than myself, is my younger sister.   With *Ego* a female, they are my brothers and sisters, elder or younger.

Ninth.   My grandfather's brother is my grandfather.

Tenth.   The grandchildren of my brothers and sisters, and the grandchildren of my collateral brothers and sisters, of my step-brothers and step-sisters, and of my male and female cousins, are, without distinction, my grandchildren.

---

[1] I think, if re-examined, it will be found that my mother's sister is my mother, and my father's brother my father, *Ego* a female; and that my sister's son, *Ego* a female, is my daughter.   In other words, the step-relationships are used by the males, whilst the females use the full terms.   The Tables show this in part.

It will be seen, by consulting the Table, that the principles of classification in the first collateral line are applied to the second, third, and fourth collateral lines, as in the Seneca and Yankton; thus, the sons and daughters of my step-brothers, and of my male cousins, *Ego* a male, are my step-sons and step-daughters, while the children of my step-sisters and of my female cousins are my nephews and nieces. With *Ego* a female, the children of the former are my nephews and nieces, and of the latter are my sons and daughters.

Amongst the Gichigamian nations the relationship of cousin is found, but restricted, as usual, to the children of a brother and sister; thus, my father's sister's son and daughter are my male and female cousins, *Ne-tä'-wis* and *Ne-ne-moo-shă'*. In like manner, my grandfather's brother's grandson and granddaughter are my cousins. On the mother's side, my mother's brother's son and daughter, and my grandmother's brother's grandson and granddaughter, are respectively my male and female cousins.

In the marriage relationship the Ojibwa system is in equally striking agreement with the Seneca and Yankton. Each of the wives of my step-sons and nephews is my daughter-in-law, *Ne-sim* ; and each of the husbands of my several step-daughters and nieces is my son-in-law, *Ne-nin-gwun'*, the same as the wife and husband of my own son and daughter. In like manner, the wives of my several step-brothers and male cousins are respectively my sisters-in-law, and the husbands of my several step-sisters and female cousins are my brothers-in-law. For a further knowledge of these relationships reference is made to the Table, in which they will be found fully presented

If the Seneca-Iroquois and Yankton-Dakota forms are placed side by side with the Ojibwa, the differences are found to be so inconsiderable, both in the relationships of consanguinity and affinity, as to excite astonishment. We have crossed from one stock language into another, and from one of the great stems of the Ganowánian family into another, and find not only the radical features of the common system intact, but their subordinate details coincident down to minute particulars. At the same time, the terms of relationship are changed beyond the reach of recognition. One set of diagrams, with scarcely the alteration of a relationship, would answer for the three forms, the classification of blood kindred and of marriage relations being substantially the same in all. The chief difference consists in the substitution of the step-relationships for a portion of the primary, which will be found to be simply a refinement upon an original system in all respects identical with the Seneca and Yankton. This is conclusively shown by the present condition of the system amongst their nearest congeners, the Mississippi nations, among whom the step-relationships are unknown in this connection. A further and still stronger impression is thus obtained of the great antiquity of this extraordinary system of relationship in the Ganowánian family, of its power to perpetuate itself, and of the fact of its transmission with the blood.

2. Otawas. 3. Potawattamies. The forms which prevail in these nations agree so closely with the Ojibwa, that it will not be necessary to consider them separately. It will also be seen, by consulting the Table, that their dialects approach each other very nearly. At the time of the settlement of Detroit, a portion of the Otawas

were settled upon the Detroit River. The largest number of them are now in Kansas; but there are small bands still upon the north shores of Lake Huron and the Georgian Bay, and still other individuals intermingled with the Ojibwas. They number collectively about two thousand. The Potawattamies occupied around the south shores of Lake Michigan at the time the settlement was commenced at Chicago, about 1830. The most of them are now established upon a reservation in Kansas. They number collectively about three thousand.

4. Crees. The Cree language is now spoken in three dialects, without any corresponding division of the people into three geographically distinct nations. They are called the Cree of the Lowlands, the Cree of the Woods, and the Cree of the Prairie, of which the former is the least and the latter is the most developed. There is a belt of thick wood country extending for about three hundred miles from the southern circuit of Hudson's Bay, reaching to Lake Winnipeg on the west, and on the south to the dividing ridge between this bay and Lake Superior and the St. Lawrence, which has been the home country of the Crees from the earliest period to which our knowledge extends. Sir George Simpson states, in his testimony before a Parliamentary commission, that this thick wood country "has a larger surface of water than of land."[1] Their occupation of the prairie regions upon the Red River of the North and the Siskatchewun was undoubtedly comparatively modern. The prairie dialect, therefore, which is the speech of the largest number of the Crees, represents that portion of the people who first emigrated from the thick wood country into the plains, and which may have been at the time in the incipient stages of its development. The differences among the three are still very slight, as will be seen by comparing the terms in the Table. Of the variations in the pronouns the following may be taken as illustrations:—

	Mine.	Thine.	His.
Cree of the Lowlands.	Ne-nä'.	We-na-wou'.	We-nä'.
" " Woods.	Ne-lä'.	We-la-wou'.	We-lä'.
" " Prairie.	Ne-yä'.	We-a-wou'.	We-yä'.

The Crees speak of each other as belonging to one of these three branches of the nation, although the dialects, colloquially, are mutually intelligible without the slightest difficulty. In the terms of relationship in the Table other differences will be observed, but they are less in the aggregate than among any other dialects given, not excepting the Dakota. This language is open and accessible to a greater extent than any other upon the American continent, from the large number of whites by whom it has been acquired, and from the unusually large number of half-bloods speaking English, to whom the Cree is the mother tongue.[2] Under the

---

[1] Report from the Select Committee on the Hudson's Bay Company, made to the British Parliament in 1857, p. 55.

[2] An exceedingly interesting experiment is now in progress at Selkirk, or Red River Settlement, near Lake Winnipeg. Along the banks of this river, from the mouth of the Asiniboine River for some twelve miles down towards the lake, there is a straggling village containing near ten thousand people, made up chiefly of half-blood Crees, but showing all shades of color, from the pure white Orkney Islander, through all the intermediate degrees of intermixture, to the full-blooded Cree. The Hudson's Bay Company, at an early day, induced Orkney men to emigrate to their territory, to act

influence of the Hudson's Bay Company, the Crees have been kept at peace among themselves, and to a great extent with contiguous nations, consequently they have made considerable progress in numbers and in civilization. With the exception, however, of the agricultural half-bloods, they are not as far advanced as many other Indian nations.

Their system of relationship was procured with unusual facility. The first schedule, that of the Lowland Cree, was obtained at the Sault St. Mary, in 1860, through a half-blood Cree from Moose Factory, on Hudson's Bay; the second, that of the Prairie Crees, in 1861, at Georgetown, on the Red River of the North, from Mrs. Alexander H. Murray, a quarter-blood Cree from Peace River, near Athapasca Lake. She was the wife of Mr. A. H. Murray, one of the factors of the Hudson's Bay Company, then stationed at Georgetown, and an educated and accomplished

---

in the service of the Company in the capacity of trappers and traders. These adventurers took the Cree women, first as companions, and afterwards, under religious influences, as wives; and when their term of service expired, took up small farms with a narrow front on the river and extending back on the prairie as far as they chose to cultivate, and became a settled agricultural people. The result, in the course of a hundred or more years, has been the development of this large population at Red River Settlement of mixed Indian and European blood, followed by the introduction among them of the habits and usages of civilized life. This population are still drawing fresh blood both from native and European sources; hence the main condition of the experiment—namely, their isolation from both stocks—has not yet been reached. But there is a permanently established half blood class, intermediate between the two; and the problem to be solved is, whether a new stock can be thus formed, able to perpetuate itself. It is too early to pronounce upon the question. There are many encouraging and some adverse indications. There is a purely physiological principle involved, which connects itself directly with this experiment. The Indian and European are at opposite poles in their physiological conditions. In the former there is very little animal passion, while with the latter it is superabundant. A pure-blooded Indian has very little animal passion, but in the half-blood it is sensibly augmented; and when the second generation is reached with a cross giving three-fourths white blood, it becomes excessive, and tends to indiscriminate licentiousness. If this be true in fact, it is a potent adverse element leading to demoralization and decay, which it will be extremely difficult to overmaster and finally escape. In his native state, the Indian is below the passion of love. It is entirely unknown among them, with the exception, to a limited extent, of the Village Indians. This fact is sufficiently proved by the universal prevalence of the custom of disposing of the females in marriage without their knowledge or participation in the arrangement. The effects produced by intermixture of European and Indian blood, although a delicate subject, is one of scientific interest. The facts above stated I obtained from traders and trappers on the Upper Missouri, who have spent their lives in the Indian country, and understand Indian life in all its relations. When at the Red River Settlement in 1861, I made this a subject of further inquiry, the results of which tended to confirm the above statements. Whether this abnormal or disturbed state of the animal passions will finally subside into a proper equilibrium, is one of the questions involved. There was much in the thrift, industry, and intelligence displayed at the Settlement to encourage the hope and the expectation of an ultimately successful solution of the problem. Among the pure Orkney men, as well as half-bloods, there were many excellent and solid men who would command respect and attain success in any community; and under such influences the probabilities of success are greatly strengthened. As far as my personal observation has extended among the American Indian nations, the half-blood is inferior, both physically and mentally, to the pure Indian; but the second cross, giving three-quarters Indian, is an advance upon the native; and giving three-fourths white is a still greater advance, approximating to equality with the white ancestor. With the white carried still further, full equality is reached, tending to show that Indian blood can be taken up without physical or intellectual detriment.

lady.   The third, that of the Cree of the Woods, was procured at the same time and place, from Mrs. Ohlson, a half-blood Cree from Pembina.   Afterwards a second Cree of the Lowlands was obtained at Red River Settlement.   Besides these, I received, in the year 1862, a second schedule of the Cree of the Prairie, from the Rev. E. A. Watkins, of Devon, on the Siskatchewan River.   These verifications of the details as well as existence of the system were more ample than usual.   The Cree language, as well as system of relationship, affiliates very closely with the dialects and systems of the remaining Gichigamian nations.

First Indicative Feature.   My brother's son and daughter, *Ego* a male, are my step-son and step-daughter.   With *Ego* a female, they are my nephew and niece.

Second.   My sister's son and daughter, *Ego* a male, are my nephew and niece. With *Ego* a female, they are my step-son and step-daughter.

Third.   My father's brother is my step-father.

Fourth.   My father's brother's son and daughter are my brother and sister, elder or younger.

Fifth.   My father's sister is my aunt.

Sixth.   My mother's brother is my uncle.

Seventh.   My mother's sister is my mother.

Eighth.   My mother's sister's son and daughter are my brother and sister, elder or younger.

Ninth.   My grandfather's brother is my grandfather.

Tenth.   The grandchildren of my brothers and sisters, and the grandchildren of my collateral brothers and sisters, and of my male and female cousins, are severally my grandchildren.

Among the Crees the relationship of cousin is also found applied by the children of a brother and sister to each other.   The relationships of step-brother and step-sister are not found in the Cree applied as in the Ojibwa.   In this respect it retains the original form of the system.

For the purpose of illustrating the degree of nearness in the vocables for common objects in the dialects of the Great Lake nations, and their relation to the Western Algonkin, a short comparative table is inserted below, compiled from unpublished vocabularies of the author.[1]

II. Mississippi Nations.   1. Miamis.   2. Illinois: (1. Weas.   2. Piankeshaws. 3. Kaskaskias.   4. Peorias.)   3. Sawks and Foxes.   4. Kikapoos.   5. Menominees. 6. Shiyans.   7. Shawnees.

The occupation of the vast prairie area in the interior of the continent, by the Indian nations, was a modern event.   It is perfectly certain, as well as obvious from the nature of these plains, that they were incapable of human habitation until after the aborigines had come into possession of the horse, and had learned to rear him as a domestic animal.   Before that event they were confined to the banks of the great rivers that traversed the prairies, leaving the remainder of these immense regions an unbroken solitude, in the exclusive possession of the herds of wild animals who grazed their inexhaustible pastures.   East of the Mississippi the

---

[1] See table at bottom of next page.

prairie area extended southward to the fringe of forest bordering the Ohio River, eastward to the central part of Indiana, and then stretching northwestward, along the forest which skirted Lake Michigan, Lake Superior, and Lake Winnipeg, it crossed Peace River near the west end of Athapasca Lake. From the plateau of Peace River southward to New Mexico for a distance of more than fifteen hundred miles, and from the Rocky Mountain chain to the great forests, east of the Mississippi, a distance of more than a thousand miles in their greatest width, these prairies lie unrolled as a carpet of verdure. They furnish the most extraordinary natural spectacle upon which the eye of man ever rested on the earth's surface. No description can realize to the mind their vastness or their magnificence. Between the western borders of Lake Superior and the Ohio the rivers and streams were bordered with forest. There were, also, patches of forest scattered here and there in the midst of the prairies, in which respect the regions east of the Mississippi differ from those west of and upon the Missouri. Throughout all the region first named there was a mixture of forest and prairie, the latter largely predominating. Within this area the Mississippi nations were found. Their habitations were along the rivers and streams, which were well supplied with fish, and also among the woodlands which afforded a shelter for game. The open prairies east of the Mississippi, as well as west of it, were destitute of inhabitants.

At the period of colonization there were eleven nations between Lake Superior and the Ohio, excluding the Winnebagoes and Potawattamies, and including the

	Cree.	Ojibwa.	Potawattamie.	Blood-Blackfoot.	Ahahnelin.
Head,	Mish'-to-gwan	O-ste'-gwan	Wa-tib'	O-too-kane'	Ah-gä'-hä
Hair,	Mis-tä'-gi-yä	We-ne-sis'-sun	Wain-sus-san'	O-to'-kwa-kin-	Be-at-ah'
Eye,	O-sk-zik'	O-ske-zhig'	Zhk-zhuk'	O-aps'-pix [is'	Pa-sa'-thä
Ear,	O-tä'-wi-gi	Tä-wäg'	O-to-uk'	Oh·-to'-kis	Wä-nä-tä'-no
Nose,	O-ske-wun'	O-jhaze'	O-jash'	Oaks-se-sis'	Ba'-sa
Mouth,	Ne-tone'	O-done'	O-tone'	Mä-aw'-ye	Ba'-ke
Arm,	Osh-pe-toon'	O-neke'	Nuk	Oh·-chim'-min	Bas'-te-na'-yä
Hand,	O-jish'-che	O-ninge'	O-nech'	O-ma-jiks-e-kin-	Bä'-kik
Bow,	Ah-chä'-le	Me-ke-gwab'	N'-ta-gwab'	Nä'-ma [ist	Bä'-ta
Arrow,	Ah-toosh'	Pe-kwack'	Wape	Ah-pe'-se	Ot'-zo
Tobacco,	Stä'-mow	Ah-sa-mä'	Sä'-mä	Pis-tä'-kä	Tza-thä'-wä
Sun,	Pee-sim	Ke-sis'	Ka-zus'	Nä-to'-ze	A-sis'
Star,	Ah-däk'	Ah-nung'	No-goke'	Kä-kä'-toase	Ah-tome'
Wind,	Yu-tin	No-din'		I'-so-po	Ne'-he-näte
Rain,	Ke-ne-wun'	Ke-nee-wun'		I-sote'	Ah-nä-thä'
Snow,	Go-nä	Kone	Kone	Ko'-nis-ko	Bä-nätz'
Fire,	E-sko'-da-o	Sko'-da		Stche	E-sit'-tä
Water,	Ne'-pe	Ne-leh'	Bish	Ah-oh·'-ke-a	Det'-za
Ice,	Mis-kwä-me'	Me-kwum'	M'-komb'	Ko-ko-to'-ä	Wä'-ho
Pigeon,	O-me'-mu	O-me'-me	Ah-me'	Kä-ko'-ä	Ne-ta'-ha
Red,	Ah-me-kwäg'	Mis-kwa'	Mas-kwäk'	Mox-e'-natch-e	Bä'-ah
Yellow,	O-sä-wäg'	O-zä-wä'	Wä-zä'-näk	Ote-ko'-e-natch-	Ne-hä'-yä
One,	Pa-yuk'		N'-goot'	Tokes'-kä [e	Na-ne'-tha
Two,	Ne-su'		Neesh	Nä'-toke	Na-ne-tha'
Three,	Nees-tŭ'		Swä	Ne-okes'-kä	Na-nä'-the
Four,	Na-woo'		Ne-ă-o'	Ne-sä-im	Ge-nä'-ne
Five,	Nee-ah-mun'		Ne-ă-nin'	Nee-se-to'-ä	Ya-nä'-tä-ne

Shawnees south of the Ohio, who dwelt upon the east bank of the Mississippi, and upon the numerous rivers which traverse the present States of Wisconsin and Illinois, and the western parts of Indiana. All of these nations spoke dialects of the Algonkin language, and were more nearly allied to each other, and nearer to the Great Lake nations, than they were to the Atlantic Algonkins. The reasons for placing the Shiyans[1] among the number will be elsewhere assigned. It is proposed to call them collectively the Mississippi Nations. At the time Father Marquette descended the Mississippi, in 1673 it is probable, from the Algonkin names upon his map, that some of these nations had establishments upon the west side of the river, from which the Dakotas were then gradually effecting their displacement. Moreover, there are reasons for supposing that the original home country of the Dakotas upon the head waters of the Mississippi, was wrested from the Algonkins, and that the Shiyans, and perhaps the Arapahoes, were the nations displaced.

1. Miamis. 2. Illinois. (1. Weas. 2. Piankeshaws. 3. Kaskaskias. 4. Peorias.)

The first group of the Mississippi Nations, consisting of the five above named, were subdivisions of the same people. This is at least certain with respect to all except the Miamis, whose dialect shows considerable divergence. During the colonial period they were so regarded both by the French and English.[2] They were sometimes styled, collectively, the "Illinois Confederacy."[3] It is a matter of doubt whether there ever was a distinct nation of Illinois Indians, as distinguished from the four bands named. None such exists at the present time, and we have no account of their extirpation. It was probably a general name for these nations or bands, which was laid aside after they became distinct under recognized names. This is not inconsistent with La Salle's account of the destruction of a large portion of the Illinois by the Iroquois. For these reasons these four nations are called collectively the Illinois. The Peorias and Kaskaskias were immediate subdivisions of the same people. In like manner, the Miamis, Weas, and Piankeshaws, as appears by the official records of the last century, were regarded as immediate subdivisions of one original nation.[4] A comparison of the terms of relationship in the Table will show the present relation of these dialects to each other.

In their system of consanguinity and affinity these nations, all of which are represented in the Table, agree very closely with each other. It will be sufficient to present one form, and that of the Miamis, who are the most numerous, will be adopted as the standard. These nations occupied the triangle between the Illinois, the Mississippi, and the Ohio Rivers, and were spread along the Wabash and the Miami into the western part of Indiana.[5]

---

[1] From the Dakota *Shi-yä*. (Cheyennes.

[2] Enumeration of Indian Nations made in 1736, Colonial History of New York, IX, 1057.

[3] Review of the Trade and Affairs of the Indians of the Northern District in 1767, by Sir William Johnson, Col. Hist. New York, IX, 966.

[4] Ib., IX, 891, and X, 248.

[5] Harvey, in his History of the Shawnees, quotes the speech of Little Turtle, a Miami chief, in which

First Indicative Feature. My brother's son and daughter, *Ego* a male, are my son and daughter, *Neen-gwase'-sä* and *Nin-dä'-na*. With *Ego* a female, they are my nephew and niece, *Lan-gwä-les'-sä* and *Shames-sä'*.

Second. My sister's son and daughter, *Ego* a male, are my nephew and niece. With *Ego* a female, they are my son and daughter.

Third. My father's brother is my father, *No-sä'*.

Fourth. My father's brother's son and daughter are my brother, elder or younger, *Ne-sä-sä'* or *Ne'-she-mä'*, and my sister, elder or younger, *Ne-mis-sä'* or *Ne-she-mä'*.

Fifth. My father's sister is my aunt, *N'-sa-gwe'-sä*.

Sixth. My mother's brother is my uncle, *Ne-zhese'-sä*.

Seventh. My mother's sister is my mother, *Nin-ge-ah'*.

Eighth. My mother's sister's son and daughter, are my brother and sister, elder or younger.

Ninth. My grandfather's brother is my grandfather, *Na-ma-sho-mä'*

The grandchildren of my brothers and sisters, and of my collateral brothers and sisters, are indiscriminately my grandchildren.

Amongst these nations the relationship of cousin is unknown. The children of a brother and sister, if males, are uncle and nephew to each other, and if females, they are mother and daughter; in which respect it is in precise agreement with the form which prevails among the Missouri nations and the Winnebagoes. As this identity is an interesting fact, the relationships may be run through specifically. My father's sister's son and daughter, *Ego* a male, are my nephew and niece, and their children are my grandchildren. With *Ego* a female, they are my son and daughter, and their children are my grandchildren. On the reverse side, my mother's brother's son is my uncle, *Ne-zhese'-sä*; his son is my uncle again, and his male descendants continue to be uncles, theoretically, in an infinite series. My mother's brother's daughter is my mother, *Nin-ge-ah'*; her children are my brothers and sisters, elder or younger; the children of these collateral brothers, *Ego* a male, are my sons and daughters; of these collateral sisters are my nephews and nieces, and their children are my grandchildren.

The progress of this particular part of the system from a lower to a higher form in branches of two independent stems of the Ganowánian family, taking in each the same direction, and reaching the same ultimate form, is a significant fact. This is seen to have been the case among the Hodenosaunian, the Dakotan, and the Great Lake nations, among whom the relationship of cousin is found. On the other hand, it is a not less striking fact that among the congeners of each respectively the same anterior form, as to the relationships between the children of a brother and sister should still prevail. Two inferences arise from the premises: first, that the radical forms of the system are stable and persistent. An obvious

---

the latter refers to the ancient area of occupation of the Miamis as follows: "My forefathers kindled the first fire at Detroit, from thence he extended his lines to the head-waters of the Scioto, from thence to its mouth, from thence down the Ohio to the mouth of the Wabash, and from thence to Chicago on Lake Michigan. These are the boundaries within which the prints of my ancestors' houses are everywhere to be seen."—*Harvey's History of the Shawnees*, p. 64.

incongruity, not to say blemish, is maintained through long periods of time among certain nations, after a portion of their congeners had corrected the defect by a change suggested by the principles of the system.   Secondly, that the system is under the absolute control of the fundamental conceptions upon which it rests, and if changed at all, the change must be in logical accordance with these conceptions, and move in a direction, as elsewhere stated, predetermined by the elements of the system.

The identity of the Miami in whatever is radical, with the common system of all the nations thus far named is sufficiently evident.[1]

2. Sawks and Foxes.   It would be inconsistent with the plan of this work to encumber its pages with historical notices of the numerous nations to whom it is necessary to refer.   A brief reference to their ancient seats, and to their present location and numbers, will yield all the information necessary to our present purpose.

The home country of the Sawks and Foxes, when they first became known to the early explorers, was upon the Fox River in Wisconsin, where they were found in 1666.   Their range was westward from this river to the Mississippi.   There is some evidence tending to show that they formerly resided upon the north shore of Lake Ontario; and subsequently upon the west side of the Mississippi in the valley of the Sawk River, within the Dakota area.   They have been distinguished among the Mississippi nations for their fighting propensities.   In 1841 they were established upon a reservation in Kansas, and were estimated at twenty-four hundred.[2]

Among the Mississippi nations there was more or less of cultivation and of village life.   This was particularly the case with the Sawks and Foxes.[3]   Their dialect affiliates very closely with the dialects of the Illinois, as will be seen by a reference to the Table.   Like all other prairie Indians, the Sawks and Foxes are very dark skinned, very much more so than the forest nations.   Some of them are but a few shades lighter than the negro.[4]

Their system of relationship, which will be found in the Table, agrees so inti-

---

[1] In 1855 the five nations above named were estimated collectively at seven hundred and eighty. Schoolcraft, Hist. Cond. & Pros. VI, 705.

[2] They are frequently referred to in the Colonial Records.   Col. Hist. N. Y., IV, 749, VII, 543, IX, 161, 889 and 1055.

[3] Carver thus speaks of a village of the Sawks on the Wisconsin River, which he visited in 1766 : "This is the largest and best built Indian town I ever saw.   It contained about ninety houses, each large enough for several families.   They are built of hewn plank, neatly jointed, and covered with bark so completely as to keep out the most penetrating rains. * * * In their plantations, which lie adjacent to their houses, and are neatly laid out, they raise great quantities of Indian corn, beans, melons, &c."—*Travels*, p. 22.

[4] I remember very distinctly the personal appearance of a Sawk woman upon the Sawk and Fox Reservation in Kansas in 1860, who assisted my interpreter in giving the details of their system of relationship.   She was short, but stout, with a very dark skin, small deep set and restless black eyes (in which the untamed animal nature was distinctly manifest), high cheek bones, narrow, high, and retreating forehead, and massive lower face, with large mouth and tumid lips.   A smile, which occasionally came and went, sat upon her imperturbable features so unnaturally that her face did not seem formed to harbor such a visitant; and it dropped out as instantaneously as a thread of light-

mately with the form which prevails in the first group of the Mississippi nations that it will be unnecessary to present the indicative relationships. The most noticeable fact connected with it is the manner of disposing of the relationships of the children of a brother and sister, who are uncle and nephew if males, and mother and daughter if females, in which respect it agrees with the Miami.

3. Kikapoos. The earliest notices of this nation placed them in the northern part of the present State of Illinois, between Lake Michigan and the Mississippi. In the enumeration of the Indian tribes made in 1736,[1] ascribed to Chauvignerie, they are located upon Fox River in Wisconsin, whilst in a later one made by Sir William Johnson in 1763,[2] they are placed upon the Wabash. They now reside upon a reservation in Kansas, and number according to the census of 1855 three hundred and forty-four.[3]

Their system of relationship, which will be found in the Table, agrees with the Miami not only in its general form, but also in the relationships between the children of a brother and sister.

4. Menominees. The original seat of this nation was upon the river of the same name, in Michigan and Wisconsin. They are mentioned by Du Chesnau, in his " Memoir on the Western Indians," made in 1681,[4] as among the Indians of Wisconsin. They remained in this region until they were removed to a reservation on Long Prairie River, one of the head tributaries of the Mississippi. In 1849 they numbered about two thousand five hundred. They have made considerable progress in civilization.

Their system of relationship is substantially identical with the Miami. It also agrees with it in making the children of a brother and sister, uncle and nephew if males, and mother and daughter if females.

5. Shiyans. Less is known of the early history of this people than of any other Mississippi nation. They were anciently seated upon the Cheyenne River, a tributary of the Red River of the North, in what afterwards became a part of the Dakota area. The Dakotas have not only preserved a tradition of their former residence upon this river, but they still point out a place, at a bend in the stream, where their village stood, and where there are still said to be traces of former occupation as well as cultivation. We are also indebted to the Dakotas for the name by which they are now known. They called them *Shi-yä'* " the people who speak an unintelligible tongue." At the time Lewis and Clarke ascended the Missouri (1804), they were established upon the Cheyenne River, a tributary of the Missouri, near the foot of the Black Hills in Nebraska.[5] They are now living

---

ning from a black cloud. The Indian eye shows neither pupil nor iris ; and is, so to speak, impenetrable and unreadable—a deep but strong unglistening black. The half bloods have glistening eyes, which, at a certain stage of further white intermixture, become the most brilliant eyes to be found in the family of mankind.

[1] Col. Hist. N. Y , IX, 1055.   [2] Ib., VII, 583.

[3] Schoolcraft, Hist. Cond. and Pros. Ind. Tribes, VI, 705. [4] Col. Hist. N. Y., IX, 161.

[5] Lewis and Clarke, speaking of this river, say : " It derives this title from the Cheyenne Indians. Their history is a short and melancholy relation of the calamities of most all the Indians. They were a numerous people, and lived on the Cheyenne, a branch of the Red River of Lake Winnipeg.

in the territory of Colorado in what was formerly the extreme western part of Kansas.   With the Arapahoes, a kindred people, they are now geographically disconnected from the Algonkin nations, the Dakotas occupying the intermediate area. Their first seat tends to show that far back of the historical period, the Algonkin area extended westward from the head of Lake Superior beyond the head-waters of the Mississippi; and that the regions afterwards occupied by the Dakotas proper were wrested, as elsewhere suggested, from the Algonkin nations.   Among the number thus displaced, were the Shiyans certainly, and probably the Arapahoes and Ahahnelins (Gros Ventres of the Prairie).   If we should seek among the Mississippi nations, the nearest congeners of the Shiyans and Arapahoes, the Menominees and Shawnees will be found to make the nearest approach to them in their dialects.   The annexed comparative Table, taken in connection with the terms of relationship, shows more or less affinity, although the amount of dialectical change is very great.[1]

First Indicative Feature.   My brother's son and daughter, *Ego* a male, are my son and daughter, *Nä* and *Nă-tun'*.   With *Ego* a female, they are my nephew and niece, *Nă-chin'e-tä* and *Ne-she'-mis*.

Second.   My sister's son and daughter, *Ego* a male, are my nephew and niece. With *Ego* a female, they are my son and daughter.

The invasion of the Sioux [Dakotas] drove them westward; in their progress they halted on the western side of the Missouri, below the Wasseconne, where their ancient fortifications still exist; but the same impulse again drove them to the heads of the Cheyenne, where they now rove, and occasionally visit the Rickarees.   They are now reduced, but still number three hundred men."—*Travels*, p. 70.

[1] COMPARATIVE VOCABULARY.

	Shawnee. Morgan.	Menominee. Bruce.	Shiyan. Smith.	Arapahoe. Smith.	Ahahnelin. (Gros Ventres of the Prairie.) Morgan.
1. Head,	We-se'	Maish	Mah-ke-o	Nee-a-tbar	At-gä'-hä
2. Ear,	Ho-tä-wä-gä'	May-tah-woc	Es-tah-vote	Won-ne-tun-a	Wä-nä-tä'-no
3. Eye,	Ske-sa-gwe'	Maish-kay-shaick	A-ch'-quin	Mee-she-shee	Pa-sa'-thä
4. Nose,	Ho-jä-se'	May-che-osh	Kune	Ner-tun-nee	Ba'-sa
5. Mouth,	Ho-do-nih'	May-tone	Marthe	Net-tee	Ba'-ke
6. Heart,	O-dă-heh'	May-tah	Es-tah	Bat-tah	It'-tä
7. Blood,	Mis-kwe'	Mainh-kee	Mah-e	Bahe	Wä'-atz-za
8. Sun,	Ge-sä-thä'	Kay-shoh	Is-she	Nee-she-ish	A-sis'
9. Day,	Ge-sä-ge'	Kay-shay-kcts	Na-vone	Ee-shee	Noh-wä-na-ho-
10. Water,	Na-be	Na-pay-we	Ma-pa	Nutch	Det'-za [sa
11. Ice,	P-gwä-mä'	Mainh-quom	Ma-omh	Wä-hoo	Wä'-h·o
12. Snow,	Mä-dä'	Koon	Es-tassa	Ee	Bä-nätz'
13. Rain,	Keem-a-won-wa'	Ke-may-won	Ho-co	Os-son-ick	
14. Elk,	Wä-pet-se'	Oh-mansh-kash	Mo-ee	Ese-wour-koo	A-was'-sa-ha
15 Beaver,	A-meex'-wä	Nah-main	Hau-mä	Ah-bash	Ah'-pis-se
16. Bear,	M'-kwä'	Ah-way-sha	Nah-quo	Whoth	Was'-see

The Menominee is taken from Schoolcraft's Hist. Cond. and Pros., II, 470; and the Shiyan and Arapahoe from the same, III, 446.   The Shawnee and Ahahnelin are from unpublished vocabularies of the authors.

Third. My father's brother is my father, Nă-o'-a.

Fourth. My father's brother's son and daughter are my brother and sister, elder or younger, Nă-ne'-ä or Nă-sim-ă', and Nă-ma' or Nă-sim-ă'.

Fifth. My father's sister is my aunt, Nă-un'.

Sixth. My mother's brother is my uncle, Nă-she'.

Seventh. My mother's sister is my mother, Nă-ko'.

Eighth. My mother's sister's son and daughter are my brother and sister, elder or younger.

Ninth. My grandfather's brother is my grandfather, Nam-a-shim'.

Tenth. The grandchildren of my brothers and sisters, and of my collateral brothers and sisters, are my grandchildren.

With respect to the relationships between the children of a brother and sister it was impossible to ascertain with certainty, and these questions are unanswered in the Table. It seemed most probable that they were uncle and nephew if males, and mother and daughter if females.[1]

The Shiyan dialect has some peculiarities which may have resulted from its long isolation from the purer forms of the Algonkin speech. It is seen in the feebleness of the accent, which renders the language monotonous, and in the shortening of the words apparently by the loss of syllables. The traders who are familiar with other Algonkin dialects regard this as the most difficult of them all; and those who are familiar with the Dakota alone, still pronounce it, as the Dakotas did, an "unintelligible tongue." Their Algonkin lineage, and their possession of the common systems of relationship of the family, are both established.

5. Shawnees. The Cumberland River in Kentucky was called the Shawnee River until 1748, when the present name was substituted.[2] In the triangular area between the Ohio and the Mississippi, watered by the lower Tennessee and the Cumberland, were the ancient seats of the Shawnees.[3] Beyond this region they have never been traced to any anterior home. They still call themselves Sä-wän-wä-ke', which signifies "southerners"—in Otawa, O-shaw-wä-noke',—a name adopted by them, probably in a boastful sense, as the southernmost band geographically of Algonkin descent.[4] They appear to have abandoned the Mississippi prior to 1650;

---

[1] I obtained the system of the Shiyans in 1860 from Joseph Tesson, a French trader at Rulo in Nebraska. He was a quarter-blood Menominee. At the age of eighteen, as he informed me, he left the Missouri River, and went out as an adventurer upon the plains. Having joined himself to the Shiyans, he learned their language, married a woman of that nation, and took an active part in all their military enterprises. In due time he was made a chief. For twenty years he had been identified with this nation, and during that time had not visited the Missouri region. Shortly before I met him he had found his way with his children to Rulo to resume civilized life. He was able to give me their system of relationship in every particular, except the part in question, upon which he was in doubt whether the relationships were those of uncle and nephew or cousin and cousin. Since he could not recall a term for cousin in the Shiyan language, with which he was perfectly familiar, it seemed reasonably certain that this relationship did not exist, and that the classification agreed with the Miami. Tesson spoke French, English, and Spanish; and had acquired five Indian languages besides the Shiyan.

[2] Col. Hist. N. Y., VIII, 113, note.   [3] Harvey's History of the Shawnees, p. 64.

[4] Ib. p. 64.

and to have moved eastward to North Carolina and Virginia, and finally, in 1678 or thereabout, to the Susquehannah River in Pennsylvania. They were a party to the second treaty with William Penn in 1701. Prior to 1786 the most of the Shawnees had removed to the Miami River in Ohio; and after several changes of residence in that State, in which they remained until 1832, they were finally removed by the general government to a reservation on the Kansas River. At the present moment they are undergoing, for the third time within a century and a half, the process of being uprooted and expatriated under the pressure of the never ending requirements of the American people.

The Shawnees, notwithstanding their trying and eventful experience in war and in peace, have preserved their nationality and made remarkable progress in agriculture and in other arts of civilized life. They have organized a representative government, founded upon a popular election of chiefs, have organized and supported schools, constructed comfortable houses, and become strictly agricultural. There are amongst them men and women of education, intelligence, and high moral worth who are striving to raise themselves to useful employments, and their families to independence. With a proper encouragement of these efforts a large portion of the remaining Shawnees would ultimately become permanently civilized and saved from extermination. It is seriously to be deplored that the Great Republic does not awaken to an intelligent as well as judicious, administration of its Indian affairs. The census of 1855 shows that they number eight hundred and fifty-one.[1]

Colloquially the Shawnee is the most beautiful dialect of the Algonkin speech. Any person who has heard these dialects, in their wide range and diversity, from the lips of the native speaker, must have noticed the superiority in smoothness of articulation of the Shawnee, the Cree, and the Ojibwa, over those of the Atlantic Algonkins, and still more over the degenerate forms of the same speech at the foot of the Rocky Mountain chain. The latter are distorted and roughened by nasal and guttural utterances from which the former are comparatively free. Amongst the central Algonkins the mental superiority was found. As compared with the Iroquois and Dakotas they were an inferior stock. Whilst the dialects of the latter are distinguished for vigor of pronunciation, and by a clear ringing accent upon the emphatic part of each word, the Algonkin, with the exceptions named, is a soft and not unmusical speech. Indian dialects unfold and contract, improve and deteriorate, as the people who hold them in their keeping increase in numbers and mental capacity, or fall back under adverse circumstances into feebleness and decay. The Shawnees have withstood the external pressure upon them with remarkable persistency and success; and have continued to advance, except in numbers, throughout the entire period of colonization and established empire.

From the fact that for upwards of two centuries they had been detached, in a great measure, from their immediate congeners, and had lived in intimate relations with the eastern Algonkins, their system of consanguinity and affinity was sought

---

[1] Schoolcraft, Hist. Cond. and Pros. &c., VI, 715.

with more than usual interest. Its present form would tend to illustrate how far, if at all, its original features might become modified in those respects in which it differed from that of the Atlantic Algonkins. Whether an established system changes with facility, under external influence, or stubbornly resists innovation from without, is a question that connects itself with the final estimate to be placed upon systems of relationship as an instrument in ethnology. The more therefore the evidence tending to establish the fact of its stability is multiplied the more reliable will the inferences drawn therefrom become.

First Indicative Feature. My brother's son and daughter, *Ego* a male, are my son and daughter, *Ne-kwe-thä'* and *Nĭ-tä-na-thä'*. With *Ego* a female, they are my nephew and niece, *Na-la-gwal-thä'* and *Na-sa-me-thä'*.

Second. My sister's son and daughter, *Ego* a male, are my nephew and niece. With *Ego* a female, they are my son and daughter.

Third. My father's brother is my father, *No-thä'*.

Fourth. My father's brother's son and daughter are my brother and sister, elder or younger, *N'-tha-thä'* or *N'-the-ma-thä'* and *Nĭ-mĭ-thä'* or *N'-the-ma-thä'*.

Fifth. My father's sister is my aunt, *Na-tha-gwe-thä'*.

Sixth. My mother's brother is my uncle, *Nĭ'sĭ-thä'*.

Seventh. My mother's sister is my mother, *Ne-ke⁻ah'*.

Eighth. My mother's sister's son and daughter are my brother and sister, elder or younger.

Ninth. My grandfather's brother is my grandfather, *Na-ma-some-thä'*.

Tenth. The grandchildren of my brothers and sisters, and of my collateral brothers and sisters, are my grandchildren.

With respect to the children of a brother and sister, they are uncle and nephew if males, and mother and daughter if females. It agrees also with the Miami as to the series of uncles. For the marriage relationships which are not less elaborately discriminated reference is made to the Table.

It thus appears that the Shawnees have not only maintained all of the radical characteristics of the system, but also that they have tenaciously held to the second form of the deviation which forms such a striking peculiarity of the system. The minute and precise agreement of the Miami, Sawk and Fox, Kikapoo and Menominee forms with each other, and with the Shawnee, is a forcible attestation of the stability of the system as a whole, and of the like stability of the relationships deviating from uniformity when they become permanently established.

It should be observed, also, that the terms of relationship amongst all of the Algonkin nations thus far considered, are, for the most part, the same original words under dialectical changes. From this fact the inference arises that the terms as well as the system, have come down to each from a common source; thus ascending to the time when all of these nations were represented by a single nation, and their dialects by a single language.[1]

---

[1] In December, 1858, I sent out the first printed schedule with an explanatory letter to the several Indian Missions, and among the number, one to Friend Simon D. Harvey, Superintendent of the Friends' Shawnee Mission School in Kansas. But three answers were returned, and the first was

III. Atlantic Algonkins.

1. Delawares. 2. Munsees. 3. Mohegans. (4. Abenakis, not in the Table.) 5. Etchemins or Malisetes. 6. Micmacs.

The eastern Algonkins were subdivided into a number of nations politically distinct; but those properly so distinguished were, in reality, less numerous than the early accounts represent. Distinctness of dialect furnishes a more reliable criterion than the nominal independence of particular bands. Separate bands of the same nation have not only received separate names, but a multiplicity of names have been given to the same nation. Our Indian nations have rarely been known by the names with which they designate themselves; but usually by those conferred upon them by contiguous nations. If classified by dialects the number having a place in our colonial history would be greatly reduced.

Between the St. Lawrence below Quebec, and Hudson's Bay, there was a scanty Algonkin population, of which Mr. Gallatin has preserved the names of the Scoffies, and the Sheshatapoosh. The country, however, was nearly destitute of inhabitants. In Nova Scotia, and in the regions bordering the Gulf of St. Lawrence, and the islands adjacent, were the Micmacs; upon the St. John's River, and south of it, were the Etchemins, now known as the Malisetes; and between the St. John's and the Kennebec were the Abenakis. These three nations were distinct, each having an independent dialect. The New England Indians occupied the remainder of New England, the eastern banks of Hudson River, and Long Island. They were closely allied in blood and language. The principal nations were the Narragansetts of Massachusetts, the Wampanoags of Rhode Island, the Pequots of Connecticut, and the Mohegans of the Hudson. They were thinly spread over these areas. Advancing southward the Delawares, of whom the Minsi were a portion, and the Munsees occupied parts of New Jersey, Delaware, and eastern Pennsylvania; whilst the Nantikokes occupied between Delaware and Chesapeake Bay in eastern and southern Maryland. In Virginia upon the Rappahannock and James Rivers, were the Powhattans and some minor bands. Still further south, upon the shores of the Atlantic along Cape Hatteras were the Pamplicos, and south of them the Cheraws, of whom but little is known. They were

from Friend Harvey, containing the Shawnee complete. This venerable and estimable gentleman, as well as his family before him, had been an active friend of the Shawnees while they resided in Ohio; and he had followed them to their new home in Kansas, where he was then laboring with zeal and perseverance for their spiritual and temporal welfare. His knowledge of the language, and the familiar acquaintance of many Shawnees with the English, enabled him to trace out their system, through all its complications, with precision and accuracy. He was the first to bring out the anomalous feature of the Indian system which established the relationship of uncle and nephew between the children of a brother and sister, which afterwards formed the basis upon which the Mississippi and Missouri nations were organized in separate groups. In 1859 I verified the work of Friend Harvey at the Shawnee Reservation, and found it correct in every particular. In 1860 he went with me to the Reservations in southern Kansas, which gave me an excellent opportunity to become acquainted with this philanthropist. I shall long retain the impression which the goodness of his character, and his noble and distinguished zeal for the welfare of the Indian family produced upon my mind. No better and no purer man than Friend Harvey lives upon the earth.

probably straggling bands from Virginia. The foregoing were the principal Atlantic Algonkin nations.

Of those enumerated, the Micmacs, the Etchemins, the Abenakis, the Mohegan, the Delawares, and the Munsees still maintain a distinct political existence. Beside these, there are about a thousand of the descendants of the New England Indians, more or less mixed in blood, still living in Massachusetts, Connecticut, and Rhode Island,[1] and about the same number in Maine.

The Atlantic Algonkins were never very numerous, although they cultivated to some extent, and possessed excellent fisheries. They were probably more numerous, in equal areas, than the Gichigamian or Mississippi nations; but still inconsiderable in numbers. Throughout the continent, with the exception of parts of Mexico and Central America, and the valley of the Columbia, the Indian population was everywhere scanty. It is impossible at the present time, under the suggestions of ample experience, to repress the tendency to exaggerated estimates. Even the census which has come in at last, to dispel these illusions, does not shed a convincing light upon the past, because the hypothesis is allowed to intervene, that they have wasted away between the estimate and the census. Experience shows that nomadic nations, and more especially nations composed of fishermen and hunters, increase slowly and waste slowly; and that the equilibrium of numbers is better preserved among them than it is among agricultural and commercial peoples. In a volume now open before me are estimates made as late as 1834, in which the Crow Indians are stated to number 45,000, the Blackfeet 30,000, and the Shoshonees 30,000. These nations were then well known to the Fur companies, and to the traders, although they had not at that time come under any direct relations to the government. In 1849, after treaties had been formed with them, and an effort had been made to ascertain their numbers, by a count of lodges, the Crows were estimated at 4000, the Blackfeet at 13,000, and the Shoshonees at 700. An actual census, when taken, will probably reduce both the Crows and Blackfeet considerably below these numbers. This is undoubtedly a fair illustration of the deceptive character of all the estimates made of our aboriginal inhabitants. With our present experience there is no further excuse for such extravagance. The early Spanish estimates of the inhabitants of Mexico and Central America reveal the same tendency to exaggeration, and upon a scale of such utter recklessness as to become insulting to common intelligence. The Indian inhabitants of these countries were undoubtedly more numerous than the northern Indians, through a higher and more productive agriculture; but their cultivation was of garden beds, and not of the field, and their occupation and use of the soil were limited to infinitesimal patches compared with the whole area held. Neither is it so assuredly true that the American Indian nations have perished at the fright-

---

[1] In the year 1862 I met on the Mississippi River a half-blood Narragansett woman, with two Pequots, her grandchildren, then on their way to Kansas, where they resided. She was descended, on the mother's side, from the Narragansetts, amongst whom descent as well as nationality follows the female line. This made her a Narragansett. She further informed me that both the Pequot and Narragansett dialects were now extinct.

ful rate generally supposed. Many Indians, indeed, were destroyed in the wars of colonization; and many others perished through vices contracted by contact with civilization; but those nations, of which no trace now remains, were rather broken up and dispersed among kindred people than annihilated. This process of dispersion and absorption has been going on continuously from the commencement of the career of the Ganowánian family upon the North American continent. It has resulted in known instances, since the epoch of colonization, from wars waged amongst themselves, as in the case of the Eries and Neutral Nation dispersed by the Iroquois; and in wars waged by the colonists, as in the case of the Natchez Indians, supposed to have been exterminated by the French, but now incorporated with the Creeks. A reinvestigation of the facts with reference to the numbers and means of subsistence of the American aborigines is necessary to correct the current impressions on these subjects.

In the Table will be found the systems of relationship of the Micmacs, Etchemins, Mohegans, Delawares, and Munsees. They represent the northern, the central, and the southern subdivisions of the eastern Algonkins. All that was peculiar in the system of these nations will presumptively be found in the forms given in the Table.

1. Delawares. The Delawares are undoubtedly one of the oldest of the Algonkin nations, and are so recognized by their congeners. They are styled " grandfathers" by the greater portion of these nations, both eastern and western, which of itself is significant of the fact. Their dialect has departed very widely from the common standards. They are now established upon a reservation in Kansas, and numbered in 1855, nine hundred persons. Through missionary instruction and agricultural pursuits, they have made as much progress as the Shawnees.

First Indicative Feature in their system of relationship. My brother's son and daughter, *Ego* a male, are my son and daughter, *N'-kweese'*, and *N'-da-nuss'*. With *Ego* a female, they are the same. These last relationships, which are a departure from the common form, result from the absence of the relationship of aunt.

Second. My sister's son and daughter, *Ego* a male, are my nephew and niece, *Longue'-kw'* and *Longue-kwä'*. With *Ego* a female, they are my son and daughter.

Third. My father's brother is my little father, *Noh·-tut*.

Fourth. My father's brother's son and daughter are my step-brother and step-sister, the males and females using different terms, *Nee-mä'-tus* and *N'-doh·-kwä-yome'* (m. s.), *N'-dun-oo-yome'*, and *Neet-koh·'-kw'* (f. s.)

Fifth. Wanting. My father's sister is my mother.

Sixth. My mother's brother is my uncle, *N'-shee'-se.*

Seventh. My mother's sister is my little mother, *N'-gä-ha'-tut.*

Eighth. My mother's sister's son and daughter are my step-brother and my step-sister, the males and the females using different terms.

Ninth. My grandfather's brother is my grandfather, *Nu-moh·'-ho-mus'.*

Tenth. The grandchildren of my brothers and sisters, and of my step-brothers and step-sisters are, without distinction, my grandchildren.

There are three peculiar features in the system of the Delawares, two of which are now met with for the first time. In the first place, the relationship of aunt is unknown among them, the father's sister being a mother. This is also the case among some other nations. Secondly. My father's brother and my mother's sister are my "little father," and my "little mother," to distinguish them from my own father and mother. This form is restricted to the eastern Algonkins, and is not universal among them. It seems probable that it was engrafted at a later period, upon the common system under influences similar to those which led them as well as the Great Lake nations to substitute the step-relationships in place of the full or primary. Thirdly and lastly, the children of a brother and sister are step-brothers and step-sisters to each other, instead of being placed in some more remote relationship, than that between the children of two or more brothers, and two or more sisters, as required by the principles of the system. This is a very great deviation from uniformity, and is the fourth and last form in which it is found. It is also a retrograde movement, since it invades the spirit if not the substance of the system. How to explain this divergence is not readily seen. When placed in the same relationships as the children of brothers and the children of sisters the effect of the classification in the last two cases is weakened. It seems probable that previously to the introduction of the step-relationships that the children of brothers were brothers and sisters to each other, and that the children of sisters were the same, whilst the children of a brother and sister were either uncle and nephew, mother and daughter, as among the Shawnees, or son and father, daughter and mother, as among the Creeks; and that the change was a modern refinement to distinguish each and all of them from own brothers and sisters. By the use of the step-relationships a singular incongruity was removed from the system, although the manner of its removal introduced even a greater blemish. In any view that may be taken of the Delaware system, it is in this one respect a deteriorated form.

A sufficient number of the radical characteristics of the common system are found in the Delaware to establish its identity with that of the other Algonkin nations, and to sustain their right of admission with all the nations previously named, into the Ganowánian family. These deviations are much less surprising than that a system so complicated should have maintained itself through so many ages, and amongst so many widely separated nations, and still be found coincident in so many of its minute details.

2. Munsees. The Munsee dialect affiliates closely with the Delaware. The two are probably immediate subdivisions of the same people. A few of the Munsees are now in Kansas, and the remainder in Wisconsin. They number but two hundred souls. Their system of relationship is, in the main, nearest to the Delaware.

First Indicative Feature. My brother's son and daughter, *Ego* a male, are my son and daughter. With *Ego* a female, they are the same. The females have neither nephews nor nieces.

Second. My sister's son and daughter, *Ego* a male, are my nephew and niece. With *Ego* a female, they are my son and daughter.

Third. My father's brother is my little father.

Fourth. My father's brother's son and daughter are my brother and sister, elder or younger.

Fifth. My father's sister is my aunt.   This relationship exists without its correlatives of nephew and niece.

Sixth. My mother's brother is my uncle.

Seventh. My mother's sister is my little mother.

Eighth. My mother's sister's son and daughter are my brother and sister, elder or younger.

Ninth. My grandfather's brother is my grandfather.

Tenth. The grandchildren of my brother and sister, and of my collateral brothers and sisters, are, without distinction, my grandchildren.

The other relationships follow in accordance with those above given, which control the remainder.

3. Mohegans.   Their original name, *Mo-he'-kun-ne-uk'*, which they still call themselves, and from which Mohegan is derived, signifies "Seaside People."   Their range at the epoch of their discovery was along the Hudson and in the western part of Connecticut.   They are closely allied in blood with the Pequots, who were probably their nearest congeners.   All of the New England Indians, it is said, spoke mutually intelligible dialects.   Upon this subject Drake remarks: "Such was the language of the Mohegans, the Pequots, the Narragansetts, and the Nipmuks; so near did they approach one another that each could understand the other throughout the united extent of their territories."[1]   Their system of relationship is still in constant use, although they number but a few more than the Munsees.

First Indicative Feature.   My brother's son and daughter, *Ego* a male, are each my step-child.   The term used is in common gender.   With *Ego* a female, they are the same.

Second. My sister's son and daughter, *Ego* a male, are my nephew and niece. With *Ego* a female, they are my son and daughter.

Third. My father's brother is my step-father.

Fourth. My father's brother's son and daughter are my step-brother and stepsister.   The males and females use different terms.

Fifth. My father's sister is my step-mother.   This is probably an error.   If correct, the Mohegans differ in this respect from all other nations.

Sixth. My mother's brother is my uncle.

Seventh. My mother's sister is my step-mother.

Eighth. My mother's sister's son and daughter are my step-brother and stepsister.

Ninth. My grandfather's brother is my grandfather.

Tenth. The grandchildren of my brothers and sisters, and of my step-brothers and step-sisters, are my grandchildren.

It will be noticed that the Mohegan form, as to the use of the step-relationships, agrees very closely with the Ojibwa.   From this fact it seems not improbable that a portion of the New England Indians, after the overthrow of their political power, found their way to the Great Lake nations, and became incorporated with them, and that it furnishes an explanation of the coincidences in special features in their

---

[1] Book of Indians of North America, Book II. p. 87.

respective systems of relationship. Intermixture of blood on a scale sufficiently large might be adequate to the introduction of minor peculiarities not inconsistent with the fundamental conceptions of the system. It is the only way in which any modification, however slight, seems likely to have been adopted. In 1849 there were about four hundred Mohegans living in Connecticut, and about fifty in Kansas.

4. Micmacs. The Micmac dialect, with which the Etchemin closely affiliates, diverges very sensibly from those of the remaining Eastern Algonkins. To produce the amount of change it now exhibits would require several centuries of separation. They are now scattered over parts of Nova Scotia, Cape Breton, Prince Edward's Island, Newfoundland, and the district of Gaspé. It is supposed that the Indians found by Cabot, in 1497, on the shores of the Gulf of St. Lawrence, were Micmacs; and that those found in the same region by Jaques Cartier, in 1534, were the same. For their system of relationship, as well as that of the Etchemins, I am indebted to Rev. Silas T. Rand, of Hantsport, Nova Scotia, who for many years has been a missionary among them, and who is intimately acquainted with their dialects.

First Indicative Feature. My brother's son and daughter, *Ego* a male, are my son and daughter. With *Ego* a female, they are my nephew and niece.

Second. My sister's son and daughter, *Ego* a male, are my nephew and niece. With *Ego* a female, they are my son and daughter.

Third. My father's brother is my little father.

Fourth. My father's brother's son and daughter are my brother and sister, elder or younger.

Fifth. My father's sister is my aunt.

Sixth. My mother's brother is my uncle.

Seventh. My mother's sister is my little mother.

Eighth. My mother's sister's son and daughter are my brother and sister, elder or younger.

Ninth. My grandfather's brother is my grandfather.

Tenth. The grandchildren of my brothers and sisters, and of my collateral brothers and sisters, are my grandchildren.

With respect to the children of a brother and sister, they are brothers and sisters, elder or younger.

5. Etchemins. Like the Micmacs and the Delawares, the Etchemins are among the oldest of the Algonkin nations. Under their modern name of Malisetes they now reside in the British province of New Brunswick, and are few in number.

First Indicative Feature. My brother's son and daughter, *Ego* a male, are my step-son and step-daughter. With *Ego* a female, they are my nephew and niece.

Second. My sister's son and daughter, *Ego* a male, are my nephew and niece. With *Ego* a female, they are my step-son and step-daughter.

Third. My father's brother is my step-father.

Fourth. My father's brother's son and daughter are my step-brother and step-sister. There is some doubt on these relationships, from the omission in the schedule of the terms for a man's and woman's step-brother.

Fifth. My father's sister is my aunt.

Sixth. My mother's brother is my uncle.

Seventh. My mother's sister's son and daughter are my step-brother and step-sister, or my brother and sister, elder or younger.

Ninth. My grandfather's brother is my grandfather.

Tenth. The grandchildren of my brothers and sisters, of my collateral brothers and sisters, and of my step-brothers and sisters are my grandchildren.

With respect to the children of a brother and sister they are cousins, as the translation of the term is given by Mr. Rand. But some doubt rests upon the fact from the omissions above referred to.

The Etchemin closes the series of schedules of the Atlantic Algonkin nations. With the exception of the Powhattans, now extinct, they show the forms of the principal, as well as most important, of these nations. It is a reasonable inference that the system of the unrepresented nations must have been in substantial agreement with them. The terms of relationship for the most part, are the same words dialectically changed, which are found in the systems of the other Algonkin nations, which, together with the identity of their radical characteristics, tends to show that all of these nations received the system, with the terms from the common source of the Algonkin speech.

IV. Rocky Mountain Nations.

1. Blackfeet. 2. Ahahnelins. (3. Arapahoes, not in the Table.)

These nations are not inhabitants of the Rocky Mountain chain; but rather of their eastern slopes and of the prairies immediately eastward. These mountains form their western boundary, and define the western limits of the spread of the Algonkins. It is not therefore an inappropriate name.

1. Blackfeet. Their range is along the base of the mountains, and between the Missouri and the south branch of the Siskatchewun. They are more numerous at the present time than any Algonkin nation, except the Crees, numbering, in 1849, about thirteen thousand. When Lewis and Clarke passed through this region, in 1805, they were established upon the Marias River, north of the Missouri; but it does not appear that they met with them. Their previous home country is supposed to have been upon the south branch of the Siskatchewan, beyond which location they have not been traced. The Blackfeet are a well formed, hardy, and courageous people. For many years they waged a continuous warfare against the Upsarokas or Crows, whom they gradually forced southward and finally expelled from the present Blackfoot area. Whether they have always lived in the vicinity of the Rocky Mountains, or were forced westward in the general retrogression of the Indian nations, which commenced at the epoch of European colonization, there are at present no means of ascertaining. Like the other prairie Indians, they are indebted to the horse for their present means of support and for their increase in numbers. They depend for subsistence upon animal food exclusively, and upon the horse for the means of pursuing the buffalo. They raise this animal in herds; and are in fact a nation of horsemen—of mounted men. As horsemen, they are equal if not superior to all other American Indians.[1] They

---

[1] All Indians are immoderate riders. They run their horses, generally when alone, or in small parties. I remember the first time I met a small party of Blackfeet near the foot of the mountains,

take excellent care of their horses, although they abuse them by immoderate use; and, it is said, that one raised among them and sold away is glad to be restored to the free and roving life of the plains.

The Blackfeet are divided into three independent bands or embryo nations—the Blackfeet proper, the Piegans, and the Bloods. Their language is spoken in three dialects, but the differences are so slight that they are mutually perfectly intelligible. The dialects of the first and third are so little changed as scarcely to deserve the distinction, whilst the Piegan has diverged considerably from both. The extent of the difference will be seen by comparing the terms of relationship in the Table. The proportion of terms of relationship which are common in the Blackfoot and in other Algonkin dialects is much larger than it is in the vocables for common objects. There is a large foreign element in the Blackfoot vocables, or a new coinage of words from common roots, one or the other, which places this language at quite a distance from the standard form. Many of the traders have acquired the Blackfoot, and a few of the Blackfeet have acquired English, but their dialects are not as yet fully open and accessible. It was my good fortune to meet the persons who were best qualified to furnish both the Piegan and Blood Blackfoot system of relationship. The first was James Bird, a half-blood Cree, who had lived twenty-five years with the Blackfeet, and had acted for many years as a government interpreter. I found him at the Red River Settlement, in 1861, and procured the Piegan system from him and his wife, who was a woman of the Piegan Blackfoot nation. The others were Alexander Culbertson, who was formerly and for twenty years the chief factor of the American Fur Company, resident at Fort Benton, in the Blackfoot country, and his wife, a Blood Blackfoot woman, from whom I procured the system of the Bloods. They happened to be at Fort Benton in 1862, at the time of my visit, and both were fluent speakers of both Blackfoot and English.

The Piegan system will be adopted as the standard form.

First Indicative Feature. My brother's son and daughter, *Ego* a male, are my step-son and step-daughter, *N'-do'-tä-ko* and *N'-do'-to-tun*. With *Ego* a female, they are my nephew and niece.

Second. My sister's son and daughter, *Ego* a male, are my nephew and niece, *N'-do'-tä-yose* and *Nee-mis'-sä*. With *Ego* a female, they are my step-son and step-daughter.

Third. My father's brother is my step-father, *N'-to'-to-mä.*

Fourth. My father's brother's son and daughter are my brother and sister, elder or younger, *Neese-sä'* or *Nïs-kan'-ä*, and *Nee-mis'-tä* or *Ne-sis'-sä*.

---

that one of them having occasion to do an unimportant errand two miles away, caught a horse from a small herd near by, put a piece of rope around his under jaw, securing it with a noose, and mounting him without a saddle, and with no other bridle than the rope, started the horse at the top of his speed, and did not slacken his pace until he had reached his destination. The same act precisely I noticed in the Sawk and Fox Indians in Kansas. When a party of mounted Indians are riding on the prairie they go two, three, and sometimes four abreast. Deep trails are thus made on their main lines of travel. I have followed them for miles in Kansas and Nebraska. They are usually about eighteen inches wide, and about nine inches deep, and are quite conspicuous in the early part of the season, before they are obscured by the growing grass.

29   March, 1870.

Fifth. My father's sister is my aunt, *Ne-to'-tarse.*

Sixth. My mother's brother is my uncle, *Ne-to'-tah·se.*

Seventh. My mother's sister is my step-mother, *N'-to'-tox-is.*

Eighth. My mother's sister's son and daughter are my brother and sister, elder or younger.

Ninth. My grandfather's brother is my grandfather, *Ne-tä-ke-ä'-sä.*

Tenth. The grandchildren of my brother and sister, and of my collateral brothers and sisters, are my grandchildren.

The children of a brother and sister are cousins. There are terms for male and female cousin used by the males, and another set for the same used by the females.

It will be noticed that the Blackfoot system, as well as dialect, approaches nearer to those of the Great Lake nations than to any other group of the Algonkin stem.

2. Ahahnelins, or Gros Ventres of the Prairie. Of the early history of this people very little is known. They appear to be a subdivision of the Arapahoes, the separation, if such were the case, having occurred at a very early period. Lewis and Clarke speak of a " great nation called Fall Indians, who occupy the intermediate country between the Missouri and the Siskatchewan, and who are known as the Minnitarees of the Missouri and the Minnitarees of Fort due Prairie."[1] Mr. Gallatin, the most thorough of American ethnologists, speaks of a confederacy of five tribes between the Missouri and the Siskatchewan, " viz., the Satsika or Blackfeet, the Kena or Blood Indians, the Piekan or Pagan Indians, the Atsina, Arapahoes, Fall Indians or Gros Ventres, and the Susses. The first three speak the same language, which belongs to the Algonkin family. The Susses speak a dialect of the Athapascan. The Arapahoes have a language of which we have as yet but a scanty vocabulary."[2] In his ethnological map, published in 1848, he locates the Arapahoes between the Missouri and Siskatchewan, with the Asiniboins on their east and the Blackfeet on their west, omitting the others, thus perhaps implying that the Arapahoes were the true nation mentioned under the four alternative names. But the Ahahnelins, now known under the vulgar name of the Gros Ventres of the Prairie, are probably the same people mentioned under the alternative name of the Gros Ventres, so that the four represented as one, were in fact two.[3]

In 1853, the Ahahnelins were established upon Milk River, between its mouth and the Bear's Paw Mountain. "This tribe," says Gov. Stephens, " numbered, in 1855, two thousand five hundred and twenty souls, and owned at least three thousand horses."[4] Their dialect has diverged greatly from the common form ; but it tends with the Arapahoe and Shiyan, in the direction of the dialects of the Mississippi nations, particularly the Menominee and Shawnee. This is shown by the terms of relationship, which are superior for comparison to ordinary vocabulary words. It was with extreme difficulty that I was able to obtain that portion of their system of relationship which is given in the Table, very few of the traders

---

[1] Travels, p. 97.   [2] Trans. Am. Eth. Soc. 11, Intro. CVI.

[3] The Minnitarees are often called the Gros Ventres of the Missouri.

[4] Explorations, Pacific Railroad, XII. Pt. 1, 239.

acquire this language, and none of the natives, as far as I could learn, spoke English. It was necessary to work it out through the Blackfoot, which many of them speak; and in this I was assisted by Mrs. Culbertson before mentioned. The woman from whom it was obtained was the wife of a French trader, and spoke the Blackfoot.[1] The work would have been made more complete if direct communication had been possible. It was carried sufficiently far to ascertain the indicative relationships, and to establish the identity of the system with the common form.

First Indicative Feature. My brother's son and daughter, *Ego* a male, are my son and daughter. With *Ego* a female, they are my nephew and niece.

Second. My sister's son and daughter, *Ego* a male, are my nephew and niece. With *Ego* a female, they are my son and daughter.

Third. My father's brother is my father.

Fourth. My father's brother's son and daughter are my brother and sister, elder or younger.

Fifth. My father's sister is my aunt.

Sixth. My mother's brother is my uncle.

Seventh. My mother's sister is my mother.

Eighth. My mother's sister's son and daughter are my brother and sister, elder or younger.

Ninth. My grandfather's brother is my grandfather.

Tenth. The grandchildren of my brothers and sisters, and the grandchildren of my collateral brothers and sisters, are my grandchildren.

With respect to the children of a brother and sister, they are also brothers and sisters to each other. This last classification is not in accordance with the principles of the system.

The Ahahnelins close the series of Algonkin nations represented in the Table.

---

[1] A very singular fact may be mentioned in connection with *E-thǎ'-be*, the Ahahnelin woman from whom it was obtained. After ascertaining that she could speak her language and the Blackfoot only, I sought her husband, supposing that I could communicate with her through him; but I found that he could neither speak her language, nor she his; and that there was no common articulate language which both understood. When asked whether she was really his wife, he replied that she was, and to the question how long they had been married, he answered three years. When finally asked how he was able to communicate with her, the singular fact was stated that "they conversed with each other by the language of signs." It may not be generally known that there is a fully developed and very expressive language of signs, in common use among the western Indian nations, by means of which they are able to communicate all of the ordinary wants of life, besides general information upon a great variety of subjects. I have seen a Minnitaree and Arickaree, who could not speak a word of each other's language, sit down together and converse for hours by signs alone. Many of the traders know this language, and speak of its efficacy in the highest terms of praise. The motions are easy and graceful, and the signs ingenious and expressive. I think we find in this sign language the germinal principle from which came, first, the pictographs of the Northern Indians, and of the Aztecs; and severally, as its ultimate development, the ideographic, and possibly, the hieroglyphic language of the Palenque and Copan monuments. When I mentioned the case of this woman to Father De Smet, he informed me that he had known a number of such instances among the nations in the valley of the Columbia.

Their system of consanguinity as it now prevails in twenty-four dialects, more or less distinct, has been presented and compared, through the indicative relationships, with the typical form.   The identity of the system of all of these nations in whatever is radical is not only manifest, but this identity continues through many minute particulars which are not essential to the unity of the system.   There is a not less striking identity in the classification of marriage relatives, amongst the widely separated Algonkin nations, which it would have been interesting to trace had it been necessary to strengthen, from this source, the principal argument for unity of origin.   The marriage relationships, standing alone, would have been sufficient to demonstrate this question.   They are fully spread out in the Table. The maintenance of the system amongst the Algonkin nations with so much fulness and precision, and through the periods of time required for the formation of these dialects, and for their divergence from each other to the extent now exhibited, yields decisive evidence of its enduring nature, and of the vital energy of the principles it embodies.   But the identity thus established does not expend its force in demonstrating the unity of origin of the Algonkin nations.   This is the least important of its revelations.   This system has shown itself capable of crossing intact the barrier that separates one stock language from another; and of maintaining itself, in each, through the still longer periods of time which the present condition and relations of the languages of these stems of the Ganowánian family implies.   Thus far, in the progress of the investigation, the radical forms of the original system have not only perpetuated themselves, unimpared, in the Dakotan and Algonkin nations, but its minute details have remained coincident to an extent, as remarkable as it is instructive.   In other words the evidence of unity is in superabundance.   It tends to show that these two stems of the family converge to a common point of union nearer, in point of time, than the other stems of the family whose systems of relationship remain to be considered.

In subsequent chapters we are to follow it amongst other great stocks of the Ganowánian family, and to subject it to still other tests of time and experience. As it is shown in the Table it will not be found with the same fulness of development, or with the same precision in subordinate details, which it has hitherto displayed.   Neither is it essential to the establishment of the identity of the system, and the consequent unity of origin of the people, that the points of agreement should be as multiform and decisive as they have been in the systems of the Algonkin and Dakotan nations.   It can lose much of its agreement in minor details, and even part with a portion of its fundamental framework, and yet be capable of identification as a common system.   The difficulties forshadowed do not arise so much from actual ascertained deviations from the typical form, as from the want of a correct knowledge of the form which does exist.   Amongst the nations whose systems are about to be considered, the facilities for investigation are less complete, and the sources of information are less accessible, than within the areas over which we have passed.   The disorganized and demoralized condition of particular nations does not imply the overthrow of their system of relationship.   There are abundant reasons for believing that it is the last domestic institution to give way.   But imperfect and incomplete schedules present a serious as well as intrinsic difficulty not easily overcome. We may be able to trace our way with tolerable assurance by means of the indicative landmarks of the common system; but not with that perfect reliance which the uniform reappearance in nation after nation, thus far, of the same identical forms carried down to minute particulars, was calculated to inspire. On passing from one great stem of the family to another it would be expected to find, in a system so elaborate and complicated, differences more or less great, and deviations from uniformity more or less marked; for no system can be held indefinitely independent of external influences. This would especially be the case where a people, less numerous than the inhabitants of a small market town, have possessed for ages an independent dialect as well as nationality. We are also to visit the valley of the Columbia, which there are cogent reasons for believing was the seminary of the Ganowánian family, and the initial point of migrations from which successive, though feeble, streams emerged for the peopling of both of the American continents; and which continued to send forth bands of emigrants down to the very epoch of European discovery. If, in point of fact, it was the original seat of the family, the domestic institutions of the modern nations residing in this valley would be expected to be heterogeneous rather than pure; whilst the separate streams, flowing therefrom at an ancient epoch, and subdividing into many as they spread abroad, would be more likely to possess homogeneous institutions. There are at the present time several stock languages in the valley of the Columbia. They are less open and accessible than those east of the mountains. Notwithstanding the inadequacy of the materials thus far obtained, the traces of the common system are not less certain and decisive upon the Pacific slopes than they have been seen to be on the Atlantic side of the continent; although the system has been worked out with much less completeness.

CHAPTER V.

SYSTEM OF RELATIONSHIP OF THE GANOWANIAN FAMILY.—Continued.

Athapasco-Apache, and other Nations.

I. Athapasco-Apache Nations—Identity of the Branches—1. Athapascan Nations—Their Area and Dialects—System of Relationship of Slave Lake Indians—Its Indicative Features—Identical with the Common Form—System of Hare Indians—Indicative Relationships—System of Red Knives—Last two in General Agreement with the First—Kŭtchin or Louchieux—Their Area and Personal Appearance—Indicative Features of their System of Relationship —It agrees with the First—Tukuthe—Their System of Relationship—It agrees with the First—2. Apache Nations —Valley of the Columbia—Remarkable Characteristics of this Region—Abundance of Natural Subsistence—The Nursery of the Ganowánian Family—Initial Point of Migrations—Great Number of Stock Languages.—II. Salish Nations—Dialects—Not fully accessible—1. Spokane System of Relationship—Opulence of the Nomenclature—Indicative Features—Special Characteristics—It possesses the Radical Features of the Common System—2. Okinaken—Schedule incomplete—Agrees with the Spokane.—III. Sahaptin Nations—Dialects—Yakama System of Relationship—Its Indicative Features—It contains the Principal Characteristics of the Common System.—IV. Kootenay System—Schedule Incomplete—Kootenays and Flatbows possess an Independent Stock Language—Elaborateness of System within this Area.—V. Shoshonee Nations—Their Area—Their Migration the last, in point of time, from the Valley of the Columbia—A Pending Migration at the Epoch of European Colonization—System of Relationship of the Tabegwaches—Fulness of the Nomenclature—Its Special Features—Contains Characteristics of the Common System—The Tabegwaches closed the series, except the Village Indians, and the Eskimo—System nearly Universal amongst the North American Indian Nations—It furnishes a substantial Basis for their Consolidation into a Great Family of Mankind.

THE Athapasco-Apache nations, in their two principal divisions, are widely separated from each other geographically. One of them, the Athapascan, occupies the chief part of the territories of the Hudson's Bay Company; and the greater part of New Caledonia, or British Columbia, west of the Rocky Mountains; whilst the other, the Apache, holds the greater part of New Mexico, and the northern parts of the Mexican State of Chihuahua. Each division consists of a number of independent nations. The identity of their languages was first shown by the late Prof. William W. Turner in 1852, and afterwards more fully in 1856.[1] It was a remarkable as well as important discovery. Their respective areas of occupancy were not comparable with those held by the Algonkin and Dakotan nations, which serves to explain their personal inferiority. But they have maintained their position, and acquired large territorial possessions by means of which they have raised themselves to an important position in the Ganowánian family. They possess a single stock language spoken in numerous dialects. None of these nations formerly cultivated, with the exception of the Navajoes. In the northern division agriculture was impossible from the coldness of the climate; and in the southern

---

[1] Explorations for a Railroad Route, &c. to the Pacific, VIII. Rep. on Ind. Tribes, p. 84.

equally impossible, without irrigation, from its dryness. The Athapascans depend for subsistence upon fish and game; the Apaches partly upon game, but chiefly upon the fruits of marauding enterprises upon their neighbors. A small portion, however, are now cultivators to some extent.

Athapasco-Apache Nations.

I. Athapascan Nations.

1. Slave Lake Indians (*A-cha'-o-tin-ne*). 2. Red Knives (*Täl-sote'-e-nä*). 3. Makenzie River Indians (*Tä-nä'-tin-ne,* possibly identical with the Hares). 4. Kŭtchin or Louchieux. 5. Takuthe. (6. Chepewyans. 7. Dog Rib. 8. Beaver Indians). 9. Noh·hannies. 10. Sheep Indians. 11. Sussees. 12. Tacullies not in the Table).

These nations occupy a broad and continuous area, extending from the Churchill River and near the north branch of the Siskatchewan, on the south, to the country of the Eskimo on the borders of the Arctic Sea on the north; and from the Barren Lands and Hudson's Bay on the east, to the Rocky Mountains on the west. They are also spread irregularly over a large area west of the mountains in British Columbia, ranging northward to the Yukon and down this river into the Russian Possessions, and westward nearly to the Pacific Ocean. Southward of these areas traces of their language have been discovered on the Umpkwa and Rogue Rivers in Oregon, and as low down as the Trinity River in the northern part of California. They are probably more numerous at the present time than at any former period, although thinly spread over these immense regions. In 1856 the officers of the Hudson's Bay Company estimated the number of "Thickwood Indians," east of the Rocky Mountains, at thirty-five thousand.[1] This would include all of the Athapascans, as well as the Crees around Hudson's Bay, and that portion of the Blackfeet without the United States. What portion of the eighty thousand Indians west of the mountains are Athapascans I am unable to state.

There are several distinct dialects of the northern branch of the Athapasco-Apache language; but, up to the present time they have not been sufficiently explored and systematized to determine their number. It is evident, from the ordinary vocabularies, that these dialects affiliate very closely; they are nearer to each other than the Algonkin, between the extremes of which there is a wide interval, and very much nearer than the Dakotan, the extremes of which are without any affinity in their vocables. If a conjecture might be indulged, founded

---

[1] Classification of Indians in the Hudson's Bay Territory.

"Thickwood Indians, east side of Rocky Mountains	. . . .	35,000
The Plain Tribes, Blackfeet, &c.	. . . .	25,000
The Eskimo	. . . .	4,000
Indians settled in Canada	. . . .	3,000
Indians in British Oregon, and on the northwest coast	. . .	80,000
		147,000
Whites and Half-breeds in Hudson's Bay Territory .	. . . .	11,000
		158,000"

"Report from Select Committee on the Hudson's Bay Company" made to the British Parliament in 1857. Report App. No. 2, p. 367.

upon a comparison of the respective dialects of these three stems of the Ganowa
nian family, it would be that the Dakotan became first detached from the common
trunk, the Algonkin second, and the Athapasco-Apache third.   For similar reasons
the Shoshonee, hereafter to be considered, must be placed subsequent to the last.
In other words, since there is no ascertainable common trunk, these three streams
of speech flowed outward from the common source of the language, in the order of
time named with respect to each other.   The subjoined comparative table of five
Athapascan dialects taken in connection with the terms of relationship in the table
(Table II), will illustrate the degree of their nearness to each other.[1]   Of these vocabularies, the first two were furnished to me by the late Robert Kennicott, who spent
several years in the Hudson's Bay Territory in scientific explorations.   The others
were taken from Richardson's Arctic Expedition.   They represent the extremes of
the Athapascan area east of the mountains.   The dialect of the Tacullies, who are
west of the mountains, shows more divergence, but the identity is obvious.   The
Sussees occupied the extreme southwestern corner of the Athapascan area east of
the mountain, and were the frontagers of the Blackfeet.   When in the Hudson's
Bay Territory in 1861, I was unable to procure either the Sussee system of rela-

	[1] ATHAPASCAN DIALECTS.				
	Slave Lake Indians. Kennicott.	Beaver Indians. Kennicott.	Chepewyan. Richardson's Coll. Vocab.	Dog Rib. Richardson's Coll. Vocabs.	Kŭtchin. Richardson's Coll. Vocabs.
1. Head,	Et-the	Et-t'-the	Zed-thi (ny)	Bet-thi & izat-	
2. Hair,	A-ga'	Ah-gä'	Thi-e-gah*	Theo-ya [the	
3. Ear,	Et-tsä'-ga	At-tsung'-ä		Setz-r-rgha (pl)	
4. Eye,	An-dä'-ga	A-tah'	Nack-hay*	Tzen-nhae (pl)	
5. Nose,	Ing-ä-goŋ'	Ing-ä-goŋ		Tin-net-ze	
6. Mouth,	A-thä'	A-thä'		Tze-thä	
7. Arrow,	Eh-ton'-ah	Eh-to'-ne	Kah		Ki-e
8. Bow,	Eh-tiŋ	Eh-tin'	El-thi, and el-tä		Net-heikh
9. Sun,	Sah	Sah	Sakh	Sa	R'-say-è
10. Stars,	Thŭm	Thŭn	Thun	Thun and thi-u	Thun
11. Day,	D-zin-d'-zen'-de	Tsä-tewh	Tzin-na	Zeu-nai	Tzin
12. Night,	Ah-tha-gä	Ka'-a-dä-ty	Het-le-ghè	Te-thi	Ta-tha
13. Rain,	Choŋ	Choŋ	Dsha	Tchon	Ahk-tsin
14. Snow,	Zäth	Zäth	Yath	Tzill and yah	
15. Water,	Tuh	T'-huh	Tu and to	To and tu	Tchu
16. Canoe,	A-lä'-tsuh	Ah-lä'	Tsi	Ki-ala	Tri
17. Good,	Na-zoŋ'	U'-cha	Ne-su & na-zu	Na-i-zou & Naa	Neer-zi
18. Bad,	Na-zu-lä	Ah-ta-u'-cho	Ne-so-ulla	Tle-nai [zo	Bets-hè-te
19. Dog,	H'-kliŋ	Kliŋ	Thling	Cle and kling	Tleine
20. Beaver,	Tsä	Tsä	Tza	Tsa	Se
21. Bear,	Säss	Säss	Sasz	Säs	So
22. Reindeer,			Bek-zi	Bed-su (male)	Bet-zey
23. Fire,	Kwon	Khun	Kkon	Kun and khun	Kon or khon

Those marked with an asterisk were taken from Gallatin's vocabularies.   Where two words are
given for the same object, they were taken from different vocabularies—Sir John Richardson's
Collection.

tionship, or a vocabulary of their language.   It seems to be generally understood that they belong to the Athapascan stock.

The degree of dialectical variation in a stock language is chiefly important for the bearing it may have upon the mutual relations of the people speaking these dialects, and also upon the further question of the time necessary for their development.   But this is subordinate to those greater questions suggested by the existence of these stock languages in certain relations to each other, as independent currents or streams of a common original speech.   Where the vocables of a language have become so completely changed that neither its words nor roots are capable of identification with those of any other language, and several such languages are found to exist, it implies centuries and decades of centuries of time, the lapse of which was necessary to work such an extraordinary transformation of the materials of an original speech.   These stock languages, as they are designated for the want of a better term, hold locked up in their time-worn forms the great problems of Indian ethnology.

The locations of the principal Athapascan nations do not appear to have changed materially since the authority of the Hudson's Bay Company became established over them.   Their ancient southern frontier was undoubtedly forced northward by the western movement of the Crees, the advance northward of the Asiniboins, and the growth of the Blackfoot nations upon their southern border; but with the particulars of these changes we are unacquainted.   The nations above enumerated, as the Athapascan, do not include all of those mentioned by Sir John Richardson, who passed through this area in 1848; neither is it certain that all of them are nationally distinct from each other.   Nearly all of these nations are found upon Mr. Gallatin's Ethnographical map published in 1848.   They are sufficiently certified for the purpose of this work.[1]   The author's materials are insufficient to trace the limits of the several dialects.   In addition to the Athapascan nations enumerated, there are still others supposed by Richardson to be of the same lineage.   From the information which he obtained, he considers the Kenaiyer of Cook's Inlet the Ugalents of King William's Sound, the Atnäer of Copper River, the Koltshaner and some

---

[1] From the work of Sir John Richardson, before referred to, the following condensed statement of their respective areas has been made.   The Chepewyans hold the regions around Athapasca Lake, and range southward to the Churchill River; the Sussees are near the mountains between the sources of the Athapasca and Siskatchewan Rivers; the Hare Indians occupy the banks of the Mackenzie River from Slave Lake downward to the Great Bear Lake; the Dog Ribs inhabit the inland country from Martin's Lake to the Coppermine River; the Red Knives are east of the latter people, and occupy a strip of country running northward from Great Slave Lake, and lying between the Great Fish River and the Coppermine; the Beaver Indians hold the area between the Peace River and the west branch of the Mackenzie; the Noh·hannies occupy the angle between the west branch and the great bend of the Mackenzie River; the Mountain Indians, or Strong Bows, and the Brushwood people, are higher up, and range back to the Rocky Mountains; the Sheep Indians range from the Mackenzie to the mountains, near the 65th parallel; the Kütchin or Louchieux confront the Eskimo on the north, and spread from the Mackenzie River westward to the Yukon, and along this river until they meet the coast tribes of Behring's Sea.   The Takuthe of Peel River affiliate closely with the Kutchin; Indians of the last stock are found on the Porcupine and Russian Rivers, as well as upon the Yukon and Mackenzie, and are estimated by Mr. Murray to number five thousand souls.

other Kolusch tribes to be of the same stock as the Kutchin.[1] If any doubt existed whether the latter nation belonged to the Athapascan branch, it is definitely settled in the affirmative by the Table.

There are five Athapascan nations represented in the Table. These are, first, the Slave Lake Indians, or the *A-cha'-o-tin-ne*, who are called " Slaves" in that region. They are probably the "Strongbows" of Richardson. Second, the Red Knives, or *Täl-sote'-e-nä*. Third, the *Tä-nä'-tin-ne*, whose common name I was unable to ascertain with certainty; but from their range, which was on Mackenzie River, and from their chief trading house, which was Fort Good Hope, they are probably the Hare Indians. In the foregoing list of nations they are mentioned separately as the Mackenzie River Indians. Fourth, the Kŭtchin, or Louchieux; and fifth, the Tukuthe of Peel River. The schedules are too limited in number for the full development of the Athapascan system of relationship; but they are sufficient to yield a general indication of its character.

1. *A-cha'-o-tin-ne*, or Slave Lake Indians. The system of relationship of this people was worked out by the late Robert Kennicott, before mentioned, at Great Slave Lake. This enterprising and lamented naturalist spent five years in the Hudson's Bay Territory, chiefly among the Athapascans, but he did not receive my schedules in time to procure the system of any other nation than this. The thorough and successful manner in which he performed the work increases the regret that it was limited to a single nation. He informed the writer, after his return, that he spent a large amount of labor upon it to make it complete and verify the results.

There are terms in this language for grandfather and grandmother, *Sa-tse'-a* and *Sa-tsun'*; for father and mother, *Sa-tä* and *En'-de*; for son and daughter *Sa-chu'-ah* and *Sa-tu'-ah* used by the males, and *Sa-yǎ'-ze* and *Sa-yä'-dze* used by the females; and a term in common gender for grandchild, *E-t'-thu'-a* used by the males, and *Sa-chä'* used by the females. All ancestors above the first are grandfathers and grandmothers, and all descendants below the last are grandchildren.

There are terms for elder brother and elder sister, *Kŭn-dig'-eh* and *Sä'-dä*; and for younger brother and younger sister, *A-cha'-a* and *A-da'-ze*, and no term for brother or sister in the abstract.

First Indicative Feature. My brother's son and daughter, *Ego* a male, are my step-son and step-daughter, *Tu-zen'-a* and *Sa-yǎ'-dze*. With *Ego* a female, they are my son and daughter. This last classification is variant from the common form; but it finds its analogue in the eastern Algonkin.

Second. My sister's son, *Ego* a male, is my nephew, *Sä'-zy*; her daughter is my grandchild, *Sa-t'-thu'-a*. This last relationship deviates from the typical form. With *Ego* a female, they are my son and daughter.

Third. My father's brother is my step-father, *En-tä'-ah*.

Fourth. My father's brother's son and daughter are my brother and sister, elder or younger.

---

[1] Arctic Expedition, Harper's ed., pp. 236–239.

Fifth. My father's sister is my aunt, *Eh-m'-ba'-dze.*

Sixth. My mother's brother is my uncle, *Thä'-tha.*

Seventh. My mother's sister is my step-mother, *San'-ga.*

Eighth. My mother's sister's son and daughter are my brother and sister, elder or younger.

Ninth. My grandfather's brother and sister, are my grandfather and grandmother, *Set-see'-a, Sa-tsun'.*

Tenth. The grandchildren of my brothers and sisters, and the grandchildren of my collateral brothers and sisters, are severally my grandchildren.

With respect to the children of a brother and sister, they are also brothers and sisters to each other, the relationship of cousin being unknown.

The principles of classification in the first collateral line are carried into the second and more remote collateral lines, *e. g.*, the children of my collateral brothers, *Ego* a male, are my step-sons and step-daughters; whilst the children of my collateral sisters are my nephews and nieces, the term *Sä'-zy* being applied to each of them. For a further knowledge of the details of the system reference is made to the Table.

The marriage relationships are fully discriminated, and are in accordance with the common form. Since we are now following the system into another, and independent stem of the Ganowánian family, the evidence from this source of identity of systems should be presented. In brief, these relationships are as follows: the wives of my several step-sons, collateral sons, and nephews are my daughters-in-law, *Sa-t'-chu'-a*, the term for this relationship, and for grandchild, being the same; and the husbands of my several step-daughters, collateral daughters, and nieces are each my son-in-law, *Se-ga'-ton.* In like manner the wives of my several collateral brothers are my sisters-in-law; and the husbands of my several collateral sisters are my brothers-in-law.

It is evident from the *A-cha'-o-tin-ne* form, that the Athapascan nations have an elaborate system of relationship which agrees, in the greater part of its fundamental conceptions, with the Algonkin and Dakotan. In some respects it falls below the highest typical form of the system. The absence of the relationship of cousin, restricted to the children of a brother and sister, and the use of that of brother and sister in its place, instead of the ruder forms found in some of the nations, tends to weaken the force of the other discriminations in the system. It will further be observed that with *Ego* a female the classification of consanguinei is less complicated than with *Ego* a male. The system on the part of the females, approaches in some respects quite near the Malayan form. There is a marked tendency in the Athapascan to a double nomenclature, one part of which belongs to the males, and the other to the females; and this again will be found a strong characteristic of the system amongst the nations in the valley of the Columbia. It has, however, been found to a moderate extent in the other stems of the family.

2. *Tä-nä'-tin-ne*, or Mackenzie River Indians. I obtained the system of this nation from a *Tä-nä'-tin-ne* woman of Fort Good Hope, whom I found at the Red River Settlement. She spoke the Cree language as well as her own, and James Bird, before mentioned, acted as interpreter. My time being then extremely

limited, I was neither able to accomplish the work in a satisfactory manner, nor to prosecute certain other inquiries necessary to my main design. This schedule, therefore, as well as the one that follows, is given without being satisfied with its correctness. For some reason she was unable to give the name of her nation among the whites. It seemed probable that she belonged to some band of a nation and could not be made to understand it was the name of the nation, and not of the band that was desired. From the place of her nativity, which was near Fort Good Hope, the chief trading post of the Hare Indians, it is probable that she belonged to a division of that nation.[1] *Tä-nä'-tin-ne*, the name by which the people called themselves, will furnish the means for their future identification.

First Indicative Feature. My brother's son and daughter, *Ego* a male, are my son and daughter. With *Ego* a female, they are the same.

Second. My sister's son and daughter, *Ego* a female, are my son and daughter. This is probably an error. With *Ego* a female, they are the same.

Third. My father's brother is my father.

Fourth. My father's brother's son and daughter are my brother and sister, elder or younger.

Fifth. My father's sister is my aunt.

Sixth. My mother's brother is probably my uncle, although the term given proved to be a translation of the question.

Seventh. My mother's sister is my mother.

Eighth. My mother's sister's son and daughter are my brother and sister, elder or younger.

Ninth. My grandfather's brother is my grandfather.

Tenth. The grandchildren of my brothers and sisters, and of my collateral brothers and sisters, are severally my grandchildren.

The relationship of cousin is unknown, and the children of a brother and sister, as in the last case, are brothers and sisters to each other.

It seems probable that I obtained only that part of the system which is used by the females, and that I failed to procure the other portion. I could not ascertain from this woman that there was any term in their language for nephew or niece, used either by the males or the females. The existence of a term for aunt, and the probable existence of a term for uncle, tends to show that these relationships were discriminated on the side of the males, although not on the part of the females. Amongst the Gulf nations it has been seen that the females have an aunt, but no nephew or niece. It is further probable that with *Ego* a male, my brother's son and daughter are my step-children, and that my father's brother is my step-father.

3. Red-Knives. *Täl-soté-e-nä*. The system of relationship of the Red-Knives was obtained from two half-blood women of that nation, whom I found at the Convent

---

[1] The Hudson's Bay Company pay little or no attention to the national or ethnic divisions of the Indians. Their posts are established with exclusive reference to certain geographical districts; and the people are known to them, chiefly, as attached to certain posts. In their classification, as we have seen *ante*, they are called " Thickwood Indians," " Plain Tribes," " Canada Indians," and " Esquimaux."

of St. Boniface, at the Red-River settlement. They were educated and intelligent, and spoke English fluently. My interview with them was short, as I was about leaving the place, and I think I fell into the same error as in the previous case, of obtaining those relationships only which pertain to *Ego* a female, the nomenclature being double. I could not find that the relationships of nephew and niece were recognized, although the question was pressed in both forms with *Ego* a male, and also a female; and although the relationship of uncle and aunt were both found to exist. If this conjecture should ultimately prove to be correct, it would become necessary so to revise the Table as to restrict most of the relationships given to *Ego* a female, and to restore the omitted terms. The system agrees so fully with that of the Hares, that it will not be necessary to give the indicative relationships.

4. Kŭtchin, or Louchieûx. Richardson's work, before referred to, contains a very full and interesting account of this Arctic people, to whom he devotes a chapter. He acknowledges his indebtedness for a share of his materials to Mr. A. H. Murray, who established the first post of the Hudson's Bay Company among the Kŭtchin, on the Yukon River, in 1845. In the year 1861 I met Mr. Murray, at Georgetown, on the Red River, and obtained from him some additional information concerning this people. This gentleman had passed through the central parts of the continent, from the Gulf of Mexico to the Arctic Sea, and had seen a large number of the North American Indian nations in their own areas, by reason of which he was well qualified to speak of their personal appearance in comparison with each other. He stated to the writer that the Kŭtchins were of lighter complexion than any other American Indians whom he had seen, although but one or two shades lighter than the Crees. In some instances they are freckled, and occasionally have gray eyes. They are of average size and height, well formed, and with regular and rather handsome features. The women also are fair, and of proportionate size. Some of them have curly hair, which falls in natural ringlets over their shoulders. Their eyes are black, narrow set, and small, and, instead of being round, are slightly elongated horizontally, but without obliquity. Their beards are slight, or wanting altogether. In their costume they were in advance of all other northern Indian nations, the severity of the climate rendering a complete dress indispensable. It consisted entirely of dressed skins, chiefly of reindeer, tanned with the hair on for winter, the hair being worn inside, and without hair for summer. The dress of the males was a full pantaloon secured around the waist and extending to the ankle, to the ends of which the moccasins were permanently attached. Over this was worn a coat or rather frock, which extended below the waist, nearly to the knees, and was pointed downwards in the centre, both before and behind. The women wore a similar pantaloon, with moccasins attached, and over it a similar frock, pointed behind, but square in front. Judging from Mr. Murray's description, and from the plates in Richardson's work, which were drawn from Mr. Murray's sketches, the Kŭtchin costume was the most complete and becoming worn by any portion of the Ganowánian family. They build round-top wigwams for winter use, whilst in summer they sleep in the open air, or under their canoes turned over for this purpose. The principal diseases amongst them are scrofula and consumption. Without the stoicism usually ascribed to the

American Indians, and which is not wholly true of other portions of them, they give vent to injured feelings, as well as physical pain, by crying, a practice shared equally by the males and females, and by the old as well as the young.[1]

The Kŭtchin mothers often nurse their children until they are four and five years old. Mrs. Murray mentioned one instance that came under her observation, of a boy ten years old who still nursed from his mother. She knew the woman and saw her often at the Fort. He was an only child, and the only one she ever had, and although well enough grown to go out to hunt with the bow and arrow, he still continued the practice. The ability of this Indian mother thus to nurse her child continuously for ten years is quite remarkable. Mrs. Murray mentioned another case of a Kŭtchin mother who nursed her youngest child until it was six years old; and still another who nursed two of her children of different ages at the same time. They usually wean them at the age of three or four years, if no other children are born in the mean time. I have observed the same practice to some extent both amongst the Mississippi and the Missouri nations. One case in particular occurs to me which I noticed on the Sawk and Fox reservation in Kansas. It was that of a boy about six years old who nursed from his mother standing on his feet, while she sat upon a stool conversing with the writer through an interpreter.

Polygamy prevails among them, and also a special form of it which is very general in the Ganowánian family, namely: when a man marries the oldest of several sisters he is entitled by custom to each and all of the remaining sisters as wives, as soon as they severally attain a marriageable age. It is an optional right which he may enforce or wave. This custom will be again referred to. I have found it a recognized usage amongst the greater portion of the nations represented in the table. Mr. Murray spoke very favorably of the intelligence of the Kŭtchin Indians, but less favorably of their honesty. They call themselves *Kŭ-tchin'*, pronounced nearly *Koo-chin'*, sometimes *Koo-tchä'*. Its signification he was unable to give. They number about five thousand.

The system of relationship of this nation was furnished by W. L. Herdisty, Esq., of Fort Liard, one of the officers of the Hudson's Bay Company. Although familiar with their language, he misconceived, in some respects, the plan of the schedule, and translated a number of the questions from English into Kŭtchin. But fortu-

---

[1] It is generally believed that the American Indians are able to restrain their emotions to a degree unknown amongst other peoples. It is true in ordinary cases of pain or suffering; but under the influence of strong excitement all of these restraints give way, and nature vindicates herself. I remember one instance in point. In the year 1862, in the Blackfoot country, I witnessed the meeting between a Blackfoot mother and her daughter, the latter recovered after twenty years of separation. The child was taken captive by the Crows, at the age of seven years, among whom she had grown up, and was then the wife of Robert Meldrum, by whom her parentage was ascertained, and the knowledge of it preserved. It was not a sudden revelation to the mother of the existence of her lost daughter, for that had been made known to her the year previous, but it was an expected meeting. The mother was an aged and shrivelled woman; but on receiving her daughter the tears streamed down her face abundantly, and it was some hours before she was sufficiently composed for quiet conversation.

nately in marginal notes, here and there, the true classification was indicated, which enabled me, by means of the correlative relationships given in the schedule, to make out quite reliably the principal characteristics of the system. For example, to the question which called for the relationships between the children of sisters, he writes in the margin, "All are brothers and sisters, no matter how far removed," and to the same questions as to the children of a brother and sister, he remarks, "Cousins are always called brothers and sisters, however far removed." In like manner he observes in another place, " Nephews and nieces are only so called when actually such by relationship." The terms nephew and niece are given without showing to what persons they are applied; and yet as my father's brother is shown to be my father, whilst my mother's brother is my uncle, it follows by correlation that my brother's son, *Ego* a male, is my son, and that my sister's son is my nephew. The lineal and a part of the first and second collateral lines will be found in the table, with such corrections as the contents of the schedule rendered substantially certain.

First Indicative Feature. My brother's son and daughter, *Ego* a male, are my son and daughter. With *Ego* a female, it is not certain whether they are my nephew and niece, or my son and daughter.

Second. My sister's son and daughter, *Ego* a male, are my nephew and niece. With *Ego* a female, they are my son and daughter.

Third. My father's brother is my father.

Fourth. My father's brother's son and daughter are my brother and sister, elder or younger.

Fifth. My father's sister is my aunt.

Sixth. My mother's brother is my uncle.

Seventh. My mother's sister is my mother.

Eighth. My mother's sister's son and daughter are my brother and sister, elder or younger.

Ninth. Not given.

Tenth. My brother's grandchildren are my grandchildren.

The remaining collateral lines are not fully extended; but without doubt they are brought into the lineal. For the marriage relationships, which are fully discriminated, and in agreement with the common form, reference is made to the Table.

5. Tukŭthe. The system of this nation was furnished by R. McDonald, Esq., of Peel River, one of the officers of the Hudson's Bay Company. It is evident from the schedule returned, every question upon which is answered, that Mr. McDonald's investigation was thoroughly made. Such is the extent of the discriminations and the opulence of the nomenclature that the series of questions in the printed schedule was not full enough to develop the whole of the system. A portion of it is still left undetermined. It arises from a tendency among the Tukŭthe, as well as other Athapascan nations, to use a double nomenclature, one part of which is used by the males, and the other by the females; and to make a further distinction of relatives of the same class into elder or younger, applying different terms to each. For the first provision was made in the schedule to a very liberal extent, but not for

the last, beyond brother and sister. As the answers in most cases are single, and limited to the elder where the distinction is made, the alternative relationship is omitted. Another difficulty in interpreting this schedule arises from the omission of Mr. McDonald to translate the terms of relationship into equivalent English. Their precise signification can usually be determined by a comparison of all of them in their particular uses. The system of the Tukŭthe in the extent of its discriminations is even more elaborate than that of the Algonkin nations.

First Indicative Feature. My brother's son, *Ego* a male, is my adopted son; and my brother's daughter is my younger sister. With myself a female, they are my step-children.

Second. My sister's son and daughter, *Ego* a male, are my step-children. With myself a female, they are the same.

Third. My father's brother is my father-in-law. This is probably an error.

Fourth. My father's brother's son and daughter are my brother and sister, elder or younger.

Fifth. With respect to the relationship of my father's sister it is not given, the question having been altered by mistake to father's sister's husband.

Sixth. My mother's brother is my uncle. The answer is given for mother's elder brother.

Seventh. My mother's sister is my step-mother.

Eighth. My mother's sister's son and daughter are my brother and sister, elder or younger.

Ninth. My grandfather's brother is my grandfather.

Tenth. The grandchildren of my brothers and sisters, and of my collateral brothers and sisters, are severally my grandchildren.

The children of a brother and sister are brothers and sisters, the relationship of cousin being unknown. In like manner the principle of classification in the first collateral line is carried into the second and more remote collateral lines.

Five of the ten indicative features are present in the Tukŭthe system; one is not given; another, the seventh, agrees with the Ojibwa; and the remaining three are variant from the common form. The precise nature of this system cannot be fully known until its remaining details are ascertained.

A comparison of the terms of relationship of the five Athapascan dialects in the Table shows not only that the Kŭtchin and the Tukŭthe belong to the Athapascan stock, but also that the five dialects thereof closely affiliate. It is a further confirmation of the superiority of terms of relationship over other words for comparison, when taken under the same pronominal forms. They are developed from a small number of roots. Several of them often being variations of the same word, and are amongst the last words in any language to be yielded or superseded.

Upon the basis of their system of relationship no doubt can reasonably be entertained of its identity with the common system of the family in whatever is ultimate and radical. The points of agreement are too numerous and significant to leave room for hesitation upon this conclusion. Although the schedules fail to develop the whole of the system in its minute parts, and fail to show some of its material characteristics, they contain sufficient to prove that the Athapascan nations, the remainder of whom presumptively possess the same system, classify their kindred in the same manner, and in accordance with the same elaborate plan which prevails amongst the Algonkin and Dakotan nations. The evidence of unity of systems seems to be sufficient for their admission into the Ganowánian family.

2. Apache Nations. 1. Jicarillo. 2. Mescaleros. 3. Mimbres. 4. Lipans. 5. Gila Apaches (Coyotes, Tontos, and Garrotes). 6. Navajoes. 7. Pinal Leños.

The Apaches held a very considerable, though much less extensive, area than their northern congeners. With the exception of the narrow strips of country occupied by the Village or Pueblo Indians, along the Rio Grande and its tributaries and the Colorado, the Apache nations hold the greater part of New Mexico, the southwestern part of Texas, and the eastern part of Arizona; and range southward into the Mexican State of Chihuahua, and from thence eastward to the Gulf. Those within the United States were estimated, in 1855, to number between eight and nine thousand.[1] The Navajoes and Pinal Leños cultivate, and are considerably advanced in civilization; but the remaining nations are the wildest of the American Indians.

After repeated and persevering efforts continued through several years, I was unable to procure the Apache system of relationship. It was sought with the more interest for comparison with the Athapascan, with which, presumptively, it agrees.

Nations of the Columbia River and its tributaries.

In natural resources for human subsistence, the region watered by the Columbia and its tributaries is the most remarkable portion of North America. This area draws to itself a sea coast line upon the Pacific of considerable extent. If from a station upon the most inland margin of Puget's Sound a semicircle is described, with a radius four hundred miles long, and the line, at each end, is protracted until it intersects the sea coast, the area referred to will be inclosed. It will include the greater part of the drainage both of the Columbia and Frazer's Rivers. The section of country thus defined can scarcely be paralleled on the face of the earth in the advantages which it afforded to a people living without agriculture, and depending exclusively upon natural subsistence. It contains a mixture of forest and prairie, of mountains, of valleys, of sea coasts, of great rivers, and of inland lakes, to which are superadded the important advantages of a mild and healthful climate. This striking combination of features made it an excellent game country. Its sea coasts, indented with numerous bays, one of which, Puget's Sound, has a shore-line fifteen hundred miles in length, afforded perpetual supplies of shell-fish; and its soil, teeming with bread-roots of various kinds, still further increased the aggregate of available subsistence. But the crowning advantage of this favored area was found in the inexhaustible salmon fisheries of the Columbia River, which, at stated seasons, filled the land with superabundance of food. If the current representations with reference to these fisheries may be credited, they

---

[1] Schoolcraft's Hist. Con. and Pros. vi. 704.

31   March, 1870.

are unequalled in any part of the earth, in the quantity and quality of fish annually supplied.   They enter this river in myriads, and penetrate its several branches, even into the mountain elevations.   The natives were expert fishermen, taking them in immense numbers in baskets, in weirs, and with the spear.   In the peculiar climate of this region, it was only necessary to split them open and hang them up in the sun to dry, to secure an ample supply of palatable and nutritious food. These natural advantages gave to the valley of the Columbia a permanent and controlling influence over all other parts of North America, and, I think it can be shown, over South America as well.   Wherever the Indian family commenced its spread it would sooner or later come into possession of this region; and from that time onward it would become the seed land of the family, and the initial point of successive streams of migration to all parts of the continent.   The abundance of subsistence in the valley of the Columbia, tending constantly to a surplus of inhabitants, determined for this region a species of supremacy over both North and South America, as the predominant centre of population, and the source from which perpetual streams of inhabitants would flow, so long as the family remained in its primitive condition.   Until its superior advantages were controlled and neutralized by the establishment of other centres of population, founded upon greater resources for subsistence, it would maintain its ascendency under the steady operation of physical causes.   How far the Village Indians, who became such through the discovery and cultivation of corn, created a surplus of numbers upon the basis of agricultural subsistence, and sent them forth as migrants to possess the continent; and whether they were sufficient in numbers and intelligence to overmaster and arrest the flow of inhabitants from the valley of the Columbia, are questions to be investigated and determined before the first proposition will become established. As these several topics will be considered in another connection, it will be sufficient here to remark that the evidence fails to show that the Village Indians ever carried agriculture far enough to obtain any sensible control over the numbers or great movements of the Indian family.   So far from this, it appears to be the actual fact, that they were unable to stem the tide of influence and power which seems always to have remained with the Roving, as distinguished from the stationary Village Indians.   All the great stems of the Ganowánian family, found upon the North American continent, point their roots to the valley of the Columbia.   This conclusion becomes demonstrated by a comparison of the means of subsistence and centres of population of the several parts of the continent, of the natural lines of migration furnished by its rivers and mountain chains, of the barrier to a free communication between the Pacific and Atlantic sides of the continent interposed by the great central prairies, by the relations and geographical positions of the several stock languages and their respective dialects, and by the traditions and systems of relationship of all of these nations collectively.   The sum of the evidence from these several sources appears to be convincing and conclusive that the valley of the Columbia was the nursery of the Ganowanian family, and the source from which both the northern and southern divisions of the continent mediately or immediately were being replenished with inhabitants, down to the epoch of their discovery; and it is my intention to present and discuss elsewhere, if space permits, both the physical causes, and the ethnological facts which relate to this interesting and important question, which for the present must be passed.

Another remarkable fact connected with this area is the unprecedented number of stock languages spoken within it, and which have been found in no other of the same limited dimensions. Mr. Gallatin, whose reduction of dialects was founded upon the vocabularies of Hale and Dana, states the number at fourteen.[1] He adopts Hale's synopsis with a change in the orthography of a single name, and thus confirms its correctness. These languages were then (in 1841) spoken in a large number of dialects, of which twenty-six are represented in his tables.

Lewis and Clarke describe in their work and locate upon their map some thirty-four distinct nations, whom they found in 1805–1806, upon the Columbia River and its tributaries, and on the neighboring sea-coasts. Most of the nations visited by them have since been identified under different names.

Although a large amount of labor has been expended upon these languages, further investigations will probably reduce their number. A very considerable reduction would leave the number disproportionately large. These languages have recently been taken up anew by George Gibbs, Esq., of New York, who spent several years in Oregon and Washington Territory as a member of the Northwestern Boundary Commission, and before that, of the Pacific Railroad Engineer Corps upon the northern parallel. From the rare facilities which he enjoyed, and from his high qualifications for linguistic investigations, we may expect in his forthcoming work a thorough elucidation of the philology of this area of Indian speech.

Mr. Gibbs has kindly furnished me with the following synopsis of the stock languages of this area as they are named and classified by him.—

1. Tinne (Athapascan, of Gal.). 2. Kootenay (Kitunaha, of Gal.). 3. Salish. 4. Maka (Wakash, of Gal.). 5. Sahaptin. 6. Kayuse (Waülatpu). 7. Chinook. 8. Shoshonee. 9. Kalapuya. 10. Yakama (Jacon, of Gal.). 11. Kalawatset. 12. Lituami. 13. Shaste.[2]

It will be observed that three or four of the stock languages of Hale and Gallatin are consolidated with others, or disappear in the synopsis of Mr. Gibbs; and that the remainder, with one or two exceptions, are the same under the old or a new name. Some of these languages are spoken in but one or two dialects, whilst others have a large number, one of them, the Salish, having upwards of fifteen.

The subdivision of the inhabitants of this area into such a large number of petty nations, which was their condition when first discovered, and which has continued to be the fact, notwithstanding their reduction in numbers, to the present time, was the inevitable result of their domestic institutions and mode of life. But the present existence of such a number of stock languages in so inconsiderable an area

---

[1]
1. Salish.	4. Kitunaha.	7. Lituami.	10. Jacon.	13. Athapascan
2. Sahaptin.	5. Waülatpu.	8. Saste.	11. Wakash.	14. Shoshonee.
3. Chinook.	6. Kalapuza.	9. Palaik.	12. Skittagets.	

[2] The remaining stock-languages in British and Russian America along the northwest coast are named by him as follows: 1. Thlinkit, or Kolosh. 2. Haida. 3. Chimsyan. 4. Belbella, or Kailt. 5. Nootka, the last two probably related.

furnishes the highest evidence of its long-continued occupation. It is explained by the hypothesis that it was the cradle land of the Ganowánian family. Under the operation of the law which tended to the disintegration of particular nations, with their increase and spread, the several dialects thus formed would widen in the long course of ages until they become hardened by use into independent stock languages, all traces of identity in their vocables having disappeared. The struggle for the possession of this area would tend to equalization by the failure of any single nation to acquire such a preponderance of numbers as would enable it to overmaster and expel the other nations. The number of these stock languages necessarily implies an occupation of the Valley of the Columbia from an antiquity as great as can be assigned, from other considerations, to the Ganowánian family upon any part of the Continent. It is also a reasonable and a probable inference that the greater part of the stock languages found upon the North American Continent were indigenous within this area, or derived from such as were immediately traceable to this source.

Judging from the more recent instead of the older vocabularies, there are peculiarities in the dialects of this area which do not exist in the dialects spoken in other parts of the Continent, and which are difficult of reduction to equivalent sounds represented by the English letters. This marked difference is surprising. It suggests, at least, the supposition that an attempt has been made by means of an improved notation to preserve minute phonetic elements in these dialects which have been disregarded in other areas. Unless great care is taken this new method will magnify and even create differences where none such to any great extent actually exist.

In 1855 the Indian nations in Washington Territory and Oregon were estimated at 27,000.[1] At the time of Lewis and Clarke's visit they were several times more numerous.

II. Salish Nations.

1. Salish or Flathead.   2. Shoushwhäp (Atna).   3. Sämenä.   4. Okinäken. 5. Schwoyelpi.   6. Sketunesh (Cœur d'Alêne).   7. Piskwous.   8. Spokäne. 9. Slkatomlch (Upper Pend d'Oreilles).   10. Kälispelm (Lower Pend d'Oreilles). 11. Balhoolä.   12. Kowooks, Sashalt, and Cowätahin.   13. Kwäntlan and Taieet.   14. Clallam, Lummi, Skagit, Chamakeem, Toanhook, and Nesqually. 15. Kwelahyate, Kwanäwult, and Chehalis.   16. Kwäwaletsk.   17. Tellamooks.

The Salish stock language, spoken in the seventeen dialects above enumerated, has a wider spread than any other within the area under consideration. Mengarini names ten nations speaking this language, most if not all whom are seated between the Rocky and Cascade Mountains;[2] but Mr. Gibbs has traced it west of the Cascade range, and quite down to the sea-coast. The above list of nations speaking dialects of the Salish language was furnished by Mr. Gibbs.

1. Spokane. Out of this large list of nations, the Spokane and Okīnäken only

---

[1] Schoolcraft, Hist. Cond. and Pres., VI. 705.
[2] Salish or Flathead Grammar, p. 120.

are represented in the Table. The system of relationship of the former nation was furnished by Mr. Gibbs, that of the latter was obtained by the author from an Okīnăken woman at Red River Settlement. Both schedules are incomplete. If an opinion may be formed from the limited portion of the system procured, it has been complicated by specializations to an extent unequalled in any form hitherto presented. The Table contains two hundred and sixty-seven distinct questions descriptive of persons in the lineal and first four collateral lines. Many of these questions are twice stated, once with *Ego* a male, and a second time with *Ego* a female, and some of them are in the alternative form of elder or younger, where relative age varied the relationship. It was also found that in some cases a double set of terms existed for the relationships of the same persons, one of which was used by the males, and the other by the females. With a schedule of questions elaborated to meet the most of these peculiarities it was found that all of the nations, whose dialects were sufficiently open and accessible to enable their system to be fully reached, answered these questions in full, the discriminations in frequent instances running beyond the compass of the schedule. Wherever blanks occur in the Table it was for want of facilities to ascertain the relationships of the persons described, and not from a failure of the system to recognize them. In other words, the Indians of all these nations know their kindred, near and remote, and preserve that knowledge by the usage of addressing each other by the term of relationship. Now the Spokane recognition and classification of kindred undoubtedly extend to and include every person described in the Table, and their nomenclature furnishes the terms of relationship applied to each and all of them. More than this, instead of leaving blanks to attest the failure of the system, a large number of the present single questions must be repeated, and some new ones added to develop the whole of the system. The tendency to a double nomenclature, and consequently to a two-fold system of relationship, one for the males and another for the females, is quite marked among the nations west of the mountains. The incompleteness of the schedules, therefore, must be attributed to the inaccessibility of these dialects, and not to a failure of the system to recognize any relationship between *Ego* and the persons described.

There is one feature in the Spokane system that has not before appeared, namely, the use of the same term in a reciprocal sense, instead of correlative terms; for example I call my father's father, *Is-hah'-pä*, and my son's son, *Is-hah'-pä*, consequently the relationship is reciprocal, as cousin and cousin, or brother and brother, instead of correlative, as grandfather and grandson. This was carried into the first collateral line male, in the first Spokane schedule of Mr. Gibbs, but in a subsequent and revised schedule the term was used in a modified form. According to the first I call my father's brother, *Is-se-mălt*, and my brother's son, *Is-se-mălt*, *Ego* in both cases being a male, which would establish between my brother's son and myself a reciprocal relationship expressed by a single term. In the revised schedule he is my son, *Kas-koo-să*, to which the other term is added for some explanatory purpose. It seems probable that the term *Is-se-mălt* is employed to indicate the relationship of these persons when speaking of their relationship to a third person; and that when they speak to each other they use the terms for father and son. The opulence of the nomenclature is such as to favor this supposition. This is one of the questions with reference to the Spokane system that remains to be determined. It will be impossible to understand this remarkable form until it is more fully developed in its details, and its unascertained parts are procured. The system of the remaining Salish nations is also desirable, since some of them may not have adopted the refinements the Spokane displays, and may, therefore, be nearer the primitive form. Notwithstanding the imperfect presentation of the Spokane system about to be made, it will not be difficult to discover decisive traces of the common system of the family.

In Mengarini's " Selish, or Flathead" Grammar, before referred to, he has collected the terms of relationship of the Flatheads, and given them with their Latin equivalents. They do not show the classification of consanguinei and marriage relations, which is the essential part of the system, and the use of some of the terms will probably be found to need correction ; but the terms show the fulness of the nomenclature, and being in another dialect, may be useful to illustrate the Spokane form.[1] Some of them will be referred to in connection with the corresponding terms in the Spokane.

---

[1] "RELATIO CONSANGUINITATIS ET AFFINITATIS.

Relatè ad viros.		Relatè ad mulieres.	
Sgelui,	Maritus.	Nòganag,	Uxor.
L'èu,	Pater	Mestm,	Pater.
Skoi,	Mater.	Tòm,	Mater.
Skokoi,	Amita (soror patris).	Tikul,	Amita (soror patris).
Sgus'mèm,	Soror.	Snkusgu,	Soror.
Tonsèh,	Nepos, neptis.	Skusèlt,	Nepos.
Szèscht,	Sororius (maritus sororis).	Sttmch'elt,	Neptis.

RELATIO COMMUNIS UTRIQUE SEXUI.

Sgaèpe,	Avus (ex parte patris).	Snkusgutèlis,	Idem, de pluribus quam duobus.
Silé,	Avus (ex parte matris).		
Kèné,	Avia (ex patre patris).*	K'ezch,	Frater natu maximus.
Ch'chièz,	Avia (ex parte matris).	Ke'eus,	Frater natu major.
Tópiè,	Abavus et abavia.	Sinze,	Frater natu minor.
Smèl,	Patruus (frater patris).	St'tènti,	Frater natu minimus.
S'sì'i,	Avunculus (frater matris).	Lch'chochèe,	Soror natu major (diminutiva).
Káge,	Matertera (soror matris).	Ikak'ze,	Soror natu minor (diminutiva).
Skusèe,	Filius.		
Sgusigult,	Filii et filiæ, the children of.	Lzzups,	Soror natu minima (diminutiva).
Sk'kusèlt,	Filiolus (generice).		
S'schitemischlt,	Filius vel filia natu major.	Sgágèe,	Socer (pater mariti vel uxoris), beau père.
Sk'eusèlt,	Filius vel filia natu minor.		
St'eutèlt,	Filius vel filia, natu minimus.	Lzesch,	Socrus (mater mariti vel uxoris), belle mère.
Stomchèlt,	Filia.		
Snkusgutèus,	Fratres vel sorores germani (de duobus).	Nluèstu,	Patruus. l'oncle (patre nepotis mortuo).

---

* "Duo relationes, Kene et ch'chioz, sunt etiam relativæ nepotibus (les petits fils), ita ut aviæ et nepotes his duobus se invicem appellent."

There are separate terms in this dialect for grandfather and grandmother. On the father's side *Is-hah'-pä*, and *In-kah'-no*, used by the males, and *In-chau'-wä* and *In-tchit-che-ä'-ä*, used by the females; and for the same relationship on the mother's side, *Is-see'-lä* and *In-chau-wä*, used by the males and females. This is the first instance yet found of the discrimination of the ancestors on the father's side from those on the mother's side, but this is limited to the maternal grandfather. There are also separate terms for father and mother, *En-le-ă'-u* and *E-sko'-i*, used by the males, and *En-ne-mes'-teem* and *En-tome'*, used by the females; for son and daughter *Is-kwoos-să* and *Is-tum-che-ălt*; and for grandson and granddaughter, namely, for son's son and son's daughter, *Is-hah'pä* and *In-chau'-wä*, and for daughter's son and daughter's daughter, *Is-se'-lä* and *In-chit-che-ă*. It will be observed that three of these terms for grandchildren are applied equally to grandparents, showing them to be reciprocal.

There are terms for elder brother, *En-kats'-tch*, used by the males, and *En'l-kahk'-tsä*, used by the females; and a common term, *En'l-chit'-shä*, for elder sister; for younger brother, *Is-sin'-sä*, used by the males, and *Is-sis'-son-sä*, used by the females; and common term, *En'l-tsits-ă-opes'*, for younger sister. Beside these there are terms for brother and sister in the abstract, *En-se-lacht'*, and *Is-soo-sin-ăm'*; and for brothers and sisters in the plural. The great number of these terms, and the tendency to minute specializations throughout the Spokane system, increase the necessity for full details of the classification, as well as the whole of the nomenclature, to a right understanding of the system itself. The Spokane nomenclature is twofold to a greater extent than any previously presented.

First Indicative Feature. My brother's son and daughter, *Ego* a male, are my son and daughter, *Kas-koo'-să* and *Ka-stum'-che-ält*. To the first *Is-se-mält* is added, as some kind of qualification. With *Ego* a female, I call my brother's son *In-tee'-kwl*, and he calls me the same. This is another instance of reciprocal relationship. In the Flathead the term *Ti-kul*, the same word dialectically changed, is applied by a female to her father's sister, and it seems probable that it is also applied by a woman to her brother's son, as in the Spokane. My brother's daughter I call

---

Sluelt,	Nepos et neptis (patre mortuo).
Znèchlgu,	Gener.
Zepu,	Nurus.
Segunèmt,	Parentes matrimonio junctorum.
Sestèm,	Levir vel fratria. le mari de sa sœur, ou la femme de sou frère.
Ischeu,	Uxor fratris uxoris. le femme du frère de sa femme.
Kolemut,	Cognatus le mari de la sœur de son mari ou la femme du frère de son mari.

Nhoiztn,	Lever et fratria (alterutro mortuo).
Luèstn,	Vetricus et noverca.
S'chélp,	Nurus (filio mortuo), la veuve de son fils.
St'mels,	Propinquus, affinis, etc.
Snkusigu,	Patruelis sobrinus, consanguineus.
Snkusgusigu,	(Plur). Les cousins, les cousines, les parens (generice), etc."

Grammar, App. 117.

Is-see'-lä, the same term I use to designate a grandmother. Here the relationship again is reciprocal.

Second. My sister's son and daughter, *Ego* a male, are my nephew and niece, for which a term in common gender, *In-toonsh'*, is employed. With *Ego* a female, they are my son and daughter. To the latter term, *In-kach'-ha* is added for some qualifying purpose.

Third. My father's brother I call *Is-se-mălt*. After the death of my own father I call him my step-parent, *Es-tlu-es-tin*. The same is true in the Flathead, in which the word is *Nluestn*.

Fourth. My father's brother's son is my brother, *Is-se-lacht'*; and his daughter is my sister, elder or younger.

Fifth. My father's sister, *Ego* a male, I call *In-kach'-ha*, and *Ego* a female, *En-tee'-kwl*. Both of these have before appeared as reciprocal terms. The first I think is erroneously used.

Sixth. My mother's brother is my uncle, *Is-să'*.

Seventh. My mother's sister I call *In-kach'-ha*, in Flathead *Kage*. After the death of my own mother I call her *Es-lu-es-tin*, my step-parent.

Eighth. My mother's sister's son and daughter are my brother and sister, elder or younger.

Ninth. My grandfather's brother is my grandfather.

Tenth. The relationships of collateral descendants are not given, beyond those previously named.

The marriage relationships are in agreement with the typical form, *e. g.*, the wives of my collateral sons and of my nephews, are my daughters-in-law; and the husbands of my collateral daughters and of my wives are my sons-in-law. In like manner the wives of my several collateral brothers are my sisters-in-law; and the husbands of my several collateral sisters are my brothers-in-law. There is one altogether novel marriage relationship recognized in a large number of Ganowánian nations, namely, between the parents of married pairs. In Yankton-Dakota the fathers of a married pair call each other *O-mä'-he-to*, in Spokane *In-teh-tum-ten*, and in Flathead, *Segunèmt*. Mr. Gibbs has furnished the signification of the Spokane term, "Dividers of the Plunder," *i. e.*, the marriage presents. It is probably a recent term, from the fact that it is still significant, and derisively bestowed.

With respect to the children of a brother and sister, they are brothers and sisters to each other. Mengarini furnishes a term for cousin in the Flathead *Sakusiga*, which is probably the Spokane *Sin-kwa-seehw*, rendered "one like my brother;" but it is extremely doubtful whether the relationship of cousin has been developed either in the Flathead or Spokane system.

Notwithstanding the insufficiency of the materials to show this system completely, an opinion may be formed upon the question of its identity with the common form. In its incomplete state, as shown in the Table, it possesses the indicative relationships, although some of them are modified and obscured by the uncertainty that rests upon the modifications. It is at least supposable that the doubtful terms are those used when speaking *of* the relationship, as before suggested, whilst the full terms may be employed when the particular persons are addressed by *Ego*, by the term of relationship. The minute discriminations of the system, and its opulent nomenclature, tend to the inference that when produced in full, it will be found to contain all of the radical characteristics of the system, and that the special use of reciprocal terms will find a rational explanation.

2. Okinaken. The fragment of the Okinaken system was obtained from Mrs. Ross, a native of this nation, at Red-River Settlement. An absence of many years from her native country had rendered her so distrustful of her knowledge of the system that she would not undertake to give its details.

III. Sahaptin Nation.

1. Sahaptin, or Nez Perce. 2. Paloos. 3. Wala-Wala and Taikh. 4. Yakama. 5. Klikitat.

The Salish and Sahaptin stock languages are spoken by a larger number of distinct nations, and in a greater number of dialects, than any other within this area. Of the Sahaptin nations only one, the Yakama, is represented in the Table. The schedule was furnished by Mr. Gibbs. A part only of the terms of relationship are given, and these are incapable of interpretation without the remainder of the nomenclature, and without a more explicit knowledge of the classification. Upon the Yakama system Mr. Gibbs, in his letter to the author, remarks: "This language, as usual, has a very complicated nomenclature of relationships, and, I believe, it is a little different from that of the Selish. In some instances, besides the name for the relationship itself, as *Pe-shet'*, father, there is the familiar one *Too-ta*, equivalent to 'papa,' which, I believe, is used only in speaking *to* the person, while the former is used exclusively in speaking *of* him. Besides these, there is an expression, the exact force of which I do not understand, further than that it is applied after a death occurs in the family, namely, *Kwuten*. It is equally applied to the father, mother, sons, or daughters, and may, therefore, have some such signification as 'bereaved.'

"The distinction that is made by the sexes in speaking to the father and mother, and certain other relatives in the Spokane, are, I understand, not made in the Yakama, though they are as between brothers and sisters, where we find not only different words used in addressing and speaking of one another, but the two sexes address one another differently, the whole being complicated by the distinctions of relative age."

"The general word 'brother' does not, I believe, exist; but as near as I can understand the word *Haigh* (plural, *thaigh-ma*), perhaps literally signifying '*friend*,' is used to denote brothers or cousins, when speaking of them at large; and the same is the case in Spokane." It will be seen, however, in the Table, that the term *En-haigh* is the term for step-brother, which explains its application to a collateral brother.

"Some of these relations," he continues, "are reciprocal. Thus grandfather and grandson are both *Poo-sha*. . . . I have not followed out to the letter your instructions about inserting the pronoun 'my,' in all cases, because it was not always given me in return, and I was not certain why. For that reason I did not change the vocative form. Neither have I always translated the word, as I am not sufficiently certain of the force of many of them."

32   March, 1870.

First Indicative Feature. My brother's son and daughter, *Ego* a male, I call *In-pit'-h*, and *Pai-ya*, the last meaning step-daughter. With *Ego* a female, they are my nephew and niece, for which a term in common gender, *In'-pote*, is used.

Second. My sister's son and daughter, *Ego* a male, I call *In-pit'-h* and *Pai-ya*, the latter step-daughter. With *Ego* a female, I call them *Pan'-ta* and *Pee'-see*, the latter meaning step-daughter.

Third. My father's brother is my step-parent, *Na-magh'-has*.

Fourth. My father's brother's son and daughter, *Ego* a male, I call *Es-hup'*, and *En'-naks*, the latter signifying my step-sister. With *Ego* a female, *Ne-pah'*, and *En'-naks*.

Fifth. My father's sister is my aunt, *Na-sis'-sas*.

Sixth. My mother's brother is my uncle, *Na-kä'-kas*.

Seventh. My mother's sister is my step-parent, *Na-magh'-has*.

Eighth. My mother's sister's son and daughter, same as in Fourth.

Ninth. The relationship of grandfather's brother is not given.

Tenth. The relationship in the collateral lines are not carried beyond collateral brothers in the Table.

With respect to the relationship between the children of a brother and sister, they are the same as between the children of two brothers.

In the Salish and Spokane, Mr. Gibbs encountered one of the most intricate and difficult of all the forms given in the Table, from the great fulness of the nomenclatures, and the minute specializations they represent. These dialects, also, are far from being as accessible as those east of the mountains through natives speaking English. Until better facilities are afforded, or these dialects are acquired by Protestant missionaries, the system of relationship of the nations of the Pacific coast in its full range and complexity will be difficult of ascertainment. That they have an elaborate system, defining the relationships of all their kindred, near and remote, and that it is both coherent and logical, there can be no reasonable doubt.[1]

From the general character of that portion of the Yakama system contained in

---

[1] Mr. Gibbs remarks upon certain Yakama relationships as follows :—

1. "Father, *Pe-shet'*; papa, *Too-ta*; child addressing him, 'my father,' *Na-too-tas*. After the death of a near relative, *Kwu-ten*.

2. Mother, *Pe-chah'*; mamma, *Eet'-la*; child addressing her, 'my mother,' *Na-eet'-las*. After the death of a relative, *Kwu-ten*.

3. Son. Both parents addressing a son use *En-meshl'*. The father, in speaking to others of a son grown up, says *Mi-an'-nash*, and the mother, *Isht*; *En-misht* = my son. To a child they use *Te-tah'*. After the death of a near relative, they use *Kwu-ten*, in speaking *of* or *to* either son or daughter. *En-kwu-ten*, my son or my daughter. The father of a grown-up daughter calls her *Isht*, and *En-misht'*; and the mother, *Päp*. To any young one they say *Is-shah'*.

I am more in doubt if I understand perfectly the following. As near as I now can give it, the names for brothers and sisters are, elder brother, addressing a brother or sister, *Piàp* or *Yai'-ya*.

Na-ai'-yas, my elder brother.

Younger brother, addressed by brothers, *Es-hap'*; by sisters, *Pat-shet*, or *Ne-kah*, or *In-kaks*, speaking of him.

Elder sister, *Päts*.

Younger sister, addressed by brothers, *Ats*; by sisters, *A-seep*. Also familiarly called *Nei'-ya*."

the Table, and the same is equally true of the Spokane, these are sufficient grounds for the admission of the Salish and Sahaptin nations into the Ganowánian family.

One other stock language belonging to the valley of the Columbia, namely, the Kootenay, is represented in the Table. The Flatbows speak a dialect of the same language, and the two together are its only ascertained representatives. Their range is along the western slopes of the Rocky Mountains immediately north of the Flathead area. Although incompletely shown, the Kootenay system of relationship is interesting as a further glimpse at the stupendous scheme of consanguinity which prevails amongst the aboriginal inhabitants of this area. Upon independent grounds a more complex system might be expected to exist in the valley of the Columbia than upon the St. Lawrence or the Mississippi. With so many nations crowded together, but held asunder by dialects and mutually unintelligible stock languages, and yet intermingling by marriage, the constant tendency would be to increase and intensify the special discriminations developed from the system, by the gradual introduction of the special features of each into all the others. These new features do not necessarily disturb the essential framework of the system, although they may greatly increase its complexity, and render it more difficult of ascertainment. Beside this a plan of consanguinity so elaborate as that of the Ganowánian family, could not be maintained pure and simple in its minute details, amongst so many nations, and over such immense areas. Additions and modifications are immaterial so long as they leave undisturbed the fundamental conceptions on which the original system rests.

V. Shoshonee Nations.

1. Shoshonees or Snake Indians. 2. Bonnacks. 3. Utahs of the Colorado (1. Tabegwaches. 2. Wemenuches. 3. Yampahs or Utahs of Grand River. 4. Unitahs. 5. Chemehuevis. 6. Capotes. 7. Mohuaches. 8. Pah-Utes). 4. Utahs of Lower California (1. Cahuillos. 2. Kechis. 3. Netelas. 4. Kizhes). 5. Comanches.

There are reasons for believing that the Shoshonee migration was the last of the series, in the order of time, which left the valley of the Columbia, and spread into other parts of the continent. It was a pending migration at the epoch of European colonization. It furnishes an apt illustration of the manner in which Indian migrations are prosecuted under the control of physical causes. They were gradual movements, extended through long periods of time, involving the forcible displacement of other migrants that had preceded them; and therefore, are without any definite direction, except such as was dictated by the exigencies of passing events. The initial point of this migration, as well as its entire course, stands fully revealed. Almost the entire area overspread, showing the general outline of a head, trunk and two legs, is still held by some one of the branches of this great stem. Upon the south branch of the Columbia River the Shoshonees still reside; south of them along the mountain wastes of the interior are the Bonnacks, a closely affiliated people, who occupy quite near to the head-waters of the Colorado. The mountains and the rugged regions drained by the Upper Colorado and its tributaries are held by the Utahs in several independent bands or embryo nations, who are spread over an area of considerable extent. Here the original stream of this migration divided into two branches; one of them, the Comanche, turned to the southeast, and occupied the western parts of the present State of Texas; whilst the other keeping the west side of the Colorado, descended towards the Gulf of California, and appropriated the regions near the Village Indians of the Lower Colorado. These are the Pah-Utes. Still other bands moved westward and southward and occupied Lower California. These are the Cahiullos, between the San Gabriel and Sante Anna Rivers; and the Mission Indians, namely, the Kizhes of San Gabriel, the Netelas of San Juan Capestrano, and the Kechis of San Louis Rey. Upon the basis of linguistic affinities the conclusion is inevitable that both the Comanches and Netelas are the descendants of original migrants from the valley of the Columbia.[1]

The Shoshonee nations are among the wildest of the American aborigines. With the exception of the Comanches, and a portion of the Shoshonees proper, they hold the poorest sections of the United States, their manners partaking of the roughness of the country they inhabit. Until quite recently they have been inaccessible to government influence. It is still nominal and precarious. The Comanches, who occupy the southern skirt of the great buffalo ranges, and are spread from the Canadian River, a branch of the Arkansas, to the Rio Grande, have become a populous Indian nation within the last century and a half. They are expert horsemen. Next to them are the Shoshonees.

It was found impossible, after repeated efforts, to procure the system of relationship of the Shoshonees or the Comanches, although much more accessible than the other nations. The time is not far distant when all the dialects on the Pacific side, as well as in the interior of the continent, will become as fully opened to us as those upon the eastern side; and when information now so difficult of attainment can be gained with ease and certainty.

An incomplete schedule of the system of the Tabegwaches, one of the Utah nations of the Colorado, was obtained unexpectedly, through my friend the late Robert Kennicott, from a delegation who visited the seat of government in 1863. It will be found in the Table. He was unable to fill out the schedule, except in its most simple parts, from the difficulty of working through interpreters imperfectly skilled in the Utah language; and, therefore, it cannot be taken as indicating to any considerable extent, the contents of the system. From the fact that a portion of the terms of relationship were not obtained, those which are, except the primary, cannot be interpreted. It is valuable as a specimen of the language; and more especially because it indicates the possession of a full nomenclature, and the presence of the minute discriminations which are characteristic of the common system. There are two special features revealed which should be noticed. First the relationship between aunt and nephew is reciprocal and expressed by a single term. The same use of reciprocal terms has been seen to exist both among the Salish and Sahaptin nations, with the language of the former, of which the Tabe-

---

[1] In 1847 the Shoshonees and Bonnacks were estimated together at 4000. Schoolcraft's Hist. Cond. and Pros. VI. 697; and the Utahs in part, at 3600. Ib. In 1855 the Comanches were estimated at 15,000. Ib. VI. 705. The numbers of the remaining Shoshonee nations on the Pacific are not known. They are not numerous.

gwach shows some affinity; and second, the discrimination of a difference in the relationship to *Ego* between the children of an elder, and the children of a younger brother.[1] This is shown by the use of different terms to express the relationships.

It is an extension of the principle of discrimination beyond any point reached in other systems as shown in the Table. The same peculiarity may exist in the Spokane, and the Yakama without having been necessarily discovered, since there were no questions on the schedule to test the fact. It may yet be found to explain the ambiguities in the system of the former nations. With the American Indians it is a peculiarity never to supplement information when answering special questions put to them by Americans. In the case in hand, if asked what he called his brother's son, he might elect to answer as to the son of his elder brother, and treat that as a sufficient answer to the question, although the son of his younger brother stood to him in different relationship.

The most that may be claimed upon this incomplete representation of the Tabegwach system of relationship is, that it is classificatory in its character, and that it tends to show the same elaborate discriminations of the relationships by blood and marriage, which are characteristic of the common system. It also furnishes sufficient grounds for the provisional admission of the Shoshonee nations into the Ganowánian family.

We have now presented the system of consanguinity and affinity of all the Indian nations represented in the Table, with the exception of the Village Indians of New Mexico, and Central America; and the Eskimo. It remains to consider separately the forms of the latter, together with some fragments of the system which prevails among a portion of the South American Indian nations. The knowledge of the system as it exists amongst the nations on the Pacific side of the continent, is not as full and precise as could have been desired; but the main fact of the nearly universal prevalence of a common system of relationship throughout all the nations, thus far enumerated, is sufficiently demonstrated, and the fundamental characteristics of the system are sufficiently ascertained, to create a definite and substantial foundation for the consolidation of all of these nations into one genealogically connected family. The further prosecution of the inquiry amongst the unrepresented Indian nations will be necessary to determine the question whether or not they belong to this great family of mankind, the unity of origin of which may now be considered established.

---

[1] In the Grammar and Dictionary of the Yakama, by Father Pandosy (Chamoisy Press, 1862), the following terms are given, which are expressive of reciprocal relationship.

Uncle,	Pitr.	[b] Pimr	Father-in-law,	Pshes
Nephew,	Pitr.	[b] Pimr	Son-in-law,	Pshes
Aunt,	Parar		Mother-in-law,	Pnash
Niece,	Pitr.	[b] Pimr. [o] Paia	Daughter-in-law,	Pnash

CHAPTER VI.

SYSTEM OF RELATIONSHIP OF THE GANOWÁNIAN FAMILY—Continued.

Village Indians of New Mexico, Arizona, and Central and South America.

Important Position of the Village Indians in American Ethnology—Their Partial Civilization—Indigenous amongst them—Its Basis—Early Knowledge of the Village Indians of New Mexico—Coronado's Expedition in 1540, 1542 —Espejo's in 1583—Spanish Missions in 1600—Reconnoissances of U. S. Army Officers since 1847—Possible Recovery of the Institutions and Mechanic Arts of the Village Indians in general, through those of the present Village Indians—Evidences of the Unity of Origin of the American Aborigines—From Unity of Physical Type —From Unity in the Grammatical Structure of their Languages—From Similarity of Arts, Inventions, Usages, and Institutions—And from Conformation in Cranial Characteristics—Dialects and Languages of the Village Indians of New Mexico and Arizona—Evidence of Ancient Occupation—Confirmed by Ruins of Ancient Pueblos— Their System of Relationship—But two Schedules obtained—1. Pueblo of Laguna—Location and Population of this Pueblo—Schedule Incomplete—Indicative Relationships—They possess, as far as it is given, the Common System—2. Pueblo of Tesuque—Schedule Incomplete—Chontal of Central America—Schedule Incomplete— Village Indians of South America—Efforts to obtain their System of Relationship, and their Failure—System of the Chibcha or Muyska Village Indians of New Granada—Partial Details of the Muyska Form—It shows five, and probably six of the Indicative Relationships—End of the Series of Indian Nations represented in the Table.

THE present Village Indians of New Mexico and Arizona are, in many respects, the most important portion of the aboriginal inhabitants of North America. Their prominent position in Indian ethnography does not arise from their numbers or their territorial possessions, both of which are inconsiderable, but from the fact that they are the living representatives of a phase of Indian society now rapidly passing away. They still possess and exhibit that species of civilization which has given to the American Indians their chief importance in the estimation of mankind. With the Village Indians in general, the transition from a roving to a stationary life had been fully consummated, and a new condition commenced. An indigenous civilization sprang up and grew apace out of this village life, which, at the epoch of discovery, was found distributed throughout parts of New Mexico, Mexico, and Central and South America. These Village Indians, however, were surrounded at all points by roving and still barbarous nations. The extent and character of this civilization, which was the same in its elements throughout all these regions, are still imperfectly understood. It is, moreover, extremely doubtful whether the facts tending to illustrate its history and development will ever be recovered from the mass of fiction and romance in which they are buried. Should an attempt be made to reinvestigate its characteristics, the key must be sought in the civil and domestic institutions, arts, usages, and customs of the present Village Indians. It is not improbable that all of its elements will be found amongst them at the present day, and that from these sources the necessary materials can be obtained for a much better elucidation of this difficult subject than any hitherto presented.

This limited and indigenous civilization was founded, in the main, upon the possession of a single cereal, Indian corn; of one textile plant, cotton; and upon one principal mechanic art, that of making sun-dried brick. Out of these, in due time, came the cultivation of irrigated garden-beds, the improved costume, and the house of more than one story high; first, with walls of sun-dried brick, then of slate and rubble-stone, the latter cemented with mud-mortar; and, finally, of cut stone laid with mortar probably without lime. Of the last class were the pueblo houses in Yucatan, now in ruins. When the transformation from fish and game to agricultural subsistence, from temporary lodges to permanent villages, and from houses of a single story constructed with perishable materials, to houses of more than one story constructed with durable materials, had become completed, the change in this, as well as in other respects, was very great intrinsically. It resulted in a degree of civilization that appeared to separate the Village Indians genetically from the remaining nations, until it was afterwards found that the Northern Indians presented all the intermediate shades of condition between the Village Indians proper and the Roving nations. The differences, it was seen, could be rationally explained as an advance by a portion of the same original family from a lower to a higher condition of life, since it was not accompanied with any radical change of domestic institutions. And yet the degree of this civilization is sufficiently remarkable to demand special evidence to establish the right of the Village Indians to admission into the Ganowánian family. If those in New Mexico could be shown to be of Ganowánian lineage, it would prepare the way for the like admission of the Village Indians of Mexico, and of Central and South America.

Our knowledge of the existence, and, to some extent, of the condition of the Village Indians of New Mexico commences within twenty years after the conquest of Mexico by Cortes, and has been substantially continuous down to the present time. It opens with the extravagant relation of Friar Marco de Neça " touching his discovery of the Kingdom of Cevola," made in 1539, which led to the expedition of Coronado in 1540–1542, for the conquest of this " kingdom," to use the common term employed by the Spanish writers of that epoch to describe a cluster of Pueblo Houses. Of the several places visited by Coronado, Acoma, and perhaps Zuñi, both existing pueblos, have been identified; but the " Seven Cities " still remain unknown. There are seven or eight remarkable Pueblo Houses of stone, now in ruins, on the cañon of the Rio de Chaco, a tributary of the San Juan, which, in location and character, answer the nearest to the " Seven Cities," of any existing or ruined Pueblos in New Mexico. They are situated about one hundred and forty miles northwest of Sante Fé. This expedition established the existence of Village Indians upon the Rio Grande, the Gila, and the Colorado; of their dependence upon agriculture for subsistence; and that they lived in houses of more than one story high, constructed of some kind of stone masonry, or adobe brick, Coronado thus speaks, in his relation of the villages he visited : " It remaineth now to testify, your honor, of the seven cities, and of the kingdoms and provinces whereof the father provincial made report to your lordship ; and, to be brief, I can assure you that he spoke the truth in nothing that he reported ; but all was quite the contrary, saving only the names of the cities and great houses of stone; for although they be not wrought with turqueses, not with lime, nor bricks, yet they are very excellent good houses of three or four or five lofts high, wherein are good lodgings and fair chambers, with ladders instead of stairs ; and certain cellars under the ground, very good and paved, which are made for winter ; they are in a manner like stoves, and the ladders which they have for their houses are all in a manner movable and portable ; which are taken away and set down when they please, and they are made of two pieces of wood with their steps as our be."[1]   This relation was written under a feeling of disappointment, as the object of the expedition was plunder, which they failed to obtain.   Other explorations followed from time to time.   Among these may be named that of Fernando Alarcon, who in 1542 ascended the Colorado River to the establishments of the Village Indians in that region ; and that of Antonio de Espejo, who in 1583 led an expedition to the Rio Grande, and visited a large number of Indian villages upon that river and its tributaries.   In the relation of this expedition several important statements are made, from which the following are selected : " Here were houses of four stories in height. * * *   Their garments were of cotton and deer skins, and the attire, both of men and woman was after the manner of Indians of Mexico. * * *   Both men and women wore shoes and boots, with good soles of neat's leather [probably of buffalo raw hide, with which the Indians of the Missouri now bottom their moccasins], a thing never seen in any other part of the Indies. * * *   There are caciques who govern the people like the caciques of Mexico."   Finally he speaks of their " good capacity, wherein they exceed those of Mexico and Peru."[2]   The late Prof. W. W. Turner collected and translated the several Spanish documents relative to the several expeditions of Coronado, Alarcon, Ruiz, and Espejo, from which the above extracts were taken ; and also appended a very interesting report upon the Indian nations of New Mexico, made by Don Jose Cortez in 1799.

The Spanish missionaries enjoyed the best facilities for becoming intimately acquainted with the institutions and domestic history of these nations.   As early as 1600, they had established a chain of missions, eleven in number, from the Gulf of California and the Colorado, to the Rio Grande, and claimed eight thousand converts.   Their relations and correspondence, if they could be collected, would probably furnish much valuable information concerning the Village Indians of that epoch.   These several expeditions and missionary establishments show conclusively that long anterior to the discovery of America, New Mexico was occupied by Village Indians in a condition of partial civilization ; and, also, that the stage of progress they had reached corresponded substantially with that in which the Village Indians of Mexico and Central and South America were found.   The differences were much less than is generally supposed.

Within the last twenty years a number of military and scientific reconnoissances through New Mexico, and westward to the Colorado and the Pacific, have been made by United States authority.   Amongst these may be mentioned that of Lieut.-Col. W. H. Emory, in 1846–1847 ; that of Lieutenant, now General J. H.

---

[1] Explorations, &c. for a Railroad Route to the Pacific, VII., Rep. on Ind. Tribes, p. 109.

Simpson, in 1849; that of Capt. Sitgreaves, in 1852; and that of Lieut. Ives, in 1857. To these must be added the expedition to determine the Mexican boundary, in 1850, under Hon. John R. Bartlett; and the exploration for a railroad route to the Pacific, on the thirty-fifth parallel, in 1854, under Lieut. Whipple. From these sources a large amount of additional information has been gained both of the country and of its inhabitants.

The present Village Indians of New Mexico are the lineal descendants of those found in the country at the Conquest. Some of them occupy the same sites, and the same identical houses which their forefathers occupied when first discovered; and such new pueblos as have since been constructed, are, many of them, upon the ancient model. They still retain the greater part of their ancient customs, usages, and arts. An opportunity, therefore, is still offered to recover their languages, their architectural, agricultural, and other mechanical arts, as well as their civil and domestic institutions, which, when procured, may prove of immense value in American ethnology. If the true history and interpretation of the civilization of the Village Indians of Mexico, Central America, and Peru are ever reached, it will probably be effected through a comparison of their arts and institutions with those of the present Village Indians. It is, therefore, a fortunate circumstance that even a fragmentary portion of this great division of the American aborigines still remain upon the continent, in the full possession of their original domestic institutions, and in the practice of many of their primitive arts. The intellectual life of a great family impresses a common stamp upon all their works. The marks of the uniform operation of minds cast in the same mould, and endowed with the same impulses and aspirations inherited from common ancestors, can be successfully traced through periods of time, and into widely separated areas. In their architecture, in their tribal organization, in their dances, in their burial customs, in their systems of relationship, the same mental characteristics are constantly revealed. It is not impossible to arrive at safe conclusions from comparisons founded exclusively upon intellectual manifestations crystallized in these several forms. These Village Indians are, at the present moment, the true and the living representatives of the indigenous civilization which was found in both North and South America; and notwithstanding the mass of fiction which has usurped the place of history, there are strong reasons for believing that they are no unfit representatives of the Village Indians in general; and that all there was of this civilization, invention for invention, institution for institution, art for art, in a word, part for part, may still be found amongst them, and in existing memorials of their past history. The great differences supposed to exist must be set down to a very considerable extent to the marvellous powers of the constructive faculty which authorship develops.

Whether or not the Village and Roving Indians are of one blood by descent, from common American ancestors has not been established in the affirmative so decidedly as to command universal acquiescence. There are several distinct and independent lines of evidence, all of which converge to an affirmative conclusion, and yield collectively such a body of testimony as to render this conclusion extremely probable. These may be briefly stated as follows:—

First. Unity of Physical Type. It cannot be denied that the Indian form and physiognomy are strikingly distinctive and peculiar. He is as definitely marked as any variety of man. The uniform testimony of all competent observers, that the individuals of these widely scattered Indian nations universally display common typical characteristics, possesses great weight. In this respect the Village Indians are not excepted, but especially included.

Secondly. Unity of Grammatical Structure in their Languages. These stock languages, so far as they have been investigated, reveal the same plan of thought, and numerous coincidences in grammatical structure. The comparison has not been coextensive with their spread; but it has been carried far enough, probably, to detect differences if more than one grammatically distinct language existed amongst them. These languages, also, have peculiarities impressed upon all of them alike, which give them a family cast. It is seen in the syllabical structure of their vocables, in the excessive use of the principle of conjugation, in the unusual amount of physical exertion required in their delivery, and possibly in the guttural and nasal utterances with which they are, more or less, roughened. It seems probable, therefore, that the analysis and comparison of these stock languages will ultimately demonstrate their unity. In these respects, also, the languages of the Village Indians are not exceptional.

Thirdly. Similarity of Arts, Usages, and Inventions. An argument based upon these considerations, and standing alone, would have but little weight, since similar conditions presuppose similar wants, and beget similar arts, usages, and inventions. And yet this objection, though unwittingly, is a powerful argument in favor of the unity of origin of the entire human family. It is only in virtue of the possession of a common mind, such as belongs to a single species, that these uniform operations are possible. Amongst all of these nations there is a striking uniformity in their manners, usages, and institutions. It is seen in those which relate to social life, to warfare, to marriage, and to the burial of the dead; but more especially in their simple mechanic arts, such as those of pottery, of weaving, whether with filaments of bark, or with threads of cotton; of the tanning of skins, and in the forms of their weapons and utensils. This is true, in a more striking sense, of their architecture, which is founded upon the communal principle in living, a principle which prevailed amongst all the Indian nations, from near the confines of the Arctic Sea to the Isthmus of Panama. The communal principle found its way into, and determined the character of this architecture. It is revealed not less distinctly in the long bark house of the Iroquois, designed for twenty families, than in the pueblo houses at Taos, New Mexico, one of which is two hundred and forty feet front, by one hundred feet deep, and five stories high, and capable of accommodating eighty families; or in the pueblo of Palenque, in Chiapa, which was two hundred and twenty-eight feet front, by one hundred and eighty feet deep, and one story high, and was capable of accommodating fifty or more families.

Fourthly. The Dance. Amongst all of these nations, without an exception, the dance is a domestic institution. Whilst barbarous nations in general indulge in this practice, often to excess, no other people on the face of the earth have raised the dance to such a degree of studied development as the American Indian nations. Each has a large number, ranging from ten to thirty, which have been handed down from generation to generation. These dances, which have special names, as the buffalo dance, the war dance, the feather dance, and the fish dance, are sometimes the recognized property of a particular society or brotherhood, but usually belong to the nation at large. Each has its own peculiar plan, steps and method, its songs and choruses and its musical instruments; and each is adapted to some particular occasion. The dance is universally recognized amongst them as a mode of worship, whence its elaborate character and wide distribution. Amongst the Village Indians of New Mexico their dances are the same to day they were centuries ago, and they are not distinguishable in their order, steps, and method, or in their songs, choruses, and musical instruments, from the dances of the Iroquois, the Dakotas, the Ojibwas, or the Blackfeet. They reveal the same conceptions, are adapted to the same condition of society, and were apparently derived from a common source.

Fifthly. The Structure of Indian Society. The evidence from the structure of Indian society bears decisively in the same direction. In the tribal organization, which prevailed very generally, though not universally, amongst them; and more especially in their form of government by chiefs and councils, a uniformity of organization prevailed throughout all the Indian nations of North America, the Village Indians inclusive.

Lastly. Conformation in Cranial Characteristics. Dr. Morton collected and presented the evidence from this source. He subdivides the "American," which is the fourth of his five great races of mankind, into two families, the American and the Toltecan, the latter embracing the Village Indians.[1] The ethnic unity of the American aborigines, with the exception of the Eskimo, was one of the principal conclusions reached by his investigations. It is proper to remark, however, that the sufficiency of the evidence from this source to sustain this conclusion has been repeatedly questioned.[2] The systems of relationship of the several nations thus far considered confirm Dr. Morton's conclusion to the extent of the number of nations represented in the Table, whether the facts upon which he relied are found inconclusive or otherwise.

From the commencement of this investigation the author has been extremely desirous to procure the evidence in full, which the system of consanguinity and affinity of the Village Indians might afford upon this important question. Its determination is of paramount importance in Indian ethnography, as well as necessary to its further advancement. So long as a doubt rests upon it, substantial progress is arrested. In the present attempt to establish the existence of an Indian family upon the basis of their system of relationship, a nucleus only has thus far been formed. Unless the Village Indians are found to be constituent members of this family, in virtue of a common descent, the family itself will lose much of its importance. The genetic connection of the two great divisions of the American aborigines is rendered so far probable by the several considerations before adduced

---

[1] Crania Americana, p. 5.

[2] Dr. J. Aitken Meigs, Trans. Acad. Nat. Sci., Philadelphia, 1860. "Observations upon the Form of the Occiput in the Various Races of Men," cf. Wilson's Prehistoric Man, sec. ed. ch. xx.

that the existence somewhere of absolute proof of the affirmative is to be presumed. It is extremely probable, not to say certain, that their systems of relationship would furnish the deficient evidence. At all events it might be expected to establish either the affirmative or the negative. Entertaining this belief, it is with much regret that I am able to furnish the system of but three nations of Village Indians, and these imperfectly worked out. Although the New Mexican Village Indians are now under the supervision of the national government, through superintendents and agents, their country seems, notwithstanding, to be hermetically sealed, so far as ethnological investigations are concerned, unless they are made in person. India and China are both much more accessible. For six years in succession the effort to procure their system of relationship was repeated until every available resource was exhausted. The two New Mexican schedules obtained are, however, of some value. They are carried far enough to show that they possess an elaborate system; and that it is coincident, substantially, with the common typical form, as far as it is given.

Some notice of the dialects and stock languages in New Mexico and Arizona should precede this limited exposition of their system of relationship. There are, at present, seven recognized stock languages spoken by the Village Indians within these areas. Lieut. Simpson furnished specimen vocabularies of the first five here-after named, and with it a classification of the nations enumerated by him.[1] Prof. Turner classified the remaining Pueblo Indians upon vocabularies furnished by Lieut. Whipple.[2] The former made six of these languages, but his first and fourth appear to be identical. It is not improbable that the present number will hereafter be reduced. The people still speak their native dialects with the single exception of the Indians of the Pueblo of Lentis, who have adopted the Spanish language. Lieut. Simpson classifies the dialects of the seven Moqui Pueblos, as one, although according to the statements of Lieut. Ives there may be some doubt upon the question. The latter remarks as follows: " A singular statement made by the Moquis is that they do not all speak the same language. At Oraybe some of the Indians actually professed to be unable to understand what was said by the Moos-hahneh chief, and the latter told me that the language of the two towns was different. At Tegwa they say that a third distinct tongue is spoken. These Indians are identical in race, manners, habits, and mode of living. They reside within a circuit of ten miles, and, save for the occasional visit of a member of some other tribe, have been for centuries isolated from the rest of the world."[3] The differences referred to may be simply dialectical.

---

[1] Report U. S. Senate, Docs. No. 64. 1st Session, 31st Congress, 1849–1850, v. 14, p. 140.
[2] Explorations, &c., for a Railroad Route to the Pacific, v. iii., Rep. Ind. Tribes, p. 94.
[3] Colorado Exploring Expedition, 1857–1858, p. 127.

I. Village Indians of New Mexico and Arizona.

Stock Languages.	Dialects.
I. Acoman.	1. Acoma. 2. Santo Domingo. 3. San Felipe. 4. Santa Anna. 5. Silla. 6. Laguna. 7. Pojuate. 8. Cochiti. 9. Jemez (old Pecos, the same).
II. Tezukan.	1. Tesuque. 2. San Juan. 3. Santa Clara. 4. Santa Ildefonso. 5. Pojuaque. 6. Nambe.
III. Isletan.	1. Isleta. 2. Taos. 3. Picoris. 4. Sandia.
IV. Zuñian.	Zuñi.
V. Mokian.	1. Oraybe. 2. Tegwa. 3. Mooshahneh, and four other Pueblos names not given.
VI. Piman.	1. Pimos (Papagos the same).
VII. Yuman.	1. Cuchan. 2. Coco-Maricopa. 3. Mohave. 4. Diegeños. 5. Yabipais.

Whether the dialects of the villages or nations above named are severally distinct I am unable to state.   The number of the stock languages within this area is unusually large.   It raises a presumption in favor of its long occupation by Village Indians.   This presumption is still further strengthened by the existence of ruins of Pueblo communal houses in various parts of the country.   The Casas Grandes upon the Colorado, the Gila and Salinas Rivers, and in the Mexican province of Chihuahua have long been known.   None of these, however, are equal in magnitude or importance with those on the Rio de Chaco, before referred to, and described by Lieut. Simpson.   These various and scattered ruins are so many standing memorials of the long-continued struggles between the Village Indians and the Roving nations for the possession of the country.   There is no evidence that the former were, in any respect, superior to the latter in the art of war, and many reasons for supposing that they were inferior to them in courage and hardihood.   There can be no doubt whatever that a large part of these areas were always in possession of the non-agricultural nations, as at the present day; and that the Village Indians were compelled to erect these communal edifices, which are in the nature of fortresses, to maintain possession of any portion of the country against the streams of migrants constantly moving down upon them from the Valley of the Columbia.

The Village Indians of the Rio Grande and its tributaries have diminished largely within the last hundred years.   In 1851 they numbered about eight thousand by census.[1]   Those upon the Colorado and its tributaries are more numerous, but the present estimate is probably exaggerated.   Mr. Charles D. Posten, Superintendent of Indian affairs for Arizona, estimated their numbers in 1863 at thirty-one thousand.[2]

1. Laguna. The first system of relationship to be presented is that of the people of the Pueblo of Laguna.   This village, consisting of a number of communal houses, is situated upon the San Jose, one of the western tributaries of the Rio Grande, about one hundred and twenty-five miles southwest of Santa Fé.   It is thus described by Dr. Ten Broeck, an Assistant Surgeon in the U. S. Army: " The town is built upon a slight rocky eminence, near the base of which runs a small stream, that supplies

---

[1] Schoolcraft's Hist. Cond. and Pros. VI. 709.

[2] President's Message and Documents 1863–1864, Dep. of Interior, p. 510.   The following are Mr. Posten's estimates: Papagos (Pimeria Alta) 7500; Pimas and Maricopas (Gila) 5000; Cocopas (Mouth of Colorado) 3000; Yumas or Cuchans (Colorado) 3500; Mohaves 5000, and Moquis (seven Pueblos) 7000.

them with water. Their lands are in the valley to the north. The population is about nine hundred. The houses are built of stone laid in mud, and, like all the other pueblos, consist of several stories built up in a terrace form; and as they have no doors opening upon the ground, one must mount to the roof by means of a ladder, and then descend through a trap-door in order to gain admittance."[1] The "terrace form" here referred to is a characteristic of the architecture of the Village Indians. A single house, not unfrequently two and three hundred feet long and a hundred feet deep, is carried up four and five stories, the second story covering the whole of the first except a space about ten feet wide along the front of the building which forms the roof of the first story. In like manner the third story stands back the same distance from the front of the second; and the fourth from the third; so that the front shows a series of stories receding as they rise, like the steps of a pyramid. The houses in the ancient Pueblo of Mexico were constructed upon the same general principles, and can probably be explained, as well as the ancient Pueblos in Yucatan, Chiapa and Guatemala, from the present architecture of the Village Indians of the Rio Grande.

There are terms in the Laguna dialect for grandfather and grandmother, *Na-nă-hash-te* and *Pä-pä-kee-you*; for father and mother, *Nish-te-ă* and *Ni-ya*; for son and daughter, *Să-mŭt* and *Să-măk*; and for grandson and granddaughter, *Să-nă-nă* and *Să-pă-pă*. A great-grandson and great-granddaughter become a son and daughter as in the Pawnee, which by correlation would make a great-grandfather a father.

There are terms for elder and younger brother, *Sät-tum-si-yă*, and *Tŭm-mŭ-hă-mäsh*; and for elder and younger sister, *Să-gwets-si-yă* and *Să-gue-sä-ha-mäsh*. As applied to collaterals, *Tŭm-mŭ* is my brother, a male speaking, and *Să-gwech* is my sister, a female speaking. The other terms are not given.

First Indicative Feature. Not given; but as the correlative relationship is that of '*father*' without much doubt my brother's son and daughter, *Ego* a male, are my son and daughter.

Second. Not given; but since the correlative relationship is that of *uncle*, it seems equally probable that my sister's son and daughter, *Ego* a male, are my nephew and niece.

Third. My father's brother is my father, *Nish-te-ă*.

Fourth. My father's brother's son is my brother, *Tum-mŭ*.

Fifth. My father's sister is my mother, *Ni-ya*.

Sixth. My mother's brother is my uncle, *Să-nou-wa*.

Seventh. My mother's sister I call *Sä-ni-ya*.

Eighth. Not given.

Ninth. My grandfather's brother is my grandfather, *Na-nă-hash-te*.

Tenth. Not given.

The relationship of cousin is unknown. My father's sister's son is my son, whence by correlation my mother's brother's son is my father. This would place the children of a brother and sister in the relationship of father and son, as amongst the Creek, Cherokees, Pawnees, and Minnitarees.

---

[1] Schoolcraft's Hist. Cond. and Pros. IV. 76.

2. Tesuque. It is impossible to form an opinion of the details of the Tesuque system of relationship upon the fragment given in the Table. The relationship of brother is in the twofold form of elder and younger, *No-vi-pa-ra*, and *No-vi-te-u*, whilst elder and younger sister are designated by a single term, *No-vi-pa-re*. The terms for father and mother are *No-vi-cen-do*, and *No-vi-ca*; for son and daughter, *No-vi-a*, and *No-vi-a-au-u-kwe*; and for grandchild, *Nau-wi-ta-te-e*. There is also, which is quite unusual, a term for great-grandchild, *Pa-pa-e*. It also appears incidentally that the children of brothers, of sisters, and of brothers and sisters, are all alike brothers and sisters to each other. Dr. Steck, who furnished what is given of the system, remarks: "If the persons addressed are younger than the speaker, they are called brother and sister; and of older, and particularly if of advanced age, they are addressed as fathers or mothers. The Indian Jose Maria Vigil, who gives me this information, is quite intelligent, and understands the system of the Spanish in this country, who recognize third and fourth, and even fifth cousins. The Indians only go to the third degree; after that they address each other as brother and sister, father or mother, according to age. Their system is very limited, and very much like that of the Iroquois. You will notice that there is no difference whether the person addressed is male or female, or whether older or younger." These remarks are too general to indicate the nature of the system, except, perhaps, the implication that it is classificatory in its character.

The Laguna schedule, although incomplete, tends very strongly to show the possession of the common system by the Laguna Village Indians, and inferentially by the remaining nations. The time is not far distant when it will become an easy matter to determine the question with certainty. In the mean time the great question of the genetic connection, or non-connection of the Village Indians with the Ganowánian family, must be left where this imperfect glimpse at their system of relationship, and the other evidence adduced, leaves it, but with a strong probability of an affirmative conclusion.

II. Village Indians of Central America.

1. Chontal. The Chontal language is allied to the Maya of Yucatan. It also affiliates with the Chol and Tzental of Chiapa. Whilst the Chontales proper inhabit the region bordering Lake Nicaragua on its east side, the branch of this stock, whose system of relationship is about to be considered, live in Mexico, in the State of Tabasco. Dr. H. Berendt, who transmitted the schedule, remarks: "The Chontal Indians live in the lower parts of that State [Tabasco], extending to the east as far as the river Tulija, and to the west to the Rio Seco, the old (now dry bed of the Orijalba, or Mescalassa, or Tabasco) river." Although great care was taken by Don Augustin Vilaseca, of the city of Tabasco, to procure the Chontal system, a misapprehension, frequently made by others, defeated the attempt. The schedule, after being translated into Spanish, was placed in the hands of Guillermo Garcia, an educated Chontal Indian living upon the Tabasco river. Misconceiving the plan of the schedule, he fell into the error of translating the questions into the Chontal language, which, of course, left them unanswered. The principal terms of relationship are given, but the manner of their use in the collateral lines remains unexplained. And since it is impossible to form any opinion of the system from

terms, apart from their use, the work, which barely failed of being complete, was entirely lost. All that appears is that the relationships of brother and sister are in the twofold form of elder and younger, and that the different relationships, both by blood and marriage, are fully discriminated.

III. Village Indians of South America.

It is with extreme regret that the author acknowledges the entire failure of his attempts to procure the system of relationship of the Indian nations of South America. The importance of the system of these nations in its bearing upon the great question whether they are constituent portions of the Ganowánian family, will at once be seen and recognized. At the outset of this investigation, as has elsewhere been stated, schedules were sent to the several diplomatic and consular representatives of the United States throughout Spanish America, with the hope that a portion at least of these nations might be reached, and their system obtained. These schedules were forwarded by the Secretary of State of the United States, with a circular commending the subject to their attention. The principal difficulty, undoubtedly, was the barrier of language, which might have been avoided, to a considerable extent, by the translation of the schedule into Spanish.[1]

One of these schedules sent to New Granada, was placed by General Jones, U. S. Minister Resident at Bogota, in the hands of Dr. Uricoechea, who filled it out, as far as he was able, in the language of the Chibcha or Muyska Indians of New Grenada. In his letter to the author, he remarks, " I send, partially filled up, one of your schedules in the language of the ancient inhabitants of this city. The nation has been long lost, and its language is nowhere spoken. However little we know of their language and customs, I believe that they have *the very same system* of consanguinity as the Iroquois. . . . As the language, besides the notices given in Trübner's Bibliotheca Glottica, I have just discovered a new grammar and vocabulary, of the year 1620. I possess three different grammars (two in MS.), and two dictionaries, which seem to be copies of an older one." Although the schedule is not sufficiently filled to develop the essential characteristics of the Muyska system, it is extremely interesting from the general conformity to the common system, which it shows, as far as its own form is displayed. Since the number of the questions he was able to answer are few in comparison with the entire list, the questions and answers will be presented in full. They are as follows, except the translations of the terms, which have been added :—

---

[1] The schedules sent to the United States Legation at Brazil were placed in the hands of an attaché, Porter C. Bliss, Esq., who afterwards visited a large number of Indian nations in Brazil, Paraguay, the Argentine Confederation, Bolivia, and Peru, for ethnological and philological purposes. He succeeded in filling out schedules in nations representing several stock languages in South America, but becoming afterwards involved in the civil disturbances in Paraguay, he was arrested and imprisoned by President Lopez, and his papers, the schedules among them, were seized and destroyed. He informed the author, after his return, that he found the system of the Northern Indians, with more or less distinctness, amongst the South American Indian nations. The principal stock languages south of the Amazon, as determined by him, are the Quichua, Aymara, Araucanian, Abipone, Toba, Ecole, Metagwaya, Guarani, Payagua, Machicuy, Chequitian, Patagonian, and Fuegian.

My Grandmother (mother's side),	Lu-e-hi'-sa,	My Grandmother.
" Father,	Pa'-ba,	" Father.
" Mother,	Gu-u-i-ra,	" Mother.
" Son (first born),	Chi-ti', others Chu-ta,	" Son or child.
" Daughter (first born),	Chu-ti', " Chu-ta,	" Daughter or child.
" Grandson,	Chu'-ne,	" Grandchild.
" Granddaughter,	Chu'-ne,	" "
" Elder brother (male speaking),	Gi'-a,	" Elder brother.
" " " (female speaking),	Ri-cu'-i,	" " "
" " sister (male speaking),	Gu-i'-a,	" " sister.
" Younger brother (male speaking),	Cu-hu'-ba,	" Younger brother.
" " " (female "),	P-cu-i-hi'-ta,	" " "
" " sister (male "),	Cu-hu'-ba,	" " sister.
" Brothers,	Gui'-as-cu-bi'-a-sa,	" Elder and younger brothers.
" Brother's son (male speaking),	Chu'-ta,	" Son.
" " son's wife,	Chu'-ta,	" Daughter.
" " daughter,	Chu'-ta,	" Daughter.
" " daughter's husband,	Chu'-ta,	" Son.
" Sister's son (male speaking),	Gwab-xi'-que,	" Nephew.
" Father's brother,	Ze-pa'-ba,	
" " brother's wife,	Zeg'-yi,	
" " " son,	The sons of two brothers call themselves brothers.	
" " sister,	Ze-pa'-ba, Fu'-cha?	
" " sister's son (m. speaking),	Ub-so,	My Male cousin.
" " " " (f. speaking),	Sa-ha-o'-a,	" " " and husband.
" " " daughter,	Pab'-cha,	" Female cousin.
" Mother's brother,	Zu-e'-cha,	" Uncle.
" " sister,	Su-a'-i-a ?	
" " sister's son,	The sons of sisters call themselves brothers.	
" Husband,	Sa-ha'-o-a,	My Husband and cousin.
" Wife,	Gu-i',	" Wife.
" Husband's father,	Gu-a'-ca,	" Father-in-law.
" " mother,	Cha-hu-a'-i-a,	" Mother-in-law.
" Wife's father,	Chi'-ca,	" Father-in-law.
" Son-in-law,	Chi'-ca (said of wife's father),	" Son-in-law.
" " "	Gu-a'-i-ca (" " mother),	" " "
" Step-son,	Ze-cu'-hi-ep-cu-a'-i-a I-chu-ta?	
" Step-daughter,	" "	
" Brother-in-law (husband's brother),	Ub-so,	" Brother-in-law and cousin
" Sister-in-law (" sister),	Gi'-ca,	" Sister-in-law.

From the foregoing fragment of the Chibcha or Muyska system of relationship, it is apparent that it possessed an elaborate nomenclature; that consanguinei and marriage relations, near and remote, were classified under the near degrees; and that the several relationships were discriminated with the same minuteness which characterizes the system of the Ganowánian family. Although it would be premature to draw an inference of genetic connection from this incomplete representation of the system of a portion of the Village Indians of South America, nevertheless it seems probable that if the system which prevailed in this nation could be fully procured, it would be found to be identical, in whatever is radical, with the typical form.

The Muyska Village Indians close the series of Indian nations represented in

34   March, 1870.

the Table, whose system of relationship is founded either upon common principles of discrimination and classification, or, in their incomplete state, show such affinities therewith as render probable their possession of the same system.   Upon this basis they have been constituted into a family.   The sufficiency of this system to sustain the conclusion of their genetic connection will elsewhere be further considered. It remains to present the system of the Eskimo, which is of such a character as to exclude this people from the Ganowánian connection, and, after that, to take up the systems of the Eastern Asiatic nations.

CHAPTER VII.

SYSTEM OF RELATIONSHIP OF THE ESKIMO.

The Eskimo a Littoral People—Their Extended Spread—Nearness of their Dialects—Their Occupation of Arctic America and Greenland comparatively Modern—Ethnic Relations of the Eskimo hitherto undetermined—Detached from the Indian Connection by Dr. Morton—Cranial Characteristics the Ground—The Habitat of Man Coextensive with the Surface of the Earth—Our Knowledge of the Eskimo still limited—Points of Agreement and of Divergence between the Eskimo and the other American Aborigines—Eskimo System of Relationship—Classificatory in Character—Details of the System—It possesses but two of the Indicative Characteristics of the Ganowánian System—Reasons for excluding the Eskimo from this Family.

THE Eskimo are a peculiar people. Dwelling exclusively in an arctic climate, beyond the region of trees, and with no vegetation around them save the lichens and the mosses, they have put themselves, for subsistence, upon the sea. As a littoral people, living upon the whale, the walrus, and the seal, they have made their homes along the bays and inlets wherever these animals are found; and have become spread, in consequence, along thousands of miles of sea coasts. Throughout Arctic America, from the Pacific to the Atlantic, and eastward in Greenland, nearly to the shores opposite ancient Scandinavia, they were found in the exclusive occupation of this extended line. It is also particularly remarkable that they still speak dialects of the same language not only, but with a less amount of dialectical variation than is found in the extremes of the Algonkin or Dakotan speech. Purity of blood, which their isolation and habits tended to maintain, would preserve homogeneity in the materials of their language; but this would neither increase nor retard the progress of dialectical change in its vocables, after the people became geographically separated. The undoubted nearness of these dialects, notwithstanding their spread over a longer continuous line than any other human speech, except, perhaps, the American Indian, tends very strongly to show that their occupation of Arctic America was a modern event in comparison with the epoch of the first occupation of the continent by the Ganowánian family. Their mode of life, after it had become permanently adopted, restricted their migrations to the sea shores, and resulted ultimately in their isolation from the remainder of the human family. Although reindeer and aquatic fowls entered their areas in their periodic migrations, and contributed to their subsistence, their principal reliance was upon fish and upon the animals of the sea. The kaiyak and the lance express the substance of their progress towards civilization. We are forced to regard them as an exclusive people, in a social condition more remarkable than that of the arctic nations of Europe or of Asia. Irrespective of their antecedent history they are at the present time a peculiar people, transformed into veritable hyperboreans, dwelling in houses of snow and ice, and living upon raw flesh like the carnivorous animals. The annexed comparative vocabularies, together with the terms of relationship in the Table (Table II), will illustrate the present relations of the several Eskimo dialects to each other.[1]

Their ethnic relations are still undetermined, unless the conclusion of Dr. Morton, which was based chiefly upon cranial characteristics, is regarded as established. In his classification the Eskimo are detached from the American Indian connection and transferred to the Mongolian race. They are placed with other arctic nations in his "Polar Family."[2] This family, which consists of all the polar nations in Europe, Asia, America, and the island of Greenland,[3] is constituted in violation of the linguistic affinities of these nations, and therefore it has not been recognized as a family by philologists. Neither has the evidence adduced by him, in favor of the separation of the Eskimo from the remainder of the American aborigines, been

[1] COMPARATIVE VOCABULARY.

	Eskimo of Behring's Sea (Kuskutchewak). Richardson.	Eskimo of Hudson's Bay. Gallatin.	Eskimo of Labrador. Latrobe.	Eskimo of Northumberland Inlet. Morgan.	Eskimo of Greenland. Cranz and Egede.
1. Head,	Ne-bä-gun	Ne-a-koke	Ne-ä-ko	Ne-ah'-ko	Ni-a-kok
2. Hair,	Nä-e-ät [(pl)	Nu-yak-ka	Nŭ-a-ak	Nŭ'-yä	Ny-ak
3. Ear,	Tchu-u-tu-ek	He-u-tin-ga	Se-ŭt	Che'-une	Si-ut
4. Eye,	Ve-ta-tŭ-ek(pl)	Ei-a-ga	E-ye	E'-ye	Ir-se
5. Nose,	Nekh	Kin-ga-ra	King-äk	Kling'-yäng	Hin-gak
6. Teeth,	Khŭ-ă-tŭ-ek	Kee-yu-teel-ka	Ke-ŭ-til	Te-u'-tee	Ki-u-tet (plu)
7. Mouth,	Kä-nek	Kan-ne-ra	Kän-nerk	Kun'-yu	Han-nek
8. Neck,	U-e-ä-nŭt	Tok-e-loo-ga	U-e-äk	Kong-i'-shil	
9. Rain,	Tchä-le-ä-le-ak	Mak-kook-poke	Sel-lä-lŭk	She-lil'-lŭ	
10 Sun,	Akk-tä	Ne-i-ya [it rains]	Ak-kee-sŭk	Suk'-ŭ-nung	Suc-a-nuk
11. Moon,	Tang-ek	Au-ning-a	Täk-kek	Tuk'-keˉung	An-ning-a
12. Wind,	A-nŭ-kä	A-no-ee	An-no-re		
13. Night,	Un-ŭk	Oo-noo-ak	U-nŭ-äk	Ood'-na	
14. Fire,	Knŭ-äk	Ik-koo-ma	Ek-o-mä		Ing-nek
15. Reindeer,	Tŭn-tŭ		Tŭk-tŭ	Tŭk'-tŭ	Tŭ-tŭ(O'Reilly)
16. White,	U-golk-kak	Kow-dlook	Kaud-lŭk-pok	Kä-goke'-to	
17. Black,	Tan-ŭlh-gät	Ker-ni-uk	Kern-gŭt	Kog-noke'-tä	
18. Red,	Ker-ä-gok	N-oo-pa-look	Au-pa-lŭk-tok [(it is red)	Aow-pat'-tŭ	
19. Blue,	Tchun-ä-e-za		Tŭng-ä-yŭk-täk	Tŭng-a-yŭ'-ge-	
20. Walrus,	Azgh-vu-ek		To-gäk	I'-ve-uk [tä	
21. Dog,	An-nä-kuk-tä	Ke-i-meg	Kem-mek	Kim'-mik	Mik-ee
22. Ice,	Tche-ko	Sik-koo	Se-ko	Sce'-koo	
23. Snow.	Kän-ekh-chäk	Kan-ne-uk-poke	Kän-nek	Ah-poon (frost)	
24. One,	A-tŭ-ŭ-chik	At-tow-se-ak	A-tou-sek	Ah-tow'-she-ang	At-tau-sek
25. Two,	Malk-khok	Ard-lek	Mar-ruk	Mok'-o	Ar-la-ek
26. Three,	Pä-e-nä-e-väk	Ping-a-hu-ke	Ping-a-sŭt	Pingᴸ-ä-shŭ	Pin-ga-ju-ak
27. Four,	Tchä-mek	Sit-ta-mat	Sct-tä-mut	She-shum'-mun	Sis-sa-mat

The Greenland Eskimo were probably emigrants from Labrador. Upon this question Cranz observes: "There can be no hesitation in affirming that Greenland was peopled from Labrador, not Labrador from Greenland." Hist. of Greenland, I, 349. Dr. Prichard expressed the same opinion, as follows: "As the Skraellings or Esquimaux of Greenland had not reached that country at the time when the Northmen had settled their early colonies in it, it may be conjectured that the progress of the race was from the west, since they had not arrived at the more distant point towards Europe till within the age of history." Nat. Hist. of Man, p. 221.

[2] Crania Americana, Philadelphia ed., 1839, folio, p. 5.

[3] Ib. p. 50.

received as conclusive. This last question is one of great importance in American ethnology. Their system of consanguinity and affinity was sought with special interest for the bearing it might have upon the solution of this problem.

The Eskimo stock are found both in Asia and America. The inhabitants of the islands of Behring's Sea, and Nammollas, or Sedentany Tshuktshi upon the shores of the Gulf of Anadyr, speak dialects of the Eskimo; and this speech has been traced as far west in Asia as the mouth of the Kolyma River, thus establishing the fact of the spread of this people on both sides of the straits of Behring. Whilst the fact furnishes evidence of an Asiatic connection, it has no necessary bearing upon the question of the blood connection or non-connection of the Eskimo with the American Indian nations. It can be explained as a migration of the same people across the straits of Behring, which interposes no obstacle to such a transit proceeding from either to the other shore; although it seems much more probable that the Eskimo were originally migrants from Asia, than that the Tshuktshi were migrants from America. Dr. Morton claims that the skulls of the Eskimo exhibit differences of such a marked and decisive character as to justify their separation from the Indian connection, and their transference to the Mongolian. He had reached this conclusion from a comparison of physical characteristics before he had examined any Eskimo skulls. "Since writing the chapter on the polar family" (page 50), he remarks: "I have been favored by George Comb, Esq., with the use of four genuine Esquimaux skulls, which are figured in the annexed plate (Plate LXX). The eye at once remarks their narrow elongated form, the projecting upper jaw, the extremely flat nasal bones, the expanded zygomatic arches, the broad and expanded cheek bones, and the full and prominent occipital regions."

"The extreme elongation of the upper jaw contracts the facial angle to a mean of seventy-three degrees, while the mean of three heads of the four gives an internal capacity of eighty-seven cubic inches, a near approach to the Caucasian average." * * * *

"The great and uniform differences between these heads, and those of the American Indians, will be obvious to any one accustomed to make comparisons of this kind, and serve as corroborative evidence of the opinion that the Esquimaux are the only people possessing Asiatic characteristics on the American continent."[1]

The separation of the Eskimo from the Indian family was one of the striking results of Dr. Morton's original and interesting investigations. Whether his premises are sufficient to sustain this inference, or otherwise, the latter is confirmed by the evidence contained in their system of relationship, which also separates them by a clearly defined line from the Ganowánian family, as well as from the Turanian and Malayan.[2] If the American aborigines came originally from Asia, it

---

[1] Crania Americana, Phila. ed. 1839, p. 247.

[2] The specific measurements given by Dr. Morton do not seem to be conclusive, taken alone, in favor of such a separation; since the differences may be neutralized by comparing the four Eskimo skulls with those of American Indians of the same internal capacity. The whole of the evidence from cranial characteristics is not contained in these specific measurements; and, therefore, if they are neutralized in this manner, it does not necessarily follow that cranial comparisons are incapable of yielding definite and trustworthy conclusions. For the purpose of illustration we may select from

would follow that two migrations from that continent to the American remain to be explained, one of which must have preceded the other by a long interval of time.

Our knowledge of the Eskimo is even more limited than it is of the other Ameri-

---

Dr. Morton's "Table of Anatomical Measurements" (page 257), certain skulls of American Indians agreeing respectively with the four Eskimo skulls in internal capacity, and ascertain the amount of difference by a comparison of their specific measurements. The following table shows the relative measurements.

Skulls.	Longitudinal diameter.	Parietal diameter.	Frontal diameter.	Vertical diameter.	Intermas. arch.	Intermast. Line.	Occipito frontal arch.	Horizontal periphery.	Facial angle.	Internal capacity.
Eskimo, No. 1 . .	7.5	5.4	4.6	5.4	14.3	4.1	15.2	20.4	72°	93.
Cayuga. . . .	7.8	5.1	4.2	5.4	14.2	4.5	15.5	20.8	78	93.5
Oneida	7.5	5.6	4.1	5.8	14.4	4.3	14.9	20.8	74	92.5
Eskimo, No. 2 . .	7.3	5.5	4.4	5.3	14.1	4.3	14.4	20.3	75	80.
Atacames . . .	7.2	5.5	4.4	5.1	14.8	4.1	13.7	20.2	76	80.
Seminole . . .	6.9	5.6	4.6	5.3	15.	4.2	13.6	19.8	75	80.
Eskimo, No. 3 . .	7.5	5.1	4.3	5.5	14.8	3.9	15.5	20.3	73	87.5
Menominee . . .	7.1	5.8	4.5	5.4	14.9	4.6	14.1	20.6	75	87.
Cherokee	7.2	5.2	4.2	5.5	15.5	4.4	14.6	20.2	77	88.

The difference of half a cubic inch in the internal capacity of a skull of eighty-seven cubic inches and upwards would scarcely be appreciated in the specific measurements. It appears, then, by the comparison of the measurements of the Eskimo, Cayuga, and Oneida skulls, that the greatest difference in any one measurement is five-tenths of an inch; and that the differences between the Cayuga and Oneida skulls are as great as between the Eskimo and Cayuga, or between the Eskimo and the Oneida. Dr. Morton refers particularly to three points of difference, the first of which is the "narrow," and the second is the "elongated" form of the Eskimo skulls, and the third is "the contraction of the facial angle." It will be observed that the Cayuga skull is narrower than the Eskimo by three-tenths of an inch, while the Oneida is wider by two-tenths. Secondly, that the Cayuga skull is longer by three-tenths of an inch, while the Oneida is of the same length as the Eskimo. The facial angles are respectively 72°, 78°, and 74°.

If we next compare the measurements of the second Eskimo skull with those of the Atacames and Seminole, it will be seen that the greatest difference in any one measurement is nine-tenths of an inch, and that the differences between the Atacames and the Seminole are less than between the Eskimo and the Seminole, and about the same as between the Eskimo and the Atacames. In parietal diameter the Eskimo and Atacames are the same, and but a tenth of an inch narrower than the Seminole; while in longitudinal diameter, the Eskimo is one-tenth of an inch longer than the Atacames, and four-tenths of an inch longer than the Seminole. The facial angles are respectively 75°, 76°, and 75.°

Lastly, a similar comparison of the measurements of the third Eskimo skull with those of the Menominee and the Cherokee will show that the greatest difference in any one measurement is one and four-tenth inches; and that the differences between the Menominee and Cherokee are less than between the Eskimo and the Menominee, and about the same as between the Eskimo and the Cherokee. The Eskimo skull is one-tenth of an inch narrower than the Menominee, and seven-tenths narcan nations. The Scandinavians colonized Greenland in 986; and when they subsequently came in contact with the Greenland Eskimo they bestowed upon them derisively the name of Skraellings, "expressive of their dwarfish and imbecile appearance."[1] About the year 1000 these enterprising navigators are supposed, in Vineland, to have discovered the coasts of Massachusetts and Rhode Island. From their description of the natives of Vineland, Von Bäer and others believed them to have been Eskimo. Be the fact as it may, when Jacques Cartier, in 1535, entered the Gulf of St. Lawrence the Eskimo dwelt upon its north shore; and subsequently to this event they were found in possession of the coast of Labrador. On the west side of Hudson's Bay they occupied as far south as Churchill River. The migration of a portion of the Eskimo from the arctic into the temperate climate, and from the treeless regions of the north into the forest areas, is a significant fact, tending to show a disposition, at least, to transfer themselves out of their polar habitat.

The physical ability of mankind, by the general process of acclimation, to endure all climates, suggests the inference that the natural habitat of man is coextensive with the surface of the earth. In this respect he differs from all other animals, whose habitats are more or less circumscribed. The spread of the Aryan family in Europe, Asia, and America, of the Turanian in Asia, and of the Ganowánian in North and South America, assuming for the present that the American aborigines, with the exception of the Eskimo, constitute a single family, contains, on the part of each family, nearly sufficient evidence to demonstrate this proposition. The

---

rower than the Cherokee, while it is three-tenths of an inch longer than the former, and four-tenths of an inch longer than the latter. The facial angles are respectively 73°, 75°, and 77°.

It should be stated that in the selection of the Indian skulls for comparison, those were taken which approximated the nearest to the Eskimo in their several measurements. Such a selection was legitimate for the purpose in view. The differences found in these several skulls appear to neutralize each other, and to leave no result, except that of general conformity, instead of essential divergence. It suggests the question whether the specific measurements adopted are such as to reveal the indicative characteristics of the human skull; and whether comparisons which are founded upon these measurements exclusively, are capable of establishing or overthrowing supposed typical forms. The seventy-two plates, and the numerous diagrams of skulls in Dr. Morton's Crania Americana show that he did not rely exclusively upon these test measurements, but connected with them, as not less important, the position of the foramen, the zygoma, the jaws, the cheek bones, and the relative proportions of the anterior and posterior parts of the skull. With the actual specimens, and with the skill and experience acquired by steady and extended cómparisons, the means of knowledge must be admitted to extend far beyond the facts expressed by these specific measurements.

Dr. Daniel Wilson, who has devoted much attention to the investigation of the cranial characteristics of the American aborigines, and who has furnished a Table of the comparative measurements of thirty-nine Eskimo skulls, besides like Tables of a large number of American Indians, states his final conclusion founded upon these extended comparisons, as follows: "They show that the form of the human skull is just as little constant among different tribes or races of the New World, as of the Old; and that so far from any simple subdivision into two or three groups sufficing for American craniology, there are abundant traces of a tendency of development into the extremes of the brachicephalic and dolichocephalic or kumbocephalic forms, and again the intermediate gradations by which the one passes into the other." This work, founded upon comprehensive and thorough researches, is a most valuable contribution to American ethnology.—*Prehistoric Man*, 2d ed., p. 483.

[1] Cranz. Hist. of Greenland, London ed., 1820, I. 128.

complement of the evidence seems to be furnished by the establishments of the commercial nations of the Aryan family in every part of the earth, with the exception of the extreme parts of the arctic area; and even these have been penetrated and occupied by Americans and Europeans for limited periods of time. Their feet have been planted in the polar regions, even beyond the farthest range of the hyperboreans themselves. To account for the spread of mankind considered as a single species over the entire surface of the earth, there is no occasion to look beyond the voluntary migrations, or compulsory flights of nations from area to area, continued through centuries of time. The first struggle would be for the possession of the temperate climates, which are the most desirable. This would increase in intensity with the multiplication of the numbers of the people. In the course of ages the weaker nations would be forced outward, toward both the tropical and polar climates. From necessary considerations the impulse from the more desirable areas outward must have been continuous and ever increasing until the polar shores, as well as the tropical plains were reached. The final results would neither be fortuitous, nor consequences of man's voluntary acts; but rather the effect of the silent and unseen operation of physical and moral causes. Subsistence and numbers go hand in hand, so that the increase of the species beyond the equilibrium established between them would enforce the dispersion of the surplus. Whence the occupation of the arctic climates is not more remarkable in itself, than the occupation of the tropical; and starting from the intermediate temperate regions the same people might have divided and taken opposite directions, as in the case of the Athapascans and Apaches. The arctic regions would probably be reached last in the order of time, but yet it might be early in the period of man's existence upon the earth. Neither was the great increase of numbers which followed upon the attainment of the pastoral, and still greater of the agricultural state, necessary to insure these results; since it is well known that nations without flocks and herds, and without agriculture, spread much the most rapidly. It is the prerogative of civilization to enable a people to grasp the soil with firmness, and to establish themselves with permanence in fixed areas. Instability upon the soil was characteristic of the nations in primitive conditions of society. The occupation by the Eskimo of their arctic habitat can be explained satisfactorily by the operation of these natural causes.

The Eskimo have been so frequently and so minutely described that very little can be added to the stock of existing information. Those who have seen the American Indian nations in their several areas, and also the Eskimo, might possibly, by means of a comparison founded upon personal observations, bring out with more distinctness the points of agreement and of difference, so far as they are revealed by external characteristics. Although I have seen and conversed with native Indians belonging to many different nations, I have met but three Eskimo, a man and woman, and their child. Whilst it is impossible to seize the characteristic features of a people from a few isolated representatives, the latter, if good specimens, as in the present case, might suggest the more general points of agreement and of divergence. Among the nations of the Ganowánian family there is no difficulty in recognizing, at a glance, a common physical type; but the Eskimo have some physical characteristics, which, although not excessively divergent, are yet sensible and marked. In a number of these characteristics they are not distinguishable from the American Indians in general; but yet they differ much more from each of these Indian nations than the latter do amongst themselves. The Eskimo referred to were brought down from the head of Baffin's Bay by the Arctic explorer, Capt. C. F. Hall, and were pronounced by him fair representatives of the Eskimo of that region. *E-pe-oke'-pe* the male, was twenty-four years of age, about five feet two inches high, straight, well formed, and with a ruddy complexion, the blood showing through his cheeks with a blush. This peculiarity I have never seen in any American Indian of pure blood. The cheek bones were high, the cheeks full, the nose rather flat at the lower extremity, and the nostrils dilated; the mouth of medium size, closed when silent, and with a pleasant expression; the lips moderately full, chin small and receding, beard nearly wanting, eyes black, of medium size, and horizontally set, but with the least perceptible obliquity. The skin was a reddish-brown, not differing from the color of the Northern Indians. The orbit of the eye externally was scarcely visible, the eye and lids filling the cavity flush with the brow, and giving the upper part of the nose a sunken appearance. This advanced position of the upper portion of the face below the skull, and which brought the line of the eyes flush with the line of the brows, was quite remarkable. Among the Ganowánian nations the orbit of the eye is rendered conspicuous by the projection of the forehead, and the sunken position of the eyes. The skull was elongated, narrow and pyramidal, with a wedge-shaped vertex, in which respect it presented a marked divergence from the common Indian type. The occiput was protuberant, and the skull relatively small. The hair was black and straight, but neither harsh nor coarse. His wife, *Tä-kä-re-tu*, was of about the same age, taller relatively, straight and not ill formed. Her general characteristics were much the same as those of her husband. The chief peculiarity of her face was the unusual length vertically, and great prominence of her cheeks, which stood out in oblong lobes on either side of her nose upon a line with its tip, and through which the blood showed with a deep blush. Whilst nursing her child I observed that her bosoms were oblong and deeply pendent, which is also characteristic of those of Ganowánian women. In the valley of the Columbia this pendency is so excessive in the females that the mother is able to nurse her child over her shoulder, the child mean time resting on her back. The Eskimo often do the same, and so do the females among the Village Indians of the Colorado.

Of the several characteristics named there are but three in which the Eskimo diverge from the common Indian type. First, the natural blush showing through the cheeks; second, the flatness of the face on the line of the eyes, together with its advance forward; and thirdly, the elongated and pyramidal structure of the skull, with the absence consequently of the flattened occiput. On the other hand, in the color of the skin, in the scantiness of the beard, in the color and character of the hair, in the smallness of the hands and feet, and in their carriage and manners they have the general appearance of American Indians. The Eskimo language, in whatever relates to articulation, accent, guttural and nasal utterances, and in the gesticulations of the persons in its delivery, is very much the same as the American Indian languages.   There were, however, some scraping sounds not easily explained, which I have never heard elsewhere.[1]

---

[1] There are some customs of such a strikingly personal character that they may, in a pre-eminent degree, be regarded as customs of the blood.   When prevalent over wide areas, and persistently maintained from generation to generation, they seem to possess some significance upon the question of the probable genetic connection of the peoples by whom they are practised.   There are three distinct customs or usages of this character, apparently transmitted with the blood, which I have taken some pains to trace, and have found them to be substantially universal in the Ganowánian family. They may possess some value as corroborative evidence of the unity of origin of these nations.   These are, first, the custom of saluting by kin; second, the usage of wearing the breech-cloth; and third, the usage of sleeping at night in a state of nudity, each person being wrapped in a separate covering. They are referred to in this connection for the purpose of comparison with the corresponding Eskimo usages.   The first of these has been definitely traced among all the principal Indian nations represented in the Table, and its universality in the Ganowánian family may be confidently affirmed. Exceptions may yet be found, but if they should it would not disturb the general rule.   Among the Eskimo the usage is found under a modified form.   They address each other when related by the term of relationship, and also by the personal name, using the former method rather more than the latter.   If the information obtained was correct, the usage, in its strictness, fails among the Eskimo. Secondly, the primitive costume of the Ganowánian family was the breech-cloth on the part of the males, and a skirt on the part of the females.   The former was a strip of skin, several inches wide, passed between the legs and thence up and under a string tied around the waist, the ends falling down before and behind; the latter was a short skirt, either of skin or vegetable materials, secured around the waist and falling nearly to the knees.   These two articles formed the costume of the Indian family, and all there was of it, except, possibly, the moccasin.   In the colder climates skin leggins and a blanket of skin were added.   At the present time the bulk of the family wear the same costume. Where American fabrics are substituted for skins they are made after the primitive pattern.   This explains the attachment of the Indians, male and female, for the woollen blanket, which has now become very generally substituted for that of skin.   Within the past hundred years a portion of each of the more advanced Indian nations have put on our dress, but the most of them still adhere to the old costume, with the addition of the woollen blanket.   Having noticed the general prevalence of the practice of wearing the cloth, it was made a subject of special inquiry, and this resulted in tracing its use among upwards of sixty Indian nations.   The simplicity and universality of this costume, and the persistency with which they have adhered to its use in the colder, and even in arctic climates, suggest two inferences which may possibly be drawn from it; first, that its use was primitive, and that it has been transmitted, as a usage, with the blood from their earliest ancestry; and secondly, that this ancestry belonged to a temperate climate.   The Eskimo do not wear it.   Thirdly, the third custom relates to their manner of sleeping, which may or may not possess significance.   Before retiring they denude themselves, with the exception of the cloth and skirt, and each one wraps up separately in a skin, covering or blanket, which usually envelops both head and feet.   Two males never sleep under the same covering in personal contact; young females, and mothers and their children do.   The Eskimo practise this custom in common with the American Indians.*   In answer to a letter of inquiry as to the usage, in this last respect, among the Tamil and Telugu people of South India, Rev. E. C. Scudder writes as follows: "All males (unless among the very high and rich ones) sleep in a state of almost entire nudity, wearing nothing but a little strip of cloth which passes between the legs, and is attached at either end to a string which is fastened about the waist.

---

* Samuel Hearne, in describing a night attack upon some Eskimo at the mouth of the Coppermine River made by the Athapascans, says, "The poor unhappy natives were surprised in the midst of their sleep, and had neither time nor power to make any resistance; men, women, and children, in all upwards of twenty, ran out stark naked, and endeavored to make their escape."

Hearne's Journey, &c. &c., Lond. ed. 4to., 1795, p. 153.   Dr. Kane, in his "Arctic Explorations," confirms this usage.

The Eskimo system of relationship contains original and distinctive features. It is classificatory in form, without being identical with the Ganowánian, Turanian, or Malayan, and it contains a number of specializations which move it in the direction of the descriptive form, but without establishing any identity between it and the Uralian or Aryan forms. Of the descriptive system, as we have seen, there are no varieties, but of the classificatory, as it will appear in the sequel, there are three, the Ganowánian and Turanian, the Malayan, and the Eskimo. As neither the Mongolian nor Tangusian nations have been reached by this investigation, and consequently their system remains unascertained, it is not improbable that they possess a system identical with the Eskimo. It has also some affinities with the Burmese and Karen, which are left without the Turanian connection.

There are three Eskimo schedules in the Table (Table II) which together present their system with sufficient fulness to exhibit its essential characteristics. The first was furnished by James R. Clare, Esq., of York Factory, one of the Factors of the Hudson's Bay Company, and contains some part of the system of the Eskimo west of Hudson's Bay. The second, that of the Greenland Eskimo, was filled out by Rev. Samuel Kleinschmidt, of Godthaab, in Greenland. It is not entirely complete, but it shows the principal part of the system. The third and last was procured by the author from the Eskimo before named, and contains the system of the Eskimo of the west side of Baffin's Bay. These persons spoke English imperfectly, but sufficiently well for ordinary purposes. They had acquired our language far enough to understand the plainest forms of speech, and possessed more than ordinary intelligence. The female Eskimo had acted as Capt. Hall's interpreter whilst in their country. The Eskimo language is by no means open and accessible, and yet I may be allowed to express confidence in the correctness of the rendering of their system as given in the Table, as I had the advantage of Captain Hall's partial knowledge of their language, as well as their knowledge of English. In the explanation of this system the nomenclature of the Eskimo of Baffin's Bay will be employed.

There are separate terms for grandfather and grandmother. *E-tŭ'-ah*, and *Ning-e-o'-wä*; for father and mother, *Ang'-o-tă*, and *Ah-nă'-nă*; for son and daughter, *En-ning'-ah*, and *Pun-ning'-ah*; and a term in common gender for grandchild,

---

This cloth is worn by day as well as night, and is concealed during the day by the waist cloth. Laborers, when at work, often take off the latter, and you will see children running about the streets constantly with nothing further on them. When sleeping the people cover themselves with a sheet which hides every part of the body, passing over the head and feet; and you often see them early in the morning lying in their verandas, presenting exactly the appearance of corpses laid out. Males never sleep in personal contact; neither do females young or old. Mothers and children do." The practice of wearing the cloth, which is found among all tropical nations, is founded upon natural suggestion, and upon climate; and it is only rendered significant by the pertinacity with which it is adhered to by the same people when transferred by migrations into cold, and even arctic climates, where a full covering of the body is rendered necessary, and the causes which led to the use of the cloth are superseded. It illustrates the difficulty of casting off, under changed conditions, these blood or hereditary usages, and upon this fact the propriety as well as the strength of any conclusions founded upon it must depend.

Eng'-o-tă. All ancestors above the first are grandfathers and grandmothers, and all children below the last are grandchildren.

There is a double set of terms for elder brother and elder sister, *Ang-a-yŭ'-äh,* and *Na-yă',* used by the males, and *An-ning'-ä,* and *Ang-a-yu'-ä,* used by the females; a single term for younger brother, *Nu'-kä,* used by both sexes; and two terms for younger sister, *Na'-yă,* used by the males, and *Nu-kä'-hä,* used by the females. It will be observed that a man calls his elder brother *Ang-a'-yu-ä,* and that a woman calls her elder sister the same; and that a man calls his elder and younger sister by the same term, *Na'-yă.* In the plural there are two terms for brothers, *Ka-tang'-o-tine* used by the males, and *Ah-ne'-kä,* used by the females; and also for sisters, *Na-yung'-ing* used by the males, and *Ang-o-yu'-kä* used by the females.

First Indicative Feature of the Ganowánian system wanting. My brother's son and daughter, *Ego* a male, are my nephew and niece, *Kung-e-ä'-gä,* the term being in common gender. With *Ego* a female, they are also my nephew and niece, but a different term, *Ung-ä'-gä,* also in common gender is employed.

Second Indicative Feature Neutralized. My sister's son and daughter, *Ego* a male, are my nephew and niece, *We-yo-o-'gwä,* the term being in common gender. With *Ego* a female, they are also my nephew and niece, *Noo-ä'-gä,* this term also being in common gender. It thus appears that there are four different terms for nephew, and as many for niece, the effect of which is to neutralize the first two indicative relationships of the Ganowánian system. But the children of these several nephews and nieces are each and all my grandchildren, thus bringing the first collateral line into the lineal, as in the Indian system.

Third Indicative Feature Wanting. My father's brother is my uncle, *Uk'-kä.*

Fourth Indicative Feature Wanting. My father's brother's son and daughter, *Ego* a male, are my cousins, *Il-lŭng'-ä,* the term being in common gender. With *Ego* a female, they are also my cousins, but a different term, *Il-lo'-ä,* also in common gender, is employed.

Fifth Indicative Feature Neutralized. My father's sister is my aunt, *At-chug'-a.* Her children are my cousins, to whom the same terms are applied as in the last case.

Sixth Indicative Feature Neutralized. My mother's brother is my uncle, *Ang-ug'-gä.* His children are my cousins as before.

Seventh Indicative Feature Wanting. My mother's sister is my aunt, *Ai-yug'-gä.*

Eighth Indicative Feature Wanting. My mother's sister's son and daughter are my cousins. Each being called, *Il-lŭng'-ä,* by the males, and *Il-lo'-ä* by the females.

Ninth Indicative Feature. My grandfather's brother and sister are my grandfather and grandmother. In all of the preceding cases the correlative terms are strictly applied, *e. g.,* the one I call my nephew calls me uncle.

Tenth Indicative Feature. The children of these several cousins are my nephews and nieces, and the terms are used as in the first collateral line, *e. g., Ego* a male, I call the son of my male cousin *Kung-e-ä-gä,* and with *Ego* a female, I call the son of my female cousin, *Noo-ä'-gä*. The children of these several collateral nephews and nieces are without distinction my grandchildren.

As near as could be ascertained the same classification was applied to the members of the third, fourth, and even more remote collateral lines; but as it was found extremely difficulty to follow the chain of relationship beyond the several branches of the first and second collateral lines, the attempt was forborne.

The Greenland Eskimo system, as far as it is given, agrees with that of the Eskimo of Baffin's Bay. The small amount of dialectical variation in the terms of relationship will also be noticed.

It will also be seen that the marriage relationships are fully discriminated, and that, in this respect the Eskimo is in general agreement with the Ganowánian form. Thus, the wives of my several nephews are my daughters-in-law, *Oo-koo'-ä'-gä*; and the husbands of my several wives are my sons-in-law, *Ning-a-ou'-gwä*. In like manner the wives of these several male cousins are my sisters-in-law, *I-e'-gä*; and the husbands of these several female cousins are my brothers-in-law, *Oo-koo-ä'-ga*. This term, it will be seen, is applied to a son-in-law as well. For the remaining marriage relationships, the nomenclature is quite full, as will be found by consulting the Table.

It thus appears that the Eskimo has but two, out of ten, of the indicative features of the system of the Ganowánian family. As it is presented in the Table it is in general agreement with the Ganowánian system in the fulness of its nomenclature, in the classification of brothers and sisters into elder or younger, and in the mergence of the collateral lines in the lineal line, ascending and descending. It is also a classificatory as distinguished from a descriptive system. But in the greater and most important fundamental characteristics of this system it is wanting. The Eskimo form not only fails in the necessary requisites for the admission of this people, upon the basis of their system of relationship, into the Ganowánian family, but furnishes positive elements to justify their exclusion. The two systems may have sprung remotely, but certainly not immediately, from the same source. After the remaining Asiatic and Polynesian forms, to which attention will next be directed, have been examined and compared, the correctness of this conclusion will be more fully appreciated.

APPENDIX TO PART II.

SYSTEM OF CONSANGUINITY AND AFFINITY OF THE GANOWÁNIAN FAMILY.

APPENDIX TO PART II.

GENEALOGICAL TABLE OF THE GANOWÁNIAN FAMILY.

Family.	Class, or Stock Language.	Branch, or Group of Dialects.	Nation, or Dialect.
GANOWANIAN	HODENOSAUNIAN .	IROQUOIS	1. Seneca, 2. Cayuga, 3. Onondaga, 4. Oneida, 5. Mohawk, 6. Tuscarora, 7. Two Mountain Iroquois.
		HURON	8. Wyandote.
	DAKOTAN . . .	DAKOTA	9. Dakota, Isauntie, 10. " Yankton, 11. " Yanktonais, 12. " Sisseton, 13. " Ogalalla, 14. " Brulè, 15. " Uncpapa, 16. " Blackfoot, 17. Asiniboine.
		MISSOURI	18. Punka, 19. Omaha, 20. Iowa, 21. Otoe, 22. Kaw, 23. Osage.
		——	24. Winnebagoe.
		UPPER MISSOURI .	25. Mandan, 26. Minnitaree, 27. Upsaroka, or Crow.
		GULF	28. Chocta, 29. Chickasa, 30. Creek, 31. Cherokee, 32. Mountain Cherokee.
	PAWNIAN . . .	PRAIRIE	33. Pawnee, 34. Arickaree.
	ALGONKIN . . .	GICHIGAMIAN . .	35. Cree, Prairie, 36. " Woods. 37. " Lowlands, 38. Ojibwa, 39. Otawa, 40. Potawattamie.

GENEALOGICAL TABLE OF THE GANOWÁNIAN FAMILY.—*Continued.*

Family.	Class, or Stock Language.	Branch, or Group of Dialects.	Nation, or Dialect.
GANOWANIAN	ALGONKIN	MISSISSIPPI	41. Miami,
			42. Peoria,
			43. Piankeshaw,
			44. Kaskaskia,
			45. Weaw,
			46. Sawk and Fox,
			47. Menominee,
			48. Shiyan,
			49. Kikapoo,
			50. Shawnee.
		ROCKY MOUNTAIN	51. Ahahnelin,
			52. Blackfoot, Piegan,
			53. " Blood.
		ATLANTIC	54. Micmac,
			55. Etchemin, or Malisete.
			56. Mohegan,
			57. Delaware,
			58. Munsee.
	ATHAPASCO-APACHE	ATHAPASCAN	59. Slave Lake Indians.
			60. Hare Indians,
			61. Red-Knives,
			62. Kutchin, or Louchieux,
			63. Tukŭthe.
	SALISH	——	64. Spokane,
			65. Okinaken.
	SAHAPTIN	——	66. Yakama.
	KOOTENAY	——	67. Kootenay.
	SHOSHONEE	YUTE	68. Utahs, Tabegwaches.
	AKOMAN	PUEBLO	69. Laguna.
	TEZUKAN	"	70. Tesuque.
	——	"	71. Chontal (Tabasco).
	——	"	72. Chibcha (New Grenada).
TUNGUSIAN	ESKIMO	——	73. Eskimo of Hudson's Bay,
			74. " of Greenland,
			75. " of Baffin's Bay.

SCHEDULES OF CONSANGUINITY AND AFFINITY OF THE GANOWANIAN FAMILY, WITH THE NAMES BY WHICH THE SEVERAL NATIONS DESIGNATE THEMSELVES, AND THE NAMES OF THE PERSONS BY WHOM THE SEVERAL SCHEDULES WERE PREPARED.

Indian Nations.	Names by which they call themselves.	Persons by whom and Places where the Schedules were filled.
1. SENECA.	Nun-da′-wä-o-no, "Great Hill People."	Lewis H. Morgan, at Tonawanda Indian Reservation, New York, December, 1858, with the assistance of Miss Caroline G. Parker (Je-go′-sä-seh), an educated Seneca woman.
2. CAYUGA.	Gwe-u′-gweh-o-no′, "People at the Mucky Land."	Lewis H. Morgan, at Tonawanda, July, 1859, with the assistance of a Cayuga woman, and Miss Parker as interpreter.
3. ONONDAGA.	O-nun′-dä-ga-o-no′, "People on the Hills."	Lewis H. Morgan, at Rochester, New York, October, 1859, with William Buck, an educated Onondaga.
4. ONEIDA.	O-na′-yote-kä-o-no′, "Granite People."	1. Lewis H. Morgan, at Oneida Centre, New York, May, 1860, with Jas. Christian, an Oneida Indian. 2. L. H. Morgan, at Albany, New York, February, 1861, with Henry Jordan, of St. Regis Reservation, half Oneida and half Mohawk.
5. MOHAWK.	Gä-ne-ä′-ga-o-no′, "People possessors of the Flint."	1. Lewis H. Morgan, at Tonawanda, January, 1860, with a Mohawk from Grand River, Canada West. 2. At Albany, February, 1861, with Henry Jordan.
6. TUSCARORA.	Dus-ga′-o-weh-o-no′, "Shirt-wearing People."	1. Lewis H. Morgan, at Tonawanda, January, 1860, with a Tuscarora woman, assisted by Isaac Doctor, interpreter. 2. From Cornelius C. Cusick, of Tuscarora Reservation, a Tuscarora Indian, August, 1860. A partial schedule.
7. TWO MOUNTAIN IROQUOIS.	(Mohawks and Oneidas.)	Lewis H. Morgan, at Pomme de Terre, Minnesota, July, 1861, with a Two Mountain Iroquois, then returning from the Hudson's Bay territory.
8. WYANDOTE.	Wane-dote′, "Calf of the Leg." This name was given to them by the Iroquois, and adopted by them. It relates to their manner of stringing buffalo-meat.	Lewis H. Morgan, at Wyandote Reservation, Kansas, June, 1859, with the assistance of Matthew R. Walker and William Walker, educated half-blood Wyandotes.
9. DAKOTA, ISAUN-TIE.	I-saun-tie′. They formerly lived at I-san-tam-de, or Knife Lake. Hence, probably, the name, as Riggs conjectures.	Rev. Stephen R. Riggs, Missionary of the American Board of Commissioners for Foreign Missions, made at the Dakota Indian Mission, Pajutaze, Minnesota, March, 1859.
10. DAKOTA, YANK-TON.	Yank-ton′, "Village at the End." (Riggs.)	Lewis H. Morgan, at Rulo Half-Breed Reservation, Nebraska Territory, June, 1859, with the assistance of a Yankton woman, and Charles Rulo as interpreter.

SCHEDULES OF CONSANGUINITY AND AFFINITY OF THE GANOWÁNIAN FAMILY.—*Continued.*

Indian Nations.	Names by which they call themselves.	Persons by whom and Places where the Schedules were filled.
11. DAKOTA, YANK-TONAIS.	E-ank'-to-wän, "End Village." (Riggs.)	Lewis H. Morgan, at Fort Abercrombie, Red River of the North, July, 1861, with the aid of Louis Roubillard (Wä-she-cho'-hos-kä), a half-blood Yanktonais, and interpreter at the fort.
12. DAKOTA, SISSE-TON.	Sis-se'-to-wän, "Village of the Marsh." (Riggs.)	Lewis H. Morgan, at Fort Abercrombie, Red River of the North, July, 1861, with the assistance of Andrew Laravie (Nä-peh'-so-tä, "Smutty Leaf"), a Sisseton half-blood.
13. DAKOTA, OGA-LALLA.	O-ga-lal'-lä, "Rovers," "Camp Movers."	Lewis H. Morgan, at Rulo Half-Breed Reservation, Nebraska Territory, June, 1860, with the aid of Joseph Tesson, a French and Indian quarter-blood and trader. He was also a chief of the Shiyans.
14. DAKOTA, BRULE.	Se-chä'-hoo, "Burnt Thighs."	Lewis H. Morgan, at St. Mary's, Missouri River, Iowa, from Um-pá-twa-ah, a Brulé woman, assisted by George Deschoutte, a half-blood, her husband, as interpreter.
15. DAKOTA, UNC-PAPA.	Unc-pä'-pä. Signification not obtained.	Lewis H. Morgan, at Uncpapa Encampment, Fort Pierre, Nebraska Territory, May, 1862, from A-ke'-che-tä-hose'-kä (Long Soldier), an Uncpapa chief, assisted by G. La Beauchamp as interpreter.
16. DAKOTA, BLACK-FOOT.	Se-ä'-sä-pä, "Blackfoot People."	Lewis H. Morgan, at Blackfoot Dakota Encampment, Fort Pierre, Nebraska Territory, May, 1862, from Wä-hät'-zum-gä'-pe (Shield Bearer), a Blackfoot Dakota warrior, assisted by same interpreter.
17. ASINIBOINE.	Yase-kä'-pe, "Stone People," from *e-es-kä'-pe,* a stone. Asiniboine is a translation of this word into the Cree language. At Selkirk Settlement they are now called "Stonies" by the half-blood Crees.	1. Lewis H. Morgan, at Fort Gerry, Selkirk Settlement, near Lake Winnipeg, July, 1861, with the aid of Mä-sä-ton'-ga (Iron Woman), an Asiniboine woman, and James Bird as interpreter. 2. At Vermillion Bluffs, Upper Missouri, Dakota Territory, June, 1862, from Tä-tan-go-mä'-ne, a half-blood Asiniboine.
18. PUNKA.	Pun-kä'. Signification not obtained.	Lewis H. Morgan, at Niobrara River, Nebraska Territory, May, 1862, from Wä-de-hah·'-ge, a Punka warrior, assisted by Catharine Woodges, a Yankton girl, acting as interpreter.
19. OMAHA.	O-mä'-hä, "Up Stream People."	1. Rev. Charles Sturges, Missionary of the Presbyterian Board of Missions, Omaha Mission, Blackbird Hills, Nebraska Territory, June, 1860. 2. Lewis H. Morgan, at Omaha, Nebraska Territory, June, 1860, assisted by Moody Martin (Ah-hiz'-ma-da, "Long Wing"), an intelligent young Omaha, and Henry Fontenelle, an educated half-blood Omaha.

SCHEDULES OF CONSANGUINITY AND AFFINITY OF THE GANOWÁNIAN FAMILY.—*Continued.*

Indian Nations.	Names by which they call themselves.	Persons by whom and Places where the Schedules were filled.
20. IOWA.	Pä-ho'-cha, "Dusty Noses."	Lewis H. Morgan, at Iowa Reservation, Nebraska Territory, June, 1859, with the assistance of Robert D. White-Cloud (Wä-n'ye-me'-na), a son of White-Cloud, the second Iowa chief of that name. Robert is a man of fine natural abilities.
21. OTOE.	O-toe'. The original name of the Otoes has a vulgar signification. They laid it aside and adopted the name of Otoe at the suggestion of the early traders. It has no signification.	1. Rev. H. A. Guthrie, Missionary of the Presbyterian Board of Missions, Otoe Mission, Kansas, April, 1859. An incomplete schedule. 2. Lewis H. Morgan, at Rulo Half-breed Reservation, Nebraska Territory, June, 1859, from an Otoe woman, the wife of M. Dupee, a French trapper, Dupee acting as interpreter.
22. KAW.	Kaw'-zä. Signification lost.	Lewis H. Morgan, at Topeka, Kansas, May, 1859, from a Kaw chief, assisted by Joseph James (Gi'-he-ga-zhiŋ'-ga, "Little Chief"), a half-blood Kaw, as interpreter.
23. OSAGE.	——	P. E. Elder, Esq., United States Indian Agent for the Osages, Neosho Agency, Fort Scott, Kansas, May, 1862.
24. WINNEBAGOE.	Ho-chun'-gä-rä. Signification not obtained. The name Winnebagoe was given them by the Great Lake Nations, and means "Scum People."	Lewis H. Morgan, at Washington, April, 1859, from a delegation of Winnebagoes, assisted by General Sylvanus B. Lowrey, of Minnesota, as interpreter.
25. MANDAN.	Me-too'-ta-häk, "South Villagers."	Lewis H. Morgan, at Mandan Village, Upper Missouri, June, 1862, with the aid of James Kipp (Mä-to-e'-kä-rup-tä'-he, "Turning the Bell"), a half-blood Mandan.
26. MINNITAREE.	E-nät'-zä, "People who come from afar." Vulgar name, "Gros Ventres of Missouri."	Lewis H. Morgan, at Minnitaree Village, Upper Missouri, Dakota Territory, from Mä-ish' (Hoop Iron) and A-rŭt-se-pish' (Beaver gnawing Wood), Minnitaree warriors, Jeffrey Smith interpreter.
27. CROW.	Ab-sär'-o-ka. Signification lost. They make the sign of the crow as their national sign, but Ab-sär'-o-ka has no relation either to the crow or raven.	Lewis H. Morgan, at Fort Union, mouth of the Yellowstone, June, 1862, with the assistance of Robert Meldrum, one of the chief traders of the American Fur Company, and his wife, a Crow woman. Meldrum is a Scotchman, and has been a chief of the Crows.

SCHEDULES OF CONSANGUINITY AND AFFINITY OF THE GANOWÁNIAN FAMILY.—*Continued.*

Indian Nations.	Names by which they call themselves.	Persons by whom and Places where the Schedules were filled.
28. CHOCTA.	Chä'-tä. Signification lost. The name was thus pronounced to me by Rev. Cyrus Byington, who for forty years has been a missionary among the Choctaws.	·Rev. John Edwards, and Rev. Cyrus Byington, Missionaries of the Presbyterian Board of Missions, Wheelock, Choctaw Nation, August, 1859, assisted by Captain Joseph Dukes, a Choctaw.
29. CHOCTA.	Chä'-tä.	Rev. Charles C. Copeland, Missionary of the Presbyterian Board of Missions, Bennington, Choctaw Nation, May, 1859. Mr. Copeland has been a missionary among this people for upwards of twenty years.
30. CHICKASA.	Not obtained.	Rev. Charles C. Copeland, above named.
31. CREEK.	Mŭs-co'-kee. Signification not obtained.	Rev. R. M. Loughridge, Missionary of the Presbyterian Board of Missions, Tallahasse Mission, Creek Agency, west of Arkansas, January, 1860. Mr. Loughridge has been a missionary for twenty years among the Creeks.
32. CHEROKEE.	Tsa-lo'-kee, "Great People."	Rev. C. C. Torrey, Missionary of the American Board of Commissioners for Foreign Missions, Park Hill, Tahlequah, Cherokee Nation, May, 1860.
33. MOUNTAIN CHEROKEE.	——	Rev. Evan Jones, Missionary of the American Baptist Board. Mr. Jones has been a missionary residing with the Cherokees upwards of thirty years.
34. REPUBLICAN PAWNEE.	Kit'-kä. Signification lost.	B. F. Lushbaugh, Esq., U. S. Indian Agent for the Pawnees, Genoa, Nebraska Territory, April, 1863.
35. GRAND PAWNEE.	Chä'-we. Signification lost.	Lewis H. Morgan, at St. Mary's, Missouri River, Iowa, with the assistance of Rev. S. S. Allis, former Missionary of the American Board among the Pawnees; and a Pawnee woman, May, 1862.
36. ARICKAREE.	Sä-nish, "The People."	Lewis H. Morgan, at Arickaree Village, Upper Missouri, June, 1862, assisted by Pierre Garrow, a half-blood Arickaree.
37. CREE OF THE PRAIRIE.	Mus-ko-ta'-we-ne-wuk', "People of the Prairie or Plains." The three divisions of the Crees by which they now distinguish themselves are based upon differences of dialect rather than geographical location.	1. Lewis H. Morgan, at Georgetown, Red River of the North, July, 1861, with the assistance of Mrs. A. H. Murray, of Peace River, Hudson's Bay Territory, wife of A. H. Murray, Esq., one of the chief factors of the Hudson's Bay Company, located at Georgetown. Mrs. Murray is an educated quarter-blood Cree. 2. Rev. E. A. Watkins, Devon, Siskachewun District, Hudson's Bay Territory, July, 1862. A very complete schedule.
38. CREE OF THE WOODS.	Na-he'-ah-wuk, "People of the Woods."	Lewis H. Morgan, at Georgetown, Red River of the North, July, 1861, with the assistance of E-she-kwa (Little Girl), the wife of Mr. Ohlson, a half-blood Cree woman from Pembina Mountain.

SCHEDULES OF CONSANGUINITY AND AFFINITY OF THE GANOWÁNIAN FAMILY.—*Continued.*

Indian Nations.	Names by which they call themselves.	Persons by whom and Places where the Schedules were filled.
39. CREE OF THE LOWLANDS.	Mus-ka'-go-wuk, "People of the Lowlands." The eastern Crees still call themselves Ke-nish-te'-no-wuk, which means the same; hence Kenistenaux, their first name among the whites.	1. Lewis H. Morgan, at Sault St. Mary, Lake Superior, August, 1860, with the assistance of Mrs. Moore, a half-blood Cree, of Moose Factory, Hudson's Bay Territory. 2. Lewis H. Morgan, at Fort Gerry, Selkirk Settlement, August, 1861, with the assistance of Angus McKay, a quarter-blood Cree, of Fort Gerry.
40. OJIBWA, LAKE SUPERIOR.	O-jib'-wa-uk', O-je'-bik, "Root" or "Stem of Peoples;" O-jib-wage' and O-jib-wa-uk', Ojibwas, or Chippewas; O-jib'-wa, an Ojibwa. Hence "Original People," or "The People."	1. Lewis H. Morgan, at Marquette, Lake Superior, July, 1858, with the assistance of William Cameron, a quarter-blood Ojibwa, and his wife. This schedule was incomplete, but sufficiently full to establish the identity of the Ojibwa system with that of the Iroquois; and it was this discovery which determined the author to follow the inquiry. 2. Rev. Edward Jacker, Missionary of the Roman Catholic Church, at Houghton, Lake Superior, Michigan, May, 1860. This schedule was elaborately and thoroughly completed.
41. OJIBWA, LAKE MICHIGAN.	Same.	Rev. P. Dougherty, Missionary of the Presbyterian Board of Missions, at the Chippewa and Otawa Mission, Grand Traverse Bay, Michigan, March, 1860.
42. OJIBWA, LAKE HURON.	Same.	Lewis H. Morgan, at Rochester, New York, March, 1860, with the assistance of Catharine B. Sutton (Nä-ne-bä'-we-kwa, "Standing Upright"), an intelligent Ojibwa woman from Owen's Sound, Lake Huron, Canada West.
43. OJIBWA, KANSAS.	Same.	Lewis H. Morgan, at Chippewa Reservation, Kansas, May, 1860, with the aid of Clear Sky (Ash-ton-kwit'), an Ojibwa chief, and his daughter, the wife of William Turner; Turner acting as interpreter.
44. OTAWA.	O-tä'-wä. Signification not obtained.	Lewis H. Morgan, at Otawa Reservation, Kansas, May, 1859, from Mr. Mills, an Otawa, and his family; John T. Jones, an educated Potawattomie, acting as interpreter. He speaks the Otawa fluently.
45. POTAWATTAMIE.	Po-tä-wät'-ä-me.	Lewis H. Morgan, at Potawattamie Reservation, Kansas, May, 1859, with the aid of J. N. Buraseau, an educated Potawattomie. I was not able to perfect this schedule, from want of time.
46. MIAMI.	Me-ä-me-ä'-ga. Signification not obtained. Wa-yä-tä-no'-ke, "Eddying Water," was an old name of the Miamis, and is still used by them. They believe they sprang from such a fountain.	Lewis H. Morgan, at Shawnee Reservation, Kansas, May, 1860, with the assistance of Moses Silver Heels (Em-bä'-whe-tä), a Miami, and Friend Simon D. Harvey as interpreter.

SCHEDULES OF CONSANGUINITY AND AFFINITY OF THE GANOWÁNIAN FAMILY.—*Continued.*

Indian Nations.	Names by which they call themselves.	Persons by whom and Places where the Schedules were filled.
47. PEORIA.	Pe-o'-ri-ă. Signification not obtained.	Lewis H. Morgan, at Peoria Reservation, Kansas, June, 1859, with the assistance of Battese Peoria.
48. PIANKESHAW.	Pe-ank'-e-shaw. Signification not obtained.	Lewis H. Morgan, at Paoli, Kansas, May, 1860, from Frank Vallé (Mă-ko-sa-tä', "Red Sun"), a half-blood Piankeshaw.
49. KASKASKIA.	Kä-kä'-ke-ah. Signification not obtained.	Lewis H. Morgan, at Paoli, Kansas, June, 1859, from Luther Paschal, a half-blood Kaskaskia.
50. WEAW.	We-ä-tä'-no. Signification not obtained.	Lewis H. Morgan, at Paoli, Kansas, May, 1860, from John Mitchel (Tek-ko-nä', "Hard Knot"), a half-blood Weaw.
51. SAWK AND FOX.	Saw-kee, "Sprouting Up," the name by which the Sawks call themselves. Mus-kwä'-ka-uk, "Red Men," the Foxes call themselves. Fox is a nick-name.	Lewis H. Morgan, at Sawk and Fox Reservation, Kansas, June, 1860, with the aid of Moh-whă'-tä (Yelping Wolf), a Sawk woman, and Antoine Gookie (Mok-kut'-up-pe, "Big-set"), a Menomine, but government interpreter of the Sawks and Foxes.
52. MENOMINE.	Not obtained. The Ojibwas call them Me-no'-me-ne-uk', "Rice People."	Lewis H. Morgan, at Sawk and Fox Reservation, Kansas, June, 1860, from Louis Gookie (Noo-nee, "Going Out"), and Antoine Gookie, educated Menomines.
53. SHIYAN.	Is-tä', "Cut Arm." The Dakotas call them Shi-yä', "The people who speak an unintelligible tongue."	Lewis H. Morgan, at Rulo Half-breed Reservation, Nebraska Territory, June, 1860, from Joseph Tesson, a quarter-blood Menomine. He lived eighteen years among the Shiyans, spoke their language fluently, became a chief, and had with him his family of Shiyan children.
54. KICKAPOO.	Not obtained. The Otawas call them Ke-gä-boge', their own name, probably, in the Otawa language.	Paschal Fish, of Wă-kä-rŭ'-sha, Kansas, and Friend Simon D. Harvey, formerly Superintendent of the Friends' Manual Labor School, Kansas, and now of Harveysburg, Ohio, November, 1861.
55. SHAWNEE.	Sä-wan-wä'-kee, "Southerners."	1. Friend Simon D. Harvey, Superintendent, &c., as above stated, Shawnee Reservation, Kansas, March, 1859. 2. Lewis H. Morgan, at Shawnee, Kansas, June, 1859, assisted (Mr. Harvey being absent) by Mrs. Chouteau and Mrs. Rogers, educated Shawnee half-blood women. Friend Harvey's schedule was thoroughly completed by him, and is the one used.
56. AH-AH-NE-LIN. ARAPAHOE THE SAME.	Ah-ah'-ne-lin. Signification not obtained. The vulgar name of this people is "Gros Ventres of the Prairie."	Lewis H. Morgan, at Judith River, near the Rocky Mountains, June, 1862, from E-thä'-be, an Ah-ah'-ne-lin woman, speaking Blackfoot, and Mrs. Alexander Culbertson, a Blood Blackfoot woman, acting as interpreter. Mrs. Culbertson speaks the English language fluently.

APPENDIX. 289

SCHEDULES OF CONSANGUINITY AND AFFINITY OF THE GANOWÁNIAN FAMILY.—*Continued.*

Indian Nations.	Names by which they call themselves.	Persons by whom and Places where the Schedules were filled.
57. PIEGAN BLACK-FOOT.	Pe-kan'-ne, "Rich People." Sik-se-kä'(Blackfeet) is the name of the Blackfeet proper. They are the least of the three bands.	Lewis H. Morgan, at Selkirk Settlement, Red River of the North, August, 1861, from the wife and daughter of James Bird, Piegan Blackfoot women, and James Bird, a half-blood Cree, as interpreter.
58. BLOOD BLACK-FOOT.	Ki-nä, "High-minded People." They formerly called themselves Ah-hi'-tä-pe, "Blood People."	Lewis H. Morgan, at Fort Benton, in the Blackfoot country at the foot of the Rocky Mountains, June, 1862, from Mrs. Alexander Culbertson (Nä-to-is'-chiks, "Medicine Snake"), above mentioned, assisted by Alexander Culbertson, Esq., formerly chief factor of the American Fur Company at Fort Benton.
59. MICMAC.	Not obtained.	Rev. Silas Tertius Rand, Missionary of the Micmac Missionary Society of Nova Scotia. Hantsport, Nova Scotia, June, 1860.
60. ETCHEMIN, OR MALISETE.	Not obtained.	Rev. Silas Tertius Rand, above named, November, 1861.
61. MOHEGAN.	Mo-he'-kun-ne-uk, "Seaside People."	Lewis H. Morgan, at Delaware Reservation, Kansas, June, 1859, with the assistance of Benjamin Toucey and sister, educated Mohegans.
62. DELAWARE.	O-puh-nar'-ke, "People of the East." Len-ä'-pe was their former name, and is still used.	1. William Adams, Delaware Reservation, Kansas, January, 1860. William Adams is a young Delaware, educated at the Delaware Mission in Kansas, under the charge of Rev. John T. Pratt. 2. Lewis H. Morgan, at Delaware Reservation, Kansas, June, 1859, with the aid of Lemuel R. Ketchum (Wool-le-kun-num, "Light of the Sun"), a Delaware.
63. MUNSEE.	Mun-see'-wuk.	Lewis H. Morgan, at Chippewa Reservation, Kansas, June, 1860, from Mrs. Haome Samuel (Mi-je-na-oke, "Plain Looking"), a Munsee woman. She spoke English fluently, as do all of the remaining Munsees.
64. SLAVE LAKE INDIANS.	A-cha'-o-tin-ne, "People of the Lowlands."	Robert Kennicott, Esq., Fort Liard, Mackenzie River District, Hudson's Bay Territory, March, 1860.
65. HARE INDIANS.	Tä-nä'-tin-ne. Signification not obtained.	Lewis H. Morgan, at Red River Settlement, Hudson's Bay Territory, August, 1861, from Angeline Irvin, a half-blood native resident at Fort Good Hope, and James Bird, interpreter.
66. RED KNIVES.	Täl-sote'-e-nä, "Red Knife."	Lewis H. Morgan, at the Convent of St. Boniface, Red River Settlement, Hudson's Bay Territory, August, 1861, from two half-blood women of that nation.
67. KUTCHIN, OR LOUCHIEUX.	Kŭ-tchin'. Signification not obtained.	W. L. Herdesty, Esq., Fort Liard, Hudson's Bay Territory, at the request of Bernard R. Ross, Esq., one of the chief factors of the company, Fort Simpson, by whom it was forwarded to the author.

37   March, 1870.

SCHEDULES OF CONSANGUINITY AND AFFINITY OF THE GANOWÁNIAN FAMILY.—*Continued.*

Indian Nations.	Names by which they call themselves.	Persons by whom and Places where the Schedules were filled.
68. TUKŬTHE.	——	R. McDonald, Esq., Peel River Fort, Hudson's Bay Territory, June, 1865, a factor of the company.
69. SPOKANE.	Sin-hu, "People wearing Red Paint on their Cheeks."	George Gibbs, Esq., of the Northwestern Boundary Survey, Steilacoom, Washington Territory, November, 1860.
70. OKINAKEN.	O-kan-ă-kan. Signification not obtained.	Lewis H. Morgan, at Red River Settlement, Hudson's Bay Territory, August, 1861, from Mrs. Ross, an Okenakan woman from Washington Territory, and her daughter.
71. YAKAMA.	——	George Gibbs, Esq., Steilacom, Washington Territory, July, 1860.
72. KOOTENAY.	——	George Gibbs, Esq., July, 1860.
73. UTAHS.	Tabegwaches. Signification not obtained.	Robert Kennicott, Esq., Washington, July, 1863, from a delegation of Utahs at the seat of government.
74. LAGUNA.	——	Rev. Samuel Gorman, Missionary of Baptist Board, Pueblo of Laguna, New Mexico, May, 1860.
75. TESUQUE.	——	Michael Steck, M. D., U. S. Indian Agent for the Pueblo Indians of New Mexico, Santa Fe, March, 1865.
76. CHONTAL.	——	Guillermo Garcia, State of Tabasco, May, 1860. It was procured at the instance of Don Augustin Vilaseca, of the city of Tabasco.
77. CHIBCHA	——	E. Uricoechea, M. D., Ph. D., Bogota, New Grenada, March, 1861.
78. ESKIMO, WEST OF HUDSON'S BAY.	——	James R. Clare, Esq., York Factory, Hudson's Bay Territory, August, 1860, at the request of Prof. Daniel Wilson, of University College, Toronto, Canada West.
79. ESKIMO, GREENLAND.	——	Samuel Kleinschmidt, Godlhaab, Greenland, August, 1862. Procured through Dr. Rink, Director-General of Greenland, and Hon. Bradford R. Wood, U. S. Minister Resident at Copenhagen.
80. ESKIMO, NORTHUMBERLAND INLET, BAFFIN'S BAY.	In-nu′-it.	Lewis H. Morgan, at New York, November, 1862, from E-pe-oke′-pe, an Eskimo from Northumberland Inlet, and Tä-kä-re′-tŭ, his wife, brought down by Capt. C. F. Hall, the Arctic explorer, who assisted in the work.

SYSTEM OF CONSANGUINITY AND AFFINITY OF THE GANOWANIAN FAMILY.

Family.	Classes.	Branches.	Nations or languages.	Persons by whom schedules were filled.	Pronoun my or mine.	Pronoun his.
GANO-WANIAN FAMILY.	DAKOTAN STEM.	Hodénosau-nian Nations.	1. Seneca	Lewis H. Morgan	Ah-gä-weh′	Ho-weh′
			2. Cayuga	" " "	Ah-gä-wä′	Ho-wä′
			3. Onondaga	" " "	E-gä′-wä	Ho′-wä
			4. Oneida	" " "	Ah-gwä-oh′-w	Lä-oh′-h′
			5. Mohawk	" " "	Ah-gwä-oh-wa′	Lä-o′-hö
			6. Tuscarora	" " "		
			7. Two Mountain Iroquois	" " "		
			8. Wyandote	" " "	Yo-mä′	
		Dakota Nations.	9. Dakota: Isauntie	Rev. Stephen R. Riggs	Me-tä′-wä	Ta′-wä
			10. Dakota: Yankton	Lewis H. Morgan	Me-tä′	Ta′-wä
			11. Dakota: Yauktonais	" " "	Me-tä′-sun-kä	Ha-tä′-wä
			12. Dakota: Sisseton	" " "	Me-tä′-sun-kä	Hä-tä′-wä
			13. Dakota: Ogalalla	" " "	Me-tä′-wä	E-a′-tä-wuk
			14. Dakota: Brulé	" " "	Me-tä′-wä	Ya-tä′-wä
			15. Dakota: Uncpapa	" " "	Me-tä′-wä	Ne-tä′-wä
			16. Dakota: Blackfoot	" " "	Me-tä′-wä	Ta′-wä
			17. Asiniboine	" " "	Me-tä′-wä	E-ä-tä′-wä
		Missouri Nations.	18. Punkä	" " "	Wa-we′-tä	
			19. Omahä	Rev. Charles Sturges	We-we′-tä	
			20. Iowä	Lewis H. Morgan	Men-tä′-weh	A-tä′-wä
			21. Otoe (Missouri the same)	" " "	Me-tä′-weh	A-tä′-weh
			22. Kaw	" " "	Be′-tä or we′-tä	
			23. Osage (Quäppä the same)	P. E. Elder, Esq.	We′-tä	
			24. Winnebagoe	Lewis H. Morgan	Hä′-rä	
		Upper Missouri Nations.	25. Mandan	" " "	Mä-wä′-ka	
			26. Minnitaree	" " "	Mat-tä-mä-itz	He-hä-it-tä-wä-itz
			27. Crow	" " "	Be′-bake	E′-dä-duk
		Gulf Nations.	28. Chocta	Rev. John Edwards	Um′-me	Im′-me
			29. Chocta	Rev. Ch. C. Copeland	Um′-me	Im′-me
			30. Chickasa	" " "	Um′-me	Im′-me
			31. Creek	Rev. R. M. Loughridge		
			32. Cherokee	Rev. C. C. Torrey		
			33. Mountain Cherokee	Rev. Evan Jones	A-gwä-tza′-re	Oo-tza′-re
		Prairie Nations.	34. Republican Pawnee	B. F. Lushbaugh, Esq.	Ko′-tä-te	
			35. Grand Pawnee	Lewis H. Morgan	Ko′-tä-te	
			36. Arickaree	" " "	Ko′-tä-te	Koo′-tä
	ALGONKIN STEM.	Great Lake Nations.	37. Cree: of the Prairie	" " "	Ne′-yä	We′-yä
			38. Cree: of the Woods	" " "	Ne-lä	We′-lä
			39. Cree: of the Lowlands	" " "	Ne-nä	We′-nä
			40. Ojibwa: Lake Superior	Rev. Father Ed. Jacker	Nin (ni-′n)	O
			41. Ojibwa: Lake Michigan	Rev. P. Dougherty	Ne or nin	O·or ween
			42. Ojibwa: Lake Huron	Lewis H. Morgan	Ne or nin	O or ween
			43. Ojibwa: Kansas	" " "	Nin	O or ween
			44. Otawa	" " "	Neen	Ween
			45. Potäwattamie	" " "	Ne-lä′	We-lä′
		Mississippi Nations.	46. Miami	" " "	Ne-lä′	We-lä′
			47. Peoria	" " "	Ne-lä′	We-lä′
			48. Piankeshaw	" " "	Ne-lä′	We-lä′
			49. Kaskaskia	" " "	Ne-lä′	We-lä′
			50. Weaw	" " "	Ne-lä′	We-lä′
			51. Sawk and Fox	" " "	Neen	Ween-nä
			52. Menomine	" " "	Na-nä′-ne-tine	Wa-neh-o-tine
			53. Shiyan (Arapahoe the same)	" " "	Nä-tuts′	His-se′-otes
			54. Kikapoo	Paschal Fish		
			55. Shawnee	Simon D. Harvey	Ne-lä′	We-lä′
		Rocky Mountain Nations.	56. Ah-ah′-ne-lin (Gros Ventres of Prairie)	Lewis H. Morgan	Na-nis-tä′	A-nis-tä′
			57. Piegan Blackfoot	" " "	Nis-to′	Yu-tse-nän′
			58. Blood Blackfoot	" " "	Nese-to′-ah	
		Atlantic-Algonkin Nations.	59. Micmac	Rev. Silas T. Rand	N′	U′
			60. Etchemin, or Malisete	" " "	Nee	Oo-ne
			61. Mohegan	Lewis H. Morgan	Ne-ä′	Oh
			62. Delaware	" " "	Nee-she-tä′	Naa
			63. Musee	" " "	Nee	Nake′-ko-mä
	ATHAPASCO-APACHE STEM.	Athapascan Nations.	64. Slave Lake Indians, or A-cha′-o-tin-ne	Robert Kennicott, Esq.		
			65. Hare Indians, or Tä-nä′-tin-ne	Lewis H. Morgan		
			66. Red Knife, or Täl-sote′-e-nä	" " "	Sä-ne-sa′che	A-ten′-ne
			67. Kütchin, or Louchieux	W. L. Herdisty, Esq.	Se	But sun
			68. Tukuthe (Peel River)			
	SALISH STEM.	—	69. Spokäne	George Gibbs, Esq.	En-te-ä′	Et-te-ä′-oos
	SAHAPTIN "	—	70. Okinäkan	Lewis H. Morgan	In-chä	Chih-milch
	KOOTENAY "	—	71. Yakama	George Gibbs, Esq.	Em-mi	Penk
	SHOSHONEE "	—	72. Kootenay	" " "	Ka	
			73. Utahs (Tabegwaches)	Robert Kennicott, Esq.		
	PUEBLO "	—	74. Laguna	Rev. Samuel Gorman		
			75. Tesuque	Michael Steck, M. D.		
			76. Chontal (Tabasco)	Guillermo Garcia.		
			77. Chibcha, or Muyska (New Grenada).	E. Uricoechea, M.D. PhD.		
ARCTIC FAMILY.		Eskimo Nations.	78. Eskimo (west of Hudson's Bay)	James R. Clare, Esq.	Kho-in-tcha-ti-ka	Um-ni-a
			79. Eskimo (Greenland)	Samuel Kleinschmidt	Suffix Ga-ra-ka	A-e
			80. Eskimo (Northumberland Inlet)	Lewis H. Morgan	Wung′-a	Ah′me-lang

NOTATION IN TABLE II.

VOWELS.

a as a in ale, mate.

ä " " " art, father.

ă " " " at, tank.

ạ " " " all, fall.

e as e in even, mete.

ĕ " " " enter, met.

ê has a nasal sound as the French *en* in mien.

i as i in idea, mite.

ĭ " " " it, pity.

o as o in over, gọ.

ŏ " " " otter, got.

u as u in use, mute.

ŭ " oo " food.

CONSONANTS.

ch as ch in chin.

g hard as in go.

ğ soft as in gem.

h· represents a deep sonant guttural.

h' represents a breathing sound of the letter.

kw' represents the same.

n̠ nasal as n in drink.

n' nasal pronounced with the tongue pressing the roof of the mouth.

r pronounced with the tip of the tongue touching the roof of the mouth.

s̠ hissing sound of s.

' An apostrophe after a word denotes an almost inaudible breathing sound of the last letter.

? An interrogation mark at the end of a term implies a doubt of its correctness.

⌢ A circumflex connecting two syllables indicates that the two are pronounced quickly with one effort of the voice.

(292)

TABLE II.—CONSANGUINITY AND AFFINITY OF THE GANOWÁNIAN FAMILY.

Nations or languages.		1. My great grandfather's father.	Translation.	2. My great grandfather's mother.	Translation.
1. Seneca	1	Hoc'-sote	My grandfather.	Oc'-sote	My grandmother.
2. Cayuga	2	Hoc'-sote	" "	Oc'-sote	" "
3. Onondaga	3	Hoc-so'-dä-hä	" "	Oc-so'-dä-hä	" "
4. Oneida	4	Lok-sote'-hä	" "	Ahk-sote'-hä	" "
5. Mohawk	5	Läk-sote'	" "	Ahk-sote'	" "
6. Tuscarora	6	Ahk-rä'-sote	" "	Ahk'-sote	" "
7. Two Mountain Iroquios	7	Lok-sote'-bä	" "	Ah-sote'-hä	" "
8. Wyandote	8	Hä-shu-tä'	" "	Ah-shu-tä'	" "
9. Dakota: Isauntie	9	Tuṇ-kaṇ'-she-daṇ	" "	Uṇ-che'	" "
10. Dakota: Yankton	10	Toon-kä'-she-nä	" "	O-che'	" "
11. Dakota: Yanktonais	11	Tun-kä'-she-lä	" "	O-che'-lä	" "
12. Dakota: Sisseton	12	To-kä'-she-lä	" "	Oh'-che	" "
13. Dakota: Ogalalla	13	Me-tonk'-ah	" "	Oo-che'	" "
14. Dakota: Brulé	14	Tŏn-kä'-she-lä	" "	Un-che'	" "
15. Dakota: Uncpapa	15	Toon-kä'-zhe-lä	" "	O-che'	" "
16. Dakota: Blackfoot	16	Toh·-kä'-she-la	" "	O-che'	" "
17. Asiniboine	17	Me-to'-gä-she	" "	O-gä'-she	" "
18. Punkä	18	Ta-ga'-hä	" "	Gä-hä'	" "
19. Omahä	19	Wee-te'-ga	" "	Wee'-kä	" "
20. Iowä	20	Hee-too'-ga	" "	Hee-koo'-n'-ye	" "
21. Otoe (Missouri the same)	21	E-tü'-kä	" "	Hiṇ-kü'-ne	" "
22. Kaw	22	Be-che'-go	" "	E-ko'	" "
23. Osage (Quäppä the same)	23	We-che'-cho	" "	E-che'	" "
24. Winnebagoe	24	E-cho'-ka	" "	E-ko-ro-ka	" "
25. Mandan	25	Tä-ta'-h·e-ha	" "	Nau·-he-a	" "
26. Minnitaree	26	Mä-toosh-ä-rü'-tä-kä	" "	Kä-rü'-hä	" "
27. Crow	27	Me-nup-h·is'-sä-ka	My old father.	Bä-sä'-kä-na	" "
28. Choota	28	Um-uh'-fo	My grandfather.	Up-puk'-nĭ	" "
29. Choota	29	Um-u'-fo	" "	Up-pok'-nĭ	" "
30. Chickasa	30	Um-u'-fo	" "	Hap-po'-sĭ	" "
31. Creek	31	Cha-pŭ-chä'	" "	Cha-pü'-se	" "
32. Cherokee	32	E-nĭ-sĭ	My grandparent.	E-nĭ-sĭ	My grandparent.
33. Mountain Cherokee	33	Ah-ge-doo'-tsĭ	My grandfather.	Ah-ge-lee'-sih	My grandmother.
34. Republican Pawnee	34	Ah-te'-is	My father.	Ah-te'-rä	My mother.
35. Grand Pawnee	35	Ah-te'-ase	" "	A-te'-rä	" "
36. Arickaree	36				
37. Cree: of the Prairie	37	Ne-mo-some'	My grandfather.	Noh·-kome'	My grandmother.
38. Cree: of the Woods	38	Ne-mo-shome'	" "	No-kome'	" "
39. Cree: of the Lowlands	39	Na-mo-shome'	" "	No-kome'	" "
40. Ojibwa: Lake Superior	40	Nĭ-mĭ-sho'-mis	" "	No'-ko-mis	" "
41. Ojibwa: Lake Michigan	41	Ne-me-sho'-mis	" "	No-ko-mis'	" "
42. Ojibwa: Lake Huron	42	Na-ma-sho'-mis	" "	No-ko-mis'	" "
43. Ojibwa: Kansas	43	Ne-mis-sho-mis	" "	No-ko-mis'	" "
44. Otäwa	44	Na-ma-sho-mis'	" "	No-ko-mis'	" "
45. Potäwattamie	45	Na-ma-sho-mis'	" "	No-ko-mis'	" "
46. Miami	46	Na-ma-sho-mä'	" "	No-ko-mä'	" "
47. Peoria	47	Na-mä-sho-mä'	" "	No-ko-mä'	" "
48. Piankeshaw	48	Na-mä-sho-mä'	" "	No-ko-mä'	" "
49. Kaskaskia	49	Na-mä-sho-mä'	" "	No-ko-mä'	" "
50. Weaw	50	Na-mä-sho-mä'	" "	No-ko-mä'	" "
51. Sawk and Fox	51	Nä-mä'-sho-mis	" "	No'-ko-mis	" "
52. Menomine	52	Na-mä'-sho	" "	No'-ko-mä	" "
53. Shiyau	53	Nam-a-shim'	" "	Na-vish'-kim	" "
54. Kikapoo	54	Nem-ma-soo'-ma-thä	" "	No-ko-ma-some-thä'	" "
55. Shawnee	55	Na-ma-some-thä'	" "	No-kome-thä'	" "
56. Ah-ah'-ne-lin (Gros Ventres of Prairie)	56	No-bes'-sib-ah	" "	Na'-e-bä	" "
57. Piegan Blackfoot	57	Na-ah'-sä	" "	Ne-tä'-ke-ä-sä	" "
58. Blood Blackfoot	58	Nä-ah·xs'	" "	Ne-tä-ke-ah·xs'	" "
59. Micmac	59	Niks-kä-mich'	" "	Nü-ga'-mich	" "
60. Etchemin, or Maliseto	60	N'-mŭke-sŭms'	" "	Nük'-mus	" "
61. Mohegan	61	Nuh-mä-home'	" "	No-ome'	" "
62. Delaware	62	Nu-moh·'-ho-mus'	" "	Noo-h·ome'	" "
63. Munsee	63	Na-mä-ho-mis'	" "	Na-no'-home	" "
64. Slave Lake Indians or A-cha'-o-tin-ne	64	Sa-tse'-a	" "	Sa-tsun'	" "
65. Hare Indians or Tä-nä'-tin-ne	65	Sa-tä'-chock	" "	Sa-cho'-na	" "
66. Red-Knife, or Täl-sote'-e-nä	66	Set-see'-a	" "	Set-sa'-nä	" "
67. Kütchin, or Louchieux	67	Set-see'	" "	Set-so'	" "
68. Tukuthe (Peel River)	68	Set-see'	" "	Set-soon'	" "
69. Spokäne	69				
70. Okinäkan	70				
71. Yakama	71				
72. Kootenay	72				
73. Utahs (Tabegwaches)	73				
74. Laguna	74				
75. Tesuque	75				
76. Chontal (Tabasco)	76				
77. Chibcha (New Granada)	77				
78. Eskimo: (West of Hudson's Bay)	78				
79. Eskimo: (Greenland)	79				
80. Eskimo: (Northumberland Inlet)	80	E-tŭ'-ah	" "	Ning-e-o'-wä	" "

TABLE II.—*Continued.*

	3. My great grandfather.	Translation.	4. My great grandmother.	Translation.	5. My grandfather.	Translation.
1	Hoc'-sote	My grandfather.	Oc'-sote	My grandmother.	Hoc'-sote	My grandfather.
2	Hoc'-sote	" "	Ov'-sote	" "	Hoc'-sote	" "
3	Hoc-so'-dä-hä	" "	Oc-so'-dä-hä	" "	Hoc-so'-dä-hä	" "
4	Lok-sote'-hä	" "	Ahk-sote'-hä	" "	Lok-sote'-hä	" "
5	Läke-sote'	" "	Ahk-sote'	" "	Läke-sote'	" "
6	Ahk-rä'-sote	" "	Ahk'-sote	" "	Ahk-rä'-sote	" "
7	Lok-sote'-hä	" "	Ak-sote'-hä	" "	Lok-sote'-hä	" "
8	Hä-shu-tä'	" "	Ah-shu-tä'	" "	Hä-shu-tä'	" "
9	Tuŋ-kaŋ-she-daŋ	" "	Uŋ-che'	" "	Tuŋ-kaŋ'-she-daŋ	" "
10	Toon-kä'-she-nä	" "	O-che'	" "	Toon-kä'-she-nä	" "
11	Tun-kä'-she-lä	" "	O-che'-lä	" "	Tun-kä-she-lä	" "
12	To-kä'-she-lä	" "	Oh'-che	" "	To-kä'-she-lä	" "
13	Me-tonk'-ah	" "	Oo-che'	" "	Me-tonk'-ah	" "
14	Tŏn-kä'-she-lä	" "	Un-che'	" "	Tŏn-kä'-she-lä	" "
15	Toon-kä'-zhe-lä	" "	O-che'	" "	Toon-kä'-zhe-lä	" "
16	Toh·-kä'-she-la	" "	O-che'	" "	Toh·-kä'-she-la	" "
17	Me-to'-gä-she	" "	O-gä'-che	" "	Me-to'-gä-she	" "
18	Ta-ga'-hä	" "	Gä-hä'	" "	Ta-ga'-hä	" "
19	Wee-te'-ga	" "	Wee-kä'	" "	Wee-te'-ga	" "
20	Hee-too'-ga	" "	Hee-koo'-n'-ye	" "	Hee-too'-ga	" "
21	E-tŭ'-kä	" "	Hiŋ-kŭ'-ne	" "	E-tŭ'-kä	" "
22	Be-che'-go	" "	E-ko'	" "	Be-che'-go	" "
23	We-che'-cho	" "	E-che'	" "	We-che'-cho	" "
24	E-cho'-ka	" "	E-ko'-ro-ka	" "	E-cho'-ka	" "
25	Tä-ta'-h·e-ba	" "	Nah·'-he-a	" "	Tä-ta'-h·e-ba	" "
26	Mä-toosh-a-rŭ'-tä-kä.	" "	Kä-rŭ'-tä-kä	" "	Mä-toosh-a-rŭ'-tä-kä	" "
27	Me-nup-h·is'-sä-ka	My old father.	Bä-sä'-kä--na	" "	Me-nup-h·is'-sä-ka	My old father.
28	Um-uh'-fo	My grandfather.	Up-puk'-nĭ	" "	Um·uh'-fo	My grandfather.
29	Um-u'-fo	" "	Up-pok'-nĭ	" "	Um-u'-fo	" "
30	Um-u'-fo	" "	Hap-pŭ'-sĭ	" "	Um-u'-fo	" "
31	Cha-pŭ-chä'	" "	Chu-pŭ'-se	" "	Cha-pŭ-chä'	" "
32	E-nĭ-sĭ	My grandparent.	E-nĭ-sĭ	My grandparent.	E-nĭ-sĭ	My grandparent.
33	Ah-ge-doo'-tsĭ	My grandfather.	Ah-ge-lee'-sih	My grandmother.	Ah-ge-doo'-tse	My grand ather.
34	Te-wä-chir-iks	My uncle.	Ah-te'-kä	My grandparent.	Ah-te'-put	" "
35	Te-watch'-e-ricks	" "	Ah-te'-kä	" "	Ah-te'-put	" "
36					Ah-te'-pot	" "
37	Ne-mo-some'	My grand father.	Noh·-kome'	My grandmother.	Ne-mo-some'	" "
38	Ne-mo-shome'	" "	No-kome'	" "	Ne-mo-shome'	" "
39	Na-mo-shome'	" "	No-kome'	" "	Na-mo-shome'	" "
40	Nĭ-mĭ-sho'-mis	" "	No'-ko-mis	" "	Nĭ-mĭ-sho'-mis	" "
41	Ne-me-sho'-mis	" "	No-ko-mis'	" "	Ne-me-sho'-mis	" "
42	Ne-ma-sho'-mis	" "	No-ko-mis'	" "	Na-ma-sho'-mis	" "
43	Ne-mis-sho'-mis	" "	No-ko-mis'	" "	Ne-mis'-sho-mis	" "
44	Na-ma-sho-mis'	" "	No-ko-mis'	" "	Na-ma-sho-mis'	" "
45	Na-ma-sho-mis'	" "	No-ko-mis'	" "	Na-ma-sho-mis'	" "
46	Na-ma-sho-mä'	" "	No-ko-mä'	" "	Na-ma-sho-mä'	" "
47	Na-mä-sho-mä'	" "	No-ko-mä'	" "	Na-mä-sho-mä'	" "
48	Na-mä-sho-mä'	" "	No-ko-mä'	" "	Na-mä-sho-mä'	" "
49	Na-mä-sho-mä'	" "	No-ko-mä'	" "	Na-mä-sho-mä'	" "
50	Na-mä-sho-mä'	" "	No-ko-mä'	" "	Na-mä-sho-mä'	" "
51	Nä-mä'-sho-mis	" "	No'-ko-mis	" "	Nä-mä'-sho-mis	" "
52	Na-mä'-sho.	" "	No'-ko-mä	" "	Na-mä'-sho	" "
53	Nam-a-shim'	" "	Na-vish-kim	" "	Nam-a-shim'	" "
54	Nem-ma-soo'-ma-thä	" "	No-ko-ma-some-thä'	" "	Nem-ma-soo'-ma-thä	" "
55	Na-ma-some-thä'	" "	No-kome-thä'	" "	Na-ma-some-thä'	" "
56	No-bes'-sib-ah	" "	Na'-e-bä	" "	No-bes'-sib-ä	" "
57	Ne-ah'-sä	" "	Ne-tä'-ke-ä'-sä	" "	Ne-ah·'-sä	" "
58	Nä-ah·xs'	" "	Ne-tä'-ke-ah·xs	" "	Ne-ahxs'	" "
59	Niks-kä-mich'	" "	Nŭ-ga'-mich	" "	Niks-kä-mich'	" "
60	N'-mŭke-sŭms'	" "	Nŭk'-mus	" "	N'-mŭke-sŭms'	" "
61	Nuh-mä-home'	" "	No-ome'	" "	Nuh-mä-home'	" "
62	Nu-moh·'-ho-mus'	" "	Noo-h·ome'	" "	Nu-moh·'-ho-mus'	" "
63	Na-mä-ho-mis'	" "	Na-no'-home	" "	Na mä-ho-mis'	" "
64	Sa-tse'-a	" "	Sa-tsun'	" "	Sa·tse'-a	" "
65	Sa-tä'-chock	" "	Sa-cho'-na	" "	Sa-tä'-chock	" "
66	Set-see'-a	" "	Set-sa'-nä	" "	Set-see'-a	" "
67	Set-see'	" "	Set-so'	" "	Set-see'	" "
68	Set-see'	" "	Set-soon'	" "	Set-seé	" "
69	Is-see'-lä (G. F. mo. side)	" "	In-chau'-wä (G. M. male	" "	{ Is-hah'-pä (m. s.)	" "
70			[speaking]		In-chau'-wä(f. s.)	" "
71	Nä-ta'-las " " "	" "	Nä-käht'-las	" "	Na-poos'-as.	" "
72					Ka-pä-pa	" "
73					Tog-go	" "
74					Na'-nä-hash-te	My grandparent.
75					Ku-pŭp-no-sheeb	My grandfather.
76						" "
77						" "
78	A-ta-ma-a-ta	My gt. grandfather.	Ah-na-cha-ga	My gt. grandfather.	Ah-tä-tä-tcha-wä	" "
79					A-ta-ga	" "
80	E-tŭ'-ah	My grandfather.	Ning-e-o'-wä	My grandfather.	E-tŭ'-ah	" "

TABLE II.—Continued.

	6. My grandmother	Translation.	7. My father.	Translation.	8. My Mother.	Translation.
1	Oc'-sote......................	My grandmother.	Hä'-nih	My father.	No-yeh'......................	My mother.
2	Oc'-sote......................	" "	Hä'-nih	" "	Kno'-hä......................	" "
3	Oc-so'-dä-hä................	" "	Kuh-ne-hä'....................	" "	Ah-ge-no'-hä	" "
4	Ahk-sote'-hä	" "	Lä'-ga-nih	" "	Ahk-nole'-hä.................	" "
5	Ahk-sote'....................	" "	Lä-ga-ne'-hä	" "	Ah-ga-nese'-tä	" "
6	Ahk-'sote...................	" "	Ahk-re'-ah	" "	Oh'-nä	" "
7	Ak-sote'-hä	" "	Lä-ga-ne'-hä	" "	Ah-ga-nese'-tä-hä	" "
8	Ah-shu-tä'..................	" "	Hi-ese'-tä	" "	Ah-nä'-uh	" "
9	Uu-che'.....................	" "	At-tay'.......................	" "	E-nah'.......................	" "
10	O-che'......................	" "	Ah-tä'........................	" "	E'-nah	" "
11	O-che'-lä	" "	Ah-ta'........................	" "	E'-nah	" "
12	Oh'-che	" "	Ah-ta'........................	" "	En'-nä.	" "
13	Oo-che'.....................	" "	Ah-ta'........................	" "	E'-nah	" "
14	Un-che'.....................	" "	Ah-ta'........................	" "	E'-nah	" "
15	O-che'......................	" "	Ah-ta'........................	" "	E'-nah	" "
16	O-che'......................	" "	Ah-ta'........................	" "	E'-nah	" "
17	O-gä'-she	" "	Ah-da'........................	" "	E-nah'.......................	" "
18	Gä-hä'......................	" "	Tä-de'-ha.. ᵇ Wä-we-tä...	" "	Nä'-hä	" "
19	Wee'-kä	" "	In-dä'-de	" "	E-nä'-ha	" "
20	Hee-koo'-n'-ye	" "	Heen'-nä	" "	Heen'-nä	" "
21	Hin-kŭ'-ne	" "	Hin'-kä	" "	He'-nah	" "
22	E-ko'.......................	" "	E-dä'-je	" "	E'-naw.	" "
23	E-che'......................	" "	In-tä'-che	" "	In-nah'......................	" "
24	E-ko'-ro-ka	" "	Chä-je'-kä. ᵇ E-un'-cha..	" "	Nä-ne'-kä. ᵇ E-oo-ne'	" "
25	Nah-'-he-a	" "	Tä-tay'.......................	" "	Nä-a'........................	" "
26	Kä-rü'-hä	" "	Tä-ta'........................	" "	Ih'-kä	" "
27	Bä-sä'-kä-na	" "	Ah-h·a'......................	" "	E'-ke-ä......................	" "
28	Up-puk'-nĭ..................	" "	A'-kĭ	" "	Ush'-kĭ	" "
29	Up-pok'-nĭ..................	" "	A'-kĭ	" "	Ush'-kĭ	" "
30	Hap-pŭ'-sĭ..................	" "	Ang'-kĭ	" "	Lush'-kĭ	" "
31	Cua-pŭ'-se	" "	Chuhl'-ke....................	" "	Chutch'-ke	" "
32	E-nĭ-sĭ	" "	E-dau-dä'....................	" "	E-tsĬ'.......................	" "
33	Ah-ge-lee'-sih	" "	Ah-ge-do'-dä	" "	Ah-gid'-ze..................	" "
34	Ah-te'-kä	My grandparent.	Ah-te'-is.....................	" "	Ah-te'-rä	" "
35	Ah-te'-kä	My grandmother.	Ah-te'-ase...................	" "	A-te'-rä	" "
36	Ah-te'-kä	" "	Ah-te'-ah	" "	At-nä'.......................	" "
37	Noh·-kome'.................	" "	Noh·-tä'-we	" "	N'-gä'-we	" "
38	No-kome'...................	" "	Noh·-tä'-we	" "	N'-gä'-we	" "
39	No-kome'...................	" "	Noh·-tä'-we	" "	N'-gä'-wa	" "
40	No'-ko-miss................	" "	Nöss.........................	" "	Nin'-gah	" "
41	No'-ko-mis.................	" "	No'-sa	" "	Nin'-gah	" "
42	No-ko'-mis.................	" "	Noss	" "	Nin-gah'.....................	" "
43	No-ko-mis'.................	" "	Noss	" "	Ne-gä-sha'..................	" "
44	No-ko-mis'..................	" "	Noss	" "	N'-gus'-sheh	" "
45	No-ko-mis'..................	" "	Noss	" "	N'-geh'......................	" "
46	No-ko-mä'..................	" "	No-sä'........................	" "	Nin-ge-ah'..................	" "
47	No-ko-mä'..................	" "	No-sä'........................	" "	Nin-ge-ah'..................	" "
48	No-ko-mä'..................	" "	No-sä'........................	" "	Nin-ge-ah'..................	" "
49	No'-ko-mä	" "	No-sä'........................	" "	Ne-ge-ah	" "
50	No'-ko-mä	" "	No-sä'........................	" "	Ne-ge-ah'...................	" "
51	No'-ko-mis	" "	Noss	" "	Nä-ke⁻ä'....................	" "
52	No'-ko-mä	" "	Noh'-neh.....................	" "	Ne-ke⁻äh'...................	" "
53	Na-vish'-kim	" "	Nä-o'-a.......................	" "	Nä'-ko	" "
54	No-ko-ma-some-thä'	" "	No-thä'.......................	" "	Nĭ-ke⁻ä'....................	" "
55	No-kome-thä'	" "	No-thä'.......................	" "	Na-ke⁻äh'...................	" "
56	Na-e'-bä....................	" "	Ne-tha'-na	" "	Na'-nä	" "
57	Ne-tä-ke-ä'-sä	" "	Nin	" "	Neex-ist'....................	" "
58	Ne-tä'-ke-ah·xs	" "	Nin'-nä	" "	Nee-crist'...................	" "
59	Nŭ-ga'-mich................	" "	Nŭch	" "	N'-keech'....................	" "
60	Núk'-mus...................	" "	Nu-me'-tonks	" "	Nee'-goos....................	" "
61	No-ome'....................	" "	Noh·.........................	" "	N'-guk'......................	" "
62	Noo-h·ome'	" "	Noh·'-h'	" "	N'-gä'-hase	" "
63	Na-no'-home	" "	Na-no'-uh....................		Nain-guk'...................	" "
64	Sa-tsun'....................	" "	Sa-tä'........................	' "	Eu'-de	" "
65	Sa-cho'-na.................	" "	Sa-tä'........................	" "	A'-na	" "
66	Set-sa'-na	" "	Set-hä'.......................	" "	A-nä'........................	" "
67	Set-so'.....................	" "	Te⁻angh'.....................	" "	En-na' or Na-aingh	" "
68	Set-soon... [chee-ä'-à (f.s.)	" "	Teh-yän..[mes'-tum(f.s.)	" "	Nu-han.............. [(f.s.)	" "
69	In-kah'-nä(m.s.), In-tchit-	" "	En-le-ä'-u (m. s.), En-ne-	" "	E-sko'-i (m. s.) En-tome'	" "
70	E-stum-te'-mä (fem.sp.)..	" "	In-mees'-tum	" "	In-toom'....................	" "
71	Nä-ah'läs	" "	Nä-too'-tas. ᵇ Pe-shit'	" "	Nä-eet'-las. ᵇ Pe-chagh .	" "
72	Ka-pä-pa	My grandparent.	Kä-ta'-to (m. s.), Kä'-to	" "	Kam-ä	" "
73	Kä-go......................	My grandmother.	Mu'-än-e............[(f. s.)	" "	Pe-än-e. ᵇ Pe'-ät-sin......	" "
74	Pä'-pä-kee-yon'	" "	Nish'-te-ä	" "	Ni'-ya......................	" "
75			No-vi-sen-do. ᵇ Ta-ra....	" "	No-vi-ca	" "
76	Ku-nä-schu-peen	" "	Ku-päp	" "	Ku-nä	" "
77	Su-e-he-sä.	" "	Pä'-bä	" "	Gä-ü-i'-ä	" "
78	A-nä-nä-tcha yä............	" "	Ah'-tä-tä-kä.................	" "	A-nä'-nä-kwä................	" "
79	A-na-ga	" "	ᵃ A-tä-ta-ga. ᵇ Aug-u-ti-ga	" "	ᵃ An-ä-na-ga. ᵇ Ar-na-ra	" "
80	Ning-e-o'-wä	" "	ᵃ Ah-tä'-tä. ᵇ Aug'-o-tä..	" "	Ah-nä'-nä...................	" "

TABLE II.—*Continued.*

	9. My son.	Translation.	10. My daughter.	Translation.	11. My grandson.	Translation.
1	Ha-ah'-wuk	My son.	Ka-ah'-wuk	My daughter.	Ha-yä'-da	My grandson.
2	Ha-hä'-wuk	" "	Ka-hä'-wuk	" "	Ha-yä'-dra	" "
3	Ha-hä'-wä	" "	Ka-hä'-wä	" "	Ha-yä'-da	" "
4	Le-yä'-hä	" "	Ka-yä'-hä	" "	Le-yä'-dla-ah	" "
5	E-yä'	" "	Ka-yä'	" "	E-yä'-dla-ah	" "
6	Kä-yä'-no-nä	My child.	Kä-yä'-no-nä	My child.	Kä-yä'-rä	My grandchild.
7	Le-yä'-ah	My son.	Ka-yä'-hä	My daughter.	Le-yä-tä-ra'-yä	My grandson.
8	A-ne-ah'	" "	E-ne-ah'	" "	Ha-tra'-ah	" "
9	Me-chink'-she	" "	Me-chunk'-she	" "	Me-tä'-ko-zhä	My grandchild.
10	Me-chink'-she	" "	Me-chounk'-she	" "	Me-tä'-ko-zhä	" "
11	Me-she'-da	" "	Me-chunk'-shä	" "	Me-tä'-ko-zhä	" "
12	Me-chink'-she	" "	Me-chunk'-she	" "	Me-tä'-ko-zha	" "
13	Me-chink'-se-la	" "	Me-chunk'-se-lä	" "	Me-tä'-ko-säk'-pok	" "
14	Me-chink'-she	" "	Me-chunk'-she	" "	Me-tä'-ko-zhä	" "
15	Me-chink'-she	" "	Me-chŭnk'-she	" "	Me-tä'-ko-zhä	" "
16	Me-chink'-she	" "	Me-chŭnk'-she	" "	Me-tä'-ko-zä	" "
17	Me-chink'-she	" "	Me-chunk'-she	" "	Me-tä'-ko-sä	" "
18	Nis-se'-hä...[zhin-go (f.sp.)	" "	Win-no'-ga	" "	Toosh'-pä-hä	" "
19	We-nis'-se .... (m. sp.), we-	" "	We-zhuņ'-ga	" "	We-tŭsh'-pä	" "
20	Hee-yin'-ga	" "	Hee-yuņ'-ga	" "	Heen-tä'-kwä	My grandson.
21	He-ne'-cha	" "	He-yuņ-ga.	" "	E-tä'-kwä	" "
22	Be-she'-gä	" "	She-me'-she-gä	My girl.	Be-chose'-pä	My grandchild.
23	We-she'-kä	" "	We-shon'-ka	My daughter.	We-chose'-pä	" "
24	E-neke'..........[ka (f. sp.)	" "	E-nook'	" "	E-chooush'-ka	My grandson.
25	Me-ne'-ka (m. sp.), Ko-ne'-	" "	Me-no'-hä-ka	" "	P-tä-we'-hä-kä	My grandchild.
26	Mä-de-shä'	" "	Mä'-kä	" "	Met-a-wä-pish'-sha	" "
27	Bot-sa'-sä	" "	Näk'-me-ä	" "	Bus-bä'-pe-ta	" "
28	Suh'-sŭh	" "	Suh-sŭh'-take	" "	Sup'-uk-nŏk'-ne	My grandson.
29	Suh'-soh	" "	Suh-soh'-take	" "	Sä'-pok-näk'-ne	" "
30	Su'-soh......[hŭs'-wä (f. s.)	" "	Su-soh'-take	" "	Sup'-pok-näk'-nĭ	" "
31	Chup-pŭ'-che (m.s.),Chuch-	" "	Chus-hus'-te (m. s.),Chuch-	" "	Um-os-sŭs'-wä	My grandchild.
32	A-gwae-tsĭ'	My child.	A-gwae-tsĭ' .. [hus'-wä(f.s.)	My child.	Aņ-gĭ-lĭ-sĭ'	My grandson.
33	Ah-gwa -tze	" "	Ah-gwa'-tze	" "	Aņ-ge-lee'-se	" "
34	Pe'-row	" "	Pe'-row	" "	Lak-te'-gish	My grandchild.
35	Pe-row. ᵇ Tik'-is	" "	Pe'-row	" "	Lak-te'-kis	" "
36	Pe'-row. ᵇ Nä-te-nä'-o	" "	Pe'-row. ᵇ Nä-te-nä'-o	" "	Nä-rä-ne-tish'-ă. ᵇ At-nuch'	" "
37	N'-go'-sis	My son.	N'-dä'-nis	My daughter.	No-se-sem'	" "
38	N'-go'-sis	" "	N'-dä'-nis	" "	No-se-sim'	" "
39	N'-koo'-sis	" "	N'-dä'-nis	" "	No-se-sem'	" "
40	Nin-dä'-niss	" "	Nin-dä'-niss	" "	No-zhĭ'-she	" "
41	Nin-gwis'	" "	Nin-dä'-niss	" "	No-she'-shä	" "
42	Neen-gwis'	" "	Neen-dä-niss	" "	No-she-shä'	" "
43	Nin-gwis'	" "	N'-dä-niss'	" "	No-she-shä'	" "
44	N'-gwis'	" "	N'-dä-niss'	" "	No-sä-seh'	" "
45	N'-gwis'	" "	N'-dä'-niss	" "	No-she-sä'	" "
46	Neen-gwase'-sä	" "	Nin-dä'-nä	" "	No-sa'-mä	" "
47	Niņ-gwa-sä'	" "	Nin-dä'-nä	" "	No-sa'-mä	" "
48	Niņ-gwa-sä'	" "	Nin-dä'-nä	" "	No-sa-mä'	" "
49	Ne-gwis-sä'	" "	N'-dä'-nä	" "	No-sa-mä'	" "
50	Ne-gwis-sä'	" "	N'-dä'-nä	" "	No-sa-mä'	" "
51	Nä-kwis'-sä	" "	Nä-tä'-niss	" "	No-she-sem'	" "
52	Ne-keese'	" "	Ne-täne'	" "	No-she-sä'	" "
53	Nä	" "	Nä-tun'	" "	Nä-h·kä'	" "
54	Nĭ-kwĕ-thä'	" "	Nĭ-tä-na-thä'	" "	Na-se-thä'-mä	" "
55	Ne-kwe-thä'	" "	Nĭ-tä-na-thä'	" "	No-stha-thä'	" "
56	Na'-hä	" "	Nä-tä'-na	" "	Nee'-sa	" "
57	Noh'-ko	" "	Ne-tan'	" "	Nee-so'-tan	" "
58	Noh'-ko'-ä	" "	Ne-tan'-ä	" "	Nee-so'-tän	" "
59	N'-kwis'	" "	N'-tŭs'	" "	Nŭ-jeech'	" "
60	N'-koos'	" "	N'-toos'	" "	N'-kway'-nus	" "
61	N'-di-ome'	" "	Ne-chune'	" "	Nä-h·ise'	" "
62	N'-kweese'	" "	N'-dä-nuss'	" "	Noh'-whese'	" "
63	Nain-gwase'	" "	Nain-dä'-ness	" "	Nain-no-whase'	" "
64	Su-chu'-ah (m. sp.), Sa-yä'	" "	Sa-tu'-ah (m. s.), Sa-yä'-dze	" "	Sa-t'-lu'-a (m.sp.), Sa-chä'-	" "
65	Sa-yä'-za............[ze (f. sp.)	" "	Sa-to'-a ....[(f. sp.)	" "	Sa-ken'-ne...........[(f. sp.)	My grandson.
66	Se-yä'-za............[(f. sp.)	" "	Sa-le'-ä	" "	Se-yä-zet'-tha-re	" "
67	Sa'-tin-ge (m. sp.), Sa-zoo'	" "	Sa-che (m.), Sa-ya-tse' (f.)	" "	Sa-chi'	My grandchild.
68	Set-een-ge (m.s.), See-zi-ou	" "	Seet-shere (m.) See-yä-tse (f.)	" "	Seet-she (m.), Seet-shai (f.)	" "
69	Is-kwoos-sä............[(f. s.)	" "	Is-tum-che-ält. ᵇ Is-shoo-te-	" "	Is-hah'-pa (sou's s.), Is-see'-	My grandson.
70	Ese-koo-see'	" "	Ese-tum'-ke-ilt........[mält	" "	Ese-in-e'-malt....[lä (d.'s s.)	My grandchild.
71	En-mesht'	" "	En-misht. ᵇ Isht (by f.), Päp	" "	Nä-poos'-as (m. s.), Nä-ä-la	" "
72	Kun-naht'-la	" "	Kas-wil.........[(by mother)	" "	Ka-pä-pa.............[(f. s.)	" "
73	To-ät'-sin	" "	Pä-chin'	" "	Kŭn'-ŭt-sin (m.s.), Nhit-sit	" "
74	Sam-mŭt'	" "	Sä-mäk'	" "	Sä-nä'-nä.........[sin (f. s.)	My grandson.
75	No-vi-a	" "	No-vi-a-au-u-kwa	" "	Nau-wi-ta-ti-e	My grandchild.
76	Ka-ash-lo		Ka-ee-she-ok		Ka-eesh	" "
77	Chib-i. ᵇ Chŭ-bä	My child.	Chibi. ᵇ Chŭb-ä	My child.	Chŭ'-ne	" "
78	E-ne-gä	My son.	Pä-ne-gä	My daughter.	E-noo-tä-kä	" "
79	Er-ne-ra	" "	Pan-ni-ga	My daughter.	Er-nu-ta-ra	" "
80	En-ning'-ah	" "	Pun-ning'-ah	" "	Eng'-o-tä	" "

TABLE II.—*Continued.*

	12 My granddaughter.	Translation.	13. My great grandson.	Translation.	14. My great grauddaughter.	Translation.
1	Ka-yä'-da	My gd. daughter.	Ha-yä'-da	My grandson.	Ka-yä'-da	My gd. daught.
2	Ka-yä'-dra	" "	Ha-yä'-dra	" "	Ka-yä'-dra	" "
3	Ka-yä'-da	" "	Ha-yä'-da	" "	Ka-yä'-da	" "
4	Ka-yä'-dla-ah	" "	Le-yä'-dla-ah	" "	Ka-yä'-dla-ah	" "
5	Ka-yä'-dla-ah	" "	E-yä'-dla-ah	" "	Ka-yä'-dla-ah	" "
6	Kä-yä'-rä	My grandchild.	Kä-yä'-rä	My grandchild.	Kä-yä'-rä	My grandchild.
7	Ka-yä-tä-ra'-yä	My gd. daughter.	Le-yä-tä-ra'-yä	My grandson.	Ka-yä-tä-ra'-yä	My gd. daught.
8	Ya-tra'-ah	" "	Ha-tra'-ah	" "	Ya-tra'-ah	" "
9	Me-tä'-ko-zhä	My grandchild.	Me-tä'-ko-zhä	My grandchild.	Me-tä'-ko-zhä	My grandchild.
10	Me-tä'-ko-zha	" "	Me-tä'-ko-zha	" "	Me-tä'-ko-zha	" "
11	Me-tä'-ko-zhä	" "	Me-tä'-ko-zhä	" "	Me-tä'-ko-zhä	" "
12	Me-tä'-ko-zha	" "	Me-tä'-ko-zha	" "	Me-tä'-ko-zha	" "
13	Me-tä'-ko-säk'-pok	" "	Me-tä-ko-säk'-pok	" "	Me-tä-ko-säk'-pok	" "
14	Me-tä'-ko-zhä	" "	Me-tä'-ko-zhä	" "	Me-tä'-ko-zhä	" "
15	Me-tä'-ko-zhä	" "	Me-tä'-ko-zhä	" "	Me-tä'-ko-zhä	" "
16	Me-tä'-ko-zä	" "	Me-tä'-ko-zä	" "	Me-tä'-ko-zä	" "
17	Me-tä'-ko-sä	" "	Me-tä'-ko-sä	" "	Me-tä'-ko-sä	" "
18	Toosh'-pä-hä	" "	Toosh'-pä-hä	" "	Toosh'-pä-hä	" "
19	Wee-tŭsh'-pä	" "	Wee-tŭsh'-pä	" "	Wee-tŭsh'-pä	" "
20	Heen-tä-kwä-me	My gd. daughter.	Heen-tä'-kwä	My grandson.	Heen-tä'-kwä-me	My gd. daught.
21	E-tä'-kwä-me	" "	E-tä'-kwä	" "	E-tä'-kwä-me	" "
22	Be-chose'-pä	My grandchild.	Be-chose'-pä	My grandchild.	Be-chose'-pä	My grandchild.
23	We-chose'-pä	" "	We-chose'-pä	" "	We-chose'-pä	" "
24	E-choon-zhunk'	My gd. daughter.	E-chooush'-ka	My grandson.	E-choon-zhunk'	My gd. daught.
25	P-tä-we'-hä-kä	My grandchild.	P-tä-we'-hä-kä	My grandchild.	P-tä-we'-hä-kä	My grandchild.
26	Met-a-wä-pish'-sha	" "	Met-a-wä-pish'-sha	" "	Met-a-wä-pish'-sha	" "
27	Bus-bä-pe-ta	" "	Bus-bä'-pe-ta	" "	Bus-bä-pe-ta	" "
28	Sup'-uk	My gd. daughter.	Sup'-uk-nŏk'-ne	My grandson.	Sup'-uk	My gd. daught.
29	Sä'-pok	" "	Sä'-pok-näk'-ne	" "	Sä'-pok	" "
30	Sup'-pok	" "	Sup'-pok-näk'-nĭ	" "	Sup'-pok	" "
31	Um-os-sŭs'-wä	My grandchild.	Um-os-sŭs'-wä	My grandchild.	Um-os-sŭs'-wä	My grandchild.
32	Uŋ-gĭ-lĭ-sĭ	" "	Uŋ-gĭ-lĭ-sĭ	" "	Uŋ-gĭ-lĭ-sĭ	" "
33	Aŋ-ge-lee'-se	" "	Aŋ-ge-lee'-se	" "	Aŋ-ge-lee'-se	" "
34	Lak-te'-gee	My gd. daughter.	Te'-wut	My nephew.	Te'-wut	My niece.
35	Lak-te'-kis	My grandchild.				
36	Nă-rä-ne-tish'-ă	" "	Ah-te'-wut	" "	Ah-te'-wut	" "
37	No-se-sem'	" "	No-se-sem'	My grandchild.	No-se-sem'	My grandchild.
38	Mo-se-sim'	" "	No-se-sim'	" "	No-se-sim'	" "
39	No-se-sem'	" "	No-se-sem'	" "	No-se-sem'	" "
40	No-zhĭ'-she	" "	No-zhĭ'-she	" "	No-zhĭ'-she	" "
41	No-she-shă	" "	No-she-shă'	" "	No-she-shă'	" "
42	No-she-shă'	" "	No-she-shă'	" "	No-she-shă'	" "
43	No-she-shă'	" "	No-she-shă'	" "	No-she-shă'	" "
44	No-she-shă'	" "	No-she-shă'	" "	No-she-shă'	" "
45	No-să-seh'	" "	No-să-seh'	" "	No-să-seh'	" "
46	No-sa-mä'	" "	No-sa-mä'	" "	No-sa-mä'	" "
47	No-sa'-mä	" "	No-sa'-mä	" "	No-sa'-mä	" "
48	No-sa-mä'	" "	No-sa-mä'	" "	No-sa-ma'	" "
49	No-sa-mä'	" "	No-sa-mä'	" "	No-sa-ma'	" "
50	No-sa-mä'	" "	No-sa-mä'	" "	No-să-ma'	" "
51	No-she-sem'	" "	No-she-sem'	" "	No-she-sem'	" "
52	No-she-să'	" "	No-she-să'	" "	No-she-să'	" "
53	Nä-h·-kä'	" "	Nä-h·-kä'	" "	Nä-h·-kä'	" "
54	Na-se-thä'-mä	" "	Na-se-thä'-mä	" "	Na-se-thä'-mä	" "
55	No-stha-thä'	" "	No-stha-thä'	" "	No-stha-thä'	" "
56	Nee'-sa	" "	Nee'-sa	" "	Nee'-sa	" "
57	Nee-so'-tan	" "	Nee-so'-tan	" "	Nee-so'-tan	" "
58	Nee-so'-tän	" "	Nee-so'-tän	" "	Nee-so'-tän	" "
59	Nŭ-jeech'	" "	Nŭ-jeech'	" "	Nŭ-jeech'	" "
60	N'-kway'-nus	" "	N'-kway'-nus	" "	N'-kway'-nus	" "
61	Nä-h·ise'	" "	Nä-h·ise'	" "	Nä-h·ise'	" "
62	Noh·-whese'	" "	Noh·-whese'	" "	Noh·-whese'	" "
63	Nain-no-whase'	" "	Nain-no-whase'	" "	Nain-no-whase'	" "
64	Sa-t'-thu'-a (m. s.), Sa-chä'	" "	Sa-t'-thu'-a (m. s.), Sa-chä'.	" "	Sa-t'-thu'-a (m. s.), Sa-chä'	" "
65	Sa-to⁻a'-bă ...... [(f. sp.)	My gd. daughter.	Sa-ken'-ne ...... [(f. s.)	My grandson.	Sa-to⁻a'-bă ...... [(w. s.)	My gd. daught.
66	Sa-le-zet'-tha-re	" "	Se-yä-zet'-tha-re	" "	Sa-le-zet'-tha-re	" "
67	Sa-chi'	My grandchild.	Sa-chi'	My grandchild.	Sa-chi'	My grandchild.
68	Seet-she	" "	Seet-she (m.), Seet shai (f.)	" "	Seet-she (m.), seet-shai (f.)	" "
69	In-chau'-wä (dau. of son), [In-chit-che-ä (dau. of d.)					
70	Ese-in-e'-malt	" "	Ese-in-e'-malt	" "	Ese-in-e'-malt	" "
71	Nä-poos'-as (m. sp.), Nä-ă-	" "				
72	Ka-pä'-pa ...... [la (f. s.)	" "	To-gŭt'-sin	My gt. grandchild.	To-gŭt'-sin	My gt. gd. child.
73	Kin-ŭt-sin (m. s.), Nhit-sit-	" "	Sam-mät'	My son.	Sä-mäk'	My daughter.
74	Să-pä'-pä ...... sin (f. s.)	My gd. daughter.	Pa-pa-e	My third child.	Pa-pa.e	My third child.
75	Nau-wi-ta-ti-e	" "				
76	Ka-eesh	My grandchild.				
77	Chŭ'-ne	" "				
78	E-noo-tä-kă	" "	Er-nu-tae-ki-u-ti-ga	My gt. gd. child...	Er-nu-tae-ki-u-ti-ga	My gt. gd. child.
79	Er-nu-ta-ra	" "	Eng'-o-tä	My grandchild.	Eng'-o-tä	My grandchild.
80	Eng'-o-tä	" "				

38

TABLE II.—*Continued.*

	15. My great grandson's son.	Translation.	16. My great grandson's daughter.	Translation.	17. My elder brother. (Male speaking.)	Translation.
1	Ha-yä′-da	My grandson.	Ka-yä′-da	My granddaughter.	Hä′-je	My elder brother.
2	Ha-yä′-dra	" "	Ka-yä′-dra	" "	Kuh-je′-ah	" " "
3	Ha-yä′-da	" "	Ka-yä′-da	" "	Kuh-je′-ah	" " "
4	Le-yä′-dla-ah	" "	Ka-yä′-dla-ah	" "	Läk-je′-hä	" " "
5	E-yä′-dla-ah	" "	Ka-yä′-dla-ah	" "	Läk-je′-hä	" " "
6	Kä-yä′-rä	My grandchild.	Kä-yä′-rä	My grandchild.	Ahk-rä′-je	" " "
7	Le-yä-tä-ra′-yä	My grandson.	Ka-yä-tä-ra′-yä	My granddaughter.	Lok-je′-hä	" " "
8	Ha-tra′-ah		Ka-tra′-ah	" "	Ha-ye′-uh	" " "
9	Me-tä′-ko-zhä	My grandchild.	Me-tä′-ko-zhä	My grandchild.	Chin-yay′	" " "
10	Me-tä-ko-zha	" "	Me-tä′-ko-zha	" "	Che-a′	" " "
11	Me-tä′-ko-zhä	" "	Me-tä′-ko-zha	" "	Che′-a	" " "
12	Me-tä′-ko-zha	" "	Me-tä′-ko-zha	" "	Che′-a	" " "
13	Me-tä′-ko-säk′-pok	" "	Me-tä′-ko-säk′-pok	" "	Che′-a	" " "
14	Me-tä′-ko-zhä	" "	Me-tä′-ko-zhä	" "	Me-che′-a	" " "
15	Me-tä′-ko-zhä	" "	Me-tä′-ko-zhä	" "	Che′-a	" " "
16	Me-tä′-ko-zä	" "	Me-tä′-ko-zä	" "	Che-a′	" " "
17	Me-tä′-ko-sä	" "	Me-tä′-ko-sä	" "	Me-chin′	" " "
18	Toosh′-pä-hä	" "	Toosh′-pä-hä	" "	Zhin-dä′-hä	" " "
19	Wee-tŭsh′-pä	" "	Wee-tŭsh′-pä	" "	Wee-zhe′-thä	" " "
20	Heen-tä′-kwä	My grandson.	Heen-tä′-kwä-me	My granddaughter.	He-yen′	" " "
21	E-tä′-kwä	" "	E-tä′-kwä-me	" "	Hee-ye′-nä	" " "
22	Be-chose′-pä	My grandchild.	Be-chose′-pä	My grandchild.	Be-zhe′-yeh	" " "
23	We-chose′-pä	" "	We-chose′-pä	" "	We-she′-lä	" " "
24	E-choonsh′-ka	My grandson.	E-choon-zhunk′	My granddaughter.	E-ne′	" " "
25	P-tä-we′-hä-kä	My grandchild.	P-tä-we′-hä-kä	My grandchild.	Moo′-tä	" " "
26	Met-a-wä-pish′-sha	" "	Met-a-wä-pish′-sha	" "	Mee-ä-kä′	" " "
27	Bus-bä′-pe-ta	" "	Bus-bä′-pe-ta	" "	Meek′-a	" " "
28	Sup′-uk-nŏk′-ne	My grandson.	Sup′-uk	My granddaughter.	Um-un′-nĭ	" " "
29	Sä′-pok-näk′-ne	" "	Sä′-pok	" "	Um-un′-nĭ	" " "
30	Sup′-pok-näk′-ni	" "	Sup′-pok	" "	Au-tik′-ä	" " "
31	Um-os-sŭs′-wä	My grandchild.	Um-os-sŭs′-wä	My grandchild.	Chu-hlä-hä	" " "
32	Uŋ-gĭ-lĭ-sĭ	" "	Uŋ-gĭ-lĭ-sĭ	" "	Uŋ-gĭ-nĭ-lĭ	" " "
33	Aŋ-ge-lee′-se	" "	Aŋ-ge.lee′-se	" "	Aŋ-ke-nee′-lĭ	" " "
34	Pe′-row	My child.	Pe-row	My child.	E-dä′-deh	My brother.
35					A-dä′-de	" "
36	Nä-te-nä′-o	" "	Nä-te-nä′-o	" "	Che-nä-tun′	My bro. (oldest).
37	No-se-sem′	My grandchild.	No-se-sem′	My grandchild.	Neese-tase′	My elder brother.
38	No-se-sim′	" "	No-se-sim′	" "	Neese-tase′	" " "
39	No-se-sem′	" "	No-se-sem′	" "	Neesh-tase′	" " "
40	No-zhĭ′-she	" "	No-zhĭ′-she	" "	Nis-sä′-yĕ	" " "
41	No-she′-shä	" "	No-she′-shä	" "	Ne-sĭ′-ya	" " "
42	No-she-shä′	" "	No-she-shä′	" "	Nĭ-sä-yä′	" " "
43	No-she-shä′	" "	No-she-shä′	" "	Nis-si-yä′	" " "
44	No-she-shä′	" "	No-she-shä′	" "	N′-sä′-yä	" " "
45	No-sä-seh′	" "	No-sä-seh′	" "	N′-seh-sä′	" " "
46	No-sa-mä′	" "	No-sa-mä′	" "	Ne-sä-sä′	" " "
47	No-sa′-mä	" "	No-sa′-mä	" "	Ne-san′-zä	" " "
48	No-sa′-mä	" "	No-sa′-mä	" "	Ne-san′-zä	" " "
49	No-sa-mä′	" "	No-sa-mä′	" "	Ne-sä-zä′	" " "
50	No-sa-mä′	" "	No-sa-mä′	" "	Ne-sä-zä′	" " "
51	No-she-sem′	" "	No-she-sem′	" "	Nä-sa′-mä	" " "
52	No-she-sä′	" "	No-she-sä′	" "	Nä-nä′	" " "
53	Nä-h·′-kä′	" "	Nä-h·′-kä′	" "	Nä-ne′-ä	" " "
54	Na-se-thä′-mä	" "	Na-se-thä′-mä	" "	Ni-tha-thä′	" " "
55	No-stha-thä′	" "	No-stha-thä′	" "	N′-tha-thä′	" " "
56	Nee-sa	" "	Nee-sa	" "	Na′-thä-hä	" " "
57	Nee-so′-tan	" "	Nee-só′-tan	" "	Neese-sä′	" " "
58	Nee-so′-tän	" "	Nee-só′-tän	" "	Nis′-sä	" " "
59	Nŭ-jeech′	" "	Nŭ-jeech′	" "	N′-sees′	" " "
60	N′-kway′-nus	" "	N′-kway′-nus	" "	N′-hay′-sees	" " "
61	Nä-h·ise′	" "	Nä-h·ise′	" "	N′-tä-kun′	" " "
62	Noh′-whese′	" "	Noh′-whese′	" "	Nah′-häns′	" " "
63	Nain-no-whase′	" "	Nain′-no-whase′	" "	Nain-n′-hans′	" " "
64	Sa-t′-thu′-a(m.s.),Sa-chä′	" "	Sa-t′-thu′-a(m.s.),Sa-chä′	" "	Kŭn′-dig-eh	" " "
65	Sa-ken′-ne......[(f. s.)	My grandson.	Sa-to¯a′-bä......[(f. s.)	My granddaughter.	Sŭn-no′-ga	" " "
66	Sa-yä-zet′-tha-re	" "	Sa-le-zet′-tha-re	" "	Sŭ-nä′-gä	" " "
67	Sa-chi′	My grandchild.	Sa-chi′	My grandchild.	Soon′-da-ga	" " "
68	Seet-she(m.),Seet-shai(f.)	" "	Seet-she(m.) Seet-shai(f.)	" "	Soon-da	" " "
69					En-kats′-tch′	" " "
70					Eel-käk-chä	" " "
71					Nä-ai′-yas. b Piap	" " "
72					Ka-tät′	" " "
73	Ko′-chin	My gt.gt.grandchild.	Ko′-chin	My gt. gt. gd. child.	Pä-ven′. b Pä-vet-sin	" " "
74					Sät-tum′	" " "
75					No-vi-pa-ra	" " "
76					Ku-su-cum	" " "
77					Gi′-ä	" " "
78					Ay-ny-yu-gä	" " "
79					An-ga-ju-ga	" " "
80	Eng′-o-tä	My grandchild.	Eng′-o-tä	My grandchild.	Ang-a-yu′-ä	

TABLE II.—*Continued.*

	18. My elder brother. (Female speaking.)	Translation.	19. My elder sister. (Male speaking.)	Translation.	20. My elder sister. (Female speaking.)	Translation.
1	Hä′ je	My elder brother.	Ah′-je	My elder sister.	Ah′-je.	My elder sister.
2	Kuh-je′-ah	" " "	Uh-je′-ah	" " "	Uh-je′-ah	" " "
3	Kuh-je′-ah	" " "	Uh-je′-ah	" " "	Uh-je′-ah	" " "
4	Läk-je′-hä	" " "	Ahk-je′-hä	" " "	Ahk-je′-hä	" " "
5	Lak-je′-ha	" " "	Ahk-je′-hä	" " "	Ahk-je′-hä	" " "
6	Ahk-rä′-je	" " "	Ahk′-je	" " "	Ahk′-je	" " "
7	Lok-je′-hä	" " "	Ak-je′-yä	" " "	Ak-je′-yä	" " "
8	Ha-ye′-uh	" " "	A-ye′-uh	" " "	A-ye′-uh	" " "
9	Te-mdo′	" " "	Taŋ-kay′	" " "	Me-chuŋ′	" " "
10	Chim′-a-do	" " "	Ton-ka′	" " "	Chu-ih′	" " "
11	Tib′-e-do	" " "	Tank′-she	" " "	Me-tank′-a-do	" " "
12	Tib′-a-do	" " "	Tank′-she	" " "	Tän′-ka	" " "
13	Tib′-a-lo	" " "	Tä-ka′	" " "	Chu-wa′	" " "
14	Tib-a-lo′	" " "	Tonk-a′	" " "	Chu-a′.	" " "
15	Tib′-a-lo	" " "	Ton′-ka	" " "	Chu′-ih	" " "
16	Tib′-a-lo	" " "	Ton-ka′	" " "	Chu-wa′	" " "
17	Me-tim′-do	" " "	Me-ton′-ga	" " "	Me-chuŋ′	" " "
18	Ton-no′-hä	" " "	Ton-ga′-hä	" " "	Zhon-da′-hä	" " "
19	Wee-te′-noo	" " "	Wee-tŏŋ-ga	" " "	Wee-zŏŋ′-thä	" " "
20	He-yen′-nä	" " "	He-yu′-nä	" " "	Heen-taŋ′-ga	" " "
21	Hee-ye′-nä	" " "	Wau-he′-cha	" " "	Heen-tang′-a	" " "
22	Be-che′-do	" " "	Be-tuŋ′-ga	" " "	Be-sho′-wa	" " "
23	We-chin′-to	" " "	We-tuŋ′-ka	" " "	We-sho′-la	" " "
24	E-che′-to	" " "	E-noo′	" " "	E-noo′	" " "
25	Me-sho′-kä	" " "	P-tä-me′-ha	" " "	Me-no′-ka	" " "
26	Má-tä-roo′	" " "	Mat-tä-we′-ä	" " "	·Mä-roo′	" " "
27	Bä-zä′-na	" " "	Bä-za′-kät	" " "	Bus-we′-nä	" " "
28	A-näk′-fī	" " "	An′-take	" " "	Um-un′-nī	" " "
29	A-näk′-fī	" " "	An′-take	" " "	Um-un′-nī	" " "
30	A-näk′-fī	" " "	An′-take	" " "	An′-tik′-bä	" " "
31	Chu-chihl′-wa	" " "	Chu-wun′-wä	" " "	Chu-hlä′-hä	" " "
32	Uŋ-gĭ-dau′	" " "	Uŋ-gĭ-dau′	" " "	Uŋ-gĭ-luŋ′-ī	" " "
33	Aŋ′-ke-doh	" " "	Aŋ′-ke-doh	" " "	Aŋ-ge-lä′-ih	" " "
34	E-rats-teh	My brother.	E-tä′-heh	My sister.	E-dä′-deh	My sister.
35	Ta-lä′-lik-tis	My brother (oldest)	A-tä′-he	" "	A-tä′-he	" "
36	A-tnas′	" " "	Ah-te′-ta	" "	Ah-te′-ta	" "
37	Neese-tase′	My elder brother.	Ne-mis′	My elder sister.	Ne-mis′	My elder sister.
38	Neese-tase′	" " "	Ne-mish′	" " "	Ne-mish′	" " "
39	Neesh-tase′	" " "	Ne-mish′	" " "	Ne-mish′	" " "
40	Nis-sä′-yĕ	" " "	Nĭ-mis′-sĕ	" " "	Nĭ-mis′-sĕ	" " "
41	Ne-sī′-ya	" " "	Ne-mis′-sa	" " "	Ne-mis′-sa	" " "
42	Nĭ-sä-yä′	" " "	Ne-mis-sä′	" " "	Ne-mis-sä′	" " "
43	Nis-si-yä′	" " "	Ne-mis-sä′	" " "	Ne-mis-sä′	" " "
44	N′-sä′-yä	" " "	N′-mis′-sä	" " "	N′-mis′-sä	" " "
45	N′-seh-sä′	" " "	N′-mis-sä′	" " "	N′-mis-sä′	" " "
46	Ne-sä-sä′	" " "	Ne-mis-sä′	" " "	Ne-mis-sä′	" " "
47	Ne-san′-zä	" " "	Ne-mis-sä′	" " "	Ne-mis-sä′	" " "
48	Ne-san′-zä	" " "	Ne-mis-sä′	" " "	Ne-mis-sä′	" " "
49	Ne-sä-zä′	" " "	Ne-me-sä′	" " "	Ne-me-sä′	" " "
50	Ne-sä-zä′.	" " "	Ne-me-sä′	" " "	Ne-me-sä′	" " "
51	Nä-sa′-mä	" " "	Nä-mis′-sä	" " "	Nä-mis′-sä	" " "
52	Nä-nä′	" " "	Ne-ma′	" " "	Ne-ma′.	" " "
53	Nä-ne′-ä	" " "	Nä-ma′	" " "	Nä-ma′	" " "
54	Ni-tha-thä′	" " "	Nĭ-mĭ-thä′	" " "	Ni-mi-thä′	" " "
55	N′-tha-thä′	" " "	Nĭ-mĭ-thä′	" " "	Nĭ-mĭ-thä′	" " "
56	Na′-thä-hä	" " "	Na′-be	" " "	Na′-be	" " "
57	Neese-sä′	" " "	Nee-mis′-tä	" " "	Nee-mis′-tä	" " "
58	Nis′-sä	" " "	Nee-his-tä	" " "	Nee-his-tä	" " "
59	N′-sees′	" " "	Nu-mees′	" " "	Nu-mees′	" " "
60	N′-hay′-sees	" " "	Nu-mu′-sees	" " "	Nu-mu′-sees	" " "
61	N′-tä-kun′	" " "	Nä-mees′	" " "	Nä-mees′	" " "
62	Nah′-häns′	" " "	Na-mese′	" " "	Na-mese′	" " "
63	Nain-n′hans	" " "	Nain-na-wase′:	" " *	Nain-na-wase′	" " "
64	Kün′-dig-eh	" " "	Sä′-dä	" " "	Sä′-dä	" " "
65	Sŭn-no′-ga	" " "	Sa-da′-za	" " "	Sa-da′-za	" " "
66	Su-nä′-gä	" " "	Set-dez′-a-ä-za	" " "	Set-dez′-a-ä-za	" " "
67	Soon′-da-ga	" " "	Sa′-che	" " "	Sa′-che	" " "
68	Soon-da	" " "	Sa-che	" " "	Sa-che	" " "
69	En′l-kählk′-tsä	" " "	En′l-chit′-shä	" " "	En′l-chit′-shä	" " "
70	Ell-käk′-chä	" " "	Eel-ke′-kä	" " "	Eel-ke′-kä	" " "
71	Nä-ai′-yas. ᵇ Piap	" " "	Päts	" " "	Päts	" " "
72	Kä-tät′	" " "	Kat′-so	" " "	Kat′-so	" " "
73	Pä-ven′	" " "	Pä′-chen	" " "	Pä′-chen	" " "
74			Sä-gwets′-sī-yä	" " "		
75	Ne-vi-pa-ra	" " "	No-vi-pa-re	" " "	No-vi-pa-re	" " "
76	Ku-su-cum	" " "	Ku-cheech	" " "	Ku-cheech	" " "
77	Ri-cu′-i	" " "	Gu-i-ä	" " "		
78			Ny-yu-gä	" " "		
79	An-i-ga	" " "	A-le-ka-ra	" " "	An-ga-ju′-ga	" " "
80	An-ning′-ä	" " "	Na-yä′	" " "	Ang-a-yu′-ä	" " "

TABLE II.—*Continued.*

	21. My younger brother. (Male speaking.)	Translation.	22. My younger brother. (Female speaking.)	Translation.	23. My younger sister. (Male speaking.)	Translation.
1	Ha'-gă	My younger brother.	Ha'-gă	My younger brother.	Ka'-gă	My younger sister.
2	Ha-gă'-ah	" " "	Ha-gă'-ah	" " "	Ka-gă'-ah	" " "
3	Ha'-gă	" " "	Ha'-gă	" " "	Ka'-gă	" " "
4	Le-gă'-ah	" " "	Le-gă'-ah	" " "	Ka-gă-ah'	" " "
5	E'-gă-hä	" " "	E'-gă-hä	" " "	Ka'-gă-hä	" " "
6	Kä'-gă	" " "	Kä'-gă	" " "	Kä'-gă	" " "
7	Le-gă'-ah	" " "	Le-gă'-ah	" " "	Ka-gă-ah'	" " "
8	Ha-ye-a'-hä	" " "	Ha-ye-a'-hä	" " "	Ya-ye-ah'-hä	" " "
9	Me-suŋ'-kä	" " "	Me-suŋ'-kä	" " "	Me-tänk'-she	" " "
10	Me-soh'-kä	" " "	Me-soh'-kä	" " "	Me-tänk'-she	" " "
11	Me-sunk'-ä	" " "	Me-sunk'-ä	" " "	Me-tank'-she	" " "
12	Me-sun'-kä	" " "	Me-sun'-ka	" " "	Me-tänk'-she	" " "
13	Me-soh'	" " "	Me-soh'-lä	" " "	Me-tunk'-she	" " "
14	Me-sunk'-ä-lä	" " "	Me-sunk'-ä-lä	" " "	Me-tunk'-she	" " "
15	Me-soh'-kä-lä	" " "	Me-soh'-kä-lä	" " "	Me-tank'-she	" " "
16	Me-son'-kä-lä	" " "	Me-son'-kä-lä	" " "	Me-tonk'-she	" " "
17	Me-soh'	" " "	Me-soh'	" " "	Me-tänk'-she	" " "
18	Kä-ga'	" " "	Kä-ga'	" " "	Wee-ha'	" " "
19	Wee-söŋ'-gä	" " "	Wee-söŋ'-gä or Kä'-gä	" " "	Wee-töŋ'-gä	" " "
20	Heen-thuŋ'-ga	" " "	E-chun'-cha	" " "	Heen-taŋ'-ya	" " "
21	Heen-thun'-ga	" " "	E-chun'-che	" " "	Heen-tän'-gä	" " "
22	Be-suŋ'-gä	" " "	Be-suŋ'-gä	" " "	Be-tuŋ'-gä-zhiŋ'-gä	" " "
23	We-son'-kä	" " "	We-son'-kä	" " "	We-tun'-ka	" " "
24	E-sŭnk'	" " "	E-sŭnk'	" " "	Wych-kä'	" " "
25	Me-sho'-kä	" " "	Me-sho'-kä	" " "	P-tä-me'-ha	" " "
26	Mat-so'-gä	" " "	Mat-so'-gä	" " "	Mä-tä-ka'-zhä	" " "
27	Bä-chŭ'-ka	" " "	Bä-chŭ'-ka	" " "	Bä-sä'.chete	" " "
28	Suh-näk'-fish	" " "	A-nak'-fī	" " "	An'-take	" " "
29	Sä-näk'-fish	" " "	A-nak'-fī	" " "	An'-take	" " "
30	Sä-näk'-fish	" " "	A-näk'-fī	" " "	An'-take	" " "
31	Chu-chŭ'-se	" " "	Chu-chihl'-wä	" " "	Chu-wun'-wä	" " "
32	Uŋ-gĭ-nuŋ'-tlĭ	" " "	Uŋ-gĭ-dau'	" " "	Uŋ-gĭ-dau'	" " "
33	Aŋ'-ke-nä-tsĭ	" " "	Aŋ'-ke-do	" " "	Aŋ'-ke-doh	" " "
34	E-dä'-deh	My brother.	E-rats'-teh	My brother.	E-tä'-heh	My sister.
35	A-dä'-de	" "	Kä'-we-ta	" "	A-tä'-ke	" "
36	Kä-wit'-ta	My bro. (1st y'nger).	Kä-wit-ta	My bro. (1st y'nger).	Ah-te'-ta	
37	Ne-seme'	My younger brother.	Ne-seme'	My younger brother.	Ne-sheme'	My younger sister.
38	Ne-sha-mish'	" " "	Ne-sha-mish'	" " "	Ne-sha-mish'	" " "
39	Ne-she-mish'	" " "	Ne-she-mish'	" " "	Ne-she-mish'	" " "
40	Nĭ-shĭ-mĕ	" " "	Nĭ-shĭ'-mĕ	" " "	Nĭ-shĭ'-mĕ	" " "
41	Ne-she'-ma	" " "	Ne-she'-ma	" " "	Ne-she'-ma	" " "
42	Ne-she'-mä	" " "	Ne-she'-mă	" " "	Ne-she'-mă	" " "
43	Ne-she-mä'	" " "	Ne-she-mä'	" " "	Ne-she-mä'	" " "
44	N'-she'-mă	" " "	N'-she'-mă	" " "	N'-she'-mă	" " "
45	Ne-she-uä'	" " "	Ne-she-uä'	" " "	Ne-she-mä'	" " "
46	Se-me-mä'?	" " "	Se-me-mä'?	" " "	Ne-go-se-mä'	" " "
47	Ne-she-mä'	" " "	Ne-she-mä'	" " "	Ne-she-mä'	" " "
48	Ne-she-mä'	" " "	Ne-she-mä'	" " "	Ne-she-mä'	" " "
49	Ne-she-mä'	" " "	Ne-she-mä'	" " "	Ne-she-mä'	" " "
50	Ne-she-mä'	" " "	Ne-she-mä'	" " "	Ne-she-mä'	" " "
51	Nă-se'-mä	" " "	Nă-se'-mä	" " "	Nă-se'-mä	" " "
52	Nă-sa'	" " "	Nă-sa'	" " "	Nă-sa'	" " "
53	Nă-sim-ă'	" " "	Nă-sim-ă'	" " "	Nă-sim-ă'	" " "
54	Kä-chä-nä-thä'-mi	" " "	Kä-chä-mä-thä'-mi	" " "	Kä-chä-mä-thä'-ni	" " "
55	N'-the-ma-thä'	" " "	N'-the-ma-thä'	" " "	N'-the-ma-thä'	" " "
56	Ta'-yä	" " "	Ta'-yä	" " "	Na-be-ă'	" " "
57	Nis-kun'-ä	" " "	Nis-kun'-ä	" " "	Ne-sis'-sä	" " "
58	Nis-kun'	" " "	Nis-kun'	" " "	Ne-sis'-sä	" " "
59	N'-chi-gu-num'	" " "	N'-chi-gu-num'	" " "	N'-kwa-jeech	" " "
60	Noo-see'-mees	" " "	Noo-see'-mees	" " "	Noo-see'-mees	" " "
61	N'-h·i-sum'	" " "	N'-h·i-sum'	" " "	N'-h·i-sum'	" " "
62	Nah·-eese'-u-miss'	" " "	Nah·-eese'-u-miss'	" " "	Nah·-eese'-u-miss'	" " "
63	Nain-hise-sa-mus'	" " "	Naine-hise'-sa-mus'	" " "	Nain-hise-sa-mus'	" " "
64	A-cha'-a	" " "	A-cha'-a	" " "	A-da'-ze	" " "
65	Sŭn-ńo'-gä-yä'-za	" " "	Sŭn-no'-gä-yä'-za	" " "	Sa-da'-za-yä'-za	" " "
66	Set-chil'-e-ä-za	" " "	Set-chil'-e-ä-za	" " "	Sä'-re	" " "
67	Sa'-chä	" " "	Sa'-chä	" " "	Sa-chith or Sit-chith'	" " "
68	Sa-chä	" " "	Sa-chä	" " "	Se-cha-the	" " "
69	Is-sis'-sä	" " "	Is-sis'-sä	" " "	En'l-tsits-ă-opes'	" " "
70	Eel-se'-sin-chä	" " "	Eel-see'-sin-chä	" " "	Eel-che-choops'	" " "
71	Es-hup'	" " "	Patsht	" " "	Ats	" " "
72	Kat'-sha	" " "	Kat'-sha	" " "	Kä-nä-nä	" " "
73	Sä-häts'-en	" " "	Sä-käts-en	" " "	Nä-mich'-en	" " "
74	Tŭm-mŭ'-ha-mäsh	" " "			Sä-gwe'-sä-hä-mash	" " "
75	No-vi-te-u	" " "	No-vi-te-u	" " "	No-vi-pa-re	" " "
76	Keet-than-äsh-lo	" " "	Keet-than-äsh-lo	" " "	Keet-than-ee-she-ok	" " "
77	Cu-hu'-bä	" " "	P-cu-i-hi'-bä	" " "	Cu-hu'-bä	" " "
78	Noo-kä-vä	" " "			Ny-ä-na-gä	" " "
79	Nu-ka-ra	" " "	Ar-ka-lu-a-ra	" " "	Na-ju'-ga	" " "
80	Nu'-kä	" " "	Nu'-kä	" " "	Na'-yä	" " "

TABLE II.—Continued.

	24. My younger sister. (Female speaking.)	Translation.	25. My brothers. (Male speaking.)	Translation.	26. My brothers. (Female speaking.)	Translation.
1	Ka'-gä..........................	My younger sister.	Da-yä'-gwä-dan'-no-dä....	My brothers.	Da-yä'-gwä-dan'-no-dä ...	My brothers.
2	Ka-gă'-ah......................	" " "	Da-yä'-gwä-dä'-no-da	" "	Da-yä'-gwä-dä-no-oa	" "
3	Ka'-gä...........................	" " "	Da-ge-ă-dä'-no-dä..........	" "	Da-ge-ă-dä'-no-dä	" "
4	Ka-gă'-ah......................	" " "	Un-gwä'-dă'-da-gä..........	" "	Un-gwä'-dä-da-gä............	" "
5	Ka'-gä-hä......................	" " "	Un-gwä'-dä-da-gä'-hä	" "	Un-gwä'-dä-da-gä-hä	" "
6	Kä'-gä...........................	" " "	Ahk-yät'-gä	" "	Ahk-yät'-gä	" "
7	Ka-gä'-ah......................	" " "				
8	Ya-ye-ah'-hä..................	" " "	Ah-wä'-ta-yeh-ä'-hä.......	" "	Ah-wä'-ta-yeh-ä'-hä.......	" "
9	Me-taŋ'-kä.....................	" " "	Me-huŋ'-kä-wäŋ-zhe......	" "		
10	Me-tuŋ'-kä.....................	" " "	Me-huŋ'-kä-wan-zhe......	" "		
11	Me-tank-a-do.................	" " "	Sun-kä'-me-tä-do..........	My elder brothers.	Tib'-e-do-i-do	My younger bros.
12	Me-tän'-kä.....................	" " "	Den-na-tank'-she-wä-a-do	My brother.	Hen-na-tib'-do-i-do........	" "
13	Me-tunk'-hä-lä................	" " "	Che-a'-wä-chä-wits........	My elder brother.	Sun-kä'-we-chä'-wits	" "
14	Me-tonk'-ä.....................	" " "	Che-a'-wä-chä'-wits........	" " "	Sun-kä'-we-chä'-wits.	" "
15	Ton'-kä	" " "	Me-hun'-kä-wä'-we-che ..	My brothers.		
16	Me-ton'-kä.....................	" " "				
17	Me-tä'...........................	" " "				
18	We-ha'..........................	" " "	Wä-gä-ke'-na................	" "	Wä-gä-ke'-na	My brothers.
19	Wee-töŋ'-gä or Wee-hä'...	" " "	O-kee'-zee	" "	E-ziŋ-thä	" "
20	Heen-tuŋ'-ga.................	" " "	E-nu'-kä-ne	" "	E-chin'-cho..................	" "
21	Heen-täu'-gä.................	" " "	E-nu'-kä-na	" "	E-chin'-cho..................	" "
22	Ah-se'-zhe-gä	" " "	Un-go'-ke-wä-kom	" "	Un-go'-ke-wä-kom'	" "
23	We-tun'-ka....................	" " "	We-she'-lä	" "	We-she'-lä	" "
24	E-chunk'.......................	" " "	Wä-ke'-no....................	" "	Wä-ke'-no	" "
25	Me-no'-ka......................	" " "				
26	Mă-tä-ka'-zhä	" " "	I-ate-sä'-we-ä'-kuts........	My elder brothers.	I-ate-sä'-wat-so'-kuts......	My younger bros.
27	Bä-so'-ka.......................	" " "	Bä-sä'-pa.....................	My brothers. [ther.	Bä-sä'-pa.....................	My bros. [gether.
28	Suh-näk'-fish.................	" " "	Et-e-bä'-pish-e	Those who suck toge-	Et-e-bä'-pish-e	Those who suck to-
29	Sä-näk'-fish..................	" " "	Et-e-bä'-pĬ-shĬ-li	" " " "	Et-e-bä'-pi-shĬ-lĬ	" " " "
30	Sä-näk'-fish..................	" " "	Et-e-bä'-pĬ-shĬ-li	" " " "	A-näk'-fĬ-u-hlĬ'-ha	My brothers.
31	Chu-chŭ'-se	" " "	Te-chäk-ke'-yäte	" " " "	Te chak-ke'-yäte	" "
32	Uŋ-gĭ-luŋ'-Ĭ	" " "	An-tsä-lĬ-nuŋ'-thĬ	My brothers.	An-tsä-lĬ-nuŋ'-thĬ	" "
33	Aŋ-ge-lä'-ih	" " "	Tsä-ke-nä'-tsĬ	" "	Tsä'-ke-nä'-tsĬ	" "
34	E-dä'-deh	My sister.	E-dä'-deh	My brother.	E-rats'-teh...................	My brother.
35	A-tä'-he	" "	A-dä'-de Kit'-to	My brother all.	A-dä'-de Kit'-to...........	My brother all.
33	Ah-te'-ta......................	" "	Nä-tä-rä-kun'-ne...........	My brothers.	Nä-tä-rä-kun'-ne...........	My brothers.
37	Ne-sheme'.....................	My younger sister.	Nees-ta-suk'	My elder brothers.	Ne-se-muk'...................	My younger bros.
38	Ne-sha-mish'.................	" " "	Gä-ka-o'-neshe-tase'......	" " " "	Gä-ka-o-ne-meshe'........	" " "
39	Ne-she-mish'.................	" " "	N'ese-ta-suk'................	" " " "	Ne-se-muk'..................	" " "
40	Ni-shĬ'-mĕ	" " "	NĬ-jĬ-kĬ-we'-yag............	My brothers.	Nin-dä-wĕ'-mäg	My brothers.
41	Ne-she'-ma...................	" " "	Ne-kä-na'-yug...............	" "	Nin-duh-wa'-mag...........	" "
42	Ne-she'-mä...................	" " "	NĬ-je-ke-wä-yuk'	" "	Nin-dä-wä'-mague	" "
43	Ne-sha-mä'...................	" " "	Ne-kä'-na-yuk'..............	My step-brothers.	N'-dä-wa'-muk..............	My step-brothers.
44	N'-she'-mä....................	" " "	N'-she'-mä-yuk	My younger brothers.	N'-she'-mä-yuk	My younger bros.
45	Ne-she'-mä....................	" " "	N'-seh'-sä-yuh	My elder brother.	N'-seh'-sä-yuh	My elder brother.
46	Ne-go-se-mä'.................	" " "	Wates-sa-mä'-ge-ka	My brothers.	Wates-sa-mä'-ge-ka	My brothers.
47	Ne-she-mä'...................	" " "	Ne-san-zä'-ke................	My elder brothers.	Ne-san-zä'-ke................	My elder brothers.
48	Ne-she-mä'...................	" " "	Ne-san-zä'-ke................	" " " "	Ne-san-zö'-ke	" " " "
49	Ne-she-mä'...................	" " "	Ne-she-mä'-ke...............	My younger brothers.	Ne-she-mä'-ke...............	My younger bros.
50	Ne-she-mä'...................	" " "	Ne-she-mä'-ke...............	" " " "	Ne-she-mä'-ke...............	" " "
51	Nä-se'-mä.....................	" " "	Nä-se-mä'-huk...............	" " " "	Nä-se-mä'-huk...............	" " "
52	Nä-sa'..........................	" " "	Nä-nä'-suk	My elder brothers.	Nä-nä'-suk...................	My elder brothers.
53	Nä-sim-ä'.....................	" " "	Nä-vis'-sim	My younger brothers.	Nä-vis'-sim...................	My younger bros.
54	Kä-chä-nä-thä-mi...........	" " "	Ni-to-ta-mä-ki'	My brothers.	Ni-to-ta-mä-ki'.............	My brothers.
55	N'-the-ma-thä'...............	" " "	N'-cha-ne-nä-ke'	" "	Nös-ke-mä-ke'...............	" "
56	Na'-be-ä.......................	" " "	Ne-tä'-ga-bä-thä	My younger brothers.	Ne-no'-pä-pe................	" "
57	Ne-sis'-sä.....................	" " "	Ne-no'-pä-pe................	My brothers.	Ne-noh'-pä-pe	" "
58	Ne-sis'-sä.....................	" " "	Ne-noh·'-pä-pe.............	" "	WĬ-je-gu-dul-teek'.........	" "
59	N'-kwa-jeech'................	" " "	WĬ-je-gu-dul-teek'.........	" "	Noo-i-jee-gud-dool-te-bin	" "
60	Noo-see'-mees	" " "	Noo-i-jee-gud-dool-te-bin	" "	N'-tä'-kun-uk(e) N'-hise'-	" "
61	N'-h·i-sum'...................	" " "	N'-tä'-kun-uk'(e.), N'-hise'	" "	{ Nah-häus-uk'(e) [nuk(y)	" "
62	Nah·-eese-u-miss'..........	" " "	{ Nah'-häus-uk'(e). [-muk ⎰ Nah'-eese-um-suk' (y.)	" "	⎱ Nah'-eese-um-suk' (y.).	" "
63	Nain-hise'-sa-mus'..........	" " "	Nain-na'-mä-dis'-uk	" "	Nain-dä'-no-yä'-muh	" "
64	A-da'-ze.......................	" " "	{ Kŭu'-dig'-eh-ka (elder). ⎰ A-cha'-a-ka (younger)..	" "	{ Kŭn'-dig-eh-ka (elder).. ⎱ A-cha'-a-ka (younger)--	" "
65	Sa-da'-za-yä'-za.............	" " "	Ah-se-u-nis'-a-no-ga......	" "	Ah-se-u-nis'-a-no-ga	" "
66	Sä'-re	" " "	{ Sŭ-nä-gä'-kra (elder).... ⎰ Set-chil'-e-ä-ze-kra (y.)	" "	{ Sŭ-nä-gä'-kra (elder) ... ⎱ Set-chil'-e-ä-za-kra (y.)	" "
67	Sa-chith' or Sit-chith'.....	" " "	Sä-chä-nä ....[nut (y.)	" "	Sä-chä-nä	" "
68	See-chath	" " "	Soon-da-kŭt(e.), Seek-ye-	" "		[my friend.
69	En'l-tsits-ä-opes'............	"· " "	Is-sin'-koo-ku-sichw'......	My bros. my friends.	Is-sin'-koo-ku-sichw'......	My brothers and [friends.
70	Eel-che-choops'..............	" " "	Yä-yat-eel-käk-chä	My elder brothers.		
71	A-seep.........................	" " "	En-haigh-mä	My bros. my friends.	En-haigh-mä................	My brothers my
72	Kä-rä-nä......................	" " "	Ko-ko-wä'-malt	My brothers.	Ko-ko-wä'-malt.............	My brothers.
73	Na-mich'-en	" " "	Pä-vwen'·e-bim	" "	Pa-vwen-e-bim	
74			Sä-tŭm-nŭ'-tee-mish.......	My brothers younger.		
75	No-vi-pa-ra	" " "	No-vi-par-a-ee...............	My brothers.	No-vi-par-a-ee...............	" "
76	Keet-than-ee-she-ok	" " "	Ku-sŭ-cum-shop	My elder brothers.		
77			Gui-as-cu-hu-bi-as-a	My elder & y'nger br.		
78			Ni-a-gä	My brothers.		
79	Na-ka-ra.......................	" " "	Ka-tang'-u-ti-ka.............	" "		
80	Nu-kä'-hä......................	" " "	Kä-tang'-o-tine..............	" "	A-ne'-kä	" "

TABLE II.—*Continued.*

	27. My sisters. (Male speaking.)	Translation.	28. My sisters. (Female speaking.)	Translation.	29. My brother's son. (Male speaking.)	Translation.
1	Da-yä′-gwä-dan′-no-dä....	My sisters.	Da-yä′-gwä-dan′-no-dä ...	My sisters.	Ha-ah′-wuk	My son.
2	Da-yä-gwä-dä′-no-dä	" "	Da-yä-gwä-dä′-no-dä	" "	Ha-hä′-wuk	" "
3	Da-ge-ä-dä′-no-dä........	" "	Da-ge-ä-dä′-no-dä..........	" "	Ha-hä′-wä	" "
4	Un-gwä′-dä-na-zä........	" "	Un-gwä′-dä-na-zä.............	" "	Le-yä′-hä	" "
5	Un-gwä′-dä-no-sä′-hä.......	" "	Un-gwä′-dä-no-sä′-hä	" "	E-yä′	" "
6	Ahk-gä-nä′-none........	" "	Ahk-gä-nä′-none............		Kä-yä′-no-nä............	My child.
7					Le-yä′-ah................	My son.
8	Ah-wä′-ta-yeh-ä′-hä......	" "	Ah-wä-ta-yeh-ä′-hä	" "	A-ne′-ah..............	" "
9	Me-tä-we-noh′-tiṇ	" "			Me-chiṇk′-she........	" "
10	Me-tä-we-noh′-tin	" "			Me-chink′-she........	" "
11	Hä-tänk-she-ha-do	My elder sisters.	Me-chu′-i-do............	My younger sisters.	Ak-she′-dä	" "
12	Den-na-tank′-she-wi-do ..	" " "	Den-na-me-tä′-wä-a-do ...	" " "	Me-chink′-she........	" "
13	Tun-kä′-we-chä-wits	" " "	Tunk-she′-we-chä′-wits...	" " "	Me-chink′-she-lä........	" "
14	Tun-kä′-we-chä-wits	" " "	Tunk-she′-we-chä′-wits...		Me-chink′-she........	" "
15	Me-tä-we-noh′-che	My sisters.			Me-chink′-she........	" "
16					Me-chink′-she........	" "
17					Nis-se′-hä	" "
18					Wee-ni′-se........	" "
19	E-töṇ′-gä..............	" "	E-töṇ′-gä..............	" "	Hee-yin′-ga........	" "
20	Wa′-he-cha.............	" "	E-nu′-kä-ne	" "	He-ne′-cha............	" "
21	E-nu′-kä-na	" "	E-nu′-kä-na	" "	Be-she′-gä........	" "
22	Un-go′-ke-wä-kom′	" "	Un-go′-ke-wä-kom′	" "	We-shen′-kä	" "
23	We-tun′-ka	" "	We-tun′-ka...............	" "	E-neke′	" "
24	Aw-ke′-no	" "	Aw-ke′-no		Me-ne′-ka............	" "
25				" "	Mä-de-shä′............	" "
26	Mä-tä-we-it′-zä	My elder sisters.	Mä-tä-ka′-zhä...........	My sisters.	Bot-sa′-sä	" "
27	Bä-koop′-me-ä	My sisters.	Bä-koop′-me-ä...........	" "	Suh′-sŭh	" "
28	Et-e-bä′-pish-e	" "	Et-e-bä′-pish-e	" "	Su′-soh	" "
29	An′-take	" "	An′-take	" "	Su′-soh	" "
30	Au′-take-u-hli′-hä........	" "	Et-e-bä′-pĭ-shĭ-lĭ.......	" "	Chup-pŭ′-che	" "
31	Chä-wun-täke′	" "	Chu-hlä-hul′-he...........	" "	A-gwae-tsĭ′........	My child.
32	An-tsä-lĭ-nuṇ′-tlĭ.......	" "	An-tsä-lĭ-nŭṇ′-tlĭ	" "	Ah-gwa′-tze	" "
33	Tsaṇ-ke-toh′..............	" "	Tsaṇ-ke-toh′.............	" "	Pe′-row................	" "
34	E-tä′-heh.............	My sister.	E-dä-heh................	My sister.	Pe-row................	" "
35	A-tä′-be Kit′-to..........	My sister all.	A-tä′-he Kit′-to	My sister all.	Nä-te-nä′-o	" "
36	Nä-na-kun′-ne	My sisters.	Nä-na-kun′-ne	My sisters.	N′-do′-sin	My step-son.
37	Ne-mis′-suk	My elder sisters.	Ne-sheme′-suk	My younger sisters.	N′-do′-zhim	" "
38	Ne-mish′-suk	" " "	Ne-mish′-suk	" " "	N′-do′-zhim	" "
39	Ne-mis′-suk.............	" " "	Ne-se-muk′		Nin-do′-zhim	" "
40	Nin-dä-wĕ′-mag.........	My sisters.	Nin-dan-gwĕ′-yag........	My sisters.	Nin-do′-zhem	" "
41	Nin-de-gek′-yug	" "	Nin-duh-wa′-mäg........	" "	N′-do′-zhim	" "
42	Nin-dä-wa′-mague	" "	Ne-dä-ki′-ko	" "	N′-do′-zhim-ä′........	" "
43	N′-dä′-wa-muk′	My step-sisters.	Ne-dä-kĭ′-ko-yuh........	" "	N′-do-zhiṇ′........	" "
44	N′-she′-mä-yuk	My younger sisters.	N′-she′-mä-yuk	My younger sisters.	N′-do′-zhe-mä........	" "
45	Ne-she′-mä-yuk...........	" " "	Ne-she′-mä-yuh...........	" " "	Neen-gwase′-sä........	My son.
46	Ne-go′-se-mä-ge-ka	" " "	Ne-go′-se-mä-ge-ka′		Niṇ-gwa-sä′........	" "
47					Niṇ-gwa-sä′........	" "
48					Ne-gwis-sä′........	" "
49	Ne-she-mä′-ke............	My sisters.	Ne-she-mä′-ke............	My sisters.	Ne-gwis-sä′........	" "
50	Ne-she-mä′-ke...........	" "	Ne-she-mä′-ke............	" "	Nä-kwis′-sä........	" "
51	Nä-tä-kwä′-muk	" "	Nä-tä-kwä′-muk		Ne-keese′	" "
52	Na-ma′-suk	My elder sisters.	Na-ma′-suk	My elder sisters.	Nä	" "
53	Nä-ma-eh............	My sisters.	Nä-ma′-eh	My sisters.	Ni-kwĕ-thä′........	" "
54	Ni-ta-kwä-ma-ki′	" "	Na-ta-tä-mä-ki′	" "	Ne-kwe-thä′........	" "
55	Nit-kwa-mä-ke′	" "	N′-cha-ne-mä-ke′........	" "	Na′-hä	" "
56	A-thä′-na-pa-na′-tine	" "			N′-do′-ta-ko	My step-son.
57	Ne-tä′-ka-nix............	" "	Ne-tä′-ka-nix............	" "	Ne-to′-to-koh′-a........	" "
58	Ne-tä′-ka-nix	" "	Wĭ-je-gu-dul-teek′.......	" "	N′-kwis′........	My son.
59	Wĭ-je-gu-dul-teek′........	" "	Noo-i-jee-gud-dool-te-bin	" "	N′-too-ä′-sum	" "
60	Noo-i-jee-gud-dool-te-bin	" "	Na-me-suk′ (e.), N′-hise′-	" "	Nä-kun′	My step-child.
61	Na-me-suk′ (e.), N′-hise′-	" "	{ Na-mese-uk′(e.)[muk(y)	" "	N′-kweese′	My son.
62	{ Na-mese-uk′(e.)[muk(y) / Noh′-eese-um-suk′ (y.).	" "	{ Noh′-eese-um-suk′ (y.). Nain-na′-to-kokue′-uk	" "	Nain-gwase′	" "
63	Nain-to′-kwa-muk′	" "	{ Sä-dä′-ka (elder)	" "	Nain-gwase′	" "
64	{ Sä-dä′-ka (elder) / A-da′-ze-ka (younger) ..	" "	{ A-da′-ze-ka (younger)...	" "	Tu-zen′-a	My step-son.
65	Ah-se-u-nis′-a-da-za	" "	Ah-se-u-nis′-a-da-za.......	" "	Sa-yä′-za	My son.
66	{ Set-dez′-a-ä-ze-kra (e.) . / Sä-ne′-kra (younger)....	" "	{ Set-dez′-a-ä-ze-kra (e.). / { Sä-ne′-kra (younger)....	" "	Se-yä′-za	" "
67	[kŭt (y.)				Sa′-tin-ge	
68	Sy-ak-e-kŭt(e.), See-chy-		Is-sin′-toot-hoos′.......	" "	Sa-chä (elder bros. son)...	My adopted son.
69	Is-soo-pelhp′-kwie	" "			Kas-koo-sä. Is-se-mält...	My son and ——
70			En-kläk′-sä-mä	" "	In-pit′h..............	(Not rendered).
71	En-kläk′-sä-mä	" "	Ne-kat-litsh-kilt	" "		
72	Ne-kat-litsh-kilt.........	" "	Pä-chen′-e-bim...........	" "	Kot′-sin(eld.br.s.),At′-sin [(y.br.son.	" "
73	Pä-chen′-e-bim...........	" "				
74	Sä-gwe′-tee-mish	My sisters younger.	No-vi-par-a-ee...........	" "	Na-vi-tu-e	
75	No-vi-par-a-ee...........	My sisters.			Ee-chäck	My nephew.
76	Ku-cheech-shop	My elder sisters.			Chu-bä	My son.
77						
78	Ni-a-kä	My sisters.			Kan-gi′-a-ra	My nephew.
79	A′-ka-ga.................	" "			Kung-e-ä′-gä	" "
80	Na-yung′-ing	" "	Ang-o-yu′-kä	" "		

TABLE II.—*Continued.*

	30. My brother's son's wife. (Male speaking.)	Translation.	31. My brother's daughter. (Male speaking.)	Translation.	32. My brother's daughter's husband. (Male speaking.)	Translation.
1	Ka'-sä	My daugh.-in-law.	Ka-ah'-wuk	My daughter.	Oc-na'-hose	My son-in-law.
2	Ka-sa-yuh'	" "	Ka-hä'-wuk	" "	Unc-na'-hose	" "
3	Ka-sä'-wä	" "	Ka-hä'-wä	" "	Ha-nane'-hose	" "
4	Ka-zä'-wä	" "	Ka-yä'-hä	" "	Ha-yale-hose'-hä	" "
5	Ka-zä'-wä	" "	Ka-yä'	" "	E-en-hü'-zä	" "
6	Ahk'-thäf	" "	Kä-yä'-no-nä	My child.	Yäk-te-he Zah'-thä	" "
7	Ka-sä'-wä	" "	Ka-yä'-äh	My daughter.	De-an-hose'-hä	" "
8	Ya-na'-mä-kwe	" "	E-ne'-ah	" "	Ha-na'-mä-kwe	" "
9	Me-tä'-kosh	" "	Me-chuṇk'-she	" "	Me-tä'-kosh	" "
10	Me-tä'-koash	" "	Me-chounk'-she	" "	Me-tä'-koash	" "
11	Me-tä'-koash	" "	Me-chink'-she	" "	Me-tä'-koash	" "
12	Me-tä'-koash	" "	Me-chunk'-she	" "	Me-tä'-koash	" "
13	Me-tä'-kosh	" "	Me-chunk'-se-lä	" "	Me-tä'-kosh	" "
14	Me-tä'-kosh	" "	Me-chunk'-she	" "	Me-tä'-kosh	" "
15	Me-tä'-koash	" "	Me-chŭnk'-she	" "	Me-tä'-koash	" "
16	Me-tä'-goash	" "	Me-chŭnk'-she	" "	Me-tä'-goash	" "
17	Me-tä'-koash	" "	Me-chunk'-she	" "	Me-tä'-goask	" "
18	Ta-ne'-hä	" "	Win-no'-ga	" "	We-tuh'-da	" "
19	We-te'-na	" "	We-zhuṇ'-ga	" "	We-töṇ-da	" "
20	Heen-toan'-ye	" "	Hee-yuṇ'-ga	" "	Wä-do'-hä	" "
21	Hin-to'-ne	" "	He-yuṇ'-ga	" "	Wan-do'-hä	" "
22	Be-je'-na	" "	She-me'-she-gä	" "	Be-tö-ja	" "
23	We-che'-ne	" "	We-shon'-ka	" "	We-ton'-chä	" "
24	E-nook-chek'-aw-chau	" "	E-nook'	" "	Wä-to'-ho	" "
25	Ko-too'-te	" "	Me-no'-hä-ka	" "	P'-too'-ta	" "
26	Mä-too'-ga	" "	Mä-kä'	" "	Mä-too'-te	" "
27	Bos-me'-ä-kun-is-ta ?	My sister-in-law.	Näk'-me-ä	" "	Boo'-sha	" "
28	Sup'-uk	My grandchild.	Suh-sŭh'-take	" "	Sai'-yup	" "
29	Su-pok'-take	My daugh.-in-law.	Suh-soh'-take	" "	Säi'-yop	" "
30	Su-pok'-take	" " [on.	Su-soh'-take	" "	Sä'-yup	" "
31	Un-hu-tis'-se	My present hanger	Chu-chus'-te	" "	Un hu-tis'-se	" "
32	E-tsän'-hī	My daugh.-in-law.	A-gwae-tsī'	My child.	E-huä-tsī	" "
33	Ah-ge-tzau'-hī	" "	Ah-gwa'-tze	" "	A-ge-h'nä'-tzī	" "
34	Scoo'-rus	" "	Pe'-row	" "	Koos-tow'-e-sŭ	" "
35	Sko'-dus	" "	Pe'-row	" "	Ko-stä'-wītch	" "
36	Sko-roo'-hoo	" "	Nä-te-nä'-o	" "	Koh-tä-wa'-suh	" "
37	Nee-tim'	" "	N'-do'-sa-mis-kwame'	My step-daughter.	Nä-häk'-sim	" "
38	Nee-stim'	" "	N'-do-zha-mis-kwame'	" "	Nä-häk'-sim	" "
39	Nee-tim'	" "	N'-do-zha-mis-kwem'	" "	N'-hä'-ke-shim	" "
40	Nis'-sim	" "	Nin-do-zhī-mī'-kwem.	" "	Nī-nin'-gwän	" "
41	Ne'-sim	" "	Nin-do'-zhe-me'-quam	" "	Ne-nin'-gwun	" "
42	Ne-sim'	" "	Nin-do-zha-mī-kwam'	" "	Ne-niṇ-gwun'	" "
43	Ne-sim'	" "	N'-do-zha-mī-kwam'	" "	Ne-niṇ-gwun'	" "
44	Ne-sim'	" "	N'-do'-zha-mi-kwam'	" "	Ne-niṇ-gwun'	" "
45	N'-ah'-ga-neh-gweh'	" "	N'-do'-zha-mis	" "	N'-do'-she-na-game'	" "
46	Lan-gwä'-lä	" "	Nin-dä'-nä	My daughter.	Na-hun'-gä-nä	" "
47	Nä-hä-gä-na'-kwa No-ko-mä'	" "	Nin-dä'-nä	" "	Ne-lä'-gwä-lä'	" "
48	Nä-hä-gä-ha'-kwä No-ko-mä'	" "	Nin-dä'-nä	" "	Ne lä'-gwä-lä'	" "
49	Nä-hä-gä-na-kwä' No-ko-mä'	" "	N'-dä'-nä	" "	N'-dä-gwä-lä'	" "
50	Nä-hä-gä-na-kwä' No-ko-mä'	" "	N'-dä'-nä	" "	N'-dä-gwä-lä'	" "
51	Nä-sem'-yä	" "	Nä-tä'-nis	" "	Nä-nä-kwem'	" "
52	No-hä'-kun-e-uk-ye-yu'	" "	Ne-täne'	" "	Ne-nä'-kwun	" "
53	Nich-ä'	" "	Nä-tun'	" "	Nich-ä'	" "
54	Na-them-mi-lä'	" "	Nī-ton-nä-thä'	" "	Na-nä-kwam-nä'	" "
55	Ni-tha-mī-ah'	" "	Nī-tä-na-thä'	" "	Nin-hä-kä-na-mä'	" "
56	Nä-tim'	" "	Nä-tä'-na	" "	Na-täs'	" "
57	Nee-mis'	" "	N'-to'-to-tun	My step-daughter.	Nis	" "
58	Nee-mis'	" "	Ne-to'-to-tun	" "	Nis	" "
59	N'-thus-wä'-skom	" "	N'-tūs'	My daughter.	N'-tlŭ'-sŭk	" "
60	N'-sum	" "	N'-su'-mus	" "	N'-tlŭ'-sŭk	" "
61	Nä-h'um'	" "	Nä-kun'	My step-child.	Wä-seen'-no-kwä	" "
62	Nah'-hun'	" "	N'-dä-nuss'	My daughter.	Nä-to-nä-mä'-kw'	" "
63	Nain-hum'	" "	Nain-dä'-niss	" "	Na-nä-toh'-na-makue'	" "
64	Sa-t'thu'-a	" "	Sa-yä'-dze	My step-daughter.	Se-ga'-ton	" "
65	Sa-tsa'-ya	" "	Sa-to'-a	My daughter.	Sa-tsa'-ya	" "
66	Set-thu'-yä	" "	Se-le'-yä	" "	Set-shi'-ya	" "
67			Sä-che'	" "		
68	Se-chy-o	—	Se-chy-o	—	Set-she-ku-in	" "
69	Is-sä'-pin	" "	Kä-stum'-che-ält	" "	Is-natche'-hu	" "
70						
71			Pai'-yä. b In pit'h	(Not rendered.)		
72						
73	E-at-sin	" "	Kot'-sin (eld.b.dau.), At'-	" "	Tä-tä'-wä-bin	" "
74			[sin (y.b.dau.)			
75	Si-ee	—			Ma-tu-too-wa	—
76						
77			Chu-bä	My child.		
78						
79			Kan-gi-a-ra	My niece.		
80	Oo-koo-ä'-gä	" "	Kung-e-ä'-gä	" "	Ning-a-ou'-gwä	" "

TABLE II.—*Continued.*

	33. My brother's grandson. (Male speaking.)	Translation.	34. My brother's granddaughter. (Male speaking.)	Translation.	35. My brother's great grandson. (Male speaking.)	Translation.
1	Ha-yä′-da	My grandson.	Ka-yä′-da	My granddaughter.	Ha-yä′-da	My grandson.
2	Ha-yä′-dra	" "	Ka-yä′-dra	" "	Ha-yä′-dra	" "
3	Ha-yä′-da	" "	Ka-yä′-da	" "	Ha-yä′-da	" "
4	Le-yä′-dla-ah	" "	Ka-yä′-dla-ah	" "	Le-yä′-dla-ah	" "
5	E-yä′-dla-ah	" "	Ka-yä′-dla-ah	" "	E-yä′-dla-ah	" "
6	Kä-yä′-rä	My grandchild.	Kä-yä′-rä	My grandchild.	Kä-yä′-rä	My grandchild.
7	Le-yä-tä-ra′-yä	My grandson.	Ka-yä-tä-ra′-yä	My granddaughter.	Le-yä-tä-ra′-yä	My grandson.
8	Ha-tra′-ah	" "	Ya-tra′-ah	" "	Ha-tra′-ah	" "
9	Me-tä′-ko-zhä	My grandchild.	Me-tä′-ko-zhä	My grandchild.	Me-tä′-ko-zhä	My grandchild.
10	Me-tä′-ko-zha	" "	Me-tä′-ko-zha	" "	Me-tä′-ko-zha	" "
11	Me-tä′-ko-zha	" "	Me-tä′-ko-zha	" "	Me-tä′-ko-zha	" "
12	Me-tä′-ko-zha	" "	Me-tä′-ko-zha	" "	Me-tä′-ko-zha	" "
13	Me-tä′-ko-säk′-pok	" "	Me-tä′-ko-säk′-pok	" "	Me-tä′-ko-säk′-pok	" "
14	Me-tä′-ko-zhä	" "	Me-tä′-ko-zhä	" "	Me-tä′-ko-zhä	" "
15	Me-tä′-ko-zhä	" "	Me-tä′-ko-zhä	" "	Me-tä′-ko-zhä	" "
16	Me-tä′-ko-zä	" "	Me-tä′-ko-zä	" "	Me-tä′-ko-zä	" "
17	Me-tä′-ko-sä	" "	Me-tä′-ko-sä	" "	Me-tä′-ko-sä	" "
18	Toosh′-pä-lä	" "	Toosh′-pä-hä	" "	Toosh′-pä-hä	" "
19	We-tŭsh′-pä	" "	Wee-tŭsh′-pä	" "	Wee-tŭsh′-pä	" "
20	Heen-tä′-kwä	My grandson.	Heen-tä′-kwä-me	My granddaughter.	Heen-tä′-kwä	My grandson.
21	E-tä′-kwä		E-tä′-kwä-me	" "	E-tä′-kwä	" "
22	Be-chose′-pä	My grandchild.	Be-chose′-pä	My grandchild.	Be-chose′-pä	My grandchild.
23	We-chose′-pä	" "	We-chose′-pä		We-chose′-pä	" "
24	E-choon′-ka-neke′	My little grandson.	E-choon-zhunk′-e-neke	My little gd. daught.	E-choon′-ka-neke	My little gd. son.
25	P-tä-we′-hä-kä	My grandchild.	P-tä-we′-hä-kä	My grandchild.	P-tä-we′-hä-kä	My grandchild.
26	Met-a-wä-pish′-sha	" "	Met-a-wä-pish′-sha	" "	Met-a-wä-pish′-sha	" "
27	Bus-bä′-pe-ta		Bus-bä′-pe-ta	" "	Bus-bä′-pe-ta	" "
28	Sup′-uk-nŏk′-ne	My grandson.	Sup′-uk	My granddaughter.	Sup′-uk-nŏk′-ne	My grandson.
29	Sä′-pok-näk′-ne	" "	Sä′-pok	" "	Sä′-pok-näk′-ne	" "
30	Sup′-pok-näk′-nĭ		Sup′-pok	" "	Sup′-pok-näk′-ni	" "
31	Um-os-sŭs′-wä	My grandchild.	Um-os-sŭs′-wä	My grandchild.	Um-os-sŭs′-wä	My grandchild.
32	Un-gĭ-lĭ-sĭ	" "	Un-gĭ-lĭ-sĭ	" "	Un-gĭ-lĭ-sĭ	" "
33	Aŋ-ge-lee′-se	" "	Aŋ-ge-lee′-se	" "	Aŋ-ge-lee′-se	" "
34	Lak-te′-gish	My grandson.	Lak-te′-gee	My granddaughter.	Te′-wŭt	My nephew.
35	Lak-te′-kis	My grandchild.	Lak-te′-kis	My child.		
36	Nä-rä-ne-tish′-ä	" "	Nä-rä-ne-tish′-ä	" "	No-se-sem′	My grandchild.
37	No-se-sem′	" "	No-se-sem′	My grandchild.	No-se-sem′	" "
38	No-se-sim′	" "	No-se-sim′	" "	No-se-sim′	" "
39	No-se-sem′	" "	No-se-sem′	" "	No-se-sem′	" "
40	No-zhĭ′-she	" "	No-zhĭ′-she	" "	No-zhĭ′-she	" "
41	No-she-shä	" "	No-she-shä	" "	No-she-shä	" "
42	No-she-shä′	" "	No-she-shä′	" "	No-she-shä′	" "
43	No-she-shä′	" "	No-she-shä′	" "	No-she-shä′	" "
44	No-she-shä′	" "	No-she-shä′	" "	No-she-shä′	" "
45	No-sä-seh′	" "	No-sä-seh′	" "	N′-seh-sä′	" "
46	No-sa-mä′	" "	No-sa-mä′	" "	No-sa-mä′	" "
47	No-sa′-mä	" "	No-sa′-mä	" "	No-sa′-mä	" "
48	No-sa′-mä	" "	No-sa′-mä	" "	No-sa′-mä	" "
49	No-sa-mä′	" "	No-sa-mä′	" "	No-sa-mä′	" "
50	No-sa-mä′	" "	No-sa-mä′	" "	No-sa-mä′	" "
51	No-she-sem′	" "	No-she-sem′	" "	No-she-sem′	" "
52	No-she-sä′	" "	No-she-sä′	" "	No-she-sä′	" "
53	Nä-h·-kä′	" "	Nä-h·-kä′	" "	Nä-h·-kä′	" "
54	Na-se-thä′-mä	" "	Na-se-thä′-mä	" "	Na-se-thä′-mä	" "
55	No-stha-thä′	" "	No-stha-thä′	" "	No-stha-thä′	" "
56	Nee′-sa	" "	Nee′-sa	" "	Nee′-sa	" "
57	Nee-so′-tan	" "	Nee-só′-tan	" "	Nee-so′-tan	" "
58	Nee-so′-tän	" "	Nee-so′-tän	" "	Nee-so′-tän	" "
59	Nŭ-jeech′	" "	Nŭ-jeech′	" "	Nŭ-jeech′	" "
60	N′-kway′-nus	" "	N′-kway′-nus	" "	N′-kway′-nus	" "
61	Nä-h·ise′	" "	Nä-h·ise′	" "	Nä-h·ise′	" "
62	Noh·-whese′	" "	Noh·-whese′	" "	Noh·-whese′	" "
63	Nain-no-whase′	" "	Nain-no-whase′	" "	Nain-no-whase′	" "
64	Sa-t′thu′-a		Sa-t′-thu′-a		Sa-t′-thu′-a	" "
65	Sa-ken′-ne	My grandson.	Sa-to⁻ä′-bä	My granddaughter.	Sa-ken′-ne	My grandson.
66	Se-yä-zet′-tha-re		Sa-le-zet′-tha-re	My grandchild.	Sa-yä-zet′-tha-re	My grandchild.
67	Sa-chi′	My grandchild.	Sa-chi′	" "	Sa-chi′	" "
68	Set-she	" "	Set-she	" "	Set-she	" "
69	Is-hah′-pä ?	My grandson.	In′-chau-wä ?	My granddaughter.		
70						
71						
72						
73	Kot-sin	(Not rendered.)				
74						
75						
76						
77						
78						
79						
80	Eng′-o-tä	My grandchild.	Eng′-o-tä	My grandchild.	Eng′-o-tä	My grandchild.

TABLE II.—*Continued.*

	36. My brother's great granddaughter. (Male speaking.)	Translation.	37. My sister's son. (Male speaking.)	Translation.	38. My sister's son's wife. (Male speaking.)	Translation.
1	Ka-yä'-da	My granddaughter.	Ha-yä'-wan-da	My nephew.	Ka'-sä	My daugh.-in-law.
2	Ka-yä'-dra	" "	Ha-yuh'-wä-deh	" "	Ka-sa-yuh'	" "
3	Ka-yä'-da	" "	Ha-yä-wä'-da	" "	Ka-sä'-wa	" "
4	Ka-yä'-dla-ah	" "	Ha-yä'-wan-dä'	" "	Ka-zä'-wä	" "
5	Ka-yä'-dla-ah	" "	E-yo-wä'dä	" "	Ka-zü'-wä	" "
6	Kä-yä'-rä	My grandchild.	Kä-yä'-wä-nä	" "	Ahk-thäf'	" "
7	Ka-yä-tä-ra'-yă	My granddaughter.	Le-wä-dä'-ah	" "	Ka-sü'-wä	" "
8	Ya-tra'-ah	" "	Ha-shone-drä'-ka	" "	Ya-na'-mäque	" "
9	Me-tä'-ko-zhä	My grandchild.	Me-tonsh'-kä	" "	Me-ta-kosh	" "
10	Me-tä'-ko-zhä	" "	Me-to͡us-ka	" "	Me-tä'-koash	" "
11	Me-tä'-ko-zhä	" "	Me-toash'-kä	" "	Me-tä'-koash	" "
12	Me-tä'-ko-zha	" "	Me-tose'-ka	" "	Me-tä'-koash	" "
13	Me-tä'-ko-säk'-pok	" "	Me-toans'-kä	" "	Me-tä'-kosh	" "
14	Me-tä'-ko-zhä	" "	Me-toase'-kä	" "	Me-tä'-kosh	" "
15	Me-tä'-ko-zhä	" "	Ne-toash'-kä	" "	Me-tä'-koash.	" "
16	Me-tä'-ko-zä	" "	Me-toas'-kä	" "	Me-tä'-goash	" "
17	Me-tä'-ko-sä	" "	Me-to'-zä	" "	Me-tä'-koash	" "
18	Toosh'-pä-hä	" "	We-toash'-kä	" "	Ta-ne-hä	" "
19	Wee-tŭsh'-pä	" "	Wee-toans'-kä	" "	We-te'-na	" "
20	Heen-tä'-kwä-me	My granddaughter.	Heen-toas'-ka	" "	Heen-toan'-ye	" "
21	E-tä'-kwä-me	" "	Hin-tose'-kee	" "	Hin-to'-ne	" "
22	Be-chose'-pä	My grandchild.	Be-chose'-kä	" "	Be-je'-na	" "
23	We-chose'-pä	" "	We-chose'-kä	" "	We-che'-ne	" "
24	E-choon-zhunk'-e-neke	My little gd. daught.	E-chonsh'-kä	" "	E-nook-chek'-au-chau	" "
25	P-tä-we'-hä-kä	My grandchild.			P-tä-we'-hä-kä	My grandchild.
26	Met-a-wä-pish'-sha	" "	Mat-so'-gä	My younger brother.	Mä-kä'	My daughter.
27	Bus-bä'-pe-ta	" "	Bä-chŭ'-ka	" "	Moo'-ä-ka	My sister-in-law.
28	Sup'-uk	My granddaughter.	Sub-ai'-yih	My nephew.	Sup'-uk	My gd.-daughter.
29	Sä'-pok	" "	Suh-bai'-yih	" "	Sä'-pok	" "
30	Sup'-pok	" "	Sä-bĭ-yih	" "	Sup'-pok	" "
31	Um-os-sŭs'-wä	My grandchild.	Un-ho-pŭe'-wä	" "	Chu-hu'-cho-wä	My daugh.-in-law.
32	Un-gĭ-lĭ-sĭ	" "	Uṇ-gĕ-wĭ-uuṇ	" "	E-tsän'-hĭ	" "
33	Aṇ-ge-lee'-se	" "	Uṇ-ge-we'-nuh	" "	Ah-ge-tzan'-hĬ	" "
34	Te'-wut	My niece.	Te'-wut	" "	Scoo'-rus	" "
35			Te'-wut	" "	Sko'-dus	" "
36			Ah-te'-wut	" "	Nä-te-nä-tä'-koo	My wife.
37	No-se-sem'	My grandchild.	N'-de-kwä-tim'	" "	Nee-tim'	My daugh.-in-law.
38	No-se-sim'	" "	N'-de-kwä-tim'	" "	Nee-stim'	" "
39	No-se-sem'	" "	N'-deh-kwä-tim'	" "	Nee-tim'	" "
40	No-zbĭ'-she	" "	Nĭ-nin-gwä-niss'	" "	Nĭ'-sim	" "
41	No-she'-shä	" "	Ne-nin-gwuh'-nis	" "	Ne'-sim	" "
42	No-she-shä'	" "	Ne-nin-gwi-nis'	" "	Ne-sim'	" "
43	No-she-shä'	" "	Ne-nin-gwi-nis'	" "	Ne-sim'	" "
44	No-she-shä'	" "	Ne-nin-gwi-nis'...	" "	Ne-sim'	" "
45	No-să-seh'	" "	Nă'-gwi-nis	" "	N'-ah'-ga-neh-gweh'	" "
46	No-sa-mä'	" "	Laṇ-gwä-les'-sä	" "	Laṇ-gwä'-lä	" "
47	No-sa'-mä	" "	Ne-lä'-gwä-la-sä'	" "	Nä-hä-ga-na-kwä' No-ko-mä'	" "
48	No-sa'-mä	" "	Ne-lä'-gwä-lo-sä'	" "	Nä-hä-ga-na-kwä' No-ko-mä'	" "
49	No-sa-mä'	" "	Ne-lä'-gwä-lis-sä'	" "	Nä-hä-gä-na-kwä' No-ko-mä'	" "
50	No-sa-mä'	" "	Ne-lä'-gwä-lis-sä'	" "	Nä-hä-ga-na-kwä' No-ko-mä'	" "
51	No-she-sem'	" "	Nă-nä'-gwä-nis'	" "	Nă-sem'-yä	" "
52	No-she-să'	" "	Ne-nä'-kwä-na	" "	No-hä'-kun-e-uk-ye-yu'	" "
53	Nä-h·kä'	" "	Nă-chin'-e-tä	" "	Nich-ä'	" "
54	Na-se-thä'-mä	" "	Nen-na-kwä-na-thä'	" "	Na-them-mi-lă	" "
55	No-stha-thä'	" "	Na-la-gwal·thä'	" "	Nĭ-tha-mi-ah	" "
56	Nee'-sa	" "	Na-tah'·ta	" "	Nä-tine'	" "
57	Nee-so'-tan	" "	N'-do'-to-yose	" "	Nee-mis'	" "
58	Nee-so'-tän	" "	No-ă'-toase	" "	Nee-mis'	" "
59	Nŭ-jeech'	" "	Nŭ-lŭks'	" "	N'-tlus-wä'-skom	" "
60	N'-kway'-nus	" "	Nu-lŭk'-nis	" "	N'-sum'	" "
61	Nä-h·ise'	" "	No-kwath'	" "	Nä-hum'	" "
62	Noh·-whese'	" "	Longue'-kw'	" "	Nah·-hum'	" "
63	Nain-no-whase'.	" "	Na-lone'-gwä-sis'	" "	Nain-hum'	" "
64	Sa-t'thu'-a	" "	Sä'-zy	" "	Sa-t'thu'-a	My grandchild.
65	Sa-to͡a'-bä	My granddaughter.	Sa-yä'-zä	My son.	Sa-tsa'-ya	My daugh.-in-law.
66	Sa-le-zet'-tha-re	" "	Se-yä'-za	" "	Set-thu'-ya	" "
67	Sa-chi'	My grandchild.	Soo	My nephew ?		
68	Seet-she	" "	Si-ou	My step-child.	See-chy-o	My y'nger sister.
69			In-toonsh'	My nephew.	Is-sä'-pin	My dau.-in-law.
70			Eese-tlilt-wi'd'	" "		
71			In-pit'h. ᵇ Pai-yä	(Not rendered.)		
72				[ᵇ Step-son.		
73						
74						
75						
76						
77						
78						
79			U-jo-ru-ga	My nephew.		
80	Eng'-o-tä	My granddaughter.	We-yo'-o-gwä	" "	Oo-koo-ä'-gä	" "

TABLE II.—*Continued.*

	39. My sister's daughter. (Male speaking.)	Translation.	40. My sister's daughter's husband. (Male speaking.)	Translation.	41. My sister's grandson (Male speaking.)	Translation.
1	Ka-yă'-wan-da	My niece.	Oc-na'-hose	My son-in-law.	Ha-yä'-da	My grandson.
2	Ka-yuh'-wä-deh	" "	Unc-na'-hose	" "	Ha-yä'-dra	" "
3	Ka-yä-wä'-da	" "	Ha-nane'-hose	" "	Ha-yä'-da	" "
4	Ka-yä'-wan-dä'	" "	Ha-yale'-hose-hä	" "	Le-yä'-dla-ah	" "
5	Ka-yo-wä'-dä	" "	E-en-hŭ'-zä	" "	E-yä'-dla-ah	" "
6	Kä-yä'-wäh-nä'	" "	Yŭk-te-he⌢ah'-thä	" "	Kä-yä'-tä	My grandchild.
7	Ka-wä-dü'-ah	" "	De-an-hose'-hä	" "	Le-yä-tä-ra'-yä	My grandson.
8	Ya-shone-drä'-ka	" "	Ha-na'-näque	" "	Ha-tra'-ah	" "
9	Me-tuŋ'-zhaŋ	" "	Me-tä'-kosh	" "	Me-tä'-ko-zhä	My grandchild.
10	Me-to⌢us'-zä	" "	Me-tä'-koash	" "	Me-tä'-ko-zhä	" "
11	Me-to'-zhä	" "	Me-tä'-koash	" "	Me-tä'-ko-zhä	" "
12	Me-to'-zhä	" "	Me-tä'-koash	" "	Me-tä'-ko-zha	" "
13	Me-toh'-zhä	" "	Me-tä'-kosh	" "	Me-tä-ko-säk'-pok	" "
14	Me-toh'-zhä	" "	Me-tä'-kosh	" "	Me-tä'-ko-zhä	" "
15	Me-to'-zä	" "	Me-tä'-koash	" "	Me-tä'-ko-zhä	" "
16	Me-to'-zä	" "	Me-tä'-goash	" "	Me-tä'-ko-zä	" "
17	Me-to'-zä	" "	Me-tä'-goash	" "	Me-tä'-ko-sä	" "
18	Tä-zhä'-dä	" "	We-tuh'-da	" "	Toosh'-pä-hä	" "
19	We-te'-zhä	" "	We-tŏn'-da	" "	Wee-tŭsh'-pä	" "
20	Heen-toas'-ka-me	" "	Wä-do'-nä	" "	Heen-tä'-kwä	My grandson.
21	Hin-tose'-kee-me	" "	Wan-do'-hä	" "	E-tä'-kwä	" "
22	Be-che'-zho	" "	Be-to'-ja	" "	Be-chose'-pä	My grandchild.
23	We-che'-zho	" "	We-ton'-chä	" "	We-chose'-pä	" "
24	E-chooŋ-zhunk'	" "	Wä-to'-ho	" "	E-chooŋ'-ka-neke	My little gd. son.
25			Wo-wä'-ke ?	My brother-in-law.		
26	Mä-tä-kä'-zhä	My younger sister.	Me-nä	" "	Met-a-wä-pish'-sha	My grandchild.
27	Bä-so'-ka	" "	Boo'-sha	My son-in-law.	Bus-bä'-pe-ta	" "
28	Sub-ih'-take	My niece.	Sai'-yup	" "	Sup'-uk-nŏk'-ne	My grandson.
29	Suh-bĭh'-take	" "	Säi'-yop	" "	Sä-pok-näk'-ne	" "
30	Su-bĭ'-take	" "	Sä'-yup	" "	Sup'-pok-näk'-nĭ	" "
31	Un-häk'-pu-te	" "	Un-chŭ-ko-wäk'-ke	" "	Um-os-sŭs'-wä	My grandchild.
32	Uŋ-gwä-duŋ'	" "	E-huä-tsĭ'	" "	Uŋ-gĭ-lĭ-sĭ	" "
33	Uŋ-gwä'-tuh	" "	A-ge-h'-nä-tzĭ'	" "	Aŋ-ge-lee'-se	" "
34	Te-wut	" "	Koos-tow'-e-su	" "	Lak-te-gish	My grandson.
35	Te'-wut	" "	Ko-stä'-witch	" "	Lak-te-kis	My grandchild.
36	Ah-te-natch	" "	Koh-tä-wa'-sah	" "	At-nuch'	" "
37	{ Nesse-tim' (older) { Neese-che-mish' (y'nger)	" "	Na-häk'-sim	" "	No-se-sem'	" "
38	{ Neesh-tim' (older) { Neeste-che-mis' (y'nger)	" "	Nä-häk'-sim	" "	No-se-sim'	" "
39	Neese-che-mis'	" "	N'-bä'-ke-shim	" "	No-se-sem'	" "
40	Nĭ-shĭ'-miss	" "	Nĭ-nin'-gwän	" "	No-zhĭ'-she	" "
41	Ne-she'-me-sha	" "	Ne-nin'-gwun	" "	No-she'-shä	" "
42	Ne-she-mis'	" "	Ne-niŋ-gwun'	" "	No-she-shä'	" "
43	Ne-she-mis'	" "	Ne-niŋ-gwun'	" "	No-she-shä'	" "
44	Ne-she-mis'	" "	Ne-niŋ-gwun'	" "	No-she-shä'	" "
45	Ne-she'-mis	" "	N'-do'-she-na-game'	" "	No-sä-seh'	" "
46	Shames-sä'	" "	Na-hun'-gä-nä	" "	No-sa-mä'	" "
47	Ne-she-mis-sä'	" "	Na-lä-gwa-lä'	" "	No-sa'-mä	" "
48	Ne-she-mis-sä'	" "	Na-lä-gwa-lä'	" "	No-sa'-mä	" "
49	Ne-she-mis-sä'	" "	N'-dä-gwä-lä'	" "	No-sa-mä'	" "
50	Ne-she-mis-sä'	" "	N'-dä-gwä-lä'	" "	No-sa-mä'	" "
51	Nä-shä'-mis	" "	Nä-nä-kwem'	" "	No-she-sem'	" "
52	Nä-nä'-mä	" "	Ne-nä-kwun	" "	No-she-sä'	" "
53	Ne-she'-mis	" "	Nich-ä'	" "	Nä-h'-kä'	" "
54	Na-sem-e-thä'	" "	Na-nä-kwam-nä	" "	Na-se-thä'-mä	" "
55	Ne-sa-me-thä'	" "	Nin-hä-kä-na-mä'	" "	No-stha-thä'	" "
56	Nä-tha'-be	" "	Na-täs'	" "	Nee'-sa	" "
57	Nee-mis'-sä	" "	Nis	" "	Nee-so'-tan	" "
58	Ne-mis'-sä	" "	Nis	" "	Nee-so'-tän	" "
59	N'-sum'	" "	N'-thŭ'-suk	" "	Nŭ-jeech'	" "
60	N'-sum'	" "	N'-thŭ'-suk	" "	N'-kway'-nus	" "
61	Nohk-soh-kwä'-oh	" "	Wä-seen'-no-kwä'	" "	Nä-h'ise'	" "
62	Longue-kwä'	" "	Nä-to-na-mä'-kw'	" "	Noh-whese'	" "
63	Na-lone'-gwä-sis'	" "	Na-nä-toh'-na-makue'	" "	Nain-whase'	" "
64	Sä'-zy	" "	Se-ga'-ton	" "	Sa-t'-thu'-a	" "
65	Sa-to-a'	My daughter.	Sa-tsa'-ya	" "	Sa-ken'-ne	My grandson.
66	Se-le'-ä	" "	Set-shi'-ya	" "	Se-yä-zet'-tha-re	" "
67	Sa'-ke ?	My niece.			Sa-chi'	My grandchild.
68	Si-ou	My step-child	Seet-she-kŭ-in	" "	Seet-she	" "
69	In-toonsh'	My niece.	Is-natchl'-hu	" "		
70						
71	In-pit'h.　ᵇ Pai-yä	My niece.　ᵇ Step- [daughter.				
72						
73						
74						
75						
76						
77						
78						
79	U-jo-ru-ga	My niece.				
80	We-yo'-o-gwä	" "	Aug-a-ou'-gwä	" "	Eng'-o-tä	" "

TABLE II.—*Continued.*

	42. My sister's granddaughter. (Male speaking.)	Translation.	43. My sister's great grandson. (Male speaking.)	Translation.	44. My sister's great granddaughter. (Male speaking.)	Translation.
1	Ka-yä'-da	My granddaughter.	Ha-yä'-da	My grandson.	Ka-yä'-da	My gd. daughter.
2	Ka-yä'-dra	" "	Ha-yä'-dra	" "	Ka-yä'-dra	" "
3	Ka-yä'-da	" "	Ha-yä'-da	" "	Ka-yä'-da	" "
4	Ka-yä'-dla-ah	" "	Le-yä'-dla-ah	" "	Ka-yä'-dla-ah	" "
5	Ka-yä'-dla-ah	" "	E-yä'-dla-ah	" "	Ka-yä'-dla-ah	" "
6	Kä-yä'-rä	My grandchild.	Kä-yä'-rä	My grandchild.	Kä-yä'-rä	My grandchild.
7	Ka-yä-tä-ra'-yä	My granddaughter.	Le-yä-tä-ra'-yä	My grandson.	Ka-yä-tä-ra'-yä	My gd. daughter.
8	Ya-tra'-ah	" "	Ha-tra'-ah	" "	Ya-tra'-ah	" "
9	Me-tä'-ko-zhä	My grandchild.	Me-tä'-ko-zhä	My grandchild.	Me-tä'-ko-zhä	My grandchild.
10	Me-tä'-ko-zha	" "	Me-tä'-ko-zha	" "	Me-tä'-ko-zha	" "
11	Me-tä'-ko-zhä	" "	Me-tä'-ko-zhä	" "	Me-tä'-ko-zhä	" "
12	Me-tä'-ko-sha	" "	Me-tä'-ko-sha	" "	Me-tä'-ko-sha	" "
13	Me-tä'-ko-säk'-pok	" "	Me-tä'-ko-säk'-pok	" "	Me-tä'-ko-säk'-pok	" "
14	Me-tä'-ko-zhä	" "	Me-tä'-ko-zhä	" "	Me-tä'-ko-zhä	" "
15	Me-tä'-ko-zhä	" "	Me-tä'-ko-zhä	" "	Me-tä'-ko-zhä	" "
16	Me-tä'-ko-zä	" "	Me-tä'-ko-zä	" "	Me-tä'-ko-zä	" "
17	Me-tä'-ko-zä	" "	Me-tä'-ko-zä	" "	Me-tä'-ko-zä	" "
18	Toosh'-pä-hä	" "	Toosh'-pä-hä	" "	Toosh'-pä-hä	" "
19	Wee-tŭsh'-pä	" "	Wee-tŭsh'-pä	" "	Wee-tŭsh'-pä	" "
20	Heen-tä'-kwä-me	My granddaughter.	Heen-tä'-kwä	My grandson.	Heen-tä'-kwä-me	My gd. daughter.
21	E-tä'-kwä-me	" "	E-tä'-kwä	" "	E-tä'-kwä-me	" "
22	Be-chose'-pä	My grandchild.	Be-chose'-pä	My grandchild.	Be-chose'-pä	My grandchild.
23	We-chose'-pä	" "	We-chose'-pä	" "	We-chose'-pä	" "
24	E-choon-zhunk'-e-neke	My little gd. daught.	E-choon'-ka-neke'	My little grandson.	E-choon-zhunk-e-neke	My little gd. dau.
25						
26						
27	Bus-bä'-he-ä					
28	Sup'-uk	My granddaughter.	Sup'-uk-nŏk'-ne	My grandson.	Sup'-uk	My gd. daughter.
29	Sä'-pok	" "	Sä'-pok-näk'-ne	" "	Sä'-pok	" "
30	Sup'-pok	" "	Sup'-pok-näk'-nĭ	" "	Sup'-pok	" "
31	Um-os-sŭs'-wä	My grandchild.	Um-os-sŭs'-wä	My grandchild.	Um-os-sŭs'-wä	My grandchild.
32	Un-gĭ-lĭ-sĭ	" "	Un-gĭ-lĭ-sĭ	" "	Un-gĭ-lĭ-sĭ	" "
33	An-ge-lee'-se	" "	An-ge-lee'-se	" "	An-ge-lee'-se	" "
34	Lak-te'-gee	My granddaughter.	Te'-wut	My nephew.	Te'-wut	My niece.
35	Lak-te'-kis	My grandchild.				
36	At-nuch'	" "	At-nuch'	My grandchild.	At-nuch'	My grandchild.
37	No-se-sem'	" "	No-se-sem'	" "	No-se-sem'	" "
38	No-se-sim'	" "	No-se-sim'	" "	No-se-sim'	" "
39	No-se-sem'	" "	No-se-sem'	" "	No-se-sem'	" "
40	No-zhĭ'-she	" "	No-zhĭ'-she	" "	No-zhĭ'-she	" "
41	No-she'-shä	" "	No-she'-shä	" "	No-sha'-shä	" "
42	No-she-shä'	" "	No-she-shä'	" "	No-she-shä'	" "
43	No-she-shä'	" "	No-she-shä'	" "	No-she-shä'	" "
44	No-she-shä'	" "	No-she-shä'	" "	No-she-shä'	" "
45	No-sä-seh'	" "	No-sä-seh'	" "	No-sä-seh'	" "
46	No-sa-mä'	" "	No-sa-mä'	" "	No-sa-mä'	" "
47	No-sa'-mä	" "	No-sa'-mä	" "	No-sa'-mä	" "
48	No-sa-mä'	" "	No-sa-mä'	" "	No-sa-mä'	" "
49	No-sa-mä'	" "	No-sa-mä'	" "	No-sa-mä'	" "
50	No-sä-mä'	" "	No-sa-mä'	" "	No-sa-mä'	" "
51	No-she-sem'	" "	No-she-sem'	" "	No-she-sem'	" "
52	No-she-sä'	" "	No-she-sä'	" "	No-she-sä'	" "
53	Nä-h·-kä'	" "	Na-h·-kä'	" "	Nä-h·-kä'	" "
54	Na-se-thä'-mä	" "	Na-se-thä'-mä	" "	Na-se-thä'-mä	" "
55	No-stha-thä'	" "	No-stha-thä'	" "	No-stha-thä'	" "
56	Nee'-sa	" "	Nee'-sa	" "	Nee'-sa	" "
57	Nee-so'-tan	" "	Nee-so'-tan	" "	Nee-so'-tan	" "
58	Nee-so'-tän	" "	Nee-so'-tän	" "	Nee-so'-tän	" "
59	Nŭ-jeech'	" "	Nŭ-jeech'	" "	Nŭ jeech'	" "
60	N'-kway'-nus	" "	N'-kway'-nus	" "	N'-kway'-nus	" "
61	Nä-h·ise'	" "	Nä-h·ise'	" "	Nä-h·ise'	" "
62	Noh·-whese'	" "	Noh·-whese'	" "	Noh·-whese'	" "
63	Nain-no-whase'	" "	Nain-no-whase'	" "	Nain-no-whase'	" "
64	Sa-t'-thu'-a	" "	Sa-t'-thu'-a	" "	Sa-t'thu'-a	" "
65	Sa-to⁻a'-bä	My granddaughter.	Sa-ken'-ne	My grandson.	Sa-to⁻a'-bä-	My gd. daughter.
66	Sa-le-zet'-tha-re	" "	Se-yä-zet'-tha-re	" "	Sa-le-zet'-tha-re	" "
67	Sa-chi'	My grandchild.	Sa-chi'	My grandchild.	Sa-chi'	My grandchild.
68	Seet-she	" "	Seet-she	" "	Seet-she	" "
69						
70						
71						
72						
73						
74						
75						
76						
77						
78						
79						
80	Eng'-o-tä	" "	Eng'-o-tä	" "	Eng'-o-tä	" "

TABLE II.—*Continued.*

	45. My brother's son. (Female speaking.)	Translation.	46. My brother's son's wife. (Female speaking.)	Translation.	47. My brother's daughter. (Female speaking.)	Translation.
1	Ha-soh'-neh	My nephew.	Ka'-sä	My daugh.-in-law.	Ka-soh'-neh	My niece.
2	Ha-hä'-wuk	My son.	Ka-sa-yuh'	" "	Ka-hä'-wuk	My daughter.
3	Ha-hä'-wa	" "	Ka-sä'-wä	" "	Ka-hä'-wä	" "
4	Le-yä'-hä	" "	Ka-zä'-wä	" "	Ka-yä'-hä	" "
5	E-yä'	" "	Ka-zä'-wä	" "	Ka-yä'	" "
6	Kä-yä'-wä-nä	My nephew.	Ahk-thäf'	" "	Kä-yä'-wä-nä	" "
7	Le-yä'-ah	My son.	Ka-sä'-wä	" "	Ka-yä'-ah	" "
8	He-wä-teh	My nephew.	Ya-na'-mäque	" "	E-wä'-teh	My niece.
9	Me-tonsh'-kä	" "	Me-tä'-kosh	" "	Me-tuŋ'-zhaŋ	My daughter.
10	Me-toⁿus'-kä	" "	Me-tä'-koash	" "	Me-to-us-zä.	My niece.
11	Me-toash'-kä	" "	Me-tä'-koash	" "	Me-to'-zhä	" "
12	Me-tose'-kä.	" "	Me-tä'-koash	" "	Me-to'-zhä	" "
13	Me-toans'-kä	" "	Me-tä'-kosh	" "	Me-toh'-zhä	" "
14	Me-toase'-kä	" "	Me-tä'-kosh	" "	Me-toh'-zhä	" "
15	Me-toash'-kä	" "	Me-tä'-koash	" "	Me-to'-zä.	" "
16	Me-toas'-kä	" "	Me-tä'-goash	" "	Me-to'-zä	" "
17	Me-to'-zä	" "	Me-tä'-koash	" "	Me-to'-zä	" "
18	We-toash'-kä	" "	Ta-ne'-lä	" "	Tä-zhä'-hä.	" "
19	Wee-toans'-kä	" "	We-te'-na	" "	We-te'-zhä	" "
20	Heen-toas'-ka	" "	Heen-toan'-ye	" "	Heen-toas'-ka-me	" "
21	Hin-tose'-kee	" "	Hin-to'-na	" "	Hin-tose'-kee-me	" "
22	Be-chose'-kä	" "	Be-je'-na	" "	Be-che'-zho.	" "
23	We-chose'-ka	" "	We-che'-ne	" "	We-che'-zho	" "
24	E-choonsh'-ka	My neph. or gd.son.	E-she-guŋ	My sister-in-law.	E-choon-zhunk'	My niece or gd.da.
25	Ko-ne'-ka ?	My son.	Ko-too'-te	My daugh.-in-law.	Me-no'-hä-ka ?	My daughter.
26	Met-a-wä-pish'-sha	My grandchild.	Mat-to'-we-ä-kä-zhe	My sister-in-law.	Met-a-wä-pish'-sha	My grandchild.
27	Bot-sa'-sä	My son.	Bos-me'-ä-kun-is-ta	" "	Näk'-me-ä	My daughter.
28	Sup'-uk-nŏk'-ne	My grandson.	Sup'-uk	My granddaughter.	Sup'-uk	My gd. daughter.
29	Sä'-pok-näk'-ne	" "	Sä'-pok	" "	Sä'-pok	" "
30	Sup'-pok-näk'-nĭ	" "	Sup'-pok.	" "	Sup'-pok	" "
31	Um-os-süs'-wä	My grandchild.	Un-hu-tis'-se	My daugh.-in-law.	Um-os-süs'-wä	" "
32	Uŋ-gĭ-wĭ-nuŋ	" "	E-tsän'-hĭ	" "	Uŋ-gwä-duŋ	My niece.
33	Un-ge-we'-nuh	My nephew.	Ah-ge-tsau'-hĭ	" "	Uŋ-gwä'-tuh	" "
34	Pe'-row	My child.	Scoo'-rus.	" "	Pe'-row	My child.
35	Pe'-row	" "	Sko'-dus	" "	Pe'-row	" "
36	At-nuch'	My grandchild.	Sko-roo'-hoo	" "	At-nuch'	My grandchild.
37	N'-de-kwä-tim'	My nephew.	Nee-tim'	" "	{ Neese-tim' (older)	My niece.
					{ Neese-che-mish' (y'nger)	" "
38	N'-de-kwä-tim'	" "	Ne-stim'	" "	{ Neesh-tim' (older)	" "
					{ Neest-che-mish' (y'nger)	" "
39	N'-deh-kwä-tim'	" "	Nee-tim'	" "	Neese-che-mis'	" "
40	Ni-ŋin-gwä'-niss	" "	Nis'-sim	" "	Nĭ-shĭ-mis'	" "
41	Ne-nin-gwuh'-nis	" "	Ne'-sim	" "	Ne-she'-me-sha	" "
42	Ne-nin-gwi-nis'	" "	Ne-sim'	" "	Ne-she-mis'	" "
43	Ne-nin-gwi-nis'	" "	Ne-sim'	" "	Ne-she-mis'	" "
44	Ne-nin-gwi-nis'	" "	Ne-sim'	" "	Ne-she-mis'	" "
45	N'-gwi-nis	" "	N'-ah'-ga-neh-gweh'	" "	Ne-she'-mis	" "
46	Lan-gwä-les'-sä	" "	Lan-gwä'-lä	" "	Shames-sä'	" "
47	Ne-lä'-gwä-la-sä'	" "	Nä-hä-ga-na'-kwä No-ko-mä	" "	Ne-she-mis-sä'	" "
48	Ne-lä'-gwä-la-sä'	" "	Nä-hä-ga-na'-kwä No-ko-mä	" "	Ne-she-mis-sä'	" "
49	Ne-lä'-gwä-lis-sä'	" "	Nä-hä-gä-na-kwä' No-ko-mä	" "	Ne-she-mis-sä'	" "
50	Ne-lä'-gwä-lis-sä'	" "	Nä-hä-gä-na-kwä' No-ko-mä	" "	Ne-she-mis-sä'	" "
51	Nä-nä'-gwa-nis	" "	Nä-hä-gä'-ne-kwam	" "	Nä-shä'-mis	" "
52	Ne-nä'-kwä-na	" "	No-hä'-kun-e-uk-ye-yu'	" "	Nä-nä'-mä	" "
53	Nä-chin'-e-tä	" "	Nich-ä'.	" "	Nä-un'	" "
54	Nen-nä-kwä-na	" "	Na-them-mi-lä'	" "	Na-sem-e-thä'	" "
55	Na-na-gwal-thä	" "	Nĭ-tha-mĭ-ah'	" "	Ne-sa-me-thä'	" "
56	Na-tah'-ta	" "	Nä-tim'	" "	Nä-thä'-be	" "
57	N'-do'-to-yose.	" "	Nee-mis'	" "	Nee-mis'-sä	" "
58	No-ä'-toase	" "	Nee-mis'	" "	Nee-mis'-sä	" "
59	Nŭ-lŭks'	" "	N'-thus-wä-skom	" "	N'-sum'	" "
60	Nu-lŭk'-nis.	" "	N'-sum'	" "	N'-sum'	" "
61	Nä-kun'	My step-child.	Nä-h·um'	" "	Nä-kun'	My step-child.
62	N'-kweese'	My son.	Näh-·hum'	" "	N'-dä-nuss'	My daughter.
63	Nain-gwase'	" "	Nain-hum'	" "	Nain-dä'-ness.	" "
64	Sa-yä'-ze	" "	Sa-chä'	" "	Sa-yä'-dze	My step-daughter.
65	Sa-yä'-za	" "	Sä-tsa'-yä	" "	Sa-to'-a	My daughter.
66	Se-yä'-za	" "	Set-thu'-ya	" "	Sa-le'-a	" "
67	Sa'-zoo ?	" "			Sa-yä-tse' ?	" "
68	Sa-chä	My y'nger brother.	See-ya-hŭt'	" "	Se-chu-the	My adopted dau.
69	In-tee'-kwl	My neph and aunt.	Is-sä'-pin	" "	Is-see'-lä	My gd. daughter.
70						
71	In'-pote	(Not rendered.)			In'-pote	(Not rendered.)
72	[Kä-gut'-sin (y.b.s.)					
73	No-pwu'-ät-sin (eld.br.s.)	" "			Kä-gut'-sin	" "
74						
75						
76						
77						
78						
79	Ang'-a-ga	My nephew.			Ang'-a-ga	My niece.
80	Ung-ä'-gä	" "	Oo-koo-ä'-gä	" "	Ung-ä'-gä	" "

TABLE II.—*Continued.*

	48. My brother's daughter's husband. (Female speaking.)	Translation.	49. My brother's grandson. (Female speaking.)	Translation.	50. My brother's granddaughter. (Female speaking.)	Translation.
1	Oc-na′-hose	My son-in-law.	Ha-yä′-da	My grandson.	Ka-yä′-da	My gd. daughter.
2	Unc-na′-hose............	" "	Ha-yä′-dra	" "	Ka-yä′-dra	" "
3	Ha-nane′-hose	" "	Ha-yä′-da	" "	Ka-yä′-da	" "
4	Ha-yale′-hose-hä	" "	Le-yä′-dla-ah	" "	Ka-yä′-dla-ah	" "
5	E-en-hŭ′-zä	" "	E-yä′-dla-ah	" "	Ka-yä′-dla-ah	" "
6	Yäk-te-he⁻ah′-thä	" "	Kä-yä′-rä	My grandchild.	Kä-yä′-rä............	My grandchild.
7	De-an-hose′-hä	" "	Le-yä-tä-ra′-yä	My grandson.	Ka-yä-tä-ra′-yä	My gd. daughter.
8	Ha-na′-mäque	" "	Ha-tra′-ah	" "	Ya-tra′-ah	" "
9	Me-tä′-kosh	" "	Me-tä′-ko-zhä	My grandchild.	Me-tä′-ko-zhä............	My grandchild.
10	Me-tä′-koash	" "	Me-tä′-ko-zha............	" "	Me-tä′-ko-zha............	" "
11	Me-tä′-koash	" "	Me-tä′-ko-zhä............	" "	Me-tä′-ko-zhä............	" "
12	Me-tä′-koash	" "	Me-tä′-ko-sha............	" "	Me-tä′-ko-sha............	" "
13	Me-tä′-kosh	" "	Me-tä′-ko-säk′-pok	" "	Me-tä′-ko-säk′-pok.	" "
14	Me-tä′-kosh	" "	Me-tä′-ko-zhä............	" "	Me-tä′-ko-zhä............	" "
15	Me-tä′-koash	" "	Me-tä′-ko-zhä............	" "	Me-tä′-ko-zhä............	" "
16	Me-tä′-goash	" "	Me-tä′-ko-zä............	" "	Me-tä′-ko-zä............	" "
17	Me-tä′-goash	" "	Me-tä′-ko-sä............	" "	Me-tä′-ko-sä............	" "
18	We-tuh′-da	" "	Toosh′-pä-hä	" "	Toosh′-pä-hä............	" "
19	Wa-toṇ′-dä	" "	Wee-tŭsh′-pä	" "	Wee-tŭsh′-pä............	" "
20	Wä-do′-hä	" "	Heen-tä′-kwä	My grandson.	Heen-tä′-kwä-me............	My gd. daughter.
21	Wan-do′-hä	" "	E-tä′-kwä	" "	E-tä′-kwä-me	" "
22	Be-to′-ja............	" "	Be-chose′-pä	My grandchild.	Be-chose′-pä	My grandchild.
23	We-toṇ′-chä	" "	We-chose′-pä	" "	We-chose′-pä	" "
24	E-she-kä′	My brother-in-law.	E-chä-h·kun	My step-child.	E-chä-h·kun	My step-daughter.
25	Ko-too′-te	My son-in-law.	P-tä-we′-hä-kä	My grandchild.	P-tä-we′-hä-kä	My grandchild.
26	Mä-too′-te	" "	Met-a-wä-pish′-sha........	" "	Met-a-wä-pish′-sha........	" "
27	Boo′-shä............	" "	Bus-bä′-pe-ta	" "	Bus-bä′-pe-ta	" "
28	Sai′-yup............	" "	Sup′-uk-nŏk′-ne	My grandson.	Sup′-uk	My gd. daughter.
29	Sai′-yop	" "	Sä′-pok-näk′-ne	" "	Sä′-pok	" "
30	Sä′-yup............	" "	Sup′-pok-näk′-hĭ	" "	Snp′-pok	" "
31	Un-hŭ-tis′-se............	" "	Um-os-sŭs′-wä............	My grandchild.	Um-os-sŭs′-wä............	My grandchild.
32	E-hua-tsĭ′	" "	Uṇ-gĭ-lĭ-sĭ′............	" "	Uṇ-gĭ-lĭ-sĭ′............	" "
33	A-ge-h·-nä′-tzĭ	" "	Aṇ-ge-lee′-se	" "	Aṇ-ge-lee′-se............	" "
34	Koos-tow′-es-sŭ	" "	Lak-te′-gish	My grandson.	Lak-te′-gee	My gd. daughter.
35	Ko-stä′-witch	" "	Lak-te′-kis	My grandchild.	Lak-te′-kis	My grandchild.
36	Koh·-tä′-wa-suh............	" "	At-nuch′............	" "	At-nuch′............	" "
37	Nä-häk-sim′	" "	No-se-sem′............	" "	No-se-sem′............	" "
38	Nä-häk-sim′	" "	No-se-sim′	" "	No-se-sim′	" "
39	N′-hä′-ke-shim′	" "	No-se-sem′	" "	No-se-sem′	" "
40	Nĭ-nin′-gwän	" "	No-zhĭ′-she	" "	No-shĭ-she............	" "
41	Ne-nin′-gwun	" "	No-she′-shä′............	" "	No-she′-shä............	" "
42	Ne-niṇ-gwun′	" "	No-she-shä′	" "	No-she′-shä............	" "
43	Ne-niṇ-gwun′	" "	No-she-shä′	" "	No-she-shä′............	" "
44	Ne-niṇ-gwun′	" "	No-she-shä′	" "	No-she-shä′............	" "
45	N′-do′-she-na-game′	" "	No-sä-seh′	" "	No-sä′-seh′............	" "
46	Na-hun′-gä-nä	" "	No-sa-mä′	" "	No-sa′-mä............	" "
47	Ne-lä′-gwä-lä′............	" "	No-sa′-mä	" "	No-sa′-mä............	" "
48	Ne-lä′-gwä-lä′............	" "	No-sa′-mä	" "	No-sa′-mä............	" "
49	N′-dä′-gwä-lä′............	" "	No-sa-mä′	" "	No-sa-mä′............	" "
50	N′-dä′-gwä-lä′............	" "	No-sa-mä′	" "	No-sa-mä′............	" "
51	Nä-nä-kwem′	" "	No-she-sem′	" "	No-she-sem′............	" "
52	Ne-nä′-kwun	" "	No-she-sä′	" "	No-she-sä′............	" "
53	Nich-ä′	" "	Nä-h·-kä′	" "	Nä-h·-kä′............	" "
54	Na-na-kwam-na	" "	Na-se-thä-mä′	" "	Na-se-thä-mä′............	" "
55	Nin-hä-kä-na-mä′	" "	No-stha-thä′	" "	No-stha-thä′............	" "
56	Na-täs′............	" "	Nee′-sa	" "	Nee′-sa	" "
57	Nis	" "	Nee-so′-tän	" "	Nee-so′-tan	" "
58	Nis	" "	Nee-so′-tän	" "	Nee-so′-tän	" "
59	N′-tlu′-sŭk............	" "	Nŭ-jeech′	" "	Nŭ-jeech′............	" "
60	N′-tlu′-sŭk............	" "	N′-kway′-nus	" "	N′-kway′-nus	" "
61	Wä-seen′-no-kwä............	" "	Nä-h·ise′............	" "	Nä-h·ise′............	" "
62	Nä-to-nä-mä′-kw′............	" "	Noh·-whese′............	" "	Noh·-whese′............	" "
63	Na-nä-toh′-na-makue	" "	Nain-no-whase′	" "	Nain-no-whase′	" "
64	Sa-chĭ′-a	" "	Sa-chä′	" "	Sa-chä′	" "
65	Sa-tsa′-yä	" "	Sa-ken′-ne............	My grandson.	Sa-to⁻a′-bä	My gd. daughter.
66	Set-shi′-ya	" "	Se-yä-zet′-tha-re	" "	Sa-le-zet′-tha-re	" "
67			Sa-chi′............	My grandchild.	Sa-chi′............	My grandchild.
68	Set-she-ku-in	" "	Set-she	" "	Set-she	" "
69	Is-natche′-hu	" "				
70						
71						
72						
73						
74						
75						
76						
77						
78						
79						
80	Ning-a-oṇ′-gwä............	' "	Eng′-o-tä	" "	Eng′-o-tä............	" "

TABLE II.—Continued.

	51. My brother's great grandson. (Female speaking.)	Translation.	52. My brother's gt. gd.daughter. (Female speaking.)	Translation.	53. My sister's son. (Female speaking.)	Translation.
1	Ha-yä'-da	My grandson.	Ka-yä'-da	My granddaughter.	Ha-ah'-wuk	My son.
2	Ha-yä'-dra	" "	Ka-yä'-dra	" "	Ha-hä'-wuk	" "
3	Ha-yä'-da	" "	Ka-yä'-da	" "	Ha-hä'-wä	" "
4	Le-yä'-dla-ah	" "	Ka-yä'-dla-ah	" "	Le-yä'-hä	" "
5	E-yä'-dla-ah	" "	Ka-yä'-dla-ah	" "	E-yä'	" "
6	Kä-yä'-rä	My grandchild.	Ka-yä'-rä	My grandchild.	Kä-yä'-no-nä	My child.
7	Le-yä-tä-ra'-yä	My grandson.	Ka-yä-tä-ra'-yä	My granddaughter.	Le-yä'-ah	My son.
8	Ha-tra'-ah	" "	Ya-tra'-ah	" "	E-ne-ah'	" "
9	Me-tä'-ko-zhä	My grandchild.	Me-tä'-ko-zhä	My grandchild.	Me-chink'-she	" "
10	Me-tä'-ko-zha	" "	Me-tä'-ko-zha	" "	Me-chink'-she	" "
11	Me-tä'-ko-zhä	" "	Me-tä'-ko-zhä	" "	Ah-she'-dä	" "
12	Me-tä'-ko-sha	" "	Me-tä'-ko-sha	" "	Me-chink'-she	" "
13	Me-tä'-ko-säk'-pok	" "	Me-tä'-ko-säk'-pok	" "	me-chink'-se-lä	" "
14	Me-tä'-ko-zhä	" "	Me-tä'-ko-zhä	" "	Me-chink'-she	" "
15	Me-tä'-ko-zhä	" "	Me-tä'-ko-zhä	" "	Me-chink'-she	" "
16	Me-tä'-ko-zä	" "	Me-tä'-ko-zä	" "	Me-chink'-she	" "
17	Me-tä'-ko-sä	" "	Me-tä'-ko-sä	" "	Me-chink'-she	" "
18	Toosh'-pä-hä	" "	Toosh'-pä-hä	" "	Nis-se'-hä	" "
19	Wee-tŭsh'-pä	" "	Wee-tŭsh'-pä	" "	Wee-zhin-ga	" "
20	Heen-tä'-kwä	My grandson.	Heen-tä'-kwä-me	My granddaughter.	Hee-yin-ga	" "
21	E-tä'-kwa	" "	E-tä'-kwä-me	" "	He-ne'-cha	" "
22	Be-chose'-pä	My grandchild.	Be-chose'-pä	My grandchild.	Be-she'-gä	" "
23	We chose'-pä	" "	We-chose'-pä	" "	We-shen'-kä	" "
24	E-chä-h·kun'-neke	My little step-child.	E cha-h·kun'-neke	My little step-child.	E-chä-h·kun'	My step-child.
25	P-tä-we'-hä-kä	My grandchild.	P-tä-we'-hä-kä	My grandchild.	Ko-ne'-ka	My son.
26	Met-a-wä-pish'-sha	" "	Met-a-wä-pish'-sha	" "	Mä-de-shä'	" "
27	Bus-bä'-pe-ta	" "	Bus-bä'-pe-ta	" "	Bot-sa'-sä	" "
28	Sup'-uk-nŏk'-ne	My grandson.	Sup'-uk	My granddaughter.	Suh'-stih	" "
29	Sä-pok-näk'-ne	" "	Sä'-pok	" "	Suh'-soh	" "
30	Sup'-pok-näk'-nĭ	" "	Sup'-pok	" "	Su'-soh	" "
31	Um-os-sŭs'-wä	My grandchild.	Um-os-sŭs'-wä	My grandchild.	Cuch-ho-sŭ-che	My little son.
32	Un-gĭ-lĭ-sĭ	" "	Un-gĭ-lĭ-sĭ	" "	A-gwal'-tsĭ	My child.
33	An-ge-lee'-se	" "	An-ge-lee'-se	" "	Ah-gwa'-tze	" "
34	Te'-wut	My nephew.	Te'-wut	My niece.	Pe'-row	" "
35					Pe'-row	" "
36	At-nuch'	My grandchild.	At-nuch'	My grandchild.	Nä-te-nä'-o	" "
37	No-se-sem'	" "	No-se-sem'	" "	N'-go'-sim	My step-son.
38	No-se-sim'	" "	No-se-sim'	" "	N'-go'-zhim	" "
39	No-se-sem'	" "	No-se-sem'	" "	N'-do'-zhim	" "
40	No-zhĭ'-she	" "	No-shĭ'-she	" "	Nin-do'-shĭ-miss	My step-child.
41	No-she'-shä	" "	No-she'-shä	" "	Nin-do'-she-mis	" "
42	No-she-shä'	" "	No-she-shä'	" "	Nin-gwis'	My son.
43	No-she-shä'	" "	No-she-shä'	" "	Nin-gwie'	" "
44	No-she-shä'	" "	No-she-shä'	" "	N'-gwis'	" "
45	No-sä-seh'	" "	No-sä-seh'	" "	N'-gwis'	" "
46	No-sa-mä'	" "	No-sa-mä'	" "	Neen-gwase'-sä	" "
47	No-sa'-mä	" "	No-sa'-mä	" "	Nin-gwa-sä'	" "
48	No-sa'-mä	" "	No-sa'-mä	" "	Nin-gwa-sä'	" "
49	No-sa-mä'	" "	No-sa-mä'	" "	Ne-gwis-sä'	" "
50	No-sa-mä'	" "	No-sa-mä'	" "	Ne-gwis-sä'	" "
51	No-she-sem'	" "	No-she-sem'	" "	Nä-kwis'-sä	" "
52	No-she-sä'	" "	No-she-sä'	" "	Ne-keese'	" "
53	Nä-h·-kä'	" "	Nä-h·-kä'	" "	Nä	" "
54	Na-the-sä'-mä	" "	Na-se-thä-mä'	" "	Ni-kwĭ-thä'	" "
55	No-stha-thä'	" "	No-stha-thä'	" "	Ne-kwe-thä'	" "
56	Nee'-sa	" "	Nee-sä	" "	Na'-hä	" "
57	Nee-so'-tan	" "	Nee-so'-tan	" "	N'-do'-to-ko	My step-son.
58	Nee-so'-tän	" "	Nee-so'-tän	" "	Ne-to'-to-koh·'-ä	" "
59	Nŭ-jeech'	" "	Nŭ-jeech'	" "	N'-kwis'	My son.
60	N'-kway'-nus	" "	N'-kway'-nus	" "	N'-too-ä'-sum	" "
61	Nä-h·ise'	" "	Nä-h·ise'	" "	N'-di-ome'	" "
62	Noh·-whese'	" "	Noh·-whese'	" "	N'-kweese'	" "
63	Nain-whase'	" "	Nain-whase	" "	Nain-gwase'	" "
64	Sa-chä'	" "	Sa-chä'	" "	Sa-yä'-ze	" "
65	Sa-ken-ne	My grandson.	Sa-to⁻a'-bä	My granddaughter.	Sa-yä'-za	" "
66	Se-yä-zet'-tha-re	" "	Sa-le-zet'-tha-re	" "	Se-yä'-za	" "
67	Sa-chi'	My grandchild.	Sa-chi'	My grandchild.	Sa'-zoo ?	" "
68	Seet-she	" "	Seet-she	" "	Si-ou	" step-child
69					Kas-koo-sä	" son
70						
71					Pam'-ta	(Not rendered.)
72						
73					Nu-pwe'-ät-sin	" "
74						
75						
76						
77						
78						
79					Nu-a-ra-lu-a-ra	My nephew.
80	Eng-o-ta'	" "	Eng-o-ta'	" "	Noo-ä'-gä	" "

TABLE II.—*Continued.*

	54. My sister's son's wife. (Female speaking.)	Translation.	55. My sister's daughter. (Female speaking.)	Translation.	56. My sister's daughter's husband. (Female speaking.)	Translation.
1	Ka'-sä....................	My daugh.-in-law.	Ka-ah'-wuk	My daughter.	Oc-na'-hose....................	My son-in-law.
2	Ka-sä'-yuh	" "	Ka-hä'-wuk	" "	Unc-na-hose	" "
3	Ka-sä'-wä	" "	Ka-hä'-wä	" "	Ha-nane'-hose	" "
4	Ka-zä'-wä	" "	Ka-yä'-hä	" "	Ha-yale-hose'-hä	" "
5	Ka-zä'-wä	" "	Ka-yä'	" "	E-en-hŭ'-zä	" "
6	Ahk'-thäf	" "	Kä-yä'-no-nä	My child.	Yäk-te-he˜ah'-thä......	" "
7	Ka-sä'-wä	" "	Ka-yä'-ăh	My daughter.	De-an-hose'-hä	" "
8	Ya-na'-mäque	" "	E-ne'-ah..............	" "	Ha-na'-mäque	" "
9	Me-tä'-kosh	" "	Me-chuŋk'-she	" "	Me-tä'-kosh	" "
10	Me-tä'-koash....................	" "	Me-chounk'-she	" "	Me-tä'-koash..............	" "
11	Me-tä'-koash....................	" "	Me-chink'-she	" "	Me-tä'-koash	" "
12	Me-tä'-koash....................	" "	Me-chunk-she	" "	Me-tä'-koash	" "
13	Me-tä'-kosh	" "	Me-chunk'-se-lä..............	" "	Me-tä'-kosh	" "
14	Me-tä'-kosh	" "	Me-chunk'-she	" "	Me-tä'-kosh	" "
15	Me-tä'-koash....................	" "	Me-chŭnk'-she	" "	Me-tä'-koash	" "
16	Me-tä'-goash	" "	Me-chŭnk'-she	" "	Me-tä'-goash	" "
17	Me-tä'-koash....................	" "	Me-chink'-she	" "	Me-tä'-goash	" "
18	Ta-ne'-hä	" "	Win-no'-ga	" "	We-tuh'-da	" "
19	We-te'-na	" "	We-zhuŋ'-ga	" "	We-töŋ'-da	" "
20	Heen-toan'-ye	" "	Hee-yuŋ'-ga	" "	Wä-do'-hä	" "
21	Hin-to'-ne....................	" "	Hey-uŋ'-ga	" "	Wan-do'-hä	" "
22	Be-je'-na	" "	She-me'-she-gä	" "	Be-tö'-ja	" "
23	We-che'-ne	" "	We-shon'-ka	" "	We-ton'-chä	" "
24	E-nook-chek'-aw-chau	" "	E-chä'-h·kun	My step-child.	Wä-to'-ho..............	" "
25	Ko-too'-te	" "	Me-no'-hä-ka	My daughter.	Ko-too'-te	" "
26	Mä-too'-ga	" "	Mä-kä'	" "	Mä-too'-te	" "
27	Mä-nä'-ka	" "	Näk'-me-ă	" "	Boo'-sha	" "
28	Sup'-uk	My gd. daughter.	Suh-sŭh'-take	" "	Sai'-yup	" "
29	Sä'-pok	" "	Suh-soh'-take..............	" "	Săi'-yop	" "
30	Su-pok'-take....................	My daugh.-in-law.	Su-soh'-take..............	" "	Sä'-yup	" "
31	Un-hu-tis'-se	" "	Chu-chus'-wä..............	" "	Un hu-tis'-se	" "
32	E-tsän'-hĭ	" "	A-gwae-tsĭ'	My child.	E-huä-tsĭ'..............	" "
33	Ah-ge-tzau'-hĭ	" "	Ah-gwa'-tze	" "	A-ge-h'nä-tzĭ	" "
34	Scoo'-rus	" "	Pe'-row	" "	Koos-tow'-e-sŭ	" "
35	Sko'-dus	" "	Pe'-row	" "	Ko-stä'-wĭtch	" "
36	Sko-roo'-hoo	" "	Nä-te-nä'-o	" "	Koh·-tä-wa'-suh	" "
37	Nee-tim'.	" "	N'-do'-sa-mis-kwame' ...	My step-daughter.	Nä-häk'-sim	" "
38	Nee-stim'	" "	N'-do'-zha-mis-kwame' ...	" "	Nä-häk'-sim	" "
39	Nee-tim'	" "	N'-do'-zha-mis-kwem'....	" "	N'-hä'-ke-shim	" "
40	Nis'-sim	" "	Nin-do'-zhĭ-miss..............	My step-child.	Nĭ-nin'-gwän	" "
41	Ne'-sim	" "	Nin-do'-zhe-mis..............	" "	Ne-nin'-gwun	" "
42	Ne-sim'	" "	Nin-dä'-niss	My daughter.	Ne-niŋ-gwun'	" "
43	Ne-sim'	" "	N'-dä-niss	" "	Ne-niŋ-gwun'	" "
44	Ne-sim'	" "	N'-dä-niss'	" "	Ne-niŋ-gwun'	" "
45	N'-ah'-ga-neh-gweh'	" "	N'-dä'-niss	" "	N'-do'-sha-na-game'	" "
46	Lan-gwä'-lä	" "	Nin-dä'-nä..............	" "	Na-hun'-gä-nä..............	" "
47	Nä-hä-gä-na'-kwa No-ko-mä'	" "	Nin-dä'-nä..............	" "	Nä-hä-gä-na'-kwä	" "
48	Nä-hä-gä-ha'-kwä No-ko-mä'	" "	Nin-dä'-nä..............	" "	Nä hä-gä-na'-kwä	" "
49	Nä-hä-gä-na-kwä' No-ko-mä'	" "	N'-dä'-nä	" "	N'-dä-gwä-lä'	" "
50	Nä-hä-gä'-na-kwä' No-ko-mä'	" "	N'-dä'-nä	" "	N'-dä-gwä-lä'	" "
51	Nä-hä-gä'-ne-kwam	" "	Nä-tä'-nis	" "	Nä-nă-kwem'	" "
52	No-hä'-kun-e-uk-ye-yu'	" "	Ne-täne'	" "	Ne-nä'-kwun	" "
53	Nich-ä'	" "	Nä-tun'	" "	Nioh-ä'	" "
54	Na-them-mi-sä	" "	Nĭ-ton-nä-thä'	" "	Nä-kwam-nä'	" "
55	Ni-tha-mĭ-ah'....................	" "	Nĭ-tä-na-thä'	" "	Nin-hä-kä-na-mä'	" "
56	Nä-tim	" "	Nä-tä'-na	" "	Na-täs'	" "
57	Nee-mis'	" "	N'-to'-to-tun	My step-daughter.	Nis	" "
58	N·e-mis'	" "	Ne-to'-to-tun	" "	Nis	" "
59	N'-thus-wä'-skom	" "	N'-tŭs'	My daughter.	N'-tlŭ'-sŭk	" "
60	N'-sum'	" "	N'-sum'	" "	N'-tlŭ'-sŭk	" "
61	Nä-h·um'	" "	Ne-chune'	" "	Wä-seen'-no-kwä..............	" "
62	Nah·-hum'	" "	N'-dä-nuss'	" "	Nä-to-nä-mä'-kwa	" "
63	Nain-hum'	" "	Nain-dä'-ness	" "	Na-nä-toh'-na-makue'	" "
64	Sa-chä'	" "	Sa-yä'-dze	" "	Sa-chĭ'-a	" "
65	Sa-tsa'-ya	" "	Sa-to'-a	" "	Sa-tsa'-ya	" "
66	Set-thu'-yä	" "	Sa-le'-yă	" "	Set-shi'-ya	" "
67			Sa-ya-tse'	" "		
68	Se-ya-hŭt....................	" "	Si-ou	My step-child.	Sa-tan-i-o'	" "
69	Is-sä'-pin	" "	Kas-toon-che-alt In-kach'-	My dau. & ——	Is-natche'-hu	" "
70			[hä			
71			Pee'-see	My step-daughter.		
72						
73			Nu-pwe'-ät-sin	(Not rendered.)	Tä-tä'-wä-be	" "
74						
75						
76						
77						
78						
79			Nu-a-ra-lu-a-ra..............	My niece.		
80	Oo-koo-ä'-gä....................	" "	Noo-ä'-gä	" "	Ning-a-ou'-gwä	" "

TABLE II.—*Continued.*

	57. My sister's grandson. (Female speaking.)	Translation.	58. My sister's granddaughter. (Female speaking.)	Translation.	59. My sister's great grandson. (Female speaking.)	Translation.
1	Ha-yă'-da	My grandson.	Ka-yă'-da	My granddaughter.	Ha-yă'-da	My grandson.
2	Ha-yă'-dra	" "	Ka-yă'-dra	" "	Ha-yă'-dra	" "
3	Le-yă'-da	" "	Ka-yă'-da	" "	Ha-yă'-da	" "
4	Le-yă'-dla-ah	" "	Ka-yă'-dla-ah	" "	Le-yă'-dla-ah	" "
5	E-yă'-dla-ah	" "	Ka-yă'-dla-ah	" "	E-yă'-dla-ah	" "
6	Kä-yă'-rä	My grandchild.	Kä-yă'-rä	" "	Kä-yă'-rä	My grandchild.
7	Le-yă-tä-ra'-yă	My grandson.	Ka-yă-tä-ra'-yă	" "	Le-yă-tä-ra'-yă	My grandson.
8	Ha-tra'-ah	" "	Ya-tra'-ah	" "	Ha-tra'-ah	" "
9	Me-tä'-ko-zhă	My grandchild.	Me-tä'-ko-zhă	My grandchild.	Me-tä'-ko-zhă	My grandchild.
10	Me-tä'-ko-zhä	" "	Me-tä'-ko-zhä	" "	Me-tä'-ko-zhä	" "
11	Me-tä'-ko-zhä	" "	Me-tä'-ko-zhä	" "	Me-tä'-ko-zhä	" "
12	Me-tä'-ko-sha	" "	Me-tä'-ko-sha	" "	Me-tä'-ko-sha	" "
13	Me-tä'-ko-säk'-pok	" "	Me-tä'-ko-säk'-pok	" "	Me-tä'-ko-säk'-pok	" "
14	Me-tä'-ko-zhä	" "	Me-tä'-ko-zhä	" "	Me-tä'-ko-zhä	" "
15	Me-tä'-ko-zhä	" "	Me-tä'-ko-zhä	" "	Me-tä'-ko-zhä	" "
16	Me-tä'-ko-zä	" "	Me-tä'-ko-zä	" "	Me-tä'-ko-zä	" "
17	Me-tä'-ko-sä	" "	Me-tä'-ko-sä	" "	Me-tä'-ko-sä	" "
18	Toosh'-pä-hä	" "	Toosh'-pä-hä	" :	Toosh'-pä-hä	" "
19	We-tŭsh'-pä	" "	Wee-tŭsh'-pä	" "	Wee-tŭsh'-pä	" "
20	Heen-tä'-kwä	My grandson.	Heen-tä'-kwä-me	My granddaughter.	Heen-tä'-kwä	My grandson.
21	E-tä'-kwä	" "	E-tä'-kwä-me	" "	E-tä'-kwä	" "
22	Be-chose'-pä	My grandchild.	Be-chose'-pä	My grandchild.	Be-chose'-pä	My grandchild.
23	We-chose'-pä	" "	We-chose'-pä	" "	We-chose'-pä	" "
24	E-choonsh'-ka	My grandson.	E-choon-zhunk'	My little gd. daught.	E-choonsh'-ka-neke'	My little gd. son.
25	P-tä-we'-hä-kä	My grandchild.	P-tä-we'-hä-kä	My grandchild.	P-tä-we'-hä-kä	My grandchild.
26	Met-a-wä-pish'-sha	" "	Met-a-wä-pish'-sha	" "	Met-a-wä-pish'-sha	" "
27	Bus-bä'-pe-ta	" "	Bus-bä'-pe-ta	" "	Bus-bä'-pe-ta	" "
28	Sup'-uk-nŏk'-ne	My grandson.	Sup'-uk	My granddaughter.	Sup'-uk-nŏk'-ne	My grandson.
29	Sä'-pok-näk'-ne	" "	Sä'-pok	" "	Sä'-pok-nak'-ne	" "
30	Sup'-pok-näk'-nĭ	" "	Sup'-pok	" "	Sup'-pok-näk'-ni	" "
31	Um-os-sŭs'-wä	My grandchild.	Um-os-sŭs'-wä	My grandchild.	Um-os-sŭs'-wä	My grandchild.
32	Uŋ-gĭ-lĭ-sĭ'	" "	Un-gĭ-lĭ-sĭ'	" "	Un-gĭ-lĭ-sĭ'	" "
33	Aŋ-ge-lee'-se	" "	Aŋ-ge-lee'-se	" "	Aŋ-ge-lee'-se	" "
34	Lak-te'-gish	My grandson.	Lak-te'-gee	My granddaughter.	Te'-wut	My nephew.
35	Lak-te'-kis	My grandchild.	Lak-te'-kis	My grandchild.		
36	At-nuch'	" "	At-nuch'	" "	At-nuch'	My grandchild.
37	No-se-sem'	" "	No-se-sem'	" "	No-se-sem'	" "
38	No-se-sim'	" "	No-se-sim'	" "	No-se-sim'	" "
39	No-se-sem'	" "	No-se-sem'	" "	No-se-sem'	" "
40	No-zhĭ'-she	" "	No-zhĭ'-she	" "	No-zhĭ'-she	" "
41	No-she-shă	" "	No-she-shă	" "	No-she-shă	" "
42	No-she-shä'	" "	No-she-shä'	" "	No-she-shă'	" "
43	No-she-shä'	" "	No-she-shä'	" "	No-she-shä'	" "
44	No-she-shä'	" "	No-she-shä'	" "	No-she-shä'	" "
45	No-să-seh'	" "	No-să-seh'	" "	No-să-seh'	" "
46	No-sa-mä'	" "	No-sa'-mä	" "	No-sa-mä'	" "
47	No-sa'-mä	" "	No-sa'-mä	" "	No-sa'-mä	' "
48	No-sa'-mä	" "	No-sa'-mä	" "	No-sa'-mä	" "
49	No-sa-mä'	" "	No-sa-mä'	" "	No-sa'-mä	" "
50	No-sa-mä'	" "	No-sa-mä'	" "	No-sa-mä'	" "
51	No-she-sem'	" "	No-she-sem'	" "	No-she-sem'	" "
52	No-she-să'	" "	No-she-să'	" "	No-she-să'	" "
53	Nä-h·-kä'	" "	Nä-h·-kä'	" "	Nä-h·-kä'	" "
54	No-se-thä'-mä	" "	Na-se-thä'-mä	" "	No-se-thä'-mä'	" "
55	No-stha-thä'	" "	No-stha-thä'	" "	No-stha-thä'	" "
56	Nee'-sa	" "	Nee'-sa	" "	Nee'-sa	" "
57	Nee-so'-tan	" "	Nee-so'-tan	" "	Nee-so'-tan	" "
58	Nee-so'-tän	" "	Nee-so'-tän	" "	Nee-so'-tän	" "
59	Nŭ-jeech'	" "	Nŭ-jeech'	" "	Nŭ-jeech'	" "
60	N'-kway'-nus	" "	N'-kway'-nus	" "	N'-kway'-nus	" "
61	Nä-h·ise'	" "	Nä-h·ise'	" "	Nä-h·ise'	" "
62	Noh·-whese'	" "	Noh·-whese'	" "	Noh·-whese'	" "
63	Nain-no-whase'	" "	Nain-no-whase'	" "	Nain-no-whase'	" "
64	Sa-chä'	" "	Sa-chä'	" "	Sa-chä'	" "
65	Sa-ken'-ne	My grandson.	Sa-to͞ä'-bă	My granddaughter.	Sa-ken-ne'	My grandson.
66	Se-yă-zet'-tha-ra	" "	Sa-le-zet'-tha-re	" "	Sa-yă-zet-tha-re	" "
67	Sa-chi'	My grandchild.	Sa-chi'	My grandchild.	Sa-chi'	My grandchild.
68	Seet-shai	" "	Seet-shai	" "	Seet-shai	" "
69						
70						
71						
72						
73	Pät'-sin	(Not rendered.)	Pät-sin	(Not rendered.)		
74						
75						
76						
77						
78						
79						
80	Eng'-o-tă	My grandchild.	Eng'-o-tă	My grandchild.	Eng'-o-tă	" "

TABLE II.—*Continued.*

	60. My sister's great grand-daughter. (Female speaking.)	Translation.	61. My father's brother.	Translation.	62. My father's brother's wife.	Translation.
1	Ka-yä′-da	My granddaughter.	Hä′-nih	My father.	Oc-no′-ese	My step-mother.
2	Ka-yä′-dra	" "	Hä′-nih	" "	Kno′-ese	My mother.
3	Ka-yä′-da	" "	Kuh-ne-hä′	" "	Uŋ-ge-noh′	My step-mother.
4	Ka-yä′-dla-ah	" "	Lä′-ga-nih	" "	Ahk-nole′-hä	My mother.
5	Ka-yä′-dla-ah	" "	Lä-ga-ne′-hä	" "	Ah-ga-nese′-tä	" "
6	Kä-yä′-rä	My grandchild.	Ahk-re′-ah	" "	Ack-we′-rä	My step-mother.
7	Ka-yä-tä-ra′-yä	My granddaughter.	Lä-ga-ne′-hä	" "		
8	Ka-tra′-ah	" "	Hi-ese′-hä	" "	Ah-rä′-hoc	My aunt.
9	Me-tä′-ko-zhä	My grandchild.	At-tay′	" "	E-nah′	My mother.
10	Me-tä′-ko-zhä	" "	Ah-ta′	" "	E′-nah	" "
11	Me-tä′-ko-zhä	" "	Ah-ta′	" "	E-nä′	" "
12	Me-tä′-ko-sha	" "	Ah-ta′	" "	Een′-nä	" "
13	Me-tä′-ko-säk′-pok	" "	Ah-ta′	" "	E-nah′	" "
14	Me-tä′-ko-zhä	" "	Ah-ta′	" "	E′-nah	" "
15	Me-tä′-ko-zhä	" "	Ah-ta′	" "	E′-nah	" "
16	Me-tä′-ko-zä	" "	Ah-ta′	" "	E′-nah	" "
17	Me-tä′-ko-sä	" "	Ah-da′	" "	E′-nah	" "
18	Toosh′-pä-hä	" "	Tä-de′-hä	" "	Nä′-hä	" "
19	Wee-tŭsh′-pä	" "	In-dä′-de	" "	E-nä′-hä	" "
20	Heen-tä′-kwä-me	My granddaughter.	Heen′-kä	" "	Heen′-nah	" "
21	E-tä′-kwä-me	" "	Hin′-kä	" "	He′-nah	" "
22	Be-chose′-pä	My grandchild.	E-dä′-je	" "	E′-naw	" "
23	We-chose′-pä	" "	In-tä′-che	" "	In-nä′	" "
24	E-chooŋ-zhunk′-neke	My little gd. daught.	E-un′-chä	" "	E-oo-ne-neke′	My step-mother.
25	P-tä-we′-hä-kä	My grandchild.	Tä-tay′	" "	Nä-a′	My mother.
26	Met-a-wä-pish′-sha	" "	Tä-ta′	" "	Ik-ka′	" "
27	Bus-bä′-pe-ta	" "	Ah-ha′	" "	E′-ke-ä	" "
28	Sup′-uk	My granddaughter.	A′-kĭ	" "	Ush′-kĭ	" "
29	Sä′-pok	" "	A′-kĭ	" "	Ush′-kĭ	" "
30	Sup′-pok	" "	Aŋg′-ki	" "	Sush-so′-kĭ	My little mother.
31	Um-os-sŭs′-wä	My grandchild.	Chul-kŭ-che′	My little father.	Chuch-kŭ-che′	" "
32	Uŋ-gĭ-lĭ-sĭ	" "	E-dau-dä′	My father.	A-gwä-tĭ-nä′-I	My step-mother.
33	Aŋ-ge-lee′-se	" "	Ah-ge-do′-dä	" "	Tä-le-na-ah-gi′-tze	" "
34	Te′-wut	My niece.	Ah-te′-is	" "	Ah-te′-rä	" "
35			A-te′-ase	" "	A-te′-rä	" "
36	At-nuch	My grandchild.	Ah-te′-ä	" "	At-nä′	" "
37	No-se-sem′	" "	No′-ko-mis	My step-father.	N′-do′-sis	" "
38	No-se-sim′	" "	No′-ko-mish	" "	N′-do′-sis	" "
39	No-se-sem′	" "	No′-ko-mis	" "	N′-do′-zis	" "
40	No-shĭ′-she	" "	Nĭ-nĭ-sho′-mĕ	" "	Nĭ-no′-shĕ	" "
41	No-she′-shä	" "	Ne-me-sho′-mä	" "	Ne-no′-shä	" "
42	No-she-shä′	" "	Ne-mis′-sho-mä	" "	Ne-no-shä′	" "
43	No-she-shä′	" "	Ne-mish-sho′-mä	" "	Ne-no′-shä	" "
44	No-she-shä′	" "	N′-mis-sho′-mä	" "	No-shä′	" "
45	No-sä-seh′	" "	Noke-mä′	" "	No-sheh′	" "
46	No-sa-mä′	" "	No-sä′	My father.	N′-sa′-gwe-sä′	My aunt.
47	No-sa′-mä	" "	No-sä′	" "	Ne-zä-gös-sä′	" "
48	No-sa′-mä	" "	No-sä′	" "	Ne-zä-gös-sä′	" "
49	Nö-sa-mä′	" "	No-sä′	" "	Ne-sä′-gwis-sä′	" "
50	No-sa-mä′	" "	No-sä′	" "	Ne-sä′-gwis-sä′	" "
51	No-she-sem′	" "	Nöss	" "	Nak-ye′-hä	" "
52	No-she-sä′	" "	Noh′-neh	" "	Ne-ke⁻ä′	" "
53	Nä-h·-kä′	" "	Nä-o′-a	" "	Nä′-ko	" "
54	Na-se-thä′-mä	" "	No-thä′	" "	Nĭ-ke⁻ä′	" "
55	No-stha-thä′	" "	No-thä′	" "	Na-ke⁻ah′	" "
56	Nee′-sa	" "	Ne-tha′-na	" "	Na′-nä	My mother.
57	Nee-so-tan	" "	Ne-to′-to-mä	My step-father.	Ne-to′-tox-is	My step-mother.
58	Nee-so′-tän	" "	Ne-to′-to-mä	" "	Ne-to′-toax-is	" "
59	Nŭ-jeech′	" "	N′-tus′	My little father.	Nŭ-gu-mich′	My grandmother.
60	N′-kway′-nus	" "	Nee-chä′-look	My step-father.	N′-kee′-sees	My little mother.
61	Nä-h·ise′	" "	Nä-jä′-ku′	" "	No-muths′	My step-mother.
62	Noh·-whese′	" "	Noh′-tut	My little father.	N′-gä-hä′-tnt	My little mother.
63	Nain-no-whase′	" "	Na-no′-whus	" "	Na-no′-ho-mus	" "
64	Sa-chä′	" "	Eh-tä′-ah	My step-father.	San′-ga	My step-mother.
65	Sa-to⁻a′-bä	My granddaughter.	Sa-tä′	My father.	A′-na	My mother
66	Sa-le-zet′-tha-re	" "	See-the′-ne	My step-father.	Set′-so	My aunt.
67	Sa-chi′	My grandchild.	Te-angh′	My father.		
68	Seet-shai	" "	Seet-ye	My father-in-law.	Sä-thŭ-i	My broth′r-in-law.
69			Is-se-mält	My uncle?	In-kach′-ha	My aunt?
70						
71			Na-magh′-has	My step-parent.	Na-magh′-has	My step-parent.
72			Kach′-ha	My step-father.		
73			Sin-ät′-sin	(Not rendered.)	E-ät-sin	(Not rendered.)
74			Nish-te′-ä	My father.	Ni′-ya	My mother.
75			Na-vi-tu-no	My uncle.	No-ves-i-e	
76						
77			Ze-pä′-bä	(Not rendered.)	Leg′-yi	(Not rendered.)
78						
79			A′-ka-ga	My uncle.		
80	Eng′-o-tä	" "	Uk′-kä	" "	U-kŭ′-ung-ä	My aunt.

40

TABLE II.—Continued.

	63. My father's brother's son—older than myself. (Male speaking.)	Translation.	64. My father's brother's son—older than myself. (Female speaking.)	Translation.	65. My father's brother's son—younger than myself. (Male speaking.)	Translation.
1	Hä'-je	My elder brother.	Hä' je	My elder brother.	Ha'-gä	My younger bro.
2	Kuh-je'-ah	" " "	Kuh-je'-ah	" " "	Ha-gä'-ah	" " "
3	Kuh-je'-ah	" " "	Kuh-je'-ah	" " "	Ha'-gä	" " "
4	Läk-je'-hä	" " "	Läk-je'-hä	" " "	Le-gä'-ah	" " "
5	Läk-je'-hä	" " "	Läk-je'-hä	" " "	E'-gä-hä	" " "
6	Ahk'-rä-je	" " "	Ahk-rä'-je	" " "	Kä'-gä	" " "
7	Lok-je'-hä	" " "	Lok-je'-hä	" " "	Le-gä'-ah	" " "
8	Ha-ye'-uh	" " "	Te-mdo'	" " "	Ha-ye-ä'-hä	" " "
9	Chiṇ-yay'	" " "	Chim'-a-do	" " "	Me-suṇ'-kä	" " "
10	Che-a'	" " "	Tib'-a-do	" " "	Me-soh'-kä	" " "
11	Che'-a	" " "	Tib'-a-do	" " "	Me-sunk'-ä	" " "
12	Che'-a	" " "	Tib-a-lo'	" " "	Me-sun'-kä	" " "
13	Che'-a	" " "	Tib-a-lo'	" " "	Me-soh'	" " "
14	Me-che'-a	" " "	Tib'-a-lo	" " "	Me-sunk'-ä-lä	" " "
15	Che'-a	" " "	Tib'-a-lo	" " "	Me-soh-'-kä-lä	" " "
16	Che-a'	" " "	Tib'-a-lo	" " "	Me-son'-kä-lä	" " "
17	Me-chin'	" " "	Me-tim'-do	" " "	Me-soh'	" " "
18	Zhin-dä'-hä	" " "	Ton-no'-hä	" " "	Kä-ga'	" " "
19	Wee-zhe'-thä	" " "	Wee-te'-noo	" " "	Wee-söṇ'-gä	" " "
20	He-yen'-nä	" " "	He-yen'-nä	" " "	Heen-thuṇ'-ga	" " "
21	He-ye'-nä	" " "	Hee-ye'-nä	" " "	Heen-thun'-ga	" " "
22	Be-zhe'-yeh	" " "	Be-che'-do	" " "	Be-suṇ'-gä	" " "
23	We-she'-lä	" " "	We-chin'-to	" " "	We-son'-kä	" " "
24	E-ne'	" " "	E-che'-to	" " "	E-sünk'	" " "
25	Moo'-kä	" " "	Me-sho'-kä	" " "	Me-sho'-kä	" " "
26	Mee-ä-kä'	" " "	Má-tä-roo'	" " "	Mat-so'-gä	" " "
27	Meek'-a	" " "	Bä-zä'-na	" " "	Bä-chü'-ka	" " "
28	Um-un'-nī	" " "	A-näk'-fī	" " "	Suh-näk'-fish	" " "
29	Et-e-bä'-pī-shī-lī	My brother. (The one I sucked with.)	A-näk'-fī	" " "	Et-e-bä'-pī-shī-lī	My brother.
30	Et-e-bä'-pī-shī-lī	My brother.	A-näk'-fī	" " "	Et-e-bä'-pī-shī-lī	" "
31	Un-it-te-chä-ke'-to	My other brother.	Chu-chihl'-wä	" " "	Um-it-te-chä-ke'-to	My other brother.
32	Tsän-sdä-dä-nuṇ'-tlī	My brother.	Uṇ-gī-nī-lī	" " "	Uṇ-gī-nuṇ'-tlī	My younger bro.
33	De-nä-da-nuh'-tsī	Thou and I, brothers.	De-nä-dä-uuh'-tsī	Thou and brothers.	De-nä-dä-uuh'-tsī	Thou and I, bros.
34	E-dä'-deh	My brother.	E-rats-teh	My brother.	E-dä'-deh	My brother.
35	A-dä'-de	" "	Ta-lä'-lik-tis	My brother (oldest)	A-dä'-de	" "
36	Che-nä-tun'	My brother (oldest).	A-tnas'	My brother.	Kä-wit'-ta	" "
37	Neese-tase'	My elder brother.	Neese-tase'	My elder brother.	Ne-seme'	My younger bro.
38	Neese-tase'	" " "	Neese-tase'	" " "	Ne-sha-mish'	" " "
39	Neesh-tase'	" " "	Neesh-tase'	" " "	Nī-shī'-mǒ	" " "
40	Nis-sä'-yĕ	" " "	Nis-sä'-yĕ	" " "	Ne-kä'-na	My step-brother.
41	Ne-kä'-na	My step-brother.	Nin-dä-wa'-mä	My step-brother.	Ne-kä'-na	" " "
42	Ne-kä'-na	" " "	Nī-sä-y'ä'	My elder brother.	Ne-kä-nis'	" " "
43	Ne-kä-nis'	" " "	Nis-si'-yä	" " "	Ne-kä'-na	" " "
44	Ne-kä'-nä	" " "	N'-sä'-yä	" " "	Ne-kä'-na	" " "
45	Ne-kä'-na	" " "	N'-seh-sä'	" " "	Se-me-mä'	My younger bro.
46	Ne-sä-sä'	My elder brother.	Ne-sä-sä'	" " "	Ne-she'-mä	" " "
47	Ne-san'-zä	" " "	Ne-san'-zä	" " "	Ne-she'-mä	" " "
48	Ne-san'-zä	" " "	Ne-san'-zä	" " "	Ne-she-mä'	" " "
49	Ne-sä-zä'	" " "	Ne-sä-zä'-	" " "	Ne-she-mä'	" " "
50	Ne-sä-zä'	" " "	Ne-sä-zä'	" " "	Nä-se'-mä	" " "
51	Nä-sa'-mä	" " "	Nä-sa'-mä	" " "	Nä-sa'	" " "
52	Nä-nä'	" " "	Nä-nä'	" " "	Nä-sim-ä'	" " "
53	Nä-ne'-ä	" " "	Nä-ne'-ä	" " "	Ni-to-ta-mä'	My brother.
54	Ni-to-ta-mä'	My brother.	Ni-to-ta-mä'	My brother.	N'-cha-ne-nä'	
55	N'-cha-ne-mä'	" "	Nos-ke'-mä	" "	Ta'-yä	My younger bro.
56	Nä'-thä-hä	My elder brother.	Nä'-thä-hä	My elder brother	Nis-kun'-ä	" " "
57	Neese-sä'	" " "	Neese-sä'	" " "	Nis-kun'	" " "
58	Nis'-sä	" " "	Nis'-sä	" " "	N'-chi-gu'-num	" " "
59	N'-sees'	" " "	N'-sees'	" " "	N'-see-wes or N'-tul-nŭm'	My brother.
60	N'-see'-wees or N'-tul-nŭm'	My brother.	N'-tul-nŭm' or Neet-see-[kes]	My brother.	N'-dä-kwus'	My step-brother.
61	N'-dä-kwus'	My step-brother.	N'-donk'	My step-brother.	Nee-mä'-tus	
62	Nee-mä'-tus		N'-dun-oo-yome'		Nain-hise'-sa-mus	My younger bro.
63	Nain-n'-hans	My elder brother.	Nain-n'-hans	My elder brother.	A-cha'-a	" " "
64	Kŭn'-dig-eh	" " "	Kŭn'-dig-eh	" " "	Sŭn-no'-gä-yä'-za	" " "
65	Sun-no'-gä	" " "	Sŭn-no'-gä	" " "	Set-chil'-e-ä-ze	" " "
66	Sä-nä'-gä	" " "	Su-nä'-gä	" " "	Sa'-chä	" " "
67	Soon'-da-ga	" " "	Soon'-da-ga	" " "	Sa-chä	" " "
68	Soon-da	" " "	Soon-da	" " "	Is-se-lacht'	My brother.
69	Is-sin-kwu-seehw'. ᵇ Is-[se-lacht]	One like my brother.	Is-sin-kwu-seehw'	One like my brother.		
70		[ᵇ My brother.				
71	Es-hup', or Ne-pah'	My younger brother.			Ko-ko-wä-malt	" " "
72	Ko-ko-wä-malt	My brother.	Ko-ko-wä-malt	My brother.		
73					Tŭm-mŭ'	My younger bro.
74					No-vi-te-u	" " "
75	No-vi-pa-ra	My elder brother	No-vi-pa-ra	My elder brother		
76					Cu-hu-bä	" " "
77	Gi'-ä	" " "	Ri-cu'-i	" " "		
78					Ig-dlo-a	My cousin.
79	Ig-dlo-ra	My cousin.	Ig-llo-ra	My cousin.	Il-lŭng'-ä	" "
80	Il-lung'-ä	" "	Il-lo'-ä	" "		

TABLE II.—*Continued.*

	66. My father's brother's son—younger than myself. (Female speaking.)	Translation.	67. My father's brother's son's wife. (Male speaking.)	Translation.	68. My father's brother's son's wife. (Female speaking.)	Translation.
1	Ha'-gă	My younger brother.	Ah-ge-ah'-ne-ah	My sister-in-law.	Ah-ge⌒äh'-ne⌒o	My sister-in-law.
2	Ha-gă'-ah	" " "	Un-ge-ah'-ne-a	" "	Uh-ge-ah'-ne-o	" "
3	Ha'-gă	" " "	Ah-ge-ah'-yeh	" "	Ah-ge-ah'-ne-o	" "
4	Le-gä'-ah	" " "	Un-ge⌒ah'-le⌒a	" "	Un-ge-ah'-le-a	" "
5	E'-gä-ha	" " "	Un-gä-le-ya'-ah	" "	Un-gä-le-a'-ah	" "
6	Kä'-gä.	" " "	Ack-gä'-re-ah	" "	Ack-gä'-re-ah	" "
7	Le-gä'-ah	" " "	Ah-go-hä'-kwä	" "	Ah-go-hä'-kwä	" "
8	Ha-ye-a'-hä	" " "	O-in-dä'-wait	" "	O-in-dä'-wait	" "
9	Me-suŋ'-kä	" " "	Häŋ-kä'	" "	E-chä'-paŋ	" "
10	Me-soh'-kä	" " "	Hä-kä'	" "	E-shä'-pä	" "
11	Me-sunk'-ä	" " "	Wä'-kä	" "	E-shä'-pä	" "
12	Me-sun'-ka	" " "	Hä'-kä	" "	E-shä'-pä	" "
13	Me-soh'-kä-lä.	" " "	Huŋ-kä'	" "	S'-cha'-pä	" "
14	Me-sunk'-ä-lä.	" " "	Huŋ-kä'	" "	S'-cha'-pä	" "
15	Me-soh'-'kä-lä	" " "	Hä'-kä	" "	E-sä'-pä	" "
16	Me-son'-kä-lä	" " "	Hä'-kä	" "	E-sä'-pä	" "
17	Me-soh'	" " "	Mä-hä'-hä	" "	Me-she'-cha-pas	" "
18	Kä-ga'.	" " "	We-hun'-gä	" "	She-kä'	" "
19	Wee-söŋ-gä	" " "	We-huŋ'-gä	" "	We-she'-kä	" "
20	E-chun'-cha	" " "	Huŋ'-gä	" "	He she'-kä	" "
21	E-chun'-cha	" " "	Häŋ'-gä	" "	Hin-she'-kä	" "
22	Be-suŋ'-gä	" " "	Be-hä'-gä	" "	Be-she'-kä	" "
23	We-son'-kä	" " "	We-hun'-kä	" "	We-she'-kä	" "
24	E-sŭnk'	" " "	E-yuŋ'-ga	" "	E-she'-ga	" "
25	Me-sho'-kä	" " "	Moo'-ha	" "	Koo-too'-min-ik	" "
26	Mat-so'-gä	" " "	Boo'-ä-kä	" "	Mat-too'	" "
27	Bä-chŭ'-ka	" " "	Moo'-ä-ka	" "	Bos-me'-ä-kun-is-ta	" "
28	A-näk'-fĭ	" " "	Suh-hai'-yă	" "	Suh-hai'-yă	" "
29	A-näk'-fĭ	" " "	Sä-hĭ'-yä	" "	Sä-hĭ'-yä	" "
30	A-näk'-fĭ	" " "	Sä-hi'-yä	" "	Sä-hi'-yä	" "
31	Chu-chihl'-wä	" " "	Chu-hu'-cho-wä	" "	Um-e-hi'-wä	" "
32	Uŋ-gĭ-dau'	" " "	Au-sdä-duŋ'-hĭ	" "	Au-sdä-lĭ-gĭ	" "
33	Aŋ'-ke-do	" " "	Ah-ke-tso'-hĭ	" "	E-nä-duh'-hĭ	" "
34	E-rats'-teh	My brother.	Tä-tee'-luk-tuk-ŭ	My wife.	Scoo'-rus	" "
35	Kä'-we-ta	" "	Sko'-dus	My sister-in-law.	Sko'-dus	" "
36	Kä-wit'-ta	" "	Nä-te'-nä-tä-koo	My wife.	Sko-roo'-hoo	" "
37	Ne-seme'	My younger brother.	Nee-tim'	My sister-in-law.	N'-jä'-koase	" "
38	Ne-sha-mish'	" " "	Nee-tim'	" "	N'-jä'-koase	" "
39	Ne-she-mish'	" " "	Nee-tim'	" "	N'-dä'-koase	" "
40	Nĭ-shĭ'-mĕ	" " "	Nĭ'-nim	" "	Nin-dän'-gwĕ	" "
41	Nin-dä-wa'-mä	My step-brother.	Ne'-nim	" "	Nin-don'-gwa	" "
42	Ne-she'-mä	My younger brother.	Ne-nim'	" "	Nin-dän-gwa'	" "
43	Ne-she-mä'	" " "	Ne-nim'	" "	N'-daŋ-gwa'	" "
44	N'-she'-mä	" " "	Ne-nim'	" "	N'-daŋ-gwa'	" "
45	Ne-she-mä'	" " "	Ne-nim'	" "	N'-dän-gwa'	" "
46	Se-me-mä'	" " "	Ne-lim-wä'	" "	N'-jän-gwa'	" "
47	Ne-she'-mä	" " "	Ne-lim-wä'	" "	Nin-jä-gwä'	" "
48	Ne-she'-mä	" " "	Ne-lim-wä'	" "	Nin-jä-gwä'	" "
49	Ne-she-mä'	" " "	Ne-le-mwä'	" "	Nin-jä-kwä'	" "
50	Ne-she-mä'	" " "	Ne-le-mwä'	" "	Nä-dä'-kwä	" "
51	Nä-se'-mä	" " "	Ne-nim'-wä	" "	Nä-dä'-kwä	" "
52	Nä-sa'	" " "	Na-nim'	" "	Wä-a'-che-uk	" "
53	Nä-sim-ä'	" " "	Nee'-tum	" "	Nee-tuu'	" "
54	Ni-to-ta-mä'	My brother.	Ni-nem-wä'	" "	Wa-se-nä-mä-kä	" "
55	Nös-ke-mä'	" "	Nĭ-lim'-wä'	" "	N'-tä-kwä'	" "
56	Ta'-yä	My younger brother.	Ne-tim'	" "	Ne-ta'-be	" "
57	Nis-kun'-ä	" " "	N'-do-to'-ke-man	" "	Nee-mis'	" "
58	Nis-kun'	" " "	Ne-to'-to-ke-man	" "	Nee-mis'	" "
59	N'-chi'-gu-num	" " "	Ne-lu-mŭs'	" "	Ne-mäk-tem'	" "
60	N'-see'-mees or N'-tul-	My brother.	Nee'-lu-mŭs	" "	Ne'-takw'	" "
61	N'-donk' ...... [num'	My step-brother.	Nee-num'	" "	N'-dä-oh-k'	" "
62	N'-dun-oo-yome'	" "	Nee-lum'	" "	Nee-tä'-wis	" "
63	Naine-hise'-sa-mus	My younger brother.	Na-nee-lim'	" "	Nain-ne-la'-kon	" "
64	A-cha'-a	" " "	Sa'-gy	" "	Sa'-gy	" "
65	Sŭn-no'-gä-yä'-ze	" " "	Sa-teŋ'-a bä-che-la	" "	Sa'-ga	" "
66	Set-chil'-e-ä-za	" " "	Set'-so	" "	Sa'-o-ga	" "
67	Sa'-chä	" " "				
68	Sa-chä	" " "	See-chy-oo	My younger sister.	See-cha-the	My younger sister.
69	Is-sin-kwu-seehw'	My brother.	Is-sas-tăm	My sister-in-law.		
70						
71			En-pe-noke'	" "		
72	Ko-ko-wä-malt	" "				
73						
74			Pe'-a	(Not rendered.)		
75	No-vi-te-u	My younger brother.				
76						
77	P-cu-i-hi-bä	" " "				
78						
79	Ig-dlo-ra	My cousin.				
80	Il-lo'-ä	" "	I-e'-gä	My sister-in-law.	Oo-koo-ä'-gä	My sister-in-law.

TABLE II.—*Continued.*

	69. My father's brother's daughter—older than myself. (Male speaking.)	Translation.	70. My father's brother's daughter—older than myself. (Female speaking.)	Translation.	71. My father's brother's daughter—younger than myself. (Male speaking.)	Translation.
1	Ah'-je......	My elder sister.	Ah'-je......	My elder sister.	Kă'-gă......	My younger sister.
2	Uh-je'-ah	" " "	Uh-je'-ah	" " "	Ka-gä'-ah	" " "
3	Uh-je'-ah	" " "	Uh-je'-ah	" " "	Ka'-gă	" " "
4	Ahk-je'-hä	" " "	Ahk-je'-hä	" " "	Ka-gä'-ah	" " "
5	Ahk-je'-hä	" " "	Ahk-je'-hä	" " "	Ka-gä'-hä	" " "
6	Ahk'-je	" " "	Ahk'-je	" " "	Kä'-gä	" " "
7	Ak-je'yä	" " "	Ak-je'-yă	" " "	Ka-gä-ah'	" " "
8	A-ye'-uh	" " "	A-ye'-uh	" " "	Ya-ye'-hä	" " "
9	Tän-kay'	" " "	Me-chuŋ'	" " "	Me-tank'-she	" " "
10	Ton-ka'	" " "	Chu-ih'	" " "	Me-tänk'-she	" " "
11	Tank'-she	" " "	Me-tank-a-do	" " "	Me-tank'-she	" " "
12	Tank'-she	" " "	Tan'-ka	" " "	Me-tänk'-she	" " "
13	Tä-ka'	" " "	Chu-wa'	" " "	Me-tunk'-she	" " "
14	Tonk-a'	" " "	Chu-a'	" " "	Me-tunk'-she	" " "
15	Ton'-ka	" " "	Chu-ih'	" " "	Me-tank'-she	" " "
16	Ton-ka'	" " "	Chu-wa'	" " "	Me-tonk'-she	" " "
17	Me-ton'-ga	" " "	Me-chun'	" " "	Me-tänk'-she	" " "
18	Ton-ga'-hä	" " "	Zhon-da'-hä	" " "	We-ha'	" " "
19	We-töŋ'-ga	" " "	Wee-zŏn'-thä	" " "	We-töŋ'-ga	" " "
20	He-yu'-nä	" " "	Heen-taŋ'-ga	" " "	Heen-tan'-ya	" " "
21	Wau-he'-cha	" " "	Heen-täng'-a	" " "	Heen-tän'-gă	" " "
22	Be-tuŋ'-ga	" " "	Be-sho'-wa	" " "	Be-tuŋ'-gă-zhiŋ'-gă	" " "
23	We-tun'-ka	" " "	We-sho'-ka	" " "	We-tun'-ka	" " "
24	E-noo'	" " "	E-noo'	" " "	Wych-kă'	" " "
25	P-tä'-me-ha	" " "	Me-no'-ka	" " "	P-tä-me'-ha	" " "
26	Mat-tä-we'-ă	" " "	Mä-rü'	" " "	Mä-tä-ka'-zhä	" " "
27	Bä-zä'-kät	" " "	Bus-we'-nä	" " "	Bä-sä'-chete	" " "
28	An'-take	" " "	Um-un'-nI	" " "	An'-take	" " "
29	An'-take	" " "	Et-e-bä'-pI-shI-lI	My sister.	An'-take	" " "
30	An'-take	" " "	Et-e-bä'-pI-shI-lI	" "	An'-take	" " "
31	Chu-wun'-wä	" " "	Chu-hlä'-hä	My elder sister.	Chu-wun'-wä	" " "
32	Uŋ-gI-dau'	" " "	Uŋ-gI-luŋ'-I	" " "	Uŋ-gI-dau'	" " "
33	Aŋ'-ke-doh	" " "	Aŋ-ge-lä'-ih	" " "	Aŋ'-ke-doh	" " "
34	E-tä'-heh	My sister.	E-dä'-deh	My sister.	E-tä'-heh	My sister.
35	A-tä'-he	" "	A-tä'-he	" "	A-tä'-ke	" "
36	Ah-te'-ta	" "	Ah-te'-ta	" "	Ah-te'-ta	" "
37	Ne-mis'	My elder sister.	Ne-mis'	My elder sister.	Ne-se'-mis	My younger sister.
38	Ne-mish'	" " "	Ne-mish'	" " "	Ne-sha-mish'	" " "
39	Ne-mish'	" " "	Ne-mish'	" " "	Ne-she-mish'	" " "
40	NI-mis'-sĕ	" " "	NI-mis'-sĕ	" " "	NI-shI'-mĕ	" " "
41	Nin-dä-wa'-mä	My step-sister.	Ne-de-ge'-ko	My step-sister.	Nin-dä-wa'-mä	My step-sister.
42	Nin-dä-wa'-mä	" " "	Ne-mis-sä'	My elder sister.	N'-dä-wa'-mä	" " "
43	N'-do-wa-mă'	" " "	Ne-mis-sä'	" " "	N'-do-wa-mä'	" " "
44	N'-dä-wa-nä'	" " "	N'-dä-kwam'	My step-sister.	N'-dä-wa-mä'	" " "
45	N'-dä-wä'-mă	" " "	N'-dä-kwam'	" " "	N'-dä-wä'-mă	" " "
46	Ne-mis-sä'	My elder sister.	Ne-mis-sä'	My elder sister.	Ne-go-se-mä'	My younger sister.
47	Ne-mis-sä'	" " "	Ne-mis-sä'	" " "	Ne-she'-mä	" " "
48	Ne-mis-sä'	" " "	Ne-mis-sä'	" " "	Ne-she'-mä	" " "
49	Ne-me-sä'	" " "	Ne-me-sä'	" " "	Ne-she-mä'	" " "
50	Ne-me-sä'	" " "	Ne-me-sä'	" " "	Ne-she-mä'	" " "
51	Nä-mis'-sä	" " "	Nä-mis'-sä	" " "	Nä-se'-mä	" " "
52	Ne-ma'	" " "	Ne-ma'	" " "	Nä-sa'	" " "
53	Nä-ma'	" " "	Nä-ma'	" " "	Nä-sim-ă'	" " "
54	Ni-tä-kwä'-mä	" " "	Ni-tä-kwä'-mä	" " "	Ni-tä-kwä'-mä	" " "
55	Net-kwa'-mä	My sister.	N'-cha-ne-nä'	My sister.	Net-kwa'-mä	My sister.
56	Na'-be	My elder sister.	Na'-be	My elder sister.	Na-be-ă'	My younger sister.
57	Nee-mis'-tä	" " "	Nee-mis'-tä	" " "	Ne-sis'-sä	" " "
58	Ne-his'-tä	" " "	Ne-his'-tä	" " "	Ne-sis'-sä	" " "
59	Nu-mees'	" " "	Nu-mees'	" " "	N'-kwa-jeech'	" " "
60	N'-pee-hen-mŭm	My sister.	N'-pee-hen-mŭm	My sister.	N'-pee-hen-mum	My sister.
61	N'-dä-kwus-oh'-kwä-oh	My step-sister.	N'-ko-kwä'	My step-sister.	N'-dä-kwus-h'-kwä-oh	My step-sister.
62	N'-do-kwä-yome'	" " "	Neet-koh'-kw'	" " "	N'-do-kwä-yome'	" " "
63	Nain-na-wase'	My elder sister.	Nain-na-wase'	My elder sister.	Nain-hise-sa-mus'	My younger sister.
64	Sä'-da	" " "	Sä'-da	" " "	A-dä'-zy	" " "
65	Sa-da'-za	" " "	Sa-da'-za	" " "	Sa-da'-za-yä'-za	" " "
66	Set-dez'-a-ä-ze	" " "	Set-dez'-a-ä-ze	" " "	Sä'-re	" " "
67	Sa'-che	" " "	Sa'-che	" " "	Sa-chith'	" " "
68	Sa-che	" " "	Sa-che	" " "	See-chy-o	" " "
69	Is-soo-se-măm	My sister.	In-chit-sha	" " "		
70						
71	In'-chats. ᵇ En'-naks	ᵇ My step-sister.				
72	Al-kat-litsh-kilt	My sister.	Al-kat-litsh-kilt	My sister.	Al-kat-litch-kilt	My sister.
73						
74					Sä-gwe'-sä	My younger sister.
75	No-vi-pa-re	My elder sister.	No-vi-pa-re	My elder sister	No-vi-pa-re ?	My younger sister.
76						
77	Gu-i'-a	" " "			Cu-hu'-ba	" " "
78						
79						
80	Il-lŭng'-ä	My cousin.	Il-lo'-ä	My cousin.	Il-lŭng'-ä	My cousin.

TABLE II.—*Continued.*

	72. My father's brother's daughter—younger than myself. (Female speaking.)	Translation.	73. My father's brother's daughter's husband. (Male speaking.)	Translation.	74. My father's brother's daughter's husband. (Female speaking.)	Translation.
1	Ka′-gă............	My younger sister.	Ah-ge⌒ăh′-ne⌒o	My brother-in-law.	Ha-yă′-o............	My brother-in-law.
2	Ka-gă′-ah	" " "	Uh-ge-ah′-ne-a	" "	Ha-yă′-ho............	" "
3	Ka′-gă	" " "	Ah-ge-ah′-ne-o	" "	Ah-ge-ah′-de-o	" "
4	Ka-gă′-ah	" " "	Un-ge⌒ah′-de⌒o	" "	Un-ge⌒ah′-le⌒o............	" "
5	Kä′-gä	" " "	Un-gä-de⌒o′-hä	" "	Un-gä-le⌒ya′-ah............	" "
6	Kä′-gä	" " "	Ack-gow′-no-ah	" "	Ack-gow′-no-ah............	" "
7	Ka-gä′-ah	" " "	Un-jă jo′-hä	" "	Un-ja-jo′-hä	" "
8	Ya-ye-ä′-hä	" " "	O-in-dä′-wait	" "	Ah-zhä′-ku	" "
9	Me-taṇ′-kä	" " "	Tä-han′............	" "	E-chä-she	" "
10	Me-tuṇ′-kä	" " "	Tä-huh′............	" "	She-cha′............	" "
11	Me-tänk′-a-do	" " "	Tä-hä′............	" "	She-cha′............	" "
12	Me-tän′-kä	" " "	Tä-hä′............	" "	She-cha′............	" "
13	Me-tunk′-hä-lä	" " "	Tä-hä′............	" "	She-cha′............	" "
14	Me-tonk′-ä	" " "	Tä-hä′............	" "	She-ches′............	" "
15	Ton′-kä	" " "	Tä-hä′............	" "	She′-cha	" "
16	Me-ton′-kä	" " "	Tä-huh′............	" "	She′-cha	" "
17	Me-tä′............	" " "	Me-hän′-kä	" "	Me-she′-cha	" "
18	We-ha′............	" " "	Tä-hä′-huh	" "	We-she′-eh	" "
19	Wee-töṇ′-ga	" " "	We-tä′-hä	" "	We-she′-kä	" "
20	Heeu-tuṇ′-ga	" " "	Heen-tä′-hä	" "	He-she′-kä	" "
21	Heen-tän′-gä	" " "	Heen-tä′-hä	" "	Hin-she′-kä	" "
22	Ah-se′-zhe-gä	" " "	Be-tä′-hä	" "	Be-she′-kä	" "
23	We-tun′-ka	" " "	We-tä′-ha	" "	We-she′-kä	" "
24	E-chunk′............	" " "	E-chun′............	" "	E-she′-ga	" "
25	Me-no′-ka	" " "	Wo-wä′-ke-a	" "	Wo-wä′-ke-a	" "
26	Mă-tä-ka′-zhä	. " " "	Mä-nä′-te	" "	Mä-rush′-ke-rash	" "
27	Bä-so′-ka............	" " "	Ma-nä′-zha	" "	Bä′-che-na	" "
28	Suh-näk′-fish	" " "	Um-ä′-lok	" "	Um-ä′-lok	" "
29	Et-e-bä′-pĭ-shĭ-lĭ............	My sister.	Um-ä′-läk	" "	Um-ä′-lak	" "
30	Et-e-bä′-pĭ-shĭ-lĭ............	" "	Um-ä′-läk	" "	Um-ä′-läk	" "
31	Chu-chŭ′-se	My younger sister.	Un-kä′-wä	" "	Chu-hu′-cho-wä............	" "
32	Uṇ-gĭ-luṇ′-ĭ	" " "	Au-sdä-lau′-sĭ	" "	Au-sä-dluṇ-hĭ	" "
33	Aṇ-ge-lä′-ih	" " "	Squä-lo′-sih	" "	Squä-lo′-sih	" "
34	E-dä′-deh	My sister.	Koos-tow′-et-sä	My son-in-law.	Koos-tow′-et-sŭ	My son-in-law.
35	A-tä′-he	" "	Ko-stä-witch	" "	Ko-stä′-witch	" "
36	Ah-te′-ta	" "	Kuh-tä′-wa-suh	" "	Kuh-tä′-wa-suh	" "
37	Ne-se′-mis	My younger sister.	Neese-tow′............	My brother-in-law.	Nee-tim′............	My brother-in-law.
38	Ne-sha-mish′............	" " "	Neese-tow′............	" "	Nee-tim′............	" "
39	Ne-she-mish′............	" " "	Neesh-tow′............	" "	Nee-tim′............	" "
40	Ni-shĭ′-me	" " "	Nĭ′-tä............	" "	Nĭ′-nim	" "
41	Ne-de-ge′-ko	My step-sister.	Ne-che-ke′-wa-ze	" "	Ne′-nim	" "
42	Ne-she′-mä	My younger sister.	Ne-tä′............	" "	Ne′-nim	" "
43	Ne-she-mä′............	" " "	Ne-tä′............	" "	Ne-nim′............	" "
44	N′-da-kwam′............	My step-sister.	Ne-tä′............	" "	Ne-nim′............	" "
45	Ne-dä-kwam′............	" "	Ne-tä′............	" "	Ne-nim′............	" "
46	Ne-go-se-mä′............	My younger sister.	Ne-tä-wä′............	" "	Ne-lim-wä′............	" "
47	Ne-she′-mä	" " "	Ne-tä-wä′............	" "	Ne-lim-wä′............	" "
48	Ne-she-mä′............	" " "	Ne-tä-wä′............	" "	Ne-lim-wä′............	" "
49	Ne-she-mä′............	" " "	Ne-tä-wä′............	" "	Ne-le-mwä′............	" "
50	Ne-she-mä′............	" " "	Ne-tä-wä′............	" "	Ne-le-mwä′............	" "
51	Nă-se′-mä	" " "	Ne-tä′-wä	" "	Ne-nim′-wä............	" "
52	Nă-sa′............	" " "	Na-tow′............	" "	Na-nim′............	" "
53	Nă-sim-ä′............	" " "	Ne-to′............	" "	Nee-tum′	" "
54	Na-tä-tä′-mä	" " "	Nen-hă-kä-ni-mä	" "	Ne-nem-wä′............	" "
55	N′-cha-ne-nä′............	" " "	Ne-tä-kwä′............	" "	Ne-lim-wä′............	" "
56	Na-be′-ä	" " "	Ne-ah′-ă............	" "	Ne-ta′-be............	" "
57	Ne-sis′-sä	" " "	Nis-tä-mo′............	" "	Ne-to′-to-yome	" "
58	Ne-sis′-sä	" " "	Nis-tä-mo′............	" "	Ne-to′-to-yome	" "
59	N′-kwa-jeech′............	" " "	Nu-mäk-tem′............	" "	Ne-lu-mŭs′............	" "
60	N′-pee-hen-mum............	My sister.	Nu-mäk-tem′............	" "	Nee′-lu-mŭs	" "
61	N′-ko′-kwä	My step-sister.	N′-dä-oh·k′............	" "	Nee-nun′............	" "
62	Neet-koh′-kw′	" "	Noh′-taṇ-kw′............	" "	Nee-lum′............	" "
63	Nain-hise′-sa-mus′.........	My younger sister.	Na-nä-donkue′............	" "	Na-ne-lim′	" "
64	A-da′-zy............	" " "	Sa′-gä	" "	Sa′-gä	" "
65	Sa-da′-za-yă′-za............	" " "	Sa′-ga	" "	Sa-ta′-za-pa-ten′-ne	" "
66	Sä′-re	" " "	Sa′-ga	" "	Set-shi′-ya............	" "
67	Sa-chith′	" " "			Sa-thŭ-i	" "
68	See-chath	" " "	Săhn	" "		
69	In-tchit-cha-opes′............	" " "	Snatch′l-hu............	" "		
70						
71			Enm-au′-wi-tahtl	" "		
72	Al-kat-litsh-kilt	My sister.				
73						
74						
75	No-vi-pa-re............	My younger sister.				
76						
77						
78						
79						
80	Il-lo′-ä............	My cousin.	Ning-ä-ou′-gwä............	" "	I-e′-gä............	" "

TABLE II.—*Continued.*

	75. My father's brother's son's son. (Male speaking.)	Translation.	76. My father's brother's son's son. (Female speaking.)	Translation.	77. My father's brother's son's daughter. (Male speaking.)	Translation.
1	Ha-ah'-wuk	My son.	Ha-soh'-neh	My nephew.	Ka-ah'-wuk	My daughter.
2	Ha-hä'-wuk	" "	Ha-hä'-wuk	My son.	Ka-hä'-wuk	" "
3	Ha-hä'-wä	" "	Ha-hä'-wa	" "	Ka-hä'-hä	" "
4	Le-yä'-hä	" "	Le-yä'-hä	" "	Ka-yä'-hä	" "
5	E-yä'	" "	E-yä'	" "	Ka-yä'	" "
6	Kä-yä'-no-nä	" "	Kä-yä'-no-na-ah	My nephew.	Kä-yä'-no-nä	" "
7	Le-yä'-ah	" "	Le-yä'-ah	My son.	Ka-yä'-ah	" "
8	A-ne-ah'	" "	He-wä'-teh	" "	E-ne-ah'	" "
9	Me-chink'-she	" "	Me-tonsh'-kä	My nephew.	Me-chunk'-she	" "
10	Me-chink'-she	" "	Me-to⁻us'-kä	" "	Me-chounk'-she	" "
11	Ak she'-dä	" "	Me-toash'-kä	" "	Me-chink'-she	" "
12	Me-chink'-she	" "	Me-tose'-kä	" "	Me-chunk'-she	" "
13	Me-chink'-se-lä	" "	Me-toans'-kä	" "	Me-chunk'-se-lä	" "
14	Me-chink'-she	" "	Me-toase'-kä	" "	Me-chunk'-she	" "
15	Me-chink'-she	" "	Me-toash'-kä	" "	Me-chŭnk'-she	" "
16	Me-chink'-she	" "	Me-toas'-kä	" "	Me-chŭnk'-she	" "
17	Me-chink'-she	" "	Me-to'-zä	" "	Me-chunk'-she	" "
18	Nis-se'-hä	" "	We-toash'-kä	" "	Win-no'-ga	" "
19	We-nĭs-se	" "	We-toans'-kä	" "	Wee-zhuŋ'-ga	" "
20	Hee-yiŋ'-ga	" "	Heen-toas'-ka	" "	Hee-yun'-ga	" "
21	He-ne'-cha	" "	Hin-tose'-kee	" "	He-yuŋ'-ga	" "
22	Be-she'-gä	" "	Be-chose'-kä	" "	She-me'-she-gä	" "
23	We-shen'-kä	" "	We-shen'-ka	" "	We-shon'-ka	" "
24	E-cha-h·kun'	My step-child.	E-choonsh'-ka	My son.	E-chä-h·kun	My step-child.
25	Me'-ne-ka	My son.	Ko'-ne-ka	" "	Me-no'-hä-ka	My daughter.
26	Mä-de-shä'	" "	Met-a-wä-pish'-sha	My grandchild.	Mä'-kä	" "
27	Bot-so'-kä	" "	Bot-so'-kä	My son.	Näk'-me-ä	" "
28	Suh'-sŭh	" "	Sup'-uk-nŏk'-ne	My grandson.	Suh-sŭh'-take	" "
29	Suh'-soh	" "	Sä'-pok-näk'-ne	" "	Suh-soh'-take	" "
30	Su'-soh	" "	Sup'-pok-näk'-nĭ	" "	Su-soh'-take	" "
31	Chup-pŭ'-ce	" "	Um-os-sŭs-wä	My grandchild.	Chu-chŭs'-te	" "
32	A-gwe-tsi'	My child.	Un-ge-wĭ'-nuŋ	My nephew.	A-gwae-tsĭ'	My child.
33	Ah-gwa'-tze	" "	Un-ge-we'-nuh	" "	Ah-gwa'-tze	" "
34	Pe'-row	" "	Pe'-row	My child.	Pe'-row	" "
35	Pe'-row	" "	Pe'-row	" "	Pe'-row	" "
36	Nä-te-nä'-o	" "	At-nuch'	My grandchild.	Nä-te-nä'-o	" "
37	N'-do'-sim	My step-son	N'-de-kwä-tim'	My nephew.	N'-do'-sa-mis-kwame'	My step-daughter.
38	N'-do'-zhim	" "	N'-de-kwä-tim'	" "	N'-do'-zha-mis-kwame'	" "
39	N'-do'-zhim	" "	N'-deh-kwä-tim'	" "	N'-do'-zha-mis-kwem'	" "
40	Nin-do'-zhim	" "	Ni-nin-gwä'-niss	" "	Nin-do-zhĭmi-kwem	" "
41	Nin-do'-zhim	" "	Ne-nin-gwuh'-nis	" "	Nin-do'-zhe-me-kwam	" "
42	N'-do-zhim	" "	Ne-nin-gwi-nis'	" "	Nin-do-zha-mĭ-kwam'	" "
43	N'-do-zhim-ä'	" "	Ne-nin-gwi-nis'	" "	N'-do'-zha-mĭ-kwam'	" "
44	N'-do-zhim'	" "	Ne-nin-gwi-nis'	" "	N'-do'-zhä-mĭ-kwam'	" "
45	N'-do'-zhe-ruä	" "	Nä'-gwi-nis	" "	N'-do-sha-mis	" "
46	Neen-gwase'-sä	My son.	Lan-gwä-les'-sä	" "	Nin-dä'-nä	My daughter.
47	Niŋ-gwa-sä'	" "	Ne-lä'-gwä-la-sä'	" "	Nin-dä'-nä	" "
48	Niŋ-gwa-sä'	" "	Ne-lä'-gwä-la-sä'	" "	Nin-dä'-nä	" "
49	Ne-gwis-sä'	" "	Ne-lä'-gwä-lis-sä'	" "	N'-dä'-nä	" "
50	Ne-gwis-sä'	" "	Ne-lä'-gwä-lis-sä'	" "	N'-dä'-nä	" "
51	Nä-kwis'-sä	" "	Nä-nä'-gwä-nis	" "	Nä-tä'-nis	" "
52	Ne-keese'	" "	Ne-nä'-kwä-na	" "	Ne-täne'	" "
53	Nä	" "	Nä-chin'-e-tä	" "	Nä-tun'	" "
54	Ni-kwĭ-thä'	" "	Na-nä-kwä-ma-thä	" "	Nĭ-ton-nä-thä	" "
55	Ne-kwe-thä'	" "	Na-la-gwal-thä'	" "	Nĭ-tä-na-thä'	" "
56	Na'-hä	" "	Na-tah'-ta	" "	Nä-tä'-na	" "
57	N'-do'-to-ko	My step-son.	N'-do'-to-yose	" "	N'-to-to-tun	My step-daughter.
58	Noh·'-ko-ä.	My son.	No-ä'-toase	" "	Ne-tan'-ä.	My daughter.
59	N'-kwis'	" "	Nŭ-lŭks'	" "	N'-tŭs'	" "
60	N'-too-ä'-sum	" "	Nu-lŭ'-knees	" "	N'-su'-mus	" "
61	Nä-kun'	My step-child.	Nä-kun'	My step-child.	Nä-kun'	My step-child.
62	N'-kweese'	My son.	N'-kweese'	My son.	N'-dä-nuss'	My daughter.
63	Nain-gwase'	" "	Nain-gwase'	" "	Nain-dä'-ness	" "
64	Tu-zen'-a	My step-son.	Sa-yä'-ze	" "	Sa-yä'-dze	My step-daughter.
65	Sa-yä'-za	My son.	Sa-yä'-za	" "	Sa-to'-a	My daughter.
66	Se-yä'-za	" "	Se-yä'-za	" "	Sa-le'-ä	" "
67						
68						
69						
70						
71						
72						
73						
74	Sam-mŭt'	" "			Sä-mäk	" "
75						
76						
77						
78						
79						
80	Kung-e-ä'-gä	My nephew.	Ung-ä'-gä	My nephew.	Kung-e-ä'-gä	My niece.

TABLE II.—*Continued.*

	78. My father's brother's son's daughter. (Female speaking.)	Translation.	79. My father's brother's daughter's son. (Male speaking)	Translation.	80. My father's brother's daughter's son. (Female speaking.)	Translation.
1	Ka-soh'-neh	My niece.	Ha-yă'-wan-da	My nephew.	Ha-ah'-wuk	My son.
2	Ka-hä'-wuk	My daughter.	Ha-yah'-wä-da	" "	Ha-hä'-wuk	" "
3	Ka-hä'-wa	" "	Ha-yă-wä'-da	" "	Ha-hä'-wa	" "
4	Ka-yä'-hä	" "	Ha-yă'-wan-dä	" "	Le-yä-hä	" "
5	Ka-yä'	" "	E-yo-wä'-da	" "	E-yä'	" "
6	Kä-yä'-no-na-ah	My niece.	Kä-yä'-wä-nä	" "	Kä-yä'-no-nä	My child.
7	Ka-yä'-ah	My daughter.	Le-wä-da'-ah	" "	Le-yä'-ah	My son.
8	E-wä'-teh	My niece.	Ha-shone-drä'-ka.	" "	A-ne-ah'	" "
9	Me-tuŋ'-zhan	My daughter.	Me-tonsh'-kä	" "	Me-chiŋk'-she	" "
10	Me-to͡us'-zä	" "	Me-to͡us'-ka	" "	Me-chink'-she	" "
11	Me-to'-zhä	" "	Me-toash'-kä	" "	Ak-she'-dä	" "
12	Me-to'-zhä	" "	Me-tose'-ka	" "	Me-chiŋk'-she	" "
13	Me-toh'-zlä	" "	Me-toans'-kä	" "	Me-chink'-se-lä	" "
14	Me-toh'-zhä	" "	Me-toase'-kä	" "	Me-chink'-she	" "
15	Me-to'-zä	" "	Ne-toash'-kä	" "	Me-chiŋk'-she	" "
16	Me-to'-zä	" "	Me-toas'-kä	" "	Me-chiŋk'-she	" "
17	Me-to'-zä	" "	Me-to'-zä	" "	Me-chiŋk'-she	" "
18	Tä-zhä'-hä	" "	We-toash'-kä	" "	Nis-se'-hä	" "
19	We-te'-zhä	" "	We-toans'-kä	" "	Wee-zhiŋ'-ga	" "
20	Heen-toas'-ka-me	" "	Heen-toas'-kä	" "	Hee-yiŋ'-ga	" "
21	Hin-tose'-kee-me	" "	Hiŋ-tose'-kee	" "	He-ne'-cha	" "
22	Be-che'-zha	" "	Be-chose'-kä	" "	Be-she'-gä	" "
23	We-shon'-ka	" "	We-chose'-kä	" "	We shon'-kä	" "
24	E-choon-zhunk'	" "	E-chonsh'-ka	" "	E-chä-h·kun'	My step-child.
25	Me-no'-hä-ka	" "			Me'-ne-ka	My son.
26	Met-a-wä-pish'-sha	My grandchild.	Mat-so-gä'	My younger brother.	Mä-de-shä'	" "
27	Näk'-me-ä	My daughter.	Bä-cha'-ka ?	" "	Bot-so'-ka	" "
28	Sup'-uk	My gd. daughter.	Sub-ai'-yih	My nephew.	Sup'-uk-nök'-ne	My grandson.
29	Sä'-pok	" "	Sä-bi'-yih	" "	Sä-pok-näk'-ne	" "
30	Sup'-pok	" "	Sä-bi'-yih	" "	Sup'-pok-näk-nĭ	" "
31	Um-os-sŭs'-wä	My grandchild.	Un-ho-pŭe'-wä	" "	Um-os-sŭs'-wä	My grandchild.
32	Uŋ-gwä-duŋ'	My niece.	Uŋ-gi-wĭ'-nuŋ	" "	A-gwae-tsĭ'	My child.
33	Uŋ-gwä'-tuh	" "	Uŋ-ge-we'-nuh	" "	Ah-gwa'-tze	" "
34	Pe'-row	My child.	Te'-wut	" "	Pe'-row	" "
35	Pe'-row	" "	Te'-wut	" "	Pe'-row	" "
36	At-nuch'	My grandchild.	Ah-te'-wut	" "	Nä-to-nä'-o	" "
37	Neese-che-mis'	My niece.	N'-de-kwä-tim'	" "	N'-go-sim	My step-son.
38	Neest-che-mis'	" "	N'-de-kwä-tim'	" "	N'-go'-zhim	" "
39	Neest-che-mish'	" "	N'-deh-kwä-tim'	" "	N'-do'-zhim	" "
40	Nĭ-shĭ-miss'	" "	Nĭ-nin-gwä'-niss	" "	Nin-do'-shĭ-miss	My step-child.
41	Ne-she'-me-sha	" "	Ne-nin-gwuh'-nis	" "	Nin-do'-zhe-mis	" "
42	Ne-she-mis'	" "	Ne-nin-gwi-nis'	" "	Nin-gwis'	My son.
43	Ne-she-mis'	" "	Ne-nin-gwi-nis'	" "	Nin-gwis'	" "
44	Ne-she-mis'	" "	Ne-nin-gwi-nis' ...	" "	N'-gwis'	" "
45	Ne-she'-mis	" "	Nä'-gwi-nis	" "	N'-gwis'	" "
46	Shame-sä'	" "	Laŋ-gwä-les'-sä	" "	Neen-gwase'-sä	" "
47	Ne-she-mis'-sä	" "	Ne-lă'-gwä-la-sä'	" "	Niŋ-gwa-sä'	" "
48	Ne-she-mis'-sä	" "	Ne-lă'-gwä-la-sä'	" "	Niŋ-gwa-sä'	" "
49	Ne-she-mis-sä'	" "	Ne-lä'-gwä-lis-sä'	" "	Ne-gwis-sä'	" "
50	Ne-she-mis-sä'	" "	Ne-lä'-gwä-lis-sä'	" "	Ne-gwis-sä'	" "
51	Nä-shä'-mis	" "	Nä-nä'-gwä-nis	" "	Nä-kwis'-sä	" "
52	Nä-nä'-mä	" "	Ne-nä'-kwä-na	" "	Ne-keese'	" "
53	Nä-un'	" "	Nä-chin'-e-tä	" "	Nä	" "
54	Na-sem-e-thä'	" "	Na-na-kwä-na-thä	" "	Ni-kwĭ-thä'	" "
55	Ne-sa-me-thä'	" "	Na-la-gwal-thä'	" "	Ne-kwe-thä'	" "
56	Nä-thä'-be	" "	Na-tah-'-ta	" "	Na'-hä	" "
57	Nee-mis'-sä	" "	N'-do'-to-yose	" "	N'-do'-to-ko	My step-son.
58	Ne-mis'-sä	" "	No-ă'-toase	" "	Noh'-ko'-ä	My son.
59	N'-sum'	" "	Nu-lŭks'	" "	N'-kwis	" "
60	N'-sum'	" "	Nu-lŭ'-knees	" "	N'-too-ä'-sum	" "
61	Nä-kun'	My step-child	No-kwath'	" "	N'-di-ome'	" "
62	N'-dä-nuss'	My daughter.	Longue'-kw'	" "	N'-kweese'	" "
63	Nain-dä'-ness	" "	Na-lone'-gwä-sis'	" "	Nain-gwase'	" "
64	Sa-yä'-dze	" "	Sä'-zy	" "	Sa-yä'-ze	" "
65	Sa-to'-a	" "	Sa-yä'-za	My son.	Sa-yä'-za	" "
66	Sa-le'-a	" "	Se-yä'-za	" "	Se-yä'-za	" "
67						
68						
69						
70						
71						
72						
73						
74						
75						
76						
77						
78						
79						
80	Ung-ä'-gä	My niece.	We-yo-o'-gwä	My nephew.	Noo-ä'-gä	My nephew

TABLE II.—*Continued.*

	81. My father's brother's daughter's daughter. (Male speaking.)	Translation.	82. My father's brother's daughter's daughter. (Female speaking.)	Translation.	83. My father's brother's great grandson.	Translation.
1	Ka-yă'-wan-da	My niece.	Ka-ah'-wuk	My daughter.	Ha-yă'-da	My grandson.
2	Ka-yuh'-wä-da	" "	Ka-bä'-wuk	" "	Ha-yă'-dra	" "
3	Ka-yă-wä'-da	" "	Ka-hä'-wä	" "	Ha-yă'-da	" "
4	Ka-yă'-wan-dä	" "	Ka-yä'-hä	" "	Le-yä'-dla-ah	" "
5	Ka-yo-wä'-dä	" "	Ka-yä'	" "	E-yä'-dla-ah	" "
6	Ka-yă'-wä-nä	" "	Ka-yä'-no-nä	My child.	Kä-yä'-rä	My grandchild.
7	Ka-wä-dä'-ah	" "	Ka-yä'-hä	My daughter.	Le-yä-tä-ra-'yä	My grandson.
8	Ya-shone-drä'-ka	" "	E-ne-ah'	" "	Ha-tra'-ah	" "
9	Me-tuŋ'-zhaŋ	" "	Me-chuŋk'-she	" "	Me-tä'-ko-zhä	My grandchild.
10	Me-to͞us'-zä	" "	Me-chunk'-she	" "	Me-tä'-ko-zhä	" "
11	Me-to'-zhä	" "	Ak-she'-dä	" "	Me-tä'-ko-zhä	" "
12	Me-to'-zhä	" "	Me-chunk'-she	" "	Me-tä'-ko-zha	" "
13	Me-toh'-zhä	" "	Me-chunk'-se-lä	" "	Me-tä'-ko-säk'-pok	" "
14	Me-toh'-zhä	" "	Me-chunk'-she	" "	Me-tä'-ko-zhä	" "
15	Me-to'-zä	" "	Me-chŭnk'-she	" "	Me-tä'-ko-zhä	" "
16	Me-to'-zä	" "	Me-chunk'-she	" "	Me-tä'-ko-zä	" "
17	Me-to'-zä	" "	Me-chŭnk'-she	" "	Me-tä'-ko-sä	" "
18	Tä-zhä'-hä	" "	Win-no'-ga	" "	Toosh'-pä-hä	" "
19	We-toans'-kä	" "	We-zbuŋ'-ga	" "	Wee-tŭsh'-pä	" "
20	Heen-toas'-ka-me	" "	Hee-yuŋ'-ga	" "	Heen-tä'-kwä	My grandson.
21	Hin-tose'-kee-me	" "	He-yuŋ'-ga	" "	E-tä'-kwä	" "
22	Be-chose'-kä	" "	She-me'-she-gä	" "	Be-chose'-pä	My grandchild.
23	We-chose'-kä	" "	We-shon'-ka	" "	We-chose'-pä	" "
24	E-chooŋ-zhunk'	" "	E-chä-h·kun	My step-child.	E-chooŋsh'-ka-neke	My little gd. son.
25			Me-no'-hä-ka	My daughter.	P-tä-we'-hä-kä	My grandchild.
26	Mä-tä-ka'-zha	My younger sister.	Mä'-kä	" "	Met-a-wä-pish'-sha	" "
27	Bä-sä'-chete ?	" "	Näk'-me-ä	" "	Bus-bä'-pe-ta	" "
28	Sub-ih'-take	My niece.	Sup'-uk	My granddaughter.	Sup'-uk-nŏk'-ne	My grandson.
29	Sä-bĭh'-take	" "	Sä'-pok	" "	Sä'-pok-näk'-ne	" "
30	Su-bĭ'-take	" "	Sup'-pok	" "	Sup'-pok-näk'-nĭ	" "
31	Un-häk'-pu-te	" "	Um-os-sŭs'-wä	My grandchild.	Um-os-sŭs'-wä	My grandchild.
32	Uŋ-gwä-duŋ'	" "	A-gwae-tsĭ'	My child.	Uŋ-gĭ-lĭ-sĭ	" "
33	Uŋ-gwaä'-tuh	" "	Ah-gwa'-tze	" "	Aŋ-ge-lee'-se	" "
34	Te'-wut	" "	Pe'-row	" "	Lak-te'-gish	My grandson.
35	Te'-wut	" "	Pe-row	" "	Lak-te'-kis	My grandchild.
36	Ah-te-natch	" "	Nä-te-nä'-o	" "	At-nuch'	" "
37	Neese-che-mis'	" "	N'-do'-za-mis-kwame'	My step-daughter.	No-se-sem'	" "
38	Neest-che-mish'	" "	N·-do'-zha-mis-kwame'	" "	No-se-sim'	" "
39	Nees-che-mish'	" "	N'-do'-zha-mis-kwem'	" "	No-se-sem'	" "
40	Nĭ-zhĭ'-miss	" "	Niu-do'-zhĭ-miss	My step-child.	No-zhĭ'-she	" "
41	Ne-she'-me-sha	" "	Nin-do'-zhe-mis	" "	No-she-shă	" "
42	Ne-she-mis'	" "	Nin-da'-niss	My daughter.	No-she-shä'	" "
43	Ne-she-mis'	" "	N'-dä-niss	" "	No-she-shä'	" "
44	Ne-she-mis'	" "	N'-dä-niss'	" "	No-she-shä'	" "
45	Ne-she'-mis	" "	N'-dä'-niss	" "	No-sä-seh'	" "
46	Shames-sä'	" "	Nin-dä'-nä	" "	No-sa-mä'	" "
47	Ne-she'-mis-sä'	" "	Nin-dä'-nä	" "	No-sa-'mä	" "
48	Ne-she'-mis-sä'	" "	Nin-dä'-nä	" "	No-sa-'mä	" "
49	Ne-she-mis-sä'	" "	N'-dä'-nä	" "	No-sa-mä'	" "
50	Ne-she-mis-sä'	" "	N'-dä'-nä	" "	No-sa-mä'	" "
51	Nä-shä'-mis	" "	Nä-tä'-nis	" "	No-she-sem'	" "
52	Nä-nä'-mä	" "	Ne-täne'	" "	No-she-sä'	" "
53	Ne-she'-mis	" "	Nä-tun'	" "	Nä-h·-kä'	" "
54	Na-sem-e-thä'	" "	Nĭ-ton-nä-thä'	" "	Na-se-thä'-mä	" "
55	Ne-sa-me-thä'	" "	Nĭ-tä-ua-thä'	" "	No-stha-thä'	" "
56	Nä-tha'-be	" "	Nä-tä'-na	" "	Nee'-sa	" "
57	Ne-mis'-sä	" "	N'-to'-to-tun	My step-daughter.	Nee-so'-tan	" "
58	Ne-mis'-sä	" "	Ne-tan'-ä	My daughter.	Nee-so'-tän	" "
59	N'-sum'	" "	N'-tŭs'	" "	Nŭ-jeech'	" "
60	N'-sum'	" "	N'-su'-mus	" "	N'-kway'-nus	" "
61	Noh·k-soh-kwä'-oh	" "	Nee-chune'	" "	Nä-h·ise'	" "
62	Longue'-kwä'	" "	N'-dä-nuss'	" "	Noh·-whese'	" "
63	Na-lone'-gwä-sis'	" "	Nain-dä'-niss	" "	Nain-no-whase'	" "
64	Sä'-zy	" "	Sa-yä'-dze	" "	Sa-t'-thu'-a(man),Sa'-chä	" "
65	Sa-to-a'	My daughter.	Sa-to'-a	" "	Sa-ken'-ne .....[(woman)	My grandson.
66	Se-le'-ă	" "	Sa-le'-ă	" "	Se-yä-zet'-tha-re	" "
67						
68						
69					Seet-shee	My child.
70						
71						
72						
73						
74						
75						
76						
77						
78						
79						
80	We-yo-o'-gwä	My niece.	Noo-ä'-gă	My niece.	Eng'-o-tä	My grandchild.

TABLE II.—*Continued.*

	84. My father's brother's great granddaughter.	Translation.	85. My father's brother's great grandson's son.	Translation.	86. My father's brother's great grandson's daughter.	Translation.
1	Ka-yä'-da	My granddaughter.	Ha-yä'-da	My grandson.	Ka-yä'-da	My gd.-daughter.
2	Ka-yä'-dra	" "	Ha-yä'-dra	" "	Ka-yä'-dra	" "
3	Ka-yä'-da	" "	Ha-yä'-da	" "	Ka-yä'-da	" "
4	Ka-yä'-dla-ah	" "	Le-yä'-dla-ah	" "	Ka-yä'-dla-ah	" "
5	Ka-yä'-dla-ah	" "	E-yä'-dla-ah	" "	Ka-yä'-dla-ah	" "
6	Kä-yä'-rä	My grandchild.	Kä-yä'-rä	My grandchild.	Kä-yä'-rä	My grandchild.
7	Ka-yä-tä-ra'-yä	My granddaughter.	Le-yä-tä-ra'-yä	My grandson.	Ka-yä'-tä-ra'-yä	My gd. daughter.
8	Ya-tra'-ah	" "	Ha-tra'-ah	" "	Ya-tra'-ah	" "
9	Me-tä'-ko-zhä	My grandchild.	Me-tä'-ko-zhä	My grandchild.	Me-tä'-ko-zhä	My grandchild.
10	Me-tä'-ko-zhä	" "	Me-tä'-ko-zhä	" "	Me-tä'-ko-zhä	" "
11	Me-tä'-ko-zhä	" "	Me-tä'-ko-zhä	" "	Me-tä'-ko-zhä	" "
12	Me-tä'-ko-zha	" "	Me-tä'-ko-zha	" "	Me-tä'-ko-zha	" "
13	Me-tä'-ko-säk'-pok	" "	Me-tä'-ko-säk'-pok	" "	Me-tä'-ko-säk'-pok	" "
14	Me-tä'-ko-zhä	" "	Me-tä'-ko-zhä	" "	Me-tä'-ko-zhä	" "
15	Me-tä'-ko-zhä	" "	Me-tä'-ko-zhä	" "	Me-tä'-ko-zhä	" "
16	Me-tä'-ko-zä	" "	Me-tä'-ko-zä	" "	Me-tä'-ko-zä	" "
17	Me-tä'-ko-sä	" "	Me-tä'-ko-sä	" "	Me-tä'-ko-sä	" "
18	Toosh'-pä-hä	" "	Toosh'-pä-hä	" "	Toosh'-pä-hä	" "
19	Wee-tŭsh'-pä	" "	Wee-tŭsh'-pä	" "	Wee-tŭsh'-pä	" "
20	Heen-tä'-kwä-me	My granddaughter.	Heen-tä'-kwä	My grandson.	Heen-tä'-kwä-me	My gd. daughter.
21	E-tä'-kwä-me	" "	E-tä'-kwä	" "	E-tä'-kwä-me	" "
22	Be-chose'-pä	My grandchild.	Be-chose'-pä	My grandchild.	Be-chose'-pä	My grandchild.
23	We-chose'-pä	" "	We-chose'-pä	" "	We-chose'-pä	" "
24	E-choon-zhunk'-e-neke	My little gd. daught.	E-choonsh'-neke'	My little grandson.	E-choon-zhunk-e-neke	My little gd. dau.
25	P-tä-we'-hä-kä	My grandchild.	P-tä-we'-hä-kä	My grandchild.	P-tä-we'-hä-kä	My grandchild.
26	Met-a-wä-pish'-sha	" "	Met-a-wä-pish'-sha	" "	Met-a-wä-pish'-sha	" "
27	Bus-bä'-pe-ta	" "	Bus-bä'-pe-ta	" "	Bus-bä'-pe-ta	" "
28	Sup'-uk	My granddaughter.	Sup'-uk-nŏk'-ne	My grandson.	Sup'-uk	My gd. daughter.
29	Sä'-pok	" "	Sä'-pok-näk'-ne	" "	Sä'-pok	" "
30	Sup'-pok	" "	Sup'-pok-näk'-nĭ	" "	Sup'-pok	" "
31	Um-os-sŭs'-wä	My grandchild.	Um-os-sŭs'-wä	My grandchild	Um-os-sŭs'-wä	My grandchild.
32	Uŋ-gĭ-lĭ-sĭ	" "	Un-gĭ-lĭ-sĭ	" "	Un-gĭ-lĭ-sĭ	" "
33	Aŋ-ge lee'-se	" "	Aŋ-ge-lee'-se	" "	Aŋ-ge-lee'-se	" "
34	Lak-te-gee	My granddaughter.	Te'-wut	My nephew.	Te-wut	My niece.
35	Lak-te-kis	My grandchild.				
36	At-nuch	" "				
37	No-se-sem'	" "	No-se-sem'	My grandchild.	No-se-sem'	My grandchild.
38	No-se-sim'	" "	No-se-sim'	" "	No-se-sim'	" "
39	No-se-sem'	" "	No-se-sem'	" "	No-se-sem'	" "
40	No-zhĭ'-she	" "	No-zhĭ'-she	" "	No-zhĭ'-she	" "
41	No-she'-shä	" "	No-she'-shä	" "	No-she'-shä	" "
42	No-she-shä'	" "	No-she-shä'	" "	No-she-shä'	" "
43	No-she-shä'	" "	No-she-shä'	" "	No-she-shä'	" "
44	No-she-shä'	" "	No-she-shä'	" "	No-she-shä'	" "
45	No-sä-seh'	" "	No-sä-seh'	" "	No-sä-seh'	" "
46	No-sa-mä'	" "	No-sa-mä'	" "	No-sa-mä'	" "
47	No-sa'-mä	" "	No-sa'-mä	" "	No-sa'-mä	" "
48	No-sa'-mä	" "	No-sa'-mä	" "	No-sa'-mä	" "
49	No-sa'-mä	" "	No-sa'-mä	" "	No-sa'-mä	" "
50	No-sa-mä'	" "	No-sa-mä'	" "	No-sa-mä'	" "
51	No-she-sem'	" "	No-she-sem'	" "	No-she-sem'	" "
52	No-she-sä'	" "	No-she-sä'	" "	No-she-sä'	" "
53	Nä-h·-kä'	" "	Nä-h·-kä'	" "	Nä-h·-kä'	" "
54	Na-se-thä'-mä	" "	Na-se-thä'-mä	" "	Na-se-thä'-mä	" "
55	No-stha-thä'	" "	No-stha-thä'	" "	No-stha-thä'	" "
56	Nee'-sa	" "	Nee'-sa	" "	Nee'-sa	" "
57	Nee-so'-tan	" "	Nee-so'-tan	" "	Nee-so'-tan	" "
58	Nee-so'-tän	" "	Nee-so'-tän	" "	Nee-so'-tän	" "
59	Nŭ-jeech'	" "	Nŭ-jeech'	" "	Nŭ-jeech'	" "
60	N'-kway'-nus	" "	N'-kway'-nus	" "	N'-kway'-nus	" "
61	Nä-h·ise'	" "	Nä-h·ise'	" "	Nä-h·ise'	" "
62	Noh·-whese'	" "	Noh·-whese'	" "	Noh·-whese'	" "
63	Nain-no-whase'	" "	Nain-no-whase'	" "	Nain-no-whase'	" "
64	Sa-t'thu'-a(man), Sa'-chä	" "	Sa-t'thu'-a (man), Sa'-chä	" "	Sa-t'thu'-a (man), Sa'-chä	" "
65	Sa-to⁻a'-bä .... [(woman)	My granddaughter.	Sa-ken'-ne...... [(woman)	My grandson.	Sa-to⁻a'-bä.....[(woman)	" "
66	Sa-le-zet'-tha-re	" "	Se-ya-zet'-tha-re	" "	Sa-le-zet'-tha-re	" "
67						
68	Seet-she	My child.	Seet-she	My child.	Seet-she	" "
69						
70						
71						
72						
73						
74						
75						
76						
77						
78						
79						
80	Eng'-o-tä	My grandchild.	Eng'-o-tä	My grandchild.	Eng'-o-tä	My grandchild.

TABLE II.—*Continued.*

	87. My father's sister.	Translation.	88. My father's sister's husband.	Translation.	89. My father's sister's son—older than myself. (Male speaking.)	Translation.
1	Ah-ga'-huc	My aunt.	Hoc-no'-ese	My step-father.	Ah-găre'-seh	My cousin.
2	Kno'-hä	My mother.	Hoc-no'-nese	" "	Ah-ge-ah'-seh	" "
3	Ah-ge-no'-hä	" "	Hä-ge-no'	" "	Ah-gare'-seh	" "
4	Ahk-nole'-hä	" "	Lä-ga-nih'	My father.	Un-gă-lä'-seh	" "
5	Ah-ga-nese'-tä	" "	Lä-ga-ne'-hä	" "	Un-gă-läss'	" "
6	Ahk-kaw'-rack	My aunt.	Ack-we'-rä	My step-father.	Ahk-gă-rä'-sthar	
7	Ah-ga-nese-tä'-hä	My mother	Le-an-hose'-hä	" "	Lak-je'-hä	My elder brother.
8	Ah-rä'-hoc	My aunt.	Hä-wä-te-no'-rä	My uncle.	Jä-rä'-seh	My cousin.
9	Tun-win'	" "	Dak-she'	My step-father.	Tan-han'-she	" "
10	Toh'-we	" "	Dake'-she	My father.	Tä'-she	" "
11	Tonk'-wa	" "	A-dik'-she	My uncle.	Kä'-zha	" "
12	Tonk'-wa	" "	Ah-dik'-she	" "	Tä'-she	" "
13	Toh-we'	" "	Lake-she'	" "	Tä'-she	" "
14	Toh'-we	" "	Lake'-she	" "	Tä-hä'-she	" "
15	Toh'-we	" "	Lake-she'	" "	Tä'-she	" "
16	Toh'-we	" "	Lake'-she	" "	Tä-hä'-she	" "
17	Me-toh'-we	" "	Me-nake'-she	" "	Tä-hä'-she	" "
18	Te-na'-hä	" "	Na-ge'-hä	" "	We-toash'-kä	My nephew.
19	Wee-tee'-me	" "	Wee-nä'-gee	" "	We-toans'-kä	" "
20	Heen-too'-me	" "	Heen-ja'-kä	" "	Heen-toas'-ka	" "
21	E-tŭ'-me	" "	Hin-chä'-kä	" "	Hin-tose'-kee	" "
22	Be-je'-me	" "	Be-tä'-hä	My brother-in-law.	Be-chose'-kä	" "
23	We-je'-me	" "	We-tä'-ha	" "	We-chose'-kä	" "
24	E-choon'-we	" "	E-chun'	" "	E-choonsh'-ka	" "
25	P-to'-me-nick (m.)	" "	Ta-tay'	My father.		
	Mä-sa'-we (male speaking)	" "				
	Nä-a (woman speaking) ..	My mother.				
26	Kä-ru'-hǎ	My grandmother.	Mä-toosh-ǎ-rŭ'-tä-kä	My grandfather.	Tä-ta'	My father.
27	E'-ke-ă .... [nǐ (w. sp.)	My mother.	Ah-h'a'	My father.	Ah-h'a'	" "
28	A-huk'-ne (m.s.), Up-puk'-	My aunt, My gd. mo.	Um-uh'-fo	My grandfather.	A'-kǐ	" "
29	A-huc'-nǐ (m.s.), Up-pok'-	" "	Um-ă'-fo	" "	A'-kǐ	" "
30	Hap-po'-sǐ ..... [ni(w.sp.)	My grandmother.	Um-u-fo-sǐ	My little gd. father.	Aug-kǐ	
31	Chu-pŭ'-se	" "	Chu-pŭ-chä	My grandfather.	Chuhl'-kŭ-che'	My little father.
32	E-hlän'-gǐ	My aunt.	A-gwä-tǐ-nä'-ǐ	My step-parent.	E-dau-dä' (?)	My father.
33	Ah-ge-h'lo'-gih	" "	Tä-le-na-ah-ge-do-dä	My second father.	Ah-ge-do'-dä	" "
34	Ah-te'-rä	My mother.	Ah-te'-put	My grandfather.	Ah-te'-is	" "
35	A-te'-rä	" "	Ah-te'-pot	" "	A-te'-ase	" "
36	At-nä	" "	Ah-te'-ǎ	My father.		
37	Nis-sǐ-goos'	My aunt.	Ne-sis'	My uncle.	Nees'-chäs	My cousin.
38	Nis-se-goos'	" "	Ne-sis'	" "	Nee-säs'	" "
39	Nǐ-se-goos'	" "	Nee-sis'	" "	Nees'-chäs	" "
40	Nin-sǐ'-goss	" "	Nǐ-zhi-shě	" "	Nǐ-tä'-wiss	" "
41	Ne-ze-gŭs'	" "	Ne-zhe-sha'	" "	Ne-tä'-wis	" "
42	Ne-zee-goss'	" "	Ne-she-shǎ	" "	Ne-tä'-wis'	" "
43	Nis-zee-gŭss'	" "	Ne-zhish'-shǎ	" "	Ne-tä'-wis	" "
44	Nis-sa-gose'	" "	Ne-zhish-shǎ'	" "	Ne-tä'-wis	" "
45	N'-si-gwis'	" "	N'-jeh-shǎ'	" "	Lan-gwä-les'-sä	My nephew.
46	N'-sa'-gwe-sä'	" "	Ne-zhese'-sä	" "	Ne-lä'-gwä-la-sä'	" "
47	Ne-za'-gos-sä'	" "	Ne-zhe'-sä	" "	Ne-lä'-gwä-la-sä'	" "
48	Ne-za'-gos-sä'	" "	Ne-zhe'-sä	" "	Ne-lä'-gwa-lis-sä	" "
49	Ne-sǎ'-gwis-sä'	" "	Ne-zhe'-saw	" "	Ne-lä'-gwa-lis-sä	" "
50	Ne-sǎ'-gwis-sä'	" "	Ne-zhe'-saw	" "	Nä-nǎ'-gwä-nis	" "
51	Nak-ye'-hä	" "	Nä-zhe-sǎ'	" "	Ne-nǎ'-kwä-na	" "
52	Ne-ne'	" "	Ne-zha'	" "		
53	Nǎ-un'	" "	Nǎ'-she	" "		
54	Na-tha-kwi-thǎ'	" "	Na-si-thǎ'	" "	Nen-na-kwǎ-na-thǎ	" "
55	Na-tha-gwe-thǎ'	" "	Nǐ-sǐ-thǎ'	" "	Na-la-gwal-thä	" "
56	Nǎ-ha'	" "	Na'-see	" "	Nǎ'-thä-hä ?	My elder brother.
57	Ne-to'-tarse	" "	Ne-to-tah-se'	" "	N'-to-tes-tä-mo'	My cous. & bro.-in-law.
58	Ne-to'-tahxs	" "	Nee'-sä	" "	Noh-sä-kin'-ame.	My cousin. [law.
59	N'-su-gwis'	" "	Nikes-kä-mich'	" "	N'-sees'	My elder brother.
60	Noo-kum' or N'-kee-sees'	" "	N'-kn-lä-mook'-sis	" "	N'-tä-gus'?.	My cousin.
61	No-muths'	My step-mother.	Nä-jä'-kw''	My step-father.	N'-dä-kwus'	My step-brother.
62	N'-gä-hä'-tut	My little mother.	N'-me-lu-täk-tut	My little step-father.	Nee-mä'-tus	" "
63	Na-ma-la'-däkue	My aunt.	Na-ne-mo'-whome	My step-father.	Nain-n'-hans'	My elder brother.
64	Kh-m'ba'-dza	" "	Thä-tha'	My uncle.	Kün'-dig-eh	" "
65	Ba-tso'-na	" "	Sa-che'-na-pa'-te-na ?	My aunt's husband.	Sa-ga-yǎ'-za ?	My cousin.
66	Set'-so	" "	Sel-the'-ne	My step-father.	Sü-nä'-gä	My elder brother.
67	Sä-ki'	" "			Soon'-da-ga	" " "
68	[kwl (f.s.)					
69	In-kach'-ha (m.s.), En-tee'-	" "	Is-se-mält	My uncle?	Is-se-lacht. ᵇIs-sin-kwa-	My brother. ᵇOne
70	Kse-wǎ'-wä-sä	" "			[seehw'	[like my bro.
71	Nä-sis'-sas	(Not rendered.)	Swagh	(Not rendered.)	Es-hup or Ne-pah'	My younger bro.
72	Nu-pwe'-ä-tsin	" "				
73						
74						
75						
76						
77	Ze-pa-bä-fu-chä				Ub-so	My cousin.
78						
79	At-sa-ga	My aunt.			Ig-dlo-ra	My cousin.
80	At-chung'-ä	" "			Il-lŭng'-ä	" "

TABLE II.—*Continued.*

	90. My father's sister's son—older than myself. (Female speaking.)	Translation.	91. My father's sister's son. younger than myself. (Male speaking.)	Translation.	92. My father's sister's son—younger than myself. (Female speaking.)	Translation.
1	Ah-găre'-seh	My cousin.	Ah-găra'-seh	My cousin.	Ah-găre'-seh	My cousin.
2	Ah-ge-ah'-seh	" "	Ah-ge-ah'-seh	" "	Ah-ge-ah'-seh	" "
3	Ah-gare'-seh	" "	Ah-gare'-seh	" "	Ah-gare'-seh	" "
4	Un-gă-lä'-seh	" "	Un-gă-lä'-seh	" "	Un-gă-lä'-seh	" "
5	Un-gă-lăss'	" "	Un-gă-lass'	" "	Un-gă-lass'	" "
6	Ahk-gă-rä'-sthar	" "	Ahk-gă-rä'-sthar	" "	Ahk-gă-rä'-sthar	" "
7	Lok-je'-hä	My elder brother.	Le-gä-ah	My younger brother.	Le-gä-ah	My younger bro.
8	Ja-rä'-seh	My cousin.	Ja-rä'-seh	My cousin.	Jä-rä-seh	My cousin.
9	She-chay'-she	" "	Taṇ-haṇ'-she	" "	She chay'-she	" "
10	She-chä'-she	" "	Tä'-she	" "	She-chä'-she	" "
11	She-cha'-ze	" "	Hä-kä'	" "	She-chä'-ze	" "
12	She-cha'-she	" "	Tä'-she	" "	She-cha'-she	" "
13	S'cha-pa'-she	" "	Tä'-she	" "	S'cha-pa'-she	" "
14	She-cha'-she	" "	Tä-hä'-she	" "	She-cha'-she	" "
15	She-cha'-she	" "	Tä'-she	" "	She-cha'-she	" "
16	She-cha'-she	" "	Tä-hä'-she	" "	She-cha'-she	" "
17	Me-hä'-gä-she	" "	Tä-hä'-she	" "	Me-hä'-gä-she	" "
18	Nis-se'-hä	My son.	We-toash'-kä	My nephew.	Nis-se'-hä	My son.
19	We-zhuṇ'-ga	" "	We-toans'-kä	" "	We-zhiṇ'-ga	" "
20	Hee-yiṇ'-ga	" "	Heen-toas'-kä	" "	Hee-yiṇ'-ga	" "
21	He-ne'-cha	" "	Hin-tose'-kee	" "	He-ne'-cha	" "
22	Be-she'-gä	" "	Be-chose'-kä	" "	Be-she'-gä	" "
23	We-shen'-kä	" "	We-chose'-kä	" "	We-shén'-kä	" "
24	E-neke'	" "	E-choonsh'-ka	" "	E-neke'	" "
25						
26	Tä-ta'	My father.	Tä-ta'	My father.	Tä-ta'	My father.
27	Ah-h·a'	" "	Ah-h·a'	" "	Ah-h·a'	" "
28	A'-kĭ	" "	A'-kĭ	" "	A'-kĭ	" "
29	A'-kĭ	" "	A'-kĭ	" "	A'-kĭ	" "
30	Ang-kĭ	" "	Ang-kĭ			
31	Chuhl'-kŭ-che'	My little father.	Chuhl'-kŭ-che'	My little father.	Chuhl'-kŭ-che'	My little father.
32	E-dau-dä'	My father.	E-dau-dä'	My father.	E-dau-dä'	My father.
33	Ah-ge-do'-dä	" "	Ah-ge-do'-dä	" "	Ah-ge-do'-dä	" "
34	Ah-te'-is	" "	Ah-te'-is	" "	Ah-te'-is	" "
35	Ah-te'-ase	" "	Ah-te'-ase	" "	Ah-te'-ase	" "
36						
37	Nee'-che-moos	My cousin.	Neese'-chäs	My cousin.	Nee'-che-moos	My cousin.
38	Nee'-che-moosh	" "	Nee-säs'	" "	Nee'-che-moosh	" "
39	Nee'-ta-moos	" "	Nees'-chäs	" "	Nee'-ta-moos	" "
40	Nĭ-nĭ-mo'-she	" "	Nĭ-tä'-wiss	" "	Nĭ-nĭ-mo'-she	" "
41	Ne-ne-mo'-sha	" "	Ne-tä'-wis	" "	Ne-ne-mo'-sha	" "
42	Ne-ne-moo-shä'	" "	Ne-tä-wis'	" "	Ne-ne-moo-shä'	" "
43	Ne-ne-moo-shä'	" "	Ne-tä'-wis	" "	Ne-ne-moo-shä'	" "
44	Ne-ne-moo-shä'	" "	Ne-tä'-wis	" "	Ne-ne-moo-shä'	" "
45						
46	Neen-gwase-sä'	My son.	Laṇ-gwä-les'-sä	My nephew.	Neen-gwase-sä'	My son.
47	Niṇ-gwa-sä'	" "	Ne-lä'-gwä-la-sä'	" "	Niṇ-gwa-sä'	" "
48	Niṇ-gwa-sä'	" "	Ne-lä'-gwä-la-sä'	" "	Niṇ-gwa-sä'	" "
49	Ne-gwis-sä'	" "	Ne-lä'-gwä-lis-sä'	" "	Ne-gwis-sä'	" "
50	Ne-gwis-sä'	" "	Ne-lä'-gwa-lis-sä	" "	Ne-gwis-sä'	" "
51	Nă-kwis'-sä	" "	Nă-nä'-gwä-nis	" "	Nă-kwis'-sä	" "
52	Ne-keese'	" "	Ne-nä'-kwä-na	" "	Ne-keese'	" "
53						" "
54	Ni'-kwĭ-thä	" "	Nen-na-kwă-na-thä	" "	Ni-kwĭ-thä	" "
55	Ne-kwe-thä'	" "	Na-la-gwal-thä'	" "	Ne-kwe-thä'	" "
56	Nă-thä-hä'?	My elder brother.	Ta'-yä?	My younger brother.	Ta'-yä?	My younger bro.
57	N'-do'-to-ke-man'	My cousin.	N'-to'-tes-ta-mo	My cousin & bro.-in-	N-do-to-ke-man'	My cousin.
58	No-in'-nä	" "	Noh'-să-kin'-ame	My cousin. [law.	No-in'-nä	" "
59	N'-sees	My elder brother.	N'-chi-gu-num'	My younger brother.	N'-chi-gu-num'	My younger bro.
60	N'-tul-nŭm?	My cousin.	N'-tä-gus	My cousin.	N'-tul-num	My cousin.
61	N'-donk	My step-brother.	N'-da-kwus	My step-brother.	N'-donk	My step-brother.
62	N'-dun-oo-yome'	" "	Nee-mä'-tus	" "	N'-dun-oo-yome'	
63	Nain-n'-haus'	My elder brother.	Nain-hise-sa-mus	My younger brother.	Nain-hise-sa-mus	My younger bro.
64	Kŭn'-dig-eh	" " "	A-cha'-a	" "	A-cha'-a	" "
65	Sa-tso-yä'-ză?	My cousin.	Sa-ga-yä'-za?	My cousin.	Sa-tso-yä'-za?	My cousin.
66	Sŭ-nä'-gä	My elder brother.	Set-chil'-e-ä-ze	My younger brother.	Set-chil'-e-ä-ze	My younger bro.
67	Soon'-da-ga	" " "	Sa'-chä	" " "	Sa'-chä	" " "
68	Soon-dä'	" " "	Sa-chä	" " "	Sa-chä	" " "
69	Is-sin-kwa-seehw'	One like my brother.				
70						
71						
72						
73						
74						
75						
76						
77	Sä-hä-o-ä	My husband.				
78						
79	Ig-dlo-ra	My cousin.				
80	Il-lo'-ä	" "	Il-lŭng'-ä	My cousin.	Il-lo'-ä	My cousin.

TABLE II.—*Continued.*

	93. My father's sister's son's wife. (Male speaking.)	Translation.	94. My father's sister's son's wife. (Female speaking.)	Translation.	95. My father's sister's daughter —older than myself. (Male speaking.)	Translation.
1	Ah-ge-ah′-ne-ah	My sister-in-law.	Ah-ge⌢ah′-ne⌢a...............	My sister-in-law.	Ah-găre′-seh	My cousin.
2	Uh-ge-ah′-ne-a...................	" "	Uh-ge⌢ah′-ne⌢o	" "	Ah-ge-ah′-seh	" "
3	Ah-ge-ah′-yeh	" "	Ah-ge-ah′-ne-o	" "	Ah-gare′-seh	" "
4	Un-ge⌢ah′-le⌢a...................	" "	Un-ge⌢ah-le⌢a	" "	Un-gä-lä′-seh	" "
5	Un-gä-le-ya-ah...................	" "	Un-gä-le-ya′-ah	" "	Un-gä-läss′...................	" "
6	Ack-gä-se′-ah...................	" "	Ack-gä-re′-ah	" "	Ahk-gä-rä′-sthar	" "
7	Ah-go-hä′-kwä	" "	Ah-go-hä-kwä	" "	Ak-je-yä...................	My elder sister.
8	O-in-dä′-wait...................	" "	O-in-dä′-wait	" "	Jä-rä′-seh	My cousin.
9	Häṇ-kä′..................	" "	E-cha-paṇ	" "	Häṇ-kä′-she	" "
10	Hä-kä′..................	" "	E-shä′-pä	" "	Hä-kä′-she	" "
11	Hä-kä′..................	" "	E-shä′-pä	" "	Ah-kä′-zha	" "
12	Hä-kä′..................	" "	E-shä′-pä	" "	Hä-kä′-she	" "
13	Huṇ-kä′..................	" "	S′-cha′-pä	" "	Hun-kä′-she	" "
14	Hun-kä′..................	" "	S′-cha′-pä	" "	Hun-kä′-she	" "
15	Hä-kä′..................	" "	E-sä′-pä	" "	Ha-kä′-she	" "
16	Hä-kä′..................	" "	E-sä′-pä	" "	Ha-kä′-she	" "
17	Me-hä′-gä..................	" "	Me-she′-cha-pä	" "	Zä-hä′-she	" "
18	Ta-ne′-hä..................	My daught.-in-law.	Ta-ne′-hä	My daught.-in-law.	Tä-zhä′-hä	My niece.
19	We-te′-na..................	" "	We-te′-na	" "	We-te′-zhä	" "
20	Heen-toan′-ye..................	" "	Heen-toan′-ye	" "	Heen-toas′-ka-me	" "
21	Hin-to′-ne..................	" "	Hin-to′-ne	" "	Hin-tose′-kee-me	" "
22	Be-je′-na..................	" "	Be-je′-na..................	" "	Be-che′-zho	" "
23	We-che′-ne..................	" "	We-che′-ne	" "	We-che′-zho	" "
24	E-nook-chek-aw-chan	" "	E-nook-chek′-aw-chau′	" "	E-chooṇ-zhunk′	" "
25						
26	Ih′-kä	My mother.	Ih′-kä	My mother.	Ih′ kä.....................	My mother.
27	E′-ke-ä.....................	" "	E′-ke-ä.....................	" "	E′-ke-ä.....................	" "
28	Ush′-kï.....................	" "	Ush′-kï.....................	" "	A-huc′-ne	My aunt.
29	Ush′-kï.....................	" "	Ush′-kï.....................	" "	Ush′-kï	My mother.
30	Sush-ko′-sï.....................	My little mother.	Ush-ko′-sï.....................	My little mother.	Hap-po′-sï	My grandmother.
31	Chuch′-kŭ-che′.....................	" " "	Chuch′-kŭ-che′.....................	" " "	Chu-pŭ′-se	" " "
32	A-gwä-tï-nä′-ï.....................	My step-parent.	A-gwä-tï-nä′-ï.....................	My step-parent.	E-hlau′-gï	My aunt.
33					Ah-ge-h′lo′-gih	" "
34	Ah-te′-rä.....................	My mother.	Ah-te′-rä.....................	My mother.	Ah-te′-rä	My mother.
35	A-te-rä.....................	" "	A-te′-rä.....................	" "	A-te′-rä	" "
36						
37	Nee-tim′.....................	My sister-in-law.	N′-jä′-koase	My sister-in-law	Nee′-che-moos	My cousin.
38	Nee-tim′.....................	" "	N′-jä′-koase	" "	Nee′-che-moosh	" "
39	Nee-tim′.....................	" "	N′-dä′-koase	" "	Nee′-ta-moos	" "
40	Nï′-nim.....................	" "	Nin-dän′-gwe	" "	Nï-nï-mo′-she	" "
41	Ne′-nim.....................	" "	Nin-don′-gwa	" "	Ne-ne-mo′-sha	" "
42	Ne-nim′.....................	" "	Nin-dän-gwa′	" "	Ne-ne-moo-shä′	" "
43	Ne-nim′.....................	" "	N′-däṇ-gwä′	" "	Ne-ne-moo-shä′	" "
44	Ne-nim′.....................	" "	N′-däṇ-gwa′	" "	Ne-ne-moo-shä′	" "
45						
46	Laṇ-gwä-lä.....................	My daught.-in-law.	Laṇ-gwä-lä	My daught.-in-law.	Shame-sä′	My niece.
47	Nä-hä-gä-na′-kwa No-ko-mä′	" "	Nä-hä-gä-na′-kwa No-ko-mä′	" "	Ne-she′-mis-sä′	" "
48	Nä-hä-gä-na′-kwa No-ko-mä′	" "	Nä-hä-gä-na′-kwä No-ko-mä′	" "	Ne-she′-mis-sä′	" "
49	Nä-hä-gä-na-kwa′ No-ko-mä′	" "	Nä-hä-gä-na-kwä No-ko-mä′	" "	Ne-she-mis-sä′	" "
50	Nä-hä-gä-na-kwa′ No-ko-mä′	" "	Nä-hä-gä-na-kwä′ No-ko-mä′	" "	Ne-she-mis-sä′	" "
51	Nä-sem′-yä.....................	" "	Nä-hä-gä′-ne-kwam	" "	Nä-shä-mis′	" "
52	Mo-hä′-kun-e-uk-ye-yu′.....	" "	No-hä′-kun-e-uk-ye-yu′	" "	Nä-nä′-mä	" "
53	Nee-tum′.....................	My sister-in-law.	Nach-a-ma′.....................	My sister-in-law.		
54					Ni-sem-e-thä′	" "
55	Nï-tha-mï-ah′.....................	My daught.-in-law.	Ni-tha-mï-ah′.....................	My daught.-in-law.	Ne-sa-me-thä′	" "
56	Nee-tim′.....................	My sister-in-law.	Ne-ta′-be.....................	My sister-in-law.	Na′-be	My elder sister.
57	N′-do′-to-ke-man′.............	" "	Ne-nis′.....................	" "	Ne′-tä-kame ?	My cousin.
58	N′-do′-to-ke-man′.............	" "	Ne-mis′.....................	" "		
59	Ne-lu-mŭs′.....................	" "	Nu-mak-tem′.....................	" "	Nu-mees	My elder sister.
60	Nee-lu-mus′.....................	" "	Nu-täkwe.....................	" "	Nu-tä-kw-sus′-kw	My step-sister.
61	Nee-num′.....................	" "	N′-dä-oh·k′.....................	" "	N′-dä-kwus-oh′-kwä-oh ..	" " "
62	Nee-lum′.....................	" "	Nee-tä′-wis.....................	" "	N′-doh-kwä-yome′	" " "
63	Na-nee-lim′.....................	" "	Nain-ne-la′-kon	" "	Nain-na-wase′	My elder sister.
64	Sa′-gy.....................	" "	Sa′-gy.....................	" "	Sä′-dä	" " "
65	Sa-ten′-a-bä′-che-la...........	" "	Sa′-ga.....................	" "	Sa-tso-yä′-za ?	My cousin.
66	Set′-so	" "	Sa′-o-ga.....................	" "	Set-dez′-a-ä-ze	My elder sister.
67					Sa′-che	" " "
68	Se-ya-ut.....................	My daught.-in-law.	Se-ya-ut	My daught.-in-law.	Sa-che	" " "
69	Is-säs-täm	My sister-in-law.			Is-soo-se-mäm	My sister.
70						
71	In-matsh.....................	" "			In-chats or En-naks	(Not rendered.) [My step-sister.
72						
73						
74						
75						
76						
77					Päb′-chä	My cousin.
78						
79					Ig-dlo-ra.....................	" "
80	I-e′-gä	My sister-in-law.	Oo-koo-ä′-gä.....................	My sister-in-law.	Il-lŭng′-ä.....................	" "

TABLE II.—*Continued.*

	96. My father's sister's daughter—older than myself. (Female speaking.)	Translation.	97. My father's sister's daughter—younger than myself. (Male speaking.)	Translation.	98. My father's sister's daughter—younger than myself. (Female speaking.)	Translation.
1	Ah-găre'-seh	My cousin.	Ah-găre'-seh	My cousin.	Ah-găre'-seh	My cousin.
2	Ah-ge-ah'-seh	" "	Ah-ge-ah'-seh	" "	Ah-ge-ah'-seh	" "
3	Ah-gare'-seh	" "	Ah-gare'-seh	" "	Ah-gare'-seh	" "
4	Un-gă-lä'-seh	" "	Un-gă-lä'-seh	" "	Un-gă-lä'-seh	" "
5	Un-gă-läss'	" "	Un-gă-läss'	" "	Un-gă-läss'	" "
6	Ahk-gä-rä'-sthar	" "	Ahk-gä-rä'-sthar	" "	Ahk-gä-rä'-sthar	" "
7	Ak-je'-yä	My elder sister.	Ka-gä'-ah	My younger sister.	Ka-gä'-ah	My younger sister.
8	Jä-rä'-seh	My cousin.	Jä-rä'-seh	My cousin.	Jä-rä'-seh	My cousin.
9	E-cha'-pan-she	" "	Hän-kä-she	" "	E-cha'-pän-she	" "
10	Cha'-pä-she	" "	Hä-kä'-she	" "	Cha'-pä-she	" "
11	Pä'-zha	" "	Ah-kä'-zha	" "	Pä'-zha	" "
12	A-cha-pä'-zhe	" "	Hä-kä'-she	" "	A-cha-pä'-zhe	" "
13	S'cha-pä-she	" "	Hun-kä'-she	" "	S'-cha-pä'-she	" "
14	Cha-pä'-she	" "	Hun-kä'-she	" "	Cha-pä'-she	" "
15	Cha-pä'-she	" "	Ha-kä'-zhe	" "	Cha-pä'-she	" "
16	Cha-pä'-she	" "	Ha-kä'-she	" "	Cha-pä'-she	" "
17	Mä-hä'-gä-she	" "	Zä-hä'-she	" "	Ma-hä'-gä-she	" "
18	Win-no'-ga	My daughter.	Tä-zhä'-hä	My niece.	Win-no'-ga	My daughter.
19	Wee-zhun'-ga	" "	We-te'-zhä	" "	Wee-zhun'-ga	" "
20	Heen-yun'-ga	" "	Heen-toas'-ka-me	" "	Heen-yun'-ga	" "
21	He-yun'-ga	" "	Hin-tose-kee-me	" "	He-yun'-ga	" "
22	She-me'-she-gä	" "	Be-che'-zho	" "	She-me'-she-gä	" "
23	We-shon'-ka	" "	We-che'-zho	" "	We-shon'-ka	" "
24	E-nook'	" "	E-choon-zhuuk'	" "	E-nook'	" "
25						
26	Ih'-kä	My mother.	Ih'-kä	My mother.	Ih'-kä	My mother.
27	E'-ke-ä	" "	E'-ke-ä	" "	E'-ke-ä	" "
28	Up-puk'-ne	My grandmother.	A-huc'-ne	My aunt.	Up-puk'-ne	My grandmother.
29	Ush'-kĭ	" "	Ush'-kĭ	My mother.	Ush'-kĭ	My mother.
30	Hap-po'-sĭ	" "	Hap-po'-sĭ	My grandmother.	Hap-po'-sĭ	My grandmother.
31	Chu-pŭ'-se	" "	Chu-pŭ'-se	" "	Chu-pŭ'-se	" "
32	E-hlan'-gĭ	My aunt.	E-hlan'-gĭ	My aunt.	E-hlan'-gĭ	My aunt.
33	Ah-ge-h'lo'-gih	" "	Ah-ge-h'lo'-gih	" "	Ah-ge-h'lo'-gih	" "
34	Ah-te'-rä	My mother.	Ah-te'-rä	My mother.	Ah-te'-rä	My mother.
35	A-te'-rä	" "	A-te'-rä	" "	A-te'-rä	" "
36						
37	N'-jä'-koase	My cousin.	Nee'-che-moos	My cousin.	N'-jä'-koase	My cousin.
38	N'-jä'-koase	" "	Nee'-che-moosh	" "	N'-dä'-koase	" "
39	N'-dä'-koase	" "	Nee'-ta-moos	" "	N'-jä'-koase	" "
40	Nin-dän'-go-she	" "	Nĭ-nĭ-mo'-she	" "	Nin-dän'-go-she	" "
41	Ne-don'-go-sha	" "	Ne-ne-mo'-sha	" "	Ne-don'-go-sha	" "
42	N'-dä-n'-go-shä'	" "	Ne-ne-moo-shä'	" "	N'-dä-n'-go-shä'	" "
43	N'-dan-gwush-ä'	" "	Ne-ne-moo-shä'	" "	N'-dan-gwush-ä'	" "
44	N'-dä-kwam'	" "	Ne-ne-moo-shä'	" "	N'-dä-kwam'	" "
45						
46	Nin-dä'-nä	My daughter.	Shame-sä'	My niece.	Nin-dä'-nä	My daughter.
47	Nin-dä'-nä	" "	Ne-she'-mis-sä'	" "	Nin-dä'-nä	" "
48	Nin-dä'-nä	" "	Ne-she'-mis-sä'	" "	Nin-dä'-nä	" "
49	N'-dä'-nä	" "	Ne-she-mis-sä'	" "	N'-dä'-nä	" "
50	N'-dä'-nä	" "	Ne-she-mis-sä'	" "	N'-dä'-nä	" "
51	Nä-tä'-nis	" "	Nä-shä-mis'	" "	Nä-tä'-nis	" "
52	Ne-tane'	" "	Nä-nä'-mä	" "	Ne-tane'	" "
53						
54	Ni-ton-na-thä	" "	Ni-sem-e-thä'	" "	Ni-ton-na-thä	" "
55	Nĭ-tä-na-thä'	" "	Ne-sa-me-thä'	" "	Nĭ-tä-na-thä'	" "
56	Na'-be	My elder sister.	Na'-be-ä	My younger sister.	Na'-be-ä	My younger sister.
57	Ne-mis'-tä	" " "	Ne'-tä-kame ?	My cousin.	Ne-sis'-sä	" " "
58						
59	Nu-mees'	" " "	N'-kwa-jeech	My younger sister.	N'-kwa-jeech'	" " "
60	N'-tul-nŭ'	My step-sister.	Nu-tä-kw-sus'-kw	My step-sister.	N'-tul-nŭ'	My step-sister.
61	N'-ko-kwä'	" "	N'-dä-kwus-oh'-kwä-oh..	" "	N'-ko-kwä'	" "
62	Neet-koh-kw'	" "	N'-doh'-kwä-yome'	" "	Neet -koh-'-kw'	" "
63	Nain-na-wase'	My elder sister.	Nain-hise-sa-mus'	My younger sister.	Nain-hise'-sa-mus'	My younger sister.
64	Sä'-dä	" "	A-da'-ze	" "	A-da'-ze	" "
65	Sa'-ga	My sister-in-law.	Sa-tso-yä'-za ?	My cousin.	Sa'-ga	My sister-in-law.
66	Set-dez'-a-ä-ze	My elder sister.	Sä'-re	My younger sister.	Sä'-re	My younger sister.
67	Sa-che'	" " "	Sa-chith'	" " "	Sa-chith'	" " "
68	Sa-che	" " "	Se-chy-o	" " "	Sa-cha-the	" " "
69	In-chit'-sha	" " "			In-tchit-chä-opes'	" " "
70						
71						
72						
73						
74						
75						
76						
77	Päb'-chä	My cousin.	Päb-chä	My cousin.	Päb'-chä	My cousin.
78						
79	Ig-dlo-ra	" "				
80	Il-lo'-ä	" "	Il-lüng'-ä	" "	Il-lo'-ä	" "

TABLE II.—*Continued.*

	99. My father's sister's daughter's husband. (Male speaking.)	Translation.	100. My father's sister's daughter's husband. (Female speaking.)	Translation.	101. My father's sister's son's son. (Male speaking.)	Translation.
1	Ah-ge͡ah'-ne͡o	My brother-in-law.	Ha-yă'-o	My brother-in-law.	Ha-ah'-wuk	My son.
2	Uh-ge͡ah'-ne͡o	" "	Ha-yă'-ho	" "	Ha-hä'-wuk	" "
3	Ah-ge-ah'-ne-o	" "	Ah-ge-ah'-de-o	" "	Ha-hä'-wä	" "
4	Un-ge͡ah'-de͡o	" "	Un-ge͡ah'-le-o	" "	Le-yä'-hä	" "
5	Un-gä-de͡o'-hä	" "	Un-gä-le-yä'-ah	" "	E-yä'	" "
6	Ack-gaw'-na-ah	" "	Ack-gaw'-na-ah	" "	Kä-yä'-no-nä	My child.
7	Un-jä-go'-hä	" "	Un-jä-go'-hä	" "	Le-yä'-ah	My son.
8	O-in-dä'-wait	" "	Ah-zhä'-ku	" "	A-ne-ah'	" "
9	Tä-häŋ'	" "	She-chay'	" "	Me-chink'-she	" "
10	Tä-hä'	" "	She-cha'	" "	Me-chink'-she	" "
11	Tä-hä'	" "	She-cha'	" "	Ah-she'-dä	" "
12	Tä-hä'	" "	She-cha'	" "	Me-chink'-she	" "
13	Tä-hä'	" "	She-cha'	" "	Me-chink'-se-lä	" "
14	Tä-hä'	" "	She-ches'	" "	Me-chink'-she	" "
15	Tä-hä'	" "	She'-cha	" "	Me-chink'-she	" "
16	Tä-huh'	" "	She cha'.	" "	Me-chink'-she	" "
17	Mä-hä'-gä		Me-she'-cha		Me-chink'-she	
18	We-tuh'-da	My son-in-law.	We-tuh'-da	My son-in-law.	Toosh'-pä-hä	My grandchild.
19	We-tä'-da	" "	We-tä'-da	" "	Wee-tŭsh'-pä	My grandson.
20	Wä-do'-hä	" "	Wä-do'-hä	" "	Heen-tä'-kwä	" "
21	Wan-do'-hä	" "	Wan-do'-hä	" "	E-ta'-kwä	
22	Be-to'-ja	" "	Be-to'-ja	" "	Be-chose'-pä	My grandchild.
23	We-ton'-chä	" "	We-ton'-chä	" "	We-chose'-pä	
24	E-wong'-o		Wä-to-ho'		E-choonsh'-ka-neke'	My little gd. son.
25						
26	Tä-ta'	My father.	Tä-ta'	My father.	Bus-bä'-he-ä	
27	Ah-h·a'	" "	Ah-h·a'	" "		
28	Um-uh'-fo	My grandfather.	Um-uh'-fo	My grandfather.	A'-kĭ	My father.
29	A'-kĭ	My father.	A'-kĭ	My father.		" "
30	Um-u-fo'-sĭ	My little gd. father.	Um-u-fo'-sĭ	My little gd. father.	Et-e-bä'-pĭ-shĭ-li	My brother.
31	Chu-pŭ-cha'	" " "	Chu-pŭ-cha'	" " "	Chuhl-kŭ-che'	My little father.
32	A-gwä-tĭ-nä'-ĭ	My step-parent.	A-gwä-tĭ-nä'-ĭ	My step-parent.	E-dan-dä'	My father.
33					Ah-ge-do'-dä	
34	Ah-te'-put	My grandfather.	Ah-te'-put	My grandfather.	E-dä'-deh	My brother.
35					A-te'-ase	My father.
36						
37	Neese-tow'	My brother-in-law.	Nee-tim'	My brother-in-law.	N'-do'-sim	My step-son.
38	Neese-tow'	" "	Nee-tim'	" "	N'-do'-zhim	" "
39	Neesh-tow'	" "	Nee-tim'	" "	N'-do'-zhin	" "
40	Nĭ'-tä	" "	Nĭ'-nim	" "	Nin-do'-zhin	" "
41	Ne-che-ke'-wă-ze	" "	Ne'-nim	" "	Nin-do'-shim	" "
42	Ne-tä'	" "	Ne-nim'	" "	N'-do-zhim'	" "
43	Ne-tä'	" "	Ne-nim'	" "	N'-do-zhim-ä'	" "
44	Ne-tä'	" "	Ne-nim'	" "	N'-do-zhim'	" "
45						
46	Na-hun'-gä-nä	My son-in-law.	Na-han'-gä-nä	My son-in-law.	No-sa-mä'	My grandchild.
47	Ne-lä'-gwä-lä'	" "	Ne-lä'-gwä-lä'	" "	No-sa-mä	
48	Ne-lä'-gwä-lä'	" "	Ne-lä'-gwä-lä'	" "	No-sa-mä	
49	N'-dä'-gwä-lä'	" "	N'-dä'-gwä-lä'	" "	No-sa-mä'	
50	N'-dä'-gwä-lä'	" "	N'-dä'-gwä-lä'	" "	No-sa-mä'	
51	Nä-nä-gwun'	" "	Nä-nä-gwun'	" "	No-she-sem'	
52	Ne-nä'-kwun	" "	Ne-nä'-kwun	" "	No-she-sä'	
53	Na-to'	My brother-in-law.	Nee-tum'	My brother-in-law.		
54					No-se-thä'-mä	" "
55	Nin-hä-kä-na-mä'	My son-in-law.	Nin-hä-kä-na-mä	My son-in-law.	No-stha-thä'	
56	Ne-ah'-ă	My brother-in-law.	Ne-ta'-be	My brother-in-law.		
57	Nis'-tä-no	" "	Ne-to'-to-yome	" "	N'-do'-to-ko	My step-son.
58					Noh'-ko'-ä	My son.
59	Nu-mäk-tem'	" "	Ne-lu-mŭs'	" "	N'-kwis'	" "
60	Nu-mäk-tem'	" "	Nee-lu-mŭs'	" "	N'-too-ä'-sum	" "
61	N'-dä-oh k'	" "	Nee-num'	" "	Nä-kun'	My step-child.
62	Noh'-tau̯-kw'	" "	Nee-lum'	" "	N'-kweese'	My son.
63	Na-nä̯donkue'	" "	Na-ne-lim'	" "	Nain-gwase'	" "
64	Sä'-gä	" "	Sä'-gä	" "	Tu-zen'-a	My step-son.
65	Sa'-ga	" "	Sa'-ga	" "	Sa-yä'-za	My son.
66	Sa'-o-ga	" "	Set-shi'-ya	" "	Se-yä'-za	" "
67						
68	Sa-cha-koon-du-i	(Not rendered.)	Set-shai	My grandchild.	Set-she	My grandchild.
69	Snatch'l-hu	My brother-in-law.				
70						
71	Enm-au'-wi-tahtl	" "				
72						
73						
74						
75						
76						
77						
78						
79						
80	Ning-a-ou'-gwä	My brother-in-law.	I-e'-gä	My brother-in-law.	Kung-e-ä'-gä	My nephew.

TABLE II.—*Continued.*

	102. My father's sister's son's son. (Female speaking.)	Translation.	103. My father's sister's son's daughter. (Male speaking.)	Translation.	104. My father's sister's son's daughter. (Female speaking.)	Translation.
1	Ha-soh'-neh	My nephew.	Ka-ah'-wuk	My daughter.	Ka-soh'-neh	My niece.
2	Ha-hä'-wuk	My son.	Ka-hä'-wuk	" "	Ka-hä'-wuk	My daughter.
3	Ha-hä'-wä	" "	Ka-hä'-wä	" "	Ka-hä'-wa	" "
4	Le-yä'-hä	" "	Ka-yä'-hä	" "	Ka-yä'-hä	" "
5	E-yä'	" "	Ka-yä'	" "	Ka-yä'	" "
6	Kä-yä'-no-nä	My child.	Kä-yä'-no-nä	My child.	Kä-yä'-no-nä	My child.
7	Le-yä'-ah	My son.	Ka-yä'-hä	My daughter.	Ka-yä'-ah	My daughter.
8	He-wä'-teh	" "	E-ne-ah'	" "	E-wä'-teh	My niece.
9	Me-toush'-kä	" "	Me-chunk'-she	" "	Me-tun'-zhan	My daughter.
10	Me-to͡us'-kä	" "	Me-chounk'-she	" "	Me-to͡us'-zä	My niece.
11	Me-toash'-kä	" "	Me-chunk'-shä	" "	Me-to'-zhä	" "
12	Me-toze'-kä	" "	Me-chunk'-she	" "	Me-to'-zhä	" "
13	Me-toans'-kä	" "	Me-chunk'-se-lä	" "	Me-toh'-zhä	" "
14	Me-toaze'-kä	" "	Me-chunk'-she	" "	Me-toh'-zhä	" "
15	Me-toash'-kä	" "	Me-chŭnk'-she	" "	Me-to'-zä	" "
16	Me-toas'-kä	" "	Me-chŭnk'-she	" "	Me-to'-zä	" "
17	Me-to'-zä	" "	Me-chunk'-she	" "	Me-to'-zä	" "
18	Toosh'-pä-hä	My grandchild.	Toosh-pä-hä	My grandchild.	Toosh-pä-hä	My grandchild.
19	Wee-tŭsh'-pä	" "	Wee-tŭsh'-pä	" "	Wee-tŭsh'-pä	" "
20	Heen-tä'-kwä	My grandson.	Heen-tä'-kwä-me	My granddaughter.	Heen-tä'-kwä-me	My gd. daughter.
21	E-tä'-kwä		E-tä'-kwä-me	" "	E-tä'-kwä-me	
22	Be-chose'-pä	My grandchild.	Be-chose'-pä	My grandchild.	Be-chose'-pä	My grandchild.
23	We-chose'-pä	" "	We-chose'-pä	" "	We-chose'-pä	" "
24	E-choon-zhunk'-e-neke	My little gd. daught.	E-choonsh'-ka-neke	My little grandson.	E-choon-zhunk'-e-neke'	My little gd. dau.
25						
26						
27	Bus-bä'-he-ä		Bus-bä'-he-ä		Bus-bä'-he-ä	
28	A'-kï	My father.	An'-take	My younger sister.	Suh-näk'-fish	My y'nger sister.
29	A'-kï	" "	An'-take	" " "	Et-e-bä'-pï-shï-lï	My sister.
30	A-näk-fï	My elder brother.	An'-take	" " "	Et-e-bä'-pï-shï-lï	" "
31	Chuhl-kŭ-che'	My little father.	Chu-pŭ'-se	My grandmother.	Chu-pŭ'-se	My grandmother.
32	E-dau-dä'	My father.	Un-gï-dau'	My younger sister.	Un-gï-lun'-ï	My y'nger sister.
33	Ah-ge-do'-dä	" "	An-ke-doh	" " "	An-ge-lä'-ih	" "
34	E-rats'-teh	My brother.	E-tä'-heh	My sister.	E-dä'-deh	My sister.
35	A-te'-ase	My father.	A-tä'-he	" "	A-tä'-he	" "
36						
37	N'-de-kwä-tim'	My nephew.	N'-do-sa-mis-kwame'	My step-daughter.	Neese-che-mis'	My niece.
38	N'-de-kwä-tim'	" "	N'-do-zha-mis-kwame'	" "	Neest-che-mish	" "
39	N'-deh-kwä-tim'	" "	N'-do-zhï-mis-kwem'	" "	Neest-che-mis'	" "
40	Nï-nin-gwä'-niss	" "	Nin-do-zhï-mï'-kwem	" "	Nï-shï'-miss	" "
41	Ne-nin-gwuh'-nis	" "	Nin-do'-zhe-mi-quam	" "	Ne-she'-me-sha	" "
42	Ne-nin-gwi-nis'	" "	Nin-do'-zha-mi-kwam'	" "	Ne-she-mis'	" "
43	Ne-nin-gwi-nis'	" "	N'-do'-zha-mï-kwam'	" "	Ne-she-mis'	" "
44	Ne-nin-gwi-nis'	" "	N'-do'-zha-mï-kwem'	" "	Ne-she-mis'	" "
45						
46	No-sa-mä'	My grandchild.	No-sa-mä'	My grandchild.	No-sa-mä'	My grandchild.
47	No-sa'-mä	" "	No-sa'-mä	" "	No-sa'-mä	" "
48	No-sa'-mä	" "	No-sa'-mä	" "	No-sa'-mä	" "
49	No-sa-mä'	" "	No-sa-mä'	" "	No-sa-mä'	" "
50	No-sa-mä'	" "	No-sa-mä'	" "	No-sa-mä'	" "
51	No-she-sem'	" "	No-she-sem'	" "	No-she-sem'	" "
52	No-she-sä'	" "	No-she-sä'	" "	No-she-sä'	" "
53						
54	No-se-thä'-mä	" "	Na-se-thä'-mä	" "	Na-se-thä'-mä	" "
55	No-stha-thä'	" "	No-stha-thä'	" "	No-stha-thä'	" "
56						
57	N'-do'-to-yose	My nephew.	N'-to'-to-tun	My step-daughter.	Nee-mis'-sä	My niece.
58	No-ä'-toase	" "	Ne-tan'-ä	My daughter.	Nee-mis'-sä	" "
59	Nu-lüks'	" "	N-tŭs'	" "	N'-sum'	" "
60	Nu-lü'-knees	" "	N'-su'-mus	" "	N'-sum'	" "
61	Nä-kun'	My step-child.	Nä-kun'	My step-child.	Nä-kun'	My step-child.
62	N'-kweese'	My son.	N'-dä-nuss'	My daughter.	N'-dä-nuss'	My daughter.
63	Nain-gwase'	" "	Nain-dä'-ness	" "	Nain-dä'-ness	" "
64	Sa-yä'-ze	My step-son.	Sa-yä'-dze	My step-daughter.	Sa-yä'-dze	" "
65	Sa-yä'-za	My son.	Sa-to'-a	My daughter.	Sa-to'-a	" "
66	Se-yä'-za	" "	Sa-le'-ä	" "	Sa-le'-ä	" "
67						
68	Set-shai	My grandchild.	Set-she	My grandchild.	Ses-shai	My grandchild.
69						
70						
71						
72						
73						
74						
75						
76						
77						
78						
79						
80	Ung-ä'-gä	My nephew.	Kun-e-ä'-gä	My niece.	Ung-ä'-gä	My niece.

TABLE II.—*Continued.*

	105. My father's sister's daughter's son. (Male speaking.)	Translation.	106. My father's sister's daughter's son. (Female speaking.)	Translation.	107. My father's sister's daughter's daughter. (Male speaking.)	Translation.
1	Ha-yă′-wan-da............	My nephew.	Ha-ah′-wuk	My son.	Ka-yă′-wan-da............	My niece.
2	Hä-yuh′-wä-deh	" "	Ha-hä′-wuk	" "	Ka-yuh′-wä-deh	" "
3	Ha-yä-wä′-da............	" "	Ha-hä′-wä	" "	Ka-yä-wä′-da............	" "
4	Ha-yä′-wan-dä	" "	Le-yä′-hä	" "	Ka-yä′-wan-dä..........	" "
5	E-yo-wä′-dä............	" "	E-yä′....................	" "	Ka-yo-wä′-dä...........	" "
6	Kä-yä′-wä-nä............	" "	Kä-yä′-no-nä............	My child.	Kä-yä′-wä-nä............	" "
7	Le-wä-dä′-ah............	" "	Le-yä′...................	My son.	Ka-wä-dä′-ah............	" "
8	Ha-shone-drä′-ka........	" "	A-ne-ah′.................	" "	Ya-shone-drä′-kä	" "
9	Me-tonsh′-kä............	" "	Me-chink′-she...........	" "	Me-tuṇ′-zhaṇ	" "
10	Me-to⌢us′-kä	" "	Me-chink′-she...........	" "	Me-to⌢us′-zä...........	" "
11	Me-toash′-kä............	" "	Ak-she′-da.............	" "	Me-to′-zhä	" "
12	Me-tose′-kä.............	" "	Me-chink′-she...........	" "	Me-to′-zhä	" "
13	Me-toans′-kä............	" "	Me-chink′-se-lä.........	" "	Me-toh′-zhä	" "
14	Me-toase′-kä............	" "	Me-chink′-she...........	" "	Me-toh′-zhä	" "
15	Mĕ-toash′-kä............	" "	Me-chink′-she...........	" "	Me-to′-zä	" "
16	Me-toas′-kä.............	" "	Me-chink′-she...........	" "	Me-to′-zä	" "
17	Me-to′-zä...............	" "	Me-chink′-she...........	" "	Me-to′-zä	" "
18	Toosh′-pä-hä............	My grandchild.	Toosh′-pä-hä............	My grandchild.	Toosh′-pä-hä............	My grandchild.
19	Wee-tŭsh′-pä...........	" "	Wee-tŭsh′-pä...........	" "	Wee-tŭsh′-pä...........	" "
20	Heen-tä′-kwä...........	My grandson.	Heen-tä′-gwä...........	My grandson.	Heen-tä′-kwä-me	My gd. daughter.
21	E-tä′-kwä..............	" "	E-tä′-kwä..............	" "	E-tä′-kwä-me	" "
22	Be-chose′-pä...........	My grandchild.	Be-chose′-pä...........	My grandchild.	Be-chose′-pä...........	My grandchild.
23	We-chose′-pä...........	" "	We-chose′-pä...........	" "	We-chose′-pä...........	" "
24	E-choonsh′-ka-neke′.......	My little grandson.	E-choonsh-ka′-neke′.......	My little grandson.	E-chooṇ-zhunk′-e-neke′.......	My little gd. dau.
25						
26						
27	Bus-bä′-he-ä............		Bus-bä′-he-ä............		Bus-bä′-he-ä............	
28	Suh-näk′-fish.	My younger brother.	A-näk′-fĭ...............	My younger brother.	An′-take	My y'nger sister.
29	Et-e-bä′-pĭ-shĭ-lĭ...........	My brother.	A-näk′-fĭ...............	" " "	An′-take	" " "
30	Aug-ko′-sĭ.............	My little father.	Ang-ko′-si.............	My little father.	Hap-po′-sĭ.............	My grandmother.
31	Chuhl′-kŭ-che′...........	" " "	Chuhl-kŭ-che′..........	" " "	Chu-pŭ′-se.............	" " "
32	E-dan-dä′...............	My father.	E-dau-dä′.............	My father.	E-hlau′-gĭ.............	My aunt.
33	Ah-ge-do′-dä...........	" "	Ah-ge-do′-dä	" "	Ah-ge-h′lo′-gih.........	" "
34	Ah-te′-is..............	" "	Ah-te′-is..............	" "	Ah-te′-rä	My mother.
35	A-dä′-de...............	My brother.	A-dä′-de...............	My brother.		
36						
37	N'-de-kwä-tim′..........	My nephew.	N'-go′-sim.............	My step-son.	Neese-che-mis′............	My niece.
38	N'-de-kwä-tim′..........	" "	N'-go′-zhim............	" "	Neest-che-mish′...........	" "
39	N'-deh-kwä-tim′.........	" "	N'-do′-zhim............	" "	Neest-che-mis′...........	" "
40	Nĭ-nin-gwä′-niss........	" "	Nin-do′-zhĭ-miss........	My step-child.	Nĭ-shĭ′-miss............	" "
41	Ne-nin-gwuh′-nis........	" "	Nin-do′-zhe-mis.........	" "	Ne-she′-me-sha..........	" "
42	Ne-nin-gwi-nis′.........	" "	Nin-gwis′..............	My son.	Ne-she-mis′.............	" "
43	Ne-nin-gwi-nis′.........	" "	Nin-gwis′..............	" "	Ne-she-mis′.............	" "
44	Ne-nin-gwi-nis′.........	" "	N'-gwis′...............	" "	Ne-she-mis′.............	" "
45						
46	No-sa-mä′...............	My grandchild.	No-sa-mä′...............	My grandchild.	No-sa-mä′...............	My grandchild.
47	No-sa′-mä	" "	No-sa′-mä..............	" "	No-sa′-mä..............	" "
48	No-sa′-ma	" "	No-sa′-mä..............	" "	No-sa′-mä..............	" "
49	No-sa-mä′...............	" "	No-sa-mä′..............	" "	No-sa-mä′..............	" "
50	No-sa-mä′...............	" "	No-sa-mä′..............	" "	No-sa-mä′..............	" "
51	No-she-sem′.............	" "	No-she-sem′............	" "	No-she-sem′............	" "
52	No-she-sä′..............	" "	No-she-sä′	" "	No-she-sä′.............	" "
53						
54	Na-se-thä′-mă	" "	Na-se-thä′-mä	" "	Na-se-thä′-mă	" "
55	No-stha-thä′............	" "	No-stha-thä′............	" "	No-stha-thä′............	" "
56						
57	N'-do′-to-yose..........	My nephew.	N'-do′-to-ko	My step-son.	Nee-mis′-sä............	My niece.
58	No-ă′-toase	" "	Noh-ko′-ä..............	My son.	Nee-mis′-sa............	" "
59	Nu-lŭks′...............	" "	N'-kwis................	" "	N'-sum	" "
60	Nu-lŭ′-knees...........	" "	N'-tŭ-ă′-sum...........	" "	N'-sum′................	" "
61	No-kwath′..............	" "	N'-di-ome′.............	" "	Noh·k-soh·-kwä′-oh.......	" "
62	Longue′-kw′............	" "	N'-kweese′.............	" "	Longue-kwä	" "
63	Na-lone′-gwä-sis′.......	" "	Nain-gwase′............	" "	Na-lone-gwä-sis′.......	" "
64	Sä′-zy.................	" "	Sa-yä′-ze..............	" "	Sä′-zy.................	" "
65	Sa-yä′-za..............	My son.	Sa-yä′-za..............	" "	Sa-te′-a...............	" "
66	Se-yä′-za..............	" "	Se-yä′-za..............	" "	Sa-le′-ă...............	My daughter.
67						
68	Set-she................	My grandchild.	Set-shai	My grandchild.	Set-she	My grandchild.
69						
70						
71						
72						
73						
74						
75						
76						
77						
78						
79						
80	We-yo-o′-gwä..............	My nephew.	Noo-ä-gä......................	My nephew.	We-yo-o′-gwä..............	My niece.

TABLE II.—*Continued.*

	108. My father's sister's daughter's daughter. (Female speaking.)	Translation.	109. My father's sister's great grandson.	Translation.	110. My father's sister's great granddaughter.	Translation.
1	Ka-ah'-wuk	My daughter.	Ha-yä'-da	My grandson.	Ka-yä'-da	My gd. daughter.
2	Ka-hä'-wuk	" "	Ha-yä'-dra	" "	Ka-yä'-dra	" "
3	Ka-hä'-wä	" "	Ha-yä'-da	" "	Kä-yä'-da	" "
4	Ka-yä'-hä	" "	Le-yä'-dla-ah	" "	Ka-yä'-dla-ah	" "
5	Ka-yä'	" "	E-yä'-dla-ah	" "	Ka-yä'-dla-ah	" "
6	Kä-yä'-no-nä	My child.	Kä-yä'-rä	My grandchild.	Ka-yä'-rä	My grandchild.
7	Ka-yä'-hä	My daughter.	Le-yä-tä-ra-yä	My grandson.	Ka-yä-tä-ra-yä	My gd. daughter.
8	E-ne-ah'	" "	Ha-tra'-ah	" "	Ya-tra'-ah	" "
9	Me-chunk'-she	" "	Me-tä'-ko-zhä	My grandchild.	Me-tä'-ko-zhä	My grandchild.
10	Me-chounk'-she	" "	Me-tä'-ko-zha	" "	Me-tä'-ko-zha	" "
11	Ak-she'-dä	" "	Me-tä'-ko-zhä	" "	Me-tä'-ko-zha	" "
12	Me-chunk'-she	" "	Me-tä'-ko-zha	" "	Me-tä'-ko-zha	" "
13	Me-chunk'-se-lä	" "	Me-tä'-ko-säk-pok	" "	Me-tä'-ko-säk-pok	" "
14	Me-chunk'-she	" "	Me-tä'-ko-zhä	" "	Me-tä'-ko-zhä	" "
15	Me-chŭnk'-she	" "	Me-tä'-ko-zhä	" "	Me-tä'-ko-zä	" "
16	Me-chŭnk'-she	" "	Me-tä'-ko-zä	" "	Me-tä'-ko-sä	" "
17	Me-chunk'-she	" "	Me-tä'-ko-sä	" "	Me-tä'-ko-sä	" "
18	Toosh'-pä-hä	My grandchild.	Toosh'-pä-hä	" "	Toosh'-pä-hä	" "
19	Wee-tŭsh'-pä	" "	Wee-tŭsh'-pä	" "	Wee-tŭsh'-pa	" "
20	Heen-tä'-kwä-me	My granddaughter.	Heen-tä'-kwä	My grandson.	Heen-tä'-kwä-me	My gd. daughter.
21	E-tä'-kwä-me	" "	E-tä'-kwä	" "	E-tä'-kwä-me	" "
22	Be-chose'-pä	My grandchild.	Be-chose'-pä	My grandchild.	Be-chose'-pä	My grandchild.
23	We-chose'-pä	" "	We-chose'-pä	" "	We-chose'-pä	" "
24	E-choon-zhunk'-e-neke'	My little gd. daught.	E-choonsh'-ka-neke'	My little grandson.	E-choon-zhunk'-e-neke'	My little gd. dau.
25						
26						
27	Bus-bä'-he-ä				Suh-sŭh'-take	My daughter.
28	Suh-näk'-fish	My younger sister.	A'-kĭ	My father	Suh-soh'-take	" "
29	Et-e-bä'-pĭ-shĭ-lĭ	My sister.	A'-kĭ	" "		
30	Hap-po'-sĭ	My grandmother.	Ang-ko'-sĭ	My father little.	Hap-po'-sĭ	My gd. mother.
31	Chu-pŭ'-se	" "	Chuhl-kŭ'-che	" " "	Chu-pŭ'-se	" "
32	E-hlau'-gĭ	My aunt.	E-dau-dä'	My father.	A-gwae-tsi'	My child.
33	Ah-ge-h'lo'-gih	" "	Ah-ge-do'-dä	" "	Ah-gwa'-tzse	" "
34	Ah-te'-rä	My mother.	Ah-te'-is	" "	Ah-te'-rä	My mother.
35						
36						
37	N'-do-sa-mis-kwame'	My step-daughter.	No-se-sem'	My grandchild.	No-se-sem'	My grandchild.
38	N'-do-zha-mis-kwame'	" "	No-se-sim'	" "	No-se-sim'	" "
39	N'-do-zha-mis-kwem'	" "	No-se-sem'	" "	No-se-sem'	" "
40	Nin-do'-zhĭ-miss	My step-child.	No-zhĭ'-she	" "	No-zhi'-she	" "
41	Nin-do'-zhe-mis	" "	No-she'-shä	" "	No-she'-shä	" "
42	Nin-dä'-niss	My daughter.	No-she-shä'	" "	No-she-shä'	" "
43	N'-dä-niss'	" "	No-she-shä'	" "	No-she-shä'	" "
44	N'-dä-niss'	" "	No-she-shä'	" "	No-she-shä'	" "
45						
46	No-sa-mä'	My grandchild.	No-sa-mä'	" "	No-sa-mä'	" "
47	No-sa'-mä	" "	No-sa'-mä	" "	No-sa'-mä	" "
48	No-sa'-mä	" "	No-sa'-mä	" "	No-sa'-mä	" "
49	No-sa-mä'	" "	No-sa-mä'	" "	No-sa-mä'	" "
50	No-sa-mä'	" "	No-sa-mä'	" "	No-she-sem'	" "
51	No-she-sem'	" "	No-she-sem'	" "	No-she-sä'	" "
52	No-she-sä'	" "	No-she-sä'	" "		
53						
54	Na-se-thä'-mä	" "	Na-se-thä'-mä	" "	Na-se-thä'-mä	" "
55	No-stha-thä'	" "	No-stha-thä'	" "	No-stha-thä'	" "
56						
57	N'-to'-to-tun	My step-daughter.	Nee-so'-tan	" "	Nee-so'-tan	" "
58	Ne-tan'-ä	My daughter.	Nee-so'-tän	" "	Nee-so'-tän	" "
59	N'-tŭs'	" "	Nŭ-jeech'	" "	Nŭ-jeech'	" "
60	N'-su'-mus	" "	N'-kway'-nus	" "	N'-kway'-nus	" "
61	Nee-chune'	" "	Nä-h·ise'	" "	Nä-h·ise'	" "
62	N'-dä-nuss'	" "	Noh'-whese'	" "	Noh'-whese'	" "
63	Nain-dä'-ness	" "	Nain-no-whase'	" "	Nain-no-whase'	" "
64	Sa-ya'-dze	" "	Sa-t'thu'-a	" "	Sa-t'thu'-a	" "
65	Sa-to'-ä	" "	Sa-ken'-ne	My son.	Sa-to⁻a'-bä	My gd. daughter.
66	Sa-le'-ä	" "	Se-yä-zet'-tha-re	My grandson.	Sa-le-zet'-tha-re	" "
67						
68	Set-shai	My grandchild.	Set-she	" "	Set-she	" "
69						
70						
71						
72						
73						
74						
75						
76						
77						
78						
79						
80	Noo-ä'-gä	My niece.	Eng'-o-tä	My grandchild.	Eng'-o-tä	My grandchild.

TABLE II.—*Continued.*

	111. My father's sister's great grandson's son.	Translation.	112. My father's sister's great grandson's daughther.	Translation.	113. My mother's brother.	Translation.
1	Ha-yä'-da	My grandson.	Ka-yä'-da	My granddaughter.	Hoc-no'-seh	My uncle.
2	Ha-yä'-dra	" "	Ka-yä'-dra	" "	Kuḥ-no'-seh	" "
3	Ha-yä'-da	" "	Ka-yä'-da	" "	Ge-no'-sä-ha	" "
4	Le-yä'-dla-ah	" "	Ka-yä'-dla-ah	" "	Läg-nole'-hä	" "
5	E-yä'-dla-ah	" "	Ka-yä'-dla-ah	" "	Lä-ga-nole'-hä	" "
6	Kä-yä' rä'	My grandchild.	Kä-yä'-rä	My grandchild.	Ahk-rä'-do-no'-re-ah	" "
7	Le-yä-tä-ra'-yä	My grandson.	Ka-yä-tä-ra'-yä	My granddaughter.	Lä-ga-no-hä'-ah	" "
8	Ha-tra'-ah	" "	Ya-tra'-ah	" "	Hä-wä-te-no'-rä	" "
9	Me-tä'-ko-zhä	My grandchild.	Me-tä'-ko-zhä	My grandchild.	Dak-she'	" "
10	Me-tä'-ko-zhä	" "	Me-tä'-ko-zhä	" "	Dake'-she	" "
11	Me-tä'-ko-zhä	" "	Me-tä'-ko-zhä	" "	A-dik'-she	" "
12	Me-tä'-ko-zha	" "	Me-tä'-ko-zha	" "	Ah-dik'-she	" "
13	Me-tä'-ko-säk-pok	" "	Me-tä'-ko-säk-pok	" "	Lake'-she	" "
14	Me-tä'-ko-zhä	" "	Me-tä'-ko-zhä	" "	Lake'-she	" "
15	Me-tä'-ko-zhä	" "	Me-tä'-ko-zhä	" "	Lake'-she	" "
16	Me-tä'-ko-zä	" "	Me-tä'-ko-zä	" "	Lake'-she	" "
17	Me-tä'-ko-sä	" "	Me-tä'-ko-sä	" "	Me-nake'-she	" "
18	Toosh'-pä-hä	" "	Toosh'-pä-hä	" "	Na-ge'-hä	" "
19	Wee-tŭsh'-pä	" "	Wee-tŭsh'-pä	" "	Wee-nä'-gee	" "
20	Heen-tä'-kwä	My grandson.	Heen-tä'-kwä-me	My granddaughter.	Heen-ja'-kä	" "
21	E-tä'-kwä	" "	E-tä'-kwä-me	" "	Hin-chá'-kä	" "
22	Be-chose'-pä	My grandchild.	Be-chose'-pä	My grandchild.	Be-ja'-ga	" "
23	We-chose'-pä	" "	We-chose'-pä	" "	We-ja'-ga	" "
24	E-choonsh'-ka-neke'	My little grandson.	E-choon-zhunk-e-neke'	My little gd. daught.	E-take'	" "
25					Tä-wä'-rä-to-ra	" "
26					Me-ä'-ka (m. s.), Mä-tä-	My elder brother.
27					Bä-sä'-na......[roo' (w. s.)	" " "
28	A'-kĭ	My father.	Sup'-uk	My granddaughter.	Um-ush'-ĭ	My uncle.
29	Sä'-pok-näk'-ne	My grandson.	Sä'-pok	" "	Um-u'-shĭ	" "
30	Ang-ko'-sĭ	My father little.	Hap-po'-sĭ	My grandmother.	Um-o'-shĭ	" "
31	Chuhl-kŭ'-che	" " "	Chu-pŭ'-se	" "	Chu-pä'-wä	" "
32	E-dau-dä'	My father.	Un-gĭ-lĭ-sĭ	My grandchild.	E-dŭ-tsĭ	" "
33	Ah-ge-do'-dä	" "	Aŋ-ge-lee'-se	" "	Ah-ge-doo'-dzĭ	" "
34	Ah-te'-is	" "	Ah-te'-rä	My mother.	Te-wä'-cḥir-iks	" "
35					Te-watch'-e-riks	" "
36					Ah-te-wä-se'-rish	" "
37	No-se-sem'	My grandchild.	No-se-sem'	My grandchild.	Nee-sis'	" "
38	No-se-sim'	" "	No-se-sim'	" "	Nee-sis'	" "
39	No-se-sem'	" "	No-se-sem'	" "	Nee-sis'	" "
40	No-zhi-she	" "	No-zhĭ'-she	" "	Nĭ-zhĭ-she	" "
41	No-she'-shä	" "	No-she'-shä	" "	Ne-zhe-sha	" "
42	No-she-shä	" "	No-she-shä'	" "	Ne-zhe'-shä	" "
43	No-she-shä'	" "	No-she-shä'	" "	Ne-zhish'-shä	" "
44	No-she-shä'	" "	No-she-shä'	" "	Ne-zhish-shä'	" "
45					N'-jeh-shä'	" "
46	No-sa-mä'	" "	No-sa-mä'	" "	Ne-zhese'-sä	" "
47	No-sa'-mä	" "	No-sa'-mä	" "	Ne-zhe'-sä	" "
48	No-sa'-mä	" "	No-sa'-mä	" "	Ne-zhe'-sä	" "
49	No-sa-mä'	" "	No-sa-mä'	" "	Ne-zhe-sän'	" "
50	No-sa-mä'	" "	No-sa-mä'	" "	Ne-zhe-sän	" "
51	No-she-sem'	" "	No-she-sem'	" "	Nä-zhe-sä'	" "
52	No-she-sä'	" "	No-she-sä'	" "	Ne-zha'	" "
53					Nä-she'	" "
54	Na-se-thä'-mä	" "	Na-se-thä'-mä	" "	Na-si-thä'	" "
55	No-stha-thä'	" "	No-stha-thä'	" "	Nĭ-sĭ-thä'	" "
56					Na'-see	" "
57	Nee-so'-tan	" "	Nee-so'-tan	" "	Ne-to-tah'se'	" "
58	Nee-so'-tän	" "	Nee-so'-tän	" "	Nee'-sä	" "
59	Nŭ-jeech'	" "	Nŭ-jeech'	" "	N'-ku-lä-mŭk'-sis	" "
60	N'-kway'-nus	" "	N'-kway'-nus	" "	N'-ku-lä-mook'-sis	" "
61	Nä-h·ise'	" "	Nä-h·ise'	" "	Nee-zeeth'	" "
62	Noh·-whese'	" "	Noh·-whese'	" "	N'-shee'-se	" "
63	Nain-no-whase'	" "	Nain-no-whese'	" "	Nee-zhese'	" "
64	Sa-t'thu'-a	" "	Sa-t'thu'-a	" "	Thä-tha'	" "
65	Sa-ken'-ne	My grandson.	Sa-toⁿä'-bä	" "	A-na-bä'-che-la?	My mother's bro.
66	Se-yä-zet'-tha-re	" "	Sa-le-zet'-tha-re	" "	Ser'-a	My uncle.
67					Soo-e'	" "
68	Set-she	My grandchild.	Set-she	My grandchild.	So-he	" "
69					Is-sä' (m. & f. s.)	" "
70					E-se-see'	" "
71					Na-kah'-kas	" "
72						
73						
74					Sä-non'-wä	" "
75					Me-me	" "
76					Oo-sheet-than	" "
77					Zu-e'-cha	" "
78						
79					Ang-a-ga	" "
80	Eng'-o-tä	My grandchild.	Eng'-o-tä	My grandchild.	Ang-ug'-gä	" "

TABLE II.—*Continued.*

	114. My mother's brother's wife.	Translation.	115. My mother's brother's son—older than myself. (Male speaking.)	Translation.	116. My mother's brother's son—older than myself. (Female speaking.)	Translation.
1	Ah-gă'-nĭ-ah	Aunt-in-law.	Ah-găre'-seh	My cousin.	Ah-găre'-seh	My cousin.
2	Ka-ah'-ne-ha	" "	Ah-ge-ah'-seh	" "	Ah-ge-ah'-seh	" "
3	Ah-gă-ne'-hä	" "	Ah-gare'-seh	" "	Ah-gare'-seh	" "
4	Oc-no-nese'-kwä	My step-mother.	Un-gă-lä'-seh	" "	Un-gă-lä'-seh	" "
5	Ah-ga-nä-nese'-kwä	" "	Un-gă-läss'	" "	Un-gă-läss'	" "
6	Ahk-we'-rä	My aunt-in-law.	Ahk-gä-rä'-sthar	" "	Ahk-gä'-rä-sthar	" "
7	Ah-go-hä'-kwä	My aunt.	Lok-je'-hä	My elder brother.	Lok-je'-ah	My elder brother.
8	Ah-rä'-hoc	" "	Jä-rä'-seh	My cousin.	Jä-rä'-seh	My cousin.
9	Tuṇ-wiṇṇ'	" "	Täṇ-haṇ'-she	" "	She-chay'-she	" "
10	Toh'-we	" "	Tä'-she	" "	She-chä'-she	" "
11	Tonk'-wa	" "	Kä'-zha	" "	She-cha'-ze	" "
12	Tonk'-wa	" "	Tä'-she	" "	She-cha'-she	" "
13	Toh-we'	" "	Tä'-she	" "	S'cha-pa'-she	" "
14	Toh'-we	" "	Tä'-hä-she	" "	She-cha'-she	" "
15	Toh'-we	" "	Tä'-she	" "	She-cha'-she	" "
16	Toh'-we	" "	Tä-hä'-she	" "	She-cha'-she	" "
17	Me-toh'-we	" "	Tä-hä'-she	" "	Me-hä'-gä-she	" "
18	Te-na'-hä	" "	Na-ge'-hä	My uncle.	Na-ge'-hä	My uncle.
19	Wee-tee'-me	" "	Wee-nä'-gee	" "	Wee-nä'-gee	" "
20	Heen-too'-me	" "	Heen-ja'-kä	" "	Heen-ja'-kä	" "
21	E-tŭ'-me	" "	Hin-chä'-kä	" "	Hin-chä'-kä	" "
22	Be-je'-me	" "	Be-ja'-ga	" "	Be-ja'-ga	" "
23	We-je'-me	" "	We-ja'-ga	" "	We-ja'-ga	" "
24	E-chooṇ'-we	" "	E-take'	" "	E-take'	" "
25						
26	Boo-ä-kä'	My sister-in-law.	Mă-de-shä'	My son.	Mă-de-shä'	My son.
27	Moo'-ä-ka	" "	Bot-so'-kă	" "	Bot-so'-kă	" "
28	Suh-hai'-yă	" "	Suh'-sŭh	" "	Suh'-sŭh	" "
29	Sä-hi'-ya	" "	Suh'-soh	" "	Suh'-soh	" "
30	Sush-ho'-sĭ	My little mother.	Su'-soh	" "	Sup'-pok-näk'-nĭ	My grandson.
31	Chu-hu-cho-wä'	My sister-in-law.	Chup-pŭ'-che	" "	Um-os-sŭs'-wä	My grandchild.
32	A-gwä-tĕ-nä'-ĭ	My step-parent.	A-gwae-tsĭ'	My child.	A-gwae-tsĭ'	My child.
33	Tä-le-na-ah-ge-do'-dä	" "	A-gwa'-tze	" "	A-gwa'-tze	" "
34	Tä-te'-luk-tuk-ŭ	My wife.	Pe'-row	" "	Pe'-row	" "
35	Sko'-dus	My daughter-in-law.	Pe'-row	" "	Pe'-row	" "
36						
37	Nis-sĭ-goos'	My aunt.	Neest-chäs'	My cousin.	Nee'-che-moos	My cousin.
38	Nis-se-goos'	" "	Nee-säs'	" "	Nee'-che-moosh	" "
39	Nĭ-se-goos'	" "	Neest-chäs'	" "	Nee'-ta-moos	" "
40	Nin-sĭ'-goss	" "	Nĭ-tä'-wiss	" "	Nĭ-nĭ-mo'-she	" "
41	Ne-ze-gŭs'	" "	Ne-tä'-wis	" "	Ne-ne-mo'-sha	" "
42	Ne-see-goss'	" "	Ne-tä'-wis	" "	Ne-ne-moo-shä'	" "
43	Nis-za-gwis'	" "	Ne-tä'-wis	" "	Ne-ne-moo-shä'	" "
44	Nis-sa-gose'	" "	Ne-tä'-wis	" "	Ne-ne-moo-shä'	" "
45	N'-si-gwis'	" "				
46	N'-sa'-gwe-sä'	" "	Ne-zhese'-sä	My uncle.	Ne-zhese'-sä	My uncle.
47	Ne-ză'-gŏs-sä'	" "	Ne-zhe'-sä	" "	Ne-zhe'-sä	" "
48	Ne-ză'-gŏs-sä'	" "	Ne-zhe'-sä	" "	Ne-zhe'-sä	" "
49	Ne-să'-gwis-sä'	" "	Ne-zhe'-san	" "	Ne-zhe'-san	" "
50	Ne-să'-gwis-sä'	" "	Ne-zhe'-san	" "	Ne-zhe'-san	" "
51	Nak-ye'-hä	" "	Nă-zhe-sä'	" "	Nă-zhe-sä'	" "
52	Ne-ne'	" "	Ne-zha'	" "	Ne-zha'	" "
53	Nă-un'	" "				
54	Na-thä-kwi-thä'	" "	Na-si-thä'	" "	Na-si-thä'	" "
55	Na-tha-gwe-thä'	" "	Nĭ-sĭ-thä'	" "	Nĭ-sĭ-thä'	" "
56	Na-ha'	" "	Nă'-thä-hä?	My elder brother.	Nă'-thä-hä?	My elder brother.
57	Ne-to'-tarse	" "	N'-to'-tes-tä-mo'	My cousin.	N'-do'-to-ke-man'	My cousin.
58	Ne-to'-tah·xs	" "	Noh'-sä-kin'-ame	" "	No-in'-nä	" "
59	Nu-gu'-mich	My grandmother.	N'-sees'	My elder brother.	N'-sees	My elder brother.
60	Noo'-kun	" "	Nu-tä'-gus	My cousin.	Neet-see-kes'	My cousin.
61	No-muths'	My aunt.	N'-dä-kwus'	My step-brother.	N'-donk'	My step-brother.
62	Nooh'-muss	My great aunt.	Nee-mä'-tus	" "	N'-dun-oo-yome'	" "
63	Na-no'-ho-mus	My step-mother.	Nain-n'-hans'	My elder brother.	Nain-n'-hans	My elder brother.
64	Eh-m'-ba-dze	My aunt.	Kŭn'-dig-eh	" " "	Kun'-dig-eh	" " "
65	Bo-nä-ba'-je-kwa?	My aunt.	Sa-ga-yă'-za?	My cousin.	Sa-ga-yă'-za?	My cousin.
66	Set'-so	" "	Sŭ-nä'-gä	My elder brother.	Sŭ-nä'-gä	My elder brother.
67			Soon'-da-ga	" " "	Soon'-da-ga	" " "
68	So-tre	My mother-in-law.	Soon-da	" " "	Soon-da	" " "
69	In-kach'-hä	My aunt.	Is-lacht'. [b]Sin-koo-sä'-hu	My bro. [b] One like [my brother.		
70						
71	Na-sis'-sas	" "	Pee-tu (m. s.). In-pats (f. s.)	(Not rendered.)		
72						
73						
74						
75						
76						
77						
78						
79			Ig-dlo-ra	My cousin.	Ig-dlo-ra	My cousin.
80	Ai-yug'-gä	My aunt.	Il-lŭng'-ä	" "	Il-lo'-ä	" "

TABLE II.—*Continued.*

	117. My mother's brother's son —younger than myself. (Male speaking.)	Translation.	118. My mother's brother's son —younger than myself. (Female speaking.)	Translation.	119. My mother's brother's son's wife. (Male speaking.)	Translation.
1	Ah-găre'-seh	My cousin.	Ah-găre'-seh	My cousin.	Ah-ge-ah'-ne-ah	My sister-in-law.
2	Ah-ge-ah'-seh	" "	Ah-ge-ah'-seh	" "	Un-ge-ah'-ne-a	" "
3	Ah-gare'-seh	" "	Ah-gare'-seh	" "	Ah-ge-ah'-yeh	" "
4	Un-gă-lä'-seh	" "	Un-gă-lä'-seh	" "	Un-ge͡-ah'-le͡-a	" "
5	Un-gă-läss'	" "	Un-gă-lass'	" "	Un-gă-le-ya'-ah	" "
6	Ahk-gä'-rä-sthar	" "	Ahk-gä'-rä-sthat	" "	Ack-gä'-re-ah	" "
7	Le-gä'-ah	My younger brother.	Le-gä-ah	My younger brother.	Uh-go-hä'-kwä	" "
8	Jä-rä'-seh	My cousin.	Jä-rä'-seh	My cousin.	O-in-dä'-wait	" "
9	Taṇ-haṇ'-she	" "	She-chay'-she	" "	Häṇ-kä'	" "
10	Tä'-she	" "	She-chä'-she	" "	Hä-kä'	" "
11	Kä'-zha	" "	She-cha'-ze	" "	Wä-kä'	" "
12	Tä'-she	" "	She-cha'-she	" "	Hä-kä'	" "
13	Tä'-she	" "	S'cha-pa'-she	" "	Huṇ-kä'	" "
14	Tä'-hä-she	" "	She-cha'-she	" "	Ha-kä'	" "
15	Tä'-she	" "	She-cha'-she	" "	Hä-kä'	" "
16	Tä-hä'-she	" "	She-cha'-she	" "	Hä-kä'	" "
17	Tä-hä'-she	" "	Me-hä'-gä-she	" "	Mä-hä'-gä	" "
18	Na-ge'-hä	My uncle.	Na-ge'-hä	My uncle.	Te-na'-hä	My aunt.
19	Wee-nä'-gee	" "	Wee-nä'-gee	" "	Wee-tee'-me	" "
20	Heen-ja'-kä	" "	Heen-ja'-kä	" "	Heen-too'-me	" "
21	Hin-chä'-kä	" "	Hin-chä'-kä	" "	E-tŭ'-me	" "
22	Be-ja'-ga	" "	Be-ja'-ga	" "	Be-je'-me	" "
23	We-ja'-ga	" "	We-ja'-ga	" "	We-je'-me	" "
24	E-take'	" "	E-take'	" "	E-chooṇ'-we	" "
25						
26	Mă-de-shä'	My son.	Mă-de-shä'	My son.	Mä-to'-gä	My dau.-in-law.
27	Bot-so'-kä	" "	Bot-so'-kä	" "	Bos-me'-ä-kun-is-tä	My sister-in-law.
28	Suh'-sŭh	" "	Suh'-sŭh	" "	Sup'-uk	My gd. daughter.
29	Suh'-soh	" "	Suh'-soh	" "	Sä'-pok	" "
30	Su'-soh	" "	Sup'-pok-näk'-nĭ	My grandson.	Snp'-pok	" "
31	Chup-pŭ'-che	" "	Um-os-sŭs'-wä	My grandchild.	Un-hu-tis'-se	My dau.-in-law.
32	A-gwae·tsĭ'	My child.	A-gwae-tsĭ'	My child.	E-tsän'-hĭ	" "
33	A-gwa'-tze	" "	A-gwa'-tze	" "	Ah-ge-tzau'-hĭ	" "
34	Pe'-row	" "	Pe'-row	" "	Scoo'-rus	" "
35	Pe'-row	" "	Pe'-row	" "	Sko'-dus	" "
36						
37	Neest-chäs'	My cousin.	Nee'-che-moos	My cousin.	Nee-tim'	My sister-in-law.
38	Nee-säs'	" "	Nee'-che-moosh	" "	Nee-tim'	" "
39	Neest-chäs'	" "	Nee'-ta-moos	" "	Nee-tim'	" "
40	Nĭ-tä'-wiss	" "	Nĭ-nĭ-mo'-she	" "	Nĭ'-nim	" "
41	Ne-tä'-wis	" "	Ne-ne-mo'-sha	" "	Ne'-nim	" "
42	Ne-tä'-wis	" "	Ne-ne-moo-shä'	" "	Ne-nim'	" "
43	Ne-tä'-wis	" "	Ne-ne-moo-shä'	" "	Ne-nim'	" "
44	Ne-tä'-wis	" "	Ne-ne-moo-shä'	" "	Ne-nim'	" "
45						
46	Ne-zhese'-sä	My uncle.	Ne-zhese'-sä	My uncle.	N'-sa'-gwe-sä'	My aunt.
47	Ne-zhe'-sä	" "	Ne-zhe'-sä	" "	Ne-zä'-gös-sä'	" "
48	Ne-zhe'-sä	" "	Ne-zhe'-sä	" "	Ne-zä'-gös-sä'	" "
49	Ne-zhe'-san	" "	Ne-zhe'-san	" "	Ne-sä'-gwis-sä'	" "
50	Ne-zhe'-san	" "	Ne-zhe'-san	" "	Ne-sä'-gwis-sä'	" "
51	Nă-zhe-sä'	" "	Nă-zhe-sä'	" "	Nak-ye'-hä	" "
52	Ne-zha'	" "	Ne-zha'	" "	Ne-ne'	" "
53					Nee'-tum	My sister-in-law.
54	Na-si-thä'	" "	Na-si-thä'	" "	Na-tha-kwi-thä'	My aunt.
55	Nĭ-sĭ-thä'	" "	Nĭ-sĭ-thä'	" "	Na-tha-gwe-thä'	" "
56	Ta'-yä ?	My younger brother.	Ta'-yä	My younger brother.	Nee-tim'	My sister-in-law.
57	N'-to'-tes-tä-mo	My cousin.	N'-do'-to-ke-man'	My cousin.	N'-do'-to-ke-man	" "
58	Noh'-sä-kin'-ame	" "	No-in'-nä	" "	Ne-to'-to-ke-man	" "
59	N'-che'-gu-num	My younger brother.	N'-chi-gu-num'	My younger brother.	Ne-lu-mŭs'	" "
60	Nu-tä'-gus	My cousin.	Neet-see-kes'	My cousin.	Ne-lu-mŭs'	" "
61	N'-dä-kwus	My step-brother.	N'-donk'	My step-brother.	Nee-num'	" "
62	Nee-mä'-tus	" "	N'-dun-oo-yome'	" "	Nee-lum'	" "
63	Nain-hise'-sa-mus'	My younger brother.	Nain-hise'-sa-mus'	My younger brother.	Na-nee-lim'	" "
64	A-cha'-a	" " "	A-cha'-a	" " "	Sa'-gy	" "
65	Sa-ga-yä'-za ?	My cousin.	Sa-ga-yă'-za ?	My cousin.	Sa-ten-a-bä'-che-la	" • "
66	Set-chil'-e-ä-za	My younger brother.	Set-chil'e-ä-za	My younger brother.	Set'-so	" "
67	Sa'-chä	" " "	Sa'-chä	" " "		
68	Sa-chä	" " "	San-do-hu-hä	" " "	Soo-tre (o.), Sa-chuth (y.)	ᵇ Half-sister.
69						
70						
71						
72						
73						
74						
75						
76						
77						
78						
79	Ig-dlo-ra	My cousin.	Ig-dlo-ra	My cousin.		
80	Il-lŭng'-ä	" "	Il-lo'-ä	" "	I-e'-gä	My sister-in-law.

TABLE II.—*Continued.*

	120. My mother's brother's son's wife. (Female speaking.)	Translation.	121. My mother's brother's daughter—older than myself. (Male speaking.)	Translation.	122. My mother's brother's daughter—older than myself. (Female speaking.)	Translation.
1	Ah-ge͡äh'-ne͡o............	My sister-in-law.	Ah-găre'-seh................	My cousin.	Ah-găre'-seh................	My cousin.
2	Uh-ge-ah'-ne-o..............	" "	Ah-ge-ah'-seh..............	" "	Ah-ge-ah'-seh..............	" "
3	Ah-gare-ah'-ne-o..............	" "	Ah-gare'-seh..............	" "	Ah-gare'-seh..............	" "
4	Un-ge͡ah'-le͡a..............	" "	Un-gä-lä'-seh..............	" "	Un-gä-lä'-seh..............	" "
5	Un-gä-le-ya'-ah.............	" "	Un-gä-läss'..............	" "	Un-gä-läss'..............	" "
6	Ack-gä'-re-ah.............	" "	Ahk-gä'-rä-sthar........	" "	Ahk-gä'-rä-sthar........	" "
7	Uh-go-hä'-kwä	" "	Ak-je'-yä	My elder sister.	Ak-je'-yä	My elder sister.
8	O-in-dä'-wait	" "	Jä-rä'-seh..............	My cousin.	Jä-rä'-seh	My cousin.
9	E-chä'-paṇ	" "	Häṇ-kä'-she..............	" "	E-chay'-pän-she	" "
10	E-shä'-pä	" "	Hä-kä'-she..............	" "	E-cha-pä'-she..............	" "
11	E-shä'-pä	" "	Ah-kä'-zha..............	" "	Pä'-zhe	" "
12	E-shä'-pä	" "	Hä-kä'-she..............	" "	Ah-cha'-pä-zhe............	" "
13	S'-cha-pä	" "	Hun-kä'-she..............	" "	S'cha-pä'-she..............	" "
14	S'-chä'-pä	" "	Hun-kä'-she..............	" "	Cha-pä'-she..............	" "
15	E-sä'-pä	" "	Hä-kä'-zhe	" "	Cha-pä'-she..............	" "
16	E-sä'-pä	" "	Hä-kä'-she	" "	Cha-pä'-she..............	" "
17	Me-she'-cha-pä........	" "	Tä-kä'-she..............	" "	Mä-hä'-gä-she..............	" "
18	Te-na'-hä	My aunt.	Nä'-hä..............	My mother.	Nä'-hä..............	My mother.
19	Wee-tee'-me..........	" "	E-nä'-hä	" "	E-nä'-hä..............	" "
20	Heen-too'-me..........	" "	Heen'-nah..............	" "	Heen'-nah..............	" "
21	E-tŭ'-me	" "	He'-nah	" "	He'-nah..............	" "
22	Be-je'-me	" "	E'-naw	" "	E'-naw..............	" "
23	We-je'-me	" "	In-nah'..............	" "	In-nah'..............	" "
24	E-chooṇ-we	" "	Nä-ne'-kä..............	" "	Nä-ne'-kä..............	" "
25						
26	Mä-to'-gä..............	My daught.-in-law.	Mä'-kä..............	My daughter.	Mä'-kä..............	My daughter.
27	Bos-me'-ä-kun-is-tä........	My sister-in-law.	Näk'-me-ä	" "	Näk'-me-ä	" "
28	Sup'-uk	My granddaughter.	Suh-suh'-take	" "	Suh-suh'-take..............	" "
29	Sä'-pok	" "	Suh-soh'-take	" "	Suh-soh'-take..............	" "
30	Sup'-pok	" "	Su-soh'-take	" "	Sup'-pok	My gd. daughter.
31	Un-hu-tis'-se	My daught.-in-law.	Chuch-hus'-te	" "	Um-os-süs'-wä..............	My grandchild.
32	E-tsän'-hĭ	" "	A-gwae-tsi'	My child.	A-gwae-tsi'	My child.
33	Ah-ge-tzau'-hĭ	" "	A-gwa'-tze	" "	A-gwa'-tze	" "
34	Scoo'-rus	" "	Pe'-row	" "	Pe'-row	" "
35	Sko'-dus.	" "	Pe'-row	" "	Pe'-row..............	" "
36						
37	N'-jä'-koase	My sister-in-law.	Nee'-che-moos..............	My cousin.	N'-jä'-koase	My cousin.
38	N'-jä'-koase	" "	Nee'-che-moosh..............	" "	N'-jä'-koase	" "
39	N'-dä'-koase	" "	Nee'-ta-moos..............	" "	N'-dä'-koase	" "
40	Nin-dan'-go-she	" "	Nĭ-nĭ-mo'-she..............	" "	Nin-dän'-go-she	" "
41	Nin-dan'-gwa	" "	Ne-ne-mo'-sha..............	" "	Nin-don'-go-sha..............	" "
42	Nin-däṇ-gwa'..............	" "	Ne-ne-moo-shä'..............	" "	N'-dä-n'-go-shä'..............	" "
43	N'-däṇ-gwä'	" "	Ne-ne-moo-shä'..............	" "	N'-däṇ-gwush-ä'..............	" "
44	N'-däṇ-gwa'..............	" "	Ne-ne-moo-shä'..............	" "	N'-dä-kwam'..............	" "
45						
46	N'-sa'-gwe-sä'	My aunt.	Niṇ-ge-ah'..............	My mother.	Niṇ-ge-ah'..............	My mother.
47	Ne-zä'-gos-sä'	" "	Niṇ-ge-ah'..............	" "	Niṇ-ge-ah'..............	" "
48	Ne-zä'-gos-sä'	" "	Niṇ-ge-ah'..............	" "	Niṇ-ge-ah'..............	" "
49	Ne-sä'-gwis-sä'	" "	Ne-ge-ah'..............	" "	Ne-ge-ah'..............	" "
50	Ne-sä'-gwis-sä'	" "	Ne-ge-ah'..............	" "	Ne-ge-ah'..............	" "
51	Näk-ye'-hä	" "	Na-ke͡ä'..............	" "	Nă-ke͡ä'..............	" "
52	Ne-ne'	" "	Ne-ke͡ah'..............	" "	Ne-ke͡ah'..............	" "
53	Nach-a-im'	My sister-in-law.				
54	Na-thä-kwi-thä'..............	My aunt.	Nĭ-ke͡ä'..............	" "	Nĭ-ke͡ä'..............	" "
55	Na-tha-gwe-thä'	" "	Na-ke͡ah'..............	" "	Na-ke͡ah'..............	" "
56	Ne-ta'-be.	My sister-in-law.	Na'-be ?..............	My elder sister.	Na'-be ?..............	My elder sister.
57	Nee-mis'	" "	N'-do'-to-ke-man'	My cousin.	Ne-wä'-toase	My cousin.
58	Nee-mis'	" "	Ne-tä'-kame..............	" "	Ne-his'-ta	My elder sister.
59	Nu-mäk-tim'..............	" "	Nu-mees	My elder sister.	Nu-mees'..............	" "
60	Nu-tä'-ku	" "	Nu-tä-kw'-sus'-ku	My step-sister.	Ne-tse-kes'..............	My cousin.
61	N'-dä-ohk'..............	" "	N'-dä-kwus-oh'-kwä-oh ..	" "	N'-ko-kwä'..............	My step-sister.
62	Nee-tä'-wis	" "	N'-doh-kwä-yome'..............	" "	Neet-koh'-kw'..............	" "
63	Nain-ne-la'-kon	" "	Nain-na-wase'..............	My elder sister.	Nain-na-wase'..............	My elder sister.
64	Sa'-gy	" "	Sä'-dä..............	" "	Sä'-dä..............	" "
65	Sa'-ga	" "	Sa-tso-yä'-za ?..............	My cousin.	Sa'-ya ?..............	My sister-in-law.
66	Sa'-o-ga	" "	Set-dez'-a-ä-za	My elder sister.	Set-dez'-a-ä-za..............	My elder sister.
67			Sa'-che..............	" " "	Sa'-che..............	" " "
68	Soo-tre (o.), Se-chuth (y.)	[b] Half-sister.	Se-chuth	My half-sister.	Se-chuth..............	My half-sister.
69						
70						
71						
72						
73						
74						
75						
76						
77						
78						
79			Ig-dlo-ra	My cousin.	Ig-dlo-ra	My cousin.
80	Oo-ko-ä'-gä..............	My sister-in-law.	Il-lŭng'-ä	" "	Il-lo'-ä..............	" "

TABLE II.—*Continued.*

	123. My mother's brother's daughter—younger than myself. (Male speaking.)	Translation.	124. My mother's brother's daughter—younger than myself. (Female speaking.)	Translation.	125. My mother's brother's daughter's husband. (Male speaking.)	Translation.
1	Ah-găre′-seh	My cousin.	Ah-găre′-seh	My cousin.	Ah-ge͡ah′-ne͡o	My bro.-in-law.
2	Ah-ge-ah′-seh	" "	Ah-ge-ah′-seh	" "	Uh-ge-ah′-ne-a	" "
3	Åh-gare′-seh	" "	Ah-gare′-seh	" "	Ah-ge-ah′-ne-o	" "
4	Un-gă-lä′-seh	" "	Un-gă-lä′-seh	" "	Un-ge͡ah′-de͡o	" "
5	Un-gă-läss′	" "	Un-gă-läss′	" "	Un-gă-de͡o-hä	" "
6	Ahk-gä′-rä-sthar	" "	Ahk-gä′-rä-sthar	" "	Ack-gaw′-na-ah	" "
7	Ka-gä′-ah	My younger sister.	Ka-gä′-ah	My younger sister.	Un-jä-jo′-hä	" "
8	Jä-rä′-seh	My cousin.	Jä-rä′-seh	My cousin.	O-in-dä′-wait	" "
9	Häņ-kä′-she	" "	E-chay′-pän-she	" "	Tä-häņ′	" "
10	Hä-kä′-she	" "	E-cha-pä′-she	" "	Tä-huh′	" "
11	Ah-kä′-zha	" "	Pä′-zhe	" "	Tä-hä′	" "
12	Hä-kä′-she	" "	Ah-cha′-pä-zhe	" "	Tä-hä′	" "
13	Hun-kä′-she	" "	S′cha-pä′-she	" "	Tä-hä′	" "
14	Hun-kä′-she	" "	Cha-pä′-she	" "	Tä-hä′	" "
15	Hä-kä′-zhe	" "	Cha-pä′-she	" "	Tä-hä′	" "
16	Hä-kä′-she	" "	Cha-pä′-she	" "	Tä-huh′	" "
17	Ta-hä′-she	" "	Mä-hä′-gä-she	" "	Mä-hä′-gä	" "
18	Nä′-hä	My mother.	Nä′-hä	My mother.	We-tuh′-da	My son-in-law.
19	E-nä′-hä	" "	E-nä-hä	" "	We-tŏņ-da	" "
20	Heen′-nä	" "	Heen′-nä	" "	Heen′-kä	My father.
21	He′-nah	" "	He′-nah	" "	Hin′-kä	" "
22	E′-naw	" "	E′-naw	" "	E-dä′-je	" "
23	In-nah′	" "	In-nah′	" "	In-tä′-che	" "
24	Nä-ne′-kä	" "	Nä-ne′-kä	" "	E-chuņ′	My bro.-in-law.
25						
26	Mä′-kä	My daughter.	Mä′-kä	My daughter.	Mä-too′-te	My son-in-law.
27	Näk′-me-ä	" "	Näk′-me-ä	" "	Boo′-sha	" "
28	Suh-suh′-take	" "	Suh-suh′-take	" "	Sai′-yup	" "
29	Suh-soh′-take	" "	Suh-soh′-take	" "	Säi′-yop	" "
30	Su-soh′-take	" "	Sup′-pok	My granddaughter.	Sä′-yup	" "
31	Chuch-hus′-te	" "	Um-os-sŭs′-wä	My grandchild.	Un-hu-tis′-se	" "
32	A-gwae-tsĭ′	My child.	A-gwae-tsĭ′	My child.	E-huä-tsĭ′	" "
33						
34	Pe′-row	" "	Pe′-row	" "	Koos-tow′-e-sŭ	" "
35	Pe′-row	" "	Pe′-row	" "	Ko-stä′-witch	" "
36						
37	Nee′-che-moos	My cousin.	N′-jä′-koase	My cousin.	Neese-tow′	My bro.-in-law.
38	Nee′-che-moosh	" "	N′-jä′-koase	" "	Neese-tow′	" "
39	Nee′-ta-moos	" "	N′-dä′-koase	" "	Neesh-tow′	" "
40	Nĭ-nĭ-mo′-she	" "	Nin-dän′-go-shĕ	" "	Ne′-tä	" "
41	Ne-ne-mo′-sha	" "	Nin-don′-go-sha	" "	Ne-che-ke′-wä-ze	" "
42	Ne-ne-moo-shä′	" "	N′-dä-n′go-shä′	" "	Ne-tä′	" "
43	Ne-ne-moo-shä′	" "	N′-däņ-gwush-ä′	" "	Ne-tä′	" "
44	Ne-ne-moo-shä′	" "	N′-dä-kwam′	" "	Ne-tä′	" "
45						
46	Niņ-ge-ah′	My mother.	Niņ-ge-ah′	My mother.	No-sä′	My father.
47	Niņ-ge-ah′	" "	Niņ-ge-ah′	" "	No-sä′	" "
48	Niņ-ge-ah′	" "	Niņ-ge-ah′	" "	No-sä′	" "
49	Ne-ge-ah′	" "	Ne-ge-ah′	" "	No-sä′	" "
50	Ne-ge-ah′	" "	Ne-ge-ah′	" "	No-sä′	" "
51	Nă-ke͡-ă′	" "	Na-ke͡-ă′	" "	Nŏss	" "
52	Ne-ke͡ah′	" "	Ne-ke͡ah′	" "	Noh′-neh	" "
53					Na-to′	" "
54	Nĭ-ke͡ă′	" "	Nĭ-ke͡ă′	" "		
55	Na-ke͡ah′	" "	Na-ke͡ah′	" "	No-thä′	" "
56	Na′-be-ă	My younger sister.	Na′-be-ă	My younger sister.	Nä-to′	My bro.-in-law.
57	N′-do′-to-ke-man′	My cousin.	Ne-wä′-toase	My cousin.	Nis-tä′-mo	" "
58	Ne-tä′-kame	" "	Ne-sis′-sä	My younger sister.	Nis-tä′-mo	" "
59	N′-kwa-jeech′	My younger sister.	N′-kwa-jeech′	" " "	Nu-mäk-tem′	" "
60	Nu-tä-kw-sus′-kw	My step-sister.	Ne-tse-kes′	My cousin.	Nu-mäk-tem′	" "
61	N′-dä-kwus-oh′-kwä-oh	" "	N′-ko-kwä′	My step-sister.	N′-dä-oh-k′	" "
62	N′-doh-kwä-yome′	" "	Neet-koh-kw′	" "	Noh′-taņ-kw′	" "
63	Nain-hise′-sa-mus′	My younger sister.	Nain-hise′-sa-mus′	My younger sister.	Na-nä-donkue′	" "
64	A-da′-ze	" " "	A-da′-ze	" " "	Sä′-gä	" "
65	Sa-tso-yä′-za ?	My cousin.	Sa′-ga	My sister-in-law.	Sa′-ga	" "
66	Sä′-re	My younger sister.	Sä′-re	My younger sister.	Sa′-o-ga	" "
67	Sa-chith′	" " "	Sa-chith′	" " "		
68						
69						
70						
71						
72						
73						
74						
75						
76						
77						
78						
79	Ig-dlo-ra	My cousin.	Ig-dlo-ra	My cousin.		
80	Il-lŭng′-ä	" "	Il-lo′-ä	" "	Ning-ä-on′-gwä	My bro.-in-law.

TABLE II.—*Continued.*

	126. My mother's brother's daughter's husband. (Female speaking.)	Translation.	127. My mother's brother's son's son. (Male speaking.)	Translation.	128. My mother's brother's son's son. (Female speaking.)	Translation.
1	Ha-yă'-o	My brother-in-law.	Ha-ah'-wuk	My son.	Ha-soh'-neh	My nephew.
2	Ha-yă'-ho	" "	Ha-hä'-wuk	" "	Ha-hä'-wuk	My son.
3	Ah-ge-ah'-de-o	" "	Ha-hä'-wä	" "	Ha-hä'-wä	" "
4	Un-ge͡-ah'-le͡-o	" "	Le-yä'-hä	" "	Le-yä'-hä	" "
5	Un-gă-le-ya'-ah	" "	E-yä'	" "	E-yo-wä'-dä	" "
6	Ack-gow'-na-ah	" "	Kä-yä'-no-nä	My child.	Kä-yä'-no-na-ah	My nephew.
7	Un-jă'-go-hä	" "	Le-yä'-ah	My son.	Le-yä'-ah	" "
8	Ah-zhă'-ku	" "	A-ne-ah'	" "	He-wä'-teh	My nephew.
9	She-chäy'	" "	Me-chiŋk'-she	" "	Me-tonsh'-kä	My son.
10	She-cha'	" "	Me-chink'-she	" "	Me-to͡-us'-kä	" "
11	She-cha'	" "	Ak-she'-dä	" "	Me-toash'-kä	" "
12	She-cha'	" "	Me-chink'-she	" "	Me-toze'-kä	" "
13	She-cha'	" "	Me-chink'-se-la	" "	Me-toans'-kä	" "
14	She-ches'	" "	Me-chink'-she	" "	Me-toase'-kä	" "
15	She-cha'	" "	Me-chink'-she	" "	Me-toash'-kä	" "
16	She-cha'	" "	Me-chink'-she	" "	Me-toas'-kä	" "
17	Me-she'-cha-pas	" "	Me-chink'-she	" "	Me-to'-zä	" "
18	We-tuh'-da	My son-in-law.	Na-ge'-hä	My uncle.	Na-ge'-hä	My uncle.
19	We-tön'-da	" "	Wee-nä'-gee	" "	Wee-nä'-gee	" "
20	Heen'-kä	My father.	Heen-ja'-kä	" "	Heen-ja'-kä	" "
21	Hin'-kä	" "	Hin-chä'-kä	" "	Hin-chä'-kä	" "
22	E-dä'-je	" "	Be-ja'-ga	" "	Be-ja'-ga	" "
23	In-tä'-che	" "	We-ja'-ga	" "	We-ja'-ga	" "
24	E-chuŋ'	My brother-in-law.	E-take'-e-neke'	My little uncle.	E-take'-e-neke	My little uncle.
25						
26	Mä-too'-te	My son-in-law.	Met-a-wä-pish'-shä	My grandchild.	Met-a-wä-pish'-shä	My grandchild.
27	Boo'-sha	" "	Bus-bä'-pe-ta	" "	Bus-bä'-pe-ta	" "
28	Sai'-yup	" "	Sup'-uk-nŏk'-ne	My grandson.	Sup'-uk-nŏk'-ne	My grandson.
29	Säi'-yop	" "	Sä'-pok-näk'-ne	" "	Sä'-pok-näk'-ne	" "
30	Sä'-yup	" "	Sup-pok-näk'-nĭ	" "	Sup-pok-näk'-nĭ	" "
31	Un-hu-tis'-se	" "	Um-os-sŭs'-wä	My grandchild.	Um-os-sŭs'-wä	My grandchild.
32	E-huä-tsĭ'	" "	Uŋ-gĭ-lĭ-sĭ'	" "	Uŋ-gĭ-lĭ-sĭ	" "
33					Aŋ-ge-lee'-se	" "
34	Koos-tow'-e-sŭ	" "	Lak-te'-gish	My grandson.	Lak-te'-gish	My grandson.
35	Ko-stä'-witch	" "	Lak-te'-kis	My grandchild.	Lak-te'-kis	My grandchild.
36						
37	Nee-tim'	My brother-in-law.	N'-do'-sim	My step-son.	N'-de-kwä-tim'	My nephew.
38	Nee-tim'	" "	N'-do'-zhim	" "	N'-de-kwä-tim'	" "
39	Nee-tim'	" "	N'-do'-zhim	" "	N'-de-kwä-tim'	" "
40	Nĭ'-nim	" "	Nin-do'-zhim	" "	Nĭ-nin-gwä'-niss	" "
41	Ne'-nim	" "	Nin-do'-zhem	" "	Ne-nin-gwuh'-nis	" "
42	Ne'-nim	" "	N'-do'-zhim	" "	Ne-nin-gwi-nis'	" "
43	Ne-nim'	" "	N'-do'-zhim-ă	" "	Ne-nin-gwi-nis'	" "
44	Ne-nim'	" "	N'-do-zhim'	" "	Ne-nin-gwi-nis'	" "
45						
46	No-sä'	My father.	Ne-zhese'-sä	My uncle.	Ne-zhese'-sä	My uncle.
47	No-sä'	" "	Ne-zhe'-sä	" "	Ne-zhe'-sä	" "
48	No-sä'	" "	Ne-zhe'-sä	" "	Ne-zhe'-sä	" "
49	No-sä'	" "	Ne-zhe'-san	" "	Ne-zhe'-san	" "
50	No-sä'	" "	Ne-zhe'-san	" "	Ne-zhe'-san	" "
51	Nŏss	" "	Nä-zhe-sä'	" "	Nä-zhe-sä'	" "
52	Noh'-neh	" "	Ne-zha'	" "	Ne-zha'	" "
53						
54			Na-si-thă'	" "	Na-si-thă'	" "
55	No-thä'	" "	Nĭ-sĭ-thä'	" "	Nĭ-sĭ-thä'	" "
56	Ne-ta'-be	My brother-in-law.				
57	N'-to'-to-yome	" "	N'-do'-to-ko	My step-son.	N'-do'-to-yose	My nephew.
58	Ne-to'-to-yome	" "	Noh'-ho'-ä	My son.	No-ä'-toase	" "
59	Ne-lu-mŭs'	" "	N'-kwis'	" "	Nu-lŭks'	" "
60	Ne-lu-mŭs'	" "	N'-too-ä'-sum	" "	Nu-lŭk'-nis	" "
61	Nee-num'	" "	Nä-kun'	My step-child.	Nä-kun'	My step-child.
62	Nee-lum'	" "	N'-kweese'	My son.	N'-kweese'	My son.
63	Na-nee-lim'	" "	Nain-gwase'	" "	Nain-gwase'	" "
64	Sä'-gä	" "	Tu'-zen-a	My step-son.	Sa-yä'-ze	" "
65	Sa-ta'-za-pa-ten'-ne	" "	Sa-yä'-za	My son.		
66	Set-shi'-ya	" "	Se-yä'-za	" "	Se-yä'-za	" "
67						
68						
69						
70						
71						
72						
73						
74						
75						
76						
77						
78						
79						
80	I-e'-gä	" "	Kun-e-ä'-gä	My nephew.	Ung-ä'-gä	My nephew.

TABLE II.—*Continued.*

	129. My mother's brother's son's daughter. (Male speaking.)	Translation.	130. My mother's brother's son's daughter. (Female speaking.)	Translation.	131. My mother's brother's daughter's son. (Male speaking)	Translation.
1	Ka-ah′-wuk	My daughter.	Ka-soh′-neh	My niece.	Ha-yä′-wan-da	My nephew.
2	Ka-hä′-wuk	" "	Ka-hä′-wuk	My daughter.	Ha-yuh′-wä-da	" "
3	Ka-hä′-wä	" "	Ka-hä′-wä	" "	Ha-yä-wä′-da	" "
4	Ka-yä′-hä	" "	Ka-yä′-hä	" "	Ha-yä′-wan-dä	" "
5	Ka-yä′	" "	Ka-yä′	" "	E-yo-wä′-dä	" "
6	Kä-yä′-no-nä	My child.	Kä-yä′-no-na-ah	" "	Kä-yä′-wä-nä	" "
7	Ka-yä′-ah	My daughter.	Ka-yä′-hä	" "	Le-wä-dä′-ah	" "
8	E-ne-ah′	" "	E-wä′-teh	My niece.	Ha-shone-drä′-ka	" "
9	Me-chunk′-she	" "	Me-tuŋ′-zhan	" "	Me-tonsh′-kä	" "
10	Me-chounk′-she	" "	Me-toꞈus′-zä	" "	Me-toꞈus′-ka	" "
11	Me-chunk′-she	" "	Me-to′-zhä	" "	Me-toash′-kä	" "
12	Me-chunk′-she	" "	Me-to′-zhä	" "	Me-tose′-kä	" "
13	Me-chunk′-se-lä	" "	Me-toh′-zhä	" "	Me-toans′-kä	" "
14	Me-chunk′-she	" "	Me-toh′-zhä	" "	Me-toase′-kä	" "
15	Me-chŭnk′-she	" "	Me-to′-zä	" "	Ne-toash′-kä	" "
16	Me-chŭnk′-she	" "	Me-to′-zä	" "	Me-toas′-kä	" "
17	Me-chunk′-she	" "	Me-to′-zä	" "	Me-to′-zä	" "
18	Nä′-hä	My mother.	Nä′-hä	My mother.	Zhin-dä′-hä	My elder brother.
19	E-nä′-ha	" "	E-nä′-hä	" "	We-zhe′-thä	" "
20	Heen′-nä	" "	Heen′-nä	" "	He-yen′-nä	" "
21	He′-nah	" "	He′-nah	" "	He-ye′-nä	" "
22	E′-naw	" "	E′-naw	" "	Be-zhe′-yeh	" "
23	In-nah′	" "	In-nah′	" "	We-she′-lä	" "
24	E-oo′-ne-neke′	My step or little mo-	E-oo′-ne-neke′	My step or little mo-	E-ne′	" "
25		[ther.		[ther.		
26	Met-a-wä-pish′-shä	My grandchild.	Met-a-wä-pish′-shä	My grandchild.	Met-a-wä-pish′-shä	My grandchild.
27	Bus-pä′-pe-ta	" "	Bus-bä-pe-ta	" "	Bus-bä′-pe-ta	" "
28	Sup′-uk	My granddaughter.	Sup′-uk	My granddaughter.	Sup′-uk-nŏk′-ne	My grandson.
29	Sä′-pok	" "	Sä′-pok	" "	Sä′-pok-näk′-ne	" "
30	Sup′-pok	" "	Sup′-pok	" "	Sup′-pok-näk′-nĭ	" "
31	Um-os-sŭs′-wa	My grandchild.	Um-os-sŭs′-wä	My grandchild.	Um-os-sŭs′-wä	My grandchild.
32	Un-gĭ-lĭ-sĭ	" "	Un-gĭ-lĭ-sĭ	" "	Un-gĭ-lĭ-sĭ	" "
33	Aŋ-ge-lee′-se	" "	Aŋ-ge-lee′-se	" "	Aŋ-ge-lee′-se	" "
34	Lak-te′-gee	My granddaughter.	Lak-te′-gee	My granddaughter.	Lak-te′-gish	My grandson.
35	Lak-te′-kis	My grandchild.	Lak-te′-kis	My grandchild.	Lak-te′-gis	My grandchild.
36						
37	N′-do′-sa-mis-kwame′	My step-daughter.	Neese-che-mish′	My niece.	N′-de-kwä-tim′	My nephew.
38	N′-do′-zha-mis-kwame′	" "	Neest-che-mish′	" "	N′-de-kwä-tim′	" "
39	N′-do′-zha-mis-kwem′	" "	Neese-che-mis′	" "	N′-deh-kwä-tim′	" "
40	Nin-do-zhĭ-mĭ′-kwem	" "	Nĭ-shĭ-miss′	" "	Nĭ-nin-gwä′-niss	" "
41	Nin-do-zhe-mi′-quam	" "	Ne-she′-me-sha	" "	Ne-nin-gwuh′-nis	" "
42	Nin-do′-zha-mĭ-kwam′	" "	Ne-she-mis′	" "	Ne-nin-gwi-nis′	" "
43	N′-do-zha-mĭ-kwam′	" "	Ne-she-mis′	" "	Ne-nin-gwi-nis′	" "
44	N′-do-zhä-mĭ-kwam′	" "	Ne-she-mis′	" "	Ne-nin-gwi-nis′	" "
45						
46	Niŋ-ge-ah′	My mother.	Niŋ-ge-ah′	My mother.	Ne-sä-sä′	My elder brother.
47	Niŋ-ge-ah′	" "	Niŋ-ge-ah′	" "	Ne-saŋ′-zä	" "
48	Niŋ-ge-ah′	" "	Niŋ-ge-ah′	" "	Ne-san′-zä	" " "
49	Ne-ge-ah′	" "	Ne-ge-ah′	" "	Ne-sä-zä′	" " "
50	Ne-ge-ah′	" "	Ne-ge-ah′	" "	Ne-sä-zä′	" " "
51	Nä-keꞈa′	" "	Nä-keꞈa′	" "	Nä-sa′-mä	" " "
52	Ne-keꞈah′	" "	Ne-keꞈah′	" "	Nä-nä′	" " "
53						
54	Nĭ-keꞈä′	" "	Nĭ-keꞈä′	" "	Ni-to-ta-mä′	My brother.
55	Na-keꞈah′	" "	Na-keꞈah′	" "	N′-tha-thä′	My elder brother.
56						
57	N′-to′-to-tun	My step-daughter.	Nee-mis′-sä	My niece.	N′-do′-to-yose	My nephew.
58	Ne-tan′-ä	My daughter.	Nee-mis′-sä	" "	No-ä′-toase	" "
59	N′-tŭs′	" "	N′-sum′	" "	Nu-lŭks′	" "
60	N′-su′-mus	" "	N′-sum′	" "	Nu-lŭ′-knees	" "
61	Nä-kun′	My step-child.	Nä-kun′	My step-child	No-kwath′	" "
62	N′-dä-nuss′	My daughter.	N′-dä-nuss′	My daughter.	Longue′-kw′	" "
63	Nain-dä′-ness	" "	Nain-dä′-ness	" "	Na-lone′-gwä-sis′	" "
64	Sa-yä′-dze	My step-daughter.	Sa-yä′-dze	" "	Sä-zy′	" "
65	Sa-to′-a	My daughter.	Sa-to′-a	" "	Sa-yä′-za	My son.
66	Sa-le′-ä	" "	Sa-le′-ä	" "	Se-yä′-za	" "
67						
68						
69						
70						
71						
72						
73						
74						
75						
76						
77						
78						
79						
80	Kun-e-ä′-gä	My niece.	Uŋg-ä′-gä	My niece.	We-yo-o′-gwä	My nephew.

TABLE II.—*Continued.*

	132. My mother's brother's daughter's son. (Female speaking.)	Translation.	133. My mother's brother's daughter's daughter. (Male speaking.)	Translation.	134. My mother's brother's daughter's daughter. (Female speaking.)	Translation.
1	Ha-ah'-wuk	My son.	Ka-yă'-wan-da	My niece.	Ka-ah'-wuk	My daughter.
2	Ha-hä'-wuk	" "	Ka-yuh'-wä-deh	" "	Ka-hä'-wuk	" "
3	Ha-hä'-wä	" "	Ka-yä-wä'-da	" "	Ka-hä'-wä	" "
4	Le-yä'-hä	" "	Ka-yă'-wan-dä	" "	Ka-yä'-hä	" "
5	E-yä'	" "	Ka-yo-wä'-dä	" "	Ka-yä'	" "
6	Kä-yä'-no-nä	My child.	Kä-yä'-wä-nä	" "	Kä-yä'-no-nä	My child.
7	Le-yä'-ah	My son.	Ka-wä-dä'-ah	" "	Ka-yä'-ah	My daughter.
8	A-ne-ah'	" "	Ya-shone-drä'-ka	" "	E-ne-ah'	" "
9	Me-chink'-she	" "	Me-tuŋ'-zhaŋ	" "	Me-chuŋk'-she	" "
10	Me-chunk'-she	" "	Me-to͡-us'-zä	" "	Me-chounk'-she	" "
11	Ak she'-dä	" "	Me-to'-zhä	" "	Me-chuuk'-she	" "
12	Me-chink'-she	" "	Me-to'-zhä	" "	Me-chunk'-she	" "
13	Me-chink'-se-lä	" "	Me-toh'-zhä	" "	Me-chunk'-se-lä	" "
14	Me-chink'-she	" "	Me-toh'-zhä	" "	Me-chunk'-she	" "
15	Me-chink'-she	" "	Me-to'-zä	" "	Me-chŭnk'-she	" "
16	Me-chink'-she	" "	Me-to'-zä	" "	Me-chŭnk'-she	" "
17	Me-chink'-she	" "	Me-to'-zä	" "	Me-chunk'-she	" "
18	Ton-no'-hä	My elder brother.	Ton-ga'-hä	My elder sister.	Zhon-da'-hä	My elder sister.
19	Wee-te'-noo	" " "	Wee-tŏn'-ga	" " "	Wee-tŏn-tha	" " "
20	He-yen'-nä	" " "	He-yu'-nä	" " "	Heen-taŋ'-ya	" " "
21	He-ye'-nä	" " "	Wan he'-cha	" " "	Heen-taŋg'-a	" " "
22	Be-che'-do	" " "	Be-tuŋ'-ga	" " "	Be-sho'-wa	" " "
23	We-chin'-to	" " "	We-tuŋ'-ka	" " "	We-sho'-la	" " "
24	E-che'-to	" " "	E-noo'	" " "	E-noo'	" " "
25						
26	Met-a-wä-pish'-sha	My grandchild.	Met-a-wä-pish'-sha	My grandchild.	Met-a-wä-pish'-sha	My grandchild.
27	Bus-bä'-pe-ta	" "	Bus-bä'-pe-ta	" "	Bus-bä'-pe-ta	" "
28	Sup'-uk-nŏk'-ne	My grandson.	Sup'-uk	My granddaughter.	Sup'-uk	My gd. daughter.
29	Sä'-pok-näk'-ne	" "	Sä'-pok	" "	Sä'-pok	" "
30	Sup'-pok-näk'-nĭ	" "	Sup'-pok	" "	Sup'-pok	" "
31	Um-os-sŭs'-wä	My grandchild.	Um-os-sŭs'-wä	My grandchild.	Um-os-sŭs'-wä	" "
32	Aŋ-gĭ-lĭ-sĭ	" "	Un-gĭ-lĭ-sĭ	" "	Un-gĭ-lĭ-sĭ	" "
33	Aŋ-ge-lee'-se	" "	Aŋ-ge-lee'-se	" "	Aŋ-ge-lee'-se	" "
34	Lak-te'-gish	My grandson.	Lak-te'-gee	My granddaughter.	Lak-te'-gee	" "
35	Lak-te'-kis	My grandchild.	Lak-te'-kis	My grandchild.	Lak-te'-kis	My grandchild.
36						
37	N'-go'-sim	My step-son	Neese-che-mish'	My niece.	N'-do'-sa-mis-kwame'	My step-daughter.
38	N'-go'-zhim	" "	Neest-che-mis'	" "	N'-do'-zha-mis-kwame'	" "
39	N'-do'-zhim	" "	Neese-che-mis'	" "	N'-do'-zha-mis-kwem'	" "
40	Nin-do'-shĭ-miss	My step-child.	Nĭ-shĭ'-mis	" "	Nin-do'-zhe-mis	My step-child.
41	Nin-do'-zhe-mis	" "	Ne-she'-me-sha	" "	Nin-do'-zhe-mis	" "
42	Neen-gwis'	My son.	Ne-she-mis'	" "	Nin-dä'-niss	My daughter.
43	Nin-gwis'	" "	Ne-she-mis'	" "	N'-dä-niss'	" "
44	N'-gwis'	" "	Ne-she-mis'	" "	N'-dä-niss'	" "
45						
46	Ne-sä-sä'	My elder brother.	Ne-mis-sä'	My elder sister.	Ne-mis-sä'	My elder sister.
47	Ne-san'-zä	" " "	Ne-mis-sä	" " "	Ne-mis-sä'	" " "
48	Ne-san'-zä	" " "	Ne-mis-sä'..	" " "	Ne-mis-sä'	" " "
49	Ne-sä-zä'	" " "	Ne-me-sä'	" " "	Ne-me-sä'	" " "
50	Ne-sä-zä'	" " "	Ne-me-sä'	" " "	Ne-me-sä'	" " "
51	Nä-sa'-mä	" " "	Nä-mis'-sä	" " "	Nä-mis'-sä	" " "
52	Nă-nä'	" " "	Ne-ma'	" " "	Ne-ma'	" " "
53						
54	Ni-to-ta-mă'	My brother.	Ne-tä-kwä-mĭ	My sister.	Na-tä-tä-mĭ	My sister.
55	N'-tha-thä'	My elder brother.	Nĭ-mĭ-thä'	My elder sister.	Nĭ-mĭ-thä'	My elder sister.
56						
57	N'-do'-to-ko	My step-son.	Nee-mis'-sä	My niece.	N'-to'-to-tun	My step-daughter.
58	Noh·-ko'-ä	My son.	Nee-mis'-sä	" "	Ne-tan'-ä	My daughter.
59	N'-kwis	" "	N'-sum'	" "	N'-tus'	" "
60	Nee-tse-kes'	" "	N'-sum'	" "	N'-su'-mus	" "
61	N'-di-ome'	" "	Noh·k-soh'-kwä'-oh	" "	Nee-chune'	" "
62	N'-kwees'	" "	Longue-kwä'	" "	N'-dä-nuss'	" "
63	Nain-gwase'	" "	Na-lone'-gwä-sis'	" "	Nain-dä'-ness	" "
64	Sa-yä'-za	" "	Sä'-zy	" "	Sa-yä'-dze	" "
65	Se-yä'-za	" "	Sa-to'-ä	My daughter.	Sa-to'-ä	" "
66	Se-yä'-za	" "	Sa-le'-ä	" "	Sa-le'-ä	" "
67						
68	So-he	" "	Set-she	My grandchild.	Set-shai	My grandchild.
69						
70						
71						
72						
73						
74						
75						
76						
77						
78						
79						
80	Noo-ä'-gä	My nephew.	We-yo-o'-gwä	My niece.	Noo-ä'-gä	My niece.

TABLE II.—Continued.

	135. My mother's brother's great grandson.	Translation.	136. My mother's brother's great granddaughter.	Translation.	137. My mother's brother's great grandson's son.	Translation.
1	Ha-yä'-da	My grandson.	Ka-yä'-da	My granddaughter.	Ha-yä'-da	My grandson.
2	Ha-yä'-dra	" "	Ka-yä'-dra	" "	Ha-yä'-dra	" "
3	Ha-yä'-da	" "	Ka-yä'-da	" "	Ha-yä'-da	" "
4	Le-yä'-dla-ah	" "	Ka-yä'-dla-ah	" "	Le-yä'-dla-ah	" "
5	E-yä'-dla-ah	" "	Ka-yä'-dla-ah	" "	E-yä'-dla-ah	" "
6	Kä-yä'-rä	My grandchild.	Kä-yä'-rä	My grandchild.	Kä-yä'-rä	My grandchild.
7	Le-yä-tä-ra'-yä	My grandson.	Ka-yä-tä-ra'-yä	My granddaughter.	Le-yä-tä-ra'-yä	My grandson.
8	Ha-tra'-ah	" "	Ya-tra'-ah	" "	Ha-tra'-ah	" "
9	Me-tä'-ko-zhä	My grandchild.	Me-tä'-ko-zhä	My grandchild.	Me-tä'-ko-zhä	My grandchild.
10	Me-tä'-ko-zhä	" "	Me-tä'-ko-zhä	" "	Me-tä'-ko-zhä	" "
11	Me-tä'-ko-zhä	" "	Me-tä'-ko-zhä	" "	Me-tä'-ko-zhä	" "
12	Me-tä'-ko-zha	" "	Me-tä'-ko-zha	" "	Me-tä'-ko-zha	" "
13	Me-tä'-ko-säk-pok	" "	Me-tä'-ko-säk-pok	" "	Me-tä'-ko-säk-pok	" "
14	Me-tä'-ko-zhä	" "	Me-tä'-ko-zhä	" "	Me-tä'-ko-zhä	" "
15	Me-tä'-ko-zhä	" "	Me-tä'-ko-zhä	" "	Me-tä'-ko-zhä	" "
16	Me-tä'-ko-zä	" "	Me-tä'-ko-zä	" "	Me-tä'-ko-zä	" "
17	Me-tä'-ko-sä	" "	Me-tä'-ko-sä	" "	Me-tä'-ko-sä	" "
18	Na-ge'-hä	My uncle.	Tä-zhä'-zä	My niece.	Na-ge'-hä	My uncle.
19	Wee-nä'-gee	" "	We te'-zhä	" "	Wee-nä'-gee	" "
20	Heen-ja'-kä	" "	Heen-toas'-kä-me	" "	Heen-ja'-kä	" "
21	Hin-chä'-kä	" "	Hin-tose'-kee-me	" "	Hin-chä'-kä	" "
22	Be-ja'-ga	" "	Be-che'-zho	" "	Be-ja'-ga	" "
23	We-ja'-ga	" "	We-che'-zho	" "	We-ja'-ga	" "
24	E-take'-e-neke	My little uncle	E-choon-zhunk'-e-neke'	My little niece or gd. [daughter.	E-take'-e-neke'	My little uncle.
25						
26	Met-a-wä-pish'-sha	My grandchild.	Met-a wä-pish'-sha	My grandchild.	Met-a-wä-pish'-shä	My grandchild.
27	Bus-bä'-pe-ta	" "	Bus-bä'-pe-ta	" "	Bus-bä'-pe-ta	" "
28	Sup'-uk-nŏk'-ne	My grandson.	Sup'-uk	My granddaughter.	Sup'-uk-nŏk'-ne	My grandson.
29	Sä'-pok-näk'-ne	" "	Sä'-pok	" "	Sä'-pok-näk'-ne	" "
30	Sup'-pok-näk'-nĭ	" "	Sup'-pok	" "	Sup'-pok-näk'-nĭ	" "
31	Um-ŏs-sŭs'-wä	My grandchild.	Um-os-sŭs'-wa	My grandchild.	Um-os-sŭs'-wä	My grandchild.
32	An-gĭ-lĭ-sĭ	" "	Un-gĭ-lĭ-sĭ	" "	An-gĭ-lĭ-sĭ	" "
33	An-ge-lee'-se	" "	An-ge-lee'-se	" "	An-ge-lee'-se	" "
34	Te'-wut	My nephew.	Te'-wut	My niece.	Pe'-row	My child.
35	Lak-te'-kis	My grandchild.	Lak-te'-kis	My grandchild.	Lak-te'-kis	My grandchild.
36						
37	No-se-sem'	My grandchild.	No-se-sem'	My grandchild.	No-se-sem'	My grandchild.
38	No-se-sim'	" "	No-se-sim'	" "	No-se-sim'	" "
39	No-se-sem'	" "	No-se-sem'	" "	No-se-sem'	" "
40	No-zhĭ'-she	" "	No-zhĭ'-she	" "	No-zhĭ'-she	" "
41	No-she'-shă	" "	No-she'-shă	" "	No-she'-shă	" "
42	No-she-shă'	" "	No-she-shă'	" "	No-she-shă'	" "
43	No-she-shă'	" "	No-she-shă'	" "	No-she-shă'	" "
44	No-she-shă'	" "	No-she-shă'	" "	No-she-shă'	" "
45	No-să-seh'	" "	No-să-seh'	" "	No-să-seh'	" "
46	Ne-zhese'-sä	My uncle.	Shames-sä'	My niece.	Ne-zhese'-sä	My uncle.
47	Ne-zhe'-sä	" "	Ne-she-mis-sä'	" "	Ne-zhe'-sä	" "
48	Ne-zhe'-sä	" "	Ne-she-mis-sä'	" "	Ne-zhe'-sä	" "
49	Ne-zhe'-san	" "	Ne-she-mis-sä'	" "	Ne-zhe'-san	" "
50	Ne-zhe'-san	" "	Ne-she-mis-sä'	" "	Ne-zhe'-san	" "
51	Nă-zhe-sä	" "	Nă-shä'-mis	" "	Nă-zhe-sä'	" "
52	Ne-zha'	" "	Nă-nă'-mä	" "	Ne-zha'	" "
53						
54	Na-si-thä'	" "	Ne-sem-e-thä'	" "	Na-si-thä'	" "
55	Nĭ-sĭ-thä'	" "	Ne-sa-me-thä'	" "	Nĭ-sĭ-thä'	" "
56						
57	Nee-so'-tan	My grandchild.	Nee-so-tan	My grandchild.	Nee-so'-tan	My grandchild.
58	Nee-so'-tän	" "	Nee-so'-tän	" "	Nee-so'-tän	" "
59	Nŭ-jeech'	" "	Nŭ-jeech'	" "	Nŭ-jeech'	" "
60	N'-kway'-nus	" "	N'-kway'-nus	" "	N'-kway'-nus	" "
61	Nä-h·ise'	" "	Nä-h·ise'	" "	Nä-h·ise'	" "
62	Noh·-whese'	" "	Noh·-whese'	" "	Noh·-whese'	" "
63	Nain-no-whase'	" "	Nain-no-whase'	" "	Nain-no-whase'	" "
64	Sa-t'-thu'-a	" "	Sa-t'thu'-a	" "	S-t'thu'-a	" "
65	Sa-ken'-ne	My grandson.	Sa-to͡a'-bä	My granddaughter.	Sa-ken'-ne	My grandson.
66	Se-yä-zet'-tha-re	" "	Sa-le-zet'-tha-re	" "	Se-yä-zet'-tha-re	" "
67						
68	Set-she	" "	Set-shai	" "	Set-she	" "
69						
70						
71						
72						
73						
74						
75						
76						
77						
78						
79						
80	Eng'-o-tä	My grandchild.	Eng'-o-tä	My grandchild.	Eng'-o-tä	My grandchild.

TABLE II.—*Continued.*

	138. My mother's brother's great grandson's daughter.	Translation.	139. My mother's sister.	Translation.	140. My mother's sister's husband.	Translation.
1	Ka-yä'-da	My granddaughter.	No-yeh'	My mother.	Hoc-no'-ese	My step-father.
2	Ka-yä'-dra	" "	Kno'-hä	" "	Hoc-no'-nese	" "
3	Ka-yä'-da	" "	Ah-ge-no'-hä	" "	Hä-ge-noh'	" "
4	Ka-yä'-dla-ah	" "	Ahk-nole'-hä	" "	Oc-no-nese'-kwä	" "
5	Ka-yä'-dla-ah	" "	Lä-ga-ne'-hä	" "	Lä-ga-nä-nese'-kwä	" "
6	Kä-yä'-rä	My grandchild.	Oh-nä	" "	Ack-we'-rä	" "
7	Ka-yä-tä-ra'-yä	My granddaughter.	Ah-ga-nese'-tä-ha	" "	Lä-ga-ne'-hä	My father.
8	Ya-tra'-ah	" "	Ah-nä'-uh	" "	Hä-wä-te-no'-ra	My uncle.
9	Me-tä'-ko-zhä	My grandchild.	E-nah'	" "	At-tay'	My father.
10	Me-tä'-ko-zhä	" "	E'-nah	" "	Ah-ta'	" "
11	Me-tä'-ko-zhä	" "	E'-nah	" "	Ah-ta'	" "
12	Me-tä'-ko-zha	" "	Een-nä'	" "	Ah-ta'	" "
13	Me-tä'-ko-säk-pok	" "	E'-nah	" "	Ah-ta'	" "
14	Me-tä'-ko-zhä	" "	E'-nah	" "	Ah-ta'	" "
15	Me-tä'-ko-zhä	" "	E'-nah	" "	Ah-ta'	" "
16	Me-tä'-ko-zä	" "	E'-nah	" "	Ah-ta'	" "
17	Me-tä'-ko-sä	" "	E-nah'	" "	Ah-da'	" "
18	Toosh'-pä-hä	" "	Nä'-hä	" "	Tä-de'-ha	" "
19	Wee-tŭsh'-pä	" "	E-nä'-hä	" "	In-dä'-de	" "
20	Heen-tä'-kwa'-me	My granddaughter.	Heen'-nä	" "	Heen'-kä	" "
21	E-tä'-kwä-me		He'-nah	" "	Hin'-kä	" "
22	Be-chose'-pa	My grandchild.	E'-naw	" "	E-dä'-je	" "
23	We-chose'-pä	" "	In-nah'	[ther.	In-tä'-che	My step-father.
24	E-choon-zhunk'-e-neke'	My little gd. daught.	E-oo'-ne-neke'	My step or little mo-	E-noo'-gos-neke'	My step-father.
25			Nä-a'	My mother.	Tä-tay'	My father.
26	Met-a-wä-pish'-sha	My grandchild.	Ih'-kä	" "	Tä-ta'	" "
27	Bus-bä'-pe-ta	" "	E'-ke-ä	" "	Ah-lra'	" "
28	Sup'-uk	My granddaughter.	Ush'-kĭ	" "	A'-kĭ	" "
29	Sä'-pok	" "	Ush'-kĭ	" "	A'-kĭ	" "
30	Sup'-pok	" "	Sush-ko'-sĭ	My little mother.	Ang-ko'-sĭ	My little father.
31	Um-os-sŭs'-wä	My grandchild.	Chuch-kŭ'-ce	" " "	Chul-kŭ-che'	" " "
32	Un-gĭ-lĭ-sĭ	" "	E-tsi'	My mother.	A-gwä-tĭ-nä'-ĭ	My step-parent.
33	An-ge-lee'-se		Ah-gid'-ze	" "	Tä-le-ra-ah-ge-do'-dä	" "
34	Pe'-row	My child.	Ah-te'-rä	" "	Ah-te'-is	" "
35	Lak-te'-kes	My grandchild.	A-te'-rä	" "	Ah-te'-rä	" "
36			At-nä'	" "	Ah-te'-ä	" "
37	No-se-sem'	My grandchild.	N'-do'-sis	My step-mother.	No'-ko-mis	My step-father.
38	No-se-sim'	" "	N'-do'-sis	" "	No'-ko-mish	" "
39	No-se-sem'	" "	N'-do'-zis	" "	No'-ko-mis	" "
40	No-zhĭ'-she	" "	Nĭ-no'-shĕ	" "	Nĭ-mĭ-sho'-me	" "
41	No-she'-shä	" "	Ne-no'-sha	" "	Ne-me-sho'-ma	" "
42	No-she-shä'	" "	Ne-no-shä'	" "	Ne-mis-sho'-mä	" "
43	No-she-shä'	" "	Ne-no'-shä	" "	Ne-mish-sho'-mä	" "
44	No-she-shä'	" "	No-shä'	" "	N'-ruis-sho'-mä	" "
45	No-sä-seh'	" "	No-sheh'	" "	Noke-mä'	" "
46	No-sa-mä'	" "	Nin-ge-ah'	My mother.	Ne-zhese'-sä	My uncle.
47	No-sa'-mä	" "	Nin-ge-ah'	" "	No-sä'	My father.
48	No-sa-mä'	" "	Nin-ge-ah'	" "	No-sä'	" "
49	No-sa-mä'	" "	Ne-ge-ah'	" "	Ne-zhe'-san	My uncle.
50	No-sa-mä'	" "	Ne-ge-ah'	" "	Ne-zhe'-san	" "
51	No-she-sem'	" "	Nä-ke⌢ä'	" "	Nä-zhe-sä'	" "
52	No-she-sä'	" "	Ne-ke⌢ah'	" "	Noh'-neh	My father.
53			Nä'-ko	" "	Nä-o'-ä	" "
54	Na-se-thä'-mä	" "	Ni-ke⌢ä'	" "	No-thä'	" "
55	No-stha-thä'	" "	Na-ke⌢ah'	" "	No-thä'	" "
56			Nä'-na	" "	Ne-tha'-na	" "
57	Nee-so'-tan	" "	N'-to'-tox-is	My step-mother.	No-to'-to-mä	My step-father.
58	Nee-so'-tän	" "	Ne-to'-toax-is	" "	Ne-to'-to-nä	" "
59	Nŭ-jeech'	" "	Nu-lis'	My little mother.	Niks-kä-mich'	My grandfather.
60	N'-kway'-nus	" "	N'-kee'-sees	" " "	Nee-chä'-loŏk	My step-father.
61	Nä-hrise'	" "	N'-guk'	My mother.	N'-jä'-kw'	" "
62	Noh-whese'	" "	N'-gä-hä'-tut	My little mother.	N'-me-lu-täk'-tut	My little step-fath.
63	Nain-no-whase'	" "	Nin-guk'-us	" "	Na-na-mo'-whome	My step-father.
64	Sa-t'thu'-a	" "	San'-ga	My step-mother.	Eh-tä-eh	My father.
65	Sa-to⌢a'-bä	My granddaughter.	A'-na	My mother.	Sä-ta'	My step-father.
66	Sa-le-zet'-tha-re	" "	Sä-kre'-a	My step-mother.	Sel-the'-na	" "
67			Na-aingh'	My mother.		
68	Set-shai	" "	Sa-ku-i	My step-mother.	Set-ye	My father-in-law.
69			In-kach'-ha	My aunt ?		
70						
71			Nä-magh'-has	My step-mother.	Swagh	(Not rendered.)
72			Ka-ko-o'kt	" "	En-kach-ha	My step-father.
73			Pä'-tsin	(Not rendered.)		
74						
75						
76						
77			Su-ä'-i-ä	" "		
78						
79			A-ja'-ga	My aunt.		
80	Eng'-o-tä	My grandchild.	Ai-yug'-gä	" "	I-e-ing'-gä	My step-father.

TABLE II.—Continued.

	141. My mother's sister's son—older than myself. (Male speaking.)	Translation.	142. My mother's sister's son—older than myself. (Female speaking.)	Translation.	143. My mother's sister's son—younger than myself. (Male speaking.)	Translation.
1	Hä'-je	My elder brother.	Hä'-je	My elder brother.	Ha'-gă	My younger bro.
2	Kuh-je'-ah	" " "	Kuh-je' ah	" " "	Ha-gä'-ah	" " "
3	Kuh-je'-ah	" " "	Kuh-je'-ah	" " "	Ha'-gä	" " "
4	Läk-je'-hä	" " "	Läk-je'-hä	" " "	Le-gä'-ah	" " "
5	Läk-je'-hä	" " "	Lak-je'-hä	" " "	E'-gä-hä	" " "
6	Ahk-rä'-je	" " "	Ahk-rä'-je	" " "	Kä'-gä	" " "
7	Lok-je'-hä	" " "	Lok-je'-hä	" " "	Lok-je'-hä	" " "
8	Ha-ye'-uh	" " "	Ha-ye'-uh	" " "	Ha-ye-a'-hä	" " "
9	Chiņ-yay'	" " "	Te-mdo'	" " "	Me-suņ'-kä	" " "
10	Che-a'	" " "	Chim'-a-do	" " "	Me-soh'-kä	" " "
11	Che'-a	" " "	Tib'-e-do	" " "	Me-sunk'-ä	" " "
12	Che'-a	" " "	Tib'-a-do	" " "	Me-sun'-kä	" " "
13	Che'-a	" " "	Tib'-a-lo	" " "	Me-soh'	" " "
14	Me-che'-a	" " "	Tib-a-lo'	" " "	Me-sunk'-ä-lä	" " "
15	Che'-a	" " "	Tib'-a-lo	" " "	Me-soh'-kä-lä	" " "
16	Che'-a	" " "	Tib'-a-lo	" " "	Me-son'-kä-lä	" " "
17	Me-chin'	" " "	Me-tim'-do	" " "	Me-soh'	" " "
18	Zhin-da'-hä	" " "	Ton-no'-hä	" " "	Kä-ga'	" " "
19	Wee-zhe'-thä	" " "	We-te'-noo	" " "	Wee-söŋ'-gä	" " "
20	He-yen'-nä	" " "	He-yen'-nä	" " "	Heen-thuņ'-ga	" " "
21	He-ye'-nä	" " "	He-ye'-nä	" " "	Heen-thuņ'-ga	" " "
22	Be-zhe'-yeh	" " "	Be-che'-do	" " "	Be-suņ'-gä	" " "
23	We-she'-lä	" " "	We-chin'-to	" " "	We-son'-kä	" " "
24	E-ne'	" " "	E-che'-to	" " "	E-sŭnk'	" " "
25	Moo'-kä	" " "	Me-sho'-ka	" " "	Me-sho'-kä	" " "
26	Mee-ä'-kä	" " "	Mä-tä-roo'	" " "	Mat-so'-gä	" " "
27	Meek'-a	" " "	Bä-zä'-na	" " "	Bä-chŭ'-ka	" " "
28	Um-un'-nĭ	" " "	A-näk'-fĭ	" " "	Suh-näk'-fish.	" " "
29	Um-un'-nĭ	" " "	A-näk'-fish	" " "	Sä-näk'-fish	" " "
30	Et-e-bä'-pĭ-shĭ-lĭ	My brother.	A-näk'-fĭ	" " "	Et-e-bä'-pĭ-shĭ-lĭ	My brother.
31	Chu-hlä'-hä	My elder brother.	Chu-chil'-wä	" " "	Chu-chŭ'-se	My younger bro.
32	Un-gĭ-nĭ'-lĭ	" " "	Uņ-gĭ-dau'	" " "	Uņ-gĭ-nuņ'-tlĕ	" " "
33	Aņ-ke-nee'-le	" " "	Aņ-ke-do	" " "	Aŭņ'-ke-nä-tsĭ	" " "
34	E-dä'-deh	My brother.	E-rats'-teh	My brother.	E-dä'-deh	My brother.
35	A-dä'-de	" "	Ta-lä'-lik-tis	" "	A-dä'-he	" "
36	Che-na-tun'	" "	A-tnas'	" "	Kä-wit'-ta	" "
37	Neese-tase'	My elder brother.	Neese-tase'	My elder brother.	Ne-seme'	My younger bro.
38	Neese-tase'	" " "	Neese-tase'	" " "	Ne-sha-mish'	" " "
39	Neesh-tase'	" " "	Neesh-tase'	" " "	Ne-she-mish'	" " "
40	Nis-sä'-ye	" " "	Nis-sä'-ye	" " "	Nĭ-shĭ'-me	" " "
41	Ne-kä'-na	My step-brother.	Nin-dä-wa'-mä	My step-brother.	Ne-kä'-na	My step-brother.
42	Ne-kä'-na	" " "	Nĭ-sä-yä'	My elder brother.	Ne-kä'-na	" " "
43	Ne-kä'-nis	" " "	Nis-si-yä'	" " "	Ne-kä'-nis	" " "
44	Ne-kä'-nä	" " "	N'-sä'-yä	" " "	Ne-kä'-nä	" " "
45	Ne-kä'-na	" " "	N'-seh-sä'	" " "	Ne-kä'-na	" " "
46	Ne-sä-sä'	My elder brother.	Ne-sä-sä'	" " "	Se-me-mä'	My younger bro.
47	Ne-san'-zä	" " "	Ne-san'-zä	" " "	Ne-she'-mä	" " "
48	Ne-san'-zä	" " "	Ne-san'-zä	" " "	Ne-she'-mä	" " "
49	Ne-sä-zä'	" " "	Ne-sä-zä'	" " "	Ne-she-mä'	" " "
50	Ne-sä-zä'	" " "	Ne-sä-zä'	" " "	Ne-she-mä'	" " "
51	Nä-sa'-mä	" " "	Nä-sa'-mä	" " "	Nä-se'-mä	" " "
52	Nä-nä'	" " "	Nä-nä'	" " "	Nä-sa'	" " "
53	Nä-ne'-ä	" " "	Nä-ne'-ä	" " "	Nä-sim-ä'	" " "
54	Ni-to-ta-mä'	My brother.	Ni-to-ta-mä'	" " "	Ni-to-ta-mä'	" " "
55	N'-tha-thä'	My elder brother.	N'-tha-thä'	" " "	N'-the-ma-thä'	" " "
56	Nä'-thä-hä	" " "	Na'-thä-hä	" " "	Ta'-yä	" " "
57	Neese-sä'	" " "	Neese-sä'	" " "	Nis-kun'-ä	" " "
58	Nis'-sä	" " "	Nis'-sä	" " "	Nis-kun'	" " "
59	N'-sees'	" " "	N'-sees'	" " "	N'-chi-gu'-num	" " "
60	N'-see'-wes	My brother.	N'-tul-mŭm'	My step-brother.	N'-see'-wes	My brother.
61	Ne-tä-kun'	" "	Ne-tä-kun'	" " "	N'-lr-i-sum'	My step-brother.
62	Nee-mä'-tus	My step-brother.	N'-dun-oo-yome'	" " "	Nee-mä'-tus	" " "
63	Nain-n'-hans'	My elder brother.	Nain-n'-hans'	" " "	Nain-hise'-sa-mus	My younger bro.
64	Kŭn'-dig-eh	" " "	Kŭn'-dig-eh	My elder brother.	A-cha'-a	" " "
65	Sŭn-no'-ga	" " "	Sŭn-no'-ga	" "	Sŭn-no'-ga-yä'-za	" " "
66	Su-nä'-ga	" " "	Su-nä'-ga	" " "	Set-chil'-e-ä-ze	" " "
67	Soon'-da-ga	" " "	Soon'-da-ga	" " "	Sa'-chä	" " "
68	Soon-da	" " "	Soon-da	" " "	Sa-chä	" "
69	Is-sin-kwu-seehw'	One like my brother.				
70						
71			Es-hup. bNe-pah'	My younger brother.		
72	Ko-ko-wä-malt	My brother.	Ko-ko-wä malt	My brother.	Ko-ko-wä-malt	My brother.
73						
74	No-vi-pa-ra	My elder brother.	No-vi-pa-ra	My elder brother.	No-vi-te-u	My younger bro.
75						
76						
77						
78						
79	Ig-dlo-ra	My cousin.	Ig-dlo-ra	My cousin.	Ig-dlo-ra	My cousin.
80	Il-lŭng'-ä	" "	Il-lo'-ä	" "	Il-lŭng'-ä	" "

TABLE II.—*Continued.*

	144. My mother's sister's son —younger than myself. (Female speaking.)	Translation.	145. My mother's sister's son's wife. (Male speaking.)	Translation.	146. My mother's sister's son's wife. (Female speaking.)	Translation.
1	Ha'-gă	My younger brother.	Ah-ge͡ah'-ne-ah	My sister-in-law.	Ah-ge͡ah'-ne͡o	My sister-in-law.
2	Ha-gă'-ah	" " "	Uh-ge-ah'-ne-a	" "	Uh-ge͡ah'-ne͡o	" "
3	Ha'-gă	" " "	Ah-ge-ah'-yeh	" "	Ah-ge-ah'-ne-o	" "
4	Le-gă'-ah	" " "	Un-ge͡ah'-le͡a	" "	Un-ge͡ah'-le͡a	" "
5	E'-gä-hä	" " "	Un-gä-le-ya'-ah	" "	Un-gä-le-a'-ah	" "
6	Kä'-gä	" " "	Ack-gä'-re-ah	" "	Ack-gä'-re-ah	" "
7	Lok-je'-hä	" " "	Ah-go-hä'-kwä	" "	Ah-go-hä'-kwä	" "
8	Ha-ye-ä'-hä	" " "	O-in-dä'-wait	" "	O-in-dä'-wait	" "
9	Me-suŋ'-kä	" " "	Häŋ-kä'	" "	E-cha'-päŋ	" "
10	Me-soh'-kä	" " "	Hä-kä'	" "	E-shä'-pä	" "
11	Me-sunk'-ä	" " "	Wä'-kä	" "	E-shä'-pä	" "
12	Me-sun'-kä	" " "	Hä-kä'	" "	E-shä'-pä	" "
13	Me-soh'-kä-lä	" " "	Hun-kä'	" "	S'cha'-pä	" "
14	Me-sunk'-ä-lä	" " "	Huŋ-kä'	" "	S'cha'-pä	" "
15	Me-soh'-kä-lä	" " "	Hä'-kä	" "	E-sä'-pä	" "
16	Me-son'-kä-lä	" " "	Hä'-kä	" "	E-sä'-pä	" "
17	Me-soh'	" " "	Me-hä'-kä	" "	Me-she'-cha-pas	" "
18	Kä-ga'	" " "	We-hun'-gä	" "	She-kä'	" "
19	Wee-soŋ'-gä	" " "	We-huŋ'-gä	" "	We-she'-kä	" "
20	E-chun'-cha	" " "	Hun'-gä	" "	Hee-she'-kä	" "
21	E-chun'-che	" " "	Häŋ'-gä	" "	Hin-she'-kä	" "
22	Be-suŋ'-gä	" " "	Be-hä'-gä	" "	Be-she'-kä	" "
23	We-son'kä	" " "	We-hun'-kä	" "	We-she'-kä	" "
24	E-sŭnk'	" " "	E-yuŋ'-ga	" "	E-she'-gä	" "
25	Me-sho'-kä	" " "	Moo'-ha	" "	Koo-too'-min-ik	" "
26	Mat-so'-gä	" " "	Boo-ä-kä'	" "	Mat-too'	" "
27	Bä-chŭ'-ka	" " "	Moo'-ä-ka	" "	Bos-me'-ä-kun-is-ta	" "
28	A-näk'-fĭ	" " "	Suh-hai'-yä	" "	Suh-hai'-yä	" "
29	A-näk'-fĭ	" " "	Sä-haĭ'-ya	" "	Sä-haĭ'-ya	" "
30	A-näk'-fĭ	" " "	Sä-hĭ'-yä	" "	Sä-hi'-yä	" "
31	Chu-chihl'-wä	" " "	Chu-hu'-cho-wä	" "	Um-e-hi'-wä	" "
32	Uŋ-gĭ-dan'	" " "	Au-sdä-duŋ'-hĭ	" "	Au-sdä-lĭ-gĭ	" "
33	Aŋ'-ke-do	" " "	Ah-ke-tso'-hĭ	" "	E-nä-duh'-hĭ	" "
34	E-rats'-teh	My brother.	Tä-te'-luk-tuk-u	My wife.	Scoo'-rus	" "
35	Kä-we'-ta	" "	Sko'-dus	My sister-in-law.	Sko'-dus	" "
36	Kä-wit'-tä	" "	Sko-roo'-hoo	" "	Sko-roo'-hoo	" "
37	Ne-seme'	My younger brother.	Nee-tim'	" "	N'-jä'-koase	" "
38	Ne-sha-mish'	" " "	Nee-tim'	" "	N'-jä'-koase	" "
39	Ne-she-mish'	" " "	Nee-tim'	" "	N'-dä'-koase	" "
40	Nĭ-shĭ'-me	" " "	Nĭ'-nim	" "	Nin-dän'-gwe	" "
41	Nin-dä-wa'-mä	My step-brother.	Ne'-nim	" "	Nin-dou'-gwa	" "
42	Ne-she'-mä	My younger brother.	Ne-nim'	" "	Niu-dän-gwa'	" "
43	Ne-she-mä'	" " "	Ne-nim'	" "	N'-dän-gwä'	" "
44	Ne-she'-mä	" " "	Ne-nim'	" "	N'-däŋ-gwa'	" "
45	Ne-she-mä'	" " "	Ne'-nim	" "	N'-dän-gwa'	" "
46	Se-me-mä'	" " "	Ne-lim-wä'	" "	N'-jan-gwä'	" "
47	N'-she-mä'	" " "	Ne-lim-wä'	" "	Nin-jä-gwa'	" "
48	Ne-she-mä'	" " "	Ne-lim-wä'	" "	Nin-jä-gwa'	" "
49	Ne-she-mä'	" " "	Ne-le-mwä'	" "	Nin-jä-kwa'	" "
50	Ne-she-mä'	" " "	Ne-le-mwä'	" "	Nin-jä-kwa'	" "
51	Nä-se'-mä	" " "	Ne-nim'-wä	" "	Nä-dä'-kwä	" "
52	Nä-sa'	" " "	Ne-nim'	" "	Wä-a'-che-uk	" "
53	Nä-sim-ä'	" " "	Nee'-tum	" "	Nach-a-im	" "
54	Ni-to-ta-mä'	" " "	Ne-nem-wä'	" "	Wa-si-nä-mä-kä	" "
55	N'-the-ma-thä'	" " "	Ne-lim-wä'	" "	N'-tä-kwä'	" "
56	Ta'-yä	" " "	Nee-tim'	" "	Ne-ta'-be	" "
57	Nis-kun'-ä	" " "	N'-do'-to-ke-man'	" "	Nee-mis'	" "
58	Nis-kun'	" " "	Ne-to'-to-ke-man	" "	Nee-mis'	" "
59	N'-chi-gu'-num	" " "	Ne-lu-mŭs'	" "	Ne-mäk-tem'	" "
60	Neet-see-kes'	My step-brother.	Ne-lu-mŭs'	" "	Ne'-tä-kw'	" "
61	N'-hri-sun'	My younger brother.	Nee-num'	" "	N'-dä-oh·k'	" "
62	N'-dun-oo-yome'	My step-brother.	Nee-lum'	" "	Ne-tä'-wis	" "
63	Nain-hise'-sa-mus	My younger brother.	Na-nee-lim'	" "	Nain-ue-la'-kon	" "
64	A-cha'-a	" " "	Sa'-gy	" "	Sa'-gy	" "
65	Sŭn-no'-ga-yä-za	" " "	Sa-teŋ'-a-bä-che-la	" "	Sa'-ga	" "
66	Set-chil'-a-ä-ze	" " "	Set'-so	" "	Sa'-o-ga	" "
67	Sa'-chä	" " "				
68	Sa-chä	" " "				
69						
70						
71			In'-matsh	" "		
72	Ko-ko-wä-malt	My brother.				
73						
74						
75						
76						
77	P-cu-i-hi'-bä	My younger brother.				
78						
76	Ig-dlo-ra	My cousin.				
80	Il-lo'-ä	" "	I-e'-gä	" "	Oo-keo-ä'-gä	" "

TABLE II.—*Continued.*

	147. My mother's sister's daughter—older than myself. (Male speaking.)	Translation.	148. My mother's sister's daughter—older than myself. (Female speaking.)	Translation.	149. My mother's sister's daughter—younger than myself. (Male speaking.)	Translation.
1	Ah′-je......................	My elder sister.	Ah′-je......................	My elder sister.	Ka′-gă......................	My younger sister
2	Uh-je′-ah..................	" " "	Uh-je′-ah..................	" " "	Ka-gă′-ah..................	" " "
3	Uh-je′-ah..................	" " "	Uh-je′-ah..................	" " "	Ka′-gă......................	" " "
4	Ahk-je′-hä................	" " "	Ahk-je′-hä................	" " "	Kä-gä′-ah.................	" " "
5	Ahk-je′-hä................	" " "	Ahk-je′-hä................	" " "	Ka-gä′-hä.................	" " "
6	Ahk′-je....................	" " "	Ahk′-je....................	" " "	Kä′-gä......................	" " "
7	Ak-je′-yä..................	" " "	Ak-je′-yä..................	" " "	Ka-gä′-ah.................	" " "
8	A-ye′-uh...................	" " "	A-ye′-uh...................	" " "	Ya-ye-ă′-hä...............	" " "
9	Tăŋ-kay′...................	" " "	Me-chuŋ′...................	" " "	Me-tänk′-she.............	" " "
10	Ton-kä′....................	" " "	Chu-ih′....................	" " "	Me-tänk′-she.............	" " "
11	Tank′-she.................	" " "	Me-tank′-a-do...........	" " "	Me-tänk′-she.............	" " "
12	Tank′-she.................	" " "	Tan′-ka...................	" " "	Me-tänk′-she.............	" " "
13	Tä-ka′.....................	" " "	Chu-wa′...................	" " "	Me-tunk′-she.............	" " "
14	Tonk-a′....................	" " "	Chu-a′....................	" " "	Me-tunk′-she.............	" " "
15	Ton′-ka....................	" " "	Chu-ih′....................	" " "	Me-tank′-she.............	" " "
16	Ton-ka′....................	" " "	Chu-wa′...................	" " "	Me-tonk′-she.............	" " "
17	Me-ton′-ga................	" " "	Me-chuŋ′...................	" " "	Me-tänk′-she.............	" " "
18	Ton-ga′-hä................	" " "	Zhon-da′-hä...............	" " "	We-ha′....................	" " "
19	Wee-töŋ′-ga...............	" " "	Wee-zön-thä...............	" " "	Wee-töŋ′-ga...............	" " "
20	Hee-u′-nä.................	" " "	Heen-taŋ′-ta	" " "	Heen-täŋ′-ya.............	" " "
21	Wau-he′-cha...............	" " "	Heen-tän′-ga	" " "	Heen-täŋ′-gä.............	" " "
22	Be-tuŋ′-ga................	" " "	Be-sho′-wa	" " "	Be-tuŋ′-gä-zhin-gä......	" " "
23	We-tuŋ′-ka................	" " "	We-sho′-la................	" " "	We-tuŋ′-ka................	" " "
24	E-noo′.....................	" " "	E-noo′.....................	" " "	Wych-kä′..................	" " "
25	P-tä′-me-ha...............	" " "	Me-no′-ha.................	" " "	P-tä′-me-ha...............	" " "
26	Mat-tä-we′-ä..............	" " "	Mä-roo′...................	" " "	Mă-tä-ka′-zhä............	" " "
27	Bä-za′-kät................	" " "	Bus-we′-nä................	" " "	Bä-sä′-chete..............	" " "
28	Aŋ′-take...................	" " "	Um-un′-nĭ.................	" " "	An′-take...................	" " "
29	Aŋ′-take...................	" " "	Um-un′-nĭ.................	" " "	An′-take...................	" " "
30	An′-take...................	" " "	Et-e-bä′-pĭ-shĭ-lĭ.........	My sister.	An′-take...................	" " "
31	Chu-wun′-wä..............	" " "	Chu-hlä′-hä...............	My elder sister.	Chu-wun′-wä..............	" " "
32	Un-gi-dau′................	" " "	Uŋ-gi-lüŋ′-ĭ..............	" " "	Un-gĭ-dau′................	" " "
33	Aŋ-ke′-doh	" " "	Aŋ-ge-lä′-ih..............	" " "	Aŋ-ke-doh.................	" " "
34	E-tä′-heh.................	My sister.	E-dä′-deh.................	My sister.	E-tä′-heh.................	My sister.
35	A-tä′-he...................	" "	A-tä′-he...................	" "	A-tä′-ke...................	" "
36	Ah-te′-ta	" "	Ah-te′-ta	" "	Ah-te′-ta	" "
37	Ne-mis′....................	My elder sister.	Ne-mish′...................	My elder sister.	Ne-sheme′.................	My younger sister.
38	Ne-mish′...................	" " "	Ne-mish′...................	" " "	Ne-she-mish′.............	" " "
39	Ne-mish′...................	" " "	Ne-mish′...................	" " "	Ne-she-mish′.............	" " "
40	Nĭ-mis′-s.................	" " "	Nĭ-mis′-s.................	" " "	Nĭ-shĭ′-me...............	" " "
41	Nin-dä-wa′-mä...........	My step-sister.	Ne-de-ge′-ko.............	My step-sister.	Nin-dä-wa′-mä...........	My step-sister.
42	Nin-dä-wa′-mä...........	" "	Ne-mis-sä′...............	My elder sister.	Ne-she′-mä...............	My younger sister.
43	N′-do-wa′-mä	" "	Ne-mis-sä′...............	" " "	Ne-she-mä′...............	" " "
44	N′-dä-wa-mä′..............	" "	N′-mis′-sä................	" " "	N′-she′-mä...............	" " "
45	N′-dä-wä′-mä..............	" "	Ne-mis-sä′...............	" " "	Ne-she-mä′...............	" " "
46	Ne-mis-sä′................	My elder sister.	Ne-mis-sä′...............	" " "	Ne-go-se-mä′..............	" " "
47	Ne-mis-sä′................	" " "	Ne-mis-sä′...............	" " "	Ne-she′-mä...............	" " "
48	Ne-mis-sä′................	" " "	Ne-mis-sä′...............	" " "	Ne-she′-mä...............	" " "
49	Ne-me-sä′.................	" " "	Ne-me-sä′.................	" " "	Ne-she′-mä...............	" " "
50	Ne-me-sä′.................	" " "	Ne-me-sä′.................	" " "	Ne-she-mä′...............	" " "
51	Nă-mis′-sä................	" " "	Na-mis′-sä................	" " "	Nă-se′-mä.................	" " "
52	Ne-ma′....................	" " "	Nă-ma′....................	" " "	Nă-sa′....................	" " "
53	Nă-ma′....................	" " "	Nă-ma′....................	" " "	Nă-sim-ä′.................	" " "
54	Ne-ta-kwă-mĭ′............	My sister.	Ne ta-kwă-mĭ′............	My sister.	Ne-ta-kwă-mĭ............	My sister.
55	Nĭ-mĭ-thä′................	My elder sister.	Nĭ-mĭ-thä′................	My elder sister.	N′-the-ma-thä′...........	My younger sister.
56	Na′-be....................	" " "	Na′-be....................	" " "	Na′-be-ă..................	" " "
57	Nee-mis′-tä...............	" " "	Nee-mis′-tä...............	" " "	Ne-sis′-sä................	" " "
58	Ne-his′-tä	" " "	Ne-his′-tä	" " "	Ne-sis′-sä................	" " "
59	Nu-mees′..................	" " "	Nu-mees′..................	" " "	N′-kwa-jeech′.............	" " "
60	Nu-tä-kw-sŭs′-kw	My step-sister.	Nee-tse-kes′..............	My step-sister.	Nu-tä-kw-sŭs′-kw........	My step-sister.
61	Na-mese′..................	" "	Na-mese′..................	" "	N′-h′i-sum′...............	" "
62	N′-doh′-kwä-yome′........	" "	Neet-koh′-kw′.............	" "	N′-doh′-kwä-yome′........	" "
63	Nain-na-wase′............	My elder sister.	Nain-na-wase′............	My elder sister.	Nain-hise′-sa-mus′.......	My younger sister.
64	Sä′-dä....................	" " "	Sä′-dä....................	" " "	A-da′-ze..................	" " "
65	Sa-da′-za.................	" " "	Sa-da′-za.................	" " "	Sa-da′-za-yă′-za.........	" " "
66	Set-dez′-a-ä-ze...........	" " "	Set-dez′-a-ä-ze...........	" " "	Sä′-re....................	" " "
67	Sa′-che...................	" " "	Sa-che′...................	" " "	Sa-chith′.................	" " "
68	Sa-che	" " "	Sa-che	" " "	Se-chy-o	" " "
69						
70		[step-sister.				
71	In-chats or En-naks	(Not rendered.) My				
72	Al-kat-kitsh-kilt...........	My sister.	Al-kat-kitsh-kilt...........	My sister.	Al-kat-kitsh-kilt	My sister.
73						
74						
75						
76						
77	Gu-i′-ä....................	My elder sister.	Gu-i′-ä....................	My elder sister.	Cu-hu′-bä.................	My younger sister.
78						
79	Ig-dlo-ra	My cousin.	Ig-dlo-ra	My cousin.	Ig-dlo-ra	My cousin.
80	Il-lŭng′-ä.................	" "	Il-lo′-ä...................	" "	Il-lŭng′ä..................	" "

TABLE II.—*Continued.*

	150. My mother's sister's daughter—younger than myself. (Female speaking.)	Translation.	151. My mother's sister's daughter's husband. (Male speaking.)	Translation.	152. My mother's sister's daughter's husband. (Female speaking.)	Translation.
1	Ka′-gă	My younger sister.	Ah-ge͡-ah′-ne͡o	My brother-in-law.	Ha-yă′-o	My broth.-in-law.
2	Ka-gă′-ah	" " "	Uh-ge͡-ah′-ne͡o	" "	Ha-yă′-bo	" "
3	Ka′-gă	" " "	Ah-ge-ah′-ne-o	" "	Ah-ge-ah′-de-o	" "
4	Ka-gä′-ah	" " "	Un-ge͡-ah′-de͡o	" "	Un-ge͡-ah′-le͡o	" "
5	Kă′-gă	" " "	Un-gă-de͡o′-hä	" "	Un-gă-le-yă′-ah	" "
6	Kă′-gă	" " "	Ack-gaw′-no-ah	" "	Ack-gä′-rä	" "
7	Ka-gä′-ah	" " "	Un-jă′-jo-hä	" "	Un-jă′-jo-hä	" "
8	Ya-ye-ă′-hä	" " "	O-in-dä′-wait	" "	Ah-zhă′-ku	" "
9	Me-tăŋ′-kă	" " "	Tä-häŋ′	" "	She-chay′	" "
10	Me-tuŋ′-kă	" " "	Tä-hä′	" "	She-cha′	" "
11	Me-tank′-ă-do	" " "	Tä-hä′	" "	She-cha′	" "
12	Me-tän′-kă	" " "	Tä-hä′	" "	She-cha′	" "
13	Me-tunk′-hä-lä	" " "	Tä-hä′	" "	She-cha′	" "
14	Me-tonk′-ă	" " "	Tä-hä′	" "	She-ches′	" "
15	Ton′-kä	" " "	Tä-hä′	" "	She-cha′	" "
16	Me-ton′-kă	" " "	Tä-huh′	" "	She-cha′	" "
17	Me-tä′	" " "	Me-hän′-kă	" "	Me-she′-cha	" "
18	We-ha′	" " "	Tä-hä′-hnh	" "	We-she′-eh	" "
19	Wee-töŋ′-ga	" " "	We-tä′-hä	" "	We-she′-kă	" "
20	Heen-tuŋ′-ga	" " "	Heen-tä′-hä	" "	Hin-she′-kä	" "
21	Heen-tän′-gä	" " "	Heen-tä′-ha	" "	Hin-she′-kä	" "
22	Ah-se′-zhe-gä	" " "	Be-tä′-hä	" "	Be-she′-kă	" "
23	We-tuŋ′-ka	" " "	We-tä′-ha	" "	We-she′-kă	" "
24	E-chunk′	" " "	E-chuŋ′	" "	E-she′-ga	" "
25	Me-no′-ka	" " "	Wo-wä′-ke-a	" "	Wo-wä′-ke-a	" "
26	Mă-tä-ka′-zhă	" " "	Mä-nä′-te	" "	Mä-nä′-te	" "
27	Bä-so′-ka	" " "	Mä-nä′-zha	" "	Bä-che′-na	" "
28	Suh-năk′-fish	" " "	Um-ă′-lŏk	" "	Um-ă′-lŏk	" "
29	Sä-năk′-fish	" " "	Um-ă′-läk	" "	Um-ă′-läk	" "
30	Et-e-bä′-pĭ-shĭ-lĭ	My sister.	Um-ă′-läk	" "	Um-ă′-läk	" "
31	Chu-chŭ′-se	My younger sister.	Un-kä′-wä⸫	" "	Chu-hu′-cho-wä	" "
32	Un-gĭ-luŋ′-Ĭ	" " "	Au-sda-lau′-sĭ	" "	Aw-să′-dluŋ′-hĬ	" "
33	Aŋ-ge-lä′-ih	" " "	Squä-lo′-sih	" "	Squa-lo′-sih	" "
34	E-dä′-deh	My sister.	Koos-tow′-et-sŭ	My son-in-law.	Koos-tow′-et-sŭ	My son-in-law.
35	A-tä′-he	" "	Ko-stä′-witch	" "	Ko-stä′-witch	" "
36	Ah-te′-ta	" "	Kuh-tä-wä′-suh	" "	Kuh-tä-wä′-suh	" "
37	Ne-sheme′	My younger sister.	Neese-tow′	My brother-in-law.	Nee-tim′	My broth.-in-law.
38	Ne-she-mish′	" " "	Neese-tow′	" "	Nee-tim′	" "
39	Ne-she-mish′	" " "	Neesh-tow′	" "	Nee-tim′	" "
40	Nĭ-shĭ′-me	" " "	Nĭ′-tä	" "	Nĭ′-nim	" "
41	Ne-de-ge′-ko	My step-sister.	Ne-che-ke-wa-ze	" "	Ne′-nim	" "
42	Ne-she-mă′	My younger sister.	Ne-tä′	" "	Ne′-nim	" "
43	Ne-she-mă′	" " "	Ne-tä′	" "	Ne-nin′	" "
44	N′-she′-mă	" " "	Ne-tä′	" "	Ne-nim′	" "
45	Ne-she-mă′	" " "	Ne-tä′	" "	Ne-nim′	" "
46	Ne-go-se-mă′	" " "	Ne-tä-wä′	" "	Ne-lim-wä′	" "
47	Ne-she-mä′	" " "	Ne-tä-wĭ′	" "	Ne-lim-wä′	" "
48	Ne-she-mä′	" " "	Ne-tä-wä′	" "	Ne-lim-wä′	" "
49	Ne-she-mä′	" " "	Ne-tä-wä′	" "	Ne-le-mwä′	" "
50	Ne-she-mä′	" " "	Ne-tä-wä′	" "	Ne-le-mwä′	" "
51	Nă-se′-mă	" " "	Ne-tä′-wä	" "	Ne-nim′-wä	" "
52	Nă-sa′	" " "	Na-tow′	" "	Ne-nim′	" "
53	Nă-sim-ă′	" " "	Ne-to′	" "	Nee-tum′	" "
54	Na-ta-tă-mă′	My sister.	Nen-hă-kă-ni-mä	" "	Ne-nem-wä′	" "
55	N′-the-ma-thä′	My younger sister.	Ne-tä-kwä′	" "	Ne-lim-wä′	" "
56	Na′-be-ă	" " "	Ne-ah′-ă	" "	Ne-ta′-be	" "
57	Ne-sis′-sä	" " "	Nis-tä-mo′	" "	N′-to′-to-yome	" "
58	Ne-sis′-sä	" " "	Nis-tä-mo′	" "	Ne-to′-to-yome	" "
59	N′-kwa-jeech′	" " "	Nu-mäk-tem′	" "	Ne-lu-müs′	" "
60	Nee-tse-kes′	My step-sister.	Nu-mäk-tem′	" "	Ne-lu-müs′	" "
61	N′-hi-sum	" "	N′-dä-oh·k′	" "	Nee-mun′	" "
62	Neet-koh′-kw′	" "	Noh·-taŋ′-kw′	" "	Nee-lum′	" "
63	Nain-hise′-sa-mus′	My younger sister.	Na-nä-donkue′	" "	Na-nee-lim′	" "
64	A-da′-ze	" " "	Sä′-gä	" "	Sä′-gä	" "
65	Sa-da′-za-yä′-za	" " "	Sa′-ga	" "	Sa-ta′-za-pa-ten′-ne	" "
66	Sä′-re	" " "	Sa′-o-ga	" "	Set-shi′-ya	" "
67	Sa-chith′	" " "				
68	Se-chy-o	" " "	Set-she-ku-in	My son-in-law.	Sa-ta-ni-o	(Not rendered.)
69						
70						
71			Enm-au′-wi-tahll	My brother-in-law.		
72	Al-kat-kitsh-kilt	My sister.				
73						
74						
75						
76						
77	Cu-hu′-bä	My younger sister.				
78						
79	Ig-dlo-ra	My cousin.				
80	Il-lo′-ä	" "	Ning-a-ou′-gwä	My son-in-law.	I-e′-gä	My son-in-law.

TABLE II.—*Continued.*

	153. My mother's sister's son's son. (Male speaking.)	Translation.	154. My mother's sister's son's son. (Female speaking.)	Translation.	155. My mother's sister's son's daughter. (Male speaking.)	Translation.
1	Ha-ah′-wuk	My son.	Ha-soh′-neh	My nephew.	Ka-ah′-wuk	My daughter.
2	Ha-hä′-wuk	" "	Ha-hä′-wuk	My son.	Ka-hä′-wuk	" "
3	Ha-hä′-wä	" "	Ha-hä′-wä	" "	Ka-hä′-wä	" "
4	Le-yä′-hä	" "	Le-yä′-hä	" "	Ka-yä′-hä	" "
5	E-yä′	" "	E-yä′	" "	Ka-yä′	" "
6	Kä-yä′-no-nä	My child.	Kä-yä-no′-na-ah	My nephew.	Kä-yä′-no-nä	My child.
7	Le-yä′-ah	My son.	Le-yä′-ah	My son.	Ka-yä′-ah	My daughter.
8	A-ne-ah′	" "	He-wä′-teh	My nephew.	E-ne-ah′	" "
9	Me-chink′-she	" "	Me-tonsh′-kä	" "	Me-chunk′-she	" "
10	Me-chink′-she	" "	Me-to͞us′-kä	" "	Me-chounk′-she	" "
11	Ak-she′-dä	" "	Me-toash′-kä	" "	Me-chink′-she	" "
12	Me-chink′-she	" "	Me-tose′-kä	" "	Me-chunk′-she	" "
13	Me-chink′-se-lä	" "	Me-toans′-kä	" "	Me-chunk′-se-lä	" "
14	Me-chink′-she	" "	Me-toase′-kä	" "	Me-chunk′-she	" "
15	Me-chink′-she	" "	Me-toash′-kä	" "	Me-chunk′-she	" "
16	Me-chink′-she	" "	Me-toas′-kä	" "	Me-chŭnk′-she	" "
17	Me-chink′-she	" "	Me-to′-zä	" "	Me-chunk′-she	" "
18	Nis-se′-hä	" "	We-toash′-kä	" "	Win-no′-ga	" "
19	We-nĭs′-se	" "	We-toans′-kä	" "	We-zhun′-ga	" "
20	Hee-yiŋ′-ga	" "	Heen-toas′-kä	" "	Hee-yuŋ′-ga	" "
21	He-ne′-cha	" "	Hin-tose′-kee	" "	He-yuŋ′-ga	" "
22	Be-she′-gä	" "	Be-chose′-kä	" "	She-me′-she-gä	My girl.
23	We-she′-kä	" "	We-chose′-ka	" "	We-shon′-ka	My daughter.
24	E-neke′	" "	E-choonsh′-ka-neke′	My little nephew.	E-nook′	" "
25	Me-ne′-ka	" "	Ko′-ne-ka	My son.	Me-no′-hä-ka	" "
26	Mä-de-shä′	" "	Met-a-wä-pish′-sha	My grandchild.	Mä′-kä	" "
27	Bot-sa′-sä	" "	Bot-sa′-sä	My son.	Näk′-me-ă	" "
28	Suh′-sŭh	" "	Sup′-uk-nŏk′-ne	My grandson.	Suh-sŭh′-take	" "
29	Suh′-soh	" "	Sä′-pok-näk′-ne	" "	Suh-soh′-take	" "
30	Su′-soh	" "	Sup′-pok-näk′-nĭ	" "	Su-soh′-take	" "
31	Chup-pŭ′-ce	" "	Um-os-sŭs′-wä	My grandchild.	Chus-hus′-te	" "
32	A-gwae-tsĭ′	My child.	Uŋ-gĭ-wĭ′-nuŋ	My nephew.	A-gwae-tsĭ′	My child.
33	A-gwa′-tze	" "	Un-ge-we′-nuh	" "	A-gwa′-tze	" "
34	Pe′-row	" "	Pe′-row	My child.	Pe′-row	" "
35	Pe′-row	" "	Pe′-row	" "	Pe′-row	" "
36	Nä-te-nä′-o	" "	At-nuch′	My grandchild.	Nä-te-nä′-o	" "
37	N′-do′-sim	My step-son.	N′-de-kwä-tim′	My nephew.	N′-do′-sa-mis-kwame′	My step-daughter.
38	N′-do′-zhim	" "	N′-de-kwä-tim′	" "	N′-do′-zha-mis-kwame′	" "
39	N′-do′-zhim	" "	N′-deh-kwä-tim′	" "	N′-do′-zha-mis-kwem′	" "
40	Nin-do′-zhim	" "	Nĭ-nin-gwä′-niss	" "	Nin-do-zhĭ-mĭ-kweu	" "
41	N′-do′-zhim	" "	Ne-nin-gwuh′-nis	" "	Nin-do-zhe-me′-quam	" "
42	N′-do′-zhim	" "	Ne-nin-gwi-nis′	" "	Nin-do-sha-mĭ-kwam′	" "
43	N′-do′-zhim-ä	" "	Ne-nin-gwi-nis′	" "	N′-do′-zha-mĭ-kwam′	" "
44	N′-do′-zhim	" "	Ne-nin-gwi-nis′	" "	N′-do′-zha-mĭ-kwam′	" "
45	N′-do′-she-mä	" "	N′-ah′-ga-neh-gweh′	" "	N′-do′-zha-mis	" "
46	Neen-gwase′-sä	My son.	Lan-gwä-les′-sä	" "	Nin-dä′-nä	My daughter.
47	Niŋ-gwa-sä′	" "	Ne-lä′-gwä-la-sä′	" "	Nin-dä′-nä	" "
48	Niŋ-gwa-sä′	" "	Ne-lä′-gwä-la-sä′	" "	Nin-dä′-nä	" "
49	Ne-gwis-sä′	" "	Ne-lä′-gwä-lis-sä′	" "	N′-dä′-nä	" "
50	Ne-gwis-sä′	" "	Ne-lä′-gwä-lis-sä′	" "	N′-dä′-nä	" "
51	Nä-kwis′-sä	" "	Nä-nä-gwä′-nis	" "	Nä-tä′-nis	" "
52	Ne-keese′	" "	Ne-nä-kwä-na	" "	Ne-täne′	" "
53	Nä	" "	Nä-chin′-e-tä	" "	Nä-tun′	" "
54	Nĭ-kwe-thä′	" "	Neu-na-kwä-na-thä′	" "	Ni-ton-na-thä′	" "
55	Ne-kwe-thä′	" "	Na-la-gwal-thä′	" "	Nĭ-tä-na-thä′	" "
56	Na′-hä	" "	Na-tah′-ta	" "	Nä-tä′-na	" "
57	N′-do′-to-ko	My step-son.	N′-do′-to-yose	" "	N′-to′-to-tun	My step-daughter.
58	Noh′-ko′-ä	My son.	No-ä′-toase	" "	Ne-tan′-ä	" "
59	N′-kwis′	" "	Nu-lŭks′	" "	N′-tŭs′	My daughter.
60	N′-too-ä′-sum	My step-child.	Nu-lŭ′-knees	My step-child.	N′-su′-mus	My step-child.
61	Nä-kun′	" "	Nä-kun′		Nä-kun′	" "
62	N′-kweese′	My son.	N′-kweese′	My son.	N′-dä-nuss′	My daughter.
63	Nain-gwase′	" "	Nain-gwase′	" "	Nain-dä′-niss	" "
64	Tu-zen′-a	My step-son.	Sa-yä′-ze	" "	Sa-yä′-dze	My step-daughter.
65	Sa-yä′-za	My son.	Sa-yä′-za	" "	Sa-to′-a	My daughter.
66	Se-yä′-za	" "	Se-yä′-za	" "	Sa-le-ä′	" "
67						
68	Si-ou	My step-child.	Si-ou	My step-child.	Si-ou	My step-child
69						
70						
71						
72						
73						
74						
75						
76						
77						
78						
79						
80	Kun-e-ä′-gä	My nephew.	Ung-ä′-gä	My nephew.	Kun-e-ä′-gä	My niece.

TABLE II.—*Continued.*

	156. My mother's sister's son's daughter. (Female speaking.)	Translation.	157. My mother's sister's daughter's son. (Male speaking.)	Translation.	158. My mother's sister's daughter's son. (Female speaking.)	Translation.
1	Ka-soh'-neh	My niece.	Ha-yă'-wan-da	My nephew.	Ha-ah'-wuk	My son.
2	Ka-hä'-wuk	My daughter.	Ha-yuh'-wä-da	" "	Ha-hä'-wuk	" "
3	Ka-hä'-wä	" "	Ha-yä-wä'-da	" "	Ha-bä'-wä	" "
4	Ka-yä'-hä	" "	Ha-yă'-wan-dă.	" "	Le-yä'-hä	" "
5	Ka-yä'	" "	E-yo-wä'-dä	" "	E-yä'	" "
6	Kä-yä-no'-nä-ah	" "	Kä-yä-wä-no	" "	Kä-yä'-no-nä	My child.
7	Ka-yä'-ah	" "	Le-wä-dä'-ah	" "	Le-yä'-ah	My son.
8	E-wä'-teh	My niece.	Ha-shone-drä'-ka	" "	A-ne-ah'	" "
9	Me-tuṇ'-zhan	" "	Me-tonsh'-kä	" "	Me-chiṇk'-she	" "
10	Me-to⁻us'-zä	" "	Me-to⁻us'-kä	" "	Me-chink'-she	" "
11	Me-to'-zhä	" "	Me-toash'-kä	" "	Ah-she'-dä	" "
12	Me-to'-zhä	" "	Me-tose'-kä	" "	Me-chink'-she	" "
13	Me-toh'-zhä	" "	Me-toans'-kä	" "	Me-chink'-she-lä	" "
14	Me-toh'-zhä	" "	Me-toase'-kä	" "	Me-chink'-she	" "
15	Me-to'-zä	" "	Me-toash'-kä	" "	Me-chink'-she	" "
16	Me-to'-zä	" "	Me-toas'-kä	" "	Me-chink'-she	" "
17	Me-to'-zä	" "	Me-to'-zä	" "	Me-chink'-she	" "
18	Tä-zhä'-hä	" "	We-toash'-kä	" "	Nis-se'-hä	" "
19	We-te'-zhä	" "	We-toans'-kä	" "	We-zhin'-ga	" "
20	Heen-toas'-ka-me	" "	Heen-toas'-ka	" "	Hee-yiṇ-ga	" "
21	Hin-tose'-kee-me	" "	Hin-tose'-kee	" "	He-ne'-cha	" "
22	Be-che'-zho	" "	Be-chose'-kä	" "	Be-she'-gä	" "
23	We-che'-zho	" "	We-chose'-kä	" "	We-shen'-kä	" "
24	E-chooṇ-zhunk'-e-neke'	My little niece.	E-choonsh'-ka-neke'	My little nephew.	E-chä-h·kun'	My step-child.
25	Me-no'-hä-ka	My daughter.			Ko'-ne-ka	My son.
26	Mä'-kä	" "	Mat-so'-gä	My younger brother.	Mä-de-shä'	" "
27	Näk'-me-ä	" "	Ba-chŭ'-ka	" "	Bot-sa'-sä	" "
28	Sup'-uk	My granddaughter.	Sub-ai'-yih	My nephew.	Sup'-uk-nŏk'-ne	My grandson
29	Sä'-pok	" "	Suh-bai'-yih	" "	Sä'-pok-näk'-ne	" "
30	Sup'-pok	" "	Sä-bi'-yih	" "	Sup'-pok-näk'-nĭ	" "
31	Um-os-sŭs'-wä	My grandchild.	Un-ho-pŭ'-e-wä	" "	Um-os-sŭs'-wä	My grandchild.
32	Uṇ-gwä-duṇ'	My niece.	Uṇ-gĭ-wĭ'-nuṇ	" "	A-gwae-tsĭ'	My child.
33	Uṇ-gwä'-tuh	" "	Uṇ-ge-we'-nuh	" "	A-gwa'-tže	" "
34	Pe'-row	My child.	Te'-wut	" "	Pe'-row	" "
35	Pe'-row	" "	Te'-wut	" "	Pe'-row	" "
36	At-nuch'	My grandchild.	Ah-te'-wut	" "	Nä-te-nä'-o	" "
37	Neese-che-mish'	My niece.	N'-de-kwä-tim'	" "	N'-go'-sim	My step-son.
38	Neest-cha-mish'	" "	N'-de-kwä-tim'	" "	N'-go'-zhim	" "
39	Neest-che-mis'	" "	N'-deh-kwä-tim'	" "	N'-do'-zhim	" "
40	Nĭ-shĭ'-miss	" "	Nĭ-nin-gwä'-niss	" "	Nin-do'-zhĭ-miss	My step-child.
41	Ne-she'-me-sha	" "	Ne-nin-gwuh'-nis	" "	Nin-do'-she-miss	" "
42	Ne-she-mis'	" "	Ne-nin-gwi-nis'	" "	Neen-gwis'	My son.
43	Ne-she-mis'	" "	Ne-nin-gwi-nis'	" "	Nin-gwis'	" "
44	Ne-she-mis'	" "	Ne-nin-gwi-nis'	" "	N'-gwis'	" "
45	Ne-she'-inis	" "	Nă'-gwi-nis'	" "	N'-gwis'	" "
46	Shame-sä'	" "	Laṇ-gwä-les'-sä	" '	Neen-gwase'-sä	" "
47	Ne-she'-mis-sä'	" "	Ne-lä'-gwä-la-sä'	" "	Niṇ-gwa-sä'	" "
48	Ne-she'-mis-sä'	" "	Ne-lä'-gwä-la-sä'	" "	Niṇ-gwa-sä'	" "
49	Ne-she'-mis-sä'	" "	Ne-lä'-gwä-lis-sä'	" "	Ne-gwis-sä'	" "
50	Ne-she'-mis-sä'	" "	Ne-lä'-gwä-lis-sä'	" "	Ne-gwis-sä'	" "
51	Nä-shä-mis'	" "	Nä-nä'-gwä-nis	" "	Nä-kwis'-sä	" "
52	Nä-nä'-mä	" "	Ne-nä'-kwä-na	" "	Ne-keese'	" "
53	Nä-un'	" "	Nä-chin'-e-tä	" "	Nä	" "
54	Na-sem-e-thä'	" "	Nen-na-kwä-na-thä	" "	Nĭ-kwe-thä'	" "
55	Ne-sa-me-thä'	" "	Na-la-gwal-thä'	" "	Ne-kwe-thä'	" "
56	Nä'-tha-be	" "	Na-tah'-ta	" "	Na'-hä	" "
57	Nee-mis'-sä	" "	N'-do'-to-yose	" "	N'-do'-to-ko	My step-son.
58	Nee-mis'-sä	" "	No-ä'-toase	" "	Noh-ko'-ä	My son.
59	N'-sum'	" "	Nu-lŭks'	" "	N'-kwis'	" "
60	N'-sum'	" "	Nu-lŭ'-knees	" "	N'-too-ä'-sum	" "
61	Nä-kun'	My step-child.	No-kwath'	" "	N'-di-ome	" "
62	N'-dä-nuss'	My daughter.	Longue'-kw'	" "	N'-kweese'	" "
63	Nain-dä'-ness	" "	Na-lone'-gwü-sis	" "	Nain-gwase'	" "
64	Sa-yä'-dze	" "	Sä'-zy	" "	Sa-yä'-ze	My step-son.
65	Sa-to'-a	" "			Se-yä'-za	My son.
66	Sa-le'-ä	" "	Se-yä'-za	My son.	Se-yä'-za	" "
67						
68	Si-ou	My step-child.	Si-ou	My step-child.	Si-ou	My step-child.
69						
70						
71						
72						
73						
74						
75						
76						
77						
78						
79						
80	Ung-ä'-gä	My niece.	We-yo-o'-gwä	My nephew.	Noo-ä'-gä	My nephew.

TABLE II.—*Continued.*

	159. My mother's sister's daughter's daughter. (Male speaking.)	Translation.	160. My mother's sister's daughter's daughter. (Female speaking.)	Translation.	161. My mother's sister's great grandson.	Translation.
1	Ka-yä′-wan-da	My niece.	Ka-ah′-wuk	My daughter.	Ha-yä′-da	My grandson.
2	Kä-yuh′-wä-da	" "	Ka-hä′-wuk	" "	Ha-yä′-dra	" "
3	Ka-yä-wä′-da	" "	Ka-hä′-wä	" "	Ha-yä′-da	" "
4	Ka-yä′-wan-dă	" "	Ka-yä′-hä	" "	Le-yä′-dla-ah	" "
5	Ka-yo-wä′-dä	" "	Ka-yä′	" "	E-yä′-dla-ah	" "
6	Kä-yä′-wä-nä	" "	Kä-yä′-no-pä	" "	Kä-yä′-rä	My grandchild.
7	Ka-wä-dä′-ah	" "	Ka-yä′-hä	" "	Le-yä-tä-ra′-yä	My grandson.
8	Ya-shone-drä′-ka	" "	E-ne-ah′	" "	Ha-tra′-ah	" "
9	Me-tun′-zhan	" "	Me-chunk′-she	" "	Me-tä′-ko-zhä	My grandchild.
10	Me-to͡us′-zä	" "	Me-chounk′-she	" "	Me-tä′-ko-zhä	" "
11	Me-to′-zhä	" "	Me-chink′-she	" "	Me-tä′-ᴋo-zhä	" "
12	Me-to′-zhä	" "	Me-chunk′-she	" "	Me-tä′-ko-zha	" "
13	Me-toh′-zhä	" "	Me-chunk′-se-lä	" "	Me-tä′-ko-säk′-pok	" "
14	Me-toh′-zhä	" "	Me-chunk′-she	" "	Me-tä′-ko-zhä	" "
15	Me-to′-zä	" "	Me-chŭnk′-she	" "	Me-tä′-ko-zhä	" "
16	Me-to′-zä	" "	Me-chŭnk′-she	" "	Me-tä′-ko-zhä	" "
17	Me-to′-zä	" "	Me-chunk′-she	" "	Me-tä′-ko-sä	" "
18	Ta-zhä′-hä	" "	Win-no′-ga	" "	Toosh′-pä-hä	" "
19	We-te′-zhä	" "	We-zhun′-ga	" "	Wee-tŭsh′-pä	" "
20	Heen-toas′-ka-me	" "	Hee-yuŋ′-ga	" "	Heen-tä′-kwä	My grandson.
21	Hin-tose′-kee-me	" "	He-yuŋ′-ga	" "	E-tä′-kwä	" "
22	Be-che′-zho	" "	She-me′-she-gä	My girl.	Be-chose′-pä	My grandchild.
23	We-che′-zho	" "	We-shon′-ka	My daughter.	We-chose′-pä	" "
24	E-choon-zhunk′-e-neke′	My little niece.	E-chä-h′kun′	My step-child.	E-choonsh′-ka-neke	My little gd. son.
25			Me-no′-hä-ka	My daughter.	P-tä-we′-hä-kä	My grandchild.
26	Mä-tä-kä′-zhä	My younger sister.	Mä′-kä	" "	Met-a-wä-pish′-shä	" "
27	Bä-sä′-chete	" " "	Näk′-ıne-a		Bus-bä′-pe-ta	" "
28	Sub-ih′-take	My niece.	Sup′-uk	My granddaughter.	Sup′-uk-nŏk′-ne	My grandson.
29	Suh-bih′-take	" "	Sä′-pok	" "	Sä′-pok-näk′-ne	" "
30	Su-bĭ′-take	" "	Sup′-pok	" "	Sup′-pok-näk′-nĭ	" "
31	Un-häk′-pute	" "	Um-os-sŭs′-wä	My grandchild.	Um-os-sŭs′-wä	My grandchild.
32	Uŋ-gwä-duŋ′	" "	A-gwae-tsĭ′	My child.	Uŋ-gĭ-lĭ-sĭ′	" "
33	Uŋ-gwä′-tuh	" "	A-gwa′-tze	" "	Aŋ-ge-lee′-se	" "
34	Te′-wut	" "	Pe′-row	" "	Lak-te′-gish	My grandson.
35	Te′-wut	" "	Pe′-row	" "	Lak-te′-kis	My grandchild.
36	Ah-te′-natch	" "	Nä-te-nä′-o	" "	At-nuch′	" "
37	Neese-che-mish′	" "	N'-do′-sa-mis-kwame′	My step-daughter.	No-se-sem′	" "
38	Neest-che-mish′	" "	N'-do′-zha-mis-kwame′	" "	No-se-sim′	" "
39	Neest-che-mis′	" "	N'-do-zha-mis-kwem′	" "	No-se-sem′	" "
40	Ni-shĭ′-miss	" "	Nin-do′-zhĭ-she	My step-child.	No-zhĭ′-she	" "
41	Ne-she′-me-sha	" "	Nin-do′-zhe-mis	" "	No-she′-shä	" "
42	Ne-she-mis′	" "	Neen-dä′-niss	My daughter.	No-she-shä′	" "
43	Ne-she-mis′	" "	N'-dä-niss′	" "	No-she-shä′	" "
44	Ne-she-nis′	" "	N'-dä-niss′	" "	No-she-shä′	" "
45	Ne-she-mĭs′	" "	N'-dä′-niss	" "	No-sä′-seh′	" "
46	Shame-sä′	" "	Nin-dä′-nä	" "	No-sa-mä′	" "
47	Ne-she-mis-sä′	" "	Nin-dä′-nä	" "	No-sa′-mä	" "
48	Ne-she-mis-sä′	" "	Nin-dä′-nä	" "	No-sa′-mä	" "
49	Ne-she-mis-sä′	" "	N'-dä′-nä	" "	No-sa-mä′	" "
50	Ne-she-mis-sä′	" "	N'-dä′-nä	" "	No-sa-mä′	" "
51	Nä-shä′-mis	" "	Nä-tä′-nis	" "	No-she-sem′	" "
52	Nä-nä′-mä	" "	Ne-täne′	" "	No-she-sä′	" "
53	Ne-she-mis′	" "	Nä-tun′	" "	Nä-h·kä′	" "
54	Ni-sem-e-thä	" "	Ni-tä-na-thä′	" "	Na-se-thä′-mä	" "
55	Ne-sa-me-thä′	" "	Nĭ-tä-na-thä′	" "	No-stha-thä′	" "
56	Nä-thä′-be	" "	Nä-tä′-na	" "	Nee′-sa	" "
57	Nee-mis′-sä	" "	N'-to′-to-tun	My step-daughter.	Nee-so′-tan	" "
58	Nee-mis′-sä	" "	Ne-tan′-ä	My daughter.	Nee-so′-tän	" "
59	N'-sum′	" "	N-tŭs′	" "	Nŭ-jeech′	" "
60	N'-sum′	" "	N'-su′-mus	" "	N'-kway′-nus	" "
61	Noh-soh-kwä′-oh	" "	Nee-chune′	" "	Nä-h·ise′	" "
62	Longue-kwä′	" "	N'-dä′-nuss	" "	Noh-whese′	" "
63	Na-lone′-gwä-sis′	" "	Nain-dä′-ness	" "	Nain-no-whase′	" "
64	Sä′-zy	" "	Sa-yä′-dze	My step-daughter.	Sa-t'thu′-a	" "
65			Sa-to′-a	My daughter.	Sa-ken′-ne	My grandson.
66	Sa-le′-ă	My daughter.	Sa-le′-ă	" "	Sa-yä-zet′-tha-re	" "
67						
68	Si-ou	My step-child.	Si-ou	My step-child.	Set-she	" "
69						
70						
71						
72						
73						
74						
75						
76						
77						
78						
79						
80	We-yo-o′-gwä	My niece.	Noo-ä′-gä	My niece.	Eng′-o-tä	My grandchild.

TABLE II.—*Continued.*

	162. My mother's sister's great granddaughter.	Translation.	163. My mother's sister's great grandson's son.	Translation.	164. My mother's sister's great granddaughter's daughter.	Translation.
1	Ka-yä′-da	My granddaughter.	Ha-yä′-da	My grandson.	Ka-yä′-da	My gd. daughter.
2	Ka-yä′-dra	" "	Ha-yä′-dra	" "	Ka-yä′-dra	" "
3	Ka-yä′-da	" "	Ha-yä′-da	" "	Ka-yä′-da	" "
4	Ka-yä′-dla-ah	" "	Le-yä′-dla-ah	" "	Ka-yä′-dla-ah	" "
5	Ka-yä′-dla-ah	" "	E-yä′-dla-ah	" "	Ka-yä′-dla-ah	" "
6	Kä-yä′-rä	My grandchild.	Kä-yä′-rä	My grandchild.	Kä-yä′-rä	My grandchild.
7	Ka-yä-tä-ra′-yä	My granddaughter.	Le-yä-tä-ra′-yä	My grandson.	Ka-yä-tä-ra′-yä	My gd. daughter.
8	Ya-tra′-ah	" "	Ha-tra′-ah	" "	Ya-tra′-ah	" "
9	Me-tä′-ko-zhä	My grandchild.	Me-tä′-ko-zhä	My grandchild.	Me-tä′-ko-zhä	My grandchild.
10	Me-tä′-ko-zhä	" "	Me-tä′-ko-zhä	" "	Me-tä′-ko-zhä	" "
11	Me-tä′-ko-zhä	" "	Me-tä′-ko-zhä	" "	Me-tä′-ko-zhä	" "
12	Me-tä′-ko-zha	" "	Me-tä′-ko-zha	" "	Me-tä′-ko-zha	" "
13	Me-tä′-ko-säk′-pok	" "	Me-tä′-ko-säk-pok	" "	Me-tä′-ko-säk-pok	" "
14	Me-tä′-ko-zhä	" "	Me-tä′-ko-zhä	" "	Me-tä′-ko-zhä	" "
15	Me-tä′-ko-zhä	" "	Me-tä′-ko-zhä	" "	Me-tä′-ko-zhä	" "
16	Me-tä′-ko-zä	" "	Me-tä′-ko-zä	" "	Me-tä′-ko-zä	" "
17	Me-tä′-ko-sä	" "	Me-tä′-ko-sä	" "	Me-tä′-ko-sä	" "
18	Toosh′-pä-hä	" "	Toosh′-pä-hä	" "	Toosh′-pä-hä	" "
19	Wee-tŭsh′-pä	" "	Wee-tŭsh′-pä	" "	Wee-tŭsh′-pä	" "
20	Heen-tä′-kwä-me	My granddaughter.	Heeu-tä′-kwä	My grandson.	Heen-tä′-kwä-me	My gd. daughter.
21	E-tä′-kwä-me	" "	E-tä′-kwä	" "	E-tä′-kwä-me	" "
22	Be-chose′-pä	My grandchild.	Be-chose′-pä	My grandchild.	Be-chose′-pä	My grandchild.
23	We-chose′-pä	" "	We-chose′-pä	" "	We-chose′-pa	" "
24	E-chooŋ-zhunk′-e-neke′	My little gd. daught.	E-choonsh′-ka-neke′	My little grandson.	E-chooŋ-zhunk′-e-neke′	My little gd. dau.
25	P-tä-we′-hä-kä	My grandchild.	P-tä-we′-hä-kä	My grandchild.	P-tä-we′-hä-kä	My grandchild.
26	Met-a-wä-pish′-sha	" "	Met-a-wä-pish′-sha	" "	Met-a-wä-pish′-sha	" "
27	Bus-bä′-pe-ta	" "	Bus-bä′-pe-ta	" "	Bus-bä′-pe-ta	" "
28	Sup′-uk	My granddaughter.	Sup′-uk-nŏk′-ne	My grandson.	Sup′-uk	My gd. daughter.
29	Sä′-pok	" "	Sä′-pok-näk′-ne	" "	Sä′-pok	" "
30	Sup′-pok	" "	Sup′-pok-näk′-nĭ	" "	Sup′-pok	" "
31	Um-os-sŭs′-wä	My grandchild.	Um-os-sŭs′-wä	My grandchild.	Um-os-sŭs′-wä	My grandchild.
32	Uŋ-gĭ-lĭ-sĭ	" "	Uŋ-gĭ-lĭ-sĭ	" "	Uŋ-gĭ-lĭ-sĭ	" "
33	Uŋ-ge-lee′-se	" "	Aŋ-ge-lee′-se	" "	Aŋ-ge-lee′-se	" "
34	Lak-te′-gee	My granddaughter.	Te′-wut	My nephew.	Te′-wut	My niece.
35	Lak-te′-kis	My grandchild.				
36	At-nuch′	" "				
37	No-se-sem′	" "	Nose-sem′	My grandchild.	No-se-sem′	My grandchild.
38	No-se-sim′	" "	No-se-sim′	" "	No-se-sim′	" "
39	No-se-sem′	" "	No-se-sem′	" "	No-se-sem′	" "
40	No-zhĭ′-she	" "	No-zhĭ′-she	" "	No-zhĭ′-she	" "
41	No-she′-shä	" "	No-she′-shä	" "	No-she′-shä	" "
42	No-she-shä′	" "	No-she-shä′	" "	No-she-shä′	" "
43	No-she-shä′	" "	No-she-shä′	" "	No-she-shä′	" "
44	No-she-shä′	" "	No-she-shä′	" "	No-she-shä′	" "
45	No-sä-seh′	" "	No-sä-seh′	" "	No-sa-seh′	" "
46	No-sa-mä′	" "	No-sa-mä′	" "	No-sa-mä′	" "
47	No-sa′-mä	" "	No-sa-mä′	" "	No-sa′-mä	" "
48	No-sa′-mä	" "	No-sa′-mä	" "	No-sa′-mä	" "
49	No-sa-mä′	" "	No-sa-mä′	" "	No-sa-mä′	" "
50	No-sa-mä′	" "	No-sa-mä′	" "	No-sa-mä′	" "
51	No-she-sem′	" "	No-she-sem′	" "	No-she-sem′	" "
52	No-she-sä′	" "	No-she-sä′	" "	No-she-sä′	" "
53	Nä-hˑ-kä′	" "	Nä-hˑ-kä′	" "	Nä-hˑ-kä	" "
54	Na-se-thä′-mä	" "	Na-se-thä′-mä	" "	Na-se-thä′-mä	" "
55	No-stha-thä′	" "	No-stha-thä′	" "	No-stha-thä′	" "
56	Nee′-sa	" "	Nee′-sa	" "	Nee′-sa	" "
57	Nee-so′-tan	" "	Nee-so′-tan	" "	Nee-so′-tan	" "
58	Nee-so′-tän	" "	Nee-so′-tän	" "	Nee-so′-tän	" "
59	Nŭ-jeech′	" "	Nŭ-jeech′	" "	Nŭ-jeech′	" "
60	N′-kway′-nus	" "	N′-kway′-nus	" "	N′-kway′-nus	" "
61	Nä-hˑise′	" "	Nä-hˑise′	" "	Nä-hˑise′	" "
62	Nohˑ-whese′	" "	Nohˑ-whese′	" "	Nohˑ-whese′	" "
63	Nain-no-whase′	" "	Nain-no-whase′	" "	Nain-no-whase′	" "
64	Sa-t′thu′-a	" "	Sa-t′thu′-a	" "	Sa-t′thu′-a	" "
65	Sa-to⌢a′-bä	My granddaughter.	Sa-ken′-ne	" "	Sa-to⌢a′-bä	My gd. daughter.
66	Sa-le-zet′-tha-re	" "	Se-yä-zet′-tha-re	" "	Sa-le-zet′-tha-re	" "
67						
68	Set-she	My grand-child.	Set-she	" "	Set-she	" "
69						
70						
71						
72						
73						
74						
75						
76						
77						
78						
79						
80	Eng′-o-tä	My grandchild.	Eng′-o-tä	My grandchild.	Eng′-o-tä	My grandchild.

TABLE II.—*Continued.*

	165. My father's father's brother.	Translation.	166. My father's father's brother's son.	Translation.	167. My father's father's brother's son's son—older than myself. (Male speaking.)	Translation.
1	Hoc'-sote	My grandfather.	Hä'-nih	My father.	Hä'-je	My elder brother.
2	Hoc'-sote	" "	Hä'-nih	" "	Kuh-je'-ah	" " "
3	Hoc-so'-dä-hä	" "	Kuh-ne-hä'	" "	Kuh-je'-ah	" " "
4	Lok-sote'-hä	" "	Lä'-ga-nih	" "	Läk-je'-hä	" " "
5	Läke-sote	" "	Lä-ga-ne'-hä	" "	Läk-je'-hä	" " "
6	Ahk-rä'-sote	" "	Ahk-re'-ah	" "	Ahk-rä'-je	" " "
7	Lok-sote'-hä	" "	Lä-gä-ne'-hä	" "	Lok-je'-ah	" " "
8	Shu-tä'	" "	Hi-ese'-tä	" "	Ha-ye'-uh	" " "
9	Tuŋ-kaŋ-she-daŋ	" "	At-tay'	" "	Chiŋ-yay'	" " "
10	Toon-kä'-she-nä	" "	Ah-ta'	" "	Che-a'	" " "
11	Tun-kä'-she-lä	" "	Ah-ta'	" "	Che'-a	" " "
12	To-kä'-she-lä	" "	Ah-ta'	" "	Che'-a	" " "
13	Me-tonk'-ä	" "	Ah-ta'	" "	Me-che'-a	" " "
14	Tŏn-kä'-she-lä	" "	Ah-ta'	" "	Che'-a	" " "
15	Toon-kä'-zhe-lä	" "	Ah-ta'	" "	Che-a'	" " "
16	Toh·-kä'-she-la	" "	Ah-dä'	" "	Me-chin'	" " "
17	Me-to'-gä-she	" "	Tä-de'-ha	" "	Zhin-dä'-hä	" " "
18	Ta-ga'-hä	" "	In-dä'-de	" "	Wee-zhe'-thä	" " "
19	Wee-te'-ga	" "	Heen'-kä	" "	He-yen'-nä	" " "
20	Hee-too'-ga	" "	Hiŋ'-kä	" "	He-ye'-nä	" " "
21	E-tŭ'-kä	" "	E-dä'-je	" "	Be-zhe'-yeh	" " "
22	Be-che'-go	" "				
23	We-che'-cho	" "				" " "
24	E-cho'-ka	" "	Chä-je'-kä	" "	E-ne'	
25	Tä-ta'-h·e-ha	" "				
26	Mä-toosh-ä-rŭ-tä-kä	" "				
27	Me-nup-h·is-sä-ka	" "				" " "
28	Um-uh'-fo	" "	A'-kĭ	" "	Um-un'-nĭ	" " "
29	Um-u'-fo	" "	A'-kĭ	" "	Um-un'-nĭ	" " "
30	Um-u'-fo	" "	Ang'-kĭ	" "	Et-e-bä'-pĭ-shĭ-lĭ	" " "
31	Chup-pŭ-chä'	" "	Chuhl'-ke	" "	Chu-hlä'-hä	" " "
32	E-nĭ'-sĭ	My grandparent.	E-dau-dä'	" "	Ung-ĭ-nĭ'-lĭ	" " "
33	Ah-ge-doo'-tse	" " "	Ah-ge-do'-dä	" "	An-ke-nee'-lĭ	" " "
34	Ah-te'-put	My grandfather.	Ah-te'-is	" "	E-dä'-deh	My brother.
35	Ah-te'-put	" " "	A-te'-ase	" "	A-dä'-de	" "
36	Ah-te'-pot	" " "				
37	Ne-mo-some'	" "	Noh·-tä'-we	" "	Neese-tase'	My elder brother.
38	Ne-mo-shome'	" "	Noh·-tä'-we	" "	Neese-tase'	" " "
39	Na-mo-shome'	" "	Noh-tä'-we	" "	Neesh-tase'	" " "
40	Nĭ-mĭ-sho'-miss	" "	Nŏss	" "	Nis-sä'-ye	" " "
41	Ne-me-sho'-mis	" "	No'-sa	" "	Ne-kä'-na	My step-brother.
42	Na-ma-sho-mis'	" "	Nŏss	" "	Ne-kä'-na	" "
43	Ne-mis'-sho-mis'	" "	Nŏss	" "	Ne-kä'-nis	" "
44	Na-ma-sho-mis'	" "	Nŏss	" "	Ne-kä'-nä	" "
45	Na-ma-sho'-mis	" "	Nŏss	" "	Ne-kä'-na	" "
46	Na-ma-sho'-mis	" "	No-sä'	" "	Ne-sä-sä'	My elder brother.
47	Na-mä'-sho-mä'	" "	No-sä'	" "	Ne-san'-zä	" " "
48	Na-mä'-sho-mä'	" "	No-sä'	" "	Ne-san'-zä	" " "
49	Na-mä'-sho-mä	" "	No-sä'	" "	Ne-sä-zä	" " "
50	Na-mä'-sho-mä	" "	No-sä'	" "	Ne-sä-zä	" " "
51	Nä-mä'-sho-mis	" "	Nŏss	" "	Nä-sa'-mä	" " "
52	Na-mä'-sho	" "	Noh'-neh	" "	Nä-nä'	" " "
53	Nam-a-shim'	" "	Nä-o'-a	" "	Nä-ne'-ä	" " "
54	Nem-ma-soo'-ma-thä	" "	No-thä'	" "	Ni-to-ta-mä'	My brother.
55	Na-ma-some-thä'	" "	No-kome-thä'	My step-father.	N'-tha-thä'	My elder brother.
56	No-bes'-sib-ä	" "				
57	Nä-ah'-sä	" "	Nä-ahʼ'-sä	My father.	Neese-sä'	" " "
58	Nä-ahxs'	" "				
59	Niks-kä-mich'	" "	Nŭch	" "	N'-sees'	" " "
60	N'-mŭk·sŭms'	" "	Nee-chä'-look	My step-father.	N'-see'-wes	My brother.
61	Nuh-mä-home'	" "	Noh·	" "	N'-dä-kwus'	My step-brother.
62	Nu-moh·-ho-mus'	" "	Noh'-h'	" "	Nee-mä'-tus	" "
63	Na-mä-ho-mis'	" "	Na-ho'-whus	My little father.	Nain-n'-hans	My elder brother.
64	Sa-tse'-a	" "	E-tä'-eh	My step-father.	Kŭn'-dig-eh	" " "
65	Sa-tä'-chock	" "				
66	Set-see'-a	" "	Sel-the'-ne	" "	Sŭ-nä'-gä	" " "
67					Soon-da	" " "
68	Set-se	" "	Set-ye	My father-in-law.		
69	Is-hah'-pä	" "				
70						
71						
72						
73						
74						
75						
76						
77						
78						
79						
80	E-tŭ'-ah	" "				

TABLE II.—*Continued.*

	168. My father's father's brother's son's son—younger than myself. (Male speaking.)	Translation.	169. My father's father's brother's son's son's son. (Male speaking.)	Translation.	170. My father's father's brother's son's son's son. (Female speaking.)	Translation.
1	Ha'-gă	My younger brother.	Ha-ah'-wuk	My son.	Ha-soh'-neh	My nephew.
2	Ha-gă'-ah	" " "	Ha-hä'-wuk	" "	Ha-hä'-wuk	My son.
3	Ha'-gă	" " "	Ha-hä'-wä	" "	Ha-hä'-wä	" "
4	Le-gă'-ah	" " "	Le-yä'-hä	" "	Le-yä'-hä	" "
5	E'-gä-hä	" " "	E-yä'	" "	E-yä'	" "
6	Kä'-gä	" " "	Kä-yä'-no-nä	My child.	Kä-yä'-wä-nä	" "
7	Le-gä'-ah	" " "	Le-yä'-ah	My son.	Le-yä'-ah	" "
8	Ha-ye-a'-hä	" " "	A-ne-ah'	" "	He-wä'-teh	My nephew.
9	Me-suŋ'-kä	" " "	Me-chink'-she	" '	Me-tonsh'-kä	My son.
10	Me-soh'-kä	" " "	Me-chink'-she	" "	Me-toꞋus'-kä	" "
11	Me-sunk'-ä	" " "	Ak-she'-dä	" "	Me-toash'-kä	" "
12	Me-sun'-kä	" " "	Me-chink'-she	" "	Me-toze'-kä	" "
13	Me-sŏh'	" " "	Me-chink'-she-la	" "	Me-toans'-kä	" "
14	Me-sunk'-ä-lä	" " "	Me-chink'-she	" "	Me-toase'-kä	" "
15	Me-soh'-kä-lä	" " "	Me-chink'-she	" "	Mĕ-toash'-kä	" "
16	Me-son'-kä-lä	" " "	Me-chink'-she	" "	Me-toas'-kä	" "
17	Me-soh'	" " "	Me-chink'-she	" "	Me-to'-zä	" "
18	Kä-ga'	" " "	Nis-se'-hä	" "	We-toash'-kä	" "
19	We-sŏŋ'-gä	" " "	We-nis-se	" "	We-toans'-kä	" "
20	Heen-thuŋ'-ga	" " "	Hee-yiŋ'-ga	" "	Heen-toas'-ka	" "
21	Heen-thuŋ'-ga	" " "	He-ne'-cha	" "	Hin-tose'-kee	" "
22	Be-suŋ'-gä	" " "	Be-she'-gä	" "	Be-chose'-kä	" "
23						
24	E-sŭnk'	" " "	E-neke'	" "	E-choonsh'-ka-neke'	My little nephew.
25						
26						
27						
28	Suh-näk'-fish	" " "	Suh'-sŭh	" "	Sup'-uk-nŏk'-ne	My grandson.
29	Sä-näk'-fish	" " "	Suh'-soh	" "	Sä'-pok-näk'-ne	" "
30	Sä-näk'-fish	" " "	Su-soh'	" "	Sup'-pok-näk'-nĭ	" "
31	Chu-chŭ'-se	" " "	Chup-pu'-che	" "	Um-os-sŭs'-wä	My grandchild.
32	Uŋ-gĭ-nuŋ-th'	" " "	A-gwae-tsi'	My child.	Uŋ-gi-wĭ'-nuŋ	My nephew.
33	Aŋ'-ke-nä-tsĭ	" " "	A-gwa'-tze	" "	Un-ge-we'-nuh	" "
34	E-dä'-deh	My brother.	Pe'-row	" "	Pe'-row	My child.
35	A-dä'-de	" "	Pe'-row	" "	Pe'-row	" "
36						
37	Ne-seme'	My younger brother.	N'-do'-sim	My step-son.	N'-de-kwä-tim'	My nephew.
38	Ne-sha-mish'	" " "	N'-do'-zhim	" "	N'-de-kwä-tim'	" "
39	Ne-she-mish'	" " "	N'-do'-zhim	" "	N'-deh-kwä-tim'	" "
40	Nĭ-shĭ'-me	" " "	Nin-do'-zhim	" "	Nĭ-nin-gwä'-niss	" "
41	Ne-kä'-na	My step-brother.	Nin-do'-zhem	" "	Ne-nin-gwuh'-nis	" "
42	Ne-kä'-na	" "	N'-do'-zhim	" "	Ne-nin-gwi-nis'	" "
43	Ne-kä'-nis	" "	Nin-do'-zhim-ă	" "	Ne-nin-gwi-nis'	" "
44	Ne-kä'-nä	' "	N'-do'-zhim	" "	Ne-nin-gwi-nis'	" "
45	Ne-kä'-na	" "	N'-do'-zhe-mä	" "	Nä'-gwi-nis	" "
46	Se-me-mä'	My younger brother.	Neen-gwase'-sä	My son.	Lan-gwä-les'-sä	" "
47	Ne-she'-mä	" " "	Niŋ-gwa-sä'	" "	Ne-lä'-gwä-la-sä'	" "
48	Ne-she'-mä	" " "	Niŋ-gwa-sä'	" "	Ne-lä'-gwä-la-sä'	" "
49	Ne-she-mä'	" " "	Ne-gwis-sä'	" "	Ne-lä'-gwä-lis-sä'	" "
50	Ne-she-mä'	" " "	Ne-gwis-sä'	" "	Ne-lä'-gwä-lis-sä'	" "
51	Nä-se'-mä	" " "	Nä-kwis'-sä	" "	Nä-nä'-gwä-nis	" "
52	Nä-sa'	" " "	Ne-keese	" "	Ne-nä'-kwä-nis	" "
53	Nä-sim-ä'	" " "	Nä	" "	Nä-chin'-e-tä	" "
54	Ni-to-ta-mä'	My brother.	Nĭ-kwe-thä'	" "	Nen-nä-kwä-na-thä	" "
55	N'-the-ma-thä'	My younger brother.	Ne-kwe-thä'	" "	Na-na-gwal-thä'	" "
56						
57	Nis-kun'-ä	" " "	N'-do'-to-ko	My step-son.	N'-do'-to-yose	" "
58						
59	N'-chi-gu'-num	" " "	N'-kwis'	My son.	Nu-lŭks'	" "
60	N'-see'-wes	My brother.	N'-too-ä'-sum	" "	Nu-lŭ'-knees	" "
61	N'-dä-kwus'	My step-brother.	Nä-kun'	My step-child.	Nä-kun'	My step-child.
62	Nee-mä'-tus	" "	N'-kweese'	My son.	N'-kweese'	My son.
63	Nain-hise'-sa-mus'	My younger bro.	Nain-gwase'	" "	Nain-gwase'	" "
64	A-cha'-a	" " "	Tu-zen'-a	" step-son.	Sa-yä'-ze	My step-son.
65						
66	Set-chil'-e-ă-za	" " "	Se-yä'-za	My son.	Se-yä'-za	My son.
67						
68	Sa-chă	" " "	Set-en-ge	" "	Se-zi-ou	" "
69						
70						
71						
72						
73						
74						
75						
76						
77						
78						
79						
80						

TABLE II.—*Continued.*

	171. My father's father's brother's son's son's daughter. (Male speaking.)	Translation.	172. My father's father's brother's son's son's daughter. (Female speaking.)	Translation.	173. My father's father's brother's great great grandson.	Translation.
1	Ka-ah'-wuk	My daughter.	Ka-soh'-neh	My niece.	Ha-yä'-da	My grandson.
2	Ka-hä'-wuk	" "	Ka-hä'-wuk	My daughter.	Ha-yä'-dra	" "
3	Ka-hä'-wä	" "	Ka-hä'-wä	" "	Ha-yä'-da	" "
4	Ka-yä'-hä	" "	Ka-yä'-hä	" "	La-yä'-dla-ah	" "
5	Ka-yä'	" "	Ka-yä'	" "	E-yä'-dla-ah	" "
6	Kä-yä'-no-nä	My child.	Kä-yä-no'-na-ah	My niece.	Kä-yä' rä	My grandchild.
7	Ka-yä'-hä	My daughter.	Ka-yä'-ah	My daughter.	Le-yä-tä-ra'-yä	My grandson.
8	E-ne-ah'	" "	E-wä'-teh	My niece.	Ha-tra'-ah	" "
9	Me-chuṇk'-she	" "	Me-tuṇ'-zhan	My daughter.	Me-tä'-ko-zhä	My grandchild.
10	Me-chounk'-she	" "	Me-to͡us'-zä	" "	Me-tä'-ko-zhä	" "
11	Me-chink'-she	" "	Me-to'-zhä	" "	Me-tä'-ko-zhä	" "
12	Me-chunk'-she	" "	Me-to'-zhä	" "	Me-tä'-ko-zhä	" "
13	Me-chunk'-she	" "	Me-toh'-zhä	" "	Me tä'-ko-sak'-pok	" "
14	Me-chunk'-she	" "	Me-toh'-zhä	" "	Me-tä'-ko-zhä	" "
15	Me-chŭnk'-she	" "	Me-to'-zä	" "	Me-tä'-ko-zä	" "
16	Me-chŭnk'-she	" "	Me-to'-zä	" "	Me-tä'-ko-zä	" "
17	Me-chunk'-she	" "	Me-to'-zä	" "	Me-tä'-ko-zä	" "
18	Win-no'-ga	" "	Tä-zhä'-hä	" "	Toosh'-pä-hä	" "
19	Wee-zhun'-gä	" "	We-te'-zhä	" "	Wee-tŭsh'-pa	" "
20	Hee-yuṇ'-ga	" "	Heen-toas'-ka-me	" "	Heen-tä'-kwä	" "
21	He-yuṇ'-ga	" "	Hin-tose'-kee-me	" "	E-tä'-kwä	" "
22	She-me'-she-gä	" "	Be-che'-zho	" "	Be-chose'-pä	" "
23						
24	E-nook'	" "	E-chooṇ-zhunk'-e-neke'	My little niece.	E-choonsh'-ka-neke'	My little gd. son.
25						
26						
27						
28	Suh-săh'-take	" "	Sup'-uk	My granddaughter.	Sup'-uk-nŏk'-ne	My grandson.
29	Suh-soh'-take	" "	Sä'-pok	" "	Sä'-pok-näk'-ne	" "
30	Su-soh'-take	" "	Sup'-pok	" "	Sup'-pok-näk'-nĭ	" "
31	Chuch-hus'-te	" "	Um-os-sŭs'-wä	My grandchild.	Um-os-sŭs'-wä	My grandchild.
32	A-gwae-tsi'	" "	Uṇ-gwä-duṇ'	My niece.	Uṇ-gĭ-lĭ'-sĭ	" "
33	A-gwa'-tze	" "	Un-gwä'-tuh	" "	Un-ge-lee'-se	" "
34	Pe'-row	My child.	Pe'-row	My child.	Lak-te'-gish	My grandson.
35	Pe'-row	" "	Pe'-row	" "	Lak-te'-kis	My grandchild.
36						
37	N'-do-sa-mis-kwame'	My step-daughter.	Neese-che-mis'	My niece.	No-se-sem'	" "
38	N'-do-zha-mis-kwame'	" "	Neest-che-mish'	" "	No-se-sim'	" "
39	N'-do-zha-mis-kwem'	" "	Neest-che-mis'	" "	No-se-sem'	" "
40	Nin-do-zhĭ-mĭ-kwem'	" "	Ni-shĭ'-miss	" "	No-zhĭ'-she	" "
41	Nin-do'-zhe-mĭ-quam'	" "	Ne-she'-me-sha	" "	No-she'-shä	" "
42	Nin-do-sha-mĭ-kwam'	" "	Ne-she-mis'	" "	No-she-shä'	" "
43	N'-do-zha-mĭ-kwam'	" "	Ne-she-mis'	" "	No-she-shä'	" "
44	N'-do-zha-mĭ-kwam'	" "	Ne-she-mis'	" "	No-sä-seh'	" "
45	N'-do-zha-mis	" "	Ne-she'-mis	" "	No-sa-mä'	" "
46	Nin-dä'-nä	My daughter.	Shames-sä'	" "	No-sa'-mä	" "
47	Nin-dä'-nä	" "	Ne-she'-mis-sä'	" "	No-sa'-mä	" "
48	Nin-dä'-nä	" "	Ne-shi-mis-sä'	" "	No-sa-mä'	" "
49	N'-dä'-nä	" "	Ne-she-mis-sä'	" "	No-sa-mä'	" "
50	N'-dä'-nä	" "	Ne-she-mis-sä'	" "	No-she-sem'	" "
51	Nä-tä'-niss	" "	Nä-shä'-mis	" "	No-she-sä'	" "
52	Ne-täne'	" "	Nä-nä'-mä	" "	Nä-h·-kä'	" "
53	Nä-tun'	" "	Nä-un	" "	Na-se-thä'-mä	" "
54	Ni-tä-na-thä'	" "	Ni-sem-e-thä'	" "	No-stha-thä'	" "
55	Nĭ-tä-na-thä'	" "	Ne-sa-me-thä'	" "		
56						
57	N'-to'-to-tun	My step-daughter.	Ne-mis'-sä	" "	Nee-so'-tan	" "
58						
59	N'-tŭs'	My daughter.	N'-sum'	" "	Nŭ-jeech'	" "
60	N'-su'-mus	" "	N'-sum'	" "	N'-kway'-nus	" "
61	Nä-kun'	My step-child.	Nä-kun'	My step-child.	Nä-h·ise'	" "
62	N'-dä-nuss'	My daughter.	N'-dä-nuss'	My daughter.	Noh'-whese'	" "
63	Nain-dä'-ness	" "	Nain-dä'-ness	" "	Nain-no-whase'	" "
64	Sa-yä'-dze	My step-daughter.	Sa-yä'-dze	My step-daughter.	Sa-t'thu'-a	" "
65						
66	Sa-le'-ă	My daughter.	Sa-le'-ă	My daughter	Se-yä-zet'-tha-re	" "
67						
68	Set-shere	" "	Se-yat-ze	" "	Set-she	" "
69						
70						
71						
72						
73						
74						
75						
76						
77						
78						
79						
80						

TABLE II.—*Continued.*

	174. My father's father's brother's great great granddaughter.	Translation.	175. My father's father's sister.	Translation.	176. My father's father's sister's daughter. (Male speaking.)	Translation.
1	Ka-yä′-da....................	My granddaughter.	Oc′-sote.....................	My grandmother.	Ah-ga′-huc.................	My aunt.
2	Ka-yä′-dra...................	" "	Oc′-sote.....................	" "	Kuo′-hä	My mother.
3	Ka-yä′-da....................	" "	Oc-so′-dä-hä	" "	Ah-ge-no′-hä...............	" "
4	Ka-yä′-dla-ah...............	" "	Ahk-sote′-hä	" "	Ahk-nole′-hä................	" "
5	Ka-yä′-dla-ah...............	" "	Ahk-sote′....................	" "	Ah-ga-nese′-tä..............	" "
6	Kä-yä′-rä....................	My grandchild.	Ahk′-sote	" "	Ahk-kaw′-rack.............	My aunt.
7	Ka-yä-tä-ra′-yä.............	My granddaughter.	Lok-sote′-hä	" "	Ah-ga-nese′-tä-hä..........	My mother.
8	Ya-trä′-ah...................	" "	Ah-shu-tä′...................	" "	Ah-rä′-hoc.................	My aunt.
9	Me-tä′-ko-zhä...............	My grandchild.	Un-che′.....................	" "	Tuṇ-wiṇ′....................	" "
10	Me-tä′-ko-zhä...............	" "	O-che′......................	" "	Toh′-we.....................	" "
11	Me-tä′-ko-zhä...............	" "	O-che′-lä	" "	Tonk′-wa....................	" "
12	Me-tä′-ko-zha...............	" "	Oh-che′.....................	" "	Tonk′-wa....................	" "
13	Me-tä′-ko-säk′-pok	" "	Oo-che′.....................	" "	Toh-we′.....................	" "
14	Me-tä′-ko-zhä...............	" "	Un-che′.....................	" "	Toh′-we	" "
15	Me-tä′-ko-zhä...............	" "	O-che′......................	" "	Toh′-we	" "
16	Me-tä′-ko-zä................	" "	O-che′......................	" "	Toh′-we	" "
17	Me-tä′-ko-sä................	" "	O-gä′-she	" "	Me-toh′-we	" "
18	Toosh′-pä-hä................	" "	Gä-hä′	" "	Te-na′-hä	" "
19	Wee-tŭsh′-pä	" "	Wee′-kä.....................	" "	Wee-tee′-me	" "
20	Heen-tä′-kwä-me	My granddaughter.	Hee-koo′-n′-ye	" "	Hee-too′-me	" "
21	E-tä′-kwä-me	" "	Hiṇ-kŭ′-ne	" "	E-tŭ′-me	" "
22	Be-chose′-pä................	My grandchild.	E-ko′.......................	" "	Be-je′-me	" "
23			E-che′......................	" "		
24	E-choon-zhunk′-e-neke′...	My little gd. daught.	E-ko′-ro-ka.................	" "	E-choon′-we................	" "
25			Nah′-he-a	" "		
26			Kä-rŭ′-hä...................	" "		
27			Bä-sä′-kä-na................	" "		
28	Sup′-uk	My granddaughter.	Up-puk′-nĭ	" "	A-huk′-ne	My aunt.
29	Sä′-pok	" "	Up-pok′-nĭ..................	" "	A-huc′-nĭ	" "
30	Sup′-pok	" "	Hap-pŭ′-sĭ	" "	Hap-po′-sĭ	My grandmother.
31	Um-os-sŭs′-wä..............	My grandchild.	Chu-pŭ′-se..................	" "	Chu-pŭ′-se	" "
32	Uṇ-gĭ-lĭ′-sĭ.................	" "	E-nĭ′-sĭ	My grandparent.	E-hlau′-gĭ	My aunt.
33	Aṇ-ge-lee′-se...............	" "	Ah-ge-lee′-sih...............	" "	Ah-ge-h′lo′-gih	" "
34	Lak-te′-gee.................	My granddaughter.	Ah-te′-kä	" "	Ah-te′-kä	My grandmother.
35	Lak-te′-kis........	My grandchild.	Ah-te′-kä	" "	Ah-te′-kä	" "
36			Ah-te′-kä	" "		
37	No-se-sem′..................	" "	Noh′-kome′..................	My grandmother.	Nis-sĭ-goos′.................	My aunt.
38	No-se-sim′..................	" "	No-kome′....................	" "	Nis-se-goos′................	" "
39	No-se-sem′..................	" "	No-kome′....................	" "	Nĭ-se-goos′.................	" "
40	No-zhĭ′-she.................	" "	No′-ko-miss	" "	Nin-sĭ-gŏss	" "
41	No-she′-shä.................	" "	No′-ko-mis	" "	Ne-se-gŭs′..................	" "
42	No-she-shä′.................	" "	No-ko′-mis	" "	Ne-see-gŏss′................	" "
43	No-she-shä′.................	" "	No-ko-mis′..................	" "	Nis-zee-gŭss′...............	" "
44	No-she-shä′.................	" • "	No-ko-mis′..................	" "	Nis-sa-gose′................	" "
45	No-sä-seh′..................	" "	No-ko′-mis	" "	N′-si-gwis′..................	" "
46	No-sa-mä′...................	" "	No-ko-mä′...................	" "	N′-sa′-gwe-sä′...............	" "
47	No-sa′-mä	" "	No-ko-mä′...................	" "	Ne-zä′-gŏs-sä′...............	" "
48	No-sa′-mä	" "	No-ko-mä′...................	" "	Ne-zä′-gŏs-sä′...............	" "
49	No-sa-mä′...................	" "	No′-ko-mä	" "	Ne-sä′-gwis-sä′..............	" "
50	No-sa-mä′...................	" "	No′-ko-mä	" "	Ne-sä′-gwis-sä′..............	" "
51	No-she-sem′.................	" "	No′-ko-mis	" "	Nak-ye′-hä..................	" "
52	No-she-sä′..................	" "	No′-ko-mä	" "	Ne-ne′......................	" "
53	Nä-h′-kä′...................	" "	Nä-vish′-kim	" "		
54	Na-se-thä′-mä	" "	No-ko-ma-some-thä	" "	Na-tha-kwi-thä′.............	" "
55	Ne-sa-me-thä′...............	" "	No-kome-thä′................	" "	Na-tha-gwe-thä′.............	" "
56			Na′-e-bä....................	" "		
57	Nee-so′-tan.................	" "	Ne-tä-ke-ä′-sä...............	" "	Ne-to′-tarse.................	" "
58			Ne-tä′-ke-ahxs	" "		
59	Nŭ-jeech′...................	" "	Nŭ-gu′-mich	" "	N′-su-gwis′..................	" "
60	N′-kway′-nus...............	" "	Nuk′-mus...................	" "	Nŭ′-kum	" "
61	Nä-h′ise′...................	" "	No-ome′....................	" "	No-muths′..................	My step-mother.
62	Noh′-whese′................	" "	Noo-h′ome′.................	" "	N′-gä-hä′-tut	My little mother.
63	Nain-no-whase′.............	" "	Na-no′-home................	" "	Niṇ-guk′-us.................	" "
64	Sa-t′thu′-a.................	" "	Sa-tsun.....................	" "	Eh-m′-ba′-dze	My aunt.
65			Sa-cho′-na	" "		
66	Sa-le-zet′-tha-re............	" "	Set-sa′-nä	" "	Set′-so	" "
67			Set-soon....................	" "	Sa-ku-i	My step-mother.
68				" "		
69				" "		
70			In-kah′-na (m. s.). In-	" "		
71			[chau′-wa (f. s.).			
72						
73						
74						
75						
76						
77						
78						
79						
80			Ning-e-o′-wä................	" "		

TABLE II.—*Continued.*

	177. My father's father's sister's daughter's son. (Male speaking.)	Translation.	178. My father's father's sister's daughter's daughter. (Male speaking.)	Translation.	179. My father's father's sister's daughter's daughter's son. (Male speaking.)	Translation.
1	Ah-găre'-seh	My cousin.	Ah-găre'-seh	My cousin.	Hä-yä'-wan-da	My nephew.
2	Ah-ge-ah'-seh	" "	Ah-ge-ah'-seh	" "	Ha-hä'-wuk	My son.
3	Ah-gare'-seh	" "	Ah-gare'-seh	" "	Ha-hä'-wä	" "
4	Un-gă-lä'-seh	" "	Un-gă-lä'-seh	" "	Le-yä'-hä	" "
5	Un-gă-läss'	" "	Un-gă-läss'	" "	E-yä'	" "
6	Ahk-gă'-rä-sthar	" "	Ahk-gă'-rä-sthar	" "	Kä-yä'-wä-nä	My nephew.
7	Lok-jë'-hä(e.), Le-gä'-ah(y.)	My eld. or young.bro.	Ak-je'-yä(e.), Ka-gä'-ah(y.)	My eld. or young. sis.	Le-wä-dä'-ah	" "
8	Jä-rä'-seh	My cousin.	Jä-rä'-seh	My cousin.	Ha-shone-drä'-ka	" "
9	Taṇ-han'-she	" "	Häṇ-kä'-she	" "	Me-tonsh'-kä	" "
10	Tä'-she	" "	Hä-kä'-she	" "	Me-to-us'-kä	" "
11	Kä'-she	" "	Ah-kä'-zha	" "	Me-toash'-kä	" "
12	Tä'-she	" "	Hä-kä'-she	" "	Me-tose'-kä	" "
13	Tä'-she	" "	Hun-kä'-she	" "	Me-toans'-kä	" "
14	Tä-hä'-she	" "	Hun-kä'-she	" "	Me-toase'-kä	" "
15	Tä'-she	" "	Hä-kä'-zhe	" "	Me-toash'-kä	" "
16	Tä-hä'-she	" "	Hä-kä'-she	" "	Me-toas'-kä	" "
17	Tä-hä'-she	" "	Mä-hä'-gä-she	" "	Me-to'-zä	" "
18	We-toash'-kä	My nephew.	Tä-zhä'-hä	My niece.	Toosh'-pä-hä	My grandchild.
19	We-toans'-kä	" "	We-te'-zhä	" "	Wee-tŭsh'-pä	" "
20	Heen-toas'-ka	" "	Heen-toas'-ka-me	" "	Heen-tä'-kwä	My grandson.
21	Hin-tose'-kee	" "	Hin-tose'-kee-me	" "	E-tä'-kwä	" "
22	Be-chose'-kä	" "	Be-che'-zho.		Be-chose'-pä	My grandchild.
23						
24	E-choonsh'-ka-neke'	My little nephew.	E-chooṇ-zhunk'-e-neke'	My little niece.	E-choonsh'-ka-neke'	My little gd. son.
25						
26						
27						
28	A'-kĭ	My father.	A-huc'-ne	My aunt.	Suh-näk'-fish	My younger bro.
29	A'-kĭ	" "	Ush'-kĭ	My mother.	Et-e-bä'-pĭ-shĭ-lĭ	My brother.
30	Ang-ko-si	My little father.	Hap-po'-sĭ	My grandmother.	Ang-ko'-sĭ	My little father.
31	Chuhl-kŭ'-che	" " "	Chup-pŭ'-se	" "	Chuhl-kŭ-che'	" " "
32	E-dau-dä'	My father	E-hlau'-gĭ	My aunt.	E-dau-dä'	My father.
33	Ah-ge-do'-dä	" "	Ah-ze-h'lo'-gih	" "	Ah-ge-do'-dä	" "
34	Ah-te'-is	" "	Ah-te'-kä	My grandmother.	Ah-te'-put	My grandfather.
35	A-te'-ase	" "				
36						
37	Nees-chäs'	My cousin.	Nee'-che-moos	My cousin.	N'-de-kwä-tim'	My nephew.
38	Nee-säs'	" "	Nee'-che-moosh	" "	N'-de-kwä-tim'	" "
39	Neest-chäs'	" "	Nee'-ta-moos	" "	N'-deh-kwä-tim'	" "
40	Nĭ-tä'-wiss	" "	Nĭ-nĭ-mo'-she	" "	Nĭ-nin-gwä'-niss	" "
41	Ne-tä'-wis	" "	Ne-ne-mo'-sha	" "	Ne-nin-gwuh'-nis	" "
42	Ne-tä'-wis	" "	Ne-ne-moo-shä'	" "	Ne-nin-gwi-nis'	" "
43	Ne-tä'-wis	" "	Ne-ne-moo-shä'	" "	Ne-nin-gwi-nis'	" "
44	Ne-tä'-wis	" "	Ne-ne-moo-shä'	" "	Ne-nin-gwi-nis'	" "
45						
46	Laṇ-gwä-les'-sä	My nephew.	Shames-sä'	My niece.	No-sa-mä'	My grandchild.
47	Ne-lä'-gwä-la-sä'	" "	Ne-she'-mis-sä'	" "	No-sa'-mä	" "
48	Ne-lä'-gwä-la-sä'	" "	Ne-she'-mis-sä'	" "	No-sa'-mä	" "
49	Ne-lä'-gwä-lis-sä'	" "	Ne-she-mis-sä'	" "	No-sa-mä'	" "
50	Ne-lä'-gwä-lis-sä'	" "	Ne-she-mis-sä'	" "	No-sa-ṉä'	" "
51	Nă-nä'-gwä-nis	" "	Nă-shä'-nis	" "	No-she-sem'	" "
52	Ne-nä'-kwä-na	" "	Nă-nä'-mä	" "	No-she-sä'	" "
53						
54	Nen-na-kwă-na-thä	" "	Na-sem-e-thä'	" "	Nen-na-kwä-na-thä	" "
55	Na-la-gwal-thä'	" "	Ne-sa-me-thä'	" "	No-stha-thä'	" "
56						
57	N'-to'-tes-tä-mo	My cousin.	N'-to'-to-ke-man'	My cousin.	N'-do'-to-yose	My nephew.
58						
59	N'-sees'	My elder brother.	Nu-mees'	My elder sister.	Nu-lŭks'	" "
60	N'-tä'-gus	My cousin.	Nu-tä-kw-sŭs'-kw	My step-sister.	Nu-lŭ'-knees	" "
61	N'-dă-kwus'	My step-brother.	N'-dă-kwus-oh-kwä-oh	" "	No-kwath'	" "
62	Nee-mä'-tus	" " "	N'-doh-kwä-yome'	" "	Longue'-kw'	" "
63	Nain-n'-hans	My elder brother.	Nain-na-wase'	My elder sister.	Na-lone'-gwä-sis'	" "
64	Kŭn'-dig-eh	" " "	Sä'-dä	" " "	Sä'-zy	" "
65						
66	Sŭ-nä'-gä	" " "	Set-dez'-a-ä-za	" " "	Se-yä'-za	My son.
67						
68	Sa-chă	My younger brother.	Sa-che	" " "	Sa-ten-gee	" "
69						
70						
71						
72						
73						
74						
75						
76						
77						
78						
79						
80						

TABLE II.—*Continued.*

	180. My father's father's sister's daughter's daughter's son. (Female speaking.)	Translation.	181. My father's father's sister's daughter's daughter's daughter. (Male speaking.)	Translation.	182. My father's father's sister's daughter's daughter's daughter. (Female speaking.)	Translation.
1	Ha-ah′-wuk	My son.	Ka-yă′-wan-da..............	My niece.	Ka-ah′-wuk	My daughter.
2	Ha-hä′-wuk	" "	Ka-hä′-wuk	My daughter.	Ka-hä′-wuk	" "
3	Ha-hä′-wä	" "	Ka-hä′-wä.................	" "	Ka-hä′-wä.................	" "
4	Le-yä′-hä	" "	Ka-yä′-hä	" "	Ka-yä-hä.	" "
5	E-yä′	" "	Ka-yä′	" "	Ka-yä′	" "
6	Kä-yä′-no-nä	My child.	Kä-yä′-no-nä	My niece.	Kä-yä′-no-nä	My child.
7	Le-yä′-ah	My son.	Ka-wä-dä′-ah	" "	Ka-yä′-hä	My daughter.
8	A-ne-ah′..................	" "	Ya-shone-drä′-ka..........	" "	E-ne-ah′	" "
9	Me-chink′-she	" "	Me-tuṇ′-zhan	" "	Me-chuṇk′-she	" "
10	Me-chink′-she	" "	Me-to⁻us′-zä	" "	Me-chouŋk′-she	" "
11	Ak-she′-dä	" "	Me-to′-zhä	" "	Me-chink′-she	" "
12	Me-chink′-she	" "	Me-to′-zhä	" "	Me-chunk′-she	" "
13	Me-chink′-se-lä	" "	Me-toh′-zhä	" "	Me-chunk′-se-lä	" "
14	Me-chink′-she	" "	Me-toh′-zhä	" "	Me-chuŋk′-she	" "
15	Me-chink′-she	" "	Me-to′-zä	" "	Me-chŭnk′-she	" "
16	Me-chink′-she	" "	Me-to′-zä	" "	Me-chŭnk′-she	" "
17	Me-chink′-she	" "	Me-to′-zä	" "	Me-chunk′-she	" "
18	Toosh′-pä-hä	My grandchild.	Toosh′-pä-hä..............	My grandchild.	Toosh′-pü-hä..............	My grandchild.
19	Wee-tüsh′-pä	" "	Wee-tüsh′-pä	" "	Wee-tüsh′-pä..............	" "
20	Heen-tä′-kwä	My grandson.	Heen-tä′-kwä-me	My granddaughter.	Heen-tä′-kwä-me	My gd. daughter.
21	E-tä′-kwä	" "	E-tä′-kwä-me	" "	E-tä′-kwä-me	" "
22	Be-chose′-pä	My grandchild.	Be-chose′-pä	My grandchild.	Be-chose′-pä	My grandchild.
23						
24	E-choonsh′-ka-neke′	My little grandson.	E-choon-zhunk′-e-neke′ ..	My little gd. daught.	E-chooṇ-zhunk′-e-neke′..	My little gd. dau.
25						
26						
27						
28	A-näk-fĭ..................	My younger brother.	An′-take	My younger sister.	Sup′-uk	My gd. daughter.
29	A-näk-fĭ..................	" " "	An′-take	" " "	Sä′-pok..................	" "
30	Ang-ko-sĭ	My little father.	Hap-po′-sĭ	My grandmother.	Hap-po′-sĭ	My grandmother.
31	Chuhl-kŭ-che′..............	" " "	Chu-pŭ′-se	" "	Chu-pŭ′-se	" "
32	E-dau-dä′..................	My father.	E-hlan′-gĭ	My aunt.	E-hlan′-gĭ	My aunt.
33	Ah-ge-do′-dä	" "	Ah-ge-h′lo′-gih	" "	Ah-ge-h′lo′-gih..............	" "
34	Ah-te′-put	My grandfather.	Ah-te′-kä	My grandmother.	Ah-te′-kä	My grandmother.
35						
36						
37	N'-go′-sim	My step-son.	Neese-che-mis′..............	My niece.	N'-do′-sa-mis-kwame′	My step-daughter.
38	N'-go′-shim..................	" "	Neest-che-mish′............	" "	N'-do′-zha-mis-kwame′...	" "
39	N'-do′-zhim	" "	Neest-che-mis′	" "	N'-do′-zha-mis-kwem′.....	" "
40	Nin-do′-zhĭ-miss	My step-child.	Nĭ-shĭ′-miss	" "	Nin-do′-zhĭ-miss	My step-child.
41	Nin-do′-zhe-mis.............	" "	Ne-she′-me-sha..........	" "	Nin-do′-zhe-mis..............	" "
42	Nin-gwis′	My son.	Ne-she-mis′	" "	Nin-dä′-niss	My daughter.
43	Nin-gwis′	" "	Ne-she-mis′	" "	N'-dä-niss′..................	" "
44	N'-gwis′	" "	Ne-she-mis′	" "	N'-dä-niss′..................	" "
45						
46	No-sa-mä′	My grandchild.	No-sa-mä′..................	My grandchild.	No-sa-mä′..................	My grandchild.
47	No-sa′-mä	" "	No-sa′-mä	" "	No-sa′-mä	" "
48	No-sa′-mä	" "	No-sa′-mä	" "	No-sa′-mä	" "
49	No-sa′-mä′	" "	No-sa′-mä	" "	No-sa′-mä′..................	" "
50	No-sa-mä′	" "	No-sa′-mä′..................	" "	No-sa′-mä	" "
51	No-she-sem′	" "	No-she-sem′	" "	No-she-sem′..................	" "
52	No-she-sä′	" "	No-she-sä′..................	" "	No-she-sä′	" "
53						
54	Na-se-thä′-mä.	" "	No-se-thä′-mä..............	" "	Na-se-thä′-mä	" "
55	No-stha-thä′	" "	No-stha-thä′	" "	No-stha-thä′	" "
56						
57	N'-do′-to-ko	My step-son.	Ne-mis′-sä..................	My niece.	N'-to′-to-tun	My step-daughter.
58						
59	N'-kwis′	My son.	N'-sum′..................	" "	N'-tus′..................	My daughter.
60	N'-too-ä′-sum	" "	N'-sum′..................	" "	N'-su′-mus	" "
61	N'-di-ome′	" "	Noh′-soh′-kwä′-oh..........	" "	Nee-chune′..................	" "
62	N'-kweese′..................	" "	Longue-kwä′..................	" "	N'-dä-nuss′..................	" "
63	Nain-gwase	" "	Na-lone′-gwä-sis	" "	Nain-dä′-ness..............	" "
64	Sa-yä′-za	My step-son.	Sa-t'thu′-a	My grandchild.	Sa-chä′	My grandchild.
65						
66	Se-yä′-za	My son.	Sa-le-zet′-tha-re	My granddaughter.	Sa-le-zet′-tha-re............	My gd. daughter.
67						
68	Se-zi-ou	" "	Set-she	" "	Set-shai	" "
69						
70						
71						
72						
73						
74						
75						
76						
77						
78						
79						
80						

TABLE II.—*Continued.*

	183. My father's father's sister's great great grandson.	Translation.	184. My father's father's sister's great great granddaughter.	Translation.	185. My mother's mother's brother.	Translation.
1	Ha-yä'-da	My grandson.	Ka-yä'-da	My granddaughter.	Hoc'-sote	My grandfather.
2	Ha-yä'-dra	" "	Ka-yä'-dra	" "	Hoc'-sote	" "
3	Ha-yä'-da	" "	Ka-yä'-da	" "	Hoc-so'-dä-hä	" "
4	Le-yä'-dla-ah	" "	Ka-yä'-dla-ah	" "	Lok-sote'-hä	" "
5	E-yä'-dla-ah	" "	Ka-yä'-dla-ah	" "	Läke-sote'	" "
6	Kä-yä'-rä	My grandchild.	Kä-yä'-rä	My grandchild.	Ahk-rä'-sote	" "
7	Le-yä-tä-ra'-yä	My grandson.	Ka-yä-tä-ra'-yä	My granddaughter.	Lok-sote'-hä	" "
8	Ha-tra'-ah	" "	Ya-tra'-ah	" "	Hä-shu-tä'	" "
9	Me-tä'-ko-zhä	My grandchild.	Me-tä'-ko-zhä	My grandchild.	Tuŋ-käŋ'-she-dän	" "
10	Me-tä'-ko-zhä	" "	Me-tä'-ko-zhä	" "	Toon-kä'-she-nä	" "
11	Me-tä'-ko-zhä	" "	Me-tä'-ko-zhä	" "	Tun-kä'-she-lä	" "
12	Me-tä'-ko-zhä	" "	Me-tä'-ko-zhä	" "	To-ka'-she-lä	" "
13	Me-tä'-ko-säk'-pok	" "	Me-tä'-ko-säk'-pok	" "	Me-tonk'-ah	" "
14	Me-tä'-ko-zhä	" "	Me-tä'-ko-zhä	" "	Tŏn-kä'-she-lä	" "
15	Me-tä'-ko-zhä	" "	Me-tä'-ko-zhä	" "	Toon-kä'-zhe-lä	" "
16	Me-tä'-ko-zä	" "	Mo-tä'-ko-zä	" "	Toh-kä'-she-la	" "
17	Me-tä'-ko-sä	" "	Me-tä'-ko-sä	" "	Me-to'-gä-she	" "
18	Toosh'-pä-hä	" "	Toosh'-pä-hä	" "	Ta-ga'-hä	" "
19	Wee-tŭsh'-pä	" "	Wee-tŭsh'-pä	" "	Wee-te'-ga	" "
20	Heen-tä'-kwä	My grandson.	Heen-tä'-kwä-me	My granddaughter.	Hee-too'-ga	" "
21	E-tä'-kwä	" "	E-tä'-kwä-me	" "	E-tŭ'-kä	" "
22	Be-chose'-pä	My grandchild.	Be-chose'-pä	My grandchild.	Be-che'-go	" "
23					We-che'-cho	" "
24	E-choonsh'-ka-neke'	My little grandson.	E-chooŋ-zhunk'-e-neke'	My little gd. daught.	E-cho'-ka	" "
25					Tä-ta'-h·e-ha	" "
26					Mä-toosh-ä-rŭ'-tä-kä	" "
27					Me-nup-h·is'-sä-ka	" "
28	Sup'-uk-nök'-ne	My grandson.	Sup'-uk	My granddaughter.	Um-uh'-fo	" "
29	Sä'-pok-näk'-ne	" "	Sä-pok	" "	Um-u'-fo	" "
30	Ang-ko'-sī	My little father.	Hap-po'-sī	My grandmother.	Um-u'-fo	" "
31	Chuhl-kŭ-che'	" " "	Chu-pŭ'-se	" "	Chu-pŭ'-chä'	" "
32	E-dau-dä'	My father.	E-hlau-gī'	My aunt.	E-nī'-sī	My grandparent.
33	Ah-ge-do'-dä	" "	Ah-ge-h·lo'-gih	" "	Ah-ge-doo'-tse	" "
34					Ah-te'-put	" "
35					Ah-te'-put	" "
36					Ah-te'-pot	" "
37	No-se-sem'	My grandchild.	No-se-sem'	My grandchild.	Ne-mo-some'	My grandfather.
38	No-se-sim'	" "	No-se-sim'	" "	Ne-mo-shome'	" "
39	No-se-sem'	" "	No-se-sem'	" "	Na-mo-shome'	" "
40	No-zhī'-she	" "	No-zhī'-she	" "	Nī-mī-sho'-miss	" "
41	No-she'-shä	" "	No-she-shä	" "	Ne-me-sho'-mis	" "
42	No-she-shä'	" "	No-she-shä'	" "	Na-ma'-sho-mis	" "
43	No-she-shä'	" "	No-she-shä'	" "	Ne-mis'-sho-mis'	" "
44	No-she-shä'	" "	No-she-shä'	" "	Na-ma-sho'-mis	" "
45	No-sä-seh'	" "	No-sä-seh'	" "	N'-ma-sho'-mis	" "
46	No-sa-mä'	" "	No-sa-mä'	" "	Na-ma-sho'-mä	" "
47	No-sa'-mä	" "	No-sa'-mä	" "	Na-ma'-sho-mä	" "
48	No-sa'-ma	" "	No-sa'-mä	" "	Nä-ma'-sho-mä	" "
49	No-sa-mä'	" "	No-sa'-mä	" "	Ne-mä'-sho-mä	" "
50	No-sa-mä'	" "	No-sa'-mä	" "	Ne-mä'-sho-mä	" "
51	No-she-sem'	" "	No-she-sem'	" "	Nä-mä'-sho-mis	" "
52	No-she-sä'	" "	No-she-sä'	" "	Na-mä'-sho	" "
53					Nam-a-shim'	" "
54	Na-se-thä'-mä	" "	Na-se-thä'-mä	" "	Nem-ma-soo'-ma-thä'	" "
55	No-stha-thä'	" "	No-stha-thä'	" "	Na-ma-some-thä'	" "
56					No-bes'-sib-ä.	" "
57	Nee-so'-tan	" "	Nee-so'-tan	" "	Nä-ah'-sä	" "
58					Nä-ahxs'	" "
59	Nŭ-jeech'	" "	Nŭ-jeech'	" "	Niks-kä-mich'	" "
60	N'-kway'-nus	" "	N'-kway'-nus	" "	N'-mŭke-sŭms'	" "
61	Nä-h·ise'	" "	Nä-h·ise'	" "	Nuh-mä-home'	" "
62	Noh'-whese'	" "	Noh'-whese'	" "	Nu-moh'-ho-mus'	" "
63	Nain-no-whese'	" "	Nain-no-whase'	" "	Na-mä-ho-mis'	" "
64	Sa-t'thu'-a	" "	Sa-t'thu'-a	" "	Sa-tse'-a	" "
65					Sa-tä-chock	" "
66	Se-yä-zet'-tha-re	My grandson.	Sa-le-zet'-tha-re	My granddaughter.	Set-see'-a	" "
67						
68	Set-she	" "	Set-she	" "	Set-se	" "
69						
70						
71						
72						
73						
74						
75						
76						
77						
78						
79					E-tŭ'-ah	" "
80						

TABLE II.—*Continued.*

	186. My mother's mother's brother's son.	Translation.	187. My mother's mother's brother's son's son. (Male speaking.)	Translation.	188. My mother's mother's brother's son's daughter. (Female speaking.)	Translation.
1	Hoc-no′-seh	My uncle.	Ah-găre′-seh	My cousin.	Ah-găre′-seh	My cousin.
2	Kuh-no′-seh	" "	Ah-ge-ah′-seh	" "	Ah-ge-ah′-seh	" "
3	Ge-no′-sä-hä	" "	Ah-gare′-seh	" "	Ah-gare′-seh	" "
4	Läg-nole′-hä	" "	Un-gă-lä′-seh	" "	Un-gă-lä′-seh	" "
5	Lä-ga-nole′-hä	" "	Un-gă-läss′	" "	Un-gă-läss′	" "
6	Ahk-rä-do-no′-re-ah	" "	Ahk-gä-rä′-sthar	" "	Ahk-gä-rä′-sthar	" "
7	Lä-ga-no̱-hä′-ah	" "	Lok-je′-hä(e.), Le-gä′-ah(y.)	My eld. or y'nger bro.	Ak-je′-ya(e.), Ka-gä′-ah (y.)	My e. or y. sister.
8	Hä-wä-te-no′-rä	" "	Jä-rä′-sa	My cousin.	Jä-rä-sa	My cousin.
9	Dak-she′	" "	Tä̱n-ha̱n′-she	" "	Hä̱n-kä′-she	" "
10	Dake′-she	" "	Tä′-she	" "	Hä-kä′-she	" "
11	A-dik′-she	" "	Kä′-zha	" "	Wä-kä′	" "
12	Ah-dik′-she	" "	Tä′-she	" "	Hä-kä′-she	" "
13	Lake-she′	" "	Tä′-she	" "	Han-kä′-she	" "
14	Lake′-she	" "	Tä′-hä-she	" "	Hun-kä′-she	" "
15	Lake′-she	" "	Tä′-she	" "	Hä-kä′-zhe	" "
16	Lake′-she	" "	Tä-hä′-she	" "	Hä-kä′-she	" "
17	Me-nake′-she	" "	Tä-hä′-she	" "	Mä-hä′-gä-she	" "
18	Na-ge′-hä	" "	Na-ge′-hä	My uncle.	Nä′-hä	My mother.
19	Wee-nä′-gee	" "	Wee-nä′-gee	" "	E-nä′-hä	" "
20	Heen-ja′-kä	" "	Heen-ja′-kä	" "	Heen′-naẖ	" "
21	Hin-chä′-kä	" "	Hin-chä′-kä	" "	He′-nah	" "
22	Be-ja′-ga	" "	Be-ja′-ga	" "	E′-naw	" "
23						
24	E-take′-e-neke′	My little uncle.	E-take′-e-neke′	My little uncle.	E-oo′-nee-neke′	My little mother.
25						
26						
27						
28	Um-ush′-Ĭ	My uncle.	Suh′-sŭh	My son.	Suh-suh′-take	My daughter.
29	Um-u′-shĭ	" "	Suh′-soh	" "	Suh-soh′-take	" "
30	Um-o′-shĭ	" "	Su′-soh	" "	Su′-soh-take	" "
31	Chu-pä′-wä	" "	Chup-pŭ′-che	" "	Chuch-hŭs′-wä	" "
32	E-dŭ′-tsĭ	" "	A-gwae-tsĭ′	My child.	A-gwae-tsĭ′	My child.
33	Ah-ge-doo′-dzĭ	" "	A-gwa′-tze	" "	A-gwa′-tze	" "
34	Te-wä′-chir-iks	" "	Pe′-row	" "	Pe′-row	" "
35	Te-watch′-e-riks	" "	Pe′-row	" "	Pe′-row	" "
36						
37	Nee-sis′	" "	Neest-chäs′	My cousin.	Nee′-che-moos	My cousin.
38	Nee-sis′	" "	Nee-säs′	" "	Nee′-che-moosh	" "
39	Nee-sis′	" "	Neest-chäs′	" "	Nee′-ta-moos	" "
40	Nĭ-zhĭ′-she	" "	Nĭ-tä′-wiss	" "	Nĭ-nĭ-mo′-she	" "
41	Ne-zhe-sha′	" "	Ne-tä′-wis	" "	Ne-ne-mo′-sha	" "
42	Ne-zhe-shä′	" "	Ne-tä′-wis	" "	Ne-ne-moo-shä′	" "
43	Ne-zhish′-shä′	" "	Ne-tä′-wis	" "	Ne-ne-moo-shä′	" "
44	Ne-zhish-shä′	" "	Ne-tä′-wis	" "	Ne-ne-moo-shä′	" "
45	N′-jeh-shä′	" "				
46	Ne-zhese′-sä	" "	Ne-zhese′-sä	My uncle.	Ni̱n-ge-ah′-	My mother.
47	Ne-zhe′-sä	" "	Ne-zhe′-sä	" "	Ni̱n-ge-ah′	" "
48	Ne-zhe′-sä	" "	Ne-zhe′-sä	" "	Ni̱n-ge-ah′	" "
49	Ne-zhe′-saw	" "	Ne-zhe′-saw	" "	Ne-ge-ah′	" "
50	Ne-zhe′-saw	" "	Ne-zhe′-saw	" "	Ne-ge-ah′	" "
51	Nă-zhe-sä′	" "				
52	Ne-zha′	" "	Ne-zha′	" "	Ne-ke⌒ah′	" "
53	Nă-she′	" "				
54	Na-si-thä′	" "	Na-si-thä′	" "	Nĭ-ke⌒ä′	" "
55	Nĭ-sĭ-thä′	" "	Nĭ-sĭ-thä′	" "	Na-ke⌒ah′	" "
56						
57	Ne-to-tah·se′	" "	N′-to-tes′-tä-mo	My cousin.	N′-to′-to-ke-man′	My cousin.
58						
59	N′-ku-lă-mŭk′-sis	" "	N′-sees′	My elder brother.	Nu-mees′	My elder sister.
60	N′-ku-lă-mook′-sis	" "	Nu-tä′-gus	My cousin.	Nu-mu′-sees	" " "
61	Nee-zeethe′	" "	N′-da-kwus′	My step-brother.	N′-dä-kwus-oh-kwä′-oh	My step-sister.
62	N′-shee′-se	" "	Nee-mä′-tus	" "	Neet-koh′-kw′	
63	Nee-zheese′	" "	Nain-n′-hans′	My elder brother.	Nain-na-wase′	My elder sister.
64	Thä-tha′	" "	Kŭn′-dig-eh	" " "	Sä′-dä	" " "
65						
66	Ser′-a	" "	Sŭ-nä′-ga	" " "	Sŭ-nä′-gä	" " "
67						
68						
69						
70						
71						
72						
73						
74						
75						
76						
77						
78						
76						
80						

TABLE II.—*Continued.*

	189. My mother's mother's brother's son's son's son. (Male speaking.)	Translation.	190. My mother's mother's brother's son's son. (Female speaking.)	Translation.	191. My mother's mother's brother's son's son's daughter. (Male speaking.)	Translation.
1	Ha-ah'-wuk	My son.	Ha-soh'-neh	My nephew.	Ka-ah'-wuk	My daughter.
2	Ha-hä'-wuk	" "	Ha-hä'-wuk	My son.	Ka-hä'-wuk	" "
3	Ha-hä'-wä	" "	Ha-hä'-wä	" "	Ka-hä'-wa	" "
4	Le-yä'-hä	" "	Le-yä'-hä	" "	Ka-yä'-hä	" "
5	E-yä'	" "	E-yä'	" "	Ka-yä'	" "
6	Kä-yä'-no-nä	My child.	Kä-yä-no'-na-ah	My nephew.	Kä-yä'-no-na	My child.
7	Le-yä'-ah	My son.	Le-yä'-ah	My son.	Ka-yä'-ah	My daughter.
8	A-ne-ah'	" "	He-wä'-teh	My nephew	E-ne-ah'	" "
9	Me-chink'-she	" "	Me-tonsh'-kä	" "	Me-chunk'-she	" "
10	Me-chink'-she	" "	Me-to⌒us'-ka	" "	Me-chounk'-she	" "
11	Ak-she'-da	" "	Me-toash'-kä	" "	Me-chunk'-sha	" "
12	Me-chink'-she	" "	Me-tose'-kä	" "	Me-chunk'-she	" "
13	Me-chink'-se-lä	" "	Me-toans'-kä	" "	Me-chunk'-se-lä	" "
14	Me-chink'-she	" "	Me-toase'-kä	" "	Me-chunk'-she	" "
15	Me-chink'-she	" "	Me-toash'-kä	" "	Me-chŭnk'-she	" "
16	Me-chink'-she	" "	Me-toas'-kä	" "	Me-chŭnk'-she	" "
17	Me-chink'-she	" "	Me-to'-zä	" "	Me-chunk'-she	" "
18	Na-ge'-hä	My uncle.	Na-ge'-hä	My uncle.	Nä'-hä	My mother.
19	Wee-nä'-gee	" "	Wee-nä'-gee	" "	E-nä'-hä	" "
20	Heen-ja'-kä	" "	Heen-ja'-kä	" "	Heen'-nah	" "
21	Hin-ehä'-kä	" "	Hin-chä'-kä	" "	He'-nah	" "
22	Be-ja'-ga	" "	Be'-ja-ga	" "	E'-naw	" "
23						
24	E-take'-e-neke'	My little uncle.	E-take-e-neke'	My little uncle.	E-oo'-ne-neke	My step or little [mother.
25						
26						
27						
28	Sup'-uk-nŏk'-ne	My grandson.	Sup'-uk-nŏk'-ne	My grandson.	Sup'-uk	My gd. daughter.
29	Sä'-pok-näk'-ne	" "	Sä'-pok-näk'-ne	" "	Sä'-pok	" "
30	Sup'-pok-näk'-nĭ	" "	Sup'-pok-näk'-nĭ	" "	Sup'-pok	" "
31	Um-os-sŭs'-wä	My grandchild.	Um-os-sŭs'-wä	My grandchild.	Um-os-sŭs'-wä	My grandchild
32	Uŋ-gĭ-lĭ'-sĭ	" "	Un-gĭ-lĭ'-sĭ	" "	Un-gĭ-lĭ'-sĭ	" "
33	Aŋ-ge-lee'-se	" "	Aŋ-ge-lee'-se	" "	Aŋ-ge-lee-se	" "
34	Lak-te'-gish	My grandson.	Lak-te'-gish	My grandson.	Lak-te'-gee	My gd. daughter.
35	Lak-te'-kis	My grandchild.	Lak-te'-kis	My grandchild.	Lak-te'-kis	My grandchild.
36						
37	N'-do'-sim	My step-son.	N'-de-kwä-tim'	My nephew.	N'-do'-sa-mis-kwame'	My step-daughter
38	N'-do'-zhim	" "	N'-do-kwä-tim'	" "	N'-do'-zha-mis-kwame'	" "
39	N'-do'-zhim	" "	N'-deh-kwä'-tim	" "	N'-do'-zha-mis-kwem'	" "
40	Nin-do'-zhim	" "	Nĭ-nin-gwä'-niss	" "	Nin-do-zhĭ-mĭ'-kwem	" "
41	Nin-do'-zhem	" "	Ne-nin-gwuh'-nis	" "	Nin-do-zhe-me'-quam	" "
42	N'-do'-zhim	" "	Ne-nin-gwi-nis'	" "	Nin-do-sha-mĭ-kwam'	" "
43	N'-do'-zhim-ă	" "	Ne-nin-gwi-nis'	" "	N'-do'-zha-mĭ-kwam'	" "
44	N'-do-zhim'	" "	Ne-nin-gwi-nis'	" "	N'-do'-zha-mĭ-kwam'	" "
45						
46	Ne-zhese-sä'	My uncle.	Ne-zhese'-sä	My uncle.	Nin-ge-ah'	My mother.
47	Ne-zhe'-sä	" "	Ne-zhe'-sä	" "	Niŋ-ge-ah'	" "
48	Ne-zhe'-sä	" "	Ne-zhe'-sä	" "	Niŋ-ge-ah'	" "
49	Ne-zhe'-saw	" "	Ne-zhe'-saw	" "	Ne-ge-ah'	" "
50	Ne-zhe'-saw	" "	Ne-zhe'-saw	" "	Ne-ge-ah'	" "
51	Nă-zhe-sä'	" "	Nă-zhe-sä'	" "	Nă-ke-ă'	" "
52	Ne-zha'	" "	Ne-zha'	" "	Ne-ke⌒ah'	" "
53						
54	Na-si-thä'	" "	Na-si-thä'	" "	Ni-ke⌒ă'	" "
55	Nĭ-sĭ-thä'	" "	Nĭ-sĭ-thä'	" "	Na-ke⌒ah'	" "
56						
57	N'-do-to'-ko	My step-son.	N'-do'-to-yose	My nephew.	N'-to'-to-tun	My step-daughter.
58						
59	N'-kwis'	My son.	Nu-lŭks'	" "	N'-tŭs'	My daughter.
60	N'-too-ă'-sum	" "	Nu-lŭ'-knees	" "	N'-su'-mus	" "
61	N'-di-ome'	" "	Nä-kun'	My step-child.	Nä-kun'	My step-child.
62	N'-kweese'	" "	N'-kweese'	My son.	N'-dă-nuss'	My daughter.
63	Nain-gwase'	" "	Nain-gwase'	" "	Nain-dä'-ness	" "
64	Tu-zen'-a	My step-son.	Sa-yä'-ze	My step-son.	Sa-yä'-dze	My step-daughter.
65						
66	Se-yä'-za	My son.	Se-yä'-za	My son.	Sa-le'-ă	My daughter.
67						
68						
69						
70						
71						
72						
73						
74						
75						
76						
77						
78						
79						
80						

TABLE II.—*Continued.*

	192. My mother's mother's brother's son's son's daughter. (Female speaking.)	Translation.	193. My mother's mother's brother's son's son's son's son. (Male speaking.)	Translation.	194. My mother's mother's brother's son's daughter's daughter's daughter. (Male speaking.)	Translation.
1	Ka-soh'-neh	My niece.	Ha-yä'-da	My grandson.	Ka-yä'-da	My gd. daughter.
2	Ka-hä'-wuk...............	My daughter.	Ha-yä'-dra..................	" "	Ka-yä'-dra	" "
3	Ka-hä'-wä..............	" "	Ha-yä'-da	" "	La-yä'-da	" "
4	Ka-yä'-hä	" "	Le-yä'-dla-ah	" "	Ka-yä'-dla-ah	" "
5	Ka-yä'....................	" "	E-yä'-dla-ah	" "	Ka-yä'-dla-ah	" "
6	Kä-yä-no'-na-ah..........	My niece.	Kä-yä'-rä	My grandchild.	Ka-yä'-rä...................	" "
7	Ka-yä'-ah	My daughter.	Le-yä-tä-ra'-yä	My grandson.	Ka-yä-tä-ra'-yä..............	" "
8	E-wä'-teh	My niece.	Ha-tra'-ah	" "	Ka-tra'-ah...................	My grandchild.
9	Me-tuṇ'-zhaṇ..............	" "	Me-tä-ko-zhä................	My grandchild.	Me-tä'-ko-zhä................	" "
10	Me-to⌒us'-zä..............	" "	Me-tä'-ko-zhä...............	" "	Me-tä'-ko-zhä...............	" "
11	Me-to'-zhä................	" "	Me-tä'-ko-zhä...............	" "	Me-tä'-ko-zha...............	" "
12	Me-to'-zhä................	" "	Me-tä'-ko-zhä...............	" "	Me-tä'-ko-zhä...............	" "
13	Me-toh'-zhä...............	" "	Me-tä'-ko-säk'-pok..........	" "	Me-tä'-ko-säk'-pok	" "
14	Me-toh'-zhä...............	" "	Me-tä'-ko-zhä...............	" "	Me-tä'-ko-zhä...............	" "
15	Me-to'-zä.................	" "	Me-tä'-ko-zhä...............	" "	Me-tä'-ko-zä................	" "
16	Me-to'-zä.................	" "	Me-tä'-ko-za................	" "	Me-tä'-ko-sä................	" "
17	Me-to'-zä.................	" "	Me-tä'-ko-sa................	" "		
18	Nä'-hä	My mother.	Na-ge'-hä	My uncle.	Tä-zä'-hä	My niece.
19	E-nä'-hä..................	" "	Wee-nä'-gee.................	" "	We-te'-zhä..................	" "
20	Heen'-nah................	" "	Heen-jä'-ka.................	" "	Heen-toas'-ka-me	" "
21	He'-nah	" "	Hin-chä'-kä.................	" "	Hin-tose'-kee-me	" "
22	E'-naw....................	" "	Be-ja'-ga...................	" "	Be-che'-zho.................	" "
23						
24	E-oo'-ne-neke'	My step or little [mother.	E-take'-e-neke'	My little uncle.	E-oo'-ne-neke'	My step or little [mother.
25						
26						
27						
28	Sup'-uk...................	My granddaughter.	Sup'-uk-nŏk'-ne	My step-son.	Sup'-uk....................	My gd. daughter.
29	Sä'-pok	" "	Sä'-pok-näk'-ne	" "	Sä'-pok	" "
30	Sup'-pok..................	" "	Sup'-pok-näk'-nĭ............	" "	Sup'-pok....................	" "
31	Um-os-sŭs'-wä...........	My grandchild.	Um-os-sŭs'-wä..............	My grandchild.	Um-os-sŭs'-wä..............	My grandchild.
32	Uṇ-gĭ-lĭ-sĭ..............	" "	Uṇ-gĭ-lĭ-sĭ	" "	Uṇ-gĭ-lĭ-sĭ.................	" "
33	Aṇ-ge-lee'-se	" "	Aṇ-ge-lee'-se	" "	Aṇ-ge-lee'-se...............	" "
34	Lak-te'-gee	My granddaughter.	Te'-wut	My nephew.	Te'-wut	My niece.
35	Lak-te'-kis	My grandchild.				
36						
37	Neese-che-mish'	My niece.	No-se-sem'..................	My grandchild.	No-se-sem'..................	My grandchild.
38	Neest-che-mish'...........	" "	No-se-sim'..................	" "	No-se-sim'..................	" "
39	Neese-che-mis'............	" "	No-se-sem'..................	" "	No-se-sem'..................	" "
40	Nĭ-shĭ-miss'...............	" "	No-zhi'-she.................	" "	No-zhĭ'-she.................	" "
41	Ne-she'-me-sha............	" "	No-she'-shä	" "	No-she'-shä	" "
42	Ne-she-mis'...............	" "	No-she-shä'.................	" "	No-she-shä'.................	" "
43	Ne-she-mis'...............	" "	No-she-shä'.................	" "	No-she-shä'.................	" "
44	Ne-she-mis'...............	" "	No-she-shä'.................	" "		
45						
46	Niṇ-ge-ah'.................	My mother.	Ne-zhese'-sä................	My uncle.	Shames-sä'.................	My niece.
47	Niṇ-ge-ah'.................	" "	Ne-zhe'-sä..................	" "	Ne-she'-mis-sä'.............	" "
48	Niṇ-ge-ah'.................	" "	Ne-zhe'-sä..................	" "	Ne-she'-mis-sä'.............	" "
49	Ne-ge-ah'..................	" "	Ne-zhe'-saw................	" "	Ne-she-mis-sä'..............	" "
50	Ne-ge-ah'..................	" "	Ne-zhe'-saw................	" "	Nä-shä'-mis	" "
51	Nä-ke⌒ä'.................	" "	Nä-zhe-sä'..................	" "		
52	Ne-ke⌒ah'................	" "	Ne-zhä'....................	" "		
53						
54	Nĭ-ke⌒ä'.................	" "	Na-si-thä'..................	" "	Ni-sem-e-thä...............	" "
55	Na-ke⌒ah'................	" "	Nĭ-sĭ-thä'..................	" "	Ne-sa-me-tha	" "
56						
57	Ne-mis'-sä.................	My niece.	Nee-so'-tan	My grandchild.	Nee-so'-tan	My grandchild.
58						
59	N'-sum'...................	" "	Nŭ-jeech'...................	" "	Nŭ-jeech'	" "
60	N'-sum'...................	" "	N'-kway'-nus...............	" "	N'-kway'-nus...............	" "
61	Nä-kun'...................	My step step-child.	Nä-h·ise'...................	" "	Nä-h·ise'....................	" "
62	N'-da-nuss'...............	My daughter.	Noh·-whese'.................	" "	Noh·-whese'..................	" "
63	Nain-dä'-ness	" "	Nain-no-whase'.............	" "	Nain-no-whase'..............	" "
64	Sa-yä'-dze.................	My step-daughter.	Sa-t'thu'-a.................	" "	Sa-t'thu'-a.................	
65						
66	Sa-le'-ä	My daughter.	Se-yä-zet'-tha-re	My grandson.	Sa-le-zet'-tha-re............	My gd. daughter.
67						
68						
69						
70						
71						
72						
73						
74						
75						
76						
77						
78						
79						
80						

TABLE II.—*Continued.*

	195. My mother's mother's sister.	Translation.	196. My mother's mother's sister's daughter.	Translation.	197. My mother's mother's sister's daughter's daughter—older than myself. (Female speaking.)	Translation.
1	Oc′-sote....................	My grandmother.	No-yeh′.....................	My mother.	Ah′-je.....................	My elder sister.
2	Oc′-sote....................	" "	Kuh-no′-hä.................	" "	Uh-je′-ah.................	" " "
3	Oc-so′-dä-hä...............	" "	Kuh-ne-hä′.................	" "	Uh-je′-ah.................	" " "
4	Ahk-sote′-hä...............	" "	Ahk-nole′-hä	" "	Ahk-je′-hä.................	" " "
5	Ahk-sote′..................	" "	Ah-ga-nese′-tä.............	" "	Ahk-je′-hä.................	" " "
6	Ahk′-sote..................	" "	Oh′-nä......................	" "	Ahk′-je...................	" " "
7	Ak-sote′-hä................	" "	Ah-ga-nese′-tä-hä.........	" "	Ak-je′-yä.................	" " "
8	Ah-shu-tä′.................	" "	Ah-nä′-uh..................	" "	A-ye′-uh..................	" " "
9	Uṇ-che′....................	" "	E-nah′......................	" "	Me-chuṇ′..................	" " "
10	O-che′.....................	" "	E′-nah......................	" "	Chu-ih′...................	" " "
11	O-che′-lä..................	" "	E′-nah......................	" "	Me-tänk′-a-do.............	" " "
12	Oh-che′....................	" "	Een′-nä....................	" "	Tän′-ka...................	" " "
13	Oo-che′....................	" "	E′-nah......................	" "	Chu-wa′...................	" " "
14	Un-che′....................	" "	E′-nah......................	" "	Chu-a′....................	" " "
15	O-che′.....................	" "	E′-nah......................	" "	Chu-ih′...................	" " "
16	O-che′.....................	" "	E′-nah......................	" "	Chu-wa′...................	" " "
17	O-gă′-she..................	" "	E-nah′......................	" "	Me-chun′..................	" " "
18	Gä-hä′.....................	" "	Nä′-hä.....................	" "	Zhon-da′-hä...............	" " "
19	Wee′-kä....................	" "	E-nä′-hä...................	" "	Wee-zöṇ-thä...............	" " "
20	He-koo-n′-ye...............	" "	Heen′-nah..................	" "	Heen-tan′-ga..............	" " "
21	Hiṇ-kŭ′-ne.................	" "	He′-nah....................	" "	Heen-tang′-a..............	" " "
22	E-ko′-be-tä................	" "	E′-naw.....................	" "	Be-sho′-wa................	" " "
23	E-che′.....................	" "				
24	E-ko′-ro-ka................	" "	E-oo′-ne...................	" "	E-noo′.	" " "
25	Nah′-he-a..................	" "				
26	Kä-rŭ′-hä..................	" "				
27	Bä-sä′-kä-na...............	" "				
28	Up-puk′-nĭ.................	" "	Ush′-kĭ....................	" "	Um-un′-nĭ.................	" " "
29	Up-pok′-nĭ.................	" "	Ush′-kĭ....................	" "	Um-un′-nĭ.................	" " "
30	Hap-pŭ′-sĭ.................	" "	Lush′-kĭ...................	" "	An-tik′-bä................	" " "
31	Chu-pŭ′-se.................	" "	Chuch-kŭ′-ce...............	My little mother.	Chu-hlä′-hä...............	" " "
32	E-nĭ-sĭ....................	My grandparent.	E-tsĭ′......................	My mother.	Uṇ-gĭ-luṇ′-ĭ..............	" " "
33	Ah-ge-lee′-sih.............	" "	Ah-gid′-ze.................	" "	Aṇ-ge-lä′-ih..............	" " "
34	Ah-te′-kä..................	My grandmother.	Ah-te′-rä..................	" "	E-dä′-deh.................	My sister.
35	Ah-te′-kä..................	" "	A-te′-rä...................	" "	A-tä′-he..................	" "
36	Ah-te′-kä..................	" "				
37	Noh′-kome′.................	" "	N′-gä′-we..................	" "	Ne-mis′...................	My elder sister.
38	No-kome′...................	" "	N′-gä′-we..................	" "	Ne-mish′..................	" " "
39	No-kome′...................	" "	N′-gä′-wa..................	" "	Ne-mish′..................	" " "
40	No′-ko-miss................	" "	Nin′-gah...................	" "	Nĭ-mis′-sĕ................	" " "
41	No′-ko-mis.................	" "	Nin′-gah...................	" "	Ne-de-ge′-ko..............	My step-sister.
42	No-ko′-mis.................	" "	Nin-gah′...................	" "	Ne-mis-sä′................	My elder sister.
43	No-ko-mis′.................	" "	Ne-gä-sha..................	" "	Ne-mis-sä′................	" " "
44	No-ko-mis′.................	" "	N′-gus′-sheh...............	" "	N′-mis′-sä................	" " "
45	No-ko′-mis.................	" "	N′-geh′....................	" "	Ne-mis-sä′................	" " "
46	No-ko-mä′..................	" "	Niṇ-ge-ah′.................	" "	Ne-mis′-sä................	" " "
47	No-ko-mä′..................	" "	Niṇ-ge-ah′.................	" "	Ne-mis′-sä................	" " "
48	No-ko-mä′..................	" "	Niṇ-ge-ah′.................	" "	Ne-mis-sä′................	" " "
49	No-ko-mä′..................	" "	Ne-ge-ah′..................	" "	Ne-me-sä′.................	" " "
50	No′-ko-mä..................	" "	Ne-ge-ah′..................	" "	Ne-me-sä′.................	" " "
51	No′-ko-mis′................	" "	Nă-ke⁀ä′...................	" "	Nă-mis′-sä................	" " "
52	No′-ko-mä..................	" "	Ne-ke⁀ah′..................	" "	Ne-ma′....................	" " "
53	Na-vish′-kim...............	" "	Nä′-ko.....................	" "	Nä-ma′....................	" " "
54	No-ko-ma-some-thä′.......	" "	Nĭ-ke⁀ä′...................	" "	Na-ta-tä-mä...............	My sister.
55	No-kome-thä′...............	" "	Na-ke⁀ah′..................	" "	Nĭ-mĭ-thä′................	My elder sister.
56	Na′-e-bä...................	" "				
57	Ne-tä-ke-ä′-sä.............	" "	Neex-ist′..................	" "	Nee-mis′-tä...............	" " "
58	Ne-tä′-ke-ahxs.............	" "				
59	Nu-gu′-mich................	" "	N′-keech′..................	" "	Nu-mees′..................	" " "
60	Nuk′-mus...................	" "	N′-kee′-sees...............	" "	Nee-tse′-kes..............	" " "
61	No-ome′....................	" "	N′-guk′....................	" "	N′-ko-kwä′................	My step-sister.
62	Noo-h′ome′.................	" "	N′-gä-hä′-tut..............	My little mother.	Neet-kohr′-kw′............	" " "
63	Na-no′-home................	" "	Niṇ-guk′-us................	" " "	Nain-na-wase′.............	My elder sister.
64	Sa-tsun′...................	" "	San′-ga....................	My step-mother.	Sä′-dä....................	" " "
65	Sa-cho′-na.................	" "				
66	Set-sa′-nä.................	" "	Sä-kre′-a..................	" "	Set-dez′-a-ä-ze...........	" " "
67						
68	So-he......................	My uncle.	Sa-ku-i....................	" "	Sa-che....................	" " "
69						
70						
71						
72						
73						
74						
75						
76						
77						
78						
79						
80	Ning-e-o′-wä	" "				

TABLE II.—*Continued.*

	198. My mother's m'her's sister's daughter's daughter—younger than myself. (Female speaking.)	Translation.	199. My mother's mother's sister's daughter's daughter's son. (Male speaking.)	Translation.	200. My mother's mother's sister's daughter's daughter's son. (Female speaking.)	Translation.
1	Ka'-gä	My younger sister.	Ha-yä'-wan-da	My nephew.	Ha-ah'-wuk	My son.
2	Ka-gä'-ah	" " "	Ha-yuh'-wä-da	" "	Ha-hä'-wa	" "
3	Ka'-gä	" " "	Ha-yä-wä'-da	" "	Ha-hä'-wä	" "
4	Ka-gä'-ah	" " "	Ha-yä-wä'-dä	" "	Le-yä'-hä	" "
5	Ka-gä'-ha	" " "	E-yo-wä'-dä	" "	E-yä'	" "
6	Kä'-gä	" " "	Kä-yä'-wä-nä	" "	Kä-yä'-no-nä	My child.
7	Ka-gä'-ah	" " "	Le-wä-dä'-ah	" "	Le-yä'-ah	My son.
8	Ya-ye-ä'-hä	" " "	Ha-shone-drä'-ka	" "	A-ne-ah'	" "
9	Me-täṇ-kä	" " "	Me-tonsh'-kä	" "	Me-chiṇk'-she	" "
10	Me-tuṇ'-kä	" " "	Me-to͡us'-kä	" "	Me-chink'-she	" "
11	Me-tänk'-a-do	" " "	Me-toash'-kä	" "	Ak-she'-da	" "
12	Me-tän'-ka	" " "	Me-tose'-ka	" "	Me-chink'-she	" "
13	Me-tunk'-hä-lä	" " "	Me-toans'-kä	" "	Me-chink'-se-lä	" "
14	Me-tonk'-ä	" " "	Me-toase'-kä	" "	Me-chink'-she	" "
15	Ton'-ka	" " "	Me-toash'-kä	" "	Me-chink'-she	" "
16	Me-ton'-ka	" " "	Me-toas'-kä	" "	Me-chink'-she	" "
17	Me-tä'	" " "	Me-to'-zä	" "	Me-chink'-she	" "
18	We-ha'	" " "	We-toash'-kä	" "	Nis-se'-hä	" "
19	Wee-töṇ'-ga	" " "	We-toans'-kä	" "	We-zhiṇ'-ga	" "
20	Heen-tuṇ'-ga	" " "	Heen-toas'-ka	" "	Hee-yiṇ'-ga	" "
21	Heen-tän'-ga	" " "	Hin-tose'-kee	" "	He-ne'-cha	" "
22	Be-tuṇ'-ga	" " "	Be-chose'-kä	" "	Be-she'-gä	" "
23						
24	E-chunk'	" " "	E-choonsh'-ka-neke'	My little nephew.	E-chä-h·kun	My step-child.
25						
26						
27						
28	Suh-näk'-fish	" " "	Sub-ai'-yih	My nephew.	Sup'-uk-nŏk'-ne	My grandson.
29	Sä-näk'-fish	" " "	Suh-bai'-yih	" "	Sä-pok-näk'-ne	" "
30	Sä-näk'-fish	" " "	Sä-bi'-yih	" "	Sup'-pok-näk'-nĭ	" "
31	Chu-chŭ'-se	" " "	Un-ho-pŭ'-e-wä	" "	Um-os-sŭs'-wä	My grandchild.
32	Un-gĭ-luṇ'-ĭ	" " "	Uṇ-gĭ-wĭ'-nuṇ	" "	A-gwae-tsi'	My child.
33	Aṇ-ge-lä'-ih	" " "	Uṇ-ge-we'-nuh	" "	A-gwa'-tze	" "
34	E-dä'-deh	My sister.	Te'-wut	" "	Pe'-row	" "
35	A-tä'-he	" "	Te'-wut	" "	Pe'-row	" "
36						
37	Ne-sheme'	My younger sister.	N'-de-kwä-tim'	" "	N'-go'-sim	My step-son.
38	Ne-sha-mish'	" " "	N'-de-kwä-tim'	" "	N'-go'-zhim	" "
39	Neh-she-mish'	" " "	N'-deh-kwä-tim'	" "	N'-do'-zhim	" "
40	Nĭ-shĭ'-mĕ	" " "	Nĭ-nin-gwä-niss'	" "	Nin-do'-shĭ-miss	My step-child.
41	Ne-de-ge'-ko	My step-sister.	Ne-nin-gwuh'-nis	" "	Nin-do'-zhe-mis	" "
42	Ne-she-nis'	My younger sister.	Ne-nin-gwi-nis'	" "	Neen-gwis'	My son.
43	Ne-she-mä'	" " "	Ne-nin-gwi-nis'	" "	Nin-gwis'	" "
44	N'-she'-mä	" " "	Ne-nin-gwi-nis'	" "	N'-gwis'	" "
45	Ne-she-mä'	" " "	Nä'-gwi-nis	" "	N'-gwis'	" "
46	Ne-go-se-mä'	" " "	Laṇ-gwä-les'-sä	" "	Neen-gwase'-sä	" "
47	Ne-she-mä'	" " "	Ne-lä'-gwä-la-sä'	" "	Niṇ-gwa-sä'	" "
48	Ne-she-mä'	" " "	Ne-lä'-gwä-la-sä'	" "	Niṇ-gwa-sä'	" "
49	Ne-she-mä'	" " "	Ne-lä'-gwä-lis-sä'	" "	Ne-gwis-sä'	" "
50	Ne-she-mä'	" " "	Ne-lä'-gwä-lis-sä'	" "	Ne-gwis-sä'	" "
51	Nä-se'-mä	" " "	Ne-nä'-gwä-nis	" "	Nä-kwis'-sä	" "
52	Nä-sa'	" " "	Ne-nä'-kwä-na	" "	Ne-keese'	" "
53	Nä-sim-ä'	My elder sister.	Na-chin'-e-tä	" "	Nä	" "
54	Na-ta-tä-mä'	My sister.	Nen-na-kwä-na-thä	" "	Nĭ-kwa-thä'	" "
55	N'-the-ma-thä'	My younger sister.	Na-la-gwal-thä'	" "	Ne-kwe-thä'	" "
56						
57	Nee-sis'-sä	" " "	N'-do'-to-yose	" "	N'-do'-to-ko	My step-son.
58						
59	N'-kwa-jeech'	" " "	Nu-lŭks'	" "	N'-kwis	My son.
60	Nee-tse'-kes	" " "	Nu-lŭ'-knees	" "	N'-su'-mus	" "
61	N'-ko'-kwä	My step-sister.	No-kwath'	" "	N'-di-ome'	" "
62	Neet-koh'-kw'	" " "	Longue'-kw'	" "	N'-kweese'	" "
63	Nain-hise'-sa-mus'	My younger sister.	Na-lone'-gwä-sis'	" "	Nain-gwase'	" "
64	A-da'-ze	" " "	Sä'-zy	" "	Sa-yä'-ze	My step-son.
65						
66	Sä'-re	" " "	Sạ-yä'-za	My son.	Se-yä'-za	My son.
67						
68	See-chath	" " "	Set-en-ge	" "	Se-zi-ou	" "
69						
70						
71						
72						
73						
74						
75						
76						
77						
78						
79						
80						

TABLE II.—*Continued.*

	201. My mother's mother's sister's daughter's daughter's daughter. (Male speaking.)	Translation.	202. My mother's mother's sister's daughter's daughter's daughter. (Female speaking.)	Translation.	203. My mother's mother's sister's great great grandson.	Translation.
1	Ka-yă'-wan-da	My niece.	Ka-ah'-wuk	My daughter.	Ha-yă'-da	My grandson.
2	Ka-yuh'-wä-deh	" "	Ka-hä'-wuk	" "	Ha-yă'-dra	" "
3	Ka-yă-wä'-da	" "	Ka-hä'-wä	" "	Ha-yă'-da	" "
4	Ka-yă'-wan-dă	" "	Ka-yă'-hä	" "	Le-yă'-dla-ah	" "
5	Ka-yo-wä'-dä	" "	Ka-yă'	" "	E-yă'-dla-ah	" "
6	Kä-yă'-wä-nä	" "	Kä-yă'-no-nä	My child.	Kä-yă'-rä	My grandchild.
7	Ka-wä-dä'-ah	" "	Ka-yă'-ah	My daughter.	Le-yă-tä-ra'-yä	My grandson.
8	Ya-shone-drä'-ka	" "	E-ne-ah'	" "	Ha-tra'-ah	" "
9	Me-tuṇ'-zhan	" "	Me-chunk'-she	" "	Me-tä'-ko-zhä	My grandchild.
10	Me-to-us'-zä	" "	Me-chounk'-she	" "	Me-tä'-ko-zhä	" "
11	Me-to'-zhä	" "	Me-chunk'-she	" "	Me-tä'-ko-zhä	" "
12	Me-to'-zhä	" "	Me-chunk'-she	" "	Me-tä'-ko-zha	" "
13	Me-toh'-zhä	" "	Me-chunk'-se-lä	" "	Me-tä'-ko-säk'-pok	" "
14	Me-toh'-zhä	" "	Me-chunk'-she	" "	Me-tä'-ko-zhä	" "
15	Me-to'-zä	" "	Me-chŭnk'-she	" "	Me-tä'-ko-zhä	" "
16	Me-to'-zä	" "	Me-chŭnk'-she	" "	Me-tä'-ko-zä	" "
17	Me-to'-zä	" "	Me-chunk'-she	" "	Me-tä'-ko-zä	" "
18	Ta-zhä'-hä	" "	Win-no'-ga	" "	Toosh'-pä-hä	" "
19	We-te'-zhä	" "	Wee-zhuṇ'-ga	" "	Wee-tŭsh'-pä	" "
20	Heen-toas'-ka-me	" "	Hee-yuṇ'-ga	" "	Heen-tä'-kwä	My grandson.
21	Hin-tose'-kee-me	" "	He-yun'-ga	" "	E-tä'-kwä	" "
22	Be-che'-zho	" "	She-me'-she-gä	My girl.	Be-chose'-pä	My grandchild.
23						
24	E-chooṇ-zhuhk'-e-neke	My little niece.	E-chä-h·kun'	My step-child.	E-choonsh'-ka'-neke	My little gd. son.
25						
26						
27						
28	Sub-ih'-take	My niece.	Sup'-uk	My granddaughter.	Sup'-uk-nŏk'-ne	My grandson.
29	Suh-bih'-take	" "	Sä'-pok	" "	Sä'-pok-näk'-ne	" "
30	Su-bĭ'-take	" "	Sup'-pok	" "	Sup'-pok-näk'-nĭ	" "
31	Un-häk'-pu-te	" "	Um-os-sŭs'-wä	My grandchild.	Um-os-sŭs'-wä	My grandchild.
32	Uṇ-gwä-dun'	" "	A-gwae-tsĭ'	My child.	Un-gĭ-lĭ-sĭ	" "
33	Uṇ-gwä'-tuh	" "	A-gwa'-tze	" "	Aṇ-ge-lee'-se	" "
34	Te'-wut	" "	Pe'-row	" "	Lak-te'-gish	My grandson.
35	Te'-wut	" "	Pe'-row	" "	Lak-te'-kis	My grandchild.
36						
37	Neese-che-mish'	" "	N'-do'-sa-mis-kwame'	My step-daughter.	No-se-sem'	" "
38	Neest-che-mish'	" "	N'-do'-zha-mis-kwame'	" "	No-se-sim'	" "
39	Neese-che-mis'	" "	N'-do'-zha-mis-kwem'	" "	No-se-sem'	" "
40	Nĭ-shĭ'-miss	" "	Nin-do'-zhĭ-miss	My step-child.	No-zhĭ'-she	" "
41	Ne-she'-me-sha	" "	Nin-do'-zhe-mis	" "	No-she'-shä	" "
42	Ne-she-mis'	" "	Neen-dä'-niss	My daughter.	No-she-shä'	" "
43	Ne-she-mis'	" "	N'-dä-niss'	" "	No-she-shä'	" "
44	Ne-she-mis'	" "	N'-dä-niss'	" "	No-sä-seh'	" "
45	Ne-she'-mis	" "	N'-dä'-niss	" "	No-sa'-ma'	" "
46	Shames-sä'	" "	Nin-dä'-nä	" "	No-sa'-mä	" "
47	Ne-she'-mis-sä'	" "	Nin-dä'-nä	" "	No-sa'-mä	" "
48	Ne-she'-mis-sä'	" "	Nin-dä'-nä	" "	No-sa-mä'	" "
49	Ne-she-mis-sä'	" "	N'-dä'-nä	" "	No-sa-mä'	" "
50	Ne-she-mis-sä'	" "	N'-dä'-nä	" "	No-she-sem'	" "
51	Nă-shä'-mis	" "	Nä-tä'-niss	" "	No-she-sä'	" "
52	Na-nä'-mä	" "	Ne-täne'	" "	Nä-h·kä'	" "
53	Ne-she'-mis	" "	Nä-tun'	" "	Na-se-thä'-mä	" "
54	Na-sem-e-thä'	" "	Ni-tä-na-thä'	" "	No-stha-thä'	" "
55	Ne-sa-me-thä'	" "	Nĭ-tä-na-thä	" "		
56						
57	Nee-mis'-sä	" "	N'-to'-to-tun	" "	Nee-so'-tan	" "
58						
59	N'-sum'	" "	N'-tŭs'	" "	Nŭ-jeech'	" "
60	N'-sum'	" "	N'-su'-mus	" "	N'-kway'-nus	" "
61	Noh·k-soh'-kwä'-oh	" "	Nee-chune'	" "	Nä-h·ise'	" "
62	Longue-kwä'	" "	N'-dä-nuss'	" "	Noh·-whese'	" "
63	Na-lone'-gwä-sis'	" "	Nain-dä'-ness	" "	Nain-no-whase'	" "
64	Sä'-zy	" "	Sa-yä'-dze	My step-daughter.	Sa-t'thu'-a	" "
65						
66	Sa-le'-ă	My daughter.	Sa-le'-ă	My daughter.	Se-yä-zet'-tha-re	My grandson.
67						
68	Set-she	My grandchild.	Set-shai	My grandchild.	Set-she	My child.
69						
70						
71						
72						
73						
74						
75						
76						
77						
78						
79						
80						

TABLE II.—*Continued.*

	204. My mother's mother's sister's great great granddaughter.	Translation.	205. My father's father's father's brother.	Translation.	206. My father's father's father's brother's son.	Translation.
1	Ka-yä'-da	My granddaughter.	Hoc'-sote......................	My grandfather.	Hoc'-sote......................	My grandfather.
2	Ka-yä'-dra	" "	Hoc'-sote......................	" "	Hoc'-sote......................	" "
3	Ka-yä'-da	" "	Hoc-so'-dä-hä..................	" "	Hoc-so'-dä-hä..................	" "
4	Ka-yä'-dla-ah..................	" "	Lok-sote'-hä	" "	Lok-sote'-hä	" "
5	Ka-yä'-dla-ah..................	" "	Läke-sote'......................	" "	Läke-sote'......................	" "
6	Kä-yä'-rä.......................	My grandchild.	Ahk-rä'-sote	" "	Ahk-rä'-sote	" "
7	Ka-yä-tä-ra'-yä...............	My granddaughter.	Lok-sote'-hä	" "	Lok-sote'-hä	" "
8	Ya-tra'-ah......................	" "	Hä-shu-tä'......................	" "	Hä-shu-tä'......................	" "
9	Me-tä'-ko-zhä..................	My grandchild.	Tuṇ-käṇ'-she-däṇ........	" "	Tun-käṇ'-she-däṇ........	" "
10	Me-tä'-ko-zha..................	" "	Toon-kä'-she-nä	" "	Toon-kä'-she-nä	" "
11	Me-tä'-ko-zhä..................	" "	Tun-kä'-she-lä	" "	Tun-kä'-she-lä	" "
12	Me-tä'-ko-zhä..................	" "	To-kä'-she-lä..................	" "	To-kä'-she-lä..................	" "
13	Me-tä'-ko-säk'-pok........	" "	Me-tonk'-ah	" "	Me-tonk'-ah	" "
14	Me-tä'-ko-zhä..................	" "	Tŏn-kä'-she-lä	" "	Tŏn-kä'-she-lä	" "
15	Me-tä'-ko-zhä..................	" "	Toon-kä'-zhe-lä	" "	Toon-kä'-she-lä	" "
16	Me-tä'-ko-zä....................	" "	Toh·-kä'-she-la...............	" "	Toh·-kä'-she-la...............	" "
17	Me-tä'-ko-sä....................	" "	Me-to'-gä-she.................	" "	Me-to'-gä-she	" "
18	Toosh'-pä-hä	" "	Ta-ga'-hä	" "	Ta-ga'-hä	" "
19	Wee-tŭsh'-pä	" "	Wee-te'-ga	" "	Wee-te'-ga	" "
20	Heen-tä'-kwä-me	My granddaughter.	Hee-too'-ga	" "	Hee-too'-ga	" "
21	E-tä'-kwä-me	" "	E-tŭ'-kä	" "	E-tŭ'-kä	" "
22	Be-chose'-pä	My grandchild.	Be-che'-go	" "	E-ko'............................	" "
23			We-che'-cho	" "		
24	E-chooṇ-zhunk-e-neke' ...	My little gd. daught.	E-cho'-ka	" "	E-cho'-ka	" "
25			Tä-ta'-h·e-ha..................	" "	Tä-ta'-h·e-ha..................	" "
26			Mä-toosh-ä-rŭ'-tä-kä......	" "	Mä-toosh-ä-rŭ'-tä-kä......	" "
27			Me-nup-h·is'-sa-kä	" "	Me-nup-h·is'-sa-kä	" "
28	Sup'-uk	My granddaughter.	Um-uh'-fo	" "	Um-uh'-fo	" "
29	Sä'-pok	" "	Um-u'-fo	" "	Um-u'-fo	" "
30	Sup'-pok........................	" "	Um-u'-fo	" "	Um-u'-fo	" "
31	Um-os-sŭs'-wä	My grandchild.	Chu-pŭ-chä'...................	" "	Chu-pŭ-chä'...................	" "
32	Uṇ-gĭ-lĭ-sĭ	" "	E-nĭ'-sĭ	My grandparent.	E-nĭ'-sĭ	" "
33	Aṇ-ge-lee'-se..................	" "	Ah-ge-doo'-tse................		Ah-g·e-doo'-tse................	" "
34	Lak-te'-gee	My granddaughter.	Te-wä'-chir-iks..............	My uncle.	Ah-te'-put......................	" "
35	Lak-te'-kis	My grandchild.	Ah-te'-put......................	My grandfather.	Ah-te'-put......................	" "
36			Ah-te'-pot......................	" "	Ah-te'-pot......................	" "
37	No-se-sem'	" "	Ne-mo-some'...................	" "	Ne-mo-some'...................	" "
38	No-se-sim'	" "	Ne-mo-shome'	" "	Ne-mo-shome'	" "
39	No-se-seu'	" "	Na-mo-shome'	" "	Na-mo-shome'	" "
40	No-zhĭ'-she....................	" "	Nĭ-mĭ-sho'-miss..............	" "	Nĭ-mĭ-sho'-miss..............	" "
41	No-she'-shă....................	" "	Ne-me-sho'-mis	" "	Ne-me-sho'-mis	" "
42	No-she-shă'	" "	Na-ma'-sho-mis'	" "	Na-ma'-sho-mis'	" "
43	No-she-shă'	" "	Ne-mis'-sho-mis	" "	Ne-mis'-sho-mis	" "
44	No-she-shă'	" "	Na-ma-sho-mis'	" "	Na-ma-sho-mis'	" "
45	No-să-seh'	" "	Na-ma-sho-mis'	" "	Na-ma-sho-mis'	" "
46	No-so-mä'	" "	Na-ma-sho-mä'	" "	Na-ma-sho-mä'	" "
47	No-sa'-mä	" "	Na-mä-sho-mä'................	" "	Na-mä-sho-mä'................	" "
48	No-sa'-mä	" "	Na-mä-sho-mä'................	" "	Na-mä-sho-mä'................	" "
49	No-sa-mä'	" "	Na-mä'-sho-mä................	" "	Na-mä'-sho-mä................	" "
50	No-sa-mä'	" "	Na-mä'-sho-mä................	" "	Na-mä'-sho-mä................	" "
51	No-she-sem'	" "	Nä-mä'-sho-mis	" "	Nä-mä'-sho-mis	" "
52	No-she-să'	" "	Na-mä'-sho....................	" "	Na-mä'-sho....................	" "
53	Nä-h·-kä'	" "	Nam-a-shim'...................	" "	Nam-a-shim'...................	" "
54	Na-se-thä'-mä	" "	Nem-ma-soo'-ma-thä'	" "	Nem-ma-soo'-ma-thă	" "
55	No-stha-thä'	" "	Na-ma-some-thä'	" "	Na-ma-some-thä'	" "
56			No-bes'-sib-ă..................	" "	No-bes'-sib-ă..................	" "
57	Nee-so-tan......................	" "	Nä-oh'-sä......................	" "	Nä-ah'·sä......................	" "
58			Nä-ah·xs'.......................	" "	Nä-ah·xs'.......................	" "
59	Nŭ-jeech'	" "	Niks-kä-mich'.................	" "	Niks-kä-mich'.................	" "
60	N'-kway'-nus..................	" "	N'-mŭh-sums'.................	" "	N'-mŭh-sums'.................	" "
61	Nä-h·ise'	" "	Nuh-mä-home'...............	" "	Nuh-mä-home'...............	" "
62	Noh·-whese'	" "	Nu-moh·'-ho-mus'...........	" "	Nu-moh·'-ho-mus'...........	" "
63	Nain-no-whase'	" "	Na-mä-ho-mis'...............	" "	Na-mä-ho-mis'...............	" "
64	Sa-t'thu'-a.....................	" "	Sa-tse'-a			
65			Sa-tä'-chock			
66	Sa-le-zet'-tha-re.............	My granddaughter.	Set-see'-a	" "		
67						
68						
69						
70						
71						
72						
73						
74						
75						
76						
77						
78						
79						
80						

TABLE II.—*Continued.*

	207. My father's father's father's brother's son's son.	Translation.	208. My father's father's father's brother's son's son's son—older than myself. (Male speaking.)	Translation.	209. My father's father's father's brother's son's son's son. (Male speaking.)	Translation.
1	Hä'-nih	My father.	Hä'-je	My elder brother.	Ha-ah'-wuk	My son.
2	Hä'-hih	" "	Kuh-je'-ah	" " "	Ha-hä'-wuk	" "
3	Kuh-ne-hä'	" "	Kuh-je'-ah	" " "	Ha-hä'-wä	" "
4	Lä'-ga-nih	" "	Läk-je'-hä	" " "	Le-yä'-hä	" "
5	Lä-ga-ne'-hä	" "	Läk-je'-hä	" " "	E-yä'	" "
6	Ahk-re'-ah	" "	Ahk-rä'-je	" " "	Kä-yä'-no-nä	My child.
7	Lä-ga-ne'-hä	" "	Lok-je'-hä	" " "	Le-yä'-ah	My son.
8	Hi-ese'-tä	" "	Ha-ye'-uh	" " "	A-ne-ah'	" "
9	At-tay'	" "	Chin-yay'	" " "	Me-chink'-she	" "
10	Ah-ta'	" "	Che'-a	" " "	Me-chink'-she	" "
11	Ah-ta'	" "	Che'-a	" " "	Ak-she'-dä	" "
12	Ah-ta'	" "	Che'-a	" " "	Me-chink'-she	" "
13	Ah-ta'	" "	Che'-a	" " "	Me-chink'-se-la	" "
14	Ah-ta'	" "	Me-che'-a	" " "	Me-chink'-she	" "
15	Ah-ta'	" "	Che-a'	" " "	Me-chink'-she	" "
16	Ah-ta'	" "	Che-a'	" " "	Me-chink'-she	" "
17	Ah-dä'	" "	Me-chin'	" " "	Me-chink'-she	" "
18	Tä-de'-ha	" "	Zhin-dä'-hä	" " "	Nis-se'-hä	" "
19	In-da'-de	" "	Wee-zhe'-thä	" " "	We-nis-se	" "
20	Heen'-kä	" "	He-yen'-nä	" " "	Hee-yin'-ga	" "
21	Hin'-kä	" "	He-ye'-nä	" " "	He-ne'-cha	" "
22	E-dä'-je	" "	Be-zhe'-yeh	" " "	Be-she'-gä	" "
23						
24	E-un'-cha	" "	E-ne'	" " "	E-neke'	" "
25						
26						
27						
28	A'-kĭ	" "	Um-un'-nĭ	" " "	Suh'-sŭh	" "
29	A'-kĭ	" "	Um-un'-nĭ	" " "	Suh'-soh	" "
30	Ang'-kĭ	" "	Et-e-bä'-pĭ-shĭ-lĭ	My brother.	Su'-soh	" "
31	Chuhl'-ke	" "	Chu-hlä'-hä	My elder brother.	Chup-pŭ'-che	" "
32	E-dau-dä'	" "	Un-gĭ-nĭ'-lĭ	" " "	A-gwae-tsĭ'	My child.
33	Ah-ge-do'-dä	" "	An-ke-nee'-le	" " "	A-gwa'-tze	" "
34	Ah-te'-rä	" "	E-dä'-deh	My brother.	Pe'-row	" "
35						
36						
37	Noh-ta'-we	" "	Neese-tase'	My elder brother.	N'-do'-sim	My step-son.
38	Noh-tä'-we	" "	Neese-tase'	" " "	N'-do'-zhim	" "
39	Noh-'-tä'-we	" "	Neesh-tase'	" " "	N'-do'-zhim	" "
40	Noss	" "	Nis-sä'-yĕ	" " "	Nin-do'-zhim	" "
41	No'-sa	" "	Ne-kä'-nä	My step-brother.	Nin-do'-zhem	" "
42	Nŏss	" "	Ne-kä'-na	" "	N'-do'-zhim	" "
43	Noss	" "	Ne-kä'-nis	" "	N'-do'-zhim'-ă	" "
44	Noss	" "	Ne-kä'-nä	" "	N'-do-zhim'	" "
45	Noss	" "	Ne-kä'-na	" "	N'-do-zhim-ă	" "
46	No-sä'	" "	Ne-sä-sä'	My elder brother.	Neen-gwase'-sä	My son.
47	No-sä'	" "	Ne-san'-zä	" " "	Nin-gwa-sä'	" "
48	No-sä'	" "	Ne-san'-zä	" " "	Nin-gwa-sä'	" "
49	No-sä'	" "	Ne-sä-zä'	" " "	Ne-gwis-sä'	" "
50	No-sä'	" "	Ne-sä-zä'	" " "	Ne-gwis-sä'	" "
51	Noss	" "	Nä-sa'-mä	" " "	Nä-kwis'-sä	" "
52	Noh'-neh	" "	Nä-nä'	" " "	Ne-keese'	" "
53	Nä-o'-a	" "	Nä-ne'-ä	" " "	Nä	" "
54	No-thä'	" "	Ni-to-ta-mä	My brother.	Nĭ-kwă-thä'	" "
55	No-thä'	" "	N'-tha-thä'	My elder brother.	Ne-kwe-thä'	" "
56						
57	Nin	" "	Neese-sä'	" " "	N'-do'-to-ko	My step-son.
58						
59	Nŭch	" "	N'-sees'	" " "	N'-kwis'	My son.
60	Ne-cha'-look	" "	N'-see'-wes	My brother.	N'-too-ä'-sum	" "
61	Noh'	" "	N'-dä-kwus'	My step-brother.	Nä-kun'	My step-child.
62	Noh'-'h'	" "	Nee-mä'-tus	" "	N'-kweese'	My son.
63	Na-no'-whus	My little father.	Nain-n'-hans'	My elder brother.	Nain-gwase'	" "
64						
65						
66						
67						
68						
69						
70						
71						
72						
73						
74						
75						
76						
77						
78						
79						
80						

	TABLE II.—*Continued.*					
	210. My father's father's father's brother's son's son's son's son's son.	Translation.	211. My father's father's father's sister.	Translation.	212. My father's father's father's sister's daughter.	Translation.
1	Ha-yä'-da......................	My grandson.	Oc'-sote	My grandmother.	Oc'-sote......................	My grandmother.
2	Ha-yä'-dra.....................	" "	Oc'-sote	" "	Oc'-sote	" "
3	Ha-yä'-da.....................	" "	Oc-so'-dä-hä..................	" "	Oc-so'-dä-hä	" "
4	Le-yä'-dla-ah.................	" "	Ahk-sote'-hä..................	" "	Ahk-sote'-hä..................	" "
5	E-yä'-dla-ah..................	" "	Ahk-sote'......................	" "	Ahk-sote'......................	" "
6	Kä-yä'-rä......................	My grandchild.	Ahk'-sote	" "	Ahk'-sote	" "
7	Le-yä-tä-ra'-yä...............	My grandson.	Ak-sote'-hä....................	" "	Ak-sote'-hä....................	" "
8	Ha-tra'-ah....................	" "	Hä-shu-tä'....................	" "	Ah-shu-tä'....................	" "
9	Me-tä'-ko-zhä................	My grandchild.	Uṇ-che'.......................	" "	Uṇ-che'.......................	" "
10	Me-tä'-ko-zha................	" "	O-che'........................	" "	O-che'........................	" "
11	Me-tä'-ko-zhä................	" "	O-che'-lä.....................	" "	O-che'-lä.....................	" "
12	Me-tä'-ko-zha................	" "	Oh-che'.......................	" "	Oh-che'.......................	" "
13	Me-tä'-ko-säk'-pok	" "	Oo-che'.......................	" "	Oo-che'.......................	" "
14	Me-tä'-ko-zhä................	" "	Un-che'.......................	" "	Un-che'.......................	" "
15	Me-tä'-ko-zhä................	" "	O-che'........................	" "	O-che'........................	" "
16	Me-tä'-ko-zä.................	" "	O-che'........................	" "	O-che'........................	" "
17	Me-tä'-ko-sä.................	" "	O-gä'-she.....................	" "	O-ge'-she.....................	" "
18	Toosh'-pä-hä.................	" "	Gä-hä'........................	" "	Gä-hä'........................	" "
19	Wee-tŭsh'-pä.................	" "	Wee'-kä......................	" "	Wee'-kä......................	" "
20	Heen-tä'-kwä.................	My grandson.	Hee-too'-ga...................	" "	He-koo'-n'-ye.................	" "
21	E-tä'-kwä.....................	" "	Hiṇ-kŭ'-ne...................	" "	Hiṇ-kŭ'-ne...................	" "
22	Be-chose'-pä.................	My grandchild.	E-ko'.........................	" "	E-ko'-be-tä..................	" "
23			E-che'........................	" "		
24	E-choonsh'-ka-neke'.......	My little grandson.	E-ko'-ro-ka..................	" "	E-ko'-ro-ka..................	" "
25			Nah'-he-a....................	" "	Nah'-he-a....................	" "
26			Kä-rŭ'-hä....................	" "	Kä-rŭ'-hä....................	" "
27			Bä-sä'-kä-na.................	" "	Bä-sä'-kä-na.................	" "
28	Sup'-uk-nŏk'-ne	My grandson.	Up-puk'-ne....................	" "	Up-puk'-ne....................	" "
29	Sä'-pok-näk'-ne	" "	Up-pok'-nĭ....................	" "	Up-pok'-nĭ....................	" "
30	Sup'-pok-näk'-nĭ...........	" "	Hap-po'-sĭ....................	" "	Hap-po'-sĭ....................	" "
31	Um-os-sŭs'-wä	My grandchild.	Chup-pŭ'-se..................	" "	Chu-pŭ'-se..................	" "
32	Uṇ-gĭ-lĭ-sĭ	" "	E-nĭ'-sĭ	My grandparent.	E-nĭ'-sĭ	My grandparent.
33	Ah-ge-doo'-tse..............	" "	Ah-ge-lee'-sih	" "	Ah-ge-lee'-sih	" "
34	Lak-te'-gish.................	My grandson.	Ah-te'-rä.....................	My mother.	Ah-te'-kä.....................	My grandmother.
35						
36						
37	No-se-sem'...................	My grandchild.	Noh'-kome'...................	My grandmother.	Noh-kome'...................	" "
38	No-se-sim'...................	" "	No-kome'.....................	" "	No-kome'.....................	" "
39	No-se-sem'...................	" "	No-kome'.....................	" "	No-kome'.....................	" "
40	No-zhĭ'-she..................	" "	No'-ko-miss..................	" "	No'-ko-mis...................	" "
41	No-zhe'-zhä..................	" "	No'-ko-mis...................	" "	No'-ko-mis...................	" "
42	No-she-shä'..................	" "	No-ko'-mis...................	" "	No-ko'-mis...................	" "
43	No-she-shä'..................	" "	No-ko-mis'...................	" "	No-ko-mis'...................	" "
44	No-she-shä'..................	" "	No-ko-mis'...................	" "	No-ko-mis'...................	" "
45	No-sä-seh'...................	" "	No-ko'-mis...................	" "	No-ko-mis'...................	" "
46	No-sa-mä'....................	" "	No-ko'-mis...................	" "	No-ko-mä'...................	" "
47	No-sa'-mä....................	" "	No-ko-mä'....................	" "	No-ko-mä'...................	" "
48	No-sa'-mä....................	" "	No-ko-mä'....................	" "	No-ko-mä'...................	" "
49	No-sa-mä'....................	" "	No-ko'-mis...................	" "	No-ko-mä'...................	" "
50	No-sa-mä'....................	" "	No-ko'-mis'..................	" "	No-ko-mä'...................	" "
51	No-she-sem'..................	" "	No'-ko-mis...................	" "	No'-ko-mis...................	" "
52	No-she-sä'...................	" "	No'-ko-mä....................	" "	No'-ko-mä...................	" "
53	Nä-h'-kä'....................	" "	Na-vish'-kim.................	" "	Na-vish'-kim.................	" "
54	Na-se-mä'-thä...............	" "	No-ko-ma-some-thä'.......	" "	No-ko-ma-some-thä'.......	" "
55	No-stha-thä'.................	" "	No-kome-thä'................	" "	No-kome-thä'................	" "
56			Na'-e-bä......................	" "		
57	Nee-so'-tan	" "	Ne-tä-ke-ä'-sä...............	" "	Ne-tä-ke-ä'-sä...............	" "
58			Ne-tä'-ke-ahxs..............	" "	Ne-tä'-ke-ahxs..............	" "
59	Nŭ-jeech'....................	" "	Nŭ-gŭ-mich'.................	" "	Nŭ-gŭ-mich'.................	" "
60	N'-kway'-nus.................	" "	Nŭk'-mus.....................	" "	Nŭk'-mus.....................	" "
61	Nä-h'ise'....................	" "	No-ome'......................	" "	No-ome'......................	" "
62	Noh'-whese'..................	" "	Noo h'ome'...................	" "	Noo-h'ome'...................	" "
63	Nain-no-whase'..............	" "	Na-ho'-home..................	" "	Na-no'-home..................	" "
64			Sa-tsum......................	" "		
65			Sa-cho'-na....................	" "		
66			Set-sa'-nä....................	" "		
67						
68						
69						
70						
71						
72						
73						
74						
75						
76						
77						
78						
79						
80						

TABLE II.—*Continued.*

	213. My father's father's father's sister's daughter's daughter.	Translation.	214. My father's father's father's sister's daughter's daughter's daughter. (Male speaking.)	Translation.	215. My father's father's father's sister's daughter's daughter's daughter's daughter. (Male speaking.)	Translation.
1	Ah-ga'-huc	My aunt.	Ah-găre'-seh	My cousin.	Ka-yă'-wan-da	My niece.
2	Kno'-hä	My mother.	Ah-ge-ah'-seh	" "	Ka-yuh'-wä-da	" "
3	Ah-ge-no'-hä	" "	Ah-gare'-seh	" "	Ka-yă-wä'-da	" "
4	Ahk-nole'-hä	" "	Un-gä-lä'-seh	" "	Ka-yă'-wan-dă	" "
5	Ah-ga-nese'-tä	" "	Un-gä-läss'	" "	Ka-yo-wä'	" "
6	Ahk-kaw'-rack	My aunt.	Ahk-gä'-rä-sthar	" " [sister.	Kä-yä'-wä-nä	" "
7	Lä-ga-nese'-tä-hä	My mother.	Ak-je'-yä (e.), Ka-gä'-ah (y.)	My elder or younger	Ka-wä-dä'-ah	" "
8	Ah-rä'-hoc	My aunt.	Jä-rä'-sa	My cousin.	Ya-shone-drä'-ka	" "
9	Tuṇ-wiṇ'	" "	Tän-haṇ'-she	" "	Me-tuṇ'-zhän	" "
10	Toh'-we	" "	Hä-kä'-she	" "	Me-to͡-us'-zä	" "
11	Tonk'-wa	" "	Ah-ka'-zha	" "	Me-to'-zhä	" "
12	Tonk'-wa	" "	Hä-kä'-she	" "	Me-to'-zhä	" "
13	Toh-we'	" "	Hun-kä'-she	" "	Me-toh'-zhä	" "
14	Toh'-we	" "	Hun-kä'-she	" "	Me-toh'-zhä	" "
15	Toh'-we	" "	Hä-kä'-she	" "	Me-to'-zä	" "
16	Toh'-we	" "	Hä-kä'-she	" "	Me-to'-zä	" "
17	Me-toh'-we	" "	Tä-hä'-she	" "	Me-to'-zä	" "
18	Te-na'-hä	" "	Ta-zhä'-hä	My niece.	Toosh'-pä-hä	My grandchild.
19	Wee-tee'-me	" "	We-te'-zhä	" "	Wee-tŭsh'-pä	" "
20	Heen-too'-me	" "	Heen-toas'-ka-me	" "	Heen-tä'-kwä-me	My gd. daughter.
21	E-tŭ'-me	" "	Hin-tose'-kee-me	" "	E-tä'-kwä-me	" "
22	Be-je'-me	" "	Be-che'-zho	" "	Be-chose'-pä	My grandchild.
23						
24	E-chooṇ'-we	" "	E-chooṇ-zhunk'-e-neke'	My little niece.	E-chooṇ-zhunk'-e-neke'	My little gd. dau.
25						
26						
27						
28	A-huk'-ne	My aunt.	Aṇ'-take	My younger sister.	Sub-ih'-take	My niece.
29	A-huc'-ne	" "	An'-take	" " "	Suh-bih'-take	" "
30	Hap-po'-sĭ	My grandmother.	Hap-po'-sĭ	My grandmother.	Hap-po'-sĭ	My grandmother.
31	Chu-pŭ'-se	" "	Chŭ-pŭ'-se	" "	Chu-pŭ'-se	" "
32	E-hlau'-gĭ	My aunt.	E-hlau'-gĭ	My aunt.	E-hlau'-gĭ	My aunt.
33	Ah-ge-h'lo'-gih	" "	Ah-ge-h'lo'-gih	" "	Ah-ge-h'lo'-gih	" "
34						
35						
36						
37	Nis-sĭ-goos'	" "	Nee'-che-moos	My cousin.	Neese-che-mish'	My niece.
38	Nis-se-goos'	" "	Nee'-che-moosh	" "	Neest-che-mish'	" "
39	Nĭ-se-goos'	" "	Nee'-ta-moos	" "	Neese-che-mis'	" "
40	Nin'-sĭ'-goss	" "	Nĭ-nĭ-mo'-shĕ	" "	Nĭ-shĭ'-miss	" "
41	Ne-ze-gŭs'	" "	Ne-ne-mo'-sha	" "	Ne-she'-me-sha	" "
42	Ne-see-goss'	" "	Ne-ne'-moo-shă'	" "	Ne-she-mis'	" "
43	Nis-zee-gŭss'	" "	Ne-ne-moo-shä'	" "	Ne-she-mis'	" "
44	Nis-sa-gŏse	" "	Ne-ne-moo-shä'	" "	Ne-she-nis'	" "
45	N'-si-gwis'	" "			No-sa-mä'	My grandchild.
46	N'-sa'-gwe-sä'	" "	Shames-sä'	My niece.	No-sa'-mä	" "
47	Ne-zä'-gŏs-sä'	" "	Ne-she'-mis-sä'	" "	No-sa'-mä	" "
48	Ne-zä'-gŏs-sä'	" "	Ne-she'-mis-sä'	" "	No-sa-mä'	" "
49	Ne-sä'-gwis-sä	" "	Ne-she-mis-sä'	" "	No-sa-mä'	" "
50	Ne-sä'-gwis-sä	" "	Ne-she-mis-sä'	" "	No-she-sem'	" "
51	Nak-ye'-hä	" "	Nä-shä'-nis	" "	No-she-sä'	" "
52	Ne-ne'	" "	Nä-nä'-mä	" "		
53	Nä-nn'	" "				
54	Na-tha-kwi-thä	" "	Ni-sem-e-thä'	" "	No-se-thä'-mä	" "
55	Na-tha-gwe-thä'	" "	Ne-sa-me-thä'	" "	Na-stha-thä'	" "
56						
57	Ne-to'-tarse	" "	N'-to'-to-ke-man'	My cousin.	Ne-mis'-sä	My niece.
58						
59	N'-su-gwis'	" "	Nu-mees'	My elder sister.	N'-sum'	" "
60	Noo'-kum	" "	N'-tä'-gus	My cousin.	N'-sum'	" "
61	No-muths'	My step-mother.	Na-mese'	My step-sister.	Nohrk-soh-kwä'-oh	" "
62	N'-gä-hä'-tut	My little mother.	N'-doh'-kwä-yome	" "	Longue-kwä'	" "
63	Niṇ-guk'-us	" "	Nain-na-wase'	My elder sister.	Na-lone'-gwä-sis'	" "
64						
65						
66						
67						
68						
69						
70						
71						
72						
73						
74						
75						
76						
77						
78						
79						
80						

TABLE II.—*Continued.*

	216. My father's father's father's sister's daughter's daughter's daughter's daughter's daughter.	Translation.	217. My mother's mother's mother's brother.	Translation.	218. My mother's mother's mother's brother's son.	Translation.
1	Ka-yä′-da	My granddaughter.	Hoc′-sote	My grandfather.	Hoc′-sote	My grandfather.
2	Ka-yä′-dra	" "	Hoc′-sote	" "	Hoc′-sote	" "
3	Ka-yä′-da	" "	Hoc-so′-dä-hä	" "	Hoc-so′-dä-hä	" "
4	Ka-yä′-dla-ah	" "	Lok-sote′-hä	" "	Lok-sote′-hä	" "
5	Ka-yä′-dla-ah	" "	Läke-sote′	" "	Läke-sote′	" "
6	Kä-yä′-rä	My grandchild.	Ahk-rä′-sote	" "	Ahk-rä′-sote	" "
7	Ka-yä-tä-ra′-yä	My granddaughter.	Lok-sote′-hä	" "	Lok-sote′-hä	" "
8	Ya-tra′-ah	" "	Hä-shu-tä′	" "	Hä-shu-tä′	" "
9	Me-tä′-ko-zhä	My grandchild.	Tuŋ-käŋ′-she-däŋ	" "	Tuŋ-häŋ′-she-däŋ	" "
10	Me-tä′-ko-zhä	" "	Toon-kä′-she-nä	" "	Toon-kä′-she-nä	" "
11	Me-tä′-ko-zhä	" "	Tun-kä′-she-lä	" "	Tun-kä′-she-lä	" "
12	Me-tä′-ko-zha	" "	To-kä′-she-lä	" "	To-kä′-she-lä	" "
13	Me-tä′-ko-säk′-pok	" "	Me tonk′-ah	" "	Me-tonk′-ah	" "
14	Me-tä′-ko-zhä	" "	Tŏn-kä′-she-lä	" "	Tŏn-kä′-she-lä	" "
15	Me-tä′-ko-zhä	" "	Toon-kä′-zhe-lä	" "	Toon-kä′-zhe-lä	" "
16	Me-tä′-ko-zä	" "	Toh-kä′-she-la	" "	Toh′-kä′-she-la	" "
17	Me-tä′-ko-sä	" "	Me-to′-gä-she	" "	Me-to′-gä-she	" "
18	Toosh′-pä-hä	" "	Ta-gä′-hä	" "	Ta-gä′-hä	" "
19	Wee-tŭsh′-pä	" "	Wee-te′-ga	" "	Wee-te′-ga	" "
20	Heen-tä′-kwä-me	My granddaughter.	Hee-too′-ga	" "	Hee-too′-ga	" "
21	E-tä′-kwä-me	" "	E-tŭ′-kä	" "	E-tŭ′-kä	" "
22	Be-chose′-pä	My grandchild.	Be-che′-go	" "	Be-che′-go-be-tä	" "
23			We-che′-cho	" "		
24	E-chooŋ-zhunk′-e-neke′	My little gd. daught.	E-cho′-ka	" "	E-cho′-ka	" "
25			Tä-ta′-h·e-ha	" "	Tä-ta′-h·e-ha	" "
26			Mä-toosh-ä-rŭ′-tä-kä	" "	Mä-toosh-a-rŭ′-kä	" "
27			Me-nup-h·is′-sä-kä	" "	Me-nup-h·is′-sä-ka	" "
28	Sup′-uk	My granddaughter.	Um-uh′-fo	" "	Um-uh′-fo	" "
29	Sä′-pok	" "	Um-u′-fo	" "	Um-u′-fo	" "
30	Hap-po′-sĭ	My grandmother.	Um-u′-fo	" "	Um-u′-fo	" "
31	Chu-pŭ′-se	" "	Chu-pŭ-chä′	" "	Chu-pŭ·chä′	" "
32	E-hlau′-gĭ	My aunt.	E-nĭ′-sĭ	My grandparent.	E-nĭ′-sĭ	My grandparent.
33	Ah-ge-h′lo′-gih	" "	Ah-ge-doo′-tse	" "	Ah-ge-doo′-tse	" "
34			Te-wä′-chir-iks	My uncle.	Ah-te′-put	" "
35			Ah-te′-put	My grandfather.	Ah-te′-pot	" "
36			Ah-te′-pot	" "	Ah-te′-pot	" "
37	No-se-sem′	My grandchild.	Ne-mo-some′	" "	Ne-mo-some′	My grandfather.
38	No-se-sim′	" "	Ne-mo-shome′	" "	Ne-mo-shome′	" "
39	No-se-sem′	" "	Na-mo-shome′	" "	Na-mo-shome′	" "
40	No-zhĭ′-she	" "	Nĭ-mĭ-shŏ′-miss	" "	Nĭ-mĭ-shŏ′-miss	" "
41	No-she′-shä	" "	Ne-me-sho′-mis	" "	Ne-me-sho′-mis	" "
42	No-she-shä′	" "	Na-ma-sho-mis′	" "	Na-ma-sho-mis′	" "
43	No-she-shä′	" "	Ne-mis′-sho-mis′	" "	Ne-mis′-sho-mis′	" "
44	No-she-shä′	" "	Na-ma-sho-mis′	" "	Na-ma-sho′-mis	" "
45			Na-ma-sho-mis′	" "	Na-ma-sho′-mis	" "
46	No-sa-mä′	" "	Na-ma-sho′-mis	" "	Na-ma-sho-ma′	" "
47	No-sa′-mä	" "	Ne-mä-sho-mä′	" "	Ne-mä-sho-mä′	" "
48	No-sa′-mä	" "	Ne-mä-sho-mä′	" "	Ne-mä-sho-mä′	" "
49	No-sa-mä′	" "	Ne-mä′-sho-mä	" "	Ne-mä-sho-mä′	" "
50	No-sa-mä′	" "	Ne-mä′-sho-mä	" "	Ne-mä-sho-mä′	" "
51	No-she-sem′	" "	Nä-mä′-sho-mis	" "	Nä-mä′-sho-mis	" "
52	No-she-sä′	" "	Na-mä′-sho	" "	Na-mä′-sho	" "
53			Nam-a-shim′	" "	Nam-a-shim′	" "
54	Na-se-thä′-mä	" "	Nem-ma-soo′-ma-thä	" "	Nem-ma-soo′-ma-thä	" "
55	No-stha-thä′	" "	Na-ma-some-thä′	" "	Na-ma-some-thä′	" "
56			No-bes′-sib-ä	" "	No-bes′-sib-ä	" "
57	Nee-so′-tan	" "	Na-ah·′-sä	" "	Na-ah′-sä	" "
58			Nä-ah·xs′	" "	Nä-ah·xs′	" "
59	Nŭ-jeech′	" "	Niks-kä-mich′	" "	Niks-kä-mich′	" "
60	N′-kway′-nus	" "	N′-muh-sŭms′	" "	N′-muke-sŭms′	" "
61	Nä-h·ise′	" "	Nuh-mä-home′	" "	Nuh-ma-home′	" "
62	Noh·-whese′	" "	Nu-moh·′-ho-mus′	" "	Nu-moh·′-ho-mus′	" "
63	Nain-no-whase′	" "	Na-mä-ho-mis′	" "	Na-mä-ho-mis′	" "
64			Sa-tse′-a	" "		
65			Sä-tä′-choek	" "		
66			Set-see′-a	" ‘		
67						
68						
69						
70						
71						
72						
73						
74						
75						
76						
77						
78						
79						
80						

TABLE II.—*Continued.*

	219. My mother's mother's mother's brother's son's son.	Translation.	220. My mother's mother's mother's brother's son's son's son.	Translation.	221. My mother's mother's mother's brother's son's son's son.	Translation.
1	Hoc-no'-seh	My uncle.	Ah-găre'-seh	My cousin.	Ha-ah'-wuk	My son.
2	Kuh-no'-seh	" "	Ah-ge-ah'-seh	" "	Ha-hä'-wuk	" "
3	Ge-no'-sä-hä	" "	Ah-gare'-seh	" "	Ha-hä'-wä	" "
4	Läg-nole'-hä	" "	Un-gă-lä'-seh	" "	Le-yä'-hä	" "
5	Lä-ge-nole'-hä	" "	Un-gä-läss'	" "	E-yä'	" "
6	Ahk-rä-do-no'-re-ah	" "	Ahk-gä-rä'-sthär	" " [brother.	Kä-yä'-no-nä	My child.
7	Lä-ga-no-hä'-ah	" "	Lok-je'-hä(e.), Le-gä'-ah (y.)	My elder or younger	Le-yä'-ah	My son.
8	Hä-wä-te-no'-rä	" "	Jä-rä'-sa	My cousin.	A-ne-ah'	" "
9	Dak-she'	" "	Tän-hän'-she	" "	Me-chink'-she	" "
10	Dake'-she	" "	Tä'-she	" "	Me-chink'-she	" "
11	A-dik'-she	" "	Kä'-sha	" "	Ak-she'-dä	" "
12	Ah-dik'-she	" "	Tä'-she	" "	Me-chink'-she	" "
13	Lake'-she	" "	Tä'-she	" "	Me-chink'-se-lä	" "
14	Lake'-she	" "	Tä-hä'-she	" "	Me-chink'-she	" "
15	Lake'-she	" "	Tä'-she	" "	Me-chink'-she	" "
16	Lake'-she	" "	Ta-hä'-she	" "	Me-chink'-she	" "
17	Me-nake'-she	" "	Ta-hä'-she	" "	Me-chink'-she	" "
18	Na-ge'-hä	" "	Na-ge'-hä	My uncle.	Na-ge'-hä	My uncle.
19	Wee-nä'-gee	" "	Wee-nä'-gee	" "	Wee-nä'-gee	" "
20	Heen-ja'-kä	" "	Heen-ja'-kä	" "	Heen-ja -kä	" "
21	Hin-chä'-kä	" "	Hin-chä'-kä	" "	Hin-chä'-kä	" "
22	Be-ja'-ga	" "	Be-ja'-ga	" "	Be-ja'-ga	" "
23						
24	E-take'-e-neke'	My little uncle.	E-take'-e-neke'	My little uncle.	E-take'-e-neke'	My little uncle.
25						
26						
27						
28	Um-ush'-ɪ	My uncle.	Suh'-sŭh	My son.	Sup'-uk-nŏk'-ne	My grandson.
29	Um-u'-shɪ	" "	Suh'-soh	" "	Sä'-pok-näk'-ne	" "
30	Um-o'-shɪ	" "	Su'-soh	" "	Sup'-pok-näk'-nɪ	" "
31	Chu-pä'-wä	" "	Chu-pŭ'-che	" "	Um-os-sŭs'-wä	My grandchild.
32	E-dŭ'-tsɪ	" "	A-gwae-tsɪ'	" "	Un-gɪ-lɪ'-sɪ	" "
33	Ah-ge-doo'-dze	" "	A-gwa'-tse	" "	An-ge-lee'-se	" "
34						
35						
36						
37	Nee-sis'	" "	Nees'-chäs	My cousin.	N'-do'-sim	My step-son.
38	Nee-sis'	" "	Nee-säs'	" "	N'-do'-zhim	" "
39	Nee-sis'	" "	Neets-chäs'	" "	N'-do'-zhim	" "
40	Nɪ-zhɪ'-she	" "	Nɪ-tä'-wiss	" "	Nin-do'-zhim	" "
41	Ne-zhe-sha'	" "	Ne-tä'-wis	" "	Nin-do'-zhim	" "
42	Ne-zhe-shă'	" "	Ne-tä'-wis	" "	N'-do'-zhim	" "
43	Ne-zhish'-shă	" "	Ne-tä'-wis	" "	N'-do'-zhim-ă	" "
44	Ne-zhish-shă'	" "	Ne-tä'-wis	" "	N'-do-zhim	" "
45	N'-jeh-shă'	" "				
46	Ne-zhese'-să	" "	Ne-zhese'-să	My uncle.	Ne-zhese'-să	My uncle.
47	Ne-zhe'-să	" "	Ne-zhe'-să	" "	Ne-zhe'-să	" "
48	Ne-zhe'-să	" "	Ne-zhe'-să	" "	Ne-zhe'-sa	" "
49	Ne-zhe'-saw	" "	Ne-zhe'-saw	" "	Ne-zhe'-saw	" "
50	Ne-zhe'-saw	" "	Ne-zhe'-saw	" "	Ne-zhe'-saw	" "
51	Nă-zhe-să'	" "	Nă-zhe-să'	" "	Nă-zhe-să'	" "
52	Ne-zha'	" "	Ne-zha'	" "	Ne-zha'	" "
53	Nă-she'	" "				
54	Na-si-thă'	" "	Na-si-thă'	" "	Na-si-thă'	" "
55	Nɪ-sɪ-thä'	" "	Nɪ-sɪ-thä'	" "	Nɪ-sɪ-thä	" "
56						
57	Ne-to-tah·se'	" "	N'-to'-tes-tä-mo	My cousin.	N'-do'-to-ko	My step-son.
58						
59	N'-ku-lă-mŭk'-sis	" "	N'-sees	My elder brother.	N'-kwis'	My son.
60	N'-ku-lă-mook'-sis	" "	N'-tä'-gus	My cousin.	N'-too-ă'-sum	" "
61	Nee-zeethe'	" "	N'-da-kwas'	My step-brother.	Nä-kun'	My step-son.
62	N'-shee'-se	" "	Nee-mä'-tus	" "	N'-kweese'	My son.
63	Ne-zheese'	" "	Nain-n'-hans'	My elder brother.	Nain-gwase'	" "
64						
65						
66						
67						
68						
69						
70						
71						
72						
73						
74						
75						
76						
77						
78						
79						
80						

TABLE II.—*Continued.*

	222. My mother's mother's mother's brother's son's son's son's son's son.	Translation.	223. My mother's mother's mother's sister.	Translation.	224. My mother's mother's mother's sister's daughter.	Translation.
1	Ha-yä'-da	My grandson.	Oc'-sote	My grandmother.	Oc'-sote	My grandmother.
2	Ha-yä'-dra	" "	Oc'-sote	" "	Oc'-sote	" "
3	Ha-yä'-da	" "	Oc-so'-dä-hä	" "	Oc-so'-dä-hä	" "
4	Le-yä'-dla-ah	" "	Ahk-sote'-hä	" "	Ahk-sote'-hä	" "
5	E-yä'-dla-ah	" "	Ahk-sote'	" "	Ahk-sote'	" "
6	Kä-yä'-rä	My grandchild.	Ahk-rä'-sote	" "	Ahk-sote	" "
7	Le-yä-tä-ra'-yä	My grandson.	Ak-sote'-hä	" "	Ak-sote'-hä	" "
8	Ha-tra'-ah	" "	Ah-shu-tä'	" "	Ah-shu-tä'	" "
9	Me-tä'-ko-zhä	" "	Uṇ-che'	" "	Uṇ-che'	" "
10	Me-tä'-ko-zhä	" "	O-che'	" "	O-che'	" "
11	Me-tä'-ko-zhä	" "	O-che'-lä	" "	O-che'-lä	" "
12	Me-tä'-ko-zha	" "	Oh-che'	" "	Oh-che'	" "
13	Me-tä'-ko-säk'-pok	" "	Oo-che'	" "	Oo-che'	" "
14	Me-tä'-ko-zhä	" "	Un-che'	" "	Un-che'	" "
15	Me-tä'-ko-zhä	" "	O-che'	" "	O-che'	" "
16	Me-tä'-ko-zä	" "	O-che'.	" "	O-che'.	" "
17	Me-tä'-ko-sä	" "	O-gä'-she	" "	O-gä'-she	" "
18	Na-ge'-hä	My uncle.	Gä-hä'	" "	Gä-hä'	" "
19	Wee-nä'-gee	" "	Wee'-kä	" "	Wee'-kä	" "
20	Heen-ja'-kä	" "	He-koo'-n'ye	" "	He-koo'-n'ye	" "
21	Hin-chä'-kä	" "	Hiṇ-kü'-ne	" "	Hiṇ-kü'-ne	" "
22	Be-ja'-ga	" "	E-ko'	" "	E-ko.	" "
23			E-che'.	" "		
24	E-take'-e-neke'	My little uncle.	E-ko'-ro-ka	" "	E-ko'-ro-ka	" "
25			Nah·-he-a	" "	Nah'-he-a	" "
26			Kä-rü'-hä	" "	Kä-rü'-hä	" "
27			Bä-sä'-kä-na	' "	Bä-sä'-kä-na	" "
28	Sup'-uk-nŏk'-ne	My grandson.	Up-puk'-nĭ	" "	Up-puk'-ne	" "
29	Sä'-pok-näk'-ne	" "	Up-pok'-nĭ	" "	Up-pok'-ne	" "
30	Sup'-pok-näk'-nĭ	" "	Hap-po'-sĭ	" "	Hap-po'-sĭ	" "
31	Um-os-süs'-wä	My grandchild.	Chu-pŭ'-se	" "	Chu-pŭ'-se	" "
32	Uṇ-gĭ-lĭ-sĭ	" "	E-nĭ'-sĭ	My grandparent.	E-nĭ'-sĭ	My grandparent.
33	Aṇ-ge-lee'-se	" "	Ah-ge-lee'-sih	" "	Ah-ge-lee'-sih	" "
34			Ah-te'-rä	My mother.	Ah-te'-kä	" "
35			Ah-te'-kä	My grandmother.	Ah-te'-kä	" "
36			Ah-te'-kä	" "	Ah-te'-kä	" "
37	No-se-sem'	" "	Noh·-kome'	" "	Noh·-kome'	My grandmother.
38	No-se-sim'	" "	No-kome'	" "	No-kome'	" "
39	No-se-sem'	" "	No-kome'	" "	No-kome'	" "
40	No-zhĭ'-she	" "	No'-ko-miss	" "	No'-ko-miss	" "
41	No-zhe'-shä	" "	No'-ko-mis	" "	No'-ko-mis	" "
42	No-she-shä'	" "	No-ko'-mis	" "	No-ko'-mis	" "
43	No-she-shä'	" "	No-ko-mis'	" "	No-ko-nis'	" "
44	No-she-shä'	" "	No-ko-mis'	" "	No-ko-mis'	" "
45			No-ko-mis'	" "	No-ko-mis'	" "
46	Ne-zhese'-sä	My uncle.	No-ko-ma'	" "	No-ko-mä'	" "
47	Ne-zhe'-sä	" "	No-ko-mä'	" "	No-ko-mä'	" "
48	Ne-zhe'-sä	" "	No-ko-mä'	" "	No-ko-mä'	" "
49	Ne-zhe'-saw	" "	No-ko-mä'	" "	No-ko-mä'	" "
50	Ne-zhe'-saw	" "	No-ko-mä'	" "	No-ko-mä'	" "
51	Nä-zhe-sä'	" "	No'-ko-mis	" "	No-ko-mis'	" "
52	Ne-zha'	" "	No'-ko-mis	" "	No'-ko-mä	" "
53			Na-vish'-kim	" "	Na-vish'-kim	" "
54	Na-si-thä'	" "	No-ko-ma-some-thä'	" "	No-ko-ma-some-thä'	" "
55	Nĭ-sĭ-thä'	" "	No-kome-thä'	" "	No-kome-thä'	" "
56			Na'-e-bä	" "	Na'-e-bä	" "
57	Nee-so'-tan	My grandchild.	Ne-tä-ke-ä'-sä	" "	Ne-tä-ke-ä'-sä	" "
58			Ne-tä'-ke-ahxs	" "	Ne-tä'-ke-ahxs	" "
59	Nŭ-jeech'	" "	Nŭ-ga'-mich	" "	Nŭ-ga'-mich	" "
60	N'-kway'-nus	" "	Nuk'-mus	" "	Nuk'-mus	" "
61	Nä-h·ise'	" "	No-ome'	" "	No-ome'	" "
62	Noh·-whese'	" "	Noo-h·ome'	" "	Noo-h·ome'	" "
63	Nain-no-whase'	" "	Na-no'-home	" "	Na-no'-home	" "
64			Sa-tsun	" "		
65			Sa-cho'-na	" "		
66			Set-sa'-na	" "		
67						
68						
69						
70						
71						
72						
73						
74						
75						
76						
77						
78						
79						
80						

TABLE II.—*Continued.*

	225. My mother's mother's mother's sister's daughter's daughter.	Translation.	226. My mother's mother's mother's sister's daughter's daughter's daughter—older than myself. (Female speaking.)	Translation.	227. My mother's mother's mother's sister's daughter's daughter's daughter. (Female speaking.)	Translation.
1	No-yeh′....................	My mother.	Ah′-je....................	My elder sister.	Ka-ah′-wuk	My daughter.
2	Kuh⌒no′-hä..............	" "	Uh-je′-ah....................	" " "	Ka-hä′-wuk....................	" "
3	Ah-ge-no′-hä	" "	Uh-je′-ah....................	" " "	Ka-hä′-wä	" "
4	Ahk-nole′-hä	" "	Ahk-je′-hä....................	" " "	Ka-yä′-hä	" "
5	Ah-ga-nese′-tä	" "	Ahk-je′-hä....................	" " "	Ka-yä′....................	" "
6	Oh′-nä....................	" "	Ahk′-je	" " "	Kä-yä′-no-nä	My child.
7	Lä-ga-nese′-tä-hä ..	" "	Ak-je′-yä (e.), Ka-gä′-ah (y.)	My eld. or young. sis.	Ka-yä′-ah	My daughter.
8	Ah-nä-uh	" "	A-ye′-uh	" " "	E-ne-ah′....................	" "
9	E-nah′....................	" "	Me-chuŋ′....................	" " "	Me-chuŋk′-she....................	" "
10	E-nah′....................	" "	Chu-ih′....................	" " "	Me-chounk′-she....................	" "
11	E′-nah....................	" "	Me-tank′-a-do....................	" " "	Me-chunk′-she....................	" "
12	En′-nä....................	" "	Tän′-ka	" " "	Me-chunk′-she....................	" "
13	E′-nah....................	" "	Chu-wa′....................	" " "	Me-chunk′-se-lä....................	" "
14	E′-nah....................	" "	Chu-a′....................	" " "	Me-chunk′-she....................	" "
15	E′-nah....................	" "	Chu-ih′....................	" " "	Me-chŭnk′-she....................	" "
16	E′-nah....................	" "	Chu-wa′....................	" " "	Me-chŭnk′-she....................	" "
17	E-nah′....................	" "	Me-chun′....................	" " "	Me-chunk′-she....................	" "
18	Nä′-hä....................	" "	Zhon-dä′-hä....................	" " "	Win-no′-ga	" "
19	E-nä′-hä....................	" "	Wee-zöŋ′-thä....................	" " "	We-zhuŋ′-ga	" "
20	Heen′-nah	" "	Heen-taŋ′-ga....................	" " "	Hee-yuŋ′-ga	" "
21	He′-nah....................	" "	Heen-tang′-a....................	" " "	He-yuŋ′-ga	" "
22	E′-naw....................	" "	Be-sho′-wa	" " "	Se-me′-she-gä	My girl.
23						
24	E-oo′-ne....................	" "	E-noo′....................	" " "	E-nook′....................	" "
25						
26						
27						
28	Ush′-kǏ....................	" "	Um-un′-nǏ....................	My elder sister.	Suh-sŭh′-take	My daughter.
29	Ush′-kǏ....................	" "	Um-un′-nǏ....................	" " "	Suh-soh′-take....................	" "
30	Sush′-kǏ....................	" "	An′-tik-bä....................	" " "	Su-soh′-take	" "
31	Chuhl-kŭ′-che..............	My little mother.	Chu-hlä′-hä....................	" " "	Chuch-hŭs′-wä	" "
32	E-tsI′....................	My mother.	Uŋ-gǏ-luŋ-I....................	" " "	A-gwae-tsI′....................	" "
33	Ah-gid′-ze	" "	Ah-ge-lä′-ih....................	" " "	A-gwa-tze	" "
34	Ah-te′-rä....................	" "	E-tä′-he	My sister.	Pe′-row	My child.
35						
36						
37	N'-gä′-we	" "	Ne-mis′....................	My elder sister.	N'-do′-sa-mis-kwame′....	My step-daughter.
38	N'-gä′-we	" "	Ne-mish′....................	" " "	N'-do′-zha-mis-kwame′....	" "
39	N'-ga′-wa	" "	Ne-mish′....................	" " "	N'-do′-zha-mis-kwem′	" "
40	Nin′-gäh	" "	NǏ-mis′-se....................	" " "	Nin-do′-zhǏ-miss....................	My step-child.
41	Nin′-gah	" "	Ne-de-ge′-ko....................	My step-sister.	Nin-do′-zhe-mis	" "
42	Nin′-gah	" "	Ne-mis-sä′....................	My elder sister.	Neen-dä′-niss....................	My daughter.
43	Ne-gä-sha′....................	" "	Ne-mis-sä′....................	" " "	N'-dä-niss′....................	" "
44	N'-gus′-sheh	" "	Ne-mis-sä′....................	" " "	N'-dä-niss′....................	" "
45	N'-geh′....................	" "	Ne-mis-sä′....................	" " "	N'-dä′-niss....................	" "
46	Niŋ-ge-ah′....................	" "	Ne-mis-sä′....................	" " "	Nin-dä′-nä....................	" "
47	Niŋ-ge-ah′....................	" "	Ne-mis-sä′....................	" " "	Nin-dä′-nä....................	" "
48	Niŋ-ge-ah′....................	" "	Ne-mis-sä′....................	" " "	Nin-dä′-nä....................	" "
49	Ne-ge-ah′....................	" "	Ne-me-sä′....................	" " "	N'-dä′-nä....................	" "
50	Ne-ge-ah′....................	" "	Ne-me-sä′....................	" " "	N'-dä′-nä....................	" "
51	Nä-ke⌒a′....................	" "	Nä-mis′-sä....................	" " "	Nä-tä′-nis....................	" "
52	Ne-ke⌒ah′....................	" "	Ne-ma′....................	" " "	Ne-täne′....................	" "
53	Nä′-ko....................	" "	Nä-ma′....................	" " "	Nä-tun′....................	" "
54	Ni-ke⌒ä′....................	" "	Ni-ta-tä-mä′....................	My sister.	Ni-tä-na-thä′....................	" "
55	Na-ke⌒ah′....................	" "	NǏ-mǏ-thä′....................	My elder sister.	NǏ-tä-na-thä′....................	" "
56						
57	Neex-ist′....................	" "	Nee-hist′-ä	" " "	N'-to′-to-tun....................	My step-daughter.
58						
59	N'-keech′....................	" "	N'-sees′....................	" " "	N'-tŭs′....................	My daughter.
60	N'-kee′-sees	My step-mother.	Nee-tse-kes′....................	My step-sister.	N'-su′-mus....................	" "
61	N'-guk′....................	My mother.	Ne-tä-kur′....................	" " "	Nee-chune′....................	" "
62	N'-gä-hä′-tut..........	My little mother.	Neet-koh′-kw′....................	" " "	N'-dä-nuss′....................	" "
63	Niŋ-guk′-us....................	" " "	Naᴉn-na-wase′....................	My elder sister.	Nain-dä′-ness....................	" "
64						
65						
66						
67						
68						
69						
70						
71						
72						
73						
74						
75						
76						
77						
78						
79						
80						

TABLE II.—Continued.

	228. My mother's mother's mother's sister's daughter's daughter's daughter's daughter's daughter.¹	Translation.	229. My husband.	Translation.	230. My wife.	Translation.
1	Ka-yä'-da	My granddaughter.	Da-yake'-ne	My husb. (2 joined).	Da-yake'-ne	My wife (2 joined).
2	Ka-yä'-dra	" "	Da-yäke-ne-yä'-seh	Two joined.	Da-yäke-ne-yä'-seh	Two joined.
3	Ka-yä'-da	" "	Da-hä-gis'-ne-a	" "	Da-yo-gis'-ne-a	" "
4	Ka-yä'-dla-ah	" "	Da-yäke-ne'-da	" "	Da-yäke-ne'-da	" "
5	E-yä'-dla-ah	" "	Da-yä-ga-ne'-dä	" "	Da-yä-ga-ne'-dä	" "
6	Kä-yä' rä	My grandchild.	Wak-dak'-gä	" "	Wak-dak'-gä	" "
7	Ka-yä-tä-ra'-yä	My granddaughter.	Da-yä-gä-ne'-tar-o	" "	Da-yä-gä-ne'-tar-o	" "
8	Ya-tra'-ah	" "	Tä-än'-de	" "	Tä-än'-de	" "
9	Me-tä'-ko-zhä	My grandchild.	Me-he'-hnä	My husband.	Me-tä'-win	My wife, my wom.
10	Me-tä'-ko-zhä	" "	Ma-e-gin'-nä	" "	Me-tä'-we-cho	" " "
11	Me-tä'-ko-zhä	" "	E-chak'-sä-me-ta'-we-do..	" "	We-nake'-chä-me-tä'-we-	My wife.
12	Me-tä'-ko-zha	" "	We-chas'-tä-ne-tä'-wä....	" "	Me-tä'-we ....[do	" "
13	Me tä'-ko-säk'-pok	" "	Me-hï-ga-nä	" "	Me-tä'-we	" "
14	Me-tä'-ko-zhä	" "	Me-he'-gin-a	" "	Me-tä'-we-ah	" "
15	Me-tä'-ko-zhä	" "	Ma-he'-gin-nä	" "	Me-tä'-wich	" "
16	Me-tä'-ko-zä	" "	Ma-he'-gin-nä	" "	Me-tä'-we-cho	" "
17	Me-tä'-ko-sä	" "	Ma-he'-gin-nä	" "	Me-tä'-we	" "
18	Toosh'-pä-hä	" "	We-ä-ge-nun'-ge	" "	We-gä-ke-nʌ	" "
19	Wee-tŭsh'-pä	" "	Wee-ä'-grŏṇ-kä	" "	Wee-gä'-thnough	" "
20	Heen-tä'-kwä-me	My granddaughter.	Heen-gä'-me	" "	Hee-tä'-me	" "
21	E-tä'-kwa	" "	En-kr-ä'-me	" "	Een-tä'-me	" "
22	Be-chose'-pä	My grandchild.	Ne-ka'	" "	Wä-ko'	" "
23			Ne-cha'	" "	Wa-che'	" "
24	E-choonsh'-ka-neke'	My little gd. daught.	E-kun'-ʌ	" "	E-chaw'-e	" "
25			Me-mer'-ŭl	" "	Moo'-hul	" "
26			Mä-ke-rä'	" "	Mä-tä-rä-we'-ä	" "
27			Bä'-che-na	" "	Moo'-a	" "
28	Sup'-uk	My granddaughter.	A-hä'-täk	My man.	Sä-take'-chI	" "
29	Sä'-pok	" "	A-hä'-täk	" "	Sut-take'-chI	" "
30	Sup'-pok	" "	Su-lau-a'-lI	He leads me.	SI-ä-wä'-yä	" "
31	Um-os-sŭs'-wä	My grandchild.	Chu-he'	My husband.	Chu-hi'-wä	" "
32	Uṇ-gĭ-lĭ'-sĭ	" "	Ah-gĭ-ya'-hĭ	" "	Ah-gwä-dä-lI	" "
33	Aṇ-ge-lee-a'-se	" "	Ah-ge-he-a'-hih	" "	Ag-gwä-dä-le'-ih	" "
34	Lak-te'-gee	My granddaughter.	Te-kŭ'-tuk-ŭ	" "	Ta-te'-luk-tuk-ŭ	" "
35			Tow-ä'-so	" "	Chä'-pot	" "
36			Ne-ko-ta-koo'	" "	Nä-te-nä-tä-koo	" "
37	No-se-sem'	My grandchild.	Nä-pem'	My man.	Ne-wä'	Part of myself.
38	No-se-sim'	" "	Nä-bame'	" "	Ne-wä'	" " "
39	No-se-sem'	" "	Nä-bim'	" "	Ne-wä'	" " "
40	No-zhĭ'-she	" "	Nin-wä-bem	" "	Nin-wĕ-dĭ-gĕ-mä-gan	My cohabitant.
41	No-zhe'-shä	" "	Ne-nä'-ba-mun	" "	Ne-we-te-ga'-nä-gan	" "
42	No-she-shä'	" "	Nee-nä'-bam	" "	Ne-wish'	Part of myself.
43	No-she-shä'	" "	Nä'-bam	" "	Ne-wish'	" " "
44	No-she-shä'	" "	Nä-bam'	" "	Ne-wish'	" " "
45	No-sä-seh'	" "	Nä-bam'	" "	Ne-wish'	" " "
46	No-sa-mä'	" "	Ne-nä'-bame-äh	" "	Nee-we'-wä	" " "
47	No-sa'-mä	" "	Nä-ba-mä'	" "	Ne-we-wä'	" " "
48	No-sa'-mä	" "	Nä-ba-mä'	" "	Ne-we-wä'	" " "
49	No-sa-mä'	" "	Nä-ba-mä'	" "	Ne-we-wä'	" " "
50	No-sa-mä'	" "	Nä-ba-mä'	" "	Ne'-wä	" " "
51	No-she-sem'	" "	Nä'-nä-bam	" "	Ne'-wä	" " "
52	No-she-sä'	" "	Ne-nä'-pe-äm	" "	Na'-yo	" " "
53	Nä-h'-kä'	" "	Na'-am	" "	Nä-tsem	My wife.
54	No-se-thä'-mä	" "	Na-nä-pa-mä	" "	Na-wä	" "
55	No-stha-thä'	" "	Wa-se-ah'	My husband.	Ne-wä'	" "
56			Näse		Na-ta-tä'-hä	" "
57	Nee-so'-tan	" "	Nome	My man.	Ne-to-ke'-man	" "
58			No'-mä	" "	Ne-toh'-ke'-man	" "
59	Nŭ-jeech'	" "	N'-che'-nu-nŭs'	My husband.	N'-t-a-bĭ-tem'	" "
60	N'-kway'-nus	" "	Nus-kee-chä'-bem	My man.	N'-tay-pee'-tem	My woman.
61	Nä-hise'	" "	Wä-he-yuh'	My husband.	Nu-e-nä-thome'	My wife.
62	Noh'-whese'	" "	Wee-chaa'-oke	My aid through life.	Wee-chaa'-oke	My aid thro' life.
63	Nain-no-whase'	" "	Na-wä-h'-an	My male.	Na-na-h'-wh'	My wife.
64			Sa-ten'-ne	My man.	Sa-tsa'-ka	My woman.
65			Sa-ten'-ne	" "	Sa-ja'-kwe	" "
66			Set-den'-na		Set-ze'-ä-na	
67			Suk-ingh	My husband.	Sa-ut	My wife.
68			Su-ku-i. ᵇSe-te-koon-du-i	" "	Se-tran-jo. ᵇSu-hut	" "
69			Is-heh-low	" "	In-no'ch'-ho-no'ch'	" "
70			Ese-hile'-wa	" "	E-nah'-naw	" "
71			In-mäm	" "	Ask'-sham	" "
72			Kan-u-kläk-a-nak	" "	Kat'hlä-mo	" "
73			Ton-uṇ-äṇ	" "	Mä-mä-sä-gwä	" "
74			Sä'-trü	" "	Sauk'-we	" "
75			No-vis-o. ᵇNo-vi-to-wa	" "	No-vis-o	" "
76			Kee-tock	" "	Kee-tock	" "
77			Sä-hä-o'-ä	" "	Gu-i'	" "
78			Oo-ĕ-gä	" "	Oo-ly-aŭg-ä	" "
79			U-vi-ga	" "	Nu-li-a-ra	" "
80			Wing'-ä	" "	Nu-g'le-ung'-ä	" "

TABLE II.—*Continued.*

	231. My husband's father.	Translation.	232. My husband's mother.	Translation.	233. My husband's grandfather.	Translation.
1	Hä-ga'-să	My father-in-law.	Oŋ-ga'-să	My mother-in-law.	Hä-ga'-să	My father-in-law.
2	Hä-ga-să-ah	" "	Oŋ-ga'-să-ah	" "	Hä-ga'-să-ah	" "
3	Hoc-să'-wă	" "	Oc-să'-wă	" "	Hoc-să'-wă	" "
4	Hä-gwale-hose'-hă	" "	Un-gwale-hose'-hă	" "	Hä-gwale-hose'-hă	" "
5	Lä-gwen-ho'-ză	" "	Yun-gwen-ho'-ză	" "	Lä-gwen-ho'-ză	" "
6	Yä-thaf'	" "	Yä-thaf'	" "	Yä-thaf'	" "
7						
8	Hä-ya-na-mă	" "	Ah-ya'-na-mă	" "	———	Not related.
9	Tuŋ-kaŋ'-she	" "	Un-che'-she	" "	Taŋ-kăŋ'-she-dăŋ	My grandfather.
10	To-kä'-she	" "	O-che'-she	" "	Toon-kä'-she-nă	" "
11	Me-tan'-kă	" "	O-che'-she	" "	Tun-kä'-she-lă	" "
12	To-kä'-she	" "	Ko-o'-che	" "	To-kä'-she-lä	" "
13	Tŭŋ-kä'-she	" "	Oon-che'-she	" "	Me-tonk'-ah	" "
14	Tŭŋ-kä'-she	" "	Un-che'-she	" "	Tăn-kä'-she	My father-in-law.
15	To-kä'-she	" "	O-che'-she	" "	Toon-kä'-zhe-lä	My grandfather.
16	To-kä'-she	" "	O-che'-she	" "	Toh'-kä'-she-la	" "
17	Me-to'-gä-she	" "	Me-toh'-we	My aunt.	Me-to'-gä-she	" "
18	Ta-gä'-hă	My grandfather.	Gä-hä'	My grandmother.	Ta-gä'-hă	" "
19	Wee-te'-ga	" "	Wee'-te'-a	" "	Wee-te'-ga	" "
20	Hee-too'-ga	" "	He-koo-n'ye	" "	Hee-too'-ga	" "
21	E-tŭ'-kă	" "	Hiŋ-kŭ'-ne	" "	E-tŭ'-kă	" "
22	Be-che'-go	" "	E-ko'	" "	Be-che'-go	" "
23	We-che'-cho	" "	E-che'	" "	We-che'-cho	" "
24	E-cho'-ka	" "	E-ko'-ro-ka	" "	E-cho'-ro-ka	" "
25	Ko-too'-te	My father-in-law.	Ko-too'-te	My mother-in-law.		
26	Mä-nä'-tish	" "	Mä-too-tä'-kä	" "		
27	Ah-h·a'	My father.	E'-ke-ă	My mother.		
28	Um-uh'-fo	My grandfather.	Up-puk'-ne	My grandmother.	Um-uh'-fo	" "
29	Um-u'-fo	" "	Up-pok'-ne	" "	Um-u'-fo	" "
30	Um-u-fo'-sĭ	My little grandfather.	Hap-po'-sĭ	" "	Um-u'-fo-si	My little gd. father.
31	Um-mä'-he	My father-in-law.	Um-hok-tŭl'-wă	My mother-in-law.	Um-mä'-he	My father-in-law.
32	E-hnä-tsĭ'	My parent-in-law.	E-hnä-tsĭ'	My parent-in-law.	E-hnä-tsĭ'	My parent-in-law.
33	Tse-nä'-tze	" "	Tse-nä'-tze	" "	Tse-nä'-tze	
34	Kool'-er-hoos	My old man.	Chose'-tit	My old woman.	Kool'-er-hoos	My old man.
35	Kool'-er-hoose	" " "	Chose'-tit	" " "	Kool'-er-hoose	" " "
36	Nä-toot-kä'-koo	My parent-in-law.	Nä-toot-kä'-koo	My parent-in-law.	Nä-toot-kä'-koo	
37	Nee-sis'	My uncle.	Nis-sĭ-goos'	My aunt.	Ne-mo-some'	My grandfather.
38	Nee-sis'	" "	Nis-se-goos'	" "	Ne-mo-shome'	" "
39	Nee-sis'	" "	Nĭ-sĭ-goos'	" "	Na-mo-shome'	" "
40	Nĭ-sĭ'-miss	My father-in-law.	Nĭ-sĭ-go'-siss	My mother-in-law.	Nĭ-mĭ-sho'-miss	" "
41					Ne-me-sho'-mis	" "
42	Nee'n-zhe-nis'	" "	N'-za-gwä-zis'	" "	Na-ma-sho-mis'	" "
43	Ne-zhe-nis'	" "	N'-zik'-zis	" "	Ne-mis'-sho-mis'	" "
44	Ne-zha-nis'	" "	N'-za-gwä-zis'	" "	Ne-zha-nis'	My father-in-law.
45	N'-zhen-niss'	" "	N'-za-go-sis'	" "	N'-zhen-niss'	" "
46	No-sa-mah'	" "	No-sa-mah'	" "	No-sa-mah'	" "
47	No-sa-mah'	" "	No-sa-mah'	" "	No-sa-mah'	" "
48	No-sa-mah'	" "	No-sa-mah'	" "	No-sa-mah'	" "
49	No-sa-mah'	" "	No-sa-mah'	" "	No-sa-mah'	" "
50	No-sa-mah'	" "	No-sa-mah'	" "	No-sa-mah'	" "
51	Nă-mä-sho-mä	" "	No-ko'-ma	" "	Nă-mä'-sho-mä	" "
52	Na-sha'-nä	" "	Ne-shä'-ke-shä	" "	Nă-mä'-sho	" "
53	Nă-mĭ-sheme'	" "	Nă-rĭ-skim'	" "	Nam-a-shim'	My grandfather.
54	Wa-si'-na-mä-kă	" "	Wa-si'-na-mä	" "		
55	Wa-se-ah'-O-thä-le'	" "	Wa-se-ah'-O-ka-le'	" "	Wa-se-ah'-O-thä-le'	My father-in-law.
56	Na-sit'	" "	Na-ha'-hä	" "		
57	Ne-tä'-so-ko	" "	Ne-tä'-ke-äse	" "	Nä-ah'-să	My grandfather.
58	Nin'-nä	My father.	Nee-krist'	My mother.	Nä-ah·xs'	" "
59	N'-chilch'	My father-in-law.	N'-chú-gwe'-jich	My mother-in-law.	N'-chilch'	My father-in-law.
60	N'-seel'-hŭhs	" "	N'-su'-kwus	" "	N'-seel'-hŭhs	" "
61	N'-zein-noth'	" "	N'-zo-kwaths'	" "	N'-zein-noth'	" "
62	N'-zhe'-luh-looh'	" "	N'-zoo-kwese'	" "		
63	Ne-ze-la-loze'	" "	Nain-zo-kwase'	" "		
64	Sa-tse'-a	My grandfather.	Sa-tsun'	My grandmother.	Sa-tse'-a	My grandfather.
65	Sa-ten'-ne-ba-tä	My father-in-law.	Sa-cho'-na	" "	Sa-tä'-choek	" "
66	Seth'-a	" "	Set'-so	My aunt.	Set-see'-a	" "
67						
68	Set-ye	" "	So-tre	My mother-in-law.	Set-se	" "
69	Is-hah'-hä	" "	En'e-tsats'-tsh	" "		
70	Ese-h·ä'-hä	" "	Eel-cheetsk'	" "		
71	En-pe-natsh'	" "	En-pe-natsh'	" "		
72	Kan-a-wäs-patl	" "	Kan-a-wäs-patl	" "		
73	Tä-tä'-wähe-ät-sin	" "			Tä-tä'-wä-be-at-sin	" "
74	Shko'-ă-te	" "	Shko'-ă-te	" "	Nish-te'-ă	My father.
75	No-vis-ei-sen-do	" "	E-a-kwi-a	" "		
76	Oo-păp-kee-tock	" "	Oo-nă-kee-tock	" "		
77	Gu-ä'-că	" "	Chä-hu-ä'-i-ä	" "		
78	Noo-ly-ă-mä-ah-tä-tä	My husband's father.	A-kee-gă	" "	Ah-tä-tä-tchă-nä	My grandfather.
79	Sa-ki-ga	My parent-in-law.	Sa-ki-ga	My parent-in-law.		
80	Shak-ing'-ă	" "	Shak-ing'-ä	" "	E-tŭ'-ah	" "

TABLE II.—*Continued.*

	234. My husband's grandmother.	Translation.	235. My wife's father.	Translation.	236. My wife's mother.	Translation.
1	Oŋ-ga'-să	My mother-in-law.	Oc-na'-hose	My father-in-law.	Oc-na'-hose	My mother-in-law.
2	Oŋ-ga'-să-ah	" "	Unc-na'-hose	" "	Unc-na'-hose	" "
3	Oc-să'-wä	" "	Hä-ga-nane'-hose	" "	O-ga-nane'-hose	" "
4	Un-gwale-hose'-hä	" "	Hä-gwale-hose'-hä	" "	Un-gwale-hose'-hä	" "
5	Un-gwen-ho'-ză	" "	Lä-gwen-ho'-ză	" "	Un gwen-ho'-ză	" "
6	Yä-thaf'	" "	Yak-te'-he-a-tho	" "	Yak-te'-he-a-tho	" "
7			Le-an-hose'-hä	" "	Le-an-hose'-hä	" "
8	———	Not related.	Hä-ya'-na-mä	" "	Ah-ya'-na-mä	" "
9	Uŋ-che'	My grandmother.	Tuŋ-käŋ'-she	" "	Un-che'-she	" "
10	O-che'	" "	To-kä'-she	" "	O-che'-she	" "
11	O-che'-lä	" "	Me-ton'-kä	" "	Ko-o'-che	" "
12	Oh-che'	" "	To-kä'-she	" "		
13	Oo-che'	" "	Me-tonk'-ah	My grandfather.	Oo-che'	My grandmother.
14	Un-che'-she	My mother-in-law.	Tün-kä'-she	My father-in-law.	Un-che'-she	My mother-in-law.
15	O-che'	My grandmother.	To-kä'-she	" "	O-che'-she	" "
16	O-che'-she	" "	To-kä'-she	" "	O-che'-she	" "
17	O-ge'-she	" "	Me-to'-gä-she	" "	Me-toh'-we	My aunt.
18	Gä-hä'	" "	Ta-gä'-hä	My grandfather.	Gä-hä'	My grandmother.
19	Wee'-kä	" "	Ashe-ah'-ga	My old man.	Gah'-ah	My mother-in-law.
20	He-koo-n'ye	" "	Hee-too'-ga	My father-in-law.	He-koo'-n'ye	My aunt
21	Hiŋ-kŭ'-ne	" "	E-tŭ'-kä	" "	Hiŋ-kŭ'-ne	" "
22	E-ko'	" "	S'ah'-ga	My old man.	Wä-ko'-s'ah-ga	My old woman.
23	E-che'	" "				
24	E-ko'-ro-ka	" "	E-cho'-ka	" " "	E-ko'-ro-ka	" " "
25						
26			Mä-nä'-tish	My father-in-law.	Mä-too-tä'-kä	My mother-in-law.
27			Boo'-sha	My father.	Boo'-sha-gä-na	My mother.
28	Up-puk'-ne	" "	Sup-po'-chĭ	My father-in-law.	Sup-po'-chĭ. O-hoy'-oh	My mother-in-law.
29	Up-pok'-ne	" "	Sä-po'-chĭ	" "	Sä-po'-chĭ. O-ho'-yo	" "
30	Hap-po'-sĭ	" "	Sä-po'-chĭ	" "	Sä-po'-chĭ. O-ho'-yo	" "
31	Um-hok-tŭl'-wä	My mother-in-law.	Um-mä'-he	" "	Un-hok-tŭl'-wä	" "
32	E-hnä-tsĭ'	" "	E-dsau'-hĭ	" "	E-dsau'-hĭ	" "
33	Tse-nä'-tze	" "	Tse-nä'-tze	" "	Tse-nä'-tze	" "
34	Chose'-tit	My old woman.	Kool'-er-hoos	My old man.	Chose'-tit	My old woman.
35	Chose'-tit	" " "				
36			Nä-toot-kä'-koo	My parent-in-law.	Nä-toot-kä'-koo	My parent-in-law.
37	Noh'-kome'	My grandmother.	Nee-sis'	My uncle.	Nis-sĭ-goos'	My aunt.
38	No-kome'	" "	Nee-sis'	" "	Nis-se-goos'	" "
39	No-kome'	" "	Nee-sis'	" "	Nĭ-sĭ-goos'	" "
40	No'-ko-miss	" "	Nĭ-sĭ'-miss	My father-in-law.	Nĭ-sĭ-go'-sis	My mother-in-law.
41	No'-ko-mis	" "				
42	No-ko'-mis	" "	Nee'n-zhä-nis'	" "	N'-za-gwä-zis'	" "
43	No-ko-mis'	" "	Ne-zhe-nis'	" "	Ne-zeke-zis'	" "
44	N'-za-gwä-zis'	My mother-in-law.	Ne-zha-nis'	" "	N'-za-gwä-zis'	" "
45	N'-za-go-sis'	" "	N'-zhen-niss'	" "	N'-za-go-sis'	" "
46	No-sa-mah'	" "	Na-ma-sho-ma-ga'	" "		
47	No-sa-mah'	" "	Na-ma'-sho-mä'-ke-äh'	" "	Ne-zak'-ses-a-ke-ah'	" "
48	No-sa-mah'	" "	Na-ma'-sho-mä'-ke-äh'	" "	Ne-zak'-ses-a-ke-ah'	" "
49	No-sa-mah'	" "	Na-ma'-sho-mä'-ke-ah'	" "	Ne-zak'-ses-a-ke-ah'	" "
50	No-sa-mah'	" "	Na-ma'-sho-mä'-ke-ah'	" "	Ne-zak'-ses-a-ke-ah'	" "
51	No-ko'-mä	My grandmother.	Nä-mä'-sho-mä	" "	No-ko'-mä	" "
52	No'-ko-ma	" "	Na-sha'-nä	" "	Ne-shä'-ke-shä	" "
53	Nä-vish'-kim	" "	Nä-mĭ-sheme'	" "	Nä-ri-skim'	" "
54			Wa-si-na-mä-kä	" "	Wa-si-na-mä-kä	" "
55	Wa-se-ah'-O-ka-le'	My mother-in-law.	Wa-se-ah'-O-thä-le'	" "	Wä-se-ah'-O-thä-le'	" "
56			Na-sa'-ta	" "	Na-ha'-hä	" "
57	Ne-tä-ke-ä'-să	My grandmother.	Ne-tä'-so-ko	" "	Ne-tä'-ke-äse	" "
58	Ne-tä'-ke-ahxs	" "	Nä-ah'xs'	My grandfather.	Ne-tä'-ke-ah'xs	My grandfather.
59	N'-chŭ-gwe'-jich	My mother-in-law.	N'-chilch'	My father-in-law.	N'-chŭ-gwe'-jich'	My mother-in-law.
60	N'-sŭ'-kwus	" "	N'-see'-hŭhs	" "	N'-sŭ'-kwus	" "
61	N'-zo-kwaths'	" "	N'-zein-noth'	" "	N'-zo-kwaths'	" "
62			N'-zhe'-luh-looh'	" "	N'-zoo-kwatse'	" "
63			Ne-ze-la-loze'	" "	Nain-zo-kwase'	" "
64	Sa-tsun	" "	Sa-tse'-a	My grandfather.	Sa-tsun'	My grandmother.
65	Sa-cho'-na	" "	Sa-ja'-kwe-ba-tä	" "	A'-nä	My mother.
66	Set-sa'-nä	" "	Seth'-a	My father-in-law.	Set'-so	My aunt.
67						
68	Soo-tre	" "	Set-ye	" "	Soo-tre	My mother-in-law.
69			Is-hah'-hä	" "	En'l-tsats'-tsh	" "
70						
71			En-pe-shass'	" "	En-swagh'	" "
72			Kan-a-wäs-patl	" "	Kan-a-wäs-patl	" "
73	Tä-tä'-wä-le-at-sin	" "				
74	Ni'-ya	My mother.	Nish-te'-ä	My father.	Ni'-ya	My mother.
75			No-viw-a-sen-do	My father-in-law.	E-a-kwi-a	My mother-in-law.
76						
77			Chi-cä	" "		
78			Noo-ly-ä-mä-ah-tä-tä	My wife's father.	Noo-le-ä-mä-nä-nä	My wife's mother.
79			Sa-ki-ga	My parent-in-law.	Sa-ki-ga	My parent-in-law.
80	Ning-e-o'-wä	My grandmother.	Chek-ing'-ä	" "	Chek-ing'-ä	" "

TABLE II.—*Continued.*

	237. My wife's grandfather.	Translation.	238. My wife's grandmother.	Translation.	239. My son-in-law. (Male speaking)	Translation.
1	Hoo'-sote....................	My grandfather.	Oc'-sote....................	My grandmother.	Oc-na'-hose	My son-in-law.
2	Hoo'-sote....................	" "	Oc'-sote....................	" "	Unc-na'-hose................	" "
3	Hoo-so'-dä-hä.	" "	Oc-so'-dä-hä.	" "	Ha-nane'-hose...............	" "
4	Hä-gwale-hose'-hä	My father-in-law.	Un-gwale-hose'-hä	My mother-in-law.	Ha-yale-hose'-hä..........	" "
5	Läke-sote'..................	My grandfather.	Ahk-sote'...................	My grandmother.	E-en-hŭ'-zä................	" "
6	Ahk-rä'-sote	" "	Ahk-sote'...................	" "	Yäk-te-he-ah'-thä...........	" "
7	Lok-sote'-hä	" "	Ak-sote'-hä	" "	Le-an-hose'-hä..............	" "
8	———	Not related.	———	Not related.	Ha-na'-mäque..............	" "
9	Tuŋ-käŋ'-she-däŋ..........	My grandfather.	Uŋ-che'....................	My grandmother.	Me-tä'-kosh................	" "
10	Toon-kä'-she-nä...........	" "	O-che'....................	" "	Me-tä'-koash...............	" "
11	Tun-kä'-she-lä	" "	O-che'-lä.................	" "	Me-tä'-koash...............	" "
12	To-kä'-she-lä	" "	Oh-che'...................	" "	Me-tä'-koash...............	" "
13	Me-tonk'-ah................	" "	Oo-che'...................	" "	Me-tä'-kosh................	" "
14	Tŭn-kä'-she-lä	My father-in-law.	Un-che'-zhe	My mother-in-law.	Me-tä'-kosh................	" "
15	Toon-kä'-she-lä	My grandfather.	O-che'....................	My grandmother.	Me-tä'-koäsh...............	" "
16	Toh'-kä'-she-la	" "	O-che'....................	" "	Me-tä'-goash...............	" "
17	Me-to'-gä-she	" "	O-gä'-she	" "	Me-tä'-goash...............	" "
18	Ta-gä'-hä	" "	Gä-hä'....................	" "	We-tuh'-da.................	" "
19	Wee-te'-ga	" "	Wee'-kä..................	" "	We-töŋ'-da.................	" "
20	Hee-too'-ga	" "	He-koo'-n'ye	" "	Wä-do'-hä.................	" "
21	E-tŭ'-kä	" "	Hiŋ-kŭ'-ne	" "	Wan-do'-ha................	" "
22	S'ah'-ga	My old man.	Wä-ko-s'ah'-ga............	My old woman.	Be-to'-ja..................	" "
23					We-ton'-chä...............	" "
24	E-cho'-ka	" "	E-ko'-ro-ka................	" "	ªWä-to'-hö. ᵇE-wong'-o-no	" "
25					Ko-too'-te.................	" "
26					Mä-too'-te................	" "
27					Boo'-sha..................	" "
28	Sup-po'-chĭ................	My father-in-law.	Sup-po'-chĭ. O-hoy'-oh....	My mother-in-law.	Sai'-yup..................	" "
29	Sä-po'-chĭ..................	" "	Sä-po'-chĭ. O-ho'-yo.......	" "	Säi'-yop..................	" "
30	Sä-po'-chĭ..................	" "	Sä-po'-chĭ. O-ho'-yo.......	" "	Sä'-yup...................	⌠on. My present hanger
31	Um-mä'-he.................	" "	Un-hok-tŭl'-wä	" "	Un-hu-tis'-se	My son-in-law.
32	E-dsau'-hĭ.................	" "	E-dsau'-hĭ................	" "	E-hnä-tsĭ'.................	" "
33	Tse-nä'-tze	" "	Tse-nä'-tze	" "	Ah-ge-h'nä'-ṫzĕ............	" "
34	Kool'-er-hoos	My old man.	Ch·ose-tit..................	My old woman.	Koos-tow'-et-sŭ............	" "
35					Ko-stä'-witch..............	" "
36					Koh·-tä-wa'-sŭh...........	" "
37	Ne-mo-some'..............	My grandfather.	Noh'-kome'	My grandmother.	Nä-hak'-sim...............	" "
38	Ne-mo-shome'.............	" "	No-kome'	" "	Nä-hak'-sim...............	" "
39	Na-mo-shome'.............	" "	No-kome'	" "	N'-hä'-ke-shim............	" "
40	Nĭ-mĭ-sho'-miss...........	" "	No'-ko-miss...............	" "	Nĭ-nin'-gwän..............	" "
41	Ne-me-sho'-mis............	" "	No'-ko-mis................	" "	Ne-nin'-gwun.............	" "
42	Na-ma-sho'-mis............	" "	No-ko'-mis................	" "	Ne-niŋ-gwun'.............	" "
43	Ne-mis'-sho-mis'..........	" "	No-ko-mis'................	" "	Na-niŋ-gwun'.............	" "
44	Na-ma-sho'-mis............	" "	No-ko-mis'................	" "	Nə-niŋ-gwun'.............	" "
45	Na-ma-sho'-mis............	" "	No-ko-mis'................	" "	N'-do'-she-na-game'.......	" "
46	Na-ma-sho'-mis............	" "	No-ko'-mis................	" "	Nä-huŋ-gä-na.............	" "
47	Na-mä'-sho-mä'...........	" "	No-ko-mä'................	" "	Na-lä'-gwä-lä'............	" "
48	Na-mä'-sho-mä'...........	" "	No-ko-mä'................	" "	Na-lä'-gwä-lä'............	" "
49	Na-mä'-sho-mä'...........	" "	No-ko-mä'................	" "	N'-dä-gwä-lä'.............	" "
50	Na-mä'-sho-mä'...........	" "	No-ko-mä'................	" "	N'-dä-gwä-lä'.............	" "
51	Nä-mä'-sho-mis...........	" "	No-ko'-mä................	" "	Nä-nä-kwem..............	" "
52	Na-mä'-sho................	" "	No'-ko-mä................	" "	Ne-nä'-kwun..............	" "
53	Nam-a-shim'..............	" "	Nä-vish'-kim		Nich-ä'...................	" "
54					Na-nä-kwam-nä'..........	" "
55	Na-ma-some-thä'..........	" "	No-kome-thä'..............	" "	Nin-hä-kä-na-mä'.........	" "
56	No-bes'-sib-ä..............	" "	Na'-e-bä..................	" "	Na-täs'...................	" "
57	Nä-ah'-sä..................	" "	Ne-tä-ke-ä'-sä	" "	Nis.......................	" "
58	Nä-ah·xs'..................	" "	Ne-tä'-ke-ahxs	" "	Nis.......................	" "
59	N'-chilch'..................	My father-in-law.	N'-chŭ-gwe'-jich...........	My mother-in-law.	N'-tlŭ'-sŭk................	" "
60	N'-see'-chŭhs..............	" "	N'-sŭ'-kwus...............	" "	N'-tlŭ'-sŭk................	" "
61	N'-zein-noth...............	" "	N'-zo-kwaths'.............	"	Wä-seen'-no-kwä'..........	⌠benefit. My hunter for my
62					Nä-to-na'-mä'-kw'........	My son-in-law.
63					Na-nä-to'-na-makue	
64	Sa-tse'-a.ª	My grandfather.	Sa-tsun'..................	My grandmother.	Se-ga'-ton.................	" "
65	Sa-tä'-chock..............	" "	Sa-cho'-na	" "	Sa-tsä'-ya.................	" "
66	Set-see'-a	" "	Set-sa'-nä.................	" "	Set-shi'-ya................	" "
67					Sa-che-kingh..............	" "
68	Set-se.....................	" "	Soo-tre....................	" "	Set-she-ku-i...............	" "
69					Is-natch'l-hu..............	" "
70					Ees-neek'-allou	" "
71					En-pe-shass'..............	
72						" "
73					Tä-tä'-wä-bä.............	" "
74	Nish-te'-ä.................	My father.	Ni-ya.....................	My mother.	Sa-wä'-te.................	" "
75					So-eng-gi.................	" "
76					Ku-nee-u	" "
77					Chu'-ä....................	" "
78	Noo-le-ä-mä-a-tä-ta-	My wife's gd. father.			Ning-ä-oo-wä.............	" "
79	[tchang-ä	" " "	Ning-e-o'-wä..............		Ning-a-u-ga...............	" "
80	E-tŭ'-ah....................	" " "		My grandmother.	Ning-a-ou'-gwä............	

TABLE II.—*Continued.*

	240. My son-in-law. (Female speaking.)	Translation.	241. My daughter-in-law. (Male speaking.)	Translation.	242. My daughter-in-law. (Female speaking.)	Translation.
1	Oc-na'-hose..............	My son-in-law.	Ka'-sä..............	My daught.-in-law.	Ka'-sä..............	My daught.-in-law.
2	Uno-na'-hose..............	" "	Ka-sa-yuh'..............	" "	Ka-sa-yuh'..............	" "
3	Ha-nane'-hose............	" "	Ka-sä'-wä..............	" "	Ka-sä'-wä..............	" "
4	Ha-yale-hose'-hä.........	" "	Ka-zä'-wä..............	" "	Ka-zä'-wä..............	" "
5	E-en-hŭ'-zä..............	" "	Ka-zä'-wä..............	" "	Ka-zä'-wä..............	" "
6	Yak-te-he-ah'-thä........	" "	Ahk-thaf'..............	" "	Ahk-thaf'..............	" "
7	Le-an-hose'-hä..........	" "	Ka-sä'-wä..............	" "	Ka-sä'-wä..............	" "
8	Ha-na'-mäque..........	" "	Ya-nä'-mäque..........	" "	Ya-nä'-mäque..........	" "
9	Me-tä'-kosh..........	" "	Me-tä'-kosh..........	" "	Me-tä'-kosh..........	" "
10	Me-tä'-koash..........	" "	Me-ta'-koash..........	" "	Me-tä'-koash..........	" "
11	Me-tä'-koash..........	" "	Me-tä'-koash..........	" "	Me-tä'-koash..........	" "
12	Me-tä'-koash..........	" "	Me-tä'-koash..........	" "	Me-tä'-koash..........	" "
13	Me-tä'-kosh..........	" "	Me-tä'-kosh..........	" "	Me-tä'-kosh..........	" "
14	Me-tä'-kosh..........	" "	Me-tä'-kosh..........	" "	Me-tä'-kosh..........	" "
15	Me-tä'-koash..........	" "	Me-tä'-koash..........	" "	Me-tä'-koash..........	" "
16	Me-tä'-goash..........	" "	Me-tä'-goash..........	" "	Me-tä'-goash..........	" "
17	Me-tä'-goash..........	" "	Me-tä'-koash..........	" "	Me-tä'-koash..........	" "
18	We-tuh'-da..........	" "	Ta-ne'-hä..........	" "	Ta-ne'-hä..........	" "
19	We-tŏn'-da..........	" "	We-te'-na..........	" "	We-te'-na..........	" "
20	Wä-do'-hä..·..........	" "	Heen-toan'-ye..........	" "	Heen-toan'-ye..........	" "
21	Wan-do'-ha..........	" "	Hin-to'-ne..........	" "	Hin-to'-ne..........	" "
22	Be-to'-ja..........	" "	Be-je'-na..........	" "	Be-je'-na..........	" "
23	We-ton'-chä..........	" "	We-che'-ne..........	" "	We-che'-ne..........	" "
24	aWä-to'-hö. bE-wong'-o-no	" "	E-nook-chek'-aw-chau......	" "	E-nook-chek'-aw-chau......	" "
25	Ko-too'-te..........	" "	Ko-too'-te..........	" "	Ko-too'-te..........	" "
26	Ma-too'-te..........	" "	Mä-too'-gä..........	" "	Mä-too'-gä..........	" "
27	Boo'-sha..........	" "	Bos-me'-ä-kun-is-ta....	" "	Mä-nä'-ka..........	" "
28	Sai'-yup..........	" "	Sup'-uk..........	My gd. daughter.	Sup'-uk..........	My gd. daughter.
29	Säi'-yop..........	" "	Sä'-pok..........	" "	Sä'-pok..........	" "
30	Sä'-yup..........	" "	Sup-pok'-take..........	My daught.-in-law.	Sup-pok'-take..........	My daught.-in-law.
31	Un-hu-tis'-se..........	" "	Un-hu-tis'-se..........	" "	Un-hu-tis'-se..........	" "
32	E-hnä'-tsĭ'..........	" "	E-tsau'-hĭ..........	" "	E-tsau'-hĭ..........	" "
33	Ah-ge-h'nä'-tze..........	" "	Ah-ge-tzau'-hĭ..........	" "	Ah-ge-tzau'-hĭ..........	" "
34	Koos-tow'-et-sä..........	" "	Scoo'-rus..........	" "	Scoo'-rus..........	" "
35	Ko-stä'-witch..........	" "	Sko'-dus..........	" "	Sko'-dus..........	" "
36	Koh'-tä-wa'-sŭh..........	" "	Sko-roo'-hoo..........	" "	Sko-roo'-hoo..........	" "
37	Nä-hak'-sim..........	" "	Neese-tim'..........	" "	Neese-tim'..........	" "
38	Nä-hak'-sim..........	" "	Neesh-tim'..........	" "	Neesh-tim'..........	" "
39	N'-hä'-ke-shim..........	" "	Neesh-tim'..........	" "	Neesh-tim'..........	" "
40	Nĭ-nin'-gwän..........	" "	Nis'-sim..........	" "	Nis'-sim..........	" "
41	Ne-nin'-gwun..........	" "	Ne'-sim..........	" "	Ne'-sim..........	" "
42	Ne-niṇ-gwun..........	" "	Ne-sim'..........	" "	Ne-sim'..........	" "
43	Na-niṇ-gwun'..........	" "	Ne-sim'..........	" "	Ne-sim'..........	" "
44	Ne-niṇ-gwun'..........	" "	Ne-sim'..........	" "	Ne-sim'..........	" "
45	N'-do'-she-na-game'......	" "	Ne-ah'-ga-neh-gweh'..	" "	Ne-ah'-ga-neh-gweh'..	" "
46	Nä-huṇ-gä-nä..........	" "	Lan-gwä'-lä..........	" "	Lan-gwä'-lä..........	" "
47	Na-lä'-gwä-lä'..........	" "	Nä-hä'-gä-na'-kwä-No-ko-mä'	" "	Nä-hä-gä-na'-kwä-No-ko-mä'	" "
48	Na-lä'-gwä-lä'..........	" "	Nä-hä'-gä-na'-kwä-No-ko-mä'	" "	Nä-hä-gä-na'-kwä-N -ko-mä'	" "
49	N'-dä-gwä'-lä'..........	" "	Na-hä-gä-na-kwä-No-ko-mä'	" "	Nä-hä'-gä-na-kwä-No-ko-mä'	" "
50	N'-dä-gwä-lä'..........	" "	Na-hä-gä-na-kwä'-No-ko-mä'	" "	Nä-hä-gä-na-kwä-No-ko-mä'	" "
51	Nä-nä-kwem'..........	" "	Nä-sem'-yä..........	" "	Nä-hä-gä'-ne-kwam..	" "
52	Ne-nä'-kwun..........	" "	No-hä'-kun-e-uk-ye-yu'....	" "	No-hä'-kun-e-uk-ye-yu'....	" "
53	Nich-ä'..........	" "	Nich-ä'..........	" "	Nich-ä'..........	" "
54	Na-nä-kwam-nä'..........	" "	Na-them-mi-lä..........	" "	Na-them-mi-lä..........	" "
55	Nin-hä-kä-na-mä'..........	" "	Nĭ-tha-mĭ-ah'..........	" "	Ni-tha-mĭ-ah'..........	" "
56	Na-täs'..........	" "	Nä-tim'..........	" "	Nä-tim'..........	" "
57	Nis..........	" "	Ne-mis'..........	" "	Ne-mis'..........	" "
58	Nis..........	" "	Ne'-mis..........	" "	Ne'-mis..........	" "
59	N'-tlŭ'-sŭk..........	" "	N'-thus-wä'-skom..........	" "	N'-thus-wä-skom..........	" "
60	N'-tlŭ'-sŭk..........	" "	N'-sum'..........	" "	N'-sum'..........	" "
61	Wä-seen'-no-kwä'..........	My hunter.	Nä-hum'..........	My cook.	Nä-hum'..........	My cook.
62	Nä-to-na-mä'-kw'..........		Nah'-hum'..........	My cook.	Nah'-hum'..........	
63	Na-nä-to-na-makue'......	My son-in-law.	Nain-hum'..........	My daught.-in-law.	Nain-hum'..........	My daught.-in-law.
64	Sa-chĭ'-a..........	" "	Sa-t'thu'-a..........	My grandchild.	Sa-chä'-ya.	My grandchild.
65	aSa-ja'-kwe. bSa-ya-ze-la-	" "	Sa-tsä'-ya..........	My daught.-in-law.	Sa-tsä'-ya. Sa-yä-za-la-ja'-	My daught.-in-law.
66	Set-shi'-ya.......[ja'-kwe	" "	Set-thu'-ya..........	" "	Set-thu'-ya.......[kwe	" "
67						
68	Sa-tan-i-o..........	" "	Set-she..........	" "	Se-ya-ut..........	" "
69	Is-natch'l-hu..........	" "	Is-sä'-pin..........	" "	Is-sä'-pin..........	" "
70	Ees-neek'-al-lou..........	" "	E-see'-pen..........	" "	E-see'-pen..........	" "
71	En-swagh'..........	" "	En-pe-natsh'..........	" "	En-pe-natsh..........	" "
72						
73	To-ät-sin..·..........	My son.	E-ät-sin..........	" "	E-ät-sin..........	" "
74			Sä-pe'-a..........	" "		" "
75	So-eng-gi..........	My son-in-law.	Sa-ye..........	" "	Sa-ye..........	" "
76	Ku-nee-u..........	" "	Ku-reep..........	" "	Ku-reep..........	" "
77	Guä'-l-ä..........	" "	Chu'-ä..........	" "	Guä'-i-ä..........	" "
78	Ning-ä-oo-wä..........	My son-in-law.	Oo-kvä-wä..........	" "	Oo-kvä-wä..........	" "
79	Ning-a-u-ga..........	" "	U-ku-ä'-rä..........	" "	U-ku-ä'-rä..........	" "
80	Ning-a-ou'-gwä..........	" "	Oo-koo-ä'-gä..........	" "	Oo-koo-ä'-gä..........	" "

TABLE II.—*Continued.*

	243. My step-father.	Translation.	244. My step-mother.	Translation.	245. My step-son. (Male speaking.)	Translation.
1	Hoc-no'-ese..............	My step-father.	Oc-no'-ese..............	My step-mother.	Ha'-no..............	My step-son.
2	Hoc-no'-nese..............	" "	Kuh-no'-ese..............	" "	Ha'-no..............	" "
3	Hä-ge-noh'..............	" "	Un-ge-noh'..............	" "	Ha-noh'..............	" "
4	Hoc-no-nese'-kwä	" "	Oc-no-nese'-kwä	" "	Le'-no..............	" "
5	Lä-ga-nä-nese'-kwä	" "	Ah-ga-nä-nese'-kwä	" "	E-noh'..............	" "
6	Ack-we'-rä..............	" "	Ahk-we'-rä..............	" "	Kä-we'-rä..............	My step-child.
7	Lok-no-nese'-kwä	" "	Ak-no-nese'-kwä	" "	Le'-no..............	My step-son.
8	Hoon-du'-ah..............	" "	Oon-du'-ah..............	" "	Hoon-du'-ah..............	" "
9	At-tay' Wä-ya..............	I call father.	Shäṇ-kay'..............	" "	Me-tä'-wä-gäṇ..............	" "
10	Ah-ta'..............	My father.	E'-nah..............	My mother.	Me-chink'-she..............	My son.
11	Ah-ta'..............	" "	E'-nah..............	" "	Ak-she'-da..............	" "
12	Ah-ta'..............	" "	Een'-nä..............	" "	Me-chink'-she..............	" "
13	Ah-ta'..............	" "	E'-nah..............	" "	Me-chink'-se-lä..............	" "
14	Ah-ta'..............	" "	E'-nah..............	" "	Me-chink'-she..............	" "
15	Ah-ta'..............	" "	E'-nah..............	" "	Me-chink'-she..............	" "
16	Ah-ta'..............	" "	E'-nah..............	" "	Me-chink'-she..............	" "
17	Ah-da'..............	" "	E-nah'..............	" "	Me-chink'-she..............	" "
18	Tä-de'-ha..............	" "	Nä'-hä..............	" "	Nis-se'-hä..............	" "
19	In-dä'-de..............	" "	E-nä'-hä..............	" "	We-nis'-se..............	" "
20	Heen'-kä..............	" "	Heen'-nah..............	" "	He-yiṇ'-ga..............	" "
21	Hin'-kä..............	" "	He'-nah..............	" "	He-ne'-cha..............	" "
22	E-dä'-je..............	" "	E'-naw..............	" "	Be-she'-gä..............	" "
23	In-tä'-che..............	" "	In-nah'..............	" "	We-she'-kä..............	" "
24	E-noo-go'..............	My step-father.	E-oo'-ne-neke'..............	My little mother	E-chä-h'kun..............	My step-child.
25	Tä-tay'..............	My father.	Nä-a'..............	My mother.	Me-ne'-ka..............	My son.
26	Tä-ta'..............	" "	Ih'-kä..............	" "	Mä-de-shä'..............	" "
27	E-sä'-che-ka..............	My step-father.	E'-ke-ä..............	" "	Bot-sä'-ki..............	" "
28	A'-kĭ To'-bä..............	My father become.	Ush'-kĭ Pĭ'-lä..............	Towards a mother.	Suh'-süh To-bä..............	My son become.
29	A'-kĭ To'-bä..............	" " "	Ush'-kĭ To'-bä..............	" " "	Suh'-soh To'-bä..............	" " "
30	Ang-ko'-sĭ..............	My little father.	Sush-ko'-sĭ..............	My little mother.	Su-soh' To'-bä..............	" " "
31	Chuhl-kŭ-che'..............	" " "	Chuch'-kŭ-che'..............	" " "	Chup-pŭ'-chu-hä'-ke..............	Like my son.
32	Ah-gwä-ti-nä'-ĭ..............	My step-parent.	Ah-gwä-tĭ-nä'-ĭ..............	My step-parent.	Tsi-yä-tĭ-nä'-ĭ..............	My step-child.
33	Tä-le-na'-ah-ge-do'-dä....	My step-father.	Tä-le-na-ah-ge'-tse..............	My step-mother.	Tsi-yä-tĭ-nä'-ĭ..............	" "
34	Ah-te'-is..............	My step-parent.	Ah-te'-rä..............	My step-parent.	Pe'-row..............	My child.
35	A-te'-ase..............	" "	A-te'-rä..............	" "	Pe'-row..............	" "
36						
37	No'-ko-mis..............	My step-father.	N'-do'-sis..............	My step-mother.	N'-do'-sim..............	My step-son.
38	No'-ko-mish..............	" "	N'-do'-sis..............	" "	N'-do'-zhim..............	" "
39	No'-ko-mis..............	" "	N'-do'-zis..............	" "	N'-do'-zhim..............	" "
40	Nĭ-mĭ-sho'-mĕ..............	" "	Nĭ-no'-shĕ..............	" "	Nin-do'-zhim..............	" "
41	Ne-me-sho'-ma..............	" "	Ne-no-shä'..............	" "	Nin-do'-zhim..............	" "
42	Ne-mis'-sho-mä..............	" "	Ne-no-shä'..............	" "	N'-do'-zhim..............	" "
43	Ne-mish'-sho-mä..............	" "	Ne-no'-shä..............	" "	N'-do'-zhim-ä..............	" "
44	N'-mis-sho mä'..............	" "	No-shä'..............	" "	N'-do'-zhim..............	" "
45	Noke-mä'..............	" "	No-sheh'..............	" "	N'-do-sheh-mä..............	" "
46	Na-no-ne-tä'..............	" "	Na-no-ne-tä' Niṇ-gä'......	" "	N'-jo'-sä..............	" "
47	Na-no-ne-tä'..............	" "	Na-no-ne-tä'..............	" "	Na-no nä'-kä..............	" "
48	Na-no-ne-tä'..............	" "	Na-no-ne-tä'..............	" "	Na-no-nä'-kä..............	" "
49	Na-no-ne-tä'..............	" "	Na-no-ne-tä' We-ga......	" "	Ne-gwis-sä' Nä-no-ne-kä'	" "
50	Na-no-ne-tä'..............	" "	Na-no-ne-tä' We-ga......	" "	Ne-gwis-sä' Nä-no-ne-kä'	" "
51	Nöss..............	My father.	Nä-ke⁻ä'..............	My mother.	Nä-kwis'-sä..............	My son.
52	Na-tä'..............	My step-father.	Ne-ne'..............	My step-mother.	Ne-poo-on'-a-mä..............	My step-son
53	Ne-sä-wit-sin-ne'-o-a..	" * "	Ne-sä-wit-sin'-na-ko..............			
54	Ka-sa-no-ni-tä..............	My step-parent.	Ka-sa-no-ni-tä..............	My step-parent.	Ka-so-no-ni-kä'..............	My step-child.
55	Ne-ka'-se-no-ne-tä'..............	" "	Ne-kä'-se-no-ne-tä'..............	My step-mother.	Ne-ka'-se-no-ne-kä'..............	" "
56	Na-thä'-na ?..............	My father.	Na'-mä ?..............	My mother.	Na'-hä..............	My son.
57	Ne-to'-to-mä..............	My step-father.	Ne-to-tox'-is..............	My step-mother.	N'-do'-to-ko..............	My step-son.
58	Ne-to'-to-ma..............	" "	Ne-to'-toax-is..............	" "	Ne-to'-to-koh'-a..............	" "
59	Niks-kä-mich'..............	My grandfather.	Nu-gu'-mich..............	My grandmother.	Nŭ-jeech'..............	My grandchild.
60	Nee-chä'-look..............	My step-father.	N'-kee'-sees..............	My step-mother.	N'-too-ä'-sum..............	My step-son.
61	N'-jä'-kw'..............	" "	No-muths'..............	" "	Nä-kun'..............	My step-child.
62	N'-me-lu-teh'..............	My giver of profit.	M'-bee-a-tah'..............	Saver of profit.	N'-hoh'-pä-la-kun'..............	My outside child.
63	Na-na-mo'-whome..............	My step-father.	Na-na'-ho-mus..............	My step-mother.	Na-nokue'-tone..............	My step-child.
64	E-tah'-eh..............	" "	San-ga'..............	" "	Tu-zen'-a..............	My step-son.
65	Sa-tä'..............	My father.	A'-na..............	My mother.	Sa-yä'-za..............	My son.
66	Set-the'-na..............	My step-father.	Sa-kre'-a..............	My step-mother.	Se-yä'-za..............	" "
67	Set'-he..............	" "	Sa'-ki..............	My step-mother and	Sa'-ki..............	My child.
68	Set-se..............	" "	Sa-ku-i..............	" " [aunt.	Si-ou..............	My step-child.
69	In-tlu-es'-tin..............	My step-parent.	In-tlu-es'-tin..............	My step-parent.	Is-tlu-ält'..............	" "
70						
71	Na-magh'-has..............	" "	Na-magh'-has..............	" "	Pai'-ya..............	My step-son.
72	Kach-ha..............	" "	Ka-ko-o'kt..............	My step-mother.	Hä'-nish..............	My step-child.
73	Mo-än ?..............	My father.	Pe-an ?..............	My mother.	To-ät-sin ?..............	My son.
74	Shkŭ-ni'-yŭ..............	My step-father.	Shkŭ-ni'-yŭ..............	My step-mother.	Shkŭ-ni'-yŭ..............	My step-son.
75	Qua-ta-ra..............	" "	Qua-ye-a..............	" "	Qua-e-a..............	" "
76	Ku-mä-shän-päp..............	" "	Ku-mä-shän-nä..............	" "		
77						
78	Ung-oo-te-kä-vä..............	" "	An-ah-nä-kä..............	" "	Yŭn-e-kä-vä..............	" "
79	Ang-u-tigs-sa-ra..............	" "	Ar-nags-sa-ra..............	" "	Er-nigs-sa-ra..............	" "
80	Ang-o-e-chä'..............	" "	Au-nck-chä'..............	" "	In-nik-chä'..............	" "

TABLE II.—*Continued.*

	246. My step-son. (Female speaking.)	Translation.	247. My step-daughter.	Translation.	248. My step-brother. (Male speaking.)	Translation.
1	Ha'-no......................	My step-son.	Ka'-no	My step-daughter.	Hä-je (o.), Ha'-gă (y.)..............	My e. or y. bro.
2	Ha'-no......................	" "	Ka'-no......................	" "	Kuh-je'-ah (o.), Ha-gä'-ah (y.) ..	" " "
3	Ha-noh'....................	" "	Ka-noh'....................	" "	Kuh-je'-ah (o.), Ha-gä' (y.)	" " "
4	Le'-no.....................	" "	Kä'-no	" "	Läk-je'-ha (o.), Le-gä'-ah (y.) ...	" " "
5	E-noh'.....................	" "	Ka-noh'....................	" "	Lak-je'-ha (o.), E'-gä-ha (y.)	" " "
6	Kä-we'-rä.................	My step-child.	Kä-we'-rä.................	My step-child.	Ahk-rä'-je (o.), Kä'-gä (y.)	" " "
7	Le'-no.....................	My step-son.	Ka'-no.....................	My step-daughter.	Lok-je-hä' (o.), Le-gä-ä' (y.) ...	" " "
8	Hoon-du'-ah..............	" "	Oon-du'-ah................	" "	Ha-ye'-uh (o.), Ha-ye-ä'-hä (y.)	" " "
9	Me-tä'-wä-gäŋ...........	"	Me-tä'-wä-gäŋ	" "	Chiŋ-yay' (o.), Me-suŋ-kä (y.)..	" " "
10	Me-chink'-she...........	My oŋ	Me-chounk'-she.........	My daughter.	Che-a' (o.), Me-soh'-kä (y.)	" " "
11	Ak-she'-da................	"	Me-chink'-she..........	" "	Che'-a (o.), Me-sun'-kä (y.)	" " "
12	Me-chink'-she...........	" "	Me-chunk-she	" "	Che'-a (o.), Me-sun'-kä (y.)	" " "
13	Me-chink'-se-lä..........	" "	Me-chunk'-se-lä.........	" "	Che'-a (o.), Me-soh' (y.)...........	" " "
14	Me-chink'-she...........	" "	Me-chunk'-she..........	" "	Me-che'-a (o.), Me-sunk'-a-lä (y.)	" " "
15	Me-chink'-she...........	" "	Me-chunk'-she..........	" "	Che'-a (o.), Me-soh'-kä-lä (y.) ...	" " "
16	Me-chink'-she...........	" "	Me-chŭnk'-she..........	" "	Che-a' (o.), Me-son'-kä-lä (y.) ...	" " "
17	Me-chunk'-she..........	" • "	Me-chunk'-she..........	" "	Me-chin' (o.), Me-soh' (y.)........	" " "
18	Nis-se'-hä................	" "	Win-no'-gha..............	" "	Zhin-dä'-hä (o.), Kä-ga' (y.)......	" " "
19	We-zhiŋ'-ga..............	" "	Wee-zhuŋ'-ga	" "	Wee-zhe'-thä (o.), Wee-söŋ'-gä (y.)	" " "
20	He-yiŋ'-ga	" "	Hee-yuŋ'-ga.............	" "	He-yen'-nä (o.), Heen-thuŋ'-ga (y.)	" " "
21	He-ne'-cha	" "	He-yuŋ'-ga.............	" "	Hee-ye'-nä (o.), Heen-thun'-ga (y.)	" " "
22	Be-she'-gä	" "	She-me'-she-ga..........	My girl.	Be-zhe'-yeh (o.), Be-sun'-ga (y.)	" " "
23	We-she'-kä...............	" "	We-shon'-ka.............	My daughter.	We-she'-lä (o.), We-son'-kä (y.)	" " "
24	E-chä-h'kun..............	My step-child.	E-chä-h'kun	My step-child.	E-ne' (o.), E-sunk' (y.)	" " "
25	Me-ne'-ka.................	My son.	Me-no'-hä-ka	My daughter.	Moo'-kä (o.), Me-sho'-kä (y.) ...	" " "
26	Mä-de-shä'................	" "	Mä'-kä	" "	Mee-ä-kä' (o.), Mat-so'-gä (y.) ...	" " "
27	Bot-sa'-sä.................	" "	Näk'-me-ä.................	" "	Meek'-a (o.), Bä-chü'-ka (y.)	" " "
28	Suh'-sŭh To'-bä.........	My son become.	Suh-suh'-take Pī'-lä ...	My dau. become.	Um-un'-nĭ (o.), Suh-näk'-fish (y.)	My bro. become.
29	Suh'-soh To'-bä..........	" " "	Suh-soh'-take To'-bä...	" " "	Et-e-bä'-pĭ-shĭ-lĭ To'-bä........	" " "
30	Su-soh' To'-bä...........	" " "	Sü-soh'-take To'-bä	" " "	Et-e-bä'-pĭ-shĭ-lĭ...................	My other brother.
31	Chup-pŭ'-chu-hä'-ke.....	Like my son.	Chuch'-hŭ-stu-ha'-ke ..	Like my daughter.	Um-it'-te-chä-ke'-to	My step-brother.
32	Tsi-yä-tĭ-nä'-Ι............	My step-child.	Tsi-yä-tĭ-nä'-Ι	My step-child.		
33	Tsi-yä-tĭ-nä'-Ι............	" "	Tsi-yä-tĭ-nä-Ι	" "	E-dä'-deh...........................	My brother.
34	Pe'-row	My child.	Pe'-row....................	My child.		
35	Pe'-row	" "	Pe'-row....................	" "	A-dä'-he	" "
36						
37	N'-go'-sim.................	My step-son.	N'-do'-sa-mis-kwame'..	My step-daughter.	Neese-tase' (o.)	My elder brother.
38	N'-go'-zhim...............	" "	N'-do'-zha-mis-kwame'	" "	Neese-tase' (o.).....................	" " "
39	N'-go'-zhim...............	" "	N'-do'-zha-mis-kwem'..	" "	Neesh-tase'........................	" " "
40	Nin-do'-zhe-miss.........	" "	Nin-do-zhĭ-mĭ'-kwem..	" "	Ne-kä'-na	My step-brother.
41	Nin-do'-zhe-mis..........	" "	Nin-do-zhe-me'-quam..	" "	Ne-kä'-na	" " "
42	N'-do'-sha-mis............	" "	Nin-do-sha-mĭ-kwam...	" "	Ne-kä'-na	" " "
43	N'-do'-zha-mis............	" "	N'-do'-zha-mĭ-kwam'...	" "	Ne-kä'-nis...........................	" " "
44	N'-do'-zha-mis............	" "	N'-do'-zha-mĭ-kwam ...	" "	N'-do-zha-mis'.....................	" " "
45	N'-do'-zha-mä............	" "	N'-do'-zha-mis	" "	N'-do'-zhe-mis	" " "
46	N'-jo'-sä...................	" "	Na-no'-na-gä-ne-dän'...	" "		
47	Na-no-nä'-kä..............	" "	Na-no-nä'-kä	" "		
48	No-no-nä'-kä..............	" "	Na-no-nä'-kä	" "		
49	Ne-gwis-sä' Nä-no-ne-kä'	" "	N'-dä-nä Nä-no-ne-kä'.	" "		
50	Ne-gwis-sä' Nä-no-ne-kä'	" "	N'-dä-nä Nä-no-ne-kä'.	" "		
51	Nä-kwis'-sä................	My son.	Nä-tä'-niss	My daughter.		
52	Ne-poo-oŋ-on'-a-mä......	My step-son.	Ne-poo-on'-a-mä	My step-daughter.		
53					O-nä-vi'-son	My half-brother.
54	Ka-sa-no-ni-kä............	My step-child.	Ka-sa-no-ni-kä	My step-child.	Pä-the'-ne-cha-ne-nä'...............	My elder brother.
55	Ne-ka'/-se-no-ne-kä'	" "	Ne-ka-se-no-ne-kä'......	" "	Nä'-thä-hä (o.), Ta'-yä (y.).......	My e. or y. bro.
56	Na'-hä	My son.	Nä-tä'-na	My daughter.	Ne-to'-to-pä-pe	My step-brother.
57	N'-do'-to-ko...............	My step-son.	N'-to'-to-tun	My step-daughter.	Ne-to'-toase........................	" " "
58	Ne-to'-to-koh'-a	" "	Ne-to'-to-tun.............	" "		
59	Nŭ-jeech'	My grandchild.	Nŭ-jeech'.................	My grandchild.	N'-sees'............................	My elder brother.
60	N'-too-ä'-sum.............	My step-son.	N'-su'-mus................	My step-daughter.		
61	Nä-kun'....................	My step-child.	Nä-kun'...................	My step-child.	N'-dä-kwus'........................	My step-brother.
62	N'-hoh'-pä-la-kun'.......	My outside child.	N'-hoh'-pä-la-kun'....	My outside child.	Nee-mä'-tus..............[mus (y.)	My brother.
63	Na-nokue'-tone...........	My step-child.	Na-nokue'-tone.........	My step-child.	Nain-n'-hans (o.), Nain-hise-se- [(y.)	
64	Sa-yä'-ze.................	My step-son.	Sa-yä'-dze...............	My step-daughter.	Sŭn-no'-ga (o.), Sun-no-ga-ya'-za	My bro. e. or y.
65	Sa-yä'-za.................	My son.	Sa-to'-a..................	My daughter.	Sü-nä'-za (o.), Set-chil'-e-ŭ-ze (y.)	" " "
66	Se-yä'-za.................	" "	Sa-le'-ä..................	" "	Soon'-da-ga (o.), Sa'-chä (y.).....	
67	Sa'-ki.....................	My child.	Sa'-ki....................	My child.		
68	Si-ou	My step-child.	Si-ou	My step-child.	Is-säs-täm..........................	" " "
69	Is-tlu-ält'.................	" "	Is-tlu-ält'	" "		
70						
71	A'-tee	My step-son.	{ Pach-h'yach' (m. s.) } { Pee'-see (f. s.) }	My step-daughter.	En-haigh	My brother.
72	Ko-ke'-tish	My step-child.	{ Ha'-nish (m. s.) ..... } { Ko-ke'-tish (f. s.) ... }	My step-child.		
73	To-ät-sin ?................	My son.	Pä-chin ?.................	My daughter.	Pä-chin ?...........................	My daughter.
74			Shkŭ-ri'-yŭ	My step-daughter.	Tum-mŭ'............................	My younger bro.
75	Qua-e-a....................	My step-son.	Qua-e-a	" "		
76						
77						
78	Yŭn-e-kä-vä...............	" "	Pä-ne-kä-vä..............	" "	Ung-e-oo-kä-vä (o.), Noo-kä-kä-	My step-brother.
79	Er-nigs-sa-ra	" "	Pan-igs-sa-ra	" "	Na-tang-u-tigs-sa-ra ......[vä (y.)	" " "
80	In-nik-chä'................	" "	Pen-ne-chä'..............	" "	Ang-a-yŭk-chä'...................	" "

TABLE II.—*Continued.*

	249. My step-brother. (Female speaking.)	Translation.	250. My step-sister. (Male speaking.)	Translation.
1	Ha'-je (o.), Ha-gă (y.)	My older or younger bro.	Ah'-je (o.), Ka'-gă (y.)	My elder or y'nger sister.
2	Kuh-je'-ah (o.), Ha-gă'-ah (y.)	" " " "	Uh-je'-ah (o.), Ka-gă'-ah (y.)	" " " "
3	Kuh-je'-ah (o.), Ha-gă' (y.)	" " " "	Uh-je'-ah (o.), Ka'-gă (y.)	" " " "
4	Läk-je'-ha (o.), Le-gă'-ah (y.)	" " " "	Ahk-je'-hä (o.), Ka-gä'-ah (y.)	" " " "
5	Lak-je'-ha (o.), E'-gä-hä (y.)	" " " "	Ahk-je'-hä (o.), Ka'-gä-hä (y.)	" " " "
6	Ahk-rä'-je (o.), Kä'-gä (y.)	" " " "	Ahk'-je (o.), Kä'-gä (y.)	" " " "
7	Lok-je-hä' (o.), Le-gä-ä' (y.)	" " " "	A k-je'-yä (o.), Ka-gä'-ah (y.)	" " " "
8	Ha-ye'-uh (o.), Ha-ye-ä'-hä (y.)	" " " "	A-ye'-uh (o.), Ya-ye-ah'-hä (y.)	" " " "
9	Te-mdo' (o.), Me-suɳ'-kä (y.)	" " " "	Täɳ-kay' (o.), Me-tänk'-she (y.)	" " " "
10	Chim'-a-do (o.), Me-soh'-kä (y.)	" " " "	Ton-ka' (o.), Me-tänk'-she (y.)	" " " "
11	Tib'-e-do (o.), Me-sunk'-ä (y.)	" " " "	Tank'-she (o.), Me-tänk'-she (y.)	" " " "
12	Tib'-a-do (o.), Me-sun'-kä (y.)	" " " "	T auk'-she (o.), Me-tänk'-she (y.)	" " " "
13	Tib-a-lo' (o.), Me-soh'-kä-lä (y.)	" " " "	Tä-ka' (o.), Me-tunk'-she (y.)	" " " "
14	Tib'-a-lo (o.), Me-sunk'-ä-lä (y.)	" " " "	Tonk-a' (o.), Me-tunk'-she (y.)	" " " "
15	Tib'-a-lo (o.), Me-soh'-kä (y.)	" " " "	Ton'-ka (o.), Me-tank'-she (y.)	" " " "
16	Tib'-a-lo (o.), Me-son'-kä-lä (y.)	" " " "	Ton-ka' (o.), Me-tonk'-she (y.)	" " " "
17	Me-tim'-do (o.), Me-soh (y.)	" " " "	Me-ton-ga (o.), Me-tank-she (y.)	" " " "
18	Ton-no' (o.), Kä'-ga' (y.)	" " " "	Toɳ-gä'-hä (o.), We-ha' (y.)	" " " "
19	Wee-te'-noo (o.), Wee-sŏn'-gä (y.)	" " " "	Wee-tŏɳ'-ga (o.), Wee-tŏɳ'-gä (y.)	" " " "
20	He-yen'-nä (o.), E-chun'-cha (y.)	" " " "	He-yu'-nä (o.), Heen-taɳ'-ya (y.)	" " " "
21	He-ye'-nä (o.), E-chun'-cha (y.)	" " " "	Wan-he'-cha (o.), Heen-täɳ'-gä (y.)	" " " "
22	Be-che'-do (o.), Be-suɳ'-gä (y.)	" " " "	Be-tuɳ-ga (o.), Be-tuɳ'-gä-zhiɳ'-gä (y.)	" " " "
23	We-chin'-to (o.), We-son'-kä (y.)	" " " "	We-tun-ka (o.), We-tuɳ'-ka (y.)	" " " "
24	E-che'-to (o.), E-sŭnk' (y.)	" " " "	E-noo' (o.), Wych-kä' (y.)	" " " "
25	Me-sho'-kä (o.), Me-sho'-kä (y.)	" " " "	P-tä-me'-ha.	
26	Mä-tä-roo' (o.), Mat-so'-gä (y.)	" " " "	Mat-tä-we'-ä (o.), Mä-tä-kä-zhä (y.)	" " " "
27	Bä-zä'-na (o.), Bä-chĭ'-ka (y.)	" " " "	Bä-za'-kät (o.), Bä-sä'-chete (y.)	" " " "
28	A-näk'-fĭ (o.), A-näk'-fĭ (y.)	" " " "	An'-take (o.), An'-take (y.)	" " " "
29	Et-e-bä'-pĭ-shĭ-lĭ To'-bä	My brother become.	Et-e-bä'-pĭ-shĭ-lĭ To'-bä	My sister become.
30	A-näk-fĭ	My elder brother.	An-take'	My elder sister.
31	Chu-chihl'-wä	" " "	Chu-wun'-wä	" " "
32				My step-sister.
33				
34	E-rats'-teh	My step-brother.	E-tä'-heh	My sister.
35	A-dä'-he	My brother.	A-tä'-he	" "
36				
37	Neese-tase' (o.)	My elder brother.	Ne-mis' (o.)	My elder sister.
38	Neese-tase' (o.)	" " "	Ne-mish' (o.)	" " "
39	Neesh-tase'.	" " "	Ne-mish' (o.)	" " "
40	Nin-dä-wa'-mä	My step-brother.	Nin-dä-wa'-mä	My step-sister.
41	Nin-dä-wa'-mä	" " "	Nin-dä-wa'-mä	" " "
42	Nin-dá-wa'-mä	" " "	Nin-dä-wa'-mä	" "
43	N'-do-wa-mä'	" " "	N'-do-wa-mä'	" "
44	N'-dä-wa-mä'	" " "	N'-dä-wa-mä'	" "
45	N'-dä-wä'-mä	" " "	N'-dä-wä'-mä	" "
46				
47				
48				
49				
50				
51				
52				
53	O-nă-vĭ'-son	My half-brother.	O-nă-vĭ'-son	My half-sister.
54				
55	Pä-the-ne-cha-ne-nä'	My elder brother.	Pä-the'-ne-nit-kwa-a-mä'	My elder sister.
56	Nä'-thä-hä (o.), Tä'-yä (y.)	My elder or younger bro.	Na'-be (o.), Na'-be-ä (y.)	My elder or y'nger sister.
57	Ne-to'-to-pä-pe	My step-brother.	N'-to'-to-kame	My step-sister.
58	Ne-to'-toase.	" " "	Ne-to'-toax-is	" "
59	N'-chi-gu'-num	My younger brother.	Nu-mees	My elder sister.
60			Na-tä-kw-sŭs'-kw	My step-sister.
61	N'-donk'	My step-brother.	N'-dä-kwus-oh'-kwä-oh	" "
62	N'-dun-oo-yome'	" " "	N'-doh-kwä-yome'	" "
63	Nain-n'-hans' (o.), Nain-hise-se-mus' (y.)	My brother.	Nain-na-wase' (o.), Nain-hise'-se-mus' (y.)	My sister.
64				
65	Sŭn-no'-ga (o.), Sŭn-no-ga-yă'-za (y.)	My bro. elder or younger.	Sä-dä'-za (o.), Sa-dä'-za-yă'-za (y.)	My sister elder or y'nger.
66	Sŭ-nä'-gä (o.), Set-chil'-e-ä-ze (y.)	" " " "	Set-dez'-a-ä-ze (o.), Sä'-ze (y.)	" " " "
67	Soon'-da-ga (o.), Sa-chä (y.)	" " " "	Sa'-che (o.), Sa-chith' (y.)	" " " "
68				
69				
70				
71	En-haigh'	My step-brother.		
72				
73				
74			Sä-gwech'	My sister.
75				
76				
77				
78	Ung-e-oo-kä-vä (o.), Noo-kä-kä-vä (y.)	" " "	Ny-yä-kä	My step-sister.
76			Na-tang-u-tigs-sa-ra	" "
80	An-ne-chä'	" " "	Na-yŭk-chä'	" "

TABLE II.—*Continued.*

	251. My step-sister. (Female speaking.)	Translation.	252. Two fathers-in-law to each other.	Translation.	253. Two mothers-in-law to each other.	Translation.
1	Ah'-je (o.), Ka'-gă (y.)	My o. or y. sister.				
2	Uh-je'-ah (o.), Ka-gă'-ah (y.)	" " "				
3	Uh-je'-ah (o.), Ka'-gă (y.)	" " "	Ho-nă-dä-no'-wä	Same.	O-nă-dä-no'-wä	Same.
4	Ahk-je'-hä (o.), Ka-gä'-ah (y.)	" " "	Un-gä-dä'-no-hä	"	O-nă-dä'-nole	"
5	Ahk-je'-hä (o.), Ka-gä'-hä (y.)	" " "	Un-gä'-dä-nole	"	O-nä'-dä-nole	"
6	Ahk'-je (o.), Kä'-gä (y.)	" " "	Nä-yo'-the-ath	"	Na-yo'-thof	"
7	Ak-je'-yä (o.), Ka-gä'-ah (y.)	" " "				
8	A-ye'-uh (o.), Ya-ye-ah'-hä (y.)	" " "				
9	Me-chuŋ' (o.), Me-taŋ'-kä (y.)	" " "	O-mä'-wä-he-toŋ	"	O-mä'-wä-he-toŋ	"
10	Chu-ih' (o.), Me-tuŋ'-kä (y.)	" " "	O-mä'-he-to	"	O-mä'-he-to	"
11	Me-tank'-a-do (o.), Me-tank'-a-do (y.)	" " "	O-mä'-he-to	"	O-mä'-he-to	"
12	Tän-ka (o.), Me-tän'-kä (y.)	" " "	O-mä'-he-to	"	O-mä'-he-to	"
13	Chu-wa' (o.), Me-tunk'-hä-lä (y.)	" " "	Ho-mo'-i-to	"	Ho-mo'-i-to	"
14	Chu-a' (o.), Me-tonk'-ä (y.)	" " "	O-mä'-he-to	"	O-mä'-he-to	"
15	Chu'-ih (o.), Ton'-kä (y.)	" " "	O-mä'-he-to	"	O-mä'-he-to	"
16	Chu-wa' (o.), Me-ton'-kä (y.)	" " "	O-mä'-he-to	"	O-mä'-he-to	"
17	Me-chun (o.), Me-tä' (y.)	" " "	O-mä'-he-to	"	O-mä'-he-to	"
18	Zhon-da'-hä (o.), We-ha' (y.)	" " "				
19	Wee-zŏŋ'-thä (o.), Wee'-hä (y.)	" " "	O-kee'-yee	"	O-kee'-yee	"
20	Heen-taŋ'-ga (o.), Heen-tuŋ'-ga (y.)	" " "				
21	Heen-tang'-a (o.), Heen-tän'-gä (y.)	" " "				
22	Be-sho'-wa (o.), Ah-se'-zhe-gä (y.)	" " "				
23	We-sho'-la (o.), We-tun'-ka (y.)	" " "				
24	E-noo' (o.), E-chunk' (y.)	" " "				
25	Me-no'-ka (o.), Me-no'-ka (y.)	" " "	Kote'-he-a	"	Me-ho-he-a	"
26	Mä-roo' (o.), Mă-tä-ka'-zhä (y.)	" " "				
27	Bus-we-nä (o.), Bä-so'-ka (y.)	" " "	Me-nä-pä'-che	"	Ha'-nä	"
28	Um-un'-nĭ (o.), Suk-năk'-fish (y.)	" " "				
29	Et-e-bä-pĭ-shĭ-lĭ To'-bä	My sister become.				
30	Et-e-bä'-pĭ-shĭ-lĭ	" " "				
31	Chu-hlä'-hä	My elder sister.	Um-mä'-he	"	Un-hok-tŭl'-wä	"
32		My step-sister.				
33						
34	E-dä'-deh	My sister.	Kool-er-hoas	My old man.	Chose'-tit	My old woman.
35	A-tä'-he	"				
36						
37	Ne-mis' (o.)	My elder sister.	N'-dä'-wä	Same.	N'-dä'-wä	Same.
38	Ne-mish' (o.)	" " "	N'-de-tä'-wä	"	N'-de-tä'-wä	"
39	Ne-mish' (o.)	" " "	N'-de-tä'-wä	"	N'-de-tä'-wä	"
40	Nee-de-gĭ'-ko	My step-sister.	Nin-din-dä'-wä	"	Nin-din-dä'-wä	"
41	Nee-de-ge'-ko	" "	Nin-din-dä'-wä	"	Nin-din-dä'-wä	"
42	Nee-de-gĭ-ko	" "	Nin-din-dä-wä'	"	Nin-din-dä-wä'	"
43	Ne-da-gĭ-ko'	" "	N'-din'-dä-wä'	"	N'-din'-dä-wä'	"
44	N'-da-kwam'	" "	N'-din-dä-wä'	"	N'-din-dä-wä'	"
45	N'-dä-kwam'	" "	N'-din-dä-wä'	"	N'-din-dä-wä'	"
46			No relation of different nations, when they are brothers.		No relation unless of different nations, when they are sisters.	
47			No-sa'-mä	Same.	No-sa'-mä	Same.
48						
49						
50						
51			Nă-tel'-tä-wä	"	Nă-tel'-tä-wä	"
52			Ne-tä'-tä-won	"	Ne-tä'-tä-won	"
53	O-nă-vĭ'-son	My half-sister.	——	Not related.	——	Not related.
54						
55	Pä-the'-ne-nit-kwa-a-mä'	My elder sister.	——	" "		" " "
56	Na'-be (o.), Na'-be-ă (y.)	My e. or y. sister.	Nä-tä-nake'	Same.	Nä-tä-nake'	Same.
57	N'-to'-to-kame	My step-sister.	Ne-tä'-so-ko	"	Ne-tä'-so-ko	"
58	Ne-to'-toax-is	" "	Ne-tah'-soh-ko	" [in-law.	Ne-tah'-soh-ko	" [-in-law.
59	N'-kway-jeech'	My younger sister.	N'-tŭ-dem'	My child's father-	N'-tŭ-te-me'-skw	My child's mother
60	N'-tul'-mŭ	My step-sister.	N'-tu'-tem	" " "	N'-tu-te-mees'-kw	" " "
61	N'-ko-kwä'	" "				
62	Neet-koh'-kw'	" "				
63	Nain-na-wase' (o.), Nain-hise-se-mus' (y.)	My sister.				
64		[(y.)				
65	Sä-dä'-za (o.), Sa-dä'-za-yä'-za (y.)	My sister e. or y.				
66	Set-dez'-a-ä-ze (o.), Sä'-re (y.)	" " "			Sa-ga'-u-nä	
67	Sa'-che (o.), Sa-chith' (y.)	" " "				
68			Sahn		Su-thu-i	
69			In-ta'-tum-ten	Dividers of the	In-ta'-tum-ten	Dividers of the
70				plunder, *i. e.*, the		[plunder.
71			Păn'-wash	marriage presents.	Păn'-wash	
72						
73						
74	Kă-o'-wa	My step-sister.				
75						
76						
77						
78	Ny-yŭ-kä	" "				
79						
80	Ang-a-yŭk-chä'	" "	Nŭ-l'ug'-ing	——	Nŭ-l'ug'-ing	——

TABLE II.—*Continued.*

	254. Brother-in-law. My husband's brother.	Translation.	255. Brother-in-law. My sister's husband. (Male speaking.)	Translation.	256. Brother-in-law. My sister's husband. (Female speaking.)	Translation.
1	Ha-yă'-o	My brother-in-law.	Ah-ge͡ah'-ne͡o	My brother-in-law.	Ha-yă'-o	My bro.-in-law.
2	Ha-yă'-ho	" "	Uh-ge͡ah'-ne͡o	" "	Ha-yă'-ho	" "
3	Ah-ge-ah'-yeh	" "	Uh-ge-ah'-ne-o	" "	Ah-ge-ah'-de-o	" "
4	Un-gă'-le-a-hä	" "	Un-ge͡ah'-de͡o	" "	Un-ge͡ah'-le͡o	" "
5	Un-gă-le-ya'-ha	" "	Un-gă-de͡o'-hä	" "	Un-gă-le-ya'-hä	" "
6	Ack-gä'-rä	" "	Ack-gaw'-no-ah	" "	Ack-gaw'-we-ri-o	" "
7	Lä-go-hä'-kwä	" "	Un-jä'-jo-hä	" "		
8	Ah-zhä'-ku	" "	O-in-dä'-wait	" "	Ah-zhă'-kŭ	" "
9	She-chay'	" "	Tä-hän'	" "	She-chay'	" "
10	She-cha'	" "	Tä-huh'	" "	She-cha'	" "
11	She-cha'-do	" "	Tä-hä'	" "	She-cha'	" "
12	She-cha'	" "	Tä-hä'	" "	She-cha'	" "
13	She-hä'	" "	Tä-hä'	" "	She-cha'	" "
14	She-ches'	" "	Tä-hä'	" "	She-ches'	" "
15	She-cha'	" "	Tä-hä'	" "	She-cha'	" "
16	She-cha'	" "	Tä-huh'	" "	She-cha'	" "
17	Me-she'-cha	" "	Me-hä'-gä	" "	Me-she'-cha	" "
18	We-she'-eh	" "	Tä-hä'-huh	" "	We-she'-eh	" "
19	We-she'-ă	" "	We-tä'-hä	" "	We-she'-ă	" "
20	Hee-she'-kä	" "	Heen-tä'-hä	" "	Hee-she'-kä	" "
21	Hin-she'-kä	" "	Heen-tä'-ha	" "	Hin-she'-kä	" "
22	Be-she'-kä	" "	Be-tä'-hä	" "	Be-she'-kä	" "
23	We-she'-kä	" "	We-tä'-hä	" "	We-she'-kä	" "
24	E-she'-gä	" "	E-chun'	" "	E-she'-gä	" "
25	Wo-wä'-ke-a	" "	Wo-wä'-ke-a	" "	Wo-wä'-ke-a	" "
26	Boo-ä-kä'	" "	Mä-nä'-te	" "	Ma-ensh'-ke-rash	" "
27	Bos-che'-ta	" "	Mä-nä'-zha	" "	Bä'-che-na	" "
28	Um-ome-buh'-la-hä	" "	Um-ä'-lok	" "	Um-ä'-lok	" "
29	Um-ome-buh'-lä-hä	" "	Um-ä'-läk	" "	Um-ä'-läk	" "
30	Um-ä-läk'-o-sĭ	" "	Um-ä'-läk	" "	Um-ä'-läk	" " [pant.
31	Chu-hu'-cho-wä	My present occupant.	Un-kä'-wä	" "	Chu-hu'-cho-wä	My present occu-
32	An-sdä-duŋ'-hĭ	My brother-in-law.	Au-sdä-lau'-sĭ	" "	Aw-sä-dluŋ'-hĭ	My bro.-in-law.
33	E-nä-duh'-hĭ	" "	Squä'-o-sĭ	" "	Aw-sä-dluŋ'-hĭ	
34	Tä-kŭ-tuk-ŭ	My husband.	Koos-tow'-et-sŭ	My son-in-law	Tä-kŭ-tuk-ŭ	My husband.
35	Tow-ä'-ra	" "	Ko-stä'-witch	" "		
36			Kuh-tä'-wa-suh	" "	Kuh-tä'-wa-sŭh?	My bro.-in-law.
37	Nee-tim'	My brother-in-law.	Neese-tow'	My brother-in-law.	Nee-tim'	" "
38	Nee-tim'	" "	Neese-tow'	" "	Nee-tim'	" "
39	Nee-tim'	" "	Neesh-tow'	" "	Nee-tim'	" "
40	Nĭ'-nim	" "	Nĭ-tä	" "	Nis'-sim	" "
41	Ne'-nim	" "	Ne-che-ke'-wä-ze	My old friend.	Ne'-nim	" "
42	Ne-nim'	" "	Ne-tä'	My brother-in-law.	Ne-nim'	" "
43	Ne-nim'	" "	Ne-tä'	" "	Ne-nim'	" "
44	Ne-nim'	" "	Ne-tä'	" "	Ne-nim'	" "
45	Ne-nim'	" "	Ne-tä'	" "	Ne-nim'	" "
46	Ne-lim-wä'	" "	Ne-tä-wä'	" "	Ne-lim-wä'	" "
47	Ne-lim-wä'	" "	Ne-tä-wä'	" "	Ne-lim-wä'	" "
48	Ne-lim-wä'	" "	Ne-tä-wä'	" "	Ne-lim-wä'	" "
49	Ne-le-mwä'	" "	Ne-tä-wä'	" "	Ne-le-mwä'	" "
50	Ne-le-mwä'	" "	Ne-tä-wä'	" "	Ne-le-mwä'	" "
51	Ne-nim'-wä	" "	Ne-tä-wä'	" "	Ne-nim'-wä	" "
52	Na-nim'	" "	Na-tow'	" "	Na-nim'	" "
53	Ne-tum'	" "	Ne-to'	" "	Ne-tum'	" "
54	Ne-nem-wä'	" "	Nen-hä-kä-ni-mä	" "	Ne-nem-wä'	" "
55	Ne-lim-wä'	" "	N'-tä-kwä	" "	Ne-lim-wä'	" "
56	Ne-ta'-be	" "	Ne-ah'-ä	" "	Ne-ta'-be	" "
57	N'-to'-to-yome	" "	Nis-tä'-mo	" "	N'-to'-to-yome	" "
58	Ne-to'-to-yome	" "	Nis-tä'-mo	" "	Ne-to'-to-yome	" "
59	Ne-lu-mŭs'	" "	Nu-mäk'-tem	" "	Ne-lu-mŭs'	" "
60	Nee'-lu-mŭs	" "	Nu-mä-ku-tem	" "	Nee'-lu-mŭs	" "
61	Ne-num'	" "	N'-dä-oh·k'	" "	Nee-num'	" "
62	Nee-lum'	" "	Noh·taŋ'-kw'	" "	Nee-lum'	" "
63	Na-nee-lim'	" "	Na-nä-donkue'	" "	Na-nee-lim'	" "
64	Sa'-gä	" "	Sa'-gä	" "	Sa'-ga	" "
65	Sa-ten'-a-bă-che-la	" " [in-law.	Sa'-ga	" "	Sa-ten'-a-bă-che-la	" "
66	Set-shi'-ya	My bro. in-law & son-	Sa'-o-ga	" "	Set-shi'-ya	" "
67	Längh	My brother-in-law.	Längh	" "	Längh	" "
68	Su-thu-i	" "	Sahn	" "	Su-thu-igh	" "
69	Is-säs'-tăm	" "	Ist-sasht'	" "	Is-säs'-tăm	" "
70	E-sas-tan'	" "			E-sas-tan'	
71	En-pe-noke'	" "	En-pe-noke'	" "		
72			Kash-kat	" "		
73	Tä-tä'-wä-be	" "	Tä-tä'-wä-be	" "		
74						
75						
76						
77	Ub-so	" "				
78	Ay-e-gä	" "	Ning-oo-wä	" "		
79	Sa-ki-ah-si-a-ra	" "	Ning-a-u-ga	" "	Ning-a-u-ga	" "
80	I-e'-gä	" "	Ning-a-ou'-gwä	" "	I-e'-gä	" "

TABLE II.—*Continued.*

	257. Brother-in-law. My wife's brother.	Translation.	258. My wife's sister's husband.	Translation.	259. My husband's sister's husband.	Translation.
1	Ah-ge⌢ah′-ne⌢o	My brother-in-law.	——	Not related.	——	Not related.
2	Uh-ge⌢ah′-ne-o	" "	——	" "	——	" "
3	Ah-ge-ah′-ne-o	" "	——	" "	——	" "
4	Un-gä-de⌢o′-hä	" "	——	" "	——	" "
5	Un-gä-de⌢o′-hä	" "	——	" "	——	" "
6	Ack-gaw′-we-ri-o′-ah	" "	——	" "	——	" "
7	U′-jä′-jo-hä	" "	——	" "	——	" "
8	O-in-dä-wait	" "	——	" "	——	" "
9	Tä-hän′	" "	Tä-hän′	My brother-in-law.	She-chay′	My bro.-in-law.
10	Tä-huh′	" "	Che-a′ (o.), Me-soh-kä′ (y.)	My brother.	Che-a′ (o.), Me-soh′-kä (y.)	My brother.
11	Tä-hä′	" "	Tä-hä′	My brother-in-law.	She-cha′	My bro.-in-law.
12	Tä-hä′	" "	Tä-hä′	" "	She-cha′	" "
13	Tä-hä′	" "	Tä-hä′	" "	She-cha′	" "
14	Tä-hä′	" "	Tä-hä′	" "	She-ches′	" "
15	Tä-hä′	" "	Tä-hä′	" "	She-chas′	" "
16	Tä-hä′	" "	Tä-hä′	" "	She-cha′	" "
17	Me-tä′-hä	" "	Me-tä′-hä	" "	Me-she′-cha	" "
18	Ta-hä′-huh	" "	[gä		We-tä′-hä	" "
19	We-tä′-hä	" "	Wee-she′-thä or Wee-söŋ′-	My e. or y. brother.	We-tä′-hä	" "
20	Heen-tä′-hä	" "	He-yen′-na	My elder brother.	He-she′-kä	" "
21	Heen-tä′-hä	" "	He-ye′-nä	" " "	He-she′-ka	" "
22	Be-tä′-bä	" "	Be-zhe′-yeh or Be-suŋ′-gä	My e. or y. brother.	Be-she′-kä	" "
23	We-tä′-hä	" "				
24	E-chun′	" "	ᵃE-ne. ᵇE-sunk′	My e. bro. if married and y. if married first.	Kee-nomb′	My brother.
25	Wo-wä′-ke-a	" "				
26	Mä-nä′-te	" "				
27	Mä′-zhe	" "				
28	Um-ä-lok′-o-sĭ	My little br.-in-law.				
29	Um-ä-läk′-o-sĭ	" " "				
30	Um-ä-läk′-o-sĭ	" " "	A-ka-noh′-mĭ	My relative.	A-ka-noh′-mĭ	My relative.
31	Un-kä-pŭ′-che	My little separator.	Un-kä-pŭ′-che	My little separator.	Chu-hu′-oho-wä	My pre. occupant.
32	Au-sdä-law′-sĭ	My brother-in-law.	Sĭ-dä-nä′-luŋ	My brother-in-law.	Au-sdä-duŋ′-hĭ	My bro.-in-law.
33	Gä-yä-loh′-si	" "			Gä-yä-loh′-sih	" "
34	Tä-koot-scoo-rus	Male marriage rela- [tive.	Sä-toot-kä-kŭ	" "	Lä-kŭ′-tuk-ä	My husband.
35						
36						
37	Neese-tow′	My brother-in-law.	——	Not related.	——	Not related.
38	Neese-tow′	" "	——	" "	——	" "
39	Neese-tow′	" "	Neech′-ke-wä	My brother-in-law.	——	" "
40	Nĭ′-tä	" "	Nĭ′-tä	" "	Nĭ′-nim	My bro.-in-law.
41	Ne-che-ke′-wä-ze	My old friend.	Ne-kä′-na	My step-brother.	Nin-dä-wä′-mä	My step-brother.
42	Ne-tä′	My brother-in-law.	Ne-kä′-na	" "	Nin-dä-wä′-mä	" "
43	Ne-tä′	" "	Ne-kä′-nis	" " "	N'-dä-wa′-mä	" "
44	Ne-tä′	" "	Ne-tä-wa-mä′	My brother.		Not related.
45	Ne-tä′	" "	Ne-tä	My brother-in-law.	Ne-nim′	My bro.-in-law.
46	A-mä-kä	" "	——	Not related.	——	Not related.
47	Em-mä′-kä	" "	——	" "	——	" "
48	Em-mä′-kä	" "	——		——	" "
49	Em-mä′-kä	" "	——			
50	Em-mä′-kä	" "				
51	Ne-tä′-wä	" "	Mäs-sä-wik	My brother.	Ne-nim′-wä	My bro.-in-law.
52	Na-tow′	" "			Nä-ɒä′	My elder brother.
53	Na-to′	" "	——	Not related.		Not related.
54	Wa-si-nä-mä-kä	" "	Ne-nem-wă′	My brother-in-law.	——	" "
55	Ne-tä-kwä′	" "		Not related.	——	" "
56	Ne-ah′-ä	" "				
57	Nis-tä-moh′-ko	" "				
58	Nis′-tä-mo	" "	Nis′-tä-mo	My brother-in-law.	Nis′-tä-mo	My bro.-in-law.
59	Nu-mäk-tem′	" "	Nit-chŭs′	" "	Nit-chŭs′	" "
60	Nu-mä′-ku-tem	" "	Nit-chus′	" "	Nee′-lu-mŭs	" "
61	N'-dä-oh·k′	" "				
62	Noh·-taŋ′-kw'	" "				
63	Na-na-donkue′	" "	Nain-jose′	My friend.	Nain-jose′	My friend.
64	Sa′-gä	" "	Kŭn′-dig-eh	My elder brother.	Kŭn′-dig-eh	My elder brother.
65	Sa′-ga	" "				
66	Sa′-o-ga	" "				
67						
68	Sahn	" "	Ha-thon-a-ga-gech-el-che	My brother-in-law.	Su-thu-igh	My bro -in-law.
69	Ist-sasht′	" "			Eu-koo′-la-moot	" "
70						
71	Au′-wi-ta-atl	" "				
72	Al-käsh-kat	" "				
73	Tä-tä′-wä-le	" "				
74						
75						
76						
77						
78	Noo-ly-ä-mä-ŭn-yă	" "	Ang-a-jor-no-ra (o.), Nu-[ha-or-no-ra (y.)	My brother-in-law.	I-ega	" "
79	Sa-ki-at-si-a-ra	" "			Ning-a-u-ga	" "
80	Shuk-i-ä′-gä	" "				

TABLE II.—*Continued.*

	260. Sister-in-law. My wife's sister.	Translation.	261. Sister-in-law. My husband's sister.	Translation.	262. Sister-in-law. My brother's wife. (Male speaking.)	Translation.
1	Ka-yă'-o	My sister-in-law.	Ah-ge⁀ah'-ne⁀o	My sister-in-law.	Ah-ge⁀ah'-ne-ah	My sister-in-law.
2	Ka-yă'-ho	" "	Uh-ge⁀ah'-ne⁀o	" "	Uh-ge⁀ah'-ne-a	" "
3	Ah-ge-ah'-yeh	" "	Ah-ge-ah'-ne-o	" "	Ah-ge-ah'-yeh	" "
4	Un-ge⁀ah'-le⁀a	" "	Un-ge⁀ah'-le⁀a	" "	Un-ge⁀ah'-le⁀a	" "
5	Un-gă-le-ya'-hä	" "	Un-gă-le-ya'-hä	" "	Un-gă-le-ya'-hä	" "
6	Yack-gaw'-we-ri-o'-ah	" "	Ack-gä'-re-ah	" "	Ack-gä'-re-ah	" "
7	Uh-ge-hä'-kwä	" "	Uh-go-hä'-kwä	" "	Ah-go-hä'-kwä	" "
8	E-zhä-ku	" "	O-in-dä'-wait	" "	O-in-dä'-wait	" "
9	Häṇ-kä'	" "	E-cha'-päṇ	" "	Häṇ-kä'	" "
10	Hä'-kä	" "	E-shä'-pä	" "	Hä-kä'	" "
11	Wä'-kä	" "	E-shä'-pä	" "	Wä'-kä	" "
12	Hä'-kä	" "	E-shä'-pä	" "	Hä'-kä	" "
13	Hun'-kä	" "	S'-cha'-pä	" "	Hun'-kä	" "
14	Huṇ-kä'	" "	S'-cha'-pä	" "	Huṇ-kä'	" "
15	Hä-kä'	" "	E-sä'-pä	" "	Hä-kä'	" "
16	Hä-kä'	" "	Scha'-pä	"	Hä-kä'	" "
17	Mä-hä-gä'	" "	Me-she'-cha	" "	Mä-hä'-gä	" "
18	We-hun'-gä	" "	She-kä'	" "	We-hun'-gä	" "
19	We-hun'-gä	" "	We-she-kä'	" "	We-hun'-gä	" "
20	Huṇ'-gä	" "	Hee-she'-kä	" "	Huṇ'-gä	" "
21	Häṇ'-gä	" "	Hin-she'-kä	" "	Häṇ'-gä	" "
22	Be-hä'-gä	" "	Be-she-kä	" "	Be-hä'-gä	" "
23	We-hun'-kä	" "	We-she'-kä	" "	We-huṇ'-kä	" "
24	E-yun'-ga	" "	A-she-gun	" "	E-yun'-ga	" "
25	Noo'-ko-ho-mus	" "			Moo'-ha	My wife.
26	Ma-tä-rä-we'-a	My wife.	Mä-too'	" "	Boo-ä-kä'	My sister-in-law.
27	Moo'-a	" "	Bä-koo'-a	" "	Moo'-ä-ka	" "
28	Um-ä-lok'-o-sĭ	My sister-in-law.	Sup'-o	" "	Suh-hai'-yä	" "
29	Um-ä-läk'-o-sĭ	" "	Suh'-po	" "	Sä-hi'-yä	" "
30	Um-ä-läk'-o-sĭ	" "	Um-ä-läk'-o-sĭ	" "	Sä-hi'-yä	" "
31	Chu-hu'-cho-wä	" "	Chu-hu'-cho-wä	" "	Chu-hu'-cho-wä	" "
32	Au-sdä-duṇ'-hĭ	" "	Au-sdä-lĭ-gĭ	" "	Au-sdä-duṇ'-hĭ	" "
33	Ah-ke-tso'-hĭ	" "	Ah-ke-tso'-hĭ	" "	Ah-ge-tso'-hĭ	" "
34	Tä'-te-luk-tuk-ŭ	My wife.	Scoo'-rus	" "	Tä'-te-luk-tuk-ŭ	My wife.
35	Chä'-pot	" "	Sko'-dus	" "		
36	Nă-te-nä-tä-koo'	" "	Sko-roo'-hoo	" "	Nă'-te-nä-tä-koo'	" "
37	Nee-tim'	My sister-in-law.	N'-jä'-koase	" "	Nee-tim'	My sister-in-law.
38	Nee-tim'	" "	N'-jä'-koase	" "	Nee-tim'	" "
39	Nee-tim'	" "	N'-dä'-koase	" "	Nee-tim'	" "
40	Nĭ'-nim	" "	Nin-dan'-gwĕ	" "	Nĭ'-nim	" "
41	Ne'-nim	" "	Nin-don'-gwa	" "	Ne'-nim	" "
42	Ne-nim'	"	Nin-dän-gwa'	" "	Ne'-nim	" "
43	Ne-nim'	" "	N'-daṇ-gwä'	" "	Ne-nim'	" "
44	Ne-nim'	" "	N'-däṇ-gwa'	" "	Ne-nim'	" "
45	Ne-nim'	" "	N'-dän-gwa'	" "	Ne-nim'	" "
46	Ne-lim-wä'	" "	N'-da'-gwä-sa-n'yu'	" "	Ne-lim-wä'	" "
47	Ne-lim-wä'	" "	N'-da'-kwä-sa-mä	" "	Ne-lim-wä'	" "
48	Ne-lim-wä'	" "	N'-dä'-kwä-sa-mä'	" "	Ne-lim-wä'	" "
49	Ne-le-mwä'	" "	N'-dä'-kwä-sa-mä'	" "	Ne-le-mwä'	" "
50	Ne-le-mwä'	" "	N'-dä'-kwä-sa-mä'	" "	Ne-le-mwä'	" "
51	Ne-nim'-wä	" "	Nä-dä'-kwä	" "	Ne-nim'-wä	" "
52	Na-nim'	" "	Wä⁀a'-che-uk	" "	Na-nim'	" "
53	Nă-tsem'	My wife.	Nach-a-im'	" "	Nee-tum'	" "
54	Ne-nem-wä'	My sister-in-law.	Wa-si-nä-mä-kä	" "	Ne-nem-wä'	" "
55	Ne-lim-wä'	" "			Ne-lim-wä'	" "
56	Ne-tim'	" "	Nä-to'	" "	Ne-tim'	" "
57	N'-do'-to-ke-man'	" "	Nee-mis'	" "	N'-do'-to-ke-man'	" "
58	Ne-to'-to-yome	" "	Nee-mis'	" "	Ne-to'-to-ke-man'	" "
59	Ne-lu-mŭs'	" "	Nu-mäk-tem'	" "	Ne-lu-mŭs'	" "
60	Nee'-lu-mŭs	" "	Nu-mä'-ku-tem	" "	Nee'-lu-mŭs	" "
61	Nee-num'	" "	N'-dä-ohˑk'	" "	Nee-num'	" "
62	Nee-lum'	" "	Ne-tä'-wis	" "	Nee-lum'	" "
63	Na-nee-lim'	" "	Nain-ne-la'-kon	" "	Na-nee-lim'	" "
64	Sa'-gä	" "	Sa'-gä	" "	Sa'-gä	" "
65	Sa'-ga	" "	Sa'-ga	" "	Sa-ten'-a-bă-che-la	" "
66	Set'-so	" "	Sa'-o-ga	" "	Set'-so	" "
67	Sug-gingh	" "	Sug-gingh	" "	Sug-gingh	" "
68	Su-thu-igh	" "	Su-thu-igh	" "	Su-thu-igh	" "
69	Is-säs'-tăm	" "			Is-säs'-tăm	" "
70					E-sas-tan'	" "
71	En-pe-noke'	" "	En-matsh	" "	En-pe-noke'	" "
72			Al-kat-shau-wat	" "	Kat-shau-wats	" "
73	Pä-ven-e-benk	" "	E-ät-sin	" "	E-ät-sin	" "
74						
75						
76						
77						
78	Noo-ly-ă-mä-no-kä	" "	Ah-ke-yä-oo-ă	" "	Nä-kä-mä-noo-ly-ang-ă	" "
79	Sa-ki-ah-si-a-ra	" "	Sa-ki-at-si-a-ra	" "	U-ku-a-ra	" "
80	I-e'-gä	" "	Shuk-e-ä'-gä	" "	I-e'-gä	" "

TABLE II.—*Continued.*

	263. Sister-in-law. My brother's wife. (Female speaking.)	Translation.	264. My husband's brother's wife.	Translation.	265. My wife's brother's wife.	Translation.
1	Ah-ge͡ah'-ne͡o	My sister-in-law.	―――	Not related.	―――	Not related.
2	Uh-ge͡ah'-ne͡o	" "	―――	" "	―――	" "
3	Ah-ge-ah'-ne-o	" "	―――	" "	―――	" "
4	Un-ge͡ah'-le͡a	" "	―――	" "	―――	" "
5	Un-gä-le-ya'-hä	" "	―――	" "	―――	" "
6	Ack-gä'-re-ah	" "	―――	" "	―――	" "
7				" "	―――	" "
8	O-in-dä'-wait	" "	―――	" "	―――	" "
9	E-cha'-päṇ	" "	E-cha-päṇ'-she	My sister-in-law.	Häṇ-kä'	My sister-in-law.
10	E-shä'-pä	" "	E-shä'-pä	" "	Hä-kä'	" "
11	E-shä'-pä	" "	E-shä'-pä	" "	Wä'-kä	" "
12	E-shä'-pä	" "	E-shä'-pä	" "	Hä'-kä	" "
13	S'cha'-pä	" "	S'cha'-pä	" "	Hun'-kä	" "
14	S'cha'-pä	" "	S'cha'-pä	" "	Haṇ-kä'	" "
15	E-sä'-pä	" "	E-sä'-pä	" "	Hä-kä'	" "
16	E-sä'-pä	" "	Scha'-pä	" "	Hä-kä'	" "
17	Me-she'-cha-pä	" "	―――	Not related.		Not related.
18	She-kä'	" "				
19	We-she-kä'	" "	We-she'-kä	My sister-in-law.	Wee'-kä	My grandmother.
20	He-she'-kä	" "		Not related.		Not related.
21	Hin-she'-kä	" "		" "	―――	" "
22	Be-she'-kä	" "	Be-sho'-wa or Be-tuṇ'-ga.	My elder or younger [sister.	Me-wi'-huh-hä	My sister-in-law.
23	We-she'-kä	" "				
24	E-she-gun'	" "	Aw-kee'-nomb	My sister.	Aw-kee'-nomb	My sister.
25	Koo-too'-min-ik	" "				
26	Mä-too'	" "				
27	Bos-me'-ä-kun-is-ta	My young woman.	Bot-ze'-no-pä-che	My comrade.	Bot-ze'-no-pä-che	My comrade.
28	Suh-hai'-yä	My sister-in-law.				
29	Sä-hi'-yä	" "				
30	Sä-hi'-yä	" "	A-ka-noh'-mĭ	My relative.	A-ka-noh'-mĭ	My relative.
31	Um-e-hi'-wä	" "	Chu-hu'-cho-wä	My present occupant.	Chu-hu'-cho-wä	Present occupant.
32	Au-sdä-lĭ'-gĭ	" "	Au-sdä-duṇ'-hĭ	My sister-in-law.	Au-sdä-lĭ'-gĭ	My sister-in-law.
33	E-nä-duh'-hĭ	" " lative.	E-nä-duh'-hĭ	" "	E-nä-duh'-hĭ	" " [relative.
34	Kee-rut-koo'-rus-täk	My fem. marriage re-			La-koot'-scoo-rus	My male marriage
35	Sko'-dus	My sister-in-law.	―――	Not related.		
36	Sko-roo'-hoo	" "	―――	" "		
37	N'-jä'-koase	" "	―――	" "	―――	Not related.
38	N'-jä'-koase	" "	―――	" "	―――	" "
39	N'-dä'-koase	" "	―――	" "		" "
40	Nin-dan'-gwe	" "	Nin-dän'-gwĕ	My sister-in-law.	Nᴉ'-nim	My sister-in-law.
41	Niu-don'-gwa	" "	Nin-de-ge'-ko	My step-sister.	Nin-dä-wa'-mä	My step-sister
42	Nin-dän-gwa'	" "	Nin-de-gĭ'-ko	" "	Nin-dä-wa-mä'	" "
43	N'-daṇ-gwä'	" "	N'-da-gĭ'-ko	" "	N'-do-wa-mä'	" "
44	N'-däṇ-gwa'	" "		Not related.	N'-dä-wa-mä'	" "
45	N'-dän-gwa'	" "	―――	" "	Ne-nim'	" "
46	N'-jan-gwä'	" "	―――	" "		Not related.
47	Nin-jä-gwä'	" "	―――	" "	―――	" "
48	Nin-jä-gwä'	" "	―――	" "	―――	" "
49	Nin-jä-kwa'	" "	―――	" "	―――	" "
50	Niu-jä-kwa'	" "		" "	―――	" "
51	Nä-dä-kwä	" "	Nä-sa'-mä	My elder sister.	―――	" "
52	Wä-a'-che-uk	" "	Ne-ma'	" " "	―――	" "
53	Nach-a-im'	" "		Not related.	Ne-ma'	My elder sister.
54	Wa-si-nä-mä-kä	" "	―――	" "		Not related.
55	Ne-tä-kwä	" "	―――	" "		" "
56	Nä-to' or Ne-ta'-be	" "				
57	Nee-mis'	" "				
58	Nee-mis'	" "	Nee-mis'	My sister-in-läw.	O-mis'	My sister-in-law.
59	Ne-mäk-tem'	" "	Nit-chŭs'	" "	Nit-chŭs'	" "
60	Na-tä'-kw'	" "	Nee-tse-kes'	" "	Neet-chus'	" "
61	N'-dä-oh·k'	" "				
62	Ne-tä'-wis	" "				
63	Nain-ne-la'-kon	" "	Nain-jose'	My friend.	Nain-jose'	My friend.
64	Sa'-gä	" "	Sä-dä	My elder sister.	Sa'-dä	My elder sister.
65	Sa'-ga	" "				
66	Sa'-o-ga	" "				
67	Sug-gingh	" "				
68	Su-thu-igh	" "			Sa-un-do	My sister-in-law.
69	In-is-cha'-oo	" "				
70						
71						
72						
73	E-ät-sin					
74						
75						
76						
77	Gi-cä	" "	Nu-kow-now-ga	My sister-in-law.		
78			Ang-a-jos-no-ra (o.), Nu-[ka-or-no-ra (y.)	" "		
79	U-ku-a-ra	" "			U-ku-a-ra	" "
80	Oo-koo-ä'-gä	My sis. & da.-in-law.				

TABLE II.—*Continued.*

	266. Widow.	Translation.	267. Widower.	Translation.	268. Twins.	Translation.
1	Go-no-kwă′-yes-hă′-ah....	Widow.	Ho-no-kwă′-yes-hă-ah	Widower.	Ta-geek′-hă	Twins.
2						"
3	Go-da-ha′-e................	"	Ho-da-ha′-e..............	"	Da-yake′-hă..............	"
4	U-dä-la′-ose..............	"	Lo-dä-la′-ose...........	"	Da-yake′.................	"
5	U-da-la′-ose..............	"	Lo-dä-la′-ose...........	"	Da-yake′.................	"
6	As-there′-oth............	"	Ras-there′-oth..........	"	Nä-yăk′-he-ah...........	"
7	Ya-dä-rä-ose′-ko..........	"	Ro-dä-ra-ose′-ko........	"	Da-yake′-hă..............	"
8						"
9	We-wä′-ze-chă............	"	We- wä′-ze-chă..........	"	Chä-kpä′-pe.............	Attached navels.
10	We-tä′-zhe-na............	"	Ta-zhe′-nä-ho...........	"	Chek-pä′................	" "
11	We-wä′-ze-chă............	"	We-chä-zeet............	"	Chak-pä′-pe-do..........	" "
12	We-wä′-ze-chă............	"	We-chä-wä′-ze-chă......	"	Chak-pä′-pe.............	" "
13	Wa-wä′-ze-chă′-we-ah....	"	We-wä′-ze-chă-we-ah.....	"	Chake′-pä...............	" "
14	We-wä -ze-jah............	"	We-chä′-we-wä′-ze-chă ...	"	Chek-pä′................	"
15	Wä-tä′-zhe-no...........	"	Wä-zhe′-nä-ho..........	"	Chek-pä′................	"
16	We-tä′-zhe-no...........	"	Tä-she-nä-ho............	"	Num-pä′-pe.............	Twins.
17	We-tä′-zhe-na...........	"	Tä-zhe-nä-hä............	"	She′-pä.................	"
18	Ta-kä′-te-a-go...........	"	Ta-kä′-te-a-go..........	"	Nome-ba′-ak-dä.........	"
19	Wä-the-hä′-zhe..........	"	Me-glä′-zhe.............	"	No-wä′-tä...............	"
20	Wan-za-ke′-chă..........	"	He-nu′-ta-ke′-chă.......	Wife dead.		
21						
22						
23	Wä-cho-ne-ka-ket-so.....	"	Ne-ko-no-cho-ket-so	Widower.	No-po′-tä...............	"
24						
25	Ko-bo′-ro-ta	"	Ko-ha-mik′..............	"	Noh·′-kă...............	"
26	We-ă-kid-e-nash-it......	"			Doots-kă′..............	"
27	Me′-ă-sha	"	Bot-she′-sheke.........	"	Natch′-ka..............	"
28	I-hät-ăk Il-lĭ...........	Her man dead.	O-ho′-yo In-il′-lĭ.......	Woman dead to him.	He′-yup................	"
29	I-hät-ăk Il-lĭ...........	" " "	O-ho′-yo In-il′-lĭ.......	" " "	He′-yop................	"
30	A-tak′-un-ai Il-lĭ.........	" " "	E-ho′-yo-im-ai Il′-lĭ....	" " "	Hä-täk-luk′-lo..........	Double men.
31	O′-ye...................	A mourner.	O′-ye..................	A mourner.	Pok-tul′-ke............	Twins.
32	Oo-wau′-sä-lau-tsuŋ......	Widow.	Oo-wau′-sä-lau-tsuŋ......	Widower.	Dĭ-nĭ-lă′-wĭ...........	"
33	Oo-wo-su-lo-tsä′-hĭ......	"	Oo-wo-su-lo-tsä′-hĭ......	"	Da-ne-h′lă′-wih........	"
34	Se-kaw-ka-luk-tuk-ŭ......	Without a husband.	Kaw-ka-hä-lä-lik-ŭ.......	Without a wife.	Ter-rok′-ee............	"
35					Tä-lă′-ke..............	"
36					Tä-rä′.................	"
37	See-kow′................	Widow.	See-kow′...............	Widower.	Ne-su′-da-wuk.........	Two hearts.
38	See-kow′................	"	See-kow′...............	"	Ne-su′-da-wuk.........	"
39	She-gow′................	"	She-gow′...............	"	Na-zho′-ja-zhuk.......	"
40	Zhĭ′-găb................	"	Zhĭ′-găb...........[nĭ-	"	Nĭ-zho-dĕ′-yag........	Twins.
41	She-gä. ᵇZhä-gä-wid Ik-wĕ	"	She′-gä. ᵇZha-gä′-wid I-nĭ-	"	Nee-zho-da′-ĭg........	Two hearts.
42	She-gä′-kwa.............	"	She-gä-ae-ne′-ne.........	"	Ne-zho′-da-yuk........	"
43	She-gä′.................	"	She-gä′................	"	Ne-zho-dä′-yuk........	"
44	She-gä′.................	"	She-gä′................	"	Ne-zho-dä′-yuk........	"
45	She-gä′.................	"	She-gä′................	"	Ne-zho-dä′-yuk........	"
46	Ke-so′-ze-tä............	"	Ke-so′-ze-tä............	"	Che-kom-wä′-ke.......	Twins.
47	K′-sho-se-ah′...........	"	K′-sho-se-ah′..........	"	Chick-sä′-ke..........	"
48	K′-sho-se-ah′...........	"	K′-sho-se-ah′..........	"	Chick-sä′-ke..........	"
49	K′-sho-se-ah′...........	"	K′-sho-se-ah′..........	"	Chick-sä′-ke..........	"
50	K′-sho-se-ah′...........	"	K′-sho-se-ah′..........	"	Chick-sä′-ke..........	"
51	She-kä′-wis.............	"	She-kä′-wă.............	"	Ne-sho′-dä-huk........	"
52	Shä-ya′-kow-it..........	"	Sha-kow′...............	"	Me-tä′-suk............	"
53					Es-tä′-ke.............	"
54	Shi-kä-wi-wă...........	"	Sho-kä-wi-wă′..........	"	No-si-ta-thä-ki.......	"
55	Sä-kä′-we-tä	"	Sä-kä′-we-tä	"	Na-swe-ta-thä′-ke.....	"
56	Ah-ke-he′-tha..........	"	A-ne′-nä Wä-ke′-wit	"	Ne-thän′-nä..........	"
57	Ne-po′-mim............	"	A-po-ke′-min...........	"	Ne-steme′-mix........	"
58	Na′-po-me	"	Na′-po-kim............	"	Neese′-che-me........	"
59	Se-gŭs′-kw′............	"	Se-gŭ-ŏp′..............	"	Ne-jit-ko-bach′.......	My twin brothers.
60	See-gŭs′-kw′...........	"	See-gŭ-op′.............	"	Tu-kwes′..............	Twins.
61	Se-kä-kwä′-wä.........	"	Se-kä′-wä.............	"	Kwäs-wuk′............	"
62	Kot-hoo′...............	"	Kot-hoo′-hose.........	"	Kä-paa′-suk..........	"
63	Sa-go′-kwă.............	"	Sa′-ko.................	"	Kä-paze′-suk.........	"
64						
65	Ja-kwe′-ba-te-no-la......	"	Ja-na-u′-cha-kwe-e-la.....	"	Nä′-ka-ten-e-ă′-za......	"
66				Est-whet′-le............	"		
67						
68	Kon-ta-tu-gu...........	"	Kon-ta-tu-gu...........	"	Nun-a-chy-o..........	"
69	Slu-el′-lumt	"	Slu-el′-lumt	"	Snäs′-säl..............	"
70						
71						
72						
73	Lä-pe-wät′..............	"	Tä-wäts′-lä-pe-wät′	"	Wä′-bäts...............	"
74						
75	Pi-so-gu................	"	Pi-so-gu................	"	Wee-e-i	"
76					Ash-he-ee-ă-sä........	"
77						
78						
79	U-vig-dlar-neu	"	Nu-lêr-sok..............	"	Mai-dlu-li-at	"
80	We-got′-tŭ	"	Nu-le-uk′-to............	"	Nult-ee′-ka............	"

PART III.

CLASSIFICATORY SYSTEM OF RELATIONSHIP.—Continued.

TURANIAN AND MALAYAN FAMILIES.

WITH A TABLE.

(383)

CHAPTER I.

SYSTEM OF RELATIONSHIP OF THE TURANIAN FAMILY.

Turanian Family as newly constituted, consists principally of three Asiatic Stocks—The People speaking the Drâvidian Language—The People speaking the Gaura Language—And the Chinese—I. Drâvidian Nations—Highest Type of the Turanian System found amongst them—They still possess their Original Domestic Institutions. 1. Tamil —Tamilian System the Standard—Its General Characteristics—Lineal and First Collateral Lines—Diagrams—Marriage Relationships—Second Collateral Line—Diagrams—Marriage Relationships—Other Collateral Lines—Diagrams—Tamilian System substantially identical with that of the Seneca-Iroquois—Importance of this Discovery—The Tamil People salute by Kin—Evidences of the Antiquity of the System—Its Ability to perpetuate itself. 2. Telŭgŭ System—Indicative Relationships—It agrees with the Tamilian. 3. Canarese—Indicative Relationships—It agrees with the Tamilian—Further Evidence of the Antiquity of the Turanian System—Presumptively the same System prevails in the six remaining Drâvidian Dialects—A Domestic Institution—One of the Oldest Institutions of the Human Family.

IN Max Müller's Genealogical Table of the Turanian family of languages, the Ugrian and Turkish dialects form a part of its northern division, and the Malayan a part of its southern.[1] It has been seen that it was found necessary, using their system of relationship as the basis of classification, to remove the former from the Turanian connection, and to organize them into an independent family, the Uralian; and, for the same reasons, it will hereafter be found necessary to detach the Malayan, and to place them also in the position of an independent family. Of the remaining dialects of the northern division, the Mongolian and Tungusian are not represented in the Table; and but a small portion of those belonging to the southern. So material an innovation upon the Turanian family, as formerly constituted, has not been made without hesitation and solicitude. A comparison, however, of the systems of relationship of the nations herein classified as Turanian, with the systems of the other families of mankind, will disclose ample reasons to justify the proposed classification upon the basis assumed. The sufficiency of this basis, as of any other, must be accepted or rejected upon its merits. It so happens that the most remarkable and distinctive system of consanguinity and affinity yet discovered in Asia prevails in a portion of the old Turanian family, and also amongst a number of other nations hitherto excluded from that connection. The quarter in which it is found seemed sufficiently commanding after the Ugrian and Turkish stocks had been removed, to carry with it the Turanian name. Whether there is a sufficient foundation for the proposed innovations can be better determined after the systems of relationship of the Turanian nations, which are herein classified as such, have been presented and considered.

The four principal Asiatic stocks comprised in the Turanian family, as newly constituted, are the people of South India, who speak the Drâvidian language, and number upwards of thirty millions; the people of North India, who speak the

---

[1] Science of Language, pp. 397, 398.

Gaura language, and number upwards of one hundred millions; the Chinese, who are supposed to number upwards of three hundred millions; and the Japanese, who are included provisionally, numbering about thirty millions. Of the systems of relationship of these great branches, that of the first is the highest and most perfectly developed, and the Tamilian form of this system will be taken as the standard or typical form of the Turanian family. The admission into this family of the people speaking the Gaura language, the present speech of the Brahmins, will excite some surprise. Their system of relationship is classificatory. Although it falls in some respects below the Tamilian, the variance seems to be explainable by Sanskritic influence, the system itself being still Turanian in the greater part of its radical characteristics. The restoration of the northern branch of the great Hindŭ stem to a connection with the southern, in the same family is in accordance with philological evidence, notwithstanding the intrusion of Aryan elements in excessive measure into the materials of the Gaura language. With respect to the Chinese, whose introduction into this family will seem still more novel and extraordinary, the reasons drawn from their system of relationship are equally decisive. Aside from the barrier interposed by the differences between a monosyllabical and an agglutinated language, such an affiliation was to have been expected on general ethnological grounds, rather than assumed to be impossible. As thus constituted the Turanian family numbers upwards of four hundred and fifty millions of people, and is, therefore, much the largest, numerically, of all the families of mankind.

Drâvidian Language. 1. Tamil. 2. Telŭgŭ. 3. Canarese (and 4. Malayâlâm. 5. Tulu. 6. Tuda. 7. Kota. 8. Gônd. 9. Ku; not in the Table).

The highest type of the Turanian system of relationship, as before remarked, is found amongst the people of South India, who speak the Drâvidian language.[1] Five of its nine dialects are cultivated, namely, the Tamil, Telŭgŭ, Canarese, Malayâlam, and Tulu. The system of relationship of the first three, fully and minutely presented, will be found in the Table. The people, to a very great extent, are still unmixed in blood, and in possession of their original domestic institutions. Their position in the southern part of the peninsula of Hindustan, hemmed in on three sides by an ocean barrier, tends to the inference that they had been forced southward from a more northern location.[2] Presumptively they are amongst the oldest,

---

[1] Dr. Caldwell estimates the number of people speaking the several dialects of the Drâvidian language as follows:—

1. Tamil.	. . .	10,000,000
2. Telugu	. . .	14,000,000
3. Canarese .	. .	5,000,000
4. Malayâlam	. .	2,500,000
5. Tulu	. . .	150,000

6. Tuda,		
7. Kota,	. . .	500,000
8. Gond,		
9. Ku		

Drâvidian Comparative Grammar, Intro., p. 9, Lond. Ed., 1856.

[2] "The existence of a distinctively Drâvidian element in these aboriginal dialects of Central India [the Râjmahal and Urâon] being established, the Drâvidian race can now be traced as far north as the banks of the Ganges; and the supposition (which was deduced from other considerations) that this race was diffused at an early period throughout India is confirmed. The Brahui, the language of the Belûchi mountaineers of the khanship of Kelat, enables us to trace the Drâvidian race beyond the Indus to the southern confines of Central Asia. The Brahui language, considered as a whole,

in the duration of their political existence, of the Asiatic stocks. For these reasons their system of consanguinity and affinity would be invested with special importance. This importance is greatly enhanced by its extraordinary character.

1. Tamil. The Tamilian system of relationship will be first considered. An analysis sufficiently complete to develop its fundamental characteristics would be nearly a literal transcript of that previously given of the system of the Seneca-Iroquois. For the purpose of comparison, this analysis is given in the subjoined note, to which reference is made.[1]

---

is derived from the same source as the Panjábi and Sindhi, but it unquestionably contains a Drá-vidian element, an element which has probably been derived from a remnant of the ancient Drá-vidian race incorporated with the Brahuis. The discovery of this Drávidian element in a language spoken beyond the Indus proves that Drávidians, like the Aryans, the Græco-Scythians, and the Turco-Mongolians, entered India by the northwestern route." Caldwell's Drávidian Comp. Gram. Intr., p. 23.

[1] Analysis of the Tamilian System of Relationship:—

I. Relatives by blood or marriage are not described by a combination of the primary terms, but each and all are so classified as to fall under the recognized relationships, for each of which there is a special term. Exceptions elsewhere stated.

II. The several collateral lines are ultimately merged in the lineal line.

III. All the brothers and sisters of my grandfather and of my grandmother are my grandfathers and grandmothers; but they are distinguished into elder or younger, as they are older or younger than my own grandparents. All the brothers and sisters of my several ancestors above grand-parents are distinguished in the same manner, and also numerically, according to the degree of removal. All of my descendants below grandchildren are also distinguished from each other numerically.

IV. The relationship of brother and sister is conceived in the twofold form of elder and younger. There is one term for elder brother, and another for younger brother; one term for elder sister, and another for younger sister; and no term for brother or sister in the abstract.

V. All the children of several brothers are brothers and sisters to each other, and they use inter-changeably the same terms which they apply to an own brother and sister.

VI. All the sons of the sons of several brothers are brothers to each other, and the sons of the latter are brothers again; and the same relationship of males, in the male line, continues downward theoretically, *ad infinitum*, so long as the persons stand at equal removes from the original brothers; but when one is further removed than the other, by a single degree, the rule which turns the col-lateral into the lineal line at once applies; thus, the son of one of these, my elder or younger brothers, becomes my son, and the son of the latter my grandson.

VII. All the children of several sisters are brothers and sisters to each other, and the terms of relationship are applied in the same manner as before stated in the case of the children of several brothers.

VIII. All the daughters of the daughters of several sisters are sisters to each other; and the relationship of females, in the female line, continues to be that of sisters, elder or younger, at equal removes, theoretically, *ad infinitum*, as in the case of the male descendants of brothers, and with the same consequences if one of them is further removed than another by a single degree from the original sisters.

IX. All the children of several brothers, on the one hand, are cousins to all the children of their several sisters on the other.

X. All the sons of several male cousins, and all the daughters of several female cousins, are them-selves cousins respectively to each other; and the same relationship of males, in the male line, and of females, in the female line, continues to be that of cousins at equal removes, theoretically, *ad infinitum*.

XI. With *Ego* a male, the children of my male cousins are my nephews and nieces, and of my female cousins are my sons and daughters. With *Ego* a female, the children of my male cousins are

It is advisable to take up this form in detail, and to trace the circuit of each branch of the first five collateral lines from the point of their emergence from the lineal until they are again restored to its descending stream, that we may seize and hold its distinctive features.   As we are now to pass from the American to the Asiatic continent, and from one family of mankind to another, which families, if in fact descended from common ancestors, must have been separated for thousands of

---

my sons and daughters, and of my female cousins are nephews and nieces; and the children of these nephews and nieces, sons and daughters, are, without distinction, my grandchildren.

XII. All the brothers of my father are my fathers, and they are fathers to each other's children. In like manner all the sisters of my mother are my mothers, and they are mothers to each other's children, but distinguished into *great* and *little*.

XIII. All the brothers of my mother are my uncles, and my mother is an aunt to the children of all her brothers.   In like manner all the sisters of my father are my aunts, and my father is an uncle to the children of all his sisters.   The relationship of uncle is restricted to the brothers of my mother, and to the brothers of such other persons as stand to me in the relation of a mother; and the relationship of aunt is restricted to my father's sisters, and to such other persons as stand to my father in the relation of sisters.

XIV. All the children of my several brothers, *Ego* a male, are my sons and daughters; and all the children of my several sisters are my nephews and nieces.

XV. All the children of my several brothers, *Ego* a female, are my nephews and nieces; and all the children of my several sisters are my sons and daughters.

XVI. All the grandchildren of my several brothers, and of my several sisters, are, without distinction, my grandchildren, and I apply to them the same terms used to designate my own grandchildren.

XVII. It has been stated in effect, and is now repeated, that all the children of the several brothers of my father, and all the children of the several sisters of my mother, are my brothers and sisters, elder or younger, the same as my own brothers and sisters.   With *Ego* a male, all the children of these several collateral brothers are my sons and daughters, and all the children of these several collateral sisters are my nephews and nieces.   With *Ego* a female, these relationships are respectively reversed.   All the grandchildren of these several collateral brothers and sisters are my grandchildren without distinction.

XVIII. The principle of discrimination as to relative nearness where the two are equally removed from the common ancestors appears to be the following: From *Ego* a male to the children of a male, and from *Ego* a female to the children of a female, the relationship of these children to *Ego* approaches in the degree of its nearness.   But from *Ego* a male to the children of a female, and from *Ego* a female to the children of a male, it recedes.   This rule is reversed as to the children of a male or female cousin.

XIX. As a general consequence the descendants of an original pair cannot, in theory, ever pass outside the relationship of cousin, which is the most remote collateral relationship recognized, and the greatest divergence allowed from the lineal line.   Hence the bond of consanguinity which can never, in fact, be broken by lapse of time is not suffered to be broken in principle.

XX. All the wives of these several collateral brothers are my sisters-in-law, or female cousins (the term used signifying a cousin as well); and all the wives of these several male cousins are my younger sisters.

XXI. All the husbands of these several collateral sisters are my brothers-in-law, or male cousins (the terms being the same for both relationships), and all the husbands of these several female cousins are my elder or younger brothers, according to relative age.

XXII. All the wives of these several collateral sons, if *Ego* is a male, are my daughters-in-law (the term for niece and daughter-in-law being the same); and if *Ego* is a female, they are my daughters.   All the wives of these several nephews are my daughters, whether *Ego* is a male or a female.   All the husbands of these several collateral daughters, *Ego* being a male, are my sons-in-law

years, it is desirable to go through the system as it now prevails in Turanian lands, although it may be a close repetition of the Ganowánian form.

The relationships of collateral kindred, in many cases, are very different with *Ego* a male from what they are with *Ego* a female, as was also the fact in the American Indian system. This characteristic cannot be too distinctly apprehended. In a family consisting of several brothers and sisters, each having children, these children stand to the brothers in one relation, and to the sisters in another, of which the converse is true with respect to the relationships of these brothers and sisters to each other's children. Collateral brothers and sisters and their children exhibit the same differences in their relationships. A chart of consanguinity with *Ego* a male, which would be true as to each of these brothers and their collateral consanguinei, would be untrue as to each of these sisters and the same persons also their consanguinei; and therefore two charts are required for the same group of persons, one for the males and the other for the females. It introduces diversity of relationships as well as complexity into the system; but since these changes are made in accordance with the established principles of discrimination they are easily understood and followed.

The lineal line admits of but little diversity, and, therefore, it is substantially the same under all systems. Ancestors above grandfather and grandmother, to the third degree in Tamil, are distinguished as second and third grandfather and grandmother, *e. g.*, *Păddăn*, *Pûddăn*, and *Muppaddăn*. Descendants below grandson are distinguished to the third degree as second and third grandsons and granddaughters, *e. g.*, *Pêrăn*, *Irandam Pêrăn*, and *Mŭndam Pêrăn*. In common intercourse the first terms only are used. There are also terms for father and mother, *Tŭkkăppăn* and *Tăy*, and for son and daughter, *Măkăn* and *Măkăl*.

There is no term in the Tamil dialect for brother or sister in the abstract. These relationships are conceived in the twofold form of elder and younger, and there are separate terms for each. To all of my brothers and sisters who are older than myself I apply the respective terms for elder brother and elder sister; and to those who are younger than myself the respective terms for younger brother and younger sister. There are two terms of synonymous import for elder brother, *Tămaiyăn* and *Annăn;* two for elder sister, *Akkărl* and *Tămăkay*, and two for younger sister, *Tangaichchi* and *Tangay;* and but one term for younger brother, *Tambi*. It seems probable that one set of these terms was originally used by the males, and the other by the females; but whether so used or otherwise, they are now used indiscriminately.

In the first collateral line male, with *Ego* a male, my brother's son and daughter I call my son and daughter, *Măkăn* and *Măkăl*. This is the first indicative feature

---

(the term for son-in-law and nephew being the same); and if *Ego* is a female, then they are my sons. And all the husbands of these several nieces, whether *Ego* is a male or female, are my sons.

XXIII. In all of the preceding cases the principle of correlative relationship is strictly applied; thus, the one I call elder brother, calls me younger brother; the one I call cousin, calls me cousin; the one I call nephew, calls me uncle; the one I call son-in-law, calls me father-in-law; and thus onward through every recognized relationship. The only exceptions are those to whom the words "great" and "little" are applied; the one I call great father calls me son.

of the Tamilian system.   My brother's grandchildren are my grandchildren, *Pêran* and *Pêrtti*.   With *Ego* a female, my brother's son and daughter are my nephew and niece, *Mărumăkăn* and *Mărumăkăl*; and their children are my grandchildren.

In the same line, female branch, with *Ego* a male, my sister's son and daughter are my nephew and niece, *Mărumăkăn* and *Mărumăkăl*.   This is the second indicative feature.   With *Ego* a female, my sister's son and daughter are my son and daughter, *Măkăn* and *Măkăl;* and my sister's grandchildren are my grandchildren, whether *Ego* be a male or female.

In the diagram Plate X. the lineal and first collateral line, male and female, are represented with *Ego* a male.   It would require a second diagram to exhibit the relationships of the same persons to *Ego* a female; but the only changes required would be the substitution of nephew and niece in the place of son and daughter, and *vice-versa*.   This diagram, and those which follow, are constructed upon the same plan as those used to illustrate the Seneca-Iroquois system, and the explanations previously given apply equally to the diagrams of the Tamilian system.

The marriage relationships in this line are as follows: the wife of my brother's son, *Ego* a male, is my daughter-in-law, *Mărumăkăl;* the wife of my sister's son is my daughter, *Măkăl;* the husband of my brother's daughter is my son-in-law, *Mărumăkăn;* and of my sister's daughter is my son, *Măkăn*.   With *Ego* a female, these relationships are reversed; the wife of my brother's son is my daughter, and of my sister's son is my daughter-in-law; whilst the husband of my brother's daughter is my son, and of my sister's daughter is my son-in-law.   It will be observed that the terms for nephew and niece are used for son-in-law and daughter-in-law as well.   This disposes of the first collateral line.

In all of the preceding relationships, as well as in all of those which follow, the principle of correlative relationship is strictly applied; the one I call my son calls me father, the one I call my nephew calls me uncle, the one I call grandfather calls me grandson, and the one I call my son-in-law calls me father-in law, and so onward through all the recognized relationships.

The principle of classification found in the first collateral line is applied to the second, third, and each successive collateral line, as far as the connection of consanguinei can be traced; that is to say, wherever a brother or sister is found in either of these lines, and however remote in numerical degrees, their children and descendants stand in the same relationship to *Ego* as the children and descendants of an own brother and sister, as above stated.

In the second collateral line male, on the father's side, my father's brother I call my father, *Tăkkăppăn*.   This is the third indicative feature.   He is also distinguished as my *great* or *little* father, as he is older or younger than my own father, by prefixing the words *Pêriyă* or *Sĕriyă*, which signify *great* and *little*.   In ordinary intercourse I call him my father.   My father's brother's son and daughter, if older than myself, are my elder brother and elder sister *Tămaiyăn* and *Akkărl*, and if younger, are my younger brother and younger sister *Tambi* and *Tăngay*.   This is a fourth indicative feature of the Tamilian system.   The son and daughter of this collateral brother, *Ego* a male, are my son and daughter; of this collateral sister are my nephew and niece; and the children of these sons and daughters, nephews and nieces, are, without distinction, my grandchildren. With *Ego* a female the former relationships are reversed; my brother's son and daughter are my nephew and niece, whilst my sister's son and daughter are my son and daughter. The children of each are my grandchildren.

My father's sister is my aunt, *Attai*. This is the fifth indicative feature. My father's sister's son and daughter are my male and female cousins. For these relationships there is a double set of terms, *Măittŭnăn* and *Măchchän*, with their feminines, *Măittŭni* and *Machchi;* and also *Attän* for male cousin. The son and daughter of my male cousin, *Ego* a male, are my nephew and niece; and of my female cousin are my son and daughter. With *Ego* a female the son and daughter of my male cousin are my son and daughter, and of my female cousin are my nephew and niece. The grandchildren of these cousins are severally my grandchildren.

The discrimination of the relationship of cousin is a remarkable fact in the Tamilian system. It is now found in the systems of but a small portion of the Turanian family. From the structure and principles of the Turanian system, as has before been remarked with reference to the Ganowánian, it was predetermined that when developed this relationship would be applied and restricted to the children of a brother and sister.[1] It was probably unknown in the primitive system.

In the male branch of the same line, on the mother's side, my mother's brother is my uncle, *Mämăn*. This is a sixth indicative feature. My mother's brother's son and daughter are my male and female cousins. The children of my male cousins, *Ego* a male, are my nephews and nieces; of my female cousins are my sons and daughters; and their children are my grandchildren. With *Ego* a female the children of my male cousins are my sons and daughters, and of my female cousins are my nephews and nieces; and the children of each are my grandchildren.

It is a little singular that the children of my male cousin, *Ego* a male, should be my nephews and nieces, instead of my sons and daughters, and that the children of my female cousins should be my sons and daughters instead of my nephews and nieces, as required by the analogies of the system. It is the only particular in which it differs materially from the Seneca-Iroquois form; and in this the Seneca is more in logical accordance with the principles of the system than the Tamilian. It is difficult to find any explanation of the variance.

My mother's sister is my mother, *Täy*. This is the seventh indicative feature. My mother's sister's son and daughter are my brother and sister, elder or younger. This is the eighth indicative feature. The son and daughter of this collateral brother, *Ego* a male, are my son and daughter; of this collateral sister are my nephew and niece; and the children of each are my grandchildren. With *Ego* a female, the children of my collateral brother are my nephew and niece; of my collateral sister, are my son and daughter; and the children of each are my grand-

---

[1] It may be conjectured that the system of the Hill Tribes of South India, when obtained, will be found without this relationship; and that its place is supplied by some ruder form, as that of uncle and nephew, or father and son.

children. In this branch of the line on the mother's side, and in the male branch on the father's side, it will be noticed that the rule of classification established in the first collateral line is fully applied; whilst in the other two branches the places of nephew and son and of niece and daughter are reversed.

Diagram Plate XI. represents the lineal and second collateral line, male and female, on the father's side; and Diagram Plate XII. represents the same lines and branches on the mother's side, with *Ego* in both cases a male. It would require two other diagrams to represent the relationships of the same persons to *Ego* a female, with changes in the lower horizontal line of figures, where son and daughter would give place to nephew and niece, and the latter to the former.

The marriage relationships in this line are discriminated with equal particularity. The wife of my father's brother is my mother, and of my mother's brother is my aunt; and the husband of my father's sister is my uncle, and of my mother's sister is my father. At the next degree, the wives of my several collateral brothers are my sisters-in-law, the term used being that for female cousin; but the wives of my several male cousins are my younger sisters. In like manner the husbands of my several collateral sisters are my brothers-in-law, the term used being that for male cousin; and the husbands of my several female cousins are my brothers, elder or younger. Whether the husbands and wives of my several collateral nephews and nieces stand to me in any recognized relationship does not appear in the Table, as no questions were introduced into the schedule to determine that question; but it is probable that they were embraced within the comprehensive folds of the system.

The four branches of the second collateral line have now been traced from the point of their emergence from the lineal, first as divergent, then as parallel, and lastly as convergent, until they were reunited with its descending stream. It is seen that the descendants of my collateral kindred, after passing beyond a certain numerical degree, are placed in the same category as my own direct posterity. The chain of consanguinity has been followed with great particularity, that the artificial and complicated character of the system might be exhibited, as well as the rigorous precision with which its minute details are adjusted. Nearly all the indicative features of the system, together with its most important principles of classification are contained in the first and second collateral lines. In those more remote the classification is the same as far as the connection of consanguinei can be traced. With this fact in mind the relationships in the remaining lines will be readily understood as a descending series.

In the third collateral line male, on the father's side, my grandfather's brother is my grandfather. This is the ninth indicative feature of the system. He is also distinguished from my lineal grandfather by prefixing the terms for great or little, as he is older or younger than my own grandfather. The son of this grandfather is my father; his son and daughter are my brother and sister, elder or younger; the son of this collateral brother, *Ego* a male, is my son, and of this collateral sister is my niece; and their children are my grandchildren. With *Ego* a female the relationships of the children of this collateral brother and sister are reversed.

My grandfather's sister is my grandmother, great or little; her son and daughter are my uncle and aunt, and their children are my cousins. The children of my male cousins, *Ego* a male, are my nephews and nieces, of my female cousins are my sons and daughters, and their children are my grandchildren. With *Ego* a female, the changes are as before.

My grandmother's brother is my grandfather; his son and daughter are my uncle and aunt, and the children of the latter are my cousins. The descendants of these cousins stand to me in the same relationships as in the last case.

Lastly, my grandmother's sister is my grandmother; her son and daughter are my father and mother, and their children are my brothers and sisters, elder or younger. The descendants of these collateral brothers and sisters stand to me in the same relationships as those named in the first branch of this line.

For all practical purposes the lineal and first three collateral lines, which include the body of our kindred whose relationships are traceable, carries the system as far as its ordinary use extends. These lines, however, neither exhaust its range, nor reach the limits of its application. It extends to the fourth, fifth, and even more remote collateral lines, without any limitation whatever upon its all embracing character, and without any change in the relationships of collaterals because of their remoteness in numerical degrees. When the position of any given person, with reference to *Ego*, is precisely ascertained, even though found in the twelfth collateral line, the relationship of such person would be at once determined. He would fall into one of the great classes found in the lineal and second collateral lines. In other words, the system is theoretically unlimited.

It will be sufficient to pass through one branch of the fourth and fifth collateral lines, proceeding from the parent to one only of his or her children, which will give the following series: My great-grandfather's brother is my grandfather in the second degree; his son is my grandfather; the son of the latter is my father, great or little; his son is my brother, elder or younger; and the son and grandson of this brother are my son and grandson. In the fifth, my great-great-grandfather's brother is my grandfather in the third degree; his son is my grandfather in the second degree; his son is my grandfather; his son is my father, great or little; the son of the latter, is my brother, elder or younger; and his son and grandson are my son and grandson.

In all of the preceding illustrations the collateral lines are ultimately brought into the lineal line, which gives the tenth indicative feature of the Tamilian system.

Diagram Plate XIII. represents the lineal, and second, third, and fourth collateral lines, male and female, on the father's side; and Diagram Plate XIV. the same on the mother's side, with *Ego* in both cases a male. Each line is restricted to a single person at each degree. The second collateral line, which was shown in previous diagrams, is retained for comparison with the third and fourth. It would require two others to exhibit the relationships of the same persons to *Ego* a female, but the changes, as before, would be limited to persons in the horizontal line of figures below *Ego*, and would be the same as indicated with reference to the other diagrams. The explanations and mode of testing these diagrams are the same as those previously given with respect to those illustrative of the Seneca-Iroquois system. The only failure in the verification will be found when the relationships to

Ego of the children of his cousins intervene, wherein the true principles of the system, as elsewhere stated, are contravened.

All of the maternal parts of the Tamilian system of relationship have now been presented with fulness and particularity. There were reasons for so doing which reach beyond any importance this form of consanguinity might possess as a local domestic institution. It is seen to be the same system, in fulness, precision, and complexity, as well as in radical characteristics, with that which now prevails in the principal branches of the Ganowánian family. For the purpose of showing this great fact amongst others, and of making it expressive, the mass of materials in the several Tables have been accumulated. It is in great part with reference to the ultimate uses to be made of this fact of identity of system upon the American and Asiatic continents that such an elaborate presentation of the systems of the several families of mankind was believed to be necessary.

Several general considerations remain to be noticed. It is apparent from the foregoing exposition that the Tamilian system proceeds with the utmost regularity, and that it is coherent, self-sustaining, and harmonious throughout, although it creates the largest conceivable diversity in the relationships of blood-kindred. As a plan of consanguinity it is stupendous in form, and complicated in its details, and seemingly arbitrary and artificial in its structure, when judged by ordinary standards. The fundamental conceptions upon which it rests are not only clearly defined, but they are enforced with rigorous precision. From the manner of their use the primary terms are divested of their strict signification, whence father and mother cease to convey the idea of progenitors, son and daughter, grandson and granddaughter that of direct lineal descent from *Ego*; and brother and sister that of birth from common parents, unless we assume the prevalence of a wide-spread system of intermarriage or cohabitation amongst relatives, which would render these relationships those which actually existed.

It will be observed, as another prominent feature of the system, that a proper classification of kindred under it involved an exact knowledge of the degrees of consanguinity numerically, since the several collateral relationships depend upon the distance in degree of related persons from the common ancestor. For example, the collateral brother of *Ego*, to stand in this relation, must be equally distant with himself from the common ancestor, the collateral father one degree less, the collateral son one degree further, and the collateral grandson two degrees further removed. To apply the proper terms with facility and correctness required a knowledge of the chain of connection as well as of the principles of the system, and also the certainty of parentage.

There are also three fundamental conceptions embodied in the Tamilian system, which were previously found in the Ganowánian, which, if they do not form its basis, contain the principal part of its substance. These are, first, that the children of own brothers should be brothers and sisters to each other; that the sons of these collateral brothers should be brothers again, and the daughters of these collateral sisters should be sisters again; and that the same rule should continue downwards amongst their descendants at equal removes in an infinite series. Second, that the children of own sisters should, in like manner, be brothers and sisters; and that their descendants at equal degrees, and under the same limitations, should also be brothers and sisters to each other in a like infinite series. And, third, that the children of a brother on the one hand, and of his own sister on the other, should stand to each other in a more remote relationship than that of brother and sister. If in that of cousin and cousin, then this relationship should continue amongst their descendants at equal removes, and under like limitations, in a like infinite series. These provisions are far from constituting the whole of this remarkable system, but a knowledge of their existence tends to render it more intelligible.

Finally, two inquiries naturally suggest themselves, of which the first is, What assurances can be given that this elaborate system of relationship, precisely as herein detailed, exists at the present moment, in actual practical use, amongst the people of South India? And the second is, By what means has such a complicated classification of consanguinei been maintained understandingly amongst the masses of the people? If it holds the rank of a domestic institution, it must be not only permanently established, and of great antiquity, but there must also be constantly operating causes by means of which a knowledge of it is both acquired and preserved. These questions may be properly answered before we present the Telŭgŭ and Canarese forms, which agree essentially with the Tamilian.

The Tamil and Telŭgŭ schedules, as given in the Table, were filled out by the Rev. Ezekiel C. Scudder, of Vellore, South India, a son of the late distinguished American missionary, Dr. John Scudder, the founder of the Arcot mission. He was born and raised in India, within the area of the Tamil speech, which thus became as much his mother tongue as the English. His qualifications as a Tamil scholar, to work out and verify the minute details of this elaborate system of relationship, were of the highest order. It was esteemed by the writer a peculiar instance of good fortune that the verification of the existence as well as of the details of the Tamilian system, upon the truthfulness of which one of the main results of this research must hinge, was to rest upon such distinguished authority. It may be further stated that when his brother, the Rev. Dr. Henry W. Scudder, was in this country in 1859, I obtained from him a synopsis of both the Tamil and Telŭgŭ systems, which he had investigated far enough to ascertain their principal indicative characteristics, but as he was unable, without native assistance, to furnish its details, he placed the schedule in the hands of his brother upon his return to India. Having thus discovered the identity of the Ganowánian and Tamilian systems, it became a matter of the utmost importance that the latter should be thoroughly explored, and its structure and principles verified beyond a contingency of doubt. In addition to the Scudder schedule, I have a second one of the Tamil filled out very completely by the late Rev. Dr. Miron Winslow, American missionary at Madras; and still a third furnished by the Rev. William Tracey, one of the English missionaries at Madras. The three schedules agree in all particulars which are fundamental to the system, and thus verify each other; but as the first was the most complete in its details, it was inserted in the Table.

The answer to the second question brings to light an unexpected usage, which is thus found to prevail in two, at least, of the great families of mankind. It has been shown to be a universal usage in the Ganowánian family for relatives to salute by kin. In familiar, as well as in formal, intercourse they address each other by the term of relationship, and never by the personal name. It was seen that this custom contributed powerfully both to the knowledge and maintenance of the system, for to use it thus it must be understood. That the same usage prevailed in India was a reasonable conjecture; and if so, it was important that the fact should be ascertained. In answer to inquiries upon this subject the Rev. E. C. Scudder writes: " You ask me first, ' Do the Tamil and Telŭgŭ people in familiar intercourse and in formal salutation address each other, when related, by the term of relationship or by the personal name, or in both forms.' The younger can *never* address the elder relative by the personal name, but always by the term of relationship, i. e., the son *must* say father, the younger brother *must* say elder brother, and so on throughout. In the case of the elder the matter is left optional. A father *may* call his son by his personal name, or by the term of relationship as he chooses. An elder brother may address a younger brother in the same way. The rule is, a younger relative *cannot* address an elder relative by the personal name; an elder may. * * * Your question in reference to correlative relationship, viz., ' Does the one I call elder brother call me younger brother?' etc. etc., is covered by the answer to your first question, I call my elder brother *anna only*, he calls me *tambi*, or by my personal name as he chooses. In this there is no variation." The difference between the American Indian and Tamil Indian usages does not impair the general result, since the necessity for addressing the elder relative by the term of relationship requires as well as teaches a complete knowledge of the system. The large number of persons brought by its provisions within the near relationships intensifies the influence of the custom. It also tends to strengthen the integrity of the bond of kindred.

2. Telŭgŭ. The system of this people agrees with the Tamilian in minute as well as general particulars, the extent of which will be seen by consulting the Table. It will, therefore, be unnecessary to do more than state the indicative relationships, which determine those that follow.

First Indicative Feature. My brother's son and daughter, *Ego* a male, are my son and daughter. With *Ego* a female, they are my nephew and niece. The children of each are my grandchildren.

Second. My sister's son and daughter, *Ego* a male, are my nephew and niece. With *Ego* a female, they are my son and daughter. The children of each are my grandchildren.

Third. My father's brother is my father. He is also distinguished as great or little father, as he is older or younger than my own father.

Fourth. My father's brother's son and daughter are my brother and sister, elder or younger.

Fifth. My father's sister is my aunt. Her children are my cousins.

Sixth. My mother's brother is my uncle. His children are my cousins.

Seventh. My mother's sister is my mother.

Eighth. My mother's sister's son and daughter are my brother and sister, elder or younger.

Ninth. My grandfather's brother is my grandfather.

Tenth. The children of my collateral brothers, and of my female cousins, *Ego* a male, are my sons and daughters; and of my collateral sisters, and of my male cousins, are my sons and daughters; and the children of each are my grand-children. In this manner the collateral line is merged in the lineal.

It is impossible to mistake the identity of the Telŭgŭ with the Tamilian form, or to fail of perceiving the same rigorous application of the principles of classifica-tion. Some changes have occurred in their nomenclatures of relationship in the lapse of ages; but the terms, for the most part, are the same words dialectically changed. The two dialects have been distinct for centuries, and the two systems independent of each other for the same period of time; but it is still manifest that both the system and the terms were derived from the same original source. From this fact an impression is obtained of the antiquity as well as permanence of the Turanian system. It is seen to have perpetuated itself, in two independent channels, from the period when these dialects became distinct; and that the two forms, in whatever is radical, are still identical not only but also coincident in nearly all of their subordinate details.

3. Canarese. Whatever has been said of the Telŭgŭ is substantially true with respect to the Canarese. The three peoples numbering upwards of twenty-seven millions, have subjected the system through force of numbers to an unusual test. If a system so elaborate in its structure has been able to maintain itself for ages without material innovation it affords decisive evidence of the vitality of its radi-cal forms, and of its ability to perpetuate itself through long periods of time. It will be sufficient for a comparison of the Canarese with the Tamilian system to present the indicative relationships.

First Indicative Feature. My brother's son and daughter, *Ego* a male, are my son and daughter. With *Ego* a female, they are my nephew and niece.

Second. My sister's son and daughter, *Ego* a male, are my nephew and niece. With *Ego* a female, they are my son and daughter.

Third. My father's brother is my father. He is also distinguished as my great or little father, as he is older or younger than my own father.

Fourth. My father's brother's son and daughter are my brother and sister, elder or younger.

Fifth. My father's sister is my aunt. Her children are my cousins.

Sixth. My mother's brother is my uncle. His children are my cousins.

Seventh. My mother's sister is my mother. She is also distinguished as great or little, as she is older or younger than my own mother.

Eighth. My mother's sister's son and daughter are my brother and sister, elder or younger.

Ninth. My grandfather's brother is my grandfather.

Tenth. The grandchildren of my own brothers and sisters, of my collateral brothers and sisters, and of my cousins, are, without distinction, my grandchildren.

The marriage relationships in both Canarese and Telŭgŭ are in general agree-ment with the Tamilian.

Presumptively the same system of relationship prevails amongst the peoples who speak the six remaining dialects of the Drâvidian language. The form, as it now exists, amongst the Hill Tribes of South India would be especially interesting, since it might be found less developed, and consequently nearer the primitive Turanian form.   If any difference exists upon a principal relationship, it will probably be found to occur in the relationship between the children of a brother and sister.   This relationship of cousin is the last developed in the order of time, and, as we have seen, is frequently wanting.

The preservation of this system in the three principal dialects of the Drâvidian language since the period of their formation, and through such changes of condition, attests in a remarkable manner the permanence of the system, and its power of self-perpetuation.   These facts can only be explained by the recognition of the system as a domestic institution.   As such it must be regarded as one of the oldest existing institutions of the human family.

CHAPTER II.

SYSTEM OF RELATIONSHIP OF THE TURANIAN FAMILY.—Continued.

Gaura Language of North India—Its Dialects—Grammatical Structure Turanian—Vocabulary mostly Sanskritic—Gaura System of Relationship—A Classificatory System. 1. Hindî Form—Explanation in Detail—Original Characteristics in which it agrees with Polish and Bulgarian—Nomenclature of Relationships—Source of same—Turanian Characteristics in the System—Absence of Others—Severe Ordeal through which it has Passed. 2. Bengâlî Form—Agrees with the Hindî. 3. Gujârathî Form—Agrees with the Hindî. 4. Marâthî Form—It also agrees with the Hindî—Evidences of the Stability of the System—First Hypothesis: Whether it is an independent Variety of the Classificatory System—Second Hypothesis: Whether it was originally Turanian, and modified under Sanskritic Influences into its present Form—The latter the most satisfactory—Reasons for placing the Gaura System in the Turanian Connection.

THE Sanskrit grammarians divided the colloquial languages of India into two classes, each containing five dialects, of which those of South India were called the "five Drâviras," and those of North India the "five Gauras." Later researches have led to the correction of this arrangement, which was found to be erroneous both in classification and in the number of dialects. There are nine dialects, as we have seen, of the Drâvidian language, and there are, also, seven of the Gaura. The latter are the Hindî, with its daughter the Hindûstânî, the Bengâlî, the Uriya, the Panjâbî, the Marâthî, the Gujârathî, and the Sindhî. To these Dr. Caldwell proposes to add the Cashmirian, and the language of Nipâl.[1]

In their formation the dialects of the Gaura language have a history somewhat remarkable. When the Sanskrit branch of the Aryan family entered India they found the countries bordering the Indus and the Ganges in the possession of rude aboriginal tribes, speaking a language or dialects of a language radically different from their own, and probably exceeding them several times in number. These tribes, whose dialects may have originated the present dialects of North India, were conquered by the Sanskrit speaking invaders. As conquerors they imposed upon the aborigines their religious system, their laws, and to some extent their usages and customs; and by the device of caste they further sought to keep themselves forever pure and unmixed in blood, whilst they retained the natives of the country in a position of political and social inferiority. But the former failed to wrest from the latter the grammatical structure of their language along with their civil liberties. In the final result the grammatical forms of the aboriginal speech conquered the polished and cultivated Sanskrit, and gave its own structure to the new dialects, which were destined to become the vernacular idioms of both invaders and invaded. The Sanskrit, in the course of time, became a dead language, and was superseded throughout North India by the Gaura speech.

---

[1] Drâvidian Comp. Gram. Intro., p. 27.

In the formation of the Hindî and Bengâlî, and other dialects of this language, by the joint contributions of two radically distinct languages, a remarkable illustration is afforded of the results of an ethnic struggle between two dissimilar peoples for the mastery of the common speech. The preponderance of numbers, or of the blood, in such cases, usually carries with it the grammatical structure, and confers it upon the resulting language. In the present case the Sanskrit element overwhelmed and enveloped the primitive speech so completely, and impressed its character upon it in so many particulars, that these dialects are still placed in the Aryan family of languages; although by the true criterion of classification, that of grammatical structure, they are not admissible into this connection. Their vocables are in the extraordinary disproportions of ninety per centum of Sanskrit to ten per centum of aboriginal words, with the exception of the Marâthî, which is estimated to contain ninety-five per centum of the former against five per centum of the latter.[1] This ratio is without a parallel in cases where the grammatical forms followed the minority of the vocables. It is explained, to some extent, by the opulence in vocables of the highly developed Sanskrit, and a corresponding scantiness of the same, for want of development, in the aboriginal tongues. Since grammatical structure must determine the classification, the source and proportion of the vocables are immaterial. Upon the manner of the formation of these dialects, which is a matter of theory, some difference of opinion exists among oriental scholars; but upon the question of their grammatical structure they generally concur in representing it to be that of the aboriginal speech. Dr. Stevenson supposes " that the North India vernaculars have been derived from the Sanscrit, not so much from the natural process of corruption and disintegration, as through the overmastering remoulding power of the un-Sanscrit element which is contained in them;" and Dr. Caldwell observes that " the grammatical *structure* of the spoken idioms of Northern India was from the first, and always continued to be, in the main Scythian [using this term generically], and the change which took place when Sanscrit acquired the predominance, as the Aryans gradually extended their conquests and their colonies, was rather a change of vocabulary than of grammar, a change not so much in arrangement and vital spirit as in the *matériel* of the language."[2] These statements are so specific and rest upon such competent authority as to leave no doubt upon the principal question. This fact, also, must be received as conclusive evidence that the aborigines exceeded their conquerers in numbers. Under the operation of the law of caste the blood of the Aryans has, in the main, continued unmixed to the present day; but the two stocks have become one people, notwithstanding, by diffusion of blood, as well as by a common

---

[1] Drâvidian Comp. Gram. Intro., p. 38.

[2] Ib. Intro., p. 38. The context is as follows: " Nevertheless, as the grammatical structure of the Scythian tongues possesses peculiar stability and persistency; and as the Pre-Âryan tribes, who were probably more numerous than the Aryans, were not annihilated, but only reduced to a dependent position, and eventually, in most instances, incorporated in the Âryan community, the large Sanscrit addition which the Scythian vernaculars received, would not alter their essential structure, or deprive them of the power of influencing and assimilating the speech of the conquering race. According to this theory the grammatical structure of the Spokane idioms," &c., as above.

language, and a common civilization, with a preponderance of the blood from aboriginal veins. If this be true, the novel spectacle is presented of a conquering and cultivated people of the Aryan lineage forced to yield their language to a people whom they had subjugated, and to become transferred linguistically to an inferior family.

Several interesting questions are presented by the system of consanguinity and affinity of the people speaking the Gaura language, the most important of which is, whether or not it is Turanian. It is certainly not Sanskritic. With the exception of three, and perhaps four, terms of relationship, the nomenclature is drawn exclusively from the Sanskrit. It has the apparel of the system of consanguinity of the latter people without its form, and the question is whether its form, originally Turanian, has been modified by Sanskritic influences, or whether it was originally a system differing from both. The weight of the evidence is in favor of the first hypothesis. Where two radically different languages become consolidated by natural processes into one resulting language it does not follow that the system of relationship would be imposed by the people who contributed the great body of the vocables; but, on the contrary, it would be more apt to be furnished by the one that conferred the grammar, since the grammatical structure of the newly developed language would represent the preponderance of the blood. It has before been shown that the Sanskrit system of relationship is descriptive. The Gaura system is classificatory. And although it is much less elaborate and discriminating than the Turanian, it embodies several of its fundamental conceptions, and perhaps it may be satisfactorily explained as originally Turanian, but modified into its present form by the overpowering influence of the Sanskrit element arrayed against it.

In the Table will be found the Hindî, the Bengâlî, the Gujarâthî, and the Marâthî, exhibiting fully and minutely the system of relationship which now prevails amongst the people speaking these dialects. They are the most important of the nine idioms, and, without doubt, these schedules exhibit substantially the form which prevails in the five remaining dialects. To illustrate fully the Gaura system, the others need examination, since each may retain some one or more features of the original system which the others have yielded, and thus from all together the original form might be satisfactorily ascertained. A sufficient number of the radical features of the Turanian system are present, taken in connection with the history of these dialects, to render extremely probable its Turanian origin.

Gaura System of Relationship. 1. Hindî. 2. Bengâlî. 3. Gujarâthî. 4. Marâthî.

It will be sufficient to present the Gaura system as it now exists among the people speaking one of these dialects. But inasmuch as its characteristics can neither be shown by means of the indicative relationships, nor by indicating the points of difference between it and the Tamilian, it will be necessary to take it up with some degree of detail. After the system has been once explained, the points of agreement and of difference between it and the systems which are found in the other dialects can be readily shown.

1. Hindî. The Hindî will be adopted as the standard form of the Gaura system of relationship. The four schedules, however, are in such full agreement with each

other that either might have been taken for the same purpose.   This schedule was filled out by the Rev. James L. Scott, of Futtehgurh, North India, a missionary of the American Presbyterian Board.[1]   The care with which it was executed is shown by his letter, which is appended in a note as a verification of the work.[2]   This system is specially interesting because it seems to embody the history and the results of a conflict between the descriptive and the classificatory forms, which are the opposites of each other in their fundamental conceptions.

The first noticeable feature of the Hindî system appears in the fraternal and sororal relationships.   Their conception in the twofold form of elder and younger, which is the rule rather than the exception amongst Asiatic nations, gives place to

---

[1] I cannot mention the name of this distinguished scholar without improving the same moment to acknowledge my great obligations to him for his courtesy, and for the very efficient aid which he has rendered me in India in procuring material for the illustration of my subject.   Beside working out the Hindi system, I am indebted to him for procuring the Marâthi, the Gujarâthi, the Canarese, and one of the Tamil schedules.   He also endeavored to obtain for me the system of the people of Nïpâl, of the Assamese, and of the Malays.   Without his friendly co-operation the materials for illustrating the systems of consanguinity of the Asiatic nations would have been quite insufficient.   If these lines should ever meet the eyes of my friend in his distant field of labor, I trust he will regard them as but a faint expression of my grateful appreciation of his friendship.   A person at all familiar with the excessive and exhausting labors of the American missionaries, in the enervating climate of India, will understand the measure of the obligation imposed, by the voluntary assumption on their part of additional labor, in the interests of science.

FUTTEHGURH, April 30, 1860.

[2] MY DEAR SIR: It has given me much pleasure to fill the schedule which you have sent, and I now return it, having done the best I could to make it accurate.   I have gone over it two or three times in company with a maulwi, a moushee, a pundit, and one or two others, besides having had the assistance of an elderly female whom I found skilled in relationships.   I have besides had it revised by a friend of mine, assisted by his pundit, who pronounced it correct.   Under these circumstances I may be allowed to express the hope that no mistake has been made, and that you may depend upon the accuracy of the Table.

The language which I have used is the Hindi.   Had I used the Urdú, which is the language introduced by the Mussulmen conquerors of India, the system would have been substantially the same, with here and there a Persian instead of a Hindi term.   The explanation of this I suppose is, that the Mussulmen have, in the main, adopted the Hindi system.   The Hindi language is, I am persuaded, the one in which it was the most important that the schedule should be prepared.   It is the language of the great mass of the people, and is derived immediately from the Sanskrit.   Hence it represents the system of relationship adopted by the Aryan race, who are shown by affinities of language to be the same race as our own.

And yet I see that their system of relationship is, in some points, strikingly similar to that which you have found among the American Indians, and which is represented as existing among the aborigines of Southern India.   I hope you will be able to explain how this has happened.

The Hindi language is spoken with slight variation over a large portion of Northern India, and I should expect to find that the same system of relationship prevails in the Punjaub or the Mahratta country, and in Bengal, the languages of these countries being only different dialects, all looking up to the Sanskrit as their common parent.

The system of notation which I have used is that adopted by Sir William Jones, and extensively used in this country.   By attending to the directions I have given, you will, I think, have no difficulty in reading it.   Wishing you every success in your investigations,

I remain, dear sir, yours sincerely,

J. L. SCOTT.

To L. H. MORGAN, Esq., Rochester, New York.

a different form—to descriptive phrases in the place of original terms—which recognize a difference in relationship, but without expressing it in the concrete. In the Hindî an elder brother is described as *bara bhai*, greater brother, and younger brother as *chota bhai*, lesser brother; and elder and younger sister by the feminine form of these terms. An explanation of this form appears to be found in the Bengâlî, in which a younger brother calls his oldest brother *burro dada*, the next to the oldest *majo dada*, third *shejo dada*, and the fourth *mono dada*, whilst the oldest brother calls the youngest by his personal name. Sisters are distinguished from each other in the same manner. Whether the youngest brother and sister are distinguished by descriptive phrases to be used at the option of the speaker does not appear. As a method of discriminating these relationships, it is radically different from the Tamilian. In the Marâthî, however, the regular form is found, namely, *agraz*, elder brother; *agraza*, elder sister; *anuz*, younger brother; and *awarza*, younger sister. But we have words from the same root in the Sanskrit system of relationship previously given, namely, *agrajar*, elder brother; *agrajri*, elder sister; *amujar*, younger brother; and *amujri*, younger sister. Whether these terms were indigenous in the Marâthî dialect, and were borrowed thence into the Sanskrit, or were derived from pure Sanskrit roots, I am unable to state. From the absence of this method of discriminating the fraternal and sororal relationships in the Aryan family, and its general prevalence among the non-Aryan Asiatic nations, the presumption would be strongly in favor of their origin in the aboriginal language.

Another peculiarity in the Gaura system is the absence of any difference in the relationships of the same persons with a change of the sex of *Ego*. This striking feature of the Turanian system, and which produces its principal diversities, has been entirely eradicated from the Gaura form, if it ever formed a part of its structure. The terms used, however, are sometimes different.

In the first collateral line male, in the Hindî system, my brother's son and daughter are my nephew and niece, *Bhatija* and *Bhavji*, and their children are my grandchildren, *Pota* and *Poti*.

In the female branch my sister's son and daughter are my nephew and niece, but different terms are used. *Bhavja* and *Bhavji* with *Ego* a male, and *Bahinauta* and *Bahinauti*, with *Ego* a female. The children of each are my grandchildren.

The wives of these several nephews are my daughters-in-law, and the husbands of these several nieces are my sons-in-law; but these relationships are qualified by prefixing the terms for nephew and niece, to indicate the precise manner of the connection, *e. g.*, *Batij Damad*, nephew-son-in-law. The recognized relationship is seen to be Turanian, but the qualification, as well as the terms, are Sanskritic.

In the second collateral line my father's brother is my uncle, *Chachá*. This is one of the few terms in the nomenclature which is not Sanskritic but aboriginal. The Vaisyas often use *Tâú*, and the Kshatriyas *Dâú* in its place. If the Sûdras also used the latter term, it would at least suggest the probability that it was the aboriginal term for father, which was retained as an appellative for father's brother after the Sanskrit *pita* had become substituted to distinguish an own father. In addition to the term *Chachá*, which expresses the recognized relationship, he is also called, by courtesy, "great" or "little" father, as he is older or younger than the real father, which, as we have seen, is the Tamilian form. At the next degree the most remarkable feature of the Hindî system is found. My father's brother's son and daughter are my brother and sister, *Bhai* and *Bahin*, the terms being the same as those applied to an own brother and sister. But there is still another form of expressing these relationships, of which the counterpart is found in the Polish and Bulgarian. They are described by the phrase, *Chachera Bahi*, and *Chacheri Bahin*, literally " paternal uncle brother," and " paternal uncle sister," or " brother through paternal uncle," and "·sister through paternal uncle." In the Polish we have Styj paternal uncle, *Stryjeczna Brat*-brother through paternal uncle, and *Stryjeczna Siostra*-sister through paternal uncle. The two forms, both as to relationship and method of expressing it, are the same. If a parallel is run between the Hindî and Polish systems, the coincidences will be found to be sufficiently remarkable to challenge inquiry concerning the probable Gaura origin of the Slavonic form. But to proceed, the children of these collateral brothers and sisters are my nephews and nieces, discriminated from each other as in the first collateral line, and their children are my grandchildren.

My father's sister is my aunt, *Phuphi*. This term is also aboriginal. Her son and daughter are my brother and sister, but they are also distinguished as a brother through paternal aunt, *Phuphera Bhai*, and sister through paternal aunt, *Phupheri Bahin*. The children of these collateral brothers and sisters are my nephews and nieces, and their children are my grandchildren.

My mother's brother is my uncle, *Mamú*. This term is probably aboriginal, although Mr. Scott suggests a Sanskrit derivation. His son and daughter are my brother and sister. They are also distinguished as *Mamera Bahai* and *Mameri Bahin*, as in the previous cases. The children of these collateral brothers and sisters are my nephews and nieces, and their children are my grandchildren.

In the remaining branch of this line my mother's sister is my aunt, *Mausi*. This term is from the Sanskrit *Matri Susi*, and has nearly the signification of mother. To the extent in which it carries this meaning it is used in accordance with the Turanian system, and tends to restore the other term for aunt to its primitive and restricted application. Her children are my brothers and sisters. They are also distinguished as *Mauseta Bhai*, brother through maternal aunt, and *Mauseti Bahin*, sister through maternal aunt. The children of this collateral brother and sister are my nephews and nieces, and the children of the latter are my grandchildren.

The wives of these several collateral brothers are my sisters-in-law, and the husbands of these several collateral sisters are my brothers-in-law. In these marriage relationships the Hindî agrees substantially with the Tamilian form.

With respect to the remaining collateral lines they can be sufficiently shown by taking a single branch of each. In the third, my grandfather's brother is my grandfather, *Dada*. His son is my paternal uncle, *Chachá*; the son of this uncle is my brother, his son is my nephew, and the son of the latter is my grandson. In like manner, in the fourth, my great grandfather's brother is my great grandfather, *Pardada*; his son is my grandfather, *Dada*, and the son of the latter is my paternal uncle, *Chachá*. The son of this uncle is my brother, his son is my nephew, and the son of the latter is my grandson. The fifth collateral line is also extended in the Table, and gives the following series: *Sardada, Pardada, Dada, Chachá, Bhai, Bhatija*, and *Pota*.

It now remains to examine the source of the nomenclature of relationships, and to indicate the principal points of agreement and of disagreement between the Hindî and the Turanian systems.

The Rev. Mr. Scott has furnished me with a table showing the derivation of the several terms, together with his observations upon the same, which will be found in the note.[1] It is quite remarkable how completely the Sanskritic have displaced

---

[1] HINDI TERMS OF RELATIONSHIP WITH THEIR SANSKRIT ORIGINALS.

Terms.	Hindi.	Sanskrit.	Remarks.
1. Father	Pitá. ᵇ Báp	Pitá. ᵇ Bábá	
2. Mother	Má. ᵇ Máta. ᵇ Ammá	Mátá. ᵇ Ambá	
3. Son	Betá	———	No connection with Sanskrit; must be original words.
4. Daughter . . .	Beti		
5. Grandson . . .	Potá	Potá	
6. Brother	Bhái	Bhrátá	In Hindi the *r* often falls out, as *krishn—kishn*; and the i is a Hindi termination.
7. Sister	Bahin	Bhagni	*Bahin* is the shortening of *bháí ín*.
8. Sister-in-law . .	Bhawaj	Bhrátra jáyá	*Bhrátrá* becomes *bhá*; the j is the radical j of *jaya*, wife; *wa* is a connecting link.
9. Son-in-law . .	Dámád	Iámtrí	
10. Daughter-in-law .	Bahú	Badhú	The *d* is easily dropped.
11. Grandfather . .	Dádá	———	Must be Sanskrit; a natural word.
12. Husband . . .	Ádmí. ᵇ Pat	Pat (master)	AAdmí is Arabic, meaning *man*, son of Abram.
13. Wife	Jarú	———	Hindi *jor*, join, from Sanskrit *jukt*, joined.
14. Father-in-law . .	Sasur	Sasur	
15. Mother-in-law .	Sás	Sás	
16. Widow	Ránd	Ránd	
17. Widower . . .	Bidwá	Bidwa	
18. Father's brother .	Chacha	———	Not Sanskrit. The Vaishyas often say *táee*, and the Chatrias *dáeé*, neither of which is Sanskrit.
19. Mother's brother .	Mámú	Matul ?	Evidently from *má*.
20. Father's sister .	Phúphá	———	Not Sanskrit.
21. Mother's sister .	Mausi	Mátri súsi	Matr, =mother.
22. Brother's son . .	Bhatija	Bhrátrá já	Born of a brother: a man's or a woman's brother's son.
23. Sister's son (m.s.)	Bháujá. ᵇ Bhauijá	Bhagni ja	Born of a sister. (A man's sister's son.)
24. Sister's son (f. s.)	Bahenautá	Bhagneyá	Born of a sister. (A woman's sister's son.)

"From the foregoing table it appears that all these words, and they include I believe all the terms of relationship, are derived from the Sanskrit, except three, viz., *Betá, Chachá*, and *Phúphá*. I think I am safe in saying that these are not, and that the probability is they are original.

"I think Caldwell's explanation of the sources of the Hindi, and its cognate dialects exceedingly ingenious and probable. I believe that most of our low caste people are of aboriginal descent, and

the aboriginal terms; and the fact is rendered still more extraordinary by the presumption that the native idioms were opulent in terms of relationship, however scant in other vocables. Out of twenty-two radical terms in the nomenclature, exclusive of *Taú*, Mr. Scott was able to recognize but three of undoubted origin in the aboriginal speech. To these it is suggested that *Mámú*, maternal uncle, should probably be added, which, aside from the difficulty of deriving it from the Sanskrit *Matul*, may prove to be from the same root as *Mămăn* of the Tamil, *Mama*, of the Bengâlî, and *Mara*, of the Canarese dialect, for the same relationship. Four of the indicative features of the Turanian system are involved in the relationship of the father's and mother's brothers and sisters. The presence of aboriginal terms for one, and perhaps two of these relationships, and the qualifications which attach to the other two reveal distinct traces of the Turanian system. We must suppose that the principal point of controversy between the Aryan and Turanian or aboriginal form was upon the classification of kindred. Upon the assumption of the existence of marriage between single pairs, the former was true to the nature of descents, whilst the latter was false in respect to it in more than half of its provisions. If the latter system was originally true to the nature of descents through compound marriages or a custom of wide-spread cohabitation amongst relatives, and it had survived the epoch in which society had extricated itself from this condition, and had reached the marriage relation between single pairs, the system itself would have been vulnerable upon this part of the classification. The reasons for calling a father's brother a father, and a mother's sister a mother; and also for a man calling his brother's son his son, and a woman calling her sister's son her son could not be defended (the causes justifying this classification having disappeared), when it was resisted and questioned by a portion of the people speaking the same language and desiring a common system. And yet the surrender of the Turanian and the adoption of the Aryan system, or the reverse, would not be expected, but rather a modification of both into one resulting system. Such appears to have been the issue of the conflict between the two antagonistic forms. Traces of compromise are seen throughout its details. The principal points in which it has been influenced from each source may be briefly stated as follows.

In the first place the Hindî system is classificatory. Consanguinei are arranged in an arbitrary manner under a few principal relationships, or into a limited number of great classes, without regard, in most cases, to nearness or remoteness in degree, or to the obvious divergence of the streams of the blood. This is distinctively Turanian.

Secondly. The son of a man's brother becomes his nephew instead of his son; and as if to mark the falsity of the Turanian classification, the Sanskrit term em-

---

it is not surprising that they have moulded the Sanskrit, into what we now find it in Hindi, with an infusion of words of their own.

"On the question whether the system of consanguinity has followed that of the Aryan, or of the original race, I am not able to judge. From the Table it will be manifest that the *words* have been mostly taken from the Sanskrit, with a small element from the original language. This, however, is what might have been expected. The aboriginal system may have remained notwithstanding."

ployed signifies "born of a brother." This modification obliterates two of the indicative features of the Turanian system. It is also extended to the second and more remote collateral lines, in which the sons of collateral brothers become nephews and nieces instead of sons and daughters.

Thirdly. The children of two or more brothers continue to be brothers and sisters to each other, notwithstanding the falsity of the classification under the principles of the Aryan system. This is equally true with respect to the children of two or more sisters. It is also a Turanian characteristic, and would give two of the indicative features of the latter system but for the admission of the children of a brother and sister into the same relationships. The Sanskrit also intervenes again at this point, and discriminates these collateral brothers from each other, as well as from own brothers, by the phrases "brother through paternal uncle," brother through paternal aunt," without making it the exclusive form.

Fourthly. The brotherhood of consanguinei in a perpetual series, which is one of the striking characteristics of the Turanian system, is also preserved. For example, the sons of brothers are brothers to each other, the sons of the latter are brothers again, and the same relationship continues downward indefinitely among their descendants at equal removes from the common ancestor. The same is equally true of the children of two sisters, and of the children of a brother and sister.

Fifthly. The several collateral lines are ultimately merged in the lineal line, so that the posterity of my collateral consanguinei are placed in the same category with my own posterity. This is also a Turanian characteristic.

Sixthly. In the ascending series, the collateral lines are not allowed to become detached from the lineal. None of the brothers, for example, of my several ancestors above father could fall without the relationship of grandfather. Grandfather, uncle, brother, nephew, and grandson mark the external boundaries of the system, within which all of a person's consanguinei, near and remote, were embraced. This is another and a marked characteristic of the Turanian system.

Seventhly. The relationships of uncle and aunt, applied to the mother's brother and the father's sister are Turanian in form; and although the force of these relationships is weakened by placing the father's brother and the mother's sister in the same relationships, thus tending to obliterate two other indicative features of the former system, yet there are special circumstances leading to the supposition that they were modifications from the Aryan source imperfectly suppressing the original form, as to the latter, whilst the former remained unchanged.

Lastly. The marriage relationships are Turanian.

The ability of the original system to resist the powerful influence of the language and form of consanguinity of the Aryan invaders, and retain, with so small a part of its nomenclature, so many of its aboriginal features, is to be ascribed to its internal vigor and resisting force, supported as it was by a majority of the people. If the modifications introduced from Sanskrit sources could be separated, and the displaced parts restored, there might still be some question whether the system thus reproduced was Turanian, or an independent form, although the former supposition is much the most probable. It cannot, in any event, be classed with the descriptive systems of the Aryan, Semitic, or Uralian families. But as there are three distinct varieties of the classificatory form, the Turanian, Malayan, and Eskimo, so there may be still others among the remaining Asiatic nations. However this may be, it can be confidently affirmed that no other form of consanguinity given in the Tables has been subjected to such an ordeal as that now under consideration. Its preservation as a classificatory system, possessed of so many Turanian characteristics, against the pressure brought to bear upon it by the superior intelligence and cultivation of the Sanskrit colonists, to whom its provisions must have been exceedingly offensive, is a striking confirmation of the persistency of the fundamental conceptions upon which it rests.

With respect to the identity of a portion of the Hindî system of relationship with the corresponding part of the Polish and Bulgarian, the supposition of accidental coincidence is not so convincing as to repress speculation. It may be conjectured, with some degree of plausibility, that after the Sanskrit branch of the Aryan family had become incorporated with the native tribes beyond the Indus, their blood undoubtedly going downward through the masses, whether that of the latter penetrated their ranks or otherwise, and after the new vernaculars, and the new system of relationship had commenced their formation, a portion of this amalgamated stock broke off and emigrated westward, carrying with them the system as it then existed, and becoming, in the course of time, the Slavonic branch of the Aryan family.

2. Bengâlî. This form follows the Hindî so closely, both in its nomenclature, and in its classification of persons, that it does not require a notice in detail. The schedule was prepared by the late Rev. Gopenath Nundy, a Bengalese by birth, and a missionary of the American Presbyterian Board, stationed at Futtehpore, North India. It was executed with care and precision. His letter to the author, which presents the essential parts of the system, and contains some valuable information, will be found entire to the note.[1] Some of his answers, however, need qualification.

FUTTEHPORE, NORTHERN INDIA, July 26, 1860.

[1] DEAR SIR: I have the pleasure to acknowledge the receipt of your printed letter, and some printed forms, which were forwarded by Rev. J. C. Lowrie, Secretary of the A. B. of Foreign Missions, requesting me to fill up the printed forms, and to answer your letter, which I herewith beg to do.

By reading over all the printed papers I find that there is a great likeness and similarity in relationships between the Indian nations of North America, and the nations of this country. When I say nations of this country I do not mean the Mohamedans, but the Hindus, who are the original natives of India. They are called by different names, such as Toybunguis (People of South India), Marhatos, Hindustanies, Bengalies, &c. &c. They all have pretty much the same religion, and in most parts agree in their relationships. I, as a Bengali, born and brought up in Calcutta, speak from my own experience and knowledge when I say there is a great similarity in the various degrees of consanguinity between the Indian nations of North America and the natives of this country, as the answers to your questions will show. How they came to agree I cannot understand, for there must have been some sort of communication with each other.

Now I will answer [the propositions resulting from an analysis of the system of relationship] as they stand in your printed letter, page 4.

"I. All the brothers and sisters of a man's grandfather, and of his grandmother, and all his ancestors above grandfather and grandmother, together with all their brothers and sisters, are equally

It appears that there are two terms for paternal uncle, *Ja'ta* when older than my father, and *Khoro* when younger, which give to these terms the signification of elder and younger paternal uncle. His son is my brother. He is also distinguished as in Hindi as my brother through this uncle, *Jatoto Bhrata*, and *Khortoto Bhrata*. My father's sister is my aunt, *Pishi;* my mother's brother is my uncle, *Mama;* and

---

his grandfathers and grandmothers. Some of the nations discriminate among them as second and third grandfathers, &c., but practically, they are all grandfathers and grandmothers. There are no great uncles or great aunts, as with us."

We also call them all grandfathers and grandmothers, as a matter of courtesy.

"II. All the brothers of a father are equally fathers to his children, and he is a father to the children of all his brothers. In like manner, all the sisters of a mother are equally mothers to her children, and she is a mother to the children of all her sisters. These are not uncles and aunts, nephews and nieces, as with us."

We call them *Játa* and *Khoro* (uncles). *Játa* is the elder brother, and *Khoro* is the younger brother of a father. But as a matter of courtesy they are called elder and younger fathers. The sister of a mother, whether elder or younger, is called *Mashi* (*Mash*, aunt-mother). The children of a mother to her sister are, if male, *Bonpo*, and if female, *Bonjhi*, nephew and niece.

"III. On the contrary, all the brothers of a mother are uncles to her children, and all the sisters of a father are aunts to his children, as with us; so that of the father's brothers and sisters, and of the mother's brothers and sisters, the mother's brothers and the father's sisters are the true and the only uncles and aunts recognized under this system."

All the brothers of a mother are called *Mama*, equivalent to uncle; and all the sisters of a father are called *Pishi*, aunt.

"IV. There is one term for elder brother; another for younger brother; one term for elder sister, and another for younger sister; and no term either for brother or sister, except in the plural number. These separate terms are not applied to the oldest or the youngest specifically, but to each and all, who are older or younger than the person speaking."

The younger calls their oldest brother *Burro Dada*, next to him *Majo Dada*, third, *Shejo Dada*, and fourth, *Nono Dada*, but elder call their younger brothers by name. In the same way sisters are called *Burro Didy* (eldest sister); *Majo Didy* (second); *Shejo Didy* (third); *Nono Didy* (fourth), and so on; but elder sister calls her younger brothers and sisters by name. All brothers and sisters, whether older or younger, also call each other by the general name *Bhrata* (brother), and *Bhogny* (sister).

"V. All the children of several brothers are brothers and sisters to each other, and all the children of several sisters are brothers and sisters to each other, and they use, in each case, the respective terms for elder and younger brother, and for elder and younger sister, the same as in the case of own brothers and sisters. Whilst all the children of brothers on the one hand, and of sisters on the other, are cousins to each other, as with us. To this last rule there are exceptions. When you cross from one sex to the other, the degree of relationship is farther removed."

As a general rule they are called brothers and sisters to each other, and the same with the children of sisters. But when required to particularize, the former (*i. e.*, the children of my father's brother) are called *Játoto Bhrata*, and *Játoto Bhogny*, or *Khortoto Bhrata*, and *Khortoto Bhogny*, according to their birth; and the latter (*i. e.*, the children of my mother's sisters) *Mashtoto Bhrata*, and *Mashtoto Bhogny*.

"VI. All the sons of a man's brothers, as before stated, are his sons; so that all the grandsons of a man's brothers are his grandsons. The sons of a man's sisters are his nephews, but the grandsons of a man's sisters are his grandsons. In the next collateral line the son of a man's female cousin is his nephew, and the son of this nephew is grandson."

The grandson of a man's brothers are his *Pautra* (grandsons), and the granddaughters his granddaughters, *Pautry*. According to Bengali usage, the sons of a man's sisters are called *Bhagna* (nephews), and the grandsons of a man's sisters are also grandsons to him. In the next collateral

my mother's sister is my aunt, *Mausi* = aunt-mother.   All of these terms but the last are from the aboriginal speech; and they seem to indicate that the true uncle and aunt, as in the Tamilian form, were the mother's brother, and the father's sister, and that the other are but qualified forms of the previous relationships of father and mother.

A comparison of the Bengâli with the Hindî form shows that they are in full agreement with each other, with slight deviations, in their minute details; and that the terms of relationship are the same words dialectically changed.   If the Gaura speech was divided into its present dialects at the epoch of the Sanskrit colonization of India, then the modifications of the original system, under Sanskritic influences, have taken the same precise direction in each dialect; thereby illustrating the uniformity of the operation of intellectual and moral causes in its formation.   On the other hand, if the present system antedates the formation of these dialects it is a not less significant attestation of the permanency of the system

---

line, the son of a man's female cousin (here his sister) is his *Bhagua* (nephew); the grandson of this female cousin is also a grandson to him.

"VII. All the grandsons of brothers are brothers to each other, and the same of all the grandsons of sisters, while all the grandsons of brothers on the one hand, and of sisters on the other, are cousins; and the same relationship continues to the remotest generation in each case, so long as these persons stand in the same degree of nearness to the original brothers and sisters.   But when one is farther removed than the other, by a single degree, the rule which changes the collateral line into the lineal at once applies; thus the son of one cousin becomes a nephew to the other cousin, and the son of this nephew a grandson.   In like manner the son of one brother becomes a son to the other brother, and the son of this son a grandson."

Among us they are also called brothers to each other, and the same with the grandsons of sisters. And so also all the grandsons of brothers on the one hand, and of sisters on the other, are called brothers; and the same relationships continue to the remotest generations.

"VIII. Consequently the descendants of brothers and sisters, or of an original pair, could not, in theory, ever pass beyond the degree of cousin, that being the most remote degree of relationship recognized, and the greatest divergence allowed from the lineal line.   Hence the bond of consanguinity which can never, in fact, be broken by lapse of time, was not, as a fundamental idea of the Indian system, suffered to be broken in principle."

It is exactly the same among us.

"IX. All the wives of these several brothers, without discrimination, and all the wives of these several male cousins, are interchangeably sisters-in-law to the brothers and cousins of their respective husbands; and all the husbands of these several sisters, without distinction, and of these several female cousins, are in like manner brothers-in-law to the sisters and cousins of their respective wives. All the wives of these several sons and nephews are daughters-in-law alike, to the fathers and mothers, uncles and aunts of their respective husbands; and all the husbands of these several daughters and nieces are sons-in-law alike to the fathers and mothers, uncles and aunts of their respective wives.

"This system, which, from its complexity and unlikeness to our own, is embarrassing to us, is yet perfectly natural and readily applied by the Indian, to whom any other than this is entirely unknown."

It is substantially the same among us.

    *   *   *   *   *   *   *   *   *   *

I believe I have answered all your inquiries.   Should you need any further information, I shall be happy to give it.   I remain yours very truly,

GOPENATH NUNDY.

through centuries of time, demonstrated by its preservation in such a number of independent channels.

3. Gujârâthî. This system is also in full and and minute agreement with the Hindî and Bengâlî, as will be seen by consulting the Table. It is chiefly interesting as confirmatory of the truthfulness of the latter; and for the additional testimony which it furnishes of the stability of the system in its present condition. The features in which it deviates from, as well as those in which it agrees with the Tamilian are also constant in the Gujârâthî.

4. Marâthî. The same remarks that have been made with reference to the last form are equally true of the Marâthî. There are but two particulars in which there is any noticeable difference between the Marâthî and those previously explained. The first consists in the presence and use of special terms in the Marâthî system, for elder and younger brother, and for elder and younger sister, which have before been considered; and the other of the absence of the Polish method of distinguishing the children of uncles and aunts. The failure to adopt this method tends to confirm the inference of the Sanskritic origin of this method of discrimination. For a further knowledge of this form, reference is made to the Table.

From the foregoing exposition of the Gaura system of relationship a definite impression of its present characteristics has been obtained. The form which prevails in the five remaining dialects must be ascertained and compared with those given before the question of the true position of the Gaura system can be fully determined. Presumptively the same form prevails in all of the dialects; but at the same time if the original system were the same as the Tamilian, other traces than those already found may still exist in the unrepresented dialects. There are two hypotheses, as before intimated, with reference to this system, each of which has some basis of probability. First, that it is an independent variety of the classificatory system, and has remained unchanged, in its radical features, since the advent in India of the Sanskrit stock; or, Second, that it was originally Turanian of the Tamilian type, and has been modified to the extent of losing several of its radical characteristics under the long-continued pressure of Sanskritic influence. Upon the first hypothesis, in addition to what has previously been stated, it may be remarked that it would exclude all influence from Sanskrit sources upon its formation. If adopted, we must suppose that they voluntarily abandoned their own descriptive system and accepted, in its place, the form of a barbarous people, contenting themselves with the substitution of their own terms of relationship in the place of the aboriginal. Upon the second, which is much the strongest hypothesis, it may be said, first of all, that the system is un-Sanskritic, and, therefore, must have taken its origin without the Aryan family. Secondly, that when the two peoples became united, two radically different systems of consanguinity were brought into collision, and held in antagonistic relations until a new system was constructed. Thirdly, that the resulting system would represent in the source of its several parts the amount of influence each was able to impress upon it. Lastly, That the Sanskritic influence would be directed with greater force against the objectionable parts of the aboriginal system which they sought to eradicate. It is certain that the indigenous form held the mastery to the end, and that it yielded the very features, and no others, that would be most offensive to Sanskritic tastes For these and other reasons the latter hypothesis is the most satisfactory.

There seemed, therefore, to be sufficient reasons for placing the Gaura system in the Turanian connection.

CHAPTER III.

SYSTEM OF RELATIONSHIP OF THE TURANIAN FAMILY—Continued.

1. Chinese—Antiquity of the Chinese Nation—Immobility of their Civilization—Its tendency to arrest Changes in their Domestic Institutions—Their System of Relationship—Fully Exhibited in the Table—Classificatory in Character—Possesses a number of Turanian Characteristics—The System consists of Two Parts—First, the Terms of Relationship—Second, Qualifying Terms to distinguish the Branches—In the last respect it differs from all other Forms—This part evidently Supplemented by Scholars—The " Nine Grades of Relations"—Elaborate and Artificial Characters of the Chinese System—Lineal Line—Fraternal and Sororal Relationships—First Collateral Line—Second and Third Collateral Lines—Reasons for placing the Chinese in the Turanian Family—Their System midway between the Turanian and Malayan. 2. Japanese—Their System of Relationship—Details of the System—Reasons for placing the Japanese provisionally in the Turanian Connection—Addenda: Observations of Hon. Robert Hart, upon the Chinese System—Table.

THE acknowledged antiquity of the Chinese nation invests their system of relationship with special importance. Notwithstanding the tendency of later opinion has been to lessen the extravagant age claimed for their literature and civilization, there can be no doubt whatever that the distinct political existence of this singular people ascends to a period of time, in the past, coeval, at least, with the oldest nations of which we have any knowledge. No existing nation has perpetuated itself, with unbroken identity, through the same number of centuries, or developed from one stem or stock an equal number of people. In numbers of the same lineage, and in years of political duration, the Chinese are the first among the nations of mankind.

Within the historical period immobility has been the characteristic of their civilization. This hereditary jealousy of innovation has tended to preserve their domestic institutions within the narrowest limits of change. If, then, there is found among them a clearly defined and perfectly developed domestic institution, which is founded upon fixed necessities of the social state, and which satisfies as well as regulates these necessities, it would be expected to partake of the permanence and stability such immobility implies. It would also follow as a legitimate inference, that the institution itself, in virtue of its identification with primary needs, originated in the earliest periods of the national existence.

The Chinese system of consanguinity and affinity is a domestic institution of this description. As a system it belongs to the classificatory division, and to the Turanian branch of this division, although it falls below the highest type of the Turanian form, and affiliates wherever it diverges with the Malayan. If the Drâvidiàn speaking people of India are placed in the centre of the Turanian family, the Chinese nation is an outlying member. Their system of relationship possesses some features which distinguish it from every other, but these will be seen, in the end, to relate to external rather than to radical characteristics. In its method it is cumbersome and highly artificial; yet in the completeness of its plan for the separation of the several lines, and branches of lines, from each other, and for the specialization of the relationships of every kinsman to the central *Ego*, it is second only to the Roman form; and, in many respects, is not surpassed by any existing system. It has accomplished the difficult task of maintaining a principle of classification which confounds the natural distinctions in the relationships of consanguinei, and, at the same time, of separating these relationships from each other in a precise and definite manner. Certain individuals in each of the several collateral lines are placed upon the same level in the degree of their nearness to *Ego*, and yet their relationships are distinguished one from another. The collateral lines are maintained divergent from the lineal, and yet are finally merged within it. These seemingly inconsistent results have been produced in a manner altogether peculiar to the Chinese form.

There are two distinct parts of the system of relationship, by the joint operation of which the results indicated have been effected, and which, to a great extent, may yet be separated from each other. The first consists of the terms of relationship which are used, to a great extent, in accordance with the Turanian principle of classification. Consanguinei, near and remote, are arranged into great classes, and the members of each class are admitted into the same relationship, irrespective of nearness or remoteness in degree. This is the original as well as radical portion of the system. The second part consists of independent qualifying terms, which are used to distinguish the several branches of each collateral line from each other, and consequently the relationship of each individual. By means of these additional terms the branch of the line in every case, and, usually, the line itself, are definitely indicated; and collateral consanguinei are thus discriminated from the lineal. In some instances these qualifying terms have superseded the terms of relationship; but in all such cases the latter are probably understood. The precise manner in which these results are produced will become apparent as the several branches of each line are presented in detail. All that is peculiar in the Chinese system will be readily apprehended by following the chain of relationship from parent to child, observing the terms that are employed to express the series of these relationships to *Ego*, and, also, the specific additions by which the branches of particular lines are distinguished from each other. It will thus be found that that part of the framework of the system which specializes the several branches of each line was engrafted upon the radical portion; that it was the afterwork of scholars or civilians to clear up or qualify the primitive classification; and that it probably originated in the necessity for a code of descents to regulate the inheritance of property.

The Chinese system of relationship, as given in the Table, was furnished by Hon. Robert Hart, an English gentleman of Canton, now at the head of the Chinese Bureau of Marine Customs. It was especially fortunate that the difficult labor of spreading out in detail this elaborate and artificial form of consanguinity and affinity was undertaken by one so abundantly qualified as Mr. Hart to trace it to its limits in this peculiar language, and to bestow upon its nomenclature the etymological observations so necessary to its interpretation. It is evident, from his work, that his investigations covered its entire range, and developed all of its material characteristics. The schedule gives the system in the Pekin or Mandarin dialect. It will be found at the end of this chapter in a form more convenient for special examination than in the Table, together with Mr. Hart's observations upon the Chinese system.

The Chinese classify the consanguinei of any given person under nine grades of relationship, four of which are above, and four below *Ego*. It would seem that collateral consanguinei are included to some extent in the nine grades, and stand in the same relationship to *Ego*, respectively, as the person in the lineal line does who is at the same distance in degree from the common ancestor. For example, my first, second, and third cousins, male, under our system, are my brothers under the Chinese, and the sons of the latter are my sons; and they stand in the same grades respectively as my own brothers and my own sons. Mr. Hart furnishes, in his observations, the following translation from a Chinese author upon this subject:

"(*A*) All men who are born into the world have nine ranks of relations. My own generation is one grade, my father's is one, my grandfather's is one, that of my grandfather's father is one, and that of my grandfather's grandfather is one; thus above me are four grades: my son's generation is one grade, my grandson's is one, that of my grandson's son is one, and that of my grandson's grandson is one; thus below me are four grades of relations; including myself in the estimate, there are in all nine grades. These are brethren, and though each grade belongs to a different house or family, yet they are all my relations, and these are called the nine grades of relations."

"(*B*) The degrees of kindred in a family are like the streamlets of a fountain, or the branches of a tree; although the streams differ in being more or less remote, and the branches in being more or less close, yet there is but one trunk, and one fountain head."

The chief question of interest in the interpretation of this fragment is, whether the members of each grade of relations stand upon a level and fall under the same relationship to *Ego* as the person in the lineal line at the same remove from the common ancestor, *e. g.*, whether my father's brother and my mother's brother are equally my fathers, my brother's son and my sister's son are equally my sons; or whether it is a division of a man's kindred into generations simply, founded upon the degrees in the lineal line. In the former case all consanguinei, near and remote, would stand to *Ego* in the relation either of fathers or mothers, brothers or sisters, sons or daughters, grandparents or grandchildren of different degrees. This would render the Chinese and Malayan forms identical, and tend to show that the true ethnic position of the Chinese is at the head of the Malayan family. In the latter case, if consanguinei are merely classified into generations according to the distance of particular persons from common ancestors, whilst the division has but little significance, it would leave the relationships of persons unaffected. The system itself does not fully sustain either interpretation, although it contains abundant internal evidence of an original affinity with the Malayan form.

It is now proposed to take up the several lines in their order, and present them with fulness of detail that a complete knowledge of this singular system may be obtained.

The Chinese differs from other forms in possessing a double set of terms for ancestors, one for those on the father's side, and another for those on the mother's, which was rendered necessary by the descent of the family name in the male line. Also for the further reason that the term for grandfather on the father's side, *tsŭ-fŭ* = ancestral father, contained the idea that he was the founder or beginner of a family; whence *wae-kung* = "outside grandfather," is employed to distinguish the grandfather on the mother's side. To discriminate the several ancestors for four degrees above *Ego*, qualifying terms are added to indicate the relative nearness of each; thus, on the father's side we have for the series, father, *fŭ-tsin* = "my father relation" (*wo-te* = "my" being understood as prefixed in this and each succeeding illustration); grandfather, *tsŭ-fŭ* = "my ancestral father;" great-grandfather, *tsung-tsŭ* = "my additional ancestor;" and grandfather's grandfather, *kaon-tsŭ* = "my far removed ancestor." On the mother's side we have for mother, *mo-tsin* = my mother relation; grandmother, *wae-po* = my outside mother; great-grandmother, *wae-tsŭ-po* = "my outside ancestral old mother;" and grandmother's grandmother, *wae-tsung-tsŭ-mo* = "my outside more remote ancestral mother." In the descending series we have son, *ir-tsze* = "my child-boy;" grandson, *sun-tsze* = "my growing for the second time boy;" great-grandson, *tsung-sun* = "my additional growing for the second time boy;" and grandson's grandson, *yuen-san* = "my great growing for the second time."

There is a double set of terms for elder and younger brother and for elder sister, and a single term for younger sister, but no term either for brother or sister in the abstract. It will be observed that one of the terms for elder brother, *ko-ko*, one for elder sister, *tsea-tsea*, and the term for younger sister, *mei-mei*, are each duplications of the same term. No explanation is given why they were thus formed; *heung-te* is the term for younger brother. The other terms are *heung*, my elder brother, literally "senior;" *a-te*, my younger brother, literally "junior;" and *tsze* my elder sister, literally "an experienced woman." All of these are used indiscriminately by the males and females. The term *heung-te* is employed to designate each of the collateral brothers, and *tse-mei* each of the collateral sisters, which are equivalent respectively to elder-younger brother and elder-younger sister. They also apply to collateral brothers and sisters the full terms for our brothers and sisters.

In the first collateral line male, *Ego* a male, I call my brother's son *chih-ir*, my child of the *chih* class, or branch, or grade; my brother's daughter, *chih-neu*, my girl of the *chih* class; my brother's grandson, *chih-sun*, my grandson of the *chih* class; and my brother's granddaughter, *chih-sun-neu*, my granddaughter of the *chih* class.

It is difficult to find a proper definition for the term *chih*, which is here employed to distinguish the descendants of the brothers of *Ego*, and elsewhere of his collateral brothers. The word "class" is adopted by Mr. Hart, and although not perfectly expressive of the idea, is preferable to "branch" or "grade." This, and similar terms, will be best understood by the manner of their use. In the previous relationships *ir* and *neu* express kin. *Ir-tsze* = child-boy, is the term for son, and *neu-ir* = girl-child, that for daughter; *ir*, therefore, is a strict term of relationship, whilst *tsze* and *neu* seem to express more than gender. Whether or not the last two, standing apart from *ir*, are the equivalents of son and daughter, or whether *ir* is understood in each case, I am unable to determine. The reciprocal relationships in the above cases appear to be those of father and son, father and daughter, grandfather and grandson, and grandfather and granddaughter. If this be so, the Chinese possesses the first indicative feature of the Turanian system. Notwithstanding the discrimination of my brother's descendants from my own by means of the term *chih*, this branch of the first collateral line is merged in the lineal line by force of the terms of consanguinity, which is an indicative feature of the Turanian system, and also of the Malayan.

My sister's son, *Ego* a male, I call *wae-sung*, which is rendered by Mr. Hart, " outside nephew." *Wae* signifies " outside," and *sung*, which originally signified a " daughter's child," with *wae* prefixed expresses " sister's son." A better rendering, perhaps, would be " outside child"=nephew. My sister's daughter I call *wae-sung-neu*, translated by Mr. Hart, " my daughter of the *wae-sung* class." Rendered as suggested above, it would be " my outside female child"=niece. As the correlative relationship is that of uncle, it favors the latter form. My sister's grandson I call *wae-sung-sun*, and her granddaughter *wae-sung-neu*, my grandson and granddaughter of the *wae-sung* class. Whether these several renderings are correct is important only so far as it tends to show that the Chinese has a third distinctive and indicative feature of the Turanian system, namely; that whilst my brother's children are my sons and daughters, my sister's children are my nephews and nieces, *Ego* being a male. It will be seen in the sequel that this feature does not run through the system as it does in the typical Turanian form.

On the other hand, with *Ego* a female, my brother's son I call *wae-chih*, my " outer nephew," or *ir* being understood, " my child of the *wae-chih* class;" his daughter I call *wae-chih-neu*, my " outer niece," or my child of the *wae-chih* class; and the children of this nephew and niece are my grandchildren of the same class. The correlative relationship in the first cases is that of " aunt-mother," sometimes " aunt." If we find here, in fact, the relationship of aunt and nephew, another Turanian characteristic is revealed; but with *ir* understood in each case, my brother's children are my children by force of the terms of consanguinity, whilst the force of the discrimination comes from the qualifying terms which have no counterpart in any other known system. It also tends to show that the Chinese form is still in a transition state from the Malayan to the Turanian.

My sister's son, *Ego* a female, I call *e-sung*, which is not rendered. Mr. Hart remarks that the *E* here used is composed of two characters, one of which signifies " woman," and the other " foreign," and that it appears in the word *E-ma*, applied to a mother's sister. *Sung* is the same term before considered. This branch of the first collateral line is the same, whether *Ego* be a male or female, except that in the former case *wae*, and in the latter *E* is prefixed. It follows that my sister's children stand to me a female in the same relationship of consanguinity that they do to my brother a male, except that they are made nearer or more remote in grade, as the terms *wae* and *E* are interpreted. My sister's daughter I call *e-sung-neu*; and her grandchildren my grandchildren of the *e-sung* class.

The wives of these several sons and nephews are my daughters-in-law; and the husbands of these several daughters and nieces are my sons-in-law, each of them addressing me by the correlative terms, which last usage runs through the system; but they are distinguished from each other, and from my own sons-in-law and daughters-in-law, by the terms expressive of the class to which they severally belong. This disposes of the first collateral line.

A digression may be here allowed to observe that descent, amongst the Chinese, as to the family name, is limited to the male line, and followed strictly. Family names are still used in the primitive sense. They call themselves, as a nation or people, *Pih-sing*, which signifies "The Hundred Families." The idea of the family and of the family name, as it now exists in the Aryan family, was comparatively modern, and of slow growth. It appears to have been imperfectly reached outside of this great family. Originally the idea expressed itself in tribes, the family being then unknown. The descendants of an original pair, or of the founder of a family, assumed a distinctive name to perpetuate the memory of their common descent. Into this general name, the names of individuals and of immediate consanguinei were absorbed. They thus became a tribe, or a great family, united by the bond of kin, and distinguished by a common tribal name. Such, in all probability, were the original "hundred families" of the Chinese. Under this organization the names of persons, whilst they might indicate the tribe, would not show that the members of the same household, or children of the same parents, were related to each other, except generally as the members of a great family or circle of kindred. To the all-creative Roman mind the Aryan family is chiefly indebted for the full development of the idea of the *gens* with its subordinate distinctions as expressed by the *prenomen*, *nomen*, and *cognomen*, out of which, at a later day, came the family as now constituted, with the Christian and surname, the latter descending in the male line. Mr. Hart further states that at present there are but four hundred family names in China,[1] or about that number. It seems probable, particularly from the prohibition of intermarriage in the same family, that the "Hundred Families" of the Chinese were the remains or the result of their ancient tribal subdivisions. With them, therefore, in a more marked sense than with us, the females were regarded as transferred to the families of their respective husbands. The male descendants of a man's brothers would retain his family name; whilst his sisters, and their female descendants would assume those of their respective husbands.

In the second collateral line male, on the father's side, and irrespective of the sex of *Ego*, I call my father's brother, if older than my own father, *poh-fŭ*, my

---

[1] "In some parts of the country," he remarks, "large villages are met with, in each of which there exists but one family name; thus, in one district will be found, say, three villages, each containing two or three thousand people, the one of the 'horse,' the second of the 'sheep,' and the third of the 'ox' family name." The Rev. J. V. N. Talmadge, a returned American missionary from Amoy, mentioned the same fact to the writer. He spoke of one village of five thousand inhabitants, all of whom had the same name, with a few exceptions. The most interesting fact connected with this matter is the prohibition of intermarriage amongst all of those who bear the same family name, for reason of consanguinity.

senior father, and if younger, *shuh-fŭ*, my junior father. This is a fourth indicative feature of the Turanian system. My father's brother's son I call *tang-heung-te,* " my Hall brother," or my brother of the *tang* class ; and my father's brother's daughter, *tang-tsze-mei,* my " Hall sister," or my sister of the *tang* class, each of them calling me the same. As the children of brothers we bear the same family name. I also call them elder and younger brother and sister, according to our relative ages. Since the three remaining male cousins are my brothers in Chinese, the system in these relationships agrees with the Malayan. The son and daughter of this collateral brother I call *tang-chih* and *tang-chih-neu,* my son and daughter of the *tang-chih* class ; and his grandson and granddaughter, *tang-chih-sun* and *tang-chih-sun-neu,* my grandchildren of the same class. It will be observed that the *chih* class of the first collateral line here reappears, thus showing that the son of my own brother and of my collateral brother fall into the same class, although in different branches. In like manner the son and daughter of this collateral sister I call *tang-wae-sung* and *tang-wae-sung-neu,* my outside nephew and outside niece of the *tang* class, and their children are my grandchildren of the same class. Up to this point the method of the system is coherent, and its parts are in self-agreement. But a deviation now occurs with respect to the children of this collateral brother and sister, *Ego* a female, which is difficult of explanation ; they are the same as above given with *Ego* a male. It has been seen that the principle of classification, *Ego* a male, established in the first collateral line, is carried into the second, *Ego* still a male ; but with *Ego* a female, the principle established in the first is not carried into the second, as it should be in accordance with the logic of the system. In other words, the second collateral line should be in its male and female branches a counterpart of the first, with the addition of the word *tang,* expressive of the class, and it is not. It is one of those particulars in which the original Malayan form at the basis of the system still manifests itself.

My father's sister, if older than my father, and irrespective of the sex of *Ego,* I call *kŭ-mo* = aunt-mother, and if younger, *kŭ-tseay* = aunt-elder-sister ; but in common usage, simply *kŭ* = aunt. This is a fifth indicative relationship of the Turanian system. My father's sister's son and daughter I call *peaon-heung-te,* and *peaon-tsze-mei,* my external brother and my external sister of the *peaon* class. I also call them my elder or younger brother and sister, according to relative age, using the same terms I apply to own brothers and sisters. In these relationships the system is again Malayan. The son and daughter of this collateral brother I call *peaon-chih* and *peaon-chih-neu,* my son and daughter of the *peaon* class. Mr. Hart renders these terms nephew and niece ; but inasmuch as they are the same terms applied by a man to his brother's children, with *peaon* added to distinguish the branch and line, the former appears to be the preferable translation. The children of the latter are my grandchildren of the same class. The son and daughter of this collateral sister I call *peaon-chih-wae-sung* and *peaon-chih-wea-sung-neu,* my nephew and niece of the *peaon* class. The children of the latter are my grandchildren of the same class. With *Ego* a female, these relationships are the same. From the precision with which the same terms are applied in this line which are used in the first, with *Ego* a male, it still appears singular that the discriminations made in the former, with *Ego* a female, are not applied in the latter with *Ego* the same. Without any reason for supposing that any part of this intricate system escaped the critical attention of Mr. Hart, to maintain its consistency with itself the principles of classification adopted in the first collateral line should be carried into the second, third, and even more remote. Wherever a collateral brother and sister are found, however distant in degree, their children should fall into the same relationships of consanguinity as those of an own brother and sister, but distinguished from each other by the class terms. Notwithstanding the apparently arbitrary character of the system, it rests upon definite ideas which stand to each other in fixed relations; and the relations thus created must constantly assert their integrity, or the system becomes blemished.

Irrespective of the sex of *Ego*, I call my mother's brother *mo-kew* = my mother-uncle, or commonly *kew*, uncle. Sometimes *kew-fŭ* = uncle-father, is used. The relationship of uncle, restricted to my mother's brother, is a sixth indicative characteristic of the Turanian system. It was the presence of this relationship, together with that of aunt, which is equally positive, followed, but with much less distinctness, by the correlative relationships of nephew and niece, that furnished the preponderating reason for placing the Chinese in the Turanian rather than in the Malayan connection. When the Malayan form is presented it will be found that the Chinese system stands on the confines between the Malayan and Turanian forms. In determining the question of its true position the terms of consanguinity, which represent the original as well as the radical parts of the system, must govern; and the qualifying terms, which represent the afterwork of scholars, must be laid out of view. If this is done, the Chinese form, with the exception of the relationships named, will be seen to affiliate more closely with the Malayan than with the Turanian. On the other hand, with those relationships which mark the transition from the former to the latter stage of development, the preponderance of internal evidence is in favor of the Turanian connection. When the systems of relationship of the remaining Asiatic nations, as well as of the assemblage of nations inhabiting Oceanica, are collected and compared it is not improbable, as elsewhere intimated, that the rightful position of the Chinese nation will be in the Malayan family. This subject will be referred to again. To resume: my mother's brother's son and daughter I call *peaon-heung-te* and *peaon-tsze-mei*, my external brother and sister, or my brother and sister of the *peaon* class. I call them also my elder or younger brother and sister, according to our relative ages; the son and daughter of this collateral brother *peaon-chih* and *peaon-chih-neu*, my son and daughter of the *peaon* class, and the children of the latter my grandchildren of the same class. The son and daughter of this collateral sister I call *wae-peaon-chih*, and *wae-peaon-chih-neu*, my son and daughter of the *wae* branch of the *peaon* class. Mr. Hart renders this phrase as equivalent to nephew and niece of the same branch and class. Their children are my grandchildren of the *peaon-chih* class.

Mr. Hart remarks in a note that " relationship on the father's side transmitted from male to male is of the *tang* class; the moment it passes out, by the marriage of a female to another family, it is characterized as *peaon*; and if it passes from that to another family, by the marriage of another female, it becomes *wae-peaon*."

My mother's sister, if older than my mother, I call *ta-e-ma*, and if younger, *leaon-e-ma*, which is rendered by Mr. Hart my " great" or " little outside mama." Whether in common usage she is called mother does not appear. Her son and daughter I call *e-peaon-heung-te*, and *e-peaon-tsze-mei*, my brother and sister of the *e-peaon* class. The force of the *E*, appears to be, to make this class more remote than the *peaon*, which is another departure from the spirit of the Turanian form. As phrases, they are equivalent to " outside external," brother and sister. I also call them elder or younger brother and sister. The children of this brother are my sons and daughters of the *e-peaon* class; and the children of the latter are my grandchildren of the same class. On the other hand, the son and daughter of this collateral sister I call *wae-e-peaon-chih* and *wae-e-peaon-chih-neu*, which Mr. Hart translates my nephew and niece of the *wae* branch of the *e-peaon* class. Their children are my grandchildren of the same class.

It will be observed that the children of brothers are placed upon the same level under the relationship of " Hall brothers" and " Hall sisters;" that the children of sisters are placed upon equality as " external outside brothers and sisters;" and that the children of a brother and sister are similarly placed as " outside brothers and sisters." The members of each of the three classes are equal amongst themselves, but stand in different relationships as classes, the difference being made in the qualifying terms. By the terms of consanguinity they are all brothers and sisters to each other, which is another departure from the Turanian system.

The wives of these several collateral brothers in each of the four branches of the second collateral line, are each my sister-in-law; and the husbands of each of these collateral sisters are my brothers-in-law, each of them addressing me by the correlative term; but they are distinguished from each other, in the same manner as blood relations, by the qualifying terms expressive of the class with which they are respectively connected by marriage. This disposes of the second collateral line.

It will be sufficient to present in detail one of the four branches of the third collateral line. My father's father's sister I call *kū-mo*, my aunt-mother the same as my father's sister; her son if older than my father I call *peaon-poh*, if younger *peaon-shuh*, my " senior" or " junior," of the *peaon* class. If the relationship in this case was that of uncle, it would be more consistent. My father's sister's daughter I call *peaon-kŭ*, my aunt of the *peaon* class. The children of each I call *peaon-heung-te*, and *peaon-tsze-mei*, my brother and sister of the *peaon* class. The son and daughter of this collateral brother are my children, and the children of the latter are my grandchildren of the same class.

We have now, with tedious minuteness, presented the material parts of the Chinese system of relationship. Although the contents of this remarkable system are by no means exhausted by the explanations given, they exhibit its form sufficiently to illustrate its elaborate and artificial character. It embodies a well-considered plan, which works out its results in a coherent and harmonious manner. If we eliminate from the system the supplemental portion which renders specific the classes, and their branches, and examine the terms of relationship which remain, together with the classification of consanguinei under them, the primitive system of the people will be revealed with considerable certainty. It will thus be seen that it was originally Malayan in form, but with positive and distinct Turanian elements engrafted upon it, which in the sequel will be found equally true of the Turanian system as a whole.   The Chinese is more complicated than any system contained in the Tables, and yet not so difficult as to forbid its universal use amongst the people.   If they address each other, in familiar intercourse, by the terms of relationship, instead of their personal names, this usage would impart as well as preserve a knowledge of the system.   Whether or not this mode of address generally prevails the writer is not able to state.   In the immediate family they speak to each other by the terms of relationship, and not by personal names.   This fact is stated upon the authority of Rev. Mr. Talmadge before mentioned, who had observed the usage at Amoy in Chinese families with whom he was in constant intercourse.

There are said to be barbarous tribes in the interior and mountain districts of China who are imperfectly controlled by the government, and who enjoy some measure of independence.   In this class of the population the primitive system of this ancient nation, unencumbered with the qualifying terms, might be expected to be found.   If the form now in use among them is ever procured, it will settle the question of the character of the original system, as well as explain its present characteristics.

Below, in a note,[1] will be found the letter of Mr. Hart, which accompanied

---

CANTON, CHINA, Sept. 18, 1860.

DEAR SIR : In compliance with the request made by you in your circular letter dated 1st October, 1859, and which has been placed in my hands by Mr. Perry, U. S. Consul at this port, I have much pleasure in forwarding, through that gentleman, for your perusal, a schedule (with remarks) of the system of relationship in existence in China.

My comparison of the Chinese system with the results of your inquiries amongst the American Indian tribes, inclines me to think that it not merely *possesses* the radical features of the Indian system, but that it further possesses those features in such a manner as to give ground for the supposition that, while most intimately connected, it—the Chinese system—precedes, as it were, and is much nearer the parent relationship system than is the Indian system.

If, from the examination of the schedule now forwarded, you should wish further inquiries to be made, I shall most willingly give my assistance ; the subject already interests me not a little.

Very faithfully, yours,   ROBERT HART.

LEWIS H. MORGAN, ESQ., New York.

Observations by Hon. Robert Hart, upon the annexed Schedule, &c.

1. The Chinese system of relationship is, as will be seen, based upon definite ideas, standing in fixed and intelligent relations to each other.   The bond of consanguinity does not lose itself in the diverging collateral lines, while these collateral lines revert into, or are merged in the lineal, the merging process acting upwards as well as downwards.

2. The groundwork of the system, judging from the nomenclature employed, is to be found in the terms used to designate the immediate or nearest relations of any individual, viz., father, mother, brother, sister, son, daughter.   All the persons related by consanguinity to such an individual are regarded by him as standing in some one or other of these relationships to himself ; but while the *true* father is styled simply father, the *true* brother, brother, and the *true* son, son, the others are styled class fathers, class brothers, and class sons ; the word for "class" being in each case one authorized by both rule and practice, and which expresses clearly the manner in which such a relationship originated.

3. The brothers and sisters of one's grandparents are styled "class grandparents," the word for

the Chinese schedule, together with his observations upon the Chinese system of relationship. These are followed, at the end of the chapter, with the schedule

---

"class" showing, on the paternal side, whether the individual spoken of is senior or junior to the *true* grandparent; and on the maternal side, that the person referred to is, like the maternal *true* grandfather, not a real *lineal* progenitor.

4. The brothers and sisters of one's parents are with the true parents, equally styled parents, characterized, however, as "class parents," the word for "class" on the father's side showing their seniority or juniority to the true father, and on the mother's side explaining, as it were, that they are parents by relationship with the mother, as her brothers and sisters. In some instances, however, there appears to be a trace of distinction made between the relationships in which a father's brother and a mother's sister stand to an individual, when compared with that in which a father's sister and a mother's brother are situated, showing that while in the former case they are called "class parents," they are in the latter distinguished by terms—the words for father and mother being omitted—equivalent, seemingly, to "uncle and aunt."

5. There is no one word for brother, but there is one expression used for elder, and another for younger brother, and these are employed, not to designate the oldest and youngest brother, but respectively for such brothers as may be older or younger than the person speaking or spoken of. In the same way, while there is one term signifying sister generally, there are in use two expressions, the one for older, and the other for younger sister.

6. The children of several brothers of several sisters, as well as of brothers on the one hand, and sisters on the other, are brothers and sisters to each other, and they in each case use the respective terms for elder and younger brother, and for elder and younger sister, the same as in the case of own brothers and sisters. Such relatives, however, style each other "class brothers," "class sisters," the word signifying "class" showing whether the person in question is the child of a father's brother, of a father's sister, or of a mother's brother, or of a mother's sister; the fraternal relationship being of three classes, *Tang*, Peaon, and *E-peaon*. The children of these class brothers, &c., are again class brothers and class sisters to each other, as are also their children's children, the bond of consanguinity continuing the same so long as the parties concerned are equally removed by descent from the original pair of brothers, &c. The degree or intensity of relationship is, however, lessened or farther removed, when it passes from one to another family by the going out of a female in marriage.

7. The children of an individual's brothers and sisters, as also of class brothers and sisters, are that individual's children likewise, but characterized as class children of various classes, according to fixed rule and practice; and the children of such class children are that individual's class grandchildren. Thus, for instance:—

Said by a man.	A brother's child is the individual's child of the Chih class.
" " "	A sister's " " " " " Wae-sung class.
Said by a woman.	A brother's child is the individual's child of the Wae-chih class.
" " "	A sister's " " " " " E-sung class.

It is here worth noticing that the *wae* in *wae-sung*, and *wae-chih* signifies external, so that the words made use of by a man to designate a sister's son and daughter, and by a woman to designate a brother's child, might be considered equivalent in some degree to our words nephew and niece. In this way a kind of confirmation is given of the remark made in No. 4, that traces seem to exist of occasions on which one's father's sisters, and one's mother's brothers are regarded as uncles and aunts, rather than as class parents.

8. The grandchildren of brothers, of sisters, and of brothers and sisters are, as already stated, class brothers and sisters to each other; and the same relationship continued to exist to the remotest generation, so long as the parties concerned stand in the same degree of nearness to the original brothers and sisters. But when one is further removed than another by a single degree, the rule which changes the collateral line into the lineal at once applies. It is, however, to be remarked that as regards *remoteness* in respect of ancestors and descendants, the Chinese system recognizes, *practically*, only such either way, as with an individual form *five* generations; thus above me, my

itself, which contains also his etymological observations upon the nomenclature of relationships.   They were evidently prepared with much care and labor, and treat

---

great-great-grandfather is the most remote of my practically recognized forefathers; while, in the same way, my most remote practically recognized descendant is my great-great-grandson.   By *practical* recognition two things are expressed: first, within these limits each individual has a separate name of relationship, while beyond them relations are classed generally as "ancestors" and "descendants" respectively; and secondly, it would be only for relatives within such limits that, according to usage, I should be obliged to wear mourning in the event of their decease during my lifetime.

9. Thus, the descendants of an original pair do not, in theory, pass beyond the degree of class brother, and hence results a recognized tie of consanguinity which no lapse of time can effect, but which, practically, the brethren do not consider worth observing after the fifth generation.

10. The wives of these several brothers and class brothers, as also the husbands of these several sisters and class sisters are interchangeably sisters-in-law and class sisters-in-law, brothers-in-law and class brothers-in-law to the brothers and class brothers, as to the sisters and class sisters of their respective wives and husbands.   Likewise all the wives of these several sons and class sons are daughters-in-law and class daughters-in-law to the parents and class parents of their respective husbands, and the husbands of these several daughters and class daughters are alike sons-in-law and class sons-in-law to the parents and class parents of their respective wives.

11. The nomenclature employed in the designation of two brothers-in-law and two sisters-in-law, *i. e.*, by a wife towards the brothers and sisters of her husband, and by a husband towards the brothers and sisters of his wife, seems to have its origin in the names applied to such people by the children (their class children, or nephews and nieces) born of the marriage.   Thus, an individual's wife's brother is the *kew* of that individual's children, and that individual in speaking of him as his brother-in-law, employs the same word, *kew*, to designate him as such.   So with the others.

12. As regards "Division into Tribes," I am not aware that the Chinese, amongst whom the preceding form of relationship is in existence, recognize at this day any such tribal distinctions.   There are, it is true, in some parts of the country wild aboriginal mountain tribes, but the people composing such tribes speak languages differing entirely (I believe) from that from which the schedule nomenclature is drawn, and they likewise ignore the authority of the Chinese officials in their country. Their system of relationship, with their habits and customs, are unknown to me, and have not, so far as I am aware, as yet been investigated by foreigners.   The Chinese expression, however, for the people is "*Pih-sing*," which means "the hundred family names;" but whether this is merely word-painting, or had its origin at a time when the Chinese general family consisted of one hundred sub-families or tribes, I am unable to determine.   At the present day there are about four hundred family names in this country, amongst which I find some that have reference to animals, fruits, metals, natural objects, &c., and which may be translated as Horse, Sheep, Ox, Fish, Bird, Phœnix, Plum, Flower, Leaf, Rice, Forest, River, Hill, Water, Cloud, Gold, Hide, Bristles, &c. &c.   In some parts of the country large villages are met with in each of which there exists but one family name: thus, in one district will be found, say, three villages, each containing two or three thousand people, the one of the "Horse," the second of the "Sheep," and the third of the "Ox" family name; and two of the three will in all probability have a kind of reciprocity treaty, offensive and defensive, and be continually at feud with the third.   In this way may perhaps be detected traces of a recognition, at some former period, of tribal divisions.

13. Just as among the North American Indians, husbands and wives are of different tribes, so in China, husband and wife are always of different families, *i. e.*, of different surnames.   Custom and law alike prohibit intermarriage on the part of people having the same family surname.

14. The children are of the father's family, that is they take the family surname.   The only case in which a child is of its mother's family, taking her family surname, is when a father, having only a female child, instead of marrying her out, brings to his own house a husband for her, then if more sons than one are the fruit of the marriage, the second one generally takes the mother's family name and is considered as continuing literally her father's race.

the several subjects named in a thorough and scholarly manner. It should be stated that the order in which he discusses the radical features of the Chinese system follows step by step the series of propositions deduced by an analysis of the Ganowánian system which accompanied the blank schedule. These several productions of the pen of Mr. Hart are worthy of careful examination.

2. Japanese Nation.

The insular situation of the Japanese, their numbers and their civilization give to them an important position among oriental nations. Since their language is now becoming generally accessible their domestic institutions and early history, as well as their ethnic relations, will soon become understood. It is evident that they have made considerable progress in the direction of a true civilization. They are also a teachable as well as an appreciative and improvable people. From such customs and institutions as have been ascertained to exist amongst them a presumption arises of their great antiquity as a nation. They likewise tend to show that in their upward progress they have extricated themselves from the worst evils

---

15. The Chinese, by national custom, change the names of individuals at different periods. Thus, a child at the breast and during its early years has its "milk name;" it goes to school, and is then called by another name; it arrives at puberty, or is married, and it receives another name. There are, besides, amongst the Chinese a few other occasions on which an additional name is taken or given.

16. When a father dies intestate the property generally remains undivided, but under the control of the oldest son during the life of the widow. On her death the oldest son divides the property between himself and his brothers, the shares of the juniors depending entirely upon the will of the elder brother.

17. The following translation from the Chinese may not be out of place here.

"A. All men who are born into the world have nine ranks of relations. My own generation is one grade, my father's is one, my grandfather's is one, that of my grandfather's father is one, and that of my grandfather's grandfather is one; thus above me are four grades. My son's generation is one grade, my grandson's is one, that of my grandson's son is one, and that of my grandson's grandson is one; thus below are four grades of relations. Including myself in the estimate, there are in all nine grades. These are brethren, and though each grade belongs to a different house or family, yet they are all my relations, and these are called the nine grades of relations.

"B. The degrees of kindred in a family are like the streamlets of a fountain or the branches of a tree; although the streams differ in being more or less remote, and the branches in being more or less close, yet there is but one trunk and one fountain head."

18. The natives of the province of *Keang-se* are celebrated through the other Chinese provinces for the mode or form used by them in address, which is *Laon-peaon*. This may be paraphrastically translated as "O you old fellow! brother mine by some of the ramifications of female relationship."

19. In conclusion, it merely remains to be remarked that the Chinese system of relationship, judging from its nomenclature, and that nomenclature one that has existed for some thousands of years, must have had its origin in the earliest days, and in the cradle-lands of humanity—in the days when all existing looked upon each other as being equally members of the one increasing family—when each successive birth was considered as increasing the *one* family, and as being in relationship with every individual composing that family; and when from the original pair or parents down to their coeval great-great-grandchildren, the relationship of each to the other, through every successive grade, and upwards and downwards, could be distinctly traced, accurately expressed, and was in actual being, having a personal interest for, and being patent to the observation of all.

N. B.—The Mandarin dialect, or, more properly expressed, the "Pekin dialect," is the standard spoken language of China.

The Table of Consanguinity and Affinity of the Chinese, in the Mandarin dialect, will be found at the end of the chapter, p. 432.

54   April, 1870.

of barbarism. When they have learned to put aside their exclusiveness as well as jealousy of foreign influence, and have experienced the advantages of a wisely regulated commercial intercourse, which has contributed so largely to the material and intellectual advancement of the civilized nations, there is every reason to believe that the Japanese will attain to a respectable and creditable position among the nations of the earth.

The Japanese islands sustain a peculiar physical relation to the northwest coast of the United States. A chain of small islands (the Kurilian) breaks the distance which separates Japan from the peninsula of Kamtschatka; and from thence the Aleutian chain of islands stretches across to the peninsula of Alaska upon the American continent, forming the boundary between the north Pacific and Behring's Sea. These islands, the peaks of a submarine mountain chain, are thickly studded together within a continuous belt, and are in substantial communication with each other, from the extreme point of Alaska to the island of Kyska, by means of the ordinary native boat in use among the Aleutian islanders. From the latter to Attou island the greatest distance from island to island is less than one hundred miles. Between Attou island and the coast of Kamtschatka, there are but two islands, Copper and Behring's, between which and Attou the greatest distance occurs, a distance of about two hundred miles; whilst from Behring's island to the main land of Asia it is less than one hundred miles. These geographical features alone would seem to render possible a migration, in the primitive and fishermen ages, from one continent to the other. But superadded to these is the great thermal ocean current, analogous to the Atlantic gulf stream, which, commencing in the equatorial regions near the Asiatic continent, flows northward along the Japan and Kurilian islands, and then bearing eastward divides itself into two streams. One of these, following the main direction of the Asiatic coast, passes through the straits of Behring and enters the Arctic Ocean; whilst the other, and the principal current, flowing eastward, and skirting the southern shores of the Aleutian islands, reaches the northwest coast of America, whence it flows southward along the shores of Oregon and California, where it finally disappears. This current, or thermal river in the midst of the ocean, would constantly tend, by the mere accidents of the sea, to throw Asiatics from Japan and Kamtschatka upon the Aleutian islands, from which their gradual progress eastward to America would become assured. It is common at the present time to find trunks of camphor wood trees from the coasts of China and Japan upon the shores of the island of Ounalaska, one of the easternmost of the Aleutian chain, carried thither by this ocean current. It also explains the agency by which a disabled Japanese junk with its crew was borne directly to the shores of California but a few years since. Another remarkable effect produced by this warm ocean current is the temperate climate which it bestows upon this chain of islands and upon the northwest coast of America. These considerations assure us of a second possible route of communication besides the straits of Behring, between the Asiatic and American continents.[1]

---

[1] The Eskimo now occupy the Aleutian islands; but it seems probable that it is a retrogression westward of this people under the pressure upon them of the Athapascan nations. As a matter of

Whilst our knowledge of the Japanese is in a fragmentary state every new fact concerning their domestic institutions possesses value. Since the completion of this work an opportunity was unexpectedly offered, through the visit to this country of a Japanese troupe, to obtain not only their system of relationship, but also to extend the inquiry to some other particulars. The results in the latter respect, although not especially important, may be worth inserting for the reason first above stated. They will be limited to three particulars: the family, the burial of the dead, and the divisions of the people into classes. The interpreter of this troupe, *Man-kï'-chi Kä-wä'-be*, a young man of intelligence and of education in the Japanese sense, had acquired our language in Japan through Mr. Smith, who brought the troupe to this country to exhibit their performances in our cities. In this respect he had made sufficient progress to use it for ordinary colloquial purposes. I am indebted to him for the Japanese system of relationship contained in the Table, for a vocabulary of the language, and for the information given upon the subjects named. After a fruitless effort to procure the former from the American Legation at Yedo, and which resulted in obtaining but a fragment of the system, it seemed not a little singular that this troupe of adventurers should have brought it to my door at the last moment before publication.[1]

The Japanese have not only reached the state of marriage between single pairs, which is now common in nearly all barbarous nations, but they have also developed the family in the civilized and modern sense of this term, with the distinctions of the family and the personal name. This is rarely the case in barbarous nations, and is, in itself, decisive evidence of the substantial progress of the Japanese in the scale of civilization. Amongst the former class of nations, while in the lowest condition, a single personal name for each individual is the extent of the development of the modern family distinctions, the tribe supplying the place of the family. The family name arises after the dawn of civilization. Our Saxon ancestors within the historical period had the personal name only, and were without the family name. Whilst the latter names are numerous amongst the Japanese, they have not been multiplied to such an extent as in civilized nations. The father bestows personal names upon his children, in addition to which they take his family name and retain it so long as they remain members of a common family.

In describing a person the surname precedes the personal, thus reversing our custom. The following are examples:—

Family.	Names of Males.			Family.	Names of Females.	
Kä-wä'-be,	Man-kï'-chï.	My Interpreter.		Kä-wä'-be,	O-kä'-ma.[2]	His Mother.
"	To'-yen.	His Father.		She-rä'-tä,	O-ee'-che.	
"	To-dä'-ro.	His Brother.		Nong-oo'-che,	O-ka'-ee.	
No'-dä,	Ska-ro'-ko.			No'-dä,	O-ee'-ro.	
Tä'-rook,	Ju'-ba.			She-wä'-yä,	O'-sen.	
Nung'-ich,	Gen'-zo			No'-za-wä,	Oaf'-kŭ.	

---

speculation the straits of Behring was the more probable route of the Eskimo migration as hyperboreans; whilst that by the Aleutian islands is the more probable route of the much older migration of the Ganowánian family.

[1] May, 1867.   [2] Female personal names universally commence with the vowel *O*.

In the higher classes marriages are arranged by the parents for their sons and daughters; amongst the lower, by the parties themselves. Polygamy is unknown. Individuals of the privileged classes take to themselves concubines, but recognize only one lawful wife. The eldest son, who inherits the property, is not allowed to leave the paternal home. When he marries he takes his wife to his father's house and she assumes his family name. In like manner the eldest daughter is not allowed, when she marries, to leave the paternal home, but her husband removes thereto, and takes her family name. It follows, and such is the established custom, that the eldest son of one family cannot marry the eldest daughter of another, as the latter cannot leave her home. Neither can the second son of one family marry the second daughter of another, as he would be excluded from the houses of both families, and so of each of the remaining children, unless a separate house is provided for them. If the father buys a house for his second or other younger son, and he marries, his wife takes his family name; but if the wife's father provides the house, then he loses his family name, and takes that of his wife. The eldest son may marry the second or other younger daughter of another family, and the eldest daughter the second or other younger son of another family. Upon the death of the eldest son, the next, or oldest remaining son, if married, returns to the paternal home and resumes the family name. Cousins are allowed to intermarry, but within this degree marriage is forbidden. The purchase or sale of women for wives is unknown amongst the Japanese. Females are marriageable at seventeen.

They still practise the custom of changing their personal names. It may be done by the father, or by the person, and is limited to one change. It is not unusual, however, for persons to carry the same name through life. In this custom is recognized the very ancient Asiatic and American Indian usage of the " milk name" for childhood, followed by a different one for adult life. The modern or family name has direct relation to the house or home, and consequently must have originated after property had become stable, and its transmission by inheritance had become established by law. This is sufficiently shown by the term itself, E'-a, a house; E-a'-no, a family; E-a'-no-no, a family name. The clear and perfect development of the idea, as well as the realization of the family, with the personal and family name distinctions, it may be here repeated, is very high evidence of the progress of the Japanese in a true civilization.

The Japanese bury their dead in a sitting posture. After the body is dressed in its ordinary apparel, it is placed in an urn of earthenware, about three feet and a half high, with the legs flexed and the arms folded. This urn is then covered and inclosed in a coffin of wood, and buried in the ground, in a grave four feet square and eight feet deep. No personal articles are buried with the deceased, except he is a person of rank entitled to wear two swords, in which case two wooden swords, as insignia of his rank, are deposited in the urn by his side. A tombstone or obelisk is erected near the grave inscribed with the family and personal name of the deceased.[1]

---

[1] The cemeteries of the Japanese are not much unlike our own. In Perry's Japan Expedition, I, 407, there is a representation of a Japanese graveyard and temple which fully sustains this statement.

The political or class divisions of the people are more difficult to be understood. They have, in vigorous development, those cunningly devised gradations of rank which spring up in the transition period from barbarism to civilization, and which the privileged classes are certain to perpetuate long after the absurdity as well as criminal injustice of legalized rank is perfectly understood by all classes. The entire scheme of hereditary rank and titles, having its roots in barbarism, is still essentially a barbarous institution, violative of the brotherhood which should unite the people of the same immediate lineage. The privileged classes in Japan whose mastery over the people is complete, illustrate in a striking manner the injurious operations of the principle.

With respect to the civil head of the Japanese empire the common opinion that it is under the joint sway of a spiritual and a temporal emperor does not appear to be correct. The Japanese regard the *Me-kă'-do* as the true emperor and supreme ruler of Japan, and the *Ty'-koon* as his prime minister or vicegerent. *Man-ki-chi*, illustrated to the writer their relative positions by that of a merchant and his chief clerk. Notwithstanding the fact that the people regard the *Ty'-koon* as the subordinate of the *Me-kă'-do*, he has the substance of power, and for most practical purposes is the emperor. For several generations the office has been hereditary in the same family. He resides in the chief city of the empire, whilst the *Me-kă'-do* lives at *Ke-o'-to*, some three hundred miles distant. The former levies and collects taxes, commands and supports the military forces, and appoints and controls all the subordinate officers of the empire. In all these particulars he appears to be left substantially to his own direction. He is bound, however, to obey the requisitions of the *Me-kă'-do* in every particular, as *Man-ki-chi* affirms. The treaty with the United States was negotiated by the *Ty'-koon*, but it was also signed, I am told, by the *Me-kă'-do*, who was waited upon by the *Ty-koon* and his ministers, to solicit his signature, which he was reluctant to give, and also professed their readiness to commit *hari-kari* if he so directed. The position of the *Ty'-koon* appears to be analogous to that of the Mayor of the Palace, in the early days of the French monarchy.

The remaining orders of nobility and gradations of the people are, 1. The *Koo'-gih* class. Of their numbers, privileges, and position I could obtain no satisfactory information, except that they are higher in rank than the princes. 2. *Koke'-she Di'-me-o* class, or the Eighteen Princes. These Dimeos are under the *Ty'-koon*, and are the persons to whom the great districts or provinces of the empire are farmed out for the letting of the land and the collection of the taxes. They receive their titles from the *Me-kă'-do*, but whether it is hereditary in their families I did not ascertain. They are called the *Koke'-she* Dimeos, to distinguish them from an inferior class of princes. 3. *Di'-me-o* class. Of these princes, called Dimeos[1] simply, there are several thousand. 4. *Hă'-tä-mo'-to* class. These are the officers of the *Ty'-koon* in the various departments of the public service. They are of the

---

[1] In the Japanese language there is no plural for words signifying objects or things. To such words the number is prefixed. For persons, it is made by adding *do'-mo*, e. g. *O-to'-ko*, a man; *O-to'-ko do'-mo*, men.

class of nobles, are entitled to wear two swords, and number eighty-eight thousand. Man-ki̇̆-chi̇̆ belongs to this class, as he assured me. 5. Farmers. 6. Artisans, as goldsmiths, carpenters, blacksmiths, &c. &c. 7. Shopkeepers. 8. Common people.

The Japanese language is syllabical, of the Turanian type, but apparently in an advanced stage of development. Its verbs are regularly inflected, and its nouns appear to have a systematic declension.[1] It is entirely free from guttural and nasal tones if the ordinary vocabulary words are sufficient to determine that question. In speaking the lips rarely close, but they have most, if not all, the labial letters. The Lew Chewans speak a dialect of the Japanese.[2]

When related the Japanese address each other by the term of relationship, and when not related, by the personal name. Their system of relationship is classific, and embraces all collateral consanguinei as far as the connection can be traced. It is an interesting form for the reason especially that it has passed under the powerful influences arising from the possession of fixed property, and the establishment of laws for its transmission by inheritance. Property rights alone appear to possess sufficient power to overthrow the classificatory system.

In the lineal line there are terms for grandfather and grandmother, *o-jee'-sang* and *o-bä'-san;* for great-grandfather and mother, *she-jee'-je* and *she-bä'-bä;* for grandson and granddaughter, *mä'-go* and *ma'-ee;* for great-grandchild, *zhe'-ko;* and for grandchild's grandchild, *yă-shang'-o.* There are also separate terms for elder and younger brother and for elder and younger sister, but no term for brother or sister in the abstract. The plural is formed, as before stated, by adding *do'-mo,* e. g., *ă'-nee,* elder brother; *ă'-nee do'-mo* elder brothers. These terms are used both by the males and females.

My brother's son and daughter are my nephew and niece, *e-to-ko* and *o-nä e-to'-ko;* their children are my grandsons and granddaughters; and the children of the latter are my grandchildren. My sister's children, and their descendants, stand to me in the same relationships; and these are the same whether *Ego* is a male or a female.

The wife of this nephew is my daughter-in-law, *yo'-mä;* and the husband of this niece is my son-in-law, *moo'-ko.*

My father's brother is my uncle, *o'-jee.* This term was rendered by the late Mr. H. J. S. Heusken, U. S. Secretary of Legation at Yedo, from whom I received an imperfectly filled schedule, "my little father." The son of this uncle, if older than myself, is my elder brother, *ă'-nee;* if younger, my younger brother, *o-to'-to;* his daughter, in like manner, is my elder or younger sister, *ă'-nih* or *e-mo'-to.* Each of the sons and daughters of this collateral brother and sister is my nephew, *e-to'-ko,* or my niece, *o'-nä e-to'-ko;* each of their children is my grandson or granddaughter, *mä'-go* or *mä'-ee;* and each of the children of the latter is my great-grandchild, *she'-ko.*

---

[1] Oo'-mä.   A horse.   Oo'-mä.   A horse.
　　Mä'-mo.   Of a horse.   Oo'-mä-to.   With a horse.
　　Mä'-me.   To or for a horse.
[2] Japan Expedition, under Commodore Perry, 2, 47.

OF THE HUMAN FAMILY. 431

My father's sister is my aunt, *o'-bä*, which is also rendered by Mr. Heusken, "my little mother." Her children and descendants stand to me in the same relationships as those of my uncle last above mentioned.

My mother's brother is also my uncle, *o'-jee*, and my mother's sister is my aunt, *o'-bä*. The relationships of their respective children and descendants are the same as those above given, no difference whatever being made in the several branches of this line.

The wives of my several collateral brothers are my elder or younger sisters, according to our relative ages; and the husbands of my several collateral sisters are severally my elder or younger brothers.

In the third collateral line, my grandfather's brother is my grandfather, *o-jee'-sang ;* his son is my uncle, *o'-jee ;* the son of this uncle is my elder or younger brother, *ă'-nee* or *o-to'-to ;* his son and daughter are my nephew and niece; and the children of the latter are my grandsons and granddaughters. In the other branches of this line the relationships are the same after that of the first person.

The fourth and more remote collateral lines are counterparts of the second and third, but with additional ancestors.

With respect to the position of this system it will be seen, when the Malayan form is presented, that there is a strong probability that it was originally Malayan in form. Whilst the Chinese appears to be in a transition state between the Malayan and the Turanian, the Japanese is passing out of the Turanian in the direction of the Aryan form, but without giving sufficient evidence to determine the question whether it passed into the Turanian in its progressive development from the Malayan into its present form. It is placed, provisionally, in the Turanian connection.

TABLE OF CONSANGUINITY AND AFFINITY OF THE CHINESE, IN THE MANDARIN DIALECT.

By Hon. Robert Hart, of Canton.

Description of persons.	Relationships in Chinese.	Translation.	Etymological explanations.
1. My great great grandfather (father's side).	Wo-tĕ kaon-tsŭ	My far removed ancestor.	*Kaon* = high or lofty.
2. " great great grandmother	" kaon-tsŭ-mo	" far removed ancestral mother.	
3. " great grandfather	" tsung-tsŭ.........	" additional ancestor, i. e., more remote.	
4. " great grandfather's brother......	" tsung-poh/shuh-tsŭ....	" more remote ancestor.	Of the *poh* or *shuh* paternal relationship, see "father's brother."
5. " great grandfather's sister	" kŭ-po...........	" old mother of the *kŭ* class.	*Kŭ* is a term applied alike to a woman's husband's mother, and to a father's sisters. *Po* = old mother. Thus *kŭ-po* is my old mother of the *kŭ* class.
6. " great grandmother	" tsung-tsŭ-mo	" more remote ancestral mother.	
7. " great grandmother's brother.....	" kew-tae-kung.....	" very old gentleman.	*Kew-kung* is my grandmother's brother. *Tae* means great. *Kew-tae-kung* is thus my mother's brother (my father of the *kew* class), that *very* old gentleman.
8. " great grandmother's sister	" kŭ-tae-po.........	" old great mother.	Same *kŭ-po* as above, and the same *tae*.
9. " grandfather	" tsŭ-fŭ	" ancestral father.	*Tsŭ* is one who begins or founds a family.
10. " grandfather's elder brother......	" poh-tsŭ	" senior ancestral relation.	The same *poh* and *shuh* are met with in my father's brother.
" grandfather's younger brother...	" shuh-tsŭ	" junior ancestral relation.	
11. " grandfather's sister.............	" kŭ-mo	" aunt mother.	Same as father's sister.
12. " grandmother	" tsŭ-mo	" ancestral mother.	
13. " grandmother's brother..........	" wae-tsŭ-kung	" outer ancestral old gentleman.	
" mother's brother	" kew-kung	" mother's brother; the old gentleman.	
14. " mother's sister.................	" wae-e-po	" mother of the wae-e class.	*E* is a mother's sister; *po* is an "old mother;" *wae-po*, without the *e*, is my mother's mother. *Kung* and *po* are used for father and mother towards persons who stand in that relationship without being the *real* parents.
15. " great great grandfather (mother's side).	" wae-tsung-tsŭ.....	" more remote ancestor.	
16. " great great grandmother	" wae-tsung-tsŭ-mo .	" more remote ancestral mother.	
17. " great grandfather	" wae-tsŭ-kung	" out of the family ancestral old father.	
18. " great grandmother	" wae-tsu-po	" out of the family ancestral old mother.	
19. " grandfather	" wae kung	" out of the family old father.	*Kung* and *po* are likewise used by a woman to designate her husband's parents. They mean, originally, old or venerable people of either sex. *Wae* is outer, external. *Wae-kung* is thus my out of the family old father, *kung* showing that the person spoken of is not the real begetter.
20. " grandmother	" wae-po	" out of the family old mother.	
21. " father	" fŭ-tsin	" father relation.	
" "	" [b]teay-teay; [c]kea-fŭ.	" [a]daddy; [b]housefather.	
22. " mother	" mo-tsin; [b]kea-mo..	" mother relation; [b]housemother.	
23. " son.........................	" Ir-tsze	" child-boy.	
24. " daughter	" neu-ir	" girl child.	
25. " grandson....................	" sun-tsze	" growing for the second time boy.	
26. " granddaughter................	" sun-neu	" growing for the second time girl.	
27. " great grandson	" tsung-sun	" additional growing for the second time boy (grandson).	
28. " great granddaughter............	" tsung-sun-neu	" additional growing for the second time girl (granddaughter).	
29. " great great grandson............	" yuen-sun	" great growing for the third time boy (grandson).	
30. " great great granddaughter	" yuen-sun-neu	" great growing for the third time girl (granddaughter).	
31. " elder brother	" ko-ko; [b]heung....	" elder brother; [b]senior.	*Ko* originally means "to sing;" repeated, *ko-ko*, is simply an untranslatable word for *elder brother.* *Heung* means senior. *Tseay* was originally applied to a "mother." It is now a simple term for "elder sister," and it is likewise the equivalent for our word "miss." *Tsze* = an experienced woman.
32. " elder sister	" tseay-tseay; [b]tsze.	" elder sister;[b] an experienced woman.	
33. " younger brother	" heung-te; [b]a-te....	" senior little junior; [b]little brother.	
34. " younger sister	" mei-mei	" younger sister.	
35. " brothers	" heung-te-mun.....	" seniors-juniors; that is, brothers.	*Mun* is sign of plural.
36. " sisters	" tsze-mei..........	" elder sister, younger sister; i. e., sisters.	
37. " brother's son (*male speaking*)....	" chih-ir	" nephew child, or my child boy of the *chih* class.	
38. " brother's son's wife (*male speak'g*)	" chih-fŭ	" nephew child's wife.	
39. " brother's daughter " ..	" chih-neu	" niece girl, or my child daughter of the *chih* class.	

TABLE OF CONSANGUINITY AND AFFINITY OF THE CHINESE, IN THE MANDARIN DIALECT.—*Continued.*

Description of persons.	Relationships in Chinese.	Translation.	Etymological explanations.
40. My bro.'s daughter's husband (*m. s.*)	Wo-tŏ chih-neu-se.......	My niece girl's superior, or my son-in-law.	
41. " brother's grandson (*male speak'g*)	" chih-sun	" grandson of the *chih* class.	A man's brother's children and their descendants are thus styled his descendants of the *chih* class.
42. " brother's granddaughter " ..	" chih-sum-neu.....	" granddaughter of the *chih* class.	
43. " brother's great grandson " ..	" chih-tsung-neu....	" great grandson of the *chih* class.	
44. " bro.'s gt. granddaughter " ..	" chih-tsung-sun-neu	" great granddaughter of the *chih* class.	
45. " sister's son " ..	" wae-sung........	" outside nephew.	*Sung* originally is a daughter's child; with "*wae*" (outside) prefixed, it expresses sister's son, and forms a *wae-sung* class. "Daughter-in-law." "*Seih-fŭ*" is a son's wife.
47. " sister's son's wife " ..	" wae-sung-seih-fŭ ..	" son's wife of the *wae-sung* class.	
48. " sister's daughter " ..	" wae-sung-neu.....	" daughter of the *wae-sung* class.	
49. " sister's daughter's husb. " ..	" wae-sung-neu-se ..	" son-in-law of the *wae-sung* class.	
50. " sister's grandson " ..	" wae-sung-sun	" grandson of the *wae-sung* class.	
51. " sister's granddaughter " ..	" wae-sung-sun-neu .	" granddaughter of the *wae-sung* class.	
52. " sister's great grandson " ..	" wae-sung-tsung-sun	" great grandson of the *wae-sung* class.	
53. " sist.'s gt. granddaughter " ..	" wae-sung-tsung-sun-neu.	" great granddaughter of the *wae-sung* class.	
54. " brother's son (*female speaking*)..	" wae-chih.........	" outer nephew, or, ĭr being understood, my child of the *wae-chih* class.	
55. " brother's son's wife (*fem. speak'g*)	" wae-chih-seih-fŭ ..	" outer nephew's wife.	
56. " brother's daughter " ..	" wae-chih-neu.....	" niece of the *wae* class, or my daughter of the *wae-chih* class.	
57. " bro.'s daughter's husband " ..	" wae-chih-neu-se...	" son-in-law of the *wae-chih* class.	
58. " brother's grandson " ..	" wae-chih-sun.....	" grandson of the *wae-chih* class.	
59. " brother's granddaughter " ..	" wae-chih-sun-neu .	" granddaughter of the *wae-chih* class.	
60. " brother's great grandson " ..	" wae-chih-tsung-sun	" great grandson of the *wae-chih* class.	
61. " bro.'s gt. granddaughter " ..	" wae-chih-tsung-sun-neu.	" great granddaughter of the *wae-chih* class.	
62. " sister's son " ..	" e-sung	" son of the *e-sung* class.	This *e* is the word already used in "my mother's sister," and the *sung* as in *wae-sung* above. Thus, while a man calls his sister's sons *wae*, a woman styles them *e-sung*.
63. " sister's son's wife " ..	" e-sung-seih-fŭ.....	" daughter-in-law of the *e-sung* class.	
64. " sister's daughter " ..	" e-sung-neu	" daughter of the *e-sung* class, *i. e.*, through her sister.	
65. " sister's daughter's husb. " ..	" e-sung-neu-se.....	" son-in-law of the *e-sung* class.	
66. " sister's grandson " ..	" e-sung-sun	" grandson of the *e-sung* class.	
67. " sister's granddaughter " ..	" e-sung-sun-neu ...	" granddaughter of the *e-sung* class.	
68. " sister's great grandson " ..	" e-sung-tsung-sun..	" great grandson of the *e-sung* class.	
69. " sist.'s gt. granddaughter " ..	" e-sung-tsung-sun neu.	" great granddaughter of the *e-sung* class.	
70. " father's elder brother..........	" poh-fŭ	" senior father.	One's father's brothers are styled father, but distinguished as senior and junior from the real begetter. *Shuh* is a term of respect applied by one to their juniors.
71. " father's younger brother........	" shuh-fŭ	" junior father.	
72. " father's elder brother's wife.....	" poh-mo	" senior mother.	
73. " father's younger brother's wife..	" shin-neang	" father's younger brother's wife.	*Shin* is the wife of one's younger brother. *Shin-neang* is the wife of one's father's younger brother. *Neang* is a word often used for mother, meaning originally a young female.
74. " father's brother's son (males and females use same terms).	" tang-heung-te.....	" hall brother, or brother of the *tang* class.	*Tang* means hall or family; my hall brother, *i. e.*, my brother of the *tang* class, of the same family, descended from the same grandfather, of the same surname.
75. " father's brother's son's wife.....	" tang-saon	" sister-in-law of the *tang* class.	
76. " father's brother's daughter......	" tang-tsze-mei	" hall sister, or sister of the *tang* class.	
77. " father's bro.'s daughter's husb'd	" tang-ᵗˢᶻᵉ₋ₘₑᵢ-fŭ.......	" brother-in-law, *i. e.*, elder younger sister's husband of the *tang* class.	
78. " father's brother's son's son......	" tang-chih........	" nephew of the *tang* class.	
79. " father's brother's son's daughter.	" tang-chih-neu.....	" niece of the *tang* class.	
80. " father's brother's daughter's son.	" tang-wae-sung	" wae-sung child of the *tang* class.	My sister's child is my *wae-sung*; my paternal uncle's daughter's child is my *wae-sung* of the *tang* class. Thus my sister's child is my child of the *wae-sung* class; my *wae-sung* daughter of the *tang* class is my father's brother's daughter's daughter.

TABLE OF CONSANGUINITY AND AFFINITY OF THE CHINESE, IN THE MANDARIN DIALECT.—*Continued.*

Description of persons.	Relationships in Chinese.	Translation.	Etymological explanations.
81. My father's bro.'s daugh.'s daughter	Wo-tĕ tang-wae-sung-neu	My wae-sung daughter of the *tang* class.	
82. " father's brother's gt. grandson..	" tang-chih-sun	" grandson of the *tang-chih* class, or in the *tang-chih* line.	My hall nephew reproduced.
83. " father's bro.'s gt. granddaughter	" tang-chih-sun-neu.	" granddaughter in the *tang-chih* line of relationship.	My hall niece reproduced.
84. " father's bro.'s gt. gt. grandson..	" tang-chih-tsung-sun.	" great grandson of the *tang-chih* class.	
85. " father's bro.'s great great grand-daughter.	" tang-chih-tsung-sun-neu.	" great granddaughter of the *tang-chih* class.	
86. " father's elder sister	" kŭ-mo	" aunt's mother.	A father's sister is called *kŭ, i. e.,* aunt.
87. " father's younger sister.........	" kŭ-tseay	" aunt's elder sister.	
88. " father's sister's husband.......	" kŭ-chang........	" aunt's husband.	
89. " father's sister's son (males and females use same terms).	" peaon-heung-te ...	" brother of the *peaon* class.	My external brother, *i. e.,* not of the same surname.
90. " father's sister's son's wife......	" peaon-saon	" sister-in-law of the *peaon* class.	
91. " father's sister's daughter.......	" peaon-tsze-mei	" sister of the *peaon* class.	
92. " father's sister's daughter's husband.	" peaon-tseay-mei-fŭ	" elder younger sister's husband of the *peaon* class.	
93. " father's sister's son's son	" peaon-chih	" nephew of the *peaon* class.	
94. " father's sister's son's daughter..	" peaon-chih-neu ...	" niece of the *peaon* class.	
95. " father's sister's daughter's son .	" peaon-chih-wae-sung.	" nephew of the *wae-sung* branch of the *peaon* class.	
96. " father's sister's daugh.'s daughter.	" peaon-chih-wae-sung-neu.	" niece of the *wae-sung* branch of the *peaon* class.	
97. " father's sister's great grandson..	" peaon-chih-sun ...	" grandson of the *peaon-chih* class.	
98. " father's sist.'s gt. granddaughter	" peaon-chih-sun-neu.	" granddaughter of the *peaon-chih* class.	
99. " father's sister's gt. gt. grandson .	" peaon-chih-tsung-sun.	" great grandson of the *peaon-chih* class.	
100. " father's sister's great gt. grand-daughter.	" peaon-chih-tsung-sun-neu.	" great granddaughter of the *peaon-chih* class.	
101. " mother's brother..............	" mŏ-kew	" mother uncle.	A mother's brothers are called *kew, i. e.,* uncle. *Mo-kew* = mother-uncle. Sometimes *kew-fŭ* is used = uncle-father. *Kew* is pronounced like the *gu* in the Scotch word "gude" (good).
102. " mother's brother's wife	" kew-mo	" uncle mother.	
103. " mother's brother's son (males and females use same terms).	" peaon-heung-te ...	" brother of the *peaon* class.	Same as my father's sister's son. In this way the descendants of my father's brothers are my brothers; the children of my mother's brothers and my father's sisters are my cousins; the children of my mother's sisters are my second cousins. This distinction between brothers and cousins is but fanciful; all the children of the brothers and sisters of my parents are my brothers and sisters, but distinguished as belonging to the *tay-peaon* or *e-peaon* class, according to the relationship in which their parents stood to mine
104. " mother's brother's son's wife ...	" peaon-saon	" sister-in-law of the *peaon* class.	
105. " mother's brother's daughter....	" peaon-tsze-mei	" sister of the *peaon* class.	
106. " mother's bro.'s daughter's husband.	" peaon-tsze-mei-fŭ	" sister's husband of the *peaon* class.	
107. " mother's brother's son's son....	" peaon-chih	" nephew of the *peaon* class.	
108. " mother's bro.'s son's daughter..	" peaon-chih-neu ...	" niece of the *peaon* class.	
109. " mother's bro.'s daughter's son..	" wae-peaon-chih ...	" nephew of the *wae* branch of the *peaon* class.	
110. " mother's brother's daughter's daughter.	" wae-peaon-chih-neu.	" niece of the *wae* branch of the *peaon* class.	
111. " mother's bro.'s great grandson..	" peaon-chih-sun	" grandson of the *peaon-chih* class.	
112. " mother's brother's great grand-daughter.	" peaon-chih-sun-neu.	" granddaughter of the *peaon-chih* class.	
113. " mother's brother's great great grandson.	" peaon-chih-tsung-sun.	" great grandson of the *peaon-chih* class.	
114. " mother's brother's great great granddaughter.	" peaon-chih-tsung-sun-neu.	" great granddaughter of the *peaon-chih* class.	
115. " mother's elder sister	" ta-e-ma	" great outside mamma.	The sisters of a mother, as also the sisters of one's wife, are designated *e.* As written by the Chinese, the character for *e* is composed of two other characters, meaning "woman" and "foreign." *Tae* and *seaon* are "great" and "small." *Ta-e-ma* is thus "great outside mamma," and *seaon-e-ma* = small outside mamma.
116. " mother's younger sister........	" seaon-e-ma	" small outside mamma.	
117. " mother's sister's husband......	" e-fŭ.............	" mother's sister-father.	The *e* is the same word as in *e-ma* = mother's sister.
118. " mother's sister's son (males and females use same terms).	" e-peaon-heung-te..	" brother of the *e-peaon* class.	
119. " mother's sister's son's wife	" e-peaon-saon......	" sister-in-law of the *e-peaon* class.	
120. " mother's sister's daughter	" e-peaon-tsze-mei ..	" sister of the *e-peaon* class.	

TABLE OF CONSANGUINITY AND AFFINITY OF THE CHINESE, IN THE MANDARIN DIALECT.—*Continued.*

Description of persons.	Relationships in Chinese.	Translation.	Etymological explanations.
121. My mother's sister's daughter's husband.	Wo-te e-peaon-tsze-mei-fŭ....	My sister's husband older younger of the *e-peaon* class.	My son and daughter of the *chih* kind in the *e-peaon* class.
122. " mother's sister's son's son......	" e-peaon-chih......	" nephew of the *e-peaon* class.	
123. " mother's sister's son's daughter.	" e-peaou-chih-neu..	" niece of the *e-peaon* class.	
124. " mother's sister's daughter's son.	" wae-e-peaon-chih..	" nephew of the *wae* branch of the *e-peaon* class (*wae* = outside).	
125. " mother's sister's daughter's daughter.	" wae-e-peaon-chih-neu.	" niece of the *wae* branch of the *e-peaon* class.	
126. " mother's sister's great grandson	" e-peaon-chih-sun..	" grand-son of the *chih* kind of the *e-peaon* class.	
127. " mother's sister's great grand-daughter.	" e-peaon-chih-sun-neu.	" granddaughter of the *chih* kind of the *e-peaon* class.	
128. " mother's sister's great gt. grand-son.	" e-peaon-chih-tsung-sun.	" great grandson of the *chih* kind of the *e-peaon* class.	
129. " mother's sister's great gt. grand-daughter.	" e-peaon-chih-tsung-sun-neu.	" great granddaughter of the *chih* kind of the *e-peaon* class.	
130. " father's father's sister.........	" kŭ-mo..........	" aunt mother.	
131. " father's father's sister's son....	" peaon-poh-shuh......	" —— of the *peaon* class.	The same *poh* and *shuh* as in father's brother, *peaon* denoting that the individual is related to my father's house through a female who has by marriage entered another family.
132. " father's father's sister's daughter.	" peaon-kŭ........	" —— of the *peaon* class.	Father's sisters are called *kŭ*. *Peaon-kŭ* is thus a female relation of mine in the *peaon* class, but of the same kind as is my father's sister.
133. " father's father's sister's son's son	" peaon-heung-te....	" brother of the *peaon* class.	Same relation to me as is my father's sister's or my brother's brother's son.
134. " father's father's sister's son's daughter.	" peaon-tsze-mei	" sister " " "	
135. " father's father's sister's daughter's son.	" peaon-heung-te ...	" brother " " "	
136. " father's father's sister's daughter's daughter.	" peaon-tsze-mei	" sister " " "	
137. " father's father's sister's great grandson.	" peaon-chih	" nephew " " "	
138. " father's father's sister's great granddaughter.	" peaon-chih-neu ...	" niece " " "	
139. " father's father's sister's great gt. grandson.	" peaon-chih-sun ...	" grandson of the *peaon-chih* class.	
140. " mother's mother's sister......	" wae-e-po.........	" mother of the *wae-e* class.	
141. " mother's mother's sister's son ..	" kew-chang.......	" uncle of the *peaon* class.	Same *kew* as in mother's brother.
142. " mother's moth.'s sist.'s daughter	" peaon-e..........	" aunt " " "	Same *e* as in mother's sister.
143. " mother's mother's sister's son's son.	" peaon-heung-te ...	" brother " " "	
144. " mother's mother's sister's son's daughter.	" peaon-tsze-mei	" sister " " "	
145. " mother's mother's sist.'s daughter's son.	" wae-e-peaon-heung-te.	" brother of the *wae-e* branch of the *peaon* class.	
146. " mother's mother's sist.'s daughter's daughter.	" wae-e-peaon-tsze-mei.	" sister of the *wae-e* branch of the *peaon* class.	
147. " mother's mother's sister's great grandson.	" peaon-chih	" nephew of the *peaon* class.	
148. " mother's mother's sister's great granddaughter.	" peaon-chih-neu ...	" niece " " "	
149. " mother's mother's sister's great great grandson.	" peaon-chih-sun ...	" grandson of the *peaon-chih* class.	
150. " husband....................	" laon-kung; ᵇchang-fŭ.	" old man.	
151. " wife........................	" laon-po-ᵇtsee-tsze..	" old woman or wife.	*Tsëĕ* is one's equal.
152. " husband's father.............	" kung-kung	" old, old man.	My husband's father.
153. " husband's mother............	" po-po	" old, old woman.	My husband's mother.
154. " husband's grandfather..... ...	" tae-kea-yung	" great family venerable.	*I.e.* the venerable old gentleman of our family.
155. " wife's father.............	" qŭe-fŭ...........	" wife's father.	*Que* is used to designate the parents of one's
156. " wife's mother...........	" qŭe-mo..........	" wife's mother.	*Fŭ*, father ; *mo*, mother. [wife.
157. " wife's grandfather............	" wae-tsu-kung.....	" out of the family ancestral old father.	*Wae-tsŭ-kung* is also used for father's grand-mother's brother, and mother's great grand-father.
158. " son-in-law..................	" nen-se	" daughter's superior.	
159. " daughter-in-law..............	" seih-fŭ	" son's wife, lady.	
160. " step-father	" how-fŭ	" subsequent father.	
161. " step-mother	" how-mo	" subsequent mother.	
162. " step-son....................	" peën-e-tsze	" easily gotten child.	Though this is the expression in existence, people do not like to make use of it.
162.* " step-daughter..	" peën-e-neu.	" easily gotten daughter.	This form of relationship is of very rare oc-currence. Brothers and sisters by the same
163. " step-brother...	" e-fŭ-heung-te	" of a different father brother.	father, but of different mothers, are simply
164. " step-sister..................	" e-fŭ-tsze-mei......	" of a different father sister.	brothers and sisters—*heung-te* and *taze-mei.*
165. Two fathers-in-law to each other....	Tsin-kea	Related family.	
166. " mothers-in-law to each other...	Tsin-kea-neang-mo	Related family's lady mother.	

TABLE OF CONSANGUINITY AND AFFINITY OF THE CHINESE, IN THE MANDARIN DIALECT.—*Continued.*

Description of persons.	Relationships in Chinese.	Translation.	Etymological explanations.
167. My brother-in-law (husband's bro.)	Wo-tĕ ta-poh-yay........ " seaon-shuh-tsze ...	My husband's elder brother. " " junior "	The words *poh* and *shuh* are applied to the brothers of a father, as also to those of a husband. These names for brother-in-law seem taken from the relationship in which they will stand to the children of the lady speaking.
168. " brother-in-law (sister's husb'd)	" taze/mei-fŭ	" elder/younger sister's husband.	
169. " brother-in-law (wife's sister's husband).	" kin-heung/te	The husband of a wife's sister. " " " " younger sister.	*Kin* is that part of a garment which, folding over, is joined and fastened by clasps or buttons.
170. " brother-in-law (wife's brother) .	" ta/seaon-kew........	My elder or younger brother.	This same *kew* is used for "mother's brother." Thus, while a wife designates her husband's brothers by the same terms she applies to her *paternal* uncles, a husband applies to his wife's brothers the word (*kew*) he would use in speaking of his *maternal* uncle. Again, my wife's brother will be to my child in a *kew* relationship.
171. " brother-in-law (husband's sister's husband).	" kŭ-chang-kung ...	" husband's sister's husband.	*Ku* is applied to the mother and sisters of one's husband, and also to the sisters of one's father—*chang-kung*, husband.
172. " sister-in-law (wife's sister).....	" ta-ĕ .... " seaon-ĕ..........	" elder sister of wife. " younger sister of wife.	The sisters of one's mother and wife go by the same name "*ĕ*"; *ta* and *seaon* = large and small = elder and younger.
173. " sister-in-law (husband's sister)	" ta-kŭ (o) seaon-kŭ-tsey. (y)	" great and little sister-in-law.	
174. " sister-in-law (bro.'s wife, *male speaking*).	" saon-tsze .... " shin-tsze	" elder brother's wife. " younger brother's wife.	*Saon* is an elder brother's wife; *shuh* a younger brother's wife. The wife of a *shuh-fŭ*, father's younger brother, is also styled *shin*.
175. " sister-in-law (bro.'s wife, *female speaking*).	" tsin-tsze..........	" brother's wife.	
176. " sister-in-law (husband's bro.'s wife).	" ta-mo .... " a-shin	" husband's older brother's wife. " " younger " "	My great mother, *i. e.*, wife of one's husband's elder brother. *A-shin* as above in *shin-tsze*.
177. " sister-in-law (wife's brother's wife).	" tsin-tsze..........	" wife's brother's wife.	From this it would appear that the names by which people address their brothers and sisters-in-law are derived from the names which would be applied to such individuals by the children born, their nephews and nieces.
178. Twins	Shwang-sung	Double, or rather a pair birth.	
179. Widow	Kwa-fŭ	Lone woman.	
180. Widower	Kwa-nan	Lone man.	
1. The daughter of the daughter of one sister to the daughter of the daughter of the other sister.	E-peaon-tsze-mei	Sisters of the *e-peaon* class.	
2. The son of the son of one sister to the son of the son of the other sister.	E-peaon-heung-te........	Brothers " " "	
3. The son of the son of one sister to the daughter of the daugh'r of the other sister.	E-peaon-heung-mei......	Brother and sister of the *e-peaon* class.	
4. The daughter of the son of one sister to the son of the daughter of the other sister.	E-peaon-heung mei	Brother and sister of the *e-peaon* class.	
5. The daughter of the daughter of the daughter of one sister to the daughter of the daughter of the daughter of the other sister.	E-peaon-tsze-mei	Sisters of the *e-peaon* class.	
1. The son of the son of one brother to the son of the son of the other brother.	Tsung-tang-heung-te.....	Brothers of the *tang* class.	The point from which anything begins is called *tsung*. Thus, while these two people are brothers of the *tang* class, the *tsung* prefixed shows that they are some generations removed from their common progenitor—their great grandfather.
2. The daughter of the daughter of one brother to the daughter of the daughter of the other brother.	Peaon-tsze-mei	Sisters " " "	
3. The son of the son of one brother to the daughter of the daughter of the other brother.	Peaon-heung-mei	Brother and sister of the *tang* class.	
4. The son of the son of the son of one brother to the son of the son of the son of the other brother.	Woo-she-tang-heung-te ..	Brothers of the *tang* class, fifth generation.	

TABLE OF CONSANGUINITY AND AFFINITY OF THE CHINESE, IN THE MANDARIN DIALECT.—*Continued.*

Description of persons.	Relationships in Chinese.	Translation.	Etymological explanations.
1. The son of the son of a brother to the son of the son of the brother's sister.	Peaon-heung-te	Brothers of the *peaon* class.	
2. The daughter of the daughter of a brother to the daughter of the daughter of the brother's sister.	Peaon-tsze-mei	Sisters " " "	
3. The son of the son of a brother to the daughter of the daughter of the brother's sister.	Peaon-heung-mei	Brother and sister of the *peaon* class.	
4. The son of the son of the son of a brother to the son of the son of the son of the brother's sister.	Peaon-heung-te	Brothers of the *peaon* class.	
1. The daughter of the daughter of one sister to the daughter of the daughter of the daugh'r of the other sister.	The second is the *e-sung-new* of the first.	A woman's sister's daughter is her *e-sung-neu.*	
2. The son of the son of one brother to the daughter of the son of the son of the other brother.	The second is the *chih-ĭr* of the first.	The nephew, or son of the *chih* class.	
3. The daughter of the daughter of one brother to the son of the son of the son of the brother's sister.	The first is the *peaon-kŭ-mo* of the second.	A father's sisters are called *kŭ-mo.*	In the present relationship, the first is a *kŭ-mo* of the *peaon* class to the second.

CHAPTER IV.

SYSTEM OF RELATIONSHIP OF UNCLASSIFIED ASIATIC NATIONS.

Burmese and Karens—Their System of Relationship classificatory—Whether an Independent or a Subordinate Form of the Turanian uncertain. 1. Burmese—Not Ancient within their present Area—Their System of Relationship —It possesses a number of Turanian Characteristics—Lineal Line—First Collateral Line—Second and other Collateral Lines—Marriage Relationships—Recapitulation of its Radical Characteristics. 2. Karens—The People without Nationality—Dialects of the Karen Language—Mr. Judson's Description of the Karens—Their System closely allied to the Burmese—Three Schedules in the Table—Lineal and Collateral Lines—Marriage Relationships—Burmese and Karen complete the Series of Asiatic Schedules—Concluding Observations.

THERE are two other Asiatic nations represented in the Table, (Table III.) which remain to be noticed, the Burmese and the Karen. They are left, for the present, as unclassified, for the reason that their system of relationship, although it belongs to the classificatory division, does not affiliate decisively with any form hitherto, or hereafter, to be presented. It approaches very closely to that of the people of North India, but differs from it in some particulars which are material. There were reasons for placing the Gaura form in the Turanian connection which do not exist in the present case. The nomenclature of relationships in the Hindî, Bengâlî, and other dialects of the Gaura language, as we have seen, has been so greatly changed under Sanskritic influence that it was a more reasonable supposition that the system itself had been modified from a higher to a lower Turanian form, than that it had remained unchanged under the pressure of the modifying causes which had supplanted its aboriginal terms of relationship. From these considerations the Gaura form was placed in the Turanian connection. There is no evidence, and but little probability, that the system of consanguinity of the Burmese or of the Karens has been influenced from without, and it has, without doubt, continued in its present condition for a long period of time. It has also been stated that all the systems of relationship of the human family fall under two general divisions, the descriptive and the classificatory. Of the first there is no subordinate form, that of the Aryan, the Semitic, and the Uralian families being identical; but of the second there are three which may be regarded as distinct, the Turanian, the Malayan, and the Eskimo; and there may be a fourth form, of which the Burmese and the Karen are representatives, which may yet be found to be widely distributed amongst Asiatic nations not represented in the Tables. Until after the forms which prevail among these nations have been investigated, it is preferable to leave unclassified the systems about to be presented.

1. Burmese. The Burmese are not regarded by ethnologists as a very ancient people within their present area. They first came into prominence as a nation about the middle of the last century. The ethnic relations of the native popula-

tions that inhabit the extensive regions between Chinese Tartary, China, and Siam on the north and east, and Hindustan on the south and west, are still very imperfectly understood. In connection with them may be placed the inhabitants of Bhotan and Asam. They are broken up into tribes, more or less intermixed, and can only be treated in groups, which are formed upon slender affiliations. The principal of these are the Bhot, Asamese, and the Burmese. In the latter are placed the Karens. Among all of these native populations the Burmese have attained to the highest national rank; and, as a people, they have been made quite familiar to us on this side of the Atlantic, by the life and labors of the illustrious Judson.

The Burmese system of relationship is regular in its form and clearly defined. It has a number of Turanian characteristics, but is wanting in some of its arbitrary and artificial principles of classification. Some of its generalizations are the same as those found in the system of the Aryan family. The points of agreement and disagreement with the forms before presented will be seen as its details are given.

In the lineal line, male, the series is as follows: *a-bă*, father; *bo*, grandfather; *ba*, great-grandfather; *bee*, great-great-grandfather; and descending, *thä*, son; *my-a*, grandchild; *my-eet*, great-grandchild; and *tee*, great-great-grandchild.

There is a double set of terms for elder and younger brother, and for elder and younger sister, one of which is used by males, and the other by females.

	Elder Brother.	Elder Sister.	Younger Brother.	Younger Sister.
Said by a male.	E-ko',	E-mă',	Ny-ee'.	Hnee-mă'.
Said by a female.	Mo-ung' Ky-ee',	E-mă',	Mo-ung Ga-ta',	Ny-ee-mă'.

The term for elder and younger brother, which is used by females, is the same, a separate word being added expressive of elder and younger; and the term used for younger sister is the same as that used by a male for younger brother, with the addition of a particle expressive of the female gender. In the formation of the plural of brother, the terms for elder and younger brother are united, *ny-ee-e'-ko-to'*, literally, younger-elder brother = brothers, *to* being the sign of the plural; in like manner, for sisters we have *e-mă' hne-mă'-to*, literally, elder-younger sister. The plural is formed in the Chinese in precisely the same way, *e. g.*, *heung*, elder brother, literally, senior; *a-te*, little brother or junior, which give *heung-te-mun*, senior-junior = brothers; *mun* being the sign of the plural; and for sisters, *tsze-mei* = elder-younger sister = sisters.

In the first collateral line male, irrespective of the sex of *Ego*, my brother's son is my nephew, *too*. Inasmuch as the correlative here used is that of father, it may be doubtful whether the latter word is in strictness equivalent to nephew. My brother's daughter I call *too-mă'*, my niece. Each of the children of this nephew and niece I call my grandchild, *my-a*. My sister's son and daughter, *Ego* being still a male, are my nephew and niece, using the same terms, and their children are my grandchildren.

The principal Turanian characteristics are wanting with the exceptions that my father's brother is my father, and my father's sister is my aunt, and with the further exception that this line is merged in the lineal line.

In the second collateral line male, on the father's side, irrespective of the sex of *Ego*, my father's brother is my father, great or little, his son and daughter are my elder or younger brother, or my elder or younger sister, as they are respectively older or younger than myself. The sons and daughters of this collateral brother and sister are my nephews and nieces, the terms used being *too* and *too-mă'*, and the children of the latter are my grandchildren.

In the female branch of the same line, my father's sister, is my great or little aunt, as she is older or younger than my father. Here we find a distinct Turanian characteristic, namely the relationship of aunt, restricted to the sisters of a father to the exclusion of those of a mother. My father's sister's son and daughter are my elder or younger brother, and my elder or younger sister in all respects as in the former case; their children are my nephews and nieces, and the children of the latter are my grandchildren.

On the mother's side, my mother's brother is my uncle, *oo-men*. He is also my great or little father, as he is older or younger than my mother; and this appears to be the prevailing relationship over that of uncle. The presence of an original term for uncle, restricted to the mother's brothers, is a significant fact, especially when considered in connection with the other term *tau*, aunt, restricted to a father's sister. It may be found, on further investigation, that the latter terms are used exclusively when the Burmese system is strictly interpreted. Should this prove to be the fact, it would give to the system two other important Turanian characteristics. My mother's brother's son and daughter are my brother and sister, elder or younger, according to our relative ages; the children of this collateral brother and sister are my nephews and nieces, and the children of the latter are my grandchildren.

My mother's sister is my mother, great or little, as in other cases; her son and daughter are my brother and sister, elder or younger; the children of this collateral brother and sister are my nephews and nieces, and the children of the latter are my grandchildren.

The third, and more remote, collateral lines are counterparts of the first and second in all respects, with the exception of additional ancestors. In respect to the latter, we find that the brothers and sisters of the grandfather and of the grandmother are all alike grandfathers and grandmothers, which is a characteristic of the Turanian system.

The coincidences between the Burmese form, and the Tamilian will be at once observed. Its close agreement with the Gaura form will also be noticed, as well as the points in which it differs from both. Its principal characteristics may be recapitulated as follows: first, it has a double set of terms for elder and younger brother, and for elder and younger sister, one of which is used by males, and the other by females. Secondly, it has but one term for nephew and one for niece, which are not only applied to the children of an own brother, as well as to the children of an own sister, but also to the children of a collateral brother and sister. Thirdly, that while these terms have strict correlatives in *oo-men*, uncle, and *tau*, aunt, and do not find a proper correlative in great or little father and mother, they are used indiscriminately as correlatives of both, which is, at least, a defect in the principles of the system.   Fourthly, the relationship of cousin is unknown.   Fifthly, the children of brothers, of sisters, and of brothers and sisters, are all alike brothers and sisters to each other.   Sixthly, the several collateral lines are ultimately merged in the lineal, by means of which remote consanguinei are brought within the fold of the near relationships.   And lastly it is a classificatory system.[1]

2. Karens.   The Karen language, which is now spoken in nine dialects, is an uncultivated speech, except that it has been reduced to a written form by the American missionaries.   The people are subdivided into a number of tribes, and the area of their occupation extends beyond the boundaries of the Tenasserim province into Burmah, into Siam, and even into the southern part of China; but this occupation is not continuous.   They are a rude, but gentle and teachable people, and are without nationality.[2]

---

[1] The Burmese have a strong resemblance to the American Indians.   It is seen in the color of the skin the character and color of the hair, and in the eyes.   In their features and in the shape of the head the resemblance fails.   I met a Burmese accidentally in a railway car, and upon asking him to what Indian nation he belonged, was surprised to be informed, in good English, that he was a Burmese.   He is now a student in Madison University.

[2] The following general description of the Karens from the pen of the second Mrs. Judson, as they appeared about the year 1830, when the now venerable Dr. Francis Mason and Dr. Jonathan Wade founded the American missions amongst them, furnishes an interesting picture of this singular people. "The Karens," she says, "are a meek, peaceful race, simple and credulous, with many of the softer virtues, and few flagrant vices.   Though greatly addicted to drunkenness, extremely filthy and indolent in their habits, their morals, in other respects, are superior to many civilized races.   Their traditions, like those of several tribes of American Indians, are a curious medley of truth and absurdity; but they have some tolerably definite ideas of the Great Being who governs the universe; and many of their traditionary precepts bear a striking resemblance to those of the gospel.   They have various petty superstitions; but, with the exception of a small division, known to the Burmans as the Talingkarens, and to the missionaries as the Pwos or Shos, they have never adopted Boodhism; the oppressive treatment which they have received at the hands of their Burmese rulers probably contributing to increase their aversion to idolatry.

"Soon after the arrival of the first Burmese missionary [Dr. Judson] in Rangoon, his attention was attracted by small parties of strange wild-looking men, clad in unshapely garments, who from time to time straggled past his residence.   He was told that they were called Karens; that they were more numerous than any other similar tribe in the vicinity, and as untamable as the wild cow of the mountains.   He was further told that they shrunk from association with other men, seldom entering a town, except on compulsion; and that, therefore, any attempt to bring them within the sphere of his influence would prove unsuccessful.   His earnest inquiries, however, awakened an interest in the minds of the Burmese converts; and one of them, finding, during the war, a poor Karen bond-servant in Rangoon, paid his debt, and thus became, according to the custom of the country, his temporary master.   When peace was restored, he was brought to the missionaries on the Tenasserim coast, and instructed in the principles of the Christian religion.   He eventually became the subject of regenerating grace, and proved a faithful and efficient evangelist.   Through this man, who will be recognized as Ko-thah-byu, access was gained to others of his countrymen, and they listened with ready interest.   They were naturally docile: they had no long-cherished prejudices and time-honored customs to fetter them; and their traditions taught them to look for the arrival of white-faced foreigners from the west, who would make them acquainted with the true God.   The missionaries, in their first communications with the Karens, were obliged to employ a Burmese interpreter; and notwithstanding the disadvantages under which they labored, the truth spread with great rapidity.   Soon, however, Messrs. Wade and Mason devoted themselves to the acquisition of the language, and the former conferred an inestimable boon on the race by reducing it to writing.   This gave a fresh

The Rev. H. L. Van Meter in a letter to the author which accompanied one of the Karen schedules of relationships, dated at Bassein in 1861, remarks: "The Karens are not an independent united people, and, if they ever were, the fact is not certainly known to those now living. Those in Pegu, and near the sea coast, have long been in subjection to the Burmese, while the tribes inhabiting the mountains of Toungoo and beyond, though not acknowledging any other government, if we except their subjection to the English, within a few years past have been in a constant state of warfare with each other, and with adjacent powers. Their tribal divisions are numerous. The two principal divisions in Southern Burmah are the Sgaus and the Pwos, indicated in Karen as *Pah-tee* and *Mo-tee*, the former signifying, *of descent from the father's side*, and the latter, *of descent from the mother's side;* but how, or when these divisions originated cannot be discovered. The former are all known as Burmese Karens, and the latter as Talaing Karens, from the nations with which they have associated. There are also White Karens, Red Karens, and Black Karens. Dr. Mason says, ' All the Karen tribes between the mouth of the Tenasserim and the sources of the Sittang resolve themselves into three classes, the Sgau tribes, the Pwo tribes, and the Bhgai tribes.' In reference to the schedule, the answers elicited have been prompt and unhesitating with very few exceptions, showing that the system of consanguinity, as here presented, is well established among them, and one with which all are more or less familiar."

From the highly primitive character thus ascribed to the Karens their system of relationship is very important. It has remained uninfluenced by the development of civilization from within, and doubtless unchanged from external causes, as a consequence of their free and roving habits. Their system is classificatory; and it is not a little singular, that whilst it does not possess the extraordinary characteristics which distinguish the Tamilian, it affiliates, in its fundamental features, very closely with the Burmese, and also with the Gaura form, although variant from both in some particulars. The nomenclature is rude and rather scant. Many of the terms are in common gender, which is an unfailing indication of the undeveloped condition of a language. It is, however, in the systems of the rude and uncultivated

impulse to the spread of Christianity. The wild men and women in their mountain homes found a new employment; and they entered upon it with enthusiastic avidity. They had never before supposed their language capable of being represented by signs, like other languages; and they felt themselves, from being a tribe of crushed, down-trodden slaves, suddenly elevated into a nation, with every facility for possessing a national literature. This had a tendency to check their roving propensities; and under the protection of the British government, they began to cultivate a few simple arts, though the most civilized among them still refused to congregate in towns, and it is unusual to find a village that numbers more than five or six houses. Their first reading books consisted of detached portions of the gospel; and the Holy Spirit gave to the truth thus communicated, regenerating power. Churches sprang up, dotting the wilderness like so many lighted tapers; and far back among the rocky fastnesses of the mountains, where foreign foot has never trod, the light is already kindled, and will continue to increase in brilliancy, till one of the darkest corners of the earth shall be completely illuminated."*

* Wayland's Life of Judson, I. 542.

nations and tribes that we must look for the most ancient and unaltered forms of consanguinity. However undeveloped any language may be it will be found that the system of relationship in daily use among the people is clearly defined and perfectly familiar to all. As a domestic institution it is invested with a peculiar stability and persistency. Its deviations from other forms with which it is nearly allied embody a record of ancient affilations, which a comparison of forms will still reveal; and these deviations thus become a source of evidence of the ethnic connection of widely separated stocks.

There are three schedules in the Table, each giving the system of relationship of the Karens. The first was prepared by the Rev. Dr. Francis Mason, of Toungoo; the second by Rev. Dr. Jonathan Wade, of Maulmain; and the third by Rev. H. L. Van Meter, of Bassein. For upwards of thirty years the first two have been engaged in the Karen missionary field. The first schedule is in the Sgau dialect, as Dr. Mason states in his letter; the second is conjectured to be in the Pwo dialect, although the fact is not stated by Dr. Wade; in what dialect the third is written does not appear.

The Karen language is very difficult to represent by any system of notation which can be prepared, from the unusual number of vowel sounds, and the inability of English letters fully to indicate the native consonants. Dr. Wade says upon this subject: " The Karen language has nine vowel sounds, and each of these five inflections, making, in all, fifty-four vowel sounds. Every change in these fifty-four sounds involves a change in the signification. It is plain, therefore, that with all the diacritical marks with which we are able to invest our English vowels, the exact sound, and, of necessity, difference of signification between some words and others will not be comprehendible. There is, also, as great an impossibility of indicating the native consonants by English letters; and it is equally important that they should be indicated, in order to avoid wrong deductions from apparent identity of syllables, where really no identity exists. I have, therefore, great aversion to writing native words in Roman characters, where scientific questions are involved. Erroneous conclusions will very often be the consequence."[1] Dr. Wade furnished

---

[1] Dr. Mason, in the letter which accompanied his schedule, and which was dated at Toungoo, June 6, 1860, after premising that " it seems necessary to append a few remarks that could not be introduced into the schedule," proceeds as follows :—

" I. *Karen Dialects.*

"There are three or four written Karen dialects, and several more unwritten. It matters nothing, for the purposes of the schedule, which is adopted in filling it up. The Sgau has been used because it is the most cultivated. The difference of dialect may be illustrated by the word for *man* which occurs in the schedule.

Dialects.	Man.	Dialects.	Man.
Sgau,	Phä-kă-my-an.	Pwo,	Hen-phlung.
Red Karen,	Pray-kă-yä.	"	Ghen.
Paku,	Gha-yan.	Ka,	Han.
"	Pie-yan.	Shopgha,	Plan.
Bhgai,	Pie-yä.	Tarn,	Pln.
		Sham-phie,	Pă-lu.

a special notation for the Karen schedule filled by him, with appropriate characters to indicate the high, low, and middle sounds of the vowels, but it was deemed advisable to reduce it to the notation adopted in the schedule, for the sake of uniformity.

It is now proposed to take up the Karen system of relationship, and pass through the several lines for the purpose of comparing it with other forms.

The lineal line in the descending series is distinguished, as to its members, in much the same manner as the Burmese. The whole series, beginning with grandfather, and ending with great-great-grandchild, is as follows: *phŭ, pä, phō, le, lō,* and *lä.*

" 2. *Additional Letters.*

ō, as o in note.

n, as pronounced on the continent.

eu,   "   "   "

ei, as pronounced in German.

au and *ay,* as pronounced in English.

kh, like the German ch, or the Scotch in loch.

gh, like the Northumberland *r.*

" 3. *Terms of Consanguinity.*

" The only independent terms which distinguish difference of sex are

Father,	Pä.	Mother,	Mŏ.	Son-in-law,	Mă.
Grandfather,	Phŭ.	Grandmother,	Ph*ie.*	Daughter-in-law,	Day.
Uncle,	Phä-*tie.*	Aunt,	Mu-ghä.		

The other primitive terms are

Phŏ, a child, male or female.

L*ie,* a grandchild, male or female.

Lŏ, a great-grandchild, male or female.

Lä, a great-great-grandchild, male or female.

Way, an elder brother or sister.

Pu, a younger brother or sister.

Mue-pghä, a father or mother-in-law.

Tă-khwa, or Dan-tă-khwa, cousin.

" Cousins are distinguished, as first, second, third, as in English.

"Words of common gender are made masculine or feminine by affixes. Pŏ-khwa, or khwa, masculine ; po-mu, or mu, feminine. *Dan* denotes relationship, and is prefixed to some of the compound terms. For instance, as in the Indian languages, there are independent words for elder brother and younger brother, but none for brother or sister; so the words for elder and younger are inverted, *dăn* prefixed, and the compound is used for brother or sister. Thus, *way,* elder brother or sister, becomes *dan-pu-way,* a brother or sister younger or older.

" 4. *Karen Tribes.*

" The Karens are broken up into many tribes, but nothing like the tribal organization of the American Indians is known among them. The names of some of the principal tribes are

Sgau.	Mop-gha.	Sho.	Ka, or Kay.
Pa-ku.	Klm-hxa.	Bghai.	Hash-wie.

" It is remarkable that no satisfactory signification of any one of these names can be given.

" 5. *Marriage Customs.*

" In the matter of marriages the rule among the Karens is diametrically opposite to that among the American Indians. Marriages must always, among the Karens, be contracted by relations. First cousins marry, but that is deemed undesirably near. Second cousins are considered the most suitable matches, but third cousins may marry without impropriety, though that is considered undesirably remote. Beyond third cousins marriages are forbidden.

"These rules are not carried out very strictly, but sufficiently so to produce a weakly people, owing to the intermarriages of near relations."

A peculiar feature is found in the fraternal and sororal relationships, the terms for which are still significant. They are conceived in the duplex form of elder and younger, but the terms are in common gender, and require the addition of *khwa* and *mu* to express the sex of the person. The term for elder brother and elder sister is *wai*, which signifies " predecessor in birth ;" and for younger brother and sister, *pu*, which signifies " successor in birth." With the connecting particle *po*, we have for elder brother, *wai-po-khwa*, for elder sister, *wai-po-mu*, and for younger brother, *pu-po-khwa*, and for younger sister, *pu-po-mu*. The method here used for expressing these relationships is evidently founded upon natural suggestion. A form somewhat analogous obtains in the Hawaiian system.

In the first collateral line, irrespective of the sex of *Ego*, I call my brother's son *phō-do-khwa*, and my brother's daughter *pho-do-mu*, which are rendered nephew and niece by Dr. Mason. The children of this nephew and niece are my grandchildren. In the female branch, my sister's son and daughter are my nephew and niece, the same terms being used as before; and their children are my grandchildren. It will be observed that the relationships of uncle and aunt are applied to the father's and mother's brothers, and to the father's and mother's sisters, as the correlatives of nephew and niece; but the term for uncle, *phä-te*, the literal signification of which is not given, is evidently based upon the radical term *pä*, father, and in like manner, the term for aunt, *mu-ghä*, upon that for mother, which is *mo*. At the same time the terms which are rendered nephew and niece are the same as those for son and daughter (*phō-khwa* and *phō-mu*), with the exception of the particle *do*. The point of the observation is this, that the relationships of uncle and aunt, nephew and niece, in Karen, are but slight variations of the relationships of father and mother, son and daughter, which may have been the previously recognized connections, and which by this variation of the terms they sought to change. If such were in fact the original form, it was identical with the present Malayan form. The etymologies of the terms of consanguinity possess great value for the proper interpretation of systems of relationship, and particularly of their modifications; but unfortunately these are seldom preserved, and when they are, the terms themselves are usually found to be recent.

In the second collateral line male, on the father's side, irrespective of the sex of *Ego*, my father's brother is my uncle, the son and daughter of this uncle are my male and female cousins, *tă-khwa* if a male, and *tă-khwa-mu*, if a female. The presence of this relationship is another remarkable feature of the Karen system. Among the Turanian nations it is only found among the people speaking the Drâvidian language, and it has also been found among a portion of the Ganowánian family. Mr. Van Meter remarks upon this relationship as follows: " The descendants of brothers and sisters are generally designated by the term given in the schedule, viz., *t'-khwä*, cousin; but the terms brother and sister are occasionally used in speaking of or to each other, the term for elder or younger brother or sister being used according to the relative ages of the persons." This is a very significant suggestion, tending to show a concurrent, and perhaps, originally, an exclusive use of the latter terms. To resume, the sons and daughters of these cousins are my nephews and nieces, and the children of these nephews and nieces are my grandchildren.

The three remaining branches of this line are the same in all respects as the one just described, with a change of the first person in the line. My father's sister is my aunt, my mother's brother is my uncle, and my mother's sister is my aunt; and the relationships of the children of each, and their respective descendants, is such as to make each branch of the line a counterpart of the other, with the single exception of changing uncle to aunt, or the reverse.

The marriage relationships in the first and second collateral line are also peculiar in the Karen. By courtesy the wife of a nephew becomes a niece, the husband of a niece becomes a nephew, and the husband and wife of a female and male cousin in like manner are regarded as cousins. These deviations from uniformity, even in slight particulars, will be found to subserve an important purpose when the systems of many nations are brought together for comparison. These forms are not taken up and laid aside inconsiderately, but tend, when adopted, to become permanent, and to perpetuate themselves in all of the off-shoots of a particular branch of a family which become detached from the parent connection after these deviations were made; and thus they will often reappear in the separate subdivisions of such a branch after long intervals of time.

The third and more remote collateral lines, so far as they are extended in the Table, are counterparts, in their several branches, of the corresponding branches of the second collateral line; and it will not, for this reason, be necessary to consider them in detail. My father's father's brother is my grandfather; his son is my uncle, the son of this uncle is my male cousin, and the remainder of the line is the same as the second. My father's father's sister is my grandmother; her daughter is my aunt, the daughter of this aunt is my female cousin; and the remainder of this line is the same as the corresponding part of the second. The male and female branches, on the mother's side, are counterparts of those on the father's side.

The close approximation of that part of the system of a portion of the Aryan family, which is classificatory, to the corresponding part of the Karen will at once be noticed; but when we pass beyond such portion, the remainder of the Karen system continues classificatory, while that of the Aryan nations referred to is descriptive.

We have now considered in this, and in previous chapters, the series of Asiatic schedules, contained in the Table, which fall under the classificatory form. They are much too limited in number to represent fairly the great body of the Asiatic nations, considered with reference to the number of nationalities; but they are abundantly sufficient to establish the existence of one most remarkable form, the Turanian, as exemplified by the system of the people of South India, who speak the Drâvidian language. This form, of which the Tamilian is selected as the type, rises to the rank of a domestic institution in the highest sense of that term, by reason of its elaborate and complicated character, and of its uses for the organization of the family upon the broadest scale of numbers. This remarkable system of consanguinity and affinity embodies important testimony concerning the ethnic affinities of nations among whom its fundamental conceptions can be definitely traced.

Whether this peculiar form, under different degrees of modification, prevails among the remaining Asiatic nations, or whether one or more forms radically distinct from the Turanian will yet be discovered, remains to be determined. Whichever may be the case, it will be found, in the sequel, that any form, endowed with radical and distinctive characteristics, is able, within certain limits, to survive radical mutations of language, and, having crossed intact the boundary line which separates one stock language from another, will remain unimpaired after the vocables of the disunited languages (not to say their grammatical structure) have become so entirely changed as to be unrecognizable. The schedules referred to exhibit, at most, but two forms, both of which are classificatory. Of these, the Turanian, as exemplified by the Tamil, Telugu and Canarese, is the highest and the most artificial, and the other, whether independent or a subordinate form of the Turanian as exemplified by the Burmese and the Karen, is the lowest and least artificial. It will be necessary to bring together the systems of consanguinity and affinity of the remaining Asiatic nations, and to compare their radical forms with each other, and with those herein presented, before the true position of the latter nations can be definitely ascertained.

The principal object of the author has been attained in the discovery among the people of South India, who speak the Drâvidian language, of a system of relationship which is at once original, clearly defined, and elaborate. The fact of the actual present existence of such a system in practical operation upon the Asiatic continent was the main fact to be established in the third part of this work. The extent of the ramifications of the system in Asia is of much less importance than the knowledge of its present existence among some portion of the continental Asiatic populations. Should the uses of such a system of consanguinity and affinity be found important, as well as successful, in advancing our knowledge of the families of mankind, it will be comparatively easy, hereafter, to bring together the forms which prevail in Central and Northern Asia, for the purpose of gathering up the testimony which they may be able to deliver concerning the affiliations of these nations with each other, and with those herein named, as well as with reference to the order of their separation from each other. The principal object of developing with so much particularity the Turanian system of consanguinity and affinity has been to prepare the way for a comparison of its radical forms with those which now exist in the system of the Ganowánian family.

CHAPTER V.

SYSTEM OF RELATIONSHIP OF THE MALAYAN FAMILY.

Continental and Island Life—Difference in their Advantages for National Development—Malayan Family—Its Principal Branches—Malayan System of Relationship—I. Polynesian.—1. Hawaiian—Analysis of the System—Consanguinei Reduced to Great Classes—These Restricted to the Primary Relationship—The Malayan Realizes the "Nine Grades" of the Chinese—System Classificatory—Lineal Line—Collateral Lines—Marriage Relationships—Simplicity and Regularity of the System—Older than the Turanian—Latter probably Engrafted upon it—The Hawaiian Custom or Pinaluanic Bond—It Tends to Explain the Origin of the Malayan System of Relationship. 2. Maori of New Zealand—Details of the System—Identical with the Hawaiian.—II. Micronesian Form. 1. Kusaien—Lineal Line—Collateral Lines—Marriage Relationships. 2. Kingsmill Island—Lineal Line—Collateral Lines—Marriage Relations—Micronesian Form identical with the Hawaiian—Failure to procure System of Negroid Nations—III. Amazulu or Kafir—Zulu-Kafir Language—Their System of Relationship—Lineal Line—Collateral Lines—Marriage Relationships—Agrees substantially with the Hawaiian—The Amazulu concludes the Series of Schedules.

FROM continental to island life the change for the worse is very great with respect to opportunities and incitements to progress. Primitive peoples, having the range of a continent, must of necessity have commenced their career as fishermen, in dependence upon this great primary source of human subsistence, and with but incidental support from the proceeds of the hunt. In the course of time they would learn to domesticate young animals captured in the chase, out of which would come a discovery of the uses of flocks and herds, as a more abundant and more invigorating means of subsistence. This again, in the lapse of time and through migrations, would be followed by the discovery of cereals, and of the art of cultivation, which would lead inevitably to village life, out of which would spring the first germs of civilization. In addition to this known sequence of the means of progress, the stages of which were doubtless separated from each other by centuries and decades of centuries of time, every nation upon a continent had one or more contiguous nations between whom and itself there was more or less of intercourse. Amongst contiguous nations there would be a free propagation of arts and inventions, which would tend to the general advancement of society throughout the entire area in which these influences were felt. Nations are apt to share in the more important elements of each other's progress.

On the other hand, the islands of the Pacific, except those adjacent to the main land, may be likened to so many cages in which their insulated occupants were shut in from external influences, as well as denied a knowledge of the uses of flocks and herds and of the principal cereals. Intercourse, at most, was limited to the inhabitants of particular groups of islands, who were thus compelled to sustain their national growth upon the development of their own intelligence exclusively, and without the great instruments of progress afforded by continental areas. They were also denied the advantages of numbers which is a most important element in the progress of human society. Under such circumstances it would be expected that isolated populations would remain in a stationary condition through longer periods of time than the inhabitants of continents. Immigrants, presumptively, from original continental homes, their posterity would be expected to reflect the condition of their ancestors at the epoch of their migration, since the probabilities of retrograding in knowledge would be at least equal to those of progress, under the physical limitations with which they were subsequently surrounded. These hindrances would tend to preserve their domestic institutions within narrow limits of change.

Dr. Prichard's classification and description of the assemblage of nations inhabiting Oceanica will bring them before us in their proper relations. "The inhabitant of Oceanica," he remarks, "divide themselves into three groups. * * * The first is the race termed by different writers Malayan, Polynesian, and Oceanic. * * * I shall term these people the Malayo-Polynesian, or, in short, the Malayan race. * * * The second group consists of tribes of people of darker complexion, with hair crisp, and more or less resembling African negroes. * * * I shall call them Pelagian negroes. They have often been called Papuas. * * * A third distinct group consists of tribes who differ in physical characters from the two former. * * * They are savages of dark color, lank hair, and prognathous heads. To this group the natives of Australia belong. I shall term them collectively Alforas." * * *

"The Malayan stock may be subdivided in a manner that will facilitate the description, into three branches. The first branch is the Indo-Malayan, comprehending the Malays proper of Malacca, and the islands of the Indian Archipelago, as the inhabitants of Sumatra, Java, Celebes, the Moluccas, and the Philippines. The last nations resemble the proper Malays both in language and in physical characters much more nearly than they do the Polynesian tribes. To the Indo-Malayan branch may, perhaps, be associated the nations of the Caroline Islands, and the Ladrones, who appear to be nearly related to their neighbors, the natives of the Philippines. To the second or Polynesian branch belong the Tonga Islanders, the New Zealanders, the Tahitians, and the Hawaii; these are the four principal groups of the Polynesian family, arranged according to the indications of their languages. The third branch are the Madacasses, or people of Madagascar."[1]

The Rev. Artemus Bishop, an American missionary, resident during the last forty years at the Sandwich Islands, thus remarks upon the Polynesian branch of the Malayan family, in a letter to the author, dated in April, 1860, at Honolulu: "It has been pretty well ascertained that the Polynesian race is not from Northern Asia, but from the Indian Archipelago. They are the same people as the Malays, and include, also, the inhabitants of Madagascar. In the Pacific, among the western islands, they pass into another race who speak a radically different language, in which enter many words of Polynesian origin. But through the Eastern and Southern Pacific they belong to the same branch. The same contour of features, the same structure of sentences in the language, and in perhaps half the words or more, the same words in their radical letters, but slightly varying by the omission

---

[1] Nat. Hist. of Man, 326–328.

of some of the letters, and the substitution of others. But they are all dialects of the same language. A native of New Zealand, of the Fejee, the Navigators, the Tahitian, or the Marquesas Islands can, in a few days, interchange thoughts as freely with Hawaiians as if he were among his own people. I mentioned, in a note, an Indian girl from Chili, who lived in my family a few years ago. She had the perfect contour of features which mark the Hawaiian women, and the same copper color, but a shade lighter. After being here a few months she spoke with the same fluency and intonation of voice as if she had been born here. Yet she was ignorant of the grammar of language, and of letters. She told me her native tongue was a little like the Hawaiian, but could give me no further information. The words in many cases may differ, but, as the structure of sentences is the same in both cases, it is easy, as in her case, to quickly get hold of the tongue.

"When I visited the Marquesas, two years ago, I found the people essentially Hawaiian. In a week after landing I could talk with them on any common subject. I found they held traditions that their ancestors came originally from Hawaii, and the name of the first ancestor of their race was Mawi of Hawaii, which is the same traditional name the Hawaiians boast of as their first ancestor.

"But the question, how the Polynesian race became so widely scattered, I fear will never be fully solved. In coming from Southern Asia they must have sailed to the windward all the way. The only manner in which I can solve it is to suppose that the ancient Southern Asiatics were civilized, and sailed in ships rather than in canoes; and that they had a sufficient knowledge of navigation to traverse a pathless ocean to windward. If so, they have long lost it. They have no traditions of their Asiatic origin. But there are intimations of the original Hawaiians having come here direct from the Navigators' Islands. The name of the principal island of that group corresponds to the name of our principal island. Svaii there. Hawaii here. The v and w are interchangeable letters in all Polynesia; s and h are exchangeable, although there is no s in Hawaiian."

The Malayan family possess an original and distinctive system of relationship; a system not less clearly limited and defined than the highest form of the Turanian. Its importance is much enhanced by the relation in which it stands to the Ganowánian and Turanian forms, although separated from them by a wide interval. It is an older, and so far as the tables show, the first stage of the classificatory system. Whatever form may have existed antecedent to · the Malayan, the latter is probably the oldest form of consanguinity and affinity now existing upon the earth. In the natural order of the subject it should have been first presented; but as the question of the probable origin of the system, and the relation of its several forms, does not arise until after a knowledge of these forms has been obtained, it has been reserved for the last place.

In the table will be found the system of relationship of the Hawaiians, and New Zealanders of Polynesia, and also of the Kusaiens and Kingsmill islanders of Micronesia. For a family of nations so numerous and so widely scattered geographically as the Malayan, this number of schedules furnish a narrow basis for a final induction determinative of the system of this family. The Hawaiian form herein presented prevails, presumptively, amongst the Tonga, Samoan, Navigators, and Marquesas islanders, and the Tahitians; and the Kusaien and Kingsmill among the Caroline, Ladrone and Pelew islanders, representing very favorably two of the great branches of the Malayan family, and leaving the inhabitants of Madagascar unrepresented. The system of the Malays proper, however, is wanting in the Table. To this we should naturally look for the typical form of the family. Repeated and persevering efforts, continued through a period of several years, to procure this system proved unsuccessful, although the Malays apparently are more accessible than any other branch of the family. If it had been obtained, and on comparison had been found identical in form with the Hawaiian, it would have rendered the proposition reasonably certain that the Malayan family, as constituted of the Malayan race of Dr. Prichard, possessed a common system, of which the Hawaiian was typical. The Malay terms of relationship were procured from a returned missionary from Borneo, and are given in the note,[1] but he was unable, without native assistance, to fill out a schedule. It should be observed, however, that the terms for nephew and niece, uncle and aunt, are descriptive phrases. It is not probable that these relationships are discriminated; but that the persons thus described are son and daughter, and father and mother, under the system. From the nomenclature the close approximation if not identity of the Malay and Hawaiian forms may be inferred with some degree of probability. The system of relationship of the Zulus or Kafirs of South Africa is also Malayan in form. Upon the basis of these schedules, which reveal an independent and distinctive system of consanguinity, the Malayan family has been constituted, and into which may be admitted all such nations as hereafter furnish evidence of common blood, through the possession of the same system of relationship.

I. Polynesian. 1. Hawaiian. The language and domestic institutions of these islanders have been rendered thoroughly accessible through the labors of the American missionaries. It is well known that the language is now written, and that it has become to some extent a cultivated language. Three schedules of the Hawaiian system of relationship were obtained. One of them was furnished by the Hon. Thomas Miller, United States Consul at Hilo, Island of Hawaii; the second by

---

[1] Malay Terms of Relationship by the Rev. William H. Steele.

1. Grandfather,	Nenek.	15. Husband,	Swami or Laki.
2. Grandmother,	Nenek Parampuan.	16. Wife,	Bini or Istri.
3. Father,	Bapa.	17. Father-in-law,	Mintua Laki Laki.
4. Mother,	Mak or Ibu.	18. Mother-in-law,	Mintua Parampuan.
5. Son (Anak child),	Anak Laki Laki.	19. Wife's brother,	Biras.
6. Daughter,	Anak Parampuan.	20. Brother-in-law,	Ipat.
7. Grandson,	Chuchu Laki Laki.	21. Step-father,	Bapa Tiri.
8. Granddaughter,	Chuchu Parampuan.	22. Step-mother,	Mak Tiri.
9. Elder brother,	Abañg.	23. Step-child,	Anak Tiri.
10 Younger brother,	Adik.	24. Adopted child,	Anak Añgkat.
11. Uncle,	Bapa Sudara.	25. First born,	Anak Sulung.
12. Aunt,	Mak Sudara.	26. Last born,	Anak Bongsu.
13. Nephew,	Anak Sudara Laki Laki.	27. Cousin,	Sudar Sa-pupu.
14. Niece,	Anak Sudara Parampuan.	28. Twins,	Anak Kumbar.

the Hon. Lorin Andrews, of Honolulu, Island of Oahu, one of the judges of the Supreme Court of Hawaii, under Kamchameha IV.; and the third by Rev. Artemus Bishop, before mentioned. They furnish a full and complete exposition of the Hawaiian system. The schedule of Mr. Miller was adopted for the table, with some modification of the orthography of the terms of relationship from that of Judge Andrews. The valuable observations of the gentleman last named, upon the nomenclature, as well as upon the system, which were evidently prepared with great care, will be found in the subjoined note, to which attention is invited.[1]

---

[1] *Notes on the Hawaiian Degrees of Relationship, by Judge Andrews.*

"1. Captain Cook, on the discovery of these islands, named them Sandwich Islands, after Lord Sandwich, and the English and most travellers continue the appellation to the present day. But he found the islands not only inhabited, but regular governments existing under chiefs or rulers, and each of the islands had its specific name, and there was, also, a general name for the whole group. This name was Hawaii, from the name of the larger island. 'Na aina o Hawaii,' the lands or country of Hawaii; 'Na moku o Hawaii,' the Islands of Hawaii. These have been the names appropriated by the inhabitants themselves from time immemorial; and it seems proper that that name should be continued rather than a name given by a discoverer. Especially as no untaught Hawaiian can pronounce the epithet *Sandwich Islands*, until after a long training of his vocal organs. In all laws and legal documents the word Hawaii is used to denote this group of islands.

"2. Where there is an elision of a vowel it is indicated by an apostrophe. Thus, *ko' u* or *ka' u* stands for *ko ou* and *ka au*, and is the genitive of *ou* and *au;* the same applies to *o'u* and *a'u*. The pronunciation is effected by a slight break where the apostrophe occurs, to distinguish it from *kou* and *kau*, of the second person, *thy* or thine, *ou, au*, of thee, of thine, &c. The form *kua*, my or mine, is used when it is not certain whether *ko' u* or *ka' u* ought to be used in order to be grammatically correct.

"In Hawaiian printed books no accents or other diacritical signs are used, except the above apostrophe. I have, therefore, marked the accented syllables by a simple inclined dash over the vowel. The sounds of the vowels, it will be perceived, are those of the languages of Southern Europe, in distinction from the English. The vowel *u* may, perhaps, be an exception.

"3. The Hawaiians have no definite word for *father*, *mkúa* signifies parent, either male or female. If we wish to say *father* or *mother*, we must add *káne*, male, or *wahína*, female. When used as nouns *káne* signifies husband, and *wahíne* a wife.

"4. For *máku wahíne*, mother, a slightly different orthography is often used; thus, *makúahíne*, the syllable *wa* is thrown out, and the two words united in one, the pronunciation continuing nearly the same.

"5. The Hawaiian has no specific word for *son*. *Keíki* signifies *child*, or originally *the little;* *ikí*, little, small; the article *ke* has, in modern times, become prefixed, that is attached, and the word thus compounded takes at present another article, *ke;* hence the present form, *ke keíki*, the little one, the junior, &c. To express the idea *son*, the adjective *káne*, male, must be added.

"6. The form *kaíkamahíne* is an anomaly which I have never heard a native (though often asked) account for. According to the analogy of the language, the word for daughter would be *keikí wahíne;* but Hawaiians never use that phrase. *Kaíkamahíne* signifies a female child, girl, daughter, young woman, &c.

"7. The Hawaiian has no term for grandson. *Moopuna* signifies a grandchild of either sex. Hence *kane*, male, or *wahíne*, female, is added. *Moopuna*, however, is not always restricted to a descendant of the second generation, but is often used of several degrees.

"8. *Moopuna kualua*, that is *ku*, fitting, belonging to, *alua*, two, the second, &c. This assumes that *moopuna*, grandchild, is the first in a series of that title. Hence *moopúna kualúa* signifies a great-grandchild.

The Hawaiian system is classificatory in the strict sense of the term; but more simple and inartificial than any other form which obtains in the several families of mankind. Its simplicity is caused by the adoption of the primary relationships as the basis of the system, and by bringing collateral consanguinei within one or the other of these relationships. In this fundamental provision can be clearly recognized the "nine ranks of relatives" which form the basis of the Chinese system (*supra*, page 415), but reduced to five. The Chinese text reduced accordingly,

---

"9. *Moopúna kúakólu*, great-great-grandchild, from *ku*, belonging to, and *akolu*, three, or these, &c., as above.

"10. *Kaíkuaána.* The Hawaiian has no definite general word for *brother* in common use. (See *hoahanau* below.) *Kaikuaána* signifies any one of my brothers older than myself; that is an older brother of a brother. The same applies to females. If a woman speaks of a sister older than herself, she calls her *kaikuaána*.

"11. *Kuíkunáne*, thus spoken by a female, applies to any of her brothers, older or younger than herself.

"12. *Kaíkuwahine*, said by a male, means a sister older than himself.

"13. *Kaíkaína*, a younger brother of a brother, or a younger sister of a sister. Thus, a brother speaks of a brother either as *kaikuaáne*, elder brother, or *kaikuaína*, younger brother The terms apply to any number older or younger. The same applies to a sister. When a sister speaks of a younger brother she calls him *kaikunáne*. See No. 11.

"14. Brothers. See No. 10. The Hawaiian has no word for brother in the sense of the languages of Western Europe. The word *hóahánau*, from *hóa*, companion, and *hanau*, born, *i. e.*, a companion in birth, is used in a loose sense, and is now mostly applied to those belonging to the church, or church members. They seldom use it of one born of the same parents. The word is in common gender, and needs *káne* or *wahine* in order to specify the sex. I have used the terms *hóahánau* and *hóahánau wahine*, for brothers and sisters, because they may be so used, and because without them I could not go on with the degrees of relationship.

"15. The Hawaiian has no words for uncle or aunt. All *uncles* and *aunts* are *makúa*, *i. e.*, fathers or mothers.

"16. *Makúahíne.* See No. 4.

"17. See No. 15. This admits of another form in Hawaiian, but the phrase in the line is the most common.

"18. Hawaiians have no words for *nephew* or *niece*. Nephews and nieces are all *sons* and *daughters*.

"19. Hawaiians have no term for *cousin*. All cousins are *brothers* and *sisters*, and the same distinguishing epithets of older and younger apply as in the case of own brothers and sisters. See Nos. 10–13. This applies to cousins of any degree.

"20. The word *kupuna*=more, literally means a grandparent, and with *káne* or *wáhine*, grandfather or grandmother. This was, probably, the original idea; but in common use it means an ancestor of any degree.

"21. The *hunóna* has no corresponding term in English. It applies to a man who has married my daughter, or to a woman who has married my son.

"22. *Kolea* has no corresponding term in English.

"23. *Hunai* (fed, nursed) is equivalent in practice to our word adoption, though it has no such legal form. If a child lived to grow up in the family of one in no way related to it, or was sustained at their expense, it was entitled by common law to inherit as if a real child.

"24. *Puliena* expresses the relationship of a man's parents to those of his wife.

"25. *Kaikoéke* is a brother-in-law or sister-in-law, according as *káne* or *wahine* is added.

"26. The relationship of *pínalúa* is rather amphibious. It arose from the fact that two or more brothers, with their wives, or two or more sisters with their husbands, were inclined to possess each other in common; but the modern use of the word is that of *dear friend*, an intimate companion."

would read as follows in Hawaiian: "All men who are born into the world have five ranks of relatives. My own generation is one grade; my father's is one; and my grandfather's is one; thus above me are two grades. My son's generation is one grade, and my grandson's is one; thus below me are two grades of relations; including myself in the estimate, there are five grades. These are brethren, and though each grade belongs to a different house or family, yet they are all my relations; and these are called the five grades of relations." The difference consists in this, that whilst the Chinese have departed from the literal classification of consanguinei into nine grades, by the introduction into their system of what may be called distinctive Turanian elements, the Hawaiians have held, pure and simple, to the five primary grades of relatives. When compared with the highest type of the Turanian system the Hawaiian is found to be classific without being Turanian; and the difference between them is the precise element which constitutes the Turanian system, as distinguished from other classificatory forms. In about half of the Hawaiian relationships the classification is identical with the Turanian, but the remaining parts of the two are wholly different. It will be seen in the sequel that the Turanian might have been, and probably was, engrafted upon an original form in all respects agreeing with the Hawaiian; but that the latter could not have been derived from the former, whence the inference that the Hawaiian is the oldest form.

An analysis of the system will develop in a few propositions the limited number of ideas upon which it is founded.

I. All the brothers and sisters of my grandfather and of my grandmother on the father's side, and on the mother's side, are, without distinction, my grandparents; and the same is true of the several ancestors above grandparents, and their brothers and sisters. They are distinguished from each other as second or third grandparents, but practically stand in the relationship of grandparents.

II. All the children and descendants of my sons and daughters are my grandchildren, but distinguished from each other in the manner last above named.

III. Brothers are distinguished into elder and younger, by the males, but not by the females; and sisters are distinguished into elder and younger by the females, but not by the males.

IV. All the children of my several brothers, and all the children of my several sisters are my children, and all the children of the latter are my grandchildren. A change in the sex of *Ego* makes no difference in relationships under the Hawaiian system.

V. All the brothers of my father, and all the brothers of my mother are my fathers, and all the sisters of my father, and all the sisters of my mother are my mothers.

VI. All the children of several brothers, of several sisters, and of several brothers and sisters, are themselves brothers and sisters to each other, elder or younger; and they apply to each other the same terms they would use to designate own brothers and sisters. The children of these collateral brothers and sisters are also brothers and sisters to each other, elder or younger; and the same relationships continue, theoretically, amongst their descendants, at equal removes, indefinitely.

VII. All the children of these, my collateral brothers and sisters, are my sons and daughters; and the children of the latter are my grandchildren.

VIII. The wives of my collateral sons are my daughters-in-law, and the husbands of my collateral daughters are my sons-in-law. The wives of my several collateral brothers are my wives, and the husbands of my collateral sisters are my brothers-in-law.

IX. In each and all of these relationships the correlative terms are applied to *Ego*; *e. g.*, the one I call father calls me son, the one I call grandfather calls me grandson, the one I call elder brother calls me younger brother, and the one I call father-in-law calls me son-in-law.

X. The several collateral lines are ultimately merged in the lineal line, ascending as well as descending.

From the foregoing propositions it appears, first, that the relationships of uncle and aunt, nephew and niece, and cousin are unknown in the Hawaiian system; secondly, that consanguinei are never described; and, lastly, that they are generalized into as many great classes or categories as there are primary relationships. All the members of each class are thus reduced to the same level in the rank of their relationships to each other, and to *Ego*, without regard to nearness or remoteness in degree. It exhibits, as before stated, a perfect realization of the "Grades of Relatives" described by the Chinese author, and which the Chinese system now fails to illustrate. If we make the application, commencing with grandfather, it will be seen that my grandparents, and such kinsmen of theirs as stand to me in the relation of grandparents, form one grade or class; that my parents, and such relatives of theirs as stand to me in the relationship of parents, form a second grade or class; that myself, with my brothers and sisters, and my collateral brothers and sisters, form a third grade or class; that my children, and the children of my collateral brothers and sisters form a fourth grade or class; and that my grandchildren and my collateral grandchildren form a fifth grade or class. Those of each grade stand to *Ego* in the same identical relationship, and the individuals of the same grade or class stand to each other in the relationships of brothers and sisters. It follows, also, that a knowledge of the degrees of consanguinity, numerically, is an integral part of the Hawaiian system, without which it would be impossible to determine to which of the great classes any given person belonged. The simple and distinctive character of the Hawaiian system will at once arrest attention. It has positive elements, which contravene natural suggestion, on the assumption of marriage between single pairs, and it is also classificatory without the special discriminations of the Turanian system.

The Malayan form holds such an important relation both to the Turanian and Ganowánian that it should be presented with some degree of detail. It affords a probable solution of the origin of the classificatory system.

There are terms in Hawaiian for grandparent, *Kŭpŭnä*, for parent, *Mäkŭä*, for child, *Kaikee*, and for grandchild, *Moopŭnă*. The gender is expressed by adding the terms for male and female, *Käna* and *Wäheena*. Ancestors and descendants above and below those named, are distinguished numerically, when it is necessary

to be specific, as second, third, and so on. But in common usage *Kŭpŭnä* is ap
plied to all ancestors above father, and *Moopŭnă* to all descendants below son.[1]

In the manner of indicating the fraternal and sororal relationships, there are
peculiar characteristics which deserve special notice.

Elder brother, said by a male,	Kaikuaana.	Said by a female,	Kaikunana.
Younger brother, "	"	Kaikaina.	"	"	Kaikunana.
Elder sister, "	"	Kaikuwahina.	"	"	Kaikuaana.
Younger sister "	"	Kaikuwahina.	"	"	Kaikaina.

It will be observed that a man calls his elder brother *Kaikuaana*, and that a
woman calls her elder sister the same ; a man calls his younger brother *Kaikaina*,
a woman calls her younger sister the same ; hence these terms are in common
gender, and the manner of their use suggests the idea found in the Karen system,
of predecessor and successor in birth, although limited to the brothers of the male,
and to the sisters of the female. To this extent these relationships are conceived
in the twofold form of elder and younger. But a single term is used by the males
for elder and younger sister, and a single term by the females for elder and younger
brother. It thus appears that with *Ego* a male his brothers are classified into elder
and younger, whilst his sisters are placed in one class ; and that with *Ego* a female
her sisters are distinguished into elder and younger, whilst her brothers are placed
in one class. A double set of terms are in this way developed, one of which is
used by the males, and the other by the females. This arrangement is quite artificial as well as peculiar, and wherever it prevails will furnish evidence of
ethnic connection with the Hawaiians. Deviations from the common form, in
which two or more independent nations concur, very often suggest the order of the
separation of these nations from each other, and from the common stem.

In the first collateral line, and irrespective of the sex of *Ego*, my brother's and
sister's children are my sons and daughters, and their children are my grandchildren.

The husbands and wives of these several collateral sons and daughters are my
daughters-in-law and my sons-in-law, the terms used being in common gender, and
having the word for male or female added to each respectively.

In the second collateral line my father's brother is my father ; his children are
my brothers and sisters, the same terms being used which are applied to own
brothers and sisters ; their children are my sons and daughters ; and the children
of the latter are my grandchildren. My father's sister is my mother ; her children
are my brothers and sisters ; the children of the latter are my sons and daughters ;
and their children are my grandchildren.

In like manner, my mother's brother is my father ; his children are my brothers
and sisters ; the children of the latter are my sons and daughters ; and their children are my grandchildren. My mother's sister is my mother ; her children are
my brothers and sisters ; the children of the latter are my sons and daughters ; and
their children are my grandchildren.

The wives of these several collateral brothers are, without distinction, my own

---

[1] See Judge Andrews's statement. Note, *supra*, 7, 820.

wives, the same term being still used to designate them, which I apply to my own wife; and the husbands of these several collateral sisters are my brothers-in-law.

In the third collateral line, my grandfather's brother is my grandfather; his son is my father; the children of this father are my brothers and sisters; their children are my sons and daughters; and the children of the latter are my grandchildren. The remaining branches of this line give the same series. If the connection of consanguinei is traced into the fourth and more remote collateral lines, the same principle of classification is applied.

From the foregoing analysis and detailed presentation of the Hawaiian form its simplicity and originality are apparent. It is a clearly defined system, comprehensive in its range, and uniform in its classification. The generalizations upon which it rests are fundamentally different from those which underlie the Aryan, Semitic, and Uralian; but they agree in part with those which organize the Turanian system. In other words, half of the Hawaiian is Turanian, and the other half is not; and that part which is not Turanian is a duplicate of the part which is. The differences will be seen by placing the two forms side by side. Several interesting problems are suggested by the comparison which will come up for discussion in another place.

It is important, in this connection, that particular attention should be directed to the Hawaiian custom, or Pinaluanic bond which is mentioned by Judge Andrews in the last section of his notes (supra, p. 453.) "The relationship of *Pinalua*," he remarks, "is rather amphibious. It arose from the fact that two or more brothers with their wives, or two or more sisters, with their husbands, were inclined to possess each other in common; but the modern use of the word is that of dear friend or intimate companion." The Rev. Artemus Bishop refers to the same usage in the following language: "This confusion of relationships is the result of the ancient custom among relatives of the living together of husbands and wives in common."

In this singular usage, which is now for the first time announced, so far as the writer is aware, we recognize a custom older in point of time than polygamy and polyandria, and yet involving the essential features of both. The several brothers, who thus cohabited with each other's wives, lived in polygynia; and the several sisters, who thus cohabited with each other's husbands, lived in polyandria. It also presupposes *communal families*, with communism in living, which, there are abundant reasons for supposing, were very general in the primitive ages of mankind; and one of the stages through which human society passed before reaching the family in its proper sense, founded upon marriage between single pairs.

The Hawaiian custom affords a probable solution of the Hawaiian system of relationship. After this is determined a probable explanation of the origin of the Turanian may be obtained through other customs which together will be considered in a subsequent chapter.

2. Maori, of New Zealand. The dialects of New Zealand affiliate closely with the Hawaiian, and the two peoples were evidently derived from the same immediate stem. As far as the Maori system of relationship is given in the Table, it is identical with the Hawaiian.

In the manner of indicating the fraternal and sororal relationships the same method is found.

Elder brother.	Said by a male,	Tu-a-ka-na.		Said by a female,	Tun-ga-ne.
Younger brother.	" " "	Te-i-na.		" " "	Tun-ga-ne te-i-na.
Elder sister.	" " "	Tu-a-hi-ne.		" " "	Tu-a-ka-na.
Younger sister.	" " "	Tu-a-hi-na te-i-na.		" " "	Te-i-na.

A man calls his elder brother *Tu-a-ka-na*, and a woman calls her elder sister the same; a man calls his younger brother *Te-i-na*, and a woman calls her younger sister the same; hence these terms are in common gender. This is analogous to the Hawaiian method (*supra*, 456).

In the first collateral line, and irrespective of the sex of *Ego*, my brother's children and my sister's children are my sons and daughters, and their children are my grandchildren.

In the second and third collateral lines the questions on the schedule were, by a misapprehension, translated into Maori, which would have left the relationships in these lines in doubt, but for a marginal note by Mr. Taylor, as follows: "A cousin of any degree is a brother or sister." It appears, also, that the same relationship continues downward indefinitely at equal removes, for he remarks further: "To one descended from an elder brother he or she is a *Te-i-na*, and the descendant of the elder branch is a *Tu-a-ka-na* to the younger."[1]

It is rendered probable from the Maori schedule in its imperfect state that the system is identical with the Hawaiian. And since New Zealand is at the southern, as the Sandwich Islands are at the northern, extreme of Polynesia, it seems probable that the Hawaiian system will be found prevalent in the intermediate Tonga, Samson, Society, and Marquesas Islands, as elsewhere suggested. In like manner the existence of the same system, as will next appear, in the Kingsmill or Tarawan Islands will lead to a similar inference that it will also be found in the Caroline, Ladrone, and Pelew Islands, which are the principal groups in Micronesia.

II. Micronesian. 1. Kusaien, of Strong's Island. 2. Kingsmill, of Kingsmill Island.

The Micronesian Islands are near the equator, and nearer to the coast of Asia than to the Hawaiian group. Judging from the nomenclature of relationships these dialects are radically distinct from the Hawaiian, although in grammatical structure the two languages are said to be the same.

From two of these island schedules were obtained. One, that of the Kusaiens, was prepared by the Rev. B. G. Snow, and the other, that of the Kingsmill Islanders, by the Rev. Hiram Bingham, Jr., both American Missionaries to the Micronesian Islands. They had at the time resided upon these islands about two years, not long enough to master the dialects, but sufficiently long to use them for ordinary colloquial purposes. Neither schedule was completely filled, but the work,

---

[1] Mr. Taylor further observes, that "a descendant of the elder branch of a family is a *pa-pa* [father] to all other branches, and the eldest child of the main branch is an *a-ri-ki*, lord, to all that family, and is supposed to have the spirits of all his or her ancestors embodied in himself or herself, and to be able to converse with them at pleasure."

in each case, was far enough advanced to reveal the principal features of the system, and to show its substantial identity with the Hawaiian.

1. Kusaien. No terms exist for ancestors above father and mother, and none for descendants below son and daughter. They are indicated by a reduplication of the primary terms.[1]

Whether the relationships of brother and sister are in the twofold form of elder and younger, is left in some uncertainty by the schedule.

My elder brother, said by a male,	Lek läss, or mätŭ.	My brother, larger or older.
My younger brother, " "	Lék Srik, or fwos.	" " smaller or younger.
My elder sister, " "	Louk läss, or mätŭ.	" sisters, larger or older.
My younger sister, " "	Louk Srik, or fwos.	" " smaller or younger.
My brothers,	Mä leh=my brother.	The number is indicated by numerals.
My sisters,	Ma läuk=my sister.	" " "

The terms used by females are not given. It is not improbable that the above terms are the mere equivalents of the questions in the schedule, for which reason these relationships require further investigation.

In the first collateral line, my brother's son and daughter are my son and daughter, which is all that is given in this line.

In the second, my father's brother is my father; his son and daughter are my brother and sister; and the children of this collateral brother and sister are my sons and daughters. This is the extent to which this branch of the line is carried. My father's sister is my mother, her children are my brothers and sisters, and their children are my sons and daughters.

My mother's brother is my father, his children are my brothers and sisters, and their children are my sons and daughters. My mother's sister is my mother, her children are my brothers and sisters, and their children are my sons and daughters. The foregoing is all that is given of the Kusaien form. It is reasonably inferable that the children of these collateral sons and daughters are my grandchildren, which is all that is needed to establish its identity with the Hawaiian form.

---

[1] In the letter which accompanied the schedule, dated at Kusaie, March, 1860, Mr. Snow remarks: "You will readily see, when you once get the run of the pronominal suffixes, that you can carry the relationships on ad infinitum, e. g., päpä, father; päppä tŭmmŭk=my father; päpä tŭmmum=your father; päpä tŭmmäl=his or her father. Nenĕ, mother; nenĕ keyŭk=my mother; nenĕ keyum=your mother; nenĕ keyäl=his or her mother. Then we have päpä tŭmmŭn päpä=father of my father; nenĕ keyën nenĕ=mother of my mother.

"The paradigms for the filial relationships are quite uniform, though different as to their forms; e. g., muĕn, son; muĕn mŭttĭk=my son; muĕn mŭttĭn muen mŭttik=my grandson; ăn, daughter; ăn mŭttik=my daughter; ăn muttin ăn mŭttik=my granddaughter.

"A form for gender in the third person is wanting. It is always indicated not with persons, but with animals, fish, fowls, &c., by the word which signifies male and female respectively; male, mogul; female, mŭtăn.

"The forms for the relationships of brother and sister differ of course from the foregoing, e. g., mä lek=my brother; mä leum=your brother; mä lal=his brother. Mä louk=my sister; mä loum=your sister; mä loŭl=his sister. Then there is a form used only for the brother of a brother, as tämŭlal; also, for the sister of a sister, as tämŭläel. I have not been able to ascertain that these two forms mean anything more than to indicate the relationship of a brother's brother and a sister's sister."

2. Kingsmill. The system of relationship of these Islanders is more fully developed than the Kusaien, but it is limited to the lineal and first and second collateral lines.

With respect to the fraternal and sororal relationships it agrees in some respects and differs in others from the Hawaiian.

My elder brother, said by a male,	Taru te Karimoa.	Said by a female,	Mänu te karimoa.
" younger brother, " "	Taru te karimwi.	" "	Mänu te karimwi.
" elder sister, " "	Mänu te karimoa.	" "	Taru te karimoa.
" younger sister, " "	Mänu te karimwi.	" "	Taru te karimwi.

They are also expressed in another manner as follows :—

My elder, a male.	Said by a male or a female,	Karimoau te mane.
" younger, a male.	" " "	Karimwin te mane.
" elder, a female.	" " "	Karimoau te aine.
" younger, a female.	" " "	Karimwin te aine.

The true test by which to discover whether these relationships are held in the mind in the twofold form of elder and younger, is the manner in which they address each other, which I am unable to give.[1]

In the first collateral line, and irrespective of the sex of *Ego*, my brother's children and my sister's children are my sons and daughters. The term *Nätu* = my child, is in common gender, and is followed by *mane* = male, for son, and *aine* = female, for daughter. These last words appear to be the Hawaiian *käna* = male, and *wäheena* = female, dialectically changed. Whether my brother's children are my grandchildren was not shown in the schedule; but there can be no doubt that this is the classification.

In the second collateral line my father's brother is my father, his children are my brothers and sisters, and the children of the latter are my sons and daughters.

---

[1] In Mr. Bingham's first letter to the author, dated at Apaiang, Nov. 1859, and which preceded the schedule, he says: " Our terms of relationship, so far as I am acquainted with them, are as follows :—

Tămä=father or uncle.
Tämäu=my father or uncle.
Tinä=mother or aunt.
Tinäu=my mother or aunt.
Näti or Näje=child.
Nätu=my child.
Nätŭ te mäne=my child, the male.
Nätŭ te aine=my child, the female.
Jinăpaŭ=my daughter-in-law.
　　my (a man's) mother-in-law.
　　my (a woman's) father-in-law.
Aŭ bŭ=my relations in general.
Aŭ käro　my parents.
Täde or Tari=man's brother and male cousin.
　　woman's sister and female cousin.
" I presume other terms exist."

Tädu or Tära=my brother, &c.
Märu=man's sister and female cousin.
　　woman's brother and male cousin.
Mäna=My sisters, &c.
Tibŭ=my grandparent and grandchild.
　　foster parent and foster child.
Bŭ=my husband or wife.
Bŭjikäŭ=my wife's brother and my (a man) sister's husband.
Käenăpaŭ=my husband's sister, and my (a woman's) brother's wife.
Eadekŭ=my wife's sister, my (a woman's) sister's husband, and my (a man's) brother's wife, and my husband's brother.

My father's sister is my mother, her children are my brothers and sisters, and their children are my sons and daughters.

On the mother's side, my mother's brother is my father, his children are my brothers and sisters, and the children of the latter are my grandchildren. In like manner my mother's sister is my mother, her children are my brothers and sisters, and their children are my grandchildren. This is the extent to which the several branches of this line are carried.

The husbands and wives of these several collateral sons and daughters are my sons-in-law and my daughters-in-law, and the husbands and wives of these several collateral brothers and sisters are my brothers-in-law and my sisters-in-law.

The identity of this system with the Hawaiian admits of no doubt. It is not surprising that this peculiar classification of consanguinei wore the appearance of an abuse of terms. The "confusion of relationships," as Rev. Mr. Bishop expressed it, was still more strongly insisted upon by Rev. Mr. Bingham. In his first letter to the author, dated at Apiang, in 1859, he observes: "The terms for father, mother, brother, and sister, and for other relationships, are used so loosely we can never know, without further inquiry, whether the real father, or the father's brother is meant, the mother or the mother's sister, the brother or the cousin, the grandfather or the godfather." In his subsequent letter, dated in August, 1860, which accompanied the schedule, he remarks: "You think I will find that the terms to which you refer are not used loosely, but in the most precise, regular, and uniform manner. * * * They are so loosely used that in common conversation I am often much puzzled to know who is referred to, until I have put specific questions. A man comes to me and says *e mote tamau*, my father is dead. Perhaps I have just seen his father alive and well, and I say, 'No, not dead?' He replies, 'I mean my father's brother,' or 'my mother's brother.'" These quotations are introduced to verify their work, and to show how distinctly the prominent features of this system of relationship met their attention at every point, and that it is both a real and a living form.

These schedules complete the series from the Pacific Islands. Each one is sufficient to bring to our notice a system distinct and original in its character, however limited their united testimony may be with reference to the extent of its distribution. Notwithstanding the extreme simplicity of its plan it produces a definite and coherent system, capable of answering the ordinary purposes of life. That it descended to each of these nations, with the streams of the blood, from a common source, and has been perpetuated by them through all the centuries of their separation from each other, would seem to be a necessary inference from the continued agreement of their radical characteristics. If the forms which now prevail amongst the members of the widely scattered Malayan family could be brought together for comparison, it would undoubtedly lead to singular and interesting results. The system is radically different from the Aryan, Semitic, and Uralian; and, although classificatory, it is widely divergent from the Turanian. It is sufficiently *sui generis* to be capable of self-perpetuation, in this precise condition, through indefinite periods of time, and after crossing, unaffected, the barrier which separates one stock language from another, and even one family of languages from another, of remaining constant in each after the identity of the vocables and of the grammatical forms of these languages have ceased to be recognizable. The materials in the table, however, as before stated, are perhaps too limited to show the range, and, inferentially, the permanence throughout the family of the Malayan system of relationship.

An attempt was made to reach the Negroid nations of Africa, but it proved entirely unsuccessful. The people of pure negro stock are known to be limited in numbers on the African continent. To such a degree is this now understood to be the fact that Dr. Latham remarks that "the negro is an exceptional African."[1] A portion of the west coast, between the Senegal and the Congo, and some other small and isolated portions of the interior are in possession of this family, leaving the remainder of the continent in the occupation of nations of more or less immediate Asiatic affiliations. Unimportant in numbers, feeble in intellect, and inferior in rank to every other portion of the human family, they yet centre in themselves, in their unknown past and mysterious present, one of the greatest problems in the science of the families of mankind. They seen to challenge and to traverse all the evidences of the unity of origin of the human family by their excessive deviation from such a standard of the species as would probably be adopted on the assumption of unity of origin. The primitive condition of the red and brown races, as revealed in their domestic institutions of consanguinity and affinity, involves successive stages of barbarism, each more profound and unrelieved than we have been accustomed to conceive as possible; but it would scarcely imply a condition of physical and mental inferiority such as the remote ancestors of the present negro race must have exhibited. In the light of our present knowledge the negro is the chief stumbling block in the way of establishing the unity of origin of the human family, upon the basis of scientific proofs. The monuments of Egypt determine the fact of the existence of Negroes in nations in Africa at least fifteen hundred years before the Christian era, according to the chronological dynasties of Lepsius;[2] thus showing that the whole amount of this divergence had then occurred. It is difficult to know even the direction in which to look for a discovery of the causes which produced such an excessive amount of divergence from a common typical standard of the species. The element of time, if measured out upon a scale sufficiently ample, may contribute to a solution; but it would manifestly require such a series of ages upon ages as would greatly overstep our present conceptions with respect to the antiquity of man upon the earth.

Inasmuch as the Tables of consanguinity and affinity contained in this work are presented in a great measure as an experiment to test the uses of systems of relationship in ethnological investigations; and since the inquiry, if found deserving of further prosecution, must be carried far beyond its present limits before the system of the Negroid family will become material, the absence of their system from the tables is, in a great measure, unimportant. It will be found, however, that they have a system, and that it will furnish evidence of their relations to each other, and possibly to the other families of mankind.

---

[1] Descriptive Ethnology, II. 184.   [2] See plate 117, Book III., Lepsius's Egypt and Ethiopia.

III. Amazulu or Kafir. One African schedule will be found in the table exhibiting the system of relationship of the Amazulus or Kafirs. The Kafir stock is one of the largest, in the number of people, as well as most widely distributed in Africa. Under this name, says the Rev. J. L. Döhne, is included, "all the tribes to the eastward of Cape Colony, along the coast, as far as Delagoa."[1] He afterwards enumerates twenty-nine of these tribes under seven general divisions.[2] He remarks upon the language as follows: "Generally speaking the Zulu distinguishes only two dialects, the high language, Ukukuluma, and the low, Amalala. To the first belong the Zulu, Tembu, and Xosa; to the second, the languages of all the other tribes of Natal, the frontier Fingoes, the Seetos," &c.[3] The Bechuanas, and some other tribes of the interior are said to speak closely allied languages. It is probable, therefore, that the Amazulu schedule exhibits the system of relationship of the Kafirs proper, not only, but also that which prevails over a large portion of Southern and Eastern Africa. Their system of relationship is classificatory in form, and essentially Malayan in its characteristics. It is distinguished from the latter in two particulars only, one of which is the discrimination of the relationship of uncle, restricted to the mother's brother; and the other that of cousin, which is limited in its application to the children of this uncle. Its agreement with the Malayan system in all other particulars will be at once recognized.

The first African Mission of the American Board was established among the Kafirs in the province of Natal, about the year 1835; and it has been eminently successful. Amongst the fruits of missionary labor upon the language is the complete lexicon of the language before referred to, together with the reduction of the language to a written form by the translation of portions of the Scriptures, and of some entire works into the vernacular tongue.

The schedule in the Table was filled out by the Rev. A. Abraham, one of the oldest members of this mission, and a resident of Mapumulo in Natal. It was executed with such fulness as to illustrate in the most satisfactory manner the details of the system. He also furnished, with it, a number of valuable observations upon the nomenclature of relationships, and upon the Amazulu classification of kindred, which will be found in the note, and to which attention is invited.[4]

---

[1] Döhne's Tulu Kafir Dictionary, Intro., p. viii. Cape Town ed., 1857.
[2] Ib. Intro., p. xvi. [3] Ib. Intro., p. xv.
[4] "Notes on the Schedule" by the Rev. A. Abraham, Mapumulo, January, 1866.
"The vowels are not always of the same length. They are longer on the accented syllables. Sometimes the final vowel of a word is scarcely heard. The consonants are the same as in English, except the hl, represents a sound peculiar to this language. We have other characters which I have not had occasion to use in filling up the schedule. The accent is on the penultimate; and generally every syllable ends with a vowel, as u-bä'-bä, u-mä'-ma, u'-mna or um'-na.
"a. The pronouns are not generally used in connection with the words for father and mother. U-bä'-bä is my father, u-ye-hlo thy father, u'-yese his father, u-mä'-ma my mother, u-my-o'-ko thy mother, ŭ-ne'-nä his mother.
"For grandfather and grandmother we suffix ku-lu = great, to the above words; thus, ubäbä kulu, my grandfather; wyise kulu, his grandfather. Ukulu is either grandfather or grandmother, and is used with the pronouns thus, ukulu wäme, my grandparent; ukulu wäka, his grandparent.

These explanations are so specific as to render a detailed presentation of the Amazulu form, for the most part, unnecessary; but from the great importance which attaches to this system, the several lines should be briefly considered.

"*b. Umetshä, umetshänä, umzukulu,* and *umzukulwänä* are usually synonymous. Grandchildren and all below grandchildren are designated by either of these words.

"*c. Umma, umnäwa,* and *udäda* are never used alone, *i. e.,* without the pronouns. We may say *bä lämänä, i. e.,* they were born one after the other (having the same father or mother). From the verb we have the noun, *ezalämäna,* (own) brothers and sisters.

"There is another peculiarity to be observed here. *Umna* and *udäda* always require the plural pronoun. We must say *umna wetu,* our brother; and not *umna wäme,* my brother. So also we never hear a native say *udäda wäme,* my sister, but *udäda natu,* our sister.

"*Umfo* is very much used for brother, and it is a very convenient term, as it may be used either for elder or younger brother. It must be used with a plural pronoun, thus *umfo natu,* our brother; never *umfo wäme,* for my brother. *Umfo* without a pronoun means an enemy or stranger or foreigner. Thus, if people come in from a neighboring nation, they may be called *äbäfo* (plural), whether they come as enemies, or on any business. With a singular pronoun, *umfo* means son, thus *umfo wäme,* my son; *umfo wäka,* his son. *Abafo watu* = my brothers, *abafo bäme* = my sons; but this is not the usual term for son.

"*d.* My father's brothers are my fathers, and my father's sisters are my fathers (not my mothers). *Aze* may be added, thus, *ubäbäkäze.*

"My mother's sisters are my mothers, *umäma* or *umämäkäze,* but her brothers are not my fathers. My mother's sister's husband is my father *ubäbä,* and not *ubäbäkäze.*

"*e. Umäluma* is my uncle, *i. e.,* my mother's brother. The pronouns are not necessary, *unyokoluma,* thy uncle; *uninäluma,* his uncle. There is no special term for mother's brother's wife, unless it be the same, *umäluma.* In speaking to her she might be addressed as *umäluma;* but in speaking of her a native would generally say, *umkä mäluma,* wife of my uncle.

"*f.* My father's brother's son is the same to me as my father's son, *i. e., unfo natu,* my (own) brother. The same is the rule as respects the other relations; my father's brother's son's wife is the same as my father's son's wife; *i. e.,* my brothers wife, which is *umkawe,* 'my wife.'

"*g.* It will be observed that *umzälä* is the son or daughter of the *umäluma.* The relationship is not reciprocal here, as with us, where both are cousins. My *umzälä* (cousin) calls me his brother.

"*h. Umkwanyäna* = *umkwanyä* is the name given to a man who marries into a family. The father and mother call him *umkwayännä wäme,* my son; but a brother or sister will always use the plural pronoun, thus, *umkwayänä watu,* our brother-in-law; never *umkwayänä wame,* my brother-in-law. From the same root we have *unkwa,* father-in-law; and *umkuakäze,* mother-in-law, *i. e.,* the males father-in-law and mother-in-law, *ebakwame* (locative case from *ebukwa*), at the wife's house. A man generally calls his wife's father and mother, *ubäbä* and *umäma,* father and mother.

"*i. Umyana* is the proper term for husband. A woman also calls her husband's brothers and sisters by the same term, *i. e.,* her husbands; she also calls them brothers and sisters.

"*j. Umkäme* is a compound word, composed of a noun and pronoun, and hence changes with the person, thus, *umkäme,* my wife; *umkäko,* thy wife; *umkäka,* his wife; *umkä'nkäze,* wife of the king; *umka fäka,* wife of *ufäku.* The noun is never used except with a pronoun or noun as above. *Umfäze* is another term, used for wife, which may be used without a pronoun or noun. A man's brother's wife is his wife, and a woman's brother's wife is her wife.

"*k. Unyänä* is a term by which one wife of a polygamist addresses another wife, using the plural pronoun, thus, *unyänä watu.* The husband's brother's wives are addressed in the same way.

"*l. Umfalskäze* is a woman who has lost either her husband or children. I am not aware that there is any term for widower. It is not often that we meet with a widower. If a man loses one or two wives he usually has several left. It is common to use the verb thus, *ufalwa umkäka,* 'he is died for by his wife,' *i. e.,* he has lost his wife.

"*m.* These relationships will be understood if we keep in mind that my father's father's sister's son

Amongst the Amazulu the relationship of brother is conceived in the twofold form of elder and younger, whilst that of sister is in the abstract. *Umna watŭ*, " elder brother of us," *watŭ* being the pronoun; *umnawa wamu*, " younger brother of me;" *udada watŭ*, " sister of us," whether elder or younger. The near approach of this form to the Hawaiian will be noticed. The fraternal and sororal relationships have not been treated as indicative, although in many respects they deserve this distinction. Beside these there is a term in the abstract for brother, *abäfo*, which with *udada*, are also applied to collateral brothers and sisters.

In the first collateral line, and irrespective of the sex of *Ego*, the children of my brother, and the children of my sister are my sons and daughters, and the children of the latter are my grandchildren.

In the second, my father's brother is my father, *ubäbäkaze*, instead of *ubäbä*, but the addition of the particle, *aze*, does not change the signification of the term; his children are my brothers and sisters; the children of the latter are my sons and daughters, and their children are my grandchildren. My father's sister is my *father*, *ubäbä*, instead of my mother, *umäme*. No explanation is given of this singular use of the term. It is probably used in the sense of *parent*. Her children are my brothers and sisters, the children of the latter are my sons and daughters, and their children are my grandchildren.

My mother's brother is my uncle, *umälŭma*, but he calls me his son. The relationship, therefore, is not reciprocal, and it raises a presumption that the relationship originally was that of father. His children are each my cousins, *umzäla*, but they call me brother. Here again the relationship is not reciprocal, and it leads to the same inference. The children of these cousins are my sons and daughters, and their children are my grandchildren. My mother's sister is my mother, her children are my brothers and sisters, the children of the latter are my sons and daughters, and their children are my grandchildren.

The wives and husbands of my several collateral sons and daughters are my daughters-in-law and my sons-in-law; the wives of my several collateral brothers, and of my several male cousins are my wives, and the husbands of my several collateral sister, and of my several female cousins are my brothers-in-law.

The third collateral line, in its four branches, is a counterpart of the second, with the exception of one additional ancestor. It will be sufficient to give the series in one branch. My father's father's brother is my grandfather, his son is my father, his children are my brothers and sisters, the children of the latter are my sons and daughters, and their children are my grandchildren.

It thus appears that the Amazulu system of relationship is clearly defined as well

---

= my father's father's son = my father's brother = my father = *rebäbä*; and that my mother's mother's brother's son = my mother's mother's son = my mother's brother = *umäluma*, my uncle.

" Many of the proper terms of relationship are not used in common conversation. A man calls his wife *comtäname*, my child, or he may call her 'mother of his child,' or 'child of her father.' So also a woman calls her husband by the name of her child; father of ——. We have *boy* instead of *son*; *girl* instead of *daughter*. We often hear *umtänä ka bäbä*, child of my father, *i. e.*, father's brother; *umtänä wodäda wäbo kä bäbä* = child of the sister of my father."

as fully developed, and that in its principles and structure it is in radical agreement with the Malayan. This fact is immensely significant, if identity of systems proves unity of origin. It suggests the possibility that the ancestors of the Kafirs and of the Hawaiians, once an Eastern Asiatic stock, had divided into branches, one of which ventured upon the ocean and became spread over the Polynesian Islands, whilst the other, holding to continental life, had, through the exigencies and migrations of the centuries, finally reached the southern confines of the African continent. Such a supposition is not improbable in view of what must necessarily have been the rapid spread of mankind in the fisherman age.

With the Amazulu system the examination of the schedules contained in the Tables is concluded. The contents of these Tables have by no means been exhausted, although the more important characteristics of each particular form have been brought into notice. It has been a tedious and unattractive labor to follow the course of these time-worn forms of consanguinity and affinity through so many nations; and yet, without an investigation and comparison of the details and structure of the system of the several families of mankind, as it now exists in the largest number of nations capable of being reached, it was impossible to secure comprehensive results. The investigation has brought to light a mass of singular and suggestive facts relating to the oldest existing domestic institution of mankind. It also illustrates, in a forcible manner, the power of ideas and conceptions to perpetuate themselves long after the causes which produced them have disappeared by becoming incorporated with our primary necessities, and thus acquiring possession, for their transmission, of the channels of the blood.

It now remains to gather up and bring together the final results of a comparison of these forms, to test the validity of these results, and to indicate some of the conclusions which they appear to authorize.

CHAPTER VI.

GENERAL RESULTS.

General Results considered in a Series of Propositions—Two Radically Distinct Forms, the Descriptive and the Classificatory—Peculiarities of each—Both Domestic Institutions—The Descriptive System is explicable from the Nature of Descents upon the Assumption of the Existence of Marriage between Single Pairs—Classificatory not so Explicable—Causes which might be supposed to have influenced the formation of the Latter—Uses of the Bond of Kin for Mutual Protection—Influence of the Tribal Relationships—Of Polygamy and Polyandria—Insufficient separately or collectively to account for the Origin of the System—Series of Customs and Institutions the assumed Existence of which will explain the Origin of the Classificatory System from the Nature of Descents. 1. Promiscuous Intercourse—2. The Intermarriage or Cohabitation of Brothers and Sisters—3. The Communal Family—4. The Hawaiian Custom—These explain the Origin of the Malayan System from the Nature of Descents—5. The Tribal Organization ; breaking up the Cohabitation of Brothers and Sisters—This explains the Origin of the Remainder, or Turanian portion of the System—6. Marriage between Single Pairs—7. Polygamy—8. The Patriarchal Family—9. Polyandria—10. Rise of Property with the Establishment of Lineal Succession to Estates—11. The Civilized Family—12. Overthrow of the Classificatory System, and Substitution of the Descriptive—Evidence from the System of the Unity of Origin of the American Indian Nations—Evidence of Its Transmission with the Blood—Stability of Its Radical Forms—Coeval with the first Appearance of the Ganowánian Family upon the American Continent—Turanian Family organized upon the Basis of the same System—Systems of the Turanian and Ganowánian Families Identical—Evidence from this Source of the Asiatic Origin of the Ganowánian Family—But Four Ways of accounting for this Identity—By borrowing from each other—By Accidental Invention in Disconnected Areas—By Spontaneous Growth in like Areas—By Transmission with the Blood from a Common Source—First Three Hypotheses incapable of explaining the Facts—Reasons which appear to render the Fourth sufficient—Adequacy of this Channel of Transmission—Stability of the Radical Features of the System—Verification of its Mode of Propagation—Final Inference of the Asiatic Origin of the Ganowánian Family—Malayan System not Derivable from the Turanian—Latter might have been Engrafted upon the Former—Malayan the Older Form—But Malayan Family not necessarily the Oldest—Malayan the Original System of the Turanian Family—Its Turanian Element introduced after the Malayan Migration—Ganowánian Family probably derived from the Turanian after the Separation of the Malayan—The Ganowánian consequently the Youngest of the three Families—Eskimo System—Mongolian and Tungusian Systems not in the Tables—Probability that the Eskimo will affiliate with one of them.

THE systems of consanguinity and affinity of six of the great families of mankind, the Aryan, Semitic, and Uralian, the Ganowánian, Turanian, and Malayan have now been presented, together with a series of Tables illustrative of the forms of each. In these Tables all of the principal, and many of the inferior nations of the earth are represented. They contain the systems of relationship of eighttenths and upwards, numerically, of the entire human family. And notwithstanding the absence of the Mongolian, Tungusian, Australian and Negroid nations, the materials which they contain are sufficient to determine the nature and objects of systems of relationship, considered as domestic institutions, the mode of their propagation, and their ultimate uses for ethnological purposes.

In order to develop the general results which are derived from an investigation of these several forms of consanguinity and affinity, and from their comparison with each other, the following series of propositions will be considered: First. How many systems of relationship, radically distinct from each other, exist amongst the nations represented in the Tables? Secondly. Whether or not their several forms rest upon and embody clearly-defined ideas and principles, and contain the essential qualities of a domestic institution.   Thirdly.   Whether or not the origin of the descriptive system can be accounted for and explained from the nature of descents, and upon the principle of natural suggestion, on the assumption of the existence of the state of marriage between single pairs.   Fourthly.   Whether or not the origin of the classificatory system can be accounted for and explained from the nature of descents and upon the principle of natural suggestion, on the assumption of the existence of a series of customs and institutions antecedent to the state of marriage between single pairs, of which the Hawaiian custom is one.   Fifthly. Whether or not the present existence of such a system as that found amongst the American Indian nations furnishes, in itself, conclusive evidence that it was derived by each and all from a common source; and, therefore, that the nations themselves are of common origin; or, in other words, whether the genealogical connection of certain nations may be inferred from the fact of their joint possession of this particular system of relationship, the radical characteristics of which are found to be constant and identical amongst them all.   Sixthly.   Whether or not the genealogical connection of two or more families, separately constituted upon the basis of such a system, may be inferred from their joint possession of the same, when these families are found in disconnected areas.   And lastly.   When the forms which prevail in different families are to a limited extent radically the same, whether any, and what, inference may be drawn from this partial identity.   Upon these several propositions, which are believed to comprehend the material facts contained in the Tables, some observations will be submitted, as a proper conclusion to this investigation.

I.) How many systems of consanguinity and affinity, radically distinct from each other, do the Tables present?

In a general sense there are but two, the *descriptive* and the *classificatory*.   Of the first, the Celtic, and of the second, the Seneca-Iroquois is an example.   They rest upon conceptions fundamentally different, and are separated from each other by a line so clearly defined as to admit of no misapprehension.   In the first, which is the form of the Aryan, Semitic, and Uralian families, consanguinei are, in the main, described by a combination of the primary terms of relationship, the collateral lines are maintained distinct and divergent from the lineal, and the few special terms employed are restricted to particular persons, and to those nearest in degree.   The generalizations of kindred into classes, with special terms to express the relationships, are few in number, were an aftergrowth in point of time, and are exceptional in the system.   These facts have been shown in previous chapters. The original system of these families, or rather their present system in its origin, was purely descriptive, as it appears from the Sanskritic when it ceased to be a living form, and as it is still exemplified by the Celtic and the Scandinavian forms in the Aryan family, by the Arabic in the Semitic family, and by the Esthonian in the Uralian.   As a system it is based upon a true and logical appreciation of the natural outflow of the streams of the blood, of the distinctiveness and perpetual divergence of these several streams, and of the difference in degree, numerically, and by lines of descent, of the relationship of each and every person to the central *Ego*. It is, therefore, a natural system, founded upon the nature of descents, and may be supposed to have been of spontaneous growth. But it manifestly proceeds upon the assumption of the existence of marriage between single pairs, and of the certainty of parentage through this marriage relation. Hence it must have come into existence after the establishment of marriage between single pairs.

The systems of relationship of these families are identical. There are some discrepancies in the several forms in each family, but the character and extent of the coincidences are such as to leave no doubt that in general plan and in fundamental conceptions the system is one and the same amongst them all. The Celtic, the Scandinavian, and the Sanskritic forms are in closer agreement with the Arabic and the Esthonian than they are with the Romaic the Germanic or the Slavonic, whilst all alike proceed upon the idea of a rigorous discrimination of the degrees of consanguinity according to their value, and in maintaining the natural distinctions between the several lines of descent.

Whether the possession of the same system furnishes any evidence of the unity of origin of these families, and to what extent it may be supposed to have a bearing upon this question, it is not necessary here to inquire, as it is not proposed to draw any inference as to these families from this identity of forms. It may be remarked, however, that if the system is to be regarded as exclusively natural and spontaneous, the argument for unity of origin would be without force; since, as such, it would be the form to which all nations must insensibly gravitate under the exercise of ordinary intelligence. But if to reach the descriptive system these families have struggled out of a previous system, altogether different, through a series of customs and institutions which existed antecedently to the attainment of the state of marriage between single pairs, then it becomes a result, or ultimate consequence of customs and institutions of man's invention, rather than a system taught by nature. The evidence drawn from the classificatory system tends to show that marriage between single pairs was unknown in the primitive ages of mankind. If this conclusion is sustained, a strong presumption arises that these families once possessed the classificatory system, and that it was overthrown by the progressive development of their institutions. Considered in this light it is the institution of marriage between single pairs which teaches the descriptive system of relationship; whilst this form of marriage has been taught by nature through the slow growth of the experience of ages. In the second place the adoption and maintenance of the descriptive system required both intelligence and discernment which endowed it with affirmative elements. The joint possession of the same system by the three families implies a similar antecedent condition, and a similar progressive experience, which cannot be divested of a deep significance. Moreover the preservation of this form for so many centuries, through so many independent channels, and under such eventful changes of condition, is, in itself, a remarkable fact. It is now, and has been for ages, a transmitted system. It is not at all improbable that marriage in its high sense was the culminating institution by means of which these families emerged from barbarism, and commenced their civilized career.

On the other hand, the classificatory system contains one principal and one subordinate form, which are separate stages of growth of the same system; and a third form which differs from both.   In the Turanian and Ganowánian families is found the principal or highest form in full and perfect development, whilst in the Malayan the same system is recognized in a lower stage.   The Eskimo represents the third. The three forms are distinct and independent of each other, although the first two stand to each other in intimate relations.   As complicated and apparently artificial systems they are capable of delivering decisive testimony concerning the ethnic connection of the nations by whom they are severally possessed.   Under the classificatory system consanguinei are not described by a combination of the primary terms, but each and all, however remote in degree, fall under some one of the recognized relationships.   The *gradus* yields to the *nexus*.   By comprehensive, as well as apparently arbitrary, generalizations they are reduced to great classes or categories, the members of each of which, irrespective of nearness or remoteness in-degree, are placed upon the same level, and admitted into the same relationship. In this manner, if marriage existed between single pairs, persons whose relationships would be obviously dissimilar are confounded together.   In the next place, persons who would stand in the same degree of nearness are placed in different relationships by a generalization true to the nature of descents as to one, and false as to the other, in consequence of which those who should be classed together are separated from each other; and lastly, the several collateral lines are ultimately merged in the lineal line, by means of which the otherwise natural outflow of the streams of the blood is arrested, and diverted from several channels into a single stream.   The classificatory system becomes, in these several particulars, arbitrary, artificial and complicated.

When it is considered that the domestic relationships of the entire human family, so far as the latter is represented in the Tables, fall under the descriptive or the classificatory form, and that they are the reverse of each other in their fundamental conceptions, it furnishes a significant separation of the families of mankind into two great divisions.   Upon one side are the Aryan Semitic and Uralian, and upon the other the Ganowánian the Turanian and the Malayan, which gives nearly the line of demarcation between the civilized and uncivilized nations.   Although both forms are older than civilization, it tends to show that the family, as now constituted, and which grew out of the development of a knowledge of property, of its uses, and of its transmission by inheritance, lies at the foundation of the first civilization of mankind.   Whilst the division introduces no new barriers between the recognized families, it tends to draw nearer together the members of each division.

II.   Do these systems of relationship rest upon and embody clearly defined ideas and principles; and do they contain the essential requisites of a domestic institution?

Some method of distinguishing the different degrees of consanguinity is an absolute necessity for the daily purposes of life.   The invention of terms to express the primary relationships, namely, those for father and mother, brother and sister, son and daughter, and husband and wife, would probably be one of the earliest acts of human speech.   With these terms all of the remaining relatives, both by blood and marriage, may be described by using the possessive case of the several terms. The Erse and Gaelic systems were never carried beyond this stage. After a descriptive system was adopted it would have a form, a method of distinguishing relatives one from another, and, as a consequence, an arrangement of kindred into lines of descent. The application of this method involves a series of conceptions which become, at the same time, clothed with definite forms. If this simple plan of consanguinity became permanently introduced into practical use, its transmission, through a few generations, would convert it into an indurated system capable of resisting radical innovations. The Erse and Gaelic are illustrations in point. The ideas embodied are few in number, but their association in fixed relations creates a system, as well as organizes a family. In its connection with the family, and in its structure as a system, its power of self-perpetuation resides. By these considerations it is raised to the rank of a domestic institution.

The invention of terms for collateral relationships must of necessity have been extremely difficult under the descriptive system. This is shown by the present condition of these forms in the several Aryan and Semitic nations, none of which developed their system far beyond the Erse. In process of time the relationship of paternal and maternal *uncle* and *aunt* might be turned from the descriptive into the concrete form by the invention of special terms, making each of the four distinct. This is the extent of the advance made in the Arabic and Hebraic forms. The discrimination of the relationships of *nephew* and *niece* in the concrete would be still more difficult, since it involves a generalization of the children of an individual's brothers and sisters into one class, and the turning of two descriptive phrases into a single concrete term with a masculine and feminine form. These relationships, as now used, were reached among such of the Aryan nations as possess them within the modern period. That of *cousin* was still more difficult of attainment, as it involved a generalization of four different classes of persons into a single class, and the invention of a term to express it in the concrete. Amongst the nations of the Aryan family the Roman and the German alone reached this, the ultimate stage of the system. Such of the remaining nations as possess this relationship borrowed it, with the term, from the Roman source; and it is probable that the Germans derived the conception from the same quarter, although their term was indigenous in the German speech. These terms were designed to relieve the inconvenience of the descriptive method as far as they applied. In so far as they were founded upon generalizations they failed, with some exceptions, to indicate with accuracy the manner of the relationships; whence it became necessary to resort to explanatory words, or to the descriptive method, to be specific. These considerations tend still further to show the stability of the system as a domestic institution, although the ideas which it embodies are limited in number.

In marked contrast with the *descriptive* is the *classificatory* system, which is complex in its structure, elaborate in its discriminations, and opulent in its nomenclature. A very different and more striking series of ideas and principles here present themselves, without any existing causes adequate for their interpretation or explanation. With marriage between single pairs, with the family in a modified sense, with the tribal organization still unimpaired in certain nations and abandoned in others, with polygamy polyandria and the Hawaiian custom either unknown or of limited practice, and with promiscuous intercourse substantially eradicated, the classificatory system of relationship still exists in full vigor in a large portion of the human family, ages upon ages after the sequence of customs and institutions in which it apparently originated have ceased to exercise any influence upon its form or upon its preservation. This system as it now stands is seen to magnify the bond of consanguinity into stupendous proportions, and to use it as an organic instrument for the formation of a communal family upon the broadest scale of numbers. Differences in the degree of nearness are made to yield to the overmastering strength of the kindred tie. Its generalizations traverse the natural lines of descent, as they now exist through the marriage of single pairs, disregard equalities in the degree of nearness of related persons, and create relationships in contravention of those actually existing. There are upwards of twenty of these particulars, each of which develops a distinct idea, all uniting in the formation of a coherent intelligible and systematic plan of consanguinity. From the excessive and intricate specializations embodied in the system it might be considered difficult of practical use; but it is not the least singular of its characteristics that it is complicated without obscurity, diversified without confusion, and understood and applied with the utmost facility. With such a number of distinct ideas associated together in definite relations, a system has been created which must be regarded as a domestic institution in the highest sense of this expression. No other can properly characterize a structure the framework of which is so complete, and the details of which are so rigorously adjusted.

III. Can the origin of the *descriptive system* be accounted for and explained from the nature of descents, and upon the principle of natural suggestion, on the assumption of the existence of the state of marriage between single pairs?

Natural suggestions are those which arise spontaneously in the mind with the exercise of ordinary intelligence. As suggestions from nature they might spring from internal sources or from the subject; from external sources or from the object; or from both united.

In the formation of a plan of consanguinity reflection upon the nature of descents, where society recognized the marriage relation, would reveal the method of nature in evolving generations of mankind from common ancestors, through a series of marriages, and thus develop the suggestions of nature from the subject. On the other hand, the uses of a system, when formed, would reach outward upon the condition and wants of society and induce reflection upon the objects to be gained. Whatever deliverances may thus be supposed to come from the voice of nature they are necessarily uniform in all time and to all men, the conditions of society being similar.[1]

---

[1] The phrase, "similar conditions of society," which has become technical, is at least extremely vague. It is by no means easy to conceive of two peoples, in disconnected areas, living in conditions precisely similar. The means of subsistence would vary, and this would create diversity in the mode of life. But we may regard the condition of agricultural nations as similar, as well as that of pastoral nations; and going back of these, the same may be said of such nations as subsist by fishing and hunting. Their domestic institutions, however, might be materially different. It is only in the

The descriptive and the classificatory systems of relationship cannot both be explained from the nature of descents, and as arising by natural suggestion, if a similar condition of society is assumed to have existed at the time of their formation. The same argument which proved one of them to be true to the nature of descents would demonstrate the untruthfulness of the other. And yet there are grounds for believing that both can be explained from the nature of descents by recognizing, not improbable, conditions of society suggestive of their respective forms. If they can be thus explained, the two systems will rise into striking prominence as domestic institutions, since they will be found to represent and embody the vast and varied experience of mankind through the unrecorded ages of barbarism.

The descriptive system can be readily shown to be in accordance with the nature of descents, as they now exist, with marriage between single pairs. The very method by which the generations of mankind are reproduced, through marriage, creates a lineal line consisting of such persons as are derived immediately one from the other, proceeding from parent to child, in an infinite series. Each person in this line becomes in turn the centre of a group of kindred, the stationary *Ego*, who represents and sustains to his lineal and collateral kindred, at one and the same time, every relationship which can possibly exist. Out of the lineal line emerge the several collateral lines, one beyond the other, each consisting of branches. The first consists of the brothers and sisters of *Ego* and their descendants; the second of the brothers and sisters of the father, and of the brothers and sisters of the mother of *Ego*, and of their respective descendants; and beyond these there are as many other collateral lines as there are ancestors of *Ego*; each leaving brothers and sisters and descendants. It is thus made obvious that consanguinei are bound together in virtue of their descent from common ancestors; and that the manner of the relationship can be expressed by ascending from *Ego* to the common ancestor, counting each person a degree, and then by descending, in the same manner through the collateral line, to the person whose relationship is sought. The descriptions of persons thus made produce the descriptive system of relationship. It also indicates a numerical system founded upon the units of separation between *Ego* and his several kinsmen. A classification of consanguinei, into lineal and collateral lines, is thus taught from the nature of descents, as well as the perpetual divergence of the latter from the former; followed by a decrease in the value of the relationship of each person as he recedes from *Ego*. A system both numerical and descriptive thus arises from marriage between single pairs which nature may be said to teach to mankind with unerring certainty. It gives a classification of persons into lines, with an indication of the value of each relationship in numerical degrees; but no classification of persons into grades, with an indication of the relationship of each in the abstract. The discrimination of collateral relationships in the

---

most general sense that nations can be said to live in similar conditions of society; thus, the stone age, which antedates agriculture and the possession of domestic animals, necessitated and developed a mode of life which led to the simultaneous invention, in disconnected areas, of similar implements and contrivances to answer similar wants. In this comprehensive sense, the one in which the phrase is used, two peoples may be said to live in similar conditions of society.

concrete was the growth of experience. It has been seen that such special terms as were subsequently brought into use were employed in accordance with the principles of the descriptive system. The truth of the general proposition is so far manifest that it does not require further discussion except to remark, that the adoption and maintenance of this system required an exercise of intelligence. It seems probable, also, that marriage between single pairs and the descriptive system of relationship had become established institutions in the Aryan and Semitic families prior to or simultaneous with the commencement of the civilization of their several branches. Neither is it improbable that in the preceding ages of barbarism they possessed a classificatory system.

IV. Can the origin of the classificatory system be accounted for, and explained from the nature of descents, upon the assumption of the existence of a series of customs and institutions antecedent to a state of marriage between single pairs, of which the Hawaiian custom is one?

It is perfectly evident that the origin of the classificatory system cannot be explained from the nature of descents as they now exist amongst civilized nations. And yet a state of society might have existed in the primitive ages, and might exist at the present time, in which this system would be in strict accordance with the nature of descents, and explainable as the product of natural suggestion. It is for this reason, among others, that it becomes important to inquire whether in any portion of uncivilized society, as now organized, there are at present operating causes adequate to the production and therefore to the constant reproduction of this remarkable system of relationship; and secondly, if no such causes are now found to exist, whether its origin can be explained by any supposable antecedent condition of society, however contrary that condition may be to our conceptions of the early state of mankind. Should the first hypothesis become established, the possession of this system by different nations of the same family would lose much of its significance, since it might have sprung up spontaneously in each under the operating force of these causes. On the other hand, should the last hypothesis be sustained it must be treated as a transmitted system from the earliest epoch of its complete establishment, and its origin would be contemporaneous with the introduction of the customs, or the birth of the institutions, from which it sprung. A presumption would arise, from the fact of its possession by different nations of the same family, that it was derived by each from a common source; and a like presumption where it was found in different families; provided the system could be shown to be stable in its forms, and capable of self-perpetuation. That such causes do not now exist will be made to appear in the discussion of the second hypothesis, which will supersede the necessity of considering the first.

There are two external causes which might be supposed to have exercised some influence upon the formation of the system, the bearing of which should be considered before those are taken up which spring from the nature of descents. These are the uses of the bond of kin for mutual protection, and the tribal organization.

In the primitive ages the uses of the blood tie for the mutual protection of related persons could not fail to arrest attention, and to rise to pre-eminent importance. It would be more natural to intrust personal rights to the protection of near kindred, than to the community at large ; whence, the larger the circle of blood relatives the greater the assurance of safety. A more cordial recognition of collateral consanguinei would be expected to prevail in such a state of society than in civilized communities, where the law or the state is the source of protection. Whilst it is certain that the system does preserve the relationships of remote consanguinei by bringing them within the near degrees, thus making the kindred tie more authoritative than the divergence of descents, it does not follow that relationships would be created in the system which found no sanction in the nature of descents. And finally, since these considerations would neither suggest this particular plan of consanguinity, nor any definite plan, they are rather results of the system, than operative causes in its production.

The tribal organization stands in a much nearer connection with this system of relationship. This organized form of society has existed in all ages, and amongst the greater portion of the nations of mankind in the early periods of their history. It prevails at the present time, to a greater or less extent, amongst the uncivilized nations of Asia, Africa, and America. Within the historical period it has been found so wide spread as to leave no doubt whatever that it is one of the oldest institutions of the human family. In a general sense a tribe is a group of consanguinei, not including all of the descendants of a supposed original ancestor, but usually such only as are embraced within the line through which descent is reckoned. If descent is limited to the male line, then it is composed of the children of a supposed male ancestor, and his descendants in the male line forever. It would include the sons and daughters of this ancestor, the children of his sons ; and all the children of his lineal male descendants. The children of the males only belong to the tribe, whilst the children of the females would be transferred to the tribe of their respective fathers. In like manner, when descent is limited to the female line, the tribe would consist of a supposed female ancestor, and her descendants in the female line forever. It would include the children of this ancestor, the children of her daughters, and all the children of her lineal female descendants ; the children of the females only belonging to the tribe, whilst the children of the males would be transferred to the tribe of their respective mothers. These results were produced by the prohibition of intermarriage in the tribe, and by assigning the children to the tribe of the father, or to the tribe of the mother, as descent was in the male or in the female line. The last two characteristics of the tribal organization were fundamental. Modified forms of the tribe, as thus explained, may have existed, but this is the substance of the institution. Other incidents pertaining to the tribe have elsewhere (*supra*, page 139) been explained.

Inasmuch as the tribal organization is founded upon consanguinity, and furthermore, since all the members of a tribe are, theoretically, brothers and sisters to each other it might seem probable that it had exercised some influence upon the formation of the classificatory system of relationship. To show how the fact is the tribal relationships must be placed by the side of those established by the system of consanguinity, in doing which the illustrations will be drawn from the tribes and system of the Seneca-Iroquois. Two sisters and their children are of the same tribe, and these children are brothers and sisters to each other in virtue of their common tribal name. They are also brothers and sisters under this system of relationship. It is at least a plausible supposition that the tribal connection, superadded to their nearness of kin as the children of sisters, might have suggested the relationship of brother and sister as eminently proper, and thus have laid the foundation of one of the indicative features of the system. The same thought developed a step further might, from analogy, establish the two sisters in the relation of a mother to each other's children, which would give a second indicative feature of the system. But these influences are set aside by running the parallel in other cases. Thus two brothers, born of the same mother, are of the same tribe; but since they must marry out of the tribe, and since descent is in the female line, their children are of a different tribe from themselves, and seven chances out of eight of two different tribes, each differing from their own, and yet their children who are not tribal brothers and sisters are such under the system. If the principle of the tribal connection suggested these relationships in the former case, it would, for the want of that connection, forbid it in the latter. Again, *Ego* being a female, my sister's son is my son; we are also both of the same tribe, whilst my brother's son, who is not of my tribe, is placed in the more remote relationship of nephew. Conformity with the tribal connection is here preserved. But on the other hand, with *Ego* a male, my brother's son is my son, although he is not of my tribe, whilst my sister's son, who is of my tribe, stands in the more remote relationship of nephew. Conformity with the tribal organization is here disregarded. To the same effect it may be added that my father's brother, who is not of my tribe, is my father; whilst my mother's brother, who is of my tribe, is placed in the more remote relationship of uncle. Contrariwise, my father's sister, who is not of my tribe, is my aunt; whilst my mother's sister, who is of my tribe, is my mother. It thus appears when the tribal relationships are run parallel with those established by the system that the former traverse the latter quite as frequently as they affirm the connection. This will be found to be the case throughout the entire range of the system. In some Indian nations descent is in the male line, in which cases the tribal relationships, as above given, would be reversed; in still others it does not now exist, and yet the same system of relationship prevails amongst them all alike, irrespective of the existence or non-existence of the tribal organization, and whether descent is in the male or female line. There is, however, another aspect of the case in which this tribal organization, as one of a series of institutions affecting the conditions of society, may have exercised a decisive influence upon the formation of the classificatory system. This will be considered in another connection.

Among existing customs which touch the domestic relationships, and thus become sources of influence upon the system, are polygamy and polyandria. They are incapable of explaining, from the nature of descents, the origin of the classificatory system as a whole; but they seem to afford an explanation of one or more of its indicative features. Inasmuch as polygamy has prevailed, more or less, amongst the principal nations of mankind in the early periods of their history, and since it is an existing custom in a large number of nations at the present time, the nature and limits of its influence must be ascertained before other causes of the origin of the system are sought; and it is further important in order to show that the true causes must be found in a state of society which existed antecedently to the introduction of both polygamy and polyandria. Polygamy may claim the position of a domestic institution. In its highest and regulated form it presupposes a considerable advance of society, together with the development of superior and inferior classes, and of some kinds of wealth. The means of subsistence must have become enlarged as well as stable, and individual ownership of property recognized, before a single person would be able to maintain more than one household, or several sets of children by several different mothers. In its high form it must have been limited to the privileged few, whilst the mass of the people were debarred, by poverty, from its practice. In a lower and unregulated form it has probably prevailed from a very early period in man's history. Polyandria, on the other hand, is scarcely entitled to the rank of a domestic institution. It is an excrescence of polygamy, and its repulsive converse. Traces of it have been found in many polygamous nations in various parts of Asia, in Africa, and, according to Hearne and Humboldt, in occasional instances in North and South America. The countries in which it has prevailed most extensively, as is well known, are Thibet, and the Nilgherry Hills of South India. It presupposes either a scarcity of unappropriated females, or of the means of subsistence, or of both together. The Thibetan polyandria, where several brothers possess one wife in common, is the highest form of the usage; and the lowest, that in the Nilgherry Hills, where several unrelated persons possess one wife in common. There are no reasons for supposing that the mass of the people in any country were involved in the practice of these customs, after polygamy had become a settled usage, although their joint existence in a particular nation would be a most unfavorable indication of the condition of the remainder of the people. There is no evidence that polyandria was ever an established practice of the American aborigines. On the contrary there are reasons which render its practice improbable. The females are usually more numerous than the males from the destruction of the latter in war.[1] Polygamy has prevailed among them very generally, and is still practised; but it is under a permanent check amongst the greater portion of the people from the inability of an individual to support more than one set of children. Consequently throughout this family there never has been a necessity for the practice of polyandria.

With respect to the influence of general polygamy upon the formation of the system it is very slight; but there is a special form of this usage existing in theory, and to some extent in practice, in the Ganowánian family, which reaches some of the domestic relationships. It embraces all of the influence of general polygamy, and also reaches beyond it. When a man marries the eldest daughter he becomes, by that act, entitled to each and all of her sisters as wives when they severally attain the marriageable age. The option rests with him, and he may enforce the

---

[1] In some nations, as the Blackfoot and the Shiyann, they are said to be two to one.

claim, or yield it to another.[1] Taking such a case of polygamy as an illustration, the children of sisters thus married would naturally apply to each other the full terms for brother and sister. They are own brothers and sisters with respect to their father, and half-brothers and half-sisters with respect to the wives of their father, one of whom is their mother. This might explain one of the most important indicative features of the system. Advancing a step beyond this, the children of one sister might apply the term mother to each sister of their mother, although the true relationship is neither that of mother, nor strictly that of step-mother, since the own mother is still living. Assuming this to have occurred, it would give a second indicative feature. For the same reason it might be supposed that the several sisters would call each other's children their sons and daughters, which would explain the origin of half of a third indicative feature. Here the influence of this form of polygamy, which may or may not have existed in other families of mankind, terminates. Turning next to the Thibetan form of polyandria, where several brothers have children by a common wife, these children would necessarily call themselves brothers and sisters, first because they are such with respect to their mother, and, secondly, because with respect to the several brothers who are the husbands of their mother, it would be unknown which of them was their father. This would explain the probable origin of a fourth indicative relationship. Again, these children would call the several husbands of their mother indiscriminately fathers. If they so called either one, then all would receive the appellation. For the same reasons the several brothers would call these children their sons and daughters without distinction, thus explaining a fifth and sixth indicative relationship, as well as a seventh and eighth with more or less distinctness, namely, that the children of these children would be called grandchildren by each of these brothers, and be called grandfathers in return. Here the influence of polyandria ceases. It will be seen that these special forms of polygamy and polyandria approach the system very closely, and tend to render it explainable as a natural system drawn from the nature of descents as they actually existed at the time the system was formed. But it must be remembered, first, that these relationships are the same in the Malayan, Turanian, and Ganowánian forms; secondly, that they are not indicative relationships in the Malayan system; and thirdly, that they become such in the latter by virtue of the remaining indicative relationships, which polygamy and polyandria are incapable of explaining. Why my mother's brother is my uncle, my father's sister is my aunt, my sister's son and daughter, *Ego* a male, are my nephew and niece, and why the children of this uncle and aunt are placed in the more remote relationship of cousin, still remain unexplained. At the same time, it is to these relationships that the Ganowánian and Turanian systems are indebted for their striking characteristics. But there is another and a general objection to the sufficiency of these customs to explain the origin of those parts of the system first above named. It is their restriction in practice to a small portion of the people. The number of children of sisters, and also of brothers, in

[1] I have found this practice among the Shyannes, Omahas, Iowas, Kaws, Osages, Blackfeet, Crees, Minnitarees, Crows, and several other nations.

every nation unaffected by these customs would far outnumber, in any event, those included within their operation. In other words the reasons for these relationships, which should be as universal as their adoption, would fail for want of universality. If these forms of polygamy and polyandria suggested the relationships named in a certain number of cases, the reasons for them would fail in a much larger number of other cases in the same community, and thus the chances would preponderate against their adoption.

This view of the possible influence of these customs upon the formation of certain parts of the classificatory system is as important as it is significant. It shows that we are drawing near to the causes from which it originated, and an increasing probability that it sprung, by organic growth, from the nature of descents as they actually existed. I think it will appear in the sequel, that whilst its origin antedates the first existence of these customs in the primitive nations of mankind, the latter have contributed materially to the perpetuation of the system, through the intervening ages, by means of the principles which polygamy and polyandria have tended to preserve.

I propose now to take up the Malayan system of relationship, as the earliest stage of the classificatory, and to submit a conjectural solution of its origin. This solution will be founded upon the Hawaiian custom,[1] and upon the assumption of the existence of antecedent promiscuous intercourse, involving the cohabitation of brothers and sisters. After this I shall present a further conjectural solution of the origin of the remainder, or Turanian portion of the system, upon the basis of the tribal organization. These solutions will render necessary an assumption of the existence and general prevalence of a series of customs and institutions which sprang up at intervals along the pathway of man's experience, and which must of necessity have preceded a knowledge of marriage between single pairs, and of the family itself, in the modern sense of the term; but which led, step by step, as so many organic movements of society, to the realization of the latter. Mankind, if one in origin, must have become subdivided at a very early period into independent nations. Unequal progress has been made by their descendants from that day to the present; some of them still remaining in a condition not far removed from the primitive, and now revealing many of the intervening stages of progress. It must be supposed, therefore, that these customs and institutions, taken as a complete series or sequence, must have been of slow growth, and of still slower diffusion amongst the nations, as they progressed in experience; and that they are but the great remaining landmarks of this experience, whilst the mass of minor influences which contributed to their adoption have fallen out of knowledge. This series, originating in the order named, and brought down to an epoch long subsequent to the complete establishment of the classificatory system, may be stated as follows:—

---

[1] I am indebted to my learned friend, Rev. Dr. J. H. McIlvaine, Prof. of Political Science in the College of New Jersey, for the suggestion of a probable solution of the origin of the classificatory system upon the basis of the Hawaiian custom.

I. Promiscuous Intercourse.

II. The Intermarriage or Cohabitation of Brothers and Sisters.

III. The Communal Family.   (First Stage of the Family.)

IV. The Hawaiian Custom.   Giving

V. The Malayan form of the Classificatory System of Relationship.

VI. The Tribal Organization.   Giving

VII. The Turanian and Ganowánian System of Relationship.

VIII. Marriage between Single Pairs.   Giving

IX. The Barbarian Family.   (Second Stage of the Family.)

X. Polygamy.   Giving

XI. The Patriarchal Family.   (Third Stage of the Family.)

XII. Polyandria.

XIII. The Rise of Property with the Settlement of Lineal Succession to Estates. Giving

XIV. The Civilized Family.   (Fourth and Ultimate Stage of the Family.)   Producing.

XV. The Overthrow of the Classificatory System of Relationship, and the Substitution of the Descriptive.

The first four customs and institutions being given, the origin of the Malayan system can be demonstrated from the nature of descents, and the several relationships shown to be those actually existing.   In like manner the first six being given (although IV. is not material), the origin of the Turanian system can be explained on the principle of natural suggestion, and the relationships proved to be in accordance with the nature of descents.   Whether, given the Turanian system of relationship, the antecedent existence of these customs and institutions can be legitimately inferred, will depend upon the probability of their prevalence, from the nature of human society, and from what is known of its previous conditions.   It may be confidently affirmed that this great sequence of customs and institutions, although for the present hypothetical, will organize and explain the body of ascertained facts, with respect to the primitive history of mankind, in a manner so singularly and surprisingly adequate as to invest it with a strong probability of truth.

Although the universal prevalence of promiscuous intercourse in the primitive ages, involving the cohabitation of brothers and sisters as its most common form, rests, for the present, upon an assumption, evidence is not wanting in many barbarous nations of such a previous condition.   In several civilized nations the intermarriage of brother and sister continued long after civilization had supervened upon barbarism.   Without multiplying cases, one of the Herods was married to his sister, and Cleopatra was married to her brother.   Even these modern cases are more satisfactorily explained as the remains, as well as the evidence, of an ancient custom, than as a lapsed condition of private morals.

The Hawaiian custom is neither a matter of conjecture nor of assumption. Traces of its prevalence were found by the American missionaries in the Sandwich Islands when they established their missions, and its antecedent universal prevalence amongst this people is unquestionable.   This custom, which has elsewhere (*supra*, page 453, note) been explained, is a compound form of polygynia and polyandria, since under one of its branches the several brothers live in polygynia, and their wives in polyandria; and under the other, the several sisters live in polyandria, and their husbands in polygynia. In other words, it is promiscuous intercourse within prescribed limits. The existence of this custom necessarily implies an antecedent condition of promiscuous intercourse, involving the cohabitation of brothers and sisters, and perhaps of parent and child; thus finding mankind in a condition akin to that of the inferior animals, and more intensely barbarous than we have been accustomed to regard as a possible state of man. It will be seen in the sequel that this custom springs naturally out of the communal family founded upon the intermarriage of brothers and sisters. Seen in this light it is at least supposable that the Hawaiian custom still embodies the evidence of an organic movement of society to extricate itself from a worse condition than the one it produced. For it may be affirmed, as a general proposition, that the principal customs and institutions of mankind have originated in great reformatory movements. The Pinaluanic Bond must, therefore, be regarded as a compact between several brothers to defend their common wives, and a like compact between the husbands of several sisters to defend their common wives against the violence of society, thus implying a perpetual struggle amongst the males for the possession of the females. If this supposed origin of the custom is accepted as real, it must be regarded as one of a series of similar movements by means of which mankind emerged from a state of promiscuous intercourse, and afterwards, step by step, and through a long and varied experience, attained to marriage between single pairs, and finally to the family as it now exists. In this series the two, holding the position of paramount importance, are 1st, the intermarriage of brothers and sisters, and 2d, the tribal organization. Repulsive and distasteful as every suggestion must be that assumes an antecedent condition of man in which the propensity to pair and live in the family relation, now so powerfully developed, did not exist; in which both marriage in the proper sense and the family were unknown, and in which the mental and moral powers of man must have been extremely feeble in comparison with his present; yet such a condition is rendered extremely probable from the fact that it explains the origin of the Malayan system, which, as the first stage of the Turanian and Ganowánian, must have sprung from the relations actually subsisting between the several members of the communal family as it then existed. This, at least, would be the first presumption.

Whether brothers and sisters intermarried and cohabited amongst the Hawaiians we have, at present, no evidence to submit. The fact will be assumed, and if by its assumption the origin of their system of relationship can be fully and completely explained, the existence of the system will tend to prove the fact.

In the order adopted the Malayan system will be first explained from the nature of descents, by the Hawaiian custom, and the intermarriage of brothers and sisters with antecedent promiscuous intercourse; and after that the Turanian, by the tribal organization.

It will be remembered that under the former system the primary relationships only are recognized and named. To these must be added the relationships of grandparent and grandchild. These terms are applied to consanguinei in a definite manner, by means of which they are reduced to as many great classes as there are primary relationships, including those last named. No distinction is made between lineal and collateral consanguinei except that they are distributed into classes. In a word all consanguinei are either fathers or mothers to each other, or brothers or sisters, sons or daughters, grandparents or grandchildren. It follows that a knowledge of the degrees numerically forms an integral part of the system, with certainty of parentage within prescribed limits.

1. All the children of my several brothers, myself a male, are my sons and daughters.

Reason. I cohabit with all my brothers' wives, who are my wives as well (using the terms *husband*, *wife*, and *marriage* in the sense of the custom). As it would be impossible to discriminate my children from those of my brothers, if I call any one my child I must call them all my children. One is as likely to be mine as another.

2. All the grandchildren of my several brothers are my grandchildren.

Reason. They are the children of my sons and daughters. With myself a female the relationships of my brothers' children and descendants are the same. The reason must be sought in the analogy of the system. Since my brothers are my husbands their children by other wives would be my step-children, which relationship being unrecognized they naturally fall into the category of my sons and daughters. These must be the relationships or none.

3. All the children of my several sisters, myself a male, are my sons and daughters.

Reasons. I cohabit with all my sisters, who are my wives. Explanation when fully given as in 1.

4. All the grandchildren of my several sisters are my grandchildren.

Reason. They are the children of my sons and daughters. With myself a female, the relationships in the last two cases are the same. Reason. I cohabit with all the husbands of my sisters, who are my own husbands as well. This difference, however, exists, I can distinguish my own children from those of my own sisters, to the latter of whom I am a step-mother. But since the step-relationships are not discriminated they fall into the category of sons and daughters.

5. All the children of several own brothers are brothers and sisters to each other.

Reason. These brothers cohabit with all the mothers of these children. Among their reputed fathers these children cannot distinguish their own father; but among the wives of these brothers they can distinguish their own mother; whence, as to the former, they are brothers and sisters to each other, but, as to the latter, while the children of a common mother are brothers and sisters to each other, these are step-brothers and step-sisters to the children of their mother's sisters. Therefore, for reasons stated in similar cases, they fall into the relationship of brothers and sisters.

6. The children of these collateral brothers are also brothers and sisters to each other; the children of the latter are brothers and sisters again; and these relationships continue downward, amongst their descendants, indefinitely.

An infinite series is thus created which forms a fundamental part of the system.

It is not easily explained. The Hawaiian custom, as stated, is restricted to several own brothers and their wives, and to several own sisters and their husbands. To account for this infinite series it must be further assumed that this privilege of barbarism extended wherever the relationship of brother and sister was recognized to exist; each brother having as many wives as he had sisters, and each sister as many husbands as she had brothers, whether own or collateral.

7. All the children of several own sisters are brothers and sisters to each other; all their children are brothers and sisters again; and so downward indefinitely.

Reasons as in 5 and 6.

8. All the children of several own brothers on one hand, and of their several own sisters on the other, are brothers and sisters to each other; the children of the latter are brothers and sisters again; and so downward indefinitely.

Reasons as in 5 and 6.

9. All the brothers of my father are my fathers.

Reasons as in 1.

10. All the sisters of my mother are my mothers.

Reasons as in 1 and 3.

11. All the sisters of my father are my mothers.

Reasons as in 2.

12. All the brothers of my mother are my fathers.

Reason. My mother is the wife of all her brothers.

13. All the children of my several collateral brothers and sisters are, without distinction, my sons and daughters.

Reasons as in 1, 3, and 6.

14. All the children of the latter are my grandchildren.

Reasons as in 2.

15. All the brothers and sisters of my grandparents are likewise my grandparents.

Reasons. They are the fathers and mothers of my father and mother.

Every blood relationship recognized under the Malayan system is thus explained from the nature of descents, and is seen to be the one actually existing, as near as the parentage of individuals could be known. The system, therefore, follows the flow of the blood instead of thwarting or diverting its currents. It is a natural rather than an arbitrary and artificial system. As thus explained it appears to have originated in the intermarriage of brothers and sisters in a communal family, the assumption of which custom is necessary to explain its origin from the nature of descents. When the Hawaiian custom, which finds its antetype in the former, supervened it brought other males and females into the family, but it must have left the previous custom unaffected; otherwise several of the Malayan relationships would have been untrue to the nature of descents as they existed.

The several marriage relationships may be explained with more or less of certainty upon the same principles.

This solution of the origin of the Malayan system, although it rests, aside from the Hawaiian custom, upon the assumption of the intermarriage of brothers and sisters, is sufficiently probable in itself to deserve serious attention. It uncovers and reveals a state of society in the primitive ages, not confined to the islands of the Pacific, with the evidence of its actual existence still preserved in this system of relationship, which we shall be slow and reluctant to recognize as real; and yet towards which evidence from other and independent sources has long been pointing. It finds mankind, during the periods anterior to the Hawaiian custom, in a barbarism so profound that its lowest depths can scarcely be imagined; but which is partially shadowed forth by the fact that neither the propensity to pair, nor marriage in its proper sense, nor the family except the communal, were known; and, above all, that the sacredness of the tie which binds brother and sister together, and raises them above the temptations of animal passion, had not dawned upon the barbarian mind.

In the next place the origin of the Turanian system is to be explained from the nature of descents. No evidence has been presented of the prevalence of the Hawaiian custom in any part of Asia or America, or of the intermarriage of brothers and sisters as a general custom. Neither is it necessary for the purpose in hand that such evidence should exist. The solution to be offered proceeds upon the assumed existence of these customs, together with the tribal organization; and if these are sufficient to explain the origin of the Turanian system, the system itself, to some extent, becomes evidence of their antecedent existence.

The Turanian was undoubtedly engrafted upon an original form agreeing in all essential respects with the Malayan; the latter being the first permanent, and the former the second permanent stage of the classificatory system. About half of the Malayan relationships must be changed, leaving the other half as they are, to produce the Turanian system. It is clear that the Malayan could not be derived from the Turanian, since it is the simpler, and, therefore, the older form. Neither could the Turanian be developed out of the Malayan, since the former contains additional and distinctive elements; but a great change of social condition might have occurred which would supply the new elements, and such, in all probability, is the history of the transition from the one into the other. It will be seen, at a glance, that it is only necessary to break up the cohabitation of brothers and sisters to turn the Malayan into the Turanian form, provided the changes in parentage, thus produced, are followed to their logical results.

Following step by step the supposed sequence of customs and institutions which developed the classificatory system by organic growth, it will next be assumed that the Malayan form, as its first stage, prevailed upon the continent of Asia among the ancestors of the present Turanian family at the epoch of the Malayan migration to the islands of the Pacific. In other words it may be conjectured that the Malayan family took with them the form which then prevailed, and preserved it to the present time, whilst they left the same form behind them amongst the people from whom they separated. With the Malayan system thus prevalent in Asia, it may be supposed that another great organic movement of society occurred which resulted, in the course of time, in the tribal organization. This institution is so ancient and so wide spread that its origin must ascend far back towards the primitive ages of mankind. It is explainable, and only explainable in its origin, as a reformatory movement to break up the intermarriage of blood relatives, and particularly of brothers and sisters, by compelling them to marry out of the tribe who were constituted such as a band of consanguinei. It will be seen at once that with the prohibition of intermarriage in the tribe this result was finally and permanently effected. By this organization the cohabitation of brothers and sisters was permanently abolished, since they were necessarily of the same tribe, whether descent was in the male or the female line. It would neither overthrow the Hawaiian custom, although it abridged its range, nor the communal family, which was not inharmonious with the tribal organization; but it struck at the roots of promiscuous intercourse by abolishing its worst features, and thus became a powerful movement towards the ultimate realization of marriage between single pairs, and the true family state.

If the principles resulting from the tribal organization, so far as they relate to parentage, are now applied to that part of the Turanian system which is distinctively Turanian, the relationships will be found to be in accordance with the nature of descents, and explainable by natural suggestion. It will also tend to show in what manner the Turanian element became incorporated in the system.

1. All the children of my several sisters, myself a male, are my nephews and nieces.

Reason. Under the tribal organization brothers and sisters not being allowed to intermarry or cohabit, the children of my sisters can no longer be my children, but must stand to me in different and more remote relationships. Whence the relationships of nephew and niece.

2. All the children of these nephews and nieces are my grandchildren.

The reason must be sought in the analogy of the system. No relationships outside of grandfather, uncle, cousin, nephew, and grandson, are recognized under the system, wherefore they must fall into the class of nephews and nieces or grandchildren. That of grandchild being the relationship under the previous system, would naturally remain until a new relationship was created.

On the other hand, the children of my several brothers are still my sons and daughters, because I cohabit with all the wives of my brothers, who are my own wives as well. It will be found that the changes in the system are restricted to those relationships which depended upon the intermarriage of brothers and sisters.

3. All the children of my several brothers, myself a female, are my nephews and nieces.

Reason as in 1.

4. All the children of these nephews and nieces are my grandchildren.

Reason as in 2.

On the other hand, all the children of my several sisters, myself still a female, are my sons and daughters, and their children are my grandchildren, as in the Malayan, and for the reasons there assigned.

5. All the sisters of my father are my aunts.

Reason. Since, under the tribal organization, my father cannot marry his sisters, they can no longer stand to me in the relation of mothers, but must be placed in one more remote. Whence the relationship of aunt.

6. All the brothers of my mother are my uncles.

Reason. As my mother's brothers no longer cohabit with my mother, they cannot stand to me in the relation of a father, but must be placed in one more remote. Whence the relationship of uncle.

My father's brothers are still my fathers, and my mother's sisters are still my mothers, as in the Malayan, and for the reasons there given. The tribal organization does not prevent my father and his brothers from cohabiting with each other's wives, nor my mother and her sisters from cohabiting with each other's husbands.

7. All the children of these several uncles and aunts are my cousins.

Reasons as in 5 and 6. Since they cannot be my brothers and sisters for the reasons named, they must be placed in a more remote relationship.

But the children of brothers are brothers and sisters to each other, and so are the children of sisters, as in the Malayan, and for the reasons there given.

All the children of my male cousins, myself a male, are my nephews and nieces; and all the children of my female cousins are my sons and daughters.

Such is the classification amongst the Drâvidian nations of South India. Unless I cohabit with all my female cousins, and am excluded from cohabitation with the wives of all my male cousins, these relationships cannot be explained from the nature of descents. In the Ganowánian family this classification is reversed; the children of my male cousins, myself a male, are my sons and daughters, and of my female cousins are my nephews and nieces. These are explainable from the principles, and from the analogy of the system. It is a singular fact that the deviation upon these relationships is the only one of any importance between the Tamil and the Seneca-Iroquois, which in all probability has a logical explanation of some kind. If it is attributable to the slight variation upon the privilege of barbarism above indicated a singular solution of the difference in the two systems is thereby afforded.

8. All the children of these nephews and nieces are my grandchildren.

Reasons as in 2.

9. All the children of these collateral sons and daughters are my grandchildren.

It is the same in Malayan, and for the reasons there given.

10. All the brothers and sisters of my grandfather, and of my grandmother, are my grandfathers and grandmothers.

Reasons. As to the brothers of my grandfather, and the sisters of my grandmother, the reasons are as given in the Malayan, where the relationships are the same. In the other cases they must be sought in the analogy of the system.

The same course of investigation and of explanation may be applied to the more remote collateral lines, and to several of the marriage relationships, with substantially similar results; but the solution of the origin of that part of the classificatory system which is distinctly Turanian has been carried sufficiently far for my present purpose. All of the indicative relationships have been explained, and shown to be those which actually existed in the communal family as it was constituted under the tribal organization, and the other prevailing customs and institutions. If the progressive conditions of society, during the ages of barbarism, from which this solution is drawn are partly hypothetical, the system itself, as thus explained, is found to be simple and natural, instead of an arbitrary and artificial creation of human intelligence. The probable existence of the series of customs and institutions, so far as their existence is assumed, is greatly strengthened by the simplicity of the solution which they afford of the origin of the classificatory system in two great stages of development.

An exposition of the entire series of customs and institutions upon which these solutions are founded, together with a discussion of the historical evidence of their existence and spread are necessary to a full appreciation of the probable correctness of these solutions. But they cover too wide a field, and embrace too many considerations to be treated in this connection. I am, therefore, reluctantly compelled to limit myself to what seem to be the controlling propositions, although the conclusions reached are thereby open to the charge of being too sweeping in their character. In any event this discussion is but the introduction of the subject of which it treats. Further investigations, in its various departments, will modify the positions here taken, as well as the conclusions reached, or confirm their truthfulness.

The present existence of the classificatory system of relationship, with the internal evidence of its transition from the Malayan to the Turanian form, is, of itself, a powerful argument in favor of the prevalence of these customs and institutions, and of their origination substantially in the order stated. All except the first and second, and perhaps the fourth, still prevail in portions of the human family, and are known to have existed as far back, in the past, as the oldest historical records ascend; with abundant evidence of the existence of some of them from time immemorial. Evidence is not wanting in many barbarous nations, at the present time, of an antecedent state of promiscuous intercourse involving the cohabitation of brothers and sisters as its primary form. It will not be difficult, hereafter, to accumulate such a body of evidence upon this subject as to leave no doubt upon the question.

It remains to notice the order of origination of these customs and institutions as a great progressive series founded upon the growth of man's experience; and to consider their reformatory character. The establishment of this series as a means of recovering the thread of man's history through the primitive ages is the principal result of this solution of the origin of the classificatory system. Upon these questions some suggestions will be submitted, in doing which it will be necessary to recapitulate the series.

I. Promiscuous Intercourse.

This expresses the lowest conceivable stage of barbarism in which mankind could be found. In this condition man could scarcely be distinguished from the brute, except in the potential capacity of his endowments. Ignorant of marriage in its proper sense, of the family, except the communal, and with the propensity to pair still undeveloped, he was not only a barbarian but a savage; with a feeble intellect and a feebler moral sense. His only hope of elevation lay in the fierceness of his passions, and in the improvable character of his nascent mental and moral powers. The lessening volume of the skull and its low animal characteristics as we recede in the direction of the primitive man, deliver decisive testimony concerning his immense inferiority to his civilized descendants. The implements of stone and flint found over the greater part of the earth, attest the rudeness of his condition when he subsisted chiefly upon fish, leaving it doubtful whether to become a fisherman he had not raised himself from a still more humble condition. That the ancestors of the present civilized nations were, in the primitive ages, savages of this description, is not improbable; neither is it a violent supposition that they, as well as the ancestors of the present barbarous nations, once lived in a state of promiscuous intercourse, of which, as to the latter, their systems of consanguinity and affinity still embody the evidence. To raise mankind out of this condition could only be accomplished by a series of reformatory movements, resulting in the development of a series of customs and institutions for the government of their social life.

II. Intermarriage or Cohabitation of Brothers and Sisters.

This practice, which the previous condition necessarily involved, would tend to regulate as well as to check the gregarious principle. It would, probably, be the normal condition of society under this principle; and, when once established, would be apt to perpetuate itself through indefinite, or at least immensely long periods of time. It gives the starting point and the foundation of the Malayan system of relationship, which, in turn, is the basis of the Turanian and Ganowánian. Without this custom it is impossible to explain the origin of the system from the nature of descents. There is, therefore, a necessity for the prevalence of this custom amongst the remote ancestors of all the nations which now possess the classificatory system, if the system itself is to be regarded as having a natural origin.

III. The Communal Family.

Such a family resulted necessarily from the custom last considered. The union of effort to procure subsistence for the common household, led to communism in living. This probable organization of society, in the primitive ages, into communal families, and which continued long after the intermarriage of brothers and sisters was abolished, has not been sufficiently estimated in its bearings upon the early condition of mankind. Without being able to assert the fact, there are strong grounds for supposing that most barbarous nations at the present time, although marriage between single pairs exists, are now organized into such families, and practise communism as far as the same can be carried out in practical life. The American aborigines have lived, and still live to a greater or less extent, in communal families, consisting of related persons, and practise communism within the household. This feature of their ancient mode of life can still be definitely and widely traced amongst them. It also entered into and determined the character of their architecture.[1]

---

[1] This principle entered into and determined the character of their architecture, as soon as they gathered in villages. This may be illustrated by a brief reference to the character of their houses. Tiotohatton, one of the ancient Seneca villages near Rochester, is thus described by Mr. Greenhalgh, who visited it in 1677. (Doc. Hist. N. Y., I, 13.) "It lyes to the westward of Canagora [Canandaigua] about 30 miles, contains about 120 houses, being the largest of all the houses we saw; the ordinary being 50 to 60 feet long, with twelve and thirteen fires in one house." A house with ten fires would be about seventy feet long and eighteen wide, and comparted at intervals of seven feet, with a hall through the centre, and a door at each end. The fire-pits were in the centre of the hall, one between each two compartments. Each family or married pair used one compartment, and each pair of families on opposite sides of the hall used the fire in common. Such a house would accommodate twenty families, usually consisting of related persons who shared their provisions in common. Some years ago I had a model of one of these ancient houses constructed to ascertain

In the communal family, consisting of several brothers and sisters, and their children, the family in its *first stage* is recognized.

IV. The Hawaiian Custom.

The existence of this custom is not necessary to an explanation of the origin of the Malayan system. All it contains bearing upon this question is found in the intermarriage of brothers and sisters, where the brothers live in polygynia, and the sisters in polyandria; but it holds a material position in the series, for the reason that it was an existing and still prevalent custom in the Sandwich Islands at the epoch of their discovery. It finds its type in the previous custom out of which it naturally arose, and for which reason it may be expected that it will yet be found in other barbarous nations. So far as it brought unrelated persons into the house-

---

its mechanism. Mr. Caleb Swan, who visited the Creeks in 1790, thus describes their houses: "These houses stand in clusters of four, five, six, seven, and eight together, . . . each cluster of houses containing a clan or family of relatives, who eat and live in common." (Schoolcraft, Hist. Cond. and Pros. Ind. Tribes, 5, 262.) Lewis and Clarke thus speak of a village of the Chopunnish (Nez Perces) in the valley of the Columbia. (Travels, Lond. ed., 1814, p. 548.) "The village of Tumachemootool is in fact only a single house one hundred and fifty feet long. . . . It contains twenty-four fires, about double that number of families, and might, perhaps, muster one hundred fighting men." In like manner the Dirt Lodge of the Mandans and Minnitares is a communal house, about forty feet in diameter, and polygonal in form, and capable of accommodating seven or eight families. It is comparted with willow screens; each apartment being open towards the fire-pit in the centre. These specimens illustrate the principle. If we now turn to the architecture of the Village Indians of New Mexico, Mexico, Chiapa, and Yucatan, it will be found that their houses were great communal edifices, constructed of adobe brick, or of rubble stone and mud mortar, or of slate stone, or of stone fractured or cut, and laid with mortar, possibly in some cases of lime and sand. The pueblo of Taos, in New Mexico, consists of two such houses, one of which is 260 feet long, 100 feet deep, and five stories high, the stories being in the retreating or terrace form; and the second is 140 feet long, 220 feet deep, and six stories high. They are built of adobe brick, and each capable of accommodating about four hundred persons. They are now occupied by 361 Taos Indians. In the cañon of the Rio de Chaco, about one hundred and forty miles northwest of Santa Fé, there is a remarkable group of some seven pueblos, now in ruins (they answer very well to the seven cities of Cibola), constructed of stone, a thin tabular limestone. That of Hungo Pavie is built on three sides of a court, is 300 feet long, by 130 deep on the two sides, and three stories high. It contained 144 chambers, each about 15 by 18 feet, and would accommodate seven or eight hundred persons. It was built in the terraced form, the stories retreating from the court backward, and the court was protected by a low stone wall. If this communal edifice is compared with the so-called palaces of Mexico, as they are imperfectly described by the early Spanish writers, a very satisfactory explanation of the latter will be found in the former, and the reason why the communal houses of Mexico were mistaken for palaces will also be made apparent. By the light of the same testimony the so-called palaces of Palenque, Uxmal, and Chi-Chen-Itza fade away into communal houses, crowded with Indians throughout all their apartments.*

---

* In an article upon the "Seven Cities of Cibola," published in the April number of the *North American Review* for 1869, I pointed out, with some minuteness of detail, the characteristics of the architecture of the Village Indians; and in two subsequent articles in the same *Review*, published in the October number, 1869, and in the January number, 1870, I treated at length the subject of "Indian Migrations." The latter was considered under three principal divisions: First, the influence of physical causes, including the geographical features of North America, and the natural subsistence afforded by its different areas; second, the influence of Indian agriculture; and third, their known migrations, together with such as might be inferred to have occurred from the relations in which the several Indian stocks were found. These articles form a proper supplement to Part II., and this reference is made to them as such.

62   April, 1870.

hold it was a positive advance upon the previous condition, tending to check promiscuous intercourse, and to relieve society from some of the evils of intermarriage amongst blood-relatives. It also tended to develop still further the idea of the communal family, and to move society in the direction of marriage between single pairs. Its reformatory character is plainly indicated by the fact that it imposed upon the several brothers, who shared their wives in common, the joint obligation of their defence against the violence of society, the necessity for which would be apt to exist in such a state of society as this custom presupposes.

V. The Malayan System of Relationship.

This system has been sufficiently explained. It holds the rank of a domestic institution, and takes its place in the series as the basis of the Turanian and Ganowánian systems. The argument, when fully developed, tends very strongly to show that this form of consanguinity must have prevailed over Asia at the epoch of the institution of the tribal organization.

VI. The Tribal Organization.

It is to be inferred that this institution was designed to work out a reformation with respect to the intermarriage of brothers and sisters, from the conspicuous manner in which it accomplishes this result. Its necessity is demonstrated by the state of society revealed by the Malayan system. The origin of this ancient wide-spread and most remarkable institution seems, from the stand point of this discussion, to find a full explanation, the first yet found in all respects adequate and satisfactory. It is not supposable that it came into existence all at once as a completed institution; but rather that it was of organic growth, and required centuries upon centuries for its permanent establishment, and still other great periods of time for its spread amongst existing nations. The existence of this organization, with the prohibition of intermarriage in the tribe, implies the antecedent intermarriage of blood relatives, together with a knowledge of its evils. From the very constitution of society, in the primitive ages, into small and independent bands the introduction of the tribal organization, with the prohibition of intermarriage, would make neighboring bands dependent upon each other for wives, and thus produce a radical change of social condition. For this and other reasons it seems extremely probable that it can only be explained as a reformatory movement. It was probably the greatest of all the institutions of mankind in the primitive ages, in its influence upon human progress, particularly toward the true family state, as well as the most widely distributed in the human family. This also gave the Turanian system of relationship.

VII. The Turanian System of Relationship.

This has elsewhere been sufficiently explained. With the changes in parentage thereby introduced the necessary additional materials are supplied to demonstrate its origin from the nature of descents. It fixes the seventh great epoch in the progress through barbarism, and becomes one of the permanent landmarks of man's advancement toward civilization. We cannot fail to notice the extremely ancient date at which the Turanian system must have become established.

VIII. Marriage between Single Pairs.

The observations made upon the previous customs and institutions have reference to the condition of the body of the people. Instances of marriage between single pairs may have, and probably did occur in all periods of man's history; but they must have been exceptional from the necessity of the case in the primitive ages. After the tribal organization came into existence, and the cohabitation of brothers and sisters was broken up, as well as all intermarriage in the tribe, there must have been a very great curtailment of the license of barbarism. Women for wives became objects of negotiation out of the tribe, of barter, and of capture by force. The evidence of these practices in Asia and America is ample. Wives thus gained by personal effort, and by personal sacrifices for their purchase, would not be readily shared with others. In its general tendency it would lead to individual contracts to procure a single wife for a single husband, and thus inaugurate marriage between single pairs. Such must have been the direct result of the tribal organization; but these marriages were followed down the ages with polygynia and polyandria of the Hawaiian and other types.[1] This argument upon the basis of authenticated facts, will bear great amplification, and would tend in a remarkable manner to confirm the conclusion that marriage between single pairs cannot be placed earlier in the sequence than the place here assigned.

IX. The Barbarian Family.

The family in its second stage thus developed is far removed from the family in its modern sense, or the civilized family. It is rather an aggregation of families, with communism in living more or less prevalent, and with tribal authority holding the place of parental. The family name, in addition to the personal, and the idea of property and of its transmission by inheritance were still unknown.

X. Polygamy.

In its relation to pre-existing customs and institutions polygamy is essentially modern. It presupposes, as elsewhere stated, a very great advance of society from its primitive condition, with settled governments, with stability of such kinds of property as existed, and with enlargement of the amount, as well as permanence of subsistence. It seems to spring, by natural suggestion, out of antecedent customs akin to the Hawaiian. With strength and wealth sufficient to defend and support several wives the strongest of several brothers takes them to himself, and refuses to share them longer with his brothers. Regarded from this stand point polygamy becomes a reformatory instead of a retrograde movement, and a decisive advance in the direction of the true family.

XI. The Patriarchal Family.

Polygamy resulted in the establishment of the patriarchal family, or the family in its third stage. A family, having a single male head, was an immense advance upon the communal, and even upon the barbarian. It necessitated to some extent a privileged class in society before one person would be able to support several sets of children by several different mothers. Polygamy in its higher forms belongs to the ages of dawning civilization.

---

[1] The passion of *love* was unknown amongst the North American aborigines of pure blood. The fact is sufficiently established by their marriage customs. They were given in marriage without being consulted, and often to entire strangers. Such, doubtless, is also the fact and the usage among barbarous nations in general.

XII. Polyandria.

This custom, a consequence of polygamy, requires no further notice.

XIII. The Rise of Property and the Settlement of Lineal Succession to Estates.

It is impossible to over-estimate the influence of property upon the civilization of mankind. It was the germ, and is still the evidence, of his progress from barbarism, and the ground of his claim to civilization. The master passion of the civilized mind is for its acquisition and enjoyment. In fact governments, institutions, and laws resolve themselves into so many agencies designed for the creation and protection of property. Out of its possession sprang immediately the desire to transmit it to children, the consummation of which was the turning point between the institutions of barbarism and those of civilization. When this desire, which arose with the development of property, was realized by the introduction of lineal succession to estates, it revolutionized the social ideas inherited from the previous condition of barbarism. Marriage between single pairs. became necessary to certainty of parentage; and thus, in the course of time, became the rule rather than the exception. The interests of property required individual ownership to stimulate personal exertion, and the protection of the state became necessary to render it stable. With the rise of property, considered as an institution, with the settlement of its rights, and, above all, with the established certainty of its transmission to lineal descendants, came the first possibility among mankind of the true family in its modern acceptation. All previous family states were but a feeble approximation. The subject involved in this proposition is one of vast range and compass. A passing glance is all that can be given to it for the purpose of indicating its position in the series of customs and institutions, by means of which mankind have traversed the several epochs of barbarism, until they finally, in some families, crossed the threshold which ushered them into the commencement of their civilized career. It is impossible to separate property, considered in the concrete, from civilization, or for civilization to exist without its presence, protection, and regulated inheritance. Of property in this sense, all barbarous nations are necessarily ignorant.[1]

XIV. The Civilized Family.

As now constituted, the family is founded upon marriage between one man and one woman. A certain parentage was substituted for a doubtful one; and the family became organized and individualized by property rights and privileges. The establishment of lineal succession to property as an incident of descent overthrew, among civilized nations, every vestige of pre-existing customs and institutions inconsistent with this form of marriage. The persistency with which the classificatory system has followed down the families of mankind to the dawn of civilization furnishes evidence conclusive that property alone was capable of furnishing an adequate motive for the overthrow of this system and the substitution of the descriptive. There are strong reasons for believing that the remote ancestors of the

---

[1] Under the tribal organization property usually descended in the tribe, and was distributed amongst the tribal kinsmen, resulting substantially in the disinheritance of the children. Lands were usually held in common.

Aryan, Semitic, and Uralian families possessed the classificatory system, and broke it up when they reached the family state in its present sense.

Upon this family, as now constituted, modern civilized society is organized and reposes. The whole previous experience and progress of mankind culminated and crystallized in this one great institution. It was of slow growth, planting its roots far back in the ages of barbarism; a final result, to which the experience of the ages had steadily tended. The family, which in this view of the case is essentially modern, is the offspring of this vast and varied experience of the ages of barbarism.

Since the family was reached, it has also had its stages of progress, and a number of them. The rise of family names, as distinguished from the single personal name common in barbarous nations, is comparatively modern in the Aryan family. The Roman GENS is one of the earliest illustrations. This people produced the triple formula to indicate the *name of the individual*, of the *Gens* or *great family*, and of the *particular family* within the *Gens*. Out of this arose, in due time, the doctrine of agnation, to distinguish the relationship of the males, who bore the family name, from that of the females of the same family. Agnatic relationship was made superior to cognatic, since the females were transferred, by marriage, to the families of their husbands. This overthrew the last vestige of tribalism, and gave to the family its complete individuality.

XV. The Overthrow of the Classificatory System of Relationship, and the Substitution of the Descriptive.

It is not my intention to discuss the fragments of evidence yet remaining here and there, tending to show that the Aryan, Semitic, and Uralian families once possessed the classificatory system. I shall content myself with remarking that if such were the fact, the rights of property and the succession to estates would insure its overthrow. Such an hypothesis involves the concession that the remote ancestors of the Celts, and of the Esthonians, and Finns as well, had once attained to the earliest stages of civilization. It is more than probable that the Uralian nations, after reaching the first stages of civilization, were forced out of their area by Aryan nations, and were never afterwards able to recover their lost advantages. Their system of consanguinity seems to require, for its interpretation, such an antecedent experience. Property alone is the only conceivable agency sufficiently potent to accomplish so great a work as the overthrow of the classificatory, and the substitution of the descriptive system. This is shown by the present condition of the classificatory system in the partially civilized nations.

Finally, in considering the relations of these several customs and institutions to each other, and their order of origination, it cannot be supposed that there was a trenchant line of demarcation between them. They must have sprung up gradually, prevailed more or less concurrently, and been modified in different areas under special influences. In the midst of unequal degrees of development, there must have been a constant tendency, under their operative force, from a lower to a higher condition. Remains of each and all of these customs and institutions are still found in some of the nations of mankind. The first seven were probably reached at a very early epoch after substantial progress had commenced.

If this solution of the origin of the classificatory system is accepted, another question will at once arise, namely, whether any limit would exist to the constant reproduction of the system in barbarous nations. Should its reproduction in disconnected areas become even probable, the system must lose its value for certain branches of ethnological investigation. The discussion of this question belongs in another connection. It may be remarked, however, that the adoption of this sequence of customs and institutions to explain its origin from the nature of descents, plants the roots of the system in the primitive ages of mankind. It then follows it down to the epoch of the institution of the tribal organization which perfected the Turanian form, since which time it has, in all probability, been a transmitted system to all the descendants of the Turanian family.

V. Does the present existence of such a system as that found amongst the American Indian nations furnish, in itself, conclusive evidence that it was derived by each and all from a common source, and, therefore, that the nations themselves are of common origin; or, in other words, can the genealogical connection of certain nations be inferred from the fact of their joint possession of this particular system of relationship, the radical characteristics of which are found to be constant and identical amongst them all?

Whether this system can be made of any use for the purposes named must depend upon the stability of its radical forms, and upon its power of self-perpetuation. If these are found to be attributes of the system it will lead the way to far-reaching and important conclusions. There is no occasion to assume either the stability or the self-perpetuating power of these radical forms. The Table contains abundant material to test the system in both these respects; either to overthrow its testimony or to place it upon a solid foundation. Whether this system of relationship may be employed in corroboration of other evidence tending to establish the unity of origin of the American Indian nations is not the question; but whether, as principal evidence thereof it is convincing and conclusive. The number of truths implicitly accepted, which rest upon mathematical demonstration, are few in number compared with those which are received with equal confidence when drawn by legitimate deduction from sufficient premises. Up to a certain point, which is far enough advanced to include the great practical questions submitted to individual judgment, the processes of moral reasoning are as trustworthy as those of mathematical reasoning, and their results not less conclusive. Conclusions thus founded enforce their own acceptance. In disposing of the questions, now under consideration, the quantity and quality of the evidence must be the same that would be required to form an opinion in any other case.

If, then, as a matter of research, the system of relationship of the Seneca-Iroquois were taken up, it would be our first care to trace it out in its entire range, and to acquaint ourselves with its structure and principles. When the contents of the system are mastered we ask the Senecas from whence its was obtained, and they answer: "We and our ancestors before us have used it from time immemorial; it has remained unchanged within the period to which our knowledge extends; it answers every want a system of relationship could supply; and we know nothing of its origin." We next pursue the inquiry in the five remaining Iroquois nations, amongst whom we find the same elaborate and stupendous system in full operation.

The same question is asked of each of these nations, and the same answer is given. Two other facts are now determined; first, that the system exists in six nations speaking as many dialects of a common stock language; and second, that the terms of relationship are the same original words dialectically changed. From these facts the first inference arises, namely, that they severally obtained the system, with the common terms, from the parent nation from which they were derived. Next we turn to the Wyandotes or ancient Hurons, who spoke another dialect of the same stock language, but who are known to have been detached from the Iroquois political connection for several centuries. Amongst them we find not only the same system, but, also, the same nomenclature of relationships, almost term for term, changed dialectically like the other vocables of the language. From this fact comes a second inference, corroborative of the first, and reaching back of it in point of time, namely, that the Wyandotes and the Iroquois derived the system, with the terms, from a common parent nation, and that it had been transmitted to each with the streams of the blood. Since the forms of the system among these nations are radically the same it follows that the system was coeval, in point of time, with the existence of a single original nation from which they are mediately or immediately derived. We thus obtain our first impression of its stability as a domestic institution, as it can now claim an antiquity of several centuries, and also a verification of its mode of transmission. Up to this point the argument for its stability, for its antiquity, and for its mode of transmission is corroborated by the parallel argument from unity of language.

Having thus traced the system throughout one stock language, we next cross the Mississippi and enter the area of the Dakotas. It is a change from the forest to the prairie, begetting, to some extent, a change in the mode of life. Here we find twelve or more nations, in embryo, occupying an area of immense extent. We take up their system of relationship and spread it out, in its several lines, upon diagrams, and then compare it with the Seneca-Iroquois. Every term of relationship, with perhaps two exceptions, are different from the corresponding Seneca terms; so completely transformed, indeed, that no " letter changes," however ingenious, can break through the indurated crust produced by the lapse of centuries. Although the words have lost the power to avow their common parentage with the Seneca, the relationships of persons are still the same. Every indicative feature of the Seneca system is found in the Dakota. This is not only true with reference to fundamental particulars, but throughout their minute details the two systems are identical with unimportant exceptions. If the same question is asked the Dakotas with reference to the origin of the system, the same answer will be received. Having now crossed the barrier which separates one stock language from another; and found the system present as well as intact in each, the question arises how shall this fact be explained ? The several hypotheses of accidental concurrent invention, of borrowing from each other, and of spontaneous growth are entirely inadequate. Of these hypotheses the first two need no discussion, and the third may be disposed of with the single remark that it is not possible these two Indian stocks should have passed independently through the same identical experiences, developing the same sequence of customs and institutions with the long intervals of time between each which this sequence presupposes, and finally have wrought out, by organic growth and development, the same identical system of relationship. The length of time required would far outrun any supposable period during which these stocks have maintained an independent existence.   The terms in the several Dakota dialects are still the same original words changed dialectically, thus furnishing conclusive proof that both the system and the terms were derived immediately by each from a common parent nation.   If the inquiry were extended so as to include the remaining nations speaking dialects of the same stock language, the same conclusion would be obtained, thus moving back the system to a point of time coeval with the first appearance of the parent nation from which they were severally derived.   The antiquity of the Iroquois and Dakota systems being thus established, the inference arises that it was derived by each stock from some other stock back of both, from which they were alike descended; and that it had been transmitted with the blood to the several branches of each.   When the Iroquois and Dakota forms are placed side by side every thought and principle embodied in each ring out an audible affirmation of their descent from a common original.

Turning northward, we next enter that portion of the Algonkin area occupied by the Ojibwas and the Crees, and having ascertained their system of relationship, it is, in like manner, spread out upon diagrams.   A third stock language is now before us.   The terms of relationship are equally numerous but each and all of them differ from the corresponding Seneca and Dakota terms.   Moreover, whilst there is a slight, and perhaps traceable, family resemblance between the Seneca and Dakota nomenclatures, the Cree and Ojibwa are so pointedly unlike them as to stand in marked contrast.   Yet the personal relationships, with deviations in unessential particulars, are the same.   Every indicative feature of the common system is present, and the greater part of its subordinate details.   There is no possibility of mistaking in each the same fundamental conceptions.   The system exists in full vigor and in constant practical use.   To the same question concerning its origin a similar answer is given.   In these dialects the terms of relationship are the same words, dialectically changed, which proves, as in the other cases, that they inherited the system, with the terms, from a common parent nation.   If the inquiry were extended so as to include the remaining Algonkin nations, the same results would be reached, namely, that it was transmitted to each with the blood from the parent Algonkin nation.   Its great antiquity in this stock is thus established.   Up to this stage of the inquiry the number of special features which are identical in the three forms of the system, beyond those which are radical, is very great.   Hence the possibility of simultaneous invention, or of spontaneous growth decreases with the increase of the number of these special characteristics which are constant.   There are now three distinct and independent currents of Indian speech, each subdivided into a large number of dialects, which are found to possess the system in all its fulness and complexity; thus leading us, by a threefold chain of testimony, to refer the system, the languages, and the peoples to a common original source.   This carries back the system to a point of time coeval with the separation and development of these three currents of language.

The same course of statement and of inference may be applied to each of the remaining stock languages represented in the Table. In the south was the Creek and its several cognate dialects, and the Cherokee; in the west the Pawnee, also spoken in several dialects. These languages have been distinct for many centuries. If the forms of consanguinity prevailing in each are spread out in diagrams and compared with those before presented, the indicative features of the common system will be found definitely and distinctly preserved. The terms of relationship in each stock language have lost their identity; but those in the same are still readily identified, although dialectically changed; thus showing that each nation received the system, with the terms, from a common source; and that the system is as ancient as the first development of each independent language. There are now six great currents of Indian speech, subdivided into sixty independent dialects, giving six different lines of evidence supported in the aggregate by sixty qualified witnesses, all testifying to the same great fact, namely; that this system of relationship, in its radical characteristics, existed in the original stock, from which these several stocks were mediately or immediately derived; and that it was transmitted to each, and to their several subdivisions, with the streams of the blood.

Upon the evidence of unity of origin contained in this system of relationship these several stocks have been organized into the Ganowánian family, and a position is now claimed for them as a family of nations, whose common origin has been established.

There are several other stock languages yet remaining the concurrent testimony of whose system of relationship to the same effect might be added. These are the Athapasco-Apache, the Salish, the Sahaptin, the Shoshonee, the Kootenay, and the Village Indians of New Mexico, which would increase the number of independent lines of evidence to ten or more, and the number of independent witnesses to upwards of one hundred. Whilst these are important to illustrate the general prevalence of the system, and to determine the right of these several stocks to be admitted into the Ganowánian family, they are not necessary to the completeness of the argument. It cannot be made more convincing by adding to its fulness. It has been demonstrated that the system has been propagated, in repeated instances, into several dialects of the same language from an original parent dialect. Further than this, it has been shown that it is still the same system in all the dialects of ten or more stock languages. The inference from these facts is unavoidable, that it was propagated into these several languages from a common parent language lying back of all of them. This conclusion is not only reasonable and probable, but there seems to be no alternative. Thus the great antiquity and mode of propagation of the system become fully demonstrated.

From the foregoing considerations the following conclusions are deemed established :—

First, that.the present existence of this system of relationship amongst the nations comprised in the Ganowánian family is conclusive evidence that these nations were derived from a common source; and are, therefore, genealogically connected

Second, that the system was transmitted to each of these nations with the streams of the blood.

Third, that the stability of its radical forms through centuries of time is verified by its perpetuation in such a number of independent channels, and through such periods of unknown duration as must have elapsed whilst these stock languages and their several dialects were forming.

And fourth, that the system is, presumptively, coeval with the first appearance of the Ganowánian family upon the North American Continent.

VI. Where two or more families, constituted independently upon the basis of such a system of relationship, are found in disconnected areas or upon different continents, can their genealogical connection be legitimately inferred from their joint possession of the same system?

The question involved in this proposition is of deep importance. It covers the great problem of the Asiatic origin of the Ganowánian family. In the solution of this problem, about to be submitted, the conclusions previously reached must be applied on a more comprehensive scale, and the stability and mode of propagation of the system must be subjected to a severer test than any hitherto employed. This interesting question it is now proposed to consider upon the basis of the identity of the Ganowánian and the Turanian systems of relationship.

The Asiatic origin of the Ganowánian family is no new hypothesis. It has long been rendered probable from the physical characteristics of the American aborigines, and from philological considerations; but it is rather a belief than an established proposition. The evidence has not assumed that direct and tangible form which sustains conviction. It has not, at least, been rendered so entirely probable as to leave further evidence undesirable, from whatever source it can be obtained. The question is sufficiently open, as well as important, to insure an impartial consideration of any new current of testimony which may be adduced; and which, if it tends to support the affirmative, will have the advantage of following in the same general direction to which previous evidence has pointed.

There is another, and independent class of facts, which tend to render probable their Asiatic origin. A careful study of the geographical features of the continent of North America, with reference to its natural lines of migration and to the means of subsistence afforded by its several parts to populations of fishermen and hunters, together with the relations of their languages and systems of relationship all unite, as elsewhere stated, to indicate the valley of the Columbia as the nursery of the Ganowánian family, and the initial point of migration from which both North and South America received their inhabitants. If the outflow of the several branches of this family can be retraced to the valley of the Columbia, of which there can be little doubt, it carries them to a region above all others within the possible reach of adventurers from Asia. The Amoor River stands very much in the same relation to the coasts of Northeastern Asia as the Columbia does to the coasts of Northwestern America. Both are celebrated for their fisheries and both undoubtedly became, from this fact, centres of population at an early day, and initial points of migration upon each continent. Dependence upon fish for subsistence, which, prior to the pastoral and agricultural periods, was the chief means of subsistence of the human family, begets a knowledge of boat craft. A glance at the map shows the relation which nations of fishermen and hunters established in the valley of the Amoor would sustain to the shores of the sea of Ochotsk and Kamtschatka, and to the first islands of the Aleutian chain ; and another inspection shows the relation of the valley of the Columbia to the peninsula of Alaska, and the easternmost islands of the same chain. There is no evidence whatever that the feet of the American Indians were ever planted on these islands; or, if they came in fact from Asia, of the route by which they came. But the fact is not immaterial that a possible route exists without forcing the ancestors of the Ganowánian family first to become an arctic people, as a preparatory step to a migration across the straits of Behring, and afterwards to become reacclimated to a lower latitude. It is important to know of a possible line of communication unembarrassed by this consideration. Whilst adventurers, originally from Asia, may have reached this continent in some other way by the accidents of the sea, or by an ancient actual continental connection, it is yet not impossible that they may have come by way of the Aleutian chain. This hypothesis, and it is nothing more, will occupy the strongest position until it is superseded by one having superior claims to adoption.

Before entering upon the question of the Asiatic origin of the Ganowánian family there is a preliminary fact to be determined, upon which the discussion must be founded ; namely, whether the systems of consanguinity and affinity of the Ganowánian and Turanian families are identical in their radical elements, and in their fundamental characteristics. This fact must be ascertained, beyond the possibility of a doubt, before any ground whatever from this source is obtained, from which such an inference may be drawn. A general impression of the close approximation of the two forms must have been obtained from the previous chapters. It now remains to place the two side by side for comparison throughout their entire range, that it may be seen not only how far their indicative relationships are coincident, but also the extent of their agreement in subordinate details. It will thus be found that the application of the same principles of classification, inherent in the two forms, have produced precisely the same results. The typical forms of the two families will be selected for comparison; since in these the principles of discrimination have been most rigorously applied, and because organic structures are more successfully studied in elaborate, than in the restricted development. A comparative Table of the Seneca and Tamil systems will be found at the end of the present chapter, in which the relationships of persons are presented on a scale sufficiently ample to exhibit all the features and principles of each system.

An attentive examination of the two forms, as they stand side by side, will satisfy the reader of their complete identity. It is not only revealed in a manner sufficiently comprehensive and absolute, but it includes minute as well as general characteristics. No argument is necessary to render more apparent this fact of identity in whatever is material in the common system, since a bare inspection of the table determines the question.[1] The question now arises how shall this identity be explained ?

The same proof exists with respect to the great antiquity of this system in Asia,

---

[1] There is another manner of showing this identity, namely, by comparing the analysis of the Seneca Iroquois system (*supra*, page 145) with that of the Tamil (*supra*, page 387, note). The several points in which they are identical and in which they are divergent are thus made to appear.

which has before been adduced in relation to its antiquity in America. Its present existence among the people who speak the three principal dialects of the Drâvidian language (and it is presumptively in the six remaining) carries it back to the primitive stock from which these nations were derived, or of which they are sub-divisions. The terms of relationships in the three dialects, with unimportant exceptions, are still the same words, dialectically changed, like the other vocables of the language; thus showing conclusively that it has been a transmitted system from the epoch of the formation of these dialects. Next, its parallel existence amongst the Gangetic nations gives the same inference of an antiquity coeval with the formation of the dialects out of which the Gaura speech was partly formed. And finally, if the Chinese system is regarded as identical in its radical characteristics with the Drâvidian and Gaura forms, its great antiquity in Asia is still further illustrated. The materials in the Tables are more abundant for the verification of its antiquity and mode of propagation upon the American continent than upon the Asiatic; but with an equal number of schedules, in the latter case, the results of the agreement would be equally convincing. The fact of its perpetuation in the Ganowánian family would render probable its like perpetuation in the Turanian, in which the old ideas of barbarous society are not yet overthrown.

There would seem to be but four conceivable ways of accounting for the joint possession of this system of relationship by the Turanian and Ganowánian families; and they are the following: First, by borrowing from each other; secondly, by accidental invention in disconnected areas; thirdly, by spontaneous growth in like disconnected areas, under the influence of suggestions springing from similar wants in similar conditions of society; and fourthly, by transmission with the blood from a common original source. These four hypotheses are sufficiently comprehensive to exhaust the subject. If then three of the four are insufficient, separately or collectively, to explain the fact of their joint possession of the system, and a fourth is shown to be sufficient, it ceases to be an hypothesis and becomes an established proposition.

1. By borrowing from each other. It appears from the Tables that the terms of relationship in the several dialects of each of the Ganowánian stock languages, changed dialectically like other vocables, have been transmitted with the system to each nation, thus tending to show that each received it from the same source from which each stock language was derived, and that in each case it was a transmitted system. If the system had been borrowed from one stock language into another, the terms themselves would reveal the fact, whereas their identity is as completely lost as that of other vocables. This fact holds as well with respect to the Turanian as the Ganowánian languages. The manner of its propagation, as a domestic in-stitution, forbids the supposition of its spread by borrowing. This hypothesis, therefore, is incapable of furnishing an explanation. Moreover, the supposition that the Ganowánian family borrowed the system from the Turanian would presup-pose a direct and long-continued territorial connection between them, thus admitting their Asiatic origin.

2. By accidental invention in disconnected areas. If there were a multiplicity of systems, radically different, amongst the nations of the earth such a fact might

encourage an inference of accidental invention, where two or more of these forms were found to be in radical agreement; but since the number is but two, the descriptive and the classificatory, of the first of which there is no subordinate form, and of the last but one principal and two subordinate forms, this hypothesis is seen to rest upon a weak foundation. There is, however, a much greater difficulty than this, and it is found in the elaborate and complicated structure of the system. The improbability of an accidental invention of the same system in disconnected areas increases with the addition of each special feature, from the first to the last; becoming finally an impossibility. A system of consanguinity which, upon analysis, yields upwards of twenty distinct particulars must be acknowledged to stand entirely beyond the possibility of accidental invention. This hypothesis, therefore, like the preceding one, must be dismissed as untenable.

3. By spontaneous growth in disconnected areas under the influence of suggestions springing from similar wants in similar conditions of society.

This method of accounting for the origin of the classificatory system, by repeated reproduction, possesses both plausibility and force. It suggests itself at once as a presumption, and as the readiest solution of its origin independently in different families of mankind. From the commencement of this research it has seemed to the author to be the essential and the only difficulty that stood in the pathway between this extraordinary system of relationship and the testimony it might deliver, unincumbered by this objection, upon ethnological questions. It has, therefore, been made a subject of not less careful study and reflection than the system itself. Not until after a patient analysis and comparison of its several forms, upon the extended scale in which they are given in the Tables, and not until after a careful consideration of the functions of the system, as a domestic institution, and of the evidence of its mode of propagation from age to age, did these doubts finally give way, and the insufficiency of this hypothesis to account for the origin of the system many times over, or even a second time, become fully apparent. Every attempt to account for the simultaneous or concurrent production of the system in the several subdivisions of a particular family is met with insuperable difficulties, and these are equally great with respect to its production independently in different families. Whether the reasons herein assigned against the sufficiency of this hypothesis are convincing or otherwise is neither material nor final, since the Tables remain to declare for themselves. They stand unaffected by argument or inference, and hold their own facts and testimony uninfluenced by the theories or speculations of particular persons.

The discussion of this hypothesis resolves itself into two distinct arguments. The first proceeds upon the rejection of the proposed solution of the origin of the system from the nature of descents, as they would exist in virtue of the series of assumed customs and institutions (*supra*, 480), thus leaving the system to have sprung from unknown causes. And the second, accepting this solution as probable and recognizing the said series as having actually existed, meets the final question whether or not it originated in disconnected areas, through the rise and development independently of the same series of customs and institutions.

Under the first branch the system is unexplainable and fortuitous in its origin;

and, having nothing in the nature of descents to uphold its classification of consanguinei, it stands before us as a purely artificial system. The only existing causes which could have exercised any influence upon its formation are polygamy and polyandria, since there are no traces of the Hawaiian custom either in the Turanian or Ganowánian families as yet produced. Polygamy, as has been seen, must have been restricted to the privileged few, whilst polyandria came in, as its consequence, to repair the disturbed balance of the sexes, so far as it was caused by the former, leaving the masses of the people unaffected by either custom. As to the latter, and their children, who were living in a state of marriage between single pairs, the reasons for the relationships established by the system would not exist, and, therefore, the latter must be supposed to have been adopted without any reference to polygamy and polyandria. Considered as an arbitrary and purely artificial system, without ascertained causes of its origin, similar conditions and similar wants are voiceless with respect to the manner of its production. In whatever direction this argument is produced nothing can be elicited, because the reasoning must be disconnected from a probable cause of its origin. It is contrary to the nature of descents as they now exist both in the Turanian and Ganowánian families, amongst whom marriage between single pairs is now recognized, and has been as far back as our direct knowledge extends. If it sprang up spontaneously in two disconnected families, the causes must have operated with remarkable power and uniformity to have produced two systems so complicated and elaborate, and yet in such minute agreement as the Seneca and the Tamil. Causes adequate to produce and maintain such results must necessarily be within reach of discovery. It will not be necessary to pursue this branch of the argument further than to remark that if the question of the Asiatic origin of the Ganowánian family turned upon the necessary adoption of one of the two following alternative propositions, namely; either that the system sprang up in the two families by spontaneous growth, from similar wants in similar conditions of society, or; that it was transmitted to each with the streams of the blood from a common original source, the latter must of necessity be adopted, provided it can be shown that the channel of its transmission is adequate, the common origin of the two families being for that purpose assumed.

The second branch of the argument whether this system originated in Asia, and also in America, through the rise and development independently of the same series of customs and institutions, presents several difficult questions. It has been seen that the influence of the bond of kin for mutual protection, and of the tribal relationships have no connection with the origin of the system. Further than this, it has been shown that polygamy and polyandria, whilst they touch the family relationships, quite nearly, are incapable of explaining its origin, from the necessary limitations upon their influence. And, finally, it has been rendered extremely probable, so probable as scarcely to admit of a doubt, that the tribal organization by breaking up the intermarriage of brothers and sisters produced an epoch in the growth of the system which developed its Turanian element. With these points considered established the first appearance of the Turanian system is carried back to a period of time coeval with the introduction of the tribal organization, thus giving to it an antiquity in Asia immensely remote. It must be accepted as a truth that the families who now occupy Europe and Asia shared a common experience, and lived in direct relations during the ages of barbarism; and that they participated in the benefits, to a greater or less extent, of each other's discoveries, customs, and institutions. Another fact seems not less certain, namely, that there is progress in barbarism. With some oscillation forward and backward there is a constant and prevailing tendency upward to a higher and improved condition. This is an inevitable consequence of the development, through reformatory movements, of customs and institutions, the benefits of which when once secured were never lost. Their progress may have been substantially imperceptible for ages upon ages; but any supposed perpetual tendency to relapse into a deeper barbarism was permanently arrested by their influence. They were so many sheet anchors against the surging waves of barbarism. Indestructible elements of progress are incorporated in the improvable nature of man. The tribal organization, which was by far the most important reformatory institution conceived in the ages of barbarism, was common alike to the Aryan, Semitic, Uralian, and Turanian families. It originated with some one of their respective ancestral stocks, and was propagated from thence into all the others; or it may, and it is not a violent supposition, have originated in a primitive family from which they are all alike descended. This gives to the system of relationship an antiquity without known limits, and probably reaching back to a point of time which preceded the independent existence of these families. And yet the tribal organization gave a supplementary part of the system only, the body of it with its displaced portions extending back through unmeasured periods beyond this epoch. If it is now assumed, for the time being, that the Ganowánian family came out of Asia, the period of their migration or expulsion must be fixed long subsequent to the establishment of the tribal organization. The whole period since its first introduction is much too long for the relative conditions of these families at the present time, physical and linguistic on any other assumption. Within its lifetime four great families of mankind, and perhaps a fifth, the Mongolian, have been developed in Asia, with clearly defined lines of separation between them, whilst the American aborigines are still of the same type, and without such marked diversities as to break their ethnic connection. Every fact in man's physical history points to a much longer occupation of the Asiatic continent by man, than of the American. Herein is found an insuperable difficulty in ascribing to the Ganowánian family an occupation of the American continent anterior to or even coeval with the introduction of the tribal organization. It follows that if they came, in fact, from Asia, they must have brought the tribal organization with them, and also the system of relationship then fully developed. The further progress of the argument seems now to be shut in to one of two alternative theories of the origin of the human species. First, that man was created in Asia, and has spread from thence over the surface of the earth; or, second, that he was created, the same species, several different times in independent zoological provinces. The first theory, as it assumes the Asiatic origin of the Ganowánian family, needs no discussion; but the second requires some notice.

Whilst this last theory is open to the objection that it is entirely unnecessary to explain the physical history of man, it will be considered exclusively in its relations to the question in hand.   If it is assumed, then, that the Turanian and Ganowánian families were created independently in Asia and America, would each, by impera tive necessity, have passed through the same experience, have developed the same sequence of customs and institutions, and, as a final result, have produced the same identical system of relationship?   The statement of the proposition seems to work its refutation on the ground of excessive improbability.   It is evident that the whole of this experience is but partially represented by the series of customs and institutions named; they are but the prominent landmarks of man's progress from one stage of barbarism into another.   The accidents, the struggles and the neces- sities connected with the rise and adoption of each custom and institution must remain unknown.   If the tribal organization is taken as an illustration, it is neither so obvious nor so simple that two people would originate it by natural suggestion, or fall into it without design.   It contains one refinement contravening the prin- ciple upon which it may be supposed to rest as à natural organism; namely, it excludes a portion of the descendants of the supposed common ancestor, by the limitation of descent to the male or to the female line, whereas nature would sug- gest the inclusion of all.   The series given involves great changes of social condi- tion, and the intervention of long periods of time between the establishment of each, during which the people, if the exclusive occupants of North and South America, must have broken up into independent stocks, and scattered far asunder. Besides this, the system must pass through two widely different and distinctly marked stages, and change in the same precise direction in both.   In its first stage promiscuous intercourse inaugurates some system adapted to the state of society it produced; then comes the intermarriage or cohabitation of brothers and sisters, as a partial check upon the former, with the introduction of the communal family. This should be followed by the Hawaiian custom, bringing unrelated persons to some extent into these communal families, and tending still further to check pro- miscuous intercourse.   Out of this experience arises the Malayan system of rela- tionship, at once definite and complete.   From this to the Ganowánian the transi- tion is very great.   It can only be reached by breaking up the cohabitation of brothers and sisters, and whatever device was resorted to, it must leave unimpaired existing institutions, except so far as they affected this particular practice.   If the tribal organization was then introduced, it is by no means a necessary inference that two families, created independently upon different continents, would reform their respective systems of relationship in precisely the same manner, and after- wards maintain them unchanged down to the present time.   After this it must further be supposed that each family, with their progressive experience, attained to marriage between single pairs, and to the family state in a limited sense, together with the practice of polygamy; and also that they encountered the dis- turbing influence of property so far as it existed and the question of its inheritance, and yet maintained the system unbroken on both continents.   These are but a few of the difficulties in the way of explaining the simultaneous origin of the system in two independent families of mankind.   The present existence of this system of relationship in the Turanian and Ganowánian families is a decisive argument, as it seems to the author, against the theory of the separate creation of man upon the

Asiatic and American continents; and also against the possibility of his having reached the American continent before the epoch of the tribal organization. It may be said that if these causes produced the system once they might again. This is true, but it involves a further condition that two primitive families in disconnected areas shall have their lives through unnumbered ages graduated to the same experiences. Without pursuing other branches of the argument, I may confidently leave the conclusion of the Asiatic origin of the Ganowánian family to turn upon the naked question of the probability or improbability of the production of the system in America by natural growth, from suggestions springing from the nature of descents, its antecedent existence in Asia having been established. If the two families commenced on separate continents in a state of promiscuous intercourse, having such a system of consanguinity as this state would beget of the character of which no conception can be formed, it would be little less than a miracle if both should develop the same ultimate system of relationship. Upon the doctrine of chances it is not supposable that each would pass through the same experience, develop the same series of customs and institutions, and finally produce for themselves the same system of consanguinity, which would be found, on comparison, to be identical in radical characteristics, as well as coincident in minute details. A slight divergence in customs, an imperfect development of a particular institution, or a difference in social condition would be apt to be represented by corresponding divergencies in their respective systems of relationship. And finally, from what is known of the mode of propagation of the system in different stocks of the same family, and of its power of self-perpetuation when once established, the hypothesis of its transmission with the blood from a common original source is found to be both adequate and satisfactory; thus leaving no occasion for the violent hypothesis under discussion. It remains to consider this final proposition.

4. By transmission with the blood from a common original source. If the four hypotheses named cover and exhaust the subject, and the first three are incapable of explaining the present existence of the system in the two families, then the fourth and last, if capable of accounting for its transmission, becomes transformed into an established conclusion. Its joint possession by the Turanian and Ganowánian families having been demonstrated, and no causes adequate for its repeated reproduction either in the same, or in disconnected areas, being found it follows that it is only necessary to find an instrumentality capable of its propagation, from a single beginning, to conclude the discussion. When such a vehicle is found, it yields a solution of the problem. The system once established finds in the diverging streams of the blood an instrument and a means for its transmission through periods of indefinite duration. As these innumerable lines ascend through the ages they converge continually until they finally meet in a common point, and whatever was in the original blood, capable of flowing in its currents, was as certain to be transmitted as the blood itself. Could anything have existed in the ancient human brain more likely to follow down in these streams of existence, through all vicissitudes, than those simple ideas, in their fixed relations, by which man sought to distinguish his several kinsmen? These ideas were seeds planted in the beginning, and perpetually germinating. Language has rolled along

the same diverging lines; first breaking up into dialects each of which in course of time became the fountain of still other dialects, until this not less wonderful attendant of the blood in all its multitudinous branches has become worn by the friction of time, into indurated forms. These now interpose serious obstacles to a reascent along the several lines of outflow beyond certain points of demarcation. The ideas deposited in its grammatical structure, and the laws governing the development of its grammatical forms, are analogous to the ideas contained in a system of relationship, and to the laws which govern its development; but language has been subjected to more subtle, long-continued, and powerful influences than consanguinity. Whilst the instrument for the perpetuation of their respective ideas was the same in both cases, the ability of this instrument to hold and transmit the original indicative features of language was greatly less than in the other case, from the magnitude of the burden imposed; and also from the nature of language, which must advance and unfold with the growth of knowledge. Consanguinity advances by great stages, and these are few in number with immense intervals between; but language changes imperceptibly and continuously, the change stamping it with a monotonous flow. The terms of relationship have passed through the same ordeal as the other vocables of language, and have lost themselves as completely; but the ideas and conceptions they represent are independent of the mutations of language, and they have lived without essential modification, because they were defined and made perfect once for all, both separately, and in their relations to each other.

It is a striking as well as instructive fact that all the nations of mankind have been traced, by conclusive linguistic evidence, to a few primitive stems or families. If philologers could possess themselves of their several languages precisely as they existed when they represented the speech of the entire human family, they could readily determine the question whether these languages were derived from a single original; but inasmuch as they are limited to the forms in which the several dialects of each are at present found, after the great changes produced by the wear of centuries, their efforts have hitherto been arrested by the barrier which separates one grammatically distinct language from another. No grammatical analysis, however minute and searching, has been able to reveal the subtle processes by which the radical structure of these languages has been changed. The achievements of comparative philology have been so brilliant and so remarkable as to justify the expectation that, with its augmented means and improved methods, it will yet be able to solve the great problem of the linguistic unity of mankind, of which, as a science, she has assumed the charge. In this great work philology will welcome any assistance, however slight, which may be offered from other sources. The object of this investigation was to determine the question whether an instrumentality could be found, in systems of consanguinity and affinity, which was able to take up the problem at the point where philology is now arrested; and having crossed the barrier which separates these languages from each other, find the links of connection between any two or more of these stocks or families through the constancy of the ideas embodied in this system of relationship as an organic structure, and as the oldest existing institution of mankind.

It now remains to present a summary of the argument, which the facts contained in the Tables appear to sustain, together with the final conclusion to which it appears to lead, so far as the classificatory system is concerned. It has been seen that this system was transmitted, with the terms of relationship, to the several dialects of the Iroquois stock language from a common original source, the terms having been changed dialectically like the other vocables of the language; but that the system, as well as the terms, remained constant, and its forms identical. Next it was shown that in the Dakota stock language corresponding terms for the same relationship existed, entirely unlike the former, and that these were changed dialectically like its other vocables, thus showing that it was a transmitted system in each dialect from a common parent nation; and yet the system in its radical forms, and in the greater part of its subordinate details, was identical with the first. Its propagation into two stock languages from some other lying back of both was thus rendered apparent. The Algonkin, the Creek, the Cherokee, and the Pawnee, four other distinct and independent currents of Indian speech, were then examined in their several dialects, and were found to deliver, respectively, the same concurrent testimony as to the identity and mode of transmission of the common system to each from a common source. A further examination of the system which prevails in several other stock languages tended to the same conclusions. The prevalence of the system in upwards of a hundred Indian nations not only furnished a sufficient basis for their classification together as one family of nations, but it also appeared to show conclusively that the system was coeval, in point of time, with the first appearance of the Ganowánian family upon the North American Continent. If, then, this family came in fact originally from Asia, they must have brought the system with them from the Asiatic continent, and have left it behind them amongst the stock from which they separated; and further than this, its perpetuation upon the American continent rendered probable its like perpetuation upon the Asiatic. We next entered the area of the Turanian family, and traced their system of relationship through its several branches, by the same chain of facts and inferences, to a common original form, which gave to the system in Asia an antiquity equally great. Up to this point the argument appears to encounter neither difficulty nor doubt. Whether the proposed solution of the origin of the system is accepted or rejected, it was made apparent that, instead of a constantly reproduced, it had been a transmitted system from the earliest epoch of the separate existence of the Turanian and Ganowánian families; and if the solution is accepted, then from the period of the introduction of the tribal organizations in the Turanian family. Having ascended, by a chain of facts and inferences, from the several systems of the several branches of the Ganowánian family to a common original form; and, by a like chain, from the several systems in the several branches of the Turanian family to a common original form, the two ultimate forms were then placed side by side and found to be identical in their radical characteristics. From this ascertained identity the final induction follows as a necessary consequence, namely, that if the preceding facts and inferences are true of each form and of each family separately, they are equally true of both forms and of both families unitedly; and thus the two ascend to a common fountain and source, from which both were derived. In other words, the Turanian and Ganowánian families drew their common system of consanguinity and affinity from the same parent nation or stock, from whom both were derived; and that each family has propagated it, with the streams of the blood, to each of its subdivisions upon their respective continents through all the centuries of time by which their separation from each other is measured.

The magnitude and importance of this final conclusion are sufficiently obvious. Before it will be admitted and recognized, as a demonstrated proposition, the facts contained in the Tables will be subjected to a more rigid analysis and to a severer scrutiny than they have yet received. By that ordeal this conclusion of the Asiatic origin of the Ganowánian family must abide.

The whole question seems to turn upon the point whether the radical forms of the system are stable, and capable of self-perpetuation through the immense period which has elapsed since the supposed separation of these families from each other. It is believed that the affirmative has been established by the undoubted fact of its perpetuation in the several branches of each family from a common source. And this conclusion is further strengthened by the extraordinary circumstance that the system, in virtue of its organic structure, has survived for ages the causes in which it originated, and is now in every respect an artificial system, because it is contrary to the nature of descents as they actually exist in the present state of Indian society. It is also confirmed by the negative proposition that it is found impossible to account for the present existence of the same system in the two families except through its transmission with the blood. If the facts show that the Iroquois, Algonkin, and Dakota nations derived their system from a common source, the remaining facts show, in a manner equally conclusive, that the Turanian and Ganowánian families derived their systems from a common source; and also, that it was a transmitted system in each of their several branches.

Should the main conclusion of the Asiatic origin of the Ganowánian family abide the test of criticism it will furnish an additional illustration of the toilsome processes by which we strive to discover hidden truths when they lie open before us in the pathway upon which we tread. Although separated from each other by continents in space, and by unnumbered ages in time, the Tamilian Indian of the Eastern hemisphere, and the Seneca Indian of the Western, as they severally address their kinsmen by the conventional relationships established in the primitive ages, daily proclaim their direct descent from a once common household. When the discoverers of the New World bestowed upon its inhabitants the name of *Indians*, under the impression that they had reached the Indies, they little suspected that children of the same original family, although upon a different continent, stood before them. By a singular coincidence error was truth.

VII. When the forms which prevail in different families are, to a limited extent, radically the same, can any inference be drawn from this partial identity, and to what effect?

Several interesting questions are suggested with respect to the relation of the Malayan system of relationship to the Turanian and Ganowánian. The Malayan family were foreordained to a stationary condition from the moment their fortunes became permanently identified with the islands of the sea. Without the range of a continent, which, sooner or later, leads to the possession of flocks and herds, or to the discovery of the cereals together with the art of cultivation, the first germs of civilization were beyond their reach. With the exception of that portion of the family who maintained some connection with the Asiatic continent, they have remained in a stationary condition through a longer period of time than any other family of mankind. It must be inferred, as a consequence, that their domestic institutions have undergone the minimum amount of change. The extent of the agreement and of the differences between the Malayan and the Turanian systems of relationship have elsewhere been indicated. In constructing the latter, the former was apparently used as the basis, and after substituting certain new relationships here and there, and such only as were necessarily suggested by the principles of the tribal organization, the remainder of the system was retained unaltered. An inference of great importance arises from this undoubted identity of a part of the Malayan system with the corresponding part of the Turanian, namely, that whilst the former cannot be derived from the latter, the latter may have been engrafted upon the former, which, if actually done, would make the Malayan the older form. It is not probable that the Turanian form would ever revert into the Malayan; neither could that part which is distinctly Turanian be developed out of any ideas or principles contained in the Malayan. The great change from the latter to the former could only be effected by the introduction into the Malayan system of a new and independent class of conceptions in harmony with those which were retained. It will be seen by a comparison of the two systems that they stand to each other in the precise relations indicated. The same is true with respect to the Ganowánian as compared with the Malayan.

This probable connection of the two forms raises the question of their relative antiquity. It does not necessarily follow because the Malayan is the oldest form that the Malayan family is also the oldest. On the contrary, if the supposed connection of the two forms is real, it might follow, and the inference is both reasonable and probable, that both families sprang from the same stock, amongst whom the present Malayan system prevailed; and that when this family broke off and migrated to their insular homes, they carried with them the system as it then existed and perpetuated it to the present time, as well as left it behind them amongst the people from whom they separated. And finally, that the Turanian element was engrafted upon the common form subsequent to the separation. Another inference of great significance necessarily and immediately follows, namely, that the Ganowánian family became detached from the Turanian, subsequently to the establishment of the Turanian system of relationship, and consequently, as a family, are younger than the Malayan. If these conclusions should be sustained, it will follow, as a further consequence, that America was not peopled from the Polynesian Islands, the system of relationship having been completely developed in Asia after the Malayan migration.

Another result of this investigation was the discovery among the Eskimo of an independent classificatory system of consanguinity, differing radically from the Ganowánian, Turanian, and Malayan. It appears to remove any remaining doubt with respect to the non-connection of the Eskimo with each and all of the families.

so far as any evidence in their respective systems bears upon the question. The systems of the Tungusian and Mongolian stocks yet remain to be ascertained. They are the only important Asiatic stocks not represented in some of their branches in the Tables. When their several systems are procured it is not improbable that the Eskimo form will find its type in one of them, although the supposition is conjectural. It would be remarkable if it did not. The Eskimo are comparatively a recent people upon the American continent, at least to the eastward of Mackenzie River. This fact is attested by the present nearness of the dialects of the Greenland, Labrador, and Western Eskimo, in all of which the identity of the vocables is still recognized with facility; whilst the Ganowánian language has fallen into a large number of stock languages, the vocables of each of which are different and distinct.

The Eskimo form agrees with the Ganowánian in being classificatory, and in merging the collateral lines in the lineal line; but it differs from it in the classification of kindred. Its generalizations are true to the nature of descents in every particular, as they now exist with marriage between single pairs, and as they are found in the Aryan family, with the exception of those which relate to the merging of the collateral lines in the lineal line. In many respects it approaches quite near to the systems of the Aryan and Uralian families, to both of which it is nearer than to the Turanian or Ganowánian, thus implying an advance in their experience at some anterior period far beyond either of the latter. In the absence of all knowledge of the forms which prevail in Northeastern Asia, it is premature to indulge in conjectures, but there are features in the Eskimo which suggest, at least, the possibility that when traced to its limits it may furnish the connecting links between the Turanian and Uralian forms.

COMPARISON OF THE SYSTEM OF RELATIONSHIP OF THE SENECA-IROQUOIS WITH THAT OF THE TAMIL PEOPLE OF SOUTH AMERICA.

Description of persons.	Relationships in Seneca. (Morgan.)	Translation.	Relationships in Tamil. (Scudder)	Translation.
1. My great grandfather's father	Hoc'-sote	My grandfather.	En muppáddan	My 3d grandfather.
2. " great grandfather's mother	Oc'-sote	" grandmother.	" muppáddi	" " grandmother.
3. " great grandfather	Hoc'-sote	" grandfather.	" pûddǎn	" 2d father.
4. " great grandmother	Oc'-sote	" grandmother.	" pûddi	" " mother.
5. " grandfather	Hoc'-sote	" grandfather.	" pǎddǎn	" grandfather.
6. " grandmother	Oc'-sote	" grandmother.	" pǎddi	" grandmother.
7. " father	Hä'-nih	" father.	" tǎkkǎppǎn	" father.
8. " mother	No-yeh'	" mother.	" tǎy	" mother.
9. " son	Ha-ah'-wuk	" son.	" mǎkǎn	" son.
10. " daughter	Ka-ah'-wuk	" daughter.	" mǎkǎl	" daughter.
11. " grandson	Ha-yǎ'-da	" grandson.	" pěrǎn	" grandson.
12. " granddaughter	Ka-yǎ'-da	" granddaughter.	" pěrtti	" granddaughter.
13. " great grandson	Ha-yǎ'-da	" grandson.	" irandǎm pěran	" 2d grandson.
14. " great granddaughter	Ka-yǎ'-da	" granddaughter.	" irandǎm pěrtti	" " granddaughter.
15. " great grandson's son	Ha-yǎ'-da	" grandson.	" mǔndam pěran	" 3d grandson.
16. " great grandson's daughter	Ka-yǎ'-da	" granddaughter.	" mǔndam pěrtti	" " granddaughter.
17. " elder brother (*male speaking*)	Hä'-je'	" elder brother.	" tǎmaiyǎn. ᵇ Aṇṇǎn	" elder brother.
18. " " " (*female speaking*)	Hä'-je	" " "	" tǎmaiyǎn. ᵇ Aṇṇǎn	" " "
19. " elder sister (*male speaking*)	Ah'-je	" elder sister.	" akkǎrl. ᵇ Tǎmǎkay.	" elder sister.
20. " " " (*female speaking*)	Ah'-je	" " "	" akkǎrl. ᵇ Tǎmǎkay.	" " "
21. " younger brother (*male speaking*)	Ha'-gǎ	" younger brother.	" tambi	" younger brother.
22. " " " (*female speaking*)	Ha'-gǎ	" " "	" tambi	" " "
23. " younger sister (*male speaking*)	Ka'-gǎ	" younger sister.	" tangaiohchi. ᵇ Tǎngay	" younger sister.
24. " " " (*female speaking*)	Ka'-gǎ	" " "	" tangaiohchi. ᵇ Tǎngay	" " "
25. " brothers (*male speaking*)	Da-yǎ'-gwä-dan'-no-dä	" brothers.	" aṇṇan tambi mär	" brothers.
26. " " (*female speaking*)	Da-yǎ'-gwä-dan'-no-dä	" "	" sǎkothǎrer	" brothers (Sanskrit).
27. " sisters (*male speaking*)	Da-yǎ'-gwä-dan'-no-dä	" sisters.	" tǎmǎkay tǎngay mär	" sisters.
28. " " (*female speaking*)	Da-yǎ'-gwä-dan'-no-dä	" "	" sǎkötharckǎl	" sisters (Sanskrit).
29. " brother's son (*male speaking*)	Ha-ah'-wuk	" son.	" mǎkǎn	" son.
30. " brother's son's wife (*male speaking*)	Ka'-sǎ	" daughter-in-law.	" mǎrūmǎkǎl	" dau.-in-law & niece.
31. " brother's daughter	Ka-ah'-wuk	" daughter.	" mǎkǎl	" daughter.
32. " brother's daughter's husband (*m. s.*)	Oc-na'-hose	" son-in-law.	" mǎrūmǎkǎn	" son-in-law & neph.
33. " brother's grandson "	Ha-yǎ'-da	" grandson.	" pěran	" grandson.
34. " brother's granddaughter "	Ka-yǎ'-da	" granddaughter.	" pěrtti	" granddaughter.
35. " brother's great grandson "	Ha-yǎ'-da	" grandson.	" irandǎm pěran	" 2d grandson.
36. " brother's great granddaughter "	Ka-yǎ'-da	" granddaughter.	" irandǎm pěrtti	" " granddaughter.
37. " sister's son "	Ha-yǎ'-wan-da	" nephew.	" mǎrūmǎkǎn	" nephew.
38. " sister's son's wife "	Ka'-sǎ	" daughter-in-law.	" mǎkǎl	" daughter.
39. " sister's daughter "	Ka-yǎ'-wan-da	" niece.	" mǎrūmǎkǎl	" niece.
40. " sister's daughter's husband "	Oc-na'-hose	" son-in-law.	" mǎkǎn	" son.
41. " sister's grandson "	Ha-yǎ'-da	" grandson.	" pěrǎn	" grandson.
42. " sister's granddaughter "	Ka-yǎ'-da	" granddaughter.	" pěrtti	" granddaughter.
43. " sister's great grandson "	Ha-yǎ'-da	" grandson.	" irandǎm pěrǎn	" 2d grandson.
44. " sister's great granddaughter "	Ka-yǎ'-da	" granddaughter.	" irandǎm pěrtti	" " granddaughter.
45. " brother's son (*female speaking*)	Ha-soh'-neh	" nephew.	" mǎrūmǎkǎn	" nephew.
46. " brother's son's wife (*female speaking*)	Ka'-sǎ	" daughter-in-law.	" mǎkǎl	" daughter.
47. " brother's daughter "	Ka-so'-neh	" niece.	" mǎrūmǎkǎl	" niece.
48. " brother's daughter's husband (*f. s.*)	Oc-na'-hose	" son-in-law.	" mǎkǎn	" son.
49. " brother's grandson "	Ha-yǎ'-da	" grandson.	" pěrǎn	" grandson.
50. " brother's granddaughter "	Ka-yǎ'-da	" granddaughter.	" pěrtti	" granddaughter.
51. " brother's great grandson "	Ha-yǎ'-da	" grandson.	" irandǎm pěrǎn	" 2d grandson.
52. " brother's great granddaughter "	Ka-yǎ'-da	" granddaughter.	" irandǎm pěrtti	" " granddaughter.
53. " sister's son "	Ha-ah'-wuk	" son.	" mǎkǎn	" son.
54. " sister's son's wife "	Ka'-sǎ	" daughter-in-law.	" mǎrūmǎkǎl	" dau.-in-law & niece.
55. " sister's daughter "	Ka-ah'-wuk	" daughter.	" mǎkǎl	" daughter.
56. " sister's daughter's husband "	Oc-na'-hose	" son-in-law.	" mǎkǎn	" son.
57. " sister's grandson "	Ha-yǎ'-da	" grandson.	" pěrǎn	" grandson.
58. " sister's granddaughter "	Ka-yǎ'-da	" granddaughter.	" pěrtti	" granddaughter.
59. " sister's great grandson "	Ha-yǎ'-da	" grandson.	" irandǎm pěrǎn	" 2d grandson.
60. " sister's great granddaughter "	Ka-yǎ'-da	" granddaughter.	" irandǎm pěrtti	" " granddaughter.
61. " father's brother	Hä'-nih	" father.	" periya tǎkkǎppǎn	" great father if older than my father.
			" serīya tǎkkǎppǎn	" little father if y'nger than my father.
62. " father's brother's wife	Oc-no'-ese	" step-mother.	" tǎy	" mother.
63. " father's brother's son (*older than myself*)	Hä'-je	" elder brother.	" tǎmaiyǎn	" elder brother.
64. " " " (*younger than myself*)	Ha'-gǎ	" younger brother.	" tambi	" younger brother.
65. " father's brother's son's wife (*male speaking*)	Ah-ge-ah'-ne-ah	" sister-in-law.	" mǎittǔni(o.), aṇṇi(y.)	" cousin & sis.-in-law.
66. " " " " " (*fem. speaking*)	Ah-ge͡-ah'-ne͡-o	" "	" mǎittǔni(o.), aṇṇi(y.)	" " " "
67. " father's brother's daughter (*older than myself*)	Ah'-je	" elder sister.	" Akkǎrl. ᵇ Tǎmǎkay.	" elder sister.
68. " father's brother's daughter (*younger than myself*)	Ka'-gǎ	" younger sister.	" tangaichchi ᵇTǎngay	" younger sister.
69. " father's brother's daughter's husb'd (*m. s.*)	Ah-ge͡-ah'-ne͡-o	" brother-in-law.	" mǎittǔnǎn	" bro.-in-law & cous.
70. " " " " (*f. s.*)	Ha-yǎ'-o	" "	" mǎittǔnǎn	" " " "
71. " father's brother's son's son (*male speaking*)	Ha-ah'-wuk	" son.	" mǎkǎn	" son.
72. " " " " " (*fem. speaking*)	Ha-soh'-neh	" nephew.	" mǎrūmǎkǎn	" nephew.
73. " father's brother's son's daughter (*m. s.*)	Ka-ah'-wuk	" daughter.	" mǎkǎl	" daughter.
74. " " " " " (*f. s.*)	Ka-soh'-neh	" niece.	" mǎrūmǎkǎl	" niece.
75. " father's brother's daughter's son (*m. s.*)	Ha-yǎ'-wan-da	" nephew.	" mǎrūmǎkǎn	" nephew.
76. " " " " " (*f. s.*)	Ha-ah'-wuk	" son.	" mǎkǎn	" son.

COMPARISON OF THE SYSTEM OF RELATIONSHIP OF THE SENECA-IROQUOIS WITH THAT OF THE TAMIL PEOPLE.—*Continued.*

Description of persons.	Relationships in Seneca.	Translation.	Relationships in Tamil.	Translation.
77. My father's bro.'s daughter's daughter (*m. s.*)	Ka-yă′-wan-da	My niece.	En mărŭmăkăl	My niece.
78. " " " " " (*f. s.*)	Ka-ah′-wuk	" daughter.	" măkăl	" daughter.
79. " father's brother's great grandson	Ha-yă′-da	" grandson.	" pĕrăn	" grandson.
80. " father's brother's great granddaughter	Ha-yă′-da	" granddaughter.	" pĕrtti	" granddaughter.
81. " father's sister	Ah-gă′-huc	" aunt.	" attai	" aunt.
82. " father's sister's husband	Hoc-no′-ese	" step-father.	" mămăn	" uncle.
83. " father's sister's son (*male speaking*)	Ah-găre′-seh	" cousin.	" Attăn. ᵇ Măittŭnăn	" cousin.
84. " " " " (*female speaking*)	Ah-găre′-seh	" "	" măchchăn	" "
85. " father's sister's son's wife (*male speaking*)	Ah-ge-ah′-ne-ah	" sister-in-law.	" tăngay	" younger sister.
86. " " " " (*fem. speaking*)	Ah-ge⌢ah′-ne⌢o	" "	" tăngay	" "
87. " father's sister's daughter (*male speaking*)	Ah-găre′-seh	" cousin.	" măittuni	" cousin.
88. " " " " (*fem. speaking*)	Ah-găre′-seh	" "	" măchchi. ᵇ Măchchărl	" "
89. " father's sister's daughter's husband (*m. s.*)	Ah-ge⌢ah′-ne⌢o	" brother-in-law.	" aṇnan (o.), tambi(y.)	" bro. older or y'nger.
90. " " " " " (*f. s.*)	Ha-yă′-o	" "	" aṇnan (o.), tambi(y.)	" " " "
91. " father's sister's son's son (*male speaking*)	Ha-ah′-wuk	" son.	" mărŭmăkăn	" nephew.
92. " " " " " (*fem. speaking*)	Ha-soh′-neh	" nephew.	" măkăn	" son.
93. " father's sister's son's daughter (*m. s.*)	Ka-ah′-wuk	" daughter.	" mărŭmăkăl	" niece.
94. " " " " " (*f. s.*)	Ka-soh′-neh	" niece.	" măkăl	" daughter.
95. " father's sister's daughter's son (*m. s.*)	Ha-yă′-wan-da	" nephew.	" măkăn	" son.
96. " " " " " (*f. s.*)	Ha-ah′-wuk	" son.	" mărŭmăkăn	" nephew.
97. " father's sister's daught.'s daughter (*m. s.*)	Ka-yă′-wan-da	" niece.	" măkăl	" daughter.
98. " " " " " (*f. s.*)	Ka-ah′-wuk	" daughter.	" mărŭmăkăl	" niece.
99. " father's sister's great grandson	Ha-yă′-da	" grandson.	" pĕrăn	" grandson.
100. " father's sister's great granddaughter	Ka-yă′-da	" granddaughter.	" pĕrtti	" granddaughter.
101. " mother's brother	Hoc-no′-seh	" uncle.	" mămăn	" uncle.
102. " mother's brother's wife	Ah-gă′-nĭ-ah	" aunt-in-law.	" mămĕ	" aunt.
103. " mother's brother's son (*male speaking*)	Ah-găre′-seh	" cousin.	" măittŭnăn	" cousin.
104. " " " " (*female speaking*)	Ah-găre′-seh	" "	" măchchăn	" "
105. " mother's brother's son's wife (*m. s.*)	Ah-ge-ah′-ne-ah	" sister-in-law.	" tăngay	" younger sister.
106. " " " " " (*f. s.*)	Ah-ge⌢ah′-ne⌢o	" "	" tăngay	" "
107. " mother's brother's daughter (*m. s.*)	Ah-găre′-seh	" cousin.	" Măittŭni	" cousin.
108. " " " " (*f. s.*)	Ah-găre′-seh	" "	" măchchărl.	" "
109. " mother's brother's daughter's husb.	Ah-ge⌢ah′-ne⌢o	" brother-in-law.	" aṇnan (o.), tambi(y.)	" bro. elder or y'nger.
110. " " " " " (*f. s.*)	Ha-yă′-o	" "	" aṇnan (o.), tambi(y.)	" " " "
111. " mother's brother's son's son (*m. s.*)	Ha-ah′-wuk	" son.	" mărŭmăkăn	" nephew.
112. " " " " " (*f. s.*)	Ha-soh′-neh	" nephew.	" măkăn	" son.
113. " mother's brother's son's daughter (*m. s.*)	Ka-ah′-wuk	" daughter.	" mărŭmăkăl	" niece.
114. " " " " " (*f. s.*)	Ka-soh′-neh	" niece.	" măkăl	" daughter.
115. " mother's brother's daughter's son (*m. s.*)	Ha-yă′-wan-da	" nephew.	" măkăn	" son.
116. " " " " " (*f. s.*)	Ha-ah′-wuk	" son.	" mărŭmăkăn	" nephew.
117. " mother's bro.'s daught.'s daughter (*m. s.*)	Ka-yă′-wan-da	" niece.	" măkăl	" daughter.
118. " " " " " (*f. s.*)	Ka-ah′-wuk	" daughter.	" mărŭmăkăl	" niece.
119. " mother's brother's great grandson	Ha-yă′-da	" grandson.	" pĕrăn	" grandson.
120. " mother's brother's great granddaughter	Ka-yă′-da	" granddaughter.	" pĕrtti [than my mo.).	" granddaughter.
121. " mother's sister	No-yeh′	" mother.	" pĕriyă tăy (if older) sĕriyă tăy (if y'nger).	" mother great or little.
122. " mother's sister's husband	Hoc-no′-ese	" step-father.	" takăppăn (P. or S.).	" father great or little.
123. " mother's sister's son (*older than myself*)	Hă′-je	" elder brother.	" tămăiyăn. ᵇ Aṇnăn.	" elder brother.
124. " " " " (*younger than myself*)	Ha′-gă	" younger brother.	" tambi	" younger brother.
125. " mother's sister's son's wife (*m. s.*)	Ah-ge-ah′-ne-ah	" sister-in-law.	" măittŭni	" sist.-in-law & cous.
126. " " " " " (*f. s.*)	Ah-ge⌢ah′-ne⌢o	" "	" annatăvi	" " "
127. " mother's sister's daughter (*older than myself*).	Ah′-je	" elder sister.	" akkărl. ᵇ Tămăkăy	" elder sister.
128. " mother's sister's daughter (*younger than myself*).	Ka′-gă	" younger sister.	" tăngăichchi. ᵇ Tăngay.	" younger sister.
129. " mother's sister's daughter's husb'd (*m. s.*)	Ah-ge⌢ah′-ne⌢o	" brother-in-law.	" măittŭnăn	" bro.-in-law & cous.
130. " " " " " (*f. s.*)	Ha-yă′-o	" "	" măittŭnăn	" " " "
131. " mother's sister's son's son (*m. s.*)	Ha-ah′wuk	" son.	" măkăn	" son.
132. " " " " " (*f. s.*)	Ha-soh′-neh	" nephew.	" mărŭmăkăn	" nephew.
133. " mother's sister's son's daughter (*m. s.*)	Ka-ah′-wuk	" daughter.	" măkăl	" daughter.
134. " " " " " (*f. s.*)	Ka-soh′-neh	" niece.	" mărŭmăkăl	" niece.
135. " mother's sister's daughter's son (*m. s.*)	Ha-yă′-wan-da	" nephew.	" mărŭmăkăn	" nephew.
136. " " " " " (*f. s.*)	Ha-ah′-wuk	" son.	" măkăn	" son.
137. " mother's sister's daught.'s daughter (*m. s.*)	Ka-yă′-wan-da	" niece.	" mărŭmăkăl	" niece.
138. " " " " " (*f. s.*)	Ka-ah′-wuk	" daughter.	" măkăl	" daughter.
139. " mother's sister's great grandson	Ha-yă′-da	" grandson.	" pĕran	" grandson.
140. " mother's sister's great granddaughter	Ka-yă′-da	" granddaughter.	" pĕrtti	" granddaughter.
141. " father's father's brother	Hoc′-sote	" grandfather.	" păddăn (P. & S.).	" gd. father gt. or lit.
142. " father's father's brother's son	Hă′-nih	" father.	" takăppăn (P. & S.).	" father gt. or little.
143. " father's father's brother's son's son (*older than myself*).	Hă′-je	" elder brother.	" aṇnan. ᵇ Tămăiyăn	" elder brother.
144. " father's father's bro.'s son's son (*younger than myself*).	Ha′-gă	" younger brother.	" tambi	" younger brother.
145. " father's father's brother's son's son's son (*m. s.*).	Ha-ah′-wuk	" son.	" măkăn	" son.
146. " father's father's brother's son's son's son (*f. s.*).	Ha-soh′-neh	" nephew.	" mărŭmăkăn	" nephew.
147. " father's father's bro.'s son's son's daughter (*m. s.*).	Ka-ah′-wuk	" daughter	" măkăl	" daughter.
148. " father's father's bro.'s son's son's daughter (*f. s.*).	Ka-soh′-neh	" niece.	" mărŭmăkăl	" niece.

COMPARISON OF THE SYSTEM OF RELATIONSHIP OF THE SENECA-IROQUOIS WITH THAT OF THE TAMIL PEOPLE.—*Continued.*

Description of persons.	Relationships in Seneca.	Translation.	Relationships in Tamil.	Translation.
149. My father's father's brother's great gt. grandson.	Ha-yä'-da	My grandson.	En pêran	My grandson.
150. " father's father's brother's great gt. granddaughter.	Ka-yä'-da	" granddaughter.	" pêrtti	" granddaughter.
151. " father's father's sister.	Oc'-sote	" grandmother.	" pǎddi (P. & S.)	" gd. mother gt. or lit.
152. " father's father's sister's daughter	Ah-ga'-huc	" aunt.	" täy ? (P. & S.)	" mother gt. or little.
153. " father's father's sister's daught.'s daughter (m. s.).	Ah-gäre'-seh	" cousin.	" tämäkay (o.), tangay (y.)	" sister elder or younger.
154. " father's father's sister's daught.'s daughter (f. s.).	Ah-gäre'-seh	" "	" tämäkay (o.), tangay (y.)	" sister elder or younger.
155. " father's father's sister's daught.'s daughter's son (m. s.).	Ha-yä'-wan-da	" nephew.	" märümäkän	" nephew.
156. " father's father's sister's daught.'s daughter's son (f. s.).	Ha-ah'-wuk	" son.	" mäkän ?	" son.
157. " father's father's sister's daught.'s daughter's daughter (m. s.).	Ka-yä'-wan-da	" niece.	" märämäkäl ?	" niece.
158. " father's father's sister's daught.'s daughter's daughter (f. s.) .	Ka-ah'-wuk	" daughter.	" mäkäl ?	" daughter.
159. " father's father's sister's great gt. grandson.	Ha-yä'-da	" grandson.	" pêrän	" grandson.
160. " father's father's sister's great gt. granddaughter.	Ka-yä'-da	" granddaughter.	" pêrtti	" granddaughter.
161. " mother's mother's brother	Hoc'-sote	" grandfather.	" paddan (P. & S.)	" gd. father gt. or lit.
162. " mother's mother's brother's son	Hoc-no'-seh	" uncle.	" mämän	" uncle.
163. " mother's mother's bro.'s son's son (m. s.)	Ah-gäre'-seh	" cousin.	" mäittünän	" cousin.
164. " mother's mother's bro.'s son's son (f. s.)	Ah-gäre'-seh	" "	" mächchän	" "
165. " mother's mother's brother's son's son's son (m. s.).	Ha-ah'-wuk	" son.	" märümäkän	" nephew.
166. " mother's mother's brother's son's son's son (f. s.).	Ha-so'-neh	" nephew.	" mäkän	" son.
167. " mother's mother's brother's son's son's daughter (m. s.).	Ka-ah'-wuk	" daughter.	" märümäkäl	" niece.
168. " mother's mother's brother's son's son's daughter (f. s.).	Ka-so'-neh	" niece.	" mäkäl	" daughter.
169. " mother's mother's brother's great great grandson.	Ha-yä'-da	" grandson.	" pêrän	" grandson.
170. " mother's mother's brother's great great granddaughter.	Ka-yä'-da	" granddaughter.	" pêrtti	" granddaughter.
171. " mother's mother's sister.	Oc'-sote	" grandmother.	" pǎddi (P. & S.)	" gd. mother gt. or lit.
172. " mother's mother's sister's daughter	No-yeh'	" mother.	" täy (P. & S.)	" mother gt. or little.
173. " mother's mother's sister's daugh.'s daughter (older than myself).	Ah'-je	" elder sister.	" tämäkäy	" elder sister.
174. " mother's mother's sister's daugh.'s daughter (younger than myself).	Ka'-gä	" younger sister.	" tängäy	" younger sister.
175. " mother's mother's sister's daugh.'s daughter's son (m. s.).	Ha-yä'-wan-da	" nephew.	" märümäkän	" nephew.
176. " mother's mother's sister's daugh.'s daughter's son (f. s.).	Ha-ah'-wuk	" son.	" mäkän	" son.
177. " mother's mother's sister's daugh.'s daughter's daughter (m. s.).	Ka-yä'-wan-da	" niece.	" märümäkäl	" niece.
178. " mother's mother's sister's daugh.'s daughter's daughter (f. s.).	Ka-ah'-wuk	" daughter.	" mäkäl	" daughter.
179. " mother's mother's sister's great great grandson.	Ha-yä'-da	" grandson.	" pêrän	" grandson.
180. " mother's mother's sister's great great granddaughter.	Ka-yä'-da	" granddaughter.	" pêrtti	" granddaughter.
181. " father's father's father's brother	Hoc'-sote	" grandfather.	" irandäm päddän	" 2d grandfather.
182. " father's father's father's brother's son	Hoc'-sote	" "	" päddän (P. & S.)	" gd. father gt. or litt.
183. " father's father's father's bro.'s son's son	Hä'-nin	" father.	" täkäppän (P. & S.)	" father great or little.
184. " father's father's father's brother's son's son's son (older than myself).	Hä'-je	" elder brother.	" annan	" elder brother.
185. " father's father's father's brother's son's son's son's son (m. s.).	Ha-ah'-wuk	" son.	" mäkän	" son.
186. " father's father's father's brother's son's son's son's son.	Ha-yä'-da	" grandson.	" pêrän	" grandson.
187. " father's father's father's sister	Oc'-sote	" grandmother.	" irandäm päddi	" 2d grandmother.
188. " father's father's father's sister's daughter	Oc'-sote	" "	" päddi (P. & S.)	" gd.mother gt. or lit.
189. " father's father's father's sister's daught.'s daughter.	Ah-ga'-huc	" aunt.	" täy ? (P. or S.)	" mother gt. or little.
190. " father's father's father's sister's daught.'s daughter's daughter (m. s.).	Ah-gäre'-seh	" cousin.	" tämäkäy. b Tängäy ?	" sister elder or younger.
191. " father's father's father's sister's daught.'s daughter's daughter's daughter (f. s.).	Ka-ah'-wuk	" daughter.	" märümäkäl	" niece.
192. " father's father's father's sister's daughter's daughter's daughter's daughter.	Ka-yä'-da	" granddaughter.	" pêrtti	" granddaughter.
193. " mother's mother's mother's brother	Hoc'-sote	" grandfather.	" irandäm päddän	" 2d grandfather.
194. " mother's mother's mother's brother's son	Hoc'-sote	" "	" päddän (P. or S.)	" gd. mother gt. or lit.
195. " mother's mother's mother's brother's son's son.	Hoc-no'-seh	" uncle.	" mämän	" uncle.
196. " mother's mother's mother's brother's son's son's son (m. s.).	Ah-gäre'-seh	" cousin.	" mäittünän	" cousin.

COMPARISON OF THE SYSTEM OF RELATIONSHIP OF THE SENECA-IROQUOIS WITH THAT OF THE TAMIL PEOPLE.—*Continued.*

Description of persons.	Relationships in Seneca.	Translation.	Relationships in Tamil.	Translation.
197. My mother's mother's mother's brother's son's son's son son (m. s.).	Ha-ah'-wuk	My son.	En mărŭmăkăn	My nephew.
198. " mother's mother's mother's brother's son's son's son's son.	Ha-yä'-da	" grandson.	" pĕrăn	" grandson.
199. " mother's mother's mother's sister	Oc'-sote	" grandmother.	" irandăm păddĭ	" 2d grandmother.
200. " mother's mother's mother's sist.'s daughter.	Oc'-sote	" "	" puddi (P. or S.)	" gd. mother gt. or lit.
201. " mother's mother's mother's sist.'s daughter's daughter.	No-yeh'	" mother.	" täy (P. or S.)	" mother gt. or little.
202. " mother's mother's mother's sist.'s daughter's daughter's daughter (older than myself).	Ah'-je	" elder sister.	" akkärl	" elder sister.
203. " mother's mother's mother's sist.'s daughter's daughter's daughter's daughter (f. s.).	Ka-ah'-wuk	" daughter.	" măkăl	" daughter.
204. " mother's mother's mother's sist.'s daughter's daughter's daughter's daughter.	Ka-yä'-da	" granddaughter.	" pĕrtti	" granddaughter.
205. " husband	Da-yake'-ne	" husband (2 joined).	" kănavăn. ᵇPurushan	" husband.
206. " wife	Da-yake'-ne	" wife (2 joined).	" mănaivĭ. ᵇPernchätti	" wife.
207. " husband's father	Hä-ga'-sä	" father-in-law.	" mämän. ᵇMämanär.	" uncle & fath.-in-law.
208. " husband's mother	Oŋ-ga'-sä	" mother-in-law.	" mämi. ᵇMämiar	" aunt & mo.-in-law.
209. " husband's grandfather	Hä-ga'-sä	" father-in-law.	" păddăn	" grandfather.
210. " husband's grandmother	Oŋ-ga'-sä	" mother-in-law.	" păddi	" grandmother.
211. " wife's father	Oc-na'-hose	" father-in-law.	" mämăn	" uncle.
212. " wife's mother	Oc-na'-hose	" mother-in-law.	" mämi	" aunt.
213. " wife's grandfather	Hoc'-sote	" grandfather.	" păddăn	" grandfather.
214. " wife's grandmother	Oc'-sote	" grandmother.	" păddi [kăn	" grandmother.
215. " son-in-law	Oc-na'-hose	" son-in-law.	" mäpellai. ᵇMărŭmă-	" son-in-law. ᵇ Neph.
216. " daughter-in-law	Ka'-sä	" daughter-in-law.	" mărŭmăkăl	" dau.-in-law niece. (Widow cannot marry.)
217. " step-father	Hoc-no'-ese	" step-father.	" sĕrĭyă täy	My little mother.
218. " step-mother	Oc-no'-ese	" step-mother.	" măkăn	" son.
219. " step-son	Ha'-no	" step-son.	" măkăl	" daughter.
220. " step-daughter	Ka'-no	" step-daughter.	" annan (o.), tambi (y.)	" bro. older or y'nger.
221. " step-brother	Hä'-je (o.), Ha'-gä (y.)	" e. or y. brother.	" akkärl (o.), tăngay (y.)	" sist. older or y'nger.
222. " step-sister	Ah'-je (o.), Ka'-gä (y.)	" e. or y. sister.	" mäittunăn	" bro.-in-law & cous.
223. " brother-in-law (husband's brother)	Ha-yä'-o	" brother-in-law.	" mäittŭnăn [(y.)	" " " "
224. " " " (sister's husband, m. s.)	Ah-ge͡ah'-ne͡o	" " "	" attan (o.), maichchăn	" " " "
225. " " " (" " f. s.)	Ha-yä'-o	" " "	" mäittŭnăn	" " " "
226. " " " (wife's brother)	Ah-ge͡ah'-ne͡o	" " "	" sakälăn	" " " "
227. " " " (wife's sister's husband)	———	Not related.	" sakotaran [tŭmi	" " " "
228. " " " (husband's sister's husband)	———	Not related.	" korlunti (o.) ᵇMäit-	" sist.-in-law. ᵇ Cous.
229. " sister-in-law (wife's sister)	Ka-yä'-o	My sister-in-law.	" năttănar [(y.)	" sister-in-law.
230. " " " (husband's sister)	Ah-ge͡ah-ne͡o	" sister-in-law.	" anni (o.), mäittŭni	" "
231. " " " (brother's wife, m. s.)	Ah-ge-ah'-ne-ah	" "	" anni (o.), mäittŭni	" "
232. " " " (" " f. s.)	Ah-ge͡ah'-ne͡o	" "	" orakatti [(y.)	" "
233. " " " (husband's brother's wife)	———	Not related.	" tămăkăy (o.), tangay	" sister old. or y'nger.
234. " " " (wife's brother's wife)		" "	Kiempun [(y.)	Widow.
235. Widow	Go-no-kwä'-yes-hä-ah	Widow.	———	No term.
236. Widower	Ho-no-kwä'-yes-hä-ah	Widower.	Dithambathie	Twins (Sanskrit.)
237. Twins	Tä-geek'-hä	Twins.		

Relationships to each other of the descendants of two brothers, of two sisters, and of a brother and sister.

1. The son of the son of one brother to the son of the son of the other brother.	Hä'-je and Hä'-gä	Brothers elder and younger.	Annăn and Tambi	Brothers elder and younger.
2. The son of the son of the son of one brother to the son of the son of the son of the other brother.	Hä'-je and Ha'-gä	" " " "	Annan and Tambi	" " " "
3. The daughter of the daughter of the daughter of one brother to the daughter of the daughter of the daughter of the other brother.	Ah'-je and Ka'-gä	Sisters elder and younger.	Tămăkăy and Tăngay	Sisters elder and younger.
1. The daughter of the daughter of one sister to the daughter of the daughter of the other sister.	Ah'-je and Ka'-gä	" " " "	Tămăkăy and Tăngay	" " " "
2. The daughter of the daughter of the daughter of one sister to the daughter of the daughter of the daughter of the other sister.	Ah'-je and Ka'-gä	" " " "		
3. The son of the son of one sister to the son of the son of the son of the other sister.	Hä'-je and Ha'-gä	Brothers elder and younger.	Annăn and Tambi	Brothers elder and younger.
1. The son of the son of a brother to the son of the son of the brother's sister.	Ah-găre'-seh and Ah-găre'-seh.	Cousin and cousin.	Attăn and Mäittŭnăn	Cousin and cousin.
2. The son of the son of the son of a brother to the son of the son of the son of the brother's sister.	Ah-găre'-seh and Ah-găre'-seh.	" " "	Attăn and Mäittŭnăn	" " "
3. The daughter of the daughter of the daughter of a brother to the daughter of the daughter of the daughter of the brother's sister.	Ah-găre'-seh and Ah-găre'-seh.	" " "	Măchchi and Măchchărl	" " "

APPENDIX TO PART III.

TABLE OF CONSANGUINITY AND AFFINITY OF THE TURANIAN AND MALAYAN FAMILIES.

APPENDIX TO PART III.

Family.	Class.	Dialects.
TURANIAN	DRÂVIDIC	1. Tamil, 2. Telŭgŭ, 3. Canarese.
	GAURAIC	4. Hindi, 5. Bengâli, 6. Gujârâthi, 7. Marâthi.
	CHINESE	8. Chinese.
	JAPANESE	9. Japanese.
	UNCLASSIFIED	10. Burmese, 11. Karen (Sgau dialect), 12. Karen (Pwo dialect), 13. Karen.
MALAYAN	OCEANIC	14. Kingsmill Island, 15. Kusaien, 16. Hawaiian. 17. Maori (New Zealand). 18. Tongan[1] (Friendly Islands). 19. Rewan[1] (Fiji Islands). 20. Amazulu (Kafir).

[1] These schedules were received too late for insertion in the Table, and will be found in a note appended to Table III.

(517)

SCHEDULES OF CONSANGUINITY AND AFFINITY OF THE TURANIAN FAMILY, AND OF SEVERAL UNCLASSI-
FIED NATIONS OF ASIA, AND ALSO OF THE MALAYAN FAMILY; WITH THE NAMES AND RESIDENCES
OF THE PERSONS BY WHOM THE SAME WERE SEVERALLY PREPARED.

Nations and Dialects.	Persons by whom and Places where Schedules were filled.
1. TAMIL	1. Rev. Ezekiel C. Scudder, Missionary of the American Board of Foreign Missions of the Dutch Reformed Church, Vellore, South India, August 1, 1862. 2. Rev. Miron Winslow, D. D., Missionary of the American Board of Commissioners for Foreign Missions, Madras, South India, October, 1860. 3. Rev. William Tracey, English Missionary, Madura, South India, December, 1862. Procured through Rev. James L. Scott, of Futtehghur, North India.
2. TELUGU	Rev. Ezekiel C. Scudder, before mentioned, Vellore, South India, April, 1863.
3. CANARESE	Rev. B. Rice, English Missionary, Bangalore, South India, December, 1862. Procured through Rev. Jas. L. Scott, of Futtehghur, North India.
4. HINDI	Rev. James L. Scott, Missionary of the American Presbyterian Board, Futtehghur, North India, April, 1860.
5. BENGALI	Rev. Gopenath Nundy, Missionary of the same Board, Futtapore, North India, July, 1860. A native Bengali.
6. GUJARÂTHI	Rev. Joseph S. Taylor, Irish Presbyterian Mission, Borsaa, Gujarat, North India, July, 1862. Procured through Rev. James L. Scott, of Futtehghur, North India.
7. MARÂTHI	Rev. S. B. Fairbank, Missionary of the American Board of Commissioners for Foreign Missions, Wadale, District of Ahmednuggur, North India, April, 1862. Procured through Rev. James L. Scott, of Futtehghur, North India.
8. CHINESE	Hon. Robert Hart, Department of Marine Customs, Canton, China, September, 1860.
9. JAPANESE	Lewis H. Morgan, Rochester, N. Y. From Man-kĭ-chĕ Kä-wä-be, a native Japanese from Yedo, May, 1867.
10. BURMESE	Rev. E. A. Stephens, Missionary of the American Baptist Missionary Union, Rangoon, India, August, 1860.
11. KAREN (Sgau dialect)	Rev. Francis Mason, D. D., Missionary of the Board last named, Toungoo, India, June, 1860.
12. KAREN (Pwo dialect) .	Rev. Jonathan Wade, D. D., Missionary of the Board last named, Maulmain, India, June, 1860.
13. KAREN	Rev. H. L. Van Meter, Missionary of the Board last named, Bassein, India, November, 1861.
14. KINGSMILL ISLAND .	Rev. Hiram Bingham, Jr., Missionary of the American Board of Commissioners for Foreign Missions, Kingsmill Island, Micronesia, August, 1860.
15. KUSAIEN (STRONG'S ISLAND.)	Rev. B. G. Snow, Missionary of the Board last named, Kusai, Strong's Island, March, 1860.

SCHEDULES OF CONSANGUINITY AND AFFINITY OF THE TURANIAN FAMILY, ETC.—*Continued.*

Nations and Dialects.	Persons by whom and Places where Schedules were filled.
16. HAWAIIAN	1. Hon. Thomas Miller, United States Consul, Sandwich Islands, Hilo, Island of Hawaii, May, 1860. 2. Hon. Lorin Andrews, one of the Judges of the King's Courts, Honolulu, Sandwich Islands, May, 1860. 3. Rev. Artemus Bishop, Missionary of the Board last named, Honolulu, Sandwich Islands, April, 1860.
17. MAORI	Rev. Richard Taylor, M. A., F.S.L., Wanganni, New Zealand, August, 1862. Procured by the late Hon. G. W. Leavenworth, U. S. Consul, Bay of Islands.
18. TONGAN	Rev. Lorimer Fison, English Missionary to the Fiji Islands, Rewa, Fiji, December, 1869. Procured through Prof. Goldwin Smith, of Cornell University, New York.
19. REWAN	Rev. Lorimer Fison, Rewa, Fiji, December, 1869. Procured through Prof. Goldwin Smith.
20. AMAZULU, or KAFIR .	Rev. Andrew Abraham, Missionary of the Board last named, Mapumalo, Natal, East Africa, January, 1861.

TABLE III.—Systems of Consanguinity and Affinity of the Turanian and Malayan Families.

Families.	Classes.	Branches.	Dialects.	Persons by whom schedules were filled.	Pronoun *my* or *mine*.
TURANIAN,	DRAVIDIC,	Dravidian,	1. Tamil	Rev. Ezekiel C. Scudder	En.
			2. Telugu	" " " "	
			3. Canarese	Rev. B. Rice	Nănnă.
	GAURAIC,	Gauran,	4. Hindi	Rev. James L. Scott . .	Masc. merá; fem. meri.
			5. Bengáli	Rev. Gopenath Nundy .	" amar
			6. Maráthi	Rev. S. B. Fairbank . .	" mäzhä; " mäzhi.
			7. Gujáráthi	Rev. Joseph S. Taylor .	" märo; " märi.
		—	8. Chinese	Hon. Robert Hart . .	Wo-tĕ.
			9. Japanese	Lewis H. Morgan . . .	Wä-tä⌒k'-se-no
MALAYAN,	Unclassified,	—	10. Burmese	Rev. E. A. Stephens .	{ Masc. Ky-u-nok'. / Fem. Ky-uu-mä.
			11. Karen. (Sgau dialect)	Rev. Francis Mason, D. D.	Yă.
			12. Karen. (Pwo ")	Rev. Jonath'n Wade, D.D.	Y'
			13. Karen.	Rev. H. L. Van Meter .	Yeh.
	OCEANIC,	Micronesian,	14. Kings Mill Islands .	Rev. Hiram Bingham .	Suffix u.
			15. Kusaien (Strong's Is'd)	Rev. B. G. Snow . . .	Suffix uk or ik.
		Polynesian,	16. Hawaiian	Hon. Thomas Miller . .	Kŭ-ŭ and ko'ŭ.
			17. Maori (New Zealand)	Rev. Rich'd Taylor, F.S.L.	Ta'-ku (sing.), a'-ku (pl.)
			18. Tongan (Friendly Is'ds)	Rev. Lorimer Fison . .	E-ku or ho-ku.
			19. Fijian (Rewa Nation)	" " "	Suffix Nŏ'ng-gu or Nĕ'ng-gu.
		Kafrarian,	20. Amazulu (Kafir) . .	Rev. Andrew Abraham .	Wa'-me or ya'-me.

NOTATION IN TABLE III.

VOWELS.

a as a in ale, mate.
ä " " " art, father.
ă " " " at, tank.
a̤ " " " all, fall.

e as e in even, mete.
ĕ " " " enter, met.
ê has a nasal sound as the French *en*
    in mien.

i as i in idea, mite.
ĭ " " " it, pity.

o as o in over, go.
ŏ " " " otter, got.

u as u in use, mute.
ŭ " oo " food.

CONSONANTS.

ch as ch in chin.
d pronounced harshly by curving back
    the tongue and bringing it forcibly
    against the roof of the mouth.
g hard as in go.
ğ soft as in gem.
h· a sonant guttural.
ṇ nasal as in drink.

t' prefixed indicates that the tongue is
    to be pressed forcibly against the
    teeth in its pronunciation.
' An apostrophe after a final syllable
    denotes a slight breathing sound.
? An interrogation mark in the Table
    indicates that the answer is con-
    jectural.

The notation of the cultivated languages is left unchanged. The following is
much used in India:—

a short as in cat.
á as in far.
e long a as in pale.
ì short as in pit.
í long as e in mete.
o as in note.
u as in bull.

ú as oo in food.
t dental.
  palatal.
n as French non.
ch as in church.
au as ow in how.

(522)

TABLE III.—CONSANGUINITY AND AFFINITY OF THE TURANIAN AND MALAYAN FAMILIES.

		1. My great grandfather's father.	Translation.	2. My great grandfather's mother.	Translation.
1.	Tamil	En muppaddan	My third grandfather.	En muppäddi	My third grandmother.
2.	Telugu				
3.	Canarese				
4.	Hindî	Merá sardádá	My great great grandfather.	Meri sardadï	My great gt. grandmother.
5.	Bengâlî	Amar oty broh pse pté mohu	" " " "	Amar oty broh pse pitá mohy	" " " "
6.	Marâthî	Mázhä nipanazä panazä	" " "	Mäzhi nipanaze panaze	" " " "
7.	Gujârâthî	Märo purvaj	My forefather or ancestor.	Märi purvaj	My ancestor.
8.	Chinese	Wo-te-kaon-tsŭ	My far removed ancestor.	Wo-tĕ kaon-tsŭ-mo	Far removed ancestral mo.
9.	Japanese	Ko-o-so-foo	High beginning father.	Ko-o-so-bo	High beginning mother.
10.	Burmese	K: bee. ᵇA-bee	My great great grandfather.	K: bee-mä'. ᵇA-bee-mä	My great gt. grandmother.
11.	Karen (Sgau dial'ct)	Yä phu-pgha	" " " "	Yä phiè-pgha	" " " "
12.	Karen (Pwo ")	Y' phu	My grandfather.	Y' phe	My grandmother.
13.	Karen	Yeh-pü-pa-do	My great grandfather.	Yeh pee-pa-do	My great grandmother.
14.	Kings Mill Islands	Jïbŭ	My ancestor.		My ancestor.
15.	Kusaien	[kó-lŭ	generation.	[ä kó-lŭ	[generation.
16.	Hawaiian	Kŭ'-ŭ kŭ'-pŭ-nä kä'-na kŭ'-ä	My grand parent male, third	Kŭ'-ŭ kŭ'-pŭ-nä wä-heé-na kŭ'	My gd. parent female, third
17.	Maori				
18.	Amazulu (Kafir)	U-ko'-ko wa'-me	My ancestor.	U-ko'-ko wa'-me	My ancestor.

		3. My great grandfather.	Translation.	4. My great grandmother.	Translation.
1.	Tamil	En pûddan	My second grandfather.	En pûddì	My second grandmother.
2.	Telugu	Müttäta	Great grandfather.	Muttävvä	Great grandmother.
3.	Canarese	Nännä muttätä	My great grandfather.	Nännä muttäwwä	My great grandmother.
4.	Hindî	Merá pardádá	" " "	Meri pardádi	" " "
5.	Bengâlî	Amar pse pitá mohu	" " "	Amar oty pitá mohy	" " "
6.	Marâthî	Mäzhä panazä	" " "	Mäzhi panaze	" " "
7.	Gujârâthî	Märo purvaj	My ancestor.	Märi purvaj	My ancestor. [mother.
8.	Chinese	Wo-tĕ tsung-tsŭ	My additional ancestor.	Wo-tĕ tsung-tsŭ-mo	My more remote ancestral
9.	Japanese	She'-je-je	Great grandfather.	She'-bä-ba	Great grandmother
10.	Burmese	K: ba. ᵇA-bá	My great grandfather.	K: a-bá-mä. ᵇBá-mä	My great grandmother.
11.	Karen (Sgau dial'ct)	Yä phu-phga	" " "	Yä phiè-pgha	" " "
12.	Karen (Pwo ")	Y' phu	My grandfather.	Y' phe	My grandmother.
13.	Karen	Yeh pü-pa-do.	My great grandfather.	Yeh pee-pa-do	My great grandmother.
14.	Kings Mill Islands	Jïbŭ [päpä-tummuk	My ancestor. [my.		[keyŭk [ther my.
15.	Kusaien	Päpä-tummun-päpä-tummun	Father of the father of father	Nenĕ-keyĕn-nenĕ-keyĕn-nenĕ	Mother of the mother of mo-
16.	Hawaiian	Kŭ'-ŭ ku'-pu-nä kä'-na kŭ'- [lŭ'-ä	My gd. parent male, second [generation.	Kŭ'-ŭ kŭ-pŭ'-nä wä-hee-na kŭ'- [ä-lŭ'-ä	My gd.parent female, second [generation.
17.	Maori				
18.	Amazulu (Kafir)	U-ko'-ko wa'-we	My ancestor.	U-ko'-ko wa'-me	My ancestor.

		5. My grandfather.	Translation.	6. My grandmother.	Translation.
1.	Tamil	En paddan	My grandfather.	En paddi	My grandmother.
2.	Telugu	Tatä	Grandfather.	Avvä	Grandmother.
3.	Canarese	Nännä tätäna	My grandfather.	Nännä äwwä	My grandmother.
4.	Hindî	Merá dádá	" "	Meri dádi	" "
5.	Bengâlî	Amar dádá	" "	Amar didy	" "
6.	Marâthî	Mäzhä äzä	" "	Mäzhi äze	" "
7.	Gujârâthî	Märo vadova	" "	Märi yardi ma	My elder brother.
8.	Chinese	Wo-tĕ tsŭ-fŭ	My ancestral father.	Wo-tĕ tsŭ-mo	My ancestral mother.
9.	Japanese	O-je'-sang	Grandfather.	O-bä'-sän	Grandmother.
10.	Burmese	K: bo. ᵇA-pó	My grandfather.	K: a-pwä. ᵇBwää. ᶜBwä	My grandmother.
11.	Karen (Sgau dial'ct)	Yä phu	" "	Yä phie	" "
12.	Karen (Pwo ")	Y' phu.	" "	Y' phe	" "
13.	Karen	Yeh pü	" "	Yeh pee	" "
14.	Kings Mill Islands	Jïbŭ	My ancestor.		
15.	Kusaien	Päpä-tummun-päpä-tummuk.	Father of the father my.	Nenĕ-keyĕn-nenĕ-keyŭk	Mother of the mother my.
16.	Hawaiian	Kŭ'-ŭ kŭ-pŭ'-nä kä'-na	My grandparent male.	Kŭ'-ŭ kŭ-pŭ'-nä wä-hee-na	My grandparent female.
17.	Maori	Tá-ku tu-pu-na	My grandfather.	Tá-ku ku-i-a	My grandmother.
18.	Amazulu (Kafir)	U-bä'-bä kŭ'-lŭ	My grandfather.	U-mä'-me kŭ'-lŭ	My grandmother.

TABLE III.—*Continued.*

		7. My father.	Translation.	8. My mother.	Translation.
1. Tamil	1	En tăkkăppăn	My father.	En tăy	My mother.
2. Telugu	2	Taṇḍrĭ	Father.	Tăllĭ	Mother.
3. Canarese	3	Nănnă tănde	My father.	Nănnă tăi	My mother.
4. Hindî	4	Merá pitá	" "	Meri mátá	" "
5. Bengâlî	5	Amar pitah	" "	Amar mátah	" "
6. Marâthî	6	Măzhă băp-	" "	Măzhi äe	" "
7. Gujârâthî	7	Măro băpă. [b] Pită.... [c] Kea-fŭ	" "	Mări mă	" "
8. Chinese	8	Wo-tĕ fŭ-tsin. [b] Teay-teay	My father relation. [b] Daddy.	Wo-tĕ mo-tsin. [b] Kea-mo	My mother relation. [b] House
9. Japanese	9	O-to'-tsang. [b] Tsee-tsee	Father. [c] House father.	O-ka-tsan. [b] Hă-hă	Mother. [mother.
10. Burmese	10	K: a-bă'. [b] A-pă'	My father.	K: a-me'. [b] A-ma'	My mother.
11. Karen (Sgau dial'ct)	11	Yă pä	" "	Yă mo	" "
12. Karen (Pwo ")	12	Y' pä	" "	Y' mo	" "
13. Karen	13	Yeh pah	" "	Yeh mo	" "
14. Kings Mill Islands	14	Táman	" "	Tínău	" "
15. Kusaien	15	Pä-pä-tum-muk	Father, male my.	Ne-nĕ-keyŭk	Mother female my.
16. Hawaiian	16	Kŭ'-ŭ mä-kŭ'-ă kä'-na	My parent male.	Kŭ'-ŭ mä-kŭ'-ă kä'-na	My parent female.
17. Maori	17	Ta-ku pa-pa	My father.	Ta-ku wa-e-a	My mother.
18. Amazulu (Kafir)	18	U-bä'-bä	My father.	U-mä'-me	My mother.

		9. My son.	Translation.	10. My daughter.	Translation.
1. Tamil	1	En măkăn	My son.	En măkăl	My daughter.
2. Telugu	2	Kŏḍŭkŭ	Son.	Kutŭrŭ	Daughter.
3. Canarese	3	Nănnă măgănu	My son.	Nănnă măgălu	My daughter.
4. Hindî	4	Merá betá	" "	Meri' beti'	" "
5. Bengâlî	5	Amar putro	" "	Amar kouyah	" "
6. Marâthî	6	Măzhă putra. [b] Lank. [c] Mulagă	" "	Măzhi kamyă. [b] Lek. [c] Mulage	" "
7. Gujârâthî	7	Măro dikaro. [b] Pŭtră	" "	Mări dikari. [b] Putri	" "
8. Chinese	8	Wo-tĕ ir-tsze	My child boy.	Wo-tĕ neu-ir	My girl child.
9. Japanese	9	Moos'-ko	Son.	Moo'-soo-mă	Daughter.
10. Burmese	10	K: thă	My son.	K: tha-neĕ	My daughter.
11. Karen (Sgau dial'ct)	11	Yă pho-khwă	My male child.	Yă pho-mu	My female child.
12. Karen (Pwo ")	12	Y' pho-khwá	" " "	Y' pho-mu	" " "
13. Karen	13	Yeh pó-khwa	" " "	Yeh po-mŭ	" " "
14. Kings Mill Islands	14	Nátu-te-máne	Child my a male.	Nátu-te-áine	Child my a female.
15. Kusaien	15	Mwĕn-nŭttik	Son my.	Au-nŭttik	Daughter my.
16. Hawaiian	16	Kŭ'-ŭ kaĭ'-kee kä'-na. [b] Kä'-	My child male	Kŭ'-ŭ kaĭ-kee wă-heĕ-na	My child female.
17. Maori	17	Tá-ku ta-ma ......[mă kä'-na	My son.	Tá-ku ta-ma-hi-ne.... [tom-be	My daughter.
18. Amazulu (Kafir)	18	In-do-dä'-nä yä'-me	Son of me.	In-do-dä-kä'-ze yä'-me. [b] In-	Daughter of me. A daughter.

		11. My grandson.	Translation.	12. My granddaughter.	Translation.
1. Tamil	1	En pĕrăn	My grandson.	En pĕrtti	My granddaughter.
2. Telugu	2	Mănămăḍŭ	Grandson.	Mănămărălŭ	Granddaughter.
3. Canarese	3	Nănnă mommăgănu	My grandson.	Nănnă mommăgălu	My granddaughter.
4. Hindî	4	Merá potá	" "	Meri poti'	" "
5. Bengâlî	5	Amar naty [b] Powutro	My grandson. [b] Son's son.	Amar natuy [b] Dowutir	My gd. daught. [b] Dau. dau.
6. Marâthî	6	Măzhă nătŭ	My grandson.	Măzhi nät	My granddaughter.
7. Gujârâthî	7	Măro pautră	My born of a son.	Mări pautri	My born of a daughter.
8. Chinese	8	Wo-tĕ sun-tsze	My growing for the second	Wo-tĕ sun-neu	My growing for the 2d time
9. Japanese	9	Mä'-go	Grandson. [time boy.	Ma'-ee	Granddaughter. [girl.
10. Burmese	10	K: my-a'	My grandchild.	K: my-a'	My grandchild.
11. Karen (Sgau dial'ct)	11	Yă lie-pŏ-khwă	My grandson.	Yă lie-pŏ-mu	My granddaughter.
12. Karen (Pwo ")	12	Y' le-po-khwä	" "	Y' le-po-mu	" "
13. Karen	13	Yeh lee'-khwa	My grandchild male.	Yeh-leĕ-mu	My grandchild female.
14. Kings Mill Islands	14	Tibu-te-mane	Grandchild my a male.	Tíbu-te-aine	My grandchild a female.
15. Kusaien	15	Mwĕn-nŭttin-nŭttik	Grandson my.	An-nŭttin-nŭttik	Granddaughter my.
16. Hawaiian	16	Kŭ'-ŭ moo-pŭ'-nä kä'-na	My grandchild male.	Kŭ'-ŭ moo-pŭ'-nä wă-heĕ-na	My grandchild female.
17. Maori	17	Tá-ku mo-ko-pu-na	My grandchild.	Tá-ku mo-ko-pu-na	My grandchild.
18. Amazulu (Kafir)	18	U-me-tshä'-nä yä'-me	Grandchild of me.	U-me-tshä'-nä yä'-ne	Grandchild of me.

TABLE III.—*Continued.*

		13. My great grandson.	Translation.	14. My great granddaughter.	Translation.
1. Tamil	1	En irandām pêran	My second grandson.	En irandām pêrtti	My second granddaughter.
2. Telugu	2	Münimännämädŭ	Great grandson.	Münimännärälŭ	Great granddaughter
3. Canarese	3	Nännä mümmäganu	My great grandson.	Nännä mümmägälu	My great granddaughter.
4. Hindî	4	Merá parotá	" " "	Merí paroti	" " "
5. Bengâlî	5	Amar powutro	" " "	Amar powtry	" " "
6. Marâthî	6	Mazhä paṇatŭ	" " "	Mäzhi panate	" " "
7. Gujârâthî	7		[the second time boy.		[the second time girl.
8. Chinese	8	Wo-tĕ tsung-sun	My additional growing for	Wo-tĕ tsung-sun-neu	My additional growing for
9. Japanese	9	She'-ko	Great grandchild.	She'-ko	Great grandchild.
10. Burmese	10	K : my-eet'	My great grandchild.	K : my-eet'	My great grandchild.
11. Karen (Sgau dial'ct)	11	Yă lo-pŏ-khwă	My great grandson.	Yă lo-pŏ-mu	My great granddaughter.
12. Karen (Pwo ")	12	Y' lo-po-khwä	" " "	Y' lo-po-mu	" " "
13. Karen	13	Yeh ló-khwa	My greăt grandchild male.	Yeh ló-mü,	My great grandchild female.
14. Kings Mill Islands	14	Tibun-natu [nŭttik	Grandchild of my child.	Tibun-natu	Grandchild of my child.
15. Kusaien	15	Mwĕn - nŭttin - mwĕn - nŭttin -	Great grandson my.	Au-nŭttin-ăn-nŭttin-nŭttik	Great granddaughter my.
16. Hawaiian	16	Kŭ'-ă moo-pŭ'-nă kä'-na ku'-ä-	My great grandchild male.	Kŭ'-ŭ moo-pŭ'-nă wä-hée-na-	My great grandchild female.
17. Maori	17	Tă-ku mo-ko-pu-na [hi-ä	My grandchild.	Tă-ku mo-ko-pu-na.[kŭ-ä-lü-ä	My grandchild.
18. Amazulu (Kafir)	18	U-mzŭ-kŭ'-lŭ wä'-me	Great grandchild of me.	U-mzŭ-kŭ-lŭ wä'-me	Great grandchild of me.

		15. My great grandson's son.	Translation.	16. My great grandson's daughter.	Translation.
1. Tamil	1	En mŭndam pêran	My third grandson.	En mŭndam pertti	My third granddaughter.
2. Telugu	2				
3. Canarese	3				
4. Hindî	4	Merá sarotá	My great great grandson.	Merá saroti	My gt. gt. granddaughter.
5. Bengâlî	5	Amar powutro	My great grandson.	Amar powtry	My granddaughter.
6. Marâthî	6	Mäzhä nipanatu	My great great grandson.	Mäzhi nipanazĕ	My gt. gt. granddaughter.
7. Gujârâthî	7		[cond time boy.		[second time girl.
8. Chinese	8	Wo-tĕ yuen-sun	My great growing for the se-	Wo-tĕ yuen-sun-neu	My great growing for the
9. Japanese	9	Yă-shang'-o	Great grandson's child.	Yă-shang'-o	Gt. gd. daughter's child.
10. Burmese	10	K : tee.	My great great grandchild.	K : tee.	My great great grandchild.
11. Karen (Sgau dial'ct)	11	Yă lä-pŏ-khwă	My great great grandson.	Yă lä-pŏ-mu	My gt. gt. granddaughter.
12. Karen (Pwo ")	12	Y' la-po-khwä	" " " "	Y' la-po-mu	" " " "
13. Karen	13	Yeh lá-khwa.	My gt. gt. grandchild male.	Yeh lá-mü	My gt. gt. gd. child female.
14. Kings Mill Islands	14	Tibnn-natn [tik	Grandchild of my child.	Tibun-natu	Grandchild of my child.
15. Kusaien	15	Mwĕn-nŭttin-n.-n.-n.-n.-nŭt-	Great great grandson my.	Au-nŭttin-ă-nuttin-ă-n.-nŭttik	Gt. gt. granddaughter my.
16. Hawaiian	16	Kŭ'-ŭ moo-pŭ'-nă kä'-na kŭ-ä	My gt. gt. grandchild male.	Kŭ'-ŭ moo-pŭ'-nă wä-há-na kĕ-	My gt. gt. gd. child female.
17. Hawaiian	17	Tă-ku mo-ko-pu-na [kó-lü	My grandchild.	Ta-ku mo-ko-pu-ne [ä kó-lü	My grandchild.
18. Amazulu (Kafir)	18	U-mzŭ-kŭ-lŭ wä'-me	Great grandchild of me.	U-mzŭ-kŭ'-lŭ wä'-me tä-ren-ty-[tär	Great grandchild of me.

		17. My elder brother. (Male speaking.)	Translation.	18. My elder brother. (Female speaking.)	Translation.
1. Tamil	1	En tămaiyăn. b Aṇṇăn	My elder brother.	En tămaiyăn. b Aṇṇăn	My elder brother.
2. Telugu	2	Annă	Elder brother.	Annă	Elder brother.
3. Canarese	3	Nănnä änna	My elder brother.	Nănnä änna	My elder brother.
4. Hindî	4	Merá bará bhái.	My greater brother.	Merá bará bhái	My greater brother.
5. Bengâlî	5	Amar burro dádá	My eldest brother.	Amar burro dádá	My oldest brother.
6. Marâthî	6	Mäzhá wadēl bhäu. b Agraz..	" " "	Mäzhá wadēl bhäu. b Agraz.	" " "
7. Gujârâthî	7	Märo bhäi	My brother.	Märo bhäi	My brother.
8. Chinese	8	Wo-te ko-ko. b Heung	My elder brother. Senior.	Wo-tĕ ko-ko. b Heung	My elder brother. b Senior.
9. Japanese	9	A'-nee	Elder brother.	A'-nee	Elder brother.
10. Burmese	10	K : e-ko.	My elder brother. [cessor.	K : mo-ung ky-ee	My brother elder. [cessor.
11. Karen (Sgau dial'ct)	11	Yă way-khwă	My elder bro. (male prede-	Yă way-khwă	My elder bro. (male prede-
12. Karen (Pwo ")	12	Y' wai-po-khwä	" " " " "	Y' wai-po-khwä	" " " " "
13. Karen	13	Yeh wĕh-pau-khwa	My elder brother.	Yeh-wĕh-pau-khwä	My elder brother.
14. Kings Mill Islands	14	Tăru-te-karimoä	Brother my elder.	Manu-te-karimoä	Brother my older.
15. Kusaien	15	Lĕk-lass. b Mä-tŭ	Brother my larger.	Lĕk-lass. b Mä-tŭ	Brother my larger.
16. Hawaiian	16	Kŭ'-ŭ käï'-kŭ-ä-ä'-nä	My bro. older than myself.	Kŭ'-ŭ-käï' kŭ-nä'-na	My bro. older than myself.
17. Maori	17	Ta-ku tu-a-ka-na.	My elder brother.	Ta-ku tun-go-ne	My elder brother.
18. Amazulu (Kafir)	18	U'-mna wa'-tŭ	Elder brother of us.	U'-mna wa'-tŭ	Elder brother of us.

TABLE III.—*Continued.*

		19. My elder sister. (Male speaking.)	Translation.	20. My elder sister. (Female speaking.)	Translation.
1. Tamil	1	En akkärl. [b] Tămăkay	My elder sister.	En akkäl. [b] Tămăkay	My elder sister.
2. Telugu	2	Akkă	Elder sister.	Akkă	Elder sister.
3. Canarese	3	Nănnă ăkkă	My elder sister.	Nănnă ăkkă	My elder sister.
4. Hindî	4	Merí barí bahin	My greater sister.	Meri barí bahin	My greater sister.
5. Bengalî	5	Amar burro didy	My eldest sister.	Amar burro diddy	My eldest sister.
6. Marâthî	6	Măzhi wadel bahen. [b] Agrază	" " "	Măzhi wadel bahen. [b] Agrază	" " "
7. Gujârâthî	7	Märi băhen.	My sister. [enced woman.	Märi băhen.	My sister. [enced woman.
8. Chinese	8	Wo-tĕ tseay-tseay. [b] Tsze.	My elder sist. [b] An experi-	Wo-tĕ tseay-tseay. [b] Tsze.	My elder sist. [b] An experi-
9. Japanese	9	A'-nih.	Elder sister.	A'-nih	Elder sister.
10. Burmese	10	K: e-mă'.	My elder sister. [decessor.	K: e-mă'.	My elder sister. [decessor.
11. Karen (Sgau dial'ct)	11	Yă way-mu	My elder sister (female pre-	Yă way-mu	My elder sister (female pre-
12. Karen (Pwo ")	12	Y' wai-po-mu.	" " " " "	Y' wai-po-mu.	" " " " "
13. Karen	13	Yeh-wĕh-pau-mü	My elder sister.	Yeh wĕh-pau-mü	My elder sister.
14. Kings Mill Islands	14	Manu-te-karimoă	Sister my older.	Taru-te-karimoă	Sister my older.
15. Kusaien	15	Loŭk-lass. [b] Mătŭ	Sister my larger.	Loŭk-lass. [b] Mătŭ	Sister my larger.
16. Hawaiian	16	Kŭ'-ŭ kăĭ'-kŭ wä-hee'-na	My sister older than myself.	Kŭ'-ŭ kăĭ'-kŭ-ă-ă'-nă	My sister older than myself.
17. Maori	17	Ta-ku tu-a-hi-ne	My elder sister.	Ta-ku tu-a-ka-na.	My elder sister.
18. Amazulu (Kafir)	18	U-dă'-da wa'-tŭ	Sister of us.	U-dă'-da wa'-tŭ	Sister of us.

		21. My younger brother. (Male speaking.)	Translation.	22. My younger brother. (Female speaking.)	Translation.
1. Tamil	1	En tambí.	My younger brother.	En tambí	My younger brother.
2. Telugu	2	Tămmŭdŭ	Younger brother.	Tămmŭdŭ	Younger brother.
3. Canarese	3	Nănnă tămmă	My younger brother.	Nănnă tămmă	My younger brother.
4. Hindî	4	Merá chotá bhái.	My lesser brother.	Merá chotá bhái.	My lesser brother.
5. Bengalî	5	Amar chota bratah	" " "	Amar chota bratah	" " "
6. Marâthî	6	Măzhă dhăkata bhăŭ. [b] Anŭz	My brother. [brother.	Măzhă dhăkată bhăŭ. [b] Anŭz	My brother. [brother.
7. Gujârâthî	7	Măro bhăi.	My sen.little junior. [b] Little	Măro bhăi.	My sen.little junior. [b] Little
8. Chinese	8	Wo-tĕ heung-te. [b] A-te	Younger brother.	Wo-tĕ heung-te. [b] A-te	Younger brother.
9. Japanese	9	O-to'-to	My younger bro. [cessor.	O-to'-to	My bro. younger. [cessor.
10. Burmese	10	K: ny-eé	My younger bro. (male suc-	K: mo-ung ga-ta'.	My younger bro. (male suc-
11. Karen (Sgau dial'ct)	11	Yă pu-khwă	" " " " "	Yă pu-khwă	" " " " "
12. Karen (Pwo ")	12	Y' pu-po-khwă.		Y' pu-po-khwă.	
13. Karen	13	Yeh pü' pau-khwa	My younger brother.	Yeh pü'-pau-khwa	My younger brother.
14. Kings Mill Islands	14	Taru-te-kărimwi	Brother my younger.	Taru-te-karimwi	Brother my younger.
15. Kusaien	15	Lik-srik. [b] Fwos.	Brother my smaller.	Lik-srik. [b] Fwos.	Brother my smaller.
16. Hawaiian	16	Kŭ'-ŭ kăĭ' kăĭ'-nă.	My brother younger than	Kŭ'-ŭ kăĭ'-kŭ-nă'-nă.	My brother younger than
17. Maori	17	Ta-ku te-i-na.	My younger bro. [myself.	Tᵢ-ku tun-ga-ne te-i-na.	My younger bro. [myself.
18. Amazulu (Kafir)	18	U-mnä'-wa wä'-ma	Younger brother of me.	U-mnä'-wa wä'-ma	Younger brother of me.

		23. My younger sister. (Male speaking.)	Translation.	24. My younger sister. (Female speaking.)	Translation.
1. Tamil	1	En tangaichchi. [b] Tangay	My younger sister.	En tangaichchi. [b] Tangay	My younger sister.
2. Telugu	2	Chĕllĕlŭ.	Younger sister.	Chĕllĕlŭ.	Younger sister
3. Canarese	3	Nănnă tănga	My younger sister.	Nanna tăngi	My younger sister.
4. Hindî	4	Meri chotí bahin	My lesser sister.	Meri chotá bahin	My lesser sister.
5. Bengalî	5	Amar chota bhuguy	" " "	Amar choto bhuguy	" " "
6. Marâthî	6	Măzhi dhăkate bahen. [b] Aw-	My sister.	Măzhi dhăkate bahen. [b] Aw-	[arză
7. Gujârâthî	7	Mări băhen. [arză	My sister.	Wo-tĕ mei-mei.	My younger sister.
8. Chinese	8	Wo-tĕ mei-mei.	My younger sister.	E-mo'-to.	Younger sister.
9. Japanese	9	E-mo'-to.	Younger sister.	K: ny-ee-mă.	My younger sist. [cessor).
10. Burmese	10	K: hnee-mă	My younger sist. [cessor).	Yă pu-mu	My younger sist. (fem. suc-
11. Karen (Sgau dial'ct)	11	Yă-pu-mu	My younger sist. (fem. suc-	Y' pu-po-mu.	" " " "
12. Karen (Pwo ")	12	Y' pu-po-mu.	" " " "	Yeh pü'-pau-mü	My younger sister.
13. Karen	13	Yeh pü'-pau-mü	My younger sister.	Taru-te-karimwi	Sister my younger.
14. Kings Mill Islands	14	Manu-te-karimwi	Sister my younger.	Loŭk-srik	Sister my smaller.
15. Kusaien	15	Loŭk-srik	Sister my smaller.	Kŭ-ŭ' kăĭ-lăĭ-nă	My sister younger.
16. Hawaiian	16	Kŭ'-ŭ kăĭ-kŭ wä-heć-nă	My sister younger.	Ta-ku te-i-na	My younger sister.
17. Maori	17	Ta-ku tu-a-hi-ne te-i-na.	My younger sister.	U-dá'da wa'-tŭ	Sister of us.
18. Amazulu (Kafir)	18	U-dă' da wa'-tŭ	Sister of us.		

TABLE III.—Continued.

		25. My brothers. (Male speaking.)	Translation.	26. My brothers. (Female speaking.)	Translation.
1. Tamil	1	En aṇṇan tambi män	My elder younger brothers.	En sakothärer	My brother's (Sanskrit).
2. Telugu	2	Annä tämmŭlŭ	My brothers.	Annä tämmŭlŭ	Elder younger brothers.
3. Canarese	3	Săhodărărŭ	Brothers (Sanskrit).	Săhodărărŭ	Brothers (Sanskrit).
4. Hindî	4	Merä bhái	My brothers.	Merä bhaí	My brothers.
5. Bengâlî	5	Amar bratah	" "	Amar bratah	" "
6. Marâthî	6	Mäzhä bhăw. ᵇ Bhäwaṇde	" "	Mäzhä bhäw. ᵇ Bhäwande	" "
7. Gujârâthî	7				
8. Chinese	8	Wo-tĕ heung-te-mun	My seniors and juniors.	Wo-tĕ heung-te-mun	My seniors juniors.
9. Japanese	9	A'-nee-do'-mo	Elder brothers.	A'-nee-do'-mo	Elder brothers.
10. Burmese	10	K: ny-ee-é-ko-to'	My older and younger bros.	K: ny-ee-e'-ko-to'	My older and younger bros.
11. Karen (Sgau dial'ct)	11	Yă dau-pu-way-khwă	" " " " "	Yä dau-pu-way-khwă	" " " " "
12. Karen (Pwo ")	12	Y' du-pu-waí-khwä	" " " " "	Y' du-pu-waí-khwä	" " " " "
13. Karen	13	Yeh pü-yeh-wĕh pan-khwa-t-	" " " " "	Yeh pü-yeh-wĕh-pau-khwa-t-	" " " " "
14. Kings Mill Islands	14	Taru-nako [pa	Brother my all of.	Manu-nako [pa	Brothers my all of.
15. Kusaien	15	Mä-lĕk	Brothers my.	Mä-lĕk	Brothers my.
16. Hawaiian	16	Kŭ-ŭ' maŭ-käï'-ku-ä-ä'-nä	My brothers.	Kŭ-ŭ' maŭ-käï'-käï-nä	My brothers.
17. Maori	17	A-ku tu-a-ka-na	My brothers (elder)	A-ku te-i-na	My brothers (younger).
18. Amazulu (Kafir)	18	U'-mfo wa'-tŭ	Brother our.	U'-mfo wa'-tŭ	Brother our.

		27. My sisters. (Male speaking.)	Translation.	28. My sisters. (Female speaking.)	Translation.
1. Tamil	1	En tämäkay tängay mäi	My sisters.	En săköthärkäl	My sisters (Sanskrit).
2. Telugu	2	Săköthärŭlŭ	Sisters (Sanskrit).	Săkothärŭlŭ	Sisters (Sanskrit).
3. Canarese	3	Sähodängälu	" "	Sähodărigälu	" "
4. Hindî	4	Meri bahin	My sisters.	Meri bahin	My sisters.
5. Bengâlî	5	Amar bhoguy	" "	Amar bhogny	" "
6. Mârâthî	6	Mäzhi bahiṇe	" "	Mäzhi bahiṇe	" "
7. Gujârâthî	7				
8. Chinese	8	Wo-tĕ tsze-mei	My elder younger sisters.	Wo-tĕ tsze-mei	My elder younger sister.
9. Japanese	9	A-nih-do'-mo	Elder sisters.	E-mo-to-do'-mo	Younger sisters.
10. Burmese	10	K: e-mä' hnee-mä'-to	My elder and younger sists.	K: e-mä' hnee-mä'-to	My older and younger sists.
11. Karen (Sgau dial'ct)	11	Yă-dau-pu-way-mu	" " " " "	Yă dau-pu-way-mu	" " " " "
12. Karen (Pwo ")	12	Y' du-pu-waí-mu	" " " " "	Y' dŭ-pu-waí-mu	" " " " "
13. Karen	13	Yeh pü-yeh-weh-pau-mü-t-pa	" " " " "	Yeh pü-yeh-wĕh-pau-mü-t-pa	" " " " "
14. Kings Mill Islands	14	Manu-nako	Sisters my all of.	Taru-nako	Sisters my all of.
15. Kusaien	15	Mä-laŭk	Sister my.	Mä-laŭk	Sister my.
16. Hawaiian	16	Kŭ-ŭ' maŭ-käï'-ku-wä-heé-na	My sisters.	Kŭ-ŭ' maŭ-käï'-ku-wä-heé-na	My sisters.
17. Maori	17	A-ku tu-a-hi-ne	My sisters (elder).	A-ku te-i-na	My sisters (younger).
18. Amazulu (Kafir)	18	U-dä'-da wa'-tŭ	Sister our.	U-dä'-da wa'-tŭ	Sister our.

		29. My brother's son. (Male speaking.)	Translation.	30. My brother's son's wife. (Male speaking.)	Translation.
1. Tamil	1	En mäkän	My son.	En mărŭmäkäl	My dau.-in-law and niece.
2. Telugu	2	Kădŭkŭ	Son.	Kŏdälŭ	Daughter-in-law.
3. Canarese	3	Nännä mägänu	My son.	Nännä sŏsĕ	My daughter-in-law.
4. Hindî	4	Merä bhatija	My nephew.	Merí bhatij bahú	My nephew. Dau.-in-law.
5. Bengâlî	5	Amar bhypo	" "	Amar bohu	My daughter-in-law.
6. Marâthî	6	Müzhä putanyä	" "	Mäzhi sŭn. ᵇ Chŭlat sŭn	" " "
7. Gujârâthî	7	Märo bhrätijo.	My nephew (born of bro.)	Märi bhrätija vabu	My nephew. Dau.-in-law.
8. Chinese	8	Wo-tĕ chih-ïr	My nephew child or child boy	Wo-tĕ chih-fŭ	My nephew child's wife.
9. Japanese	9	E-to'-ko. ᵇ O-ee	Nephew. [of the *chih* class.	Yo'-mä	Daughter-in-law.
10. Burmese	10	K: too	My nephew.	K: too-mä	My niece.
11. Karen (Sgau dial'ct)	11	Yă pho-do	" "	Yă pho-do-mu	" "
12. Karen (Pwo ")	12	Y' pho-do-khwä	" "	Y' pho-do-mu	" "
13. Karen	13	Yeh pó-do-khwa	" "	Yeh pó-do-mü	" "
14. Kings Mill Islands	14	Nätu-te-mäne	Son my a male.	Tinapau	Daughter-in-law my.
15. Kusaien	15	Mwĕn-nŭttik	Son my.	Au-nŭttik	Daughter my.
16. Hawaiian	16	Kŭ-ŭ'- käï'-hee kä'-na	My child male.	Kŭ-ŭ' hŭ-no'-nä	My child-in-law female.
17. Maori	17	Ta-ku ta-ma	My son.		
18. Amazulu (Kafir)	18	In-do-dä'-nä yä'-me	Son of me.	U-ä'-nä wä'-me	My daughter-in-law.

TABLE III.—*Continued.*

		31. My brother's daughter. (Male speaking.)	Translation.	32. My brother's daughter's husband. (Male speaking.)	Translation.
1. Tamil	1	En măkăl	My daughter.	En mărŭmakăn	My son-in-law and nephew.
2. Telugu	2	Kŭthŭrŭ	Daughter.	Allŭdŭ	Son-in-law.
3. Canarese	3	Nănnă măgălu	My daughter.	Nănnă aliyă	My son-in-law.
4. Hindî	4	Meri bhatijî	My niece.	Merā bhatij damad	My nephew son-in-law.
5. Bengâlî	5	Amar bhyjhe	" "	Māzhă zawai. ᵇ Chûlat zawai	My son-in-law.
6. Marâthî	6	Māzhi putani. ᵇ Dhade	" "	Māro bhrătijo jamăi	My nephew son-in-law.
7. Gujârâthî	7	Mări bhrătiji	My niece (born of sister).	Wo-tĕ chih-neu-se	Niece girl's superior or son-
8. Chinese	8	Wo-tĕ chih neu	My dau. of the *chih* class or	Moo'-ko	Son-in-law. [in-law.
9. Japanese	9	O-nä'-e-to-ko. ᵇ Mă-o-e	Nephew. [niece girl.	K : too	My nephew.
10. Burmese	10	K : too-mă	My niece.	Yă pho-do	" "
11. Karen (Sgau dial'ct)	11	Yă pho-do-mu	" "	Y' pho-do	" "
12. Karen (Pwo ")	12	Y' pho-do-mu	" "	Yeh pó-do-khwa	" "
13. Karen	13	Yeh pó-do-mŭ	" "	Jinăpăŭ	Son-in-law my.
14. Kings Mill Islands	14	Natu-te-aine	Daughter my a female.	Mwĕn-nŭttik	Son my.
15. Kusaien	15	Au-nŭttik	Daughter my.	Kŭ-ŭ'-hŭ-nó-nă kă'-na	My child-in-law male.
16. Hawaiian	16	Kŭ-ŭ' kăï -kĕe-wa heé·nă	My child female.		
17. Maori	17	Ta-ku tam-a-hi-ne	My daughter.		
18. Amazulu (Kafir)	18	In-do-dä-kä'-se yä'-me	Daughter of me.	U-mkwā-ny-ä'-na-wä'-tă	Son-in-law of us.

		33. My brother's grandson. (Male speaking.)	Translation.	34. My brother's granddaughter. (Male speaking.)	Translation.
1. Tamil	1	En pēran	My grandson.	En pērtti	My granddaughter.
2. Telugu	2	Mănămădŭ	Grandson.	Mănămărălu	Granddaughter.
3. Canarese	3	Nănnă mŏmmăgănu	My grandson.	Nănni mŏmmăgălu	My granddaughter.
4. Hindî	4	Merá potá	" "	meri potí	" "
5. Bengâlî	5	Amar naty	" "	Amar natny	" "
6. Marâthî	6	Māzhi nätŭ	" "	Māzhi nät	" "
7. Gujârâthî	7	Māro pₐwtră	" "	Māri pautri	" "
8. Chinese	8	Wo-tĕ chih-sun	My grandson of the *chih*	Wo-tĕ chih-sun-neu	My granddaughter of the
9. Japanese	9	Mā'-go	Grandson. [class.	Ma'-ee	Granddaughter. [*chih* class.
10. Burmese	10	K : my-a'	My grandchild.	K : my-a'	My grandchild.
11. Karen (Sgau dial'ct)	11	Yă liè-khwă	My grandson.	Yă liè-mu	My granddaughter.
12. Karen (Pwo ")	12	Y' le-khwă	" "	Y' le-mu	" "
13. Karen	13	Yeh leé-khwa	" "	Yeh leé-mŭ	" "
14. Kings Mill Islands	14	Tibu-te-máne	Grandchild my a male.	Tibu-te-aine	Grandchild my a female.
15. Kusaien	15	Mwĕn-nŭttin-nŭttik	Grandson my.	Au-nŭttin-nŭttik	Grandchild my.
16. Hawaiian	16	Kŭ-ŭ' moo-pŭ'-na kă' na	My grandchild male.	Kŭ-ŭ' moo-pŭ'-na wä-heé-na	My grandchild female.
17. Maori	17	Ta-ku mo-ko-pu-na	My grandchild.	Ta-ku mo-ko-pu-na	
18. Amazulu (Kafir)	18	U-me-tshä'-na wä'-me	Grandchild of me.	U-me-tshä'-nä wä'-me	Grandchild of me.

		35. My brother's great grandson. (Male speaking.)	Translation.	36. My brother's great granddaughter. (Male speaking.)	Translation.
1. Tamil	1	En irandăm pēran	My second grandson.	En irandăm pērtti	My second granddaughter.
2. Telugu	2	Mŭnĭmănămădŭ	Great grandson.	Mŭnĭmănămărălŭ	Great granddaughter.
3. Canarese	3	Nănnă mŭmmăngănu	My great grandson.	Nănni mŭmmăgălu	My great granddaughter.
4. Hindî	4	Merá parotá	" " "	Meri parotí	" " "
5. Bengâlî	5	Amar naty	My grandson.	Amar natny	My granddaughter.
6. Marâthî	6	Māzhi pănaẗŭ	My great grandson.	Māzhi pänati	My great granddaughter.
7. Gujârâthî	7				
8. Chinese	8	Wo-tĕ chih-tsung-new	My great grandson of the	Wo-tĕ chih-tsung-sun neu	My great granddaughter of
9. Japanese	9	She'-ko	Grandchild. [*chih* class.	She'-ko	Grandchild. [the *chih* class.
10. Burmese	10	K : my-eet'	My great grandchild.	K : my-eet'	My great grand child.
11. Karen (Sgau dial'ct)	11	Yă lo-khwă	My great grandson.	Yă lo-mu	My great granddaughter.
12. Karen (Pwo ")	12	Y' lo-khwa	" " "	Y' lo-mu	" " "
13. Karen	13	Yeh ló-khwa	" " "	Yeh ló-mŭ	" " "
14. Kings Mill Islands	14	Tibun-natu [nŭttik	Grandchild of my child.	Tibun-nalu	Grandchild of my child.
15. Kusaien	15	Mwĕn - nŭttin - mwĕn - nŭttin-	Great grandson my.	Au-nŭttin-ăn-nŭttin-nŭttik	Great granddaughter my.
16. Hawaiian	16	Kŭ-ŭ' moo-pŭ'-na kă'-na kŭ'-ä-	My great grandchild male.	Kŭ-ŭ moo-pŭ'-na- wä-heé-na	My great grandchild female.
17. Maori	17	[lŭ'-ä		[kŭ-ä-lŭ'-ä	
18. Amazulu (Kafir)	18	U-mzŭ-kŭ'-lŭ wä'-me	Great grandchild of me.	U-mzŭ-kŭ'-lu wä'-me ta-ren- ty-tăr	Great grandchild of me.

TABLE III.—Continued.

		37. My sister's son. (Male speaking.)	Translation.	38. My sister's son's wife. (Male speaking.)	Translation.
1. Tamil	1	En mărŭnmăkăn	My nephew.	En măkăl	My daughter.
2. Telugu	2	Měnăllŭdu	Nephew.	Kŭthŭrŭ	Daughter.
3. Canarese	3	Nănnă sodărălĭyă	My nephew.	Nănnă södărănăgălu	My niece.
4. Hindî	4	Merá bháujá	" "	Meri bhauej bahú	My nephew dau.-in-law.
5. Bengâlî	5	Amar bhagna	" "	Amar bhagna bohu	My daughter-in-law.
6. Marâthî	6	Mázhă patanyă	" "	Măzhi chache sŭn	" " " "
7. Gujârâthî	7	Märo bhouej	My neph. (born of a sister).	Märi bhouej vahu	My nephew dau.-in-law.
8. Chinese	8	Wo-tĕ wae-sung	My outside neph.or son of the	Wo-tĕ wae-sung-suh-fŭ	My son's wife of the wae-
9. Japanese	9	E-to'-ko. ᵇ O'-e	Nephew. [wae-sung class.	Yo'-mä	Dau.-in-law. [sung class.
10. Burmese	10	K : too	My nephew.	K : too-mă'	My niece.
11. Karen (Sgau dial'ct)	11	Yă pho-do	" "	Yă pho-do-mu	" "
12. Karen (Pwo ")	12	Y' pho-do-khwă	" "	Y' pho-do-mu	" "
13. Karen	13	Yeh pó-do-khwa	" "	Yeh pó-do-mü	" "
14. Kings Mill Islands	14	Nătu-te-mäne	Child my a female.	Tinapau	Daughter-in-law my.
15. Kusaien	15	Mwĕn-nŭttik	Son my.	Au nŭttik	Daughter my.
16. Hawaiian	16	Kŭ-ŭ' käï'-kee-kä'-na	My child a male.	Kŭ-ŭ' hŭ-nó-na wä-heé na	My child-in-law female.
17. Maori	17	Ta-ku ta-ma	My son.		
18. Amazulu (Kafir)	18	In-do-dä'-nä yä'-me	Son of me.	U-mä-lo-kä-zä'-nä wä'-me	Daughter-in-law of me.

		39. My sister's daughter. (Male speaking.)	Translation.	40. My sister's daughter's husband. (Male speaking.)	Translation.
1. Tamil	1	En mărŭmăkăl	My niece.	En măkăn	My son.
2. Telugu	2	Měnăkŏdălŭ	Niece.	Kŏdŭkŭ	Son.
3. Canarese	3	Nănnă sodărăsöse	My niece.	Nănnă măgănu	My son.
4. Hindî	4	Meri bhaunjé	" "	Merá bhauej dámád	My nephew son-in-law.
5. Bengâlî	5	Amar bhagny	" "	Amar jamye	My son-in-law.
6. Marâthî	6	Mäzhi pŭtani	" "	Mäzhă putanyä zawai	" " " "
7. Gujârâthî	7	Märi bhoueji	My niece (born of a sister).	Märo bouej jamăi	My nephew-son-in-law.
8. Chinese	8	Wo-tĕ wae-sung-nen	My daught. of the wae-sung	Wo-tĕ wae-sung-neu-se	My son-in-law of the wae-
9. Japanese	9	O-nä'-e-to'-ko. ᵇ Mä-o-e	Niece. ᵇ Fem. neph. [class.	Moo'-ko	Son-in-law. [sung class.
10. Burmese	10	K : too-mă'	My niece.	K : too	My nephew.
11. Karen (Sgau dial'ct)	11	Yă pho-do-mu	" "	Yă pho-do	" "
12. Karen (Pwo ")	12	Y' pho-do-mu	" "	Y' pho-do-khwă	" "
13. Karen	13	Yeh pó-do-mü	" "	Yeh pó-do-khwa	" "
14. Kings Mill Islands	14	Nătu-te-aine	Child my a female.	Jinapau	Son-in-law my.
15. Kusaien	15	Au-nŭttik	Daughter female my.	Mwĕn-nŭttik	Son male my.
16. Hawaiian	16	Kŭ-ŭ' käï-kä-wä-hee-na	My child female.	Kŭ-ŭ' hŭ-no'-na-kä-ne	My child-in-law male.
17. Maori	17	Ta-ku ta-ma-hi-ne	My daughter.		
18. Amazulu (Kafir)	18	In-do-dä-kä'-ze yä'-me	Daughter of me.	U-mkwa-ny-ä'-nä-wä'-me	Son-in-law of me.

		41. My sister's grandson. (Male speaking.)	Translation.	42. My sister's granddaughter. (Male speaking.)	Translation.
1. Tamil	1	En pêrăn	My grandson.	En pêrtti	My granddaughter.
2. Telugu	2	Mănămădŭ	Grandson.	Mănămărălŭ	Granddaughter.
3. Canarese	3	Nănnă mŏmmăgănu	My grandson.	Nănni mommăgalu	My granddaughter.
4. Hindî	4	Merá potá	" "	Meri poti	" "
5. Bengâlî	5	Amar naty	" "	Amar natny	" "
6. Marâthî	6	Mäzhä nătŭ	" "	Mäzhi năt	" "
7. Gujârâthî	7	Märo pautră	" "	Märi pautri	" "
8. Chinese	8	Wo-tĕ wae-sung sun	My grandson of the wae-sung	Wo-tĕ wae-sung sun-neu	My granddaughter of the
9. Japanese	9	Mä'-go	Grandson. [class.	Ma'-ee	Gd. dau. [wae-sung class.
10. Burmese	10	K : my-a'	My grandchild.	K : my-a'	My grandchild.
11. Karen (Sgau dial'ct)	11	Yă lie-khwă	My grandson.	Yă liè-mu	My granddaughter.
12. Karen (Pwo ")	12	Y' le-khwă	" "	Y' leé-mu	" "
13. Karen	13	Yeh lee'-khwa	" "	Y' leé-mü	" "
14. Kings Mill Islands	14	Tibu-te-máne	Grandchild my a male.	Tibu-te-aine	Grandchild my a female.
15. Kusaien	15	Mwĕn-nŭttin-nŭttik	Grandson my.	Au-nŭttin-nŭttik	Granddaughter my.
16. Hawaiian	16	Kŭ-ŭ' moo-pŭ'-nä-kä'na	My grandchild male.	Kŭ-ŭ' moo-pŭ-na-wä-heé-na	My-grandchild female.
17. Maori	17	Ta-ku mo-ko-pu-na	My grandchild.	Ta-ku mo-ko-pu-na	My grandchild.
18. Amazulu (Kafir)	18	U-me-tshä'-nä wä'-me	Grandchild of me.	U-me-tshä'-nä wä'-me	Grandchild of me.

TABLE III.—*Continued.*

			43. My sister's great grandson. (Male speaking.)	Translation.	44. My sister's great granddaughter. (Male speaking.)	Translation.
1.	Tamil	1	En irandäm pĕrän	My second grandson.	En irandäm pĕrtti	My second granddaughter.
2.	Telugu	2	Mŭnĭmänăḍŭ	Great grandson.	Mŭnĭmänămärälŭ	Great granddaughter.
3.	Canarese	3	Nănnă mummăgănu	My great graudson.	Nănnă mummăgălu	My great granddaughter.
4.	Hindî	4	Merá parotá	" " "	Meri paroti	" " "
5.	Bengâlî	5	Amar naty	My grandson.	Amar natury	My granddaughter.
6.	Marâthî	6	Mäzhä pänatŭ	My great grandson.	Mäzhi pänati	My great granddaughter.
7.	Gujârâthî	7				
8.	Chinese	8	Wo-tĕ wae-sung-tsung-sun	My g.gd.son of the *wae-sung* Gt. gd. child. [class.	Wo-tĕ wae-sung-tsung-sun	My gt. gd. dau. of the *wae-sung* class. Gt. gd. child. [neu
9.	Japanese	9	She'-ko	Gt. gd. child. [class.	She'-ko	Gt. gd. child. [sung class.
10.	Burmese	10	K: my-eet'	My great grandchild.	Yă lo-mu	My great grandchild.
11.	Karen (Sgau dial'ct)	11	Yă lo-khwă	My great grandson.	Y' lo-mu	My great granddaughter.
12.	Karen (Pwo ")	12	Y' lo-khwă	" " "	Yeh lo-mü	" " "
13.	Karen	13	Yeh ló-khwa	" " "	Tibun-natu	Grandchild of my child.
14.	Kings Mill Islands	14	Tibun-natu[nŭttik	Grandchild of my child.	Au-nŭttin-än-nŭttin-nŭttik	Great granddaughter my.
15.	Kusaien	15	Mwĕn – nŭttin – mwĕn – nŭttin-	Great grandson my.	Kŭ-ŭ' moo-pŭ-na – wä-hĕĕ-na-	My great grandchild female.
16.	Hawaiian	16	Kŭ-ŭ' moo-pŭ-na-kä'-na-kŭ'- [ä-lŭ-a	My great grandchild male.	[kŭ'-ä-lŭ-ä	
17.	Maori	17				
18.	Amazulu (Kafir)	18	U-mzu-kŭ'-lŭ wä'-me	Great grandchild of me.	U-mzŭ-kŭ'-lŭ wä'-me	Great grandchild of me.

			45. My brother's son. (Female speaking.)	Translation.	46. My brother's son's wife. (Female speaking.)	Translation.
1.	Tamil	1	En märŭmäkän	My nephew.	En mäkäl	My daughter.
2.	Telugu	2	Mĕnăllŭḍŭ	Nephew.	Kŭthŭrŭ	Daughter.
3.	Canarese	3	Nănnă aliyänu	My nephew.	Nănnă mägălu	My daughter.
4.	Hindî	4	Merá bhatijá	" "	Meri bhatij bahú	My daughter-in-law.
5.	Bengâlî	5	Amar bhaypo	" "	Amar bohu	" " " "
6.	Marâthî	6	Mäzhä chächä	" "	Mäzhi chächä sŭn	" " " "
7.	Gujârâthî	7	Märo bhătrijo	My nephew (born of bro.).	Märi bhătrija vahu	My nephew daught.-in-law.
8.	Chinese	8	Wo-tĕ wae-chih	My outer neph. or my son of	Wo-tĕ wae-chih-seih-fŭ	My outer nephew's wife.
9.	Japanese	9	E-to'-ko. ᵇ O'-ĕ	Neph. [the *wae-chih* class.	Yo'-mä	Daughter-in-law.
10.	Burmese	10	K: too	My nephew.	K: too-mä'	My niece.
11.	Karen (Sgau dial'ct)	11	Yă pho-do	" "	Yă pho-do-mu	" "
12.	Karen (Pwo ")	12	Y' pho-do-khwă	" "	Y' pho-do-mu	" "
13.	Karen	13	Yeh pó-do-khwa	" "	Yeh pó-do-mü	" "
14.	Kings Mill Islands	14	Nátu-te-máne	Child my a male.	Tinapau	Daughter-in-law my.
15.	Kusaien	15	Mwĕn-nŭttik	Son my.	Au-nŭttik	Daughter my.
16.	Hawaiian	16	Kŭ-ŭ' käï-kee-kä'-na	My child male.	Kŭ-ŭ' hu-no'-nä-wä-hee'-na	My child-in-law female.
17.	Maori	17	Ta-ku ta-ma	My son.		
18.	Amazulu (Kafir)	18	In-do-dä'-nä yä'-me	Son of me.	U-mä-lo-kä-zä'-nä wä'-me	Daughter-in-law of me.

			47. My brother's daughter. (Female speaking.)	Translation.	48. My brother's daughter's husband. (Female speaking.)	Translation.
1.	Tamil	1	En märŭmäkäl	My niece.	En mäkän	My son.
2.	Telugu	2	Mĕnäkŏḍälŭ	Niece.	Kŏḍŭkŭ	Son.
3.	Canarese	3	Nanna sodărăsose	My niece.	Nănnă mägänu	My son.
4.	Hindî	4	Meri bhatijé	" "	Merá bhatij dámád	My nephew son-in-law.
5.	Bengâlî	5	Amar bhyjhe	" "	Amar jamye	My son-in-law.
6.	Marâthî	6	Mäzhi chäche	" "	Mäzhä chächä zwai	" " " "
7.	Gujârâthî	7	Märi bhătrije	My niece (born of a brother).	Märo bhătrijo jamai	My nephew son-in-law.
8.	Chinese	8	Wo-tĕ wae-chih neu	My dau. of the *wae-chih* class.	Wo-tĕ-wae-chih neu-se	My son-in-law of the *wae-chih* class.
9.	Japanese	9	O-nä'-e-to-k. ᵇ Mä-ó-é	Niece. ᵇ Female nephew.	Moo'-koo	Son-in-law. [chih class.
10.	Burmese	10	K: too-mä'	My niece.	K: too-mä'	My nephew.
11.	Karen (Sgau dial'ct)	11	Yă pho-do-mu	" "	Ya pho-do	" "
12.	Karen (Pwo ")	12	Y' pho-do-mu	" "	Y' pho-do-khwä-	" "
13.	Karen	13	Yeh pó-do-mü	" "	Yeh pó-do-khwa	" "
14.	Kings Mill Islands	14	Nátu-te-aine	Child my a female.	Jinepau	Son-in-law my.
15.	Kusaien	15	Au-nŭttik	Daughter my.	Mwĕn-nŭttik	Son my.
16.	Hawaiian	16	Kŭ-ŭ' käï-kä-wä-heé'-na	My child female.	Kŭ-ŭ' hŭ-no'-nä-kä'-na	My child-in-law male.
17.	Maori	17	Ta-ku ta-ma-hi-ne	My daughter.		
18.	Amazulu (Kafir)	18	In-do-dä-kä'-ze yä'-me	Daughter of me.	U-mkwä-ny-ä'-nä wä'-me	Son-in-law of me.

TABLE III.—*Continued.*

		49. My brother's grandson. (Female speaking.)	Translation.	50. My brother's granddaughter. (Female speaking.)	Translation.
1. Tamil	1	En pĕrăn.............................	My grandson.	En pĕrtti.............................	My granddaughter.
2. Telugu.................	2	Mănămădŭ	Grandson.	Mănămărălŭ.........................	Granddaughter.
3. Canarese	3	Nănnă mommăgănu	My grandson.	Nănnă mommăgălu...............	My granddaughter.
4. Hindî	4	Meră potă	" "	Meri poti	" "
5. Bengâlî	5	Amar naty	" "	Amar natny.........................	" "
6. Marâthî	6	Măzhă nătŭ	" "	Măzhă năt	" "
7. Gujârâthî............	7	Măro pautră.........................	" "	Mări pautri.........................	" "
8. Chinese	8	Wo-tĕ wae-chih-sun............	Grandson of the *wae chih*	Wo-tĕ wae-chih-sun-neu......	My granddaughter of the Gd. dau. [*wae-chih* class.
9. Japanese	9	Mă'-go	Grandson. [class.	Ma' ee	
10. Burmese	10	K : my-a'	My grandchild.	K : my-a'	My grandchild.
11. Karen (Sgau dial'ct)	11	Yă liĕ-khwă.........................	My grandson.	Yă lĕ-mu.........................	My granddaughter.
12. Karen (Pwo ")	12	Y' le-khwă	" "	Y' le mu.........................	" "
13. Karen	13	Yeh leĕ-khwa.....................	" "	Yeh leĕ-mŭ.....................	" "
14. Kings Mill Islands..	14	Tibu-te-mane.....................	Grandchild my a male.	Tibu-te-aine.....................	Grandchild my a female.
15. Kusaien	15	Mwĕn-nŭttin-nŭttik	Grandson my.	Au-nŭttin-nŭttik	Granddaughter my.
16. Hawaiian...............	16	Kŭ-ŭ' moo-pŭ'-nä-kä'-na......	My grandchild male.	Kŭ-ŭ' moo-pŭ'-nä-wä-heĕ-na..	My grandchild female.
17. Maori	17	Ta-ku mo ku-pu-na............	My grandchild.	Ta-ku mo-ko-pu-na............	
18. Amazulu (Kafir)....	18	U-me-tshä'-nä wä'-me..........	Grandchild of me.	U-me-tshä'-nä wä'-me..........	Grandchild of me.

		51. My brother's great grandson. (Female speaking.)	Translation.	52. My brother's great granddaughter. (Female speaking.)	Translation.
1. Tamil	1	En irandäm pĕrăn	My second grandson.	En irandäm pĕrtti...............	My second granddaughter.
2. Telugu	2	Mŭnīmănămădŭ	Great grandson.	Mŭnīmănămărălŭ	Great granddaughter.
3. Canarese	3	Nănnă mummăgănu............	My great grandson.	Nănnă mummăgălu...............	My great granddaughter.
4. Hindî	4	Meră parotă.........................	" " "	Merī paroti	" " "
5. Bengâlî	5	Amar naty	My grandson.	Amar natny.........................	My granddaughter.
6. Marâthî	6	Măzhă panatŭ	My great grandson. [*wae-chih* class.	Măzhă pănati	My great granddaughter. [the *wae-chih* class.
7. Gujârâthî............	7				
8. Chinese	8	Wo-tĕ wae-chih-tsung-sun.....	My great grandson of the	Wo-tĕ wae-chih-tsung-sun-neu	My great granddaughter of
9. Japanese	9	She-ko.............................	Great grandchild.	She'-ko.............................	Great grandchild.
10. Burmese	10	K : my-eet'	My great grandchild.	K : my-eet'	My great grandchild.
11. Karen (Sgau dial'ct)	11	Yă lo-khwă.........................	My great grandson.,	Yă lo-mu.........................	My great granddaughter.
12. Karen (Pwo ")	12	Y' lo-khwă	" " "	Y' lo-mu.........................	" " "
13. Karen	13	Yeh lo-khwa.....................	" " "	Yeh lo-mŭ	" " "
14. Kings Mill Islands..	14	Tibun-natu.................[nŭttik	Grandchild of my child.	Tibun-aine.....................	Grandchild of my child.
15. Kusaien	15	Mwĕn - nŭttin - mwĕn - nŭttin-	Great grandson my.	Au-nŭttin-ăn-nŭttin-nŭttik ...	Great granddaughter my.
16. Hawaiian.............	16	Kŭ-ŭ' moo-pŭ-nä-kä-ne-kŭ'-ä- [lŭ'-ä	My great grandchild male.	Kŭ-ŭ' moo-pŭ'-nä-wä-heĕ-na- [ku-ŭ'-ä-lŭ'-ä	My great grandchild female.
17. Maori	17				
18. Amazulu (Kafir)....	18	U-mzŭ-kŭ'-lŭ wä'-me..........	Great grandchild of me.	U-mzŭ-kŭ'-lu wä'-me..........	Great grandchild of me.

		53. My sister's son. (Female speaking.)	Translation.	54. My sister's son's wife. (Female speaking.)	Translation.
1. Tamil	1	En măkăn.........................	My son.	En mărŭmăkăl,....................	My dau.-in-law and niece.
2. Telugu.................	2	Kōdălŭ.........................	Son.	Kōdălŭ.........................	Daughter-in-law.
3. Canarese	3	Nănnă măgănu	My son.	Nănnă sose.........................	My Daughter in-law.
4. Hindi	4	Meră bhahinaută.................	My nephew.	Merī bahinaut bahú............	My nephew dau.-in-law.
5. Bengâlî	5	Amar boupo.........................	" "	Amar bohu.........................	My daughter-in-law.
6. Marâthî	6	Măzhă chăchă	" "	Măzhi chăcha sŭn	" " " "
7. Gujârâthî............	7	Măro bhouej.........................	My neph. (born of a sister).	Mări bhouej vahu	My nephew dau.-in-law.
8. Chinese	8	Wo-tĕ e-sung.....................	My son of the *e-sung* class.	Wo-tĕ e-sung-seih-fŭ	My daughter-in-law of the Dau.-in-law. [*e-sung* class.
9. Japanese	9	E-to-ko. ᵇ O'-ĕ	Nephew.	Yo'-mă.........................	
10. Burmese	10	K : too.........................	My nephew.	K : too-mă'	My niece.
11. Karen (Sgau dial'ct)	11	Yă pho-do.........................	" "	Yă pho-do-mu	" "
12. Karen (Pwo ")	12	Y' pho-do-khwă	" "	Y' pho-do-mu	" "
13. Karen	13	Yeh pó-do-khwa	" "	Yeh pó-do-mŭ	" "
14. Kings Mill Islands..	14	Natŭ te-mane.....................	Child my a male.	Tinapau	Daughter-in-law my.
15. Kusaien	15	Mwĕn-nŭttik.....................	Son my.	Au-nŭttik.........................	Daughter my.
16. Hawaiian.............	16	Kŭ-ŭ' käï-kee-kä'-na............	My child male.	Kŭ-ŭ' hŭ-no'-nä-wä-hee'-na...	My child-in-law female.
17. Maori	17	Ta-ku ta-ma	My son.		
18. Amazulu (Kafir)....	18	In-do-dä'-nä yä' me	Son of me.	U-mä-lo-kä-zä'-na wä'-me.....	My daughter-in-law.

TABLE III.—*Continued.*

		55. My sister's daughter. (Female speaking.)	Translation.	56. My sister's daughter's husband. (Female speaking.)	Translation.
1. Tamil	1	En măkăl	My daughter.	En măkăn	My son.
2. Telugu	2	Kŭthŭrŭ	Daughter.	Allŭdŭ	Son of law.
3. Canarese	3	Nănnă măgălu	My daughter.	Nănnă aliyănu	My nephew.
4. Hindî	4	Merï bahinanti'	My niece.	Merá bahinant dámád	My niece, son-in-law.
5. Bengâlî	5	Amar boujhe	" "	Amar jamye	My son-in-law.
6. Marâthî	6	Măzhi chăche	" "	Măzhă chăchă zawai	" "
7. Gujârâthî	7	Märi bhoneji	My niece (born of a sister).	Mari bonej jamäi	My niece, son-in-law.
8. Chinese	8	Wo-tĕ e-sung-nen	My daughter of the *e-sung*	Wo-tĕ e-sung-neu-se	My son-in-law of the *e-sung*
9. Japanese	9	O-mä'-e-to'-ko	Niece. [class.	Moo'-ko	My son-in-law. [class.
10. Burmese	10	K: too-mä'	My niece.	K: too	My nephew.
11. Karen (Sgan dial'ct)	11	Yă pho-do-mu	" "	Yă pho-do	" "
12. Karen (Pwo ")	12	Y' pho-do-mu	" "	Y' pho-do-khwä	" "
13. Karen	13	Yeh pó-do-mu	" "	Yeh pó-do-khwa	" "
14. Kings Mill Islands	14	Nătu-de-äine	Child my, a female.	Jinapau	Son-in-law my.
15. Kusaien	15	Au-nuttik	Daughter my.	Mwĕn-nuttik	Son my.
16. Hawaiian	16	Kŭ-ŭ' kăï-kă-wă-hee'-na	My child, a female.	Kŭ-ŭ' hŭ-nó-nă-kă'-na	My child-in-law male.
17. Maori	17	Ta-ku tam-ă-hi-ne	My daughter.		
18. Amazulu (Kafir)	18	In-do-da-kä'-ze yä'-me	Daughter of me.	U-mkwa-ny-ä'-na wä'-me	Son-in-law of us.

		57. My sister's grandson. (Female speaking.)	Translation.	58. My sister's granddaughter. (Female speaking.)	Translation.
1. Tamil	1	En pĕrăn	My grandson.	En pĕrtti	My granddaughter.
2. Telugu	2	Mănămădŭ	Grandson.	Mănămărălŭ	Granddaughter.
3. Canarese	3	Nănnă mommăgănŭ	My grandson.	Nănnă mommăgălu	My granddaughter.
4. Hindî	4	Merá potá	" "	Merä poti'	" "
5. Bengâlî	5	Amar naty	" "	Amar natny	" "
6. Marâthî	6	Măzhă natŭ	" "	Măzhi năt	" "
7. Gujârâthî	7	Märo pautră	" "	Märi pautri	" "
8. Chinese	8	Wo-te e-sung-sun	My grandson of the *e-sung*	Wo-te e-sung-sun-neu	My granddau. of the *e-sung*
9. Japanese	9	Mä'-go	My grandson. [class.	Ma'-ee	My granddaughter. [class.
10. Burmese	10	K: my-a'	My grandchild.	K: my-a'	My grandchild.
11. Karen (Sgau dial'ct)	11	Yă lie-khwă	My grandson.	Yă lie-mu	My granddaughter.
12. Karen (Pwo ")	12	Y' le-khwä	" "	Y' le-mu	" "
13. Karen	13	Yeh-lee'-khwa	" "	Yeh lee'-mü	" "
14. Kings Mill Islands	14	Tibu-te-máne	Grandchild my a male.	Tibu-te-aine	Grandchild my a female.
15. Kusaien	15	Mwĕn-nuttin-nuttik	Grandson my.	Au-nuttin-nuttik	Granddaughter my.
16. Hawaiian	16	Kŭ-ŭ' moo-pŭ'-nă-kă'-na	My grandchild male.	Kŭ-ŭ' moo-pŭ'-nă-wă-hee'-na.	My grandchild female.
17. Maori	17	Ta-ku mo-ko-pu-na	My grandchild.	Ta-ku mo-ko-pu-na	My grandchild.
18. Amazulu (Kafir)	18	U-me-tshă'-na wä'-me	Grandchild of me.	U-me-tshä'-nä wä'-me	Grandchild of me.

		59. My sister's great grandson. (Female speaking.)	Translation.	60. My sister's great granddaughter. (Female speaking.)	Translation.
1. Tamil	1	En irandäm pĕrăn	My second grandson.	En irandäm pĕrtti	My second granddaughter.
2. Telugu	2	Mŭ-nĭ-mă-nă-mă-dŭ	Great grandson.	Mŭnĭmănămărălŭ	Great granddaughter.
3. Canarese	3	Nănnă mummăgănu	My great grandson.	Nănnă mummăgălu	My great granddaughter.
4. Hindî	4	Merá parotá	" " "	Merï paroti'	" " "
5. Bengâlî	5	Amar naty	My grandson.	Amar natny	My granddaughter.
6. Marâthî	6	Măzhă pănatŭ	My great grandson.	Măzhi pănati	My great granddaughter.
7. Gujârâthî	7				
8. Chinese	8	Wo-tĕ e-sung-tsung-sun	My gt. gd. son of the *e-sung*	Wo-tĕ e-sung-tsung-sun-neu..	My gt. gd.dau. of the *e-sung*
9. Japanese	9	She'-ko	My gt. grandchild. [class.	She'-ko	My gt. grandchild. [class.
10. Burmese	10	K: my-eet'	" "	K: my-eet'	" "
11. Karen (Sgau dial'ct)	11	Yă lo-khwă	My great grandson.	Yă lo-mu	My great granddaughter.
12. Karen (Pwo ")	12	Y' lo-khwä	" " "	Y' lo-mu	" " "
13. Karen	13	Yeh ló-khwa	" " "	Yeh lo-mü	" " "
14. Kings Mill Islands	14	Tibun-natu............[nuttik	Grandchild of my child.	Tibun-natu	Grandchild of my child.
15. Kusaien	15	Mwĕn-nuttin·mwĕn-nuttin-	Great grandson my.	An-nuttin-ăn-nuttin-nuttik	Great granddaughter my.
16. Hawaiian	16	Kŭ-ŭ' moo-pŭ'-nă-kă'-na-kŭ'-a-lŭ'-ä.	My great grandchild male.	Kŭ-ŭ' moo-pŭ'-nă-wă-hee'-na-ku'-ä-lŭ'-ä.	My great grandchild female.
17. Maori	17				
18. Amazulu (Kafir)	18	U-mzu-kŭ'-lŭ wä'-me	Great grandchild of me.	U-mzŭ-kŭ'-lŭ wä'-me	Great grandchild of me.

TABLE III.—*Continued.*

			61. My father's brother.	Translation.	62. My father's brother's wife.	Translation.
1.	Tamil	1	En periya tăkkăppăn ...; " seriya " ...	My great father (if older.) / My lit. fa. (if y. than my fa.)	En täy...	My mother.
2.	Telugu	2	Pĕttăndrĭ (o.), Pĭnatăndri (y.)	" " " " "	Pĕtăllĭ (o.), Pĭnătăllĭ (y.)...	Great or little mother. " " "
3.	Canarese	3	Nănnă Doddăppă. bChikkăppă	" " " " "	N. Doddăppă (o.), Chikkappa	" " "
4.	Hindî	4	Merá chachá...	My uncle paternal.	Merá chachi'...[(y.)	My aunt paternal.
5.	Bengâlî	5	Amar jata (o.), Khoro (y.)...	" "	Amar jataye.-	
6.	Marâthî	6	Mázhĭ chŭlata...	My uncle.	Mäzhĭ chŭlate...	My aunt.
7.	Gujârâthî	7	Măro kako...	" "	Märi kaki...	" "
8.	Chinese	8	Wo-tĕ poh shuh -fŭ	My senior/junior father.	Wo-tĕ poh-mo shin-neang...	My senior mother.
9.	Japanese	9	Ne-băn-mă-no-o-asee...; bO-je / So-ree-o-no-o-asee...	My little father. / bUncle. / Father's elder brother.	O-bä...	My father's younger bro-[ther's wife. / My aunt.
10.	Burmese	10	K: bă-ky-ee (o.), Bă-twă (y.)	My great or little father.	K: mee-ky-ee...	My great mother.
11.	Karen (Sgau dial'ct)	11	Yă phă-tie...	My uncle.	Yă mu-ghä...	My aunt.
12.	Karen (Pwo ")	12	Y' pha-te-te...	My own uncle.	Y' m'-gä...	" "
13.	Karen	13	Yeh páh-tee...	My uncle.	Yeh-mü'-gah...	" "
14.	Kings Mill Islands	14	Täman...	My father.	Eirikin tamau...	Sister-in-law of father my.
15.	Kusaien	15	Pä-pä-tummuk...	Father male my.	Nĕne-kyŭk...	Mother female my.
16.	Hawaiian	16	Kŭ-ŭ' mä-kŭ-ă-kä'-na.	My parent male.	Kŭ-ŭ' mä-kŭ-ă-wä-hee'-na....	My parent female.
17.	Maori	17	Ta-ku pa-pa-ke-ke	My other father.	U-mä'-mä...	My mother.
18.	Amazulu (Kafir)	18	U-bä-bä-kä'-sa ...	My paternal uncle.		

			63. My father's brother's son—older than myself. (Male speaking.)	Translation.	64. My father's brother's son—older than myself. (Female speaking.)	Translation.
1.	Tamil	1	En tămaiyan. bAṇṇan	My elder brother.	En tămaiyăn. bAṇṇan	My elder brother.
2.	Telugu	2	Annă	Elder brother.	Annä	Elder brother.
3.	Canarese	3	Nănnă Annă	My elder brother.	Nănnă ănnă	My elder brother. [uncle.
4.	Hindî	4	Merá bhai'. bChacherá bhai'..	Bro. or bro. thro' pat. uncle.	Merá bhai'. bChacherá bhai'..	My bro. or bro. thro' pat'nal
5.	Bengâlî	5	Amar. Jattoto bhye	" " " " "	Amar. Jattoto bhye	" " " " "
6.	Marâthî	6	Mázhă chŭlat bhäü	" " " " "	Mäzhä chŭlat bhäü	" " " " "
7.	Gujârâthî	7	Măro bhäi	My brother.	Märo bhäi	My brother.
8.	Chinese	8	Wo-tĕ tang-heung-te	My bro. of the *tang* class.	Wo-tĕ tang-heung-te	My bro. of the *tang* class.
9.	Japanese	9	A'-nee	My elder brother.	A'-nee	My brother.
10.	Burmese	10	K: e-ko	My elder brother.	K: e-ko	My older brother.
11.	Karen (Sgau dial'ct)	11	Yă tă-khwă	My male cousin.	Yă tă-khwă	My male cousin.
12.	Karen (Pwo ")	12	Y' t'-khwä-sau	" " "	Y' t'-khwä-sau	
13.	Karen	13	Yeh t'-khwa	My cousin.	Yeh t'-khwa	My cousin.
14.	Kings Mill Islands	14	Taru-te-karimoa	Brother my elder.	Manu-te-karimoa	Brother my elder.
15.	Kusaien	15	Mä-lĕk	My brother.	Mä-lĕk	Brother my.
16.	Hawaiian	16	Kŭ-ŭ' käï'-kŭ-ă'-nä	My brother elder.	Kŭ-ŭ käï'-kŭ-ă'-nä	My brother elder.
17.	Maori	17	Ta-ku tu-a-ka-na	My elder brother.	Ta-ku tun-ga-ne	My elder brother.
18.	Amazulu (Kafir)	18	U'-mfo wá-tŭ	Brother of us.	U'-mfo wá-tŭ	Brother of us.

			65. My father's brother's son—younger than myself. (Male speaking.)	Translation.	66. My father's brother's son—younger than myself. (Female speaking.)	Translation.
1.	Tamil	1	En tambi	My younger brother.	En tambi	My younger brother.
2.	Telugu	2	Tămmŭlŭ	Younger brother.	Tămmŭlŭ	Younger brother.
3.	Canarese	3	Nănnă tămmă	My younger brother. [uncle.	Merá bhai'. bChacherá bhai'..	My younger bro. [uncle.
4.	Hindî	4	Merá bhai'. bChacherá bhai'..	My bro. or bro. thro' pat'nal	Amar. Jattoto bhye	My bro. or bro. thro' pat'nal
5.	Bengâlî	5	Amar. Jattoto bhye	" " " " "	Mäzhä chŭlat bhäü	" " " " "
6.	Marâthî	6	Mázhă chŭlat bhäü	My brother.	Märo bhäi	My brother.
7.	Gujârâthî	7	Măro bhäi	My bro. of the *Tang* class.	Wo-tĕ tang-heung-te	My bro. of the *Tang* class.
8.	Chinese	8	Wo-tĕ tang-heung-te	My younger brother.	O-to'-to	My younger brother.
9.	Japanese	9	O-to'-to	" " "	K: ny-ee-taw	" " "
10.	Burmese	10	K: ny-ee-taw	My male cousin.	Yă tă-khwă	My male cousin.
11.	Karen (Sgau dial'ct)	11	Yă tă-khwă	" " "	Y' t'-khwä-sau	" " "
12.	Karen (Pwo ")	12	Y' t'-khwä-sau	My cousin.	Yeh t'-khwa	My cousin.
13.	Karen	13	Yeh t'-khwa	Brother my younger.	Manu-te-karimwi	Brother my younger.
14.	Kings Mill Islands	14	Taru-te-karimwi	Brother my.	Mä-lĕk	Brother my.
15.	Kusaien	15	Mä-lĕk	My brother younger.	Kŭ-ŭ' käï'-kŭ-nä	My brother younger.
16.	Hawaiian	16	Kŭ-ŭ' käï'-kŭ-nä	" " "	Ta-ku tun-ga-ne-te-i-na	" " "
17.	Maori	17	Ta-ku te-i-na	Younger brother of me.	U-mwä'-wä wä'-me	Younger brother of me.
18.	Amazulu (Kafir)	18	U-mnä'-wä Wä'-me			

TABLE III.—*Continued.*

		67. My father's brother's son's wife. (Male speaking.)	Translation.	68. My father's brother's son's wife. (Female speaking.)	Translation.
1. Tamil	1	En maittuni (o.), Aṇṇi (y.)	My sister-in-law & cousin.	Maittuni (o.), Aṇṇi (y.)	My sister-in-law and cousin.
2. Telugu	2	Vă-dĭnĕ (o.), Mărădălŭ (y.)	Sister-in-law.	Vădĭnĕ (o.), Mărădălŭ (y.)	My sister-in-law.
3. Canarese	3	Nănnă attige (o.), Nadini (y.)	My sister-in-law & cousin.	Nănnă attige (o.), Nadini (y.)	My sister-in-law and cousin.
4. Hindî	4	Merï bháwaj	My sister-in-law.	Merï bháwaj	" "
5. Bengalî	5	Amar bhaj	" "	Amar bhaj	" "
6. Marâthî	6	Mäzhä bhäŭzai	" "	Mäzhe bhäŭzai	" "
7. Gujârâthî	7	Märï bhävi	" "	Wo-tĕ tang-saon	" "
8. Chinese	8	Wo-tĕ tang-saon	My sister-in-law of the *tang* class.	A'-nih	My sister-in-law of the *tang* class.
9. Japanese	9	A'-nih	My elder sister. [class.	K: kai-mä	My elder sister. [class.
10. Burmese	10	K: kai-mä	My sister-in-law.	Yă ta-khwä-mu	My sister-in-law.
11. Karen (Sgau dial'ct)	11	Yă ta-khwä-mu	My female cousin.	Y' t'-khwä-mu	My female cousin.
12. Karen (Pwo ")	12	Y' t'-khwä-mu	" " "	Yeh dan-t'-khwa-a-mä.	" " "
13. Karen	13	Yeh dan-t'-khwa-a-mä	My cousin's wife.	Eiriku	My cousin's wife.
14. Kings Mill Islands	14	Eiriku	Sister-in-law my.	Mä-läŭk	Brother's wife my.
15. Kusaien	15	Mä-läŭk	Sister my.	Kŭ-ŭ' wä-hee'-na	Sister my.
16. Hawaiian	16	Kŭ-ŭ' wä-hee'-na	My wife or my female.		·My wife or my female.
17. Maori	17				
18. Amazulu (Kafir)	18	U-mkä'-mä	My wife.		

		69. My father's brother's daughter— older than myself. (Male speaking.)	Translation.	70. My father's brother's daughter— older than myself. (Female speaking.)	Translation.
1. Tamil	1	En akkärl. ᵇTămăkay	My elder sister.	En akkärl. ᵇTămăkay	My elder sister.
2. Telugu	2	Akkă	Elder sister.	Akkă	Elder sister.
3. Canarese	3	Nănnă ăkkă	My elder sister.	Nănnă ăkkă	My elder sister.
4. Hindî	4	Merï bahin. ᵇChacheri bahin.	My sis. or sis. thro' pat. unc.	Merï bahin. ᵇChacheri bahin.	My sis. or sis. thro' pat. unc.
5. Bengalî	5	Amar. Jattoto bhugny	" " " " "	Amar. Jattoto bhugny	" " " " "
6. Marâthî	6	Mäzhi chûlat bahin	" " " " "	Mäzhi chûlat bahin	" " " " "
7. Gujârâthî	7	Märi bähen	My sister.	Märi bähen	My sister.
8. Chinese	8	Wo-tĕ tang-tse-mei	My sister of the *Tang* class.	Wo-tĕ tang-tsze-mei	My sister of the *Tang* class.
9. Japanese	9	A'-nih	My elder sister.	A'-nih	My elder sister.
10. Burmese	10	K: e-ma	" " "	K: e-ma	" " "
11. Karen (Sgau dial'ct)	11	Yă tă-khwä-mu	My female cousin.	Yă tă-khwä-mu	My female cousin.
12. Karen (Pwo ")	12	Y' t'-khwä-mŭ	" " "	Y' t'-khwä-mu	" " "
13. Karen	13	Yeh dan-t'-khwa-mü	" " "	Yeh dan-t'-khwa-mü	
14. Kings Mill Islands	14	Männu-te-karimoa	Sister my elder	Taru-te-karimoa	Sister my elder.
15. Kusaien	15	Mä-läŭk	Sister my.	Mä-läŭk	Sister my.
16. Hawaiian	16	Kŭ-ŭ' käï'-kŭ-ä-hee'-na	My sister elder.	Kŭ-ŭ' käï'-kŭ-ä-hee'-na	My sister elder.
17. Maori	17	Ta-ku tu-a-hi-ne	" " "	Ta-ku tu-a-ka-na	" " "
18. Amazulu (Kafir)	18	U-dä'-dä wä'-tŭ	Sister of us.	U-dä'-dä wä'-tŭ	Sister of us.

		71. My father's brother's daughter— younger than myself. (Male speaking.)	Translation.	72. My father's brother's daughter— younger than myself. (Female speaking.)	Translation.
1. Tamil	1	En tangaichchi. ᵇTăngay	My younger sister.	En tangaichchi. ᵇTăngay	My younger sister.
2. Telugu	2	Chĕllĕlŭ	Younger sister.	Chĕllĕlŭ	Younger sister.
3. Canarese	3	Nănä tungi	My younger sister.	Nănnă tungi	My younger sister.
4. Hindî	4	Merï bahin. ᵇChacheri bahin.	My sis. or sis. thro' pat. unc.	Merä bahin. ᵇChacheri bahin.	My sis. or sis. thro' pat. unc.
5. Bengalî	5	Amar. Jattoto bhugny	" " " " "	Amar. Jattoto bhugny	" " " " "
6. Marâthî	6	Mäzhi chûlat bahin	" " " " "	Mäzhi chûlat bahin	" " " " "
7. Gujârâthî	7	Märi bähen	My sister.	Mari bähen	My sister.
8. Chinese	8	Wo-tĕ tang-tsze-mei	My sister of the *tang* class.	Wo-tĕ tang-tsze-mei	My sister of the *tang* class.
9. Japanese	9	E-mo'-to	My younger sister.	E-mo'-to	My younger sister.
10. Burmese	10	K: hnee-mä	" " "	K: hnee-mä	" " "
11. Karen (Sgau dial'ct)	11	Yă tă-khwä-mu	My female cousin.	Yă tă-khwä-mu	My female cousin.
12. Karen (Pwo ")	12	Y' t'-khwä-mu	" " "	Y' t'-khwä-mu	" " "
13. Karen	13	Yeh dan-t'-khwa-mü	" " "	Yeh dan-t'-khwa-mü	
14. Kings Mill Islands	14	Männu-te-karimwi	Sister my younger.	Taru-te-karimwi	Sister my younger.
15. Kusaien	15	Mä-läŭk	Sister my.	Mä-läŭk	Sister my.
16. Hawaiian	16	Kŭ-ŭ' käï'-ku-ä-hee'-na	My sister younger.	Kŭ-ŭ käï'-kŭ-ä-hee'-na	My sister younger.
17. Maori	17	Ta-ku tu-a-hi-na-te-i-na	" " "	Ta-ku-te-i-na	" " "
18. Amazulu (Kafir)	18	U-dä'-dä wä'-tŭ	Sister of us.	U-dä'-dä wä'-tŭ	Sister of us.

TABLE III.—Continued.

		73. My father's brother's daughter's husband. (Male speaking.)	Translation.	74. My father's brother's daughter's husband. (Female speaking.)	Translation.
1. Tamil	1	En maittŭnăn	My bro.-in-law and cousin.	En Măittŭnăn	My bro.-in-law and cousin.
2. Telugu	2	Băvă (o.), Mărădĭ (y.)	Bro.-in-law (e. or y.) & cous.	Băvă (o.), Mărădi (y.)	Bro.-in-law (e. or y.) & cous.
3. Canarese	3	N. Bhăva (o.), Meidănă (y.)	My bro.-in-law(e.& y.)& cos.	N. Bhăva (o.), Meidănă (y.)	My br.-in-law (e. or y.) & cos.
4. Hindî	4	Merǎ bahínoí	My brother-in-law.	Merǎ bahínoí	My brother-in-law.
5. Bengâlî	5	Amar bhugny poty	" " "	Amar bhugny poty	" " "
6. Marâthî	6	Mǎzhǎ mǎhŭnǎ	" " "	Mǎzhǎ mehŭnǎ	" " "
7. Gujârâthî	7	Mǎro baneni	" " "	Mǎro baneni	" " "
8. Chinese	8	Wo-tĕ tang-$\frac{tsze}{mei}$-fŭ	My brother-in-law elder. younger.	Wo-tĕ tang-$\frac{tsze}{mei}$-fŭ	My brother-in-law elder. y'nger.
9. Japanese	9	A'-nee	My elder brother.	A'-nee	My elder brother.
10. Burmese	10	K: yonk-pǎ	My brother-in law.	D: youk-pǎ	My male cousin.
11. Karen (Sgau dial'ct)	11	Yǎ tǎ-khwǎ	My male cousin.	Yǎ tǎ-khwǎ	" " "
12. Karen (Pwo ")	12	Y' t'-khwǎ	" " "	Y' t'-khwǎ	My cousin.
13. Karen	13	Yeh t'-khwa	My cousin.	Yeh t'-khwa	Brother-in-law my.
14. Kings Mill Islands	14	Butikau	Brother-in-law my.	Butikau	Brother my.
15. Kusaien	15	Mǎ-lĕk	Brother my.	Mǎ-lĕk	My brother-in-law.
16. Hawaiian	16	Kŭ-ŭ' kǎĭ'-ko-ee'-ka	My brother-in-law.	Kŭ-ŭ' kǎĭ'-ko-ee'-ka	My brother-in-law.
17. Maori	17				
18. Amazulu (Kafir)	18	U-mkwǎ-ny-ǎ'-nǎ wǎ'-tŭ	Brother-in-law of us.	U-mkwa-ny-ǎ'-nǎ wǎ'-tŭ	Brother-in-law of us.

		75. My father's brother's son's son. (Male speaking.)	Translation.	76. My father's brother's son's son. (Female speaking.)	Translation.
1. Tamil	1	En Mǎkǎn	My son.	En mǎrŭmǎkǎn	My nephew.
2. Telugu	2	Kŏdŭkŭ	Son.	Allŭdŭ	Nephew.
3. Canarese	3	Nǎnnǎ mǎgǎnu	My son.	Nǎnnǎ aliyǎnu	My nephew.
4. Hindî	4	Merǎ bhatijǎ	My nephew.	Merǎ bhatijǎ	" "
5. Bengâlî	5	Amar bhypo	" "	Amar bhypo	" "
6. Mârâthî	6	Mǎzhǎ pŭtanyǎ	" "	Mǎzhǎ pŭtanyǎ	" "
7. Gujârâthî	7	Mǎro bhrǎtijo	" "	Mǎro bhrǎtijo	" "
8. Chinese	8	Wo-tĕ tang-chih	My nephew of the *tang* class.	Wo-tĕ tang-chih	My neph. of the *tang* class.
9. Japanese	9	E-to-ko	Nephew.	E-to-ko	Nephew.
10. Burmese	10	K: too	My nephew.	K: too	My nephew.
11. Karen (Sgau dial'ct)	11	Yǎ pho-do	" "	Yǎ pho-do	" "
12. Karen (Pwo ")	12	Y' pho-do-khwǎ	" "	Y' pho-do-khwǎ	" "
13. Karen	13	Yeh po-do-khwa	" "	Yeh po-do-khwa	" "
14. Kings Mill Islands	14	Nǎtu-te-mane	Child my a male.	Nǎtu-te-aine	Child my a female.
15. Kusaien	15	Mwĕn-nuttik	Son my.	Mwĕn-nuttik	Son my.
16. Hawaiian	16	Kŭ-ŭ' kaĭ'-kee-kǎ'-na	My child male.	Kŭ-ŭ' kaĭ'-kee-kǎ'-na	My child male.
17. Maori	17				
18. Amazulu (Kafir)	18	In-do-dǎ'-nǎ yǎ'-mǎ	Son of me.	In-do-dǎ'-nǎ yǎ'-mǎ	Son of me.

		77 My father's brother's son's daughter. (Male speaking.)	Translation.	78. My father's brother's son's daughter. (Female speaking.)	Translation.
1. Tamil	1	En mǎkǎl	My daughter.	En marumǎkǎl	My niece.
2. Telugu	2	Kŭthŭrŭ	Daughter.	Kŏdǎlŭ	Niece.
3. Canarese	3	Nǎnnǎ mǎgǎlu	My daughter.	Nǎnnǎ sodǎrǎsose	My niece.
4. Hindî	4	Merǎ bhatijĕ	My niece.	Merǎ bhatíjí	" "
5. Bengâlî	5	Amar bhyjhe	" "	Amar bhyjhe	" "
6. Marâthî	6	Mǎzhi pŭtanï	" "	Mǎzhi pŭtanï	" "
7. Gujârâthî	7	Mǎri bhrǎtiji	" "	Mǎri bhrǎtiji	" "
8. Chinese	8	Wo-tĕ tang-chih-neu	My niece of the *tang* class.	Wo-tĕ tang-chih-neu	My niece of the *tang* class.
9. Japanese	9	O-mǎ'-e-to'-ko	Niece.	O-mǎ'-e-to'-ko	Niece.
10. Burmese	10	K: too-mǎ'	My niece.	K: too-mǎ'	My niece.
11. Karen (Sgau dial'ct)	11	Yǎ pho-do-mu	" "	Yǎ pho-do-mu	" "
12. Karen (Pwo ")	12	Y' pho-do-mu	" "	Y' pho-do-mu	" "
13. Karen	13	Yeh po-do-mŭ	" "	Yeh po-do-mŭ	" "
14. Kings Mill Islands	14	Nǎtu-te-aine	Child my a female.	Nǎtu-te-mane	Child my a male.
15. Kusaien	15	Au-nuttik	Daughter my.	Au-nuttik	Daughter my.
16. Hawaiian	16	Kŭ-u' kǎĭ'-kǎ-wǎ-hee'-na	My child female.	Kŭ-ŭ' kǎĭ'-kǎ-wǎ-hee'-na	My child female.
17. Maori	17				
18. Amazulu (Kafir)	18	In-do-dǎ-kǎ'-ze yǎ'-me	Daughter of me.	In-do-dǎ-kǎ'-ze yǎ'-me	Daughter of me.

TABLE III.—*Continued.*

		79. My father's brother's daughter's son. (Male speaking.)	Translation.	80. My father's brother's daughter's son. (Female speaking.)	Translation.
1. Tamil	1	En mărŭmăkăn	My nephew.	En măkăn	My son.
2. Telugu	2	Allŭdŭ	Nephew.	Kŏdŭkŭ	Son.
3. Canarese	3	Nănnă ăliyă	My nephew.	Nănnă măgănu	My son.
4. Hindî	4	Meră bhánjá	" "	Meră bhaánja	My nephew.
5. Bengâlî	5	Amar bhagna	" "	Amar bhagna	" "
6. Marâthî	6	Măzhă pŭtanyă	" "	Măzhă pŭtanyă	" "
7. Gujârâthî	7	Măro bhrătijo	" " [*tang* class.	Măro bhrătijo	" " [*tang* class.
8. Chinese	8	Wo-tĕ tang-wae-sung	My *wae-sung* child of the	Wo-tĕ tang-wae-sung	My *wae-sung* child of the
9. Japanese	9	E-to-ko	Nephew.	E-to-ko	Nephew.
10. Burmese	10	K: too	My nephew.	K: too	My nephew.
11. Karen (Sgau dial'ct)	11	Yă pho-do-khwă	" "	Yă pho-do-khwă	" "
12. Karen (Pwo ")	12	Y' pho-do-khwă	" "	Y' pho-do-khwa	" "
13. Karen	13	Yeh po-do-khwa	" "	Yeh po-do-khwa	" "
14. Kings Mill Islands	14	Nătu-te-măne	Child my, a male.	Nătu-te-mane	Child my, a male.
15. Kusaien	15	Mwĕn-nuttik	Son my.	Mwĕn-nuttik	Son my.
16. Hawaiian	16	Kŭ-ŭ' kăĭ'-kee-kă'-na	My child, male.	Kŭ-ŭ' kăĭ'-kee-kă'-na	My child, male.
17. Maori	17				
18. Amazulu (Kafir)	18	In-do-dă'-nă yă' ma	Son of me.	In-do-dă'-nă yă'-mă	Son of me.

		81. My father's brother's daughter's daughter. (Male speaking.)	Translation.	82. My father's brother's daughter's daughter. (Female speaking.)	Translation.
1. Tamil	1	En mărŭmăkăl	My niece.	En măkăl	My daughter.
2. Telugu	2	Kŏdălu	Niece.	Kŭthŭrŭ	Daughter.
3. Canarese	3	Nănnă sodărăsose	My niece.	Nănnă măgălu	My daughter.
4. Hindî	4	Merï' bhanje'	" "	Merï bahinautí	My niece.
5. Bengâlî	5	Amar bhagny	" "	Amar bhagny	" "
6. Marâthî	6	Măzhe pŭtanï	" "	Măzhe putanï	" "
7. Gujârâthî	7	Mări bhrătiji	" " [*tang* class.	Mări bhrătiji	" " *tang* class.
8. Chinese	8	Wo-tĕ tang-wae-sung-neu	My *wae-sung* daughter of the	Wo-tĕ tang-wae-sung-neu	My *wae-sung* daughter of the
9. Japanese	9	E-mă'-e-ko-ko	Niece.	E-mă'-e-to'-ko	Niece.
10. Burmese	10	K: too-mă'	My niece.	K: too-mă'	My niece.
11. Karen (Sgau dial'ct)	11	Yă pho-do-mu	" "	Yă pho-do-mu	" "
12. Karen (Pwo ")	12	Y' pho-do-mu	" "	Y' pho-do-mu	" "
13. Karen	13	Yeh po-do-mŭ	" "	Yeh po-do-mŭ	" "
14. Kings Mill Islands	14	Nătu-te-aine	Child my, a female.	Nătu-te-aine	Child my, a male.
15. Kusaien	15	Au-nuttik	Daughter my.	Au-nuttik	Daughter my.
16. Hawaiian	16	Kŭ-ŭ' kăĭ'-kă-wă-hee'-na	My child, female.	Kŭ-ŭ' kăĭ'-kă-wă-hee'-na	My child, female.
17. Maori	17				
18. Amazulu (Kafir)	18	In-do-dă-kă'-ze	Daughter of me.	In-do-dă-kă'-ze	Daughter of me.

		83. My father's brother's great grandson.	Translation.	84. My father's brother's great granddaughter.	Translation.
1. Tamil	1	En pĕrăn	My grandson.	En pĕrtti	My granddaughter.
2. Telugu	2	Mănămădŭ	Grandson.	Mănămărălŭ	" "
3. Canarese	3	N. marimăgănu	My grandson.	N. marimăgălu	" "
4. Hindî	4	Meră potá	" "	Merï potí	" "
5. Bengâlî	5	Amar naty	" "	Amar natny	" "
6. Marâthî	6	Măzhă nătŭ	" "	Măzhi năt	" "
7. Gujârâthî	7		[class.		[*tang-chih* class.
8. Chinese	8	Wo-tĕ tang-chih-sun	My grandson of the *tang-chih*	Wo-tĕ tang-chih-sun-neu	My granddaughter in the
9. Japanese	9	Mă'-go	My grandson.	Mă'-ee	My granddaughter.
10. Burmese	10	K: my-a'	My grandchild.	K: my-a'	My grandchild.
11. Karen (Sgau dial'ct)	11	Yă lie-khwă	My grandson.	Yă lie-mu	My granddaughter.
12. Karen (Pwo ")	12	Y' le-khwă	" "	Y' le-mu	" "
13. Karen	13	Yeh lee-khwa	" "	Yeh lee-mŭ	" "
14. Kings Mill Islands	14	Tibu-te-mane	Grandchild my, a male.	Tibu-te-mane	Grandchild my, a male.
15. Kusaien	15	Mwĕn-nuttin-nuttik	Grandson my.	Au-nuttin-nuttik	Grandson my.
16. Hawaiian	16	Kŭ-ŭ' moo-pŭ'-nă-kă'-na	My grandchild, male.	Kŭ-ŭ' moo-pŭ'-nă-wa-hee'-na	My grandchild, female.
17. Maori	17				
18. Amazulu (Kafir)	18	U-me-tshă'-nă wă'-me	Grandchild of me.	U-me-tshă'-nă wă'-me	Grandchild of me.

TABLE III.—*Continued.*

		85. My father's brother's great grandson's son.	Translation.	86. My father's brother's great grandson's daughter.	Translation.
1. Tamil......	1	En pêrăn......................	My grandson.	En pêrtti.......................	My granddaughter.
2. Telugu............	2	Mŭnĭmănămădŭ	Great grandson	Mŭnĭmănămărălŭ	Great granddaughter.
3. Canarese............	3				
4. Hindî..............	4				
5. Bengâlî............	5				
6. Marâthî............	6				
7. Gujârâthî............	7		[*tang-chih* class.		[the *tang-chih* class.
8. Chinese............	8	Wo-tĕ tang-chih-tsung-sun....	My great grandson of the	Wo-tĕ tang-chih-tsung-sun-neu	My great granddaughter of
9. Japanese............	9	She'-ko......................	My great grandchild.	She'-ko......................	My great grandchild.
10. Burmese............	10	K: my-a'....................	My grandchild.	K: my-a'....................	My grandchild.
11. Karen (Sgau dial'ct)	11	Yă lo-khwă	My great grandson.	Tă lo-mu	My great granddaughter.
12. Karen (Pwo ")	12	Y' lo-khwä	" " "	Y' lo-mu	" " "
13. Karen............	13	Yeh lo-khwa..................	" " "	Yeh lo-mü..................	" " "
14. Kings Mill Islands..	14	Tibun-natu............[nuttik	Grandchild of my child.	Tibun-natu............	Grandchild of my child.
15. Kusaien..............	15	Mwĕn - nuttin - mwĕn - nuttin-	Great grandson my.	An-nuttin-ăn-nuttin-nuttik ...	Great granddaughter my.
16. Hawaiian............	16	Kŭ-ŭ' moo-pŭ'-nä-kä-na-kŭ'-ä-	My great grandchild, male.	Kŭ-ŭ' moo-pŭ'-nä-wa-hee'-na-	My gt. grandchild, female.
17. Maori............	17	[lu'-ä		[kŭ'-ä-lu'-ä	
18. Amazulu (Kafir)....	18	U-mzŭ-kŭ'-lŭ wä'-me...........	Great grandchild of me.	U-mzŭ-kŭ'-lŭ wä'-me..........	Great grandchild of me.

		87. My father's sister.	Translation.	88. My father's sister's husband.	Translation.
1. Tamil..................	1	En attai	My aunt.	En mämăn	My uncle.
2. Telugu..................	2	Mĕnăttä	Aunt.	Mämă....................[pan (y.)	Uncle.
3. Canarese............	3	Nănnă ătte....................	My aunt.	N. doddăppăn (o.), Chikkap-	My father great or small.
4. Hindî..................	4	Meri phuphi'..................	My paternal aunt.	Merá phuphá...................	My paternal uncle.
5. Bengâlî..................	5	Amar pishi..................	" " "	Amar pishe...................	" " "
6. Marâthî..................	6	Măzhi ät. ᵇMäwalan...........	" " "	Măzhă mäwală. ᵇMämä...........	" " "
7. Gujârâthî............	7	Märi phoi	My aunt. [der sister.	Märo phuo.....................	My uncle.
8. Chinese..................	8	Wo-tĕ kŭ-mo. ᵇKŭ-tseay......	My aunt mother. ᵇAunt el-	Wo-tĕ kŭ-chang	My aunt's husband.
9. Japanese..............	9	O-bä.........................	Little mother or aunt.	E-to'-ko	" " " [father.
10. Burmese..............	10	K: ky-ee-tan (o.), Twa-tan (y.)	My gt. aunt, my little aunt.	K: bă-ky-ee (o.), Bă-twa (y.)	My great father, my y'nger
11. Karen (Sgau dial'ct)	11	Yă mu-ghä...................	My aunt.	Yă phä-tie....................	My uncle.
12. Karen (Pwo ")	12	Y' n'-gä-te-te	My own aunt.	Y' pha-te....................	" " "
13. Karen..................	13	Yeh mü'-gah.................	My aunt.	Yeh păh-tee..................	" " "
14. Kings Mill Islands..	14	Tinau	Mother my.	Butikau-tamau	Brother-in-law of my father.
15. Kusaien..............	15	Nenĕ keyŭk..................	" "	Päpä-tummuk	Father my.
16. Hawaiian............	16	Kŭ-ŭ' mä-kŭ'-ä-wä-hee-na.....	My parent, female.	Kŭ-ŭ' mä-kŭ'-ä-kä'-na.........	My parent, male.
17. Maori............	17	Ta'-ku wa-e-a	My mother.		
18. Amazulu (Kafir)....	18	U-bä'-bä.	My father (so used).	U-bä'-bä.	My father.

		89. My father's sister's son—older than myself. (Male speaking.)	Translation.	90. My father's sister's son—older than myself. (Female speaking.)	Translation.
1. Tamil..................	1	En attän. ᵇMăittŭnăn...........	My cousin.	En măchchăn....................	My cousin.
2. Telugu..............	2	Bävä	Cousin.	Märădi	Cousin.
3. Canarese............	3	Nănnă bhăvămeidă.............	My cousin. [pat. uncle.	Nănnă bhăvămeidă.............	My cousin. [pat. uncle.
4. Hindî..................	4	Merá bhaí. ᵇPhuphera bhaí...	My brother. ᵇ Brother thro'	Merá bhaí. ᵇPhuphera bhaí...	My brother. ᵇ Brother thro'
5. Bengâlî..................	5	Amar bhye. ᵇPishtoto bhye...	" " "	Amar bhye. Pishtoto bhye...	" " "
6. Marâthî..................	6	Măzhă ätĕ bhäû. ᵇMahŭnä....	My brother.	Măzhă ätĕ bhäû. ᵇMahŭnä....	My brother.
7. Gujârâthî............	7	Märo bhäi		Märo bhäi	
8. Chinese..................	8	Wo-tĕ peaon-heung-te	My bro. of the *peaon* class.	Wo-tĕ peaon-heung-te	My bro. of the *peaon* class.
9. Japanese..............	9	A'-nee	My elder brother.	A'-nee	My elder brother.
10. Burmese..............	10	K: e-ko-tau	My elder brother.	K: e-ko-tau	My elder brother.
11. Karen (Sgau dial'ct)	11	Yă tä-khwä	My male cousin.	Yă tä-khwä	My male cousin.
12. Karen (Pwo ")	12	Y' t'-khwä-sau	" " "	Y' t'khwä-sau	" " "
13. Karen..................	13	Yeh t'-khwa	" " "	Yeh t'-khwa	" " "
14. Kings Mill Islands..	14	Tăru-te-karimoa	Brother, my elder.	Manu-te-karimoa............	Brother, my elder.
15. Kusaien..............	15	Mä-lĕk	Brother my.	Mä-lĕk	Brother my.
16. Hawaiian............	16	Kŭ-ŭ' käï'-kŭ-ä'-nä'...........	My brother, elder.	Kŭ-ŭ käï'-kŭ-ä'-nä	My brother, elder.
17. Maori............	17	Ta'-ku tua-ka-na	" " "	Ta'-ku tun-ga-ne............	" " "
18. Amazulu (Kafir)....	18	U-mnä wä'-tŭ	Elder brother of us.	U'-mwä wä'-tŭ	Elder brother of us.

TABLE III.—*Continued.*

		91. My father's sister's son—younger than myself. (Male speaking.)	Translation.	92. My father's sister's son—younger than myself. (Female speaking.)	Translation.
1. Tamil	1	En attän. ᵇMăittŭnăn..........	My cousin.	En Machchăn......................	My cousin.
2. Telugu	2	Băvă	Cousin.	Mărădi	Cousin.
3. Canarese	3	Nănnă bhăvămeidă....	My cousin. [pat. uncle.	Nănnă bhăvămeidă..	My cousin. [pat. uncle.
4. Hindî	4	Merá bhaí. ᵇPhuphera bhaí...	My brother or brother thro'	Merá bhaí. ᵇPhupera bhaí...	My brother or brother thro'
5. Bengálî	5	Amar bhye. ᵇPishtoto bhye ...	" " " " "	Amar bhye. ᵇ Pishtoto bhye...	" " " " "
6. Marâthî	6	Măzhă ătĕ bhăŭ. ᵇMahŭna....	My brother.	Măzhă ătĕ bhăŭ. ᵇMahŭnă....	My brother.
7. Gujârâthî	7	Măro bhăi	" "	Măro bhăi	" "
8. Chinese	8	Wo-tĕ peaon-heung-te..........	My bro. of the *peaon* class.	Wo-tĕ peaon-heung-te..........	My bro. of the *peaon* class.
9. Japanese	9	O-to'-to	My younger brother.	E-to'-ko	My younger brother.
10. Burmese	10	K: ny-ee-tau	" " "	K: ny-ee-tau	" " "
11. Karen (Sgau dial'ct)	11	Yă tă-khwă	My male cousin.	Yă tă-khwă	My male cousin.
12. Karen (Pwo ")	12	Y' t'-khwă-sau	" " "	Y' t'-khwă-sau	" " "
13. Karen	13	Yeh t'-khwa	" " "	Yeh t'-khwa	" " "
14. Kings Mill Islands	14	Taru-te-kärimwi	Brother my, younger.	Manu-te-kärimwi	Brother my, younger.
15. Kusaien	15	Mä-lĕk	Brother my.	Mä-lĕk	Brother my.
16. Hawaiian	16	Kŭ-ŭ' kăï'-kăï'-nă	My brother, younger.	Kŭ-ŭ' kăï'-kăï'-nă	My brother, younger.
17. Maori	17	Ta'-ku te-t-na	" " "	Ta'ku tun-ga-ne-te-i-na	" " "
18. Amazulu (Kafir)	18	U'-mfo wä'-tŭ	Brother of us.	U'-mfo wä'-tŭ	Brother of us.

		93. My father's sister's son's wife. (Male speaking.)	Translation.	94. My father's sister's son's wife. (Female speaking.)	Translation.
1. Tamil	1	En tăngay	My younger sister.	En tăngay	My younger sister.
2. Telugu	2	Akkă (o.), Chĕllĕlŭ (y.).	Elder or younger sister.	Akkă (o.), Chĕllĕlŭ (y.).	Elder or younger sister.
3. Canarese	3	N. ăkkă (o.), Tăngi (y.)	My elder or younger sister.	N. ăkkă (o.), Tăngi (y.)	My elder or younger sister.
4. Hindi	4	Merí bhăwáj	My sister-in-law.	Merí bhăwáj	" "
5. Bengálî	5	Amar bhaj	" "	Amar bhaj	" "
6. Marâthî	6	Măzhi ătĕ bhăŭzai	" "	Măzhe ătĕ bhăŭzoi	" "
7. Gujârâthî	7	Mări bhojai. ᵇBabi	" " [class.	Măro bhojai. ᵇ Babi	" " [class.
8. Chinese	8	Wo-tĕ peaon saon	My sister-in-law of the *peaon*	Wŏ-tĕ peaon saon	My sister-in-law of the *peaon*
9. Japanese	9	A'-nih. ᵇEm-o-to	My sister elder or younger.	A'-nih (o.), E-mo'-to	My sister elder or younger.
10. Burmese	10	K: kai-mă'	My sister-in-law.	K: kai-mă'	My sister-in-law.
11. Karen (Sgau dial'ct)	11	Yă tă-khwă-mu	My female cousin.	Yă tă-khwă-mu	My female cousin.
12. Karen (Pwo ")	12	Y' t'-khwă-mu	" " "	Y' t'-khwă-mu	" " "
13. Karen	13	Yeh dan-t'khwa-a-mä	My cousin's wife.	Yeh dan-t'-khwă-a-mä	" " "
14. Kings Mill Islands	14	Eiriku	Sister-in-law my.	Eiriku	Sister-in-law my.
15. Kusaien	15	Mä-loŭk	Sister my.	Mä-loŭk	Sister my.
16. Hawaiian	16	Kŭ-ŭ wä-hee'-na	My wife, my female.	Kŭ-ŭ' wä-hee'-na	My wife, my female.
17. Maori	17				
18. Amazulu (Kafir)	18	U-mkä' me	My wife.		

		95. My father's sister's daughter—older than myself. (Male speaking.)	Translation.	96. My father's sister's daughter—older than myself. (Female speaking.)	Translation.
1. Tamil	1	En măittuni	My cousin.	En măchchi. ᵇMachcharl	My cousin.
2. Telugu	2	Vădĭnĕ	Cousin.	Vădĭnĕ	Cousin.
3. Canarese	3	Nănnă attige	My cousin. [pat. uncle.	Nănnă attigï	My cousin. [pat. uncle.
4. Hindî	4	Merí bahin. ᵇPhupherí bahin.	My sister. ᵇSister through	Merí bahin. ᵇPhupherí bahin	My sister. ᵇSister through
5. Bengálî	5	Amar bhugny. ᵇPistoto bhugny	" " " " "	Amar bhugny. ᵇPistoto bhugny	" " " " "
6. Marâthî	6	Măzhi ătĕ bahin. ᵇMahuni....	My sister.	Măzhi ătĕ bahin. ᵇMahuni....	My sister.
7. Gujârâthî	7	Mări băhin	" "	Mări băhin	" "
8. Chinese	8	Wo-tĕ peaon tsze-mei	My sister of the *peaon* class.	Wo-tĕ peaon-tsze-mei	My sister of the *peaon* class.
9. Japanese	9	A'-nih	My elder sister.	A-nih	My elder sister.
10. Burmese	10	K: e-ma'	My elder sister.	K: e-ma'	" " "
11. Karen (Sgau dial'ct)	11	Yă tă-khwă-mu	My female cousin.	Yă tă-khwă-mu	My female cousin.
12. Karen (Pwo ")	12	Y' t'-khwă-mu	" " "	Y' t'-khwă-mu	" " "
13. Karen	13	Yeh dan-t'-khwa-mü	" " "	Yeh dan-t'-khwa-mü	" " "
14. Kings Mill Islands	14	Mănu-te-karimoa	Sister my, elder.	Taru-te-karimoa	Sister my, elder.
15. Kusaien	15	Mä-loŭk	Sister my.	Mä-loŭk	Sister my.
16. Hawaiian	16	Kŭ-ŭ' kăï'-kŭ-wa-hee'-na	My sister, elder.	Kŭ-ŭ' kăï'-kŭ-ä-ă'-ʟa	My sister, elder.
17. Maori	17	Ta'-ku te-a-hi-ne	" " "	Ta'-ku te-a-ka-na	" " "
18. Amazulu (Kafir)	18	U-dä'-dä wä'-tŭ	Sister of us.	U-dä'-dä wä'-tŭ	Sister of us.

TABLE III.—*Continued.*

		97. My father's sister's daughter—younger than myself. (Male speaking.)	Translation.	98. My father's sister's daughter—younger than myself. (Female speaking.)	Translation.
1. Tamil	1	Eu măittuni	My cousin.	En machchi. ᵇMăchchărĭ	My cousin.
2. Telugu	2	Mărădălŭ	Cousin.	Mărădălŭ	Cousin.
3. Canarese	3	Nănnă nădini	My cousin. [pat. uncle.	Nănnă nădini	My cousin. [pat. uncle.
4. Hindî	4	Merî bahin. ᵇPhupherî bahin.	My sister. ᵇ Sister through	Merî bahin. ᵇPhupherî bahin.	My sister or sister through
5. Bengâlî	5	Amar bhugny. ᵇPistoto bhugny	" " " " "	Amar bhugny. ᵇPistoto bhugny	" " " " "
6. Marâthî	6	Măzhi ătĕ bahïn. ᵇMahŭni....	My sister.	Măzhi ătĕ bahïn. ᵇMahŭni....	My sister.
7. Gujârâthî	7	Mări băhen	" "	Mări băhin	" "
8. Chinese	8	Wo-tĕ peaon-tsze-mei	My sister of the *peaon* class.	Wo-tĕ peaon-tsze-mei	My sister of the *peaon* class.
9. Japanese	9	E-mo'-to.	My younger sister.	E-mo'-to.	My younger sister.
10. Burmese	10	K: hne-nă	My younger sister.	K: hne-nă	My younger sister.
11. Karen (Sgau dial'ct)	11	Yă tă-khwă-mu	My female cousin.	Yă tă-khwă-mu	My female cousin.
12. Karen (Pwo ")	12	Y' t'-khwä-mu	" " "	Y' t'-khwä-mu	" " "
13. Karen	13	Yeh dan-t'-khwa-mü	" " "	Yeh dan-t'-khwa-mü	" " "
14. Kings Mill Islands	14	Mănu-te-karimwi	Sister my, younger.	Taru-te-karimwi	Sister my, younger.
15. Kusaien	15	Mä-louk	Sister my.	Mä-loŭk	Sister my.
16. Hawaiian	16	Kŭ-ŭ' käï'-kŭ-wä-hee'-nă	My sister, younger.	Kŭ-ŭ' käï'-läï'-na	My sister younger.
17. Maori	17	Ta'-ku tu-o-hi-na-te-i-na	" " "	Ta'-ku te-i-na	" " "
18. Amazulu (Kafir)	18	U-dä'-dä wä'-tŭ	Sister of us.	U-dä'-dä wä'-tŭ	Sister of us.

		99. My father's sister's daughter's husband. (Male speaking.)	Translation.	100. My father's sister's daughter's husband. (Female speaking.)	Translation.
1. Tamil	1	En aṇnan (o.), Tambi (y.)	My elder or younger bro.	En aṇnan (o.), Tamăi (y.)	My elder or younger brother.
2. Telugu	2	Annă (o.), Tammudu (y.)	Elder or younger brother.	Annă (o.), Tămmŭdŭ (y.)	Elder or younger brother.
3. Canarese	3	Nanna ănnă (o.), Tămmă (y.)	My elder or younger bro.	Nănnă ănnă (o.), Tămmă (y.)	My elder or younger brother.
4. Hindî	4	Merá bahïnoi	My brother-in-law.	Merá bahïnoi	My brother-in-law.
5. Bengâlî	5	Amar bhugny poty	" "	Amar bhugny poty	" "
6. Marâthî	6	Măzhă mahŭnă	" "	Măzhă mahŭnă	" "
7. Gujârâthî	7	Măro baneni	" " [the *peaon* class.	Măro baneni	" " [the *peaon* class.
8. Chinese	8	Wo-tĕ tseay mei -fŭ	My elder younger sister's husb. of	Wo-tĕ tseay mei -fŭ	My elder younger sister's husb. of
9. Japanese	9	A'-nee (o.), O-to'-to (y.)	My brother elder or y'nger.	A'-nee (o.), O-to'-to.	My brother elder or y'nger.
10. Burmese	10	K: youk-pă	My brother-in-law.	K: youk-pă	My brother-in-law.
11. Karen (Sgau dial'ct)	11	Yă tă-khwă	My male cousin.	Yă tă-khwă	My male cousin.
12. Karen (Pwo ")	12	Y' t'-khwä-sau	" " "	Y' t'-khwä-sau	" " "
13. Karen	13	Yeh dan-t'-khwa-a-wä	My cousin's husband.	Yeh dan-t'-khwa-a-wä	My cousin's husband.
14. Kings Mill Islands	14	Butikau	Brother-in-law my.	Butikau	Brother-in-law my.
15. Kusaien	15	Mä-lĕk	Brother my.	Mä-lĕk	Brother my.
16. Hawaiian	16	Kŭ-ŭ' käï'-ko-ee'-ka	My brother in-law.	Kŭ-ŭ' käï'-ko-ee'-ka	My brother-in-law.
17. Maori	17				
18. Amazulu (Kafir)	18	U-mkwä-ny-ă'-nä wä'-tŭ	Brother-in-law of us.	U-mkwä-ny-ă'-nä wä'-tŭ	Brother-in-law of us.

		101. My father's sister's son's son. (Male speaking.)	Translation.	102. My father's sister's son's son. (Female speaking.)	Translation.
1. Tamil	1	En mărŭmăkăn	My nephew.	En măkăn	My son.
2. Telugu	2	Allŭdŭ	Nephew.	Kŏdŭkŭ	Son.
3. Canarese	3	Nanna sodărăliyă	My nephew.	Nanna măgănu	My son.
4. Hindî	4	Merá bhatijá	" "	Merá bhatija	My nephew.
5. Bengâlî	5	Amar bhaypo	" "	Amar bhaypo	" "
6. Marâthî	6	Măzhă chächä	" "	Măzhă chächä	" "
7. Gujârâthî	7	Măro bhrătijo	My brother (born of aunt).	Măro bhrătijo	My brother (born of aunt.)
8. Chinese	8	Wo-tĕ peaon-chih	My neph. of the *peaon* class.	Wo-tĕ peaon-chih	My neph. of the *peaon* class.
9. Japanese	9	E-to'-ko.	My nephew.	E-to'-ko.	My nephew.
10. Burmese	10	K: too	" "	K: too	" "
11. Karen (Sgau dial'ct)	11	Yă pho-do	" "	Yă pho-do	" "
12. Karen (Pwo ")	12	Y' pho-do-khwä	" "	Y' phe-do-khwä	" "
13. Karen	13	Yeh po-do-khwa	" "	Yeh po-do-khwa	" "
14. Kings Mill Islands	14	Nătu-te-mäne	Child my, a male.	Nătu-te-mane	Child my, a male.
15. Kusaien	15	Mwĕn-nuttik	Son my.	Mwĕn-nuttik	Son my.
16. Hawaiian	16	Kŭ-ŭ' käï'-kee-kä-na	My child, male.	Kŭ-ŭ' käï'-kee-kä-na	My child, male.
17. Maori	17				
18. Amazulu (Kafir)	18	In-do-dä'-nä yă'-me	Son of me.	In-do-dä'-nä yă'-me	Son of me

TABLE III.—*Continued.*

		103. My father's sister's son's daughter. (Male speaking.)	Translation.	104. My father's sister's son's daughter. (Female speaking.)	Translation.
1. Tamil	1	En mărŭmăkăl	My niece.	En măkăl	My daughter.
2. Telugu	2	Kō-dä-lŭ	Niece.	Kŭthŭrŭ	Daughter.
3. Canarese	3	Nănnä sodărăsose	My niece.	Nănnä măgalu	My daughter.
4. Hindî	4	Meri bhatiji	" "	Meri bhatiji	My niece.
5. Bengâlî	5	Amar bhyghi	" "	Amar bhyghi	" "
6. Marâthî	6	Mäzhi chăche	" "	Mäzhi chăche	My sister (born of aunt).
7. Gujârâthî	7	Mări bhrătiji	My sister (born of uncle).	Mări bhrătiji	My niece of the *peaon* class.
8. Chinese	8	Wo-tĕ peaon-chih-neu	My niece of the *peaon* class.	Wo-tĕ peaon-chih-neu	My niece.
9. Japanese	9	O-nä'-e-to'-ko	My niece.	O-nä'-e-to-ko	" "
10. Burmese	10	K: too-mä'	" "	K: too-mä'	" "
11. Karen (Sgau dial'ct)	11	Yă-pho-do-mu	" "	Yä pho-do-mu	" "
12. Karen (Pwo ")	12	Y' pho-do-mu	" "	Y' pho-do-mu	" "
13. Karen	13	Yeh po-do-mü	" "	Yeh po-do-mü	" "
14. Kings Mill Islands	14	Nätu-te-äine	Child my, a female.	Nätu--te-äine	Child my, a female.
15. Kusaien	15	Au-nuttik	Daughter my.	Au-nuttik	Daughter my.
16. Hawaiian	16	Kŭ-ŭ' kăï'-kă-wă-hee'-na	My child, female.	Kŭ-ŭ' kăï'-kă-wă-hee'-na	My child, female.
17. Maori	17				
18. Amazulu (Kafir)	18	In-do-dä-kă'-ze yä'-me	Daughter of me.	In-do-dä-kă'-ze yä'-me	Daughter of me.

		105. My father's sister's daughter's son. (Male speaking.)	Translation.	106. My father's sister's daughter's son. (Female speaking.)	Translation.
1. Tamil	1	En măkăn	My son.	En mărŭmăkăn	My nephew.
2. Telugu	2	Kōdŭkŭ	Son.	Allŭdŭ	Nephew.
3. Canarese	3	Nănnä măgănu	My son.	Nănnä măgănu ?	My son.
4. Hindî	4	Merá bháujá	My nephew.	Merá bháujá	My nephew.
5. Bengâlî	5	Amar bhagna	" "	Amar bhagna	" "
6. Marâthî	6	Mäzhä chăchä	" "	Mäzhä chăchä	" "
7. Gujârâthî	7	Măro bhrătijo	My brother (born of aunt).	Măro bhrătijo	My brother (born of aunt).
8. Chinese	8	Wo-tĕ peaon-chih-wae-sung	My nephew of the *wae-sung* branch of the *peaon* class.	Wo-tĕ peaon-chih-wae-sung	My nephew of the *wae-sung* branch of the *peaon* class.
9. Japanese	9	E-to'-ko	My nephew.	E-to'-ko	My nephew.
10. Burmese	10	K: too	" "	K: too	" "
11. Karen (Sgau dial'ct)	11	Yă pho-do	" "	Yä pho-do	" "
12. Karen (Pwo ")	12	Y' pho-do-khwä	" "	Y' pho-do-khwä	" "
13. Karen	13	Yeh po-do-khwa	" "	Yeh po-do-khwa	" "
14. Kings Mill Islands	14	Nätu-te-mäne	Child my, a male.	Nätu-te-mäne	Child my, a male.
15. Kusaien	15	Mwĕn-nuttik	Son my.	Mwĕn-nuttik	Son my.
16. Hawaiian	16	Kŭ-ŭ' kăï'-kee-kä-na	My child, male.	Kŭ-ŭ' kăï'-kee-kä-na	My child, male.
17. Maori	17				
18. Amazulu (Kafir)	18	In-do-dä'-nä yä'-me	Son of me.	In-do-dä'-nä yä'-me	Son of me.

		107. My father's sister's daughter's daughter. (Male speaking.)	Translation.	108. My father's sister's daughter's daughter. (Female speaking.)	Translation.
1. Tamil	1	En măkăl	My daughter.	En mărŭmăkăl	My niece.
2. Telugu	2	Kŭthŭrŭ	Daughter.	Kōdălŭ	Niece.
3. Canarese	3	Nănnä măgalu	My daughter.	Nănnä măgalu ?	My daughter.
4. Hindî	4	Meri bháuji	My niece.	Meri bháuji	My niece.
5. Bengâlî	5	Amar bhagny	" "	Amar bhagny	" "
6. Marâthî	6	Mäzhi chăche	" "	Mazhi chăche	My sister (born of an aunt.)
7. Gujârâthî	7	Mări bhrătiji	My sister (born of an aunt).	Mări bhrătiji	My niece of the *wae-sung* branch of the *peaon* class.
8. Chinese	8	Wo-tĕ peaou-chih-wae-sung-neu.	My niece of the *wea-sung* branch of the *peaon* class.	Wo-tĕ peaon-chih-wae-sung-neu.	
9. Japanese	9	O-nä'-e-to'-ko	My niece.	O-nä'-e-to'-ko	My niece.
10. Burmese	10	K: too-mä'	" "	K: too-mä	" "
11. Karen (Sgau dial'ct)	11	Yă pho-do-mu	" "	Yä pho-do-mu	" "
12. Karen (Pwo ")	12	Y' pho-do-mu	" "	Y' pho-do-mu	" "
13. Karen	13	Yᵉh po-do-mü	" "	Yeh po-do-mü	" "
14. Kings Mill Islands	14	Nätu-te-äine	Child my, a female.	Nätu-te-mäne	Child my, a female.
15. Kusaien	15	Au-nuttik	Daughter my.	Au-nuttik	Daughter my.
16. Hawaiian	16	Kŭ-ŭ' kăï'-kă-wă-hee'-na	My child, female.	Kŭ-ŭ' kăï'-kă-wă-hee'-na	My child, female.
17. Maori	17				
18. Amazulu (Kafir)	18	In-do-dä-kă'-ze yä'-me	Daughter of me.	In-do-dä-kă'-ze yä'-me	Daughter of me.

TABLE III.—Continued.

		109. My father's sister's great grandson.	Translation.	110. My father's sister's great granddaughter.	Translation.
1. Tamil	1	En pêran	My grandson.	En pêrtti	My granddaughter.
2. Telugu	2	Mănămădŭ	Grandson.	Mănămărălŭ	Granddaughter.
3. Canarese	3	Nănnă mommăgănu	My grandson.	Nănnă mommăgălu	My granddaughter.
4. Hindî	4	Merá potá	" "	Meri poti	" "
5. Bengâlî	5	Amar naty	" "	Amar natny	" "
6. Marâthî	6	Mázhă nătŭ	" "	Mázhi năt	" "
7. Gujârâthî	7	Măro pautră	" " [class.	Mări pautri	" " [peaon class.
8. Chinese	8	Wo-tĕ peaon-chih-sun	My grandson of the peaon	Wo-tĕ peaon-chih-sun-neu	My granddaughter of the
9. Japanese	9	Mă'-go	My grandson.	Ma'-ee	My granddaughter.
10. Burmese	10	K: my-a'	My grandchild.	K: my-a'	My grandchild.
11. Karen (Sgau dialect)	11	Yă lie-khwă	My grandson.	Yă lie-mu	My granddaughter.
12. Karen (Pwo ")	12	Y' le-khwă	" "	Y' le-mu	" "
13. Karen	13	Yeh lee-khwa		Ye lee-mü	" "
14. Kings Mill Islands	14	Tibu-te-mäne	Grandchild my, a male.	Tibu-te-aine	Grandchild my, a female.
15. Kusaien	15	Mwĕn-nuttin-nnttik	Grandson my.	Au-nuttin-nuttik	Granddaughter my.
16. Hawaiian	16	Kŭ-ŭ' moo-pŭ'-nă-kä-na	My grandchild, male.	Kŭ-ŭ' moo-pŭ'-nă-wă-hee-na	My grandchild female.
17. Maori	17				
18. Amazulu (Kafir)	18	U-mzŭ-kŭ'-lŭ wä'-me	Grandchild of me.	U-mzŭ-kŭ'-lŭ wä'-me	Grandchild of me.

		111. My father's sister's great grandson's son.	Translation.	112. My father's sister's great grandson's daughter.	Translation.
1. Tamil	1	En pêran	My grandson.	En pêrtti	My granddaughter.
2. Telugu	2	Mŭnĭmănămădŭ	My great grandson.	Mŭnĭmănămărălŭ	Great granddaughter.
3. Canarese	3	Nănnă mummăgănu	My great grandson.	Nănnă mummăgălu	My great granddaughter.
4. Hindî	4	Merá parotá	" " "	Meri paroti	" " "
5. Bengâlî	5	Amar naty	My grandson.	Amar natny	My granddaughter.
6. Marâthî	6	Mázhă nătŭ	" "	Mázhi nătŭ	" "
7. Gujârâthî	7				
8. Chinese	8	Wo-tĕ peaon-chih-tsung-sun	My great grandson of the [peaon class.	Wo-tĕ peaon-chih-tsung-sun-neu	My great granddaughter of [the peaon-chih class.
9. Japanese	9	She'-ko	My great grandchild.	She'-ko	My great grandchild.
10. Burmese	10	K: my-a'	My grandchild.	K: my-a'	My grandchild.
11. Karen (Sgau dialect)	11	Yă lo-khwă	My great grandson.	Yă lo-mu	My great granddaughter.
12. Karen (Pwo ")	12	Y' lo-khwă	" " "	Y' lo-mu	" " "
13. Karen	13	Yeh lo-khwa	" " "	Yeh lo-mü	" " "
14. Kings Mill Islands	14	Tibun-natu [nuttik	Grandchild of my child.	Tibun-natu	Grandchild of my child.
15. Kusaien	15	Mwĕn-nuttin-äu-nuttin-nuttik	Great grandson my.	Au-nuttin-äu-nuttin-nuttik	Great granddaughter my.
16. Hawaiian	16	Kŭ-ŭ moo-pŭ-nă-kä'-na kŭ'-ă- [lu'-ă	My great grandchild, male.	Kŭ-ŭ moo-pŭ'-nă wă-hee'-na [kŭ'-ă-lu'-ă	My gt. grandchild, female.
17. Maori	17				
18. Amazulu (Kafir)	18	U-mzŭ-kŭ'-lŭ wä'-me	Great grandchild of me.	U-zmŭ-kŭ-lŭ wä'-me	Great grandchild of me.

		113. My mother's brother.	Translation.	114. My mother's brother's wife.	Translation.
1. Tamil	1	En mămăn	My uncle.	En mămĕ	My aunt.
2. Telugu	2	Mĕnămămă	Uncle.	Mĕnăttă. bĂttă	Aunt.
3. Canarese	3	Nanna măva	My uncle.	Nanna atte	My aunt.
4. Hindî	4	Merá mámú	My uncle maternal.	Meri mamani	" "
5. Bengâlî	5	Amar mămă	My uncle.	Amar mami	" "
6. Marâthî	6	Mázhă mămă	" "	Mázhi măme	" "
7. Gujârâthî	7	Măro mămo	" "	Mări mămi	" "
8. Chinese	8	Wo-tĕ mo-kew	My mother uncle.	Wo-tĕ kew-mo	My uncle mother.
9. Japanese	9	O'-je		O'-bă	My aunt.
		Nebän-mä-no-o-asee	Second little father.		
10. Burmese	10	K: bă-tyee (o.), Bă-twă (y.). bOo-men.	My great or little father. b Uncle.	K: ky-ee-tau (o.), Twa-tau (y.)	My great or little aunt.
11. Karen (Sgau dialect)	11	Yă pha-tie	My uncle.	Yă mu-ghă	My aunt.
12. Karen (Pwo ")	12	Y' pha-te-te	My own uncle.	Y' m'-gă	" "
13. Karen	13	Yeh páh-tee	My uncle.	Yeh mü'-gah	" "
14. Kings Mill Islands	14	Tămau	My father.	Kain-opan-tinau	My mother-in-law.
15. Kusaien	15	Păpă-tummuk	Father my.	Nĕnĕ-lĕyŭk	Mother my.
16. Hawaiian	16	Kŭ-ŭ' mä-kŭ-ă-ka'-nă	My parent, male.	Kŭ-ŭ' mä-kŭ'-ă-wä-hee'-na	My parent, female.
17. Maori	17				
18. Amazulu (Kafir)	18	U-mä-lŭ'-mä	My maternal uncle.	U-mä-lŭ'-mä	My aunt or uncle.

TABLE III.—*Continued.*

			115. My mother's brother's son —older than myself. (Male speaking.)	Translation.	116. My mother's brother's son —older than myself. (Female speaking.)	Translation
1.	Tamil	1	En mäittŭnän	My cousin.	En mǎchchǎn	My cousin.
2.	Telugu	2	Bävă	Cousin.	Bävă	Cousin.
3.	Canarese	3	Nännä bhävămeidă	My cousin. [ternal uncle.	Nanna bhävămeidă	My cousin. [ternal uncle.
4.	Hindî	4	Merá bhái. ᵇ Mamere bhái	My bro. ᵇ Bro. through pa-	Merá bhai. ᵇ Mamera bhái	My bro. ᵇ Bro. through pa-
5.	Bengâlî	5	Amar mamato bhye	" " " " "	Mäzhä mämä bhäŭ. ᵇMehŭna.	" " " " " "
6.	Marâthî	6	Mäzhä mämä bhäŭ. ᵇMehŭna.		Märo bhäi	My brother.
7.	Gujârâthî	7	Märo bhäi	My brother.	Wo-tĕ peaon-heung-te	My bro. of the *peaon* class.
8.	Chinese	8	Wo-tĕ peaon-heung-te	My bro. of the *peaon* class.	A'-nee	My elder brother.
9.	Japanese	9	A'-nee	My elder brother.	K: e-ko'	" " "
10.	Burmese	10	K: e-ko'	" " "	Yă tä-khwă	My male cousin.
11.	Karen (Sgau dialect)	11	Yă tä-khwă	My male cousin.	Y' t'-khwä-sau	" " "
12.	Karen (Pwo ")	12	Y' t'-khwä-sau	" " "	Yeh t'-khwa	" " "
13.	Karen	13	Yeh t'-khwa	" " "	Mänu-te-karimoa	Brother my older.
14.	Kings Mill Islands	14	Taru-te-karimoa	Brother my older.	Mä-lĕk	Brother my.
15.	Kusaien	15	Mä-lĕk	Brother my.	Kŭ-ŭ' käï'-kŭ-nä'-na	My brother, elder.
16.	Hawaiian	16	Kŭ-ŭ' käï'-kŭ-ä-ä'-nä	My brother, elder.	Ta'-ku tun-ga-ne	" " "
17.	Maori	17	Ta'-ku tu-a-ka-na	" " "	U-mzä'-lä wä'-me	Cousin of me.
18.	Amazulu (Kafir)	18	U-mzä'-lä wä'-me	Cousin of me.		

			117. My mother's brother's son —younger than myself. (Male speaking.)	Translation.	118. My mother's brother's son —younger than myself. (Female speaking.)	Translation.
1.	Tamil	1	En mäittŭnän	My cousin	En mǎchchǎn	My cousin.
2.	Telugu	2	Mărädĭ	Cousin.	Mărädĭ	Cousin.
3.	Canarese	3	Nännä bhävămeida	My cousin. [ternal uncle.	Nannä bhävămeidă	My cousin. [ternal uncle.
4.	Hindî	4	Merá bhái. ᵇ Mamera bhái	My bro. ᵇ Bro. through pa-	Merá bhái. ᵇ Mamera bhái	My bro. ᵇ Bro. through pa-
5.	Bengâlî	5	Amar mamato bhye	" " " " "	Amar mamato bhye	" " " " "
6.	Marâthî	6	Mäzhä mämä bhäŭ. ᵇMehŭnä.	" " " " " "	Mäzhä mämä bhäŭ. ᵇMehŭnä.	" " " " " "
7.	Gujârâthî	7	Maro bhäi	My brother.	Märo bhäi	My brother.
8.	Chinese	8	Wo-tĕ peaon-heung-te	My bro. of the *peaon* class.	Wo-tĕ peaon-heung-te	My bro. of the *peaon* class.
9.	Japanese	9	O-to'-to	My younger brother.	O-to'-to	My younger brother.
10.	Burmese	10	K: ny-ee'	" " "	K: ny-ee'	" " "
11.	Karen (Sgau dialect)	11	Yă tä-khwă	My male cousin.	Yă tä-khwă	My male cousin.
12.	Karen (Pwo ")	12	Y' t'-khwä-sau	" " "	Y' t'-khwä-sau	" " "
13.	Karen	13	Yeh t'-khwa	" " "	Yeh t'-khwa	" " "
14.	Kings Mill Islands	14	Manu-te-karimoa	Brother my younger.	Taru-te-karimoa	Brother my younger.
15.	Kusaien	15	Mä-lĕk	Brother my.	Mä-lĕk	Brother my.
16.	Hawaiian	16	Kŭ-ŭ' käï'-käï-nä	My brother, younger.	Kŭ-ŭ' käï'-kŭ-nä'-nä	My brother, younger.
17.	Maori	17				
18.	Amazulu (Kafir)	18	U-mzä'-lä wä'-me	Cousin cf me.	U-mzä'-lä wä'-me	Cousin of me.

			119. My mother's brother's son's wife. (Male speaking.)	Translation.	120. My mother's brother's son's wife. (Female speaking.)	Translation.
1.	Tamil	1	En Tăngay	My younger sister.	En tăngay	My younger sister.
2.	Telugu	2	Akkă (o.), Chĕllĕlŭ (y.)	Elder or younger sister.	Akka (o.), Chĕllĕlŭ	Elder or younger sister.
3.	Canarese	3	Nänkä tangi	My younger sister.	Nännä tängi	My younger sister.
4.	Hindî	4	Meri bháwaj	My sister-in-law.	Meri bháwaj	My sister-in-law.
5.	Bengâlî	5	Amar bhaj	" " "	Amar bhaj	" " "
6.	Marâthî	6	Mazhi bhaŭzai	" " "	Mäzhi bhaŭzai	" " "
7.	Gujârâthî	7	Märi bhäzi	" " " [class.	Märi bhäzi	" " " [class.
8.	Chinese	8	Wo-tĕ peaon-saon	My sist.-in-law of the *peaon*	Wo-tĕ peaon-saon	My sist.-in-law of the *peaon*
9.	Japanese	9	A'-nih (o.), E-mo'-to (y.)	My sister elder or y'nger.	A'-nih (o.), E-mo'-to (y.)	My sister elder or y'nger.
10.	Burmese	10	K: kai-mă	My sister-in-law.	K: kai-mă	My sister-in-law.
11.	Karen (Sgau dialect)	11	Yă tä-khwä-mu	My female cousin.	Yă tä-khwä-mu	My female cousin.
12.	Karen (Pwo ")	12	Y' t'-khwä-mu	" " "	Y' t'-khwä-mu	" " "
13.	Karen	13	Yeh dan-t'-khwa-a-mä	My cousin's wife.	Yeh dan-t'-khwa-a-mä	My cousin's wife.
14.	Kings Mill Islands	14	Eiriku	Sister-in-law my.	Eiriku	Sister-in-law my.
15.	Kusaien	15	Mä-loŭk	Sister my.	Mä-loŭk	Sister my.
16.	Hawaiian	16	Kŭ-ŭ' wä-hee'-na	My wife or female.	Kŭ-ŭ' wä-hee'-na	My wife or female.
17.	Maori	17				
18.	Amazulu (Kafir)	18	U-mkä'-me	My wife.		

TABLE III.—*Continued.*

		121. My mother's brother's daughter —older than myself. (Male speaking.)	Translation.	122. My mother's brother's daughter —older than myself. (Female speaking.)	Translation.
1. Tamil	1	En măittŭni..................	My cousin.	En măchchărl.................	My cousin.
2. Telugu..............	2	Vădĭně	Cousin.	Vadine	Cousin.
3. Canarese	3	Nănnă nădini..............	My cousin.	Nănnă nădini..............	My cousin.
4. Hindî	4	Meri bahin..............	My sister. [ternal uncle.	Meri bahin..............	My sister. [ternal uncle.
5. Bengâlî	5	Amar mamato bhugny	My sister or sister thro' ma-	Amar mamato bhugny	My sister or sister thro' ma-
6. Marâthî	6	Măzhi mămă bahïn. ᵇMahŭne.	" " " " "	Măzhi mămă bahïn. ᵇMahŭne.	" " " " "
7. Gujârâthî...........	7	Mări băhĕn..............	My sister.	Mări băhĕn..............	My sister.
8. Chinese	8	Wo-tĕ peaon-tsze-mei.........	My sister of the *peaon* class.	Wo-tĕ peaon-tsze-mei.........	My sister of the *peaon* class.
9. Japanese	9	A'-nih	My elder sister.	A'-nih	My elder sister.
10. Burmese	10	K : e-mă..............		K : e-mă..............	" " "
11. Karen (Sgau dialect)	11	Yă tă-khwă-mu..............	My female cousin.	Yă tă-khwă-mu..............	My female cousin.
12. Karen (Pwo ")	12	Y' t'-khwă-mu..............	" " "	Y' t'-khwă-mu..............	" " "
13. Karen	13	Yeh dan-t'-khwa-mu..............	" " "	Yeh dan-t'-khwa-mu..............	
14. Kings Mill Islands..	14	Mănu-te-karimoa..........	Sister my elder.	Taru-te-karimoa..........	Sister my elder.
15. Kusaien	15	Mă-loŭk	Sister my.	Mă-loŭk	Sister my.
16. Hawaiian	16	Kŭ-ŭ' kăï'-kŭ-wa-hee'-na	My sister, elder.	Kŭ-ŭ' kăï'-kŭ-ă-ĕ-nă......	My sister, elder.
17. Maori	17				
18. Amazulu (Kafir)...	18	U-mză'-lă wă'-me.................	Cousin of me.	U-mză'-lă wă'-me	Cousin of me.

		123. My mother's brother's daughter —younger than myself. (Male speaking.)	Translation.	124. My mother's brother's daughter —younger than myself. (Female speaking.)	Translation.
1. Tamil	1	En măittŭni..................	My cousin.	En măchchărl.................	My cousin.
2. Telugu..............	2	Mărădălŭ	Cousin.	Mărădălŭ	Cousin.
3. Canarese	3	Nănnă nădini..............	My cousin.	Nănnă nădini..............	My cousin.
4. Hindî	4	Meri bahin..............	My sister. [ternal uncle.	Meri bahin..............	My sister. [ternal uncle.
5. Bengâlî	5	Amar mamato bhugny.........	My sister or sister thro' ma-	Amar mamato bhugny.........	My sister or sister thro' pa-
6. Marâthî	6	Măzhi mămă bahïn. ᵇMahune.	" " " " "	Măzhi mămă bahïn. ᵇMahŭne.	" " " " "
7. Gujârâthî.............	7	Mări băhĕn..............	My sister.	Mări bahen..............	My sister.
8. Chinese	8	Wo-tĕ peaon-tsze-mei.........	My sister of the *peaon* class.	Wo-tĕ peaon-tsze-mei.........	My sister of the *peaon* class.
9. Japanese	9	E-mo'to..............	My younger sister.	E-mo'to..............	My younger sister.
10. Burmese	10	K : ny-ee-nă..............	" " "	K : ny-ee-nă..............	" " "
11. Karen (Sgau dialect)	11	Yă tă-khwă-mu..............	My female cousin.	Yă tă-khwă-mu..............	My female cousin.
12. Karen (Pwo ")	12	Y' t'-khwă-mu..............	" " "	Y' t'-khwă-mu..............	" " "
13. Karen	13	Yeh dan-t'-khwa-mŭ..............	" " "	Yeh dan-t'-khwa-mŭ..............	" " "
14. Kings Mill Islands..	14	Taru-te-karimwi..............	Sister my younger.	Taru-te-karmwi..............	Sister my younger.
15. Kusaien	15	Mă-loŭk	Sister my.	Mă-loŭk	Sister my.
16. Hawaiian	16	Kŭ-ŭ' kăï'-kŭ-wa-hee'-nă	My sister, younger.	Kŭ-ŭ' kăï'-lăï-nă..............	My sister, younger.
17. Maori...............	17				
18. Amazulu (Kafir)....	18	U-mză'-lă wă'-me.................	Cousin of me.	U-mză'-lă wă'-me	Cousin of me.

		125. My mother's brother's daughter's husband. (Male speaking.)	Translation.	126. My mother's brother's daughter's husband. (Female speaking.)	Translation.
1. Tamil	1	En aṇṇan (o.), Tambi (y.)....	My elder or younger brother.	En aṇṇan (o.), Tambi (y.)....	My elder or younger brother.
2. Telugu..............	2	Annă (o.), Tămmŭdĭ (y.)	Elder or younger brother.	Anna (o.), Tammudi (y.)......	Elder or younger brother.
3. Canarese.............	3	N. Annă (o.), Tămmă (y.).....	My elder or younger brother.	N. Annă (o.), Tămmă (y.).....	My elder or younger brother.
4. Hindî	4	Meră bahinoi	My brother-in-law.	Meră bahinoi	My brother-in-law.
5. Bengâlî	5	Amar bhugny poty..............	" " "	Amar bhugny poty..............	" " "
6. Marâthî	6	Măzhă mahŭna..............	" " "	Măzhă mahŭna..............	" " "
7. Gujârâthî.............	7	Măro baneni	" " " [*peaon* class.	Măro baneni	" " " [*peaon* class.
8. Chinese..............	8	Wo-tĕ peaon ᵗˢᶻᵉ_ₘₑᵢ-fŭ......	My sister's husband of the	Wo-tĕ peaon ᵗˢᶻᵉ_ₘₑᵢ-fŭ......	My sister's husband of the
9. Japanese	9	A'-nih (o.) O-to'-to (y.).......	My brother elder or young'r.	A'-nih (o.), O-to'-to (y.).....	My brother, eld'r or young'r.
10. Burmese	10	K : youk-pă'..............	My brother-in-law.	K : youk-pă'..............	My brother-in-law.
11. Karen (Sgau dialect)	11	Yă tă-khwă	My male cousin.	Yă tă-khwă	My female cousin.
12. Karen (Pwo ")	12	Y' t'-khwă sau..............	" " "	Y' t'-khwă-sau..............	
13. Karen	13	Yeh dan-t'-khwa-a-wă..............	My cousin's husband.	Yeh dan-t'-khwa-a-wă..............	My cousin's husband.
14. Kings Mill Islands..	14	Butikau..............	Brother-in-law my.	Butikau..............	Brother-in-law my.
15. Kusaien	15	Mă-lĕk	Brother my.	Mă-lĕk	Brother my.
16. Hawaiian	16	Kŭ-ŭ' kăï-ko-ee'-ka..............	My brother-in-law.	Kŭ-ŭ' kăï-ko-ee'-ka..............	My brother-in-law.
17. Maori...............	17				
18. Amazulu (Kafir)....	18	U-mkwă-ny-ă'-nă	Brother-in-law of us.	U-mkwă-ny-ă'-nă..............	Brother-in-law of us.

TABLE III.—*Continued.*

		127. My mother's brother's son's son. (Male speaking.)	Translation.	128. My mother's brother's son's son. (Female speaking.)	Translation.
1. Tamil	1	En mărămŭkăn	My nephew.	En măkăn	My son.
2. Telugu	2	Allŭdĭ	Nephew.	Kŏdŭkŭ	Son.
3. Canarese	3	Nănnă sodăraliyă	My nephew.	Nănnă sodăraliyă ?	My nephew.
4. Hindî	4	Merá bhatijá	" "	Mera bhatijá	" "
5. Bengâlî	5	Amar bhypo	" "	Amar bhypo	" "
6. Marâthî	6	Mäzhä pûtanyă	" "	Mäzhä pûtanyä	" "
7. Gujârâthî	7	Märo bhrătijo	" "	Märo bhrătijo	" "
8. Chinese	8	Wo-tě peaon-chih	My neph. of the *peaon* class.	Wo-tě peaon-chih	My neph. of the *peaon* class.
9. Japanese	9	E-to'-ko	My nephew.	E-to'-ko	My nephew.
10. Burmese	10	K : too	" "	K : too	" "
11. Karen (Sgau dialect)	11	Yă pho-do	" "	Yă pho-do	" "
12. Karen (Pwo ")	12	Y' pho-do-khwä	" "	Y' pho-do-khwä	" "
13. Karen	13	Yeh po-do-khwa		Yeh po-do-khwa	
14. Kings Mill Islands	14	Nätu-te-mänu	Child my, a male.	Nätu-te-mänu	Child my, a male.
15. Kusaien	15	Mwěn-nuttik	Son my.	Mwěn-nuttik	Son my.
16. Hawaiian	16	Kŭ-ŭ' käї'-kee-kä'-na	My child, male.	Kŭ-ŭ' käї'-kee-kä'-na	My child, male.
17. Maori	17				
18. Amazulu (Kafir)	18	In-do-dä'-nä yä'-me	Son of me.	In-do-dä'-nä yä'-me	Son of me.

		129. My mother's brother's son's daughter. (Male speaking.)	Translation.	130. My mother's brother's son's daughter. (Female speaking.)	Translation.
1. Tamil	1	En mărŭmăkăl	My niece.	En măkăl	My daughter.
2. Telugu	2	Kŏdălŭ	Niece.	Kŭthŭrŭ	Daughter.
3. Canarese	3	Nănnă sodărăsose	My niece.	Nănnă sodărăsose ?	My niece.
4. Hindî	4	Meri bhatiji	" "	Meri bhatiji	" "
5. Bengâlî	5	Amar bhyjhe	" "	Amar bhyjhe	" "
6. Marâthî	6	Mäzhi pûtani	" "	Mäzhi pûtani	" "
7. Gujârâthî	7	Märi bhrătiji	" "	Märi bhrătiji	" "
8. Chinese	8	Wo-tě peaon-chih-neu	My niece of the *peaon* class.	Wo-tě peaon-chih-neu	My niece of the *peaon* class.
9. Japanese	9	O-mä-e-to'-ko	My niece.	O-mä-e-to'-ko	My niece.
10. Burmese	10	K : too-mä'	" "	K : too-mä'	" "
11. Karen (Sgau dialect)	11	Yă pho-do-mu	" "	Yă pho-do-mu	" "
12. Karen (Pwo ")	12	Y' pho-do-mu	" "	Y' pho-do-mu	" "
13. Karen	13	Yeh po-do-mü		Yeh po-do-nü	" "
14. Kings Mill Islands	14	Nätu-te-äine	Child my, a female.	Nätu-te-äine	Child my, a female.
15. Kusaien	15	Au-nuttik	Daughter my.	Au-nuttik	Daughter my.
16. Hawaiian	16	Kŭ-ŭ' käї'-kä-wă-hee'-na	My child, female.	Kŭ-ŭ' käї'-kä-wă-hee'-na	My child, female.
17. Maori	17				
18. Amazulu (Kafir)	18	In-do-dä-kä'-ze yä'-me	Daughter of me.	In-do-dä-kä'-ze yä'-me	Daughter of me.

		131. My mother's brother's daughter's son. (Male speaking.)	Translation.	132. My mother's brother's daughter's son. (Female speaking.)	Translation.
1. Tamil	1	En măkăn	My son.	En mărŭmăkăn	My nephew.
2. Telugu	2	Kŏdŭkŭ	Son.	Allŭdŭ	Nephew.
3. Canarese	3	Nănnă măgănu	My son.	Nănnă sodărăliya	My nephew.
4. Hindî	4	Merá bhăujá	My nephew.	Merá bhăujá	" "
5. Bengâlî	5	Amar bhagna	" "	Amar bhagna	" "
6. Marâthî	6	Mäzhä chăchä	My son or nephew.	Mäzhä chăchä	My son or nephew.
7. Gujârâthî	7	Märo bhrătijo	My nephew. [the *peaon* class.	Märo bhrătijo	My nephew. [the *peaon* class.
8. Chinese	8	Wo-tě wae-peaon-chih	My neph. of the *wae* br'ch of	Wo-tě wae-peaon-chih	My neph. of the *wae* br'ch of
9. Japanese	9	E-to'-ko	My nephew.	E-to'-ko	My nephew.
10. Burmese	10	K : too	" "	K : too	" "
11. Karen (Sgau dialect)	11	Yă pho-do	" "	Yă pho-do	" "
12. Karen (Pwo ")	12	Y' pho-do-khwä	" "	Y' pho-do-khwä	" "
13. Karen	13	Yeh po-do-khwa		Yeh po-do-khwa	" "
14. Kings Mill Islands	14	Nätu-te-mäne	Child my, a male.	Nätu-te-mäne	Child my, a male.
15. Kusaien	15	Mwěn-nuttik	Son my.	Mwěn-nuttik	Son my.
16. Hawaiian	16	Kŭ-ŭ' käї'-kee-kä'-na	My child, male.	Kŭ-ŭ' käї'-kee-kä'-na	My child, male.
17. Maori	17				
18. Amazulu (Kafir)	18	In-do-dä'-nä yä'-me	Son of me.	In-do-dä'-nä yä'-me	Son of me.

TABLE III.—*Continued.*

		133. My mother's brother's daughter's daughter. (Male speaking.)	Translation.	134. My mother's brother's daughter's daughter. (Female speaking.)	Translation.
1. Tamil	1	En măkăl............................	My daughter.	En marumakal....................	My niece.
2. Telugu....................	2	Kŭthŭrŭ	Daughter.	Kodalu	Niece.
3. Canarese	3	Nănnă sodărăsose?	My niece.	Nănnă sodărăsose................	My niece.
4. Hindî	4	Merá bhauji........................	" "	Meri bhauji	" "
5. Bengâlî..................	5	Amar bhagny......................	" "	Amar bhagny	" "
6. Marâthî................	6	Măzhi chăchi	My daughter or niece.	Măzhi chăchi......................	My daughter or niece.
7. Gujârâthî............	7	Mări bhrătiji......................	My niece. [the *peaon* class.	Mări bhrătiji......................	My niece. [the *peaon* class.
8. Chinese................	8	Wo-tĕ wae-peaon-chih-neu....	My niece of the *wae* br'ch of	Wo-tĕ wae-peaon-chih-neu....	My niece of the *wae* br'ch of
9. Japanese................	9	O-mä-e-to'-ko.	My niece.	O-mä-e-to'-ko......................	My niece.
10. Burmese................	10	K : too-mä'........................	" "	K : too-mä'........................	" "
11. Karen (Sgau dialect)	11	Yă pho-do-mŭ	" "	Yă pho-do-mŭ	" "
12. Karen (Pwo ")	12	Y' pho-do-mu	" "	Y' pho-do-mu	" "
13. Karen..................	13	Yeh po-do-mŭ......................	" "	Yeh po-do-mü......................	" "
14. Kings Mill Islands..	14	Nătu-te-aine......................	Child my, a female.	Nătu-te-aine......................	Child my, a female.
15. Kusaien	15	Au-nuttik........................	Daughter my.	Au-nuttik........................	Daughter my.
16. Hawaiian	16	Kŭ-ŭ' käĭ'-kă-wă-hee'-na......	My child, female.	Kŭ-ŭ' käĭ'-kă-wă-hee'-na.......	My child, female.
17. Maori	17				
18. Amazulu (Kafir)....	18	In-do-dä-kä'-ze yä'-me..........	Daughter of me.	In-do-dä-kä'-ze yä'-me..........	Daughter of me.

		135. My mother's brother's great grandson.	Translation.	136. My mother's brother's great granddaughter.	Translation.
1. Tamil	1	En pêran............................	My grandson.	En pêrtti............................	My granddaughter.
2. Telugu....................	2	Mănămădŭ	Grandson.	Mănămărălŭ	Granddaughter.
3. Canarese	3	Nănnă mommăgănu	My grandson.	Nănnă mommăgălu..............	My granddaughter.
4. Hindî	4	Merá potá	" "	Meri poti..........................	" "
5. Bengâlî..................	5	Amar naty	" "	Amar natny........................	" "
6. Marâthî................	6	Măzhă nătŭ	" "	Măzhi năt..........................	" "
7. Gujârâthî............	7	Măro pautră	" " [*chih* class.	Măro pautri	" " [*chih* class.
8. Chinese................	8	Wo-tĕ peaon-chih-sun........	My grandson of the *peaon-*	Wo-tĕ peaon-chih-sun-neu....	My g'ddaughter of the *peaon-*
9. Japanese................	9	Mä-'go............................	My grandson.	Ma'-ee	My granddaughter.
10. Burmese................	10	K : ny-a'..........................	My grandchild.	K : ny-a'..........................	My grandchild.
11. Karen (Sgau dialect)	11	Yă lie-khwă	My grandson.	Yă lie-mu..........................	My grandchild.
12. Karen (Pwo ")	12	Y' le-khwă	" "	Y' le-mu	My granddaughter.
13. Karen..................	13	Yeh lee-khwa......................		Yeh lee-mu	" "
14. Kings Mill Islands..	14	Tibu-te-mäne......................	Grandchild my, a male.	Tibu-te-aine......................	Grandchild my, a female.
15. Kusaien	15	Mwĕn-nuttin-nuttik............	Grandson my.	Au-nuttin-nuttik................	Granddaughter my.
16. Hawaiian	16	Kŭ-ŭ' moo-pŭ'-nä-kä'-na.......	My grandchild, male.	Yŭ-ŭ' moo-pŭ'-nä-wa-hee'-na.	My grandchild, female.
17. Maori..................	17				
18. Amazulu (Kafir)....	18	U-me-tshä'-nä wä'-me...........	Grandchild of me	U-me-tshä'-nä wä'-me..........	Grandchild of me.

		137. My mother's brother's great grandson's son.	Translation.	138. My mother's brother's great grandson's daughter.	Translation.
1. Tamil	1	En pêran............................	My grandson.	En pêrtti............................	My granddaughter.
2. Telugu..................	2	Mŭnĭmănădŭ	Great grandson.	Mŭnĭmănămărălŭ	Great granddaughter.
3. Canarese..............	3	Nănnă mummăgănu..............	" " "	Nănnă mummăgălu	My great granddaughter.
4. Hindî	4	Merá parotá	My grandson.	Meri paroti	My granddaughter.
5. Bengâlî..................	5	Amar naty	" "	Amar natny	" "
6. Marâthî................	6	Măzhă nătŭ........................	" "	Măzhi năt..........................	" "
7. Gujârâthî............	7		[*chih* class.		[*peaon-chih* class.
8. Chinese................	8	Wo-tĕ peaon-chih-tsung-sun..	My gt. grandson of the *peaon*	Wo-tĕ peaon-chih-tsung-sun-	My gt. granddaughter of the
9. Japanese................	9	She'-ko............................	My great grandchild.	She'-ko............................	My great grandchild.
10. Burmese	10	K : ny-a'..........................	My grandchild.	K : ny-a'..........................	My grandchild.
11. Karen (Sgau dialect)	11	Yă lo-khwă	My great grandson.	Yă lo-mu..........................	My great granddaughter.
12. Karen (Pwo ")	12	Y' lo-khwă........................	" " "	Y' lo-mu	" " "
13. Karen..................	13	Yeh lo-khwa......................		Yeh lo-mü	
14. Kings Mill Islands..	14	Tibun-natu..............[nuttik	Grandchild of my child.	Tibun-natu........................	Grandchild of my child.
15. Kusaien	15	Mwĕn - nuttin - mwĕn - nuttin-	Great grandson my.	Au nuttin-ău-nuttin-nuttik...	Great granddaughter my.
16. Hawaiian	16	Kŭ-ŭ' moo-pŭ'-nä-kä-na-ku'- [ä-lu'-ä	My great grandchild, male.	Kŭ-ŭ' moo-pŭ'-nä-wa-hee-na- [kŭ'-ä-lŭ-ä	My gt. grandchild, female.
17. Maori	17				
18. Amazulu (Kafir)....	18	U-mzu-kŭ'-lŭ wä'-me	Great grandchild of me.	U-mzu-kŭ'-hŭ wä'-me..........	Great grandchild of me.

TABLE III.—*Continued.*

		139. My mother's sister.	Translation.	140. My mother's sister's husband.	Translation.
1. Tamil	1	En pĕriyă tăy (if older than my mother), En sĕriyă tăy (if younger).	My mother, great or little.	En Takăppăn (p. or s.)	My father, great or little.
2. Telugu	2	Pĕtăllĭ (o.), Pĭnătăllĭ (y.)	Mother, great or small.	Pettandri (o.), Pĭnatăndri (y.)	Father, great or small.
3. Canarese	3	N. doddămmă (o.), Chickkăm-mă (y.).	My mother, great or small.	N. Doddăppă (o.), Chickkăppă (y.).	My father, great or small.
4. Hindî	4	Meri mausi	My aunt maternal.	Merá Mausá	My uncle.
5. Bengâlî	5	Amar mashi	" " "	Amar masho	" "
6. Marâthî	6	Mäzhi mäwase	" " "	Mäzhă mäwasă	" "
7. Gujârâthî	7	Märi mäsi	" " "	Märo mäso	" "
8. Chinese	8	Wo-tĕ ta-e-ma. ᵇLeaon-e-ma.	My great outside mamma. ᵇLittle outside mamma.	Wo-tĕ e-fŭ	My mother's sister's father
9. Japanese	9	O-bă	Little mother or aunt.	O'-je	My uncle.
10. Burmese	10	K: mee-ky-ee (o.), Mee-kwa (y.).	My great or little mother.	K: bă-ky-ee (o.), Oo-men or Bă-twa (y.).	My great or little father.
11. Karen (Sgau dialect)	11	Yă mu-ghă	My aunt.	Yă phä-tie	My uncle.
12. Karen (Pwo ")	12	Y' m'-gä-te-te	My own aunt.	Y' phä-te	" "
13. Karen	13	Yeh mŭ'-gah	My aunt.	Yeh păh-tee	Bro.-in-law of my mother.
14. Kings Mill Islands	14	Tinau	Mother my.	Păpă tummuk	Father my.
15. Kusaien	15	Nĕnĕ keyŭk	" " "	Kŭ-ŭ' mä-kŭ'-ă-kă'-na	My parent, male.
16. Hawaiian	16	Kŭ-ŭ' mä-kŭ'-ă-wä-hee'-na	My parent, female.		
17. Maori	17		[ther.		My father.
18. Amazulu (Kafir)	18	U-mä'-mä kă'-ze. ᵇU-mä'-mä..	My maternal aunt. ᵇMy mo-	U-bä'-bä	My father.

		141. My mother's sister's son— older than myself. (Male speaking.)	Translation.	142. My mother's sister's son— older than myself. (Female speaking.)	Translation.
1. Tamil	1	En tămăiyăn. ᵇAnnăn	My elder brother.	En tămăiyăn. ᵇAnnăn	My elder brother.
2. Telugu	2	Annă	Elder brother.	Annă	Elder brother.
3. Canarese	3	Nănnă ănnă	My elder brother.	Nănnă ănnă	My elder brother.
4. Hindî	4	Merá bhái. ᵇMauseta bhái	My brother or aunt brother.	Merá bhái. ᵇMauseta bhái	My brother or aunt brother.
5. Bengâlî	5	Amar mashtoto bhye	" " " "	Amar mashtoto bhye	" " " "
6. Marâthî	6	Mäzhä mäŭs bhăŭ	" " " "	Mäzhă mäŭs bhăŭ	My brother.
7. Gujârâthî	7	Märo bhäi	My brother.	Märo bhäi	My bro. of the *e-peaon* class.
8. Chinese	8	Wo-tĕ e-peaon-heung-te	My bro. of the *e-peaon* class.	Wo-tĕ e-peaon-heung-te	My elder brother.
9. Japanese	9	A'-nee	My elder brother.	A'-nee	" " "
10. Burmese	10	K: e-ko'	" " "	K: e-ko'	My male cousin.
11. Karen (Sgau dialect)	11	Yă tă-khwă	My male cousin.	Yă tă-khwă	" " "
12. Karen (Pwo ")	12	Y' t'-khwä-sau	" " "	Y' t'-khwä-sau	" " "
13. Karen	13	Yeh t'-khwa	" " "	Yeh t'-khwa	Brother my, an elder.
14. Kings Mill Islands	14	Tăru-te-karimoa	Brother my, an elder.	Mănu-te-karimoa	Brother my.
15. Kusaien	15	Mä-lĕk	Brother my.	Mä-lĕk	My brother, elder.
16. Hawaiian	16	Kŭ-ŭ kăĭ'-kŭ-ă-nä'-nä	My brother, elder.	Kŭ-ŭ' kăĭ'-kŭ-nä'-na	[of me.
17. Maori	17		[tŭ		[tŭ
18. Amazulu (Kafir)	18	U'-mna wä'-me. ᵇU'-mfo wä'-	My elder brother. ᵇBrother [of me.	U'-mna wä'-me. ᵇU'-mfo wä'-	My elder brother. ᵇBrother

		143. My mother's sister's son— younger than myself. (Male speaking.)	Translation.	144. My mother's sister's son— younger than myself. (Female speaking.)	Translation.
1. Tamil	1	En tambi	My younger brother.	En tambi	My younger brother.
2. Telugu	2	Tămmŭdŭ	Younger brother.	Tămmŭdŭ	Younger brother.
3. Canarese	3	Nănnă tămmă	My younger brother.	Nănnă tămmă	My younger brother.
4. Hindî	4	Merá bhái. ᵇMausetu bhai	My brother or aunt brother.	Merá bhái. ᵇMauseta bhái	My brother or aunt brother.
5. Bengâlî	5	Amar mashtoto bhye	" " " "	Amar mashtoto bhye	" " " "
6. Marâthî	6	Mäzhä mäŭs bhăŭ		Märo bhäi	My brother.
7. Gujârâthî	7	Maro bhäi		Wo-tĕ e-peaon-heung-te	My bro. of the *e-peaon* class.
8. Chinese	8	Wo-tĕ e-peaon-heung-te	My bro. of the *e-peaon* class.	O-to'-to	My younger brother.
9. Japanese	9	O-to'-to	My younger brother.	K: ny-ee	
10. Burmese	10	K: ny-ee	" " "	Yă tă-khwă	My male cousin.
11. Karen (Sgau dialect)	11	Ya tă-khwă	My male cousin.	Y' t'-khwä-sau	" " "
12. Karen (Pwo ")	12	Y' t'-khwä-sau	" " "	Yeh t'-khwa	
13. Karen	13	Yeh t'-khwa		Manu-te-karimwi	Brother my, a younger.
14. Kings Mill Islands	14	Tăru-te-karimwi	Brother my, a younger.	Mä-lĕk	Brother my.
15. Kusaien	15	Mä-lĕk	Brother my.	Kŭ-ŭ' kăĭ'-kŭ-nä'-nä	My brother, younger.
16. Hawaiian	16	Kŭ-ŭ' kăĭ'-kăĭ-nä	My brother, younger.		
17. Maori	17				
18. Amazulu (Kafir)	18	U-mnă'-wä wä'-me	My younger brother.	U-mnă'-wä	My younger brother.

TABLE III.—*Continued.*

		145. My mother's sister's son's wife. (Male speaking.)	Translation.	146. My mother's sister's son's wife. (Female speaking.)	Translation.
1. Tamil	1	En măittŭni	My sister-in-law and cousin.	En annatâvi	My sister-in-law and cousin.
2. Telugu	2	Vădĭnĕ	Sister-in-law and cousin.	Vădĭnĕ	Sister-in-law and cousin.
3. Canarese	3	Nănnă attige (o.), Nădini (y.)	My sister-in-law and cousin.	Nănnă attigi (o.), Nădini (y.)	My sister-in-law and cousin.
4. Hindî	4	Meri bháwaj	My sister-in-law.	Meri bháwaj	My sister-in-law.
5. Bengâlî	5	Amar bhaj	" " "	Amar bhaj	" " "
6. Marâthî	6	Mäzhi mäŭs bhäŭzaë	" " "	Mäzhi mäŭs bhäŭzaë	" " "
7. Gujârâthî	7	Märi bhäzi	" " " [class.	Märi bhäzi	" " " [class.
8. Chinese	8	Wo-tĕ e-peaon-saon	My sist.-in-law of the *e-peaon*	Wo-tĕ e-peaon-saon	My sist.-in-law of the *e-peaon*
9. Japanese	9	A'-nih (o.), e-mo'to (y.)	My sister elder or younger.	A'-nih (o.), e-mo'-to (y.)	My elder or younger sister.
10. Burmese	10	K: ma-yee (o.), Kai-mă (y.)	My eld. or y'ger sist.-in-law.	K: ma-yee (o.), Kai-mă (y.)	" " " "
11. Karen (Sgau dialect)	11	Yă tă-khwă-mu	My female cousin.	Yă tă-khwă-mu	My female cousin.
12. Karen (Pwo ")	12	Y' t'-khwă-mu	" " "	Y' t'-khwă-mu	" " "
13. Karen	13	Yeh dan-t'-khwa-a-mă	My cousin's wife.	Yeh dan-t'-klwa-a-mă	My cousin's wife.
14. Kings Mill Islands	14	Eiriku	Sister-in-law my.	Eiriku	Sister-in-law my.
15. Kusaien	15	Mä-loŭk	Sister my.	Mä-loŭk	Sister my.
16. Hawaiian	16	Kŭ-ŭ' wä-hee'-na	My wife or female.	Kŭ-ŭ' wä-hee'-na	My wife or female.
17. Maori	17				
18. Amazulu (Kafir)	18	U-mkä'-me	My wife.		

		147. My mother's sister's daughter —older than myself. (Male speaking.)	Translation.	148. My mother's sister's daughter —older than myself. (Female speaking.)	Translation.
1. Tamil	1	En akkärl. ᵇTămăkay	My elder sister.	En akkärl. ᵇTămăkay	My elder sister.
2. Telugu	2	Akkă	Elder sister.	Akkă	Elder sister.
3. Canarese	3	Nănnă ăkkă	My elder sister.	Nănnă ăkkă	My elder sister.
4. Hindî	4	Meri bahin	My sister.	Meri bahin	My sister.
5. Bengâlî	5	Amar mashtoto bhugny	My cousin sister.	Amar mashtoto bhugny	My cousin sister.
6. Marâthî	6	Mäzhi mäŭs bahïn	My sister or sister through	Mäzhi mäŭs bahïn	My sister or sister thro' my
7. Gujârâthî	7	Märi băhen	My sister. [maternal aunt.	Märi băhen	My sister. [maternal aunt.
8. Chinese	8	Wo-tĕ e-peaon-tsze-mei	My sist. of the *e-peaon* class.	Wo-tĕ e-peaon-tsze-mei	My sist. of the *e-peaon* class.
9. Japanese	9	A'-nih	My elder sister.	A'-nih	My elder sister.
10. Burmese	10	K: e-mă'	" " "	K: e-mă'	" " "
11. Karen (Sgau dialect)	11	Yă tă-khwă-mu	My female cousin.	Yă tă-khwă-mu	My female cousin.
12. Karen (Pwo ")	12	Y' t'-khwă-mu	" " "	Y' t'-khwă-mu	" " "
13. Karen	13	Yeh dan-t'-khwa-mü	" " "	Yeh dan-t'-khwa-mü	" " "
14. Kings Mill Islands	14	Manu-te-karimoa	Sister my, an elder.	Taru-te-karimoa	Sister my, au elder.
15. Kusaien	15	Mä-loŭk	Sister my.	Mä-loŭk	Sister my.
16. Hawaiian	16	Kŭ-ŭ' käï'-kŭ-wä-hee'-na	My sister, elder.	Kŭ-ŭ' käï'-kŭ-ä-ä'-nä	My sister, elder.
17. Maori	17				
18. Amazulu (Kafir)	18	U-dä'-dä wä'-tŭ	Sister of us.	U-dä'-dä wä'-tŭ	Sister of us.

		149. My mother's sister's daughter —younger than myself. (Male speaking.)	Translation.	150. My mother's sister's daughter —younger than myself. (Female speaking.)	Translation.
1. Tamil	1	En tăngăichchi. ᵇTăngay	My younger sister.	En tăngăichchi. ᵇTăngay	My younger sister.
2. Telugu	2	Chĕllĕlŭ	Younger sister.	Chĕllĕlŭ	Younger sister.
3. Canarese	3	Nănnă tăngi	My younger sister.	Nănnă tăngi	My younger sister.
4. Hindî	4	Meri bahin	My sister.	Meri bahin	My sister.
5. Bengâlî	5	Amar mashtoto bhugny	My cousin sister.	Amar mashtoto bhugny	My cousin sister.
6. Marâthî	6	Mäzhi mäŭs bahïn	My sister or sister thro' my	Mäzhi mäŭs bahïn	My sister or sister thro' my
7. Gujârâthî	7	Märi băhen	My sister. [maternal aunt.	Märi băhen	My sister. [maternal aunt.
8. Chinese	8	Wo-tĕ e-peaon-tsze-mei	My sist. of the *e-peaon* class.	Wo-tĕ e-peaon-tsze-mei	My sist. of the *e-peaon* class.
9. Japanese	9	E-mo'-to	My younger sister.	E-mo'-to	My younger sister.
10. Burmese	10	K: my-ee-mă'	" " "	K: my-ee-mă'	" " "
11. Karen (Sgau dialect)	11	Yă tă-khwă-mu	My female cousin.	Yă tă-khwă-mu	My female cousin.
12. Karen (Pwo ")	12	Y' t'-khwă-mu	" " "	Y' t'-khwă-mu	" " "
13. Karen	13	Yeh dan-t'-khwa-mü	" " "	Yeh dan-t'-khwa-mü	" " "
14. Kings Mill Islands	14	Tărŭ-te-karimwi	Sister my, a younger.	Mănu-te-karimwi	Sister my, a younger.
15. Kusaien	15	Mä-loŭk	Sister my.	Mä-loŭk	Sister my.
16. Hawaiian	16	Kŭ-ŭ' käï'-kŭ-wä-hee'-nä	My sister, younger.	Kŭ-ŭ käï'-käï-nä	My sister, younger.
17. Maori	17				
18. Amazulu (Kafir)	18	U-dä'-dä wä'-tŭ	Sister of us.	U-dä'-dä wä'-tŭ	Sister of us.

TABLE III.—*Continued.*

		151. My mother's sister's daughter's husband. (Male speaking.)	Translation.	152. My mother's sister's daughter's husband. (Female speaking.)	Translation.
1. Tamil	1	En mäittŭnän	My bro.-in-law or cousin.	En mäittŭnän	My bro.-in-law or cousin.
2. Telugu	2	Bävä	Brother-in-law or cousin.	Bävä	Brother-in-law or cousin.
3. Canarese	3	Nännä bhävämeidănĕ	My bro.-in-law or cousin.	Nännä bhävämeidănĕ	My bro.-in-law or cousin.
4. Hindî	4	Merá bahinoi	My brother-in-law.	Merá bahinoi	My brother-in-law.
5. Bengâlî	5	Amar bhugny poty	" " "	Amar bhugny poty	" " "
6. Marâthî	6	Mäzhä mäŭs mehŭnä	" " "	Mäzhä mäŭs mehŭnä	" " "
7. Gujârâthî	7	Märi baneni	" " "	Märi baneni	" " "
8. Chinese	8	Wo-tĕ e-peaon-tsze/mei-fŭ	My son of the *chih* kind older/y'ger of the *e-peaon* class.	Wo-tĕ e-peaon-tsze/mei-fŭ	My son of the *chih* kind older/y'ger of the *e-peaon* class.
9. Japanese	9	A'-nee (o.), o-to'-to (y.)	My sister elder or younger.	A'-nee (o.), o-to'-to	My elder or y'nger brother.
10. Burmese	10	K: youk-pä	My brother-in-law.	K: youk-pä	My brother-in-law.
11. Karen (Sgau dialect)	11	Yä tä-khwä	My male cousin.	Yä tä-khwä	My male cousin.
12. Karen (Pwo ")	12	Y' t'-khwä-sau	" " "	Y' t'-khwä-sau	" " "
13. Karen	13	Yeh dan-t'-khwa-a-wä	My cousin's husband.	Yeh dan-t'-khwa-a-wä	My cousin's husband.
14. Kings Mill Islands	14	Butikau	Brother-in-law my.	Butikau	Brother-in-law my.
15. Kusaien	15	Mä-lĕk	Brother my.	Mä-lĕk	Brother my.
16. Hawaiian	16	Kŭ-ŭ' käï'-ko-ee'-ka	My brother-in-law.	Kŭ-ŭ' käï'-ko-ee'-ka	My brother-in-law.
17. Maori	17				
18. Amazulu (Kafir)	18	U-mkwä-ny-ä-nä wä'-tŭ	Brother-in-law of us.	U-mkwä-ny-ä-nä wä'-tŭ	Brother-in-law of us.

		153. My mother's sister's son's son. (Male speaking.)	Translation.	154. My mother's sister's son's son. (Female speaking.)	Translation.
1. Tamil	1	En mäkän	My son.	En märŭmäkän	My nephew.
2. Telugu	2	Kodŭkŭ	Son.	Allŭdŭ	Nephew.
3. Canarese	3	Nännä mäganu	My son.	Nännä sodärăliya	My nephew.
4. Hindî	4	Merá bhatijá	My nephew.	Merá bhatija	" "
5. Bengâlî	5	Amar bhypo	" "	Amar bhypo	" "
6. Marâthî	6	Mäzhä putanyä	" "	Mäzhä putanyä	" "
7. Gujârâthî	7	Märi bhatijo	" " [the *e-peaon* class.	Märo bhrätijo	" " [the *e-peaon* class.
8. Chinese	8	Wo-tĕ e-peaon-chih	My son of the *chih* kind of	Wo-tĕ e-peaon chih	My son of the *chih* kind of
9. Japanese	9	E-to'-ko	My nephew.	E-to'-ko	My nephew.
10. Burmese	10	K: too	" "	K: too	" "
11. Karen (Sgau dialect)	11	Yä pho-do	" "	Yä pho-do	" "
12. Karen (Pwo ")	12	Y' pho-do-khwä	" "	Y' pho-do-khwä	" "
13. Karen	13	Yeh po-do-khwa		Yeh po-do-khwa	
14. Kings Mill Islands	14	Nätu-te-mäne	Child my, a male.	Nätu-te-mäne	Child my, a male.
15. Kusaien	15	Mwĕn-nuttik	Son my.	Mwĕn-nuttik	Son my.
16. Hawaiian	16	Kŭ-ŭ' käï'-kee-ka-na	My child, male.	Kŭ-ŭ' käï'-kee-kä'-na	My child, male.
17. Maori	17				
18. Amazulu (Kafir)	18	In do-dä'-nä yä'-me	Son of me.	In-do-dä'-nä yä'-me	Son of me.

		155. My mother's sister's son's daughter. (Male speaking.)	Translation.	156. My mother's sister's son's daughter. (Female speaking.)	Translation.
1. Tamil	1	En mäkäl	My daughter.	En märŭmäkäl	My niece.
2. Telugu	2	Kŭthŭrŭ	Daughter.	Kŏdälŭ	Niece.
3. Canarese	3	Nännä mägälu	My daughter.	Nännä sodäräsose	My niece.
4. Hindî	4	Meri bhatiji	My niece.	Meri bhatiji	" "
5. Bengâlî	5	Amar bhyjhe	" "	Amar bhyjhe	" "
6. Marâthî	6	Mäzhi putani	" " [of the *e-peaon* class.	Mäzhi putani	" " [of the *e-peaon* class.
7. Gujârâthî	7	Märi bhrätiji		Märi bhrätiji	
8. Chinese	8	Wo-tĕ e-peaon-chih-neu	My daugh'r of the *chih* kind	Wo-tĕ e-peaon-chih-neu	My daugh'r of the *chih* kind
9. Japanese	9	O-mä'-e-to-ko	My niece.	O-mä'-e-to-ko	My niece.
10. Burmese	10	K: too-mä'	" "	K: too-mä'	" "
11. Karen (Sgau dialect)	11	Yä pho-do-mu	" "	Yä pho-do-mu	" "
12. Karen (Pwo ")	12	Y' pho-do-mu	" "	Y' pho-do-mu	" "
13. Karen	13	Yeh po-do-mü		Yeh po-do-mü	
14. Kings Mill Islands	14	Nätu-te-äine	Child my, a female.	Nätu-to-äine	Child my, a female.
15. Kusaien	15	Au-nuttik	Daughter my.	Au-nuttik	Daughter my.
16. Hawaiian	16	Kŭ-ŭ' käï'-kä-wä-hee'-na	My child, female.	Kŭ-ŭ' käï'-kä-wä-hee'-na	My child, female.
17. Maori	17				
18. Amazulu (Kafir)	18	In-do-dä-kä'-ze yä'-me	Daughter of me.	In-do-dä-kä'-ze yä'-me	Daughter of me.

TABLE III.—*Continued.*

		157. My mother's sister's daughter's son. (Male speaking.)	Translation.	158. My mother's sister's daughter's son. (Female speaking.)	Translation.
1. Tamil	1	En mărŭmăkăn	My nephew.	En măkăn	My son.
2. Telugu	2	Allŭdŭ	Nephew.	Kŏdŭkŭ	Son.
3. Canarese	3	Nănnă sodărăliya	My nephew.	Nănnă măgălu	My son.
4. Hindî	4	Merá bháujá	" "	Merá bháujá	My nephew.
5. Bengálî	5	Amar bhagna	" "	Amar bhagna	" "
6. Maráthî	6	Mázhä putanyä	" "	Mázhä putanyä	" "
7. Gujârâthî	7	Märo bhrätijo	" "	Märo bhrätijo	" "
8. Chinese	8	Wo-tĕ wae-e-peaon-chih	My nephew of the *wae* br'ch of the *e-peaon* class.	Wo-tĕ wae-e-peaon-chih	My nephew of the *wae* br'ch of the *e-peaon* class.
9. Japanese	9	E-to′-ko	My nephew.	E-to′-ko	My nephew.
10. Burmese	10	K : too	" "	K : too	" "
11. Karen (Sgau dialect)	11	Yă pho-do	" "	Yă pho-do	" "
12. Karen (Pwo ")	12	Y′ pho-do-khwä	" "	Y′ pho-do-khwä	" "
13. Karen	13	Yeh po-do-khwa	" "	Yeh po-do-khwa	" "
14. Kings Mill Islands	14	Nätu-te-mäne	Child my, a male.	Nätu-te-mäne	Child my, a male.
15. Kusaien	15	Mwĕn-nuttik	Son my.	Mwĕn-nuttik	Son my.
16. Hawaiian	16	Kŭ-ŭ′ käï′-kee-kä-na	My child, male.	Kŭ-ŭ′ käï′-kee-kä-na	My child, male.
17. Maori	17				
18. Amazulu (Kafir)	18	In-do-dä′-nä yä′-me	Son of me.	In-do-dä′-nä yä′-me	Son of me.

		159. My mother's sister's daughter's daughter. (Male speaking.)	Translation.	160. My mother's sister's daughter's daughter. (Female speaking.)	Translation.
1. Tamil	1	En mărŭmăkăl	My niece.	En măkăl	My daughter.
2. Telugu	2	Kŏdălŭ	Niece.	Kŭthŭrŭ	Daughter.
3. Canarese	3	Nănnă sodărăsose	My niece.	Nănnă măgălu	My daughter.
4. Hindî	4	Meri bháuji	" "	Meri bháuji	My niece.
5. Bengálî	5	Amar bhagny	" "	Amar boujhe	" "
6. Maráthî	6	Mäzhi putani	" "	Mäzhi putani	" "
7. Gujârâthî	7	Märi bhrätiji	" "	Märi bhrätiji	" "
8. Chinese	8	Wo-tĕ wae-e-peaon-chih-neu	My niece of the *wae* branch of the *e-peaon* class.	Wo-tĕ wae-e-peaon-chih-neu	My niece of the *wae* branch of the *e-peaon* class.
9. Japanese	9	O-mä′-e-to-ko	My niece.	O-mä′-e-to-ko	My niece.
10. Burmese	10	K : too-mä	" "	K : too-mä	" "
11. Karen (Sgau dialect)	11	Yă pho-do-mu	" "	Yă pho-do-mu	" "
12. Karen (Pwo ")	12	Y′ pho-do-mu	" "	Y′ pho-do-mu	" "
13. Karen	13	Yeh po-do-mü	" "	Yeh po-do-mü	" "
14. Kings Mill Islands	14	Nätu-te-äine	Child my, a female.	Nätu-te-äine	Child my, a female.
15. Kusaien	15	Au-nuttik	Daughter my.	Au-nuttik	Daughter my.
16. Hawaiian	16	Kŭ-ŭ′ käï′-kä-wä-hee′-na	My child, female.	Kŭ-ŭ′ käï′-kä-wä-hee′-na	My child, female.
17. Maori	17				
18. Amazulu (Kafir)	18	In-do-dä-kä′-ze yä′-me	Daughter of me.	In-do-dä-kä′-ze yä′-me	Daughter of me.

		161. My mother's sister's great grandson.	Translation.	162. My mother's sister's great granddaughter.	Translation.
1. Tamil	1	En pêran	My grandson.	En pêrtti	My granddaughter.
2. Telugu	2	Mănămădŭ	Grandson.	Mănămärălŭ	Granddaughter.
3. Canarese	3	Nănnă mommăgănu	My grandson.	Mănnă mommăgălu	My granddaughter.
4. Hindî	4	Merá potá	" "	Meri poti	" " "
5. Bengálî	5	Amar naty	" "	Amar natny	" " "
6. Maráthî	6	Mázhä nätu	" "	Mäzhi nät	" " "
7. Gujârâthî	7	Märo pautră	" "	Märi pautri	" " "
8. Chinese	8	Wo-tĕ e-peaon-chih-sun	My grandson of the *chih* kind in the *e-peaon* class.	Wo-tĕ e-peaon-chih-sun-neu	My granddaugh'r of the *chih* kind of the *e-peaon* class.
9. Japanese	9	Mä′-go	My grandson.	Ma′-ee	My granddaughter.
10. Burmese	10	K : ny-a′	My grandchild.	K : ny-a′	My grandchild.
11. Karen (Sgau dialect)	11	Yă lie-khwä	My grandson.	Yă lie-mu	My granddaughter.
12. Karen (Pwo ")	12	Y′ le-khwä	" "	Y′ le-mu	" " "
13. Karen	13	Yeh lee-khwa		Yeh lee-khwa	
14. Kings Mill Islands	14	Tibu-te-mäne	Grandchild my, a male.	Tibu-te-aine	Grandchild my, a female.
15. Kusaien	15	Mwĕn-nuttin-nuttik	Grandson my.	Au-nuttin-nuttik	Granddaughter my.
16. Hawaiian	16	Kŭ-ŭ′ moo-pŭ′-nä-kä-na	My grandchild, male.	Kŭ-ŭ′ moo-pŭ′-nä-wä-hee′-na	My grandchild, female.
17. Maori	17				
18. Amazulu (Kafir)	18	U-me-tshä′-nä wä′-me	Grandchild of me.	U-me-tshä′-nä wä′-me	Grandchild of me.

TABLE III.—Continued.

		163. My mother's sister's great grandson's son	Translation.	164. My mother's sister's great granddaughter's daughter.	Translation.
1. Tamil	1	En pĕran	My grandson.	En pĕrtti	My granddaughter.
2. Telugu	2	Mŭnĭmănămădŭ	Great grandson.	Mŭnīmănămārălŭ	Great granddaughter.
3. Canarese	3	Nănnă mummăgănu	My great grandson.	Nănnă mummăgălu	My great granddaughter.
4. Hindî	4	Merà parotá	" " "	Meri paroti	" " " "
5. Bengâlî	5	Amar naty	" " "	Amar natny	" " " "
6. Marâthî	6	Măzhă panătŭ	" " "	Măzhi panati	" " " "
7. Gujârâthî	7				
8. Chinese	8	Wo-tĕ e-peaon-chih-tsung-sun	My gt. grandson of the *chih* kind of the *e-peaon* class.	Wo-tĕ e-peaon-chih-tsung-sun-neu.	My gt. g'ddaugh'r of the *chih* kind of the *e-peaon* class.
9. Japanese	9	Mă'-go	My grandson.	Ma'-ee	My granddaughter.
10. Burmese	10	K: ny-a'	My grandchild.	K: ny-a'	My grandchild.
11. Karen (Sgau dial'ct)	11	Yă lo-khwă	My great grandson.	Yă lo-mu	My great granddaughter.
12. Karen (Pwo ")	12	Y' lo-khwă	" " "	Y' lo-mu	" " " "
13. Karen	13	Yeh lo-khwa		Yeh lo-mu	
14. Kings Mill Islands	14	Tibun-natu [nuttik	Grandchild of my child.	Tibun-natu	Grandchild of my child.
15. Kusaien	15	Mwĕn - nuttin - mwĕn - nuttin	Great grandson my.	Au-nuttin-ăn-nuttin-nuttik	Great granddaughter my.
16. Hawaiian	16	Kŭ-ŭ' moo-pŭ'-nă-kă-na-ku'-ă- [lu'-ă	My great grandchild, male.	Kŭ-ŭ' moo-pŭ'-nă-wă-hee'-na- [ku'-ă-lu'-ă	My gt. grandchild, female.
17. Maori	17				
18. Amazulu (Kafir)	18	U-mzŭ-kŭ'-lŭ wă-me	Great grandchild of me.	U-mzŭ-kŭ'-lŭ wă'-me	Great grandson of me.

		165. My father's father's brother.	Translation.	166. My father's father's brother's son.	Translation.
1. Tamil	1	En păddăn (p. or s.)	My grandfather, gt. or little.	En tăkăppăn (p. or s.)	My father, great or little.
2. Telugu	2	Pĕttăta (o.), Pĭntătă (y.)	Grandfather, great or little.	Pĕttăndrī (o.), Pĭnătăndri (y.)	Father, great or small.
3. Canarese	3	N. doddă tătă (o.), Chikka tătă (y.)	My grandfather, gt. or little.		
4. Hindî	4	Merá dádá	My grandfather.	Merá chăchá	My paternal uncle.
5. Bengâlî	5	Amar pitar moku	" " "	Amar játá	My father.
6. Marâthî	6	Măzhă chŭlat ăză	" " "	Măzhă chŭlat	My paternal uncle.
7. Gujârâthî	7	Măro vadova	" " "	Măro phoi	" " " " [class
8. Chinese	8	Wo-tĕ poh-tsŭ (o.), Shuh-tsŭ (y.)	My senior junior ancestral relation.	Wo-tĕ tang-poh?	My senior father of the *tang*
9. Japanese	9	O-je'-sang	My grandfather.	O'-je.	My uncle.
10. Burmese	10	K: a-po'	" " "	K: bă-ky-lee'	My great father.
11. Karen (Sgau dial'ct)	11	Yă phu	" " "	Yă phă-tai	My uncle.
12. Karen (Pwo ")	12	Y' phu	" " "	Y' pha-tee	" "
13. Karen	13	Yeh pü	" " "	Yeh pa-tee	" "
14. Kings Mill Islands	14	Jĭbú	" " "	Tamau.	Father my.
15. Kusaien	15	Păpă-tŭmmun-păpă-tummuk.	" " "	Păpă-tummuk.	" "
16. Hawaiian	16	Kŭ-ŭ' kŭ-pŭ'-nă-kă'-na	My grandparent, male.	Kŭ-ŭ' mă-kŭ'-ă-kă'-na.	My parent, male.
17. Maori	17				
18. Amazulu (Kafir)	18	U-bă'-bă kŭ'-lŭ	My grandfather.	U-bă'-bă kă'-ze	My uncle paternal.

		167. My father's father's brother's son's son—older than myself. (Male speaking.)	Translation.	168. My father's father's brother's son—younger than myself. (Male speaking.)	Translation.
1. Tamil	1	En annan. ᵇTămăiyăn	My elder brother.	En tambi	My younger brother.
2. Telugu	2	Annă	Elder brother.	Tămmŭlŭ	Younger brother.
3. Canarese	3				
4. Hindî	4	Merá bară bhái	My greater brother.	Merá chota bhái	My lesser brother.
5. Bengâlî	5	Amar buro dádá	My elder brother.	Amar choto bratah	My younger brother.
6. Mârâthî	6	Măzhă wadel bhăŭ	" " "	Măzhă dhak e-ata bhăŭ	" " "
7. Gujârâthî	7	Măro bhái	" " "	Măro bhăi	" " "
8. Chinese	8	Wo-tĕ tang-heung-te	My brother of the *tang* class.	Wo-tĕ tang-heung-te	My brother of the *tang* class.
9. Japanese	9	A'-nee	My elder brother.	O-to'-to	My younger brother.
10. Burmese	10	K: eko.	" " "	K: ny-ee	" " "
11. Karen (Sgau dial'ct)	11	Yă tă-khwă	My male cousin.	Yă tă-khwă	My male cousin.
12. Karen (Pwo ")	12	Y' t'-khwă-sau.	" " "	Y' t'-khwa	" " "
13. Karen	13	Yeh t'-khwa	" " "	Yeh t'-khwa	
14. Kings Mill Islands	14	Tărn-te-karimoa	Brother my, elder.	Mănu-te-karimoa	Brother my, younger.
15. Kusaien	15	Ma-lĕk	Brother my.	Mă-lĕk	Brother my.
16. Hawaiian	16	Kŭ-ŭ' kăĭ'-kŭ-ă-ă'-nă	My brother, elder.	Kŭ-ŭ' kăĭ'-kăĭ-nă	My brother, younger.
17. Maori	17				
18. Amazulu (Kafir)	18	U'-mfo wă'-tŭ	Brothers of us.	U'-mfo wă'-tŭ	Brothers of us.

TABLE III.—*Continued.*

		169. My father's father's brother's son's son's son. (Male speaking.)	Translation.	170. My father's father's brother's son's son's son. (Female speaking.)	Translation.
1. Tamil..................	1	En măkăn...........................	My son.	En mărŭmăkăn.....................	My nephew.
2. Telugu	2	Kădŭkŭ.	Son.	Mĕnăllŭdŭ.........................	Nephew.
3. Canarese.............	3				
4. Hindî.................	4	Merá bhatija.....................	My nephew.	Merá bhatija.....................	My nephew.
5. Bengâlî	5	Amar bhagna....................	" "	Amar bhagna....................	" "
6. Marâthî..............	6	Mäzhä pûtanyä................	" "	Mäzhä pûtanyä................	" "
7. Gujârâthî	7	Märo bhatrijo.................	" "	Märo bhătrijo.................	" "
8. Chinese..............	8	Wo-tĕ tang-chih..............	My son of the *tang* class.	Wo-tĕ tang-chih..............	My son of the *tang* class.
9. Japanese.............	9	E-to'-ko.......................	My nephew.	E-to'-ko	My nephew.
10. Burmese.............	10	K: too........................	" "	K: too	" "
11. Karen (Sgan dial'ct)	11	Yă pho-do	" "	Yă pho-do	" "
12. Karen (Pwo ")	12	Y' pho-do-khwä	" "	Y' pho-do-khwä	" "
13. Karen................	13	Yeh po-do-khwä..............	" "	Yeh po-do-khwa	" "
14. Kings Mill Islands	14	Nätu-te-mane..................	Grandchild my, a male.	Nätu-te-mäne..................	Child my, a male.
15. Kusaien...............	15	Mwĕn-nuttik...................	Son my.	Mwĕn-nuttik...................	Son my.
16. Hawaiian.............	16	Kŭ-ŭ' käï'-kee-kä'-na	My child, male.	Kŭ-ŭ' käï'-kee-kä'-na	My child, male.
17. Maori	17				
18. Amazulu (Kafir)...	18	In-do-dä'-nä yä'-me............	Son of me.	In-do-dä'-än yä'-me.............	Son of me.

		171. My father's father's brother's son's son's daughter. (Male speaking.)	Translation.	172. My father's father's brother's son's son's daughter. (Female speaking.)	Translation.
1. Tamil..................	1	En măkăl...........................	My daughter.	En mărŭmăkăl.....................	My niece.
2. Telugu	2	Kŭthŭrŭ	Daughter.	Mĕnăkōdălŭ.....................	Niece.
3. Canarese.............	3				
4. Hindî.................	4	Meri bhatiji.....................	My niece.	Meri bhatiji	My niece.
5. Bengâlî	5	Amar bhagny....................	" "	Amar bhagny....................	" "
6. Marâthî..............	6	Mäzhi pûtani	" "	Mäzhi pûtani	" "
7. Gujârâthî	7	Märi bhătriji.................	" "	Märi bhătriji.................	" "
8. Chinese..............	8	Wo-tĕ tang-chih-neu..........	My daugh'r of the *tang* class.	Wo-tĕ tang-chih-neu	My daugh'r of the *tang* class.
9. Japanese.............	9	O-mä-e-to'-ko.................	My niece.	O-mä-e-to'-ko.................	My niece.
10. Burmese.............	10	K: too-mä	" "	K: too-mä...................	" "
11. Karen (Sgau dial'ct)	11	Yă pho-do-mu.................	" "	Yă pho-do-mu.................	" "
12. Karen (Pwo ")	12	Y' pho-do-mu	" "	Y' pho-do-mu	" "
13. Karen................	13	Yeh po-do-mü..................	" "	Yeh po-do-mü..................	" "
14. Kings Mill Islands	14	Nätu-te-aine	Child my, a female.	Nätu-te-aine	Child my, a female.
15. Kusaien...............	15	Au nuttik......................	Daughter my.	Au-nuttik......................	Daughter my.
16. Hawaiian.............	16	Kŭ-ŭ' käï'-kä-wă-hee'-na	My child, female.	Kŭ-ŭ' käï'-kä-wă-hee'-na.......	My child, female.
17. Maori	17				
18. Amazulu (Kafir)...	18	In-do-dä-kä'-ze yä-me..........	Daughter of me.	In-do-dä-kä'-ze yä'-me..........	Daughter of me.

		173. My father's father's brother's great great grandson.	Translation.	174. My father's father's brother's great great granddaughter.	Translation.
1. Tamil..................	1	En pêran.....................	My grandson.	En pêrtti	My granddaughter.
2. Telugu................	2	Măυămädŭ.....................	Grandson.	Măυămärälŭ	Granddaughter.
3. Canarese.............	3				
4. Hindî.................	4	Merá pota....................	My grandson.	Meri poti	My granddaughter.
5. Bengâlî	5	Amar naty	" "	Amar natny	" " "
6. Marâthî..............	6	Mäzhä natû	" "	Mäzhi nät...................	" " "
7. Gujârâthî	7	Märo pautră.................	" " [class.	Mäzhi pautri.................	" " " [*chih* class.
8. Chinese	8	Wo-tĕ tang-chih-sun	My grandson of the *tang-chih*	Wo-tĕ tang-chih-şun-neu	My g'ddaughter in the *tang-*
9. Japanese.............	9	Mä'-go.......................	My grandson.	Ma'-ee.......................	My granddaughter.
10. Burmese.............	10	K: my-a'.....................	My grandchild.	K: my-a'.....................	My grandchild.
11. Karen (Sgau dial'ct)	11	Yă lie-khwä	My grandson.	Yă lie-mu....................	My granddaughter.
12. Karen (Pwo ")	12	Y' le-khwä	" "	Y' le-mu.....................	" " "
13. Karen................	13	Yeh lee-khwa	" "	Yeh lee-mü...................	" " "
14. Kings Mill Islands	14	Tibu-te-mäne.................	Grandchild my, a male.	Tibun-nätu...................	Grandchild my, a female.
15. Kusaien...............	15	Mwĕn-nutt in-nuttik...........	Grandson my.	Au-nuttin-nuttik....	Granddaughter my.
16. Hawaiian.............	16	Kŭ-ŭ' moo-pŭ'-nä-kä-na........	My grandchild, male.	Kŭ-ŭ' moo-pŭ'-na-wa-hee'-na.	My grandchild, female.
17. Maori	17				
18. Amazulu (Kafir)...	18	U-me-tshä'-nä wä'-me..........	Grandson of me.	U-me-tshä'-nä wä'-me	Granddaughter of me.

TABLE III.—*Continued.*

		175. My father's father's sister.	Translation.	176. My father's father's sister's daughter. (Male speaking.)	Translation.
1. Tamil	1	En pǎddi (p. or s.)	My grandmother (great or	En Täy (p. or s.)?	My mother, great or little.
2. Telugu	2	Avvǎ ......[ka awwǎ (y.)	Grandmother. [little).	Měnättä	Aunt.
3. Canarese	3	Nǎnnǎ doddǎ awwǎ (o.), Chik-	My grandmother (great or		
4. Hindî	4	Meri dadi	My grandmother. [little).	Meri phuphi	My aunt.
5. Bengalî	5	Amar mata mohy	" "	Amar pushi	" "
6. Marâthî	6	Mǎzhi chǔlat äzě	" "	Mǎzhi mäme	" "
7. Gujârâthî	7	Märi yardi ma	" "	Märi phoi	" " [class.
8. Chinese	8	Wo-tě kǔ-mo	My aunt mother.	Wo-tě peaon-kǔ	My aunt mother of the *peaon*
9. Japanese	9	O-bä′-san	My grandmother.	O′-bä	My aunt.
10. Burmese	10	K: a-pwä′	" "	K: ky-ee-tau′	My great mother.
11. Karen (Sgau dial'ct)	11	Yǎ pḥie	" "	Yǔ mu-ghä	My aunt.
12. Karen (Pwo ")	12	Y′ phe	" "	Y′ m′-gä	" "
13. Karen	13	Yeh pee	" "	Yeh mü-gaḥ	" "
14. Kings Mill Islands	14			Tinau	Mother my.
15. Kusaien	15	Něně-keyěn-neně-keyǔk	Grandmother my.	Neně-keyǔk	Mother my.
16. Hawaiian	16	Kŭ-ŭ′ kŭ-pŭ′-nä-wä-hee′-na...	My grandparent, female.	Kŭ-ŭ′ mä-kŭ′-ȧ-wä-hee′-na...	My parent, female.
17. Maori	17				
18. Amazulu (Kafir)	18	U-mä′-mä-kŭ′-lǔ wä′-me	Grandmother of me.	U-bä′-bä	My father (so used).

		177. My father's father's sister's daughter's son. (Male speaking.)	Translation.	178. My father's father's sister's daughter's daughter. (Male speaking.)	Translation.
1. Tamil	1	En aṇṇan (o.), Tambi (y.)?	My elder or y'ger brother.	En tǎmǎkǎy (o.), Tǎngǎy (y.)?	My elder or younger sister.
2. Telugu	2	Bävǎ (o.), Märǎdi (y.)	Elder or younger cousin.	Vǎdǐně (o.), Mǎrǎdǎlǔ (y.)	Elder or younger cousin.
3. Canarese	3				
4. Hindî	4	Merá bhái	My brother.	Meri bahin	My sister
5. Bengalî	5	Amar mashtoto bhye	My cousin.	Amar mashtoto bhugny	My cousin sister.
6. Marâthî	6	Mǎzhä waděl bhǎǎ	My elder brother.	Mǎzhi wadel bahin	My elder sister.
7. Gujârâthï	7	Märi bhäi	My brother.	Märi bähen	My sister.
8. Chinese	8	Wo-tě peaon-heung-te	My bro. of the *peaon* class.	Wo-tě peaon-tsze-mei	My sister of the *peaon* class.
9. Japanese	9	A′-nee (o.), O-to′-to (y.)	My elder or younger brother.	A′-nih (o.), E-mo′-to (y.)	My elder or younger sister.
10. Burmese	10	K: e-ko (o.), Ny-ee (y.)	" " " "	K: e-mä (o.), Hnee-ma (y.)	" " " "
11. Karen (Sgau dial'ct)	11	Yǎ tä-khwǎ	My male cousin.	Yǎ tä-mu	My female cousin.
12. Karen (Pwo ")	12	Y′ t′-khwä-sau	" " "	Y′ t′-khwä-mu	" " " "
13. Karen	13	Yeh t′-khwa	" " "	Yeh dan-t′khwa-mü	" " "
14. Kings Mill Islands	14	Täru	Brother my.	Mänu	Sister my.
15. Kusaien	15	Mä-lčk	" "	Mä-loǔk	" "
16. Hawaiian	16	Kŭ-ŭ′ käï′-kŭ-ä-ä′-nä	My elder brother.	Kŭ-ŭ′ käï′-kŭ-wä-hee′-na	My elder sister.
17. Maori	17				
18. Amazulu (Kafir)	18	U′-mfo wä′-tǔ	Brothers of us.	U-dä′-dä wä′-tǔ	Sister of us.

		179. My father's father's sister's daughter's daughter's son. (Male speaking.)	Translation.	180. My father's father's sister's daughter's daughter's son. (Female speaking.)	Translation.
1. Tamil	1	En mǎrǔmǎkǎn?	My nephew.	En mäkǎn?	My son.
2. Telugu	2	Kǒdǔkǔ	Son.	Allǔdǔ	Nephew.
3. Canarese	3				
4. Hindî	4	Merá bhaujá	My nephew.	Merá bhaujá	My nephew.
5. Bengalî	5	Amar bhagna	" "	Amar bhagna	" "
6. Marâthî	6	Mǎzhä pûtanyä	" "	Mǎzhä pûtanyä	" "
7. Gujârâthî	7	Märo bhätrijo		Märo bhatrijo	
8. Chinese	8	Wo-tě peaon-chih	My neph. of the *peaon* class.	Wo-tě peaon-chih	My neph. of the *peaon* class.
9. Japanese	9	E-to′-ko	My nephew.	E-to′-ko	My nephew.
10. Burmese	10	K: too	" "	K: too	" "
11. Karen (Sgau dial'ct)	11	Yǎ pho-do	" "	Yǎ pho-do	" "
12. Karen (Pwo ")	12	Y′ pho-do-khwa	" "	Y′ pho-do-khwä	" "
13. Karen	13	Yeh po-do-khwa		Yeh po-do-khwa	
14. Kings Mill Islands	14	Nätu-te-mäne	Child my, a male.	Nätu-te-mäne	Child my, a male.
15. Kusaien	15	Mwěn-nuttik	Son my.	Mwěn-nuttik	Son my.
16. Hawaiian	16	Kŭ-ŭ′ käï′-kee-kä′-na	My child, male.	Kŭ-ŭ′ käï′-kee-kä′-na	My child, male.
17. Maori	17				
18. Amazulu (Kafir)	18	In-dä′-dä yä′-me	Son of me.	In-dä′-dä yä′-me	Son of me.

OF THE HUMAN FAMILY.

553

TABLE III.—*Continued.*

		181. My father's father's sister's daughter's daughter. (Male speaking.)	Translation.	182. My father's father's sister's daughter's daughter. (Female speaking.)	Translation.
1. Tamil	1	En marumakal ?	My niece.	En măkăl ?	My daughter.
2. Telugu	2	Kŭthŭrŭ	Daughter.	Kŏdălŭ	Niece.
3. Canarese	3				My niece.
4. Hindî	4	Meră bhaují	My niece.	Merä bhauji	" "
5. Bengâlî	5	Amar bhugny	" "	Amar bhugny	" "
6. Marâthî	6	Mäzhi pŭtani	" "	Mäzhi pûtani	" "
7. Gujârâthî	7	Märi bhătriji	" "	Märi bhătriji	" " [class.
8. Chinese	8	Wo-tĕ peaon-chih-sun-neu	My gd. dau. of the *peaon* class.	Wo-tĕ peaon-chih-sun-neu	My gd. daughter of the *peaon*
9. Japanese	9	O-mä-e-to'-ko	My niece.	O-mä-e-to'-ko	My niece.
10. Burmese	10	K: too-mä'	" "	K: too-mä'	" "
11. Karen (Sgau dial'ct)	11	Yă pho-do-mu	" "	Yă pho-do-mu	" "
12. Karen (Pwo ")	12	Y' pho-do-mu	" "	Y' pho-do-mu	" "
13. Karen	13	Yeh po-do-mü	" "	Yeh po-do-mü	" "
14. Kings Mill Islands	14	Nätu-te-aine	Child my, a female.	Nätu-te-aine	Child my, a female.
15. Kusaien	15	Au-nuttik	Daughter my.	Au-nuttik	Daughter my.
16. Hawaiian	16	Kŭ-ŭ' käï'-kee-wă-hee'-na	My child, a female.	Kŭ-ŭ' käï'-kee-wă-hee'-na	My child, female.
17. Maori	17				
18. Amazulu (Kafir)	18	In-do-dä-kä'-ze yä'-me	Daughter of me.	In-dä-dä-kä'-ze yä'-me	Daughter of me.

		183. My father's father's sister's great great grandson.	Translation.	184. My father's father's sister's great great granddaughter.	Translation.
1. Tamil	1	En pĕrän	My grandson.	En pĕrtti	My granddaughter.
2. Telugu	2	Mănămădŭ	Grandson.	Mănămärälŭ	Granddaughter.
3. Canarese	3				
4. Hindî	4	Merá potá	My grandson.	Meri poti	My granddaughter.
5. Bengâlî	5	Amar naty	" "	Amar natny	" "
6. Marâthî	6	Mäzhă natŭ	" "	Mäzhe nät	" "
7. Gujârâthî	7	Märo pautră	" " [class.	Märi pautri	" "
8. Chinese	8	Wo-te peaon-chih-tsung-sun	My gd. son of the *peaon-chih*	Wo-tĕ peon-chih-tsung-sun-Ma'-ee [neu	My gd. daught. of the *peaon-chih* class.
9. Japanese	9	Mä'-go	My grandson.		My gd. daught. [chih class.
10. Burmese	10	K: my-a'	My grandchild.	K: my-a'	" "
11. Karen (Sgau dial'ct)	11	Yă lie-khwă	My grandson.	Yă lie-mu	My granddaughter.
12. Karen (Pwo ")	12	Y' le-khwä	" "	Y' le-mu	" "
13. Karen	13	Yeh-lee'-khwa	" "	Yeh lee'-mu	" "
14. Kings Mill Islands	14	Tibu-te-mäne	Grandchild my, a male.	Tibu-te-aine	Grandchild my, a female.
15. Kusaien	15	Mwĕn-nuttin-nuttik	Grandson my.	Au-nuttin-nuttik	Granddaughter my.
16. Hawaiian	16	Kŭ-ŭ' moo-pŭ'-nä-kä'-na	My grandchild, male.	Kŭ-ŭ' moo-pŭ'-na-wä-hee'-na	My grandchild, female.
17. Maori	17				
18. Amazulu (Kafir)	18	U-me-tshä'-na wä' me	Grandson of me.	U-me-tshä'-na wä'-me	Granddaughter of me.

		185. My mother's mother's brother.	Translation.	186. My mother's mother's brother's son.	Translation.
1. Tamil	1	En paddan (p. or s.)	My grandfather gt. or little.	En mämän	My uncle.
2. Telugu	2	Pĕttätä (o.), Pïntätä	Grandfather great or little.	Mĕnämämä	Uncle.
3. Canarese	3	N. daddä tättä (o.), Chikkă	My grandfather gt. or little.		
4. Hindî	4	Merä dädá [tattä (y.)	My grandfather.	Merá mámú	My uncle.
5. Bengâlî	5	Amar pita mohu	" "	Amar mämä	" "
6. Marâthî	6	Mäzhä chŭlat äsä	" "	Mäzhä mämä	" "
7. Gujârâthî	7	Märo vadova	" "	Märo mämo	" "
8. Chinese	8	Wo-tĕ wae-kung ?	My outside venerable.	Wo-tĕ peaon-poh ?	My senior of the *peaon* class.
9. Japanese	9	She-je'-je	My great grand brother.	O'-je	My uncle.
10. Burmese	10	K: a-po	My grandfather.	K: oomen'. ᵇ Oo-ky-ee	" "
11. Karen (Sgau dial'ct)	11	Yă phu	" "	Yă phä-tie	" "
12. Karen (Pwo ")	12	Y' phu	" "	Y' phä-te	" "
13. Karen	13	Yeh pü	" "	Yeh-pa-tee	" "
14. Kings Mill Islands	14	Tibü		Täman	Father my.
15. Kusaien	15	Päpä-tummun-päpä-tummuk	Grandfather my.	Päpä-tummuk	
16. Hawaiian	16	Kŭ-ŭ' kŭ-pŭ'nä-kä'-na	My grandparent, male.	Kŭ-ŭ' mä-kŭ'-ă-kä'-na	My parent, male.
17. Maori	17				
18. Amazulu (Kafir)	18	U-bä-bä-kŭ'-lŭ	My grandfather.	U-mä-lŭ'-mä	My maternal uncle.

70   May. 1870.

TABLE III.—*Continued.*

		187. My mother's mother's brother's son's son. (Male speaking.)	Translation.	188. My mother's mother's brother's son's daughter. (Female speaking.)	Translation.
1. Tamil	1	En măittŭnăn	My cousin.	En măchchăn	My cousin.
2. Telugu	2	Bävă (o.), Mărădĭ (y.)	Cousin elder or younger.	Bävă (o.), mărădĭ (y.)	Cousin older or younger.
3. Canarese	3				
4. Hindî	4	Mera bhái	My brother.	Meri bahin	My sister.
5. Bengâlî	5	Amar mamoto bhye	My cousin.	Amor mamoto bhugny	My cousin sister.
6. Marâthî	6	Mäzhä waddĕl bhäŭ	My elder brother.	Mäzhé wadĕl bahin	My elder sister.
7. Gujârâthî	7	Märo bhäi	" " "	Márá băhen	My sister.
8. Chinese	8	Wo-tĕ peaon-heung-te	My broth. of the *peaon* class.	Wo-tĕ peaon tse-mei	My sister of the *peaon* class.
9. Japanese	9	A'-nee (o), o-to'-to (y.).	My brother elder or y'nger.	A'-nih (o.), E-mo'-to (y.)	My elder or younger sister.
10. Burmese	10	K: e-ko (o.), Ny-ee (y.)	My elder or y'nger brother.	K: e-ına (e.), Hnee ma (y.)	" " " " "
11. Karen (Sgau dialect)	11	Yă tä-khwä	My male cousin.	Yă tä-khwä mu	My female cousin.
12. Karen (Pwo ")	12	Y' t'-khwä-sau	" " "	Y' t'-khwä-mu	" " "
13. Karen	13	Yeh t'-khwa	" " "	Yeh dau-t'-khwa-mü	" " "
14. Kings Mill Islands	14	Täru	Brother my.	Mänu	Sister my.
15. Kusaien	15	Mă-lĕk	" "	Mä-loŭk	" "
16. Hawaiian	16	Kŭ-ŭ' kăĭ'-kŭ'-ä-ä'-nä	My elder brother.	Kŭ-ŭ' kăĭ'-kŭ-wä-hee'-na	My elder sister.
17. Maori	17				
18. Amazulu (Kafir)	18	U-mzä'-lä	My cousin.	U-mzä'-lä	My cousin.

		189. My mother's mother's brother's son's son's son. (Male speaking.)	Translation.	190. My mother's mother's brother's son's son's son. (Female speaking.)	Translation.
1. Tamil	1	En mărŭmăkăn	My nephew.	En Măkăn	My son.
2. Telugu	2	Allŭdŭ	Nephew.	Kŏdŭkŭ	Son.
3. Canarese	3				
4. Hindî	4	Merá bháujá	My nephew.	Merá bháujá	My nephew.
5. Bengâlî	5	Amar bhypo	" "	Amar bhypo	" "
6. Marâthî	6	Mäzhä chächä	" "	Mäzhä chächä	" "
7. Gujârâthî	7	Märo bhătrijo	" "	Märo bhătrijo	" "
8. Chinese	8	Wo-tĕ peaon-chih	My son of the *peaon* class.	Wo-tĕ peaon-chih	My son of the *peaon* class.
9. Japanese	9	E-to'-ko	My nephew.	E-to'-ko	My nephew.
10. Burmese	10	K : too	" "	K: too.	" "
11. Karen (Sgau dialect)	11	Yă pho-do	" "	Yă pho-do	" "
12. Karen (Pwo ")	12	Y' pho-do-khwä	" "	Y' pho-do-khwä	" "
13. Karen	13	Yeh po-do-khwa	" "	Yeh po-do-khwa	" "
14. Kings Mill Islands	14	Nätu-te-mäne.	Child my, a male.	Nätu-te-mäne.	Child my, a male.
15. Kusaien	15	Mwĕn-nuttik	Son my.	Mwĕn-nuttik	Son my.
16. Hawaiian	16	Kŭ-ŭ' kăĭ'-kee-kä'-na	My child, male.	Kŭ-ŭ' kăĭ'-kee-kä'-na	My child, male.
17. Maori	17				
18. Amazulu (Kafir)	18	In-do-dä'-nä yä'-me	Son of me.	In-do-dä'-nä yä'-me	Son of me.

		191. My mother's mother's brother's son's son's daughter. (Male speaking.)	Translation.	192. My mother's mother's brother's son's son's daughter. (Female speaking.)	Translation.
1. Tamil	1	En mărämăkăl	My niece.	En măkăl	My daughter.
2. Telugu	2	Kŏdŭlŭ	Niece.	Kŭthŭrŭ	Daughter.
3. Canarese	3				
4. Hindî	4	Meri bháuji	My niece.	Merá bháuji	My daughter.
5. Bengâlî	5	Amar bhyjhe	" "	Amar bhyjhe	" "
6. Marâthî	6	Mäzhé chäché	" "	Mäzhä chächi	My niece.
7. Gujârâthî	7	Märi bhătriji	" "	Mari bhătriji	" "
8. Chinese	8	Wo-tĕ peaon-chih-neu	My niece of the *peaon* class.	Wo-tĕ peaon-chih-neu	My niece of the *peaon* class.
9. Japanese	9	O-mä-e-to'-ko.	My niece.	O-mä-e-to'-ko.	My niece.
10. Burmese	10	K : too-mä'	" "	K : too-mä	" "
11. Karen (Sgau dialect)	11	Yă pho-do-mu	" "	Yă pho-do-mu	" "
12. Karen (Pwo ")	12	Y' pho-do-mu	" "	Y' pho-do-mu	" "
13. Karen	13	Yeh po-do-mü	" "	Yeh po-do-mü	" "
14. Kings Mill Islands	14	Nätu-te-aine	Child my, a female.	Nätu-te-aine	Child my, a female.
15. Kusaien	15	Au-nuttik	Daughter my.	Au-nuttik	Daughter my.
16. Hawaiian	16	Kŭ-ŭ' kăĭ'-kee-wä-hee'-na	My child, female.	Kŭ-ŭ' kăĭ'-kee'-wä hee'-na	My child, female.
17. Maori	17				
18. Amazulu (Kafir)	18	In-do-dä-kä'-ze yä'-me	Daughter of me.	In do-dä-kä'-ze yä'-me	Daughter of me.

TABLE III.—*Continued.*

		193. My mother's mother's brother's son's son's son's son. (Male speaking.)	Translation.	194. My mother's mother's brother's son's daughter's daughter's daughter. (Male speaking.)	Translation.
1. Tamil..................	1	En pêran.............................	My grandson.	En pêrtti...........................,.....	My granddaughter.
2. Telugu...............	2	Mănămădŭ	Grandson.	Mănămărălŭ.......................	Granddaughter.
3. Canarese.............	3				
4. Hindî	4	Merá potá........................	My grandson.	Meri poti............................	My granddaughter.
5. Bengâlî	5	Amar naty	" "	Amar natny	" "
6. Marâthî	6	Mázhä nätŭ.......................	" "	Mázhi nät............................	" "
7. Gujârâthî	7	Mära pautră......................	" " [*chih* class.	Märi pautri........................	" " [*chih* class.
8. Chinese..............	8	Wo-tĕ peaon-chih-sun	My grandson of the *peaon-*	Wo-tĕ peaon-chih-sun-neu	My gd.daught. of the *peaon-*
9. Japanese	9	Mä'-go	My grandson.	Ma'-ee	My granddaughter.
10. Burmese..............	10	K: my-a'.............................	My grandchild.	K: my-a'.............................	My grandchild.
11. Karen (Sgau dial'ct)	11	Yă lie-khwă	My grandson.	Yă lie-mu	My granddaughter.
12. Karen (Pwo ")	12	Y' le-khwä	" "	Y' le-mu	" "
13. Karen.................	13	Yeh lee-khwa	" "	Ye lee-mü	" "
14. Kings Mill Islands	14	Tibu-te-mane.....................	Grandchild my, a male.	Tibu-te-aine	Grandchild my, a female.
15. Kusaien..............	15	Mwĕn-nutĭn-nuttik.............	Grandson my.	An-nuttin-ăn-nuttin-nuttik ..	Granddaughter my.
16. Hawaiian.............	16	Kŭ-ŭ' moo-pŭ'-nä-kä-na.......	My grandchild, male.	Kŭ-ŭ' moo-pŭ'-nä-wä-hee-na..	My grandchild, female.
17. Maori.................	17				
18. Amazulu (Kafir) ...	18	U-me-tshä'-nä wä'-me	Grandchild of me.	U-me-tshä'-nä wä'-me..........	Grandchild of me.

		195. My mother's mother's sister.	Translation.	196. My mother's mother's sister's daughter.	Translation.
1. Tamil..................	1	En paddi (p. or s.)	My gd. mother (gt. or little).	En täy (p. or s.)....................	My mother (great or little).
2. Telugu...............	2	Avvă	Grandmother (gt. or little).	Tăllĭ....................................	Mother great or little.
3. Canarese.............	3	N. doddă awwa (o.), Chikkă	My gd. mother (gt. or little).		
4. Hindî	4	Meri dadi.............[awwa y.)	My grandmother.	Meri mausi	My aunt maternal.
5. Bengâlî	5	Amar mata mohy................	" "	Amar mashi	" " "
6. Marâthî	6	Mázhĕ chŭlăt äzĕ	" "	Mäshi mäŭs mäwase	" " "
7. Gujârâthî	7	Märi yardi mä	" "	Märi mäsi...........................	" " "
8. Chinese	8	Wo-tĕ wae-e-po	My mother of the *wae-e* class.	Wo-tĕ peaon-e	My aunt of the *peaon* class.
9. Japanese	9	She-bä'-ba.........................	My grandmother.	O'-bä.................................	My aunt.
10. Burmese..............	10	K: apwä. ᵇ Bwä..........,,	" "	K: kyee-tau	My great mother.
11. Karen (Sgau dial'ct)	11	Yă phie	" "	Yă mu-ghă	My aunt.
12. Karen (Pwo ")	12	Y' phe	" "	Y' m'-gä	" "
13. Karen.................	13	Yeh pee..............................	" "	Yeh mü-gah	" "
14. Kings Mill Islands	14			Tinau................................	Mother my.
15. Kusaien..............	15	Nenĕ keyĕn-nenĕ-keyŭk.......	Grandmother my.	Nenĕ-keyŭh........................	" "
16. Hawaiian.............	16	Kŭ-ŭ' ku-pŭ'-na-wä-hee'-na..	My grandparent, female.	Kŭ-ŭ' mä-kŭ'-ă-wa-hee-na	My parent, female.
17. Maori.................	17				
18. Amazulu (Kafir) ...	18	U-mä'-nä kŭ'-lŭ	My grandmother.	U-mä-mä-kä'-ze...................	My aunt.

		197. My mother's mother's sister's daughter's daughter—older than myself. (Female speaking.)	Translation.	198. My mother's mother's sister's daughter's daughter—younger than myself. (Female speaking.)	Translation.
1. Tamil..................	1	En tămăkay	My elder sister.	En tăngăy	My younger sister.
2. Telugu...............	2	Akkă	Elder sister.	Chĕllĕlŭ.............................	Younger sister.
3. Canarese.............	3				
4. Hindî	4	Meri baari bahin	My elder sister.	Merĭ chhoti bahin...............	My younger sister.
5. Bengâlî	5	Amar boro didy...................	" " "	Amar choto bhugny	" " "
6. Marâthî	6	Mázhĕ wadel bahin.............	" " "	Mäzhi dhakate bahin...........	" " "
7. Gujârâthî	7	Märi bähen	My sister.	Mari bähen	" " "
8. Chinese	8	Wo-tĕ peaon-tsze mei	My sister of the *peaon* class.	Wo-tĕ peaon-tsze-mei...........	My sister of the *peaon* class.
9. Japanese	9	A'-nih	My elder sister.	E-mo'-to	My younger sister.
10. Burmese..............	10	K: e-mä	" " "	K: hnee-mä........................	" " "
11. Karen (Sgau dial'ct)	11	Yă tă-khwă-mu....................	My female cousin.	Yă tă-khwă-mu....................	My female cousin.
12. Karen (Pwo ")	12	Y' t'-khwä-mu....................	" " "	Y' t'-khwä-mu....................	" " "
13. Karen.................	13	Yeh dan-t'-khwa-mü	" " "	Yeh dan-t'-khwa-mu............	" " "
14. Kings Mill Islands	14	Tăru-te-karimoa.................	Sister my, elder.	Taru-te-karimwi	Sister my, younger.
15. Kusaien..............	15	Mä-loŭk............................	Sister my.	Mä-loŭk............................	Sister my.
16. Hawaiian.............	16	Kŭ-ŭ' käï'-kŭ-wä-hee'-na......	My sister elder.	Kŭ-ŭ' käï'-käï-nä	My sister younger.
17. Maori.................	17				
18. Amazulu (Kafir)....	18	U-dä'-dä	Sister of us.	In-do-dä-kä'-ze. Yă'-me	Daughter of us.

TABLE III.—*Continued.*

		199. My mother's mother's sister's daughter's daughter's son. (Male speaking.)	Translation.	200. My mother's mother's sister's daughter's daughter's son. (Female speaking.)	Translation.
1. Tamil	1	En mărŭmăkăn	My nephew.	En măkăn	My son.
2. Telugu	2	Allŭdŭ	Nephew.	Kŏdŭkŭ	Son.
3. Canarese	3				
4. Hindî	4	Merá bhatijá	My nephew.	Merá bhatijá	My nephew.
5. Bengâlî	5	Amar bhagna	" "	Amar bhagna	" "
6. Marâthî	6	Mázhä chächä	" "	Mázhä chächä	" "
7. Gujârâthî	7	Märo bhätrijo	" "	Märo bhätrijo	" "
8. Chinese	8	Wo-tĕ peaon-chih	My neph. of the *peaon* class.	Wo-tĕ peaon-chih	My neph. of the *peaon* class.
9. Japanese	9	E-to'-ko	My nephew.	E-to'-ko	My nephew.
10. Burmese	10	K : too	" "	K : too	" "
11. Karen (Sgau dialect)	11	Yă pho-do	" "	Yă pho-do	" "
12. Karen (Pwo ")	12	Y' pho-do-khwä	" "	Y' pho-do-khwä	" "
13. Karen	13	Yeh po-do-khwa	" "	Yeh po-do-khwa	" "
14. Kings Mill Islands	14	Nătu-te-mäne	Child my, a male.	Nătu-te-mäne	Child my, a male.
15. Kusaien	15	Mwĕn-nuttik	Son my.	Mwĕn-nuttik	Son my.
16. Hawaiian	16	Kŭ-ŭ' kăï'-kee-kä-na	My child, male.	Kŭ-ŭ' kăï'-kee-kä-na	My child, male.
17. Maori	17				
18. Amazulu (Kafir)	18	U-me-tshä'-na. Wä'-me	Grandson of me.	U-me-tshä'-na. Wä'-me	Grandson of me.

		201. My mother's mother's sister's daughter's daughter's daughter. (Male speaking.)	Translation.	202. My mother's mother's sister's daughter's daughter's daughter. (Female speaking.)	Translation.
1. Tamil	1	En mărŭmăkăl	My niece.	En măkăl	My daughter.
2. Telugu	2	Kŏdălŭ	Niece.	Kŭthŭrŭ	Daughter.
3. Canarese	3				
4. Hindî	4	Meri bhatiji	My niece.	Meri bhatiji	My niece.
5. Bengâlî	5	Amar bhagny	" "	Amar bhagny	" "
6. Marâthî	6	Mazhe chäché	" "	Mázhé chäché	" "
7. Gujârâthî	7	Märi bhätriji	" "	Märi bhätriji	" "
8. Chinese	8	Wo-tĕ peaon-chih-neu	My niece of the *peaon* class.	Wo-tĕ peaon-chih-neu	My niece of the *peaon* class.
9. Japanese	9	O-mä'-e-to'-ko	My niece.	O-mä'-e-to'-ko	My niece.
10. Burmese	10	K : too-mä'	" "	K : too-mä'	" "
11. Karen (Sgau dialect)	11	Yă pho-do-mu	" "	Yă pho-do-mu	" "
12. Karen (Pwo ")	12	Y' pho-do-mu	" "	Y' pho-do-mu	" "
13. Karen	13	Yeh po-do-mü	" "	Yeh po-do-mü	" "
14. Kings Mill Islands	14	Nătu-te-aine	Child my, a female.	Nătu-te-aine	Child my, a female.
15. Kusaien	15	An-nuttik	Daughter my.	An-nuttik	Daughter my.
16. Hawaiian	16	Kŭ-ŭ' kăï'-kă-wä-hee'-na	My child, female.	Kŭ-ŭ' kăï'-kă-wä-hee'-na	My child, female.
17. Maori	17				
18. Amazulu (Kafir)	18	U-me-tshä'-nă. Wä'-me	Granddaughter of me.	U-me-tshä'-nă. Wä'-me	Granddaughter of me.

		203. My mother's mother's sister's great great grandson.	Translation.	204. My mother's mother's sister's great great granddaughter.	Translation.
1. Tamil	1	En pĕran	My grandson.	En pĕrtti	My granddaughter.
2. Telugu	2	Mănămădŭ	Grandson.	Mănămärălŭ	Granddaughter.
3. Canarese	3				
4. Hindî	4	Merá potá	My grandson.	Meri poti	My granddaughter.
5. Bengâlî	5	Amar naty	" "	Amar natny	" "
6. Marâthî	6	Mázhä nätŭ	" "	Mäzhi nät	" "
7. Gujârâthî	7	Märo pauträ	" "	Märi pautri	" " [*chih* class.
8. Chinese	8	Wo-tĕ peaon-chih-sun	My grandson of the *peaon* [class.	Wo-tĕ peaon-chih-sun-neu	My gd.daught. of the *peaon*-
9. Japanese	9	Mä'-go	My grandson.	Má'-go	My granddaughter.
10. Burmese	10	K : my-a'	My grandchild.	K : my-a'	My grandchild.
11. Karen (Sgau dialect)	11	Yă lie-khwä	My grandson.	Yă lie-mu	My granddaughter.
12. Karen (Pwo ")	12	Y' le-khwa	" "	Y' le-mu	" "
13. Karen	13	Yeh lee-khwa		Yeh lee-mü	
14. Kings Mill Islands	14	Tibu-te-mäne	Grandchild my, a male.	Tibu-te-aine	Grandchild my, a female.
15. Kusaien	15	Mwĕn-nuttin-nuttik	Grandson my.	An-nuttin-nuttik	Granddaughter my.
16. Hawaiian	16	Kŭ-ŭ moo-pŭ-nä-kä'-na-kä-na	My grandchild, male.	Kŭ-ŭ moo-pŭ'-nä wä-hee'-na	My grandchild, female.
17. Maori	17				
18. Amazulu (Kafir)	18	U-mzŭ-kŭ'-lŭ wä'-me	Great grandson of me.	U-zmŭ-kŭ-lŭ wä'-me	Great granddaughter of me.

TABLE III.—*Continued.*

		205. My father's father's father's brother.	Translation.	206. My father's father's father's brother's son.	Translation.
1. Tamil	1	En irandām păddăn	My second grandfather.	En păddăn (p. or s.)	My gd. father (gt. or little).
2. Telugu	2	Mŭttäta	Great grandfather.	Tata	Grandfather.
3. Canarese	3	N. doddă muttäta (o.), chikkă	My great grandfather.		
4. Hindî	4	Merà pardádá	" " "	Mera-dádá	My grandfather.
5. Bengâlî	5	Amar pre píta mohu	" " "	Amar pita mohu	" "
6. Marâthî	6	Mäzhä chŭlat panaza	" " "	Mäzhä Bäpäza	My paternal grandfather.
7. Gujârâthî	7	Märo purvaj	My ancestor.	Märo vado¨a	My grandfather.
8. Chinese	8	Wo-tĕ tsung-ʰᵒʰ_ₛₕᵤₕ -tsŭ	My more remote ancestor of the *poh* or *shuh* class.	Wo-tĕ tsŭ-fŭ	My ancestral father.
9. Japanese	9	She'-je-je	My great grandfather.	O-jee'-sang	My grandfather.
10. Burmese	10	K: Ba'. ᵇA-ba'.	" " "	K: a-po'.	" "
11. Karen (Sgau dialect)	11	Yă phu-pgha.	" " "	Yă phu	" "
12. Karen (Pwo ")	12	Y' phu	My grandfather.	Y' phu	" "
13. Karen	13	Yeh pŭ-pa-do.	My great grandfather.	Yeh pü	" "
14. Kings Mill Islands	14	Jïbü	My ancestor. [cond generation.	Jïbü	" "
15. Kusaien	15				
16. Hawaiian	16	Kŭ-ŭ' kŭ-pŭ-na-kä'-na-kŭ-ă- [lŭ'-ă	My grandparent, male, se-	Kŭ-ŭ' kŭ-pŭ-na-kä'-na	My grandparent, male.
17. Maori	17				
18. Amazulu (Kafir)	18	U-bä-bä-kŭ'-lŭ	My grandfather.	U-bä-bä-kŭ'-lŭ	My grandfather.

		207. My father's father's father's brother's son's son.	Translation.	208. My father's father's father's brother's son's son's son—older than myself. (Male speaking.)	Translation.
1. Tamil	1	En takappan (p. or s.)	My father (great or little.)	En Annan	My elder brother.
2. Telugu	2	Tandri	My father.	Annă	Elder brother.
3. Canarese	3				
4. Hindi	4	Merá cháchá	My uncle paternal.	Merá bara bhái	My elder brother.
5. Bengâlî	5	Amar pítah bratah	" " "	Amar buro dádá	" " "
6. Marâthî	6	Mäzhä chälatä	" " "	Mäzhä wadel bhaŭ	" " "
7. Gujârâthî	7	Märo kako	" " "	Märo bhäi	" " "
8. Chinese	8	Wo-tĕ poh-fu (o.), shuh-fu (y.)	My senior or junior father.	Wo tĕ tang-heung-te	My brother of the *tang* class.
9. Japanese	9	O-to'-tsang	My father.	A'-nee	My elder brother.
10. Burmese	10	K: bä-ky-eé	My great father.	K: e-ko	" "
11. Karen (Sgau dial'ct)	11	Yă phä-tie	My uncle.	Yă tä-khwa	My male cousin.
12. Karen (Pwo ")	12	Y' phä-te	" "	Y't'-khwä-san	" " "
13. Karen	13	Yeh pa-tee	" "	Yeh t'-khwa	" " "
14. Kings Mill Islands	14	Täman	Father my.	Taru te karimoa	Brother my, elder.
15. Kusaien	15				
16. Hawaiian	16	Kŭ-ŭ mä-kŭ'-ä-kä'-na	My parent, male.	Kŭ-ŭ' käï'-kŭ'-ä-ä'-nä	My brother elder.
17. Maori	17				
18. Amazulu (Kafir)	18	U-bä-bä-kä'-ze	My uncle (paternal).	U'-mfo wä'-tŭ	Brother of us.

		209. My father's father's father's brother's son's son's son's son. (Male speaking.)	Translation.	210. My father's father's father's brother's son's son's son's son's son.	Translation.
1. Tamil	1	En mäkän	My son.	En pĕran	My grandson.
2. Telugu	2	Kädăkŭ	Son.	Mănămädŭ	Grandson.
3. Canarese	3				
4. Hindî	4	Merá bhatijá	My nephew.	Merá potá... ?	My grandson.
5. Bengâlî	5	Amar bhypo	" "	Amar powutro	" "
6. Marâthî	6	Mäzhä putanyä	" "	Mäzhä natŭ	" "
7. Gujârâthî	7	Märo bhätrijo	" "	Märo pauträ	" "
8. Chinese	8	Wo-tĕ tang-peon-heung-te	My nephew of the *tang* class.	Wo-tĕ tang-chih-sun	My grandson of the *tang-chih* class.
9. Japanese	9	E-to'-ko		Mä'-go	My grandson.
10. Burmese	10	K: too	My nephew.	K: my-ä	" "
11. Karen (Sgau dial'ct)	11	Yă pho-do	" "	Yă lie-khwä	" "
12. Karen (Pwo ")	12	Y' pho-do-khwä	" "	Y' le-khwä	" "
13. Karen	13	Yeh po-do-khwa	" "	Yeh lee-khwa	" "
14. Kings Mill Islands	14	Nätu-te-mane	Child my, a male.	Tibu-te-mäne	Grandchild my, a male.
15. Kusaien	15				
16. Hawaiian	16	Kŭ-ŭ' käï'-kee-kä'-na	My child, male.	Kŭ-ŭ' moo-pŭ'-nä-kä'-ga	My grandchild, male.
17. Maori	17				
18. Amazulu (Kafir)	18	In-dó-dä'-nä yä'-me	Son of me.	U-me-tshä'-nä wä'-me	Grandson of me.

TABLE III.—*Continued.*

		211. My father's father's father's sister.	Translation.	212. My father's father's father's sister's daughter.	Translation.
1. Tamil	1	En irandām pǎddi	My second grandmother.	En pǎddi (p. or s.)	My grandmother (gt. or lit.)
2. Telugu	2	Mǔttǎvva [(y.)	My great grandmother.	Avvǎ	Grandmother.
3. Canarese	3	N. dodda ajje (e.), chikkä ajje	My gt. gd.mother (gt. or lit.)	Meri dadi	My grandmother.
4. Hindî	4	Meri pardádi	My great grandmother.	Amar matu mohy	" "
5. Bengâlî	5	Amar oty pita mohy	" " "	Mǎzhē bǎyǎzu	My paternal grandmother.
6. Marâthî	6	Mǎzhi punazë	" " "	Mǎri yardi ma	" " "
7. Gujârâthî	7	Mǎri purvaj	My ancestor.	Wo-tě kǔ-mo	My aunt mother.
8. Chinese	8	Wo-tě phǔ-po	My old mother of the *ku*	O'-bä-san	My grandmother.
9. Japanese	9	She-bǎ'-ba	My grandmother. [class.	K: apwǎ'. ᵇBwa	" "
10. Burmese	10	K: a-bǎ-mǎ. ᵇBǎ-mǎ	My great grandmother.	Yǎ phie	" "
11. Karen (Sgau dialect)	11	Yǎ phie-pgha	" " "	Y' phe	" "
12. Karen (Pwo ")	12	Y' phe	My grandmother.	Yeh pee	" "
13. Karen	13	Yeh pee	My great grandmother.		
14. Kings Mill Islands	14				
15. Kusaien	15	[kǔ'-ä	[cond generation.		
16. Hawaiian	16	Kǔ-ǔ' kǔ-pǔ'-nä-wa-hee'-na-	My grandparent, female, se-	Kǔ-u' kǔ-pǔ'-nä'-wä-hee'-na.	My grandparent, female.
17. Maori	17				
18. Amazulu (Kafir)	18	U-mä-mä-kǔ'-lǔ	My grandmother.	U-mä-mä-kǔ'-lǔ	My grandmother.

		213. My father's father's father's sister's daughter's daughter.	Translation.	214. My father's father's father's sister's daughter's daughter's daughter. (Male speaking.)	Translation.
1. Tamil	1	En täy ? (p. or s.)	My mother (great or little).	En tǎmakǎy (o.), tangay (y.)	My elder or younger sister.
2. Telugu	2	Tallī	My mother.	Akka (o.), chěllělǔ (y.)	Elder or younger sister.
3. Canarese	3				
4. Hindî	4	Meri phuphi	My aunt paternal.	Merá bará bahin or chhota bahin	My elder or younger sister.
5. Bengâlî	5	Amar pishi	" " "	Amar boro didy. ᵇChoto bhugny	" " " " "
6. Marâthî	6	Mǎzhi ǎt	" " "	Mǎzhi wadel bahin	My elder sister.
7. Gujârâthî	7	Mǎri phoi	" " "	Mǎri bǎhen	My sister.
8. Chinese	8	Wo-tě peaon-kǔ	My aunt of the *peaon* class.	Wo-tě peaon-tsze-mei	My sister of the *peaon* class.
9. Japanese	9	O-bä	My aunt.	A'-nih (o.), E-mo'-to (y.)	My elder or younger sister.
10. Burmese	10	K: ky-ee-tau	My great aunt.	K: E-ma' (o.), hnee-ma' (y.)	" " " "
11. Karen (Sgau dialect)	11	Yǎ mu-ghǎ	My aunt.	Yǎ tǎ-khwǎ-mu	My female cousin.
12. Karen (Pwo ")	12	Y' m ?-gǎ	" "	Y' t'-khwǎ-mu	" " "
13. Karen	13	Yeh mǔ-gah	" "	Yeh-dan-t'-khwa-mǔ	" " "
14. Kings Mill Islands	14	Tinǎu	Mother my.	Manu	Sister my.
15. Kusaien	15				
16. Hawaiian	16	Kǔ-ǔ' mä-kǔ' ǎ-wä hee'-na	My parent, female.	Kǔ-ǔ' maǔ-käǐ'-kǔ wä-hee'-na	My sister.
17. Maori	17				
18. Amazulu (Kafir)	18			U-dä'-dä wä'-tǔ	Sister of us.

		215. My father's father's father's sister's daughter's daughter's daughter. (Male speaking.)	Translation.	216. My father's father's father's sister's daughter's daughter's daughter's daughter.	Translation.
1. Tamil	1	En mǎrǔmǎkǎl	My niece.	En pěrtti	My granddaughter.
2. Telugu	2	Kōdǎlǔ	Niece.	Mǎnǎmǎrǎlu	Granddaughter.
3. Canarese	3				
4. Hindî	4	Meri bhauji	My niece.	Meri poti	My granddaughter
5. Bengâlî	5	Amar bhvjhe	" "	Amar natny	" "
6. Marâthî	6	Mǎzhi pûtani	" "	Mǎzhi nǎt	" "
7. Gujârâthî	7	Mǎri bhǎtriji	" "	Mǎri pautri	My gd.daught of the *peaon*
8. Chinese	8	Wo-tě peaon-chih-neu	My niece of the *peaon* class.	Wo-tě peaon-chih-sun-neu	My grandchild. [*chih* class.
9. Japanese	9	E-to'-ko	My niece.	Mǎ'-go	" "
10. Burmese	10	K: too-mǎ'	" "	K: my-a'	
11. Karen (Sgau dial'ct)	11	Yǎ-pho-do-mu	" "	Yǎ lie'-mu	My granddaughter.
12. Karen (Pwo ")	12	Y' pho-do-mu	" "	Y' le-mu	" "
13. Karen	13	Yeh po-do-mǔ	" "	Yeh lee-mǔ	" "
14. Kings Mill Islands	14	Nǎtu-te-aine	Child my, a female.	Tibu-te-aine	Grandchild my, a female.
15. Kusaien	15				
16. Hawaiian	16	Kǔ-ǔ' käǐ' kǎ' wä-hee'-na	My child, female.	Kǔ-ǔ' moo-pǔ'-na wä-hee-na	My grandchild, female.
17. Maori	17				
18. Amazulu (Kafir)	18	In-do-dä-kä'-ze yǎ'-me	Daughter of me.	U-mzu-kǔ'-lǔ wä'-ne	Granddaughter of me.

TABLE III.—*Continued.*

		217. My mother's mother's mother's brother.	Translation.	218. My mother's mother's mother's brother's son.	Translation.
1. Tamil..	1	En irandäm păddăn	My second grandfather.	En păddăn (p. or s.)............	My grandfather (gt. or lit.)
2. Telugu.................	2	Müttäta............[muttäta (y.)	Great grandfather.	Tätä	Grandfather.
3. Canarese	3	N. dóddä muttäta (o.), chikkä	My gt. gd. fath. (gt. or lit.)		
4. Hindî	4	Merá pardádá.................	My great grandfather.	Merá dádá..........................	My grandfather.
5. Bengâlî................	5	Amar pre péta mohu	" " "	Amar péta mohu	" " "
6. Marâthî................	6	Mozha paṇazä.....................	" " "	Mäzhä mäyäzä.....................	My maternal grandfather.
7. Gujârâthî..............	7	Märo purvaj.....................	My ancestor. [old gentl'n.	Märo yardi ma.....................	" " "
8. Chinese	8	Wo-tĕ kew-tae-kung	My mother's bro., that very	Wo-tĕ wae-tsŭ-kung............	My outer ancestral old
9. Japanese	9	She-jee'-je	My great grandfather.	O-jee'-sang	My grandfather. [gentl'n.
10. Burmese	10	K: bä. ᵇ A-bä	" " "	K: a-po'	" "
11. Karen (Sgau dial'ct)	11	Yä phu-pgha	" " "	Yä phu.............................	" "
12. Karen (Pwo ")	12	Y' phu............................	My grandfather.	Y' phu	" "
13. Karen	13	Yeh pä-pa-do.....................	My great grandfather.	Yeh pŭ	" "
14. Kings Mill Islands..	14	Jïbŭ	Ancestor my.	Jïbŭ	" "
15. Kusaien	15		[lŭ'-ä [tion.		
16. Hawaiian	16	Kŭ-ŭ' kŭ-pu'-nä-kä-na-kŭ'-ä-	My grandparent, 2d genera-	Kŭ-ŭ' kŭ-pŭ'-nä-kä'-na........	My grandparent, male.
17. Maori	17				
18. Amazulu (Kafir)....	18	U-bä'-bä kŭ'-lŭ	My grandfather.	U-bä'-bä kŭ'-lŭ	My grandfather.

		219. My mother's mother's mother's brother's son's son.	Translation.	220. My mother's mother's mother's brother's son's son's son.	Translation.
1. Tamil	1	En mämăn	My uncle.	En mäittŭnăn	My cousin.
2. Telugu.................	2	Mämä	Uncle.	Bävä	Cousin.
3. Canarese	3				
4. Hindî	4	Merá mámá	My uncle paternal.	Merá mamera bhái............	My brother.
5. Bengâlî................	5	Amar mama	" " "	Mera mamoto bhye............	My cousin.
6. Marâthî................	6	Mäzhä mämä	" " "	Mäzhä bhäwandĕ...............	My brother.
7. Gujârâthî..............	7	Märo mämo	" " "	Märo bhäi.........................	" " "
8. Chinese	8	Wo-tĕ kew-chang	My uncle of the *chang* class.	Wo-tĕ peaon-heung-te	My bro. of the *peaon* class.
9. Japanese	9	O'-jee	My uncle.	A'-nee (o.), E-to'-to (y.)......	My elder or younger bro.
10. Burmese	10	K: oo-meŭ.......................	" "	K: e-kó (o.), ny-ee (y.).......	" " "
11. Karen (Sgau dial'ct)	11	Yä phä-tie.......................	" ." "	Yä tä-khwä	My female cousin.
12. Karen (Pwo ")	12	Y' phä-te	" "	Y' t'-khwä-sau...................	" " "
13. Karen	13	Yeh pa-tee	" "	Yoh t'-khwa......................	" " "
14. Kings Mill Islands..	14	Taman............................	Father my.	Nätu-te-mäne	Child my, a male.
15. Kusaien	15				
16. Hawaiian	16	Kŭ-ŭ' mä-kŭ'-ä-kä'-na	My parent, male.	Kŭ-ŭ' käi'-kee-kä'-na...........	My child, male.
17. Maori	17				
18. Amazulu (Kafir)....	18	U-mä-lŭ'-mä	My uncle.	U-mzä'-lä wä'-me	Cousin of me.

		221. My mother's mother's mother's brother's son's son's son's son.	Translation.	222. My mother's mother's mother's brother's son's son's son's son's son.	Translation.
1. Tamil	1	En Märümăkăn	My nephew.	En pĕran........................	My grandson.
2. Telugu.................	2	Allŭdī	Nephew.	Mănămădŭ	Grandson.
3. Canarese	3				
4. Hindî	4	Mera bhatijé.....................	My nephew.	Merá potá........................	My grandson.
5. Bengâlî................	5	Mera bhypo......................	" "	Amar naty	" "
6. Marâthî................	6	Mäzhä pütanyä..................	" "	Mäzhä natú	" "
7. Gujârâthî..............	7	Märo bhätrijo....................	" "	Märo pautră......................	" "
8. Chinese	8	Wo-tĕ peaon-chih................	My neph. of the *peaon* class.	Wo-tĕ peaon-chih-sun	My grandson of the *peaon-*
9. Japanese	9	E-to'-ko	My nephew.	Mä'-go............................	[*chih* class.
10. Burmese	10	K: too...........................	" "	K: my-á	My grandchild.
11. Karen (Sgau dial'ct)	11	Yä pho-do........................	" "	Yä lie-khwä	My grandson.
12. Karen (Pwo ")	12	Y' pho-do-khwä..................	" "	Y' le-khwä	" "
13. Karen	13	Yeh po-do-khwa..................	" "	Yeh lee-khwa	" "
14. Kings Mill Islands..	14	Taru	Brother my.	Tibu-te-mane.....................	Grandchild my, a male.
15. Kusaien	15				
16. Hawaiian	16	Kŭ-ŭ' käi'-kŭ'-ä-ä-na	My elder brother.	Kŭ-ŭ' moo-pŭ'-nä-kä'-na	My grandchild, male.
17. Maori	17				
18. Amazulu (Kafir)....	18	U-me-tshä'-na-wä'	Grandson of me.	U-mzŭ-kŭ'-lŭ wä'-me...........	Great grandson of me.

TABLE III.—*Continued.*

		223. My mother's mother's mother's sister.	Translation.	224. My mother's mother's mother's sister's daughter.	Translation.
1. Tamil	1	En irandäm päddi	My second grandmother.	En päddi (p. or s.)	My grandmother (gt. or lit.)
2. Telugu	2	Müttävvä [(y.)	Great grandmother.	Avvä	Grandmother.
3. Canarese	3	N. doddä ajje (o.), chekkä ajje	Gt. grandmother (gt. or lit.)		
4. Hindî	4	Meri pardädi	My great grandmother.	Meri dädi	My grandmother.
5. Bengâlî	5	Amar oty pita mohy	" " "	Amar mata mohy	" " "
6. Marâthî	6	Mäzhi panazï	" " "	Mäzhi mäyäzi	My maternal grandmother.
7. Gujârâthî	7	Märi purvaj	My ancestor. [old lady.	Märi yardi ma	" " "
8. Chinese	8	Wo-tĕ kŭ-tae-po	My mother's sister, that very	Wo-tĕ wae-e-po	My mother of the *wae-e* class.
9. Japanese	9	She-bä'-ba	My great grandmother.	O-bä'-san	My grandmother.
10. Burmese	10	K : bä-mä	" " "	K : a pwä'. Bwä	" "
11. Karen (Sgau dial'ct)	11	Yä phie-pgha	" " "	phie	" "
12. Karen (Pwo ")	12	Y' phe	My grandmother.	I' phe	" "
13. Karen	13	Yeh pee	My great grandmother.	Yeh pee	" "
14. Kings Mill Islands	14				
15. Kusaien	15	[hŭ'-ä-lŭ'-ä	[generation.		
16. Hawaiian	16	Kŭ-ŭ' kŭ-pŭ'-nä wä-hee'-na-	My grandparent, female, 2d	Kŭ-ŭ' kŭ-pŭ'-nä wä-hee-ha	My grandparent, female.
17. Maori	17				
18. Amazulu (Kafir)	18	U-mä-mä-kù'-lŭ	My grandmother.	U-mä-mä-kŭ'-lŭ	My grandmother.

		225. My mother's mother's mother's sister's daughter's daughter.	Translation.	226. My mother's mother's mother's sister's daughter's daughter's daughter—older than myself. (Fem. sp.)	Translation.
1. Tamil	1	En tây (p. or s.)	My mother (great or little.)	En akkarl	My elder sister.
2. Telugu	2	Tǎllï	My mother.	Akkä	Elder sister.
3. Canarese	3				
4. Hindî	4	Meri mausi	My aunt maternal.	Meri bahin	My sister.
5. Bengâlî	5	Amar mashi	" " "	Amar bhugny	" "
6. Marâthî	6	Mäzhi mäwasï	" " "	Mäzhi bahine	" "
7. Gujârâthî	7	Märi mäsi	" " "	Märi bähen	" "
8. Chinese	8	Wo-tĕ wae-po	My out of the family mother.	Wo-tĕ o-peaon-tsze-mei	My sister of the *peaon* class.
9. Japanese	9	O'-bä	My aunt.	A'-nih (o.), E-mo'-to (y.)	My sister elder or younger.
10. Burmese	10	K : mee-hy-ee (o.), K : mee-	My great or little mother.	K : e-mä	My elder sister.
11. Karen (Sgau dial'ct)	11	Yä mu-ghä [kwa (y.)	My aunt.	Yä tä-khwä-mu	My female cousin.
12. Karen (Pwo ")	12	Y' m'-gä	" "	Y' t'-khwä-mu	" " "
13. Karen	13	Yeh mü-gah		Yeh dan-t'-khwä-mü	" " "
14. Kings Mill Islands	14	Täman	Mother my.	Täru-te-karimoa	Sister my, elder.
15. Kusaien	15				
16. Hawaiian	16	Kŭ-ŭ' mä-hŭ'-äwä-hee'-na	My parent, female.	Kŭ-ŭ' käï'-kŭ-ä-ä'-nä	My sister, elder.
17. Maori	17				
18. Amazulu (Kafir)	18	U-mä-mä-kä'-ze	My aunt (maternal).	U-dä'-dä wä'-tŭ	Our sister.

		227. My mother's mother's mother's sister's daughter's daughter's daughter's daughter. (Female speaking.)	Translation.	228. My mother's mother's mother's sister's daughter's daughter's daughter's daughter's daughter.	Translation.
1. Tamil	1	En mäkäl	My daughter.	En pêrtti	My granddaughter.
2. Telugu	2	Küthürü	Daughter.	Mänämärälü	Granddaughter.
3. Canarese	3				
4. Hindî	4	Meri bhauji	My niece.	Meri poti	My granddaughter.
5. Bengâlî	5	Amar bhyjhe	" "	Amar natny	" " "
6. Marâthî	6	Mäzhé chächi	" "	Mäzhé nät	" " "
7. Gujârâthî	7	Märi bhatriji	" "	Märi pautri	" " "
8. Chinese	8	Wo-tĕ e-peaon-chih-neu	My daughter of the *chih* kind in the *e-peaon* class.	Wo-tĕ e-peaon-chih-sun-neu	My granddaugh'r of the *chih* kind in the *e-peaon* class.
9. Japanese	9	O-nä-e-to'-ko	My niece.	Ma'-ee	My granddaughter.
10. Burmese	10	K : too-mä'	" "	K : my-á	My grandchild.
11. Karen (Sgau dial'ct)	11	Yä pho-do-mu	" "	Yä lie-mu	My granddaughter.
12. Karen (Pwo ")	12	Y' pho-do-mu	" "	Y' le-mu	" " "
13. Karen	13	Yeh po-do-mu	" "	Yeh lee-mu	" " "
14. Kings Mill Islands	14	Nätu-te-aine	Child my, a female.	Tibu-te-aine	Grandchild my, a female.
15. Kusaien	15				
16. Hawaiian	16	Kŭ-ŭ' käï'-keĕ wä-hee'-na	My child, female.	Kŭ-ŭ' moo-pŭ'-na wä-hee'-na	My grandchild, female.
17. Maori	17				
18. Amazulu (Kafir)	18	In-do-dä-kä'-ze	My daughter.	U-kŭ'-lŭ wä'-me	My grandchild.

TABLE III.—*Continued.*

		229. My husband.	Translation.	230. My wife.	Translation.
1. Tamil	1	En kănavăn. ᵇ Purushan	My husband.	En manaivi. ᵇ Pernchätti	My wife.
2. Telugu	2	Măgădŭ. ᵇ Mŏgădŭ	Husband.	Pĕndlāmā	Wife.
3. Canarese	3	Năuuă găndăna	My husband.	Nănnă hendăti	My wife.
4. Hindî	4	Merá pat	" "	Meri patui	" "
5. Bengâlî	5	Amar poty	" "	Amar potuy	" "
6. Maràthî	6	Măzhä nawarä. ᵇDädalä. ᶜWar		Măzhi băyako. ᵇPatrus	" "
7. Gujârâthî	7	Măro dhaui	My lord.	Mări dhaniani	My lady.
8. Chinese	8	Wo-tĕ laon-kung. ᵇ Chang-fŭ	My old man.	Wo-tĕ laon po. ᵇ Tsee-tsze	My old woman or wife.
9. Japanese	9	Ote'-to	My husband.	Si	My wife.
10. Burmese	10	K : liu	" "	K : ma-yä	" "
11. Karen (Sgau dialect)	11	Yă wä	" "	Yă-mä	" "
12. Karen (Pwo ")	12	Y' wä	" "	Y' mä	" "
13. Karen	13	Yeh wah.	" "	Yeh mah	" "
14. Kings Mill Islands	14	Bŭ	Husband my.	Bŭ	Husband my.
15. Kusaien	15				
16. Hawaiian	16	Kŭ-ŭ' kä'-na	My husband.	Kŭ-ŭ' wä-hee'-na	My wife.
17. Maori	17	Ta-ku. Ta-hu		Ta-ku. Ho-a	
18. Amazulu (Kafir)	18	U-myä' nä wä-me	Husband of me.	U-mkä'-me. ᵇ U-mfä'-ze	" "

		231. My husband's father.	Translation.	232. My husband's mother.	Translation.
1. Tamil	1	En mämăn. ᵇ Mämanär	My uncle and father-in-law.	En mämi. ᵇ Mämar	My aunt and mother-in-law
2. Telugu	2	Mämă	Father-in-law.	Attă	Mother-in-law.
3. Canarese	3	Nănă mävănu	My father-in-law.	Nănnă atte	My mother-in-law.
4. Hindî	4	Merá sasur	" "	Meri los	" "
5. Bengâlî	5	Amar shoshur	" "	Amar sha shuri	" "
6. Maràthî	6	Măshä Säsarä	" "	Măzhä săsû	" "
7. Gujârâthî	7	Măro sasaro	" "	Mări säsü	" "
8. Chinese	8	Wo-tĕ kung-kung	My old, old man.	Wo-tĕ po-po	My old old woman.
9. Japanese	9	O-tote'-sä	My father-in-law.	O-ka'-săn	My mother-in-law.
10. Burmese	10	K : youk-a-mä	" "	K : yonk-a-mä	" "
11. Karen (Sgau dialect)	11	Yă mie-pghä-pŏ-khwä	" "	Yă mie-pgha-po-mu	" "
12. Karen (Pwo ")	12	Y' me-p'-gä-khwä	" "	Y' me-p'-gä-mu	" "
13. Karen	13	Yeh mee-pghä-khwa	" "	Yeh mee-pghä-mü	" "
14. Kings Mill Islands	14	Jïnapaŭ	Father-in-law my.	Jïnapaŭ	Mother-in-law my.
15. Kusaien	15				
16. Hawaiian	16	Kŭ-ŭ' mä-kŭ'-ă-hŭ-nä-äl kä'-na	My parent-in-law.	Kŭ-ŭ' mä-kŭ'-ă-hŭ-nä-äl wä-[hee'-na	My parent-in-law.
17. Maori	17				
18. Amazulu (Kafir)	18	U-mä-mä-zä'-lä. ᵇ U-bä'-bä	My father-in-law. ᵇ My father.	U-mkwä kä'-ze. Wä'-me	Mother-in-law of me.

		233. My husband's grandfather.	Translation.	234. My husband's grandmother.	Translation.
1. Tamil	1	En păddăn	My grandfather.	En păddi	My grandmother.
2. Telugu	2	Tätä	Grandfather.	Avvă	Grandmother.
3. Canarese	3	Nanna tättä	My grandfather.	Nănnă awwă	My grandmother.
4. Hindî	4	Merá sasur	My grandfather-in-law.	Meri nanuja sas	My grandmother-in-law.
5. Bengâlî	5	Amar dádá shoshur	" "	Amar diny shosury	" "
6. Maràthî	6	Măzhä äzë-säsarä	" "	Măzhi panaze säsarä	" "
7. Gujârâthî	7	Măro vada säsarŏ	" "	Mări vada säsari	" "
8. Chinese	8	Wo-tĕ tae-kea-yung	My great family venerable.		
9. Japanese	9	O-jee'-sang	My grandfather.	O-bä'-san	My grandmother.
10. Burmese	10	K : a-pó	" "	K : a-pwä	" "
11. Karen (Sgau dialect)	11	Yă-phu	" "	Yă phie	" "
12. Karen (Pwo ")	12	Y' phu	" "	Y' phe	" "
13. Karen	13	Yeh pä	" "	Yeh pee	" "
14. Kings Mill Islands	14	Jïbŭ	" "		
15. Kusaien	15				
16. Hawaiian	16	Kŭ-ŭ' kŭ-pŭ'-nä kä'-na	My grandparent, male.	Kŭ-ŭ' kŭ-pŭ'-nä wä-hee'-na	My grandparent, female.
17. Maori	17				
18. Amazulu (Kafir)	18	U-bä-bä-kŭ'-lŭ	My grandfather.	U-mä-mä-kŭ'-lŭ	My grandmother.

TABLE III.—*Continued.*

		235. My wife's father.	Translation.	236. My wife's mother.	Translation.
1. Tamil	1	En mämän	My uncle.	En mämi	My aunt.
2. Telugu	2	Mämä	Uncle.	Attä	Aunt.
3. Canarese	3	Nanua mävä	My uncle.	Nännä atte	My aunt.
4. Hindî	4	Merá sosur	My father-in-law.	Merí lás	My mother-in-law.
5. Bengâli	5	Amar shoshur	" "	Amar sha shuri	" "
6. Marâthî	6	Mäzhä säsärä	" "	Mäzhi säsû	" "
7. Gujârâthî	7	Märo vevai	" "	Märi veväni	" "
8. Chinese	8	Wo-tĕ qŭĕ-fŭ	My wife's father.	Wo-tĕ qŭĕ-mo	My wife's mother.
9. Japanese	9	O-tote'-sä	My father-in-law.	O-kä'-sän	My mother-in-law.
10. Burmese	10	K : yonk-a-mä	" "	K : yonk-a-mä	" "
11. Karen (Sgau dialect)	11	Yä mie-pghä-po-khwä	" "	Yä mie-pgha-po-mu	" "
12. Karen (Pwo ")	12	Y' me-p'-gä-khwä	" "	Y' me-p'-gä-mu	" "
13. Karen	13	Yeh mee-pghá-khwa	" "	Yeh mee-pgha-mü	" "
14. Kings Mill Islands	14				
15. Kusaien	15				
16. Hawaiian	16	Kŭ-ŭ'mä-kŭ'-ă-hŭ-nä-äi kä'-na	My parent-in-law, **male.**	Kŭ-ŭ' mä-kŭ-ă-hŭ-nä-äi wä-[hee'	My parent-in-law, female.
17. Maori	17				
18. Amazulu (Kafir)	18	U'-mkwä	My father-in-law.	U-mkwä-kä'-ze wä'-me'	Mother-in-law of me.

		237. My wife's grandfather.	Translation.	238. My wife's grandmother.	Translation.
1. Tamil	1	En päddän	My grandfather.	En päddi	My grandmother.
2. Telugu	2	Tätä	Grandfather	Avvä	Grandmother.
3. Canarese	3	Nännä tätä	My grandfather.	Nännä awwä	My grandmother.
4. Hindî	4	Merá (daduja) sasw	My grandfather-in-law.	Merí (navinya) sas	My grandmother-in-law.
5. Bengâli	5	Amar dádá shoshur	" " "	Amar didy shosung	" " "
6. Marâthî	6	Mäzhä äza säsarä	" " "	Mäzhi-aze säsü	" " "
7. Gujârâthî	7	Märo veda vevai	" " "	Mäi vada vevani	" " "
8. Chinese	8	Wo-tĕ wae-tsŭ-kung	My out of the family ances-	O-bä'-san	My grandmother.
9. Japanese	9	O-jee'-sang	My grandfather. [tral old fa.		" "
10. Burmese	10	K : a-pó	" "	K : a-pwä	" "
11. Karen (Sgau dialect)	11	Yä phu	" "	Ya phie	" "
12. Karen (Pwo ")	12	Y' phu	" "	Y' phe	" "
13. Karen	13	Yeh pü	" "	Yeh pee	" "
14. Kings Mill Islands	14	Jîbŭ	" "		
15. Kusaien	15				
16. Hawaiian	16	Kŭ-ŭ' mä-pŭ'-nä kä-na	My grandparent, male.	Kŭ-ŭ' kŭ-pŭ'-nä wä-hee'-na	My grandparent, female.
17. Maori	17				
18. Amazulu (Kafir)	18	U- bä'-bä-kŭ'-lŭ	My grandfather.	U-mä-mä-kŭ'-lŭ	My grandmother.

		239. My son-in-law. (Male speaking.)	Translation.	240. My son-in-law. (Female speaking.)	Translation.
1. Tamil	1	En Mäpillai. ᵇ Märŭmakän	My son-in-law. ᵇ Nephew.	En mäpillai. ᵇ Märŭmakän	My son-in-law. ᵇ Nephew.
2. Telugu	2	Allŭdŭ	Son-in-law.	Allŭdŭ	Son-in-law.
3. Canarese	3	Nännä aleyänu	My son-in-law and nephew.	Nännä aleyänu	My son-in-law and nephew.
4. Hindî	4	Merá dámád	My son-in-law.	Merá dámád	My son-in-law.
5. Bengâli	5	Amar jamotu	" "	Amar jamotu	" "
6. Marâthî	6	Mäzhä zäwär	" "	Mäzhä zäwär	" "
7. Gujârâthî	7	Märo jamäi	" "	Märi jamäi	" "
8. Chinese	8	Wo-tĕ neu-se	My daughter's superior.	Wo-tĕ neu-se	My daughter's superior.
9. Japanese	9	Moo'-ko	My son-in-law.	Moo'-ko	My son-in-law.
10. Burmese	10	K : tha-met	" "	K : tha-met	" "
11. Karen (Sgau dialect)	11	Yä mä	" "	Yä mä	" "
12. Karen (Pwo ")	12	Y' mä	" "	Y' mä	" "
13. Karen	13	Yeh mä	" "	Yeh mä	" "
14. Kings Mill Islands	14	Jînapaŭ	Son-in-law my.	Jînapaŭ	Son-in-law my.
15. Kusaien	15				
16. Hawaiian	16	Kŭ-ŭ' hŭ-no-nä kä'-na	My child-in-law, male.	Kŭ-ŭ' hŭ-no'-nä kä'-na	My child-in-law, male.
17. Maori	17				
18. Amazulu (Kafir)	18	U-mkwä'-nyä wä'-me	My son-in-law.	U-mkwä'-nyä wä'-me	My son-in-law.

TABLE III.—*Continued.*

		241. My daughter-in-law. (Male speaking.)	Translation.	242. My daughter-in-law. (Female speaking.)	Translation.
1. Tamil	1	En mărŭmăkăl	My daughter-in-law & niece.	En mărŭmăkăl	My daughter-in-law & niece.
2. Telugu	2	Kŏdălŭ	Daughter-in-law.	Kŏdălŭ	Daughter-in-law.
3. Canarese	3	Nănnă sose	My daughter-in-law.	Nănnă sose	My daughter-in-law.
4. Hindî	4	Merí bahú	" "	Meri bahú	" "
5. Bengâlî	5	Amar pootru bodhu	" "	Amar pootru bodhu	" "
6. Marâthî	6	Măzhi sŭn	" "	Mäzhi sŭn	" "
7. Gujârâthî	7	Märi vahu'	" "	Märi vahu	" "
8. Chinese	8	Wo-tĕ seih-fŭ	Son's wife. Lady.	Wo-tĕ seih-fŭ	My son's wife. Lady.
9. Japanese	9	Yo'-ma	My daughter-in-law.	Yo'-ma	My daughter-in-law.
10. Burmese	10	K : ky-na-mă	" "	K : ky-na-mă	" "
11. Karen (Sgau dialect)	11	Yă way	" "	Yă way	" "
12. Karen (Pwo ")	12	Y' dai	" "	Y' dai	" "
13. Karen	13	Yeh deh	" "	Yeh deh	" "
14. Kings Mill Islands	14	Jinapaŭ	Daughter-in-law, my.	Jinapaŭ	Daughter-in-law my.
15. Kusaien	15				
16. Hawaiian	16	Kŭ-ŭ' hŭ-nó-nä wä-hee'-na	My child-in-law, female.	Kŭ-ŭ' hŭ-nó-nä wä-hee'-na	My child-in-law, female.
17. Maori	17				
18. Amazulu (Kafir)	18	U-mä-lo-kä-zä'-nä wä'-me	My daughter-in-law.	U-mä-lo-kä-zä'-nä wä'-me	My daughter-in-law.

		243. My step-father.	Translation.	244. My step-mother.	Translation.
1. Tamil	1		Widow cannot marry.	En sĕrïyă. Täy	My little mother.
2. Telugu	2		" "	Sävïtï tăllï	Step-mother.
3. Canarese	3	Nănnă tănde	My father.	Nănnă täi	My mother.
4. Hindî	4	Merá sasur	My step-father.	Merí sâs	My step-mother.
5. Bengâlî	5			Amar shut maah	" "
6. Marâthî	6	Măzhä dŭsară bäp	" "	Mäzhi säwatra äĕ	" "
7. Gujârathî	7	Märo hormaio bäpa	My other father.	Märi hornai ma	My other mother.
8. Chinese	8	Wo-tĕ how-fŭ	My subsequent father.	Wo-tĕ how-mo	My subsequent mother.
9. Japanese	9	O-to'-tsang	My father.	O-kä'-tsan	My mother.
10. Burmese	10	K : po-twa. ᵇ Badwa	My younger father.	K : mee-dwă. ᵇ Mee-twă	My younger mother.
11. Karen (Sgau dialect)	11	Yă pä-yä	My step-father.	Yä mo-pho-thă	My step-mother (little mo.).
12. Karen (Pwo ")	12	Y' po-yä	" "	Y' mo-yä	My step-mother.
13. Karen	13	Yeh pah-yah	" "	Yeh mo-po-tha	My little mother.
14. Kings Mill Islands	14				
15. Kusaien	15				
16. Hawaiian	16	Kŭ-ŭ' mä-kŭ'-ă kä'-na ko-la'-ä	My step-parent, male.	Kŭ-ŭ' mä-kŭ'-ă wä-hee'-na	My step-parent, female.
17. Maori	17				
18. Amazulu (Kafir)	18	U-bä'-bä	My father.	U-mä'-mä	My mother.

		245. My step-son. (Male speaking.)	Translation.	246. My step-son. (Female speaking.)	Translation.
1. Tamil	1	En mäkän	My son.	En mäkän	My son.
2. Telugu	2	Kŏdŭkŭ	Son.	Kŏdŭkŭ	Son.
3. Canarese	3	Nănnă măgänu	My son.	Nănnă măgänu	My son.
4. Hindî	4	Merá (santela) betá	My (rival) son.	Merá (santela) betá	My (rival) son.
5. Bengâlî	5	Amar shotuto pootra	My step-son.	Amar shotuto pootra	My step-son.
6. Marâthî	6	Mäzhä adalyă gharachă mulaga	" "	Mäzhä adalyă gharachă mulaga	" "
7. Gujârâthî	7	Märo hermaio dikaro	My other son.	Märo hermaio dikaro	My other son.
8. Chinese	8	Wo-tĕ peĕn-e-tsze	My easily gotten child.	Wo-tĕ peĕn-e-tsze	My easily gotten child.
9. Japanese	9	Moo'ko	My son. [son.	Moo'-ko	My son. [son.
10. Burmese	10	K : lin-bä-thä. ᵇ Ma-yä-bä-thä	My husband's son. ᵇ Wife's	K : lin-bä-thä. ᵇMa-yä-bä-thä	My husband's son. Wife's
11. Karen (Sgau dialect)	11	Yă pho-yä-khwă	My step-son (little son).	Yă-pho-yä-khwă	My step-son (little son).
12. Karen (Pwo ")	12	Y' pho-yä-khwă	" " " "	Y' pho-yä-khwă	" " " "
13. Karen	13	Yeh nau-pŭ-wĕh-yah	My step-son.	Yeh dan-pŭ-wĕh-yah	My step-son.
14. Kings Mill Islands	14				
15. Kusaien	15				
16. Hawaiian	16	Kŭ-ŭ' kaï'-kee kä'-na	My child, male.	Kŭ-ŭ' kaï'-kee kä'-na	My child, male.
17. Maori	17				
18. Amazulu (Kafir)	18	In-do-dä'-nä yä'-me	Son of me.	In-do-dä'-nä yä'-me	Son of me.

TABLE III.—*Continued.*

		247. My step-daughter.	Translation.	248. My step-brother. (Male speaking.)	Translation.
1. Tamil	1	En măkăl	My daughter.	En annan (o.), Tambí (y.)....	My older or younger brother.
2. Telugu	2	Kŭthŭrŭ	Daughter.	Annă (o.), Tămmŭdĭ	Older or younger brother.
3. Canarese	3	Nănnă măgălu	My daughter.	Nănnă annă (o.), Tămmă (y.)	My older or younger brother.
4. Hindî	4	Merí (santelí) beti	My (rival) daughter.	Meră (santela) bhai	My (rival) brother.
5. Bengâlî	5	Amar shututo pootry	My step-daughter.	Amar brata	My brother.
6. Marâthî	6	Măzhi adalyă gharachi mulagí	" "		
7. Gujârâthî	7	Mări hermai dikari	My other daughter.	Măro hermaio bhăi	My other brother.
8. Chinese	8	Wo-tĕ peĕn-e-neu	My easily gotten daughter.	Wo-tĕ e-fŭ-heung-te	My of a different father bro.
9. Japanese	9	Moos'-ma	My daughter. [dau.	[khwă	
10. Burmese	10	K: lin-bă-tha-neé. Ma-yă-bă	My husband's dau. Wife's	Yă dan-pu-way-du-khwa-po-	My half-brother.
11. Karen (Sgau dial'ct)	11	Yă pho-yă-mu.........[tha-neé	My step-dau. (little dau.).	Y' dan-pu-wai-khwă-du-khlu	" "
12. Karen (Pwo ")	12	Y' pho-yă-mu	" " " "	Yeh pü-khwa	My younger brother.
13. Karen	13	Yeh dan-pü-wĕh-du-a-pau-mü	My step-daughter.		
14. Kings Mill Islands	14				
15. Kusaien	15				
16. Hawaiian	16	Kŭ-ŭ' kăĭ'-kee wă-hee'-na	My child, female.	Kŭ-ŭ' kăĭ'-kŭ-ă-ă'-nă	My brother.
17. Maori	17				
18. Amazulu (Kafir)	18	In-do-dă-kă'-ze yă'-me	Daughter of me.	U-mfă'-nă wă'-tŭ	Brother of us.

		249. My step-brother. (Female speaking.)	Translation.	250. My step-sister. (Male speaking.)	Translation.
1. Tamil	1	En annan (o.), Tambi (y.)....	My older or younger brother.	En akkärĭ (o.), Tăngay (y.)..	My older or younger sister.
2. Telugu	2	Annă (o.), Tămmŭdĭ	Older or younger brother.	Akkă (o.), Chĕllŭlŭ (y.)	Older or younger sister.
3. Canarese	3	Nănnă annă (o.), Tămmă (y.)	My older or younger brother.	Nănnă akkă (o.), Tăngi (y.).	My older or younger sister.
4. Hindî	4	Meră (santela) bhaí	My (rival) brother.	Merí (santelí) bahin	My (rival) sister.
5. Bengâlî	5	Amar brata	My brother.	Amar bhugny	My sister.
6. Marâthî	6				
7. Gujârâthî	7	Măro hermaio bhăi	My other brother.	Mări hermai băhen	My other sister.
8. Chinese	8	Wo-tĕ e-fŭ-heung-te	My of a different father bro.	Wo-tĕ e-fŭ-tsze-mei	My of a different fath. sister.
9. Japanese	9	[khwă		[mu	
10. Burmese	10	Yă dan-pu-way-du-khwă-po-	My half-brother.	Yă dan-pu-way-du-khwă-po-	My half-sister
11. Karen (Sgau dial'ct)	11	Y' dan-pu-wai-khwă-du-khlu	" "	Y' dan-pu-wai-mu-du-khlu	" "
12. Karen (Pwo ")	12	Yeh pü-khwa	" "	Yeh pü-mü	My younger sister.
13. Karen	13				
14. Kings Mill Islands	14				
15. Kusaien	15				
16. Hawaiian	16	Kŭ-ŭ' kŭ-nă'-na	My brother.	Kŭ-ŭ' kăĭ-kŭ wă-hee'-na	My sister.
17. Maori	17				
18. Amazulu (Kafir)	18	U'-mfă'-nă wă'-tŭ	Brother of us.	U-dă'-dă wă'-tŭ	Sister of us.

		251. My step-sister. (Female speaking.)	Translation.	252. Two fathers-in-law to each other.	Translation.
1. Tamil	1	En Akkärĭ (o.), Tăngay (y.)..	My older or younger sister.	Vĭyyăngkŭdă	Same.
2. Telugu	2	Akka (o.), Chĕllŭlŭ (y.)	" " " "	Băgăra	"
3. Canarese	3	Nănnă ăkkă (o.), Tăngi (y.).	" " " "		
4. Hindî	4	Merí (santelí) băhin	My (rival) sister.	Bhye	Brothers.
5. Bengâlî	5	Amar bhugny	My sister.	Vyăhĭ	
6. Marâthî	6			Vavar	
7. Gujârâthî	7	Mări hermai băhen	My other sister.	Tsin-kĕa	Related family.
8. Chinese	8	Wo-tĕ e-fŭ-tsze-mei	My of a different fath. sister.		Not related.
9. Japanese	9			Ka-mee ka-met	Equal of me.
10. Burmese	10			Dan-do-po-khwă	" "
11. Karen (Sgau dial'ct)	11	Yă dan-pu-way-du-khwa-po-mu	My half-sister.	Y' do-khwă	
12. Karen (Pwo ")	12	Y' dan-pu-wai-mu-du-khlu	" "	Dan-do	
13. Karen	13	Yeh pü-mü	My younger sister.		
14. Kings Mill Islands	14				
15. Kusaien	15			Pă-lŭ'-nă	
16. Hawaiian	16	Kŭ-ŭ' kŭ-ă-ă'-na	My sister.		
17. Maori	17				
18. Amazulu (Kafir)	18	U-dă'-dă wă'-tŭ	Sister of us.	U-mle-ngă'-ne wă'-me	My equal.

TABLE III.—*Continued.*

		253. Two mothers-in-law to each other.	Translation.	254. Brother-in-law. (My husband's brother.)	Translation.
1. Tamil	1			En mäittunän	My brother-in-law & cousin.
2. Telugu.............	2	Viyyămpŭrălu......................	Same.	Băvă (o.), Mărădĭ (y.).........	Brother-in-law and cousin.
3. Canarese	3	Băgăra	"	N. bhäva, meidănă (y.)	My brother-in-law & cousin.
4. Hindî................	4			Merä dewar	My brother-in-law.
5. Bengâlî	5	Bayen.............................	Sisters.	Amar bhashue (o.), Dăwor (y.)	" "
6. Marâthî..............	6	Vihin.............................		Măzhä bhäwä (o.), Dïr (y.)..	" "
7. Gujârâthî	7	Vavari.............................		Măro jetto (o), Diar (y.)....	" "
8. Chinese	8	Tsin-kea-neang-mo.............	Related family's lady moth.	Wo-tĕ ta-poh-yay..............	My husband's elder brother.
				Wo-tĕ leaon-shuh-tsze..........	My husband's junior bro.
9. Japanese	9	——	Not related.	O-to'-to	My younger brother.
10. Burmese.............	10	Ka-mee-ka-met....................	Equal of me.	K: kai-o (o.), Mat (y.).........	My brother-in-law e. or y.
11. Karen (Sgau dial'ct)	11	Dan-do-po-mu.....................	" "		My brother.
12. Karen (Pwo ")	12	Y'do-mu	——	Y' do..............................	My brother-in-law.
13. Karen..............	13	Dan-do-mu		Yeh khjee-neh-pan-khwa	" "
14. Kings Mill Islands	14				
15. Kusaien..............	15				
16. Hawaiian	16	Pă-lŭ'-nä...........................	——	Kŭ-ŭ' kä'-na....................	My husband.
17. Maori	17				
18. Amazulu (Kafir)...	18	U-mle-ngă'-ne wă'-me	My equal.	U-myă'-nä wä'-tŭ	Husband of us.

		255. Brother-in-law. (My sister's husband.) (Male speaking.)	Translation.	256. Brother-in-law. (My sister's husband.) (Female speaking.)	Translation.
1. Tamil..............	1	En mäittunän	My bro.-in-law and cousin.	En attan (o.), Maichchăn (y.)	My bro.-in-law and cousin.
2. Telugu.............	2	Băvă	Brother-in-law and cousin.	Băvă	Brother-in-law and cousin.
3. Canarese	3	N. bhäva (o.), Meidănă (y.) .	My bro.-in-law and cousin.	N. bhäva (o.), Meidănă (y.).	My bro.-in-law and cousin.
4. Hindî................	4	Merä bahïnoi......................	My brother-in-law.	Merä bahïnoi......................	My brother-in-law.
5. Bengâlî	5	Amar bhugny poty..............	" "	Amar bhugny poty..............	" "
6. Marâthî..............	6	Mäzhä mëhunä.....................	" "	Mäzhä bhäwajï.....................	" "
7. Gujârâthî	7	Märo baneni.......................	" "	Märo baneni.......................	" "
8. Chinese..............	8	Wo-tĕ taze/mei -fŭ	My elder/younger sister's husb.	Wo-tĕ taze/mei -fŭ.	My elder/younger sister's husb.
9. Japanese	9	A'-nee	My elder brother.	A'-nee	My elder brother.
10. Burmese.............	10	K : Youk-pä.......................	My brother-in-law.	K : kai-o	My brother-in-law.
11. Karen (Sgau dial'ct)	11		My brother.		My brother.
12. Karen (Pwo ")	12	Y' do..............................	My brother-in-law.	Y' do..............................	My brother-in-law.
13. Karen..............	13	Yeh khyée-neh-pan-khwa......	" "	Yeh khyée-neh-pan-khwa......	" "
14. Kings Mill Islands	14	Eïdïkŭ..............................	Sister's husband my.	Eïdïkŭ..............................	Sister's husband my.
15. Kusaien..............	15				
16. Hawaiian.............	16	Kŭ-ŭ' käï'-ko-á-ka..............	My brother-in-law.	Kŭ-ŭ' kä'-na....................	My husband.
17. Maori	17				
18. Amazulu (Kafir)...	18	U-mkwä-myä'-nä wä'-tŭ......	Brother-in-law of us.	U-mkwä-myä'-nä wä'-tŭ........	Brother-in-law of us.

		257. Brother-in-law. (My wife's brother.)	Translation.	258. My wife's sister's husband.	Translation.
1. Tamil..............	1	En mäittunän	My bro.-in-law and cousin.	En sakălăn.........................	My bro.-in-law and cousin.
2. Telugu	2	Băvă	Brother-in-law and cousin.	Săddăkŭdŭ........................	Brother-in-law.
3. Canarese	3	Nănnä bhävameidă..............	My bro.-in-law and cousin.	Nănnä shäddăgănu..............	My brother-in-law.
4. Hindî................	4	Merä sálá	My brother-in-law.	Merä sárú	" "
5. Bengâlî	5	Amar shala	" "	Amar bhoyra bhye..............	" "
6. Mârâthî..............	6	Mäzhä mëhunä. ᵇ Sala	" "	Mäzhä sadu. ᵇ Sad bhäŭ	" "
7. Gujârâthî	7	Märo salo	" "	Märo sadhu	" "
8. Chinese..............	8	Wo-tĕ ta/leaon -kew	My elder or y'nger brother.	Wo-tĕ-kin-heung.................	My husb. of a wife's sister.
				Wo-tĕ-kin-te.....................	My husb. of a y'nger sister.
9. Japanese	9	A'-nee	My elder brother.		
10. Burmese.............	10	K : youk-pä.......................	My brother-in-law.	K : e-ko-tau.....................	My related brother.
11. Karen (Sgau dial'ct)	11		My brother.		My brother.
12. Karen (Pwo ")	12	Y' deo	My brother-in-law.		
13. Karen..............	13	Yeh khyée-neh-pan-khwa	" "	Yeh khyée-neh-pan-khwa.....	My brother-in-law.
14. Kings Mill Islands	14	Bŭjïkau.............................	Wife's brother my.		
15. Kusaien..............	15				
16. Hawaiian.............	16	Kŭ-ŭ' käï-ko-á-ka...............	My brother-in-law.	Kŭ-ŭ' pŭ-nä-lŭ'-ä..............	My intimate companion.
17. Maori	17				
18. Amazulu (Kafir)...	18	U-mlä'-mŭ wä'-ne.................	Wife's brother of me.	U-mkwä-myä'-nä wä'-tŭ.......	Brother-in-law of us.

TABLE III.—*Continued.*

		259. My husband's sister's husband.	Translation.	260. Sister-in-law. (My wife's sister.)	Translation.
1. Tamil	1	En sakotaran	My bro.-in-law and cousin.	En korlunti (o.), Mäittŭni (y.)	My sister-in-law and cousin.
2. Telugu	2	Annä (o.) Tămmŭdŭ (y.)	Older or younger brother.	Vădŭiĕ (o.), Mărădălă (y.)	Sis.-in-law (o. or y.) & cous.
3. Canarese	3	Nanna ännä (o.), Tămmä (y.)	My older or younger brother.	N. attige (o.), Nädini (y.)	My sister-in-law (o. or y.) &
4. Hindî	4			Merí sáli	My sister-in-law. [cousin.
5. Bengalî	5			Amar shaly	" "
6. Marâthî	6	Mäzhä nanandă	My brother-in-law.	Mäzhi mehŭnï. ᵇ Sali	" "
7. Gujârâthî	7	Märo nandoi	" "	Märi sali	" "
8. Chinese	8	Wo-tĕ kŭ-chang-kung	My husband's sister's husb.	Wo-tĕ ta-ĕ (o.), Leaon-ĕ (y.)	My wife's eld. or y. sister.
9. Japanese	9	A'-nih	My elder sister.	A'-nih	My elder sister.
10. Burmese	10	K: kai-o	My brother-in-law.	K: ma-see (o.), Kai-mă (y.)	My sister-in-law (e. or y.)
11. Karen (Sgau dial'ct)	11		My brother.		My sister.
12. Karen (Pwo ")	12			Y' do	My sister-in-law.
13. Karen	13	Yeh khyée-neh-pan-klïwa	My brother-in-law.	Yeh khyée-neh-pan-mŭ	" "
14. Kings Mill Islands	14	Büjïkau	Husband's sister's husband.	Eïdïkŭ	Wife's sister my.
15. Kusaien	15				
16. Hawaiian	16			Kŭ-ŭ' wä-hee'-na	My wife.
17. Maori	17				
18. Amazulu (Kafir)	18	U-mkwä-myä'-nä wä'-tŭ	Brother-in-law of us.	U-mlä'-mŭ wä'-me	Wife's sister of me.

		261. Sister-in-law. (My husband's sister.)	Translation.	262. Sister-in-law. (My brother's wife.) (Male speaking.)	Translation.
1. Tamil	1	En nättänar	My sister-in-law.	En anni (o.), Mäittŭni (y.)	My sister-in-law.
2. Telugu	2	Adä bïddă. ᵇ Vädïnĕ	Sister-in-law and cousin.	Vădŭiĕ	My sister-in-law and cousin
3. Canarese	3	Nännä attige (o.), Nädini (y.)	My sister-in-law and cousin.	N. attige (o.), Nädini (y.)	" " "
4. Hindî	4	Merï nand	My sister-in-law.	Meri bhánaj	My sister-in-law.
5. Bengâlî	5	Amar nonod	" "	Amar bhaj	" "
6. Marâthî	6	Mäzhi nanand	" "	Mäzhé bhäuzaï	" "
7. Gujârâthî	7	Märi nanäd	" "	Märi bhävi	" "
8. Chinese	8	Wo-tĕ ta-kŭ (o.), Seaon-kŭ-tse	My grt. and lit. sister-in-law.	Wo-tĕ saon-tze wo-tĕ shin-tsze	My eld. or young. bro.'s wife.
9. Japanese	9				
10. Burmese	10	K: young-mä'	My sister-in-law.	K: ma-ree (o.), Kai-mä (y.)	My sister-in-law (e. or y.)
11. Karen (Sgau dial'ot)	11		My sister.		My sister.
12. Karen (Pwo ")	12	Y' do	My sister-in-law.	Y' do	My sister-in-law.
13. Karen	13	Yeh khyée-neh-pan-mü	" "	Yeh khyée-noh-pan-mŭ	" "
14. Kings Mill Islands	14	Kaïnäpaŭ	Husband's sister my.	Eïdïkŭ	Brother's wife my.
15. Kusaien	15				
16. Hawaiian	16	Kŭ ŭ' käï'-ko-á-ka wä-hee'-na	My sister-in-law.	Kŭ-ŭ' wä-hee'-na	My wife.
17. Maori	17				
18. Amazulu (Kafir)	18	U-myä'-nä wä'me	My husband (so used).	U-m-kä'-me	My wife.

		263. Sister-in-law. (My brother's wife.) (Female speaking.)	Translation.	264. My husband's brother's wife.	Translation.
1. Tamil	1	En anni (o.), Maittuni (y.)	My sister-in-law.	En orakatti	My sister-in-law.
2. Telugu	2	Vädïnĕ	My sister-in-law and cousin.	Todïködälŭ	Sister-in-law.
3. Canarese	3	N. attige (o.), Nädini (y.)	" " "	Nännä äkkä (o.), Tängi (y.)	My elder or younger sister.
4. Hindî	4	Meri bhánaj	My sister-in-law.	Merï dewarám. ᵇ Icthäni	My sister-in-law.
5. Bengâlî	5	Amar bhaj	" "	Amar ja	" "
6. Marâthî	6	Mäzhi bhäusaï	" "	Mäzhi zäŭ	" "
7. Gujârâthî	7	Märi bhävi	" "	Märi jetti	" "
8. Chinese	8	Wo-tĕ tsin-tsze	My eld. or young. bro.'s wife.	Wo-tĕ ta-mo (o.), A-shin (y.)	My hus.'s o. or y. bro.'s wife.
9. Japanese	9				
10. Burmese	10	K: young-mä.	My sister-in-law.	K: e-mä-tau	My related sister.
11. Karen (Sgau dial'ct)	11		My sister.		My sister.
12. Karen (Pwo ")	12	Y' do	My sister-in-law.		
13. Karen	13	Yeh khyée-neh-pan-mü	" "	Yeh khyée-neh-pan-mü	My sister-in-law.
14. Kings Mill Islands	14	Kaïnäpaŭ	Brother's wife my.	Eidïkŭ	Husband's brother's wife my
15. Kusaien	15				
16. Hawaiian	16	Kŭ-ŭ' käï'-ko-á-ka	My sister-in-law.	Kŭ-ŭ' pŭ-nä-lŭ'-tä	My intimate companion.
17. Maori	17				
18. Amazulu (Kafir)	18			U-myä'-nä wä'-tŭ	

TABLE III.—*Continued.*

		265. My wife's brother's wife.	Translation.	266. Widow.	Translation.
1. Tamil	1	En tamakay (o.), Tăngăy (y.)	My older or younger sister.	Kiempun.............................	Widow.
2. Telugu	2	Akkă (o.), Chĕllŭlŭ (y.)	Older or younger sister.	Munda or vĭdăvă.................	Widow (Sanskrit).
3. Canarese.............	3	Nănnă ăkkă (o.), Tăngi (y.).	My older or younger sister.	Vĕdăve.................................	" "
4. Hindî	4	Merí sarhaj	My sister-in-law.	Rănd	Widow.
5. Bengâlî	5	Amar ja...............................	" "	Rewa	"
6. Marâthî...............	6	Mazhi bahŭi.........................	My sister.	Vidawă	"
7. Gujârâthî.............	7			Vidhava	"
8. Chinese	8	Wo-te tsin-tze.....................	My wife's brother's wife.	Kwa-fŭ	Lone woman.
9. Japanese.............	9			Yă-mo'-me-on-mä	Widow.
10. Burmese	10	K: youk-pa-ma-yă...............	My brother-in-law's wife.	Mok-so-ınă............................	"
11. Karen (Sgau dialect)	11		My sister.	Mu-kă-may...........................	A bereaved female.
12. Karen (Pwo ")	12			Mu-k'-mai.............................	" " "
13. Karen	13	Yeh kbyĕe-neh-pan-mŭ.........	My sister-in-law.	Mŭ-k-meh.............................	
14. Kings Mill Islands..	14	Eidikŭ.................................	Wife's brother's wife.		
15. Kusaien	15				
16. Hawaiian	16	Kŭ-ŭ' wä-hee'-na.................	My wife.	Wä-hee'-na kä'-na mä'-ka.....	Woman, husband dead.
17. Maori.................	17				
18. Amazulu (Kafir)	18	U-m-lä'-mŭ wä'-mŭ.............		U-mfä-lo-kä'-ze...................	

		267. Widower.	Translation.	268. Twins.	Translation.
1. Tamil	1			Dithambathie	Twins (Sanskrit).
2. Telugu................	2	Apătnĭkŭdŭ........................	Widower.	Amădălŭ...............................	Twins.
3. Canarese.............	3	Vedăvă...............................	Widower (Sanskrit).	Avvali iăvăli	"
4. Hindî	4	Rănduă..............................	Widower.	Jwarwăṇ	"
5. Bengâlî	5			Jomuch	"
6. Marâthî	6	Vidŭr.................................	"	Zŭwal.................................	"
7. Gujârâthî..............	7			Jada....................................	Paired ones.
8. Chinese	8	Kwa-nau............................	Lone man.	Shwang-sung.......................	Double or rather a pair birth.
9. Japanese.............	9	Yă-mo'-me. O-to'-ko...........	Widower.	Fŭ-tä'-go	Twins.
10. Burmese	10	Mok-so-bo...........................	"	A-hm-wä'.............................	"
11. Karen (Sgau dialect)	11	Kă-may..............................	A bereaved male.	Ka-khie................................	"
12. Karen (Pwo ")	12	Khwä-k-mai.........................	" " "	M'-khye...............................	"
13. Karen	13	Khwa-k-meh.........................		T-lhĕk	"
14. Kings Mill Islands..	14				
15. Kusaien	15				
16. Hawaiian	16	Kä'-na wa-hee'-na mä'-ka.....	Husband, wife dead.	Mä-ho'-a	"
17. Maori	17		[ers.		
18. Amazulu (Kafir) ...	18	No tenu..............................	Polygamists seldom widow-	A-mä-wä'-lä.........................	"

SUPPLEMENT TO PART III.

Two schedules, the Tongan and the Fijian, were received after a portion of Table III. was stereotyped, and therefore too late for insertion. They were filled out with much care and precision, by the Rev. Lorimer Fison, an English missionary resident at the Fiji Islands, at the instance of Prof. Goldwin Smith, who very kindly undertook to procure for me the Fijian system of relationship. Some notice of the contents of these schedules is due to their importance, as well as to the unexpected presence of Turanian characteristics in the system of these Malayan nations. Their proper place in the Table is number 18 and 19. The interesting observations of Mr. Fison are also worthy of careful attention. These together seem to justify a formal note as a supplement to Part III.

Horatio Hale, author of the volume on the Ethnography and Philology of the United States Exploring Expedition under Charles Wilkes, U. S. N., places the Tonga Islands within, and the Fiji Islands without, the boundary line circumscribing Polynesia. The latter are also without Micronesia. With respect to the former he remarks: "The people of the Tonga or friendly group, though belonging to the Polynesian family, form a class apart from the rest. This is seen in their language, which differs strikingly in several points from the others, especially in the article, the pronouns, and the passive voice of the verb. Several of their customs are, moreover, peculiar, such as that of infant sacrifice of cutting off a finger to appease the gods. * * * It is evident that these islanders have received modifications in their language and usages which have not affected the rest." With respect to the Fijian language Dr. Prichard observes: "The grammatical structure of this language has been investigated by Mr. Norris. * * * The result to which he has arrived is that the Fijian is really a Polynesian dialect, though offering peculiarities not found in any other, and having a vocabulary so peculiarly modified that it requires some examination to perceive the resemblances, while the Polynesian idioms display the proofs of their affinity at a glance The Fijians are a very interesting people, of almost black complexion, with frizzled but not woolly hair, very rude and savage in their habits, but possessed of greater physical and mental energy than any of the fair Polynesians. In natural capabilities they seem to be superior to any other tribe of the Pacific, though perhaps descended from a mixture of the Tongan race with some Papua tribe. This hypothesis, however, was rejected by Baron Willian Von Humboldt, who observed that the Fijian language displays affinity to the western forms of the Malayo-Polynesian idiom, viz., the

Madecassian and Malayan, while receding from the peculiarities of the Eastern or Oceanic idioms." (Natural Hist. of Man, Third Ed., 664.)

These statements concerning the Tongans and Fijians may, perhaps, render less remarkable the deviations in their system of relationship from the Hawaiian form, and its sensible approximation to the Turanian.

1. Tongan. There are terms in this dialect for grand parent, *Kui;* for father and mother, *Tämai* and *Fae;* for son and daughter, *Fóha* and *Ofefíne;* and for grand child, *Mokopúna.*

As with the other Malayan dialects the Tongan fails to indicate the fraternal and sororal relationships in the twofold form of elder and younger with entire completeness.

Elder brother	(*male speaking*)	*Taokete.*	(*Female speaking*)		*Tuaga'ani.* ᵇ *Taokete.*
Younger brother	" "	*Tehina.*	" "		*Tuaga'ani.* ᵇ *Tehina.*
Elder sister	" "	*Tuofefine.* ᵇ *Taokete.*	" "		*Taokete.*
Younger sister	" "	*Tuofefine.* ᵇ *Tehina.*	" "		*Tehina.*

A man calls his elder brother *Taokete,* and a women calls her elder sister the same; so a man calls his younger brother *Tehina,* and a woman calls her younger sister the same. Precisely the same use of terms is found in the Hawaiian and also in Fijian. It thus appears that whilst the males distinguish their brothers into elder and younger, and not their sisters, the females distinguish their sisters into elder and younger, and not their brothers. The additional terms are anomolous.

In the first collateral line male, *Ego* a male, my brother's son and daughter are my son and daughter, *Fóha* and *Ofefine;* and their children are my grandchildren. But my sister's son and daughter are my nephew and niece *Ilamutu,* the term being in common gender. This is the first Turanian characteristic.

With myself a female my brother's son and daughter are my nephew and niece, *Ilamutu;* whilst my sister's son and daughter are my boy and girl, *Tama* and *Tahina.* The children of each are my grandchildren.

In the second collateral line, my father's brother is my father; his children are my brothers and sisters, elder or younger; the children of the former, myself a male, are my sons and daughters, of the latter are my nephews and nieces; and the children of each are my grandchildren. With myself a female, those above who are nephews and nieces become sons and daughters, and *vice versâ.*

My mother's sister is my mother; and her children and descendants follow in the same relationship as in the last case.

My father's sister is my aunt, *Mehikitage.* This again is Turanian. My mother's brother is my uncle, *Tuajina,* which in like manner is Turanian. For the children of my uncle and aunt there are no specific relationships. Mr. Fison remarks that " there are no specific terms for any of these, and yet they are considered relations. Thus, I being a male, my son will be *Tautehina* [*i. e.,* brother] with my father's sister's son's son. It is singular that the Tongans should have no specific term for cousin, for *Tama amekitega* = son or daughter of my aunt."

In the third collateral line my grandfather's brother is my grandfather; his son is my father; his son is my brother; the son of the latter is my son, and his son is my grandchild.

2. Fijian.   The schedule is filled in the dialect of the Rewas, one of the Fijian nations.   There are terms for grandparent, *Mbu'*; for father and mother, *Tămă'* and *Tină'*; for son and daughter *Luve'*, to which *tangane* = male, and *ălăwe* = female are added to distinguish sex.

The fraternal and sororal relationships are expressed as follows :—

Elder brother	(*male speaking*)	*Tuăkă'*.	(*Female speaking*)	*Ngănĕ'*.
Younger brother	"	" *Tăthĭ'*.	"	" *Ngănĕ'*.
Elder sister	"	" *Ngănĕ'*.	"	" *Tuăkă'*.
Younger sister	"	" *Ngănĕ'*.	"	" *Tăthĭ'*.

It will be seen, as in the Tongan and Hawaiian, that the males distinguish their brothers into elder and younger, and not their sisters; whilst the females distinguish their sisters into elder and younger, and not their brothers; and that the males use the same terms for elder and younger brother which the females apply to elder and younger sister.

In the first collateral line, *Ego* a male, my brother's son and daughter are my son and daughter, *Luvĕ'*, the term being in common gender; and their children are my grandchildren, *Măkubu'*; whilst my sister's son and daughter are my nephew and niece, *Vungo'*, the term being in common gender, each of them calling me the same, thus showing that the relationship is reciprocal.   This is the first Turanian characteristic.   The children of these nephews and nieces are my grandchildren.

With myself a female my brother's son and daughter are my nephew and niece, *Vungo'*; whilst my sister's children are my sons and daughters; and the children of the latter are my grandchildren.

In the second collateral line, my father's brother is my father, *Tămă'*; and his children are my brothers and sisters, elder or younger.   With myself a male, the children of these collateral brothers are my sons and daughters, of these collateral sisters are my nephews and nieces; and their children are my grandchildren.   With myself a female, those above who are nephews and nieces become sons and daughters, and *vice versâ*.

My mother's sister is my mother, *Tină'*; and her children and descendants follow in the same relationships as in the previous branch.

My father's sister is my aunt, *Vungo'*.   This is a second Turanian characteristic.   With myself a male the son and daughter of this aunt are my male and female cousin, *Tăvăle'* and *Dăvola'*; and with myself a female, the same, *Dăvola* and *Raivä*.   These terms are so rendered by Mr. Fison.   The term *Tăvăle'* signifies a brother-in-law, and is applied by a man to his wife's brother; and *Raivă'* signifies a sister-in-law, and is applied by a female to her brother's wife.   Such was doubtless the primary use of these terms, and it therefore must govern.   It is not probable that the relationship of cousin, as a distinct and definite relationship, is known amongst the Fijians.   The son and daughter of my male cousin, myself a male, are my nephew and niece, and of my female cousin are my son and daughter; whilst with myself a female these relationships are reversed.   In this respect the Fijian system agrees with the Tamilian, and differs from the Seneca-Iroquois.   The children of the persons last named are my grandchildren.

My mother's brother is my uncle, *Vungo'*.   This is also a Turanian characteristic.

It will be noticed that a single term is employed to express the four relationships of uncle and aunt, nephew and niece; and that it is an arrested or defective development of them. The striking fact is that the introduction of a new and perhaps foreign element into the system touched the precise relationships, and no other, which mark the transition from the Malayan into the Turanian form. The remainder of this line is a counterpart of the one last above described.

In the third collateral line my grandfather's brother is my grandfather; his son is father; his son is my brother, elder or younger; and the son and grandson of this brother are my son and grandson. The other branches of this line are counterparts of the corresponding branches of the second.

The marriage relationships both in Tongan and Fijian tend in a striking manner to confirm the position elsewhere taken that compound marriages in communal families prevailed universally in the primitive ages when the classificatory system was formed.

Take the following illustrations:—

	Tongan.	Fijian.	Hawaiian.
My brother's wife (m. s).	Unoho, My wife.	Noqu Dăqu', My back.	Wăhena, My wife.
My wife's sister (m. s).	Unoho, " wife.	Noqu Dăqu', " back.	Wăhena, " wife.
My husband's brother (f. s).	Unoho, " husband.	Wătequ', " husband.	Kane, " husband.
My sister's husband (f. s).	Unoho, " husband.	Noqu Dăqu', " back.	Kane, " husband.
My father's brother's son's wife (m. s).	Unoho, " wife.	Noqu Dăqu', " back.	Wăhena, " wife.
My mother's sister's son's wife (m. s).	Unoho, " wife.	Noqu Dăqu', " back.	Wăhena, " wife.
My father's brother's daughter's husband (f. s).	Unoho, " husband.	Noqu Dăqu', " back.	Kai-ko-e-ka, brother-in-law.
My mother's sister's daughter's husband (f. s).	Unoho, " husband.	Noqu Daqu', " back.	Kai-ko-e-ka-y, brother-in-law.

Wherever the relationship of wife is found in the collateral line that of husband must be recognized in the lineal; and more than this, if the wife of my father's brother's son is my wife as well as his, then my wife is doubtless his wife as well as mine.

With respect to the term *Noqu Dăqu* it must be understood as an express denial of the conjugal relationship; and as a probable substitute for *Wătequ* = husband or wife. Mr. Fison significantly remarks (Note E): "*Noqu Dăqu'*. This appears = brother-in-law or sister-in-law. Some natives gave me *Wătequ* in those places where *Noqui Dăqu'* appears; and it is evident *Noqui Dăqu'* is *Wătiqu* in theory from the fact that the children of *Noqu Dăqu'* are *Luvequ*," i. e., my children.

The presence of a Turanian element in the Tongan and Fijian systems is the remarkable fact concerning it. How is it to be explained? The Tongan has the relationship of uncle, restricted to the mother's brothers, that of aunt restricted to the father's sisters; and that of nephew and niece restricted to the children of a man's sisters, and of a woman's brothers. In like manner the Fijian has the four relationships restricted to the same several classes of persons, but expressed by a single term in common gender, *Vungo'*; which, as an inchoate form, might be explained by the desuetude of intermarriage between brothers and sisters followed by a partial recognition of the consequent change of descents. But the Tongan, it must be admitted, rises nearly to the Turanian standard. It presents the vital question whether this change was an organic growth within the Malayan system, through the progressive experience of the Malayan family; or an intrusive element brought in from Turanian sources. It will be seen at once that the antecedent history of both the Tongan and Fijian nations is necessary to a solution of the question. If the special linguistical and physical characteristics of these nations (who occupy groups of contiguous islands) noticed by Messrs. Hale and Prichard indicate a foreign element in their blood, and that element was Turanian, it would afford a satisfactory explanation. Again, this precise change comes through the tribal organization, which by abolishing the intermarriage of brothers and sisters touches the relationships in question, and no others. This organization is found in an incomplete form both among the Tongans and Fijians, as will be seen in the notes of Mr. Fison. It also prevails amongst the Kusaiens. From this fact it becomes also material to know whether it sprang up independently in these subdivisions of the Malayan family, or was propagated into it from Turanian sources. When the system of the Malayan family is completely ascertained it will reveal its own history.

COMPARATIVE TABLE OF THE TONGAN AND FIJIAN SYSTEM OF RELATIONSHIP.

Made by Rev. Lorimer Fison, Rewa, Fiji, December, 1869.

Native pronouns.—Tongan: *Eku* or *Hoku* = my. Fijian: *Nónggu* or *Nĕnggu* suffixed = my.

Description of persons.	Relationship in Tongan. (Friendly Islanders.)	Translation.	Relationship in Rewan. (Fijian.)	Translation.
1. My father¹	Eku tamái	My father.	Tāmă'nggu	My father.
2. " mother	Eku fa'e	" mother.	Tină'nggu	" mother.
3. " son	Hŏ'ku fŏ'ha	" son.	Luvĕ'nggu tăngă'ne	" child, male.
4. " daughter	Hŏ'ku ofefi'ne	" daughter.	Luvĕ'nggu ălăwă	" child, female.
5. " grandson	Hŏ'ku mokopū'na	" grandson.	Mă'kubū'nggu tăngăne	" grandchild, male.
6. " granddaughter	Hŏ'ku mokopū'na	" granddaughter.	Mă'kubū'nggu alăwa	" grandchild, female.
7. " great grandson	Hŏ'ku mokopuna ua	" grandson-two.	Nŏngu vū (see Remarks a)	" source.
8. " great granddaughter	Hŏ'ku mokopuna ua	" granddaughter-two.	Nŏngu vū	" "
9. " great great grandson	Hŏ'ku mokopuna tolu	" grandson-three.	Nŏngu vū	" "
10. " great great granddaughter	Hŏ'ku mokopuna tolu	" gr'ddaughter-three.	Nŏngu vū	" "
11. " elder brother (*male speaking*)	Hoku taokete	" elder brother.	Tŭăkă'nggu	" elder brother.
12. " " " (*female speaking*)	Hoku taokete, or hoku tuoga'ani	" elder brother.	Ngă'nĕ'nggu	" " "
13. " elder sister (*m. s.*)	Hoku taokete, or hoku tuofefine	" elder sister.	Ngă'nĕ'nggu	" elder sister.
14. " " " (*f. s.*)	Hoku taokete	" " "	Tŭăkă'nggu	" " "
15. " younger brother (*m. s.*)	Hoku tehina	" younger brother.	Tăthĭ'nggu	" younger brother.
16. " " " (*f. s*)	Hoku tehina, or tuoga'ani	" " "	Ngă'nénggu	" " "
17. " " sister (*m. s.*)	Hoku tehina, or tuofefine	" younger sister.	Ngă'nénggu	" younger sister.
18. " " " (*f. s.*)	Hoku tehina	" " "	Tăthĭnggu³	" " "
19. " brothers	Hoku gahi toko'ua²	" brothers, &c.		
20. " sisters	See 19.			
21. " father's brother	Eku tamai	" father.	Tămă'nggu	" father.
22. " father's elder brother	Eku tamai	" "	Tămă'nggu lăvu	" great father.
23. " father's younger brother	Eku tamai	" "	Tămă'nggu lĭlĭ	" little father.
24. " father's brother's wife	Eku fae	" mother.	Tĭ'nă'nngu lavu or lailai	" gt. (or lit.) mother.
25. " father's sister	Hoku mehékitaga	" aunt.	Vungŏ'-nggu	" aunt.
26. " father's sister's husband (*See No. 68*)	Hoku matāpula	" chief.	Vungŏ'-nggu	" uncle.
27. " mother's brother	Hoku tuajina	" uncle.	Vungŏ'-nggu	" "
28. " mother's brother's wife	Eku fae	" mother.	Vungŏ'-nggu	" aunt.
29. " mother's sister	Eku fae	" "	Tină'nggu	" mother.
30. " mother's elder sister	Eku fae	" "	Tină'nggu lăvu	" great mother.
31. " mother's younger sister	Eku fae	" "	Tină'nggu lĭlĭ	" little mother.
32. " mother's sister's husband	Eku tamai	" father.	Tămă'nggu	" father.
33. " brother's son (*m. s.*)	Eku foha	" son.	Luvénggu	" son.
34. " brother's son's wife (*m. s.*)	Eku ofefine	" daughter.	Vungŏ'nggu	" niece.
35. " brother's daughter (*m. s.*)	Eku ofefine	" "	Luvénggu	" daughter.
36. " brother's daughter's husband (*m. s.*)	Hoku foha	" son.	Vungŏ'nggu	" nephew.
37. " brother's grandson (*m. s.*)	Hoku mokopuna	" grandson.	Makubunggu	" grandson.
38. " brother's granddaughter (*m. s.*)	Hoku mokopuna	" granddaughter.	Makubunggu	" granddaughter.
39. " brother's great grandson (*m. s.*)	Hoku mokopuna ua	" great grandson.	Noqu vu	" source.
40. " brother's great granddaughter (*m. s.*)	Hoku mokopuna ua	" gt. granddaughter.	Noqu vu	" "
41. " sister's son (*m. s.*)	Hoku ilamutu	" nephew.	Vungŏ'nggu, or noqu vasu, or noqu vătŭ'vu⁴	" nephew.
42. " sister's son's wife (*m. s.*)	Eku fanau⁵	" child.	Luvĕ'nggu (?)	" daughter.
43. " sister's daughter (*m. s.*)	Hoku ilamutu	" niece.	Vungŏnggu	" niece.
44. " sister's daughter's husband (*m. s.*)	Eku fanau	" child.	Luvĕ nggu	" son.
45. " sister's grandson (*m. s.*)	Hoka mokopuna	" grandson.	Mă'kubúnggu	" grandson.
46. " sister's granddaughter (*m. s.*)	Hoka mokopuna	" granddaughter.	Mă'kubúnggu	" granddaughter.
47. " sister's great grandson (*m. s.*)	Hoka mokopuna ua	" great grandson.	Nŏnggu vu	" source.
48. " sister's great granddaughter (*m. s.*)	Hoka mokopuna ua	" gt. granddaughter.	Nŏnggu vu	" "
49. " sister's son (*f. s.*)	Eku tama⁶	" boy	Luvénggu	" son.
50. " sister's son's wife (*f. s.*)	Eku tahine⁶	" girl.	Vungŏ'nggu	" niece.
51. " sister's daughter (*f. s.*)	Eku takine	" "	Luvénggu	" daughter.
52. " sister's daughter's husband (*f. s.*)	Eku tama	" boy.	Vungŏ'nggu	" nephew.
53. " sister's grandson (*f. s.*)	Hoka mokopuna	" grandson.	Mă'kabúnggu	" grandson.
54. " sister's granddaughter (*f. s.*)	Hoka mokopuna	" granddaughter.	Mă'kabŭnggu	" granddaughter.

¹ The arrangement of the working schedule is followed in the Table.

² Gahi tokohua includes sisters also, children of father's brothers and mother's sisters, and in fact all the tautchina. Gahi is but the sign of the plural. There is no specific term for "brothers" or "sisters" separately, though, speaking loosely, I may call my brothers or my sisters hoku gahi toko'ua.

³ If I am the eldest, I can speak of them as tathinggu; if the youngest, as tuakanggu; but there is no one word by which I can speak of them all, if I be not either the eldest or the youngest. So also a woman cannot speak of her sisters by any one word, unless she be the eldest or the youngest. But a male can speak of his (all his) sisters as ngănĕ-na = his sisters. So also can a woman speak of all her brothers as ngäne-na = her brothers.

⁴ In future I shall write vungonggu only.

⁵ Eku fanau means literally my children, all my children; but it is used thus in the singular for this relationship and for others similar.

⁶ These are considered to be "my children," though they are thus called "my boy," "my girl." My son's wife is "eku tahine" only while she is betrothed to him, which may be from earliest childhood. When they are married she becomes "eku tama," though she is a female, or "eku fefine" = my woman. Tahine = an unmarried girl.

COMPARATIVE TABLE OF THE TONGAN AND FIJIAN SYSTEM OF RELATIONSHIP.—*Continued.*

Description of persons.	Relationship in Tongan. (Friendly Islanders.)	Translation.	Relationship in Rewan. (Fijian.)	Translation.
55. My sister's great grandson (*f. s.*)	Hoka mokopuna ua	My great grandson.	Nŏnggu vu	My source.
56. " sister's great granddaughter (*f. s.*)...	Hoka mokopuna ua	" gt. granddaughter.	Nŏnggu vu	" "
57. " brother's son (*f. s.*)	Hoku ilamutu..............	" nephew.	Vunŏŏnggu	" nephew.
58. " brother's son's wife (*f. s.*).............	Eku fanau.............	" child.	Luvĕ'nggu (♂) (?)	" daughter.
59. " brother's daughter (*f. s.*).............	Hoku ilamutu..............	" niece.	Vungŏ'nggu	" nephew.
60. " brother's daughter's husband (*f. s.*)	Eku fanau.............	" child.	Luvĕ'nggu (?)	" son.
61. " brother's grandson (*f. s.*)	Hoka mokopuna.........	" grandson.	Mǎkubúqu	" grandson.
62. " brother's granddaughter (*f. s.*)	Hoka mokopuna.........	" granddaughter.	Mǎkubúqu	" granddaughter.
63. " brother's great grandson (*f. s.*)......	Hoka mokopuna.........	" great grandson.	Noqu vu	" source.
64. " brother's great granddaughter (*f. s.*)	Hoka mokopuna ua.......	" gt. granddaughter.	Noqu vu	" "
65. " father's brother's son (*m. s.*)........	Hoku taokete[1]...........	" brother.	Tuǎkǎ'nggu or tǎthǐ'nggu	" brother.
66. " father's brother's son (*f. s.*)........	Hoku.taokete or tuoga'ani	" "	Ngǎnenggu..............	" "
67. " father's brother's son's wife (*m. s.*)....	Hoku unoho.............	" wife.	Noqu dǎku[2] (♀)	" back.
68. " " " " (*f. s.*)..	Hoku ma'a[3].............	" lady.	Rivǎnggu (♂)	" cousin.
69. " father's brother's daughter (*m. s.*)....	Hoku tuofefine[4]...........	" sister.	Ngǎnĕ'nggu.............	" sister.
70. " " " " (*f. s.*)....	Hoku tehina.............	" "	Tuǎkǎ'nggu.............	" "
71. " father's bro.'s daughter's husb. (*m. s.*)..	Hoku matapule...........	" chief.	Tǎvǎlĕnggu	" cousin.
72. " " " " " (*f. s.*)..	Hoku unoho.............	" husband.	Nóqu dǎ'ku	" back.
73. " father's brother's son's son (*m. s.*)...	Hoku foha..............	" son.	Luvĕ'nggu	" son.
74. " " " " " (*f. s.*)...	Eku tama.............	" boy.	Vungŏ'nggu	" nephew.
75. " father's brother's son's daught'r (*m. s.*)..	Hoku ofefine.............	" daughter.	Luvĕ'nggu	" daughter.
76. " " " " " (*f. s.*)..	Eku tahine.............	" girl.	Vungŏ'nggu	" niece.
77. " father's broth.'s daughter's son (*m. s.*)..	Hoku ilamutu.............	" nephew.	Vungŏ'nggu	" nephew.
78. " " " " " (*f. s.*)..	Eku tama.............	" boy.	Luvĕ'nggu	" son.
79. " father's bro.'s daug.'s daughter (*m. s.*)..	Hoku ilamutu.............	" niece.	Vungŏ'nggu	" niece.
80. " " " " " (*f. s.*)..	Eku takine.............	" girl.	Luvĕ'nggu	" daughter.
81. " father's brother's great grandson (*m.s.*)			Mǎ'kubúnggu	" grandson.
82. " " " " " (*f.s.*)			Mǎ'kubúnggu	" granddaughter.
83. " father's bro.'s gt. granddaughter (*m.s.*)			Mǎ'kubŭnggu	" "
84. " " " " " (*f. s.*)			Noqu vu	" source.
85. " father's bro.'s gt. gt. grandson (*m. s.*)			Noqu vu	" "
86. " father's bro.'s gtr gt. grandson (*f. s.*)			Tǎvǎlĕnggu	" cousin.
87. " father's sister's son (*m. s.*)..............	Hoku tama-amehekitaga..	My cousin.	Davolánggu	" "
88. " " " " (*f. s.*)..............	Hoku tama-amehekitaga..	" "	Ngǎnĕ'nggu	" sister.
89. " father's sister's son's wife (*m. s.*)......	No specific term.		Nónggu alĕwa dúa[5] (♀) ...	" woman-one.
90. " " " " " (*f. s.*)......	No specific term.		Dǎvolánggu	" cousin.
91. " father's sister's daughter (*m. s.*)	Hoku tama-amehekitaga.	" cousin.	Raivánggu	" "
92. " " " " (*f. s.*)......			Nóqu tǎngǎ'ne dua........	" man-one.
93. " father's sister's daughter's husb.(*m.s.*)			Ngǎnenggu	" brother.
94. " " " " " (*f. s.*)			Vungŏnggu	" nephew.
95. " father's sister's son's son (*m. s.*)			Luvĕ'nggu	" son.
96. " " " " " (*f. s.*)......			Vungŏ'nggu	" niece.
97. " father's sister's son's daughter (*m. s.*)			Luvénggu	" daughter.
98. " " " " " (*f. s.*)			Luvénggu	" son.
99. " father's sister's daughter's son (*m. s.*)			Vungŏ'nggu	" nephew.
100. " " " " " (*f. s.*)			Luvénggu	" daughter.
101. " father's sister's daugh.'s daugh.(*m.s.*)			Vungŏ'nggu	" niece.
102. " " " " " (*f.s.*)			Mǎkubúnggu	" grandson.
103. " father's sister's great grandson.........			Mǎkubúnggu	" granddaughter.
104. " " " " granddaughter..			Noqu vu	" source.
105. " father's sister's great great grandson..			Noqu vu	" "
106. " " " " " g'ddaughter.			Tuǎkǎ'nggu	" brother.
107. " mothers' sister's son (*m. s.*)	Hoku taokete...............	My brother.	Ngǎnénggu.............	" "
108. " " " " (*f. s.*)	Hoku tuoga'ani	" "	Noqu dǎ'ku	" back.
109. " mother's sister's son's wife (*m. s.*)....	Hoku unoho'.................	" wife.	Rivǎ'nggu	" cousin.
110. " " " " " (*f. s.*)....	Hoku ma'a	" lady.	Ngǎnénggu.............	" sister.
111. " mother's sister's daughter (*m. s.*)....	Hoku tuofefine.............	" sister.	Tuǎkǎ'nggu.............	" "
112. " " " " " (*f. s.*)....	Hoku taokete	" "	Tǎvǎlĕ'nggu	" cousin.
113. " mother's sister's daugh.'s husb.(*m.s.*)	Hoku matapule.............	" chief.	Noqu dǎ'ku	" back.
114. " " " " " (*f. s.*)	Hoku unoho.............	" husband.	Luvénggu	" son.
115. " mother's sister's son's son (*m. s.*)....	Hoku foha.............	" son.	Vungŏ'nggu	" nephew.
116. " " " " " (*f. s.*)....	Eku tama.............	" boy.	Luvénggu	" daughter.
117. " mother's sister's son's daughter (*m.s.*)	Hoku ofefine.............	" daughter.	Vungŏ'nggu	" niece.
118. " " " " " (*f.s.*)	Eku tahine.............	" girl.	Vungŏ'nggu	" nephew.
119. " mother's sister's daughter's son (*m.s.*)	Hoku ilamutu.............	" nephew.	Luvĕ'nggu	" son.
120. " " " " " (*f.s.*)	Eku tama.............	" boy.	Vungŏ'nggu	" niece.
121. " mother's sister's daugh.'s daugh.(*m.s.*)	Hoku ilamutu.............	" niece.	Luvĕ'nggu	" daughter.
122. " " " " " (*f.s.*)	Eku tahine.............	" girl.	Mǎ'kubúnggu	" grandson.
123. " mother's sister's gt. grandson (*m. s.*)			Mǎ'kubúnggu	" "
124. " " " " " (*f. s.*)			Mǎ'kubúnggu	" "
125. " mother's sister's great granddaughter			Noqu vu	" source.
126. " " " " gt. gt. grandson......			Noqu vu	" "
127. " " " " " granddaughter				

Text spanning under Tongan/Translation columns:

My father's brother's great grandchildren, male or female, are hoku makopuna, and his great grandchildren hoku mokopuna ua, whether I be male or female.

Hoku tama-amehekitaga. | My cousin.

There is no specific term for any one of these, and yet they are considered relations. Thus, I being male, my son will be "tautehina" with my father's sister's son's son. It is singular that the Tongans should actually have no specific term even for cousin; for hoku tamaamekitaga = daughter/son of my aunt. It should be noted that if a Tongan's grandchildren proper die out, he takes one of his father's sister's great grandchildren, who is then *called* his grandchild.

See note on 81 to 86, which will apply to these also.

[1] If he be the son of my father's *elder* brother, he is hoku taokete; if of my father's younger brother, hoku tehina; and this irrespective of our respective ages. He may be younger than I, and yet is he hoku taokete; older, and still hoku tehina.

[2] If her husband dies, she is then wǎ'tenggu = my wife.

[3] I have translated hoku ma'a "my lady," and hoku matapule (No. 26) "my chief." These are not the exact meanings of the words. The Tongans' answer, when asked the exact meaning, is always "They are words of respect."

[4] I shall give but one word for brother or for sister. The distinction between elder and younger must always be understood.

[5] See remarks.

COMPARATIVE TABLE OF THE TONGAN AND FIJIAN SYSTEM OF RELATIONSHIP — *Continued.*

Description of persons.	Relationship in Tongan. (Friendly Islanders.)	Translation.	Relationship in Rewan. (Fijian.)	Translation.
128. My mother's brother's son (*m. s.*)	Hoku tama'a tuajina	My cousin.	Tăvălénggu	My cousin.
129. " " " (*f. s.*)			Ndăvolánggu	" "
130. " mother's brother's son's wife (*m. s.*)			Ngănĕ'nggu	" sister.
131. " " " " " (*f. s.*)			Noqu alewa dua	" woman-one.
132. " mother's brother's daughter (*m. s.*)			Ndăvolă'nggu	" cousin.
133. " " " " (*f. s.*)			Raivă'nggu	" "
134. " mother's bro.'s daugh.'s husb. (*m. s.*)			Noqu tagane dua	" man-one.
135. " " " " " (*f. s.*)			Gănenggu	" brother.
136. " mother's brother's son's son (*m. s.*)			Vungŏ'nggu	" nephew.
137. " " " " " (*f. s.*)			Luvĕ'nggu	" son.
138. " mother's bro.'s son's daughter (*m. s.*)	See note on 92 to 106, which will apply to these also.		Vungŏ'nggu	" niece.
139. " " " " " (*f. s.*)			Luvĕ'nggu	" daughter.
140. " mother's bro.'s daughter's son (*m. s.*)			Luvĕ'eggu	" son.
141. " " " " " (*f. s.*)			Vungŏ'nggu	" nephew.
142. " mother's bro.'s dau.'s daugh. (*m. s.*)			Luvĕ'nggu	" daughter.
143. " " " " " (*f. s.*)			Vungŏ'nggu	" niece.
144. " mother's brother's great grandson			Măkubúnggu	" grandson.
145. " mother's brother's gt. granddaughter			Măkubúnggu	" granddaughter.
146. " mother's brother's great gt. grandson			Noqu vu	" source.
147. " mother's bro.'s gt. gt. granddaughter			Noqu vu	" "
148. " grandfather[1]	Eku kui	My grandfather.	Tumbúnggu	" grandfather.
149. " grandfather's brother	Eku kui	" "	Tumbúnggu	" "
150. " grandfather's sister	Eku kui	" grandmother.	Mbúnggu	" grandmother.
151. " grandmother	Eku kui	" "	Nă'ndămä'nggu	" "
152. " grandmother's brother	Eku kui	" grandfather.	Tukă'nggu	" grandfather.
153. " grandmother's sister	Eku kui	" grandmother.	Nă'ndămü'nggu	" grandmother.
154. " great grandfather	Eku kui-ua	" grandfather-two.	Noqu vu	" source.
155. " great grandfather's brother	Eku kui-ua	" " "	Noqu vu	" "
156. " great grandfather's sister	Eku kui-ua	" grandmother-two.	Noqu vu	" "
157. " great grandmother	Eku kui-ua	" " "		
158. " great grandmother's brother	Eku kui-ua	" grandfather-two.		
159. " great grandmother's sister	Eku kui-ua	" grandmother-two.		
160. " great great grandfather	Eku kui-tolu[2]	" grandfather-three.		
161. " great great grandmother	Eku kui-tolu	" grandmother-three.		
162. " father's father's sister's son (*m. s.*)	Eku tamai[3]	" father.	Vungŏ'nggu	" uncle.
163. " father's father's sister's daugh'r (*m. s.*)	Eku tamai[4]	" "	Tĭ'nă'nggu	" mother.
164. " father's father's sister's son's son (*m.s.*)	Hoku taokete	" brother.	Tăvălénggu	" cousin.
165. " father's father's sister's son's daughter (*m. s.*)	Hoku tuofefine	" sister.	Ndvă'volanggu	" "
166. " father's father's sister's daughter's son (*m. s.*)	Hoku taokete	" brother.	Tuăkă'nggu	" brother.
167. " father's father's sister's daughter's daughter (*m. s.*)	Hoku tuofefine	" sister.	Ngănĕ'nggu	" sister.
168. " father's father's sister's great grandson (*m. s.*) [daughter (*m.s.*)]	Hoku foha	" son.	Vungŏ'nggu	" nephew.
169. " father's father's sister's great grand-	Hoku ofefine	" daughter.	Vungŏ'nggu	" niece.
170. " mother's mother's sisters son (*m. s.*)	Eku fae[5]	" mother.	Vungŏ'nggu	" uncle.
171. " mother's mother's sis.'s daugh.(*m.s.*)	Eku fae	" "	Tĭnă'nggu	" mother.
172. " mother's mother's sister's son's son (*m. s.*)	Hoku taokete	" brother.	Tăvălĕ'nggu	" cousin.
173. " mother's mother's sis.'s son's daughter (*m. s.*)	Hoku tuofefine	" sister.	Ndăvolă'nggu	" "

[1] I will give the words for grandparents, &c., first for the father's side, and then for the mother's.

Description of persons.	Relationship in Tongan. (Friendly Islanders.)	Translation.	Relationship in Rewan. (Fijian.)	Translation.
148A. My mother's father			Tukánggu	My grandfather.
149A. " mother's father's brother			Tukánggu	" "
150A. " mother's father's sister			Nändămă'nggu	" grandmother.
151A. " mother's mother			Mbúnggu	" "
152A. " mother's mother's brother			Tubúnggu	" grandfather.
153A. " mother's mother's sister			Mbúnggu	" grandmother.
154A. " mother's mother's father			Noqu vu	" source.
155A. " mother's mother's father's brother			Noqu vu	" "
156A. " mother's mother's father's sister			Noqu vu	" "

Several natives whom I have questioned told me that "my great grandfather" is tukanggu vakarúa = my grandfather-twice, "my great grandmother" "bunggu vakarúa" = my grandmother-twice, &c. "Noqu vu" is not, properly speaking, a title of kinship, as is evident from the fact that all words expressing kinship take the pronoun affixed. Many natives could not tell me any word for great grandfather. Great grandfathers are very scarce in Fiji, and the word is but seldom used. I believe that "grandfather-twice" is the real title, though I have written "noqu vu" because the majority of my authorities gave it, and it is certainly used. My informants say that *all* ancestors beyond grandfathers are "noqu vu."

[2] My great great great grandfather would be eku kui-fa, my grandfather-four, and so on. If a Tongan wants to distinguish the sex of the grandparent of whom he speaks, he will say "eku kui tagata" = my grandparent male, or "eku kui fefine" = my grandparent female.

[3] The "grandfathers," &c., are the same on the mother's side.

[4] She is called "eku tamai," although she is a female.

[5] Though he is a man, yet is he called "eku fae."

COMPARATIVE TABLE OF THE TONGAN AND FIJIAN SYSTEM OF RELATIONSHIP.—*Continued.*

Description of persons.	Relationship in Tongan. (Friendly Islanders.)	Translation.	Relationship in Rewan. (Fijian.)	Translation.
174. My mother's mother's sister's daughter's son (*m. s.*)	Hoku tuokete	My brother.	Tuăkă'nggu	My brother.
175. " mother's mother's sister's daughter's daughter (*m. s.*)	Hoku tuofefine	" sister.	Gănénggu	" sister.
176. " mother's mother's sister's great grandson (*m. s.*)	Hoku foha	" son.	Vungō'nggu	" nephew.
177. " mother's mother's sister's great granddaughter (*m. s.*)	Hoku ofefine	" daughter.	Vungō'nggu	" niece.
178. " mother's mother's mother's sister's daughter (*m. s.*)	Eku kui	" grandmother.	Mbúnggu	" grandmother.
179. " mother's mother's mother's sister's granddaughter (*m. s.*)	Eku fae	" mother.	Tĭnă'nggu	" mother.
180. " mother's mother's mother's sister's gt. granddaughter (*m. s.*)	Hoku tuofefine	" sister.	Gănĕ'nggu	" sister.
181. " mother's mother's mother's sister's gt. great granddaughter (*m. s.*)	Hoku ofefine	" daughter.	Vungō'nggu	" niece.
182. " husband	Hoku unoho	" husband.	Wătĭnggu	" husband
183. " wife	Hoku unoho	" wife.	Wătĭnggu	" wife.
184. " husband's father	Eku tamai	" father.	Vungō'nggu	" uncle.
185. " husband's mother	Eku fae	" mother.	Vungō'nggu	" aunt.
186. " husband's grandfather	Eku kui	" grandfather.	No word	
187. " wife's father	Eku tamai	" father.	Vungō'nggu	" uncle.
188. " wife's mother	Eku fae	" mother.	Vungō'nggu	" aunt.
189. " wife's grandmother	Eku kui	" grandmother.	No word	
190. " son-in-law (*m. s.*)	Hoku foha	" son.	Vungō'nggu	" nephew.
191. " " (*f. s.*)	Eku tama	" boy.	Vungō'nggu	" "
192. " daughter-in-law (*m. s.*)	Hoku ofefine	" daughter.	Vungō'nggu	" niece.
193. " " " (*f. s.*)	Eku tahine	" girl.	Vungō'nggu	" "
194. " step-father	Eku tamai	" father.	Tămă'nggu	" father.
195. " step-mother	Eku fae	" mother.	Tĭnánggu	" mother.
196. " step-son	Eku ho'umatua,[1] or eku foha.	" step-child, or son.	Luvĕ'nggu	" son.
197. " step-daughter	Hoku hóumatua, or hoku ofefine	" step-child, or daughter.	Luvĕ'nggu	" daughter.
198. " adopted son	Eku tamaohi	" boy-adopted.	Noqu ngóne ni súsú	" child of nursing.
199. " adopted daughter	Eku tamaohi	" child-adopted.	Noqu ngóne ni súsú	" " " "
200. " half-brother	Hoku taokete	" brother.	Tuăkă'nggu	" brother.
201. " half-sister	Hoku twofefine	" my sister.	Ngănĕ'nggu	" sister.
202. " two fathers-in-law to each other	No word.		No word	
203. " two mothers-in-law to each other	No word.		No word	
204. " brother-in-law (*husband's brother*)	Hoku unoho	" husband.	Wăténggu	" husband.
205. " " " (*sister's husband, m. s.*)	Hoku metapule	" chief.	Tavalenggu	" cousin.
206. " " " (" " *f. s.*).	Hoku unoho	" husband.	Noqu daku	" back.
207. " " " (*wife's sister's husband*)	Hoku tokoua	One of my brethren.	Noqu tagane dua	" man-one.
208. " " " (*wife's brother*)	No specific term.[2]		Tăvălénggu	" cousin.
209. " " " (*husband's sister's husb.*)	Hoku tokoua	" " "	Raivánggu	" "
210. " sister-in-law (*wife's sister*)	Hoku unoho	My wife.	Noqu daku	" back.
211. " " " (*husband's sister*)	Hoku matapule[3]	" chief.	Raivánggu	" cousin.
212. " " " (*brother's wife, m. s.*)	Hoku unoho	" wife.	Noqu daku	" back.
213. " " " (" " *f. s.*)	Hoku ma'a	" lady.	Raivă'nggu	" cousin.
214. " " " (*husb.'s bro.'s wife, f. s.*)	Hoku tokoua	One of my sisters.	Noqu alewa dua	" woman-one.
215. " " " (*wife's bro.'s wife, f. s.*)	Hoku tokoua	" "	Ngă'nĕ'qu	" sister.
216. Twins (*if of the same sex*)	Mahaga	Twins.	Ndrŭ'ă	Twins.
" (*if a boy and a girl*)	Mahagala	"		
217. Widow	Uitou[4]	Widow.	Yăndă	Widow.
218. Widower	Takape	Widower.	Yăndă	Widower.

Relationship of descendants of brother and sister to each other.				
1. Daughter of daughter of one sister to daughter of daughter of other sister.	Tautehina	Sisters.	Veitacini (spelt after the Fijian manner.)	Sisters, literally "sistered together."
2. Son of son of one sister to son of son of other sister.	Tautehina	Brothers	Vătăthĕ'nĭ	Brothers, literally "brothered together."
3. Son of son of one sister to daughter of daughter of other sister.	Tautehina	Brother and sister.	Văndăvolă'nĭ	Cousins.

[1] Ho'umotu applies to all step-children.

[2] *He* would call *me* "hoku matapule."

[3] *My wife* would speak of MY *sister* as "hoku matapule," it being thereby understood that the respect is shown to *me*, the male, through her. My sister would speak of my wife as "hoku ma'a."

[4] I strongly suspect "Uitou" to be an introduced word. The missionaries have introduced many such words into the Tongan language, unnecessarily (as I venture to think). I don't know enough of the tongue to be *sure* about this word being our English "widow" in a Tongan dress, but it has a suspicious look and sound. I will inquire about it when I meet with an *old* Tongan. *Takape* applies to women as well as to men, and is used also with reference to an unmarried person. There is also a *verb* "takape," which means "to be poor as to clothing;" and hence I should suppose the *noun* to apply more properly to a *man*, because it is the woman's business to make *tapa*, or native cloth; so that takape would seem to mean "a man who had no woman to make tapa for him."

COMPARATIVE TABLE OF THE TONGAN AND FIJIAN SYSTEM OF RELATIONSHIP.—*Continued.*

Description of persons.	Relationship in Tongan. (Friendly Islanders.)	Translation.	Relationship in Rewan. (Fijian.)	Translation.
4. Daughter of son of one sister to son of daughter of other sister.	Tautehina	Sister and brother.	Vándávolä′nĭ...............	Cousins.
5. Daughter of daughter of daughter of one sister to daughter of daughter of daughter of other sister.	Tautehina....................	Sisters.	Vátáthě′nĭ	Sisters.
1. Son of son of one brother to son of son of other brother.	Tautehina....................	Brothers.	Vátăthě′nĭ	Brothers.
2. Daughter of daughter of one brother to daughter of daughter of other brother.	Tautehina....................	Sisters.	Vátathě′nĭ	Sisters.
3. Son of son of one brother to daughter of daughter of other brother.	Tautehina....................	Brother and sister.	Vándávolä′nĭ...............	Cousins.
4. Son of son of son of one brother to son of son of son of other brother.	Tautehina....................	Brothers.	Vátăthě′nĭ	Brothers.
1. Son of son of a brother to son of son of brother's sister.	Tautehina....................	Brothers.	Vátăvălě′nĭ	Cousins.
2. Daughter of daughter of a brother to daughter of daughter of brother's sister.	Tautehina....................	Sisters.	Váraivă′nĭ	"
3. Son of son of a brother to daughter of daughter of brother's sister.	Tautehina....................	Brother and sister.	Vá-ngănĕnĭ	Brother and sister.
4. Son of son of son of a brother to son of son of son of brother's sister.	Tautehina....................	Brothers.	Vátăvălě′nĭ	Cousins.
1. Daughter of daughter of one sister to daughter of daughter of daughter of other sister.	Enetahine....................	Aunt and niece.	Vátĭnă′nĭ	Mother & daughter, lit. "mothered together."
2. Son of son of one brother to son of son of son of other brother.	Honofoha	Uncle and nephew.	Vátămă′nĭ....................	Father and son.
3. Daughter of daughter of a brother to son of son of son of brother's sister.	Enetama[1]	Aunt and nephew.	Vávungö′nĭ	Aunt and nephew.

NOTE.—Va (spelt Fijian-wise vei) expresses some sort of reciprocity, thus :—

    Lomana = to love ; veilomani = mutual love.   Ravu = to slay ; veiraravui = mutual slaughter.
    Cata = to hate ; veicati = mutual hatred.   Lako = to go ; veilakovi = visiting one another.

[1] Tau answers to the Fijian vei.

Enetahine = her girl, but is used to express the kinship between aunt and niece.
Honofoha = his son, but is used to express the kinship between uncle and nephew.
Enetama = her boy, but is used to express the kinship between aunt and nephew.

This seemed strange to me, and I questioned the natives (Tongans) over and over again about it. There was no variation in their replies. I placed pens on a sheet of paper in double row, thus :—

$$\alpha \text{———} \beta \text{———} \text{ two sisters.}$$
$$\text{Daughter of } \alpha \quad \gamma \text{———} \varepsilon \text{———} \text{ daughter of } \beta.$$
$$\text{Daughter of } \gamma \quad \delta \text{———} \zeta \text{———} \text{ daughter of } \varepsilon.$$
$$\eta \text{———} \text{ daughter of } \zeta.$$

explaining them fully as in diagram, and asking for the kinship between δ and η. "Enetahine," said the Tongans. "No," said I, "that means her girl, and refers only to what δ would say of η." "Not so," they answered. "If you asked us what kin they are, both of them together, we should say, 'they are enetahine.'" I then inquired in like manner about "honofoha," and "enetama," with a like result.

REMARKS OF MR. FISON ON THE TONGAN SYSTEM.

From these relationships it seems that the Tongan system differs materially from the Fijian as to "cousinage"—all vietavaleni, veidavolani, and veiraivani, excepting the first generation, being tautehina (= veitacini) in the Tongan.

I have spelt all words after the Tongan manner, making a few exceptions for the sake of clearness, but departing slightly from the Tongan system of spelling only where that system is manifestly faulty. For instance, the Tongan language has the sound of *p* as well as that of *b* (the English *b*, not the Fijian, which is *mb*); but the framers of the alphabet have rejected *p* altogether, making *b* do double duty. I have, therefore, spelt "matapule," "takape," &c., with the *p*, though they would be spelt by a Tongan "matabule," "takabe," &c. They are sounded as I have spelt them.

Again, the framers of the Tongan alphabet have used *aa* very often where *a* only is required; and this is disastrous, because there are many words which require the *aa*, as ma'a—words in which there is a break.

Speaking of these breaks, I am inclined to think that they represent missing letters—*letters which were formerly sounded in the word.* What makes me *almost sure* of this, is the singular fact, that here in Fiji, two dialects, not differing *materially* from the Bauan, drop, one the *k*, and the other the *t*, in every word wherein these letters occur, making a break in the sound of the word where the missing letter has fallen. Thus, the Cakandrove people say "'ata'ata," where a Bauan says "kata-kata;" and the people on a part of the coast of Navitilevu pronounce the same word "ka'aka'a." I found this difference existing between two islands not ten miles apart; nay, even between two towns on the same island. Thus, on the island of Vanua Balavu, the Lomaloma folks say "kata-kata," but the Mualevu folks, "'ata'ata." The Ovalau islanders say "e tini na tamata" = ten men, while the people of the neighboring island, Naigani, say "e 'ini na 'ama'a." The break is distinctly heard, even when it occurs at the beginning of the word. Now there is no physical difficulty to account for this singular fact, no physical difficulty such as the Northumbrians have in pronouncing the letter *r*. "Au sa la'o 'i na 'oro," said a Cakandrove woman whom I met in the Bau district (= "I am going to the town"). "Vosa vaka bau mada ga," said I (= "speak Bauan"); whereupon she said at once, with a laugh, "Au sa lako ki na koro."

I can, therefore, look upon this letter dropping only as mere caprice, that is as to the origin of it. It *may* have taken its rise in the determination of some ruling chief never to pronounce a letter which was the first or predominant letter of some hated enemy's name; and he may have commanded his people to follow his example, or they may have followed his example of their own accord. It may have taken its rise, however, in mere affectation, just as I remember the gobbling sound of the letter "r" took its rise among foolish young men of the Lord Dundreary stamp.

The sound of the Tongan vowels is that of the Fijian, and the remarks which I made about the so-called Fijian diphthongs will apply to the Tongan also.

G is pronounced ng as in Fijian; but

B is *never* pronounced mb.

I subjoin a list of the words employed, with the accented syllables and the long vowels marked. I have separated certain syllables when it has seemed necessary to do so for the sake of clearness. The short vowels are unmarked.

Eku.	Tū'oga'áni.	Unō'ho.	Hónofóha.
Hō'ku.	Tūofefī'ne.	Ma'ā'.	Enetáma.
(Pron. Hogu, Eng. *g*.)	Tehī'na.	Tāhī'ne.	Olotē'le.
Hō'no.	Gáhi.	Kū'i.	Olomafū'a.
Hotán.	Tōkoū'a.	Tagáta.	Pagái.
Tamái.	Mehékitága.	Hō''umatū'a.	Hā'ātū'i.
Fáe.	(*k* like Eng. hard *g*.)	Táma-ō'hi.	Mō'lofà'ha.
Fō'ha.	Matá'pū'le.	Mahága.	Hā''atákalā'-ū'a.
Ofefī'ne.	Túajī'na.	Mahágaléi.	Hā''ágátamōtū'a.
Mō'kopū'na.	(*J* like soft *ch*.)	Takápe.	Mōtū'apuā'ka.
Ua.	Ilamū'tu.	Tàutehī'na.	Láu-áki.
Tō'lu.	Táma.	Enetāhī'ne.	Kámokubō'lu.
Tā'okéte.			

Answers to Questions p. 15 of Circular.

I. The Tonga nation is divided into the following tribes :—

1. Olotele, meaning obscure.   Olo = to ensnare, tele = an instrument used in shaving.
2. Olomafua, meaning uncertain.   Mafua is a sort of tree.
3. Pagai = the king's plaza.
4. Molofaha = the mad tramplers-underfoot.

These tribes are subdivided as follows :—

(Olotele and Olomafua have no subdivisions.)

Pagai.

1. Ha'atui = reverenced kings.   = Fijian roko tui, or sachems.
2. Ha'agatamotua = respected (or reverenced) old snake.
3. Ha'avéa.   Vea is a sort of yam.
4. Ha'agátatū'bu.   Reverenced growing snake.

Molofaha.

There are two divisions of this tribe, which have, however, no distinguishing name.

The chief of one division takes as his title of office, motuapuaka[1] = old pig, and stands on the right hand of the king on all state occasions.

The chief of the other division takes as his title, lauaki (meaning obscure), and stands on the king's left hand.

Quest. 2. A man was not forbidden to marry a woman of his own tribe.

Quest. 3. The children are of the father's tribe.

Quests. 4, 5, 6. The answers to these questions, which I gave in my paper about the Fijians, will apply word for word to the Tongans.

7. There were, in the heathen times, four kings or principal chiefs, or rather one queen and three kings, as follows :—

1. Támahā'.   This was a woman, daughter of the sister of a Tui Tonga, or of a Tui Kánokubō'lu.
2. Tui Ha'atakalaū'a.   He was of the Olomafua tribe.
3. Tui Toga.   He was of the Olotele tribe.
4. Tui Kanokubōlu.   He was of the Pagai tribe.

Of these Nos. 1, 2, 3 had little or no authority.   They were held in great reverence (especially the Tamaha), feasts were made for them, and property presented to them, but they had no voice in the government.

No. 4, the Tui Kanokubolu, had and has all the real power in his hands ; but it is a significant fact that when food or property is presented to No. 1, No. 2, or No. 3, he has to carry a part thereof on a stick which he holds over his shoulder ; and it is not a little remarkable that, on these occasions, the Molofaha, though an inferior tribe, carry no burdens, but sit around the Tui or Tamaha to whom the gifts are presented.   These facts seem to suggest a different state of things in the olden times. I have no opportunities of inquiring further into this matter, but I will write to the Tonga missionaries.

Quest. 8. As in Fiji.

Quest. 9. The descendants of two sisters, &c. &c., were brothers and sisters to each other throughout all generations.   So also with the descendants of two brothers.   But the descendants of a brother and of a sister were cousins in the first generation only.   The children of cousins were brothers and sisters.   See schedule.

Quest. 10. The birthname was not changed unless the person were adopted by a member of another tribe.

Quest. 11. On the father's death, his property descends to his children.

---

[1] This title motuapuaka must be of comparatively recent origin, for puaka is evidently an introduced word, ough introduced long before the missionaries went to Tonga.   I have a very curious, and somewhat disgusting, gend of the first coming of pigs to Tonga, wherein it is stated that there were formerly no pigs in Samoa, Tonga, d Fiji.

Quest. 12. On the mother's death, her property remained with her husband and children, not even excepting her dower-land, which did *not* revert to her own tribe, as in Fiji.

Quests. 13, 14, 15. I am unable to answer these questions.

Quest. 16. The members of *no* subdivision of any Tongan tribe are necessarily akin.

Quest. 17. Kinsfolk do not salute by the term of kinship. They do not even use the term in speaking *to* their nearest relations. Thus, a child, in calling his father, will not call "father!" but will bawl out his father's name.

REMARKS OF MR. FISON ON THE FIJIAN SYSTEM.

As to the spelling of the Fijian words I have sometimes been at a loss how to spell them so that the English sound of the letters should represent the sound of the Fijian word.

Where *a* is left without the breve, I have intended it to have the sound of *a* in *fame*, as vatăthēnī = vaytatheni.

Where *e* is left without the breve, I have intended it to have the sound of *e* in *meet*, also when have written it *ē* or *ee*.

Where *i* is left without the breve, I have meant it to have the sound of *i* in *light*, thus lili = ly-ly.

Where *o* is written ŏ, it is intended to have the sound of *o* in *stone*, as nŏnggu = noh-nggu.

I regret to see, in looking over the sheets, that I have in many cases relapsed into the Fijian spelling: thus, after spelling the word for *wife*, wătēnggu, I write the same word watiqu, nonggu, noqu; Rawa, Rewa; alawa, alewa; tathenggu, tathinggu, &c. &c. I am exceedingly sorry for this, and in order to remedy it as far as possible, I append a list of all the words, written according to the Fijian spelling, which is nearly phonetic; first explaining the sounds of the letters.

The Fijian alphabet consists of the following letters :—

a b c d e f g i j k l m n o p q r s t u v w y.

Of these, f, j, and p are used only in foreign words.

All the consonants are sounded as in English, except

b c d g q.

B has the sound of *mb*.

C has the sound of *th* in *these*, but never of *th* in *thin*.

D has the sound of *nd*.

G has the sound of *ng* in *ring*.

Q has the sound of *ng* in *younger*. Sometimes it has the sound of *nk* in *younker*; thus, waga = wanka; but this sound is not heard in any word which I have employed.

The vowels have the sound which they have in the French language, only it must be remembered that there are no diphthongs in Fijian, and that, therefore, ai, ei, &c. have not the French sound.

Ai = ah-e, which sounded quickly makes nearly the sound of *i* in *light*.

Ei = eh-e, which makes nearly the long *a* in *fame*.

Ou = O-oo, which makes Au = ah-oo = *ow* nearly.

These so-called diphthongs, though sounded quickly, and one vowel slurred as it were into the other, are not diphthongs, for a quick ear can always catch the distinct sound of each vowel. I mark the long vowels; the short are unmarked.

Rŏ′wa.	Tárotáro.	Kedáru.	Tacī′qu.	Búqu.
Vále-lē′vu.	Násimī′ti.	Nódatón.	Lŏ′vu.	Na′damáqu.
Núku-ni-tabū′a.	Naní′u.	Kéitón.	Láilái.	Gŏ′ne.
Sáuturága.	Vū′anámu.	Méitón.	Vugŏ′qu.	Sŭ′sŭ′.
Tóga-vī′ti.	Sŏ′ru.	Eda.	Mákubúqu.	Drŭ′a.
Narŭ′sa.	Cíkinŏ′vu.	Kóimámi.	Vásu.	Yáda.
Nakē′li.	Cā′kobáu.	Tamáqu.	Vatūvu.	Véitacī′ni.
Nacŏ′láse.	Nŏ′qu.	Tináqu.	Dáku.	Véigă′nēni.
Náivakacáu.	Kéqu.	Lūvequ.	Ráiváqu.	Véidavoláni.
Mákulū′va.	Qau.	Tagáne.	Távaléqu.	Véiraiváni.
Nakŏ′ro.	Méqu.	Alŏ′wa.	Dávoláqu.	Véitináni.
Navoláu.	Wai.	Vū.	Dúa.	Véitamáni.
Navū′savásu.	Nodáru	Tū′akáqu.	Tubúqu.	Véivugŏ′ni.
Nakáiréwa.	Kéiráu.	Qă′néqu.		

a. Grandchildren and grandfathers.

Some nations make a curious distinction here. One whom I questioned gave me the following :—

> Child of my daughter = makubuqu.
>
> Child of my son = noqu diva = my fencepost.

Both these children would salute me as " tubuqu."

Their children, grandchildren, great grandchildren, and so on throughout all generations, are *noqu vu.*

These remarks apply whether I be male or female, and whatever be the sex of my grandchildren.

Another of my informants says that in speaking of grandchildren the grandmother would say " ko ira na makubuqu" = " they the grandchildren-my," while the grandfather would say " ko ira na maku."

β. (Page 574.) Uncles and nephews.

Vugoqu is used for my uncle, my aunt, my nephew, or my niece. *Vasu* or *vatuvu* is a title rather of office than of kinship, for the nephew has strange rights and privileges as regards his uncle. He can take his uncle's property, and for this act the Fijians have a verb, vasuta, which applies to the thing so taken; thus, " sa vasuta na waga ko koya" = " has taken-nephew-wise the canoe he." The nephew has been known, when at war with his uncle, to go to his uncle's house and help himself to his gunpowder, none daring to say him nay.

A great lady is sometimes given in marriage by one kingdom to another. Her sons are vasu to the kingdom from which she came, and most abominably do they abuse their privileges.

γ. I have omitted to write "or taciq" after " tuakaqu," but in every case (excepting Nos. 11 and 14) " or taciqu" must be understood after " tuakaqu," whether the word mean " brother" or " sister."

δ. (Page 574.) I have marked a note of interrogation to Nos. 58 and 60, because the natives do not agree therein; but I think that " luvequ" is correct, because the children of both would be " makubuqu." There is, however, a doubt about it. I have given the opinion of the majority.

ε. (Page 574.) Noqu daku. This appears = brother-in-law or sister-in-law. Some natives gave me *watiqu* in those places where *noqu daqu* appears, and it is evident that *noqu daqu* is *watiqu* in theory, from the fact that the children of *noqu daqu* are *luvequ.*

ζ. (Page 574.) Raivaqu (No. 68), *Tavalequ* (No. 71), *Davolaqu* (No. 88). Each of these = cousins.

> If I am a male, my male cousin is tavalequ.
>
> If I am a male, my female cousin is davolaqu.
>
> If I am a female, my male cousin is davolaqu.
>
> If I am a female, my female cousin is raivaqu.
>
> Therefore male cousins are veitavaleni.
>
> Therefore female cousins are veiraivani.
>
> Therefore cousins of opposite sexes are veidavolani.[1]

θ. In comparing my schedule with that of the Seneca tribe, given p. 7 of pamphlet, I found that while " my father's brother's" descendants are the same in both systems, there is a most curious difference as regards the descendants of " my father's sister," the Senecan " son" being the Fijian " nephew," &c., thus :—

	Senecan.	Fijian.
My father's sister's son's son (said by a male)	= son.	Nephew.
" " " " " (said by a female)	= nephew.	Son.
My father's sister's son's daughter (said by a male)	= daughter.	Niece.
" " " " " (said by a female)	= niece.	Daughter.

I thought, when I first observed this, that I must have made a mistake in my schedules, and so went over them again, making repeated inquiries from many natives, the result whereof is to assure me beyond a doubt that the difference does exist. I cannot see the point of divergence, for that most curious fact of father's brothers being fathers, and mother's sisters, mothers; while mother's brothers are uncles, and father's sisters aunts; which seems to me to lie at the root, and to be the

---

[1] *Raiva* is a Rewa word. Its equivalent in the Bau dialect is *dauve.* The other words are the same in both dialects.

key of the whole system, explaining nearly all its difficulties, appears to be the same in both systems. I should be very glad to know whether any of the other Indian tribes thus differ from the Senecan ; and in the mean while I will not cease from making diligent inquiry among *all* the tribes (Fijians and others) to whom I have access.

Quest. 1. (P. 15 of pamphlet.)   Into how many tribes is the nation divided ?

In order to answer this question clearly, it will be necessary to define what we mean by "tribe," and what by "nation." I propose to take the people of Rewa as a Fijian "nation," and the divisions of this people as "tribes." The whole Fijian nation is split up into many of these smaller nations, who speak different dialects ; and perhaps, in the case of the hill tribes, different languages. I have been to a mountain tribe whose language was utterly unintelligible to a Fijian who accompanied me, although his town was not more than twenty or thirty miles distant, as the crow flies ; and in many places, even on the coast, we (missionaries) have to employ an interpreter.

The Rewa (= lofty, exalted) nation is divided into four tribes, viz :--

1. Vă'lě-lávü = great house.
2. Núku-ne-tămbúă = sand of whale's tooth.
3. Sow-turángă = lord-kings.
4. Tóngă-veétë = Tongan Fijians.

These are again subdivided into smaller tribes.

Văle-lava.

1. Nă-rúsă = destruction.
2. Nă-kălě = the moat.
3. Nă-thó-lă'sě = the grass coral.[1]
4. Ní-văkă-thów. (The meaning doubtful. It MAY mean "the accusers," or the "causers of gift-bringing.")[2]

Nukunitambua.

1. Mă'ku-lū'va =naked grandchild.
2. Na-kŏ'ro = the town.[3]

Nă-sow-turánga.

1. Nă'volów = the canoe shed.	2. Nă-vū'sa-vă'su = tribe of nephews.
3. Nă-kí-ráwă = people of Rewa.	4. Tă'ro-tă'ro = inquirers.
5. Ná-sīmeétě = the thieves.	6. Na-néw = the cocoanuts.

Tonga Veeti.

1. Tónga-nū'kū-ne-tămbū'ă = Tongan Nukunetambuans.
2. Na-vūsă-nămu = the tribe of Mosquitoes.[4]

Quest. 2. A man was *not* forbidden to marry a woman of his own tribe.

Quest. 3. The children are of the father's tribe.

Quests. 4, 5, 6 may be answered together, as follows : When the sachem dies, his successor is chosen from among his kinsfolk, whom I write down in order of preference. 1. Elder brother of deceased. 2. Younger brother. 3. Eldest son. 4. Elder brother's son. 5. Younger brother's son. That is, the elder brother *first* ; failing *all* elder brothers, then a younger brother ; failing all brothers, then sons in order according to age ; failing sons, then elder brother's sons, &c. He who stands first in order may be passed over because of mental or bodily defect, or notoriously foolish

---

[1] This tribe is extinct.

[2] The Rewa sachems were chosen from 1, 2, and 3 of these tribes, but never from the 4th (Ni-vaka-thow). That is, the royal family was of the Narusa tribe ; failing Narusa, then Nakali ; failing Nakali, then Natholase.

[3] The war-kings are of these tribes.

[4] These are not, strictly speaking, Rewans. They are a mixed race, the descendants of a band of Tongans who came down to Fiji many generations ago, and settled down under the protection of Rewa. There is a most curious legend about their coming to Fiji. I am strongly tempted to give it, but refrain.

conduct. A sister's son is *never* chosen, unless she be married into one of the royal tribes, her sons being of her husband's tribe.

Quest. 7. There is strong evidence, amounting to almost absolute certainty, that the sachem's duties were confined exclusively to affairs of peace. Thus, even now, if the sachem go with a war party, the war-king going also, it is the latter who takes command. Practically, however, in some cases the sachem has usurped the duties of both war-king and sachem; while, in others, the war-king has got into his own hands all the power of both sachem and war-king. A notable instance is that of the Mbau nation, whose war-king, Thakombau, has laid his hands upon *everything*, not even allowing a sachem to be formally appointed.

Quest. 8. The office of war-king is hereditary, the order of succession being precisely the same with that of the sachem.

Quest. 9. The descendants of two sisters, of the same sex, and standing in equal degrees from their common ancestors, are brothers and sisters to each other in theory, throughout all generations So also with the descendants of two brothers. But the descendants of brother and sister are not cousins throughout all generations; as, for instance, a Fijian's father's father's sister's daughter's daughter is his "sister," because his father's father's sister's daughter is his "mother." (See schedule Nos. 167 and 163.)

Quest. 10. The Fijians have *not* one name for childhood, another for manhood, &c.; but their names are sometimes changed in commemoration of some notable event, as slaying an enemy, &c., or because of some peculiarity either of body or of mind. Thus the Mbau king's birthname was Seru = Comb; afterwards, because of his stealthy manner of creeping upon his enemies, and the sudden sharpness of his bite, he was called "Thĭkĭnōvu" = Centipede; and, finally, during the great rebellion, when his father had to flee for his life, he was called "Tha-kombau" = Bau is in evil case.

Quest. 11. The theory is that on the death of the father his property descends to the widow and her children; but the practice is for the kinsfolk of the dead, especially his brothers, to take to themselves all they can get; and I have known many widows "loud in their wail" about property thus taken from them. This, however, is perhaps not quite so unjust as it seems to be, for the brothers of the dead are the "fathers" of his children, and so care for them. "My father's brother loves me more than my father," said a native whom I was questioning about this matter.

Quest. 12. On the death of the mother her property remains with her husband, excepting the land which she brought with her as her dower, and which now reverts to her own tribe.

Quests. 13, 14, 15. I am not able to say whether any of the castes or subdivisions among the Fijians be analogous to the tribes of the North American Indians, nor have I any books of reference to help me. If by "castes" we are to understand something similar to the "castes" of India, then, judging from the little I know of them, there are no such divisions among the Fijians. There are chiefs of various degrees, and commoners of various degrees. One tribe is "mbati" to another, *i. e.* has to follow it to war; but such tribes are paid for their services, after the fight; they are much esteemed, and moreover often not a little feared by the very tribe whose mbati they are, for they are inconstant and often rebellious.

Another tribe is nggali to the chief tribe. This class has not only to fight at the command of the chief tribe, but to present food, and to do work in times of peace. There are, moreover, degrees of the gali—the nggali kaisi being abject serfs, holding their lands, their property, their wives, their children, nay, their very lives, only at the will of their chiefs.

Quest. 16. The members of these subdivisions are not necessarily akin.

Quest. 17. Kinsfolk salute each other by the term of kinship.

INDEX.

---

74   June, 1870.

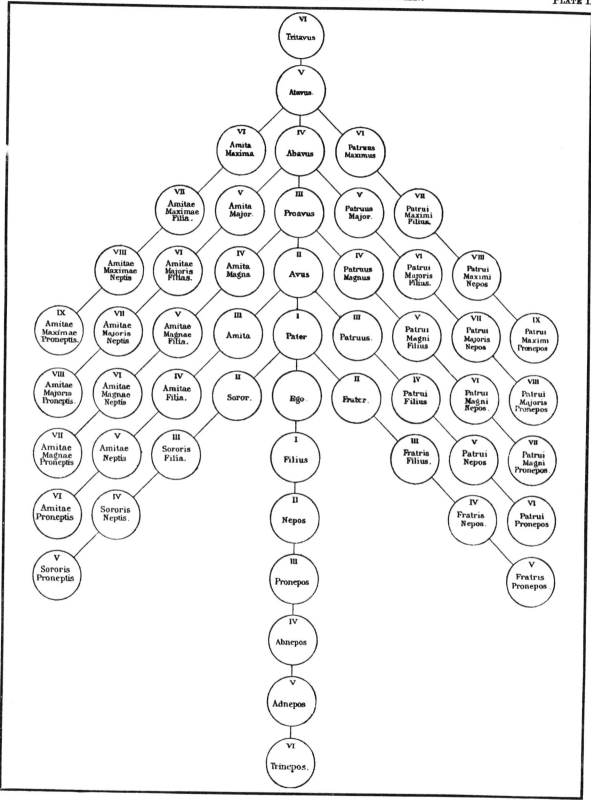

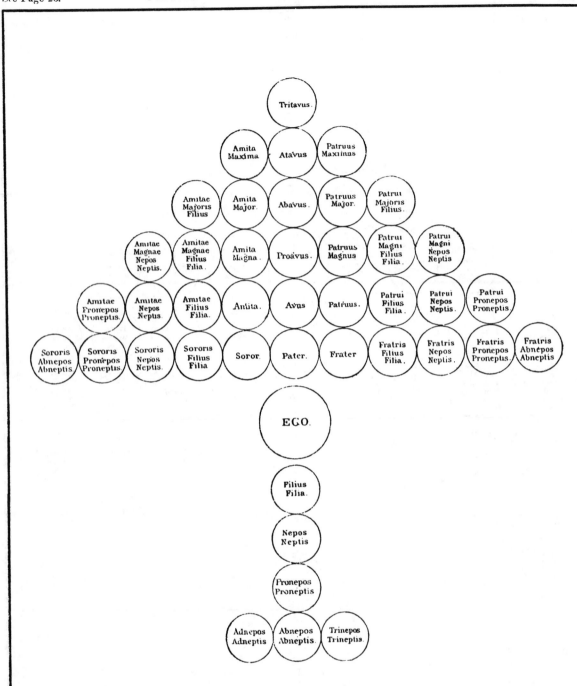

"Sed, cum magis veritas oculâ fide, quam per aures animis hominum, infigatur, ideò necessarium duximus, post narrationem graduum eos etiam præsenti libro inscribi, quatenus possint et auribus et oculorum inspectione adolescentes perfectissimam graduum doctrinam adipisci."—*Inst. Just.* Lib. iii. tit. vii. § vii.

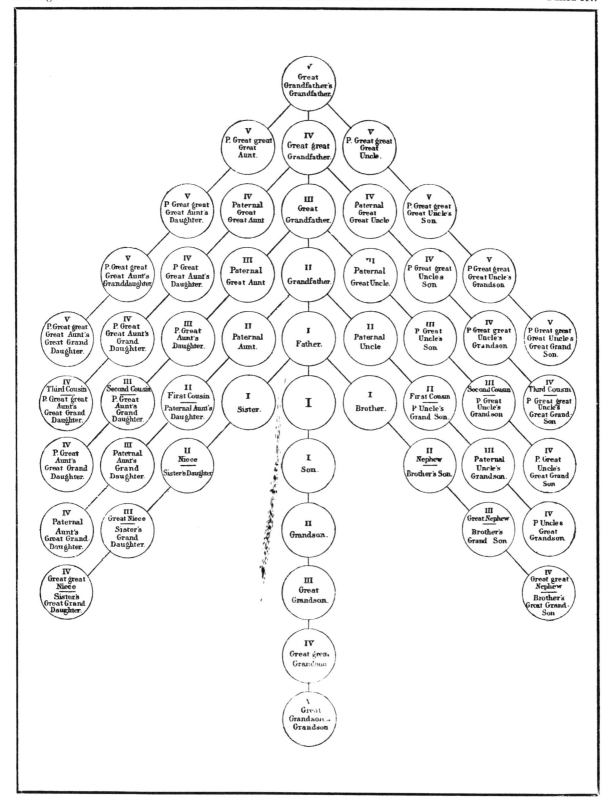

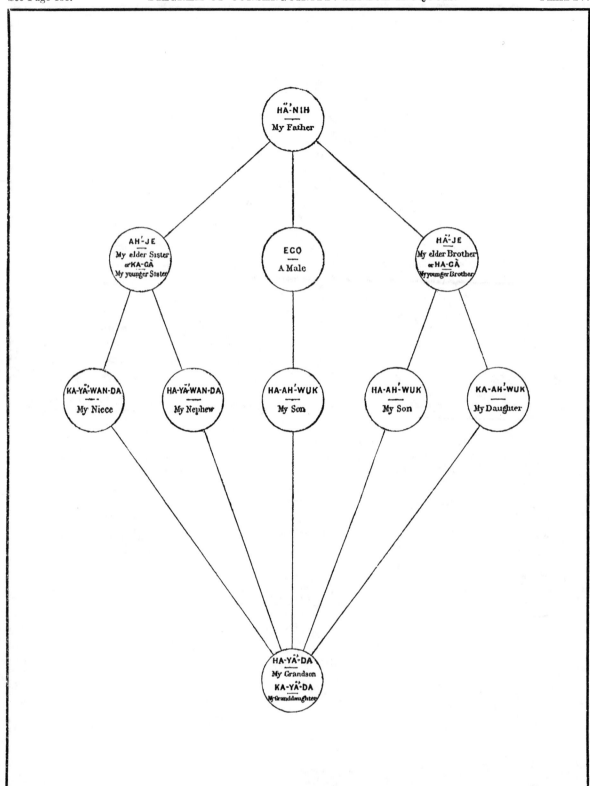

Lineal and First Collateral Lines: Male and Female
Ego, a Male.

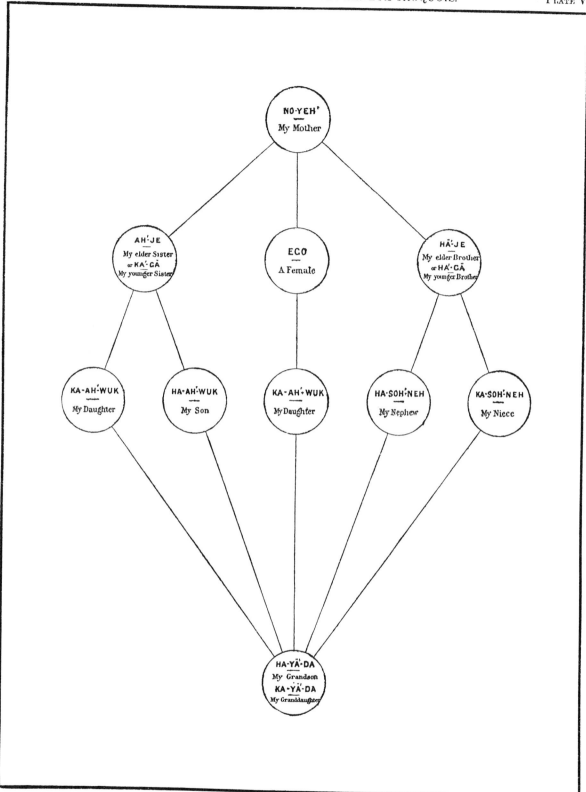

Lineal and First Collateral Lines: Male and Female.
Ego, a Female.

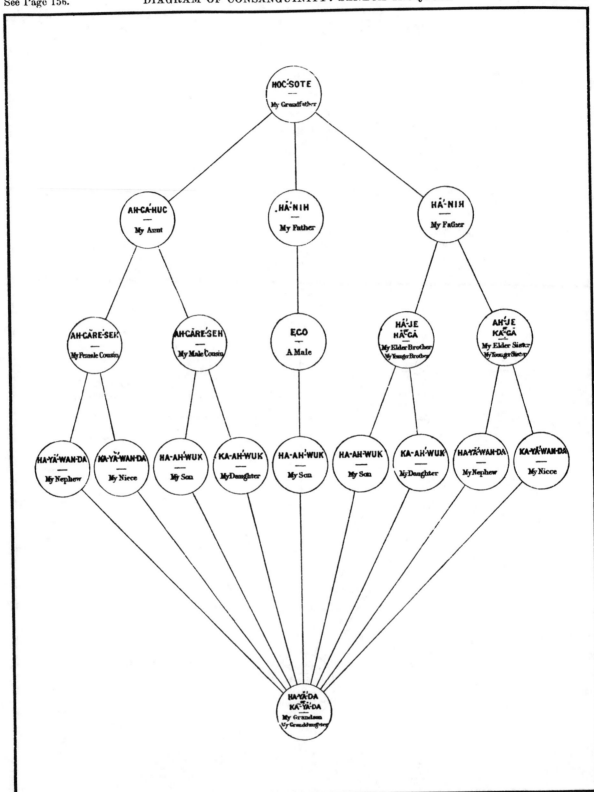

Lineal and Second Collateral Lines: Male and Female: Father's Side.
Ego, a Male.

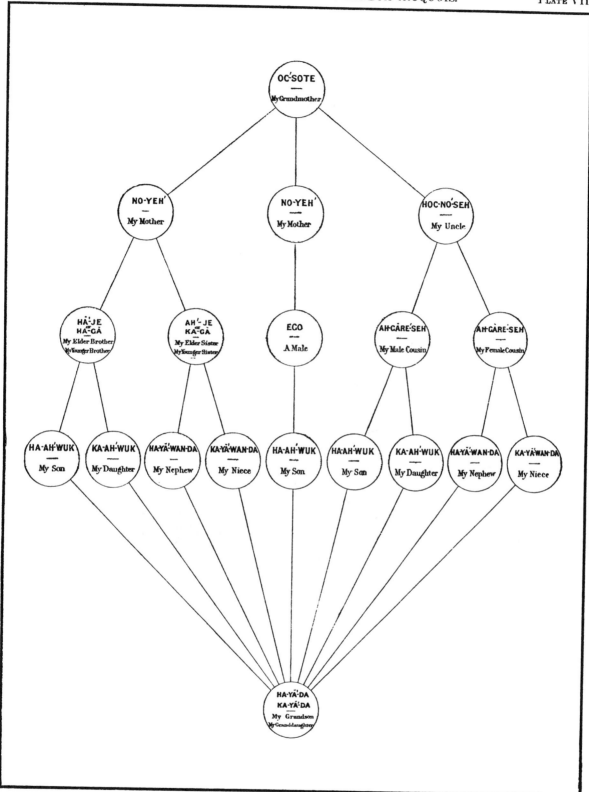

Lineal, and Second Collateral Lines: Male and Female: Mother's Side.
Ego, a Male.

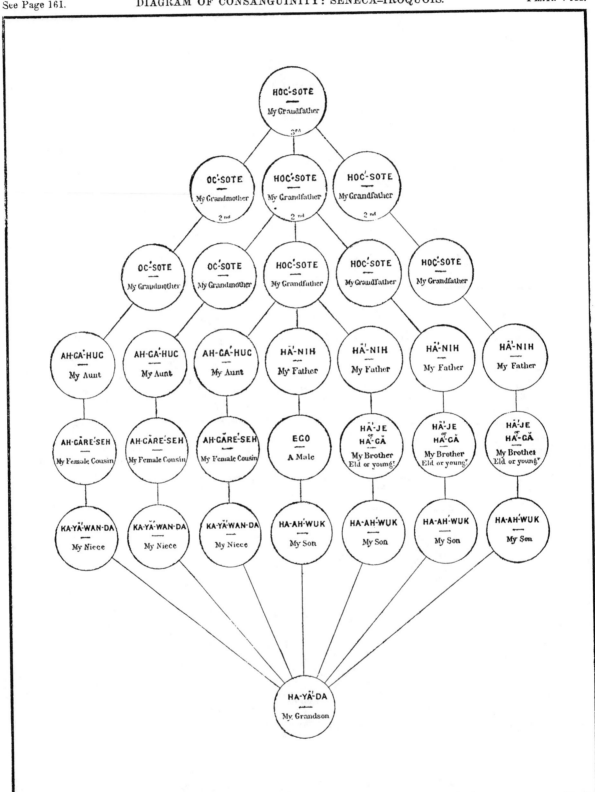

Lineal, and Second, Third, and Fourth Collateral Lines: Male and Female: Father's Side.
Ego, a Male.

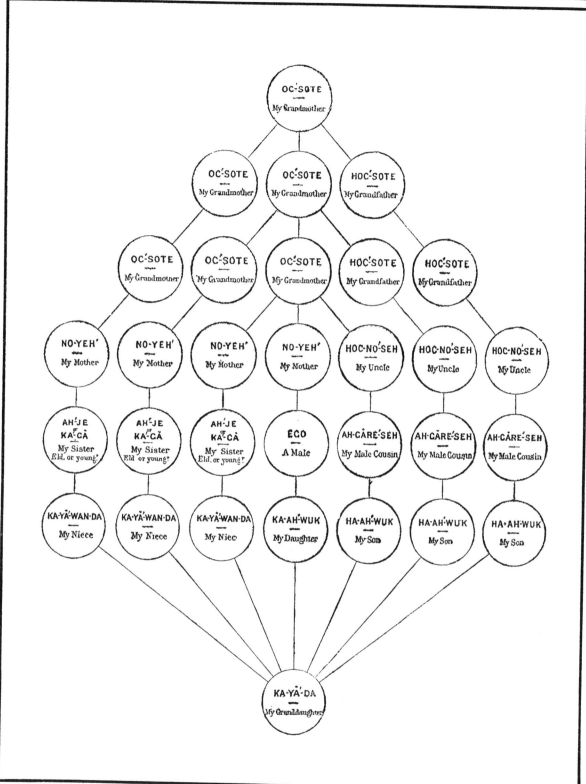

Lineal, and Second, Third, and Fourth Collateral Lines: Male and Female: Mother's Side.
Ego, a Male.

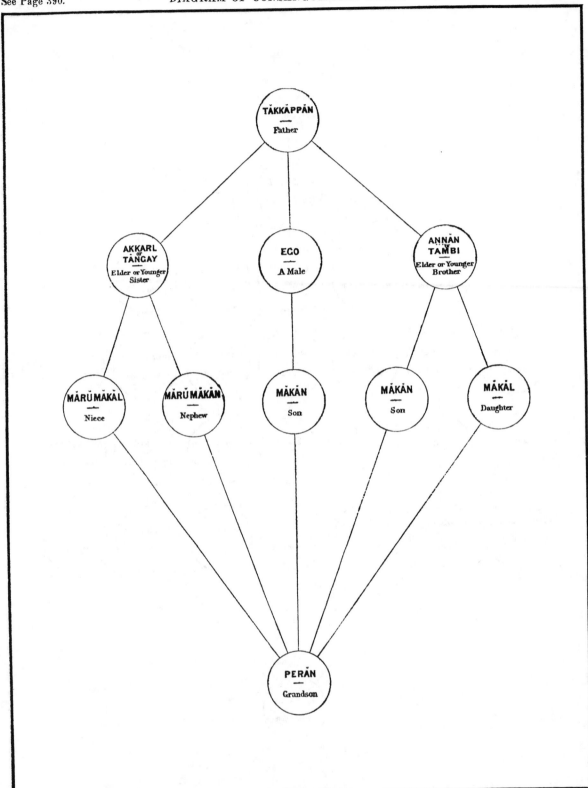

Lineal and First Collateral Lines: Male and Female.
Ego, a Male.

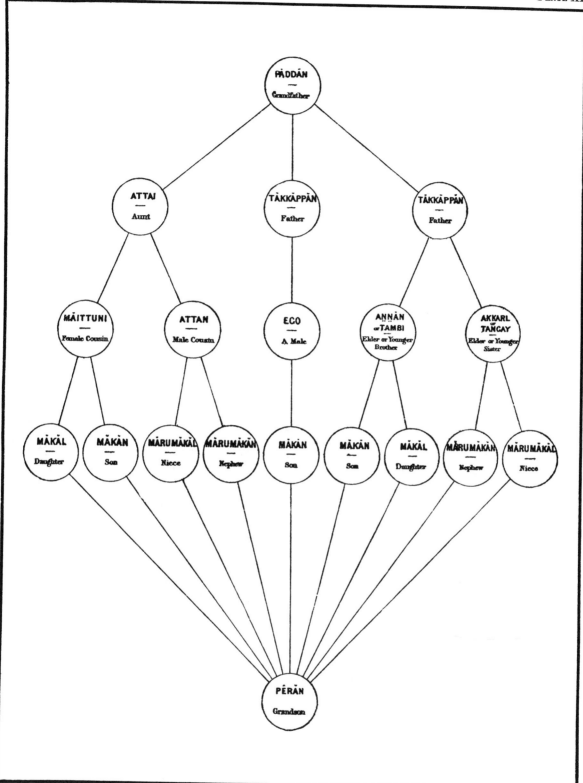

Lineal, and Second Collateral Lines: Male and Female: Father's Side.
Ego, a Male.

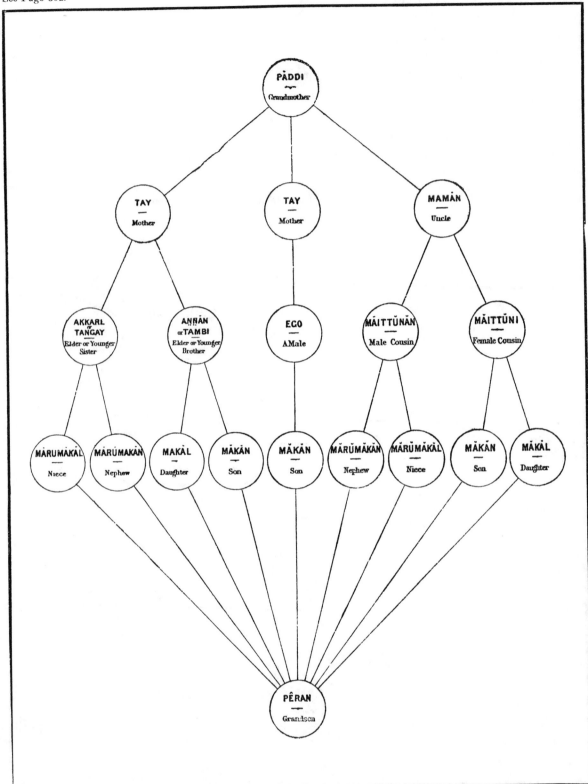

Lineal, and Second Collateral Lines: Male and Female: Mother's Side.
Ego, a Male.

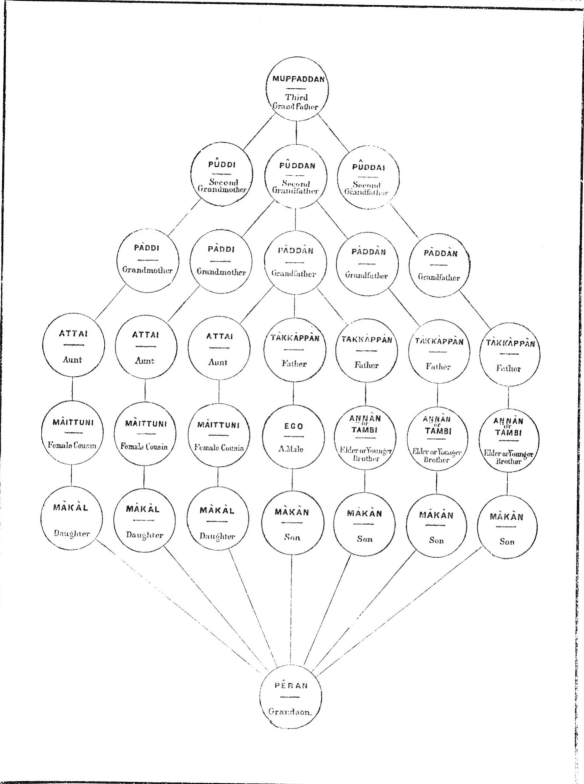

Lineal, and Second, Third, and Fourth Collateral Lines : Male and Female : Father's Side.
Ego, a Male.

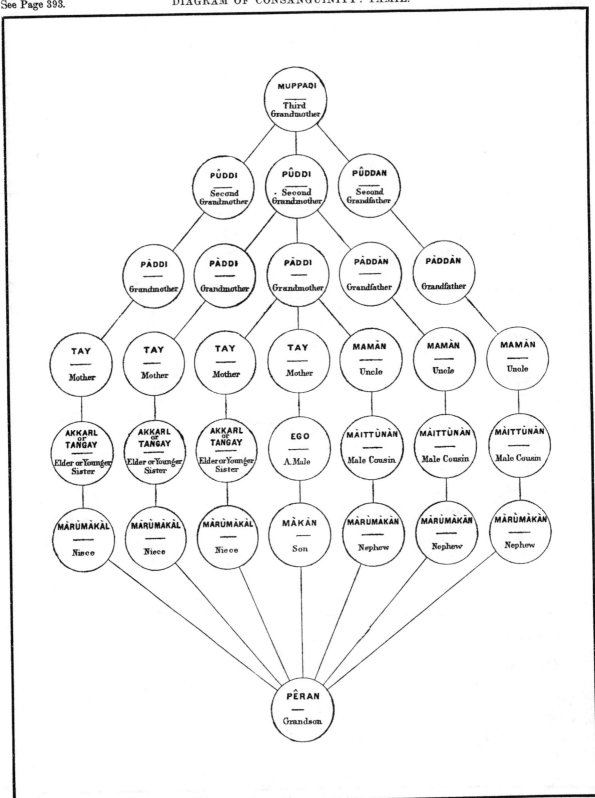

Lineal and Second, Third, and Fourth Collateral Lines: Male and Female.   Mother's Side.
Ego, a Male.